The Sporting News
HOCKEY REGISTER
2000-2001 EDITION

Editor/Hockey Register
DAVID WALTON

Editorial Director, Books
Steve Meyerhoff

Contributors
Michael Behrens, Matt Kindt, Joe Nonnenkamp,
Chris Paul, Brendan Roberts, Christen Sager,
Terry Shea, Josh Smith, Larry Wigge

ON THE COVER: 1999-2000 Hart and Norris Trophy winner Chris Pronger. (Cover designed by Michael Behrens. Action photo by Albert Dickson/THE SPORTING NEWS, portrait by Dilip Vishwanat/THE SPORTING NEWS.) Spine photo: Brendan Shanahan (File photo).

ISBN: 0-89204-638-4   10 9 8 7 6 5 4 3 2 1

CONTENTS

Veteran players and top prospects **6**
This section includes all veteran NHL players who appeared in at least one NHL game during the 1998-99 season, top prospects and other players signed with an NHL team as of July 29, 2000.

2000 top draft picks **410**
This section includes all players selected in the first two rounds of the 2000 NHL draft.

Head coaches **420**

EXPLANATION OF AWARDS

NHL AWARDS: Alka-Seltzer Plus Award: plus/minus leader. **Art Ross Trophy:** leading scorer. **Bill Masterton Memorial Trophy:** perseverance, sportsmanship and dedication to hockey. **Bud Light/NHL Man of the Year:** service to community; called Budweiser/NHL Man of the Year prior to 1990-91. **Budweiser/NHL Man of the Year:** service to community; renamed Bud Light/NHL Man of the Year in 1990-91. **Calder Memorial Trophy:** rookie of the year. **Conn Smythe Trophy:** most valuable player in playoffs. **Dodge Performance of the Year Award:** most outstanding achievement or single-game performance. **Dodge Performer of the Year Award:** most outstanding performer in regular season. **Dodge Ram Tough Award:** highest combined total of power-play, shorthanded, game-winning and game-tying goals. **Emery Edge Award:** plus/minus leader; awarded from 1982-83 through 1987-88. **Frank J. Selke Trophy:** best defensive forward. **Hart Memorial Trophy:** most valuable player. **Jack Adams Award:** coach of the year. **James Norris Memorial Trophy:** outstanding defenseman. **King Clancy Memorial Trophy:** humanitarian contributions. **Lady Byng Memorial Trophy:** most gentlemanly player. **Lester B. Pearson Award:** outstanding player as selected by NHL Players' Association. **Lester Patrick Trophy:** outstanding service to hockey in U.S. **Maurice "Rocket" Richard Trophy:** leading goal scorer. **Trico Goaltender Award:** best save percentage. **Vezina Trophy:** best goaltender; awarded to goalkeeper(s) having played minimum of 25 games for team with fewest goals scored against prior to 1981-82. **William M. Jennings Trophy:** goalkeeper(s) having played minimum of 25 games for team with fewest goals scored against.

MINOR LEAGUE AWARDS: Baz Bastien Trophy: top goaltender (AHL). **Bobby Orr Trophy:** best defenseman (CHL); awarded prior to 1984-85. **Bob Gassoff Award:** most improved defenseman (CHL); awarded prior to 1984-85. **Commissioner's Trophy:** coach of the year (IHL). **Dudley (Red) Garrett Memorial Trophy:** rookie of the year (AHL). **Eddie Shore Plaque:** outstanding defenseman (AHL). **Fred Hunt Memorial Award:** sportsmanship, determination and dedication (AHL). **Garry F. Longman Memorial Trophy:** outstanding rookie (IHL). **Governors Trophy:** outstanding defenseman (IHL). **Harry (Hap) Holmes Memorial Trophy:** goaltender(s) having played minimum of 25 games for team with fewest goals scored against (AHL); awarded to outstanding goaltender prior to 1983-84. **Jack Butterfield Trophy:** Calder Cup playoffs MVP (AHL). **Jake Milford Trophy:** coach of the year (CHL); awarded prior to 1984-85. **James Gatschene Memorial Trophy:** most valuable player (IHL). **James Norris Memorial Trophy:** outstanding goaltender (IHL). **John B. Sollenberger Trophy:** leading scorer (AHL); originally called Wally Kilrea Trophy, later changed to Carl Liscombe Trophy until summer of 1955. **Ken McKenzie Trophy:** outstanding U.S.-born rookie (IHL). **Ken McKenzie Trophy:** top rookie (CHL); awarded to scoring leader from 1992-93. **Leo P. Lamoureux Memorial Trophy:** leading scorer (IHL); originally called George H. Wilkinson Trophy from 1946-47 through 1959-60. **Les Cunningham Plaque:** most valuable player (AHL). **Louis A.R. Pieri Memorial Award:** top coach (AHL). **Max McNab Trophy:** playoff MVP (CHL); awarded prior to 1984-85. **N.R. (Bud) Poile Trophy:** playoff MVP (IHL); originally called Turner Cup Playoff MVP from 1984-85 through 1988-89. **Phil Esposito Trophy:** leading scorer (CHL); awarded prior to 1984-85. **Terry Sawchuk Trophy:** top goaltenders (CHL); awarded prior to 1984-85. **Tommy Ivan Trophy:** most valuable player (CHL); awarded prior to 1984-85. **Turner Cup Playoff MVP** (IHL); renamed N.R. (Bud) Poile Trophy in 1989-90.

MAJOR JUNIOR LEAGUE AWARDS: Association of Journalists for Major Junior League Hockey Trophy: top pro prospect (QMJHL); renamed Michael Bossy Trophy in 1983-84. **Bill Hunter Trophy:** top defenseman (WHL); called Top Defenseman Trophy prior to 1987-88 season. **Bob Brownridge Memorial Trophy:** top scorer (WHL); later renamed Bob Clarke Trophy. **Bobby Smith Trophy:** scholastic player of the year (OHL). **Bob Clarke Trophy:** top scorer (WHL); originally called Bob Brownridge Memorial Trophy. **Brad Hornung Trophy:** most sportsmanlike player (WHL); called Frank Boucher Memorial Trophy for most gentlemanly player prior to 1987-88 season. **Dave Pinkney Trophy:** top team goaltending (OHL). **Del Wilson Trophy:** top goaltender (WHL); called Top Goaltender Trophy prior to 1987-88 season. **Des Instructeurs Trophy:** rookie of the year (QMJHL); awarded to top rookie forward since 1981-82 season; renamed Michel Bergeron Trophy in 1985-86. **Dunc McCallum Memorial Trophy:** coach of the year (WHL). **Eddie Powers Memorial Trophy:** scoring champion (OHL). **Emile (Butch) Bouchard Trophy:** best defenseman (QMJHL). **Emms Family Award:** rookie of the year (OHL). **Four Broncos Memorial Trophy:** most valuable player as selected by coaches (WHL); called Most Valuable Player Trophy prior to 1987-88 season. **Frank Boucher Memorial Trophy:** most gentlemanly player (WHL); renamed Brad Hornung Trophy during 1987-88 season. **Frank J. Selke Trophy:** most gentlemanly player (QMJHL). **F.W. (Dinty) Moore Trophy:** rookie goalie with best goals-against average (OHL). **George Parsons Trophy:** sportsmanship in Memorial Cup (Can.HL). **Guy Lafleur Trophy:** most valuable player during playoffs (QMJHL). **Hap Emms Memorial Trophy:** outstanding goaltender in Memorial Cup (Can.HL). **Jacques Plante Trophy:** best goaltender (QMJHL). **Jean Beliveau Trophy:** leading point scorer (QMJHL). **Jim Mahon Memorial Trophy:** top-scoring right winger (OHL). **Jim Piggott Memorial Trophy:** rookie of the year (WHL); originally called Stewart (Butch) Paul Memorial Trophy. **Leo Lalonde Memorial Trophy:** overage player of the year (OHL). **Marcel Robert Trophy:** top scholastic/athletic performer (QMJHL). **Matt Leyden Trophy:** coach of the year (OHL). **Max Kaminsky Trophy:** outstanding defenseman (OHL); awarded to most gentlemanly player prior to 1969-70. **Michael Bossy Trophy:** top pro prospect (QMJHL); originally called Association of Journalists for Major Junior League Hockey Trophy from 1980-81 through 1982-83. **Michel Bergeron Trophy:** top rookie forward (QMJHL); awarded to rookie of the year prior to 1980-81 season. **Michel Briere Trophy:** most valuable player (QMJHL). **Most Valuable Player Trophy:** most valuable player (WHL); renamed Four Broncos Memorial Trophy during 1987-88 season. **Raymond Lagace Trophy:** top rookie defenseman or goaltender (QMJHL). **Red Tilson Trophy:** outstanding player (OHL). **Shell Cup:** awarded to offensive player of the year and defensive player of the year (QMJHL). **Stafford Smythe Memorial Trophy:** most valuable player of Memorial Cup (Can.HL). **Stewart (Butch) Paul Memorial Trophy:** rookie of the year (WHL); renamed Jim Piggott Memorial Trophy during 1987-88 season. **Top Defenseman Trophy:** top defenseman (WHL); renamed Bill Hunter Trophy during 1987-88 season. **Top Goaltender Trophy:** top goaltender (WHL); renamed Del Wilson Trophy during 1987-88 season. **William Hanley Trophy:** most gentlemanly player (OHL).

COLLEGE AWARDS: Hobey Baker Memorial Award: top college hockey player in U.S. **Senator Joseph A. Sullivan Trophy:** outstanding player in Canadian Interuniversity Athletic Union.

OTHER AWARDS: Golden Puck Award: Sweden's Player of the Year. **Golden Stick Award:** Europe's top player. **Izvestia Trophy:** leading scorer (Soviet Union).

EXPLANATION OF FOOTNOTES AND ABBREVIATIONS

*   League leader.
†   Tied for league lead.
‡   Overtime loss/shootout loss.
§   Led or tied for league lead, but total figure is divided between two different teams. Actual league-leading or league-tying figure is mentioned in "Statistical Notes" section.
. . .   Statistic unavailable, unofficial or mathematically impossible to calculate.
—   Statistic inapplicable.

POSITIONS: C: center. **D:** defenseman. **G:** goaltender. **LW:** left winger. **RW:** right winger.

STATISTICS: A: assists. **Avg.:** goals-against average. **G:** goals. **GA:** goals against. **Gms.:** games. **L:** losses. **Min.:** minutes. **PIM.:** penalties in minutes. **+/-:** plus-minus. **PP:** power-play goals. **Pts:** points. **SH:** shorthanded goals. **SO:** shutouts. **T:** ties. **W:** wins.

TEAMS: Bloom. Jefferson: Bloomington Jefferson. **Chem. Litvinov:** Chemopetrol Litvinov. **Chem. Litvinov Jrs.:** Chemopetrol Litvinov Juniors. **Culver Mil. Acad.:** Culver Military Academy. **Czech. Olympic team:** Czechoslovakian Olympic team. **Czech Rep. Oly. team:** Czech Republic Olympic team. **Czechosla. Jr. national:** Czechoslavakian Junior national team. **Det. Little Caesars:** Detroit Little Caesars. **Djur. Stockholm:** Djurgarden Stockholm. **Dynamo-Energ. Yek.:** Dynamo-Energiya Yekaterinburg. **Dyn.-Energiya 2 Yek.:** Dynamo-Energiya 2 Yekaterinburg. **Dynamo Ust-Kameno.:** Dynamo Ust-Kamenogorsk. **Fin. Olympic team:** Finnish Olympic team. **German Oly. team:** German Olympic team. **HC Ceske Bude.:** HC Ceske Budejovice. **HK 32 Lip. Mikulas:** HK 32 Liptovsky Mikulas. **IS Banska Byst.:** IS Banska Bystrica. **Kiek.-Karhut Jodusuu:** Kiekko-Karhut Jodusuu. **Krylja Sov. Moscow:** Krylja Sovetov Moscow. **Mass.-Lowell:** Massachusetts-Lowell. **Metal. Cherepovets:** Metallurg Cherepovets. **Metal. Magnitogorsk:** Metallurg Magnitogorsk. **Metallurg-2 Novok.:** Metallurg-2 Novokuznetsk. **MoDo Ornsk. Jrs.:** Modo Ornskoldsvik Jrs. **Motor Ceske Bude.:** Motor Ceske Budejovice. **N. Yarmouth Acad.:** North Yarmouth Academy. **N. Arizona Univ.:** Northern Arizona University. **N. Michigan Univ.:** Northern Michigan University. **NW Americans Jr. B:** Northwest Americans Junior B. **Poji. Pardubice Jrs.:** Pojistovna Pardubice Juniors. **Prin. Edward Island:** Prince Edward Island. **Rus. Olympic team:** Russian Olympic team. **Sault Ste. Marie:** Sault Sainte Marie. **Sever. Cherepovets:** Severstal Cherepovets. **Slovakian Oly. team:** Slovakian Olympic team. **Sov. Olympic team:** Soviet Olympic team. **Spisska N.V.:** Spisska Nova Ves. **Stad. Hradec Kralove:** Stadion Hradec Kralove. **Swed. Olympic team:** Swedish Olympic team. **Tor. Nizhny Nov.:** Torpedo Nizhny Novgorod. **Torpedo Ust-Kam.:** Torpedo Ust-Kamenogorsk. **Unif. Olympic team:** Unified Olympic team. **Univ. of New Hamp.:** University of New Hampshire. **Univ. of West. Ontario:** University of Western Ontario. **V. Frolunda Goteborg:** Vastra Frolunda Goteborg.

LEAGUES: AAHL: All American Hockey League. **ACHL:** Atlantic Coast Hockey League. **AHL:** American Hockey League. **AJHL:** Alberta Junior Hockey League. **AMHL:** Alberta Minor Hockey League. **AUAA:** Atlantic Universities Athletic Association. **BCJHL:** British Columbia Junior Hockey League. **CAHL:** Central Alberta Hockey League. **CAJHL:** Central Alberta Junior Hockey League. **Can. College:** Canadian College. **Can.HL:** Canadian Hockey League. **CCHA:** Central Collegiate Hockey Association. **CHL:** Central Hockey League. **CIS:** Commonwealth of Independent States. **CJHL:** Central Junior A Hockey League. **COJHL:** Central Ontario Junior Hockey League. **CPHL:** Central Professional Hockey League. **CWUAA:** Canada West University Athletic Association. **Conn. H.S.:** Connecticut High School. **Czech.:** Czechoslovakia. **Czech. Rep.:** Czechoslovakia Republic. **ECAC:** Eastern College Athletic Conference. **ECAC-II:** Eastern College Athletic Conference, Division II. **ECHL:** East Coast Hockey League. **EEHL:** Eastern European Hockey League. **EHL:** Eastern Hockey League. **EURO:** Euroliga. **Fin.:** Finland. **Ger.:** Germany. **GWHC:** Great Western Hockey Conference. **Hoc. East:** Hockey East. **IHL:** International Hockey League. **Ill. H.S.:** Illinois High School. **Indiana H.S.:** Indiana High School. **Int'l:** International. **KIJHL:** Kootenay International Junior Hockey League. **Mass. H.S.:** Massachusetts High School. **Md. H.S.:** Maryland High School. **Met. Bos.:** Metro Boston. **Mich. H.S.:** Michigan High School. **Minn. H.S.:** Minnesota High School. **MJHL:** Manitoba Junior Hockey League. **MTHL:** Metro Toronto Hockey League. **NAHL:** North American Hockey League. **NAJHL:** North American Junior Hockey League. **N.B. H.S.:** New Brunswick High School. **NCAA-II:** National Collegiate Athletic Association, Division II. **N.D. H.S.:** North Dakota High School. **NEJHL:** New England Junior Hockey League. **NHL:** National Hockey League. **N.H. H.S.:** New Hampshire High School. **N.J. H.S.:** New Jersey High School. **Nia. D. Jr. C:** Niagara District Junior C. **NSJHL:** Nova Scotia Junior Hockey League. **N.S. Jr. A:** Nova Scotia Junior A. **N.Y. H.S.:** New York High School. **NYMJHL:** New York Major Junior Hockey League. **NYOHL:** North York Ontario Hockey League. **ODHA:** Ottawa & District Hockey Association. **OHA:** Ontario Hockey Association. **OHA Jr. A:** Ontario Hockey Association Junior A. **OHA Mjr. Jr. A:** Ontario Hockey Association Major Junior A. **OHA Senior:** Ontario Hockey Association Senior. **OHL:** Ontario Hockey League. **O.H.S.:** Ohio High School. **OJHA:** Ontario Junior Hockey Association. **OJHL:** Ontario Junior Hockey League. **OMJHL:** Ontario Major Junior Hockey League. **OPJHL:** Ontario Provincial Junior Hockey League. **OUAA:** Ontario Universities Athletic Association. **PCJHL:** Peace Caribou Junior Hockey League. **PEIHA:** Prince Edward Island Hockey Association. **PEIJHL:** Prince Edward Island Junior Hockey League. **Penn. H.S.:** Pennsylvania High School. **QMJHL:** Quebec Major Junior Hockey League. **R.I. H.S.:** Rhode Island High School. **Rus. Div II, III:** Russian Division II, III. **SAJHL:** Southern Alberta Junior Hockey League. **SJHL:** Saskatchewan Junior Hockey League. **Sask. H.S.:** Saskatchewan High School. **SOJHL:** Southern Ontario Junior Hockey League. **Swed. Jr.:** Sweden Junior. **Switz.:** Switzerland. **TBAHA:** Thunder Bay Amateur Hockey Association. **TBJHL:** Thunder Bay Junior Hockey League. **UHL:** United Hockey League. **USHL:** United States Hockey League. **USHS:** United States High School. **USSR:** Union of Soviet Socialist Republics. **V. Frolunda Goteborg:** Vastra Frolunda Goteborg. **Vt. H.S.:** Vermont High School. **W. Germany, W. Ger.:** West Germany. **WCHA:** Western Collegiate Hockey Association. **WCHL:** Western Canada Hockey League. **WHA:** World Hockey Association. **WHL:** Western Hockey League. **Wisc. H.S.:** Wisconsin High School. **Yukon Sr.:** Yukon Senior.

VETERANS AND TOP PROSPECTS

A

AALTO, ANTTI   C   MIGHTY DUCKS

PERSONAL: Born March 4, 1975, in Lappeenranta, Finland. ... 6-2/210. ... Shoots left. ... Name pronounced AN-tee AL-toh.
TRANSACTIONS/CAREER NOTES: Selected by Mighty Ducks of Anaheim in sixth round (sixth Mighty Ducks pick, 134th overall) of NHL entry draft (June 26, 1993). ... Injured shoulder (December 16, 1998); missed one game. ... Sprained left elbow (December 4, 1999); missed 15 games. ... Suffered illness (March 2, 2000); missed three games.

		REGULAR SEASON								PLAYOFFS				
Season Team	League	Gms.	G	A	Pts.	PIM	+/-	PP	SH	Gms.	G	A	Pts.	PIM
91-92—SaiPa Jr.	Finland	19	10	10	20	38	...	...	...	—	—	—	—	—
—SaiPa	Finland	20	6	6	12	20	...	...	...	—	—	—	—	—
92-93—SaiPa	Finland	23	6	8	14	14	...	...	...	—	—	—	—	—
—TPS Turku Jr.	Finland	14	6	8	14	18	...	...	...	—	—	—	—	—
—TPS Turku	Finland	1	0	0	0	0	...	...	...	—	—	—	—	—
93-94—TPS Turku	Finland	33	5	9	14	16	...	...	...	10	1	1	2	4
94-95—TPS Turku	Finland	44	11	7	18	18	...	...	...	5	0	1	1	2
95-96—TPS Turku	Finland	40	15	16	31	22	...	...	...	11	3	5	8	14
—Kiekko-67	Finland Div. 2	2	0	2	2	2	...	...	...	—	—	—	—	—
96-97—TPS Turku	Finland	44	15	19	34	60	...	...	...	11	5	6	11	31
97-98—Cincinnati	AHL	29	4	9	13	30	...	...	...	—	—	—	—	—
—Anaheim	NHL	3	0	0	0	0	-1	0	0	—	—	—	—	—
98-99—Anaheim	NHL	73	3	5	8	24	-12	2	0	4	0	0	0	2
99-00—Anaheim	NHL	63	7	11	18	26	-13	1	0	—	—	—	—	—
NHL Totals (3 years)		139	10	16	26	50	-26	3	0	4	0	0	0	2

ABID, RAMZI   LW   COYOTES

PERSONAL: Born March 24, 1980, in Montreal. ... 6-2/195. ... Shoots left.
TRANSACTIONS/CAREER NOTES: Selected by Colorado Avalanche in second round (fifth Avalanche pick, 28th overall) of NHL entry draft (June 27, 1998). ... Returned to draft pool by Avalanche and selected by Phoenix Coyotes in third round (third Coyotes pick, 86th overall) of NHL entry draft (June 24, 2000).
HONORS: Named to Can.HL All-Star second team (1997-98). ... Named to QMJHL All-Star first team (1997-98 and 1999-2000). ... Won Jean Beliveau Trophy (1997-98). ... Won Michel Briere Trophy (1997-98). ... Named to Can.HL All-Star first team (1999-2000).

		REGULAR SEASON								PLAYOFFS				
Season Team	League	Gms.	G	A	Pts.	PIM	+/-	PP	SH	Gms.	G	A	Pts.	PIM
96-97—Chicoutimi	QMJHL	65	13	24	37	151	...	...	...	—	—	—	—	—
97-98—Chicoutimi	QMJHL	68	50	*85	*135	266	...	...	...	6	3	4	7	10
98-99—Chicoutimi	QMJHL	21	11	15	26	97	...	...	...	—	—	—	—	—
—Acadie-Bathurst	QMJHL	24	14	22	36	102	...	...	...	23	14	20	34	84
99-00—Acadie-Bathurst	QMJHL	13	10	11	21	61	...	...	...	—	—	—	—	—
—Halifax	QMJHL	59	57	80	137	148	...	...	...	10	10	13	23	18

ABRAHAMSSON, ELIAS   D   BRUINS

PERSONAL: Born June 15, 1977, in Uppsala, Sweden. ... 6-3/227. ... Shoots left. ... Full Name: Erik Elias Abrahamsson. ... Name pronounced uh-LEE-uhz ay-bruh-HAM-suhn.
TRANSACTIONS/CAREER NOTES: Selected by Boston Bruins in fifth round (sixth Bruins pick, 132nd overall) of NHL entry draft (June 22, 1996).

		REGULAR SEASON								PLAYOFFS				
Season Team	League	Gms.	G	A	Pts.	PIM	+/-	PP	SH	Gms.	G	A	Pts.	PIM
93-94—Uppsala	Sweden Dv. 2	1	0	0	0	0	...	...	...	—	—	—	—	—
94-95—Halifax	QMJHL	25	0	3	3	41	...	...	...	—	—	—	—	—
95-96—Halifax	QMJHL	64	3	11	14	268	...	...	...	6	2	2	4	8
96-97—Halifax	QMJHL	30	4	11	15	221	...	...	...	18	4	8	12	74
97-98—Providence	AHL	29	0	1	1	47	...	...	...	—	—	—	—	—
98-99—Providence	AHL	75	2	9	11	184	...	...	...	4	0	0	0	7
99-00—Providence	AHL	19	1	1	2	45	...	...	...	—	—	—	—	—
—Hamilton	AHL	56	1	3	4	90	...	...	...	10	0	1	1	4

ADAMS, BRYAN   LW   THRASHERS

PERSONAL: Born March 20, 1977, in Fort St. James, B.C. ... 6-0/185. ... Shoots left.
HIGH SCHOOL: Fort St. James (B.C.) Secondary.
COLLEGE: Michigan State.
TRANSACTIONS/CAREER NOTES: Signed as a non-drafted free agent by Atlanta Thrashers (July 1, 1999).

		REGULAR SEASON								PLAYOFFS				
Season Team	League	Gms.	G	A	Pts.	PIM	+/-	PP	SH	Gms.	G	A	Pts.	PIM
95-96—Michigan State	CCHA	42	3	8	11	12	...	...	...	—	—	—	—	—
96-97—Michigan State	CCHA	29	7	7	14	51	...	...	...	—	—	—	—	—
97-98—Michigan State	CCHA	31	9	21	30	39	...	...	...	—	—	—	—	—
98-99—Michigan State	CCHA	42	21	16	37	56	...	...	...	—	—	—	—	—
99-00—Orlando	IHL	64	16	18	34	27	...	...	...	4	0	1	1	6
—Atlanta	NHL	2	0	0	0	0	-1	0	0	—	—	—	—	—
NHL Totals (1 year)		2	0	0	0	0	-1	0	0					

ADAMS, GREG — LW

PERSONAL: Born August 15, 1963, in Nelson, B.C. ... 6-4/196. ... Shoots left. ... Full Name: Greg G. Adams. ... Son-in-law of George Swarbrick, right winger with three NHL teams (1967-68 through 1970-71).

COLLEGE: Northern Arizona.

TRANSACTIONS/CAREER NOTES: Signed as non-drafted free agent by New Jersey Devils (June 25, 1984). ... Tore tendon in right wrist (April 1986). ... Traded by Devils with G Kirk McLean to Vancouver Canucks for C Patrik Sundstrom, fourth-round pick (LW Matt Ruchty) in the 1998 draft and the option to flip second-round picks in 1988 draft; Devils exercised option and selected LW Jeff Christian and Canucks selected D Leif Rohlin (September 10, 1987). ... Fractured ankle (February 1989). ... Fractured cheekbone (January 4, 1990); missed 12 games. ... Sprained left knee (October 17, 1990); missed 12 games. ... Sprained forearm, wrist and abdomen (February 27, 1991). ... Suffered concussion (October 8, 1991); missed one game. ... Suffered charley horse (January 16, 1993); missed nine games. ... Suffered charley horse (February 15, 1993); missed 22 games. ... Suffered stress fracture in hand requiring minor surgery (December 14, 1993); missed 14 games. ... Bruised foot (February 22, 1994); missed one game. ... Traded by Canucks with RW Dan Kesa and fifth-round pick (traded to Los Angeles) in 1995 draft to Dallas Stars for RW Russ Courtnall (April 7, 1995). ... Fractured hand (March 2, 1996); missed 11 games. ... Broke toe (April 7, 1996); missed final four games of season. ... Suffered herniated disc in neck (December 21, 1996); missed 30 games. ... Strained groin (April 4, 1997); missed one game. ... Bruised ribs (November 16, 1997); missed 11 games. ... Injured knee (December 23, 1997); missed 20 games. ... Injured neck (April 6, 1998); missed two games. ... Signed as free agent by Phoenix Coyotes (September 1, 1998). ... Suffered from the flu (January 26, 1999); missed one game. ... Strained groin (February 20, 1999); missed six games. ... Suffered injury (December 11, 1999); missed two games. ... Underwent sinus surgery (December 29, 1999); missed 11 games.

HONORS: Played in NHL All-Star Game (1988).

MISCELLANEOUS: Failed to score on a penalty shot (vs. Alain Chevrier, January 7, 1988; vs. Alan Bester, January 9, 1989; vs. Jacques Cloutier, December 10, 1989; vs. Bill Ranford, December 1, 1991; vs. Curtis Joseph, January 25, 1992).

STATISTICAL PLATEAUS: Three-goal games: 1991-92 (1). ... Four-goal games: 1987-88 (1). ... Total hat tricks: 2.

		REGULAR SEASON							PLAYOFFS				
Season Team	League	Gms.	G	A	Pts.	PIM	+/-	PP	SH	Gms.	G	A	Pts.	PIM
80-81—Kelowna	BCJHL	47	40	50	90	16	...	...	...	—	—	—	—	—
81-82—Kelowna	BCJHL	45	31	42	73	24	...	...	...	—	—	—	—	—
82-83—N. Arizona Univ.	Indep.	29	14	21	35	46	...	...	...	—	—	—	—	—
83-84—N. Arizona Univ.	Indep.	47	40	50	90	16	...	...	...	—	—	—	—	—
84-85—Maine	AHL	41	15	20	35	12	...	...	...	11	3	4	7	0
—New Jersey	NHL	36	12	9	21	14	-14	5	0	—	—	—	—	—
85-86—New Jersey	NHL	78	35	42	77	30	-6	10	0	—	—	—	—	—
86-87—New Jersey	NHL	72	20	27	47	19	-16	6	0	—	—	—	—	—
87-88—Vancouver	NHL	80	36	40	76	30	-24	12	0	—	—	—	—	—
88-89—Vancouver	NHL	61	19	14	33	24	-21	9	0	7	2	3	5	2
89-90—Vancouver	NHL	65	30	20	50	18	-8	13	0	—	—	—	—	—
90-91—Vancouver	NHL	55	21	24	45	10	-5	5	1	5	0	0	0	2
91-92—Vancouver	NHL	76	30	27	57	26	8	13	1	6	0	2	2	4
92-93—Vancouver	NHL	53	25	31	56	14	31	6	1	12	7	6	13	6
93-94—Vancouver	NHL	68	13	24	37	20	-1	5	1	23	6	8	14	2
94-95—Vancouver	NHL	31	5	10	15	12	1	2	2	—	—	—	—	—
—Dallas	NHL	12	3	3	6	4	-4	1	0	5	2	0	2	0
95-96—Dallas	NHL	66	22	21	43	33	-21	11	1	—	—	—	—	—
96-97—Dallas	NHL	50	21	15	36	2	27	5	0	3	0	1	1	0
97-98—Dallas	NHL	49	14	18	32	20	11	7	0	12	2	2	4	0
98-99—Phoenix	NHL	75	19	24	43	26	-1	5	0	3	1	0	1	0
99-00—Phoenix	NHL	69	19	27	46	14	-1	5	0	5	0	0	0	0
NHL Totals (16 years)		996	344	376	720	316	-44	120	7	81	20	22	42	16

ADAMS, KEVYN — C — BLUE JACKETS

PERSONAL: Born October 8, 1974, in Washington, D.C. ... 6-1/195. ... Shoots right.

HIGH SCHOOL: Clarence (N.Y.).

COLLEGE: Miami of Ohio.

TRANSACTIONS/CAREER NOTES: Selected by Boston Bruins in first round (first Bruins pick, 25th overall) of NHL entry draft (June 26, 1993). ... Signed as free agent by Toronto Maple Leafs (August 1, 1997). ... Selected by Columbus Blue Jackets in NHL expansion draft (June 23, 2000).

HONORS: Named to CCHA All-Star second team (1994-95).

MISCELLANEOUS: Failed to score on a penalty shot (vs. Arturs Irbe, February 14, 2000).

		REGULAR SEASON							PLAYOFFS				
Season Team	League	Gms.	G	A	Pts.	PIM	+/-	PP	SH	Gms.	G	A	Pts.	PIM
90-91—Niagara	NAJHL	55	17	20	37	24	...	...	...	—	—	—	—	—
91-92—Niagara	NAJHL	40	25	33	58	51	...	...	...	—	—	—	—	—
92-93—Miami of Ohio	CCHA	41	17	16	33	18	...	...	...	—	—	—	—	—
93-94—Miami of Ohio	CCHA	36	15	28	43	24	...	...	...	—	—	—	—	—
94-95—Miami of Ohio	CCHA	38	20	29	49	30	...	...	...	—	—	—	—	—
95-96—Miami of Ohio	CCHA	36	17	30	47	30	...	...	...	—	—	—	—	—
96-97—Grand Rapids	IHL	82	22	25	47	47	...	...	...	5	1	1	2	4
97-98—Toronto	NHL	5	0	0	0	7	0	0	0	—	—	—	—	—
—St. John's	AHL	58	17	21	38	99	...	...	...	4	0	0	0	4
98-99—St. John's	AHL	80	15	35	50	85	...	...	...	5	2	0	2	4
—Toronto	NHL	1	0	0	0	0	0	0	0	7	0	2	2	14
99-00—St. John's	AHL	23	6	11	17	24	...	...	...	—	—	—	—	—
—Toronto	NHL	52	5	8	13	39	-7	0	0	12	1	0	1	7
NHL Totals (3 years)		58	5	8	13	46	-7	0	0	19	1	2	3	21

ADDUONO, JEREMY — RW — SABRES

PERSONAL: Born August 4, 1979, in Thunder Bay, Ont. ... 6-0/182. ... Shoots right.
TRANSACTIONS/CAREER NOTES: Selected by Buffalo Sabres in seventh round (eighth Sabres pick, 184th overall) of NHL entry draft (June 21, 1997).

		REGULAR SEASON							PLAYOFFS				
Season Team	League	Gms.	G	A	Pts.	PIM	+/-	PP	SH	Gms.	G	A	Pts.	PIM
95-96—Sudbury	OHL	66	15	22	37	14	...	...	...	—	—	—	—	—
96-97—Sudbury	OHL	66	29	40	69	24	...	...	...	—	—	—	—	—
97-98—Sudbury	OHL	66	37	69	106	40	...	...	...	10	5	5	10	10
98-99—Canadian nat'l team	Int'l	44	10	16	26	8	...	...	...	—	—	—	—	—
99-00—Rochester	AHL	51	23	22	45	20	...	...	...	21	6	11	17	2

AEBISCHER, DAVID — G — AVALANCHE

PERSONAL: Born February 7, 1978, in Fribourg, Switzerland. ... 6-1/185. ... Catches left. ... Name pronounced EH-bih-shuhr.
TRANSACTIONS/CAREER NOTES: Selected by Colorado Avalanche in sixth round (seventh Avalanche pick, 161st overall) of NHL entry draft (June 21, 1997).

		REGULAR SEASON								PLAYOFFS						
Season Team	League	Gms.	Min	W	L	T	GA	SO	Avg.	Gms.	Min.	W	L	GA	SO	Avg.
96-97—Fribourg-Gotteron	Switzerland	10	577	...	...	...	34	...	3.54	3	184	...	...	13	...	4.24
97-98—Fribourg-Gotteron	Switzerland	1	60	...	...	...	1	0	1.00	4	240	...	...	17	...	4.25
—Hershey	AHL	2	80	0	0	1	5	0	3.75	—	—	—	—	—	—	—
—Chesapeake	ECHL	17	930	5	7	‡2	52	0	3.35	—	—	—	—	—	—	—
—Wheeling	ECHL	10	564	5	3	‡1	30	1	3.19	—	—	—	—	—	—	—
98-99—Hershey	AHL	38	1932	17	10	5	79	2	2.45	3	152	1	2	6	0	2.37
99-00—Hershey	AHL	58	3259	29	23	2	*180	1	3.31	14	788	7	6	40	2	3.05

AFANASENKOV, DMITRY — LW — LIGHTNING

PERSONAL: Born May 12, 1980, in Arkhangelsk, U.S.S.R. ... 6-2/200. ... Shoots right. ... Name pronounced ah-fahn-ah-SEHN-kov.
TRANSACTIONS/CAREER NOTES: Selected by Tampa Bay Lightning in third round (third Lightning pick, 72nd overall) of NHL entry draft (June 27, 1998).

		REGULAR SEASON								PLAYOFFS				
Season Team	League	Gms.	G	A	Pts.	PIM	+/-	PP	SH	Gms.	G	A	Pts.	PIM
95-96—Torpedo-2 Yaroslavl	CIS Div. II	25	10	5	15	10	...	...	...	—	—	—	—	—
—Torpedo Yaroslavl	CIS Jr.	35	28	16	44	8	...	...	...	—	—	—	—	—
96-97—Torpedo-2 Yaroslavl	Rus. Div. III	45	20	15	35	14	...	...	...	—	—	—	—	—
97-98—Torpedo-Yaroslavl	Russian	45	19	11	30	28	...	...	...	—	—	—	—	—
98-99—Moncton	QMJHL	15	5	5	10	12	...	...	...	—	—	—	—	—
—Sherbrooke	QMJHL	51	23	30	53	22	...	...	...	13	10	6	16	6
99-00—Sherbrooke	QMJHL	60	56	43	99	70	...	...	...	5	3	2	5	4

AFINOGENOV, MAXIM — RW — SABRES

PERSONAL: Born September 4, 1979, in Moscow, U.S.S.R. ... 5-11/176. ... Shoots left. ... Name pronounced ah-FEEN-o-gin-ov.
TRANSACTIONS/CAREER NOTES: Selected by Buffalo Sabres in third round (third Sabres pick, 69th overall) of NHL entry draft (June 21, 1997).

		REGULAR SEASON								PLAYOFFS				
Season Team	League	Gms.	G	A	Pts.	PIM	+/-	PP	SH	Gms.	G	A	Pts.	PIM
95-96—Dynamo Moscow	CIS	1	0	0	0	0	...	...	...	—	—	—	—	—
96-97—Dynamo Moscow	Russian	29	6	5	11	10	...	...	...	4	0	2	2	0
—Dynamo-2 Moscow	Rus. Div. III	14	9	2	11	10	...	...	...	—	—	—	—	—
97-98—Dynamo Moscow	Russian	35	10	5	15	53	...	...	...	—	—	—	—	—
98-99—Dynamo Moscow	Russian	38	8	13	21	24	...	...	...	16	*10	6	†16	14
99-00—Rochester	AHL	15	6	12	18	8	...	...	...	8	3	1	4	4
—Buffalo	NHL	65	16	18	34	41	-4	2	0	5	0	1	1	2
NHL Totals (1 year)		65	16	18	34	41	-4	2	0	5	0	1	1	2

AITKEN, JOHNATHAN — D — BRUINS

PERSONAL: Born May 24, 1978, in Edmonton. ... 6-4/210. ... Shoots left. ... Full Name: Johnathan James Aitken. ... Name pronounced AYT-kihn.
TRANSACTIONS/CAREER NOTES: Selected by Boston Bruins in first round (first Bruins pick, eighth overall) of NHL entry draft (June 22, 1996).
HONORS: Named to WHL (East) All-Star second team (1997-98).

		REGULAR SEASON								PLAYOFFS				
Season Team	League	Gms.	G	A	Pts.	PIM	+/-	PP	SH	Gms.	G	A	Pts.	PIM
94-95—Medicine Hat	WHL	53	0	5	5	71	...	...	...	—	—	—	—	—
95-96—Medicine Hat	WHL	71	6	14	20	131	...	...	...	5	1	0	1	6
96-97—Brandon	WHL	65	4	18	22	211	...	...	...	6	0	0	0	4
97-98—Brandon	WHL	69	9	25	34	183	...	...	...	18	0	8	8	67
98-99—Providence	AHL	65	2	9	11	92	...	...	...	13	0	0	0	17
99-00—Providence	AHL	70	2	12	14	121	...	...	...	11	1	0	1	26
—Boston	NHL	3	0	0	0	0	-3	0	0	—	—	—	—	—
NHL Totals (1 year)		3	0	0	0	0	-3	0	0					

ALATALO, MIKA   LW   COYOTES

PERSONAL: Born June 11, 1971, in Oulu, Finland. ... 6-0/202. ... Shoots left. ... Full Name: Mikael Alatalo.
TRANSACTIONS/CAREER NOTES: Selected by Winnipeg Jets in 10th round (11th Jets pick, 203rd overall) of NHL entry draft (June 16, 1990). ... Jets franchise moved to Phoenix and renamed Coyotes for 1996-97 season; NHL approved move on January 18, 1996.

		REGULAR SEASON								PLAYOFFS				
Season Team	League	Gms.	G	A	Pts.	PIM	+/-	PP	SH	Gms.	G	A	Pts.	PIM
88-89—KooKoo Kouvola........	Finland Div. 2	34	8	6	14	10	...	...	...	—	—	—	—	—
89-90—KooKoo Kouvola........	Finland Div. 2	41	3	5	8	22	...	...	...	—	—	—	—	—
90-91—Lukko....................	Finland	39	10	1	11	10	...	...	...	—	—	—	—	—
91-92—Lukko....................	Finland	43	20	17	37	32	...	...	...	2	0	0	0	0
92-93—Lukko....................	Finland	48	16	19	35	38	...	...	...	3	0	0	0	0
93-94—Lukko....................	Finland	45	19	15	34	77	...	...	...	9	2	2	4	4
94-95—TPS Turku	Finland	44	23	13	36	59	...	...	...	13	2	5	7	8
95-96—TPS Turku	Finland	49	19	18	37	44	...	...	...	13	2	5	7	8
96-97—Lulea....................	Sweden	50	19	18	37	54	...	...	...	10	2	3	5	22
97-98—Lulea....................	Sweden	45	14	10	24	22	...	...	...	2	0	0	0	0
98-99—TPS Turku	Finland	53	14	23	37	44	...	...	...	10	6	3	9	6
99-00—Phoenix..................	NHL	82	10	17	27	36	-3	1	0	5	0	0	0	2
NHL Totals (1 year).............		82	10	17	27	36	-3	1	0	5	0	0	0	2

ALBELIN, TOMMY   D   FLAMES

PERSONAL: Born May 21, 1964, in Stockholm, Sweden. ... 6-1/194. ... Shoots left. ... Name pronounced AL-buh-leen.
TRANSACTIONS/CAREER NOTES: Selected by Quebec Nordiques in eighth round (seventh Nordiques pick, 152nd overall) of NHL entry draft (June 8, 1983). ... Traded by Nordiques to New Jersey Devils for fourth-round pick (LW Niclas Andersson) in 1989 draft (December 12, 1988). ... Injured right knee (March 2, 1990); missed four games. ... Injured groin (November 21, 1992); missed two games. ... Suffered from urinary infection (1993-94 season); missed nine games. ... Bruised thigh (December 16, 1995); missed six games. ... Traded by Devils with D Cale Hulse and RW Jocelyn Lemieux to Calgary Flames for D Phil Housley and D Dan Keczmer (February 26, 1996). ... Strained groin (November 9, 1996); missed four games. ... Reinjured groin (November 25, 1996); missed two games. ... Strained abdominal muscle (December 7, 1996); missed five games. ... Suffered concussion (November 11, 1997); missed three games. ... Pulled groin (November 27, 1997); missed three games. ... Reinjured groin (December 9, 1997); missed four games. ... Injured ribs (February 2, 1998); missed three games. ... Strained groin (November 20, 1998); missed six games. ... Injured shoulder (January 6, 2000); missed final 41 games of season.
HONORS: Named to Swedish League All-Star team (1986-87).
MISCELLANEOUS: Member of Stanley Cup championship team (1995).

		REGULAR SEASON								PLAYOFFS				
Season Team	League	Gms.	G	A	Pts.	PIM	+/-	PP	SH	Gms.	G	A	Pts.	PIM
82-83—Djurgarden Stockholm	Sweden	17	2	5	7	4	...	...	...	6	1	0	1	2
83-84—Djurgarden Stockholm	Sweden	37	9	8	17	36	...	...	...	4	0	1	1	2
84-85—Djurgarden Stockholm	Sweden	32	9	8	17	22	...	...	...	8	2	1	3	4
85-86—Djurgarden Stockholm	Sweden	35	4	8	12	26	...	...	...	—	—	—	—	—
86-87—Djurgarden Stockholm	Sweden	33	7	5	12	49	...	...	...	2	0	0	0	0
87-88—Quebec	NHL	60	3	23	26	47	-7	0	0	—	—	—	—	—
88-89—Halifax......................	AHL	8	2	5	7	4	...	...	...	—	—	—	—	—
—Quebec	NHL	14	2	4	6	27	-6	1	0	—	—	—	—	—
—New Jersey	NHL	46	7	24	31	40	18	1	1	—	—	—	—	—
89-90—New Jersey	NHL	68	6	23	29	63	-1	4	0	—	—	—	—	—
90-91—Utica	AHL	14	4	2	6	10	...	...	...	—	—	—	—	—
—New Jersey	NHL	47	2	12	14	44	1	1	0	3	0	1	1	2
91-92—New Jersey	NHL	19	0	4	4	4	7	0	0	1	1	1	2	0
—Utica	AHL	11	4	6	10	4	...	...	...	—	—	—	—	—
92-93—New Jersey	NHL	36	1	5	6	14	0	1	0	5	2	0	2	0
93-94—Albany	AHL	4	0	2	2	17	...	...	...	—	—	—	—	—
—New Jersey	NHL	62	2	17	19	36	20	1	0	20	2	5	7	14
94-95—New Jersey	NHL	48	5	10	15	20	9	2	0	20	1	7	8	2
95-96—New Jersey	NHL	53	1	12	13	14	0	0	0	—	—	—	—	—
—Calgary	NHL	20	0	1	1	4	1	0	0	4	0	0	0	0
96-97—Calgary	NHL	72	4	11	15	14	-8	2	0	—	—	—	—	—
97-98—Calgary	NHL	69	2	17	19	32	9	1	0	—	—	—	—	—
—Swedish Oly. team	Int'l	3	0	0	0	4	...	...	...	—	—	—	—	—
98-99—Calgary	NHL	60	1	5	6	8	-11	0	0	—	—	—	—	—
99-00—Calgary	NHL	41	4	6	10	12	-3	1	1	—	—	—	—	—
NHL Totals (13 years).........		715	40	174	214	379	29	15	2	53	6	14	20	18

ALDRIDGE, KEITH   D/RW

PERSONAL: Born July 20, 1973, in Detroit. ... 5-11/185. ... Shoots right.
COLLEGE: Lake Superior State.
TRANSACTIONS/CAREER NOTES: Signed as non-drafted free agent by Dallas Stars (September 1, 1999).
HONORS: Named to CCHA All-Star second team (1993-94). ... Named to NCAA All-Tournament team (1993-94). ... Named to CCHA All-Star first team (1994-95 and 1995-96). ... Named to NCAA All-America (West) second team (1994-95). ... Named to NCAA All-America (West) first team (1995-96).

Season Team	League	REGULAR SEASON									PLAYOFFS				
		Gms.	G	A	Pts.	PIM	+/-	PP	SH		Gms.	G	A	Pts.	PIM
92-93—Lake Superior State	CCHA	37	3	11	14	30	...	...	...		—	—	—	—	—
93-94—Lake Superior State	CCHA	45	10	24	34	86	...	...	...		—	—	—	—	—
94-95—Lake Superior State	CCHA	40	10	31	41	89	...	...	...		—	—	—	—	—
95-96—Lake Superior State	CCHA	38	14	36	50	88	...	...	...		—	—	—	—	—
—Baltimore	AHL	7	0	2	2	2	...	...	...		—	—	—	—	—
96-97—Baltimore	AHL	51	4	9	13	92	...	...	...		3	0	0	0	4
97-98—Detroit	IHL	79	13	21	34	89	...	...	...		23	1	9	10	67
98-99—Detroit	IHL	66	15	28	43	130	...	...	...		11	2	7	9	49
99-00—Michigan	IHL	55	2	10	12	55	...	...	...		—	—	—	—	—
—Dallas	NHL	4	0	0	0	0	1	0	0		—	—	—	—	—
NHL Totals (1 year)		4	0	0	0	0	1	0	0						

ALFREDSSON, DANIEL — RW — SENATORS

PERSONAL: Born December 11, 1972, in Partille, Sweden. ... 5-11/195. ... Shoots right.

TRANSACTIONS/CAREER NOTES: Selected by Ottawa Senators in sixth round (fifth Senators pick, 133rd overall) of NHL entry draft (June 29, 1994). ... Strained abdominal muscle (January 29, 1997); missed six games. ... Injured right ankle (November 3, 1997); missed eight games. ... Fractured right fibula (December 11, 1997); missed 13 games. ... Tore medial collateral ligament in left knee (September 16, 1998); missed first nine games of season. ... Injured right eye (November 12, 1998); missed four games. ... Suffered from the flu (December 30, 1998); missed one game. ... Sprained medial collateral ligament in left knee (January 26, 1999); missed five games. ... Strained abdominal muscle (March 17, 1999); missed five games. ... Tore medial collateral ligament in right knee (October 21, 1999); missed 20 games. ... Sprained left knee (February 15, 2000); missed five games. ... Bruised left foot (March 31, 2000); missed one game.

HONORS: Played in NHL All-Star Game (1996-1998). ... Won Calder Memorial Trophy (1995-96). ... Named to NHL All-Rookie team (1995-96).

MISCELLANEOUS: Captain of Ottawa Senators (1999-2000). ... Scored on a penalty shot (vs. Scott Langkow, March 4, 2000). ... Failed to score on a penalty shot (vs. Martin Biron, January 8, 2000).

STATISTICAL PLATEAUS: Three-goal games: 1995-96 (1).

Season Team	League	REGULAR SEASON									PLAYOFFS				
		Gms.	G	A	Pts.	PIM	+/-	PP	SH		Gms.	G	A	Pts.	PIM
91-92—Molndal Hockey	Sweden Dv. 2	32	12	8	20	43	...	...	...		—	—	—	—	—
92-93—Vastra Frolunda	Sweden	20	1	5	6	8	...	...	...		—	—	—	—	—
93-94—Vastra Frolunda	Sweden	39	20	10	30	18	...	...	...		4	1	1	2	...
94-95—Vastra Frolunda	Sweden	22	7	11	18	22	...	...	...		—	—	—	—	—
95-96—Ottawa	NHL	82	26	35	61	28	-18	8	2		—	—	—	—	—
96-97—Ottawa	NHL	76	24	47	71	30	5	11	1		7	5	2	7	6
97-98—Ottawa	NHL	55	17	28	45	18	7	7	0		11	7	2	9	20
—Swedish Oly. team	Int'l	4	2	3	5	2	...	...	...		—	—	—	—	—
98-99—Ottawa	NHL	58	11	22	33	14	8	3	0		4	1	2	3	4
99-00—Ottawa	NHL	57	21	38	59	28	11	4	2		6	1	3	4	2
NHL Totals (5 years)		328	99	170	269	118	13	33	5		28	14	9	23	32

ALLEN, BRYAN — D — CANUCKS

PERSONAL: Born August 21, 1980, in Kingston, Ont. ... 6-4/210. ... Shoots left.

TRANSACTIONS/CAREER NOTES: Selected by Vancouver Canucks in first round (first Canucks pick, fourth overall) of NHL entry draft (June 27, 1998). ... Injured knee (September 15, 1999); missed first 57 games of season.

HONORS: Named to OHL All-Star first team (1998-99).

Season Team	League	REGULAR SEASON									PLAYOFFS				
		Gms.	G	A	Pts.	PIM	+/-	PP	SH		Gms.	G	A	Pts.	PIM
95-96—Ernestown..................	Jr. C	36	1	16	17	71	...	...	...		—	—	—	—	—
96-97—Oshawa.....................	OHL	60	2	4	6	76	...	...	...		18	1	3	4	26
97-98—Oshawa.....................	OHL	48	6	13	19	126	...	...	...		5	0	5	5	18
98-99—Oshawa.....................	OHL	37	7	15	22	77	...	...	...		17	0	3	3	30
99-00—Syracuse	AHL	9	1	1	2	11	...	...	...		2	0	0	0	2
—Oshawa	OHL	3	0	2	2	12	...	...	...		3	0	0	0	13

ALLISON, JAMIE — D — BLACKHAWKS

PERSONAL: Born May 13, 1975, in Lindsay, Ont. ... 6-1/195. ... Shoots left.

TRANSACTIONS/CAREER NOTES: Selected by Calgary Flames in second round (second Flames pick, 44th overall) of NHL entry draft (June 26, 1993). ... Suffered concussion (December 20, 1996); missed three games. ... Fractured thumb (January 9, 1998); missed 11 games. ... Suffered concussion (March 28, 1998); missed 10 games. ... Traded by Flames with C/LW Marty McInnis and RW Erik Andersson to Chicago Blackhawks for C Jeff Shantz and C/LW Steve Dubinsky (October 27, 1998). ... Sprained wrist (November 17, 1998); missed 23 games. ... Strained groin (March 31, 1999); missed three games. ... Strained groin (December 26, 1999); missed four games. ... Injured muscle in rib cage (February 23, 2000); missed eight games. ... Suffered stiff neck (March 26, 2000); missed one game.

Season Team	League	REGULAR SEASON									PLAYOFFS				
		Gms.	G	A	Pts.	PIM	+/-	PP	SH		Gms.	G	A	Pts.	PIM
90-91—Waterloo Jr. B.............	OHA	45	3	8	11	91	...	...	...		—	—	—	—	—
91-92—Windsor.....................	OHL	59	4	8	12	52	...	...	...		4	1	1	2	2
92-93—Det. Jr. Red Wings......	OHL	61	0	13	13	64	...	...	...		15	2	5	7	23
93-94—Det. Jr. Red Wings......	OHL	40	2	22	24	69	...	...	...		17	2	9	11	35
94-95—Det. Jr. Red Wings......	OHL	50	1	14	15	119	...	...	...		18	2	7	9	35
—Calgary	NHL	1	0	0	0	0	0	0	0		—	—	—	—	—
95-96—Saint John	AHL	71	3	16	19	223	...	...	...		14	0	2	2	16
96-97—Saint John	AHL	46	3	6	9	139	...	...	...		5	0	1	1	4
—Calgary	NHL	20	0	0	0	35	-4	0	0		—	—	—	—	—
97-98—Saint John	AHL	16	0	5	5	49	...	...	...		—	—	—	—	—
—Calgary	NHL	43	3	8	11	104	3	0	0		—	—	—	—	—

Season Team	League	REGULAR SEASON								PLAYOFFS				
		Gms.	G	A	Pts.	PIM	+/-	PP	SH	Gms.	G	A	Pts.	PIM
98-99—Saint John	AHL	5	0	0	0	23	...			—	—	—	—	—
—Chicago	NHL	39	2	2	4	62	0	0	0	—	—	—	—	—
—Indianapolis	IHL	3	1	0	1	10	...			—	—	—	—	—
99-00—Chicago	NHL	59	1	3	4	102	-5	0	0	—	—	—	—	—
NHL Totals (5 years)		162	6	13	19	303	-6	0	0	—	—	—	—	—

ALLISON, JASON   C   BRUINS

PERSONAL: Born May 29, 1975, in North York, Ont. ... 6-4/205. ... Shoots right.

TRANSACTIONS/CAREER NOTES: Selected by Washington Capitals in first round (second Capitals pick, 17th overall) of NHL entry draft (June 26, 1993). ... Injured ankle (February 15, 1997); missed one game. ... Traded by Capitals with G Jim Carey, C Anson Carter and third-round pick (RW Lee Goren) in 1997 draft to Boston Bruins for C Adam Oates, RW Rick Tocchet and G Bill Ranford (March 1, 1997). ... Injured hip (March 1, 1998); missed one game. ... Injured wrist (October 30, 1999); missed two games. ... Injured wrist (December 23, 1999); missed three games. ... Injured ligaments in left thumb (January 8, 2000) and underwent surgery; missed 15 games. ... Injured wrist (February 12, 2000) and underwent surgery; missed final 25 games of season.

HONORS: Won Can.HL Player of the Year Award (1993-94). ... Won Can.HL Top Scorer Award (1993-94). ... Won Red Tilson Trophy (1993-94). ... Won William Hanley Trophy (1993-94). ... Won Eddie Powers Memorial Trophy (1993-94). ... Named to Can.HL All-Star first team (1993-94). ... Named to OHL All-Star first team (1993-94).

MISCELLANEOUS: Scored on a penalty shot (vs. Ron Tugnutt, March 24, 1999). ... Failed to score on a penalty shot (vs. Dominik Hasek, April 10, 1997).

STATISTICAL PLATEAUS: Three-goal games: 1997-98 (2), 1998-99 (1). Total: 3.

Season Team	League	REGULAR SEASON								PLAYOFFS				
		Gms.	G	A	Pts.	PIM	+/-	PP	SH	Gms.	G	A	Pts.	PIM
91-92—London	OHL	65	11	18	29	15	...	...	...	7	0	0	0	0
92-93—London	OHL	66	42	76	118	50	...	...	...	12	7	13	20	8
93-94—London	OHL	56	55	87	*142	68	...	...	...	5	2	13	15	13
—Washington	NHL	2	0	1	1	0	1	0	0	—	—	—	—	—
—Portland	AHL	6	2	1	3	0	...	...	...	—	—	—	—	—
94-95—London	OHL	15	15	21	36	43	...	...	...	—	—	—	—	—
—Washington	NHL	12	2	1	3	6	-3	2	0	—	—	—	—	—
—Portland	AHL	8	5	4	9	2	...	...	...	7	3	8	11	2
95-96—Washington	NHL	19	0	3	3	2	-3	0	0	—	—	—	—	—
—Portland	AHL	57	28	41	69	42	...	...	...	6	1	6	7	9
96-97—Washington	NHL	53	5	17	22	25	-3	1	0	—	—	—	—	—
—Boston	NHL	19	3	9	12	9	-3	1	0	—	—	—	—	—
97-98—Boston	NHL	81	33	50	83	60	33	5	0	6	2	6	8	4
98-99—Boston	NHL	82	23	53	76	68	5	5	1	12	2	9	11	6
99-00—Boston	NHL	37	10	18	28	20	5	3	0	—	—	—	—	—
NHL Totals (7 years)		305	76	152	228	190	32	17	1	18	4	15	19	10

AMONTE, TONY   RW   BLACKHAWKS

PERSONAL: Born August 2, 1970, in Hingham, Mass. ... 6-0/190. ... Shoots left. ... Full Name: Anthony Lewis Amonte. ... Name pronounced ah-MAHN-tee.

HIGH SCHOOL: Thayer Academy (Braintree, Mass.).

COLLEGE: Boston University.

TRANSACTIONS/CAREER NOTES: Selected by New York Rangers in fourth round (third Rangers pick, 68th overall) of NHL entry draft (June 11, 1988). ... Separated shoulder (December 29, 1990). ... Traded by Rangers with rights to LW Matt Oates to Chicago Blackhawks for LW Stephane Matteau and RW Brian Noonan (March 21, 1994). ... Pulled groin (1993-94 season); missed three games. ... Played in Europe during 1994-95 NHL lockout.

HONORS: Named to Hockey East All-Rookie team (1989-90). ... Named to NCAA All-Tournament team (1990-91). ... Named to Hockey East All-Star second team (1990-91). ... Named NHL Rookie of the Year by THE SPORTING NEWS (1991-92). ... Named to NHL All-Rookie team (1991-92). ... Played in NHL All-Star Game (1997-2000).

MISCELLANEOUS: Failed to score on a penalty shot (vs. Kelly Hrudey, January 27, 1994; vs. Guy Hebert, February 1, 1998).

STATISTICAL PLATEAUS: Three-goal games: 1991-92 (1), 1995-96 (1), 1996-97 (2), 1998-99 (2), 1999-00 (1). Total: 7.

Season Team	League	REGULAR SEASON								PLAYOFFS				
		Gms.	G	A	Pts.	PIM	+/-	PP	SH	Gms.	G	A	Pts.	PIM
86-87—Thayer Academy	Mass. H.S.	25	25	32	57	...	...	...	...	—	—	—	—	—
87-88—Thayer Academy	Mass. H.S.	28	30	38	68	...	...	...	...	—	—	—	—	—
88-89—Team USA Juniors	Int'l	7	1	3	4	...	...	...	...	—	—	—	—	—
—Thayer Academy	Mass. H.S.	25	35	38	73	...	...	...	...	—	—	—	—	—
89-90—Boston University	Hockey East	41	25	33	58	52	...	...	...	—	—	—	—	—
90-91—Boston University	Hockey East	38	31	37	68	82	...	...	...	—	—	—	—	—
—New York Rangers	NHL	—	—	—	—	—				2	0	2	2	2
91-92—New York Rangers	NHL	79	35	34	69	55	12	9	0	13	3	6	9	2
92-93—New York Rangers	NHL	83	33	43	76	49	0	13	0	—	—	—	—	—
93-94—New York Rangers	NHL	72	16	22	38	31	5	3	0	—	—	—	—	—
—Chicago	NHL	7	1	3	4	6	-5	1	0	6	4	2	6	4
94-95—Fassa	Italy	14	22	16	38	10	...	...	...	—	—	—	—	—
—Chicago	NHL	48	15	20	35	41	7	6	1	16	3	3	6	10
95-96—Chicago	NHL	81	31	32	63	62	10	5	4	7	2	4	6	6
96-97—Chicago	NHL	81	41	36	77	64	35	9	2	6	4	2	6	8
97-98—Chicago	NHL	82	31	42	73	66	21	7	3	—	—	—	—	—
—U.S. Olympic team	Int'l	4	0	1	1	4	...	...	...	—	—	—	—	—
98-99—Chicago	NHL	82	44	31	75	60	0	14	3	—	—	—	—	—
99-00—Chicago	NHL	82	43	41	84	48	10	11	5	—	—	—	—	—
NHL Totals (10 years)		697	290	304	594	482	95	78	18	50	16	19	35	32

A

PERSONAL: Born May 10, 1966, in Malmo, Sweden. ... 5-11/184. ... Shoots left. ... Full Name: Bo Mikael Andersson. ... Brother of Niklas Andersson, left winger, New York Islanders. ... Name pronounced mih-KEHL AN-duhr-suhn.

TRANSACTIONS/CAREER NOTES: Selected by Buffalo Sabres in first round (first Sabres pick, 18th overall) of NHL entry draft (June 9, 1984). ... Sprained ankle (March 3, 1987); missed three weeks. ... Twisted ankle (March 1988). ... Sprained neck and shoulder (December 1988). ... Selected by Hartford Whalers in 1989 NHL waiver draft (October 2, 1989). ... Bruised left knee (December 13, 1989). ... Reinjured knee (February 9, 1990). ... Pulled right hamstring (March 8, 1990). ... Reinjured hamstring (March 17, 1990). ... Reinjured hamstring (April 1990). ... Suffered from the flu (October 4, 1990); missed two games. ... Pulled groin (January 1991). ... Injured toe (October 26, 1991); missed one game. ... Injured groin (December 17, 1991); missed three games. ... Suffered chip fracture to foot (April 12, 1992). ... Signed as free agent by Tampa Bay Lightning (July 8, 1992). ... Suffered back spasms (November 21, 1992); missed four games. ... Injured left rotator cuff (October 27, 1993); missed three games. ... Played in Europe during 1994-95 NHL lockout. ... Injured groin (March 4, 1995); missed four games. ... Sprained ankle (April 8, 1995); missed six games. ... Injured left knee (November 25, 1995); missed two games. ... Injured left knee (December 3, 1995); missed one game. ... Suffered tendinitis in left knee (December 19, 1995); missed two games. ... Pulled hamstring (November 19, 1996); missed two games. ... Bruised shoulder (December 16, 1996); missed six games. ... Injured back (April 5, 1997); missed remainder of season. ... Suffered from the flu (October 29, 1997); missed one game. ... Strained groin (December 21, 1997); missed three games. ... Suffered from the flu (January 31, 1998); missed five games. ... Sprained medial collateral ligament in knee (February 3, 1999); missed 24 games. ... Traded by Lightning with RW Sandy McCarthy to Philadelphia Flyers for LW Colin Forbes and fifth-round pick (G Michal Lanicek) in 1999 draft (March 20, 1999). ... Traded by Flyers with fifth-round pick (F Kristofer Ottoson) in 2000 draft to New York Islanders for LW Gino Odjick (February 15, 2000). ... Injured back (March 18, 2000); missed two games.

MISCELLANEOUS: Scored on a penalty shot (vs. Robb Stauber, December 15, 1992).

STATISTICAL PLATEAUS: Three-goal games: 1992-93 (1).

					REGULAR SEASON						PLAYOFFS			
Season Team	League	Gms.	G	A	Pts.	PIM	+/-	PP	SH	Gms.	G	A	Pts.	PIM
82-83—Vastra Frolunda	Sweden	1	1	0	1	...	...	...	...	—	—	—	—	—
83-84—Vastra Frolunda	Sweden	12	0	2	2	6	...	...	...	—	—	—	—	—
84-85—Vastra Frolunda	Sweden	32	16	11	27	18	...	...	...	6	3	2	5	2
85-86—Rochester	AHL	20	10	4	14	6	...	...	...	—	—	—	—	—
—Buffalo	NHL	32	1	9	10	4	0	0	0	—	—	—	—	—
86-87—Rochester	AHL	42	6	20	26	14	...	...	...	9	1	2	3	2
—Buffalo	NHL	16	0	3	3	0	-2	0	0	—	—	—	—	—
87-88—Rochester	AHL	35	12	24	36	16	...	...	...	—	—	—	—	—
—Buffalo	NHL	37	3	20	23	10	7	0	1	1	1	0	1	0
88-89—Buffalo	NHL	14	0	1	1	4	-1	0	0	—	—	—	—	—
—Rochester	AHL	56	18	33	51	12	...	...	...	—	—	—	—	—
89-90—Hartford	NHL	50	13	24	37	6	0	1	2	5	0	3	3	2
90-91—Hartford	NHL	41	4	7	11	8	0	0	0	—	—	—	—	—
—Springfield	AHL	26	7	22	29	10	...	...	...	18	†10	8	18	12
91-92—Hartford	NHL	74	18	29	47	14	18	1	3	7	0	2	2	6
92-93—Tampa Bay	NHL	77	16	11	27	14	-14	3	2	—	—	—	—	—
93-94—Tampa Bay	NHL	76	13	12	25	23	8	1	1	—	—	—	—	—
94-95—Vastra Frolunda	Sweden	7	1	0	1	31	...	...	...	—	—	—	—	—
—Tampa Bay	NHL	36	4	7	11	4	-3	0	0	—	—	—	—	—
95-96—Tampa Bay	NHL	64	8	11	19	2	0	0	0	6	1	1	2	0
96-97—Tampa Bay	NHL	70	5	14	19	8	1	0	3	—	—	—	—	—
97-98—Tampa Bay	NHL	72	6	11	17	29	-4	0	1	—	—	—	—	—
—Swedish Oly. team	Int'l	4	1	1	2	0	...	...	...	—	—	—	—	—
98-99—Tampa Bay	NHL	40	2	3	5	4	-8	0	0	—	—	—	—	—
—Philadelphia	NHL	7	0	1	1	0	1	0	0	6	0	1	1	2
99-00—Philadelphia	NHL	36	2	3	5	0	-2	0	1	—	—	—	—	—
—New York Islanders	NHL	19	0	3	3	4	-1	0	0	—	—	—	—	—
NHL Totals (15 years)		761	95	169	264	134	0	6	14	25	2	7	9	10

ANDERSSON, NIKLAS   LW   ISLANDERS

PERSONAL: Born May 20, 1971, in Kunglav, Sweden. ... 5-9/175. ... Shoots left. ... Brother of Mikael Andersson, left winger, New York Islanders.

TRANSACTIONS/CAREER NOTES: Selected by Quebec Nordiques in third round (fifth Nordiques pick, 68th overall) of NHL entry draft (June 17, 1989). ... Signed as free agent by New York Islanders (July 15, 1994). ... Sprained shoulder (February 5, 1997); missed two games. ... Suffered sore foot (March 29, 1997); missed two games. ... Signed as free agent by San Jose Sharks (September 10, 1997). ... Signed as free agent by Toronto Maple Leafs (September 4, 1998). ... Traded by Maple Leafs to New York Islanders for F Craig Charron (August 17, 1999). ... Claimed on waivers by Nashville Predators (January 20, 2000). ... Claimed on waivers by Islanders (February 19, 2000).

HONORS: Named to IHL All-Star second team (1999-2000).

STATISTICAL PLATEAUS: Three-goal games: 1995-96 (1).

					REGULAR SEASON						PLAYOFFS			
Season Team	League	Gms.	G	A	Pts.	PIM	+/-	PP	SH	Gms.	G	A	Pts.	PIM
87-88—Frolunda	Sweden	15	5	5	10	...	...	...	...	—	—	—	—	—
88-89—Frolunda	Sweden	30	13	24	37	...	...	...	...	—	—	—	—	—
89-90—Frolunda	Sweden	38	10	21	31	14	...	...	...	—	—	—	—	—
90-91—Frolunda	Sweden	22	6	10	16	16	...	...	...	—	—	—	—	—
91-92—Halifax	AHL	57	8	26	34	41	...	...	...	—	—	—	—	—
92-93—Halifax	AHL	76	32	50	82	42	...	...	...	—	—	—	—	—
—Quebec	NHL	3	0	1	1	2	0	0	0	—	—	—	—	—
93-94—Cornwall	AHL	42	18	34	52	8	...	...	...	—	—	—	—	—
94-95—Denver	IHL	66	22	39	61	28	...	...	...	15	8	13	21	10
95-96—Utah	IHL	30	13	22	35	25	...	...	...	—	—	—	—	—
—New York Islanders	NHL	47	14	12	26	12	-3	3	2	—	—	—	—	—
96-97—New York Islanders	NHL	74	12	31	43	57	4	1	1	—	—	—	—	—

Season Team	League	REGULAR SEASON								PLAYOFFS				
		Gms.	G	A	Pts.	PIM	+/-	PP	SH	Gms.	G	A	Pts.	PIM
97-98—Kentucky	AHL	37	10	28	38	54	...	...	...	—	—	—	—	—
—San Jose	NHL	5	0	0	0	2	-1	0	0	—	—	—	—	—
—Utah	IHL	21	6	20	26	24	...	...	...	4	3	1	4	4
98-99—Chicago	IHL	65	17	47	64	49	...	...	...	10	2	2	4	10
99-00—Chicago	IHL	52	20	21	41	59	...	...	...	9	6	1	7	4
—New York Islanders	NHL	17	3	7	10	8	-3	1	0	—	—	—	—	—
—Nashville	NHL	7	0	1	1	0	0	0	0	—	—	—	—	—
NHL Totals (5 years)		153	29	52	81	81	-3	5	3					

ANDERSSON-JUNKKA, JONAS D BLUE JACKETS

PERSONAL: Born May 4, 1975, in Kiruna, Sweden. ... 6-2/170. ... Shoots right.
TRANSACTIONS/CAREER NOTES: Selected by Pittsburgh Penguins in fourth round (fourth Penguins pick, 104th overall) of NHL entry draft (June 26, 1993). ... Selected by Columbus Blue Jackets in NHL expansion draft (June 23, 2000).

Season Team	League	REGULAR SEASON								PLAYOFFS				
		Gms.	G	A	Pts.	PIM	+/-	PP	SH	Gms.	G	A	Pts.	PIM
92-93—Kiruna	Sweden Dv. 2	30	3	7	10	32	...	...	...	—	—	—	—	—
93-94—Kiruna	Sweden Dv. 2	32	6	10	16	84	...	...	...	—	—	—	—	—
94-95—Vastra Frolunda	Sweden	19	0	2	2	2	...	...	...	—	—	—	—	—
95-96—Vastra Frolunda	Sweden	31	3	1	4	20	...	...	...	13	1	0	1	6
96-97—MoDo Ornskoldsvik	Sweden	12	1	3	4	10	...	...	...	—	—	—	—	—
97-98—MoDo Ornskoldsvik	Sweden	35	5	5	10	12	...	...	...	1	0	0	0	0
98-99—HPK Hameenlinna	Finland	50	5	9	14	36	...	...	...	8	3	1	4	8
99-00—HPK Hameenlinna	Finland	54	13	18	31	72	...	...	...	8	1	4	5	20

ANDREYCHUK, DAVE LW SABRES

PERSONAL: Born September 29, 1963, in Hamilton, Ont. ... 6-4/220. ... Shoots right. ... Full Name: David Andreychuk. ... Name pronounced AN-druh-chuhk.
TRANSACTIONS/CAREER NOTES: Selected by Buffalo Sabres as underage junior in first round (third Sabres pick, 16th overall) of NHL entry draft (June 9, 1982). ... Sprained knee (March 1983). ... Fractured collarbone (March 1985). ... Twisted knee (September 1985). ... Injured right knee (September 1986). ... Strained left knee ligaments (November 27, 1988). ... Fractured left thumb (February 18, 1990). ... Suspended two off-days and fined $500 by NHL for cross-checking incident (November 16, 1992). ... Traded by Sabres with G Daren Puppa and first-round pick (D Kenny Jonsson) in 1993 draft to Toronto Maple Leafs for G Grant Fuhr and fifth-round pick (D Kevin Popp) in 1995 draft (February 2, 1993). ... Injured knee (December 27, 1993); missed one game. ... Separated shoulder (December 2, 1995); missed five games. ... Suffered from the flu (December 27, 1995); missed one game. ... Underwent thumb surgery (January 15, 1996); missed two games. ... Traded by Maple Leafs to New Jersey Devils for second-round pick (D Marek Posmyk) in 1996 draft and third-round pick (traded back to New Jersey) in 1999 draft (March 13, 1996). ... Bruised left foot (October 23, 1997); missed six games. ... Bruised sternum (November 7, 1998); missed six games. ... Fractured right ankle (January 5, 1999); missed 21 games. ... Signed as free agent by Boston Bruins (July 28, 1999). ... Injured knee (January 11, 2000); missed two games. ... Traded by Bruins with D Ray Bourque to Colorado Avalanche for LW Brian Rolston, D Martin Grenier, C Samual Pahlsson and first-round pick (LW Martin Samuelsson) in 2000 draft (March 6, 2000). ... Signed as free agent by Sabres (July 13, 2000).
HONORS: Played in NHL All-Star Game (1990 and 1994). ... Named to THE SPORTING NEWS All-Star second team (1993-94).
MISCELLANEOUS: Failed to score on a penalty shot (vs. Clint Malarchuk, November 22, 1986; vs. Darcy Wakaluk, February 7, 1992; vs. Tim Cheveldae, April 8, 1995).
STATISTICAL PLATEAUS: Three-goal games: 1987-88 (3), 1988-89 (1), 1989-90 (1), 1991-92 (1), 1992-93 (1). Total: 7. ... Four-goal games: 1991-92 (1), 1992-93 (1), 1999-00 (1). Total: 3. ... Five-goal games: 1985-86 (1). ... Total hat tricks: 11.

Season Team	League	REGULAR SEASON								PLAYOFFS				
		Gms.	G	A	Pts.	PIM	+/-	PP	SH	Gms.	G	A	Pts.	PIM
80-81—Oshawa	OMJHL	67	22	22	44	80	...	...	...	10	3	2	5	20
81-82—Oshawa	OHL	67	58	43	101	71	...	...	...	3	1	4	5	16
82-83—Oshawa	OHL	14	8	24	32	6	...	...	...	—	—	—	—	—
—Buffalo	NHL	43	14	23	37	16	6	3	0	4	1	0	1	4
83-84—Buffalo	NHL	78	38	42	80	42	20	10	0	2	0	1	1	2
84-85—Buffalo	NHL	64	31	30	61	54	-4	14	0	5	4	2	6	4
85-86—Buffalo	NHL	80	36	51	87	61	3	12	0	—	—	—	—	—
86-87—Buffalo	NHL	77	25	48	73	46	2	13	0	—	—	—	—	—
87-88—Buffalo	NHL	80	30	48	78	112	1	15	0	6	2	4	6	0
88-89—Buffalo	NHL	56	28	24	52	40	0	7	0	5	0	3	3	0
89-90—Buffalo	NHL	73	40	42	82	42	6	18	0	6	2	5	7	2
90-91—Buffalo	NHL	80	36	33	69	32	11	13	0	6	2	2	4	8
91-92—Buffalo	NHL	80	41	50	91	71	-9	*28	0	7	1	3	4	12
92-93—Buffalo	NHL	52	29	32	61	48	-8	*20	0	—	—	—	—	—
—Toronto	NHL	31	25	13	38	8	12	*12	0	21	12	7	19	35
93-94—Toronto	NHL	83	53	46	99	98	22	21	5	18	5	5	10	16
94-95—Toronto	NHL	48	22	16	38	34	-7	8	0	7	3	2	5	25
95-96—Toronto	NHL	61	20	24	44	54	-11	12	2	—	—	—	—	—
—New Jersey	NHL	15	8	5	13	10	2	2	0	—	—	—	—	—
96-97—New Jersey	NHL	82	27	34	61	48	38	4	1	1	0	0	0	0
97-98—New Jersey	NHL	75	14	34	48	26	19	4	0	6	1	0	1	4
98-99—New Jersey	NHL	52	15	13	28	20	1	4	0	4	2	0	2	4
99-00—Boston	NHL	63	19	14	33	28	-11	7	0	—	—	—	—	—
—Colorado	NHL	14	1	2	3	2	-9	1	0	17	3	2	5	18
NHL Totals (18 years)		1287	552	624	1176	892	84	228	8	115	38	36	74	134

ANDRUSAK, GREG   D

PERSONAL: Born November 14, 1969, in Cranbrook, B.C. ... 6-1/200. ... Shoots right. ... Full Name: Greg Frederick Andrusak. ... Name pronounced AN-druh-sak.
COLLEGE: Minnesota-Duluth.
TRANSACTIONS/CAREER NOTES: Selected by Pittsburgh Penguins in fifth round (fifth Penguins pick, 88th overall) of NHL entry draft (June 11, 1988). ... Separated shoulder (March 15, 1995); missed eight games. ... Signed as free agent by Toronto Maple Leafs (July 9, 1999).
HONORS: Named to WCHA All-Star first team (1991-92).

Season Team	League	REGULAR SEASON								PLAYOFFS				
		Gms.	G	A	Pts.	PIM	+/-	PP	SH	Gms.	G	A	Pts.	PIM
86-87—Kelowna	BCJHL	45	10	24	34	95	...	...	...	—	—	—	—	—
87-88—Minnesota-Duluth	WCHA	37	4	5	9	42	...	...	...	—	—	—	—	—
88-89—Minnesota-Duluth	WCHA	35	4	8	12	74	...	...	...	—	—	—	—	—
—Canadian nat'l team	Int'l	2	0	0	0	0	...	...	...	—	—	—	—	—
89-90—Minnesota-Duluth	WCHA	35	5	29	34	74	...	...	...	—	—	—	—	—
90-91—Canadian nat'l team	Int'l	53	4	11	15	34	...	...	...	—	—	—	—	—
91-92—Minnesota-Duluth	WCHA	36	7	27	34	125	...	...	...	—	—	—	—	—
92-93—Cleveland	IHL	55	3	22	25	78	...	...	...	2	0	0	0	2
—Muskegon	Col.HL	2	0	3	3	7	...	...	...	—	—	—	—	—
93-94—Cleveland	IHL	69	13	26	39	109	...	...	...	—	—	—	—	—
—Pittsburgh	NHL	3	0	0	0	2	-1	0	0	—	—	—	—	—
94-95—Cleveland	IHL	8	0	8	8	14	...	...	...	—	—	—	—	—
—Detroit	IHL	37	5	26	31	50	...	...	...	—	—	—	—	—
—Pittsburgh	NHL	7	0	4	4	6	-1	0	0	—	—	—	—	—
95-96—Detroit	IHL	58	6	30	36	128	...	...	...	—	—	—	—	—
—Pittsburgh	NHL	2	0	0	0	0	-1	0	0	—	—	—	—	—
—Minnesota	IHL	5	0	4	4	8	...	...	...	—	—	—	—	—
98-99—Eisbaren Berlin	Germany	19	2	5	7	12	...	...	...	—	—	—	—	—
—Houston	IHL	3	0	1	1	2	...	...	...	6	1	4	5	16
—Pittsburgh	NHL	7	0	1	1	4	4	0	0	12	1	0	1	6
99-00—Chicago	IHL	54	2	23	25	50	...	...	...	11	1	5	6	20
—Toronto	NHL	9	0	1	1	4	1	0	0	3	0	0	0	2
NHL Totals (5 years)		28	0	6	6	16	2	0	0	15	1	0	1	8

ANTROPOV, NIKOLAI   C   MAPLE LEAFS

PERSONAL: Born February 18, 1980, in Vost, U.S.S.R. ... 6-5/203. ... Shoots left.
TRANSACTIONS/CAREER NOTES: Selected by Toronto Maple Leafs in first round (first Maple Leafs pick, 10th overall) of NHL entry draft (June 27, 1998). ... Suffered injury (November 27, 1999); missed seven games. ... Suffered injury (January 5, 2000); missed two games. ... Suffered injury (March 29, 2000); missed one game.
STATISTICAL PLATEAUS: Three-goal games: 1999-00 (1).

Season Team	League	REGULAR SEASON								PLAYOFFS				
		Gms.	G	A	Pts.	PIM	+/-	PP	SH	Gms.	G	A	Pts.	PIM
95-96—Torpedo Ust-Kam.	CIS Jr.	20	18	20	38	30	...	...	...	—	—	—	—	—
96-97—Torpedo Ust-Kam.	Rus. Div. II	8	2	1	3	6	...	...	...	—	—	—	—	—
97-98—Torpedo Ust-Kam.	Rus. Div. II	42	15	24	39	62	...	...	...	—	—	—	—	—
98-99—Dynamo Moscow	Russian	30	5	9	14	30	...	...	...	11	0	1	1	4
99-00—St. John's	AHL	2	0	0	0	4	...	...	...	—	—	—	—	—
—Toronto	NHL	66	12	18	30	41	14	0	0	3	0	0	0	4
NHL Totals (1 year)		66	12	18	30	41	14	0	0	3	0	0	0	4

ARMSTRONG, DEREK   C   RANGERS

PERSONAL: Born April 23, 1973, in Ottawa. ... 6-0/193. ... Shoots right.
HIGH SCHOOL: Lo-Ellen Park Secondary School (Sudbury, Ont.).
TRANSACTIONS/CAREER NOTES: Selected by New York Islanders in sixth round (fifth Islanders pick, 128th overall) of NHL entry draft (June 20, 1992). ... Suffered food poisoning (January 28, 1997); missed one game. ... Signed as free agent by Ottawa Senators (July 10, 1997). ... Signed as free agent by New York Rangers (July 20, 1998).
HONORS: Won Jack Butterfield Trophy (1999-2000). ... Named to AHL All-Star second team (1999-2000).

Season Team	League	REGULAR SEASON								PLAYOFFS				
		Gms.	G	A	Pts.	PIM	+/-	PP	SH	Gms.	G	A	Pts.	PIM
89-90—Hawkesbury	COJHL	48	8	10	18	30	...	...	...	—	—	—	—	—
90-91—Hawkesbury	COJHL	54	27	45	72	49	...	...	...	—	—	—	—	—
—Sudbury	OHL	2	0	2	2	0	...	...	...	—	—	—	—	—
91-92—Sudbury	OHL	66	31	54	85	22	...	...	...	9	2	2	4	2
92-93—Sudbury	OHL	66	44	62	106	56	...	...	...	14	9	10	19	26
93-94—Salt Lake City	IHL	76	23	35	58	61	...	...	...	—	—	—	—	—
94-95—Denver	IHL	59	13	18	31	65	...	...	...	6	0	2	2	0
95-96—Worcester	AHL	51	11	15	26	33	...	...	...	4	2	1	3	0
—New York Islanders	NHL	19	1	3	4	14	-6	0	0	—	—	—	—	—
96-97—New York Islanders	NHL	50	6	7	13	33	-8	0	0	—	—	—	—	—
—Utah	IHL	17	4	8	12	10	...	...	...	6	0	4	4	4
97-98—Detroit	IHL	10	0	1	1	2	...	...	...	—	—	—	—	—
—Hartford	AHL	54	16	30	46	40	...	...	...	15	2	6	8	22
—Ottawa	NHL	9	2	0	2	9	1	0	0	—	—	—	—	—
98-99—Hartford	AHL	59	29	51	80	73	...	...	...	7	5	4	9	10
—New York Rangers	NHL	3	0	0	0	0	0	0	0	—	—	—	—	—
99-00—Hartford	AHL	77	28	54	82	101	...	...	...	23	7	16	23	24
—New York Rangers	NHL	1	0	0	0	0	0	0	0	—	—	—	—	—
NHL Totals (5 years)		82	9	10	19	56	-13	0	0					

ARNOTT, JASON C DEVILS

PERSONAL: Born October 11, 1974, in Collingwood, Ont. ... 6-4/225. ... Shoots right. ... Name pronounced AHR-niht.
HIGH SCHOOL: Henry Street (Whitby, Ont.).
TRANSACTIONS/CAREER NOTES: Selected by Edmonton Oilers in first round (first Oilers pick, seventh overall) of NHL entry draft (June 26, 1993). ... Suffered from tonsillitis (November 3, 1993); missed one game. ... Bruised sternum (November 27, 1993); missed one game. ... Sprained back (December 7, 1993); missed one game. ... Underwent appendectomy (December 28, 1993); missed three games. ... Suffered from the flu (February 22, 1995); missed one game. ... Suffered concussion (March 23, 1995); missed two games. ... Strained knee (April 19, 1995); missed two games. ... Suspended one game by NHL for game misconduct penalties (April 22, 1995). ... Suffered concussion and lacerated face (October 8, 1995); missed seven games. ... Sprained knee (February 11, 1996); missed nine games. ... Strained knee (March 19, 1996); missed one game. ... Suffered inner ear infection (April 8, 1996); missed one game. ... Fractured ankle (December 27, 1996); missed seven games. ... Injured ankle (January 22, 1997); missed two games. ... Suffered from the flu (February 12, 1997); missed two games. ... Strained lower back (March 23, 1997); missed four games. ... Separated right shoulder (December 10, 1997); missed five games. ... Reinjured shoulder (January 2, 1998); missed two games. ... Traded by Oilers with D Bryan Muir to New Jersey Devils for RW Bill Guerin and RW Valeri Zelepukin (January 4, 1998). ... Suffered back spasms (March 21, 1998); missed one game. ... Bruised hip (April 8, 1998); missed three games. ... Reinjured hip (April 16, 1998); missed two games. ... Underwent offseason finger surgery; missed first game of 1998-99 season. ... Bruised thigh (December 28, 1998); missed one game. ... Suffered from the flu (January 15, 1999); missed two games ... Bruised foot (January 20, 1999); missed one game ... Bruised hip (March 28, 1999); missed one game. ... Reinjured hip (April 4, 1999); missed two games. ... Suffered mouth injury (October 23, 1999); missed three games. ... Suffered from the flu (February 21, 2000); missed two games. ... Bruised ribs (March 17, 2000); missed one game.
HONORS: Named NHL Rookie of the Year by THE SPORTING NEWS (1993-94). ... Named to NHL All-Rookie team (1993-94). ... Played in NHL All-Star Game (1997).
MISCELLANEOUS: Member of Stanley Cup championship team (2000).
STATISTICAL PLATEAUS: Three-goal games: 1994-95 (1), 1995-96 (1). Total: 2.

Season Team	League	REGULAR SEASON								PLAYOFFS				
		Gms.	G	A	Pts.	PIM	+/-	PP	SH	Gms.	G	A	Pts.	PIM
89-90—Styaner	Jr. C	34	21	31	52	12	...	...	...	—	—	—	—	—
90-91—Lindsay Jr. B	OHA	42	17	44	61	10	...	...	...	—	—	—	—	—
91-92—Oshawa	OHL	57	9	15	24	12	...	...	...	—	—	—	—	—
92-93—Oshawa	OHL	56	41	57	98	74	...	...	...	13	9	9	18	20
93-94—Edmonton	NHL	78	33	35	68	104	1	10	0	—	—	—	—	—
94-95—Edmonton	NHL	42	15	22	37	128	-14	7	0	—	—	—	—	—
95-96—Edmonton	NHL	64	28	31	59	87	-6	8	0	—	—	—	—	—
96-97—Edmonton	NHL	67	19	38	57	92	-21	10	1	12	3	6	9	18
97-98—Edmonton	NHL	35	5	13	18	78	-16	1	0	—	—	—	—	—
—New Jersey	NHL	35	5	10	15	21	-8	3	0	5	0	2	2	0
98-99—New Jersey	NHL	74	27	27	54	79	10	8	0	7	2	2	4	4
99-00—New Jersey	NHL	76	22	34	56	51	22	7	0	23	8	12	20	18
NHL Totals (7 years)		471	154	210	364	640	-32	54	1	47	13	22	35	40

ARONSON, STEVE RW WILD

PERSONAL: Born July 15, 1978, in Minnetonka, Minn. ... 6-1/205. ... Shoots right.
COLLEGE: St. Thomas (N.B.).
TRANSACTIONS/CAREER NOTES: Signed as non-drafted free agent by Minnesota Wild (May 4, 2000).

Season Team	League	REGULAR SEASON								PLAYOFFS				
		Gms.	G	A	Pts.	PIM	+/-	PP	SH	Gms.	G	A	Pts.	PIM
96-97—Univ. of St. Thomas	MIAC	27	11	25	36	44	...	...	...	—	—	—	—	—
97-98—Univ. of St. Thomas	MIAC	28	32	25	57	41	...	...	...	—	—	—	—	—
98-99—Univ. of St. Thomas	MIAC	31	23	37	60	73	...	...	...	—	—	—	—	—
99-00—Univ. of St. Thomas	MIAC	33	38	53	91	72	...	...	...	—	—	—	—	—

ARVEDSON, MAGNUS LW SENATORS

PERSONAL: Born November 25, 1971, in Karlstad, Sweden. ... 6-2/198. ... Shoots left. ... Name pronounced AHR-vihd-suhn.
TRANSACTIONS/CAREER NOTES: Selected by Ottawa Senators in fifth round (fourth Senators pick, 119th overall) of NHL entry draft (June 21, 1997). ... Strained groin (October 17, 1997); missed seven games. ... Strained groin (November 29, 1997); missed three games. ... Suffered concussion (December 16, 1997); missed five games. ... Strained left shoulder (January 11, 1998); missed one game. ... Strained groin (March 20, 1998); missed three games. ... Suffered back spasms (October 20, 1998); missed two games. ... Bruised hip (October 14, 1999); missed one game. ... Injured abdomen (January 20, 2000) and underwent surgery; missed 34 games.
STATISTICAL PLATEAUS: Three-goal games: 1998-99 (1).

Season Team	League	REGULAR SEASON								PLAYOFFS				
		Gms.	G	A	Pts.	PIM	+/-	PP	SH	Gms.	G	A	Pts.	PIM
91-92—Orebro	Sweden Dv. 2	32	12	21	33	30	...	...	...	7	4	4	8	4
92-93—Orebro	Sweden Dv. 2	36	11	18	29	34	...	...	...	6	2	1	3	0
93-94—Farjestad Karlstad	Sweden	16	1	7	8	10	...	...	...	—	—	—	—	—
94-95—Farjestad Karlstad	Sweden	36	1	7	8	45	...	...	...	4	0	0	0	6
95-96—Farjestad Karlstad	Sweden	39	10	14	24	42	...	...	...	8	0	3	3	10
96-97—Farjestad Karlstad	Sweden	48	13	11	24	36	...	...	...	14	4	7	11	8
97-98—Ottawa	NHL	61	11	15	26	36	2	0	1	11	0	1	1	6
98-99—Ottawa	NHL	80	21	26	47	50	33	0	4	3	0	1	1	2
99-00—Ottawa	NHL	47	15	13	28	36	4	1	1	6	0	0	0	6
NHL Totals (3 years)		188	47	54	101	122	39	1	6	20	0	2	2	14

ASHAM, AARON RW/C CANADIENS

PERSONAL: Born April 13, 1978, in Portage-La-Prairie, Man. ... 5-11/195. ... Shoots right.
TRANSACTIONS/CAREER NOTES: Selected by Montreal Canadiens in third round (third Canadiens pick, 71st overall) of NHL entry draft (June 21, 1996). ... Injured back (October 23, 1999); missed one game. ... Suffered from the flu (December 27, 1999); missed one game. ... Strained groin (January 22, 2000); missed 23 games.

Season Team	League	Gms.	G	A	Pts.	PIM	+/-	PP	SH		Gms.	G	A	Pts.	PIM
94-95—Red Deer	WHL	62	11	16	27	126	...	...	...		—	—	—	—	—
95-96—Red Deer	WHL	70	32	45	77	174	...	...	...		10	6	3	9	20
96-97—Red Deer	WHL	67	45	51	96	149	...	...	...		16	12	14	26	36
97-98—Red Deer	WHL	67	43	49	92	153	...	...	...		5	0	2	2	8
—Fredericton	AHL	2	1	1	2	0	...	...	...		2	0	1	1	0
98-99—Fredericton	AHL	60	16	18	34	118	...	...	...		13	8	6	14	11
—Montreal	NHL	7	0	0	0	0	-4	0	0		—	—	—	—	—
99-00—Montreal	NHL	33	4	2	6	24	-7	0	1		—	—	—	—	—
—Quebec	AHL	13	4	5	9	32	...	...	...		2	0	0	0	2
NHL Totals (2 years)		40	4	2	6	24	-11	0	1						

ASTASHENKO, KASPARS   D   LIGHTNING

PERSONAL: Born February 7, 1975, in Riga, U.S.S.R. ... 6-2/183. ... Shoots left. ... Name pronounced KAHS-phar ahs-tah-SHEHN-koh.

TRANSACTIONS/CAREER NOTES: Selected by Tampa Bay Lightning in fifth round (fifth Lightning pick, 127th overall) of NHL entry draft (June 26, 1999). ... Suffered concussion (April 8, 2000); missed final game of season.

Season Team	League	Gms.	G	A	Pts.	PIM	+/-	PP	SH		Gms.	G	A	Pts.	PIM
93-94—Pardaugava Riga	CIS	4	0	0	0	10	...	...	...		—	—	—	—	—
94-95—Pardaugava Riga	CIS	25	0	0	0	24	...	...	...		—	—	—	—	—
95-96—CSKA Moscow	CIS	26	0	1	1	10	...	...	...		—	—	—	—	—
96-97—HC CSKA Moscow	Russian	41	0	0	0	48	...	...	...		2	0	1	1	4
97-98—HC CSKA Moscow	Russian	25	1	3	4	6	...	...	...		—	—	—	—	—
98-99—Cincinnati	IHL	74	3	11	14	166	...	...	...		3	0	2	2	6
—Dayton	ECHL	2	0	1	1	4	...	...	...		—	—	—	—	—
99-00—Detroit	IHL	51	1	10	11	86	...	...	...		—	—	—	—	—
—Long Beach	IHL	14	0	3	3	10	...	...	...		—	—	—	—	—
—Tampa Bay	NHL	8	0	1	1	4	-2	0	0		—	—	—	—	—
NHL Totals (1 year)		8	0	1	1	4	-2	0	0						

ATCHEYNUM, BLAIR   RW   BLACKHAWKS

PERSONAL: Born April 20, 1969, in Estevan, Sask. ... 6-2/198. ... Shoots right. ... Name pronounced ATCH-ih-nuhm.

TRANSACTIONS/CAREER NOTES: Selected by Hartford Whalers in third round (second Whalers pick, 52nd overall) of NHL entry draft (June 17, 1989). ... Suffered concussion (January 12, 1991). ... Selected by Ottawa Senators in NHL expansion draft (June 18, 1992). ... Signed as free agent by St. Louis Blues (August 12, 1997). ... Fractured finger (March 1, 1998); missed 17 games. ... Selected by Nashville Predators in NHL expansion draft (June 26, 1998). ... Tore anterior cruciate knee ligament (November 7, 1998); missed 15 games. ... Traded by Predators to Blues for sixth-round pick (F Zbynek Irgl) in 2000 draft (March 23, 1999). ... Signed as free agent by Chicago Blackhawks (September 30, 1999). ... Suffered sore back (November 27, 1999); missed four games.

HONORS: Won Brad Hornung Trophy (1988-89). ... Named to WHL (East) All-Star first team (1988-89). ... Named to AHL All-Star first team (1996-97).

Season Team	League	Gms.	G	A	Pts.	PIM	+/-	PP	SH		Gms.	G	A	Pts.	PIM
85-86—North Battleford	SJHL	35	25	20	45	50	...	...	...		—	—	—	—	—
—Saskatoon	WHL	19	1	4	5	22	...	...	...		—	—	—	—	—
86-87—Saskatoon	WHL	21	0	4	4	4	...	...	...		—	—	—	—	—
—Swift Current	WHL	5	2	1	3	0	...	...	...		—	—	—	—	—
—Moose Jaw	WHL	12	3	0	3	2	...	...	...		—	—	—	—	—
87-88—Moose Jaw	WHL	60	32	16	48	52	...	...	...		—	—	—	—	—
88-89—Moose Jaw	WHL	71	70	68	138	70	...	...	...		7	2	5	7	13
89-90—Binghamton	AHL	78	20	21	41	45	...	...	...		—	—	—	—	—
90-91—Springfield	AHL	72	25	27	52	42	...	...	...		13	0	6	6	6
91-92—Springfield	AHL	62	16	21	37	64	...	...	...		6	1	1	2	2
92-93—New Haven	AHL	51	16	18	34	47	...	...	...		—	—	—	—	—
—Ottawa	NHL	4	0	1	1	0	-3	0	0		—	—	—	—	—
93-94—Portland	AHL	2	0	0	0	0	...	...	...		—	—	—	—	—
—Springfield	AHL	40	18	22	40	13	...	...	...		6	0	2	2	0
—Columbus	ECHL	16	15	12	27	10	...	...	...		—	—	—	—	—
94-95—Minnesota	IHL	17	4	6	10	7	...	...	...		—	—	—	—	—
—Worcester	AHL	55	17	29	46	26	...	...	...		—	—	—	—	—
95-96—Cape Breton	AHL	79	30	42	72	65	...	...	...		—	—	—	—	—
96-97—Hershey	AHL	77	42	45	87	57	...	...	...		13	6	11	17	6
97-98—St. Louis	NHL	61	11	15	26	10	5	0	1		10	0	0	0	2
98-99—Nashville	NHL	53	8	6	14	16	-10	2	0		—	—	—	—	—
—St. Louis	NHL	12	2	2	4	2	2	0	0		13	1	3	4	6
99-00—Chicago	NHL	47	5	7	12	6	-8	0	0		—	—	—	—	—
NHL Totals (4 years)		177	26	31	57	34	-14	2	1		23	1	3	4	8

AUBIN, JEAN-SEBASTIEN   G   PENGUINS

PERSONAL: Born July 19, 1977, in Montreal. ... 5-11/176. ... Catches right. ... Name pronounced AH-ban.

TRANSACTIONS/CAREER NOTES: Selected by Pittsburgh Penguins in third round (second Penguins pick, 76th overall) of NHL entry draft (July 8, 1995). ... Strained hamstring (April 3, 1999); missed six games. ... Injured shoulder (November 23, 1999); missed two games. ... Sprained ankle (April 3, 2000); missed final three games of season.

MISCELLANEOUS: Holds Pittsburgh Penguins all-time record for goals-against average (2.50). ... Stopped a penalty shot attempt (vs. Teemu Selanne, October 27, 1999). ... Allowed a penalty shot goal (vs. Keith Tkachuk, January 12, 2000; vs. Tim Connolly, March 21, 2000).

Season	Team	League	Gms.	Min	W	L	T	GA	SO	Avg.	Gms.	Min.	W	L	GA	SO	Avg.
				REGULAR SEASON								PLAYOFFS					
94-95	Sherbrooke	QMJHL	27	1287	13	10	1	73	1	3.40	3	185	1	2	11	0	3.57
95-96	Sherbrooke	QMJHL	40	2084	18	14	2	127	0	3.66	4	174	1	3	16	0	5.52
96-97	Sherbrooke	QMJHL	4	249	3	1	0	8	0	1.93	—	—	—	—	—	—	—
	Moncton	QMJHL	23	1311	9	13	0	72	1	3.30	—	—	—	—	—	—	—
	Laval	QMJHL	11	532	2	6	1	41	0	4.62	2	128	0	2	10	0	4.69
97-98	Syracuse	AHL	8	380	2	4	1	26	0	4.11	—	—	—	—	—	—	—
	Dayton	ECHL	21	1177	15	2	‡2	59	1	3.01	3	142	1	1	4	0	1.69
98-99	Kansas City	IHL	13	751	5	7	‡1	41	0	3.28	—	—	—	—	—	—	—
	Pittsburgh	NHL	17	756	4	3	6	28	2	2.22	—	—	—	—	—	—	—
99-00	Wilkes-Barre/Scranton	AHL	11	538	2	8	0	39	0	4.35	—	—	—	—	—	—	—
	Pittsburgh	NHL	51	2789	23	21	3	120	2	2.58	—	—	—	—	—	—	—
NHL Totals (2 years)			68	3545	27	24	9	148	4	2.50							

AUBIN, SERGE — C — BLUE JACKETS

PERSONAL: Born February 15, 1975, in Val d'Or, Que. ... 6-0/190. ... Shoots left. ... Name pronounced AH-ban.
TRANSACTIONS/CAREER NOTES: Selected by Pittsburgh Penguins in seventh round (ninth Penguins pick, 161st overall) of NHL entry draft (June 29, 1994). ... Signed as free agent by Colorado Avalanche (December 18, 1998). ... Signed as free agent by Columbus Blue Jackets (July 11, 2000).
HONORS: Named to AHL All-Star first team (1999-2000).

Season	Team	League	Gms.	G	A	Pts.	PIM	+/-	PP	SH	Gms.	G	A	Pts.	PIM
				REGULAR SEASON								PLAYOFFS			
92-93	Drummondville	QMJHL	65	16	34	50	30	...	...	...	8	0	1	1	16
93-94	Granby	QMJHL	63	42	32	74	80	...	...	...	7	2	3	5	8
94-95	Granby	QMJHL	60	37	73	110	55	...	...	...	11	8	15	23	4
95-96	Cleveland	IHL	2	0	0	0	0	...	...	...	2	0	0	0	0
	Hampton Roads	ECHL	62	24	62	86	74	...	...	...	3	1	4	5	10
96-97	Cleveland	IHL	57	9	16	25	38	...	...	...	2	0	0	0	0
97-98	Syracuse	AHL	55	6	14	20	57	...	...	...	—	—	—	—	—
	Hershey	AHL	5	2	1	3	0	...	...	...	7	1	3	4	6
98-99	Hershey	AHL	64	30	39	69	58	...	...	...	3	0	1	1	2
	Colorado	NHL	1	0	0	0	0	0	0	0	—	—	—	—	—
99-00	Hershey	AHL	58	42	38	80	56	...	...	...	—	—	—	—	—
	Colorado	NHL	15	2	1	3	6	1	0	0	17	0	1	1	6
NHL Totals (2 years)			16	2	1	3	6	1	0	0	17	0	1	1	6

AUCOIN, ADRIAN — D — CANUCKS

PERSONAL: Born July 3, 1973, in Ottawa. ... 6-2/210. ... Shoots right. ... Name pronounced oh-COYN.
COLLEGE: Boston University.
TRANSACTIONS/CAREER NOTES: Selected by Vancouver Canucks in fifth round (seventh Canucks pick, 117th overall) of NHL entry draft (June 20, 1992). ... Sprained shoulder (January 10, 1997); missed six games. ... Strained groin (October 30, 1997); missed five games. ... Reinjured groin (November 12, 1997); missed 10 games. ... Sprained ankle (December 13, 1997); missed seven games. ... Injured groin (December 4, 1999); missed four games. ... Fractured finger (February 9, 2000); missed 20 games.
MISCELLANEOUS: Member of silver-medal-winning Canadian Olympic team (1994).

Season	Team	League	Gms.	G	A	Pts.	PIM	+/-	PP	SH	Gms.	G	A	Pts.	PIM
				REGULAR SEASON								PLAYOFFS			
91-92	Boston University	Hockey East	33	2	10	12	62	...	...	...	—	—	—	—	—
92-93	Canadian nat'l team	Int'l	42	8	10	18	71	...	...	...	—	—	—	—	—
93-94	Canadian nat'l team	Int'l	59	5	12	17	80	...	...	...	—	—	—	—	—
	Can. Olympic team	Int'l	4	0	0	0	2	...	...	...	—	—	—	—	—
	Hamilton	AHL	13	1	2	3	19	...	...	...	4	0	2	2	6
94-95	Syracuse	AHL	71	13	18	31	52	...	...	...	—	—	—	—	—
	Vancouver	NHL	1	1	0	1	0	1	0	0	4	1	0	1	0
95-96	Syracuse	AHL	29	5	13	18	47	...	...	...	—	—	—	—	—
	Vancouver	NHL	49	4	14	18	34	8	2	0	6	0	0	0	2
96-97	Vancouver	NHL	70	5	16	21	63	0	1	0	—	—	—	—	—
97-98	Vancouver	NHL	35	3	3	6	21	-4	1	0	—	—	—	—	—
98-99	Vancouver	NHL	82	23	11	34	77	-14	18	2	—	—	—	—	—
99-00	Vancouver	NHL	57	10	14	24	30	7	4	0	—	—	—	—	—
NHL Totals (6 years)			294	46	58	104	225	-2	26	2	10	1	0	1	2

AUDETTE, DONALD — RW — THRASHERS

PERSONAL: Born September 23, 1969, in Laval, Que. ... 5-8/184. ... Shoots right. ... Name pronounced aw-DEHT.
TRANSACTIONS/CAREER NOTES: Selected by Buffalo Sabres in ninth round (eighth Sabres pick, 183rd overall) of NHL entry draft (June 17, 1989). ... Broke left hand (February 11, 1990); missed seven games. ... Bruised thigh (September 1990). ... Bruised thigh (October 1990); missed five games. ... Tore left knee ligaments (November 16, 1990). ... Underwent surgery to left knee (December 10, 1990). ... Sprained ankle (December 14, 1991); missed eight games. ... Injured knee (March 31, 1992). ... Underwent knee surgery prior to 1992-93 season; missed first 22 games of season. ... Tore knee cartilage (September 23, 1995); missed 11 games. ... Broke tip of right thumb (November 8, 1995); missed two games. ... Injured right knee (December 1, 1995); missed seven games. ... Underwent right knee surgery (January 26, 1996); missed remainder of season. ... Strained groin (October 26, 1996); missed five games. ... Suffered concussion (October 22, 1997); missed seven games. ... Missed first 25 games of 1998-99 season due to contract dispute. ... Traded by Sabres to Los Angeles Kings for second-round pick (RW Milan Bartovic) in 1999 draft (December 18, 1998). ... Suffered back spasms (April 8, 1999); missed one game. ... Suffered from the flu (April 18, 1999); missed one game. ... Sprained left ankle (January 6, 2000); missed 15 games. ... Traded by Kings with D Frantisek Kaberle to Atlanta Thrashers for RW Kelly Buchberger and RW Nelson Emerson (March 13, 2000).

HONORS: Won Guy Lafleur Trophy (1988-89). ... Named to QMJHL All-Star first team (1988-89). ... Won Dudley (Red) Garrett Memorial Trophy (1989-90). ... Named to AHL All-Star first team (1989-90).

MISCELLANEOUS: Failed to score on a penalty shot (vs. Felix Potvin, November 21, 1996).

STATISTICAL PLATEAUS: Three-goal games: 1994-95 (1), 1995-96 (1). Total: 2.

Season Team	League	REGULAR SEASON								PLAYOFFS				
		Gms.	G	A	Pts.	PIM	+/-	PP	SH	Gms.	G	A	Pts.	PIM
86-87—Laval	QMJHL	66	17	22	39	36	...	...	...	14	2	6	8	10
87-88—Laval	QMJHL	63	48	61	109	56	...	...	...	14	7	12	19	20
88-89—Laval	QMJHL	70	76	85	161	123	...	...	...	17	*17	12	29	43
89-90—Rochester	AHL	70	42	46	88	78	...	...	...	15	9	8	17	29
—Buffalo	NHL	0	0	0	0	0	0	0	0	2	0	0	0	0
90-91—Rochester	AHL	5	4	0	4	2	...	...	...	—	—	—	—	—
—Buffalo	NHL	8	4	3	7	4	-1	2	0	—	—	—	—	—
91-92—Buffalo	NHL	63	31	17	48	75	-1	5	0	—	—	—	—	—
92-93—Buffalo	NHL	44	12	7	19	51	-8	2	0	8	2	2	4	6
—Rochester	AHL	6	8	4	12	10	...	...	...	—	—	—	—	—
93-94—Buffalo	NHL	77	29	30	59	41	2	16	1	7	0	1	1	6
94-95—Buffalo	NHL	46	24	13	37	27	-3	13	0	5	1	1	2	4
95-96—Buffalo	NHL	23	12	13	25	18	0	8	0	—	—	—	—	—
96-97—Buffalo	NHL	73	28	22	50	48	-6	8	0	11	4	5	9	6
97-98—Buffalo	NHL	75	24	20	44	59	10	10	0	15	5	8	13	10
98-99—Los Angeles	NHL	49	18	18	36	51	7	6	0	—	—	—	—	—
99-00—Los Angeles	NHL	49	12	20	32	45	6	1	0	—	—	—	—	—
—Atlanta	NHL	14	7	4	11	12	-4	0	1	—	—	—	—	—
NHL Totals (11 years)		521	201	167	368	431	2	71	2	48	12	17	29	32

AXELSSON, P.J. RW BRUINS

PERSONAL: Born February 26, 1975, in Kungalv, Sweden. ... 6-1/174. ... Shoots left. ... Full Name: Per-Johan Axelsson. ... Name pronounced AK-sihl-suhn.

TRANSACTIONS/CAREER NOTES: Selected by Boston Bruins in seventh round (seventh Bruins pick, 177th overall) of NHL entry draft (June 8, 1995). ... Suffered concussion (October 28, 1998); missed one game. ... Suffered concussion (November 3, 1998); missed three games. ... Suffered from the flu (April 17, 1999); missed one game. ... Suffered from charleyhorse (October 23, 1999); missed one game.

Season Team	League	REGULAR SEASON								PLAYOFFS				
		Gms.	G	A	Pts.	PIM	+/-	PP	SH	Gms.	G	A	Pts.	PIM
93-94—Frolunda	Sweden	11	0	0	0	4	...	...	...	4	0	0	0	0
94-95—Frolunda	Sweden	8	2	1	3	6	...	...	...	—	—	—	—	—
95-96—Frolunda	Sweden	36	15	5	20	10	...	...	...	13	3	0	3	10
96-97—Vastra Frolunda	Sweden	50	19	15	34	34	...	...	...	3	0	2	2	0
97-98—Boston	NHL	82	8	19	27	38	-14	2	0	6	1	0	1	0
98-99—Boston	NHL	77	7	10	17	18	-14	0	0	12	1	1	2	4
99-00—Boston	NHL	81	10	16	26	24	1	0	0	—	—	—	—	—
NHL Totals (3 years)		240	25	45	70	80	-27	2	0	18	2	1	3	4

BABENKO, YURI C AVALANCHE

PERSONAL: Born January 2, 1978, in Penza, U.S.S.R. ... 6-0/185. ... Shoots left.

TRANSACTIONS/CAREER NOTES: Selected by Colorado Avalanche in second round (second Avalanche pick, 51st overall) of NHL entry draft (June 22, 1996).

Season Team	League	REGULAR SEASON								PLAYOFFS				
		Gms.	G	A	Pts.	PIM	+/-	PP	SH	Gms.	G	A	Pts.	PIM
95-96—Soviet Wings	CIS	21	0	0	0	16	...	...	...	—	—	—	—	—
96-97—Soviet Wings	USSR	4	1	0	1	4	...	...	...	—	—	—	—	—
—Soviet Wings 2	Rus. Div. III	26	8	10	18	24	...	...	...	—	—	—	—	—
—CSKA	Rus. Div. II	24	3	3	6	12	...	...	...	—	—	—	—	—
97-98—Plymouth	OHL	59	22	34	56	22	...	...	...	15	3	7	10	24
98-99—Hershey	AHL	74	11	15	26	47	...	...	...	2	0	1	1	0
99-00—Hershey	AHL	75	20	25	45	53	...	...	...	14	4	3	7	37

BALMOCHNYKH, MAXIM LW MIGHTY DUCKS

PERSONAL: Born March 7, 1979, in Lipetsk, U.S.S.R. ... 6-1/200. ... Shoots left. ... Name pronounced bal-MOTCH-nick.

TRANSACTIONS/CAREER NOTES: Selected by Mighty Ducks of Anaheim in second round (second Mighty Ducks pick, 45th overall) of NHL entry draft (June 21, 1997).

Season Team	League	REGULAR SEASON								PLAYOFFS				
		Gms.	G	A	Pts.	PIM	+/-	PP	SH	Gms.	G	A	Pts.	PIM
94-95—HC Lipetsk	CIS Div. II	3	0	1	1	4	...	...	...	—	—	—	—	—
95-96—HC Lipetsk	CIS Div. II	40	15	5	20	60	...	...	...	—	—	—	—	—
96-97—Lada Togliatti	Russian	18	6	1	7	22	...	...	...	—	—	—	—	—
97-98—Lada Togliatti	Russian	37	10	4	14	46	...	...	...	—	—	—	—	—
—Traktor Chelyabinsk	Russian	2	0	0	0	2	...	...	...	—	—	—	—	—
98-99—Lada Togliatti	Russian	15	2	1	3	10	...	...	...	4	0	1	1	8
99-00—Cincinnati	AHL	40	9	12	21	82	...	...	...	—	—	—	—	—
—Anaheim	NHL	6	0	1	1	2	2	0	0	—	—	—	—	—
NHL Totals (1 year)		6	0	1	1	2	2	0	0					

BANHAM, FRANK — RW

PERSONAL: Born April 14, 1975, in Calahoo, Alta. ... 6-0/210. ... Shoots right.
TRANSACTIONS/CAREER NOTES: Selected by Washington Capitals in sixth round (fourth Capitals pick, 147th overall) of NHL entry draft (June 26, 1993). ... Signed as free agent by Mighty Ducks of Anaheim (January 22, 1996).
HONORS: Named to WHL (Central/East) All-Star first team (1995-96).

Season Team	League	Gms.	G	A	Pts.	PIM	+/-	PP	SH	Gms.	G	A	Pts.	PIM
92-93—Saskatoon	WHL	71	29	33	62	55	...	...	...	9	2	7	9	8
93-94—Saskatoon	WHL	65	28	39	67	99	...	...	...	16	8	11	19	36
94-95—Saskatoon	WHL	70	50	39	89	63	...	...	...	8	2	6	8	12
95-96—Saskatoon	WHL	72	*83	69	152	116	...	...	...	4	6	0	6	2
—Baltimore	AHL	9	1	4	5	0	...	...	...	7	1	1	2	2
96-97—Baltimore	AHL	21	11	13	24	4	...	...	...	—	—	—	—	—
—Anaheim	NHL	3	0	0	0	0	-2	0	0	—	—	—	—	—
97-98—Cincinnati	AHL	35	7	8	15	39	...	...	...	—	—	—	—	—
—Anaheim	NHL	21	9	2	11	12	-6	1	0	—	—	—	—	—
98-99—Cincinnati	AHL	66	22	27	49	20	...	...	...	3	0	1	1	0
99-00—Cincinnati	AHL	72	19	22	41	58	...	...	...	—	—	—	—	—
—Anaheim	NHL	3	0	0	0	2	0	0	0	—	—	—	—	—
NHL Totals (3 years)		27	9	2	11	14	-8	1	0					

BARCH, KRYS — LW — CAPITALS

PERSONAL: Born March 26, 1980, in Guelph, Ont. ... 6-2/199. ... Shoots left. ... Full Name: Krystofer Barch.
TRANSACTIONS/CAREER NOTES: Selected by Washington Capitals in fourth round (third Capitals pick, 106th overall) of NHL entry draft (June 27, 1998).

Season Team	League	Gms.	G	A	Pts.	PIM	+/-	PP	SH	Gms.	G	A	Pts.	PIM
96-97—Georgetown	Tier II Jr. A	51	18	26	44	58	...	...	...	—	—	—	—	—
97-98—London	OHL	65	9	27	36	62	...	...	...	16	4	3	7	16
98-99—London	OHL	66	18	20	38	66	...	...	...	25	9	17	26	15
99-00—London	OHL	56	23	26	49	78	...	...	...	—	—	—	—	—
—Portland	AHL	—	—	—	—	—	...	...	...	4	0	2	2	2

BARNABY, MATTHEW — LW — PENGUINS

PERSONAL: Born May 4, 1973, in Ottawa. ... 6-0/189. ... Shoots left.
TRANSACTIONS/CAREER NOTES: Selected by Buffalo Sabres in fourth round (fifth Sabres pick, 83rd overall) of NHL entry draft (June 20, 1992). ... Suffered lower back spasms (March 28, 1995); missed one game. ... Suspended one game by NHL for accumulating three game misconduct penalties (March 31, 1996). ... Injured groin (April 3, 1996); missed five games. ... Sprained knee ligament (April 2, 1997); missed final six games of regular season and four playoff games. ... Injured sternum (October 10, 1997); missed five games. ... Strained shoulder (February 2, 1998); missed one game. ... Suspended four games and fined §1,000 by NHL for striking another player in the head (November 5, 1998). ... Suffered back spasms (December 12, 1998); missed one game. ... Injured ankle (December 18, 1998); missed one game. ... Suffered from flu (January 11, 1999); missed one game. ... Traded by Sabres to Pittsburgh Penguins for C Stu Barnes (March 11, 1999). ... Strained shoulder (November 2, 1999); missed five games. ... Suffered concussion (December 15, 1999); missed seven games. ... Suffered concussion (January 13, 2000); missed one game. ... Suspended five games by NHL for fighting incident (February 13, 2000).

Season Team	League	Gms.	G	A	Pts.	PIM	+/-	PP	SH	Gms.	G	A	Pts.	PIM
90-91—Beauport	QMJHL	52	9	5	14	262	...	...	...	—	—	—	—	—
91-92—Beauport	QMJHL	63	29	37	66	*476	...	...	...	—	—	—	—	—
92-93—Victoriaville	QMJHL	65	44	67	111	*448	...	...	...	6	2	4	6	44
—Buffalo	NHL	2	1	0	1	10	0	1	0	1	0	1	1	4
93-94—Buffalo	NHL	35	2	4	6	106	-7	1	0	3	0	0	0	17
—Rochester	AHL	42	10	32	42	153	...	...	...	—	—	—	—	—
94-95—Rochester	AHL	56	21	29	50	274	...	...	...	—	—	—	—	—
—Buffalo	NHL	23	1	1	2	116	-2	0	0	—	—	—	—	—
95-96—Buffalo	NHL	73	15	16	31	*335	-2	0	0	—	—	—	—	—
96-97—Buffalo	NHL	68	19	24	43	249	16	2	0	8	0	4	4	36
97-98—Buffalo	NHL	72	5	20	25	289	8	0	0	15	7	6	13	22
98-99—Buffalo	NHL	44	4	14	18	143	-2	0	0	—	—	—	—	—
—Pittsburgh	NHL	18	2	2	4	34	-10	1	0	13	0	0	0	35
99-00—Pittsburgh	NHL	64	12	12	24	197	3	0	0	11	0	2	2	29
NHL Totals (8 years)		399	61	93	154	1479	4	5	0	51	7	13	20	143

BARNES, RYAN — LW — RED WINGS

PERSONAL: Born January 30, 1980, in Dunnville, Ont. ... 6-1/201. ... Shoots left.
TRANSACTIONS/CAREER NOTES: Selected by Detroit Red Wings in second round (second Red Wings pick, 55th overall) of NHL entry draft (June 27, 1998).
STATISTICAL NOTES: Led OHL in penalty minutes with 399 (1998-99).

Season Team	League	Gms.	G	A	Pts.	PIM	+/-	PP	SH	Gms.	G	A	Pts.	PIM
96-97—Quinte	Tier II Jr. A	46	15	19	34	245	...	...	...	—	—	—	—	—
97-98—Sudbury	OHL	46	13	18	31	111	...	...	...	10	0	2	2	24
98-99—Sudbury	OHL	8	2	0	2	§23	...	...	...	—	—	—	—	—
—Toronto St. Michael's..	OHL	31	11	14	25	§215	...	...	...	—	—	—	—	—
—Barrie	OHL	24	16	14	30	§161	...	...	...	12	2	4	6	40
99-00—Barrie	OHL	31	17	12	29	98	...	...	...	25	7	7	14	49

B

BARNES, STU   C   SABRES

PERSONAL: Born December 25, 1970, in Spruce Grove, Alta. ... 5-11/186. ... Shoots right. ... Full Name: Stu D. Barnes.

TRANSACTIONS/CAREER NOTES: Selected by Winnipeg Jets in first round (first Jets pick, fourth overall) of NHL entry draft (June 17, 1989). ... Traded by Jets to Florida Panthers for C Randy Gilhen (November 26, 1993). ... Strained left calf (January 1, 1994); missed one game. ... Suffered lacerations and bruises in and around left eye (February 15, 1995); missed seven games. ... Sprained left knee (March 10, 1996); missed 10 games. ... Traded by Panthers with D Jason Woolley to Pittsburgh Penguins for C Chris Wells (November 19, 1996). ... Injured hip (April 11, 1997); missed one game. ... Suffered back spasms (October 9, 1997); missed one game. ... Strained hip flexor (April 16, 1998); missed one game. ... Traded by Penguins to Buffalo Sabres for RW Matthew Barnaby (March 11, 1999).

HONORS: Won Jim Piggott Memorial Trophy (1987-88). ... Named to WHL All-Star second team (1987-88). ... Won Four Broncos Memorial Trophy (1988-89). ... Named to WHL All-Star first team (1988-89).

MISCELLANEOUS: Failed to score on a penalty shot (vs. Peter Sidorkiewicz, February 23, 1993; vs. Ron Hextall, March 8, 1998).

STATISTICAL PLATEAUS: Three-goal games: 1991-92 (1), 1997-98 (1), 1998-99 (1). Total: 3.

						REGULAR SEASON						PLAYOFFS			
Season Team	League	Gms.	G	A	Pts.	PIM	+/-	PP	SH		Gms.	G	A	Pts.	PIM
86-87—St. Albert	AJHL	57	43	32	75	80	...	...	...		—	—	—	—	—
87-88—New Westminster	WHL	71	37	64	101	88	...	...	...		5	2	3	5	6
88-89—Tri-City	WHL	70	59	82	141	117	...	...	...		7	6	5	11	10
89-90—Tri-City	WHL	63	52	92	144	165	...	...	...		7	1	5	6	26
90-91—Canadian nat'l team	Int'l	53	22	27	49	68	...	...	...		—	—	—	—	—
91-92—Winnipeg	NHL	46	8	9	17	26	-2	4	0		—	—	—	—	—
—Moncton	AHL	30	13	19	32	10	...	...	...		11	3	9	12	6
92-93—Moncton	AHL	42	23	31	54	58	...	...	...		—	—	—	—	—
—Winnipeg	NHL	38	12	10	22	10	-3	3	0		6	1	3	4	2
93-94—Winnipeg	NHL	18	5	4	9	8	-1	2	0		—	—	—	—	—
—Florida	NHL	59	18	20	38	30	5	6	1		—	—	—	—	—
94-95—Florida	NHL	41	10	19	29	8	7	1	0		—	—	—	—	—
95-96—Florida	NHL	72	19	25	44	46	-12	8	0		22	6	10	16	4
96-97—Florida	NHL	19	2	8	10	10	-3	1	0		—	—	—	—	—
—Pittsburgh	NHL	62	17	22	39	16	-20	4	0		5	0	1	1	0
97-98—Pittsburgh	NHL	78	30	35	65	30	15	15	1		6	3	3	6	2
98-99—Pittsburgh	NHL	64	20	12	32	20	-12	13	0		—	—	—	—	—
—Buffalo	NHL	17	0	4	4	10	1	0	0		21	7	3	10	6
99-00—Buffalo	NHL	82	20	25	45	16	-3	8	2		5	3	0	3	2
NHL Totals (9 years)		596	161	193	354	230	-28	65	4		65	20	20	40	16

BARON, MURRAY   D   CANUCKS

PERSONAL: Born June 1, 1967, in Prince George, B.C. ... 6-3/225. ... Shoots left. ... Full Name: Murray D. Baron.

HIGH SCHOOL: Kamloops (B.C.).

COLLEGE: North Dakota.

TRANSACTIONS/CAREER NOTES: Selected by Philadelphia Flyers as underage player in eighth round (seventh Flyers pick, 167th overall) of NHL entry draft (June 21, 1986). ... Separated left shoulder (October 5, 1989). ... Underwent surgery to have bone spur removed from foot (April 1990). ... Traded by Flyers with C Ron Sutter to St. Louis Blues for C Rod Brind'Amour and C Dan Quinn (September 22, 1991). ... Injured shoulder (December 3, 1991); missed seven games. ... Fractured foot (March 22, 1993); missed remainder of regular season. ... Injured groin (December 1, 1993); missed three games. ... Injured groin (December 11, 1993); missed three games. ... Injured knee (March 7, 1994); missed one game. ... Injured knee (April 18, 1995); missed last nine games of regular season. ... Traded by Blues with LW Shayne Corson and fifth-round pick (D Gennady Razin) in 1997 draft to Montreal Canadiens for C Pierre Turgeon, C Craig Conroy and D Rory Fitzpatrick (October 29, 1996). ... Bruised eye (November 21, 1996); missed one game. ... Traded by Canadiens with RW Chris Murray to Phoenix Coyotes for D Dave Manson (March 18, 1997). ... Fractured foot (April 6, 1997); missed remainder of regular season. ... Tore triceps muscle (November 17, 1997); missed 37 games. ... Signed as free agent by Vancouver Canucks (July 14, 1998).

						REGULAR SEASON						PLAYOFFS			
Season Team	League	Gms.	G	A	Pts.	PIM	+/-	PP	SH		Gms.	G	A	Pts.	PIM
84-85—Vernon	BCJHL	37	5	9	14	93	...	...	...		—	—	—	—	—
85-86—Vernon	BCJHL	49	15	32	47	176	...	...	...		7	1	2	3	13
86-87—Univ. of North Dakota	WCHA	41	4	10	14	62	...	...	...		—	—	—	—	—
87-88—Univ. of North Dakota	WCHA	41	1	10	11	95	...	...	...		—	—	—	—	—
88-89—Univ. of North Dakota	WCHA	40	2	6	8	92	...	...	...		—	—	—	—	—
—Hershey	AHL	9	0	3	3	8	...	...	...		—	—	—	—	—
89-90—Hershey	AHL	50	0	10	10	101	...	...	...		—	—	—	—	—
—Philadelphia	NHL	16	2	2	4	12	-1	0	0		—	—	—	—	—
90-91—Hershey	AHL	6	2	3	5	0	...	...	...		—	—	—	—	—
—Philadelphia	NHL	67	8	8	16	74	-3	3	0		—	—	—	—	—
91-92—St. Louis	NHL	67	3	8	11	94	-3	0	0		2	0	0	0	2
92-93—St. Louis	NHL	53	2	2	4	59	-5	0	0		11	0	0	0	12
93-94—St. Louis	NHL	77	5	9	14	123	-14	0	0		4	0	0	0	10
94-95—St. Louis	NHL	39	0	5	5	93	9	0	0		7	1	1	2	2
95-96—St. Louis	NHL	82	2	9	11	190	3	0	0		13	1	0	1	20
96-97—St. Louis	NHL	11	0	2	2	11	-4	0	0		—	—	—	—	—
—Montreal	NHL	60	1	5	6	107	-16	0	0		—	—	—	—	—
—Phoenix	NHL	8	0	0	0	4	0	0	0		1	0	0	0	0
97-98—Phoenix	NHL	45	1	5	6	106	-10	0	0		6	0	2	2	6
98-99—Vancouver	NHL	81	2	6	8	115	-23	0	0		—	—	—	—	—
99-00—Vancouver	NHL	81	2	10	12	67	8	0	0		—	—	—	—	—
NHL Totals (11 years)		687	28	71	99	1055	-59	3	0		44	2	3	5	52

BARRASSO, TOM   G

PERSONAL: Born March 31, 1965, in Boston. ... 6-3/210. ... Catches right. ... Full Name: Thomas Barrasso. ... Name pronounced buh-RAH-soh.
HIGH SCHOOL: Acton (Mass.)-Boxborough.
TRANSACTIONS/CAREER NOTES: Selected by Buffalo Sabres in first round (first Sabres pick, fifth overall) of NHL entry draft (June 8, 1983). ... Suffered chip fracture of ankle (November 1987). ... Pulled groin (April 9, 1988). ... Traded by Sabres with third-round pick in 1990 draft (RW Joe Dziedzic) to Pittsburgh Penguins for D Doug Bodger and LW Darrin Shannon (November 12, 1988). ... Pulled groin muscle (January 17, 1989). ... Injured shoulder (March 1989). ... Underwent surgery to right wrist (October 30, 1989); missed 21 games. ... Pulled groin (February 1990). ... Granted leave of absence to be with daughter as she underwent cancer treatment in Los Angeles (February 9, 1990). ... Rejoined the Penguins (March 19, 1990). ... Bruised right hand (October 29, 1991); missed two games. ... Bruised right ankle (December 26, 1991); missed three games. ... Suffered back spasms (March 1992); missed three games. ... Suffered from chicken pox (January 14, 1993); missed nine games. ... Strained groin (October 7, 1993); missed four games. ... Injured hip (November 18, 1993); missed 12 games. ... Underwent surgery on right wrist (January 20, 1995); missed first 43 games of season. ... Suffered sore wrist (May 3, 1995); missed one game. ... Pulled groin (December 7, 1995); missed eight games. ... Pulled groin and injured shoulder (February 6, 1996); missed four games. ... Suffered recurring shoulder problem (October 25, 1996); missed remainder of season. ... Strained leg muscle (November 5, 1997); missed one game. ... Strained quadriceps (December 29, 1997); missed five games. ... Hyperextended elbow (March 5, 1998); missed three games. ... Suffered from the flu (March 26, 1998); missed three games. ... Bruised knee (April 7, 1998); missed one game. ... Bruised finger (April 16, 1998); missed one game. ... Strained groin (October 17, 1998); missed six games. ... Strained hip (December 21, 1998); missed two games. ... Strained neck (January 26, 1999); missed three games. ... Strained hip flexor (February 11, 1999); missed two games. ... Fractured hand (March 3, 1999); missed 18 games. ... Sprained knee (October 7, 1999); missed 16 games. ... Suspended four games by NHL for slashing incident (December 6, 1999). ... Injured back (December 18, 1999); missed 12 games. ... Traded by Penguins to Ottawa Senators for G Ron Tugnutt and D Janne Laukkanen (March 14, 2000). ... Bruised finger (April 4, 2000); missed final three games of season.
HONORS: Won Vezina Trophy (1983-84). ... Won Calder Memorial Trophy (1983-84). ... Named to THE SPORTING NEWS All-Star second team (1983-84, 1984-85 and 1987-88). ... Named to NHL All-Star first team (1983-84). ... Named to NHL All-Rookie team (1983-84). ... Shared William M. Jennings Trophy with Bob Sauve (1984-85). ... Named to NHL All-Star second team (1984-85 and 1992-93). ... Played in NHL All-Star Game (1985). ... Named to THE SPORTING NEWS All-Star first team (1992-93).
RECORDS: Shares NHL single-season playoff records for most wins by a goaltender—16 (1992); and most consecutive wins by a goaltender—11 (1992). ... Holds NHL record for most points by goaltender, career—48.
MISCELLANEOUS: Member of Stanley Cup championship teams (1991 and 1992). ... Holds Pittsburgh Penguins all-time records for most games played by goalie (440), most wins (221) and most shutouts (22). ... Stopped penalty shot attempt (vs. Bryan Trottier, January 5, 1985; vs. Doug Smail, October 10, 1989; vs. Sami Kapanen, January 7, 1999). ... Allowed penalty shot goal (vs. Marcel Dionne, March 9, 1984; vs. Scott Pearson, March 16, 1991; vs. Robert Reichel, October 24, 1996).

			REGULAR SEASON								PLAYOFFS						
Season Team	League	Gms.	Min	W	L	T	GA	SO	Avg.	Gms.	Min.	W	L	GA	SO	Avg.
81-82—Acton-Boxborough HS..	Mass. H.S.	23	1035	...	...	...	32	7	1.86	—	—	—	—	—	—	—
82-83—Acton-Boxborough HS..	Mass. H.S.	23	1035	...	...	...	17	10	.99	—	—	—	—	—	—	—
83-84—Buffalo	NHL	42	2475	26	12	3	117	2	2.84	3	139	0	2	8	0	3.45
84-85—Rochester	AHL	5	267	3	1	1	6	1	1.35	—	—	—	—	—	—	—
—Buffalo	NHL	54	3248	25	18	10	144	*5	*2.66	5	300	2	3	22	0	4.40
85-86—Buffalo	NHL	60	*3561	29	24	5	214	2	3.61	—	—	—	—	—	—	—
86-87—Buffalo	NHL	46	2501	17	23	2	152	2	3.65	—	—	—	—	—	—	—
87-88—Buffalo	NHL	54	3133	25	18	8	173	2	3.31	4	224	1	3	16	0	4.29
88-89—Buffalo	NHL	10	545	2	7	0	45	0	4.95	—	—	—	—	—	—	—
—Pittsburgh	NHL	44	2406	18	15	7	162	0	4.04	11	631	7	4	40	0	3.80
89-90—Pittsburgh	NHL	24	1294	7	12	3	101	0	4.68	—	—	—	—	—	—	—
90-91—Pittsburgh	NHL	48	2754	27	16	3	165	1	3.59	20	1175	12	7	51	†1	*2.60
91-92—Pittsburgh	NHL	57	3329	25	22	9	196	1	3.53	*21	*1233	*16	5	*58	1	2.82
92-93—Pittsburgh	NHL	63	3702	*43	14	5	186	4	3.01	12	722	7	5	35	2	2.91
93-94—Pittsburgh	NHL	44	2482	22	15	5	139	2	3.36	6	356	2	4	17	0	2.87
94-95—Pittsburgh	NHL	2	125	0	1	1	8	0	3.84	2	80	0	1	8	0	6.00
95-96—Pittsburgh	NHL	49	2799	29	16	2	160	2	3.43	10	558	4	5	26	1	2.80
96-97—Pittsburgh	NHL	5	270	0	5	0	26	0	5.78	—	—	—	—	—	—	—
97-98—Pittsburgh	NHL	63	3542	31	14	13	122	7	2.07	6	376	2	4	17	0	2.71
98-99—Pittsburgh	NHL	43	2306	19	16	3	98	4	2.55	13	787	6	7	35	1	2.67
99-00—Pittsburgh	NHL	18	870	5	7	2	46	1	3.17	—	—	—	—	—	—	—
—Ottawa	NHL	7	418	3	4	0	22	0	3.16	6	372	2	4	16	0	2.58
NHL Totals (17 years)		733	41760	353	259	81	2276	35	3.27	119	6953	61	54	349	6	3.01

BARRIE, LEN   C   PANTHERS

PERSONAL: Born June 4, 1969, in Kimberley, B.C. ... 6-0/200. ... Shoots right.
TRANSACTIONS/CAREER NOTES: Selected by Edmonton Oilers in sixth round (seventh Oilers pick, 124th overall) of NHL entry draft (June 11, 1988). ... Signed as free agent by Philadelphia Flyers (February 8, 1990). ... Signed as free agent by Florida Panthers (July 20, 1993). ... Signed as free agent by Pittsburgh Penguins (August 25, 1994). ... Signed as free agent by Los Angeles Kings (July 21, 1999). ... Claimed on waivers by Panthers (March 10, 2000).
HONORS: Won Can.HL Plus/Minus Award (1989-90). ... Won Bob Clarke Trophy (1989-90). ... Named to WHL (West) All-Star first team (1989-90). ... Named to IHL All-Star second team (1993-94).

			REGULAR SEASON								PLAYOFFS			
Season Team	League	Gms.	G	A	Pts.	PIM	+/-	PP	SH	Gms.	G	A	Pts.	PIM
85-86—Calgary Spurs	AJHL	23	7	14	21	86	...	...	...	—	—	—	—	—
—Calgary	WHL	32	3	0	3	18	...	...	...	—	—	—	—	—
86-87—Calgary	WHL	34	13	13	26	81	...	...	...	—	—	—	—	—
—Victoria	WHL	34	7	6	13	92	...	...	...	5	0	1	1	15
87-88—Victoria	WHL	70	37	49	86	192	...	...	...	8	2	0	2	29
88-89—Victoria	WHL	67	39	48	87	157	...	...	...	7	5	2	7	23
89-90—Philadelphia	NHL	1	0	0	0	0	-2	0	0	—	—	—	—	—
—Kamloops	WHL	70	*85	*100	*185	108	...	...	...	17	†14	23	†37	24
90-91—Hershey	AHL	63	26	32	58	60	...	...	...	7	4	0	4	12
91-92—Hershey	AHL	75	42	43	85	78	...	...	...	3	0	2	2	32

Season Team	League	REGULAR SEASON Gms.	G	A	Pts.	PIM	+/-	PP	SH	PLAYOFFS Gms.	G	A	Pts.	PIM
92-93—Hershey	AHL	61	31	45	76	162	...	...	...	—	—	—	—	—
—Philadelphia	NHL	8	2	2	4	9	2	0	0	—	—	—	—	—
93-94—Cincinnati	IHL	77	45	71	116	246	...	...	...	11	8	13	21	60
—Florida	NHL	2	0	0	0	0	-2	0	0	—	—	—	—	—
94-95—Cleveland	IHL	28	13	30	43	137	...	...	...	—	—	—	—	—
—Pittsburgh	NHL	48	3	11	14	66	-4	0	0	4	1	0	1	8
95-96—Cleveland	IHL	55	29	43	72	178	...	...	...	3	2	3	5	6
—Pittsburgh	NHL	5	0	0	0	18	-1	0	0	—	—	—	—	—
96-97—San Antonio	IHL	57	26	40	66	196	...	...	...	9	5	5	10	20
97-98—San Antonio	IHL	32	7	13	20	90	...	...	...	—	—	—	—	—
—Frankfurt	Germany	25	11	19	30	32	...	...	...	—	—	—	—	—
98-99—Frankfurt	Germany	41	24	35	59	105	...	...	...	8	2	4	6	43
99-00—Long Beach	IHL	17	10	10	20	16	...	...	...	—	—	—	—	—
—Los Angeles	NHL	46	5	8	13	56	5	0	0	—	—	—	—	—
—Florida	NHL	14	4	6	10	6	4	0	0	4	0	0	0	0
NHL Totals (6 years)		124	14	27	41	155	2	0	0	8	1	0	1	8

BARTECKO, LUBOS   LW   BLUES

PERSONAL: Born July 14, 1976, in Kezmarok, Czechoslovakia. ... 6-1/195. ... Shoots left.
TRANSACTIONS/CAREER NOTES: Signed as non-drafted free agent by St. Louis Blues (October 3, 1997).

Season Team	League	REGULAR SEASON Gms.	G	A	Pts.	PIM	+/-	PP	SH	PLAYOFFS Gms.	G	A	Pts.	PIM
95-96—Chicoutimi	QMJHL	70	32	41	73	50	...	...	...	17	8	15	23	10
96-97—Drummondville	QMJHL	58	40	51	91	49	...	...	...	8	1	8	9	4
97-98—Worcester	AHL	34	10	12	22	24	...	...	...	10	4	2	6	2
98-99—Poprad	Slovakia	1	1	0	1	0	...	...	...	—	—	—	—	—
—St. Louis	NHL	32	5	11	16	6	4	0	0	5	0	0	0	2
—Worcester	AHL	49	14	24	38	22	...	...	...	—	—	—	—	—
99-00—Worcester	AHL	12	4	7	11	4	...	...	...	—	—	—	—	—
—St. Louis	NHL	67	16	23	39	51	25	3	0	7	1	1	2	0
NHL Totals (2 years)		99	21	34	55	57	29	3	0	12	1	1	2	2

BARTEK, MARTIN   LW   PREDATORS

PERSONAL: Born July 17, 1980, in Kindgssed Jill, Czechoslovakia. ... 6-0/197. ... Shoots left.
TRANSACTIONS/CAREER NOTES: Selected by Nashville Predators in eighth round (seventh Predators pick, 202nd overall) of NHL entry draft (June 27, 1998).

Season Team	League	REGULAR SEASON Gms.	G	A	Pts.	PIM	+/-	PP	SH	PLAYOFFS Gms.	G	A	Pts.	PIM
97-98—Rouyn-Noranda	QMJHL	28	9	19	28	12	...	...	...	—	—	—	—	—
—Rimouski	QMJHL	13	3	4	7	6	...	...	...	—	—	—	—	—
—Sherbrooke	QMJHL	25	11	12	23	38	...	...	...	—	—	—	—	—
98-99—Zvolen	Slovakia	28	10	8	18	18	...	...	...	2	1	0	1	0
99-00—Moncton	QMJHL	69	32	44	76	36	...	...	...	16	10	13	23	24

BARTOVIC, MILAN   LW   SABRES

PERSONAL: Born April 20, 1981, in Trencin, Czechoslovakia. ... 5-11/183. ... Shoots left.
TRANSACTIONS/CAREER NOTES: Selected by Buffalo Sabres in second round (second Sabres pick, 35th overall) of NHL entry draft (June 26, 1999).

Season Team	League	REGULAR SEASON Gms.	G	A	Pts.	PIM	+/-	PP	SH	PLAYOFFS Gms.	G	A	Pts.	PIM
97-98—Dukla Trencin Jrs.	Slovakia Jrs.	26	2	6	8	15	...	...	...	—	—	—	—	—
98-99—Dukla Trencin Jrs.	Slovakia Jrs.	46	36	35	71	62	...	...	...	6	9	3	12	10
99-00—Tri-City	WHL	18	8	9	17	12	...	...	...	—	—	—	—	—
—Brandon	WHL	38	18	22	40	28	...	...	...	—	—	—	—	—

BASHKIROV, ANDREI   LW   CANADIENS

PERSONAL: Born June 22, 1970, in Shelekhov, U.S.S.R. ... 6-0/215. ... Shoots left.
TRANSACTIONS/CAREER NOTES: Selected by Montreal Canadiens in fifth round (fourth Canadiens pick, 132nd overall) of NHL entry draft (June 27, 1998). ... Fractured jaw (September 30, 1998); missed first 13 games of season.

Season Team	League	REGULAR SEASON Gms.	G	A	Pts.	PIM	+/-	PP	SH	PLAYOFFS Gms.	G	A	Pts.	PIM
91-92—Khimik Voskresensk	CIS	11	2	0	2	4	...	...	...	—	—	—	—	—
92-93—Yermak Angarsk	CIS Div. III				Statistics unavailable.									
93-94—Charlotte	ECHL	62	28	42	70	25	...	...	...	3	1	0	1	...
—Providence	AHL	1	0	0	0	2	...	...	...	—	—	—	—	—
94-95—Charlotte	ECHL	61	19	27	46	20	...	...	...	3	0	0	0	0
95-96—Huntington	ECHL	55	19	39	58	35	...	...	...	—	—	—	—	—
96-97—Huntington	ECHL	47	29	41	70	12	...	...	...	—	—	—	—	—
—Detroit	IHL	2	0	0	0	0	...	...	...	—	—	—	—	—
—Las Vegas	IHL	27	10	12	22	0	...	...	...	2	0	0	0	0
97-98—Las Vegas	IHL	15	2	3	5	5	...	...	...	—	—	—	—	—
—Fort Wayne	IHL	65	28	48	76	16	...	...	...	4	2	2	4	2

Season Team	League	REGULAR SEASON								PLAYOFFS				
		Gms.	G	A	Pts.	PIM	+/-	PP	SH	Gms.	G	A	Pts.	PIM
98-99—Fredericton	AHL	13	7	5	12	4	...	...	...	—	—	—	—	—
—Montreal	NHL	10	0	0	0	0	-3	0	0	—	—	—	—	—
—Fort Wayne	IHL	34	11	25	36	10	...	...	...	—	—	—	—	—
99-00—Quebec	AHL	78	28	33	61	17	...	...	...	3	0	3	3	0
—Montreal	NHL	2	0	0	0	0	0	0	0	—	—	—	—	—
NHL Totals (2 years)		12	0	0	0	0	-3	0	0	—	—	—	—	—

BASSEN, BOB — C — B

PERSONAL: Born May 6, 1965, in Calgary. ... 5-10/190. ... Shoots left. ... Son of Hank Bassen, goaltender with three NHL teams (1954-55 through 1955-56 and 1960-61 through 1967-68); and brother of Mark Bassen, center in Philadelphia Flyers (1989-90 and 1990-91) and St. Louis Blues (1991-92 through 1994-95) organizations. ... Name pronounced BAZ-ihn.

HIGH SCHOOL: Sir Winston Churchill (Calgary).

TRANSACTIONS/CAREER NOTES: Signed as non-drafted free agent by New York Islanders (October 19, 1984). ... Injured knee (October 12, 1985). ... Traded by Islanders with D Steve Konroyd to Chicago Blackhawks for D Gary Nylund and D Marc Bergevin (November 25, 1988). ... Selected by St. Louis Blues in 1990 waiver draft for $25,000 (October 2, 1990). ... Fractured right foot (December 4, 1992); missed 22 games. ... Fractured finger (January 28, 1993); missed nine games. ... Traded by Blues with C Ron Sutter and D Garth Butcher to Quebec Nordiques for D Steve Duchesne and RW Denis Chasse (January 23, 1994). ... Lacerated left eye (March 30, 1994); missed one game. ... Injured back (February 18, 1995); missed one game. ... Signed as free agent by Dallas Stars (July 18, 1995). ... Injured knee (September 30, 1995); missed first 69 games of season. ... Underwent surgery to repair herniated disc in neck (September 28, 1996); missed first 36 games of season. ... Bruised thigh (November 10, 1997); missed one game. ... Injured hand (January 12, 1998); missed four games. ... Injured knee (February 7, 1998); missed 18 games. ... Traded by Stars to Calgary Flames for C Aaron Gavey (July 14, 1998). ... Underwent arthroscopic knee surgery (September 24, 1998); missed first 23 games of season. ... Suffered back spasms (February 26, 1999); missed 17 games. ... Claimed on waivers by Blues (December 11, 1999).

HONORS: Named to WHL (East) All-Star first team (1984-85). ... Named to IHL All-Star first team (1989-90).

Season Team	League	REGULAR SEASON								PLAYOFFS				
		Gms.	G	A	Pts.	PIM	+/-	PP	SH	Gms.	G	A	Pts.	PIM
82-83—Medicine Hat	WHL	4	3	2	5	0	...	...	...	3	0	0	0	4
83-84—Medicine Hat	WHL	72	29	29	58	93	...	...	...	14	5	11	16	12
84-85—Medicine Hat	WHL	65	32	50	82	143	...	...	...	10	2	8	10	39
85-86—New York Islanders	NHL	11	2	1	3	6	...	...	...	3	0	1	1	0
—Springfield	AHL	54	13	21	34	111	...	...	...	—	—	—	—	—
86-87—New York Islanders	NHL	77	7	10	17	89	-17	0	0	14	1	2	3	21
87-88—New York Islanders	NHL	77	6	16	22	99	8	1	0	6	0	1	1	23
88-89—New York Islanders	NHL	19	1	4	5	21	0	0	0	—	—	—	—	—
—Chicago	NHL	49	4	12	16	62	5	0	0	10	1	1	2	34
89-90—Indianapolis	IHL	73	22	32	54	179	...	...	...	12	3	8	11	33
—Chicago	NHL	6	1	1	2	8	1	0	0	—	—	—	—	—
90-91—St. Louis	NHL	79	16	18	34	183	17	0	2	13	1	3	4	24
91-92—St. Louis	NHL	79	7	25	32	167	12	0	0	6	0	2	2	4
92-93—St. Louis	NHL	53	9	10	19	63	0	0	1	11	0	0	0	10
93-94—St. Louis	NHL	46	2	7	9	44	-14	0	1	—	—	—	—	—
—Quebec	NHL	37	11	8	19	55	-3	1	0	—	—	—	—	—
94-95—Quebec	NHL	47	12	15	27	33	14	0	1	5	2	4	6	0
95-96—Michigan	IHL	1	0	0	0	4	...	...	...	—	—	—	—	—
—Dallas	NHL	13	0	1	1	15	-6	0	0	—	—	—	—	—
96-97—Dallas	NHL	46	5	7	12	41	5	0	0	7	3	1	4	4
97-98—Dallas	NHL	58	3	4	7	57	-4	0	0	17	1	0	1	12
98-99—Calgary	NHL	41	1	2	3	35	-13	0	0	—	—	—	—	—
99-00—Frankfurt	Germany	14	2	9	11	6	...	...	...	—	—	—	—	—
—St. Louis	NHL	27	1	3	4	26	-3	0	0	—	—	—	—	—
NHL Totals (15 years)		765	88	144	232	1004	...	...	...	92	9	15	24	132

BATES, SHAWN — C — BRUINS

PERSONAL: Born April 3, 1975, in Melrose, Mass. ... 5-11/190. ... Shoots right.

HIGH SCHOOL: Medford (Mass.).

COLLEGE: Boston University.

TRANSACTIONS/CAREER NOTES: Selected by Boston Bruins in fourth round (fourth Bruins pick, 103rd overall) of NHL entry draft (June 26, 1993). ... Involved in car accident (November 8, 1997); missed one game. ... Suffered from the flu (December 1, 1998); missed one game. ... Injured hamstring (April 15, 1999); missed two games. ... Injured shoulder (October 30, 1999); missed four games. ... Sprained wrist (December 9, 1999); missed 23 games. ... Sprained wrist (March 25, 2000); missed seven games.

HONORS: Named to Hockey East All-Rookie team (1993-94).

Season Team	League	REGULAR SEASON								PLAYOFFS				
		Gms.	G	A	Pts.	PIM	+/-	PP	SH	Gms.	G	A	Pts.	PIM
90-91—Medford H.S.	Mass. H.S.	22	18	43	61	6	...	...	...	—	—	—	—	—
91-92—Medford H.S.	Mass. H.S.	22	38	41	79	10	...	...	...	—	—	—	—	—
92-93—Medford H.S.	Mass. H.S.	25	49	46	95	20	...	...	...	—	—	—	—	—
93-94—Boston University	Hockey East	41	10	19	29	24	...	...	...	—	—	—	—	—
94-95—Boston University	Hockey East	38	18	12	30	48	...	...	...	—	—	—	—	—
95-96—Boston University	Hockey East	40	28	22	50	54	...	...	...	—	—	—	—	—
96-97—Boston University	Hockey East	41	17	18	35	64	...	...	...	—	—	—	—	—
97-98—Boston	NHL	13	2	0	2	2	-3	0	0	—	—	—	—	—
—Providence	AHL	50	15	19	34	22	...	...	...	—	—	—	—	—
98-99—Providence	AHL	37	25	21	46	39	...	...	...	—	—	—	—	—
—Boston	NHL	33	5	4	9	2	3	0	0	12	0	0	0	4
99-00—Boston	NHL	44	5	7	12	14	-17	0	0	—	—	—	—	—
NHL Totals (3 years)		90	12	11	23	18	-17	0	0	12	0	0	0	4

BATTAGLIA, BATES — LW — HURRICANES

PERSONAL: Born December 13, 1975, in Chicago. ... 6-2/205. ... Shoots left. ... Full Name: Jon Battaglia. ... Name pronounced buh-TAG-lee-uh.
COLLEGE: Lake Superior State (Mich.).
TRANSACTIONS/CAREER NOTES: Selected by Mighty Ducks of Anaheim in sixth round (sixth Mighty Ducks pick, 132nd overall) of NHL entry draft (June 29, 1994). ... Traded by Mighty Ducks with fourth-round pick (C Josef Vasicek) in 1998 draft to Hartford Whalers for C Mark Janssens (March 18, 1997). ... Injured shoulder (January 20, 2000); missed three games.
STATISTICAL PLATEAUS: Three-goal games: 1999-00 (1).

		REGULAR SEASON								PLAYOFFS				
Season Team	League	Gms.	G	A	Pts.	PIM	+/-	PP	SH	Gms.	G	A	Pts.	PIM
93-94—Caledon	Jr. A	44	15	33	48	104	...	...	...	—	—	—	—	—
94-95—Lake Superior State	CCHA	38	6	15	21	34	...	...	...	—	—	—	—	—
95-96—Lake Superior State	CCHA	40	13	22	35	48	...	...	...	—	—	—	—	—
96-97—Lake Superior State	CCHA	38	12	27	39	80	...	...	...	—	—	—	—	—
97-98—New Haven	AHL	48	15	21	36	48	...	...	...	1	0	0	0	0
—Carolina	NHL	33	2	4	6	10	-1	0	0	—	—	—	—	—
98-99—Carolina	NHL	60	7	11	18	22	7	0	0	6	0	3	3	8
99-00—Carolina	NHL	77	16	18	34	39	20	3	0	—	—	—	—	—
NHL Totals (3 years)		170	25	33	58	71	26	3	0	6	0	3	3	8

BAUMGARTNER, NOLAN — D — BLACKHAWKS

PERSONAL: Born March 23, 1976, in Calgary. ... 6-1/195. ... Shoots right.
HIGH SCHOOL: Norkam Secondary (Kamloops, B.C.).
TRANSACTIONS/CAREER NOTES: Selected by Washington Capitals in first round (first Capitals pick, 10th overall) of NHL entry draft (June 28, 1994). ... Traded by Capitals to Chicago Blackhawks for D Remi Royer (July 21, 2000).
HONORS: Named to Memorial Cup All-Star team (1993-94 and 1994-95). ... Won Can.HL Defenseman of the Year Award (1994-95). ... Won Bill Hunter Trophy (1994-95 and 1995-96). ... Named to Can.HL All-Star first team (1994-95). ... Named to WHL (West) All-Star first team (1994-95 and 1995-96).

		REGULAR SEASON								PLAYOFFS				
Season Team	League	Gms.	G	A	Pts.	PIM	+/-	PP	SH	Gms.	G	A	Pts.	PIM
92-93—Kamloops	WHL	43	0	5	5	30	...	...	...	11	1	1	2	0
93-94—Kamloops	WHL	69	13	42	55	109	...	...	...	19	3	14	17	33
94-95—Kamloops	WHL	62	8	36	44	71	...	...	...	21	4	13	17	16
95-96—Washington	NHL	1	0	0	0	0	-1	0	0	1	0	0	0	10
—Kamloops	WHL	28	13	15	28	45	...	...	...	16	1	9	10	26
96-97—Portland	AHL	8	2	2	4	4	...	...	...	—	—	—	—	—
97-98—Portland	AHL	70	2	24	26	70	...	...	...	10	1	4	5	10
—Washington	NHL	4	0	1	1	0	0	0	0	—	—	—	—	—
98-99—Portland	AHL	38	5	14	19	62	...	...	...	—	—	—	—	—
—Washington	NHL	5	0	0	0	0	-3	0	0	—	—	—	—	—
99-00—Portland	AHL	71	5	18	23	56	...	...	...	4	1	2	3	10
—Washington	NHL	8	0	1	1	2	1	0	0	—	—	—	—	—
NHL Totals (4 years)		18	0	2	2	2	-3	0	0	1	0	0	0	10

BEAUCHEMIN, FRANCOIS — D — CANADIENS

PERSONAL: Born June 4, 1980, in Sorel, Que. ... 5-11/190. ... Shoots left.
TRANSACTIONS/CAREER NOTES: Selected by Montreal Canadiens in third round (third Canadiens pick, 75th overall) of NHL entry draft (June 27, 1998).
HONORS: Named to Can.HL All-Rookie team (1996-97). ... Named to QMJHL All-Star second team (1999-2000).

		REGULAR SEASON								PLAYOFFS				
Season Team	League	Gms.	G	A	Pts.	PIM	+/-	PP	SH	Gms.	G	A	Pts.	PIM
96-97—Laval	QMJHL	66	7	20	27	112	...	...	...	3	0	0	0	2
97-98—Laval	QMJHL	70	12	35	47	132	...	...	...	16	1	3	4	23
98-99—Acadie-Bathurst	QMJHL	31	4	17	21	53	...	...	...	23	2	16	18	55
99-00—Acadie-Bathurst	QMJHL	38	11	36	47	64	...	...	...	—	—	—	—	—
—Moncton	QMJHL	33	8	31	39	35	...	...	...	16	2	11	13	14

BEECH, KRIS — C — CAPITALS

PERSONAL: Born February 5, 1981, in Salmon Arm, B.C. ... 6-2/178. ... Shoots left.
TRANSACTIONS/CAREER NOTES: Selected by Washington Capitals in first round (first Capitals pick, seventh overall) of NHL entry draft (June 26, 1999).

		REGULAR SEASON								PLAYOFFS				
Season Team	League	Gms.	G	A	Pts.	PIM	+/-	PP	SH	Gms.	G	A	Pts.	PIM
96-97—Sicamous	Jr. A	49	34	36	70	80	...	...	...	—	—	—	—	—
—Calgary	WHL	8	1	1	2	0	...	...	...	—	—	—	—	—
97-98—Calgary	WHL	68	26	41	67	103	...	...	...	—	—	—	—	—
98-99—Calgary	WHL	58	10	25	35	24	...	...	...	—	—	—	—	—
99-00—Calgary	WHL	66	32	54	86	99	...	...	...	5	3	5	8	16

BEGIN, STEVE — LW — FLAMES

PERSONAL: Born June 14, 1978, in Trois-Rivieres, Que. ... 5-11/190. ... Shoots left.
TRANSACTIONS/CAREER NOTES: Selected by Calgary Flames in second round (third Flames pick, 40th overall) of NHL entry draft (June 22, 1996). ... Injured shoulder (October 10, 1997); missed six games. ... Dislocated fibula (March 18, 2000); missed final 10 games of season.

Season Team	League	REGULAR SEASON								PLAYOFFS				
		Gms.	G	A	Pts.	PIM	+/-	PP	SH	Gms.	G	A	Pts.	PIM
95-96—Val-d'Or	QMJHL	64	13	23	36	218	...	...	...	13	1	3	4	33
96-97—Val-d'Or	QMJHL	58	13	33	46	207	...	...	...	10	0	3	3	8
—Saint John	AHL	—	—	—	—	—	...	...	...	4	0	2	2	6
97-98—Calgary	NHL	5	0	0	0	23	0	0	0	—	—	—	—	—
—Val-d'Or	QMJHL	35	18	17	35	73	...	...	...	15	2	12	14	34
98-99—Saint John	AHL	73	11	9	20	156	...	...	...	7	2	0	2	18
99-00—Calgary	NHL	13	1	1	2	18	-3	0	0	—	—	—	—	—
—Saint John	AHL	47	13	12	25	99	...	...	...	—	—	—	—	—
NHL Totals (2 years)...........		18	1	1	2	41	-3	0	0					

BEKAR, DERÉK   LW/C   BLUES

PERSONAL: Born September 15, 1975, in Burnaby, B.C. ... 6-3/194. ... Shoots left.
COLLEGE: New Hampshire.
TRANSACTIONS/CAREER NOTES: Selected by St. Louis Blues in eighth round (seventh Blues pick, 205th overall) of NHL entry draft (July 8, 1995).
HONORS: Named to Hockey East All-Star second team (1997-98).

Season Team	League	REGULAR SEASON								PLAYOFFS				
		Gms.	G	A	Pts.	PIM	+/-	PP	SH	Gms.	G	A	Pts.	PIM
94-95—Powell River	BCJHL	46	33	29	62	35	...	...	...	—	—	—	—	—
95-96—Univ. of New Hamp.....	Hockey East	34	15	18	33	4	...	...	...	—	—	—	—	—
96-97—Univ. of New Hamp.	Hockey East	39	18	21	39	34	...	...	...	—	—	—	—	—
97-98—Univ. of New Hamp.	Hockey East	35	32	28	60	46	...	...	...	—	—	—	—	—
98-99—Worcester	AHL	51	16	20	36	6	...	...	...	4	0	0	0	0
99-00—Worcester	AHL	71	21	19	40	26	...	...	...	7	0	3	3	2
—St. Louis	NHL	1	0	0	0	0	0	0	0	—	—	—	—	—
NHL Totals (1 year).............		1	0	0	0	0	0	0	0					

BELAK, WADE   D   FLAMES

PERSONAL: Born March 7, 1976, in Saskatoon, Sask. ... 6-4/222. ... Shoots right. ... Brother of Graham Belak, defenseman, Colorado Avalanche system. ... Name pronounced BEE-lak.
HIGH SCHOOL: North Battleford (Sask.) Comprehensive.
TRANSACTIONS/CAREER NOTES: Selected by Quebec Nordiques in first round (first Nordiques pick, 12th overall) of NHL entry draft (June 28, 1994). ... Nordiques franchise moved to Colorado and renamed Avalanche for 1995-96 season (June 21, 1995). ... Pulled abdominal muscle (March 5, 1998); missed six games. ... Strained groin (October 9, 1998); missed first two games of season. ... Strained groin (October 26, 1998); missed one game. ... Reinjured groin (November 2, 1998); missed 10 games. ... Traded by Avalanche with LW Rene Corbet and future considerations to Calgary Flames for RW Theo Fleury and LW Chris Dingman (February 28, 1999); Flames acquired D Robyn Regehr to complete deal (March 27, 1999). ... Suffered concussion (November 10, 1999); missed one game. ... Injured shoulder (February 10, 2000); missed 18 games. ... Injured groin (March 22, 2000); missed three games.

Season Team	League	REGULAR SEASON								PLAYOFFS				
		Gms.	G	A	Pts.	PIM	+/-	PP	SH	Gms.	G	A	Pts.	PIM
91-92—North Battleford	SJHL	57	6	20	26	186	...	...	...	—	—	—	—	—
92-93—North Battleford	SJHL	32	3	13	16	142	...	...	...	—	—	—	—	—
93-94—Saskatoon.................	WHL	69	4	13	17	226	...	...	...	16	2	2	4	43
94-95—Saskatoon.................	WHL	72	4	14	18	290	...	...	...	9	0	0	0	36
—Cornwall	AHL	—	—	—	—	—	...	...	...	11	1	2	3	40
95-96—Saskatoon.................	WHL	63	3	15	18	207	...	...	...	4	0	0	0	9
—Cornwall	AHL	5	0	0	0	18	...	...	...	2	0	0	0	2
96-97—Colorado.................	NHL	5	0	0	0	11	-1	0	0	—	—	—	—	—
—Hershey	AHL	65	1	7	8	320	...	...	...	16	0	1	1	61
97-98—Colorado.................	NHL	8	1	1	2	27	-3	0	0	—	—	—	—	—
—Hershey	AHL	11	0	0	0	30	...	...	...	—	—	—	—	—
98-99—Colorado.................	NHL	22	0	0	0	71	-2	0	0	—	—	—	—	—
—Hershey	AHL	17	0	1	1	49	...	...	...	—	—	—	—	—
—Saint John	AHL	12	0	2	2	43	...	...	...	6	0	1	1	23
—Calgary	NHL	9	0	1	1	23	3	0	0	—	—	—	—	—
99-00—Calgary	NHL	40	0	2	2	122	-4	0	0	—	—	—	—	—
NHL Totals (4 years)...........		84	1	4	5	254	-7	0	0					

BELANGER, JESSE   C   ISLANDERS

PERSONAL: Born June 15, 1969, in St. Georges Beauce, Que. ... 6-1/190. ... Shoots right. ... Name pronounced buh-LAH-zhay.
TRANSACTIONS/CAREER NOTES: Signed as non-drafted free agent by Montreal Canadiens (October 3, 1990). ... Selected by Florida Panthers in NHL expansion draft (June 24, 1993). ... Strained right Achilles' tendon (October 12, 1993); missed one game. ... Fractured bone in left hand (February 13, 1994); missed 12 games. ... Suffered from illness (March 24, 1995); missed one game. ... Traded by Panthers to Vancouver Canucks for future considerations (March 20, 1996). ... Signed as free agent by Edmonton Oilers (August 28, 1996). ... Signed as free agent by Tampa Bay Lightning (July 30, 1998). ... Signed as free agent by Canadiens (July 9, 1999). ... Signed as free agent by New York Islanders (July 27, 2000).
MISCELLANEOUS: Member of Stanley Cup championship team (1993).

Season Team	League	REGULAR SEASON								PLAYOFFS				
		Gms.	G	A	Pts.	PIM	+/-	PP	SH	Gms.	G	A	Pts.	PIM
87-88—Granby......................	QMJHL	69	33	43	76	10	...	...	...	5	3	3	6	0
88-89—Granby......................	QMJHL	67	40	63	103	26	...	...	...	4	0	5	5	0
89-90—Granby......................	QMJHL	67	53	54	107	53	...	...	...	—	—	—	—	—
90-91—Fredericton	AHL	75	40	58	98	30	...	...	...	6	2	4	6	0

Season Team	League	REGULAR SEASON								PLAYOFFS				
		Gms.	G	A	Pts.	PIM	+/-	PP	SH	Gms.	G	A	Pts.	PIM
91-92—Fredericton	AHL	65	30	41	71	26	...	...	...	7	3	3	6	2
—Montreal	NHL	4	0	0	0	0	-1	0	0	—	—	—	—	—
92-93—Fredericton	AHL	39	19	32	51	24	...	...	...	—	—	—	—	—
—Montreal	NHL	19	4	2	6	4	1	0	0	9	0	1	1	0
93-94—Florida	NHL	70	17	33	50	16	-4	11	0	—	—	—	—	—
94-95—Florida	NHL	47	15	14	29	18	-5	6	0	—	—	—	—	—
95-96—Florida	NHL	63	17	21	38	10	-5	7	0	—	—	—	—	—
—Vancouver	NHL	9	3	0	3	0	0	1	0	3	0	2	2	2
96-97—Hamilton	AHL	6	4	3	7	0	...	...	...	—	—	—	—	—
—Quebec	IHL	47	34	28	62	18	...	...	...	9	3	5	8	13
—Edmonton	NHL	6	0	0	0	0	-3	0	0	—	—	—	—	—
97-98—SC Herisau	Switzerland	5	4	3	7	4	...	...	...	—	—	—	—	—
—Las Vegas	IHL	54	32	36	68	20	...	...	...	4	0	1	1	0
98-99—Cleveland	IHL	22	9	13	22	10	...	...	...	—	—	—	—	—
99-00—Quebec	AHL	36	15	18	33	20	...	...	...	3	0	3	3	4
—Montreal	NHL	16	3	6	9	2	2	0	0	—	—	—	—	—
NHL Totals (7 years)		234	59	76	135	54	-15	25	0	12	0	3	3	2

BELANGER, KEN — LW — BRUINS

PERSONAL: Born May 14, 1974, in Sault Ste. Marie, Ont. ... 6-4/225. ... Shoots left. ... Name pronounced buh-LAH-zhay.
TRANSACTIONS/CAREER NOTES: Selected by Hartford Whalers in seventh round (seventh Whalers pick, 153rd overall) of NHL entry draft (June 20, 1992). ... Traded by Whalers to Toronto Maple Leafs for ninth-round pick (RW Matt Ball) in 1994 draft (March 18, 1994). ... Traded by Maple Leafs with G Damian Rhodes to New York Islanders for C Kirk Muller (January 23, 1996). ... Suffered concussion (February 6, 1996); missed two games. ... Suffered concussion (February 12, 1996); missed remainder of season. ... Suffered concussion (October 13, 1997); missed four games. ... Injured hand (November 15, 1997); missed three games. ... Suffered from the flu (November 26, 1997); missed three games. ... Reinjured hand (January 8, 1998); missed two games. ... Underwent thumb surgery (January 14, 1998); missed 22 games. ... Traded by Islanders to Boston Bruins for LW Ted Donato (November 7, 1998). ... Suffered facial laceration (November 8, 1998); missed two games. ... Strained neck (December 28, 1998); missed two games. ... Injured hand (April 3, 1999); missed one game. ... Suffered concussion (November 10, 1999); missed 34 games. ... Suffered groin injury (March 29, 2000); missed final six games of season.

Season Team	League	REGULAR SEASON								PLAYOFFS				
		Gms.	G	A	Pts.	PIM	+/-	PP	SH	Gms.	G	A	Pts.	PIM
91-92—Ottawa	OHL	51	4	4	8	174	...	...	...	11	0	0	0	24
92-93—Ottawa	OHL	34	6	12	18	139	...	...	...	—	—	—	—	—
—Guelph	OHL	29	10	14	24	86	...	...	...	5	2	1	3	14
93-94—Guelph	OHL	55	11	22	33	185	...	...	...	9	2	3	5	30
94-95—St. John's	AHL	47	5	5	10	246	...	...	...	4	0	0	0	30
—Toronto	NHL	3	0	0	0	9	0	0	0	—	—	—	—	—
95-96—St. John's	AHL	40	16	14	30	222	...	...	...	—	—	—	—	—
—New York Islanders	NHL	7	0	0	0	27	-2	0	0	—	—	—	—	—
96-97—Kentucky	AHL	38	10	12	22	164	...	...	...	4	0	1	1	27
—New York Islanders	NHL	18	0	2	2	102	-1	0	0	—	—	—	—	—
97-98—New York Islanders	NHL	37	3	1	4	101	1	0	0	—	—	—	—	—
98-99—New York Islanders	NHL	9	1	1	2	30	1	0	0	—	—	—	—	—
—Boston	NHL	45	1	4	5	152	-2	0	0	12	1	0	1	16
99-00—Boston	NHL	37	2	2	4	44	-4	0	0	—	—	—	—	—
NHL Totals (6 years)		156	7	10	17	465	-7	0	0	12	1	0	1	16

BELFOUR, ED — G — STARS

PERSONAL: Born April 21, 1965, in Carman, Man. ... 5-11/192. ... Catches left. ... Full Name: Edward Belfour.
COLLEGE: North Dakota.
TRANSACTIONS/CAREER NOTES: Signed as non-drafted free agent by Chicago Blackhawks (June 18, 1987). ... Strained hip muscle (1993-94 season); missed four games. ... Sprained knee (January 31, 1996); missed one game. ... Injured back (February 19, 1996); missed three games. ... Traded by Blackhawks to San Jose Sharks for G Chris Terreri, D Michal Sykora and RW Ulf Dahlen (January 25, 1997). ... Injured knee ligament (February 1, 1997); missed 13 games. ... Suffered bulging disc in back (March 1, 1997); missed seven games. ... Signed as free agent by Dallas Stars (July 2, 1997). ... Strained lower back (February 2, 1998); missed three games. ... Strained groin (November 10, 1999); missed one game.
HONORS: Named top goaltender in MJHL (1985-86). ... Named to NCAA All-America (West) second team (1986-87). ... Named to NCAA All-Tournament team (1986-87). ... Named to WCHA All-Star first team (1986-87). ... Shared Garry F. Longman Memorial Trophy with John Cullen (1987-88). ... Named to IHL All-Star first team (1987-88). ... Named Rookie of the Year by The Sporting News (1990-91). ... Won Vezina Trophy (1990-91 and 1992-93). ... Won Calder Memorial Trophy (1990-91). ... Won William M. Jennings Trophy (1990-91, 1992-93 and 1994-95). ... Won Trico Goaltender Award (1990-91). ... Named to The Sporting News All-Star first team (1990-91). ... Named to NHL All-Star first team (1990-91 and 1992-93). ... Named to NHL All-Rookie team (1990-91). ... Played in NHL All-Star Game (1992, 1993, 1996, 1998 and 1999). ... Named to The Sporting News All-Star second team (1992-93 and 1994-95). ... Shared William M. Jennings Trophy with Roman Turek (1998-99).
RECORDS: Shares NHL single-season playoff record for most consecutive wins by goaltender—11 (1992); most wins by goaltender—16 (1999); and most minutes played by goaltender—1,544 (1999).
MISCELLANEOUS: Member of Stanley Cup championship team (1999). ... Holds Dallas Stars franchise all-time record for goals-against average (1.99). ... Stopped penalty shot attempt (vs. Steve Maltais, February 25, 1993; vs. Roman Oksiuta, February 4, 1994; vs. Mark Howe, March 22, 1994). ... Allowed penalty shot goal (vs. Philippe Bozon, April 3, 1993; vs. Steve Larmer, January 16, 1994).
STATISTICAL NOTES: Led NHL with .910 save percentage (1990-91). ... Led NHL with .669 winning percentage (1998-99). ... Tied for NHL lead in save percentage with .919 (1999-2000).

Season Team	League	REGULAR SEASON								PLAYOFFS						
		Gms.	Min	W	L	T	GA	SO	Avg.	Gms.	Min.	W	L	GA	SO	Avg.
85-86—Winkler	MJHL	48	2880	...	...	...	124	1	2.58	—	—	—	—	—	—	—
86-87—Univ. of North Dakota	WCHA	34	2049	29	4	0	81	3	2.37	—	—	—	—	—	—	—
87-88—Saginaw	IHL	61	*3446	32	25	0	183	3	3.19	9	561	4	5	33	0	3.53

Season Team	League	REGULAR SEASON								PLAYOFFS						
		Gms.	Min	W	L	T	GA	SO	Avg.	Gms.	Min.	W	L	GA	SO	Avg.
88-89—Chicago	NHL	23	1148	4	12	3	74	0	3.87	—	—	—	—	—	—	—
—Saginaw	IHL	29	1760	12	10	0	92	0	3.14	5	298	2	3	14	0	2.82
89-90—Canadian nat'l team	Int'l	33	1808	...	...	...	93	...	3.09	—	—	—	—	—	—	—
—Chicago	NHL	—	—	—	—	—	—	—	—	9	409	4	2	17	0	2.49
90-91—Chicago	NHL	*74	*4127	*43	19	7	170	4	*2.47	6	295	2	4	20	0	4.07
91-92—Chicago	NHL	52	2928	21	18	10	132	†5	2.70	18	949	12	4	39	1	*2.47
92-93—Chicago	NHL	*71	*4106	41	18	11	177	*7	2.59	4	249	0	4	13	0	3.13
93-94—Chicago	NHL	70	3998	37	24	6	178	†7	2.67	6	360	2	4	15	0	2.50
94-95—Chicago	NHL	42	2450	22	15	3	93	†5	2.28	16	1014	9	†7	37	1	2.19
95-96—Chicago	NHL	50	2956	22	17	10	135	1	2.74	9	666	6	3	23	1	*2.07
96-97—Chicago	NHL	33	1966	11	15	6	88	1	2.69	—	—	—	—	—	—	—
—San Jose	NHL	13	757	3	9	0	43	1	3.41	—	—	—	—	—	—	—
97-98—Dallas	NHL	61	3581	37	12	10	112	9	*1.88	17	1039	10	7	31	1	1.79
98-99—Dallas	NHL	61	3536	35	15	9	117	5	1.99	*23	*1544	*16	7	43	*3	*1.67
99-00—Dallas	NHL	62	3620	32	21	7	127	4	2.10	†23	1443	14	*9	*45	*4	1.87
NHL Totals (12 years)		612	35173	308	195	82	1446	49	2.47	131	7968	75	51	283	11	2.13

BELL, MARK   C/LW   BLACKHAWKS

PERSONAL: Born August 5, 1980, in St. Paul's, Ont. ... 6-3/198. ... Shoots left.
TRANSACTIONS/CAREER NOTES: Selected by Chicago Blackhawks in first round (first Blackhawks pick, eighth overall) of NHL entry draft (June 27, 1998).

Season Team	League	REGULAR SEASON								PLAYOFFS				
		Gms.	G	A	Pts.	PIM	+/-	PP	SH	Gms.	G	A	Pts.	PIM
95-96—Stratford Jr. B	OHA	47	8	15	23	32	...	...	...	—	—	—	—	—
96-97—Ottawa	OHL	65	8	12	20	40	...	...	...	24	4	7	11	13
97-98—Ottawa	OHL	55	34	26	60	87	...	...	...	13	6	5	11	14
98-99—Ottawa	OHL	44	29	26	55	69	...	...	...	9	6	5	11	8
99-00—Ottawa	OHL	48	34	38	72	95	...	...	...	2	0	1	1	0

BELLEFEUILLE, BLAKE   C   BLUE JACKETS

PERSONAL: Born December 27, 1977, in Framingham, Mass. ... 5-10/208. ... Shoots right. ... Name pronounced BELL-fay.
COLLEGE: Boston College.
TRANSACTIONS/CAREER NOTES: Signed as non-drafted free agent by Columbus Blue Jackets (May 31, 2000).
HONORS: Named to Hockey East All-Star second team (1999-2000).

Season Team	League	REGULAR SEASON								PLAYOFFS				
		Gms.	G	A	Pts.	PIM	+/-	PP	SH	Gms.	G	A	Pts.	PIM
96-97—Boston College	Hockey East	34	16	19	35	20	...	...	...	—	—	—	—	—
97-98—Boston College	Hockey East	41	19	20	39	35	...	...	...	—	—	—	—	—
98-99—Boston College	Hockey East	43	24	25	49	80	...	...	...	—	—	—	—	—
99-00—Boston College	Hockey East	41	19	32	51	28	...	...	...	—	—	—	—	—

BERANEK, JOSEF   LW   PENGUINS

PERSONAL: Born October 25, 1969, in Litvinov, Czechoslovakia. ... 6-2/195. ... Shoots left. ... Name pronounced JOH-sehf buh-RAH-nehk.
TRANSACTIONS/CAREER NOTES: Selected by Edmonton Oilers in fourth round (third Oilers pick, 78th overall) of NHL entry draft (June 17, 1989). ... Traded by Oilers with D Greg Hawgood to Philadelphia Flyers for D Brian Benning (January 16, 1993). ... Bruised left shoulder (January 30, 1994); missed three games. ... Played in Europe during 1994-95 NHL lockout. ... Traded by Flyers to Vancouver Canucks for LW Shawn Antoski (February 15, 1995). ... Sprained thumb (February 2, 1996); missed two games. ... Injured thumb (February 17, 1996); missed one game. ... Traded by Canucks to Pittsburgh Penguins for future considerations (March 18, 1997). ... Bruised shoulder (March 24, 1997); missed one game. ... Strained groin (April 8, 1997); missed two games. ... Traded by Penguins to Oilers for D Bobby Dollas and C Tony Hrkac (June 16, 1998). ... Bruised thigh (October 20, 1998); missed two games. ... Sprained shoulder (December 8, 1998); missed three games. ... Sprained knee (February 23, 1999); missed three games. ... Injured left knee (April 3, 1999) and underwent arthoscopic surgery; missed final six games of regular season and two playoff games. ... Traded by Oilers to Penguins for C German Titov (March 14, 2000).
MISCELLANEOUS: Member of gold-medal-winning Czech Republic Olympic Team (1998).
STATISTICAL PLATEAUS: Three-goal games: 1994-95 (1).

Season Team	League	REGULAR SEASON								PLAYOFFS				
		Gms.	G	A	Pts.	PIM	+/-	PP	SH	Gms.	G	A	Pts.	PIM
87-88—CHZ Litvinov	Czech.	14	7	4	11	12	...	...	...	—	—	—	—	—
88-89—CHZ Litvinov	Czech.	32	18	10	28	47	...	...	...	—	—	—	—	—
—Czechoslovakia Jr.	Czech.	5	2	7	9	2	...	...	...	—	—	—	—	—
89-90—Dukla Trencin	Czech.	49	16	21	37	...	...	...	...	—	—	—	—	—
90-91—CHZ Litvinov	Czech.	50	27	27	54	98	...	...	...	—	—	—	—	—
91-92—Edmonton	NHL	58	12	16	28	18	-2	0	0	12	2	1	3	0
92-93—Edmonton	NHL	26	2	6	8	28	-7	0	0	—	—	—	—	—
—Cape Breton	AHL	6	1	2	3	8	...	...	...	—	—	—	—	—
—Philadelphia	NHL	40	13	12	25	50	-1	1	0	—	—	—	—	—
93-94—Philadelphia	NHL	80	28	21	49	85	-2	6	0	—	—	—	—	—
94-95—Czech Rep.	Czech Rep.	16	7	7	14	26	...	...	...	—	—	—	—	—
—Philadelphia	NHL	14	5	5	10	2	3	1	0	—	—	—	—	—
—Vancouver	NHL	37	8	13	21	28	-10	2	0	11	1	1	2	12
95-96—Vancouver	NHL	61	6	14	20	60	-11	0	0	3	2	1	3	0
96-97—Vsetin	Czech Rep.	39	19	24	43	115	...	...	...	3	3	2	5	4
—Pittsburgh	NHL	8	3	1	4	4	-1	1	0	5	0	0	0	2

Season Team	League	REGULAR SEASON								PLAYOFFS					
		Gms.	Min	W	L	T	GA	SO	Avg.	Gms.	Min.	W	L	GA	SO	Avg.
97-98—Vsetin	Czech Rep.	45	24	27	51	92	...	...	...	10	2		8	10		14
—Czech Rep. Oly. team..	Int'l	6	1	0	1	4	...	...	...	—	—	—	—	—	—
98-99—Edmonton	NHL	66	19	30	49	23	6	7	0	2	0		0	0		4
99-00—Edmonton	NHL	58	9	8	17	39	-6	3	0	—	—	—	—	—	—
—Pittsburgh	NHL	13	4	4	8	18	-6	1	0	11	0		3	3		4
NHL Totals (8 years)		461	109	130	239	355	-37	22	0	44	5		6	11		22

BERARD, BRYAN — D — MAPLE LEAFS

PERSONAL: Born March 5, 1977, in Woonsocket, R.I. ... 6-1/190. ... Shoots left. ... Name pronounced buh-RAHRD.

HIGH SCHOOL: Mount St. Charles (Woonsocket, R.I.).

COLLEGE: University of Michigan-Dearborn.

TRANSACTIONS/CAREER NOTES: Selected by Ottawa Senators in first round (first Senators pick, first overall) of NHL entry draft (July 8, 1995). ... Traded by Senators with C Martin Straka to New York Islanders for D Wade Redden and G Damian Rhodes (January 23, 1996). ... Strained groin (October 16, 1997); missed one game. ... Reinjured groin (November 10, 1997); missed two games. ... Reinjured groin (November 15, 1997); missed three games. ... Bruised elbow (March 24, 1998); missed one game. ... Strained groin (December 18, 1998); missed nine games. ... Traded by Islanders with sixth-round pick (RW Jan Sochor) in 1999 draft to Toronto Maple Leafs for G Felix Potvin and sixth-round pick (C Fedor Fedorov) in 1999 draft (January 9, 1999). ... Strained groin (January 7, 1999); missed three games. ... Suffered from the flu (March 28, 1999); missed two games. ... Suspended two games by NHL for illegal check (October 19, 1999). ... Suffered injury (November 23, 1999); missed three games. ... Suffered eye injury (March 11, 2000); missed remainder of season.

HONORS: Won Can.HL Rookie of the Year Award (1994-95). ... Won Can.HL Top Draft Prospect Award (1994-95). ... Won Emms Family Trophy (1994-95). ... Won Max Kaminsky Trophy (1994-95 and 1995-96). ... Won OHL Top Draft Prospect Award (1994-95). ... Named to Can.HL All-Star first team (1994-95 and 1995-96). ... Named to Can.HL All-Rookie team (1994-95). ... Named to OHL All-Star first team (1994-95 and 1995-96). ... Won Can.HL Defenseman of the Year Award (1995-96). ... Named NHL Rookie of the Year by THE SPORTING NEWS (1996-97). ... Won Calder Memorial Trophy (1996-97). ... Named to NHL All-Rookie team (1996-97).

Season Team	League	REGULAR SEASON								PLAYOFFS				
		Gms.	G	A	Pts.	PIM	+/-	PP	SH	Gms.	G	A	Pts.	PIM
91-92—Mt. St. Charles H.S.	R.I.H.S.	32	3	15	18	10	...	...	...	—	—	—	—	—
92-93—Mt. St. Charles H.S.	R.I.H.S.	32	8	12	20	18	...	...	...	—	—	—	—	—
93-94—Mt. St. Charles H.S.	R.I.H.S.	32	11	36	47	5	...	...	...	—	—	—	—	—
94-95—Det. Jr. Red Wings	OHL	58	20	55	75	97	...	...	...	21	4	20	24	38
95-96—Det. Jr. Red Wings	OHL	56	31	58	89	116	...	...	...	17	7	18	25	41
96-97—New York Islanders	NHL	82	8	40	48	86	1	3	0	—	—	—	—	—
97-98—New York Islanders	NHL	75	14	32	46	59	-32	8	1	—	—	—	—	—
—U.S. Olympic team	Int'l	2	0	0	0	0	...	...	...	—	—	—	—	—
98-99—New York Islanders	NHL	31	4	11	15	26	-6	2	0	—	—	—	—	—
—Toronto	NHL	38	5	14	19	22	7	2	0	17	1	8	9	8
99-00—Toronto	NHL	64	3	27	30	42	11	1	0	—	—	—	—	—
NHL Totals (4 years)		290	34	124	158	235	-19	16	1	17	1	8	9	8

BEREHOWSKY, DRAKE — D — PREDATORS

PERSONAL: Born January 3, 1972, in Toronto. ... 6-2/212. ... Shoots right. ... Name pronounced BAIR-ih-HOW-skee.

TRANSACTIONS/CAREER NOTES: Selected by Toronto Maple Leafs in first round (first Maple Leafs pick, 10th overall) of NHL entry draft (June 16, 1990). ... Sprained knee (April 15, 1993); missed remainder of season. ... Underwent knee surgery prior to 1994-95 season; missed first four games of season. ... Traded by Maple Leafs to Pittsburgh Penguins for D Grant Jennings (April 7, 1995). ... Signed as free agent by Edmonton Oilers (September 29, 1997). ... Traded by Oilers with G Eric Fichaud and D Greg de Vries to Nashville Predators for F Jim Dowd and G Mikhail Shtalenkov (October 1, 1998). ... Sprained knee (February 4, 1999); missed two games. ... Injured neck (October 2, 1999); missed first game of season.

HONORS: Won Can.HL Defenseman of the Year Award (1991-92). ... Won Max Kaminsky Trophy (1991-92). ... Named to Can.HL All-Star first team (1991-92). ... Named to OHL All-Star first team (1991-92).

Season Team	League	REGULAR SEASON								PLAYOFFS				
		Gms.	G	A	Pts.	PIM	+/-	PP	SH	Gms.	G	A	Pts.	PIM
87-88—Barrie Jr. B	OHA	40	10	36	46	81	...	...	...	—	—	—	—	—
88-89—Kingston	OHL	63	7	39	46	85	...	...	...	—	—	—	—	—
89-90—Kingston	OHL	9	3	11	14	28	...	...	...	—	—	—	—	—
90-91—Toronto	NHL	8	0	1	1	25	-6	0	0	—	—	—	—	—
—Kingston	OHL	13	5	13	18	28	...	...	...	—	—	—	—	—
—North Bay	OHL	26	7	23	30	51	...	...	...	10	2	7	9	21
91-92—North Bay	OHL	62	19	63	82	147	...	...	...	21	7	24	31	22
—Toronto	NHL	1	0	0	0	0	0	0	0	—	—	—	—	—
—St. John's	AHL	—	—	—	—	—	...	...	...	6	0	5	5	21
92-93—Toronto	NHL	41	4	15	19	61	1	1	0	—	—	—	—	—
—St. John's	AHL	28	10	17	27	38	...	...	...	—	—	—	—	—
93-94—Toronto	NHL	49	2	8	10	63	-3	2	0	—	—	—	—	—
—St. John's	AHL	18	3	12	15	40	...	...	...	—	—	—	—	—
94-95—Toronto	NHL	25	0	2	2	15	-10	0	0	—	—	—	—	—
—Pittsburgh	NHL	4	0	0	0	13	1	0	0	1	0	0	0	0
95-96—Cleveland	IHL	74	6	28	34	141	...	...	...	3	0	3	3	6
—Pittsburgh	NHL	1	0	0	0	0	1	0	0	—	—	—	—	—
96-97—San Antonio	IHL	16	3	4	7	36	...	...	...	—	—	—	—	—
—Carolina	AHL	49	2	15	17	55	...	...	...	—	—	—	—	—
97-98—Edmonton	NHL	67	1	6	7	169	1	1	0	12	1	2	3	14
—Hamilton	AHL	8	2	0	2	21	...	...	...	—	—	—	—	—
98-99—Nashville	NHL	74	2	15	17	140	-9	0	0	—	—	—	—	—
99-00—Nashville	NHL	79	12	20	32	87	-4	5	0	—	—	—	—	—
NHL Totals (9 years)		349	21	67	88	573	-28	9	0	13	1	2	3	14

BERENZWEIG, BUBBA   D   PREDATORS

PERSONAL: Born August 8, 1977, in Arlington Heights, Ill. ... 6-2/218. ... Shoots left. ... Full Name: Andrew Berenzweig.
HIGH SCHOOL: Buffalo Grove (Ill.), then Loomis-Chaffee Prep School (Windsor, Conn.).
COLLEGE: Michigan.
TRANSACTIONS/CAREER NOTES: Selected by New York Islanders in fifth round (fifth Islanders pick, 109th overall) of NHL entry draft (June 22, 1996). ... Traded by Islanders to Nashville Predators for fourth-round pick (D Johan Halvardsson) in 1999 draft (April 19, 1999).
HONORS: Named to NCAA All-Tournament team (1997-98). ... Named to CCHA All-Star second team (1997-98). ... Won Ken McKenzie Trophy (1999-2000).

		REGULAR SEASON							PLAYOFFS				
Season Team	League	Gms.	G	A	Pts.	PIM	+/-	PP	SH	Gms.	G	A	Pts.	PIM
94-95—Loomis-Chaffee	Conn. H.S.	23	19	23	42	24	...	...	...	—	—	—	—	—
95-96—Univ. of Michigan.......	CCHA	42	4	8	12	4	...	...	...	—	—	—	—	—
96-97—Univ. of Michigan.......	CCHA	38	7	12	19	49	...	...	...	—	—	—	—	—
97-98—Univ. of Michigan.......	CCHA	43	6	10	16	28	...	...	...	—	—	—	—	—
98-99—Univ. of Michigan.......	CCHA	42	7	24	31	38	...	...	...	—	—	—	—	—
99-00—Milwaukee..................	IHL	79	4	23	27	48	...	...	...	3	1	2	3	0
—Nashville....................	NHL	2	0	0	0	0	-1	0	0	—	—	—	—	—
NHL Totals (1 year).............		2	0	0	0	0	-1	0	0					

BEREZIN, SERGEI   LW   MAPLE LEAFS

PERSONAL: Born November 5, 1971, in Voskresensk, U.S.S.R. ... 5-10/200. ... Shoots right. ... Name pronounced BAIR-ih-zihn.
TRANSACTIONS/CAREER NOTES: Selected by Toronto Maple Leafs in 10th round (eighth Maple Leafs pick, 256th overall) of NHL entry draft (June 29, 1994). ... Injured hand (November 19, 1996); missed one game. ... Underwent hand surgery (December 3, 1996); missed six games. ... Strained knee (December 23, 1996); missed two games. ... Suffered hip pointer (October 30, 1998); missed four games. ... Bruised foot (November 12, 1998); missed two games. ... Suffered injury (January 8, 2000); missed five games. ... Injured hamstring (January 27, 2000); missed 14 games. ... Suffered injury (April 5, 2000); missed one game.
HONORS: Named to NHL All-Rookie team (1996-97).
STATISTICAL PLATEAUS: Three-goal games: 1998-99 (2).

		REGULAR SEASON							PLAYOFFS				
Season Team	League	Gms.	G	A	Pts.	PIM	+/-	PP	SH	Gms.	G	A	Pts.	PIM
90-91—Khimik Voskresensk ...	USSR	30	6	2	8	4	...	...	...	—	—	—	—	—
91-92—Khimik Voskresensk ...	CIS	36	7	5	12	10	...	...	...	—	—	—	—	—
92-93—Khimik Voskresensk ...	CIS	38	9	3	12	12	...	...	...	2	1	0	1	0
93-94—Khimik Voskresensk ...	CIS	40	31	10	41	16	...	...	...	—	—	—	—	—
—Russian nat'l team ...	Int'l	6	2	1	3	2	...	...	...	—	—	—	—	—
—Russian Oly. team.....	Int'l	8	3	2	5	2	...	...	...	—	—	—	—	—
94-95—Koln	Germany	43	38	19	57	8	...	...	...	18	17	8	25	18
—Russian nat'l team ...	Int'l	6	7	1	8	4	...	...	...	—	—	—	—	—
95-96—Koln	Germany	45	49	31	80	8	...	...	...	14	13	9	22	4
—Russian nat'l team	Int'l	8	4	5	9	2	...	...	...	—	—	—	—	—
96-97—Toronto	NHL	73	25	16	41	2	-3	7	0	—	—	—	—	—
97-98—Toronto	NHL	68	16	15	31	10	-3	3	0	—	—	—	—	—
98-99—Toronto	NHL	76	37	22	59	12	16	9	1	17	6	6	12	4
99-00—Toronto	NHL	61	26	13	39	2	8	5	0	12	4	4	8	0
NHL Totals (4 years)...........		278	104	66	170	26	18	24	1	29	10	10	20	4

BERG, AKI   D   KINGS

PERSONAL: Born July 28, 1977, in Turku, Finland. ... 6-3/220. ... Shoots left. ... Full Name: Aki-Petteri Berg. ... Name pronounced AH-kee BUHRG.
TRANSACTIONS/CAREER NOTES: Selected by Los Angeles Kings in first round (first Kings pick, third overall) of NHL entry draft (July 8, 1995). ... Suffered charley horse (January 25, 1997); missed one game. ... Suffered concussion (February 3, 1997); missed two games. ... Sprained left ankle (April 9, 1997); missed final two games of regular season. ... Bruised right foot (December 4, 1997); missed one game. ... Sprained right wrist (March 10, 1998); missed two games. ... Injured ribs (December 23, 1999); missed two games. ... Suffered concussion (March 13, 2000); missed two games.
MISCELLANEOUS: Member of bronze-medal-winning Finnish Olympic team (1998).

		REGULAR SEASON							PLAYOFFS				
Season Team	League	Gms.	G	A	Pts.	PIM	+/-	PP	SH	Gms.	G	A	Pts.	PIM
92-93—TPS Turku Jr.	Finland	39	18	24	42	59	...	...	...	—	—	—	—	—
93-94—TPS Turku Jr.	Finland	21	3	11	14	24	...	...	...	7	0	0	0	10
—TPS Turku.................	Finland	6	0	3	3	4	...	...	...	—	—	—	—	—
94-95—Kiekko-67	Finland Div. 2	20	3	9	12	34	...	...	...	—	—	—	—	—
—TPS Turku Jr.	Finland	8	1	0	1	30	...	...	...	—	—	—	—	—
—TPS Turku.................	Finland	5	0	0	0	4	...	...	...	—	—	—	—	—
95-96—Los Angeles.............	NHL	51	0	7	7	29	-13	0	0	—	—	—	—	—
—Phoenix.....................	IHL	20	0	3	3	18	...	...	...	2	0	0	0	4
96-97—Los Angeles.............	NHL	41	2	6	8	24	-9	2	0	—	—	—	—	—
—Phoenix.....................	IHL	23	1	3	4	21	...	...	...	—	—	—	—	—
97-98—Los Angeles.............	NHL	72	0	8	8	61	3	0	0	4	0	3	3	0
—Fin. Olympic team.....	Int'l	6	0	0	0	6	...	...	...	—	—	—	—	—
98-99—TPS Turku.................	Finland	48	8	7	15	137	...	...	...	9	1	1	2	45
99-00—Los Angeles.............	NHL	70	3	13	16	45	-1	0	0	2	0	0	0	2
NHL Totals (4 years)...........		234	5	34	39	159	-20	2	0	6	0	3	3	2

B

BERGEVIN, MARC   D   BLUES

PERSONAL: Born August 11, 1965, in Montreal. ... 6-1/214. ... Shoots left. ... Name pronounced BUHR-jih-vihn.
TRANSACTIONS/CAREER NOTES: Selected by Chicago Blackhawks as underage junior in third round (third Blackhawks pick, 59th overall) of NHL entry draft (June 8, 1983). ... Sprained neck (March 18, 1987). ... Traded by Blackhawks with D Gary Nylund to New York Islanders for D Steve Konroyd and C Bob Bassen (November 25, 1988). ... Bruised ribs (November 25, 1989). ... Broke hand (May 1990). ... Traded by Islanders to Hartford Whalers for future considerations; Islanders later received fifth-round pick in 1992 draft (C Ryan Duthie) to complete deal (October 31, 1990). ... Signed as free agent by Tampa Bay Lightning (July 9, 1992). ... Injured foot (March 18, 1993); missed one game. ... Bruised back (November 19, 1993); missed one game. ... Injured elbow (March 10, 1995); missed one game. ... Suffered from sore neck (April 22, 1995); missed three games. ... Traded by Lightning with RW Ben Hankinson to Detroit Red Wings for LW Shawn Burr and third-round pick (traded to Boston) in 1996 draft (August 17, 1995). ... Suffered from the flu (November 1, 1995); missed one game. ... Injured groin (April 7, 1996); missed three games. ... Signed as free agent by St. Louis Blues (July 9, 1996). ... Injured ankle (December 13, 1997); missed one game. ... Strained abdominal muscle (January 9, 1999); missed 20 games. ... Reinjured abdominal muscle (April 3, 1999) and underwent surgery; missed remainder of season.

Season Team	League	REGULAR SEASON Gms.	G	A	Pts.	PIM	+/-	PP	SH	PLAYOFFS Gms.	G	A	Pts.	PIM
82-83—Chicoutimi	QMJHL	64	3	27	30	113	...	...	...	—	—	—	—	—
83-84—Chicoutimi	QMJHL	70	10	35	45	125	...	...	...	—	—	—	—	—
—Springfield	AHL	7	0	1	1	2	...	...	...	—	—	—	—	—
84-85—Chicago	NHL	60	0	6	6	54	-9	0	0	6	0	3	3	2
—Springfield	AHL	—					...			4	0	0	0	0
85-86—Chicago	NHL	71	7	7	14	60	0	0	0	3	0	0	0	0
86-87—Chicago	NHL	66	4	10	14	66	4	0	0	3	1	0	1	2
87-88—Chicago	NHL	58	1	6	7	85	-19	0	0	—	—	—	—	—
—Saginaw	IHL	10	2	7	9	20	...			—	—	—	—	—
88-89—Chicago	NHL	11	0	0	0	18	-3	0	0	—	—	—	—	—
—New York Islanders	NHL	58	2	13	15	62	2	1	0	—	—	—	—	—
89-90—New York Islanders	NHL	18	0	4	4	30	-8	0	0	—	—	—	—	—
—Springfield	AHL	47	7	16	23	66	...	...	...	17	2	11	13	16
90-91—Hartford	NHL	4	0	0	0	4	-3	0	0	—	—	—	—	—
—Capital District	AHL	7	0	5	5	6	...	...	...	—	—	—	—	—
—Springfield	AHL	58	4	23	27	85	...	...	...	18	0	7	7	26
91-92—Hartford	NHL	75	7	17	24	64	-13	4	1	5	0	0	0	2
92-93—Tampa Bay	NHL	78	2	12	14	66	-16	0	0	—	—	—	—	—
93-94—Tampa Bay	NHL	83	1	15	16	87	-5	0	0	—	—	—	—	—
94-95—Tampa Bay	NHL	44	2	4	6	51	-6	0	1	—	—	—	—	—
95-96—Detroit	NHL	70	1	9	10	33	7	0	0	17	1	0	1	14
96-97—St. Louis	NHL	82	0	4	4	53	-9	0	0	6	1	0	1	8
97-98—St. Louis	NHL	81	3	7	10	90	-2	0	0	10	0	1	1	8
98-99—St. Louis	NHL	52	1	1	2	99	-14	0	0	—	—	—	—	—
99-00—St. Louis	NHL	81	1	8	9	75	27	0	0	7	0	1	1	6
NHL Totals (16 years)		992	32	123	155	997	-67	5	2	57	3	5	8	42

BERTRAND, ERIC   LW   CANADIENS

PERSONAL: Born April 16, 1975, in St. Ephrem, Que. ... 6-1/205. ... Shoots left.
TRANSACTIONS/CAREER NOTES: Selected by New Jersey Devils in eighth round (ninth Devils pick, 207th overall) of NHL entry draft (June 29, 1994). ... Traded by Devils to with RW Wes Mason and seventh-round pick (LW Ken Magowan) in 2000 draft to Atlanta Thrashers for LW Jeff Williams and C Sylvain Cloutier (November 1, 1999). ... Traded by Thrashers to Philadelphia Flyers for RW Brian Wesenberg (December 9, 1999). ... Traded by Flyers to Nashville Predators for future consideration (February 14, 2000). ... Signed as free agent by Montreal Canadiens (July 7, 2000).

Season Team	League	REGULAR SEASON Gms.	G	A	Pts.	PIM	+/-	PP	SH	PLAYOFFS Gms.	G	A	Pts.	PIM
92-93—Granby	QMJHL	64	10	15	25	82	...	...	...	—	—	—	—	—
93-94—Granby	QMJHL	60	11	15	26	151	...	...	...	6	1	0	1	18
94-95—Granby	QMJHL	56	14	26	40	268	...	...	...	13	3	8	11	50
95-96—Albany	AHL	70	16	13	29	199	...	...	...	4	0	0	0	6
96-97—Albany	AHL	77	16	27	43	204	...	...	...	8	3	3	6	15
97-98—Albany	AHL	76	20	29	49	256	...	...	...	13	5	5	10	4
98-99—Albany	AHL	78	34	31	65	160	...	...	...	5	4	2	6	0
99-00—New Jersey	NHL	4	0	0	0	0	-1	0	0	—	—	—	—	—
—Atlanta	NHL	8	0	0	0	4	-5	0	0	—	—	—	—	—
—Philadelphia	AHL	15	3	6	9	67	...	...	...	—	—	—	—	—
—Milwaukee	IHL	27	7	9	16	56	...	...	...	3	0	0	0	2
NHL Totals (1 year)		12	0	0	0	4	-6	0	0					

BERTUZZI, TODD   LW   CANUCKS

PERSONAL: Born February 2, 1975, in Sudbury, Ont. ... 6-3/230. ... Shoots left. ... Name pronounced buhr-TOO-zee.
HIGH SCHOOL: Bishop MacDonnell (Guelph, Ont.).
TRANSACTIONS/CAREER NOTES: Selected by New York Islanders in first round (first Islanders pick, 23rd overall) of NHL entry draft (June 26, 1993). ... Injured eye (February 22, 1996); missed two games. ... Suspended three games by NHL for attempting to break free of a linesman (April 2, 1996). ... Suffered from bone chips in elbow (November 23, 1996); missed one game. ... Traded by Islanders with D Bryan McCabe and third-round pick (LW Jarkko Ruutu) in 1998 draft to Vancouver Canucks for C Trevor Linden (February 6, 1998). ... Bruised thigh (March 17, 1998); missed four games. ... Fractured tibia (November 1, 1998); missed 31 games. ... Tore anterior cruciate ligament in knee (March 5, 1999); missed remainder of season. ... Suffered concussion (October 20, 1999); missed one game. ... Injured thumb (February 23, 2000); missed one game.
HONORS: Named to OHL All-Star second team (1994-95).

Season Team	League	REGULAR SEASON								PLAYOFFS				
		Gms.	G	A	Pts.	PIM	+/-	PP	SH	Gms.	G	A	Pts.	PIM
91-92—Guelph	OHL	47	7	14	21	145	...	...	...	—	—	—	—	—
92-93—Guelph	OHL	59	27	32	59	164	...	...	...	5	2	2	4	6
93-94—Guelph	OHL	61	28	54	82	165	...	...	...	9	2	6	8	30
94-95—Guelph	OHL	62	54	65	119	58	...	...	...	14	*15	18	33	41
95-96—New York Islanders	NHL	76	18	21	39	83	-14	4	0	—	—	—	—	—
96-97—New York Islanders	NHL	64	10	13	23	68	-3	3	0	—	—	—	—	—
—Utah	IHL	13	5	5	10	16	...	...	...	—	—	—	—	—
97-98—New York Islanders	NHL	52	7	11	18	58	-19	1	0	—	—	—	—	—
—Vancouver	NHL	22	6	9	15	63	2	1	1	—	—	—	—	—
98-99—Vancouver	NHL	32	8	8	16	44	-6	1	0	—	—	—	—	—
99-00—Vancouver	NHL	80	25	25	50	126	-2	4	0	—	—	—	—	—
NHL Totals (5 years)		326	74	87	161	442	-42	14	1	—	—	—	—	—

BERUBE, CRAIG   LW   CAPITALS   B

PERSONAL: Born December 17, 1965, in Calahoo, Alta. ... 6-1/205. ... Shoots left. ... Name pronounced buh-ROO-bee.

TRANSACTIONS/CAREER NOTES: Signed as free agent by Philadelphia Flyers (March 19, 1986). ... Sprained left knee (March 1988). ... Traded by Flyers with RW Scott Mellanby and C Craig Fisher to Edmonton Oilers for RW Dave Brown, D Corey Foster and the NHL rights to RW Jari Kurri (May 30, 1991). ... Traded by Oilers with G Grant Fuhr and RW/LW Glenn Anderson to Toronto Maple Leafs for LW Vincent Damphousse, D Luke Richardson, G Peter Ing, C Scott Thornton and future considerations (September 19, 1991). ... Traded by Maple Leafs with D Alexander Godynyuk, RW Gary Leeman, D Michel Petit and G Jeff Reese to Calgary Flames for C Doug Gilmour, D Jamie Macoun, LW Kent Manderville, D Ric Nattress and G Rick Wamsley (January 2, 1992). ... Traded by Flames to Washington Capitals for fifth-round pick (C Darryl LaFrance) in 1993 draft (June 26, 1993). ... Suffered from the flu (March 31, 1995); missed three games. ... Injured knee (September 14, 1995); missed seven games. ... Suffered mild concussion (November 10, 1995); missed four games. ... Suspended 10 games by NHL for coming off bench to fight (December 22, 1995). ... Injured right knee (March 22, 1996); missed 11 games. ... Suspended two games and fined §1,000 by NHL for slashing incident (January 19, 1997). ... Injured hip (October 15, 1997); missed seven games. ... Suspended one game by NHL for directing a racial slur at another player (November 25, 1997). ... Traded by Capitals for Philadelphia Flyers for future considerations (March 23, 1999). ... Suffered from the flu (January 11, 2000); missed one game. ... Signed as free agent by Capitals (July 7, 2000).

Season Team	League	REGULAR SEASON								PLAYOFFS				
		Gms.	G	A	Pts.	PIM	+/-	PP	SH	Gms.	G	A	Pts.	PIM
82-83—Williams Lake	PCJHL	33	9	24	33	99	...	...	...	—	—	—	—	—
—Kamloops	WHL	4	0	0	0	0	...	...	...	—	—	—	—	—
83-84—New Westminster	WHL	70	11	20	31	104	...	...	...	8	1	2	3	5
84-85—New Westminster	WHL	70	25	44	69	191	...	...	...	10	3	2	5	4
85-86—Kamloops	WHL	32	17	14	31	119	...	...	...	—	—	—	—	—
—Medicine Hat	WHL	34	14	16	30	95	...	...	...	25	7	8	15	102
86-87—Hershey	AHL	63	7	17	24	325	...	...	...	—	—	—	—	—
—Philadelphia	NHL	7	0	0	0	57	2	0	0	5	0	0	0	17
87-88—Hershey	AHL	31	5	9	14	119	...	...	...	—	—	—	—	—
—Philadelphia	NHL	27	3	2	5	108	1	0	0	—	—	—	—	—
88-89—Hershey	AHL	7	0	2	2	19	...	...	...	—	—	—	—	—
—Philadelphia	NHL	53	1	1	2	199	-15	0	0	16	0	0	0	56
89-90—Philadelphia	NHL	74	4	14	18	291	-7	0	0	—	—	—	—	—
90-91—Philadelphia	NHL	74	8	9	17	293	-6	0	0	—	—	—	—	—
91-92—Toronto	NHL	40	5	7	12	109	-2	1	0	—	—	—	—	—
—Calgary	NHL	36	1	4	5	155	-3	0	0	—	—	—	—	—
92-93—Calgary	NHL	77	4	8	12	209	-6	0	0	6	0	1	1	21
93-94—Washington	NHL	84	7	7	14	305	-4	0	0	8	0	0	0	21
94-95—Washington	NHL	43	2	4	6	173	-5	0	0	7	0	0	0	29
95-96—Washington	NHL	50	2	10	12	151	1	1	0	2	0	0	0	19
96-97—Washington	NHL	80	4	3	7	218	-11	0	0	—	—	—	—	—
97-98—Washington	NHL	74	6	9	15	189	-3	0	0	21	1	0	1	21
98-99—Washington	NHL	66	5	4	9	166	-7	0	0	—	—	—	—	—
—Philadelphia	NHL	11	0	0	0	28	-3	0	0	6	1	0	1	4
99-00—Philadelphia	NHL	77	4	8	12	162	3	0	0	18	1	0	1	23
NHL Totals (14 years)		873	56	90	146	2813	-65	2	0	89	3	1	4	211

BICANEK, RADIM   D   BLUE JACKETS

PERSONAL: Born January 18, 1975, in Uherske Hradiste, Czechoslovakia. ... 6-1/195. ... Shoots left. ... Name pronounced RA-deem bih-CHAN-ihk.

TRANSACTIONS/CAREER NOTES: Selected by Ottawa Senators in second round (second Senators pick, 27th overall) of NHL entry draft (June 26, 1993). ... Traded by Senators to Chicago Blackhawks for sixth-round pick (G Martin Prusek) in 1999 draft (March 12, 1999). ... Selected by Columbus Blue Jackets in NHL expansion draft (June 23, 2000).

Season Team	League	REGULAR SEASON								PLAYOFFS				
		Gms.	G	A	Pts.	PIM	+/-	PP	SH	Gms.	G	A	Pts.	PIM
92-93—Jihlava	Czech	43	2	3	5	—	...	...	...	—	—	—	—	—
93-94—Belleville	OHL	63	16	27	43	49	...	...	...	12	2	8	10	21
94-95—Belleville	OHL	49	13	26	39	61	...	...	...	16	6	5	11	30
—Ottawa	NHL	6	0	0	0	0	3	0	0	—	—	—	—	—
—Prin. Edward Island	AHL	—	—	—	—	—				3	0	1	1	0
95-96—Prin. Edward Island	AHL	74	7	19	26	87	...	...	...	5	0	2	2	6
96-97—Worcester	AHL	44	1	15	16	22	...	...	...	—	—	—	—	—
—Ottawa	NHL	21	0	1	1	8	-4	0	0	7	0	0	0	8
97-98—Ottawa	NHL	1	0	0	0	0	0	0	0	—	—	—	—	—
—Detroit	IHL	9	1	3	4	16	...	...	...	—	—	—	—	—
—Manitoba	IHL	42	1	7	8	52	...	...	...	—	—	—	—	—

Season Team	League	REGULAR SEASON								PLAYOFFS				
		Gms.	G	A	Pts.	PIM	+/-	PP	SH	Gms.	G	A	Pts.	PIM
98-99—Ottawa	NHL	7	0	0	0	4	-1	0	0	—	—	—	—	—
—Grand Rapids	IHL	46	8	17	25	48	...	...	...	—	—	—	—	—
—Chicago	NHL	7	0	0	0	6	-3	0	0	—	—	—	—	—
99-00—Cleveland	IHL	70	5	27	32	125	...	...	...	9	2	2	4	8
—Chicago	NHL	11	0	3	3	4	7	0	0	—	—	—	—	—
NHL Totals (5 years)		53	0	4	4	22	2	0	0	7	0	0	0	8

BIERK, ZAC G WILD

PERSONAL: Born September 17, 1976, in Peterborough, Ont. ... 6-4/205. ... Catches left. ... Name pronounced BUHRK.
HIGH SCHOOL: Thomas A. Stewart S.S. (Peterborough, Ont.).
TRANSACTIONS/CAREER NOTES: Selected by Tampa Bay Lightning in ninth round (eighth Lightning pick, 212th overall) of NHL entry draft (July 8, 1995). ... Injured neck (April 6, 2000); missed final two games of season. ... Selected by Minnesota Wild in NHL expansion draft (June 23, 2000).
HONORS: Won Leo Lalonde Memorial Trophy (1996-97). ... Named to Can.HL All-Star second team (1996-97). ... Named to OHL All-Star first team (1996-97).
MISCELLANEOUS: Allowed a penalty shot goal (vs. Robert Reichel, January 14, 1998).

Season Team	League	REGULAR SEASON							PLAYOFFS					
		Gms.	Min	W	L	T	GA	SO	Avg.	Gms.	Min.	W	L	GA	SO	Avg.
93-94—Peterborough	Tier II Jr. A	4	205	...	...	...	17	0	4.98	—	—	—	—	—	—	—
—Peterborough	OHL	9	423	0	4	2	37	0	5.25	1	33	0	0	7	0	12.73
94-95—Peterborough	OHL	35	1798	12	15	5	118	0	3.94	6	301	2	3	24	0	4.78
95-96—Peterborough	OHL	58	3292	31	16	6	174	2	3.17	*22	*1383	*14	†7	*83	0	3.60
96-97—Peterborough	OHL	49	2744	*28	16	0	151	2	3.30	11	666	6	5	35	0	3.15
97-98—Adirondack	AHL	12	558	1	6	1	36	0	3.87	—	—	—	—	—	—	—
—Tampa Bay	NHL	13	433	1	4	1	30	0	4.16	—	—	—	—	—	—	—
98-99—Cleveland	IHL	27	1556	11	12	‡4	79	0	3.05	—	—	—	—	—	—	—
—Tampa Bay	NHL	1	59	0	1	0	2	0	2.03	—	—	—	—	—	—	—
99-00—Detroit	IHL	15	846	6	8	‡2	46	1	3.26	—	—	—	—	—	—	—
—Tampa Bay	NHL	12	509	4	4	1	31	0	3.65	—	—	—	—	—	—	—
NHL Totals (3 years)		26	1001	5	9	2	63	0	3.78							

BILLINGTON, CRAIG G CAPITALS

PERSONAL: Born September 11, 1966, in London, Ont. ... 5-10/166. ... Catches left.
TRANSACTIONS/CAREER NOTES: Selected by New Jersey Devils as underage junior in second round (second Devils pick, 23rd overall) of NHL entry draft (June 9, 1984). ... Injured hamstring (February 15, 1992); missed two games. ... Strained knee (March 11, 1992); missed six games. ... Underwent knee surgery (April 13, 1992). ... Suffered from sore throat (March 27, 1993); missed one game. ... Traded by Devils with C/LW Troy Mallette and fourth-round pick (C Cosmo Dupaul) in 1993 draft to Ottawa Senators for G Peter Sidorkiewicz and future considerations (June 20, 1993); Senators sent LW Mike Peluso to Devils to complete deal (June 26, 1993). ... Injured knee (January 27, 1995); missed 17 games. ... Traded by Senators to Boston Bruins for eighth-round pick (D Ray Schultz) in 1995 draft (April 7, 1995). ... Signed as free agent by Florida Panthers (September 4, 1996). ... Selected by Colorado Avalanche in NHL waiver draft for cash (September 30, 1996). ... Sprained knee ligament (November 19, 1996); missed seven games. ... Traded by Avalanche to Washington Capitals for future considerations (July 16, 1999).
HONORS: Won Bobby Smith Trophy (1984-85). ... Named to OHL All-Star first team (1984-85). ... Played in NHL All-Star Game (1993).
MISCELLANEOUS: Stopped penalty shot attempt (vs. Rick Tocchet, January 6, 1987).

Season Team	League	REGULAR SEASON							PLAYOFFS					
		Gms.	Min	W	L	T	GA	SO	Avg.	Gms.	Min.	W	L	GA	SO	Avg.
82-83—London Diamonds	OPJHL	23	1338	...	...	...	76	0	3.41	—	—	—	—	—	—	—
83-84—Belleville	OHL	44	2335	20	19	0	162	1	4.16	1	30	0	0	3	0	6.00
84-85—Belleville	OHL	47	2544	26	19	0	180	1	4.25	14	761	7	5	47	†1	3.71
85-86—Belleville	OHL	3	180	2	1	0	11	0	3.67	†20	1133	9	6	*68	0	3.60
—New Jersey	NHL	18	701	4	9	1	77	0	6.59	—	—	—	—	—	—	—
86-87—Maine	AHL	20	1151	9	8	2	70	0	3.65	—	—	—	—	—	—	—
—New Jersey	NHL	22	1114	4	13	2	89	0	4.79	—	—	—	—	—	—	—
87-88—Utica	AHL	*59	*3404	22	27	8	*208	1	3.67	—	—	—	—	—	—	—
88-89—New Jersey	NHL	3	140	1	1	0	11	0	4.71	—	—	—	—	—	—	—
—Utica	AHL	41	2432	17	18	6	150	2	3.70	4	219	1	3	18	0	4.93
89-90—Utica	AHL	38	2087	20	13	1	138	0	3.97	—	—	—	—	—	—	—
90-91—Canadian nat'l team	Int'l	34	1879	17	14	2	110	2	3.51	—	—	—	—	—	—	—
91-92—New Jersey	NHL	26	1363	13	7	1	69	2	3.04	—	—	—	—	—	—	—
92-93—New Jersey	NHL	42	2389	21	16	4	146	2	3.67	2	78	0	1	5	0	3.85
93-94—Ottawa	NHL	63	3319	11	*41	4	*254	0	4.59	—	—	—	—	—	—	—
94-95—Boston	NHL	8	373	5	1	0	19	0	3.06	1	25	0	0	1	0	2.40
—Ottawa	NHL	9	472	0	6	2	32	0	4.07	—	—	—	—	—	—	—
95-96—Boston	NHL	27	1380	10	13	3	79	1	3.43	1	60	0	1	6	0	6.00
96-97—Colorado	NHL	23	1200	11	8	2	53	1	2.65	1	20	0	0	1	0	3.00
97-98—Colorado	NHL	23	1162	8	7	4	45	1	2.32	1	1	0	0	0	0	...
98-99—Colorado	NHL	21	1086	11	8	1	52	0	2.87	1	9	0	0	1	0	6.67
99-00—Washington	NHL	13	611	3	6	1	28	2	2.75	1	20	0	0	1	0	3.00
NHL Totals (12 years)		298	15310	102	136	25	954	9	3.74	8	213	0	2	15	0	4.23

BIRON, MARTIN   G   SABRES

PERSONAL: Born August 15, 1977, in Lac St. Charles, Que. ... 6-1/154. ... Catches left. ... Brother of Mathieu Biron, defenseman, New York Islanders. ... Name pronounced bih-RAH.
TRANSACTIONS/CAREER NOTES: Selected by Buffalo Sabres in first round (second Sabres pick, 16th overall) of NHL entry draft (July 8, 1995).
HONORS: Won Can.HL Goaltender of the Year Award (1994-95). ... Won Raymond Lagace Trophy (1994-95). ... Won Mike Bossy Trophy (1994-95). ... Won Jacques Plante Trophy (1994-95). ... Named to Can.HL All-Star first team (1994-95). ... Named to Can.HL All-Rookie team (1994-95). ... Named to AHL All-Star first team (1998-99). ... Won Baz Bastien Trophy (1998-99). ... Shared Harry (Hap) Holmes Memorial Trophy with Tom Draper (1998-99).
MISCELLANEOUS: Stopped a penalty shot attempt (vs. Daniel Alfredsson, January 8, 2000).

		REGULAR SEASON							PLAYOFFS						
Season Team	League	Gms.	Min	W	L	T	GA	SO	Avg.	Gms.	Min.	W	L	GA	SO	Avg.
94-95—Beauport	QMJHL	56	3193	29	16	9	132	3	2.48	16	902	8	7	37	4	2.46
95-96—Beauport	QMJHL	55	3207	29	17	7	152	1	2.84	*19	1132	*12	†8	64	0	3.39
—Buffalo	NHL	3	119	0	2	0	10	0	5.04	—	—	—	—	—	—	—
96-97—Beauport	QMJHL	18	935	6	10	1	62	1	3.98	—	—	—	—	—	—	—
—Hull	QMJHL	16	972	11	4	1	43	2	2.65	6	326	3	1	19	0	3.50
97-98—Rochester	AHL	41	2312	14	18	6	113	*5	2.93	4	239	1	3	16	0	4.02
—South Carolina	ECHL	2	86	0	1	1	3	0	2.09	—	—	—	—	—	—	—
98-99—Rochester	AHL	52	3129	36	13	3	108	*6	*2.07	*20	1167	12	*8	42	†1	*2.16
—Buffalo	NHL	6	281	1	2	1	10	0	2.14	—	—	—	—	—	—	—
99-00—Rochester	AHL	6	344	6	0	0	12	1	2.09	—	—	—	—	—	—	—
—Buffalo	NHL	41	2229	19	18	2	90	5	2.42	—	—	—	—	—	—	—
NHL Totals (3 years)		50	2629	20	22	3	110	5	2.51							

BIRON, MATHIEU   D   ISLANDERS

PERSONAL: Born April 29, 1980, in Lac St. Charles, Que. ... 6-6/212. ... Shoots right. ... Brother of Martin Biron, goaltender, Buffalo Sabres.
TRANSACTIONS/CAREER NOTES: Selected by Los Angeles Kings in first round (first Kings pick, 21st overall) of NHL entry draft (June 27, 1998). ... Rights traded by Kings with C Olli Jokinen, LW Josh Green and first-round pick (LW Taylor Pyatt) in 1999 draft to New York Islanders for RW Zigmund Palffy, C Bryan Smolinski, G Marcel Cousineau and fourth-round pick (C Daniel Johansson) in 1999 draft (June 20, 1999).
HONORS: Named to QMJHL All-Rookie Team (1997-98).

		REGULAR SEASON							PLAYOFFS				
Season Team	League	Gms.	G	A	Pts.	PIM	+/-	PP	SH	Gms.	G	A	Pts.	PIM
97-98—Shawinigan	QMJHL	59	8	28	36	60	...	...	...	6	0	1	1	10
98-99—Shawinigan	QMJHL	69	13	32	45	116	...	...	...	6	0	2	2	6
99-00—New York Islanders	NHL	60	4	4	8	38	-13	2	0	—	—	—	—	—
NHL Totals (1 year)		60	4	4	8	38	-13	2	0					

BLACK, JAMES   LW   CAPITALS

PERSONAL: Born August 15, 1969, in Regina, Sask. ... 6-0/203. ... Shoots left.
TRANSACTIONS/CAREER NOTES: Selected by Hartford Whalers in fifth round (fourth Whalers pick, 94th overall) of NHL entry draft (June 17, 1989). ... Traded by Whalers to Minnesota North Stars for C Mark Janssens (September 3, 1992). ... North Stars franchise moved from Minnesota to Dallas and renamed Stars for 1993-94 season. ... Traded by Stars with seventh-round pick (RW Steve Webb) in 1994 draft to Buffalo Sabres for RW Gord Donnelly (December 15, 1993). ... Lacerated forehead (October 27, 1993); missed five games. ... Signed as free agent by Chicago Blackhawks (August 10, 1995). ... Injured hand (October 22, 1997); missed six games. ... Sprained knee (November 8, 1997); missed three games. ... Traded by Blackhawks to Washington Capitals for future considerations (October 15, 1998). ... Fractured leg (February 3, 2000); missed final 31 games of season.

		REGULAR SEASON							PLAYOFFS				
Season Team	League	Gms.	G	A	Pts.	PIM	+/-	PP	SH	Gms.	G	A	Pts.	PIM
87-88—Portland	WHL	72	30	50	80	50	...	...	...	—	—	—	—	—
88-89—Portland	WHL	71	45	51	96	57	...	...	...	19	13	6	19	28
89-90—Hartford	NHL	1	0	0	0	0	0	0	0	—	—	—	—	—
—Binghamton	AHL	80	37	35	72	34	...	...	...	—	—	—	—	—
90-91—Hartford	NHL	1	0	0	0	0	0	0	0	—	—	—	—	—
—Springfield	AHL	79	35	61	96	34	...	...	...	18	9	9	18	6
91-92—Springfield	AHL	47	15	25	40	33	...	...	...	10	3	2	5	18
—Hartford	NHL	30	4	6	10	10	-4	1	0	—	—	—	—	—
92-93—Minnesota	NHL	10	2	1	3	4	0	0	0	—	—	—	—	—
—Kalamazoo	IHL	63	25	45	70	40	...	...	...	—	—	—	—	—
93-94—Dallas	NHL	13	2	3	5	2	-4	2	0	—	—	—	—	—
—Buffalo	NHL	2	0	0	0	0	0	0	0	—	—	—	—	—
—Rochester	AHL	45	19	32	51	28	...	...	...	4	2	3	5	0
94-95—Las Vegas	IHL	78	29	44	73	54	...	...	...	10	1	6	7	4
95-96—Indianapolis	IHL	67	32	50	82	56	...	...	...	—	—	—	—	—
—Chicago	NHL	13	3	3	6	16	1	0	0	8	1	0	1	2
96-97—Chicago	NHL	64	12	11	23	20	6	0	0	5	1	1	2	4
97-98—Chicago	NHL	52	10	5	15	8	-8	2	1	—	—	—	—	—
98-99—Chicago	IHL	5	6	0	6	0	...	...	...	—	—	—	—	—
—Washington	NHL	75	16	14	30	14	5	1	1	—	—	—	—	—
99-00—Washington	NHL	49	8	9	17	6	-1	1	0	—	—	—	—	—
NHL Totals (10 years)		310	57	52	109	80	-5	7	2	13	2	1	3	4

BLAKE, JASON　　　　　　　　C　　　　　　　　KINGS

PERSONAL: Born September 2, 1973, in Moorhead, Minn. ... 5-10/180. ... Shoots left.
HIGH SCHOOL: Moorhead (Minn.).
COLLEGE: Ferris State, then North Dakota.
TRANSACTIONS/CAREER NOTES: Signed as free agent by Los Angeles Kings (April 17, 1999). ... Suffered concussion (December 19, 1999); missed four games.
HONORS: Named to NCAA All-America (West) second team (1997-98). ... Named to WCHA All-Star first team (1996-97 through 1998-99). ... Named to NCAA All-America (West) first team (1998-99).

		REGULAR SEASON								PLAYOFFS				
Season Team	League	Gms.	G	A	Pts.	PIM	+/-	PP	SH	Gms.	G	A	Pts.	PIM
94-95—Ferris State	CCHA	36	16	16	32	46	...	...	...	—	—	—	—	—
96-97—Univ. of North Dakota	WCHA	43	19	32	51	44	...	...	...	—	—	—	—	—
97-98—Univ. of North Dakota	WCHA	38	24	27	51	62	...	...	...	—	—	—	—	—
98-99—Univ. of North Dakota	WCHA	38	*28	†41	*69	49	...	...	...	—	—	—	—	—
—Orlando	IHL	5	3	5	8	6	...	...	...	13	3	4	7	20
—Los Angeles	NHL	1	1	0	1	0	1	0	0	—	—	—	—	—
99-00—Los Angeles	NHL	64	5	18	23	26	4	0	0	3	0	0	0	0
—Long Beach	IHL	7	3	6	9	2	...	...	...	—	—	—	—	—
NHL Totals (2 years)		65	6	18	24	26	5	0	0	3	0	0	0	0

BLAKE, ROB　　　　　　　　D　　　　　　　　KINGS

PERSONAL: Born December 10, 1969, in Simcoe, Ont. ... 6-4/220. ... Shoots right. ... Full Name: Robert Bowlby Blake.
COLLEGE: Bowling Green State.
TRANSACTIONS/CAREER NOTES: Selected by Los Angeles Kings in fourth round (fourth Kings pick, 70th overall) of NHL entry draft (June 11, 1988). ... Sprained knee (April 1990). ... Injured knee (February 12, 1991); missed two games. ... Injured shoulder (October 8, 1991); missed 11 games. ... Sprained knee ligaments (November 28, 1991); missed six games. ... Suffered from the flu (January 23, 1992); missed one game. ... Suffered from the flu (February 13, 1992); missed one game. ... Strained shoulder (March 14, 1992); missed four games. ... Fractured rib (December 19, 1992); missed three games. ... Bruised lower back (April 3, 1993); missed final five games of regular season and one playoff game. ... Strained groin (January 23, 1995); missed 11 games. ... Strained groin (March 11, 1995); missed 12 games. ... Strained groin (April 7, 1995); missed one game. ... Suffered partial tear of left knee ligaments (October 20, 1995); missed 76 games. ... Fractured hand (December 26, 1996); missed 11 games. ... Suspended two games and fined $1,000 by NHL for high-sticking incident (February 5, 1997). ... Suffered tendinitis in left knee (February 22, 1997); missed seven games. ... Fractured right foot (November 6, 1998); missed 15 games. ... Suspended three games and fined $1,000 by NHL for slashing incident (December 14, 1998). ... Suspended two games by NHL for cross-checking incident (April 9, 1999). ... Strained groin (December 8, 1999); missed two games. ... Bruised knee (April 1, 2000); missed three games.
HONORS: Named to CCHA All-Star second team (1988-89). ... Named to NCAA All-America (West) first team (1989-90). ... Named to CCHA All-Star first team (1989-90). ... Named to NHL All-Rookie team (1990-91). ... Played in NHL All-Star Game (1994, 1999 and 2000). ... Named to play in NHL All-Star Game (1997); replaced by LW Dimitri Khristich due to injury. ... Named to THE SPORTING NEWS All-Star team (1997-98). ... Won James Norris Memorial Trophy (1997-98). ... Named to NHL All-Star first team (1997-98). ... Named to NHL All-Star second team (1999-2000).
MISCELLANEOUS: Captain of Los Angeles Kings (1996-97 through 1999-2000). ... Failed to score on a penalty shot (vs. Dwayne Roloson, April 13, 1998).

		REGULAR SEASON								PLAYOFFS				
Season Team	League	Gms.	G	A	Pts.	PIM	+/-	PP	SH	Gms.	G	A	Pts.	PIM
86-87—Stratford Jr. B	OHA	31	11	20	31	115	...	...	...	—	—	—	—	—
87-88—Bowling Green	CCHA	36	5	8	13	72	...	...	...	—	—	—	—	—
88-89—Bowling Green	CCHA	46	11	21	32	140	...	...	...	—	—	—	—	—
89-90—Bowling Green	CCHA	42	23	36	59	140	...	...	...	—	—	—	—	—
—Los Angeles	NHL	4	0	0	0	4	0	0	0	8	1	3	4	4
90-91—Los Angeles	NHL	75	12	34	46	125	3	9	0	12	1	4	5	26
91-92—Los Angeles	NHL	57	7	13	20	102	-5	5	0	6	2	1	3	12
92-93—Los Angeles	NHL	76	16	43	59	152	18	10	0	23	4	6	10	46
93-94—Los Angeles	NHL	84	20	48	68	137	-7	7	0	—	—	—	—	—
94-95—Los Angeles	NHL	24	4	7	11	38	-16	4	0	—	—	—	—	—
95-96—Los Angeles	NHL	6	1	2	3	8	0	0	0	—	—	—	—	—
96-97—Los Angeles	NHL	62	8	23	31	82	-28	4	0	—	—	—	—	—
97-98—Los Angeles	NHL	81	23	27	50	94	-3	11	0	4	0	0	0	6
—Can. Olympic team	Int'l	6	1	1	2	2	...	...	...	—	—	—	—	—
98-99—Los Angeles	NHL	62	12	23	35	128	-7	5	1	—	—	—	—	—
99-00—Los Angeles	NHL	77	18	39	57	112	10	12	0	4	0	2	2	4
NHL Totals (11 years)		608	121	259	380	982	-35	67	1	57	8	16	24	98

BLATNY, ZDENEK　　　　　　　　C/LW　　　　　　　　THRASHERS

PERSONAL: Born January 14, 1981, in Brno, Czechoslovakia. ... 6-1/187. ... Shoots left.
TRANSACTIONS/CAREER NOTES: Selected by Atlanta Thrashers in third round (third Thrashers pick, 68th overall) of NHL entry draft (June 26, 1999).
HONORS: Named to WHL (East) All-Star first team (1999-2000).

		REGULAR SEASON								PLAYOFFS				
Season Team	League	Gms.	G	A	Pts.	PIM	+/-	PP	SH	Gms.	G	A	Pts.	PIM
97-98—Kometa Brno Jrs.	Czech. Jrs.	42	22	21	43	40	...	...	...	—	—	—	—	—
98-99—Seattle	WHL	44	18	15	33	25	...	...	...	11	4	0	4	24
99-00—Seattle	WHL	7	4	5	9	12	...	...	...	—	—	—	—	—
—Kootenay	WHL	61	43	39	82	119	...	...	...	21	10	*17	27	46

BODGER, DOUG   D

PERSONAL: Born June 18, 1966, in Chemainus, B.C. ... 6-2/210. ... Shoots left. ... Name pronounced BAH-juhr.
TRANSACTIONS/CAREER NOTES: Selected by Pittsburgh Penguins as underage junior in first round (second Penguins pick, ninth overall) of NHL entry draft (June 9, 1984). ... Underwent surgery to remove bone chip on left foot (April 1985). ... Sprained knee (December 1987). ... Strained left knee (October 1988). ... Traded by Penguins with LW Darrin Shannon to Buffalo Sabres for G Tom Barrasso and third-round pick (RW Joe Dziedzic) in 1990 draft (November 12, 1988). ... Sprained left knee (October 1989). ... Injured shoulder (December 28, 1990); missed four games. ... Separated left shoulder (February 17, 1991); missed 18 games. ... Reinjured left shoulder (March 30, 1991). ... Injured eye (February 11, 1992); missed seven games. ... Suffered sore back (December 2, 1993); missed four games. ... Suffered from the flu (March 19, 1995); missed one game. ... Bruised shoulder (April 28, 1995); missed last three games of season. ... Traded by Sabres to San Jose Sharks for RW Martin Spanhel and first- (traded to Winnipeg) and fourth-round (traded to Buffalo) picks in 1996 draft (November 16, 1995). ... Injured knee (January 17, 1996); missed three games. ... Injured groin (February 23, 1996); missed four games. ... Injured shoulder (November 8, 1997); missed two games. ... Traded by Sharks with LW Dody Wood to New Jersey Devils for RW John MacLean and D Ken Sutton (December 7, 1997). ... Fractured right index finger (February 26, 1998); missed two games. ... Traded by Devils to Los Angeles Kings for fourth-round pick (LW Pierre Dagenais) in 1998 draft (June 18, 1998). ... Fractured left hand (November 1, 1998); missed 10 games. ... Bruised shoulder (December 28, 1998); missed six games. ... Signed as free agent by Vancouver Canucks (August 4, 1999). ... Injured groin (December 7, 1999); missed two games. ... Announced retirement (December 14, 1999).
HONORS: Named to WHL All-Star second team (1982-83). ... Named to WHL (West) All-Star first team (1983-84).

Season Team	League	REGULAR SEASON								PLAYOFFS				
		Gms.	G	A	Pts.	PIM	+/-	PP	SH	Gms.	G	A	Pts.	PIM
82-83—Kamloops	WHL	72	26	66	92	98	...	...	...	7	0	5	5	2
83-84—Kamloops	WHL	70	21	77	98	90	...	...	...	17	2	15	17	12
84-85—Pittsburgh	NHL	65	5	26	31	67	-24	3	0	—	—	—	—	—
85-86—Pittsburgh	NHL	79	4	33	37	63	3	1	0	—	—	—	—	—
86-87—Pittsburgh	NHL	76	11	38	49	52	6	5	0	—	—	—	—	—
87-88—Pittsburgh	NHL	69	14	31	45	103	-4	13	0	—	—	—	—	—
88-89—Pittsburgh	NHL	10	1	4	5	7	6	0	0	—	—	—	—	—
—Buffalo	NHL	61	7	40	47	52	9	6	0	5	1	1	2	11
89-90—Buffalo	NHL	71	12	36	48	64	0	8	0	6	1	5	6	6
90-91—Buffalo	NHL	58	5	23	28	54	-8	2	0	4	0	1	1	0
91-92—Buffalo	NHL	73	11	35	46	108	1	4	0	7	2	1	3	2
92-93—Buffalo	NHL	81	9	45	54	87	14	6	0	8	2	3	5	0
93-94—Buffalo	NHL	75	7	32	39	76	8	5	1	7	0	3	3	6
94-95—Buffalo	NHL	44	3	17	20	47	-3	2	0	5	0	4	4	0
95-96—Buffalo	NHL	16	0	5	5	18	-6	0	0	—	—	—	—	—
—San Jose	NHL	57	4	19	23	50	-18	3	0	—	—	—	—	—
96-97—San Jose	NHL	81	1	15	16	64	-14	0	0	—	—	—	—	—
97-98—San Jose	NHL	28	4	6	10	32	0	0	0	—	—	—	—	—
—New Jersey	NHL	49	5	5	10	25	-1	3	0	5	0	0	0	0
98-99—Los Angeles	NHL	65	3	11	14	34	1	0	0	—	—	—	—	—
99-00—Vancouver	NHL	13	0	1	1	4	-6	0	0	—	—	—	—	—
NHL Totals (16 years)		1071	106	422	528	1007	-36	61	1	47	6	18	24	25

BOGUNIECKI, ERIC   C   PANTHERS

PERSONAL: Born May 6, 1975, in New Haven, Conn. ... 5-8/192. ... Shoots right.
HIGH SCHOOL: Westminster (Simsbury, Conn.).
COLLEGE: New Hampshire.
TRANSACTIONS/CAREER NOTES: Selected by St. Louis Blues in eighth round (sixth Blues pick, 193rd overall) of NHL entry draft (June 29, 1993). ... Signed as free agent by Florida Panthers (July 20, 1999).
HONORS: Names to Hockey East All-Star team (1996-97).

Season Team	League	REGULAR SEASON								PLAYOFFS				
		Gms.	G	A	Pts.	PIM	+/-	PP	SH	Gms.	G	A	Pts.	PIM
92-93—Westminster School	Conn. H.S.	24	30	24	54	55	...	...	...	—	—	—	—	—
93-94—Univ. of New Hamp.	Hockey East	40	17	16	33	66	...	...	...	—	—	—	—	—
94-95—Univ. of New Hamp.	Hockey East	34	12	19	31	62	...	...	...	—	—	—	—	—
95-96—Univ. of New Hamp.	Hockey East	32	23	28	51	46	...	...	...	—	—	—	—	—
96-97—Univ. of New Hamp.	Hockey East	36	26	31	57	58	...	...	...	—	—	—	—	—
97-98—Dayton	ECHL	26	19	18	37	36	...	...	...	—	—	—	—	—
—Fort Wayne	IHL	35	4	8	12	29	...	...	...	4	1	2	3	10
98-99—Fort Wayne	IHL	72	32	34	66	100	...	...	...	2	0	1	1	2
99-00—Louisville	AHL	57	33	42	75	148	...	...	...	4	3	2	5	20
—Florida	NHL	4	0	0	0	2	-1	0	0	—	—	—	—	—
NHL Totals (1 year)		4	0	0	0	2	-1	0	0	—	—	—	—	—

BOHONOS, LONNY   RW   MAPLE LEAFS

PERSONAL: Born May 20, 1973, in Winnipeg. ... 5-11/192. ... Shoots right. ... Name pronounced boh-HAH-nohz.
TRANSACTIONS/CAREER NOTES: Signed as non-drafted free agent by Vancouver Canucks (May 31, 1994). ... Traded by Canucks to Toronto Maple Leafs for C Brandon Convery (March 7, 1998).
HONORS: Won Bob Clarke Trophy (1993-94). ... Won Brad Hornung Trophy (1993-94). ... Named to Can.HL All-Star first team (1993-94). ... Named to WHL (West) All-Star first team (1993-94).

Season Team	League	REGULAR SEASON								PLAYOFFS				
		Gms.	G	A	Pts.	PIM	+/-	PP	SH	Gms.	G	A	Pts.	PIM
91-92—Moose Jaw	WHL	8	1	1	2	0	...	...	...	—	—	—	—	—
92-93—Seattle	WHL	46	13	13	26	27	...	...	...	—	—	—	—	—
—Portland	WHL	27	20	17	37	16	...	...	...	15	8	13	21	19
93-94—Portland	WHL	70	*62	*90	*152	80	...	...	...	10	8	11	19	13
94-95—Syracuse	AHL	67	30	45	75	71	...	...	...	—	—	—	—	—
95-96—Syracuse	AHL	74	40	39	79	82	...	...	...	16	14	8	22	16
—Vancouver	NHL	3	0	1	1	0	1	0	0	—	—	—	—	—
96-97—Syracuse	AHL	41	22	30	52	28	...	...	...	3	2	2	4	4
—Vancouver	NHL	36	11	11	22	10	-3	2	0	—	—	—	—	—
97-98—Vancouver	NHL	31	2	1	3	4	-9	0	0	—	—	—	—	—
—Syracuse	AHL	17	12	12	24	8	...	...	...	—	—	—	—	—
—Toronto	NHL	6	3	3	6	4	1	0	0	—	—	—	—	—
—St. John's	AHL	11	7	9	16	10	...	...	...	2	1	1	2	2
98-99—St. John's	AHL	70	34	48	82	40	...	...	...	5	2	4	6	2
—Toronto	NHL	7	3	0	3	4	3	0	0	9	3	6	9	2
99-00—Manitoba	IHL	63	18	33	51	45	...	...	...	2	0	0	0	2
NHL Totals (4 years)		83	19	16	35	22	-7	2	0	9	3	6	9	2

BOIKOV, ALEXANDRE　　　　D　　　　PREDATORS

PERSONAL: Born February 7, 1975, in Chelyabinsk, U.S.S.R. ... 6-0/198. ... Shoots left. ... Name pronounced BOY-kahf.
TRANSACTIONS/CAREER NOTES: Signed as non-drafted free agent by San Jose Sharks (August 26, 1996). ... Signed as free agent by Nashville Predators (July 26, 1999). ... Suffered injury (April 3, 2000); missed final two games of season.

Season Team	League	REGULAR SEASON								PLAYOFFS				
		Gms.	G	A	Pts.	PIM	+/-	PP	SH	Gms.	G	A	Pts.	PIM
93-94—Victoria	WHL	70	4	31	35	250	...		...	—	—	—	—	—
94-95—Prince George	WHL	46	5	23	28	115	...		...	—	—	—	—	—
—Tri-City	WHL	24	3	13	16	63	...		...	17	1	7	8	30
95-96—Tri-City	WHL	71	3	49	52	230	...		...	11	2	4	6	28
96-97—Kentucky	AHL	61	1	19	20	182	...		...	4	0	1	1	4
97-98—Kentucky	AHL	69	5	14	19	153	...		...	3	0	1	1	8
98-99—Kentucky	AHL	55	5	13	18	116	...		...	—	—	—	—	—
—Rochester	AHL	13	0	1	1	15	...		...	17	1	3	4	24
99-00—Milwaukee	IHL	58	1	6	7	120	...		...	—	—	—	—	—
—Nashville	NHL	2	0	0	0	2	0	0	0	—	—	—	—	—
NHL Totals (1 year)		2	0	0	0	2	0	0	0					

BOMBARDIR, BRAD　　　　D　　　　WILD

PERSONAL: Born May 5, 1972, in Powell River, B.C. ... 6-1/205. ... Shoots left. ... Full Name: Luke Bradley Bombardir. ... Name pronounced BAHM-bahr-deer.
COLLEGE: North Dakota.
TRANSACTIONS/CAREER NOTES: Selected by New Jersey Devils in third round (fifth Devils pick, 56th overall) of NHL entry draft (June 16, 1990). ... Bruised left knee (November 29, 1997); missed six games. ... Suffered from the flu (April 14, 1999); missed three games. ... Suffered throat injury (October 27, 1999); missed four games. ... Bruised left hand (December 9, 1999); missed six games. ... Traded by Devils to Minnesota Wild for G Chris Terreri and ninth-round pick in 2001 draft (June 23, 2000).
HONORS: Named to AHL All-Star second team (1995-96).
MISCELLANEOUS: Member of Stanley Cup championship team (2000).

Season Team	League	REGULAR SEASON								PLAYOFFS				
		Gms.	G	A	Pts.	PIM	+/-	PP	SH	Gms.	G	A	Pts.	PIM
88-89—Powell River	BCJHL	30	6	5	11	24	...	...	...	6	0	0	0	0
89-90—Powell River	BCJHL	60	10	35	45	93	...	...	...	8	2	3	5	4
90-91—Univ. of North Dakota	WCHA	33	3	6	9	18	...	...	...	—	—	—	—	—
91-92—Univ. of North Dakota	WCHA	35	3	14	17	54	...	...	...	—	—	—	—	—
92-93—Univ. of North Dakota	WCHA	38	8	15	23	34	...	...	...	—	—	—	—	—
93-94—Univ. of North Dakota	WCHA	38	5	17	22	38	...	...	...	—	—	—	—	—
94-95—Albany	AHL	77	5	22	27	22	...	...	...	14	0	3	3	6
95-96—Albany	AHL	80	6	25	31	63	...	...	...	3	0	1	1	4
96-97—Albany	AHL	32	0	8	8	6	...	...	...	16	1	3	4	8
97-98—New Jersey	NHL	43	1	5	6	8	11	0	0	—	—	—	—	—
—Albany	AHL	5	0	0	0	0	...	...	...	—	—	—	—	—
98-99—New Jersey	NHL	56	1	7	8	16	-4	0	0	5	0	0	0	0
99-00—New Jersey	NHL	32	3	1	4	6	-6	0	0	1	0	0	0	0
NHL Totals (3 years)		131	5	13	18	30	1	0	0	6	0	0	0	0

BONDRA, PETER　　　　LW　　　　CAPITALS

PERSONAL: Born February 7, 1968, in Luck, Ukraine. ... 6-1/205. ... Shoots left. ... Name pronounced BAHN-druh.
TRANSACTIONS/CAREER NOTES: Selected by Washington Capitals in eighth round (ninth Capitals pick, 156th overall) of NHL entry draft (June 16, 1990). ... Dislocated left shoulder (January 17, 1991). ... Suffered recurring shoulder problems (February 13, 1991); missed 13 games. ... Injured throat (April 4, 1993); missed one game. ... Fractured left hand (November 26, 1993); missed 12 games. ... Played in Europe during 1994-95 NHL lockout. ... Suffered from the flu (April 8, 1995); missed one game. ... Signed by Detroit Vipers of IHL during contract holdout (September 28, 1995); re-signed by Capitals (October 20, 1995). ... Separated shoulder (November 11, 1995); missed six games. ... Pulled groin (February 24, 1996); missed four games. ... Strained groin (December 4, 1996); missed three games. ... Suspended one game and fined §1,000 by NHL for kneeing incident (February 4, 1997). ... Suffered back spasms (April 1, 1997); missed foot (November 29, 1997); missed three games. ... Injured knee (April 8, 1998); missed two games. ... Injured hip (November 28, 1998); missed one game. ... Fractured hand (March 15, 1999); missed remainder of season. ... Underwent knee surgery (December 5, 1999); missed eight

games. ... Injured knee (January 4, 2000); missed seven games. ... Injured shoulder (March 30, 1999); missed five games.
HONORS: Played in NHL All-Star Game (1993 and 1996-1999).
MISCELLANEOUS: Scored on a penalty shot (vs. Stephane Fiset, January 29, 1999). ... Failed to score on a penalty shot (vs. Mikhail Shtalenkov, December 13, 1996; vs. Stephane Fiset, April 4, 1998).
STATISTICAL NOTES: Led NHL with 13 game-winning goals (1997-98).
STATISTICAL PLATEAUS: Three-goal games: 1993-94 (1), 1994-95 (1), 1995-96 (2), 1996-97 (1), 1997-98 (1), 1998-99 (2), 1999-00 (1). Total: 9. ... Four-goal games: 1995-96 (2), 1996-97 (1), 1998-99 (1). Total: 4. ... Total hat tricks: 13.

		REGULAR SEASON								PLAYOFFS				
Season Team	League	Gms.	G	A	Pts.	PIM	+/-	PP	SH	Gms.	G	A	Pts.	PIM
86-87—Kosice	Czech.	32	4	5	9	24	...	...	...	—	—	—	—	—
87-88—Kosice	Czech.	45	27	11	38	20	...	...	...	—	—	—	—	—
88-89—Kosice	Czech.	40	30	10	40	20	...	...	...	—	—	—	—	—
89-90—Kosice	Czech.	42	29	17	46		...	...	...	—	—	—	—	—
90-91—Washington	NHL	54	12	16	28	47	-10	4	0	4	0	1	1	2
91-92—Washington	NHL	71	28	28	56	42	16	4	0	7	6	2	8	4.
92-93—Washington	NHL	83	37	48	85	70	8	10	0	6	0	6	6	0
93-94—Washington	NHL	69	24	19	43	40	22	4	0	9	2	4	6	4
94-95—HC Kosice	Slovakia	2	1	0	1	0	...	...	...	—	—	—	—	—
—Washington	NHL	47	*34	9	43	24	9	12	*6	7	5	3	8	10
95-96—Detroit	IHL	7	8	1	9	0	...	...	...	—	—	—	—	—
—Washington	NHL	67	52	28	80	40	18	11	4	6	3	2	5	8
96-97—Washington	NHL	77	46	31	77	72	7	10	4	—	—	—	—	—
97-98—Washington	NHL	76	†52	26	78	44	14	11	5	17	7	5	12	12
—Slovakian Oly. team	Int'l	2	1	0	1	25	...	...	...	—	—	—	—	—
98-99—Washington	NHL	66	31	24	55	56	-1	6	3	—	—	—	—	—
99-00—Washington	NHL	62	21	17	38	30	5	5	3	5	1	1	2	4
NHL Totals (10 years)		672	337	246	583	465	88	77	25	61	24	24	48	44

BONIN, BRIAN   C   WILD

PERSONAL: Born November 28, 1973, in St. Paul, Minn. ... 5-9/187. ... Shoots left. ... Name pronounced BAH-nihn.
HIGH SCHOOL: White Bear Lake (Minn.) Area.
COLLEGE: Minnesota.
TRANSACTIONS/CAREER NOTES: Selected by Pittsburgh Penguins in ninth round (ninth Penguins pick, 211th overall) of NHL entry draft (June 20, 1992). ... Signed as free agent by Vancouver Canucks (August 25, 1999). ... Signed as free agent by Minnesota Wild (July 6, 2000).
HONORS: Named WCHA Player of the Year (1994-95 and 1995-96). ... Named to NCAA All-America (West) first team (1994-95 and 1995-96). ... Named to WCHA All-Star first team (1994-95 and 1995-96). ... Won Hobey Baker Memorial Award (1995-96).

		REGULAR SEASON								PLAYOFFS				
Season Team	League	Gms.	G	A	Pts.	PIM	+/-	PP	SH	Gms.	G	A	Pts.	PIM
91-92—White Bear Lake H.S.	Minn. H.S.	23	22	35	57	8	...	...	...	—	—	—	—	—
92-93—Univ. of Minnesota	WCHA	38	10	18	28	10	...	...	...	—	—	—	—	—
93-94—Univ. of Minnesota	WCHA	42	24	20	44	14	...	...	...	—	—	—	—	—
94-95—Univ. of Minnesota	WCHA	44	32	31	63	28	...	...	...	—	—	—	—	—
95-96—Univ. of Minnesota	WCHA	42	34	47	81	30	...	...	...	—	—	—	—	—
96-97—Cleveland	IHL	60	13	26	39	18	...	...	...	1	1	0	1	0
97-98—Syracuse	AHL	67	31	38	69	46	...	...	...	5	1	3	4	6
98-99—Kansas City	IHL	19	2	5	7	10	...	...	...	—	—	—	—	—
—Adirondack	AHL	54	19	16	35	31	...	...	...	2	0	0	0	0
—Pittsburgh	NHL	5	0	0	0	0	-2	0	0	3	0	0	0	0
99-00—Syracuse	AHL	67	19	28	47	20	...	...	...	4	0	1	1	0
NHL Totals (1 year)		5	0	0	0	0	-2	0	0	3	0	0	0	0

BONK, RADEK   C   SENATORS

PERSONAL: Born January 9, 1976, in Koprivnice, Czechoslovakia. ... 6-3/210. ... Shoots left. ... Name pronounced BAHNK.
TRANSACTIONS/CAREER NOTES: Selected by Ottawa Senators in first round (first Senators pick, third overall) of NHL entry draft (June 28, 1994). ... Injured ankle (April 26, 1995); missed last five games of season. ... Injured hand (1995-96 season); missed one game. ... Suffered abdominal strain (November 8, 1996); missed six games. ... Fractured left wrist (November 23, 1996); missed 23 games. ... Bruised knee (March 5, 1998); missed one game. ... Injured hip flexor (November 7, 1998); missed one game. ... Suffered from the flu (January 4, 2000); missed two games.
HONORS: Won Garry F. Longman Memorial Trophy (1993-94). ... Played in NHL All-Star Game (2000).
MISCELLANEOUS: Failed to score on a penalty shot (vs. Daren Puppa, January 13, 1996).

		REGULAR SEASON								PLAYOFFS				
Season Team	League	Gms.	G	A	Pts.	PIM	+/-	PP	SH	Gms.	G	A	Pts.	PIM
90-91—Opava	Czech.	35	47	42	89	25	...	...	...	—	—	—	—	—
91-92—ZPS Zlin	Czech Dv.II	45	47	36	83	30	...	...	...	—	—	—	—	—
92-93—ZPS Zlin	Czech.	30	5	5	10	10	...	...	...	—	—	—	—	—
93-94—Las Vegas	IHL	76	42	45	87	208	...	...	...	5	1	2	3	10
94-95—Las Vegas	IHL	33	7	13	20	62	...	...	...	—	—	—	—	—
—Ottawa	NHL	42	3	8	11	28	-5	1	0	—	—	—	—	—
—Prin. Edward Island	AHL	—	—	—	—	—	...	...	...	1	0	0	0	0
95-96—Ottawa	NHL	76	16	19	35	36	-5	5	0	—	—	—	—	—
96-97—Ottawa	NHL	53	5	13	18	14	-4	0	1	7	0	1	1	4
97-98—Ottawa	NHL	65	7	9	16	16	-13	1	0	5	0	0	0	2
98-99—Ottawa	NHL	81	16	16	32	48	15	0	1	4	0	0	0	6
99-00—HC Pardubice	Czech Rep.	3	1	0	1	4	...	...	...	—	—	—	—	—
—Ottawa	NHL	80	23	37	60	53	-2	10	0	6	0	0	0	8
NHL Totals (6 years)		397	70	102	172	195	-14	17	2	22	0	1	1	20

BONNI, RYAN — D — CANUCKS

PERSONAL: Born February 18, 1979, in Winnipeg. ... 6-4/190. ... Shoots left. ... Name pronounced BAH-nee.
TRANSACTIONS/CAREER NOTES: Selected by Vancouver Canucks in second round (second Canucks pick, 34th overal) of NHL entry draft (June 21, 1997).

Season Team	League	Gms.	G	A	Pts.	PIM	+/-	PP	SH	Gms.	G	A	Pts.	PIM
				REGULAR SEASON						PLAYOFFS				
95-96—Saskatoon	WHL	63	1	7	8	78	...	...	...	3	0	0	0	0
96-97—Saskatoon	WHL	69	11	19	30	219	...	...	...	—	—	—	—	—
97-98—Saskatoon	WHL	42	5	14	19	100	...	...	...	—	—	—	—	—
98-99—Saskatoon	WHL	51	6	26	32	211	...	...	...	—	—	—	—	—
—Red Deer	WHL	20	3	10	13	41	...	...	...	9	0	4	4	25
99-00—Syracuse	AHL	71	5	13	18	125	...	...	...	2	0	1	1	2
—Vancouver	NHL	3	0	0	0	0	-1	0	0	—	—	—	—	—
NHL Totals (1 year)		3	0	0	0	0	-1	0	0					

BONVIE, DENNIS — D

PERSONAL: Born July 23, 1973, in Antigonish, Nova Scotia. ... 5-11/205. ... Shoots right. ... Name pronounced BAHN-vee.
TRANSACTIONS/CAREER NOTES: Signed as free agent by Edmonton Oilers (August 26, 1994). ... Selected by Chicago Blackhawks from Oilers in NHL waiver draft (October 5, 1998). ... Traded by Blackhawks to Philadelphia Flyers for D Frank Bialowas (January 8, 1999). ... Signed as free agent by Pittsburgh Penguins (September 20, 1999).

Season Team	League	Gms.	G	A	Pts.	PIM	+/-	PP	SH	Gms.	G	A	Pts.	PIM
				REGULAR SEASON						PLAYOFFS				
90-91—Antigonish	N.S.Jr.A					Statistics unavailable.								
91-92—Kitchener	OHL	7	1	1	2	23	...	...	...	—	—	—	—	—
—North Bay	OHL	49	0	12	12	261	...	...	...	21	0	1	1	91
92-93—North Bay	OHL	64	3	21	24	316	...	...	...	5	0	0	0	34
93-94—Cape Breton	AHL	63	1	10	11	278	...	...	...	4	0	0	0	11
94-95—Cape Breton	AHL	74	5	15	20	422	...	...	...	—	—	—	—	—
—Edmonton	NHL	2	0	0	0	0	0	0	0	—	—	—	—	—
95-96—Edmonton	NHL	8	0	0	0	47	-3	0	0	—	—	—	—	—
—Cape Breton	AHL	38	13	14	27	269	...	...	...	—	—	—	—	—
96-97—Hamilton	AHL	73	9	20	29	*522	...	...	...	22	3	11	14	*91
97-98—Edmonton	NHL	4	0	0	0	27	0	0	0	—	—	—	—	—
—Hamilton	AHL	57	11	19	30	295	...	...	...	9	0	5	5	18
98-99—Chicago	NHL	11	0	0	0	44	-4	0	0	—	—	—	—	—
—Portland	AHL	3	1	0	1	16	...	...	...	—	—	—	—	—
—Philadelphia	AHL	37	4	10	14	158	...	...	...	14	3	3	6	26
99-00—Wilkes-Barre/Scranton	AHL	42	5	26	31	243	...	...	...	—	—	—	—	—
—Pittsburgh	NHL	28	0	0	0	80	-2	0	0	—	—	—	—	—
NHL Totals (5 years)		53	0	0	0	198	-9	0	0					

BORDELEAU, SEBASTIEN — C — PREDATORS

PERSONAL: Born February 15, 1975, in Vancouver. ... 5-11/185. ... Shoots right. ... Son of Paulin Bordeleau, head coach with Fredericton Canadiens of AHL (1990-91 through 1996-97). ... Name pronounced BOHR-dih-loh.
TRANSACTIONS/CAREER NOTES: Selected by Montreal Canadiens in third round (third Canadiens pick, 73rd overall) of NHL entry draft (June 26, 1993). ... Pulled groin (January 13, 1997); missed one game. ... Strained hip flexor (November 17, 1997); missed two games. ... Bruised thigh (November 24, 1997); missed four games. ... Bruised testicles (January 24, 1998); missed two games. ... Strained hip flexor (Feburary 4, 1998); missed two games. ... Traded by Canadiens to Nashville Predators for future considerations (June 27, 1998). ... Sprained thumb (January 11, 1999); missed four games. ... Injured neck (April 12, 1999) and underwent surgery; missed final three games of season. ... Suffered injury (October 2, 1999); missed first seven games of season. ... Separated shoulder (November 2, 1999); missed 11 games.
HONORS: Named to QMJHL All-Star first team (1994-95).

Season Team	League	Gms.	G	A	Pts.	PIM	+/-	PP	SH	Gms.	G	A	Pts.	PIM
				REGULAR SEASON						PLAYOFFS				
91-92—Hull	QMJHL	62	26	32	58	91	...	...	...	5	0	3	3	23
92-93—Hull	QMJHL	60	18	39	57	95	...	...	...	10	3	8	11	20
93-94—Hull	QMJHL	60	26	57	83	147	...	...	...	17	6	14	20	26
94-95—Hull	QMJHL	68	52	76	128	142	...	...	...	18	13	19	32	25
95-96—Fredericton	AHL	43	17	29	46	68	...	...	...	7	0	2	2	8
—Montreal	NHL	4	0	0	0	0	-1	0	0	—	—	—	—	—
96-97—Fredericton	AHL	33	17	21	38	50	...	...	...	—	—	—	—	—
—Montreal	NHL	28	2	9	11	2	-3	0	0	—	—	—	—	—
97-98—Montreal	NHL	53	6	8	14	36	5	2	1	5	0	0	0	2
98-99—Nashville	NHL	72	16	24	40	26	-14	1	2	—	—	—	—	—
99-00—Nashville	NHL	60	10	13	23	30	-12	0	2	—	—	—	—	—
NHL Totals (5 years)		217	34	54	88	94	-25	3	5	5	0	0	0	2

BOTTERILL, JASON — LW — FLAMES

PERSONAL: Born May 19, 1976, in Edmonton. ... 6-4/220. ... Shoots left. ... Name pronounced BAH-tuh-rihl.
HIGH SCHOOL: St. Paul's Prep (Concord, N.H.).
COLLEGE: Michigan.
TRANSACTIONS/CAREER NOTES: Selected by Dallas Stars in first round (first Stars pick, 20th overall) of NHL entry draft (June 28, 1994). ... Traded by Stars to Atlanta Thrashers for D Jamie Pushor (July 15, 1999). ... Traded by Thrashers with D Darryl Shannon to Calgary Flames for C Hnat Domenichelli and LW Dmitri Vlasenkov (February 11, 2000).
HONORS: Named to CCHA All-Rookie team (1993-94). ... Named to CCHA All-Star second team (1995-96). ... Named to NCAA All-America (West) second team (1996-97).

Season Team	League	REGULAR SEASON								PLAYOFFS				
		Gms.	G	A	Pts.	PIM	+/-	PP	SH	Gms.	G	A	Pts.	PIM
92-93—St. Paul's	USHL	22	22	26	48	...	...	...	...	—	—	—	—	—
93-94—Univ. of Michigan........	CCHA	37	21	19	40	94	...	...	...	—	—	—	—	—
94-95—Univ. of Michigan........	CCHA	34	14	14	28	117	...	...	...	—	—	—	—	—
95-96—Univ. of Michigan........	CCHA	37	32	25	57	143	...	...	...	—	—	—	—	—
96-97—Univ. of Michigan........	CCHA	42	37	24	61	129	...	...	...	—	—	—	—	—
97-98—Michigan....................	IHL	50	11	11	22	82	...	...	...	4	0	0	0	5
—Dallas........................	NHL	4	0	0	0	19	-1	0	0	—	—	—	—	—
98-99—Michigan....................	IHL	56	13	25	38	106	...	...	...	5	2	1	3	4
—Dallas........................	NHL	17	0	0	0	23	-2	0	0	—	—	—	—	—
99-00—Orlando....................	IHL	17	7	8	15	27	...	...	...	—	—	—	—	—
—Atlanta......................	NHL	25	1	4	5	17	-7	0	0	—	—	—	—	—
—Calgary	NHL	2	0	0	0	0	-4	0	0	—	—	—	—	—
—Saint John	AHL	21	3	4	7	39	...	...	...	3	0	0	0	19
NHL Totals (3 years)...........		48	1	4	5	59	-14	0	0					

BOUCHARD, JOEL — D — STARS

PERSONAL: Born January 23, 1974, in Montreal. ... 6-0/200. ... Shoots left.
TRANSACTIONS/CAREER NOTES: Selected by Calgary Flames in sixth (sixth Flames pick, 129th overall) of NHL entry draft (June 20, 1992). ... Strained abdominal muscle (September 30, 1997); missed one game. ... Suffered concussion (January 24, 1998); missed six games. ... Selected by Nashville Predators in NHL expansion draft (June 26, 1998). ... Sprained ankle (October 27, 1998); missed 11 games. ... Sprained ankle (December 19, 1998); missed seven games. ... Suffered concussion (December 15, 1999); missed nine games. ... Claimed on waivers by Dallas Stars (March 14, 2000).
HONORS: Named to QMJHL All-Star first team (1993-94).

Season Team	League	REGULAR SEASON								PLAYOFFS				
		Gms.	G	A	Pts.	PIM	+/-	PP	SH	Gms.	G	A	Pts.	PIM
90-91—Longueuil..................	QMJHL	53	3	19	22	34	...	...	...	8	0	1	1	11
91-92—Verdun.....................	QMJHL	70	9	37	46	55	...	...	...	19	1	7	8	20
92-93—Verdun.....................	QMJHL	60	10	49	59	126	...	...	...	4	0	2	2	4
93-94—Verdun.....................	QMJHL	60	15	55	70	62	...	...	...	4	1	0	1	6
—Saint John	AHL	1	0	0	0	0	...	...	...	2	0	0	0	0
94-95—Saint John	AHL	77	6	25	31	63	...	...	...	5	1	0	1	4
—Calgary	NHL	2	0	0	0	0	0	0	0	—	—	—	—	—
95-96—Saint John	AHL	74	8	25	33	104	...	...	...	16	1	4	5	10
—Calgary	NHL	4	0	0	0	4	0	0	0	—	—	—	—	—
96-97—Calgary	NHL	76	4	5	9	49	-23	0	1	—	—	—	—	—
97-98—Calgary	NHL	44	5	7	12	57	0	0	1	—	—	—	—	—
—Saint John	AHL	3	2	1	3	6	...	...	...	—	—	—	—	—
98-99—Nashville	NHL	64	4	11	15	60	-10	0	0	—	—	—	—	—
99-00—Nashville	NHL	52	1	4	5	23	-11	0	0	—	—	—	—	—
—Dallas........................	NHL	2	0	0	0	2	1	0	0	—	—	—	—	—
NHL Totals (6 years)...........		244	14	27	41	195	-43	0	2					

BOUCHER, BRIAN — G — FLYERS

PERSONAL: Born August 1, 1977, in Woonsocket, R.I. ... 6-1/190. ... Catches left. ... Name pronounced boo-SHAY.
HIGH SCHOOL: Mount St. Charles (Woonsocket, R.I.), then Kamiakin (Kennewick, Wash.).
TRANSACTIONS/CAREER NOTES: Selected by Philadelphia Flyers in first round (first Flyers pick, 22nd overall) of NHL entry draft (July 8, 1995).
HONORS: Named to WHL (West) All-Star second team (1995-96). ... Named to WHL (West) All-Star first team (1996-97). ... Won Del Wilson Trophy (1996-97). ... Named to NHL All-Rookie team (1999-2000).

Season Team	League	REGULAR SEASON							PLAYOFFS					
		Gms.	Min	W	L	T	GA	SO	Avg.	Gms.	Min.	W	L	GA	SO	Avg.
93-94—Mt. St. Charles H.S.	R.I.H.S.	23	1170	...	...	...	23	12	1.18	—	—	—	—	—	—	—
94-95—Wexford	Tier II Jr. A	8	425	...	...	...	23	0	3.25	—	—	—	—	—	—	—
—Tri-City	WHL	35	1969	17	11	2	108	1	3.29	13	795	6	5	50	0	3.77
95-96—Tri-City	WHL	55	3183	33	19	2	181	1	3.41	11	653	6	5	37	†2	3.40
96-97—Tri-City	WHL	41	2458	10	24	†6	149	1	3.64	—	—	—	—	—	—	—
97-98—Philadelphia	AHL	34	1901	16	12	3	101	0	3.19	2	31	0	0	1	0	1.94
98-99—Philadelphia	AHL	36	2061	20	8	5	89	2	2.59	16	947	9	7	45	0	2.85
99-00—Philadelphia	NHL	35	2038	20	10	3	65	4	*1.91	18	1183	11	7	40	1	2.03
—Philadelphia	AHL	1	65	0	0	1	3	0	2.77	—	—	—	—	—	—	—
NHL Totals (1 year)..............		35	2038	20	10	3	65	4	1.91	18	1183	11	7	40	1	2.03

BOUCHER, PHILIPPE — D — KINGS

PERSONAL: Born March 24, 1973, in St. Apollnaire, Que. ... 6-3/221. ... Shoots right. ... Name pronounced fih-LEEP boo-SHAY.
TRANSACTIONS/CAREER NOTES: Selected by Buffalo Sabres in first round (first Sabres pick, 13th overall) of NHL entry draft (June 22, 1991). ... Traded by Sabres with G Grant Fuhr and D Denis Tsygurov to Los Angeles Kings for D Alexei Zhitnik, D Charlie Huddy, G Robb Stauber and fifth-round pick (D Marian Menhart) in 1995 draft (February 14, 1995). ... Sprained wrist (February 25, 1995); missed final 31 games of season. ... Suffered tendinitis in right wrist (October 6, 1995); missed first 25 games of season. ... Injured left hand (February 19, 1996); missed four games. ... Sprained right shoulder (October 4, 1996); missed 10 games. ... Suffered from the flu (December 18, 1997); missed two games. ... Suffered illness (January 10, 1998); missed 12 games. ... Suffered from the flu (March 3, 1999); missed two games. ... Underwent foot surgery (April 27, 1999); missed first 71 games of 1999-2000 season.
HONORS: Won Can.HL Rookie of the Year Award (1990-91). ... Won Raymond Lagace Trophy (1990-91). ... Won Michael Bossy Trophy (1990-91). ... Named to QMJHL All-Star second team (1990-91 and 1991-92).

Season Team	League	REGULAR SEASON								PLAYOFFS				
		Gms.	G	A	Pts.	PIM	+/-	PP	SH	Gms.	G	A	Pts.	PIM
90-91—Granby	QMJHL	69	21	46	67	92	...	...	...	—	—	—	—	—
91-92—Granby	QMJHL	49	22	37	59	47	...	...	...	—	—	—	—	—
—Laval	QMJHL	16	7	11	18	36	...	...	...	10	5	6	11	8
92-93—Laval	QMJHL	16	12	15	27	37	...	...	...	13	6	15	21	12
—Rochester	AHL	5	4	3	7	8	...	...	...	3	0	1	1	2
—Buffalo	NHL	18	0	4	4	14	1	0	0	—	—	—	—	—
93-94—Buffalo	NHL	38	6	8	14	29	-1	4	0	7	1	1	2	2
—Rochester	AHL	31	10	22	32	51	...	...	...	—	—	—	—	—
94-95—Rochester	AHL	43	14	27	41	26	...	...	...	—	—	—	—	—
—Buffalo	NHL	9	1	4	5	0	6	0	0	—	—	—	—	—
—Los Angeles	NHL	6	1	0	1	4	-3	0	0	—	—	—	—	—
95-96—Los Angeles	NHL	53	7	16	23	31	-26	5	0	—	—	—	—	—
—Phoenix	IHL	10	4	3	7	4	...	...	...	—	—	—	—	—
96-97—Los Angeles	NHL	60	7	18	25	25	0	2	0	—	—	—	—	—
97-98—Los Angeles	NHL	45	6	10	16	49	6	1	0	—	—	—	—	—
—Long Beach	IHL	2	0	1	1	4	...	...	...	—	—	—	—	—
98-99—Los Angeles	NHL	45	2	6	8	32	-12	1	0	—	—	—	—	—
99-00—Long Beach	IHL	14	4	11	15	8	...	...	...	6	0	9	9	8
—Los Angeles	NHL	1	0	0	0	0	0	0	0	—	—	—	—	—
NHL Totals (8 years)		275	30	66	96	184	-29	13	0	7	1	1	2	2

BOUGHNER, BOB — D — PENGUINS

PERSONAL: Born March 8, 1971, in Windsor, Ont. ... 6-0/203. ... Shoots right. ... Name pronounced BOOG-nuhr.

TRANSACTIONS/CAREER NOTES: Selected by Detroit Red Wings in second round (second Red Wings pick, 32nd overall) of NHL entry draft (June 17, 1989). ... Signed as free agent by Florida Panthers (August 10, 1994). ... Traded by Panthers to Buffalo Sabres for third-round pick (D Chris Allen) in 1996 draft (February 1, 1996). ... Bruised left thigh (February 28, 1996); missed one game. ... Bruised shoulder (February 7, 1998); missed two games. ... Injured wrist (March 12, 1998); missed three games. ... Bruised foot (April 29, 1998); missed one game. ... Selected by Nashville Predators in NHL expansion draft (June 26, 1998). ... Suffered from the flu (October 27, 1998); missed one game. ... Suffered from the flu (January 14, 1999); missed two games. ... Suffered from the flu (November 1999); missed two games. ... Sprained ankle (December 1999); missed two games. ... Fractured finger (February 2, 2000); missed three games. ... Traded by Predators to Pittsburgh Penguins for D Pavel Skrbek (March 13, 2000).

Season Team	League	REGULAR SEASON								PLAYOFFS				
		Gms.	G	A	Pts.	PIM	+/-	PP	SH	Gms.	G	A	Pts.	PIM
87-88—St. Mary's Jr. B	OHA	36	4	18	22	177	...	...	...	—	—	—	—	—
88-89—Sault Ste. Marie	OHL	64	6	15	21	182	...	...	...	—	—	—	—	—
89-90—Sault Ste. Marie	OHL	49	7	23	30	122	...	...	...	—	—	—	—	—
90-91—Sault Ste. Marie	OHL	64	13	33	46	156	...	...	...	14	2	9	11	35
91-92—Adirondack	AHL	1	0	0	0	7	...	...	...	—	—	—	—	—
—Toledo	ECHL	28	3	10	13	79	...	...	...	5	2	0	2	15
92-93—Adirondack	AHL	69	1	16	17	190	...	...	...	—	—	—	—	—
93-94—Adirondack	AHL	72	8	14	22	292	...	...	...	10	1	1	2	18
94-95—Cincinnati	IHL	81	2	14	16	192	...	...	...	10	0	0	0	18
95-96—Carolina	AHL	46	2	15	17	127	...	...	...	—	—	—	—	—
—Buffalo	NHL	31	0	1	1	104	3	0	0	—	—	—	—	—
96-97—Buffalo	NHL	77	1	7	8	225	12	0	0	11	0	1	1	9
97-98—Buffalo	NHL	69	1	3	4	165	5	0	0	14	0	4	4	15
98-99—Nashville	NHL	79	3	10	13	137	-6	0	0	—	—	—	—	—
99-00—Nashville	NHL	62	2	4	6	97	-13	0	0	—	—	—	—	—
—Pittsburgh	NHL	11	1	0	1	69	2	1	0	11	0	2	2	15
NHL Totals (5 years)		329	8	25	33	797	3	1	0	36	0	7	7	39

BOUILLON, FRANCIS — D — CANADIENS

PERSONAL: Born October 17, 1975, in New York. ... 5-8/189. ... Shoots left.

TRANSACTIONS/CAREER NOTES: Signed as non-drafted free agent by Montreal Canadiens (August 18, 1998).

Season Team	League	REGULAR SEASON								PLAYOFFS				
		Gms.	G	A	Pts.	PIM	+/-	PP	SH	Gms.	G	A	Pts.	PIM
92-93—Laval	QMJHL	46	0	7	7	45	...	...	...	—	—	—	—	—
93-94—Laval	QMJHL	68	3	15	18	129	...	...	...	19	2	9	11	48
94-95—Laval	QMJHL	72	8	25	33	115	...	...	...	20	3	11	14	21
95-96—Granby	QMJHL	68	11	35	46	156	...	...	...	21	2	12	14	30
96-97—Wheeling	ECHL	69	10	32	42	77	...	...	...	3	0	2	2	10
97-98—Quebec	IHL	71	8	27	35	76	...	...	...	—	—	—	—	—
98-99—Fredericton	AHL	79	19	36	55	174	...	...	...	5	2	1	3	0
99-00—Montreal	NHL	74	3	13	16	38	-7	2	0	—	—	—	—	—
NHL Totals (1 year)		74	3	13	16	38	-7	2	0	—	—	—	—	—

BOULTON, ERIC — LW — SABRES

PERSONAL: Born August 17, 1976, in Halifax, Nova Scotia. ... 6-0/201. ... Shoots left.

TRANSACTIONS/CAREER NOTES: Selected by New York Rangers in ninth round (12th Rangers pick, 234th overall) of NHL entry draft (June 29, 1994). ... Signed as free agent by Buffalo Sabres (September 3, 1999).

Season Team	League	REGULAR SEASON								PLAYOFFS				
		Gms.	G	A	Pts.	PIM	+/-	PP	SH	Gms.	G	A	Pts.	PIM
93-94—Cole Harbour	NSJHL					Statistics unavailable.								
94-95—Oshawa	OHL	27	7	5	12	125	...	...	...	—	—	—	—	—
—Sarnia	OHL	24	3	7	10	134	...	...	...	4	0	1	1	10
95-96—Sarnia	OHL	66	14	29	43	243	...	...	...	9	0	3	3	29
96-97—Binghamton	AHL	23	2	3	5	67	...	...	...	3	0	0	0	4
—Charlotte	ECHL	44	14	11	25	325	...	...	...	3	0	1	1	6
97-98—Charlotte	ECHL	53	11	16	27	202	...	...	...	4	1	0	1	0
98-99—Houston	IHL	7	1	0	1	41	...	...	...	—	—	—	—	—
—Florida	ECHL	26	9	13	22	143	...	...	...	—	—	—	—	—
—Kentucky	AHL	34	3	3	6	154	...	...	...	10	0	1	1	36
99-00—Rochester	AHL	76	2	2	4	276	...	...	...	18	2	1	3	53

BOURQUE, RAY   D   AVALANCHE   B

PERSONAL: Born December 28, 1960, in Montreal. ... 5-11/215. ... Shoots left. ... Full Name: Raymond Jean Bourque. ... Name pronounced BOHRK.

TRANSACTIONS/CAREER NOTES: Selected by Boston Bruins in first round (first Bruins pick, eighth overall) of NHL entry draft (August 9, 1979). ... Broke jaw (November 11, 1980). ... Injured left shoulder (October 1981). ... Fractured left wrist (April 21, 1982). ... Refractured left wrist and fractured left forearm (summer 1982). ... Fractured bone over left eye (October 1982). ... Sprained left knee ligaments (December 10, 1988). ... Bruised hip (April 7, 1990). ... Bruised right shoulder (October 17, 1990); missed two games. ... Fractured finger (May 5, 1992); missed remainder of playoffs. ... Injured back (December 19, 1992); missed two games. ... Injured ankle (January 21, 1993); missed three games. ... Injured knee (March 22, 1994); missed 11 games. ... Bruised shoulder (October 20, 1996); missed nine games. ... Strained abdominal muscle (December 14, 1996); missed five games. ... Bruised ankle (March 6, 1997); missed three games. ... Injured ankle (March 17, 1997); missed three games. ... Strained hip flexor (January 7, 1999); missed one game. ... Traded by Bruins with LW Dave Andreychuk to Colorado Avalanche for LW Brian Rolston, D Martin Grenier, C Samual Pahlsson and first-round pick (LW Martin Samuelsson) in 2000 draft (March 6, 2000). ... Injured groin (March 7, 2000); missed one game.

HONORS: Named to QMJHL All-Star first team (1977-78 and 1978-79). ... Won Frank J. Selke Trophy (1978-79). ... Won Emile (Butch) Bouchard Trophy (1978-79). ... Named NHL Rookie of the Year by THE SPORTING NEWS (1979-80). ... Won Calder Memorial Trophy (1979-80). ... Named to NHL All-Star first team (1979-80, 1981-82, 1983-84, 1984-85, 1986-87, 1987-88, and 1989-90 through 1993-94 and 1995-96). ... Named to THE SPORTING NEWS All-Star second team (1980-81, 1982-83, 1985-86 and 1988-89). ... Named to NHL All-Star second team (1980-81, 1982-83, 1985-86, 1988-89, 1994-95 and 1998-99). ... Played in NHL All-Star Game (1981-1986, 1988-1994 and 1996-2000). ... Named to THE SPORTING NEWS All-Star first team (1981-82, 1983-84, 1984-85, 1986-87, 1987-88 and 1989-90 through 1995-96). ... Won James Norris Memorial Trophy (1986-87, 1987-88, 1989-90, 1990-91 and 1993-94). ... Won King Clancy Memorial Trophy (1991-92). ... Named All-Star Game Most Valuable Player (1996).

RECORDS: Holds NHL career record for most goals by defenseman—403. ... Shares NHL career playoff record for most years in playoffs—20 (1979-80 through 1995-96, 1997-98 and 1999-2000). ... Shares NHL career All-Star Game record for most assists—13.

STATISTICAL PLATEAUS: Three-goal games: 1982-83 (1).

MISCELLANEOUS: Co-captain of Boston Bruins (1985-86 through 1987-88). ... Captain of Bruins (1988-89 through March 6, 2000). ... Holds Boston Bruins all-time records for most games played (1,518), most assists (1,111) and most points (1,506). ... Scored on a penalty shot (vs. Chris Terreri, March 19, 1994). ... Failed to score on a penalty shot (vs. John Vanbiesbrouck, November 11, 1988).

Season Team	League	REGULAR SEASON								PLAYOFFS				
		Gms.	G	A	Pts.	PIM	+/-	PP	SH	Gms.	G	A	Pts.	PIM
76-77—Sorel	QMJHL	69	12	36	48	61	...	...	...	—	—	—	—	—
77-78—Verdun	QMJHL	72	22	57	79	90	...	...	...	4	2	1	3	0
78-79—Verdun	QMJHL	63	22	71	93	44	...	...	...	11	3	16	19	18
79-80—Boston	NHL	80	17	48	65	73	52	3	2	10	2	9	11	27
80-81—Boston	NHL	67	27	29	56	96	29	9	1	3	0	1	1	2
81-82—Boston	NHL	65	17	49	66	51	22	4	0	9	1	5	6	16
82-83—Boston	NHL	65	22	51	73	20	49	7	0	17	8	15	23	10
83-84—Boston	NHL	78	31	65	96	57	51	12	1	3	0	2	2	0
84-85—Boston	NHL	73	20	66	86	53	30	10	1	5	0	3	3	4
85-86—Boston	NHL	74	19	58	77	68	17	11	0	3	0	0	0	0
86-87—Boston	NHL	78	23	72	95	36	44	6	1	4	1	2	3	0
87-88—Boston	NHL	78	17	64	81	72	34	7	1	23	3	18	21	26
88-89—Boston	NHL	60	18	43	61	52	20	6	0	10	0	4	4	6
89-90—Boston	NHL	76	19	65	84	50	31	8	0	17	5	12	17	16
90-91—Boston	NHL	76	21	73	94	75	33	7	0	19	7	18	25	12
91-92—Boston	NHL	80	21	60	81	56	11	7	1	12	3	6	9	12
92-93—Boston	NHL	78	19	63	82	40	38	8	0	4	1	0	1	2
93-94—Boston	NHL	72	20	71	91	58	26	10	3	13	2	8	10	0
94-95—Boston	NHL	46	12	31	43	20	3	9	0	5	0	3	3	0
95-96—Boston	NHL	82	20	62	82	58	31	9	2	5	1	6	7	2
96-97—Boston	NHL	62	19	31	50	18	-11	8	1	—	—	—	—	—
97-98—Boston	NHL	82	13	35	48	80	2	9	0	6	1	4	5	2
—Can. Olympic team	Int'l	6	1	2	3	4	...	...	...	—	—	—	—	—
98-99—Boston	NHL	81	10	47	57	34	-7	8	0	12	1	9	10	14
99-00—Boston	NHL	65	10	28	38	20	-11	6	0	—	—	—	—	—
—Colorado	NHL	14	8	6	14	6	9	7	0	13	1	8	9	8
NHL Totals (21 years)..........		1532	403	1117	1520	1093	503	171	14	193	37	133	170	159

BOYLE, DAN   D   PANTHERS

PERSONAL: Born July 12, 1976, in Ottawa. ... 5-11/190. ... Shoots right.

COLLEGE: Miami of Ohio.

TRANSACTIONS/CAREER NOTES: Signed as non-drafted free agent by Florida Panthers (March 30, 1998).

HONORS: Named to NCAA All-America (West) first team (1996-97 and 1997-98). ... Named to CCHA All-Star first team (1996-97 and 1997-98). ... Named to AHL All-Star second team (1998-99 and 1999-2000).

Season Team	League	REGULAR SEASON Gms.	G	A	Pts.	PIM	+/-	PP	SH	PLAYOFFS Gms.	G	A	Pts.	PIM
94-95—Miami of Ohio	CCHA	35	8	18	26	24	...	...	...	—	—	—	—	—
95-96—Miami of Ohio	CCHA	36	7	20	27	70	...	...	...	—	—	—	—	—
96-97—Miami of Ohio	CCHA	40	11	43	54	52	...	...	...	—	—	—	—	—
97-98—Miami of Ohio	CCHA	37	14	26	40	58	...	...	...	—	—	—	—	—
—Cincinnati	IHL	8	0	3	3	20	...	...	...	5	0	1	1	4
98-99—Kentucky	AHL	53	8	34	42	87	...	...	...	12	3	5	8	16
—Florida	NHL	22	3	5	8	6	0	1	0	—	—	—	—	—
99-00—Louisville	AHL	58	14	38	52	75	...	...	...	4	0	2	2	8
—Florida	NHL	13	0	3	3	4	-2	0	0	—	—	—	—	—
NHL Totals (2 years)		35	3	8	11	10	-2	1	0					

B

BOYNTON, NICK   D   BRUINS

PERSONAL: Born January 14, 1979, in Etobicoke, Ont. ... 6-2/210. ... Shoots right. ... Full Name: Nicholas Boynton.
TRANSACTIONS/CAREER NOTES: Selected by Washington Capitals in first round (first Capitals pick, ninth overall) of NHL entry draft (June 21, 1997). ... Returned to draft pool by Capitals and selected by Boston Bruins in first round (first Bruins pick, 21st overall) of NHL entry draft (June 26, 1999).
HONORS: Named to OHL All-Rookie team (1995-96). ... Won Can.HL Plus/Minus Award (1996-97).

Season Team	League	REGULAR SEASON Gms.	G	A	Pts.	PIM	+/-	PP	SH	PLAYOFFS Gms.	G	A	Pts.	PIM
94-95—Caledon	Jr. A	44	10	35	45	139	...	...	...	—	—	—	—	—
95-96—Ottawa	OHL	64	10	14	24	90	...	...	...	4	0	3	3	10
96-97—Ottawa	OHL	63	13	51	64	143	...	...	...	24	4	24	28	38
97-98—Ottawa	OHL	40	7	31	38	94	...	...	...	13	0	4	4	24
98-99—Ottawa	OHL	51	11	48	59	83	...	...	...	9	1	9	10	18
99-00—Providence	AHL	53	5	14	19	66	...	...	...	12	1	0	1	6
—Boston	NHL	5	0	0	0	0	-5	0	0	—	—	—	—	—
NHL Totals (1 year)		5	0	0	0	0	-5	0	0					

BRADLEY, MATT   RW   SHARKS

PERSONAL: Born June 13, 1978, in Stittsville, Ont. ... 6-2/195. ... Shoots right.
TRANSACTIONS/CAREER NOTES: Selected by San Jose Sharks in fourth round (fourth Sharks pick, 102nd overall) of NHL entry draft (June 22, 1996).
HONORS: Won William Hanley Trophy (1997-98).

Season Team	League	REGULAR SEASON Gms.	G	A	Pts.	PIM	+/-	PP	SH	PLAYOFFS Gms.	G	A	Pts.	PIM
94-95—Cumberland	CJHL	49	13	20	33	18	...	...	...	—	—	—	—	—
95-96—Kingston	OHL	55	10	14	24	17	...	...	...	6	0	1	1	6
96-97—Kingston	OHL	65	24	24	48	41	...	...	...	5	0	4	4	2
—Kentucky	AHL	1	0	1	1	0	...	...	...	—	—	—	—	—
97-98—Kingston	OHL	55	33	50	83	24	...	...	...	8	3	4	7	7
—Kentucky	AHL	1	0	1	1	0	...	...	...	—	—	—	—	—
98-99—Kentucky	AHL	79	23	20	43	57	...	...	...	10	1	4	5	4
99-00—Kentucky	AHL	80	22	19	41	81	...	...	...	9	6	3	9	9

BRASHEAR, DONALD   LW   CANUCKS

PERSONAL: Born January 7, 1972, in Bedford, Ind. ... 6-2/230. ... Shoots left. ... Name pronounced brah-SHEER.
TRANSACTIONS/CAREER NOTES: Signed as free agent by Montreal Canadiens (July 28, 1992). ... Bruised knee (November 23, 1993); missed one game. ... Injured shoulder (February 27, 1995); missed one game. ... Bruised hand (March 20, 1995); missed one game. ... Suffered cut to right thigh (December 30, 1995); missed seven games. ... Traded by Canadiens to Vancouver Canucks for D Jassen Cullimore (November 13, 1996). ... Strained back (February 8, 1997); missed three games. ... Suspended four games and fined §1,000 by NHL for fighting (February 25, 1997). ... Injured shoulder (March 11, 1998); missed two games. ... Suspended two games by NHL for illegal check (October 24, 1999). ... Suffered concussion (February 21, 2000); missed 20 games.

Season Team	League	REGULAR SEASON Gms.	G	A	Pts.	PIM	+/-	PP	SH	PLAYOFFS Gms.	G	A	Pts.	PIM
89-90—Longueuil	QMJHL	64	12	14	26	169	...	...	...	7	0	0	0	11
90-91—Longueuil	QMJHL	68	12	26	38	195	...	...	...	8	0	3	3	33
91-92—Verdun	QMJHL	65	18	24	42	283	...	...	...	18	4	2	6	98
92-93—Fredericton	AHL	76	11	3	14	261	...	...	...	5	0	0	0	8
93-94—Fredericton	AHL	62	38	28	66	250	...	...	...	—	—	—	—	—
—Montreal	NHL	14	2	2	4	34	0	0	0	2	0	0	0	0
94-95—Montreal	NHL	20	1	1	2	63	-5	0	0	—	—	—	—	—
—Fredericton	AHL	29	10	9	19	182	...	...	...	17	7	5	12	77
95-96—Montreal	NHL	67	0	4	4	223	-10	0	0	6	0	0	0	2
96-97—Montreal	NHL	10	0	0	0	38	-2	0	0	—	—	—	—	—
—Vancouver	NHL	59	8	5	13	207	-6	0	0	—	—	—	—	—
97-98—Vancouver	NHL	77	9	9	18	*372	-9	0	0	—	—	—	—	—
98-99—Vancouver	NHL	82	8	10	18	209	-25	2	0	—	—	—	—	—
99-00—Vancouver	NHL	60	11	2	13	136	-9	1	0	—	—	—	—	—
NHL Totals (7 years)		389	39	33	72	1282	-66	3	0	8	0	0	0	2

BRATHWAITE, FRED   G   FLAMES

PERSONAL: Born November 24, 1972, in Ottawa. ... 5-7/175. ... Catches left. ... Name pronounced BRATH-wayt.
TRANSACTIONS/CAREER NOTES: Signed as non-drafted free agent by Edmonton Oilers (October 6, 1993). ... Signed as free agent by Calgary Flames (January 7, 1999).
MISCELLANEOUS: Holds Calgary Flames all-time record for goals-against average (2.65).
STATISTICAL NOTES: Led OHL with 3.31 goals-against average and four shutouts (1991-92).

		REGULAR SEASON								PLAYOFFS						
Season Team	League	Gms.	Min	W	L	T	GA	SO	Avg.	Gms.	Min.	W	L	GA	SO	Avg.
89-90—Oshawa	OHL	20	901	11	2	1	45	1	3.00	10	451	4	2	22	0	*2.93
90-91—Oshawa	OHL	39	1986	25	6	3	112	1	3.38	13	677	*9	2	43	0	3.81
91-92—Oshawa	OHL	24	1248	12	7	2	81	*0	*3.89	—	—	—	—	—	—	—
—London	OHL	23	1325	23	10	4	61	*4	*2.76	10	615	5	5	36	0	3.51
92-93—Det. Jr. Red Wings	OHL	37	2192	23	10	4	134	0	3.67	15	858	9	6	48	1	3.36
93-94—Cape Breton	AHL	2	119	1	1	0	6	0	3.03	—	—	—	—	—	—	—
—Edmonton	NHL	19	982	3	10	3	58	0	3.54	—	—	—	—	—	—	—
94-95—Edmonton	NHL	14	601	2	5	1	40	0	3.99	—	—	—	—	—	—	—
95-96—Cape Breton	AHL	31	1699	12	16	0	110	1	3.88	—	—	—	—	—	—	—
—Edmonton	NHL	7	293	0	2	0	12	0	2.46	—	—	—	—	—	—	—
96-97—Manitoba	IHL	58	2945	22	22	5	167	1	3.40	—	—	—	—	—	—	—
97-98—Manitoba	IHL	51	2737	23	18	4	138	1	3.03	2	73	0	1	4	0	3.29
98-99—Canadian nat'l team	Int'l	24	989	6	8	3	47	...	2.85	—	—	—	—	—	—	—
—Calgary	NHL	28	1663	11	9	7	68	1	2.45	—	—	—	—	—	—	—
99-00—Calgary	NHL	61	3448	25	25	7	158	5	2.75	—	—	—	—	—	—	—
—Saint John	AHL	2	120	2	0	0	4	0	2.00	—	—	—	—	—	—	—
NHL Totals (5 years)		129	6987	41	51	18	336	6	2.89							

BRENDL, PAVEL   RW   RANGERS

PERSONAL: Born March 23, 1981, in Opocno, Czechoslovakia. ... 6-1/197. ... Shoots right.
TRANSACTIONS/CAREER NOTES: Selected by New York Rangers in first round (first Rangers pick, fourth overall) of NHL entry draft (June 26, 1999).
HONORS: Won Bob Clarke Trophy (1998-99). ... Won Jim Piggott Memorial Trophy (1998-99). ... Won Can.HL Rookie of the Year Award (1998-99). ... Won Can.HL Top Draft Prospect Award (1998-99). ... Named to WHL (East) All-Star first team (1998-99). ... Named to Can.HL All-Star first team (1998-99). ... Named to WHL (East) All-Star second team (1999-2000).

		REGULAR SEASON								PLAYOFFS				
Season Team	League	Gms.	G	A	Pts.	PIM	+/-	PP	SH	Gms.	G	A	Pts.	PIM
96-97—Olomouc	Czech. Jrs.	40	35	17	52	...	...	...	...	—	—	—	—	—
97-98—Olomouc	Czech. Jrs.	38	29	23	52	...	...	...	...	—	—	—	—	—
—Olomouc	Czech Dv.II	12	1	1	2	...	...	...	...	—	—	—	—	—
98-99—Calgary	WHL	68	*73	61	*134	40	...	...	...	20	*21	†25	*46	18
99-00—Calgary	WHL	61	*59	52	111	94	...	...	...	10	7	12	19	8
—Hartford	AHL	—	—	—	—	—	...	...	...	2	0	0	0	0

BREWER, ERIC   D   OILERS

PERSONAL: Born April 17, 1979, in Verona, B.C. ... 6-3/220. ... Shoots left.
COLLEGE: Northern British Columbia.
TRANSACTIONS/CAREER NOTES: Selected by New York Islanders in first round (second Islanders pick, fifth overall) of NHL entry draft (June 21, 1997). ... Strained Achilles' tendon (April 8, 1999); missed four games. ... Injured toe (November 19, 1999); missed six games. ... Traded by Islanders with LW Josh Green and second-round pick (LW Brad Winchester) in 2000 draft to Edmonton Oilers for D Roman Hamrlik (June 24, 2000).
HONORS: Named to WHL (West) All-Star second team (1997-98).

		REGULAR SEASON								PLAYOFFS				
Season Team	League	Gms.	G	A	Pts.	PIM	+/-	PP	SH	Gms.	G	A	Pts.	PIM
95-96—Prince George	WHL	63	4	10	14	25	...	...	...	—	—	—	—	—
96-97—Prince George	WHL	71	5	24	29	81	...	...	...	15	2	4	6	16
97-98—Prince George	WHL	34	5	28	33	45	...	...	...	11	4	2	6	19
98-99—New York Islanders	NHL	63	5	6	11	32	-14	2	0	—	—	—	—	—
99-00—New York Islanders	NHL	26	0	2	2	20	-11	0	0	—	—	—	—	—
—Lowell	AHL	25	2	2	4	26	...	...	...	7	0	0	0	0
NHL Totals (2 years)		89	5	8	13	52	-25	2	0					

BRIERE, DANIEL   C   COYOTES

PERSONAL: Born October 6, 1977, in Gatineau, Que. ... 5-10/181. ... Shoots left.
TRANSACTIONS/CAREER NOTES: Selected by Phoenix Coyotes in first round (second Coyotes pick, 24th overall) of NHL entry draft (June 22, 1996). ... Separated shoulder (March 21, 1998); missed five games. ... Suffered concussion (October 6, 1998); missed first two games of season.
HONORS: Won Michel Bergeron Trophy (1994-95). ... Won Marcel Robert Trophy (1994-95). ... Won Jean Beliveau Trophy (1995-96). ... Named to QMJHL All-Star second team (1995-96). ... Won Frank J. Selke Trophy (1996-97). ... Named to Can.HL All-Star second team (1996-97). ... Named to AHL All-Star first team (1997-98). ... Won Dudley (Red) Garrett Trophy (1997-98).

Season Team	League	REGULAR SEASON Gms.	G	A	Pts.	PIM	+/-	PP	SH	PLAYOFFS Gms.	G	A	Pts.	PIM
94-95—Drummondville	QMJHL	72	51	72	123	54	...	...	...	—	—	—	—	—
95-96—Drummondville	QMJHL	67	*67	*96	*163	84	...	...	...	6	6	12	18	8
96-97—Drummondville	QMJHL	59	52	78	130	86	...	...	...	8	7	7	14	14
97-98—Springfield	AHL	68	36	56	92	42	...	...	...	4	1	2	3	4
—Phoenix	NHL	5	1	0	1	2	1	0	0	—	—	—	—	—
98-99—Las Vegas	IHL	1	1	1	2	0	...	...	...	—	—	—	—	—
—Phoenix	NHL	64	8	14	22	30	-3	2	0	—	—	—	—	—
—Springfield	AHL	13	2	6	8	20	...	...	...	3	0	1	1	2
99-00—Springfield	AHL	58	29	42	71	56	...	...	...	—	—	—	—	—
—Phoenix	NHL	13	1	1	2	0	0	0	0	1	0	0	0	0
NHL Totals (3 years)		82	10	15	25	32	-2	2	0	1	0	0	0	0

B BRIGLEY, TRAVIS C

PERSONAL: Born June 16, 1977, in Coronation, Alta. ... 6-1/200. ... Shoots left.
TRANSACTIONS/CAREER NOTES: Selected by Calgary Flames in second round (second Flames pick, 39th overall) of NHL entry draft (June 22, 1996). ... Traded by Flames with sixth-round pick in 2001 draft to Philadelphia Flyers for C/RW Marc Bureau (March 6, 2000).

Season Team	League	REGULAR SEASON Gms.	G	A	Pts.	PIM	+/-	PP	SH	PLAYOFFS Gms.	G	A	Pts.	PIM
93-94—Lethbridge	WHL	1	0	0	0	0	...	...	...	—	—	—	—	—
94-95—Lethbridge	WHL	64	14	18	32	14	...	...	...	—	—	—	—	—
95-96—Lethbridge	WHL	69	34	43	77	94	...	...	...	4	2	3	5	8
96-97—Lethbridge	WHL	71	43	47	90	56	...	...	...	†19	9	9	18	31
97-98—Saint John	AHL	79	17	15	32	28	...	...	...	8	0	0	0	0
—Calgary	NHL	2	0	0	0	2	0	0	0	—	—	—	—	—
98-99—Saint John	AHL	74	15	35	50	47	...	...	...	7	3	1	4	2
99-00—Calgary	NHL	17	0	2	2	4	-6	0	0	—	—	—	—	—
—Saint John	AHL	9	3	1	4	4	...	...	...	—	—	—	—	—
—Detroit	IHL	29	6	10	16	24	...	...	...	—	—	—	—	—
—Philadelphia	AHL	15	2	2	4	15	...	...	...	5	1	0	1	4
NHL Totals (2 years)		19	0	2	2	6	-6	0	0					

BRIMANIS, ARIS D ISLANDERS

PERSONAL: Born March 14, 1972, in Cleveland. ... 6-3/195. ... Shoots right. ... Full Name: Aris Aldis Brimanis. ... Name pronounced AIR-ihz brih-MAN-ihz.
HIGH SCHOOL: Culver (Ind.) Military Academy.
COLLEGE: Bowling Green State.
TRANSACTIONS/CAREER NOTES: Selected by Philadelphia Flyers in fourth round (third Flyers pick, 86th overall) of NHL entry draft (June 22, 1991). ... Signed as free agent by New York Islanders (August 12, 1999).

Season Team	League	REGULAR SEASON Gms.	G	A	Pts.	PIM	+/-	PP	SH	PLAYOFFS Gms.	G	A	Pts.	PIM
88-89—Culver Military	Indiana H.S.	38	10	13	23	24	...	...	...	—	—	—	—	—
89-90—Culver Military	Indiana H.S.	37	15	10	25	52	...	...	...	—	—	—	—	—
90-91—Bowling Green	CCHA	38	3	6	9	42	...	...	...	—	—	—	—	—
91-92—Bowling Green	CCHA	32	2	9	11	38	...	...	...	—	—	—	—	—
92-93—Brandon	WHL	71	8	50	58	110	...	...	...	4	2	1	3	12
93-94—Philadelphia	NHL	1	0	0	0	0	-1	0	0	—	—	—	—	—
—Hershey	AHL	75	8	15	23	65	...	...	...	11	2	3	5	12
94-95—Hershey	AHL	76	8	17	25	68	...	...	...	6	1	1	2	14
95-96—Hershey	AHL	54	9	22	31	64	...	...	...	5	1	2	3	4
—Philadelphia	NHL	17	0	2	2	12	-1	0	0	—	—	—	—	—
96-97—Philadelphia	AHL	65	14	18	32	69	...	...	...	10	2	2	4	13
—Philadelphia	NHL	3	0	1	1	0	0	0	0	—	—	—	—	—
97-98—Philadelphia	AHL	30	1	11	12	26	...	...	...	—	—	—	—	—
—Michigan	IHL	35	3	9	12	24	...	...	...	4	1	0	1	4
98-99—Grand Rapids	IHL	66	16	21	37	70	...	...	...	—	—	—	—	—
—Fredericton	AHL	8	2	4	6	6	...	...	...	15	3	10	13	18
99-00—Kansas City	IHL	46	5	17	22	28	...	...	...	—	—	—	—	—
—New York Islanders	NHL	18	2	1	3	6	-5	2	0	—	—	—	—	—
NHL Totals (4 years)		39	2	4	6	18	-7	2	0					

BRIND'AMOUR, ROD C HURRICANES

PERSONAL: Born August 9, 1970, in Ottawa. ... 6-1/200. ... Shoots left. ... Full Name: Rod Jean Brind'Amour. ... Name pronounced BRIHN-duh-MOHR.
COLLEGE: Michigan State.
TRANSACTIONS/CAREER NOTES: Fractured wrist (November 1985). ... Selected by St. Louis Blues in first round (first Blues pick, ninth overall) of NHL entry draft (June 11, 1988). ... Traded by Blues with C Dan Quinn to Philadelphia Flyers for C Ron Sutter and D Murray Baron (September 22, 1991). ... Lacerated elbow (November 19, 1992); missed two games. ... Bruised right hand (February 20, 1993); missed one game. ... Fractured foot (September 25, 1999) and underwent surgery; missed first 34 games of season. ... Traded by Flyers with G Jean-Marc Pelletier and second-round pick (traded to Colorado) in 2000 draft to Carolina Hurricanes for rights to C Keith Primeau and fifth-round pick (traded to New York Islanders) in 2000 draft (January 23, 2000). ... Suffered concussion (April 3, 2000); missed one game.
HONORS: Named CCHA Rookie of the Year (1988-89). ... Named to CCHA All-Rookie team (1988-89). ... Named to NHL All-Rookie team (1989-90). ... Played in NHL All-Star Game (1992).
STATISTICAL PLATEAUS: Three-goal games: 1992-93 (1).

		REGULAR SEASON								PLAYOFFS				
Season Team	League	Gms.	G	A	Pts.	PIM	+/-	PP	SH	Gms.	G	A	Pts.	PIM
87-88—Notre Dame	SJHL	56	46	61	107	136	...	...	...	—	—	—	—	—
88-89—Michigan State..........	CCHA	42	27	32	59	63	...	...	...	—	—	—	—	—
—St. Louis	NHL	—	—	—	—	—	...	...	...	5	2	0	2	4
89-90—St. Louis	NHL	79	26	35	61	46	23	10	0	12	5	8	13	6
90-91—St. Louis	NHL	78	17	32	49	93	2	4	0	13	2	5	7	10
91-92—Philadelphia	NHL	80	33	44	77	100	-3	8	4	—	—	—	—	—
92-93—Philadelphia	NHL	81	37	49	86	89	-8	13	4	—	—	—	—	—
93-94—Philadelphia	NHL	84	35	62	97	85	-9	14	1	—	—	—	—	—
94-95—Philadelphia	NHL	48	12	27	39	33	-4	4	1	15	6	9	15	8
95-96—Philadelphia	NHL	82	26	61	87	110	20	4	4	12	2	5	7	6
96-97—Philadelphia	NHL	82	27	32	59	41	2	8	2	19	13	8	21	10
97-98—Philadelphia	NHL	82	36	38	74	54	-2	10	2	5	2	2	4	7
—Can. Olympic team	Int'l	6	1	2	3	0	...	...	...	—	—	—	—	—
98-99—Philadelphia	NHL	82	24	50	74	47	3	10	0	6	1	3	4	0
99-00—Philadelphia	NHL	12	5	3	8	4	-1	4	0	—	—	—	—	—
—Carolina	NHL	33	4	10	14	22	-12	0	1	—	—	—	—	—
NHL Totals (12 years)..........		823	282	443	725	724	11	89	19	87	33	40	73	51

BRISEBOIS, PATRICE — D — CANADIENS

PERSONAL: Born January 27, 1971, in Montreal. ... 6-1/203. ... Shoots right. ... Name pronounced pa-TREEZ BREES-bwah.

TRANSACTIONS/CAREER NOTES: Selected by Montreal Canadiens in second round (second Canadiens pick, 30th overall) of NHL entry draft (June 17, 1989). ... Sprained right ankle (October 10, 1992); missed two games. ... Suffered charley horse (December 16, 1992); missed two games. ... Injured knee (October 30, 1993); missed 10 games. ... Suffered hairline fracture of ankle (December 1, 1993); missed 14 games. ... Sprained ankle (February 21, 1994); missed seven games. ... Suffered acute herniated disc (April 3, 1995); missed 12 games. ... Injured rib cage (November 1, 1995). ... Sprained back (February 17, 1996); missed four games. ... Suffered mild disc irritation (March 25, 1996); missed last nine games of regular season. ... Separated shoulder (January 4, 1997); missed 27 games. ... Strained shoulder (March 22, 1997); missed four games. ... Injured rib (April 10, 1997); missed remainder of regular season and two playoff games. ... Sprained knee (April 15, 1998); missed three games. ... Injured back (October 2, 1998); missed first six games of season. ... Separated shoulder (December 23, 1998); missed nine games. ... Sprained knee (February 20, 1999); missed one game. ... Injured shoulder (March 11, 1999); missed 12 games. ... Injured back prior to start of 1999-2000 season; missed first 27 games of season.

HONORS: Won Michael Bossy Trophy (1988-89). ... Named to QMJHL All-Star second team (1989-90). ... Won Can.HL Defenseman of the Year Award (1990-91). ... Won Emile (Butch) Bouchard Trophy (1990-91). ... Named to QMJHL All-Star first team (1990-91). ... Named to Memorial Cup All-Star team (1990-91).

MISCELLANEOUS: Member of Stanley Cup championship team (1993).

		REGULAR SEASON								PLAYOFFS				
Season Team	League	Gms.	G	A	Pts.	PIM	+/-	PP	SH	Gms.	G	A	Pts.	PIM
87-88—Laval.......................	QMJHL	48	10	34	44	95	...	...	...	6	0	2	2	2
88-89—Laval.......................	QMJHL	50	20	45	65	95	...	...	...	17	8	14	22	45
89-90—Laval.......................	QMJHL	56	18	70	88	108	...	...	...	13	7	9	16	26
90-91—Montreal	NHL	10	0	2	2	4	1	0	0	—	—	—	—	—
—Drummondville	QMJHL	54	17	44	61	72	...	...	...	14	6	18	24	49
91-92—Fredericton	AHL	53	12	27	39	51	...	...	...	—	—	—	—	—
—Montreal	NHL	26	2	8	10	20	9	0	0	11	2	4	6	6
92-93—Montreal	NHL	70	10	21	31	79	6	4	0	20	0	4	4	18
93-94—Montreal	NHL	53	2	21	23	63	5	1	0	7	0	4	4	6
94-95—Montreal	NHL	35	4	8	12	26	-2	0	0	—	—	—	—	—
95-96—Montreal	NHL	69	9	27	36	65	10	3	0	6	1	2	3	6
96-97—Montreal	NHL	49	2	13	15	24	-7	0	0	3	1	1	2	24
97-98—Montreal	NHL	79	10	27	37	67	16	5	0	10	1	0	1	0
98-99—Montreal	NHL	54	3	9	12	28	-8	1	0	—	—	—	—	—
99-00—Montreal	NHL	54	10	25	35	18	-1	5	0	—	—	—	—	—
NHL Totals (10 years)..........		499	52	161	213	394	29	19	0	57	5	15	20	60

BRODEUR, MARTIN — G — DEVILS

PERSONAL: Born May 6, 1972, in Montreal. ... 6-2/205. ... Catches left. ... Son of Denis Brodeur, goaltender with bronze medal-winning Canadian Olympic Team (1956). ... Name pronounced MAHR-tan broh-DOOR.

TRANSACTIONS/CAREER NOTES: Selected by New Jersey Devils in first round (first Devils pick, 20th overall) of NHL entry draft (June 16, 1990). ... Suffered from the flu (December 30, 1997); missed two games.

HONORS: Named to QMJHL All-Star second team (1991-92). ... Won Calder Memorial Trophy (1993-94). ... Named to NHL All-Rookie team (1993-94). ... Played in NHL All-Star Game (1996-2000). ... Shared William M. Jennings Trophy with Mike Dunham (1996-1997). ... Named to NHL All-Star second team (1996-97). ... Won William M. Jennings Trophy (1997-98).

RECORDS: Holds NHL single-season record for most minutes played by goaltender—4,434 (1995-96). ... Shares NHL single-season playoff record for most wins by goaltender—16 (1995 and 2000).

MISCELLANEOUS: Member of Stanley Cup championship teams (1995 and 2000). ... Holds New Jersey Devils franchise all-time records for most games played by a goalie (447), most wins (244), most shutouts (42) and goals-against average (2.20). ... Stopped a penalty shot attempt (vs. Valeri Zelepukin, October 30, 1999). ... Allowed a penalty shot goal (vs. Frederick Olausson, November 24, 1999).

STATISTICAL NOTES: Scored a goal (April 7, 1997, vs. Montreal [playoffs] and February 15, 2000, vs. Philadelphia).

		REGULAR SEASON							PLAYOFFS					
Season Team	League	Gms.	Min	W	L	T	GA	SO	Avg.	Gms.	Min.	W	L	GA	SO	Avg.
89-90—St. Hyacinthe..............	QMJHL	42	2333	23	13	2	156	0	4.01	12	678	5	7	46	0	4.07
90-91—St. Hyacinthe..............	QMJHL	52	2946	22	24	4	162	2	3.30	4	232	0	4	16	0	4.14
91-92—St. Hyacinthe..............	QMJHL	48	2846	27	16	4	161	2	3.39	5	317	2	3	14	0	2.65
—New Jersey	NHL	4	179	2	1	0	10	0	3.35	1	32	0	1	3	0	5.63

– 45 –

Season Team	League	REGULAR SEASON								PLAYOFFS						
		Gms.	Min	W	L	T	GA	SO	Avg.	Gms.	Min.	W	L	GA	SO	Avg.
92-93 —Utica....................	AHL	32	1952	14	13	5	131	0	4.03	4	258	1	3	18	0	4.19
93-94 —New Jersey	NHL	47	2625	27	11	8	105	3	2.40	17	1171	8	†9	38	1	1.95
94-95 —New Jersey	NHL	40	2184	19	11	6	89	3	2.45	*20	*1222	*16	4	34	*3	*1.67
95-96 —New Jersey	NHL	77	*4434	34	†30	12	173	6	2.34	—	—	—	—	—	—	—
96-97 —New Jersey	NHL	67	3838	37	14	13	120	*10	*1.88	10	659	5	5	19	2	1.73
97-98 —New Jersey	NHL	70	4128	*43	17	8	130	10	1.89	6	366	2	4	12	0	1.97
98-99 —New Jersey	NHL	*70	*4239	*39	21	10	162	4	2.29	7	425	3	4	20	0	2.82
99-00 —New Jersey	NHL	72	4312	*43	20	8	161	6	2.24	†23	*1450	*16	7	39	2	*1.61
NHL Totals (8 years).............		447	25939	244	125	65	950	42	2.20	84	5325	50	34	165	8	1.86

BROWN, BRAD   D   BLACKHAWKS

PERSONAL: Born December 27, 1975, in Baie Verte, Ont. ... 6-4/218. ... Shoots right.
HIGH SCHOOL: Chippewa (North Bay, Ont.).
TRANSACTIONS/CAREER NOTES: Selected by Montreal Canadiens in first round (first Canadiens pick, 18th overall) of NHL entry draft (June 28, 1994). ... Suffered back spasms (October 17, 1998); missed three games. ... Traded by Canadiens with G Jocelyn Thibault and D Dave Manson to Chicago Blackhawks for G Jeff Hackett, D Eric Weinrich, D Alain Nasreddine and fourth-round pick (D Chris Dyment) in 1999 draft (November 16, 1998). ... Suffered sore back (December 17, 1998); missed two games. ... Bruised foot (March 12, 1999); missed two games. ... Bruised wrist (October 4, 1999); missed three games. ... Lacerated hand (December 17, 1999); missed two games. ... Injured hand (December 26, 1999); missed 10 games. ... Bruised left hand (March 15, 2000); missed four games.

Season Team	League	REGULAR SEASON							PLAYOFFS				
		Gms.	G	A	Pts.	PIM	+/-	PP	SH	Gms.	G	A	Pts.	PIM
91-92—North Bay	OHL	49	2	9	11	170	...	...	...	18	0	6	6	43
92-93—North Bay	OHL	61	4	9	13	228	...	...	...	2	0	2	2	13
93-94—North Bay	OHL	66	8	24	32	196	...	...	...	18	3	12	15	33
94-95—North Bay	OHL	64	8	38	46	172	...	...	...	6	1	4	5	8
95-96—Regina	WHL	21	2	3	5	7	...	...	...	—	—	—	—	—
—Fredericton	AHL	38	0	3	3	148	...	...	...	10	2	1	3	6
96-97—Fredericton	AHL	64	3	7	10	368	...	...	...	—	—	—	—	—
—Montreal	NHL	8	0	0	0	22	-1	0	0	—	—	—	—	—
97-98—Fredericton	AHL	64	1	8	9	297	...	...	...	4	0	0	0	29
98-99—Montreal	NHL	5	0	0	0	21	0	0	0	—	—	—	—	—
—Chicago	NHL	61	1	7	8	184	-4	0	0	—	—	—	—	—
99-00—Chicago	NHL	57	0	9	9	134	-1	0	0	—	—	—	—	—
NHL Totals (3 years)..........		131	1	16	17	361	-6	0	0					

BROWN, CURTIS   C/LW   SABRES

PERSONAL: Born February 12, 1976, in Unity, Sask. ... 6-0/190. ... Shoots left.
TRANSACTIONS/CAREER NOTES: Selected by Buffalo Sabres in second round (second Sabres pick, 43rd overall) of NHL entry draft (June 28, 1994). ... Injured ankle prior to 1995-96 season; missed two games. ... Bruised knee (February 11, 1999); missed two games. ... Bruised knee (March 27, 1999); missed one game. ... Missed first game of 1999-2000 season due to contract dispute. ... Suffered concussion (October 22, 1999); missed one game. ... Suffered from the flu (February 10, 2000); missed five games.
HONORS: Named to Can.HL All-Star second team (1994-95). ... Named to WHL (East) All-Star first team (1994-95). ... Named to WHL (Central/East) All-Star second team (1995-96).
STATISTICAL NOTES: Tied for NHL lead in game-tying goals with 3 (1998-99).

Season Team	League	REGULAR SEASON							PLAYOFFS				
		Gms.	G	A	Pts.	PIM	+/-	PP	SH	Gms.	G	A	Pts.	PIM
92-93—Moose Jaw	WHL	71	13	16	29	30	...	...	...	—	—	—	—	—
93-94—Moose Jaw	WHL	72	27	38	65	82	...	...	...	—	—	—	—	—
94-95—Moose Jaw	WHL	70	51	53	104	63	...	...	...	10	8	7	15	20
—Buffalo	NHL	1	1	1	2	2	2	0	0	—	—	—	—	—
95-96—Buffalo	NHL	4	0	0	0	0	0	0	0	—	—	—	—	—
—Moose Jaw	WHL	25	20	18	38	30	...	...	...	—	—	—	—	—
—Prince Albert.............	WHL	19	12	21	33	8	...	...	...	18	10	15	25	18
—Rochester	AHL	—	—	—	—	—	...	...	...	12	0	1	1	2
96-97—Buffalo	NHL	28	4	3	7	18	4	0	0	—	—	—	—	—
—Rochester	AHL	51	22	21	43	30	...	...	...	10	4	6	10	4
97-98—Buffalo	NHL	63	12	12	24	34	11	1	1	13	1	2	3	10
98-99—Buffalo	NHL	78	16	31	47	56	23	5	1	21	7	6	13	10
99-00—Buffalo	NHL	74	22	29	51	42	19	5	0	5	1	3	4	6
NHL Totals (6 years)..........		248	55	76	131	152	59	11	2	39	9	11	20	26

BROWN, DOUG   RW   RED WINGS

PERSONAL: Born June 12, 1964, in New Haven, Conn. ... 5-11/185. ... Shoots right. ... Full Name: Douglas Allen Brown. ... Brother of Greg Brown, defenseman with three NHL teams (1990-91 and 1992-93 through 1994-95).
HIGH SCHOOL: St. Mark's (Southborough, Mass.).
COLLEGE: Boston College.
TRANSACTIONS/CAREER NOTES: Signed as non-drafted free agent by New Jersey Devils (August 6, 1986). ... Fractured nose (October 1988). ... Injured back (November 25, 1989). ... Bruised right foot (February 13, 1991). ... Suspended by Devils for refusing to report to Utica (November 20, 1992). ... Reinstated by Devils (November 30, 1992). ... Signed as free agent by Pittsburgh Penguins (September 29, 1993). ... Injured leg (March 26, 1994); missed seven games. ... Selected by Detroit Red Wings from Penguins in waiver draft (January 18, 1995); Penguins claimed C Micah Aivazoff as compensation. ... Suffered from the flu (December 2, 1995); missed one game. ... Separated shoulder (April 18, 1998); missed 11 playoff games ... Selected by Nashville Predators in NHL expansion draft (June 26, 1998). ... Traded by Predators

B

to Red Wings for C Petr Sykora, third- (traded to Edmonton) and fourth-round (RW Alexandre Krevsun) picks in 1999 draft (July 14, 1998). ... Fractured foot (October 30, 1999); missed 10 games. ... Reinjured foot (November 26, 1999); missed seven games. ... Strained hip flexor (January 19, 2000); missed three games.

HONORS: Named to NCAA All-America (East) second team (1984-85 and 1985-86). ... Named to Hockey East All-Star second team (1984-85 and 1985-86).

MISCELLANEOUS: Member of Stanley Cup championship team (1997 and 1998). ... Scored on a penalty shot (vs. Ken Wregget, November 23, 1991).

Season Team	League	REGULAR SEASON								PLAYOFFS				
		Gms.	G	A	Pts.	PIM	+/-	PP	SH	Gms.	G	A	Pts.	PIM
82-83—Boston College	ECAC	22	9	8	17	0	...	...	...	—	—	—	—	—
83-84—Boston College	ECAC	38	11	10	21	6	...	...	...	—	—	—	—	—
84-85—Boston College	Hockey East	45	37	31	68	10	...	...	...	—	—	—	—	—
85-86—Boston College	Hockey East	38	16	40	56	16	...	...	...	—	—	—	—	—
86-87—Maine......................	AHL	73	24	34	58	15	...	...	...	—	—	—	—	—
—New Jersey	NHL	4	0	1	1	0	-4	0	0	—	—	—	—	—
87-88—New Jersey	NHL	70	14	11	25	20	7	1	4	19	5	1	6	6
—Utica......................	AHL	2	0	2	2	2	...	...	...	—	—	—	—	—
88-89—New Jersey	NHL	63	15	10	25	15	-7	4	0	—	—	—	—	—
—Utica......................	AHL	4	1	4	5	0	...	...	...	—	—	—	—	—
89-90—New Jersey	NHL	69	14	20	34	16	7	1	3	6	0	1	1	2
90-91—New Jersey	NHL	58	14	16	30	4	18	0	2	7	2	2	4	2
91-92—New Jersey	NHL	71	11	17	28	27	17	1	2	—	—	—	—	—
92-93—New Jersey	NHL	15	0	5	5	2	3	0	0	—	—	—	—	—
—Utica......................	AHL	25	11	17	28	8	...	...	...	—	—	—	—	—
93-94—Pittsburgh................	NHL	77	18	37	55	18	19	2	0	6	0	0	0	2
94-95—Detroit....................	NHL	45	9	12	21	16	14	1	1	18	4	8	12	2
95-96—Detroit....................	NHL	62	12	15	27	4	11	0	1	13	3	3	6	4
96-97—Detroit....................	NHL	49	6	7	13	8	-3	1	0	14	3	3	6	2
97-98—Detroit....................	NHL	80	19	23	42	12	17	6	1	9	4	2	6	0
98-99—Detroit....................	NHL	80	9	19	28	42	5	3	1	10	2	2	4	4
99-00—Detroit....................	NHL	51	10	8	18	12	8	0	1	3	0	1	1	0
NHL Totals (14 years).........		794	151	201	352	196	112	20	16	105	23	23	46	24

BROWN, KEVIN — RW

PERSONAL: Born May 11, 1974, in Birmingham, England. ... 6-1/212. ... Shoots right. ... Full Name: Kevin J. Brown.

HIGH SCHOOL: Quinte Secondary School (Belleville, Ont.).

TRANSACTIONS/CAREER NOTES: Selected by Los Angeles Kings in fourth round (third Kings pick, 87th overall) of NHL entry draft (June 20, 1992). ... Strained knee and hip (April 12, 1995); missed two games. ... Sprained right shoulder (April 19, 1995); missed last seven games of season. ... Traded by Kings to Ottawa Senators for D Jaroslav Modry (March 20, 1996). ... Traded by Senators to Mighty Ducks of Anaheim for LW Mike Maneluk (July 1, 1996). ... Traded by Mighty Ducks to Hartford Whalers for rights to C Espen Knutsen (October 1, 1996). ... Sprained shoulder (February 16, 1997); missed seven games. ... Whalers franchise moved to North Carolina and renamed Carolina Hurricanes for 1997-98 season; NHL approved move on June 25, 1997. ... Signed as free agent by Edmonton Oilers (July 22, 1998). ... Injured hip (November 18, 1998); missed 13 games. ... Traded by Oilers to New York Rangers for LW Vladimir Vorobiev (March 23, 1999). ... Signed as free agent by Oilers (March 7, 2000).

HONORS: Won Jim Mahon Memorial Trophy (1992-93 and 1993-94). ... Named to OHL All-Star second team (1992-93). ... Named to Can.HL All-Star second team (1993-94). ... Named to OHL All-Star first team (1993-94).

Season Team	League	REGULAR SEASON								PLAYOFFS				
		Gms.	G	A	Pts.	PIM	+/-	PP	SH	Gms.	G	A	Pts.	PIM
89-90—Georgetown Jr. B......	OHA	31	3	8	11	59	...	...	...	—	—	—	—	—
90-91—Waterloo Jr. B............	OHA	46	25	33	58	116	...	...	...	—	—	—	—	—
91-92—Belleville	OHL	66	24	24	48	52	...	...	...	5	1	4	5	8
92-93—Belleville	OHL	6	2	5	7	4	...	...	...	—	—	—	—	—
—Det. Jr. Red Wings......	OHL	56	48	86	134	76	...	...	...	15	10	18	28	18
93-94—Det. Jr. Red Wings......	OHL	57	54	81	135	85	...	...	...	17	14	*26	*40	28
94-95—Phoenix....................	IHL	48	19	31	50	64	...	...	...	—	—	—	—	—
—Los Angeles...............	NHL	23	2	3	5	18	-7	0	0	—	—	—	—	—
95-96—Los Angeles...............	NHL	7	1	0	1	4	-2	0	0	—	—	—	—	—
—Phoenix....................	IHL	45	10	16	26	39	...	...	...	—	—	—	—	—
—Prin. Edward Island ...	AHL	8	3	6	9	2	...	...	...	3	1	3	4	0
96-97—Springfield	AHL	48	32	16	48	45	...	...	...	17	†11	6	17	24
—Hartford	NHL	11	0	4	4	6	-6	0	0	—	—	—	—	—
97-98—Carolina	NHL	4	0	0	0	0	-2	0	0	—	—	—	—	—
—New Haven	AHL	67	28	44	72	65	...	...	...	3	0	2	2	0
98-99—Edmonton.................	NHL	12	4	2	6	0	-2	2	0	—	—	—	—	—
—Hamilton..................	AHL	32	9	14	23	47	...	...	...	—	—	—	—	—
—Hartford	AHL	9	3	2	5	14	...	...	...	5	1	3	4	4
99-00—Hamilton.................	AHL	54	21	38	59	53	...	...	...	4	2	2	4	8
—Edmonton.................	NHL	7	0	0	0	0	0	0	0	1	0	0	0	0
NHL Totals (6 years)...........		64	7	9	16	28	-19	2	0	1	0	0	0	0

BROWN, ROB — LW

PERSONAL: Born April 10, 1968, in Kingston, Ont. ... 5-10/181. ... Shoots right. ... Full Name: Robert Brown.

TRANSACTIONS/CAREER NOTES: Selected by Pittsburgh Penguins as underage junior in fourth round (fourth Penguins pick, 67th overall) of NHL entry draft (June 21, 1986). ... Separated right shoulder (February 12, 1989); missed 12 games. ... Traded by Penguins to Hartford Whalers for RW Scott Young (December 21, 1990). ... Injured Adam's apple (April 5, 1991); missed one playoff game. ... Traded by Whalers to Chicago Blackhawks for D Steve Konroyd (January 24, 1992). ... Signed as free agent by Dallas Stars (August 6, 1993). ... Signed as free agent by Los Angeles Kings (June 14, 1994). ... Signed as free agent by Pittsburgh Penguins (October 1, 1997). ... Fractured foot (December 22, 1998); missed 24 games. ... Injured knee (December 15, 1999); missed 14 games.

HONORS: Won WHL (West) Most Valuable Player Trophy (1985-86 and 1986-87). ... Won Bob Brownridge Memorial Trophy (1985-86). ... Named to WHL (West) All-Star first team (1985-86 and 1986-87). ... Won Can.HL Player of the Year Award (1986-87). ... Won Can.HL Plus/Minus Award (1986-87). ... Won WHL (West) Bob Brownridge Memorial Trophy (1986-87). ... Won WHL Player of the Year Award (1986-87). ... Played in NHL All-Star Game (1989). ... Won James Gatschene Memorial Trophy (1993-94). ... Won Leo P. Lamoureux Memorial Trophy (1993-94, 1995-96 and 1996-97). ... Named to IHL All-Star first team (1993-94, 1995-96 and 1996-97). ... Named to IHL All-Star second team (1994-95).

STATISTICAL PLATEAUS: Three-goal games: 1988-89 (4), 1989-90 (3). Total: 7.

			REGULAR SEASON								PLAYOFFS				
Season Team	League	Gms.	G	A	Pts.	PIM	+/-	PP	SH		Gms.	G	A	Pts.	PIM
83-84—Kamloops	WHL	50	16	42	58	80	...	...	...		15	1	2	3	17
84-85—Kamloops	WHL	60	29	50	79	95	...	...	...		15	8	8	16	28
85-86—Kamloops	WHL	69	58	*115	*173	171	...	...	...		16	*18	*28	*46	14
86-87—Kamloops	WHL	63	*76	*136	*212	101	...	...	...		5	6	5	11	6
87-88—Pittsburgh	NHL	51	24	20	44	56	8	13	0		—	—	—	—	—
88-89—Pittsburgh	NHL	68	49	66	115	118	27	24	0		11	5	3	8	22
89-90—Pittsburgh	NHL	80	33	47	80	102	-10	12	0		—	—	—	—	—
90-91—Pittsburgh	NHL	25	6	10	16	31	0	2	0		—	—	—	—	—
—Hartford	NHL	44	18	24	42	101	-7	10	0		5	1	0	1	7
91-92—Hartford	NHL	42	16	15	31	39	-14	13	0		—	—	—	—	—
—Chicago	NHL	25	5	11	16	34	-1	3	0		8	2	4	6	4
92-93—Chicago	NHL	15	1	6	7	33	6	0	0		—	—	—	—	—
—Indianapolis	IHL	19	14	19	33	32	...	...	...		2	0	1	1	2
93-94—Kalamazoo	IHL	79	42	*113	*155	188	...	...	...		5	1	3	4	6
—Dallas	NHL	1	0	0	0	0	-1	0	0		—	—	—	—	—
94-95—Phoenix	IHL	69	34	73	107	135	...	...	...		9	4	12	16	0
—Los Angeles	NHL	2	0	0	0	0	-2	0	0		—	—	—	—	—
95-96—Chicago	IHL	79	52	*91	*143	100	...	...	...		9	4	11	15	6
96-97—Chicago	IHL	76	37	*80	*117	98	...	...	...		4	2	4	6	16
97-98—Pittsburgh	NHL	82	15	25	40	59	-1	4	0		6	1	0	1	4
98-99—Pittsburgh	NHL	58	13	11	24	16	-15	9	0		13	2	5	7	8
99-00—Pittsburgh	NHL	50	10	13	23	10	-13	4	0		11	1	2	3	0
NHL Totals (11 years)		543	190	248	438	599	-23	94	0		54	12	14	26	45

BROWN, SEAN — D — OILERS

PERSONAL: Born November 5, 1976, in Oshawa, Ont. ... 6-3/205. ... Shoots left.
HIGH SCHOOL: Quinte Secondary School (Belleville, Ont.).
TRANSACTIONS/CAREER NOTES: Selected by Boston Bruins in first round (second Bruins pick, 21st overall) of NHL entry draft (July 8, 1995). ... Traded by Boston Bruins with RW Mariusz Czerkawski and first-round pick (D Mattieu Descoteaux) in 1996 draft to Edmonton Oilers for G Bill Ranford (January 11, 1996). ... Suspended three games and fined $1,000 by NHL for high-sticking incident (November 13, 1998).
HONORS: Named to OHL All-Star second team (1995-96).

			REGULAR SEASON								PLAYOFFS				
Season Team	League	Gms.	G	A	Pts.	PIM	+/-	PP	SH		Gms.	G	A	Pts.	PIM
92-93—Oshawa	Tier II Jr. A	15	0	1	1	9	...	...	...		—	—	—	—	—
93-94—Wellington	OJHL	32	5	14	19	165	...	...	...		—	—	—	—	—
—Belleville	OHL	28	1	2	3	53	...	...	...		8	0	0	0	17
94-95—Belleville	OHL	58	2	16	18	200	...	...	...		16	4	2	6	67
95-96—Belleville	OHL	37	10	23	33	150	...	...	...		—	—	—	—	—
—Sarnia	OHL	26	8	17	25	112	...	...	...		10	1	0	1	38
96-97—Hamilton	AHL	61	1	7	8	238	...	...	...		19	1	0	1	47
—Edmonton	NHL	5	0	0	0	4	-1	0	0		—	—	—	—	—
97-98—Edmonton	NHL	18	0	1	1	43	-1	0	0		—	—	—	—	—
—Hamilton	AHL	43	4	6	10	166	...	...	...		6	0	2	2	38
98-99—Edmonton	NHL	51	0	7	7	188	1	0	0		1	0	0	0	10
99-00—Edmonton	NHL	72	4	8	12	192	1	0	0		3	0	0	0	23
NHL Totals (4 years)		146	4	16	20	427	0	0	0		4	0	0	0	33

BRUNET, BENOIT — LW — CANADIENS

PERSONAL: Born August 24, 1968, in Montreal. ... 5-11/198. ... Shoots left. ... Name pronounced BEHN-wah broo-NAY.
TRANSACTIONS/CAREER NOTES: Selected by Montreal Canadiens as underage junior in second round (second Canadiens pick, 27th overall) of NHL entry draft (June 21, 1986). ... Injured ankle (September 1987). ... Tore left knee ligaments (September 24, 1990); missed 24 games. ... Fractured ankle (December 4, 1991). ... Sprained left knee (November 21, 1992); missed 10 games. ... Fractured thumb (January 22, 1993); missed 14 games. ... Bruised knee (November 17, 1993); missed four games. ... Suffered mild concussion (February 2, 1994); missed six games. ... Suffered sore throat (April 8, 1994); missed three games. ... Pulled hamstring (March 18, 1995); missed two games. ... Bruised right knee (May 3, 1995); missed one game. ... Sprained wrist (November 11, 1995); missed five games. ... Reinjured wrist (November 25, 1995); missed 18 games. ... Sprained back (January 11, 1996); missed 28 games. ... Bruised thigh (October 24, 1996); missed one game. ... Fractured left leg (November 2, 1996); missed 21 games. ... Suffered from tonsillitis (December 21, 1996); missed one game. ... Fractured hand (January 20, 1997); missed 19 games. ... Strained shoulder (October 23, 1997); missed three games. ... Suffered concussion (November 22, 1997); missed eight games. ... Suffered from the flu (December 22, 1997); missed one game. ... Strained rib (March 19, 1998); missed two games. ... Strained rib (November 27, 1998); missed four games. ... Injured groin (February 11, 1999); missed one game. ... Injured back (March 2, 1999); missed four games. ... Reinjured back (March 22, 1999); missed 12 games. ... Injured back prior to start of 1999-2000 season; missed first 27 games of season. ... Suffered injury to face (February 14, 2000); missed three games. ... Suffered back spasms (March 18, 2000); missed two games.
HONORS: Named to QMJHL All-Star second team (1986-87). ... Named to AHL All-Star first team (1988-89).
MISCELLANEOUS: Member of Stanley Cup championship team (1993).

Season Team	League	REGULAR SEASON								PLAYOFFS				
		Gms.	G	A	Pts.	PIM	+/-	PP	SH	Gms.	G	A	Pts.	PIM
85-86—Hull................	QMJHL	71	33	37	70	81	...	...	...	—	—	—	—	—
86-87—Hull................	QMJHL	60	43	67	110	105	...	...	...	6	7	5	12	8
87-88—Hull................	QMJHL	62	54	89	143	131	...	...	...	10	3	10	13	11
88-89—Montreal	NHL	2	0	1	1	0	0	0	0	—	—	—	—	—
—Sherbrooke........	AHL	73	41	*76	117	95	...	...	...	6	2	0	2	4
89-90—Sherbrooke....	AHL	72	32	35	67	82	...	...	...	12	8	7	15	20
90-91—Fredericton	AHL	24	13	18	31	16	...	...	...	6	5	6	11	2
—Montreal	NHL	17	1	3	4	0	-1	0	0	—	—	—	—	—
91-92—Fredericton	AHL	6	7	9	16	27	...	...	...	—	—	—	—	—
—Montreal	NHL	18	4	6	10	14	4	0	0	—	—	—	—	—
92-93—Montreal	NHL	47	10	15	25	19	13	0	0	20	2	8	10	8
93-94—Montreal	NHL	71	10	20	30	20	14	0	3	7	1	4	5	16
94-95—Montreal	NHL	45	7	18	25	16	7	1	1	—	—	—	—	—
95-96—Montreal	NHL	26	7	8	15	17	-4	3	1	3	0	2	2	0
—Fredericton	AHL	3	2	1	3	6	...	...	...	—	—	—	—	—
96-97—Montreal	NHL	39	10	13	23	14	6	2	0	4	1	3	4	4
97-98—Montreal	NHL	68	12	20	32	61	11	1	2	8	1	0	1	4
98-99—Montreal	NHL	60	14	17	31	31	-1	4	2	—	—	—	—	—
99-00—Montreal	NHL	50	14	15	29	13	3	6	1	—	—	—	—	—
NHL Totals (11 years).........		443	89	136	225	205	52	17	10	42	5	17	22	32

BRUNETTE, ANDREW   LW   THRASHERS

PERSONAL: Born August 24, 1973, in Sudbury, Ont. ... 6-1/210. ... Shoots left. ... Name pronounced broo-NEHT.
TRANSACTIONS/CAREER NOTES: Selected by Washington Capitals in sixth round (sixth Capitals pick, 174th overall) of NHL entry draft (June 26, 1993). ... Selected by Nashville Predators in NHL expansion draft (June 26, 1998). ... Traded by Predators to Atlanta Thrashers for fifth-round pick (C Matt Hendricks) in 2000 draft (June 21, 1999).
HONORS: Won Eddie Powers Memorial Trophy (1992-93). ... Named to Can.HL All-Star second team (1992-93). ... Named to OHL All-Star first team (1992-93).
MISCELLANEOUS: Holds Atlanta Thrashers all-time records for most goals (23), most assists (27), and most points (50). ... Shares Atlanta Thrashers all-time record for most games played (81).

Season Team	League	REGULAR SEASON								PLAYOFFS				
		Gms.	G	A	Pts.	PIM	+/-	PP	SH	Gms.	G	A	Pts.	PIM
90-91—Owen Sound..............	OHL	63	15	20	35	15	...	...	...	—	—	—	—	—
91-92—Owen Sound..............	OHL	66	51	47	98	42	...	...	...	5	5	0	5	8
92-93—Owen Sound..............	OHL	66	*62	*100	*162	91	...	...	...	8	8	6	14	16
93-94—Portland....................	AHL	23	9	11	20	10	...	...	...	2	0	1	1	0
—Hampton..................	ECHL	20	12	18	30	32	...	...	...	7	7	6	13	18
—Providence.............	AHL	3	0	0	0	0	...	...	...	—	—	—	—	—
94-95—Portland....................	AHL	79	30	50	80	53	...	...	...	7	3	3	6	10
95-96—Portland....................	AHL	69	28	66	94	125	...	...	...	20	11	18	29	15
—Washington	NHL	11	3	3	6	5	0	0	0	6	1	3	4	0
96-97—Portland....................	AHL	50	22	51	73	48	...	...	...	5	1	2	3	0
—Washington	NHL	23	4	7	11	12	-3	2	0	—	—	—	—	—
97-98—Portland....................	AHL	43	21	46	67	64	...	...	...	10	1	11	12	12
—Washington	NHL	28	11	12	23	12	2	4	0	—	—	—	—	—
98-99—Nashville....................	NHL	77	11	20	31	26	-10	7	0	—	—	—	—	—
99-00—Atlanta	NHL	81	23	27	50	30	-32	9	0	—	—	—	—	—
NHL Totals (5 years)...........		220	52	69	121	85	-43	22	0	6	1	3	4	0

BRYLIN, SERGEI   C   DEVILS

PERSONAL: Born January 13, 1974, in Moscow, U.S.S.R. ... 5-10/190. ... Shoots left. ... Name pronounced BREE-lihn.
TRANSACTIONS/CAREER NOTES: Selected by New Jersey Devils in second round (second Devils pick, 42nd overall) of NHL entry draft (June 20, 1992). ... Suffered from tonsillitis (May 3, 1995); missed last game of season. ... Fractured hand (November 16, 1995); missed 13 games. ... Injured knee (September 19, 1997); missed 19 games.
MISCELLANEOUS: Member of Stanley Cup championship team (1995 and 2000).

Season Team	League	REGULAR SEASON								PLAYOFFS				
		Gms.	G	A	Pts.	PIM	+/-	PP	SH	Gms.	G	A	Pts.	PIM
91-92—CSKA Moscow...........	CIS	44	1	6	7	4	...	...	...	—	—	—	—	—
92-93—CSKA Moscow...........	CIS	42	5	4	9	36	...	...	...	—	—	—	—	—
93-94—CSKA Moscow...........	CIS	39	4	6	10	36	...	...	...	3	0	1	1	0
—Russian Penguins.......	IHL	13	4	5	9	18	...	...	...	—	—	—	—	—
94-95—Albany......................	AHL	63	19	35	54	78	...	...	...	—	—	—	—	—
—New Jersey...............	NHL	26	6	8	14	8	12	0	0	12	1	2	3	4
95-96—New Jersey...............	NHL	50	4	5	9	26	-2	0	0	—	—	—	—	—
96-97—New Jersey...............	NHL	29	2	2	4	20	-13	0	0	—	—	—	—	—
—Albany......................	AHL	43	17	24	41	38	...	...	...	16	4	8	12	12
97-98—New Jersey...............	NHL	18	2	3	5	0	4	0	0	—	—	—	—	—
—Albany......................	AHL	44	21	22	43	60	...	...	...	—	—	—	—	—
98-99—New Jersey...............	NHL	47	5	10	15	28	8	3	0	5	3	1	4	4
99-00—New Jersey...............	NHL	64	9	11	20	20	0	1	0	17	3	5	8	0
NHL Totals (6 years)...........		234	28	39	67	102	9	4	0	34	7	8	15	8

BUCHBERGER, KELLY   RW   KINGS

PERSONAL: Born December 2, 1966, in Langenburg, Sask. ... 6-2/210. ... Shoots left. ... Full Name: Kelly Michael Buchberger. ... Name pronounced BUK-buhr-guhr.
HIGH SCHOOL: Langenburg (Sask.).
TRANSACTIONS/CAREER NOTES: Selected by Edmonton Oilers as underage junior in ninth round (eighth Oilers pick, 188th overall) of NHL entry draft (June 15, 1985). ... Suspended six games by AHL for leaving bench to fight (March 30, 1988). ... Fractured right ankle (March 1989). ... Dislocated left shoulder (March 13, 1990). ... Reinjured shoulder (May 4, 1990). ... Strained shoulder (April 7, 1993); missed one game. ... Fractured right forearm (January 5, 1999); missed 30 games. ... Selected by Atlanta Thrashers in NHL expansion draft (June 25, 1999). ... Traded by Thrashers with RW Nelson Emerson to Los Angeles Kings for RW Donald Audette and D Frantisek Kaberle (March 13, 2000).
MISCELLANEOUS: Member of Stanley Cup championship team (1987 and 1990). ... Captain of Edmonton Oilers (1995-96 through 1998-99). ... Captain of Atlanta Thrashers (1999-March 13, 2000). ... Holds Edmonton Oilers all-time record for most penalty minutes (1,747).
STATISTICAL PLATEAUS: Three-goal games: 1992-93 (1).

Season Team	League	Gms.	G	A	Pts.	PIM	+/-	PP	SH	Gms.	G	A	Pts.	PIM
			REGULAR SEASON							PLAYOFFS				
83-84—Melville	SAJHL	60	14	11	25	139	...	...	...	—	—	—	—	—
84-85—Moose Jaw	WHL	51	12	17	29	114	...	...	...	—	—	—	—	—
85-86—Moose Jaw	WHL	72	14	22	36	206	...	...	...	13	11	4	15	37
86-87—Nova Scotia	AHL	70	12	20	32	257	...	...	...	5	0	1	1	23
—Edmonton	NHL	—	—	—	—	—	...	...	...	3	0	1	1	5
87-88—Edmonton	NHL	19	1	0	1	81	-1	0	0	—	—	—	—	—
—Nova Scotia	AHL	49	21	23	44	206	...	...	...	2	0	0	0	11
88-89—Edmonton	NHL	66	5	9	14	234	-14	1	0	—	—	—	—	—
89-90—Edmonton	NHL	55	2	6	8	168	-8	0	0	19	0	5	5	13
90-91—Edmonton	NHL	64	3	1	4	160	-6	0	0	12	2	1	3	25
91-92—Edmonton	NHL	79	20	24	44	157	9	0	4	16	1	4	5	32
92-93—Edmonton	NHL	83	12	18	30	133	-27	1	2	—	—	—	—	—
93-94—Edmonton	NHL	84	3	18	21	199	-20	0	0	—	—	—	—	—
94-95—Edmonton	NHL	48	7	17	24	82	0	2	1	—	—	—	—	—
95-96—Edmonton	NHL	82	11	14	25	184	-20	0	2	—	—	—	—	—
96-97—Edmonton	NHL	81	8	30	38	159	4	0	0	12	5	2	7	16
97-98—Edmonton	NHL	82	6	17	23	122	-10	1	1	12	1	2	3	25
98-99—Edmonton	NHL	52	4	4	8	68	-6	0	2	4	0	0	0	0
99-00—Atlanta	NHL	68	5	12	17	139	-34	0	0	—	—	—	—	—
—Los Angeles	NHL	13	2	1	3	13	-2	0	0	4	0	0	0	4
NHL Totals (14 years)		876	89	171	260	1899	-135	5	12	82	9	15	24	120

BULIS, JAN   C   CAPITALS

PERSONAL: Born March 18, 1978, in Pardubice, Czechoslovakia. ... 6-1/201. ... Shoots left. ... Name pronounced YAHN BOO-lihsh.
TRANSACTIONS/CAREER NOTES: Selected by Washington Capitals in second round (third Capitals pick, 43rd overall) of NHL entry draft (June 22, 1996). ... Suffered concussion (November 11, 1997); missed one game. ... Sprained ankle prior to 1998-99 season; missed first 13 games of season. ... Sprained ankle (November 21, 1998); missed 15 games. ... Suffered back spasms (November 11, 1999); missed one game. ... Bruised ribs (November 20, 1999); missed two games. ... Injured groin (December 15, 1999); missed three games. ... Separated shoulder (February 26, 2000); missed remainder of season.

Season Team	League	Gms.	G	A	Pts.	PIM	+/-	PP	SH	Gms.	G	A	Pts.	PIM
			REGULAR SEASON							PLAYOFFS				
94-95—Kelowna	BCJHL	51	23	25	48	36	...	...	...	17	7	9	16	...
95-96—Barrie	OHL	59	29	30	59	22	...	...	...	7	2	3	5	2
96-97—Barrie	OHL	64	42	61	103	42	...	...	...	9	3	7	10	10
97-98—Washington	NHL	48	5	11	16	18	-5	0	0	—	—	—	—	—
—Portland	AHL	3	1	4	5	12	...	...	...	—	—	—	—	—
—Kingston	OHL	2	0	1	1	0	...	...	...	12	8	10	18	12
98-99—Washington	NHL	38	7	16	23	6	3	3	0	—	—	—	—	—
—Cincinnati	IHL	10	2	2	4	14	...	...	...	—	—	—	—	—
99-00—Washington	NHL	56	9	22	31	30	7	0	0	—	—	—	—	—
NHL Totals (3 years)		142	21	49	70	54	5	3	0					

BURE, PAVEL   RW   PANTHERS

PERSONAL: Born March 31, 1971, in Moscow, U.S.S.R. ... 5-10/189. ... Shoots left. ... Brother of Valeri Bure, right winger, Calgary Flames. ... Name pronounced PA-vihl BOOR-ay. ... Nickname: The Russian Rocket.
TRANSACTIONS/CAREER NOTES: Selected by Vancouver Canucks in sixth round (fourth Canucks pick, 113th overall) of NHL entry draft (June 17, 1989). ... Strained groin (October 24, 1993); missed eight games. ... Fined §500 by NHL for hitting another player with flagrant elbow (May 6, 1994). ... Played in Europe during 1994-95 NHL lockout. ... Suffered injury (March 17, 1995); missed two games. ... Tore knee ligament (November 9, 1995); missed remainder of season. ... Suspended one game and fined §1,000 by NHL for forearm blow (December 6, 1996). ... Suffered whiplash (March 3, 1997); missed remainder of season. ... Missed first 43 games of 1998-99 season due to contract dispute. ... Traded by Canucks with D Bret Hedican, D Brad Ference and third-round pick (Robert Fried) in 2000 draft to Florida Panthers for D Ed Jovanovski, G Kevin Weekes, C Dave Gagner, C Mike Brown and first-round pick (C Nathan Smith) in 2000 draft (January 17, 1999). ... Strained right knee (February 5, 1999); missed eight games. ... Reinjured knee (March 3, 1999); missed final 21 games of season. ... Strained groin (October 12, 1999); missed five games. ... Fractured finger (November 3, 1999); missed three games.
HONORS: Named Soviet League Rookie of the Year (1988-89). ... Won Calder Memorial Trophy (1991-92). ... Named to THE SPORTING NEWS All-Star second team (1993-94). ... Played in NHL All-Star Game (1993, 1994, 1997, 1998 and 2000). ... Named to NHL All-Star first team (1993-94). ... Named to play in NHL All-Star Game (1996); replaced due to injury. ... Named All-Star Game Most Valuable Player (2000). ... Named to NHL All-Star second team (1999-2000). ... Won Maurice "Rocket" Richard Trophy (1999-2000).

MISCELLANEOUS: Member of silver-medal-winning Russian Olympic team (1998). ... Scored on a penalty shot (vs. Rick Tabaracci, February 28, 1992; vs. Mike Vernon, November 12, 1997; vs. Nikolai Khabibulin, January 26, 1998; vs. Damian Rhodes, February 28, 1998; vs. Chris Osgood, February 26, 1999). ... Failed to score on a penalty shot (vs. John Vanbiesbrouck, February 17, 1992; vs. Kelly Hrudey, October 6, 1993).
STATISTICAL NOTES: Led NHL with 329 shots (1997-98) and with 360 (1999-2000). ... Led NHL with 14 game-winning goals (1999-2000).
STATISTICAL PLATEAUS: Three-goal games: 1992-93 (1), 1993-94 (3), 1994-95 (1), 1997-98 (3), 1998-99 (2), 1999-00 (3). Total: 13. ... Four-goal games: 1992-93 (1), 1999-00 (1). Total: 2. ... Total hat tricks: 15.

Season Team	League	REGULAR SEASON								PLAYOFFS				
		Gms.	G	A	Pts.	PIM	+/-	PP	SH	Gms.	G	A	Pts.	PIM
87-88—CSKA Moscow	USSR	5	1	1	2	0	...	...	...	—	—	—	—	—
88-89—CSKA Moscow	USSR	32	17	9	26	8	...	...	...	—	—	—	—	—
89-90—CSKA Moscow	USSR	46	14	11	25	22	...	...	...	—	—	—	—	—
90-91—CSKA Moscow	USSR	46	35	12	47	24	...	...	...	—	—	—	—	—
91-92—Vancouver	NHL	65	34	26	60	30	0	7	3	13	6	4	10	14
92-93—Vancouver	NHL	83	60	50	110	69	35	13	†7	12	5	7	12	8
93-94—Vancouver	NHL	76	*60	47	107	86	1	†25	4	24	*16	15	31	40
94-95—Landshut	Germany	1	3	0	3	2	...	...	...	—	—	—	—	—
—Spartak Moscow	CIS	1	2	0	2	2	...	...	...	—	—	—	—	—
—Vancouver	NHL	44	20	23	43	47	-8	6	2	11	7	6	13	10
95-96—Vancouver	NHL	15	6	7	13	8	-2	1	1	—	—	—	—	—
96-97—Vancouver	NHL	63	23	32	55	40	-14	4	1	—	—	—	—	—
97-98—Vancouver	NHL	82	51	39	90	48	5	13	†6	—	—	—	—	—
—Russian Oly. team	Int'l	6	9	0	9	2	...	...	...	—	—	—	—	—
98-99—Florida	NHL	11	13	3	16	4	3	5	1	—	—	—	—	—
99-00—Florida	NHL	74	*58	36	94	16	25	11	2	4	1	3	4	2
NHL Totals (9 years)		513	325	263	588	348	45	85	27	64	35	35	70	74

BURE, VALERI   RW   FLAMES

B

PERSONAL: Born June 13, 1974, in Moscow, U.S.S.R. ... 5-10/185. ... Shoots right. ... Brother of Pavel Bure, right winger, Florida Panthers. ... Name pronounced BOOR-ay.
TRANSACTIONS/CAREER NOTES: Selected by Montreal Canadiens in second round (second Canadiens pick, 33rd overall) of NHL entry draft (June 20, 1992). ... Bruised forearm (April 3, 1995); missed two games. ... Bruised kidney (October 19, 1996); missed 11 games. ... Bruised wrist (December 28, 1996); missed two games. ... Suffered concussion (January 4, 1997); missed five games. ... Bruised cheekbone (January 8, 1998); missed three games. ... Traded by Canadiens to Flames with fourth-round pick (C Shaun Sutter) in 1998 draft for D Zarley Zalapski and RW Jonas Hoglund (February 1, 1998). ... Suffered concussion (March 3, 1998); missed five games. ... Hyperextended shoulder (April 5, 1998); missed final seven games of season. ... Suffered concussion (January 10, 1999); missed two games.
HONORS: Named to WHL (West) All-Star first team (1992-93). ... Named to WHL (West) All-Star second team (1993-94). ... Played in NHL All-Star Game (2000).
MISCELLANEOUS: Member of silver-medal-winning Russian Olympic team (1998).
STATISTICAL PLATEAUS: Three-goal games: 1997-98 (1).

Season Team	League	REGULAR SEASON								PLAYOFFS				
		Gms.	G	A	Pts.	PIM	+/-	PP	SH	Gms.	G	A	Pts.	PIM
90-91—CSKA Moscow	USSR	3	0	0	0	0	...	...	...	—	—	—	—	—
91-92—Spokane	WHL	53	27	22	49	78	...	...	...	10	11	6	17	10
92-93—Spokane	WHL	66	68	79	147	49	...	...	...	9	6	11	17	14
93-94—Spokane	WHL	59	40	62	102	48	...	...	...	3	5	3	8	2
94-95—Fredericton	AHL	45	23	25	48	32	...	...	...	—	—	—	—	—
—Montreal	NHL	24	3	1	4	6	-1	0	0	—	—	—	—	—
95-96—Montreal	NHL	77	22	20	42	28	10	5	0	6	0	1	1	6
96-97—Montreal	NHL	64	14	21	35	6	4	4	0	5	0	1	1	2
97-98—Montreal	NHL	50	7	22	29	33	-5	2	0	—	—	—	—	—
—Calgary	NHL	16	5	4	9	2	0	0	0	—	—	—	—	—
—Russian Oly. team	Int'l	6	1	0	1	0	...	...	...	—	—	—	—	—
98-99—Calgary	NHL	80	26	27	53	22	0	7	0	—	—	—	—	—
99-00—Calgary	NHL	82	35	40	75	50	-7	13	0	—	—	—	—	—
NHL Totals (6 years)		393	112	135	247	147	1	31	0	11	0	2	2	8

BUREAU, MARC   C/RW   FLAMES

PERSONAL: Born May 19, 1966, in Trois-Rivieres, Que. ... 6-1/203. ... Shoots right. ... Name pronounced BYOOR-oh.
TRANSACTIONS/CAREER NOTES: Signed as non-drafted free agent by Calgary Flames (May 16, 1987). ... Suffered eye contusion (March 25, 1990); missed final two weeks of season. ... Traded by Flames to Minnesota North Stars for third-round pick (RW Sandy McCarthy) in 1991 draft (March 5, 1991). ... Injured shoulder (January 13, 1992); missed four games. ... Separated shoulder (February 15, 1992); missed five games. ... Separated shoulder (March 1, 1992); missed eight games. ... Claimed on waivers by Tampa Bay Lightning (October 16, 1992). ... Bruised shoulder (November 17, 1992); missed six games. ... Bruised right knee (April 3, 1993); missed remainder of season. ... Traded by Lightning to Montreal Canadiens for LW Brian Bellows (June 29, 1995). ... Fractured foot (September 26, 1995); missed first eight games of season. ... Suffered sore neck (November 29, 1995); missed two games. ... Suspended five games and fined §1,000 by NHL for elbowing (February 3, 1996). ... Bruised foot (November 2, 1996); missed five games. ... Tore knee ligament (December 7, 1996); missed 26 games. ... Injured knee (February 10, 1997); missed five games. ... Suffered from the flu (April 1, 1997); missed one game. ... Fractured finger (April 9, 1997); missed remainder of season. ... Bruised thigh (October 25, 1997); missed two games. ... Strained neck (February 28, 1998); missed one game. ... Signed as free agent by Philadelphia Flyers (July 6, 1998). ... Sprained left wrist (January 3, 1999); missed seven games. ... Suffered stiff neck (January 2, 2000); missed five games. ... Bruised right knee (February 16, 2000); missed one game. ... Traded by Flyers to Flames for LW Travis Brigley and sixth-round pick in 2001 draft (March 6, 2000). ... Suffered concussion (March 23, 2000); missed final seven games of season.
HONORS: Named to IHL All-Star second team (1989-90 and 1990-91).
MISCELLANEOUS: Failed to score on a penalty shot (vs. Don Beaupre, November 18, 1995; vs. Mike Richter, January 10, 1998).

Season Team	League	REGULAR SEASON								PLAYOFFS				
		Gms.	G	A	Pts.	PIM	+/-	PP	SH	Gms.	G	A	Pts.	PIM
83-84—Chicoutimi	QMJHL	56	6	16	22	14	...	...	...	—	—	—	—	—
84-85—Chicoutimi	QMJHL	41	30	25	55	15	...	...	...	—	—	—	—	—
—Granby	QMJHL	27	20	45	65	14	...	...	...	—	—	—	—	—
85-86—Chicoutimi	QMJHL	19	6	17	23	36	...	...	...	—	—	—	—	—
—Chicoutimi	QMJHL	44	30	45	75	33	...	...	...	9	3	7	10	10
86-87—Longueuil	QMJHL	66	54	58	112	68	...	...	...	20	17	20	37	12
87-88—Salt Lake City	IHL	69	7	20	27	86	...	...	...	7	0	3	3	8
88-89—Salt Lake City	IHL	76	28	36	64	119	...	...	...	14	7	5	12	31
89-90—Salt Lake City	IHL	67	43	48	91	173	...	...	...	11	4	8	12	0
—Calgary	NHL	5	0	0	0	4	-1	0	0	—	—	—	—	—
90-91—Calgary	NHL	5	0	0	0	2	-4	0	0	—	—	—	—	—
—Salt Lake City	IHL	54	40	48	88	101	...	...	...	—	—	—	—	—
—Minnesota	NHL	9	0	6	6	4	-3	0	0	23	3	2	5	20
91-92—Minnesota	NHL	46	6	4	10	50	-5	0	0	5	0	0	0	14
—Kalamazoo	IHL	7	2	8	10	2	...	...	...	—	—	—	—	—
92-93—Tampa Bay	NHL	63	10	21	31	111	-12	1	2	—	—	—	—	—
93-94—Tampa Bay	NHL	75	8	7	15	30	-9	0	1	—	—	—	—	—
94-95—Tampa Bay	NHL	48	2	12	14	30	-8	0	1	—	—	—	—	—
95-96—Montreal	NHL	65	3	7	10	46	-3	0	0	6	1	1	2	4
96-97—Montreal	NHL	43	6	9	15	16	4	1	1	—	—	—	—	—
97-98—Montreal	NHL	74	13	6	19	12	0	0	0	10	1	2	3	6
98-99—Philadelphia	NHL	71	4	6	10	10	-2	0	0	6	0	2	2	2
99-00—Philadelphia	NHL	54	2	2	4	10	-1	0	1	—	—	—	—	—
—Calgary	NHL	9	1	3	4	2	-3	0	0	—	—	—	—	—
NHL Totals (11 years)		567	55	83	138	327	-47	2	6	50	5	7	12	46

B

BURKE, SEAN   G

PERSONAL: Born January 29, 1967, in Windsor, Ont. ... 6-4/210. ... Catches left. ... Name pronounced BUHRK.

TRANSACTIONS/CAREER NOTES: Selected by New Jersey Devils as underage junior in second round (second Devils pick, 24th overall) of NHL entry draft (June 15, 1985). ... Injured groin (December 1988). ... Underwent arthroscopic surgery to right knee (September 5, 1989). ... Traded by Devils with D Eric Weinrich to Hartford Whalers for RW Bobby Holik, second-round pick (LW Jay Pandolfo) in 1993 draft and future considerations (August 28, 1992). ... Sprained ankle (December 27, 1992); missed seven games. ... Suffered back spasms (March 13, 1993); missed remainder of season. ... Pulled hamstring (September 29, 1993); missed seven games. ... Reinjured hamstring (October 27, 1993); missed 14 games. ... Suffered back spasms (December 23, 1993); missed one game. ... Strained groin (February 28, 1995); missed two games. ... Suffered back spasms (November 19, 1995); missed two games. ... Suffered back spasms (February 7, 1996); missed three games. ... Dislocated thumb (November 30, 1996); missed 19 games. ... Strained hip flexor (February 26, 1997); missed one game. ... Whalers franchise moved to North Carolina and renamed Carolina Hurricanes for 1997-98 season; NHL approved move on June 25, 1997. ... Traded by Hurricanes with LW Geoff Sanderson and D Enrico Ciccone to Vancouver Canucks for LW Martin Gelinas and G Kirk McLean (January 3, 1998). ... Traded by Canucks to Philadelphia Flyers for G Garth Snow (March 4, 1998). ... Suffered lower back spasms (March 8, 1998); missed six games. ... Signed as free agent by Florida Panthers (September 11, 1998). ... Strained hip flexor (April 10, 1999); missed final three games of season. ... Traded by Panthers with fifth-round pick (D Nate Kiser) in 2000 draft to Phoenix Coyotes for G Mikhail Shtalenkov and fourth-round pick (D Chris Eade) in 2000 draft (November 19, 1999). ... Suffered partially torn thumb ligament (November 26, 1999); missed 16 games. ... Strained hip flexor (January 12, 2000); missed one game. ... Injured groin (February 1, 2000); missed one game. ... Strained groin (March 1, 2000); missed one game.

HONORS: Played in NHL All-Star Game (1989).

MISCELLANEOUS: Member of silver-medal-winning Canadian Olympic team (1992). ... Holds Carolina Hurricanes franchise all-time record for most games played by a goaltender (281). ... Stopped a penalty shot attempt (vs. Luc Robitaille, February 2, 1989; vs. Michal Pivonka, January 21, 1995; vs. Wayne Presley, March 8, 1996; vs. Brian Bradley, April 3, 1996; vs. Kevin Stevens, March 22, 1998; vs. Terry Yake, November 18, 1999). ... Allowed a penalty shot goal (vs. Brad Isbister, January 10, 2000).

Season Team	League	REGULAR SEASON								PLAYOFFS						
		Gms.	Min	W	L	T	GA	SO	Avg.	Gms.	Min.	W	L	GA	SO	Avg.
83-84—St. Michael's H.S.	MTHL	25	1482	...	...	...	120	0	4.86	—	—	—	—	—	—	—
84-85—Toronto	OHL	49	2987	25	21	3	211	0	4.24	5	266	1	3	25	0	5.64
85-86—Toronto	OHL	47	2840	16	27	3	†233	0	4.92	4	238	0	4	24	0	6.05
—Canadian nat'l team	Int'l	5	284	...	...	...	22	0	4.65	—	—	—	—	—	—	—
86-87—Canadian nat'l team	Int'l	42	2550	27	13	2	130	0	3.06	—	—	—	—	—	—	—
87-88—Canadian nat'l team	Int'l	37	1962	19	9	2	92	1	2.81	—	—	—	—	—	—	—
—Can. Olympic team	Int'l	4	238	1	2	1	12	0	3.03	—	—	—	—	—	—	—
—New Jersey	NHL	13	689	10	1	0	35	1	3.05	17	1001	9	8	*57	†1	3.42
88-89—New Jersey	NHL	62	3590	22	31	9	†230	0	3.84	—	—	—	—	—	—	—
89-90—New Jersey	NHL	52	2914	22	22	6	175	0	3.60	2	125	0	2	8	0	3.84
90-91—New Jersey	NHL	35	1870	8	12	8	112	0	3.59	—	—	—	—	—	—	—
91-92—Canadian nat'l team	Int'l	31	1721	18	6	4	75	1	2.61	—	—	—	—	—	—	—
—Can. Olympic team	Int'l	7	429	5	2	0	17	0	2.38	—	—	—	—	—	—	—
—San Diego	IHL	7	424	4	2	‡1	17	0	2.41	3	160	0	3	13	0	4.88
92-93—Hartford	NHL	50	2656	16	27	3	184	0	4.16	—	—	—	—	—	—	—
93-94—Hartford	NHL	47	2750	17	24	5	137	2	2.99	—	—	—	—	—	—	—
94-95—Hartford	NHL	42	2418	17	19	4	108	0	2.68	—	—	—	—	—	—	—
95-96—Hartford	NHL	66	3669	28	28	6	190	4	3.11	—	—	—	—	—	—	—
96-97—Hartford	NHL	51	2985	22	22	6	134	4	2.69	—	—	—	—	—	—	—
97-98—Carolina	NHL	25	1415	7	11	5	66	1	2.80	—	—	—	—	—	—	—
—Vancouver	NHL	16	838	2	9	4	49	0	3.51	—	—	—	—	—	—	—
—Philadelphia	NHL	11	632	7	3	0	27	1	2.56	5	283	1	4	17	0	3.60
98-99—Florida	NHL	59	3402	21	24	14	151	3	2.66	—	—	—	—	—	—	—
99-00—Florida	NHL	7	418	2	5	0	18	0	2.58	—	—	—	—	—	—	—
—Phoenix	NHL	35	2074	17	14	3	88	3	2.55	5	296	1	4	16	0	3.24
NHL Totals (12 years)		571	32320	218	252	73	1704	22	3.16	29	1705	11	18	98	1	3.45

BURR, SHAWN   LW/C

PERSONAL: Born July 1, 1966, in Sarnia, Ont. ... 6-1/205. ... Shoots left.

TRANSACTIONS/CAREER NOTES: Selected by Detroit Red Wings as underage junior in first round (first Red Wings pick, seventh overall) of NHL entry draft (June 9, 1984). ... Separated left shoulder (May 1988). ... Suffered lower back spasms (October 20, 1992); missed three games. ... Underwent wrist surgery (December 8, 1993); missed 18 games. ... Injured leg (January 25, 1994); missed seven games. ... Traded by Red Wings with third-round pick (traded to Boston) in 1996 draft to Tampa Bay Lightning for D Marc Bergevin and RW Ben Hankinson (August 17, 1995). ... Injured elbow (January 15, 1996); missed one game. ... Strained lower back (October 29, 1996); missed two games. ... Lacerated finger (December 19, 1996); missed six games. ... Traded by Lightning to San Jose Sharks for fifth-round pick (D Mark Thompson) in 1997 draft (June 21, 1997). ... Suffered knee injury (October 13, 1997); missed 40 games. ... Traded by Sharks with D Andrei Zyuzin, D Bill Houlder and C Steve Guolla to Tampa Bay Lightning for LW Niklas Sundstrom and third-round pick (traded to Chicago) in 2000 draft (August 4, 1999). ... Injured groin (October 9, 1999); missed seven games. ... Suffered back spasms (November 9, 1999); missed 17 games. ... Announced retirement (July 26, 2000).

HONORS: Won Emms Family Award (1983-84). ... Named to OHL All-Star second team (1985-86).

STATISTICAL PLATEAUS: Three-goal games: 1986-87 (1), 1989-90 (1). Total: 2.

			REGULAR SEASON							PLAYOFFS				
Season Team	League	Gms.	G	A	Pts.	PIM	+/-	PP	SH	Gms.	G	A	Pts.	PIM
83-84—Kitchener	OHL	68	41	44	85	50	...	...	...	16	5	12	17	22
84-85—Kitchener	OHL	38	24	42	66	50	...	...	...	4	3	3	6	2
—Detroit	NHL	9	0	0	0	2	-4	0	0	—	—	—	—	—
—Adirondack	AHL	4	0	0	0	2	...	...	...	—	—	—	—	—
85-86—Kitchener	OHL	59	60	67	127	104	...	...	...	5	2	3	5	8
—Adirondack	AHL	3	2	2	4	2	...	...	...	17	5	7	12	32
—Detroit	NHL	5	1	0	1	4	1	0	1	—	—	—	—	—
86-87—Detroit	NHL	80	22	25	47	107	2	1	2	16	7	2	9	20
87-88—Detroit	NHL	78	17	23	40	97	7	5	3	9	3	1	4	14
88-89—Detroit	NHL	79	19	27	46	78	5	1	4	6	1	2	3	6
89-90—Adirondack	AHL	3	4	2	6	2	...	...	...	—	—	—	—	—
—Detroit	NHL	76	24	32	56	82	14	4	3	—	—	—	—	—
90-91—Detroit	NHL	80	20	30	50	112	14	6	0	7	0	4	4	15
91-92—Detroit	NHL	79	19	32	51	118	26	2	0	11	1	5	6	10
92-93—Detroit	NHL	80	10	25	35	74	18	1	1	7	2	1	3	2
93-94—Detroit	NHL	51	10	12	22	31	12	0	1	7	2	0	2	6
94-95—Detroit	NHL	42	6	8	14	60	13	0	0	16	0	2	2	6
95-96—Tampa Bay	NHL	81	13	15	28	119	4	1	0	6	0	2	2	8
96-97—Tampa Bay	NHL	74	14	21	35	106	5	1	0	—	—	—	—	—
97-98—San Jose	NHL	42	6	6	12	50	2	0	0	6	0	0	0	8
98-99—San Jose	NHL	18	0	1	1	29	-3	0	0	—	—	—	—	—
—Kentucky	AHL	26	10	14	24	29	...	...	...	12	4	9	13	10
99-00—Tampa Bay	NHL	4	0	2	2	0	2	0	0	—	—	—	—	—
—Detroit	IHL	10	2	4	6	10	...	...	...	—	—	—	—	—
—Manitoba	IHL	18	3	2	5	6	...	...	...	2	1	0	1	6
NHL Totals (16 years)		878	181	259	440	1069	118	22	15	91	16	19	35	95

BURT, ADAM   D   THRASHERS

PERSONAL: Born January 15, 1969, in Detroit. ... 6-2/205. ... Shoots left.

TRANSACTIONS/CAREER NOTES: Selected by Hartford Whalers as underage junior in second round (second Whalers pick, 39th overall) of NHL entry draft (June 13, 1987). ... Separated left shoulder (September 13, 1988). ... Bruised hip (December 1989). ... Dislocated left shoulder (January 19, 1989). ... Tore right knee ligaments (February 16, 1991); missed remainder of season. ... Sprained left wrist (January 11, 1992); missed six games. ... Fractured bone in right foot (January 25, 1993); missed 13 games. ... Sprained shoulder (February 27, 1994); missed remainder of season. ... Strained groin (February 3, 1997); missed eight games. ... Sprained shoulder (March 5, 1997); missed three games. ... Whalers franchise moved to North Carolina and renamed Carolina Hurricanes for 1997-98 season; NHL approved move on June 25, 1997. ... Strained groin (October 5, 1998); missed first five games of season. ... Suffered back spasms (November 21, 1998); missed one game. ... Bruised shoulder (December 19, 1998); missed one game. ... Strained groin (February 10, 1999); missed one game. ... Traded by Hurricanes to Philadelphia Flyers for RW Andrei Kovalenko (March 6, 1999). ... Bruised right foot (December 18, 1999); missed one game. ... Suffered concussion (January 27, 2000); missed two games. ... Signed as free agent by Atlanta Thrashers (July 14, 2000).

HONORS: Named to OHL All-Star second team (1987-88).

MISCELLANEOUS: Captain of Hartford Whalers (1994-95).

			REGULAR SEASON							PLAYOFFS				
Season Team	League	Gms.	G	A	Pts.	PIM	+/-	PP	SH	Gms.	G	A	Pts.	PIM
85-86—North Bay	OHL	49	0	11	11	81	...	...	...	10	0	0	0	24
86-87—North Bay	OHL	57	4	27	31	138	...	...	...	24	1	6	7	68
87-88—North Bay	OHL	66	17	54	71	176	...	...	...	2	0	3	3	6
—Binghamton	AHL	—	—	—	—	—	—	—	—	2	1	1	2	0
88-89—North Bay	OHL	23	4	11	15	45	...	...	...	12	2	12	14	12
—Binghamton	AHL	5	0	2	2	13	...	...	...	—	—	—	—	—
—Hartford	NHL	5	0	0	0	6	-1	0	0	—	—	—	—	—
89-90—Hartford	NHL	63	4	8	12	105	3	1	0	2	0	0	0	0
90-91—Springfield	AHL	9	1	3	4	22	...	...	...	—	—	—	—	—
—Hartford	NHL	42	2	7	9	63	-4	1	0	—	—	—	—	—
91-92—Hartford	NHL	66	9	15	24	93	-16	4	0	2	0	0	0	0
92-93—Hartford	NHL	65	6	14	20	116	-11	0	0	—	—	—	—	—
93-94—Hartford	NHL	63	1	17	18	75	-4	0	0	—	—	—	—	—
94-95—Hartford	NHL	46	7	11	18	65	0	3	0	—	—	—	—	—
95-96—Hartford	NHL	78	4	9	13	121	-4	0	0	—	—	—	—	—
96-97—Hartford	NHL	71	2	11	13	79	-13	0	0	—	—	—	—	—
97-98—Carolina	NHL	76	1	11	12	106	-6	0	1	—	—	—	—	—
98-99—Carolina	NHL	51	0	3	3	46	3	0	0	—	—	—	—	—
—Philadelphia	NHL	17	0	1	1	14	1	0	0	6	0	0	0	4
99-00—Philadelphia	NHL	67	1	6	7	45	-2	0	0	11	0	1	1	4
NHL Totals (12 years)		710	37	113	150	934	-54	9	1	21	0	1	1	8

B

BUTENSCHON, SVEN   D   PENGUINS

PERSONAL: Born March 22, 1976, in Itzehoe, West Germany. ... 6-4/215. ... Shoots left. ... Name pronounced BOO-tihn-SHAHN.
HIGH SCHOOL: Crocus Plains (Brandon, Man.).
TRANSACTIONS/CAREER NOTES: Selected by Pittsburgh Penguins in third round (third Penguins pick, 57th overall) of NHL entry draft (June 29, 1994). ... Suffered from the flu (November 7, 1997); missed two games.

		REGULAR SEASON								PLAYOFFS				
Season Team	League	Gms.	G	A	Pts.	PIM	+/-	PP	SH	Gms.	G	A	Pts.	PIM
93-94—Brandon	WHL	70	3	19	22	51	...	...	...	4	0	0	0	6
94-95—Brandon	WHL	21	1	5	6	44	...	...	...	18	1	2	3	11
95-96—Brandon	WHL	70	4	37	41	99	...	...	...	19	1	12	13	18
96-97—Cleveland	IHL	75	3	12	15	68	...	...	...	10	0	1	1	4
97-98—Syracuse	AHL	65	14	23	37	66	...	...	...	5	1	2	3	0
—Pittsburgh	NHL	8	0	0	0	6	-1	0	0	—	—	—	—	—
98-99—Houston	IHL	57	1	4	5	81	...	...	...	—	—	—	—	—
—Pittsburgh	NHL	17	0	0	0	6	-7	0	0	—	—	—	—	—
99-00—Wilkes-Barre/Scranton	AHL	75	19	21	40	101	...	...	...	—	—	—	—	—
—Pittsburgh	NHL	3	0	0	0	0	3	0	0	—	—	—	—	—
NHL Totals (3 years)		28	0	0	0	12	-5	0	0					

BUTSAYEV, SLAVA   C   SENATORS

PERSONAL: Born June 13, 1970, in Togliatti, U.S.S.R. ... 6-2/220. ... Shoots left. ... Full Name: Viacheslav Butsayev. ... Name pronounced SLAH-vuh boot-SIGH-yehf.
TRANSACTIONS/CAREER NOTES: Selected by Philadelphia Flyers in sixth round (10th Flyers pick, 109th overall) of NHL entry draft (June 16, 1990). ... Traded by Flyers to San Jose Sharks for D Rob Zettler (February 1, 1994). ... Played in Europe during 1994-95 NHL lockout. ... Injured stomach (January 20, 1995); missed eight games. ... Signed as free agent by Mighty Ducks of Anaheim (October 20, 1995). ... Signed as free agent by Florida Panthers (August 12, 1998). ... Traded by Panthers to Ottawa Senators for sixth-round pick (traded to Atlanta) in 1999 draft (March 8, 1999). ... Claimed by Tampa Bay Lightning from Senators in NHL waiver draft (September 27, 1999). ... Claimed on waivers by Senators (October 28, 1999).
HONORS: Named to IHL All-Star second team (1997-98).
STATISTICAL PLATEAUS: Three-goal games: 1993-94 (1).

		REGULAR SEASON								PLAYOFFS				
Season Team	League	Gms.	G	A	Pts.	PIM	+/-	PP	SH	Gms.	G	A	Pts.	PIM
89-90—CSKA Moscow	USSR	48	14	4	18	30	...	...	...	—	—	—	—	—
90-91—CSKA Moscow	USSR	46	14	9	23	32	...	...	...	—	—	—	—	—
91-92—CSKA Moscow	USSR	36	12	13	25	26	...	...	...	—	—	—	—	—
—Unif. Olympic team	Int'l	8	1	1	2	4	...	...	...	—	—	—	—	—
92-93—CSKA Moscow	CIS	5	3	4	7	6	...	...	...	—	—	—	—	—
—Philadelphia	NHL	52	2	14	16	61	3	0	0	—	—	—	—	—
—Hershey	AHL	24	8	10	18	51	...	...	...	—	—	—	—	—
93-94—Philadelphia	NHL	47	12	9	21	58	2	2	0	—	—	—	—	—
—San Jose	NHL	12	0	2	2	10	-2	0	0	—	—	—	—	—
94-95—Lada Togliatti	CIS	9	2	6	8	6	...	...	...	—	—	—	—	—
—San Jose	NHL	6	2	0	2	0	-2	0	0	—	—	—	—	—
—Kansas City	IHL	13	4	3	7	12	...	...	...	3	0	0	0	2
95-96—Baltimore	AHL	62	23	42	65	70	...	...	...	12	4	8	12	28
—Anaheim	NHL	7	1	0	1	0	-4	0	0	—	—	—	—	—
96-97—Farjestad Karlstad	Sweden	40	6	7	13	108	...	...	...	—	—	—	—	—
97-98—Fort Wayne	IHL	76	36	51	87	128	...	...	...	4	2	2	4	4
98-99—Fort Wayne	IHL	71	28	44	72	123	...	...	...	2	1	0	1	4
—Florida	NHL	1	0	0	0	2	-1	0	0	—	—	—	—	—
—Ottawa	NHL	3	0	1	1	4	0	0	0	—	—	—	—	—
99-00—Tampa Bay	NHL	2	0	0	0	0	-2	0	0	—	—	—	—	—
—Grand Rapids	IHL	68	28	35	63	85	...	...	...	17	4	*12	16	24
—Ottawa	NHL	3	0	0	0	0	-2	0	0	—	—	—	—	—
NHL Totals (6 years)		133	17	26	43	135	-8	2	0					

BUTSAYEV, YURI   C   RED WINGS

PERSONAL: Born October 11, 1978, in Togliatti, U.S.S.R. ... 6-1/183. ... Shoots left.
TRANSACTIONS/CAREER NOTES: Selected by Detroit Red Wings in second round (first Red Wings pick, 49th overall) of NHL entry draft (June 21, 1997).

		REGULAR SEASON								PLAYOFFS				
Season Team	League	Gms.	G	A	Pts.	PIM	+/-	PP	SH	Gms.	G	A	Pts.	PIM
95-96—Lada Togliatti	CIS	1	0	0	0	0	...	...	...	—	—	—	—	—
—Lada-2 Togliatti	CIS Div. II	—	19	7	26	—	...	...	...	—	—	—	—	—
96-97—Lada Togliatti	Russian	42	13	11	24	38	...	...	...	11	2	2	4	8
97-98—Lada Togliatti	Russian	44	8	9	17	63	...	...	...	—	—	—	—	—
98-99—Lada Togliatti	Russian	39	10	7	17	55	...	...	...	7	1	2	3	14
—Dynamo Moscow	Russian	1	0	1	1	0	...	...	...	—	—	—	—	—
99-00—Detroit	NHL	57	5	3	8	12	-6	0	0	—	—	—	—	—
—Cincinnati	AHL	9	0	1	1	0	...	...	...	—	—	—	—	—
NHL Totals (1 year)		57	5	3	8	12	-6	0	0					

BUTURLIN, ALEXANDER — LW — CANADIENS

PERSONAL: Born September 3, 1981, in Moscow, U.S.S.R. ... 5-11/183. ... Shoots left.
TRANSACTIONS/CAREER NOTES: Selected by Montreal Canadiens in second round (first Canadiens pick, 39th overall) of NHL entry draft (June 26, 1999).

		REGULAR SEASON								PLAYOFFS				
Season Team	League	Gms.	G	A	Pts.	PIM	+/-	PP	SH	Gms.	G	A	Pts.	PIM
97-98—CSKA Moscow	Russian	2	0	0	0	0	...	...	...	—	—	—	—	—
—CSKA-2 Moscow	Rus. Div. III	50	12	15	27	46	...	...	...	—	—	—	—	—
98-99—CSKA Moscow	Russian	16	1	0	1	6	...	...	...	3	1	0	1	2
99-00—Sarnia	OHL	57	20	27	47	46	...	...	...	7	4	2	6	12

BUZEK, PETR — D — THRASHERS

PERSONAL: Born April 26, 1977, in Jihlava, Czechoslovakia. ... 6-0/215. ... Shoots left. ... Name pronounced BOO-zihk.
TRANSACTIONS/CAREER NOTES: Selected by Dallas Stars in third round (third Stars pick, 63rd overall) of NHL entry draft (July 8, 1995). ... Selected by Atlanta Thrashers in NHL expansion draft (June 25, 1999). ... Suffered from dehydration (October 26, 1999); missed two games. ... Suffered concussion (November 13, 1999); missed six games. ... Sprained shoulder (December 17, 1999); missed one game. ... Strained groin (January 21, 2000); missed four games.
HONORS: Played in NHL All-Star Game (2000).

		REGULAR SEASON								PLAYOFFS				
Season Team	League	Gms.	G	A	Pts.	PIM	+/-	PP	SH	Gms.	G	A	Pts.	PIM
93-94—Jihlava	Czech Rep.	29	6	16	22	...	...	...	...	—	—	—	—	—
—Dukla Jihlava	Czech Rep.	3	0	0	0	...	...	...	...	—	—	—	—	—
94-95—Dukla Jihlava	Czech Rep.	43	2	5	7	...	...	...	...	2	0	0	0	...
95-96—Jihlava	Czech Rep.					Did not play.								
96-97—Michigan	IHL	67	4	6	10	48	...	...	...	—	—	—	—	—
97-98—Michigan	IHL	60	10	15	25	58	...	...	...	2	0	1	1	17
—Dallas	NHL	2	0	0	0	2	1	0	0	—	—	—	—	—
98-99—Michigan	IHL	74	5	14	19	68	...	...	...	5	0	0	0	10
—Dallas	NHL	2	0	0	0	2	0	0	0	—	—	—	—	—
99-00—Atlanta	NHL	63	5	14	19	41	-22	3	0	—	—	—	—	—
NHL Totals (3 years)		67	5	14	19	45	-21	3	0					

BYLSMA, DAN — RW — MIGHTY DUCKS

PERSONAL: Born September 19, 1970, in Grand Haven, Mich. ... 6-2/212. ... Shoots left. ... Full Name: Daniel Brian Bylsma. ... Name pronounced BIGHLS-muh.
COLLEGE: Bowling Green State.
TRANSACTIONS/CAREER NOTES: Selected by Winnipeg Jets in fourth round (sixth Jets pick, 69th overall) of NHL entry draft (June 17, 1989). ... Signed as free agent by Los Angeles Kings (July 14, 1994). ... Injured knee (March 19, 1997); missed one game. ... Strained groin (April 3, 1997); missed one game. ... Signed as free agent by Mighty Ducks of Anaheim (July 13, 2000).

		REGULAR SEASON								PLAYOFFS				
Season Team	League	Gms.	G	A	Pts.	PIM	+/-	PP	SH	Gms.	G	A	Pts.	PIM
87-88—St. Mary's Jr. B	OHA	40	30	39	69	33	...	...	...	—	—	—	—	—
88-89—Bowling Green	CCHA	39	4	7	11	16	...	...	...	—	—	—	—	—
89-90—Bowling Green	CCHA	44	13	17	30	32	...	...	...	—	—	—	—	—
90-91—Bowling Green	CCHA	40	9	12	21	48	...	...	...	—	—	—	—	—
91-92—Bowling Green	CCHA	34	11	14	25	24	...	...	...	—	—	—	—	—
92-93—Rochester	AHL	2	0	1	1	0	...	...	...	—	—	—	—	—
—Greensboro	ECHL	60	25	35	60	66	...	...	...	1	0	1	1	10
93-94—Albany	AHL	3	0	1	1	2	...	...	...	—	—	—	—	—
—Moncton	AHL	50	12	16	28	25	...	...	...	21	3	4	7	31
—Greensboro	ECHL	25	14	16	30	52	...	...	...	—	—	—	—	—
94-95—Phoenix	IHL	81	19	23	42	41	...	...	...	—	—	—	—	—
95-96—Phoenix	IHL	78	22	20	42	48	...	...	...	4	1	0	1	2
—Los Angeles	NHL	4	0	0	0	0	0	0	0	—	—	—	—	—
96-97—Los Angeles	NHL	79	3	6	9	32	-15	0	0	—	—	—	—	—
97-98—Long Beach	IHL	8	2	3	5	0	...	...	...	—	—	—	—	—
—Los Angeles	NHL	65	3	9	12	33	9	0	0	2	0	0	0	0
98-99—Long Beach	IHL	58	10	8	18	53	...	...	...	4	0	0	0	8
—Los Angeles	NHL	8	0	0	0	2	-1	0	0	—	—	—	—	—
—Springfield	AHL	2	0	2	2	2	...	...	...	—	—	—	—	—
99-00—Los Angeles	NHL	64	3	6	9	55	-2	0	1	3	0	0	0	0
—Long Beach	IHL	6	0	3	3	2	...	...	...	—	—	—	—	—
—Lowell	AHL	2	1	1	2	2	...	...	...	—	—	—	—	—
NHL Totals (5 years)		220	9	21	30	122	-9	0	1	5	0	0	0	0

CAIRNS, ERIC — D — ISLANDERS

PERSONAL: Born June 27, 1974, in Oakville, Ont. ... 6-6/235. ... Shoots left. ... Name pronounced KAIR-ihns.
TRANSACTIONS/CAREER NOTES: Selected by New York Rangers in third round (third Rangers pick, 72nd overall) of NHL entry draft (June 20, 1992). ... Claimed on waivers by New York Islanders (December 22, 1998). ... Strained back (January 6, 2000); missed one game. ... Suspended four games by NHL for fighting incident (February 13, 2000).

Season Team	League	REGULAR SEASON								PLAYOFFS				
		Gms.	G	A	Pts.	PIM	+/-	PP	SH	Gms.	G	A	Pts.	PIM
90-91—Burlington Jr. B...........	OHA	37	5	16	21	120	...	...	...	—	—	—	—	—
91-92—Det. Jr. Red Wings......	OHL	64	1	11	12	237	...	...	...	7	0	0	0	31
92-93—Det. Jr. Red Wings......	OHL	64	3	13	16	194	...	...	...	15	0	3	3	24
93-94—Det. Jr. Red Wings......	OHL	59	7	35	42	204	...	...	...	17	0	4	4	46
94-95—Birmingham...............	ECHL	11	1	3	4	49	...	...	...	—	—	—	—	—
—Binghamton.............	AHL	27	0	3	3	134	...	...	...	9	1	1	2	28
95-96—Binghamton...............	AHL	46	1	13	14	192	...	...	...	4	0	0	0	37
—Charlotte................	ECHL	6	0	1	1	34	...	...	...	—	—	—	—	—
96-97—New York Rangers......	NHL	40	0	1	1	147	-7	0	0	3	0	0	0	0
—Binghamton.............	AHL	10	1	1	2	96	...	...	...	—	—	—	—	—
97-98—New York Rangers......	NHL	39	0	3	3	92	-3	0	0	—	—	—	—	—
—Hartford................	AHL	7	1	2	3	43	...	...	...	—	—	—	—	—
98-99—Hartford...................	AHL	11	0	2	2	49	...	...	...	—	—	—	—	—
—Lowell....................	AHL	24	0	0	0	91	...	...	...	3	1	0	1	32
—New York Islanders.....	NHL	9	0	3	3	23	1	0	0	—	—	—	—	—
99-00—Providence..................	AHL	4	1	1	2	14	...	...	...	—	—	—	—	—
—New York Islanders.....	NHL	67	2	7	9	196	-5	0	0	—	—	—	—	—
NHL Totals (4 years)............		155	2	14	16	458	-14	0	0	3	0	0	0	0

CALDER, KYLE   C   BLACKHAWKS

PERSONAL: Born January 5, 1979, in Mannville, Alta. ... 5-11/180. ... Shoots left.
TRANSACTIONS/CAREER NOTES: Selected by Chicago Blackhawks in fifth round (seventh Blackhawks pick, 130th overall) of NHL entry draft (June 21, 1997).

Season Team	League	REGULAR SEASON								PLAYOFFS				
		Gms.	G	A	Pts.	PIM	+/-	PP	SH	Gms.	G	A	Pts.	PIM
95-96—Regina	WHL	27	1	8	9	10	...	...	...	11	0	0	0	0
96-97—Regina	WHL	62	25	34	59	17	...	...	...	5	3	0	3	6
97-98—Regina	WHL	62	27	50	77	58	...	...	...	2	0	1	1	0
98-99—Regina	WHL	34	23	28	51	29	...	...	...	—	—	—	—	—
—Kamloops	WHL	27	19	18	37	30	...	...	...	15	6	10	16	6
99-00—Cleveland	IHL	74	14	22	36	43	...	...	...	9	2	2	4	14
—Chicago....................	NHL	8	1	1	2	2	-3	0	0	—	—	—	—	—
NHL Totals (1 year)..............		8	1	1	2	2	-3	0	0					

CALOUN, JAN   RW   BLUE JACKETS

PERSONAL: Born December 20, 1972, in Usti-nad-Labem, Czechoslovakia. ... 5-10/190. ... Shoots right. ... Name pronounced YAHN shah-LOON.
TRANSACTIONS/CAREER NOTES: Selected by San Jose Sharks in fourth round (fourth Sharks pick, 75th overall) of NHL entry draft (June 20, 1992). ... Traded by Sharks to with ninth-round pick (F Martin Paroulek) in 2000 draft to Columbus Blue Jackets for future considerations (June 12, 2000).
HONORS: Named to AHL All-Star second team (1996-97).

Season Team	League	REGULAR SEASON								PLAYOFFS				
		Gms.	G	A	Pts.	PIM	+/-	PP	SH	Gms.	G	A	Pts.	PIM
90-91—CHZ Litvinov...............	Czech.	50	28	19	47	12	...	...	...	—	—	—	—	—
91-92—Chemopetrol Litvinov .	Czech.	46	39	13	52	...	...	...	...	—	—	—	—	—
92-93—Chemopetrol Litvinov .	Czech.	47	45	22	67	...	...	...	...	—	—	—	—	—
93-94—Chem. Litvinov............	Czech Rep.	41	25	17	42	...	...	...	...	4	2	0	2	...
94-95—Kansas City................	IHL	76	34	39	73	50	...	...	...	21	13	10	23	18
95-96—Kansas City................	IHL	61	38	30	68	58	...	...	...	5	0	1	1	6
—San Jose..................	NHL	11	8	3	11	0	4	2	0	—	—	—	—	—
96-97—Kentucky....................	AHL	66	43	43	86	68	...	...	...	4	0	1	1	4
—San Jose..................	NHL	2	0	0	0	0	-2	0	0	—	—	—	—	—
97-98—Czech Rep. Oly. team..	Int'l	3	0	0	0	6	...	...	...	—	—	—	—	—
98-99—HIFK Helsinki.............	Finland	51	24	*57	*81	95	...	...	...	8	*8	6	*14	31
99-00—HIFK Helsinki.............	Finland	44	38	34	72	94	...	...	...	9	3	6	9	10
NHL Totals (2 years)...........		13	8	3	11	0	2	2	0					

CAMPBELL, BRIAN   D   SABRES

PERSONAL: Born May 23, 1979, in Strathroy, Ont. ... 5-11/185. ... Shoots left.
TRANSACTIONS/CAREER NOTES: Selected by Buffalo Sabres in sixth round (seventh Sabres pick, 156th overall) of NHL entry draft (June 21, 1997).
HONORS: Won Can.HL Player of the Year Award (1998-99). ... Named to Can.HL All-Star first team (1998-99). ... Won Red Tilson Trophy (1998-99). ... Won Max Kaminsky Trophy (1998-99). ... Won William Hanley Trophy (1998-99).

Season Team	League	REGULAR SEASON								PLAYOFFS				
		Gms.	G	A	Pts.	PIM	+/-	PP	SH	Gms.	G	A	Pts.	PIM
94-95—Petrolia	Jr. B	50	1	2	3	...	...	...	...	—	—	—	—	—
95-96—Ottawa	OHL	66	5	22	27	23	...	...	...	4	0	1	1	2
96-97—Ottawa	OHL	66	7	36	43	12	...	...	...	24	2	11	13	8
97-98—Ottawa	OHL	66	14	39	53	31	...	...	...	13	1	14	15	0
98-99—Ottawa	OHL	62	12	75	87	27	...	...	...	9	2	10	12	6
99-00—Buffalo	NHL	12	1	4	5	4	-2	0	0	—	—	—	—	—
—Rochester	AHL	67	2	24	26	22	...	...	...	21	0	3	3	0
NHL Totals (1 year)..............		12	1	4	5	4	-2	0	0					

CAMPBELL, JIM RW

PERSONAL: Born February 3, 1973, in Worcester, Mass. ... 6-2/205. ... Shoots right. ... Full Name: James Tower Campbell. ... Nickname: Soup.
HIGH SCHOOL: Lawrence Academy (Groton, Mass.), then Northwood School (Lake Placid, N.Y.).
TRANSACTIONS/CAREER NOTES: Selected by Montreal Canadiens in second round (second Canadiens pick, 28th overall) of NHL entry draft (June 22, 1991). ... Traded by Canadiens to Mighty Ducks of Anaheim for D Robert Dirk (January 21, 1996). ... Signed as free agent by St. Louis Blues (July 3, 1996). ... Strained thumb (February 25, 1997); missed 10 games. ... Reinjured thumb (April 6, 1997); missed remainder of regular season. ... Strained groin (December 6, 1997); missed one game. ... Injured left heel (January 20, 1998); missed five games. ... Bruised right shoulder (October 23, 1998); missed two games. ... Injured groin (February 9, 1999); missed three games. ... Injured abdominal muscle (March 18, 1999) and underwent surgery; missed remainder of season.
HONORS: Named to NHL All-Rookie team (1996-97).

		REGULAR SEASON							PLAYOFFS				
Season Team	League	Gms.	G	A	Pts.	PIM	+/-	PP	SH	Gms.	G	A	Pts.	PIM
88-89—Northwood School......	N.Y. H.S.	12	12	8	20	6	...	...	...	—	—	—	—	—
89-90—Northwood School......	N.Y. H.S.	8	14	7	21	8	...	...	...	—	—	—	—	—
90-91—Northwood School......	N.Y. H.S.	26	36	47	83	36	...	...	...	—	—	—	—	—
91-92—Hull..........................	QMJHL	64	41	44	85	51	...	...	...	6	7	3	10	8
92-93—Hull..........................	QMJHL	50	42	29	71	66	...	...	...	8	11	4	15	43
93-94—U.S. national team	Int'l	56	24	33	57	59	...	...	...	—	—	—	—	—
—U.S. Olympic team......	Int'l	8	0	0	0	6	...	...	...	—	—	—	—	—
—Fredericton	AHL	19	6	17	23	6	...	...	...	—	—	—	—	—
94-95—Fredericton	AHL	77	27	24	51	103	...	...	...	12	0	7	7	8
95-96—Fredericton	AHL	44	28	23	51	24	...	...	...	—	—	—	—	—
—Baltimore	AHL	16	13	7	20	8	...	...	...	12	7	5	12	10
—Anaheim	NHL	16	2	3	5	36	0	1	0	—	—	—	—	—
96-97—St. Louis	NHL	68	23	20	43	68	3	5	0	4	1	0	1	6
97-98—St. Louis	NHL	76	22	19	41	55	0	7	0	10	7	3	10	12
98-99—St. Louis	NHL	55	4	21	25	41	-8	1	0	—	—	—	—	—
99-00—Manitoba	IHL	10	1	3	4	10	...	...	...	—	—	—	—	—
—Worcester	AHL	66	31	34	65	88	...	...	...	9	1	2	3	6
—St. Louis	NHL	2	0	0	0	9	0	0	0	—	—	—	—	—
NHL Totals (5 years)...........		217	51	63	114	209	-5	14	0	14	8	3	11	18

CARBONNEAU, GUY C

PERSONAL: Born March 18, 1960, in Sept-Iles, Que. ... 5-11/190. ... Shoots right. ... Name pronounced GEE KAHR-buh-noh.
TRANSACTIONS/CAREER NOTES: Selected by Montreal Canadiens as underage junior in third round (fourth Canadiens pick, 44th overall) of NHL entry draft (August 9, 1979). ... Strained right knee ligaments (October 7, 1989); missed nine games. ... Fractured nose (October 28, 1989). ... Suffered concussion (October 8, 1990). ... Fractured rib (January 13, 1992); missed six games. ... Injured elbow (March 2, 1992); missed one game. ... Suffered right knee tendinitis (October 1, 1992); missed five games. ... Fractured finger (November 14, 1992); missed three games. ... Suffered knee tendinitis (February 4, 1993); missed 15 games. ... Suffered from the flu (February 11, 1994); missed one game. ... Traded by Canadiens to St. Louis Blues for C Jim Montgomery (August 19, 1994). ... Underwent knee surgery (March 31, 1995); missed six games. ... Traded by Blues to Dallas Stars for RW Paul Broten (October 2, 1995). ... Injured groin (October 17, 1995); missed five games. ... Strained groin (December 8, 1996); missed one game. ... Bruised forearm (March 31, 1997); missed two games. ... Sprained neck (October 14, 1997); missed one game. ... Strained back (October 25, 1997); missed three games. ... Strained groin (October 22, 1998); missed one game. ... Bruised ankle (February 17, 1999); missed one game. ... Injured knee (March 14, 1999); missed two games. ... Sprained ankle (March 31, 1999); missed one game. ... Strained neck (February 21, 2000); missed two games. ... Fractured wrist (March 5, 2000); missed seven games. ... Announced retirement (July 2, 2000).
HONORS: Named to QMJHL All-Star second team (1979-80). ... Won Frank J. Selke Trophy (1987-88, 1988-89 and 1991-92).
MISCELLANEOUS: Member of Stanley Cup championship team (1986, 1993 and 1999). ... Co-captain of Montreal Canadiens (1989-90). ... Captain of Canadiens (1991-92 through 1993-94).
STATISTICAL PLATEAUS: Three-goal games: 1982-83 (1), 1993-94 (1). Total: 2.

		REGULAR SEASON							PLAYOFFS				
Season Team	League	Gms.	G	A	Pts.	PIM	+/-	PP	SH	Gms.	G	A	Pts.	PIM
76-77—Chicoutimi	QMJHL	59	9	20	29	8	...	...	...	4	1	0	1	0
77-78—Chicoutimi	QMJHL	70	28	55	83	60	...	...	...	—	—	—	—	—
78-79—Chicoutimi	QMJHL	72	62	79	141	47	...	...	...	4	2	1	3	4
79-80—Chicoutimi	QMJHL	72	72	110	182	66	...	...	...	12	9	15	24	28
—Nova Scotia	AHL	—	—	—	—	—	...	...	...	2	1	1	2	2
80-81—Montreal	NHL	2	0	1	1	0	0	0	0	—	—	—	—	—
—Nova Scotia	AHL	78	35	53	88	87	...	...	...	6	1	3	4	9
81-82—Nova Scotia	AHL	77	27	67	94	124	...	...	...	9	2	7	9	8
82-83—Montreal	NHL	77	18	29	47	68	18	0	5	3	0	0	0	2
83-84—Montreal	NHL	78	24	30	54	75	5	3	7	15	4	3	7	12
84-85—Montreal	NHL	79	23	34	57	43	28	0	4	12	4	3	7	8
85-86—Montreal	NHL	80	20	36	56	57	18	1	2	20	7	5	12	35
86-87—Montreal	NHL	79	18	27	45	68	9	0	0	17	3	8	11	20
87-88—Montreal	NHL	80	17	21	38	61	14	0	3	11	0	4	4	2
88-89—Montreal	NHL	79	26	30	56	44	37	1	2	21	4	5	9	10
89-90—Montreal	NHL	68	19	36	55	37	21	1	1	11	2	3	5	6
90-91—Montreal	NHL	78	20	24	44	63	-1	4	1	13	1	5	6	10
91-92—Montreal	NHL	72	18	21	39	39	2	1	1	11	1	1	2	6
92-93—Montreal	NHL	61	4	13	17	20	-9	0	1	20	3	3	6	10
93-94—Montreal	NHL	79	14	24	38	48	16	0	0	7	1	3	4	4
94-95—St. Louis	NHL	42	5	11	16	16	11	1	0	7	1	2	3	6
95-96—Dallas	NHL	71	8	15	23	38	-2	0	2	—	—	—	—	—
96-97—Dallas	NHL	73	5	16	21	36	9	0	1	7	0	1	1	6
97-98—Dallas	NHL	77	7	17	24	40	3	0	1	16	3	1	4	6
98-99—Dallas	NHL	74	4	12	16	31	-3	0	0	17	2	4	6	6
99-00—Dallas	NHL	69	10	6	16	36	10	0	1	23	2	4	6	12
NHL Totals (19 years)..........		1318	260	403	663	820	186	12	32	231	38	55	93	161

C

PERSONAL: Born February 3, 1970, in Providence, R.I. ... 6-2/211. ... Shoots left. ... Full Name: Keith Edward Carney.
COLLEGE: Maine.
TRANSACTIONS/CAREER NOTES: Selected by Buffalo Sabres in fourth round (third Sabres pick, 76th overall) of NHL entry draft (June 11, 1988). ... Traded by Sabres to Chicago Blackhawks for D Craig Muni (October 27, 1993). ... Traded by Blackhawks with RW Jim Cummins to Phoenix Coyotes for C Chad Kilger and D Jayson More (March 4, 1998).
HONORS: Named to Hockey East All-Rookie team (1988-89). ... Named to NCAA All-America (East) second team (1989-90). ... Named to Hockey East All-Star second team (1989-90). ... Named to NCAA All-America (East) first team (1990-91). ... Named to Hockey East All-Star first team (1990-91).

		REGULAR SEASON								PLAYOFFS				
Season Team	League	Gms.	G	A	Pts.	PIM	+/-	PP	SH	Gms.	G	A	Pts.	PIM
88-89—Univ. of Maine	Hockey East	40	4	22	26	24	...	...	...	—	—	—	—	—
89-90—Univ. of Maine	Hockey East	41	3	41	44	43	...	...	...	—	—	—	—	—
90-91—Univ. of Maine	Hockey East	40	7	49	56	38	...	...	...	—	—	—	—	—
91-92—U.S. national team	Int'l	49	2	17	19	16	...	...	...	—	—	—	—	—
—Rochester	AHL	24	1	10	11	2	...	...	...	2	0	2	2	0
—Buffalo	NHL	14	1	2	3	18	-3	1	0	7	0	3	3	0
92-93—Buffalo	NHL	30	2	4	6	55	3	0	0	8	0	3	3	6
—Rochester	AHL	41	5	21	26	32	...	...	...	—	—	—	—	—
93-94—Louisville	ECHL	15	1	4	5	14	...	...	...	—	—	—	—	—
—Buffalo	NHL	7	1	3	4	4	-1	0	0	—	—	—	—	—
—Indianapolis	IHL	28	0	14	14	20	...	...	...	—	—	—	—	—
—Chicago	NHL	30	3	5	8	35	15	0	0	6	0	1	1	4
94-95—Chicago	NHL	18	1	0	1	11	-1	0	0	4	0	1	1	0
95-96—Chicago	NHL	82	5	14	19	94	31	1	0	10	0	3	3	4
96-97—Chicago	NHL	81	3	15	18	62	26	0	0	6	1	1	2	2
97-98—Chicago	NHL	60	2	13	15	73	-7	0	1	—	—	—	—	—
—U.S. Olympic team	Int'l	4	0	0	0	2	...	...	...	—	—	—	—	—
—Phoenix	NHL	20	1	6	7	18	5	1	0	6	0	0	0	4
98-99—Phoenix	NHL	82	2	14	16	62	15	0	2	7	1	2	3	10
99-00—Phoenix	NHL	82	4	20	24	87	11	0	0	5	0	0	0	17
NHL Totals (9 years)		506	25	96	121	519	94	3	3	59	2	14	16	47

CARTER, ANSON   C   BRUINS

PERSONAL: Born June 6, 1974, in Toronto. ... 6-1/175. ... Shoots right.
COLLEGE: Michigan State.
TRANSACTIONS/CAREER NOTES: Selected by Quebec Nordiques in 10th round (10th Nordiques pick, 220th overall) of NHL entry draft (June 20, 1992). ... Nordiques franchise moved to Colorado and renamed Avalanche for 1995-96 season (June 21, 1995). ... Traded by Avalanche to Washington Capitals for fourth-round pick (D Ben Storey) in 1996 entry draft (April 3, 1996). ... Sprained thumb (February 7, 1997); missed five games. ... Traded by Capitals with G Jim Carey, C Jason Allison and third-round pick (RW Lee Goren) in 1997 draft to Boston Bruins for C Adam Oates, RW Rick Tocchet and G Bill Ranford (March 1, 1997). ... Strained hip flexor (October 7, 1997); missed two games. ... Suffered from upper respiratory infection (November 22, 1997); missed two games. ... Missed first 12 games of 1998-99 season due to contract dispute; played with Utah of IHL. ... Sprained ankle (January 2, 1999); missed 15 games. ... Bruised shoulder (February 21, 2000); missed eight games. ... Underwent wrist surgery (March 10, 2000); missed final 15 games of season.
HONORS: Named to CCHA All-Star first team (1993-94 and 1994-95). ... Named to NCAA All-America (West) second team (1994-95). ... Named to CCHA All-Star second team (1995-96).
STATISTICAL PLATEAUS: Three-goal games: 1998-99 (1).

		REGULAR SEASON								PLAYOFFS				
Season Team	League	Gms.	G	A	Pts.	PIM	+/-	PP	SH	Gms.	G	A	Pts.	PIM
91-92—Wexford	OHA Jr. A	42	18	22	40	24	...	...	...	—	—	—	—	—
92-93—Michigan State	CCHA	36	19	11	30	20	...	...	...	—	—	—	—	—
93-94—Michigan State	CCHA	39	30	24	54	36	...	...	...	—	—	—	—	—
94-95—Michigan State	CCHA	39	34	17	51	40	...	...	...	—	—	—	—	—
95-96—Michigan State	CCHA	42	23	20	43	36	...	...	...	—	—	—	—	—
96-97—Washington	NHL	19	3	2	5	7	0	1	0	—	—	—	—	—
—Portland	AHL	27	19	19	38	11	...	...	...	—	—	—	—	—
—Boston	NHL	19	8	5	13	2	-7	1	1	—	—	—	—	—
97-98—Boston	NHL	78	16	27	43	31	7	6	0	6	1	1	2	0
98-99—Utah	IHL	6	1	1	2	0	...	...	...	—	—	—	—	—
—Boston	NHL	55	24	16	40	22	7	6	0	12	4	3	7	0
99-00—Boston	NHL	59	22	25	47	14	8	4	0	—	—	—	—	—
NHL Totals (4 years)		230	73	75	148	76	15	18	1	18	5	4	9	0

CASSELS, ANDREW   C   CANUCKS

PERSONAL: Born July 23, 1969, in Bramalea, Ont. ... 6-1/185. ... Shoots left. ... Name pronounced KAS-uhls.
TRANSACTIONS/CAREER NOTES: Selected by Montreal Canadiens as underage junior in first round (first Canadiens pick, 17th overall) of NHL entry draft (June 13, 1987). ... Separated right shoulder (November 22, 1989); missed 10 games. ... Traded by Canadiens to Hartford Whalers for second-round pick (RW Valeri Bure) in 1992 draft (September 17, 1991). ... Bruised kneecap (December 4, 1993); missed one game. ... Suffered facial injury (March 13, 1994); missed four games. ... Bruised forearm (December 2, 1995); missed one game. ... Suffered charley horse (March 6, 1997); missed one game. ... Whalers franchise moved to North Carolina and renamed Carolina Hurricanes for 1997-98 season; NHL approved move on June 25, 1997. ... Traded by Hurricanes with G Jean-Sebastien Giguere to Calgary Flames for LW Gary Roberts and G Trevor Kidd (August 25, 1997). ... Strained rib cage (October 9, 1997); missed one game. ... Injured groin (February 1, 1999); missed 12 games. ... Signed as free agent by Vancouver Canucks (July 13, 1999). ... Sprained thumb (October 19, 1999); missed three games.

HONORS: Won Emms Family Award (1986-87). ... Won Red Tilson Trophy (1987-88). ... Won Eddie Powers Memorial Trophy (1987-88). ... Won William Hanley Trophy (1987-88). ... Named to OHL All-Star first team (1987-88 and 1988-89).
MISCELLANEOUS: Captain of Hartford Whalers (1994-95). ... Scored on a penalty shot (vs. Ron Hextall, April 6, 1994). ... Failed to score on a penalty shot (vs. Patrick Roy, November 30, 1999).

			REGULAR SEASON							PLAYOFFS				
Season Team	League	Gms.	G	A	Pts.	PIM	+/-	PP	SH	Gms.	G	A	Pts.	PIM
85-86—Bramalea Jr. B	OHA	33	18	25	43	26	...	...	...	—	—	—	—	—
86-87—Ottawa	OHL	66	26	66	92	28	...	...	...	11	5	9	14	7
87-88—Ottawa	OHL	61	48	*103	*151	39	...	...	...	16	8	*24	†32	13
88-89—Ottawa	OHL	56	37	97	134	66	...	...	...	12	5	10	15	10
89-90—Sherbrooke	AHL	55	22	45	67	25	...	...	...	12	2	11	13	6
—Montreal	NHL	6	2	0	2	1	1	0	0	—	—	—	—	—
90-91—Montreal	NHL	54	6	19	25	20	2	1	0	8	0	2	2	2
91-92—Hartford	NHL	67	11	30	41	18	3	2	2	7	2	4	6	6
92-93—Hartford	NHL	84	21	64	85	62	-11	8	3	—	—	—	—	—
93-94—Hartford	NHL	79	16	42	58	37	-21	8	1	—	—	—	—	—
94-95—Hartford	NHL	46	7	30	37	18	-3	1	0	—	—	—	—	—
95-96—Hartford	NHL	81	20	43	63	39	8	6	0	—	—	—	—	—
96-97—Hartford	NHL	81	22	44	66	46	-16	8	0	—	—	—	—	—
97-98—Calgary	NHL	81	17	27	44	32	-7	6	1	—	—	—	—	—
98-99—Calgary	NHL	70	12	25	37	18	-12	4	1	—	—	—	—	—
99-00—Vancouver	NHL	79	17	45	62	16	8	6	0	—	—	—	—	—
NHL Totals (11 years)		728	151	369	520	308	-48	50	8	15	2	6	8	8

CECH, VRATISLAV — D — BRUINS — C

PERSONAL: Born January 28, 1979, in Tabor, Czechoslovakia. ... 6-3/196. ... Shoots left. ... Name pronounced CHECK.
TRANSACTIONS/CAREER NOTES: Selected by Florida Panthers in third round (third Panthers pick, 56th overall) of NHL entry draft (June 21, 1997). ... Signed as free agent by Boston Bruins (July 19, 1999).

			REGULAR SEASON							PLAYOFFS				
Season Team	League	Gms.	G	A	Pts.	PIM	+/-	PP	SH	Gms.	G	A	Pts.	PIM
95-96—Kometa Brno Jrs.	Czech Rep.	37	10	13	23	...	...	...	...	—	—	—	—	—
96-97—Kitchener	OHL	57	5	19	24	72	...	...	...	13	1	2	3	12
97-98—Kitchener	OHL	63	9	33	42	66	...	...	...	6	2	2	4	13
98-99—Kitchener	OHL	66	6	21	27	73	...	...	...	1	0	1	1	4
99-00—Providence	AHL	3	0	1	1	0	...	...	...	—	—	—	—	—
—Greenville	ECHL	55	7	15	22	51	...	...	...	15	0	5	5	16

CEREDA, LUCA — C — MAPLE LEAFS

PERSONAL: Born September 7, 1981, in Lugano, Switzerland. ... 6-2/203. ... Shoots left.
TRANSACTIONS/CAREER NOTES: Selected by Toronto Maple Leafs in first round (first Maple Leafs pick, 24th overall) of NHL entry draft (June 26, 1999).

			REGULAR SEASON							PLAYOFFS				
Season Team	League	Gms.	G	A	Pts.	PIM	+/-	PP	SH	Gms.	G	A	Pts.	PIM
96-97—Ambri-Piotta Jrs.	Switzerland Jr.	35	13	8	21	21	...	...	...	—	—	—	—	—
97-98—Ambri-Piotta Jrs.	Switzerland Jr.	28	17	27	44	24	...	...	...	—	—	—	—	—
98-99—Ambri-Piotta	Switzerland	38	6	10	16	8	...	...	...	15	0	6	6	4
99-00—Ambri-Piotta	Switzerland	44	1	5	6	14	...	...	...	9	0	1	1	2

CHABOT, FREDERIC — G — BLUE JACKETS

PERSONAL: Born February 12, 1968, in Hebertville, Que. ... 5-11/187. ... Catches right. ... Name pronounced shuh-BAHT.
TRANSACTIONS/CAREER NOTES: Selected by New Jersey Devils in 10th round (10th Devils pick, 192nd overall) of NHL entry draft (June 21, 1986). ... Signed as free agent by Montreal Canadiens (January 16, 1990). ... Selected by Tampa Bay Lightning in NHL expansion draft (June 18, 1992). ... Traded by Lightning to Canadiens for G Jean-Claude Bergeron (June 18, 1992). ... Traded by Canadiens to Philadelphia Flyers for future considerations (February 21, 1994). ... Signed as free agent by Florida Panthers (August 15, 1994). ... Signed as free agent by Los Angeles Kings (September 5, 1997). ... Sprained right knee (March 10, 1998); missed seven games. ... Selected by Nashville Predators in NHL expansion draft (June 26, 1998). ... Claimed on waivers by Kings (July 20, 1998). ... Selected by Montreal Canadiens from Kings in NHL waiver draft (October 5, 1998). ... Selected by Columbus Blue Jackets in NHL expansion draft (June 23, 2000).
HONORS: Named to Memorial Cup All-Star team (1981-82). ... Named to WHL (East) All-Star first team (1988-89). ... Won Aldege (Baz) Bastien Trophy (1993-94). ... Named to IHL All-Star second team (1995-96). ... Won James Gatschene Memorial Trophy (1996-97). ... Named to IHL All-Star first team (1996-97 and 1999-2000). ... Shared James Gatschene Memorial Trophy with Nikolai Khabibulin (1999-2000). ... Won James Norris Memorial Trophy (1999-2000).

			REGULAR SEASON							PLAYOFFS						
Season Team	League	Gms.	Min	W	L	T	GA	SO	Avg.	Gms.	Min.	W	L	GA	SO	Avg.
86-87—Drummondville	QMJHL	*62	*3508	31	29	0	293	1	5.01	8	481	2	6	40	0	4.99
87-88—Drummondville	QMJHL	58	3276	27	24	4	237	1	4.34	*16	1019	10	6	56	†1	*3.30
88-89—Moose Jaw	WHL	26	1385	...	...	...	114	1	4.94	—	—	—	—	—	—	—
—Prince Albert	WHL	28	1572	...	...	...	88	1	3.36	4	199	1	1	16	0	4.82
89-90—Fort Wayne	IHL	23	1208	6	13	‡3	87	1	4.32	—	—	—	—	—	—	—
—Sherbrooke	AHL	2	119	1	1	0	8	0	4.03	—	—	—	—	—	—	—
90-91—Montreal	NHL	3	108	0	0	1	6	0	3.33	—	—	—	—	—	—	—
—Fredericton	AHL	35	1800	9	15	5	122	0	4.07	—	—	—	—	—	—	—
91-92—Winston-Salem	ECHL	25	1449	15	7	‡2	71	0	*2.94	—	—	—	—	—	—	—
—Fredericton	AHL	30	1761	17	9	4	79	2	*2.69	7	457	3	4	20	0	2.63
92-93—Fredericton	AHL	45	2544	22	17	4	141	0	3.33	4	261	1	3	16	0	3.68
—Montreal	NHL	1	40	0	0	0	1	0	1.50	—	—	—	—	—	—	—

Season Team	League	REGULAR SEASON								PLAYOFFS						
		Gms.	Min	W	L	T	GA	SO	Avg.	Gms.	Min.	W	L	GA	SO	Avg.
93-94 —Fredericton	AHL	3	143	0	1	1	12	0	5.03	—	—	—	—	—	—	—
—Las Vegas	IHL	2	110	1	1	‡1	5	0	2.73	—	—	—	—	—	—	—
—Montreal	NHL	1	60	0	1	0	5	0	5.00	—	—	—	—	—	—	—
—Hershey	AHL	31	1607	13	6	7	75	2	*2.80	11	665	7	4	32	0	2.89
—Philadelphia	NHL	4	70	0	1	1	5	0	4.29	—	—	—	—	—	—	—
94-95 —Cincinnati	IHL	48	2622	25	12	‡7	128	1	2.93	5	326	3	2	16	0	2.94
95-96 —Cincinnati	IHL	38	2147	23	9	‡4	88	3	*2.46	14	854	9	5	37	1	2.60
96-97 —Houston	IHL	*72	*4265	*39	26	‡7	*180	*7	2.53	13	777	8	5	34	†2	2.63
97-98 —Los Angeles	NHL	12	554	3	3	2	29	0	3.14	—	—	—	—	—	—	—
—Houston	IHL	22	1237	12	7	‡2	46	1	2.23	4	239	1	3	11	0	2.76
98-99 —Houston	IHL	21	1259	16	4	‡1	49	3	2.34	—	—	—	—	—	—	—
—Montreal	NHL	11	430	1	3	0	16	0	2.23	—	—	—	—	—	—	—
99-00 —Houston	IHL	*62	*3695	*48	19	‡7	131	4	2.13	11	658	6	5	20	*3	1.82
NHL Totals (5 years)		32	1262	4	8	4	62	0	2.95							

CHAMBERS, SHAWN — D

PERSONAL: Born October 11, 1966, in Sterling Heights, Mich. ... 6-2/200. ... Shoots left. ... Full Name: Shawn Randall Chambers.
COLLEGE: Alaska-Fairbanks.
TRANSACTIONS/CAREER NOTES: Selected by Minnesota North Stars in NHL supplemental draft (June 13, 1987). ... Dislocated shoulder (February 1988). ... Separated right shoulder (September 1988). ... Injured left knee (September 11, 1990); missed first 11 games of season. ... Fractured left kneecap (December 5, 1990); missed three months. ... Underwent surgery to left knee to remove piece of loose cartilage (May 1991). ... Traded by North Stars to Washington Capitals for C Trent Klatt and LW Steve Maltais (June 21, 1991). ... Suffered sore knee (October 1991); missed first 47 games of season. ... Reinjured knee (January 26, 1992); missed remainder of season. ... Underwent arthroscopic knee surgery (February 4, 1992). ... Selected by Tampa Bay Lightning in NHL expansion draft (June 18, 1992). ... Underwent arthroscopic knee surgery (October 9, 1992); missed 14 games. ... Underwent arthroscopic knee surgery (October 21, 1993); missed 14 games. ... Injured shoulder (November 13, 1993); missed two games. ... Suffered facial lacerations (January 2, 1994); missed one game. ... Suffered strep throat (February 7, 1995); missed one game. ... Traded by Lightning with RW Danton Cole to New Jersey Devils for C Alexander Semak and RW Ben Hankinson (March 14, 1995). ... Suffered charley horse (November 14, 1995); missed one game. ... Bruised shoulder (December 6, 1995); missed three games. ... Fractured right hand (March 13, 1996); missed 13 games. ... Bruised right knee (November 7, 1996); missed three games. ... Injured hip (March 19, 1997); missed one game. ... Signed as free agent by Dallas Stars (July 3, 1997). ... Fractured hand (October 1, 1997); missed eight games. ... Fractured thumb (November 5, 1997); missed nine games. ... Bruised hand (March 12, 1998); missed one game. ... Bruised hand (March 18, 1998); missed seven games. ... Fractured finger (December 2, 1998); missed seven games. ... Strained hip flexor (March 16, 1999); missed 12 games. ... Sprained thumb (April 17, 1999); missed final game of regular season. ... Injured knee (October 8, 1999) and underwent knee surgery; missed remainder of season.
MISCELLANEOUS: Member of Stanley Cup championship team (1995 and 1999).

Season Team	League	REGULAR SEASON							PLAYOFFS				
		Gms.	G	A	Pts.	PIM	+/-	PP	SH	Gms.	G	A	Pts.	PIM
85-86 —Alaska-Fairbanks	GWHC	25	15	21	36	34	...	...	...	—	—	—	—	—
86-87 —Alaska-Fairbanks	GWHC	17	11	19	30	...	...	...	...	—	—	—	—	—
—Seattle	WHL	28	8	25	33	58	...	...	...	—	—	—	—	—
—Fort Wayne	IHL	12	2	6	8	0	...	...	...	10	1	4	5	5
87-88 —Minnesota	NHL	19	1	7	8	21	-6	1	0	—	—	—	—	—
—Kalamazoo	IHL	19	1	6	7	22	...	...	...	—	—	—	—	—
88-89 —Minnesota	NHL	72	5	19	24	80	-4	1	2	3	0	2	2	0
89-90 —Minnesota	NHL	78	8	18	26	81	-2	0	1	7	2	1	3	10
90-91 —Minnesota	NHL	29	1	3	4	24	2	0	0	23	0	7	7	16
—Kalamazoo	IHL	3	1	1	2	0	...	...	...	—	—	—	—	—
91-92 —Baltimore	AHL	5	2	3	5	9	...	...	...	—	—	—	—	—
—Washington	NHL	2	0	0	0	2	-3	0	0	—	—	—	—	—
92-93 —Atlanta	IHL	6	0	2	2	18	...	...	...	—	—	—	—	—
—Tampa Bay	NHL	55	10	29	39	36	-21	5	0	—	—	—	—	—
93-94 —Tampa Bay	NHL	66	11	23	34	23	-6	6	1	—	—	—	—	—
94-95 —Tampa Bay	NHL	24	2	12	14	6	0	1	0	—	—	—	—	—
—New Jersey	NHL	21	2	5	7	6	2	1	0	20	4	5	9	2
95-96 —New Jersey	NHL	64	2	21	23	18	1	2	0	—	—	—	—	—
96-97 —New Jersey	NHL	73	4	17	21	19	17	1	0	10	1	6	7	6
97-98 —Dallas	NHL	57	2	22	24	26	11	1	1	14	0	3	3	20
98-99 —Dallas	NHL	61	2	9	11	18	6	1	0	17	0	2	2	18
99-00 —Dallas	NHL	4	0	0	0	4	-2	0	0	—	—	—	—	—
NHL Totals (13 years)		625	50	185	235	364	-5	20	5	94	7	26	33	72

CHARA, ZDENO — D — ISLANDERS

PERSONAL: Born March 18, 1977, in Trencin, Czechoslovakia. ... 6-9/246. ... Shoots left. ... Name pronounced zuh-DAY-yoh CHAH-ruh.
TRANSACTIONS/CAREER NOTES: Selected by New York Islanders in third round (third Islanders pick, 56th overall) of NHL entry draft (June 22, 1996). ... Injured left shoulder (January 10, 2000); missed 16 games. ... Suffered from the flu (April 9, 2000); missed one game.

Season Team	League	REGULAR SEASON							PLAYOFFS				
		Gms.	G	A	Pts.	PIM	+/-	PP	SH	Gms.	G	A	Pts.	PIM
94-95 —Dukla Trencin Jrs.	Slovakia	2	0	0	0	2	...	...	...	—	—	—	—	—
95-96 —Dukla Trencin Jrs.	Slovakia	22	1	13	14	80	...	...	...	—	—	—	—	—
—HC Piestany	Slov. Div. II	10	1	3	4	10	...	...	...	—	—	—	—	—
—Sparta Praha Jrs.	Czech Rep.	15	1	2	3	42	...	...	...	—	—	—	—	—
—Sparta Praha	Czech Rep.	1	0	0	0	0	...	...	...	—	—	—	—	—
96-97 —Prince George	WHL	49	3	19	22	120	...	...	...	15	1	7	8	45
97-98 —Kentucky	AHL	48	4	9	13	125	...	...	...	1	0	0	0	4
—New York Islanders	NHL	25	0	1	1	50	1	0	0	—	—	—	—	—
98-99 —Lowell	AHL	23	2	2	4	47	...	...	...	—	—	—	—	—
—New York Islanders	NHL	59	2	6	8	83	-8	0	1	—	—	—	—	—
99-00 —New York Islanders	NHL	65	2	9	11	57	-27	0	0	—	—	—	—	—
NHL Totals (3 years)		149	4	16	20	190	-34	0	1					

CHARRON, CRAIG — C — KINGS

PERSONAL: Born November 15, 1967, in North Easton, Mass. ... 5-10/175. ... Shoots left.
TRANSACTIONS/CAREER NOTES: Signed as free agent by New York Islanders (August 24, 1998). ... Traded by Islanders to Toronto Maple Leafs for LW Niklas Andersson (August 17, 1999). ... Traded by Maple Leafs to Los Angeles Kings for C Don MacLean (February 23, 2000).
HONORS: Won Fred Hunt Memorial Award (1997-98).

Season Team	League	REGULAR SEASON								PLAYOFFS				
		Gms.	G	A	Pts.	PIM	+/-	PP	SH	Gms.	G	A	Pts.	PIM
90-91—Albany	IHL	5	0	2	2	0	...	...	...	—	—	—	—	—
—Winston-Salem	ECHL	30	11	16	27	10	...	...	...	—	—	—	—	—
—Fredericton	AHL	24	2	5	7	4	...	...	...	5	0	3	3	0
91-92—Cincinnati	ECHL	64	41	55	96	97	...	...	...	9	5	5	10	10
92-93—Cincinnati	IHL	27	6	8	14	8	...	...	...	—	—	—	—	—
—Birmingham	ECHL	23	9	17	26	18	...	...	...	—	—	—	—	—
93-94—						Did not play.								
94-95—Kalamazoo	IHL	2	0	0	0	0	...	...	...	—	—	—	—	—
—Fort Wayne	IHL	2	1	0	1	4	...	...	...	—	—	—	—	—
—Dayton	ECHL	48	35	47	82	82	...	...	...	9	9	13	22	10
95-96—Rochester	AHL	72	43	52	95	79	...	...	...	19	7	10	17	12
96-97—Rochester	AHL	72	24	41	65	42	...	...	...	10	8	8	16	2
97-98—Rochester	AHL	75	25	53	78	51	...	...	...	4	1	1	2	0
98-99—Lowell	AHL	71	22	39	61	41	...	...	...	3	1	2	3	8
99-00—St. John's	AHL	32	11	18	29	14	...	...	...	—	—	—	—	—
—Lowell	AHL	22	8	13	21	14	...	...	...	7	2	3	5	4
NHL Totals (1 year)		0	0	0	0	0	0	0	0					

CHARRON, ERIC — D

PERSONAL: Born January 14, 1970, in Verdun, Que. ... 6-3/200. ... Shoots left. ... Name pronounced sha-ROH.
TRANSACTIONS/CAREER NOTES: Selected by Montreal Canadiens in first round (first Canadiens pick, 20th overall) of NHL entry draft (June 11, 1988). ... Traded by Canadiens with D Alain Cote and future considerations to Tampa Bay Lightning for D Rob Ramage (March 20, 1993); Lightning acquired D Donald Dufresne to complete deal (June 18, 1993). ... Traded by Lightning to Washington Capitals for seventh-round pick (RW Eero Somervuori) in 1997 draft (November 17, 1995). ... Injured knee prior to 1996-97 season; missed first six games of season. ... Bruised ribs (December 13, 1996); missed one game. ... Traded by Capitals to Calgary Flames for future considerations (September 4, 1997). ... Suffered concussion (March 25, 1999); missed two games.

Season Team	League	REGULAR SEASON								PLAYOFFS				
		Gms.	G	A	Pts.	PIM	+/-	PP	SH	Gms.	G	A	Pts.	PIM
87-88—Trois-Rivieres	QMJHL	67	3	13	16	135	...	...	...	—	—	—	—	—
88-89—Trois-Rivieres	QMJHL	38	2	16	18	111	...	...	...	—	—	—	—	—
—Verdun	QMJHL	28	2	15	17	66	...	...	...	—	—	—	—	—
—Sherbrooke	AHL	1	0	0	0	0	...	...	...	—	—	—	—	—
89-90—St. Hyacinthe	QMJHL	68	13	38	51	152	...	...	...	11	3	4	7	67
—Sherbrooke	AHL	—	—	—	—	—	...	...	...	2	0	0	0	0
90-91—Fredericton	AHL	71	1	11	12	108	...	...	...	2	1	0	1	29
91-92—Fredericton	AHL	59	2	11	13	98	...	...	...	6	1	0	1	4
92-93—Fredericton	AHL	54	3	13	16	93	...	...	...	—	—	—	—	—
—Montreal	NHL	3	0	0	0	2	0	0	0	—	—	—	—	—
—Atlanta	IHL	11	0	2	2	12	...	...	...	3	0	1	1	6
93-94—Atlanta	IHL	66	5	18	23	144	...	...	...	14	1	4	5	28
—Tampa Bay	NHL	4	0	0	0	2	0	0	0	—	—	—	—	—
94-95—Tampa Bay	NHL	45	1	4	5	26	1	0	0	—	—	—	—	—
95-96—Tampa Bay	NHL	14	0	0	0	18	-6	0	0	—	—	—	—	—
—Portland	AHL	45	0	8	8	88	...	...	...	20	1	1	2	33
—Washington	NHL	4	0	1	1	4	3	0	0	6	0	0	0	8
96-97—Washington	NHL	25	1	1	2	20	1	0	0	—	—	—	—	—
—Portland	AHL	29	6	8	14	55	...	...	...	5	0	3	3	0
97-98—Saint John	AHL	56	8	20	28	136	...	...	...	20	1	7	8	55
—Calgary	NHL	2	0	0	0	4	0	0	0	—	—	—	—	—
98-99—Calgary	NHL	12	0	1	1	14	-6	0	0	—	—	—	—	—
—Saint John	AHL	50	10	12	22	148	...	...	...	3	1	0	1	22
99-00—Saint John	AHL	37	2	15	17	82	...	...	...	—	—	—	—	—
—Calgary	NHL	21	0	0	0	37	-3	0	0	—	—	—	—	—
NHL Totals (8 years)		130	2	7	9	127	-10	0	0	6	0	0	0	8

CHARTRAND, BRAD — RW — KINGS

PERSONAL: Born December 14, 1974, in Winnipeg. ... 5-11/191. ... Shoots left.
TRANSACTIONS/CAREER NOTES: Signed as non-drafted free agent by Los Angeles Kings (July 21, 1999).

Season Team	League	REGULAR SEASON								PLAYOFFS				
		Gms.	G	A	Pts.	PIM	+/-	PP	SH	Gms.	G	A	Pts.	PIM
88-89—Winnipeg	MAHA	24	30	50	80	40	...	...	...	—	—	—	—	—
89-90—Winnipeg	MAHA	24	26	55	81	40	...	...	...	—	—	—	—	—
90-91—Winnipeg	MAHA	34	26	45	71	40	...	...	...	—	—	—	—	—
91-92—St. James	MJHL					Statistics unavailable.				—	—	—	—	—
92-93—Cornell	ECAC	26	10	6	16	16	...	...	...	—	—	—	—	—
93-94—Cornell	ECAC	30	4	14	18	48	...	...	...	—	—	—	—	—
94-95—Cornell	ECAC	28	9	9	18	10	...	...	...	—	—	—	—	—
95-96—Cornell	ECAC	34	24	19	43	16	...	...	...	—	—	—	—	—

C

Season Team	League	REGULAR SEASON								PLAYOFFS				
		Gms.	G	A	Pts.	PIM	+/-	PP	SH	Gms.	G	A	Pts.	PIM
96-97—Canadian Nat'l Team ...	Int'l	54	10	14	24	42	...	...	...	—	—	—	—	—
97-98—Canadian Nat'l Team ...	Int'l	60	24	30	54	47	...	...	...	—	—	—	—	—
—HC Rapperswill..........	Switz.	8	2	3	5	4	...	...	...	—	—	—	—	—
98-99—St. John's.............	AHL	64	16	14	30	48	...	...	...	5	0	2	2	2
99-00—Los Angeles..............	NHL	50	6	6	12	17	4	0	1	4	0	0	0	6
—Long Beach................	IHL	1	0	0	0	0	...	...	...	3	0	0	0	0
—Lowell.....................	AHL	16	5	10	15	8	...	...	...	—	—	—	—	—
NHL Totals (1 year).............		50	6	6	12	17	4	0	1	4	0	0	0	6

CHASE, KELLY — RW

PERSONAL: Born October 25, 1967, in Porcupine Plain, Sask. ... 5-11/201. ... Shoots right. ... Full Name: Kelly Wayne Chase.
HIGH SCHOOL: Porcupine Plain (Sask.).
TRANSACTIONS/CAREER NOTES: Signed as non-drafted free agent by St. Louis Blues (May 24, 1988). ... Bruised right foot (January 1990). ... Suffered back spasms (March 1990). ... Suspended 10 games by NHL for fighting (March 18, 1991). ... Injured knee (December 11, 1991); missed two games. ... Sprained left wrist (January 14, 1992); missed three games. ... Bruised thigh (February 2, 1992); missed five games. ... Injured hand (February 23, 1992); missed four games. ... Strained groin (October 26, 1992); missed six games. ... Injured wrist (January 9, 1993); missed five games. ... Bruised lower leg (March 30, 1993); missed last six games of season. ... Suffered from the flu (December 4, 1993); missed one game. ... Injured leg (January 2, 1994); missed four games. ... Injured elbow (January 28, 1994); missed three games. ... Pulled groin (March 24, 1994); missed three games. ... Injured hand (April 5, 1994); missed one game. ... Selected by Hartford Whalers in 1994-95 waiver draft for cash (January 18, 1995). ... Suffered back spasms (February 24, 1995); missed 14 games. ... Suffered sore back (April 9, 1995); missed six games. ... Strained groin and injured neck (December 6, 1995); missed 10 games. ... Bruised hand (January 24, 1996); missed three games. ... Sprained knee (February 21, 1996); missed three games. ... Underwent arthroscopic knee surgery (December 13, 1996); missed 11 games. ... Traded by Whalers to Toronto Maple Leafs for eighth-round pick (RW Jaroslav Svoboda) in 1998 draft (March 18, 1997). ... Suffered from tendinitis in knee (March 19, 1997); missed 10 games. ... Traded by Maple Leafs to Blues for future considerations (September 30, 1997). ... Strained groin (November 6, 1997); missed two games. ... Injured thumb (December 4, 1997); missed three games. ... Strained knee (December 29, 1997); missed two games. ... Suffered sore leg (March 21, 1998); missed four games. ... Suspended one game by NHL for fighting (April 16, 1998). ... Bruised knee (October 31, 1998); missed three games. ... Injured groin (March 9, 1999); missed five games. ... Injured shoulder (April 1, 1999); missed remainder of season. ... Sprained right knee (November 7, 1999); missed 13 games.
HONORS: Won King Clancy Memorial Trophy (1997-98).

Season Team	League	REGULAR SEASON								PLAYOFFS				
		Gms.	G	A	Pts.	PIM	+/-	PP	SH	Gms.	G	A	Pts.	PIM
85-86—Saskatoon...................	WHL	57	7	18	25	172	...	...	...	10	3	4	7	37
86-87—Saskatoon...................	WHL	68	17	29	46	285	...	...	...	11	2	8	10	37
87-88—Saskatoon...................	WHL	70	21	34	55	*343	...	...	...	9	3	5	8	32
88-89—Peoria	IHL	38	14	7	21	278	...	...	...	—	—	—	—	—
89-90—Peoria	IHL	10	1	2	3	76	...	...	...	—	—	—	—	—
—St. Louis	NHL	43	1	3	4	244	-1	0	0	9	1	0	1	46
90-91—Peoria	IHL	61	20	34	54	406	...	...	...	10	4	3	7	61
—St. Louis	NHL	2	1	0	1	15	1	0	0	6	0	0	0	18
91-92—St. Louis	NHL	46	1	2	3	264	-6	0	0	1	0	0	0	7
92-93—St. Louis	NHL	49	2	5	7	204	-9	0	0	—	—	—	—	—
93-94—St. Louis	NHL	68	2	5	7	278	-5	0	0	4	0	1	1	6
94-95—Hartford	NHL	28	0	4	4	141	1	0	0	—	—	—	—	—
95-96—Hartford	NHL	55	2	4	6	230	-4	0	0	—	—	—	—	—
96-97—Hartford	NHL	28	1	2	3	122	2	0	0	—	—	—	—	—
—Toronto	NHL	2	0	0	0	27	0	0	0	—	—	—	—	—
97-98—St. Louis	NHL	67	4	3	7	231	10	0	0	7	0	0	0	23
98-99—St. Louis	NHL	45	3	7	10	143	2	0	0	—	—	—	—	—
99-00—St. Louis	NHL	25	0	1	1	118	-5	0	0	—	—	—	—	—
NHL Totals (11 years)..........		458	17	36	53	2017	-14	0	0	27	1	1	2	100

CHEBATURKIN, VLADIMIR — D — BLUES

PERSONAL: Born April 23, 1975, in Tyumen, U.S.S.R. ... 6-2/212. ... Shoots left. ... Name pronounced VLAD-ih-meer chuh-buh-TUHR-kihn.
TRANSACTIONS/CAREER NOTES: Selected by New York Islanders in third round (third Islanders pick, 66th overall) of NHL entry draft (June 26, 1993). ... Signed as free agent by St. Louis Blues (June 12, 2000).

Season Team	League	REGULAR SEASON								PLAYOFFS				
		Gms.	G	A	Pts.	PIM	+/-	PP	SH	Gms.	G	A	Pts.	PIM
92-93—Kristall Elektrostal.......	CIS Div. II						Statistics unavailable.							
93-94—Kristall Elektrostal.......	CIS Div. II	42	4	4	8	38	...	...	...	—	—	—	—	—
94-95—Kristall Elektrostal.......	CIS	52	2	6	8	90	...	...	...	—	—	—	—	—
95-96—Kristall Elektrostal.......	CIS	44	1	6	7	30	...	...	...	1	0	0	0	0
96-97—Utah.........................	IHL	68	0	4	4	34	...	...	...	—	—	—	—	—
97-98—Kentucky....................	AHL	54	6	8	14	52	...	...	...	2	0	0	0	4
—New York Islanders.....	NHL	2	0	2	2	0	-1	0	0	—	—	—	—	—
98-99—Lowell	AHL	69	2	12	14	85	...	...	...	3	0	0	0	0
—New York Islanders.....	NHL	8	0	0	0	12	6	0	0	—	—	—	—	—
99-00—Lowell	AHL	63	1	8	9	118	...	...	...	7	0	4	4	11
—New York Islanders.....	NHL	17	1	1	2	8	-3	0	0	—	—	—	—	—
NHL Totals (3 years)..........		27	1	3	4	20	2	0	0					

CHEECHOO, JONATHAN   RW   SHARKS

PERSONAL: Born July 15, 1980, in Moose Factory, Ont. ... 6-0/205. ... Shoots right.
TRANSACTIONS/CAREER NOTES: Selected by San Jose Sharks in second round (second Sharks pick, 29th overall) of NHL entry draft (June 27, 1998).

Season Team	League	REGULAR SEASON								PLAYOFFS				
		Gms.	G	A	Pts.	PIM	+/-	PP	SH	Gms.	G	A	Pts.	PIM
96-97—Kitchener Jr. B	OHA	43	35	41	76	33	...	...	...	—	—	—	—	—
97-98—Belleville	OHL	64	31	45	76	62	...	...	...	10	4	2	6	10
98-99—Belleville	OHL	63	35	47	82	74	...	...	...	21	15	15	30	27
99-00—Belleville	OHL	66	45	46	91	102	...	...	...	16	5	12	17	16

CHELIOS, CHRIS   D   RED WINGS

PERSONAL: Born January 25, 1962, in Chicago. ... 6-1/190. ... Shoots right. ... Full Name: Christos K. Chelios. ... Cousin of Nikos Tselios, defenseman, Carolina Hurricanes system. ... Name pronounced CHEH-lee-ohz.
COLLEGE: Wisconsin.
TRANSACTIONS/CAREER NOTES: Selected by Montreal Canadiens as underage junior in second round (fifth Canadiens pick, 40th overall) of NHL entry draft (June 10, 1981). ... Sprained right ankle (January 1985). ... Injured left knee (April 1985). ... Sprained knee (December 19, 1985). ... Reinjured knee (January 20, 1986). ... Suffered back spasms (October 1986). ... Fractured finger on left hand (December 1987). ... Bruised tailbone (February 7, 1988). ... Strained left knee ligaments (February 1990). ... Underwent surgery to repair torn abdominal muscle (April 30, 1990). ... Traded by Canadiens with second-round pick (C Michael Pomichter) in 1991 draft to Chicago Blackhawks for C Denis Savard (June 29, 1990). ... Lacerated left temple (February 9, 1991). ... Suspended four games by NHL (October 15, 1993). ... Suspended four games without pay and fined $500 by NHL for eye-scratching incident (February 5, 1994). ... Played in Europe during 1994-95 NHL lockout. ... Sprained knee (March 1, 1997); missed eight games. ... Suffered sore back (April 6, 1997); missed one game. ... Strained groin (November 12, 1998); missed five games. ... Traded by Blackhawks to Detroit Red Wings for D Anders Eriksson, first-round pick (D Steve McCarthy) in 1999 draft and first-round pick in 2001 draft (March 23, 1999). ... Strained groin (April 7, 1999); missed two games. ... Suffered injury (April 7, 2000); missed one game.
HONORS: Named to NCAA All-Tournament team (1982-83). ... Named to WCHA All-Star second team (1982-83). ... Named to NHL All-Rookie team (1984-85). ... Played in NHL All-Star Game (1985, 1990-1994, 1996-1998 and 2000). ... Won James Norris Memorial Trophy (1988-89, 1992-93 and 1995-96). ... Named to THE SPORTING NEWS All-Star first team (1988-89, 1992-93 and 1995-96). ... Named to NHL All-Star first team (1988-89, 1992-93, 1994-95 and 1995-96). ... Named to THE SPORTING NEWS All-Star second team (1990-91 and 1991-92). ... Named to NHL All-Star second team (1990-91). ... Named to THE SPORTING NEWS All-Star team (1996-97).
MISCELLANEOUS: Member of Stanley Cup championship team (1986). ... Captain of Chicago Blackhawks (1996-97 through March 23, 1999).

Season Team	League	REGULAR SEASON								PLAYOFFS				
		Gms.	G	A	Pts.	PIM	+/-	PP	SH	Gms.	G	A	Pts.	PIM
79-80—Moose Jaw	SJHL	53	12	31	43	118	...	...	...	—	—	—	—	—
80-81—Moose Jaw	SJHL	54	23	64	87	175	...	...	...	—	—	—	—	—
81-82—Univ. of Wisconsin	WCHA	43	6	43	49	50	...	...	...	—	—	—	—	—
82-83—Univ. of Wisconsin	WCHA	45	16	32	48	62	...	...	...	—	—	—	—	—
83-84—U.S. national team	Int'l	60	14	35	49	58	...	...	...	—	—	—	—	—
—U.S. Olympic team	Int'l	6	0	3	3	8	...	...	...	—	—	—	—	—
—Montreal	NHL	12	0	2	2	12	-5	0	0	15	1	9	10	17
84-85—Montreal	NHL	74	9	55	64	87	11	2	1	9	2	8	10	17
85-86—Montreal	NHL	41	8	26	34	67	4	2	0	20	2	9	11	49
86-87—Montreal	NHL	71	11	33	44	124	-5	6	0	17	4	9	13	38
87-88—Montreal	NHL	71	20	41	61	172	15	10	1	11	3	1	4	29
88-89—Montreal	NHL	80	15	58	73	185	35	8	0	21	4	15	19	28
89-90—Montreal	NHL	53	9	22	31	136	20	1	2	5	0	1	1	8
90-91—Chicago	NHL	77	12	52	64	192	23	5	2	6	1	7	8	46
91-92—Chicago	NHL	80	9	47	56	245	24	2	2	18	6	15	21	37
92-93—Chicago	NHL	84	15	58	73	282	14	8	0	4	0	2	2	14
93-94—Chicago	NHL	76	16	44	60	212	12	7	1	6	1	1	2	8
94-95—Biel-Bienne	Switzerland	3	0	3	3	4	...	...	...	—	—	—	—	—
—Chicago	NHL	48	5	33	38	72	17	3	1	16	4	7	11	12
95-96—Chicago	NHL	81	14	58	72	140	25	7	0	9	0	3	3	8
96-97—Chicago	NHL	72	10	38	48	112	16	2	0	6	0	1	1	8
97-98—Chicago	NHL	81	3	39	42	151	-7	1	0	—	—	—	—	—
—U.S. Olympic team	Int'l	4	2	0	2	2	...	...	...	—	—	—	—	—
98-99—Chicago	NHL	65	8	26	34	89	-4	2	1	—	—	—	—	—
—Detroit	NHL	10	1	1	2	4	5	1	0	10	0	4	4	14
99-00—Detroit	NHL	81	3	31	34	103	48	0	0	9	0	1	1	8
NHL Totals (17 years)		1157	168	664	832	2385	248	67	11	182	28	93	121	341

CHERNESKI, STEFAN   RW   RANGERS

PERSONAL: Born September 19, 1978, in Winnipeg. ... 6-0/195. ... Shoots left. ... Name pronounced chair-NEHZ-kee.
TRANSACTIONS/CAREER NOTES: Selected by New York Rangers in first round (first Rangers pick, 19th overall) of NHL entry draft (June 21, 1997). ... Injured knee (November 1998); missed remainder of season.
HONORS: Won Can.HL Scholastic Player of the Year Award (1996-97).

Season Team	League	REGULAR SEASON								PLAYOFFS				
		Gms.	G	A	Pts.	PIM	+/-	PP	SH	Gms.	G	A	Pts.	PIM
95-96—Brandon	WHL	58	8	21	29	62	...	...	...	19	3	1	4	11
96-97—Brandon	WHL	56	39	29	68	83	...	...	...	0	0	0	0	0
97-98—Brandon	WHL	65	43	38	81	127	...	...	...	18	*15	8	23	21
98-99—Hartford	AHL	11	1	2	3	41	...	...	...	—	—	—	—	—
99-00—Hartford	AHL	1	0	0	0	0	...	...	...	—	—	—	—	—

C

CHERNOV, MIKHAIL   D   FLYERS

PERSONAL: Born November 11, 1978, in Prokopjevsk, U.S.S.R. ... 6-2/196. ... Shoots right.
TRANSACTIONS/CAREER NOTES: Selected by Philadelphia Flyers in fourth round (fourth Flyers pick, 103rd overall) of NHL entry draft (June 21, 1997).

Season Team	League	Gms.	G	A	Pts.	PIM	+/-	PP	SH	Gms.	G	A	Pts.	PIM
					REGULAR SEASON							PLAYOFFS		
94-95—Metal.-2 Novok.	CIS Div. II	12	0	3	3	0	...	...	...	—	—	—	—	—
95-96—Metal.-2 Novok.	CIS Div. II	40	2	7	9	10	...	...	...	—	—	—	—	—
96-97—Torpedo-2 Yaroslavl....	Rus. Div. III	33	4	2	6	40	...	...	...	—	—	—	—	—
—Torpedo Yaroslavl	Russian	5	0	0	0	0	...	...	...	—	—	—	—	—
97-98—Torpedo Yaroslavl	Russian	7	0	0	0	4	...	...	...	—	—	—	—	—
98-99—Philadelphia	AHL	56	4	3	7	98	...	...	...	14	1	0	1	8
99-00—Philadelphia	AHL	67	10	6	16	54	...	...	...	5	1	2	3	22

CHIMERA, JASON   C   OILERS

PERSONAL: Born May 2, 1979, in Edmonton. ... 6-0/180. ... Shoots left. ... Name pronounced chih-MAIR-uh.
TRANSACTIONS/CAREER NOTES: Selected by Edmonton Oilers in fifth round (fifth Oilers pick, 121st overall) of NHL entry draft (June 21, 1997).

Season Team	League	Gms.	G	A	Pts.	PIM	+/-	PP	SH	Gms.	G	A	Pts.	PIM
					REGULAR SEASON							PLAYOFFS		
96-97—Medicine Hat..............	WHL	71	16	23	39	64	...	...	...	4	0	1	1	4
97-98—Medicine Hat..............	WHL	72	34	32	66	93	...	...	...	—	—	—	—	—
—Hamilton	AHL	4	0	0	0	8	...	...	...	—	—	—	—	—
98-99—Medicine Hat..............	WHL	37	18	22	40	84	...	...	...	—	—	—	—	—
—Brandon	WHL	21	14	12	26	32	...	...	...	5	4	1	5	8
99-00—Hamilton	AHL	78	15	13	28	77	...	...	...	10	0	2	2	12

CHORSKE, TOM   LW

PERSONAL: Born September 18, 1966, in Minneapolis. ... 6-0/212. ... Shoots right. ... Full Name: Thomas Chorske. ... Name pronounced CHOHR-skee.
HIGH SCHOOL: Southwest (Minneapolis).
COLLEGE: Minnesota.
TRANSACTIONS/CAREER NOTES: Selected by Montreal Canadiens in first round (second Canadiens pick, 16th overall) of NHL entry draft (June 15, 1985). ... Separated shoulder (November 18, 1988); missed 11 games. ... Suffered hip pointer (October 26, 1989). ... Sprained right shoulder (March 14, 1991). ... Traded by Canadiens with RW Stephane Richer to New Jersey Devils for LW Kirk Muller and G Roland Melanson (September 20, 1991). ... Suffered charley horse (January 14, 1993); missed two games. ... Injured elbow (April 14, 1994); missed one game. ... Played in Europe during 1994-95 NHL lockout. ... Pulled groin (April 1, 1995); missed one game. ... Bruised leg (April 20, 1995); missed two games. ... Claimed on waivers by Ottawa Senators (October 4, 1995). ... Injured back during 1995-96 season; missed two games. ... Suffered from the flu during 1995-96 season; missed one game. ... Bruised hip (October 9, 1996); missed four games. ... Strained hip flexor (October 28, 1996); missed three games. ... Underwent retinal surgery on left eye (December 15, 1996); missed six games. ... Claimed by New York Islanders from Senators in NHL waiver draft (September 27, 1997). ... Strained groin (October 14, 1998); missed one game. ... Traded by Islanders with eighth-round pick (C Maxim Orlov) in 1999 draft to Washington Capitals for sixth-round pick (RW Bjorn Melin) in 1999 draft (October 16, 1998). ... Strained groin (November 28, 1998); missed 45 games. ... Traded by Capitals to Calgary Flames for future considerations (March 22, 1999). ... Reinjured groin (April 4, 1999); missed two games ... Signed as free agent by Pittsburgh Penguins (September 2, 1999). ... Separated shoulder (December 18, 1999); missed 11 games. ... Bruised shoulder (February 3, 2000); missed final 28 games of season.
HONORS: Named to WCHA All-Star first team (1988-89).
MISCELLANEOUS: Member of Stanley Cup championship team (1995). ... Scored on a penalty shot (vs. Patrick Roy, March 7, 1998).

Season Team	League	Gms.	G	A	Pts.	PIM	+/-	PP	SH	Gms.	G	A	Pts.	PIM
					REGULAR SEASON							PLAYOFFS		
84-85—Southwest HS.............	Mich. H.S.	23	44	26	70	...	...	...	...	—	—	—	—	—
85-86—Univ. of Minnesota......	WCHA	39	6	4	10	6	...	...	...	—	—	—	—	—
86-87—Univ. of Minnesota......	WCHA	47	20	22	42	20	...	...	...	—	—	—	—	—
87-88—U.S. national team	Int'l	36	9	16	25	24	...	...	...	—	—	—	—	—
88-89—Univ. of Minnesota......	WCHA	37	25	24	49	28	...	...	...	—	—	—	—	—
89-90—Montreal	NHL	14	3	1	4	2	2	0	0	—	—	—	—	—
—Sherbrooke................	AHL	59	22	24	46	54	...	...	...	12	4	4	8	8
90-91—Montreal	NHL	57	9	11	20	32	-8	3	0	—	—	—	—	—
91-92—New Jersey	NHL	76	19	17	36	32	8	0	3	7	0	3	3	4
92-93—New Jersey	NHL	50	7	12	19	25	-1	0	0	1	0	0	0	0
—Utica	AHL	6	1	4	5	2	...	...	...	—	—	—	—	—
93-94—New Jersey	NHL	76	21	20	41	32	14	1	1	20	4	3	7	0
94-95—Milan	Italy	7	11	5	16	6	...	...	...	—	—	—	—	—
—New Jersey	NHL	42	10	8	18	16	-4	0	0	17	1	5	6	4
95-96—Ottawa	NHL	72	15	14	29	21	-9	0	2	—	—	—	—	—
96-97—Ottawa	NHL	68	18	8	26	16	-1	1	1	5	0	1	1	2
97-98—New York Islanders.....	NHL	82	12	23	35	39	7	1	4	—	—	—	—	—
98-99—New York Islanders.....	NHL	2	0	1	1	2	1	0	0	—	—	—	—	—
—Washington	NHL	17	0	2	2	4	-4	0	0	—	—	—	—	—
—Calgary	NHL	7	0	0	0	2	-5	0	0	—	—	—	—	—
99-00—Pittsburgh..................	NHL	33	1	5	6	2	-2	0	0	—	—	—	—	—
NHL Totals (11 years).........		596	115	122	237	225	-2	6	11	50	5	12	17	10

CHOUINARD, MARC   C   MIGHTY DUCKS

PERSONAL: Born May 5, 1977, in Charlesbourg, Ont. ... 6-5/204. ... Shoots right. ... Cousin of Eric Chouinard, center, Montreal Canadiens system; and nephew of Guy Chouinard, center with Atlanta/Calgary Flames (1974-75 through 1982-83) and St. Louis Blues (1983-84). ... Name pronounced shwee-NAHRD.

TRANSACTIONS/CAREER NOTES: Selected by Winnipeg Jets in second round (second Jets pick, 32nd overall) of NHL entry draft (July 8, 1995). ... Traded by Jets with RW Teemu Selanne and fourth-round pick (traded to Toronto) in 1996 draft to Mighty Ducks of Anaheim for C Chad Kilger, D Oleg Tverdovsky and third-round pick (D Per-Anton Lundstrom) in 1996 draft (February 7, 1996). ... Tore Achilles' tendon (October 31, 1997); missed remainder of season.

		REGULAR SEASON								PLAYOFFS				
Season Team	League	Gms.	G	A	Pts.	PIM	+/-	PP	SH	Gms.	G	A	Pts.	PIM
93-94—Beauport	QMJHL	62	11	19	30	23	...	...	...	13	2	5	7	2
94-95—Beauport	QMJHL	68	24	40	64	32	...	...	...	18	1	6	7	4
95-96—Beauport	QMJHL	30	14	21	35	19	...	...	...	—	—	—	—	—
—Halifax	QMJHL	24	6	12	18	17	...	...	...	6	2	1	3	2
96-97—Halifax	QMJHL	63	24	49	73	52	...	...	...	18	10	16	26	12
97-98—Cincinnati	AHL	8	1	2	3	4	...	...	...	—	—	—	—	—
98-99—Cincinnati	AHL	69	7	8	15	20	...	...	...	3	0	0	0	4
99-00—Cincinnati	AHL	70	17	16	33	29	...	...	...	—	—	—	—	—

CHOUINARD, MATHIEU   G   SENATORS

PERSONAL: Born April 11, 1980, in Laval, Que. ... 6-1/209. ... Catches left.

TRANSACTIONS/CAREER NOTES: Selected by Ottawa Senators in first round (first Senators pick, 15th overall) of NHL entry draft (June 27, 1998). ... Returned to draft pool by Senators and selected by Senators in second round (second Senators pick, 45th overall) of NHL entry draft (June 24, 2000).

HONORS: Named to QMJHL All-Star first team (1998-99). ... Won Michel Briere Trophy (1998-99 and 1999-2000).

		REGULAR SEASON							PLAYOFFS						
Season Team	League	Gms.	Min	W	L	T	GA	SO	Avg.	Gms.	Min.	W	L	GA	SO	Avg.
96-97—Shawinigan	QMJHL	17	793	4	7	1	51	0	3.86	4	264	1	3	15	0	3.41
97-98—Shawinigan	QMJHL	55	3055	*32	18	3	142	2	2.79	6	348	2	4	24	0	4.14
98-99—Shawinigan	QMJHL	56	3288	36	16	4	150	*5	2.74	6	392	2	4	27	0	4.13
99-00—Shawinigan	QMJHL	†59	*3338	32	20	5	186	4	3.34	13	769	7	6	41	0	3.20

CHRISTIE, RYAN   LW   STARS

PERSONAL: Born July 3, 1978, in Beamsville, Ont. ... 6-3/200. ... Shoots left.

TRANSACTIONS/CAREER NOTES: Selected by Dallas Stars in fifth round (third Stars pick, 112th overall) of NHL entry draft (June 22, 1996).

HONORS: Named to OHL All-Star second team (1995-96).

		REGULAR SEASON								PLAYOFFS				
Season Team	League	Gms.	G	A	Pts.	PIM	+/-	PP	SH	Gms.	G	A	Pts.	PIM
95-96—Owen Sound	OHL	66	29	17	46	93	...	...	...	6	1	1	2	0
96-97—Owen Sound	OHL	66	23	29	52	136	...	...	...	4	1	1	2	8
97-98—Owen Sound	OHL	66	39	41	80	208	...	...	...	11	3	5	8	13
98-99—Michigan	IHL	48	4	5	9	74	...	...	...	3	1	1	2	2
99-00—Michigan	IHL	76	24	25	49	140	...	...	...	—	—	—	—	—
—Dallas	NHL	5	0	0	0	0	-1	0	0	—	—	—	—	—
NHL Totals (1 year)		5	0	0	0	0	-1	0	0					

CHUBAROV, ARTEM   C   CANUCKS

PERSONAL: Born December 12, 1979, in Gorky, U.S.S.R. ... 6-1/189. ... Shoots left.

TRANSACTIONS/CAREER NOTES: Selected by Vancouver Canucks in second round (second Canucks pick, 31st overall) of NHL entry draft (June 27, 1998). ... Injured hip (February 19, 2000); missed nine games.

		REGULAR SEASON								PLAYOFFS				
Season Team	League	Gms.	G	A	Pts.	PIM	+/-	PP	SH	Gms.	G	A	Pts.	PIM
94-95—Tor. Nizhny Nov.	CIS Jr.	60	20	30	50	20	...	...	...	—	—	—	—	—
95-96—Tor. Nizhny Nov.	CIS Jr.	60	22	25	47	20	...	...	...	—	—	—	—	—
96-97—Tor.-2 Nizhny Nov.	Rus. Div. III	40	24	5	29	16	...	...	...	—	—	—	—	—
—Tor. Nizhny Nov.	Rus. Div. II	15	1	1	2	8	...	...	...	—	—	—	—	—
97-98—Dynamo Moscow	Russian	30	1	4	5	4	...	...	...	—	—	—	—	—
98-99—Dynamo Moscow	Russian	34	8	2	10	10	...	...	...	12	0	0	0	4
99-00—Vancouver	NHL	49	1	8	9	10	-4	0	0	—	—	—	—	—
—Syracuse	AHL	14	7	6	13	4	...	...	...	1	0	0	0	0
NHL Totals (1 year)		49	1	8	9	10	-4	0	0					

CISAR, MARIAN   RW   PREDATORS

PERSONAL: Born February 25, 1978, in Bratislava, Czechoslovakia. ... 6-0/192. ... Shoots right. ... Name pronounced say-SAHR.

TRANSACTIONS/CAREER NOTES: Selected by Los Angeles Kings in second round (second Kings pick, 37th overall) of NHL entry draft (June 22, 1996). ... Traded by Kings to Nashville Predators for future considerations (May 29, 1998).

Season Team	League	REGULAR SEASON								PLAYOFFS				
		Gms.	G	A	Pts.	PIM	+/-	PP	SH	Gms.	G	A	Pts.	PIM
94-95—Slov. Bratislava Jrs.	Slovakia	38	42	28	70	16	...	...	...	—	—	—	—	—
95-96—Slov. Bratislava Jrs.	Slovakia	16	26	17	43	2	...	...	...	—	—	—	—	—
—Slovan Bratislava	Slovakia	13	3	3	6	0	...	...	...	6	3	0	3	0
96-97—Spokane.....................	WHL	70	31	35	66	52	...	...	...	9	6	2	8	4
97-98—Spokane.....................	WHL	52	33	40	73	34	...	...	...	18	8	5	13	8
98-99—Milwaukee..................	IHL	51	11	17	28	31	...	...	...	2	0	0	0	12
99-00—Milwaukee..................	IHL	78	20	32	52	82	...	...	...	1	0	0	0	0
—Nashville................	NHL	3	0	0	0	4	-2	0	0	—	—	—	—	—
NHL Totals (1 year)............		3	0	0	0	4	-2	0	0					

CLARK, BRETT   D   THRASHERS

PERSONAL: Born December 23, 1976, in Wapella, Sask. ... 6-1/185. ... Shoots left.
COLLEGE: Maine.
TRANSACTIONS/CAREER NOTES: Selected by Montreal Canadiens in sixth round (seventh Canadiens pick, 154th overall) of NHL entry draft (June 22, 1996). ... Suffered concussion (November 19, 1998); missed four games. ... Selected by Atlanta Thrashers in NHL expansion draft (June 25, 1999).
HONORS: Named to Hockey East All-Rookie team (1995-96).

Season Team	League	REGULAR SEASON								PLAYOFFS				
		Gms.	G	A	Pts.	PIM	+/-	PP	SH	Gms.	G	A	Pts.	PIM
94-95—Melville	SJHL	62	19	32	51	77	...	...	...	—	—	—	—	—
95-96—Univ. of Maine	Hockey East	39	7	31	38	22	...	...	...	—	—	—	—	—
96-97—Canadian nat'l team	Int'l	60	12	20	32	87	...	...	...	—	—	—	—	—
97-98—Montreal	NHL	41	1	0	1	20	-3	0	0	—	—	—	—	—
—Fredericton	AHL	20	0	6	6	6	...	...	...	4	0	1	1	17
98-99—Montreal	NHL	61	2	2	4	16	-3	0	0	—	—	—	—	—
—Fredericton	AHL	3	1	0	1	0	...	...	...	—	—	—	—	—
99-00—Orlando	IHL	63	9	17	26	31	...	...	...	6	0	1	1	0
—Atlanta	NHL	14	0	1	1	4	-12	0	0	—	—	—	—	—
NHL Totals (3 years)...........		116	3	3	6	40	-18	0	0					

CLARK, CHRIS   RW   FLAMES

PERSONAL: Born March 8, 1976, in South Windsor, Conn. ... 6-0/202. ... Shoots right.
HIGH SCHOOL: South Windsor (Conn.).
COLLEGE: Clarkson (N.Y.).
TRANSACTIONS/CAREER NOTES: Selected by Calgary Flames in third round (third Flames pick, 77th overall) of NHL entry draft (June 29, 1994). ... Injured shoulder (January 15, 2000); missed one game. ... Suffered injury (March 31, 2000); missed final five games of season.
HONORS: Named to ECAC All-Star second team (1997-98).

Season Team	League	REGULAR SEASON								PLAYOFFS				
		Gms.	G	A	Pts.	PIM	+/-	PP	SH	Gms.	G	A	Pts.	PIM
93-94—Springfield Jr. B..........	NEJHL	35	31	26	57	185	...	...	...	—	—	—	—	—
94-95—Clarkson	ECAC	32	12	11	23	92	...	...	...	—	—	—	—	—
95-96—Clarkson	ECAC	38	10	8	18	108	...	...	...	—	—	—	—	—
96-97—Clarkson	ECAC	37	23	25	48	86	...	...	...	—	—	—	—	—
97-98—Clarkson	ECAC	35	18	21	39	*106	...	...	...	—	—	—	—	—
98-99—Saint John	AHL	73	13	27	40	123	...	...	...	7	2	4	6	15
99-00—Saint John	AHL	48	16	17	33	134	...	...	...	—	—	—	—	—
—Calgary	NHL	22	0	1	1	14	-3	0	0	—	—	—	—	—
NHL Totals (1 year)............		22	0	1	1	14	-3	0	0					

CLARK, WENDEL   LW

PERSONAL: Born October 25, 1966, in Kelvington, Sask. ... 5-10/194. ... Shoots left. ... Brother of Kerry Clark, right winger with New York Islanders and Calgary Flames organizations (1986-87 through 1991-92); and cousin of Joey Kocur, right winger, Detroit Red Wings.
TRANSACTIONS/CAREER NOTES: Selected by Toronto Maple Leafs as underage junior in first round (first Maple Leafs pick, first overall) of NHL entry draft (June 15, 1985). ... Suffered from virus (November 1985). ... Fractured right foot (November 26, 1985); missed 14 games. ... Suffered back spasms (November 1987); missed 23 games. ... Reinjured back (February 1988); missed final 39 games of regular season (March 1, 1989). ... Injured back prior to 1988-89 season; missed first 51 games. ... Bruised muscle above left knee (November 4, 1989); missed seven games. ... Tore ligament in right knee (January 26, 1990); missed 29 games. ... Separated left shoulder (December 18, 1990). ... Pulled rib cage muscle (February 6, 1991); missed 12 games. ... Partially tore knee ligaments (October 7, 1991); missed 12 games. ... Strained knee ligaments (November 6, 1991); missed 24 games. ... Injured groin (October 24, 1992); missed four games. ... Strained rib muscle (January 17, 1993); missed 13 games. ... Strained knee (October 13, 1993); missed two games. ... Bruised foot (December 22, 1993); missed 17 games. ... Traded by Maple Leafs with D Sylvain Lefebvre, RW Landon Wilson and first-round pick in 1994 draft (D Jeffrey Kealty) to Quebec Nordiques for C Mats Sundin, D Garth Butcher, LW Todd Warriner and first-round pick (traded to Washington Capitals) in 1994 draft (June 28, 1994). ... Injured thigh (March 18, 1995); missed 11 games. ... Fined §1,000 by NHL for elbowing (May 10, 1995). ... Nordiques franchise moved to Colorado and renamed Avalanche for 1995-96 season (June 21, 1995). ... Traded by Avalanche to New York Islanders for RW Claude Lemieux (October 3, 1995). ... Suffered back spasms (January 30, 1996); missed eight games. ... Traded by Islanders with D Mathieu Schneider and D D.J. Smith to Toronto Maple Leafs for LW Sean Haggerty, C Darby Hendrickson, D Kenny Jonsson and first-round pick (G Roberto Luongo) in 1997 draft (March 13, 1996). ... Fractured thumb (December 10, 1996); missed 16 games. ... Bruised back (April 2, 1997); missed one game. ... Strained groin (January 10, 1998); missed 29 games. ... Reinjured groin and underwent surgery (April 7, 1998); missed remainder of season. ... Signed as free agent by Tampa Bay Lightning (July 16, 1998). ... Strained groin (November 21, 1998); missed two games. ... Reinjured groin (December 20, 1998); missed one game. ... Reinjured groin (December 23, 1998); missed two games. ... Traded by Lightning with G Bill Ranford and sixth-round pick (RW Kent McDonnell) to Detroit Red Wings for G Kevin Hodson and second-round pick (RW Sheldon Keefe) in 1999 draft (March 23, 1999). ... Signed as free agent by Chicago Blackhawks (August 2, 1999). ... Injured groin (October 16, 1999); missed one game. ... Released by Blackhawks (November 18, 1999). ... Signed by Maple Leafs (January 9, 2000). ... Announced retirement (June 29, 2000).

HONORS: Won Top Defenseman Trophy (1984-85). ... Named to WHL (East) All-Star first team (1984-85). ... Named NHL Rookie of the Year by THE SPORTING NEWS (1985-86). ... Named to NHL All-Rookie team (1985-86). ... Played in NHL All-Star Game (1986 and 1999).
MISCELLANEOUS: Captain of Toronto Maple Leafs (1991-92 through 1993-94). ... Scored on a penalty shot (vs. Trevor Kidd, November 24, 1993). ... Failed to score on a penalty shot (vs. Darcy Wakaluk, December 21, 1995).
STATISTICAL PLATEAUS: Three-goal games: 1985-86 (1), 1989-90 (1), 1991-92 (2), 1993-94 (2), 1994-95 (1), 1998-99 (3). Total: 10. ... Four-goal games: 1986-87 (1), 1996-97 (1). Total: 2. ... Total hat tricks: 12.

			REGULAR SEASON								PLAYOFFS				
Season Team	League	Gms.	G	A	Pts.	PIM	+/-	PP	SH	Gms.	G	A	Pts.	PIM
83-84—Saskatoon..................	WHL	72	23	45	68	225	...	...	...	—	—	—	—	—
84-85—Saskatoon..................	WHL	64	32	55	87	253	...	...	...	3	3	3	6	7
85-86—Toronto......................	NHL	66	34	11	45	227	-27	4	0	10	5	1	6	47
86-87—Toronto......................	NHL	80	37	23	60	271	-23	15	0	13	6	5	11	38
87-88—Toronto......................	NHL	28	12	11	23	80	-13	4	0	—	—	—	—	—
88-89—Toronto......................	NHL	15	7	4	11	66	-3	3	0	—	—	—	—	—
89-90—Toronto......................	NHL	38	18	8	26	116	2	7	0	5	1	1	2	19
90-91—Toronto......................	NHL	63	18	16	34	152	-5	4	0	—	—	—	—	—
91-92—Toronto......................	NHL	43	19	21	40	123	-14	7	0	—	—	—	—	—
92-93—Toronto......................	NHL	66	17	22	39	193	2	2	0	21	10	10	20	51
93-94—Toronto......................	NHL	64	46	30	76	115	10	21	0	18	9	7	16	24
94-95—Quebec......................	NHL	37	12	18	30	45	-1	5	0	6	1	2	3	6
95-96—New York Islanders.....	NHL	58	24	19	43	60	-12	6	0	—	—	—	—	—
—Toronto......................	NHL	13	8	7	15	16	7	2	0	6	2	2	4	2
96-97—Toronto......................	NHL	65	30	19	49	75	-2	6	0	—	—	—	—	—
97-98—Toronto......................	NHL	47	12	7	19	80	-21	4	0	—	—	—	—	—
98-99—Tampa Bay.................	NHL	65	28	14	42	35	-25	11	0	—	—	—	—	—
—Detroit......................	NHL	12	4	2	6	2	1	0	0	10	2	3	5	10
99-00—Chicago......................	NHL	13	2	0	2	13	-2	0	0	—	—	—	—	—
—Toronto......................	NHL	20	2	2	4	21	-3	0	0	6	1	1	2	4
NHL Totals (15 years)........		793	330	234	564	1690	-129	101	0	95	37	32	69	201

CLEARY, DAN   LW   OILERS

PERSONAL: Born December 18, 1978, in Carbonear, Nfld. ... 6-0/203. ... Shoots left. ... Full Name: Daniel Cleary.
TRANSACTIONS/CAREER NOTES: Selected by Chicago Blackhawks in first round (first Blackhawks pick, 13th overall) of NHL entry draft (June 21, 1997). ... Traded by Blackhawks with C Chad Kilger, LW Ethan Moreau and D Christian Laflamme to Edmonton Oilers for D Boris Mironov, LW Dean McAmmond and D Jonas Elofsson (March 20, 1999).
HONORS: Named to OHL All-Star first team (1995-96 and 1996-97). ... Named to AHL All-Star second team (1999-2000).

			REGULAR SEASON								PLAYOFFS				
Season Team	League	Gms.	G	A	Pts.	PIM	+/-	PP	SH	Gms.	G	A	Pts.	PIM
93-94—Kingston	Tier II Jr. A	41	18	28	46	33	...	...	...	—	—	—	—	—
94-95—Belleville	OHL	62	26	55	81	62	...	...	...	16	7	10	17	23
95-96—Belleville	OHL	64	53	62	115	74	...	...	...	14	10	17	27	40
96-97—Belleville	OHL	64	32	48	80	88	...	...	...	6	3	4	7	6
97-98—Chicago......................	NHL	6	0	0	0	0	-2	0	0	—	—	—	—	—
—Indianapolis	IHL	4	2	1	3	6	...	...	...	—	—	—	—	—
—Belleville	OHL	30	16	31	47	14	...	...	...	10	6	*17	*23	10
98-99—Chicago......................	NHL	35	4	5	9	24	-1	0	0	—	—	—	—	—
—Portland....................	AHL	30	9	17	26	74	...	...	...	—	—	—	—	—
—Hamilton..................	AHL	9	0	1	1	7	...	...	...	3	0	0	0	0
99-00—Hamilton.....................	AHL	58	22	52	74	108	...	...	...	5	2	3	5	18
—Edmonton..................	NHL	17	3	2	5	8	-1	0	0	4	0	1	1	2
NHL Totals (3 years)...........		58	7	7	14	32	-4	0	0	4	0	1	1	2

CLOUTIER, DAN   G   LIGHTNING

PERSONAL: Born April 22, 1976, in Mont-Laurier, Que. ... 6-1/182. ... Catches left. ... Brother of Sylvain Cloutier, center, New Jersey Devils system. ... Name pronounced KLOO-tee-yay.
HIGH SCHOOL: Notre-Dame-des-Grands-Lacs (Sault Ste. Marie, Ont.).
TRANSACTIONS/CAREER NOTES: Selected by New York Rangers in first round (first Rangers pick, 26th overall) of NHL entry draft (June 28, 1994). ... Traded by Rangers with LW Niklas Sundstrom and first-(RW Nikita Alexeev) and third-round (traded to San Jose) picks in 2000 draft to Tampa Bay Lightning for first-round pick (RW Pavel Brendl) in 1999 draft (June 26, 1999). ... Strained groin (November 18, 1999); missed two games. ... Suspended four games by NHL for kicking incident (January 14, 2000). ... Strained groin (February 21, 2000); missed three games. ... Injured neck (March 14, 2000); missed four games. ... Strained medial collateral ligament in knee (March 28, 2000); missed five games.
HONORS: Named to OHL All-Star second team (1995-96). ... Won Dave Pinkney Trophy (1995-96). ... Named to AHL All-Rookie team (1996-97).
MISCELLANEOUS: Allowed a penalty shot goal (vs. Jeremy Roenick, December 2, 1999).

			REGULAR SEASON								PLAYOFFS				
Season Team	League	Gms.	Min	W	L	T	GA	SO	Avg.	Gms.	Min.	W	L	GA	SO	Avg.
91-92—St. Thomas	Jr. B	14	823	...	...	...	80	...	5.83	—	—	—	—	—	—	—
92-93—Sault Ste. Marie	OHL	12	572	4	6	0	44	0	4.62	4	231	1	2	12	0	3.12
93-94—Sault Ste. Marie	OHL	55	2934	28	14	6	174	†2	3.56	14	833	†10	4	52	0	3.75
94-95—Sault Ste. Marie	OHL	45	2517	15	25	2	184	1	4.39	—	—	—	—	—	—	—
95-96—Sault Ste. Marie	OHL	13	641	9	3	0	43	0	4.02	—	—	—	—	—	—	—
—Guelph.....................	OHL	17	1004	12	2	2	35	2	2.09	16	993	11	5	52	*2	3.14
96-97—Binghamton	AHL	60	3367	23	†28	8	199	3	3.55	4	236	1	3	13	0	3.31
97-98—Hartford	AHL	24	1417	12	8	3	62	0	2.63	8	479	5	3	24	0	3.01
—New York Rangers	NHL	12	551	4	5	1	23	0	2.50	—	—	—	—	—	—	—
98-99—New York Rangers	NHL	22	1097	6	8	3	49	0	2.68	—	—	—	—	—	—	—
99-00—Tampa Bay	NHL	52	2492	9	30	3	145	0	3.49	—	—	—	—	—	—	—
NHL Totals (3 years)............		86	4140	19	43	7	217	0	3.14							

PERSONAL: Born April 11, 1978, in Edina, Minn. ... 6-1/195. ... Shoots right.
HIGH SCHOOL: Jefferson Senior (Alexandria, Minn.).
COLLEGE: Minnesota.
TRANSACTIONS/CAREER NOTES: Selected by Boston Bruins in second round (third Bruins pick, 27th overall) of NHL entry draft (June 21, 1997). ... Signed as free agent by Tampa Bay Lightning (October 2, 1999).
HONORS: Named to WCHA All-Rookie team (1996-97).

Season Team	League	REGULAR SEASON								PLAYOFFS				
		Gms.	G	A	Pts.	PIM	+/-	PP	SH	Gms.	G	A	Pts.	PIM
93-94—Thomas Jefferson	Minn. H.S.	23	3	7	10	6	...	...	...	—	—	—	—	—
94-95—Thomas Jefferson	Minn. H.S.	28	6	20	26	26	...	...	...	—	—	—	—	—
95-96—Thomas Jefferson	Minn. H.S.	19	12	28	40	38	...	...	...	—	—	—	—	—
96-97—Univ. of Minnesota	WCHA	29	7	13	20	64	...	...	...	—	—	—	—	—
97-98—Univ. of Minnesota	WCHA	1	0	0	0	2	...	...	...	—	—	—	—	—
98-99—Seattle	WHL	70	12	44	56	93	...	...	...	11	1	5	6	12
99-00—Detroit	IHL	19	1	9	10	30	...	...	...	—	—	—	—	—
—Tampa Bay	NHL	60	2	6	8	87	-26	2	0					
NHL Totals (1 year)		60	2	6	8	87	-26	2	0					

C

PERSONAL: Born June 1, 1961, in Weston, Ont. ... 6-0/200. ... Shoots left. ... Full Name: Paul Douglas Coffey.
TRANSACTIONS/CAREER NOTES: Selected by Edmonton Oilers in first round (first Oilers pick, sixth overall) of NHL entry draft (June 11, 1980). ... Suffered recurring back spasms (December 1986); missed 10 games. ... Traded by Oilers with LW Dave Hunter and RW Wayne Van Dorp to Pittsburgh Penguins for C Craig Simpson, C Dave Hannan, D Moe Mantha and D Chris Joseph (November 24, 1987). ... Tore knee cartilage (December 1987). ... Bruised right shoulder (November 16, 1988). ... Fractured finger (May 1990). ... Injured back (February 27, 1991). ... Injured hip muscle (March 9, 1991). ... Scratched left eye cornea (April 9, 1991). ... Fractured jaw (April 1991). ... Pulled hip muscle (February 3, 1992); missed three games. ... Traded by Penguins to Los Angeles Kings for D Brian Benning, D Jeff Chychrun and first-round pick (LW Jason Bowen) in 1992 draft (February 19, 1992). ... Suffered back spasms (March 3, 1992); missed three games. ... Fractured wrist (March 17, 1992); missed five games. ... Traded by Kings with RW Jim Hiller and C/LW Sylain Couturier to Detroit Red Wings for C Jimmy Carson, RW Marc Potvin and C Gary Shuchuk (January 29, 1993). ... Injured groin (March 18, 1993); missed one game. ... Injured groin and left knee (October 18, 1993); missed four games. ... Injured back (January 28, 1995); missed two games. ... Injured back (November 4, 1995); missed two games. ... Sprained right thumb (January 6, 1996); missed two games. ... Suffered back spasms (April 7, 1996); missed one game. ... Traded by Red Wings with C Keith Primeau and first-round pick (traded to San Jose) in 1997 draft to Hartford Whalers for LW Brendan Shanahan and D Brian Glynn (October 9, 1996). ... Strained hip flexor (October 17, 1996); missed three games. ... Suffered from the flu (November 8, 1996); missed two games. ... Injured groin (November 29, 1996); missed one game. ... Injured lower back (December 14, 1996); missed one game. ... Traded by Whalers with third-round pick (D Kris Mallette) in 1997 draft to Philadelphia Flyers for D Kevin Haller and first- (traded to San Jose) and seventh-round (C Andrew Merrick) picks in 1997 draft (December 15, 1996). ... Bruised left quadricep (December 21, 1996); missed one game. ... Suffered concussion (December 31, 1996); missed five games. ... Strained hamstring (February 4, 1997); missed two games. ... Separated left shoulder (March 25, 1997); missed three games. ... Twisted knee (April 12, 1997); missed final game of regular season. ... Strained rib muscle (January 11, 1998); missed two games. ... Suffered back spasms (March 16, 1998); missed one game. ... Traded by Flyers to Chicago Blackhawks for fifth-round pick (LW Francis Belanger) in 1998 draft (June 27, 1998). ... Suffered pinched nerve in lower back (September 25, 1998); missed first 15 games of season. ... Suffered pinched nerve in back (November 22, 1998); missed nine games. ... Traded by Blackhawks to Carolina Hurricanes for RW Nelson Emerson (December 29, 1998). ... Strained hip flexor (February 20, 1999); missed one game. ... Strained neck (March 8, 1999); missed one game. ... Signed as free agent by Boston Bruins (July 13, 2000).
HONORS: Named to OMJHL All-Star second team (1979-80). ... Named to NHL All-Star second team (1980-81 through 1983-84 and 1989-90). ... Named to THE SPORTING NEWS All-Star second team (1981-82 through 1983-84, 1986-87 and 1989-90). ... Played in NHL All-Star Game (1982-1986, 1988-1994 and 1996-1997). ... Won James Norris Memorial Trophy (1984-85, 1985-86 and 1994-95). ... Named to THE SPORTING NEWS All-Star first team (1984-85, 1985-86, 1988-89 and 1994-95). ... Named to NHL All-Star first team (1984-85, 1985-86, 1988-89 and 1994-95).
RECORDS: Holds NHL career records for most assists by a defenseman—1,131; and most points by a defenseman—1,527. ... Holds NHL single-season record for most goals by a defenseman—48 (1985-86). ... Shares NHL single-game records for most points by a defenseman—8 (March 14, 1986); and most assists by a defenseman—6 (March 14, 1986). ... Holds NHL record for most consecutive games scoring points by a defenseman—28 (1985-86). ... Holds NHL single-season playoff records for most goals by a defenseman—12; assists by a defenseman—25; and points by a defenseman—37 (1985). ... Holds NHL single-game playoff record for most points by a defenseman—6 (May 14, 1985).
STATISTICAL PLATEAUS: Three-goal games: 1982-83 (1), 1984-85 (1), 1985-86 (1), 1987-88 (1). Total: 4. ... Four-goal games: 1984-85 (1). ... Total hat tricks: 5.
MISCELLANEOUS: Member of Stanley Cup championship team (1984, 1985, 1987 and 1991).

Season Team	League	REGULAR SEASON								PLAYOFFS				
		Gms.	G	A	Pts.	PIM	+/-	PP	SH	Gms.	G	A	Pts.	PIM
77-78—Kingston	OMJHL	8	2	2	4	11	...	...	...	—	—	—	—	—
—North York	MTHL	50	14	33	47	64	...	...	...	—	—	—	—	—
78-79—Sault Ste. Marie	OMJHL	68	17	72	89	99	...	...	...	—	—	—	—	—
79-80—Sault Ste. Marie	OMJHL	23	10	21	31	63	...	...	...	—	—	—	—	—
—Kitchener	OMJHL	52	19	52	71	130	...	...	...	—	—	—	—	—
80-81—Edmonton	NHL	74	9	23	32	130	4	2	0	9	4	3	7	22
81-82—Edmonton	NHL	80	29	60	89	106	35	13	0	5	1	1	2	6
82-83—Edmonton	NHL	80	29	67	96	87	52	9	1	16	7	7	14	14
83-84—Edmonton	NHL	80	40	86	126	104	52	14	1	19	8	14	22	21
84-85—Edmonton	NHL	80	37	84	121	97	55	12	2	18	12	25	37	44
85-86—Edmonton	NHL	79	48	90	138	120	61	9	*9	10	1	9	10	30
86-87—Edmonton	NHL	59	17	50	67	49	12	10	2	17	3	8	11	30
87-88—Pittsburgh	NHL	46	15	52	67	93	-1	6	2	—	—	—	—	—
88-89—Pittsburgh	NHL	75	30	83	113	195	-10	11	0	11	2	13	15	31
89-90—Pittsburgh	NHL	80	29	74	103	95	-25	10	0	—	—	—	—	—
90-91—Pittsburgh	NHL	76	24	69	93	128	-18	8	0	12	2	9	11	6
91-92—Pittsburgh	NHL	54	10	54	64	62	4	5	0	—	—	—	—	—
—Los Angeles	NHL	10	1	4	5	25	-3	0	0	6	4	3	7	2

Season Team	League	REGULAR SEASON								PLAYOFFS				
		Gms.	G	A	Pts.	PIM	+/-	PP	SH	Gms.	G	A	Pts.	PIM
92-93—Los Angeles	NHL	50	8	49	57	50	9	2	0	—	—	—	—	—
—Detroit	NHL	30	4	26	30	27	7	3	0	7	2	9	11	2
93-94—Detroit	NHL	80	14	63	77	106	28	5	0	7	1	6	7	8
94-95—Detroit	NHL	45	14	44	58	72	18	4	1	18	6	12	18	10
95-96—Detroit	NHL	76	14	60	74	90	19	3	1	17	5	9	14	30
96-97—Hartford	NHL	20	3	5	8	18	0	1	0	—	—	—	—	—
—Philadelphia	NHL	37	6	20	26	20	11	0	1	17	1	8	9	6
97-98—Philadelphia	NHL	57	2	27	29	30	3	1	0	—	—	—	—	—
98-99—Chicago	NHL	10	0	4	4	0	-6	0	0	—	—	—	—	—
—Carolina	NHL	44	2	8	10	28	-1	1	0	5	0	1	1	2
99-00—Carolina	NHL	69	11	29	40	40	-6	6	0	—	—	—	—	—
NHL Totals (20 years)		1391	396	1131	1527	1772	300	135	20	194	59	137	196	264

COMRIE, PAUL — C — OILERS

PERSONAL: Born February 7, 1977, in Edmonton. ... 5-11/192. ... Shoots left. ... Brother of Mike Comrie, center, Edmonton Oilers system.
COLLEGE: University of Denver.
TRANSACTIONS/CAREER NOTES: Selected by Tampa Bay Lightning in ninth round (12th Lightning pick, 224th overall) in NHL entry draft (June 21, 1997). ... Traded by Lightning with D Roman Hamrlik to Edmonton Oilers for D Bryan Marchment, C Steve Kelly and C Jason Bonsignore (December 30, 1997).
HONORS: Named to NCAA All-America (West) second team (1998-99). ... Named to WCHA All-Star first team (1998-99).

Season Team	League	REGULAR SEASON								PLAYOFFS				
		Gms.	G	A	Pts.	PIM	+/-	PP	SH	Gms.	G	A	Pts.	PIM
96-97—Univ. of Denver	WCHA	40	21	28	49	72	...	...	...	—	—	—	—	—
97-98—Univ. of Denver	WCHA	33	17	23	40	72	...	...	...	—	—	—	—	—
98-99—Univ. of Denver	WCHA	40	18	31	49	84	...	...	...	—	—	—	—	—
—Hamilton	AHL	7	0	1	1	0	...	...	...	8	1	3	4	2
99-00—Hamilton	AHL	12	3	3	6	6	...	...	...	—	—	—	—	—
—Edmonton	NHL	15	1	2	3	4	-2	0	0	—	—	—	—	—
NHL Totals (1 year)		15	1	2	3	4	-2	0	0					

CONNOLLY, TIM — C — ISLANDERS

PERSONAL: Born May 7, 1981, in Baldwinsville, N.Y. ... 6-0/186. ... Shoots right.
TRANSACTIONS/CAREER NOTES: Selected by New York Islanders in first round (first Islanders pick, fifth overall) of NHL entry draft (June 26, 1999).
MISCELLANEOUS: Scored on a penalty shot (vs. Jean-Sebastien Aubin, March 21, 2000).

Season Team	League	REGULAR SEASON								PLAYOFFS				
		Gms.	G	A	Pts.	PIM	+/-	PP	SH	Gms.	G	A	Pts.	PIM
96-97—Syracuse	Jr. A	50	42	62	104	34	...	...	...	—	—	—	—	—
97-98—Erie	OHL	59	30	32	62	32	...	...	...	7	1	6	7	6
98-99—Erie	OHL	46	34	34	68	50	...	...	...	—	—	—	—	—
99-00—New York Islanders	NHL	81	14	20	34	44	-25	2	1	—	—	—	—	—
NHL Totals (1 year)		81	14	20	34	44	-25	2	1					

CONROY, CRAIG — C — BLUES

PERSONAL: Born September 4, 1971, in Potsdam, N.Y. ... 6-2/193. ... Shoots right. ... Full Name: Craig Michael Conroy.
HIGH SCHOOL: Northwood (Lake Placid, N.Y.).
COLLEGE: Clarkson (N.Y.).
TRANSACTIONS/CAREER NOTES: Selected by Montreal Canadiens in sixth round (seventh Canadiens pick, 123rd overall) of NHL entry draft (June 16, 1990). ... Traded by Canadiens with C Pierre Turgeon and D Rory Fitzpatrick to St. Louis Blues for LW Shayne Corson, D Murray Baron and fifth-round pick (D Gennady Razin) in 1997 draft (October 29, 1996). ... Sprained ankle (March 12, 1999); missed 11 games. ... Reinjured ankle (April 7, 1999); missed two games. ... Suffered from the flu (October 2, 1999); missed one game.
HONORS: Named to NCAA All-America (East) first team (1993-94). ... Named to NCAA All-Tournament team (1993-94). ... Named to ECAC All-Star first team (1993-94).
STATISTICAL PLATEAUS: Three-goal games: 1998-99 (1).

Season Team	League	REGULAR SEASON								PLAYOFFS				
		Gms.	G	A	Pts.	PIM	+/-	PP	SH	Gms.	G	A	Pts.	PIM
89-90—Northwood School	N.Y. H.S.	31	33	43	76	...	...	...	...	—	—	—	—	—
90-91—Clarkson	ECAC	40	8	21	29	24	...	...	...	—	—	—	—	—
91-92—Clarkson	ECAC	31	19	17	36	36	...	...	...	—	—	—	—	—
92-93—Clarkson	ECAC	35	10	23	33	26	...	...	...	—	—	—	—	—
93-94—Clarkson	ECAC	34	26	40	66	66	...	...	...	—	—	—	—	—
94-95—Fredericton	AHL	55	26	18	44	29	...	...	...	11	7	3	10	6
—Montreal	NHL	6	1	0	1	0	-1	0	0	—	—	—	—	—
95-96—Fredericton	AHL	67	31	38	69	65	...	...	...	10	5	7	12	6
—Montreal	NHL	7	0	0	0	2	-4	0	0	—	—	—	—	—
96-97—Fredericton	AHL	9	10	6	16	10	...	...	...	—	—	—	—	—
—St. Louis	NHL	61	6	11	17	43	0	0	0	6	0	0	0	8
—Worcester	AHL	5	5	6	11	2	...	...	...	—	—	—	—	—
97-98—St. Louis	NHL	81	14	29	43	46	20	0	3	10	1	2	3	8
98-99—St. Louis	NHL	69	14	25	39	38	14	0	1	13	2	1	3	6
99-00—St. Louis	NHL	79	12	15	27	36	5	1	2	7	0	2	2	2
NHL Totals (6 years)		303	47	80	127	165	34	1	6	36	3	5	8	24

COOKE, MATT　　　　　　　C　　　　　　　CANUCKS

PERSONAL: Born September 7, 1978, in Belleville, Ont. ... 5-11/205. ... Shoots left.
TRANSACTIONS/CAREER NOTES: Selected by Vancouver Canucks in sixth round (eighth Canucks pick, 144th overall) of NHL entry draft (June 21, 1997). ... Suspended two games by AHL for attempting to injure an opponent (February 24, 1999).

				REGULAR SEASON								PLAYOFFS			
Season Team	League	Gms.	G	A	Pts.	PIM	+/-	PP	SH		Gms.	G	A	Pts.	PIM
95-96—Windsor	OHL	61	8	11	19	102	...	...	...		7	1	3	4	6
96-97—Windsor	OHL	65	45	50	95	146	...	...	...		5	5	5	10	4
97-98—Windsor	OHL	23	14	19	33	50	...	...	...		—	—	—	—	—
—Kingston	OHL	25	8	13	21	49	...	...	...		12	8	8	16	20
98-99—Vancouver	NHL	30	0	2	2	27	-12	0	0		—	—	—	—	—
—Syracuse	AHL	37	15	18	33	119	...	...	...		—	—	—	—	—
99-00—Syracuse	AHL	18	5	8	13	27	...	...	...		—	—	—	—	—
—Vancouver	NHL	51	5	7	12	39	3	0	1		—	—	—	—	—
NHL Totals (2 years)		81	5	9	14	66	-9	0	1						

CORBET, RENE　　　　　　　LW　　　　　　　PENGUINS

PERSONAL: Born June 25, 1973, in St. Hyacinthe, Que. ... 6-0/195. ... Shoots left. ... Name pronounced ruh-NAY kohr-BAY.
TRANSACTIONS/CAREER NOTES: Selected by Quebec Nordiques in second round (second Nordiques pick, 24th overall) of NHL entry draft (June 22, 1991). ... Nordiques franchise moved to Colorado and renamed Avalanche for 1995-96 season (June 21, 1995). ... Injured shoulder (April 3, 1996); missed five games. ... Suffered concussion (December 17, 1996); missed three games. ... Suffered from the flu (October 24, 1997); missed two games. ... Strained hip muscle (November 21, 1997); missed two games. ... Sprained wrist (January 3, 1998); missed three games. ... Injured shoulder (February 25, 1998); missed three games. ... Reinjured shoulder (March 14, 1998); missed four games. ... Bruised right foot (January 6, 1999); missed three games. ... Injured hamstring (February 22, 1999); missed three games. ... Traded by Avalanche with D Wade Belak and future considerations to Calgary Flames for RW Theo Fleury and LW Chris Dingman (February 28, 1999); Flames acquired D Robyn Regehr to complete deal (March 27, 1999). ... Injured groin (April 1, 1999); missed two games. ... Injured groin (October 2, 1999); missed two games. ... Injured foot (November 9, 1999); missed 18 games. ... Traded by Flames with G Tyler Moss to Pittsburgh Penguins for D Brad Werenka (March 14, 2000). ... Bruised shoulder (March 21, 2000); missed final 10 games of season.
HONORS: Won Michel Bergeron Trophy (1990-91). ... Named to QMJHL All-Rookie team (1990-91). ... Won Jean Beliveau Trophy (1992-93). ... Named to Can.HL All-Star first team (1992-93). ... Named to QMJHL All-Star first team (1992-93). ... Won Dudley (Red) Garrett Memorial Trophy (1993-94).
MISCELLANEOUS: Member of Stanley Cup championship team (1996).

				REGULAR SEASON								PLAYOFFS			
Season Team	League	Gms.	G	A	Pts.	PIM	+/-	PP	SH		Gms.	G	A	Pts.	PIM
90-91—Drummondville	QMJHL	45	25	40	65	34	...	...	...		14	11	6	17	15
91-92—Drummondville	QMJHL	56	46	50	96	90	...	...	...		4	1	2	3	17
92-93—Drummondville	QMJHL	63	*79	69	*148	143	...	...	...		10	7	13	20	16
93-94—Cornwall	AHL	68	37	40	77	56	...	...	...		13	7	2	9	18
—Quebec	NHL	9	1	1	2	0	1	0	0		—	—	—	—	—
94-95—Cornwall	AHL	65	33	24	57	79	...	...	...		12	2	8	10	27
—Quebec	NHL	8	0	3	3	2	3	0	0		2	0	1	1	0
95-96—Cornwall	AHL	9	5	6	11	10	...	...	...		—	—	—	—	—
—Colorado	NHL	33	3	6	9	33	10	0	0		8	3	2	5	22
96-97—Colorado	NHL	76	12	15	27	67	14	1	0		17	2	2	4	27
97-98—Colorado	NHL	68	16	12	28	133	8	4	0		2	0	0	0	2
98-99—Colorado	NHL	53	8	14	22	58	3	2	0		—	—	—	—	—
—Calgary	NHL	20	5	4	9	10	-2	1	0		—	—	—	—	—
99-00—Calgary	NHL	48	4	10	14	60	-7	0	0		—	—	—	—	—
—Pittsburgh	NHL	4	1	0	1	0	-4	1	0		7	1	1	2	9
NHL Totals (7 years)		319	50	65	115	363	26	9	0		36	6	6	12	40

CORKUM, BOB　　　　　　　C　　　　　　　KINGS

PERSONAL: Born December 18, 1967, in Salisbury, Mass. ... 6-0/222. ... Shoots right. ... Full Name: Robert Freeman Corkum.
HIGH SCHOOL: Triton Regional (Byfield, Mass.).
COLLEGE: Maine.
TRANSACTIONS/CAREER NOTES: Selected by Buffalo Sabres in third round (third Sabres pick, 47th overall) of NHL entry draft (June 21, 1986). ... Injured hip (March 19, 1992). ... Selected by Mighty Ducks of Anaheim in NHL expansion draft (June 24, 1993). ... Ruptured ankle tendon (March 27, 1994); missed remainder of season. ... Lacerated lower lip (November 24, 1995); missed two games. ... Traded by Mighty Ducks to Philadelphia Flyers for C Chris Herperger and seventh-round pick (LW Tony Mohagen) in 1997 draft (February 6, 1996). ... Strained right shoulder (February 17, 1996); missed three games. ... Selected by Phoenix Coyotes from Flyers in NHL waiver draft for cash (September 30, 1996). ... Suffered from the flu (January 13, 1997); missed one game. ... Strained back (October 23, 1997); missed one game. ... Suffered concussion (March 16, 1998); missed five games. ... Strained hip flexor (January 19, 1999); missed one game. ... Strained groin (March 23, 1999); missed four games. ... Signed as free agent by Los Angeles Kings (December 29, 1999).

				REGULAR SEASON								PLAYOFFS			
Season Team	League	Gms.	G	A	Pts.	PIM	+/-	PP	SH		Gms.	G	A	Pts.	PIM
84-85—Triton Regional	Mass. H.S.	18	35	36	71	...	...	...	...		—	—	—	—	—
85-86—Univ. of Maine	Hockey East	39	7	26	33	53	...	...	...		—	—	—	—	—
86-87—Univ. of Maine	Hockey East	35	18	11	29	24	...	...	...		—	—	—	—	—
87-88—Univ. of Maine	Hockey East	40	14	18	32	64	...	...	...		—	—	—	—	—
88-89—Univ. of Maine	Hockey East	45	17	31	48	64	...	...	...		—	—	—	—	—
89-90—Rochester	AHL	43	8	11	19	45	...	...	...		12	2	5	7	16
—Buffalo	NHL	8	2	0	2	4	2	0	0		5	1	0	1	4
90-91—Rochester	AHL	69	13	21	34	77	...	...	...		15	4	4	8	4

Season Team	League	Gms.	G	A	Pts.	PIM	+/-	PP	SH	Gms.	G	A	Pts.	PIM
91-92—Rochester	AHL	52	16	12	28	47	...	...	...	8	0	6	6	8
—Buffalo	NHL	20	2	4	6	21	-9	0	0	4	1	0	1	0
92-93—Buffalo	NHL	68	6	4	10	38	-3	0	1	5	0	0	0	2
93-94—Anaheim	NHL	76	23	28	51	18	4	3	3	—	—	—	—	—
94-95—Anaheim	NHL	44	10	9	19	25	-7	0	0	—	—	—	—	—
95-96—Anaheim	NHL	48	5	7	12	26	0	0	0	—	—	—	—	—
—Philadelphia	NHL	28	4	3	7	8	3	0	0	12	1	2	3	6
96-97—Phoenix	NHL	80	9	11	20	40	-7	0	1	7	2	2	4	4
97-98—Phoenix	NHL	76	12	9	21	28	-7	0	5	6	1	0	1	4
98-99—Phoenix	NHL	77	9	10	19	17	-9	0	0	7	0	1	1	4
99-00—Los Angeles	NHL	45	5	6	11	14	0	0	0	4	0	0	0	0
NHL Totals (10 years)		570	87	91	178	239	-33	3	10	50	6	5	11	24

CORSO, DANIEL   C   BLUES

PERSONAL: Born April 3, 1978, in St. Hubert, Que. ... 5-10/184.
TRANSACTIONS/CAREER NOTES: Selected by St. Louis Blues in seventh round (fifth Blues pick, 169th overall) of NHL entry draft (June 22, 1996).
HONORS: Won Michel Briere Trophy (1996-97). ... Named to Can.HL All-Star second team (1996-97). ... Named to QMJHL All-Star first team (1996-97).

Season Team	League	Gms.	G	A	Pts.	PIM	+/-	PP	SH	Gms.	G	A	Pts.	PIM
94-95—Victoriaville	QMJHL	65	27	26	53	6	...	...	...	4	2	5	7	2
95-96—Victoriaville	QMJHL	65	49	65	114	77	...	...	...	12	6	7	13	4
96-97—Victoriaville	QMJHL	54	51	68	119	50	...	...	...	—	—	—	—	—
97-98—Victoriaville	QMJHL	35	24	51	75	20	...	...	...	3	1	1	2	2
98-99—Worcester	AHL	63	14	14	28	26	...	...	...	—	—	—	—	—
99-00—Worcester	AHL	71	21	34	55	19	...	...	...	9	2	3	5	10

CORSON, SHAYNE   LW   MAPLE LEAFS

PERSONAL: Born August 13, 1966, in Barrie, Ont. ... 6-1/198. ... Shoots left.
TRANSACTIONS/CAREER NOTES: Selected by Montreal Canadiens in first round (second Canadiens pick, eighth overall) of NHL entry draft (June 9, 1984). ... Fractured jaw (January 24, 1987). ... Strained ligament in right knee (September 1987). ... Injured groin (March 1988). ... Injured knee (April 1988). ... Injured knee (April 1989). ... Bruised left shoulder (October 29, 1989). ... Fractured toe on right foot (December 1989). ... Suffered hip pointer (November 10, 1990); missed seven games. ... Pulled groin (February 11, 1991). ... Traded by Canadiens with LW Vladimir Vujtek and C Brent Gilchrist to Edmonton Oilers for LW Vincent Damphousse and fourth-round pick (D Adam Wiesel) in 1993 draft (August 27, 1992). ... Fractured fibula (February 18, 1994); missed 12 games. ... Injured leg (March 23, 1994); missed remainder of season. ... Signed by St. Louis Blues to an offer sheet (July 28, 1995); Oilers received Blues first-round picks in 1996 and 1997 drafts as compensation; Oilers then traded picks to Blues for rights to G Curtis Joseph and RW Michael Grier (August 4, 1995). ... Fractured jaw (March 26, 1996); missed five games. ... Traded by Blues with D Murray Baron and fifth-round pick (D Gennady Razin) in 1997 draft to Canadiens for C Pierre Turgeon, C Craig Conroy and D Rory Fitzpatrick (October 29, 1996). ... Injured knee (November 3, 1996) and underwent surgery; missed 10 games. ... Sprained ankle (December 26, 1996); missed 10 games. ... Strained hip flexor (February 3, 1997); missed five games. ... Strained hip flexor (January 21, 1998); missed six games. ... Strained abdominal muscle and groin (February 25, 1998); missed 13 games. ... Suffered charley horse (April 18, 1998); missed one game. ... Injured ribs (October 16, 1998); missed six games. ... Suffered nerve irritation in neck (November 19, 1998); missed four games. ... Sprained ankle (March 8, 1999); missed three games. ... Suspended six games by NHL for high-sticking incident (April 1, 1999). ... Suffered colitis (October 6, 1999); missed 10 games. ... Suffered eye injury (March 16, 2000); missed two games. ... Signed as free agent by Toronto Maple Leafs (July 4, 2000).
HONORS: Played in NHL All-Star Game (1990, 1994 and 1998).
MISCELLANEOUS: Captain of Edmonton Oilers (1994-95). ... Captain of St. Louis Blues (October 25, 1995 through February 24, 1996).
STATISTICAL PLATEAUS: Three-goal games: 1988-89 (2), 1993-94 (1). Total: 3.

Season Team	League	Gms.	G	A	Pts.	PIM	+/-	PP	SH	Gms.	G	A	Pts.	PIM
82-83—Barrie	COJHL	23	13	29	42	87	...	...	...	—	—	—	—	—
83-84—Brantford	OHL	66	25	46	71	165	...	...	...	6	4	1	5	26
84-85—Hamilton	OHL	54	27	63	90	154	...	...	...	11	3	7	10	19
85-86—Hamilton	OHL	47	41	57	98	153	...	...	...	—	—	—	—	—
—Montreal	NHL	3	0	0	0	2	-3	0	0	—	—	—	—	—
86-87—Montreal	NHL	55	12	11	23	144	10	0	1	17	6	5	11	30
87-88—Montreal	NHL	71	12	27	39	152	22	2	0	3	1	0	1	12
88-89—Montreal	NHL	80	26	24	50	193	-1	10	0	21	4	5	9	65
89-90—Montreal	NHL	76	31	44	75	144	33	7	0	11	2	8	10	20
90-91—Montreal	NHL	71	23	24	47	138	9	7	0	13	9	6	15	36
91-92—Montreal	NHL	64	17	36	53	118	15	3	0	10	2	5	7	15
92-93—Edmonton	NHL	80	16	31	47	209	-19	9	2	—	—	—	—	—
93-94—Edmonton	NHL	64	25	29	54	118	-8	11	0	—	—	—	—	—
94-95—Edmonton	NHL	48	12	24	36	86	-17	2	0	—	—	—	—	—
95-96—St. Louis	NHL	77	18	28	46	192	3	13	0	13	8	6	14	22
96-97—St. Louis	NHL	11	2	1	3	24	-4	1	0	—	—	—	—	—
—Montreal	NHL	47	6	15	21	80	-5	2	0	5	1	0	1	4
97-98—Montreal	NHL	62	21	34	55	108	2	14	1	10	3	6	9	26
—Can. Olympic team	Int'l	6	1	1	2	2	...	...	...	—	—	—	—	—
98-99—Montreal	NHL	63	12	20	32	147	-10	7	0	—	—	—	—	—
99-00—Montreal	NHL	70	8	20	28	115	-2	2	0	—	—	—	—	—
NHL Totals (15 years)		942	241	368	609	1970	25	90	4	103	36	41	77	230

COTE, PATRICK — LW — OILERS

PERSONAL: Born January 24, 1975, in Lasalle, Que. ... 6-3/218. ... Shoots left. ... Name pronounced koh-TAY.
TRANSACTIONS/CAREER NOTES: Selected by Dallas Stars in second round (second Stars pick, 37th overall) of NHL entry draft (July 8, 1995). ... Separated shoulder (November 12, 1997); missed 69 games. ... Selected by Nashville Predators in NHL expansion draft (June 26, 1998). ... Suffered from the flu (December 19, 1998); missed one game. ... Injured shoulder (March 2, 1999); missed three games. ... Strained groin (March 18, 1999); missed one game. ... Injured hand (November 5, 1999); missed nine games. ... Injured hand (January 15, 2000); missed final 37 games of season. ... Traded by Predators to Edmonton Oilers for fifth-round pick (C Matt Koalska) in 2000 draft (June 12, 2000).
MISCELLANEOUS: Holds Nashville Predators all-time record for most penalty minutes (312).

| | | | REGULAR SEASON | | | | | | | | PLAYOFFS | | | | |
Season Team	League	Gms.	G	A	Pts.	PIM	+/-	PP	SH		Gms.	G	A	Pts.	PIM
93-94—Beauport	QMJHL	48	2	4	6	230	...	...	...		12	1	0	1	61
94-95—Beauport	QMJHL	56	20	20	40	314	...	...	...		17	8	8	16	115
95-96—Michigan	IHL	57	4	6	10	239	...	...	...		3	0	0	0	2
—Dallas	NHL	2	0	0	0	5	-2	0	0		—	—	—	—	—
96-97—Michigan	IHL	58	14	10	24	237	...	...	...		4	2	0	2	6
—Dallas	NHL	3	0	0	0	27	0	0	0		—	—	—	—	—
97-98—Dallas	NHL	3	0	0	0	15	-1	0	0		—	—	—	—	—
—Michigan	IHL	4	2	0	2	4	...	...	...		—	—	—	—	—
98-99—Nashville	NHL	70	1	2	3	242	-7	0	0		—	—	—	—	—
99-00—Nashville	NHL	21	0	0	0	70	-7	0	0		—	—	—	—	—
NHL Totals (5 years)		99	1	2	3	359	-17	0	0						

C

COTE, SYLVAIN — D — CAPITALS

PERSONAL: Born January 19, 1966, in Quebec City. ... 6-0/190. ... Shoots right. ... Brother of Alain Cote, defenseman with five NHL teams (1985-86 through 1993-94). ... Name pronounced KOH-tay.
TRANSACTIONS/CAREER NOTES: Selected by Hartford Whalers as underage junior in first round (first Whalers pick, 11th overall) of NHL entry draft (June 9, 1984). ... Fractured toe on left foot (October 28, 1989). ... Sprained left knee (December 1989). ... Fractured right foot (January 22, 1990). ... Traded by Whalers to Washington Capitals for second-round pick (LW Andrei Nikolishin) in 1992 draft (September 8, 1991). ... Fractured wrist (September 25, 1992); missed six games. ... Suffered hip pointer (January 7, 1993); missed one game. ... Injured ankle (January 16, 1996); missed one game. ... Tore medial collateral ligament in right knee (October 18, 1996); missed 19 games. ... Strained knee (December 6, 1996); missed five games. ... Traded by Capitals to Toronto Maple Leafs for D Jeff Brown (March 24, 1998). ... Sprained shoulder (March 27, 1999); missed three games. ... Traded by Maple Leafs to Chicago Blackhawks for second-round pick in 2001 draft and conditional pick in 2001 draft (October 8, 1999). ... Strained hamstring (December 6, 1999); missed four games. ... Traded by Blackhawks with D Dave Manson to Dallas Stars for C Derek Plante, D Kevin Dean and second-round pick in 2001 draft (February 8, 2000). ... Signed as free agent by Capitals (July 6, 2000).
HONORS: Named to QMJHL All-Star second team (1983-84). ... Won Emile (Butch) Bouchard Trophy (1985-86). ... Shared Guy Lafleur Trophy with Luc Robitaille (1985-86). ... Named to QMJHL All-Star first team (1985-86).

| | | | REGULAR SEASON | | | | | | | | PLAYOFFS | | | | |
Season Team	League	Gms.	G	A	Pts.	PIM	+/-	PP	SH		Gms.	G	A	Pts.	PIM
82-83—Quebec	QMJHL	66	10	24	34	50	...	...	...		—	—	—	—	—
83-84—Quebec	QMJHL	66	15	50	65	89	...	...	...		5	1	1	2	0
84-85—Hartford	NHL	67	3	9	12	17	-30	1	0		—	—	—	—	—
85-86—Hartford	NHL	2	0	0	0	0	1	0	0		—	—	—	—	—
—Hull	QMJHL	26	10	33	43	14	...	...	...		13	6	*28	34	22
—Binghamton	AHL	12	2	6	8	0	...	...	...		—	—	—	—	—
86-87—Hartford	NHL	67	2	8	10	20	10	0	0		2	0	2	2	2
87-88—Hartford	NHL	67	7	21	28	30	-8	0	1		6	1	1	2	4
88-89—Hartford	NHL	78	8	9	17	49	-7	1	0		3	0	1	1	4
89-90—Hartford	NHL	28	4	2	6	14	2	1	0		5	0	0	0	0
90-91—Hartford	NHL	73	7	12	19	17	-17	1	0		6	0	2	2	2
91-92—Washington	NHL	78	11	29	40	31	7	6	0		7	1	2	3	4
92-93—Washington	NHL	77	21	29	50	34	28	8	2		6	1	1	2	4
93-94—Washington	NHL	84	16	35	51	66	30	3	2		9	1	8	9	6
94-95—Washington	NHL	47	5	14	19	53	2	1	0		7	1	3	4	2
95-96—Washington	NHL	81	5	33	38	40	5	3	0		6	2	0	2	12
96-97—Washington	NHL	57	6	18	24	28	11	2	0		—	—	—	—	—
97-98—Washington	NHL	59	1	15	16	36	-5	0	0		—	—	—	—	—
—Toronto	NHL	12	3	6	9	6	2	1	0		—	—	—	—	—
98-99—Toronto	NHL	79	5	24	29	28	22	0	0		17	2	1	3	10
99-00—Toronto	NHL	3	0	1	1	0	1	0	0		—	—	—	—	—
—Chicago	NHL	45	6	18	24	14	-4	5	0		—	—	—	—	—
—Dallas	NHL	28	2	8	10	14	6	0	0		23	2	1	3	8
NHL Totals (16 years)		1032	112	291	403	497	56	33	5		97	11	22	33	58

COURTNALL, GEOFF — LW

PERSONAL: Born August 18, 1962, in Duncan, B.C. ... 6-1/204. ... Shoots left. ... Full Name: Geoffery Courtnall. ... Brother of Russ Courtnall, right winger with six NHL teams (1983-84 through 1998-99).
HIGH SCHOOL: Oak Bay (B.C.).
TRANSACTIONS/CAREER NOTES: Signed as non-drafted free agent by Boston Bruins (September 1983). ... Traded by Bruins with G Bill Ranford to Edmonton Oilers for G Andy Moog (March 8, 1988). ... Traded by Oilers to Washington Capitals for C Greg Adams (July 22, 1988). ... Traded by Capitals to St. Louis Blues for C Peter Zezel and D Mike Lalor (July 13, 1990). ... Traded by Blues with D Robert Dirk, C Cliff Ronning, LW Sergio Momesso and fifth-round pick (RW Brian Loney) in 1992 draft to Vancouver Canucks for C Dan Quinn and D Garth Butcher (March 5, 1991). ... Lacerated foot (February 28, 1992) and suffered from chronic fatigue (March 1992); missed nine games. ... Suspended two games by NHL (November 14, 1993). ... Suffered foot injury (April 20, 1995); missed three games. ... Signed as free agent by Blues (July 14, 1995). ... Fractured thumb (February 18, 1996); missed 13 games. ... Injured groin (January 3, 1998); missed two games. ... Bruised foot (October 12, 1998); missed one game. ... Suffered post-concussion syndrome (November 27, 1998); missed 57 games. ... Suffered concussion (October 16, 1999); missed 12 games. ... Announced retirement (November 18, 1999).

MISCELLANEOUS: Member of Stanley Cup championship team (1988). ... Scored on a penalty shot (vs. Jeff Hackett, December 13, 1996; vs. Chris Osgood, October 29, 1998). ... Failed to score on a penalty shot (vs. Alain Chevrier, February 7, 1988; vs. Damian Rhodes, March 21, 1995).
STATISTICAL NOTES: Tied for NHL lead with 11 game-winning goals (1992-93).
STATISTICAL PLATEAUS: Three-goal games: 1987-88 (1), 1987-88 (1), 1988-89 (1), 1989-90 (1), 1995-96 (1), 1997-98 (1). Total: 6.

			REGULAR SEASON								PLAYOFFS				
Season Team	League	Gms.	G	A	Pts.	PIM	+/-	PP	SH	Gms.	G	A	Pts.	PIM
80-81—Victoria	WHL	11	3	5	8	6	...	...	...	15	2	1	3	7
81-82—Victoria	WHL	72	35	57	92	100	...	...	...	4	1	0	1	2
82-83—Victoria	WHL	71	41	73	114	186	...	...	...	12	6	7	13	42
83-84—Hershey	AHL	74	14	12	26	51	...	...	...	—	—	—	—	—
—Boston	NHL	4	0	0	0	0	-1	0	0	—	—	—	—	—
84-85—Hershey	AHL	9	8	4	12	4	...	...	...	—	—	—	—	—
—Boston	NHL	64	12	16	28	82	-3	0	0	5	0	2	2	7
85-86—Moncton	AHL	12	8	8	16	6	...	...	...	—	—	—	—	—
—Boston	NHL	64	21	16	37	61	1	2	0	3	0	0	0	2
86-87—Boston	NHL	65	13	23	36	117	-4	2	0	1	0	0	0	0
87-88—Boston	NHL	62	32	26	58	108	24	8	0	—	—	—	—	—
—Edmonton	NHL	12	4	4	8	15	1	0	0	19	0	3	3	23
88-89—Washington	NHL	79	42	38	80	112	11	16	0	6	2	5	7	12
89-90—Washington	NHL	80	35	39	74	104	27	9	0	15	4	9	13	32
90-91—St. Louis	NHL	66	27	30	57	56	19	9	0	—	—	—	—	—
—Vancouver	NHL	11	6	2	8	8	-3	3	0	6	3	5	8	4
91-92—Vancouver	NHL	70	23	34	57	116	-6	12	0	12	6	8	14	20
92-93—Vancouver	NHL	84	31	46	77	167	27	9	0	12	4	10	14	12
93-94—Vancouver	NHL	82	26	44	70	123	15	12	1	24	9	10	19	51
94-95—Vancouver	NHL	45	16	18	34	81	2	7	0	11	4	2	6	34
95-96—St. Louis	NHL	69	24	16	40	101	-9	7	1	13	0	3	3	14
96-97—St. Louis	NHL	82	17	40	57	86	3	4	0	6	3	1	4	23
97-98—St. Louis	NHL	79	31	31	62	94	12	6	0	10	2	8	10	18
98-99—St. Louis	NHL	24	5	7	12	28	2	1	0	13	2	4	6	10
99-00—St. Louis	NHL	6	2	2	4	6	3	0	0	—	—	—	—	—
NHL Totals (17 years)		1048	367	432	799	1465	121	107	2	156	39	70	109	262

COUSINEAU, MARCEL · G · KINGS

PERSONAL: Born April 30, 1973, in Delson, Que. ... 5-9/180. ... Catches left. ... Name pronounced KOO-sih-noh.
TRANSACTIONS/CAREER NOTES: Selected by Boston Bruins in third round (third Bruins pick, 62nd overall) of NHL entry draft (June 22, 1991). ... Signed as free agent by Toronto Maple Leafs (November 13, 1993). ... Signed as free agent by New York Islanders (July 14, 1998). ... Traded by Islanders with RW Zigmund Palffy, C Bryan Smolinski and fourth-round pick (C Daniel Johansson) in 1999 draft to Los Angeles Kings for C Olli Jokinen, LW Josh Green, D Mathieu Biron and first-round pick (LW Taylor Pyatt) in 1999 draft (June 20, 1999). ... Suffered appendicitis (March 16, 2000); missed final 12 games of season.
HONORS: Named to QMJHL All-Rookie team (1990-91).

			REGULAR SEASON							PLAYOFFS					
Season Team	League	Gms.	Min	W	L	T	GA	SO	Avg.	Gms.	Min.	W	L	GA	SO	Avg.
90-91—Beauport	QMJHL	49	2739	13	29	3	196	1	4.29	—	—	—	—	—	—	—
91-92—Beauport	QMJHL	*67	*3673	26	*32	5	*241	0	3.94	—	—	—	—	—	—	—
92-93—Drummondville	QMJHL	60	3298	20	32	2	225	0	4.09	9	498	3	6	37	1	4.46
93-94—St. John's	AHL	37	2015	13	11	9	118	0	3.51	—	—	—	—	—	—	—
94-95—St. John's	AHL	58	3342	22	27	6	171	4	3.07	3	180	0	3	9	0	3.00
95-96—St. John's	AHL	62	3629	21	26	13	192	1	3.17	4	257	1	3	11	0	2.57
96-97—St. John's	AHL	19	1053	7	8	3	58	0	3.30	11	658	6	5	28	0	2.55
—Toronto	NHL	13	566	3	5	1	31	1	3.29	—	—	—	—	—	—	—
97-98—St. John's	AHL	57	3306	17	25	*13	167	1	3.03	4	254	1	3	10	0	2.36
—Toronto	NHL	2	17	0	0	0	0	0	...	—	—	—	—	—	—	—
98-99—Lowell	AHL	53	3034	26	17	†7	139	3	2.75	3	186	0	3	13	0	4.19
—New York Islanders	NHL	6	293	0	4	0	14	0	2.87	—	—	—	—	—	—	—
99-00—Long Beach	IHL	23	1328	18	6	‡1	62	0	2.80	—	—	—	—	—	—	—
—Los Angeles	NHL	5	171	1	1	0	6	0	2.11	—	—	—	—	—	—	—
NHL Totals (4 years)		26	1047	4	10	1	51	1	2.92							

COWAN, JEFF · LW · FLAMES

PERSONAL: Born September 27, 1976, in Scarborough, Ont. ... 6-2/192. ... Shoots left. ... Name pronounced KOW-ihn.
HIGH SCHOOL: Bishop MacDonnell (Guelph, Ont.).
TRANSACTIONS/CAREER NOTES: Signed as non-drafted free agent by Calgary Flames (October 2, 1995). ... Suffered injury (March 3, 2000); missed one game. ... Suffered illness (March 25, 2000); missed final six games of season.

			REGULAR SEASON							PLAYOFFS				
Season Team	League	Gms.	G	A	Pts.	PIM	+/-	PP	SH	Gms.	G	A	Pts.	PIM
92-93—Guelph	Jr. B	45	8	8	16	22	...	...	...	—	—	—	—	—
93-94—Guelph	Jr. B	43	30	26	56	96	...	...	...	—	—	—	—	—
—Guelph	OHL	17	1	0	1	5	...	...	...	0	0	0	0	0
94-95—Guelph	OHL	51	10	7	17	14	...	...	...	14	1	1	2	0
95-96—Barrie	OHL	66	38	14	52	29	...	...	...	5	1	2	3	6
96-97—Saint John	AHL	22	5	5	10	8	...	...	...	—	—	—	—	—
—Roanoke	ECHL	47	21	13	34	42	...	...	...	—	—	—	—	—
97-98—Saint John	AHL	69	15	13	28	23	...	...	...	13	4	1	5	14
98-99—Saint John	AHL	71	7	12	19	117	...	...	...	4	0	1	1	10
99-00—Saint John	AHL	47	15	10	25	77	...	...	...	—	—	—	—	—
—Calgary	NHL	13	4	1	5	16	2	0	0	—	—	—	—	—
NHL Totals (1 year)		13	4	1	5	16	2	0	0					

C

PERSONAL: Born July 20, 1964, in Medicine Hat, Alta. ... 6-3/195. ... Shoots left.

TRANSACTIONS/CAREER NOTES: Selected by Detroit Red Wings as underage junior in first round (first Red Wings pick, 17th overall) of NHL entry draft (June 9, 1982). ... Injured left knee cartilage (January 15, 1983). ... Traded by Red Wings with LW/C Joe Paterson to Philadelphia Flyers for C Darryl Sittler (October 1984). ... Broke foot (April 16, 1987). ... Hyperextended right knee and lacerated eye (November 1988). ... Bruised right foot (January 1989). ... Fractured left wrist (February 24, 1989). ... Fractured right wrist (April 5, 1989). ... Suffered back spasms (February 1990). ... Injured rotator cuff (March 24, 1990). ... Traded by Flyers with fourth-round pick (LW Kevin Smyth) in 1992 draft to Hartford Whalers for RW Kevin Dineen (November 13, 1991). ... Injured groin (January 21, 1992). ... Traded by Whalers with fifth-round pick (C Scott Walker) in 1993 draft to Vancouver Canucks for LW Robert Kron, third-round pick (D Marek Malik) in 1993 draft and future considerations (March 22, 1993). ... Whalers acquired RW Jim Sandlak to complete deal (May 17, 1993). ... Injured hip (November 2, 1993); missed three games. ... Strained groin (November 14, 1993); missed two games. ... Traded by Canucks to Chicago Blackhawks for C Christian Ruuttu (March 10, 1995). ... Suffered from sore back (1995); missed four games. ... Bruised foot (October 10, 1995); missed one game. ... Suffered charley horse (November 12, 1995); missed two games. ... Bruised knee (January 22, 1997); missed one game. ... Bruised shoulder (February 11, 1997); missed four games. ... Suffered stiff neck (March 5, 1997); missed one game. ... Traded by Blackhawks to San Jose Sharks for LW Petri Varis and sixth-round pick (C Jari Viuhkola) in 1998 draft (July 24, 1997). ... Injured thumb (October 22, 1997). ... Injured six games. ... Suffered sore hand (November 25, 1997); missed one game. ... Strained neck (March 11, 1998); missed seven games. ... Injured leg (December 19, 1998); missed 21 games. ... Reinjured leg (February 10, 1999); missed one game. ... Reinjured leg (February 26, 1999); missed nine games. ... Reinjured leg (March 31, 1999); missed remainder of season. ... Injured thigh (October 13, 1999); missed one game. ... Injured knee (October 23, 1999); missed six games. ... Injured back (November 10, 1999); missed two games. ... Strained muscle in abdomen (November 28, 1999); missed 21 games. ... Released by Sharks (January 20, 2000).

MISCELLANEOUS: Scored on a penalty shot (vs. Don Beaupre, March 24, 1992; vs. Andre Racicot, December 23, 1990). ... Failed to score on a penalty shot (vs. Chris Terreri, October 13, 1991).

STATISTICAL PLATEAUS: Three-goal games: 1986-87 (1), 1987-88 (1), 1991-92 (1). Total: 3.

C

			REGULAR SEASON								PLAYOFFS				
Season Team	League	Gms.	G	A	Pts.	PIM	+/-	PP	SH		Gms.	G	A	Pts.	PIM
80-81—Medicine Hat	WHL	69	5	10	15	18	...	...	...		5	0	0	0	2
81-82—Medicine Hat	WHL	72	35	46	81	49	...	...	...		—	—	—	—	—
82-83—Medicine Hat	WHL	28	17	29	46	35	...	...	...		—	—	—	—	—
—Detroit	NHL	31	4	7	11	6	5	0	0		—	—	—	—	—
83-84—Medicine Hat	WHL	48	38	56	94	53	...	...	...		4	5	3	8	4
—Detroit	NHL	15	0	4	4	6	2	0	0		—	—	—	—	—
84-85—Philadelphia	NHL	80	26	35	61	30	45	2	2		19	4	6	10	11
85-86—Philadelphia	NHL	78	21	33	54	34	24	2	0		5	0	3	3	4
86-87—Philadelphia	NHL	77	19	30	49	38	1	5	3		12	3	1	4	9
87-88—Philadelphia	NHL	72	30	46	76	58	25	6	2		7	2	5	7	4
88-89—Philadelphia	NHL	51	9	28	37	52	4	0	0		1	0	0	0	0
89-90—Philadelphia	NHL	76	25	50	75	42	2	7	0		—	—	—	—	—
90-91—Philadelphia	NHL	77	19	47	66	53	-2	6	0		—	—	—	—	—
91-92—Philadelphia	NHL	12	3	3	6	8	2	1	0		—	—	—	—	—
—Hartford	NHL	61	24	30	54	38	-4	8	4		7	3	3	6	6
92-93—Hartford	NHL	67	25	42	67	20	-4	6	3		—	—	—	—	—
—Vancouver	NHL	10	0	10	10	12	3	0	0		12	4	6	10	4
93-94—Vancouver	NHL	78	15	40	55	30	5	2	1		22	4	9	13	18
94-95—Chicago	NHL	16	4	3	7	2	2	1	0		16	5	5	10	4
95-96—Chicago	NHL	66	18	29	47	36	20	5	1		9	1	4	5	2
96-97—Chicago	NHL	75	8	27	35	12	0	2	0		2	0	0	0	2
97-98—San Jose	NHL	67	12	17	29	25	4	2	3		6	1	1	2	0
98-99—San Jose	NHL	43	4	10	14	18	-3	0	1		—	—	—	—	—
99-00—San Jose	NHL	19	0	2	2	4	-2	0	1		—	—	—	—	—
NHL Totals (18 years)		1071	266	493	759	524	129	55	22		118	27	43	70	64

PERSONAL: Born July 31, 1975, in Lloydminster, Alta. ... 6-5/219. ... Shoots left. ... Full Name: Cory James Cross.

HIGH SCHOOL: Lloydminster (Alta.) Comprehensive.

COLLEGE: University of Alberta.

TRANSACTIONS/CAREER NOTES: Selected by Tampa Bay Lightning in NHL supplemental draft (June 19, 1992). ... Injured foot (November 3, 1995); missed one game. ... Bruised right foot (November 10, 1996); missed five games. ... Suffered from the flu (March 28, 1998); missed one game. ... Injured ankle (January 4, 1999); missed two games. ... Suffered hip pointer (January 30, 1999); missed 12 games. ... Traded by Lightning with seventh-round pick in 2001 draft to Toronto Maple Leafs for RW Fredrik Modin (October 1, 1999). ... Suffered injury (November 15, 1999); missed two games. ... Suffered injury (March 29, 2000); missed two games.

HONORS: Named to CWUAA All-Star second team (1992-93).

			REGULAR SEASON								PLAYOFFS				
Season Team	League	Gms.	G	A	Pts.	PIM	+/-	PP	SH		Gms.	G	A	Pts.	PIM
90-91—Univ. of Alberta	CWUAA	20	2	5	7	16	...	...	...		—	—	—	—	—
91-92—Univ. of Alberta	CWUAA	39	3	10	13	76	...	...	...		—	—	—	—	—
92-93—Univ. of Alberta	CWUAA	43	11	28	39	105	...	...	...		—	—	—	—	—
—Atlanta	IHL	7	0	1	1	2	...	...	...		4	0	0	0	6
93-94—Atlanta	IHL	70	4	14	18	72	...	...	...		9	1	2	3	14
—Tampa Bay	NHL	5	0	0	0	6	-3	0	0		—	—	—	—	—
94-95—Atlanta	IHL	41	5	10	15	67	...	...	...		—	—	—	—	—
—Tampa Bay	NHL	43	1	5	6	41	-6	0	0		—	—	—	—	—
95-96—Tampa Bay	NHL	75	2	14	16	66	4	0	0		6	0	0	0	22
96-97—Tampa Bay	NHL	72	4	5	9	95	6	0	0		—	—	—	—	—
97-98—Tampa Bay	NHL	74	3	6	9	77	-24	0	1		—	—	—	—	—
98-99—Tampa Bay	NHL	67	2	16	18	92	-25	0	0		—	—	—	—	—
99-00—Toronto	NHL	71	4	11	15	64	13	0	0		12	0	2	2	2
NHL Totals (7 years)		407	16	57	73	441	-35	0	1		18	0	2	2	24

CROWE, PHIL   LW

PERSONAL: Born April 14, 1970, in Nanton, Alta. ... 6-2/220. ... Shoots left. ... Full Name: Philip Crowe.
TRANSACTIONS/CAREER NOTES: Signed as free agent by Los Angeles Kings (November 8, 1993). ... Signed as free agent by Philadelphia Flyers (July 19, 1994). ... Suffered back spasms (October 29, 1995); missed five games. ... Signed as free agent by Ottawa Senators (July 4, 1996). ... Suffered charley horse (March 25, 1997); missed two games. ... Selected by Atlanta Thrashers in NHL expansion draft (June 25, 1999). ... Traded by Thrashers to Nashville Predators for future considerations (June 26, 1999).

			REGULAR SEASON							**PLAYOFFS**				
Season Team	League	Gms.	G	A	Pts.	PIM	+/-	PP	SH	Gms.	G	A	Pts.	PIM
91-92—Adirondack	AHL	6	0	1	1	29	...	...	...	—	—	—	—	—
—Columbus	ECHL	32	4	7	11	145	...	...	...	—	—	—	—	—
—Toledo	ECHL	2	0	0	0	0	...	...	...	5	0	0	0	58
92-93—Phoenix	IHL	53	3	3	6	190	...	...	...	—	—	—	—	—
93-94—Fort Wayne	IHL	5	0	1	1	26	...	...	...	—	—	—	—	—
—Phoenix	IHL	2	0	0	0	0	...	...	...	—	—	—	—	—
—Los Angeles	NHL	31	0	2	2	77	4	0	0	—	—	—	—	—
94-95—Hershey	AHL	46	11	6	17	132	...	...	...	6	0	1	1	19
95-96—Hershey	AHL	39	6	8	14	105	...	...	...	5	1	2	3	19
—Philadelphia	NHL	16	1	1	2	28	0	0	0	—	—	—	—	—
96-97—Detroit	IHL	41	7	7	14	83	...	...	...	—	—	—	—	—
—Ottawa	NHL	26	0	1	1	30	0	0	0	3	0	0	0	16
97-98—Detroit	IHL	55	6	13	19	160	...	...	...	20	5	2	7	48
—Ottawa	NHL	9	3	0	3	24	3	0	0	—	—	—	—	—
98-99—Ottawa	NHL	8	0	1	1	4	1	0	0	—	—	—	—	—
—Detroit	IHL	2	0	0	0	9	...	...	...	—	—	—	—	—
—Cincinnati	IHL	39	2	6	8	62	...	...	...	—	—	—	—	—
—Las Vegas	IHL	14	1	3	4	18	...	...	...	—	—	—	—	—
99-00—Nashville	NHL	4	0	0	0	10	0	0	0	—	—	—	—	—
—Milwaukee	IHL	20	3	1	4	31	...	...	...	—	—	—	—	—
NHL Totals (6 years)		94	4	5	9	173	8	0	0	3	0	0	0	16

CROZIER, GREG   LW   PENGUINS

PERSONAL: Born July 6, 1976, in Williamsville, N.Y. ... 6-3/199. ... Shoots left.
HIGH SCHOOL: Amherst (Mass.), then Lawrence Academy (Groton, Mass.).
COLLEGE: Michigan.
TRANSACTIONS/CAREER NOTES: Selected by Pittsburgh Penguins in third round (fourth Penguins pick, 73rd overall) of NHL entry draft (June 29, 1994).

			REGULAR SEASON							**PLAYOFFS**				
Season Team	League	Gms.	G	A	Pts.	PIM	+/-	PP	SH	Gms.	G	A	Pts.	PIM
90-91—Amherst	Mass. H.S.	41	52	34	86	17	...	...	...	—	—	—	—	—
91-92—Amherst	Mass. H.S.	46	61	47	108	47	...	...	...	—	—	—	—	—
92-93—Lawrence Academy	Mass. H.S.	21	22	13	35	9	...	...	...	—	—	—	—	—
93-94—Lawrence Academy	Mass. H.S.	19	22	26	48	10	...	...	...	—	—	—	—	—
94-95—Lawrence Academy	Mass. H.S.	31	45	32	77	22	...	...	...	—	—	—	—	—
95-96—Univ. of Michigan	CCHA	42	14	10	24	46	...	...	...	—	—	—	—	—
96-97—Univ. of Michigan	CCHA	31	5	15	20	45	...	...	...	—	—	—	—	—
97-98—Univ. of Michigan	CCHA	43	12	9	21	24	...	...	...	—	—	—	—	—
98-99—Univ. of Michigan	CCHA	39	7	6	13	63	...	...	...	—	—	—	—	—
99-00—Wilkes-Barre/Scranton	AHL	71	22	22	44	33	...	...	...	—	—	—	—	—

CULLEN, MATT   C   MIGHTY DUCKS

PERSONAL: Born November 2, 1976, in Virginia, Minn. ... 6-0/195. ... Shoots left.
HIGH SCHOOL: Moorhead (Minn.) Senior.
COLLEGE: St. Cloud (Minn.) State.
TRANSACTIONS/CAREER NOTES: Selected by Mighty Ducks of Anaheim in second round (second Mighty Ducks pick, 35th overall) of NHL entry draft (June 22, 1996). ... Sprained ankle (December 16, 1998); missed one game.
HONORS: Named to WCHA All-Rookie team (1995-96). ... Named to WCHA All-Star second team (1996-97).

			REGULAR SEASON							**PLAYOFFS**				
Season Team	League	Gms.	G	A	Pts.	PIM	+/-	PP	SH	Gms.	G	A	Pts.	PIM
94-95—Moorhead Senior	Minn. H.S.	28	47	42	89	78	...	...	...	—	—	—	—	—
95-96—St. Cloud State	WCHA	39	12	29	41	28	...	...	...	—	—	—	—	—
96-97—St. Cloud State	WCHA	36	15	30	45	70	...	...	...	—	—	—	—	—
—Baltimore	AHL	6	3	3	6	7	...	...	...	3	0	2	2	0
97-98—Anaheim	NHL	61	6	21	27	23	-4	2	0	—	—	—	—	—
—Cincinnati	AHL	18	15	12	27	2	...	...	...	—	—	—	—	—
98-99—Anaheim	NHL	75	11	14	25	47	-12	5	1	4	0	0	0	0
—Cincinnati	AHL	3	1	2	3	8	...	...	...	—	—	—	—	—
99-00—Anaheim	NHL	80	13	26	39	24	5	1	0	—	—	—	—	—
NHL Totals (3 years)		216	30	61	91	94	-11	8	1	4	0	0	0	0

C

CULLIMORE, JASSEN — D — LIGHTNING

PERSONAL: Born December 4, 1972, in Simcoe, Ont. ... 6-5/220. ... Shoots left. ... Name pronounced KUHL-ih-MOHR.

TRANSACTIONS/CAREER NOTES: Selected by Vancouver Canucks in second round (second Canucks pick, 29th overall) of NHL entry draft (June 22, 1991). ... Suffered knee injury (March 31, 1995); missed three games. ... Traded by Canucks to Montreal Canadiens for LW Donald Brashear (November 13, 1996). ... Bruised eye (March 1, 1997); missed one game. ... Claimed on waivers by Tampa Bay Lightning (January 22, 1998). ... Sprained knee (April 4, 1998); missed final seven games of season. ... Injured neck (October 14, 1998); missed two games. ... Injured wrist (December 11, 1998); missed one game. ... Injured knee (April 2, 2000); missed final four games of season.

HONORS: Named to OHL All-Star second team (1991-92).

		REGULAR SEASON								PLAYOFFS				
Season Team	League	Gms.	G	A	Pts.	PIM	+/-	PP	SH	Gms.	G	A	Pts.	PIM
88-89—Peterborough	OHL	20	2	1	3	6	...	...	...	—	—	—	—	—
—Peterborough	Jr. B	29	11	17	28	88	...	...	...	—	—	—	—	—
89-90—Peterborough	OHL	59	2	6	8	61	...	...	...	11	0	2	2	8
90-91—Peterborough	OHL	62	8	16	24	74	...	...	...	4	1	0	1	7
91-92—Peterborough	OHL	54	9	37	46	65	...	...	...	10	3	6	9	8
92-93—Hamilton	AHL	56	5	7	12	60	...	...	...	—	—	—	—	—
93-94—Hamilton	AHL	71	8	20	28	86	...	...	...	3	0	1	1	2
94-95—Syracuse	AHL	33	2	7	9	66	...	...	...	—	—	—	—	—
—Vancouver	NHL	34	1	2	3	39	-2	0	0	11	0	0	0	12
95-96—Vancouver	NHL	27	1	1	2	21	4	0	0	—	—	—	—	—
96-97—Vancouver	NHL	3	0	0	0	2	-2	0	0	—	—	—	—	—
—Montreal	NHL	49	2	6	8	42	4	0	1	2	0	0	0	2
97-98—Montreal	NHL	3	0	0	0	4	0	0	0	—	—	—	—	—
—Fredericton	AHL	5	1	0	1	8	...	...	...	—	—	—	—	—
—Tampa Bay	NHL	25	1	2	3	22	-4	1	0	—	—	—	—	—
98-99—Tampa Bay	NHL	78	5	12	17	81	-22	1	1	—	—	—	—	—
99-00—Providence	AHL	16	5	10	15	31	...	...	...	—	—	—	—	—
—Tampa Bay	NHL	46	1	1	2	66	-12	0	0	—	—	—	—	—
NHL Totals (6 years)		265	11	24	35	277	-34	2	2	13	0	0	0	14

CUMMINS, JIM — RW — MIGHTY DUCKS

PERSONAL: Born May 17, 1970, in Dearborn, Mich. ... 6-2/219. ... Shoots right. ... Full Name: James Stephen Cummins. ... Name pronounced KUH-mihns.

COLLEGE: Michigan State.

TRANSACTIONS/CAREER NOTES: Selected by New York Rangers in fourth round (fifth Rangers pick, 67th overall) of NHL entry draft (June 17, 1989). ... Traded by Rangers with LW Kevin Miller and D Dennis Vial to Detroit Red Wings for RW Joe Kocur and D Per Djoos (March 5, 1991). ... Suspended 11 games by NHL for leaving penalty box to join fight (January 23, 1993). ... Traded by Red Wings with fourth-round pick (traded to Boston) in 1993 draft to Philadelphia Flyers for rights to C Greg Johnson and fifth-round pick (G Frederic Deschene) in 1994 draft (June 20, 1993). ... Suffered slightly separated shoulder during 1993-94 season. ... Traded by Flyers with fourth-round pick in 1995 draft to Tampa Bay Lightning for C Rob DiMaio (March 18, 1994). ... Traded by Lightning with D Jeff Buchanan and D Tom Tilley to Chicago Blackhawks for LW Paul Ysebaert and RW Rich Sutter (February 22, 1995). ... Sprained triceps (March 16, 1995); missed five games. ... Fractured thumb (November 1, 1995); missed 16 games. ... Suspended eight games and fined $1,000 by NHL for cross checking and punching another player (March 14, 1996). ... Bruised clavicle (December 9, 1996); missed 11 games. ... Suspended one game by NHL for third game misconduct of season (January 23, 1997). ... Suffered from the flu (November 11, 1997); missed three games. ... Traded by Blackhawks with D Keith Carney to Phoenix Coyotes for C Chad Kilger and D Jayson More (March 4, 1998). ... Suspended five games by NHL for elbowing incident (February 8, 1999). ... Traded by Coyotes to Montreal Canadiens for sixth-round pick (D Erik Lewerstrom) in 1999 draft (June 26, 1999). ... Suffered concussion (September 12, 1999); missed first two games of season. ... Separated shoulder (December 20, 1999); missed three games. ... Sprained ankle (January 24, 2000); missed 22 games. ... Signed as free agent by Mighty Ducks of Anaheim (July 5, 2000).

MISCELLANEOUS: Failed to score on a penalty shot (vs. Mike Vernon, April 7, 1996).

		REGULAR SEASON								PLAYOFFS				
Season Team	League	Gms.	G	A	Pts.	PIM	+/-	PP	SH	Gms.	G	A	Pts.	PIM
87-88—Detroit Compuware	NAJHL	31	11	15	26	146	...	...	...	—	—	—	—	—
88-89—Michigan State	CCHA	36	3	9	12	100	...	...	...	—	—	—	—	—
89-90—Michigan State	CCHA	41	8	7	15	94	...	...	...	—	—	—	—	—
90-91—Michigan State	CCHA	34	9	6	15	110	...	...	...	—	—	—	—	—
91-92—Adirondack	AHL	65	7	13	20	338	...	...	...	5	0	0	0	19
—Detroit	NHL	1	0	0	0	7	0	0	0	—	—	—	—	—
92-93—Adirondack	AHL	43	16	4	20	179	...	...	...	9	3	1	4	4
—Detroit	NHL	7	1	1	2	58	0	0	0	—	—	—	—	—
93-94—Philadelphia	NHL	22	1	2	3	71	0	0	0	—	—	—	—	—
—Hershey	AHL	17	6	6	12	70	...	...	...	—	—	—	—	—
—Atlanta	IHL	7	4	5	9	14	...	...	...	13	1	2	3	90
—Tampa Bay	NHL	4	0	0	0	13	-1	0	0	—	—	—	—	—
94-95—Tampa Bay	NHL	10	1	0	1	41	-3	0	0	—	—	—	—	—
—Chicago	NHL	27	3	1	4	117	-3	0	0	14	1	1	2	4
95-96—Chicago	NHL	52	2	4	6	180	-1	0	0	10	0	0	0	2
96-97—Chicago	NHL	65	6	6	12	199	4	0	0	6	0	0	0	24
97-98—Chicago	NHL	55	0	2	2	178	-9	0	0	—	—	—	—	—
—Phoenix	NHL	20	0	0	0	47	-7	0	0	3	0	0	0	4
98-99—Phoenix	NHL	55	1	7	8	190	3	0	0	3	0	1	1	0
99-00—Montreal	NHL	47	3	5	8	92	-5	0	0	—	—	—	—	—
NHL Totals (9 years)		365	18	28	46	1193	-22	0	0	36	1	2	3	34

CZERKAWSKI, MARIUSZ   RW   ISLANDERS

PERSONAL: Born April 13, 1972, in Radomski, Poland. ... 6-0/199. ... Shoots right. ... Name pronounced MAIR-ee-uhz chuhr-KAW-skee.
TRANSACTIONS/CAREER NOTES: Selected by Boston Bruins (fifth Bruins pick, 106th overall) of NHL entry draft (June 22, 1991). ... Played in Europe during 1994-95 NHL lockout. ... Traded by Bruins with D Sean Brown and first-round pick (D Mathieu Descoteaux) in 1996 draft to Edmonton Oilers for G Bill Ranford (January 11, 1996). ... Injured finger (March 23, 1996); missed two games. ... Suffered hip pointer (January 11, 1997); missed two games. ... Traded by Oilers to New York Islanders for LW Dan Lacouture (August 25, 1997). ... Strained muscle in rib cage (December 15, 1999); missed three games.
HONORS: Played in NHL All-Star Game (2000).
MISCELLANEOUS: Failed to score on a penalty shot (vs. Rick Tabaracci, December 4, 1998).
STATISTICAL PLATEAUS: Three-goal games: 1996-97 (2), 1999-00 (1). Total: 3.

		REGULAR SEASON								PLAYOFFS				
Season Team	League	Gms.	G	A	Pts.	PIM	+/-	PP	SH	Gms.	G	A	Pts.	PIM
90-91—GKS Tychy	Poland	24	25	15	40	...	...	...	...	—	—	—	—	—
91-92—Djurgarden Stockholm	Sweden	39	8	5	13	4	...	...	...	3	0	0	0	2
—Polish Olympic Team..	Int'l	5	0	1	1	4	...	...	...	—	—	—	—	—
92-93—Hammarby	Sweden Dv. 2	32	39	30	69	74	...	...	...	—	—	—	—	—
93-94—Djurgarden Stockholm	Sweden	39	13	21	34	20	...	...	...	—	—	—	—	—
—Boston	NHL	4	2	1	3	0	-2	1	0	13	3	3	6	4
94-95—Kiekko-Espoo	Finland	7	9	3	12	10	...	...	...	—	—	—	—	—
—Boston	NHL	47	12	14	26	31	4	1	0	5	1	0	1	0
95-96—Boston	NHL	33	5	6	11	10	-11	1	0	—	—	—	—	—
—Edmonton	NHL	37	12	17	29	8	7	2	0	—	—	—	—	—
96-97—Edmonton	NHL	76	26	21	47	16	0	4	0	12	2	1	3	10
97-98—New York Islanders	NHL	68	12	13	25	23	11	2	0	—	—	—	—	—
98-99—New York Islanders	NHL	78	21	17	38	14	-10	4	0	—	—	—	—	—
99-00—New York Islanders	NHL	79	35	35	70	34	-16	16	0	—	—	—	—	—
NHL Totals (7 years)		422	125	124	249	136	-17	31	0	30	6	4	10	14

DACKELL, ANDREAS   RW   SENATORS

PERSONAL: Born December 29, 1972, in Gavle, Sweden. ... 5-10/195. ... Shoots right. ... Name pronounced AHN-dray-uhz DA-kuhl.
TRANSACTIONS/CAREER NOTES: Selected by Ottawa Senators in sixth round (third Senators pick, 136th overall) of NHL entry draft (June 22, 1996). ... Suffered concussion (October 29, 1998); missed four games. ... Injured knee (January 14, 1999); missed one game.

		REGULAR SEASON								PLAYOFFS				
Season Team	League	Gms.	G	A	Pts.	PIM	+/-	PP	SH	Gms.	G	A	Pts.	PIM
90-91—Brynas Gavle	Sweden	3	0	1	1	2	...	...	...	—	—	—	—	—
91-92—Brynas Gavle	Sweden	4	0	0	0	2	...	...	...	2	0	1	1	4
92-93—Brynas Gavle	Sweden	40	12	15	27	12	...	...	...	10	4	5	9	2
93-94—Brynas Gavle	Sweden	38	12	17	29	47	...	...	...	7	2	2	4	8
94-95—Brynas Gavle	Sweden	39	17	16	33	34	...	...	...	14	3	3	6	14
95-96—Brynas Gavle	Sweden	22	6	6	12	8	...	...	...	—	—	—	—	—
96-97—Ottawa	NHL	79	12	19	31	8	-6	2	0	7	1	0	1	0
97-98—Ottawa	NHL	82	15	18	33	24	-11	3	2	11	1	1	2	2
98-99—Ottawa	NHL	77	15	35	50	30	9	6	0	4	0	1	1	0
99-00—Ottawa	NHL	82	10	25	35	18	5	0	0	6	2	1	3	2
NHL Totals (4 years)		320	52	97	149	80	-3	11	2	28	4	3	7	4

DAFOE, BYRON   G   BRUINS

PERSONAL: Born February 25, 1971, in Sussex, England. ... 5-11/190. ... Catches left. ... Full Name: Byron Jaromir Dafoe.
TRANSACTIONS/CAREER NOTES: Selected by Washington Capitals in second round (second Capitals pick, 35th overall) of NHL entry draft (June 17, 1989). ... Traded by Capitals with RW Dimitri Khristich to Los Angeles Kings for first- (C Alexander Volchkov) and fourth-round (RW Justin Davis) picks in 1996 draft (July 8, 1995). ... Strained thumb (February 1, 1997); missed two games. ... Traded by Kings with RW Dimitri Khristich to Boston Bruins for C Jozef Stumpel, RW Sandy Moger and fourth-round pick (traded to New Jersey) in 1998 draft (August 29, 1997). ... Injured knee (February 21, 2000) and underwent surgery; missed remainder of season.
HONORS: Shared Harry (Hap) Holmes Memorial Trophy with Olaf Kolzig (1993-94). ... Named to AHL All-Star first team (1993-94). ... Named to NHL All-Star second team (1998-99).
MISCELLANEOUS: Allowed penalty shot goal (vs. Steve Chiasson, December 11, 1995).

		REGULAR SEASON								PLAYOFFS						
Season Team	League	Gms.	Min	W	L	T	GA	SO	Avg.	Gms.	Min.	W	L	GA	SO	Avg.
87-88—Juan de Fuca	BCJHL	32	1716	...	...	...	129	0	4.51	—	—	—	—	—	—	—
88-89—Portland	WHL	59	3279	29	24	3	*291	1	5.32	*18	*1091	10	8	*81	*1	4.45
89-90—Portland	WHL	40	2265	14	21	3	193	0	5.11	—	—	—	—	—	—	—
90-91—Portland	WHL	8	414	1	5	1	41	0	5.94	—	—	—	—	—	—	—
—Prince Albert	WHL	32	1839	13	12	4	124	0	4.05	—	—	—	—	—	—	—
91-92—New Haven	AHL	7	364	3	2	1	22	0	3.63	—	—	—	—	—	—	—
—Baltimore	AHL	33	1847	12	16	4	119	0	3.87	—	—	—	—	—	—	—
—Hampton Roads	ECHL	10	562	6	4	0	26	1	2.78	—	—	—	—	—	—	—
92-93—Baltimore	AHL	48	2617	16	*20	7	191	1	4.38	5	241	2	3	22	0	5.48
—Washington	NHL	1	1	0	0	0	0	0	0.00	—	—	—	—	—	—	—
93-94—Portland	AHL	47	2662	24	16	4	148	1	3.34	1	9	0	0	1	0	6.67
—Washington	NHL	5	230	2	2	0	13	0	3.39	2	118	0	2	5	0	2.54
94-95—Portland	AHL	6	330	5	0	0	16	0	2.91	7	417	3	4	29	0	4.17
—Phoenix	IHL	49	2744	25	16	‡6	169	2	3.70	—	—	—	—	—	—	—
—Washington	NHL	4	187	1	1	1	11	0	3.53	1	20	0	0	1	0	3.00
95-96—Los Angeles	NHL	47	2666	14	24	4	172	1	3.87	—	—	—	—	—	—	—

Season Team	League	REGULAR SEASON								PLAYOFFS						
		Gms.	Min	W	L	T	GA	SO	Avg.	Gms.	Min.	W	L	GA	SO	Avg.
96-97—Los Angeles	NHL	40	2162	13	17	5	112	0	3.11	—	—	—	—	—	—	—
97-98—Boston	NHL	65	3693	30	25	9	138	6	2.24	6	422	2	4	14	1	1.99
98-99—Boston	NHL	68	4001	32	23	11	133	*10	1.99	12	768	6	6	26	2	2.03
99-00—Boston	NHL	41	2307	13	16	10	114	3	2.96	—	—	—	—	—	—	—
NHL Totals (8 years)		271	15247	105	108	44	693	20	2.73	21	1328	8	12	46	3	2.08

DAHLEN, ULF — RW — CAPITALS

PERSONAL: Born January 12, 1967, in Ostersund, Sweden. ... 6-3/191. ... Shoots left. ... Name pronounced DAH-lihn.

TRANSACTIONS/CAREER NOTES: Selected by New York Rangers in first round (first Rangers pick, seventh overall) of NHL entry draft (June 15, 1985). ... Bruised shin (November 1987). ... Bruised left shoulder (November 1988). ... Separated right shoulder (January 1989). ... Traded by Rangers with fourth-round pick (C Cal McGowan) in 1990 draft and future considerations to Minnesota North Stars for RW Mike Gartner (March 6, 1990). ... North Stars franchise moved from Minnesota to Dallas and renamed Stars for 1993-94 season. ... Traded by Stars with future considerations to San Jose Sharks for D Mike Lalor and D Doug Zmolek (March 19, 1994). ... Suffered from the flu (February 20, 1995); missed two games. ... Injured groin (October 28, 1995); missed three games. ... Fractured toe (January 11, 1996); missed 20 games. ... Traded by Sharks with G Chris Terreri and D Michal Sykora to Chicago Blackhawks for G Ed Belfour (January 25, 1997). ... Suffered back spasms (March 26, 1997); missed one game. ... Signed as free agent by Washington Capitals (July 21, 1999). ... Injured neck (March 15, 2000); missed one game.

MISCELLANEOUS: Failed to score on a penalty shot (vs. Daren Puppa, March 17, 1992; vs. Curtis Joseph, April 1, 2000).

STATISTICAL PLATEAUS: Three-goal games: 1987-88 (1), 1990-91 (1), 1992-93 (1), 1993-94 (1), 1993-94 (1). Total: 5.

Season Team	League	REGULAR SEASON							PLAYOFFS				
		Gms.	G	A	Pts.	PIM	+/-	PP	SH	Gms.	G	A	Pts.	PIM
83-84—Ostersund	Sweden	36	15	11	26	10	...	...	...	—	—	—	—	—
84-85—Ostersund	Sweden	36	33	26	59	20	...	...	...	—	—	—	—	—
85-86—Bjorkloven	Sweden	22	4	3	7	8	...	...	...	—	—	—	—	—
86-87—Bjorkloven	Sweden	31	9	12	21	20	...	...	...	6	6	2	8	4
87-88—New York Rangers	NHL	70	29	23	52	26	5	11	0	—	—	—	—	—
—Colorado	IHL	2	2	2	4	0	...	...	...	—	—	—	—	—
88-89—New York Rangers	NHL	56	24	19	43	50	-6	8	0	4	0	0	0	0
89-90—New York Rangers	NHL	63	18	18	36	30	-4	13	0	—	—	—	—	—
—Minnesota	NHL	13	2	4	6	0	1	0	0	7	1	4	5	2
90-91—Minnesota	NHL	66	21	18	39	6	7	4	0	15	2	6	8	4
91-92—Minnesota	NHL	79	36	30	66	10	-5	16	1	7	0	3	3	2
92-93—Minnesota	NHL	83	35	39	74	6	-20	13	0	—	—	—	—	—
93-94—Dallas	NHL	65	19	38	57	10	-1	12	0	—	—	—	—	—
—San Jose	NHL	13	6	6	12	0	0	3	0	14	6	2	8	0
94-95—San Jose	NHL	46	11	23	34	11	-2	4	1	11	5	4	9	0
95-96—San Jose	NHL	59	16	12	28	27	-21	5	0	—	—	—	—	—
96-97—San Jose	NHL	43	8	11	19	8	-11	3	0	—	—	—	—	—
—Chicago	NHL	30	6	8	14	10	9	1	0	5	0	1	1	0
97-98—HV 71 Jonkoping	Sweden	29	9	22	31	16	...	...	...	—	—	—	—	—
—Swedish Oly. team	Int'l	4	1	0	1	2	...	...	...	—	—	—	—	—
98-99—HV 71 Jonkoping	Sweden	25	14	15	29	4	...	...	...	—	—	—	—	—
99-00—Washington	NHL	75	15	23	38	8	11	5	0	5	0	1	1	2
NHL Totals (11 years)		761	246	272	518	202	-37	98	2	68	14	21	35	10

DAIGLE, ALEXANDRE — RW

PERSONAL: Born February 7, 1975, in Montreal. ... 6-0/200. ... Shoots left. ... Name pronounced DAYG.

TRANSACTIONS/CAREER NOTES: Selected by Ottawa Senators in first round (first Senators pick, first overall) of NHL entry draft (June 26, 1993). ... Fractured left forearm (February 3, 1996); missed remainder of season. ... Traded by Senators to Flyers for C Vaclav Prospal, RW Pat Falloon and second round pick (LW Chris Bala) in 1998 draft (January 17, 1998). ... Suffered from concussion (October 29, 1998); missed two games. ... Strained left groin (November 14, 1998); missed one game. ... Traded by Flyers to Edmonton Oilers for RW Andrei Kovalenko (January 29, 1999). ... Traded by Oilers to Tampa Bay Lightning for RW Alexander Selivanov (January 29, 1999). ... Injured wrist (March 19, 1999); missed one game. ... Reinjured wrist (March 31, 1999); missed one game. ... Traded by Lightning to New York Rangers for future considerations (October 3, 1999).

HONORS: Won Can.HL Rookie of the Year Award (1991-92). ... Named QMJHL Rookie of the Year (1991-92). ... Won Michel Bergeron Trophy (1991-92). ... Named to Can.HL All-Rookie team (1991-92). ... Named to QMJHL All-Star second team (1991-92). ... Won Can.HL Top Draft Prospect Award (1992-93). ... Won QMJHL Top Draft Prospect Award (1992-93). ... Named to QMJHL All-Star first team (1992-93).

MISCELLANEOUS: Failed to score on penalty shot attempt (vs. Guy Hebert, December 30, 1996).

STATISTICAL PLATEAUS: Three-goal games: 1994-95 (1), 1997-98 (1). Total: 2.

Season Team	League	REGULAR SEASON							PLAYOFFS				
		Gms.	G	A	Pts.	PIM	+/-	PP	SH	Gms.	G	A	Pts.	PIM
91-92—Victoriaville	QMJHL	66	35	75	110	63	...	...	...	—	—	—	—	—
92-93—Victoriaville	QMJHL	53	45	92	137	85	...	...	...	6	5	6	11	4
93-94—Ottawa	NHL	84	20	31	51	40	-45	4	0	—	—	—	—	—
94-95—Victoriaville	QMJHL	18	14	20	34	16	...	...	...	—	—	—	—	—
—Ottawa	NHL	47	16	21	37	14	-22	4	1	—	—	—	—	—
95-96—Ottawa	NHL	50	5	12	17	24	-30	1	0	—	—	—	—	—
96-97—Ottawa	NHL	82	26	25	51	33	-33	4	0	7	0	0	0	2
97-98—Ottawa	NHL	38	7	9	16	8	-7	4	0	—	—	—	—	—
—Philadelphia	NHL	37	9	17	26	6	-1	4	0	5	0	2	2	0
98-99—Philadelphia	NHL	31	3	2	5	2	-1	1	0	—	—	—	—	—
—Tampa Bay	NHL	32	6	6	12	2	-12	3	0	—	—	—	—	—
99-00—Hartford	AHL	16	6	13	19	4	...	...	...	—	—	—	—	—
—New York Rangers	NHL	58	8	18	26	23	-5	1	0	—	—	—	—	—
NHL Totals (7 years)		459	100	141	241	152	-156	26	1	12	0	2	2	2

PERSONAL: Born October 12, 1965, in Montreal. ... 5-11/192. ... Shoots left. ... Full Name: Jean-Jacques Daigneault. ... Name pronounced DAYN-yoh.

TRANSACTIONS/CAREER NOTES: Selected by Vancouver Canucks as underage junior in first round (first Canucks pick, 10th overall) of NHL entry draft (June 1984). ... Fractured finger (March 19, 1986). ... Traded by Canucks with second-round pick (C Kent Hawley) in 1986 draft to Philadelphia Flyers for RW Rich Sutter, D Dave Richter and third-round pick (D Don Gibson) in 1986 draft (June 1986). ... Sprained ankle (April 12, 1987). ... Traded by Flyers to Montreal Canadiens for D Scott Sandelin (November 1988). ... Bruised shoulder (December 1990). ... Suffered hip pointer (March 16, 1991). ... Injured knee (April 7, 1991). ... Bruised left knee (November 28, 1992); missed one game. ... Injured shoulder (December 23, 1992); missed two games. ... Sprained right ankle (March 1, 1993); missed 11 games. ... Suffered injury (December 22, 1993); missed one game. ... Suspended three games and fined $500 by NHL for elbowing (January 7, 1994). ... Sprained wrist (January 10, 1994); missed six games. ... Suffered sore back (March 1, 1994); missed one game. ... Injured shoulder (February 4, 1995); missed one game. ... Suffered from cold (February 13, 1995); missed one game. ... Bruised ankle (April 12, 1995); missed one game. ... Traded by Canadiens to St. Louis Blues for G Pat Jablonski (November 7, 1995). ... Traded by Blues to Pittsburgh Penguins for sixth-round pick (G Stephen Wagner in 1996 draft) (March 20, 1996). ... Suffered back spasms (December 30, 1996); missed one game. ... Suffered back spasms (January 4, 1997); missed two games. ... Traded by Penguins to Anaheim Mighty Ducks for LW Garry Valk (February 21, 1997). ... Suspended 10 games and fined §1,000 by NHL for abusing an official (February 26, 1997). ... Traded by Mighty Ducks with C Mark Janssens and RW Joe Sacco to New York Islanders for C Travis Green, D Doug Houda and RW Tony Tuzzolino (February 6, 1998). ... Separated shoulder (March 12, 1998); missed six games. ... Reinjured shoulder (April 18, 1998); missed one game. ... Selected by Nashville Predators in NHL expansion draft (June 26, 1998). ... Traded by Predators to Phoenix Coyotes for future considerations (January 13, 1999). ... Strained shoulder (February 16, 1999); missed three games. ... Bruised hip (March 11, 1999); missed six games. ... Strained groin (October 26, 1999); missed two games. ... Strained groin (October 31, 1999); missed four games. ... Suffered lower back pain (November 20, 1999); missed one game. ... Sprained ankle (March 13, 2000); missed four games. ... Signed as free agent by Minnesota Wild (July 24, 2000).

HONORS: Won Emile (Butch) Bouchard Trophy (1982-83). ... Named to QMJHL All-Star first team (1982-83).

MISCELLANEOUS: Member of Stanley Cup championship team (1993).

Season Team	League	REGULAR SEASON								PLAYOFFS				
		Gms.	G	A	Pts.	PIM	+/-	PP	SH	Gms.	G	A	Pts.	PIM
81-82—Laval	QMJHL	64	4	25	29	41	...	...	...	18	1	3	4	2
82-83—Longueuil	QMJHL	70	26	58	84	58	...	...	...	15	4	11	15	35
83-84—Can. Olympic team	Int'l	62	6	15	21	40	...	...	...	—	—	—	—	—
—Longueuil	QMJHL	10	2	11	13	6	...	...	...	14	3	13	16	30
—Canadian nat'l team	Int'l	55	5	14	19	40	...	...	...	—	—	—	—	—
84-85—Vancouver	NHL	67	4	23	27	69	-14	2	0	—	—	—	—	—
85-86—Vancouver	NHL	64	5	23	28	45	-20	4	0	3	0	2	2	0
86-87—Philadelphia	NHL	77	6	16	22	56	12	0	0	9	1	0	1	0
87-88—Philadelphia	NHL	28	2	2	4	12	-8	2	0	—	—	—	—	—
—Hershey	AHL	10	1	5	6	8	...	...	...	—	—	—	—	—
88-89—Hershey	AHL	12	0	10	10	13	...	...	...	—	—	—	—	—
—Sherbrooke	AHL	63	10	33	43	48	...	...	...	6	1	3	4	2
89-90—Sherbrooke	AHL	28	8	19	27	18	...	...	...	—	—	—	—	—
—Montreal	NHL	36	2	10	12	14	11	0	0	9	0	0	0	2
90-91—Montreal	NHL	51	3	16	19	31	-2	2	0	5	0	1	1	0
91-92—Montreal	NHL	79	4	14	18	36	16	2	0	11	0	3	3	4
92-93—Montreal	NHL	66	8	10	18	57	25	0	0	20	1	3	4	22
93-94—Montreal	NHL	68	2	12	14	73	16	0	0	7	0	1	1	12
94-95—Montreal	NHL	45	3	5	8	40	2	0	0	—	—	—	—	—
95-96—Montreal	NHL	7	0	1	1	6	0	0	0	—	—	—	—	—
—St. Louis	NHL	37	1	3	4	24	-6	0	0	—	—	—	—	—
—Worcester	AHL	9	1	10	11	10	...	...	...	—	—	—	—	—
—Pittsburgh	NHL	13	3	3	6	23	0	2	0	17	1	9	10	36
96-97—Pittsburgh	NHL	53	3	14	17	36	-5	0	0	—	—	—	—	—
—Anaheim	NHL	13	2	9	11	22	5	0	0	11	2	7	9	16
97-98—Anaheim	NHL	53	2	15	17	28	-10	1	0	—	—	—	—	—
—New York Islanders	NHL	18	0	6	6	21	1	0	0	—	—	—	—	—
98-99—Nashville	NHL	35	2	2	4	38	-4	1	0	—	—	—	—	—
—Phoenix	NHL	35	0	7	7	32	-8	0	0	6	0	0	0	8
99-00—Phoenix	NHL	53	1	6	7	22	-16	0	0	1	0	0	0	0
NHL Totals (15 years)		898	53	197	250	685	-5	16	0	99	5	26	31	100

DAMPHOUSSE, J.F.   G   DEVILS

PERSONAL: Born July 21, 1979, in St. Alexis-des-Monts, Que. ... 6-0/175. ... Catches left. ... Full Name: Jean-Francois Damphousse. ... Name pronounced dahm-FOOZ.

TRANSACTIONS/CAREER NOTES: Selected by New Jersey Devils in first round (first Devils pick, 24th overall) of NHL entry draft (June 21, 1997).

Season Team	League	REGULAR SEASON								PLAYOFFS						
		Gms.	Min	W	L	T	GA	SO	Avg.	Gms.	Min.	W	L	GA	SO	Avg.
96-97—Moncton	QMJHL	39	2063	6	25	2	190	0	5.53	—	—	—	—	—	—	—
97-98—Moncton	QMJHL	59	3400	24	26	*6	174	1	3.07	10	595	5	5	28	0	2.82
98-99—Moncton	QMJHL	40	2163	19	17	2	121	1	3.36	4	200	0	4	12	0	3.60
—Albany	AHL	1	59	0	1	0	3	0	3.05	—	—	—	—	—	—	—
99-00—Albany	AHL	26	1326	9	11	2	62	0	2.81	2	62	0	1	4	0	3.87
—Augusta	ECHL	14	676	6	7	0	49	0	4.35	—	—	—	—	—	—	—

DAMPHOUSSE, VINCENT   C   SHARKS

PERSONAL: Born December 17, 1967, in Montreal. ... 6-1/200. ... Shoots left. ... Name pronounced dahm-FOOZ.

TRANSACTIONS/CAREER NOTES: Selected by Toronto Maple Leafs as underage junior in first round (first Maple Leafs pick, sixth overall) of NHL entry draft (June 21, 1986). ... Traded by Maple Leafs with D Luke Richardson, G Peter Ing, C Scott Thornton and future considerations to Edmonton Oilers for G Grant Fuhr, LW/RW Glenn Anderson and LW Craig Berube (September 19, 1991). ... Traded by Oilers with fourth-round pick (D Adam Wiesel) in 1993 draft to Montreal Canadiens for LW Shayne Corson, LW Vladimir Vujtek and C Brent Gilchrist (August 27, 1992). ... Played in Europe during 1994-95 NHL lockout. ... Suspended two games and fined $1,000 by NHL for cross-checking incident (March 30, 1996). ... Partially dislocated left shoulder (March 11, 1998); missed six games. ... Suffered back spasms (November 27, 1998); missed five games. ... Traded by Canadiens to San Jose Sharks for fifth-round pick (RW Marc-Andre Thinel) in 1999 draft and first-round pick (C Marcel Hossa) in 2000 draft (March 23, 1999).

HONORS: Named to QMJHL All-Star second team (1985-86). ... Played in NHL All-Star Game (1991 and 1992). ... Named All-Star Game Most Valuable Player (1991).

RECORDS: Shares NHL All-Star single-game record for most goals—4 (1991).

STATISTICAL PLATEAUS: Three-goal games: 1988-89 (1), 1989-90 (2), 1992-93 (2), 1993-94 (2), 1996-97 (1), 1997-98 (2), 1998-99 (1). Total: 11. ... Four-goal games: 1991-92 (1). ... Total hat tricks: 12.

MISCELLANEOUS: Member of Stanley Cup championship team (1993). ... Captain of Montreal Canadiens (October 29, 1996 through March 23, 1999). ... Failed to score on a penalty shot (vs. Dominik Hasek, March 8, 1997).

Season Team	League	REGULAR SEASON								PLAYOFFS				
		Gms.	G	A	Pts.	PIM	+/-	PP	SH	Gms.	G	A	Pts.	PIM
83-84—Laval	QMJHL	66	29	36	65	25	...	...	...	—	—	—	—	—
84-85—Laval	QMJHL	68	35	68	103	62	...	...	...	—	—	—	—	—
85-86—Laval	QMJHL	69	45	110	155	70	...	...	...	14	9	27	36	12
86-87—Toronto	NHL	80	21	25	46	26	-6	4	0	12	1	5	6	8
87-88—Toronto	NHL	75	12	36	48	40	2	1	0	6	0	1	1	10
88-89—Toronto	NHL	80	26	42	68	75	-8	6	0	—	—	—	—	—
89-90—Toronto	NHL	80	33	61	94	56	2	9	0	5	0	2	2	2
90-91—Toronto	NHL	79	26	47	73	65	-31	10	1	—	—	—	—	—
91-92—Edmonton	NHL	80	38	51	89	53	10	12	1	16	6	8	14	8
92-93—Montreal	NHL	84	39	58	97	98	5	9	3	20	11	12	23	16
93-94—Montreal	NHL	84	40	51	91	75	0	13	0	7	1	2	3	8
94-95—Ratingen	Germany	11	5	6	11	24	...	...	...	—	—	—	—	—
—Montreal	NHL	48	10	30	40	42	15	4	0	—	—	—	—	—
95-96—Montreal	NHL	80	38	56	94	158	5	11	4	6	4	4	8	0
96-97—Montreal	NHL	82	27	54	81	82	-6	7	2	5	0	0	0	2
97-98—Montreal	NHL	76	18	41	59	58	14	2	1	10	3	6	9	22
98-99—Montreal	NHL	65	12	24	36	46	-7	3	2	—	—	—	—	—
—San Jose	NHL	12	7	6	13	4	3	3	0	6	3	2	5	6
99-00—San Jose	NHL	82	21	49	70	58	4	3	1	12	1	7	8	16
NHL Totals (14 years)		1087	368	631	999	936	2	97	15	105	30	49	79	98

D

DANDENAULT, MATHIEU   RW/D   RED WINGS

PERSONAL: Born February 3, 1976, in Magog, Que. ... 6-1/196. ... Shoots right. ... Cousin of Eric Dandenault, defenseman in Philadelphia Flyers organization (1991-92 through 1993-94). ... Name pronounced DAN-dih-noh.

HIGH SCHOOL: CEGEP de Sherbrooke (Que.).

TRANSACTIONS/CAREER NOTES: Selected by Detroit Red Wings in second round (second Red Wings pick, 49th overall) of NHL entry draft (June 28, 1994). ... Suffered from the flu (November 11, 1995); missed one game. ... Bruised ribs (March 10, 1997); missed four games.

MISCELLANEOUS: Member of Stanley Cup championship team (1997 and 1998).

Season Team	League	REGULAR SEASON								PLAYOFFS				
		Gms.	G	A	Pts.	PIM	+/-	PP	SH	Gms.	G	A	Pts.	PIM
91-92—Gloucester	OPJHL	6	3	4	7	0	...	...	...	—	—	—	—	—
92-93—Gloucester	OPJHL	55	11	26	37	64	...	...	...	—	—	—	—	—
93-94—Sherbrooke	QMJHL	67	17	36	53	67	...	...	...	12	4	10	14	12
94-95—Sherbrooke	QMJHL	67	37	70	107	76	...	...	...	7	1	7	8	10
95-96—Detroit	NHL	34	5	7	12	6	6	1	0	—	—	—	—	—
—Adirondack	AHL	4	0	0	0	0	...	...	...	—	—	—	—	—
96-97—Detroit	NHL	65	3	9	12	28	-10	0	0	—	—	—	—	—
97-98—Detroit	NHL	68	5	12	17	43	5	0	0	3	1	0	1	0
98-99—Detroit	NHL	75	4	10	14	59	17	0	0	10	0	1	1	0
99-00—Detroit	NHL	81	6	12	18	20	-12	0	0	6	0	0	0	2
NHL Totals (5 years)		323	23	50	73	156	6	1	0	19	1	1	2	2

DANEYKO, KEN   D   DEVILS

PERSONAL: Born April 17, 1964, in Windsor, Ont. ... 6-1/215. ... Shoots left. ... Full Name: Kenneth Daneyko. ... Name pronounced DAN-ih-koh.

TRANSACTIONS/CAREER NOTES: Selected by New Jersey Devils as underage junior in first round (second Devils pick, 18th overall) of NHL entry draft (June 1982). ... Fractured right fibula (November 2, 1983). ... Suspended one game and fined $500 by NHL for playing in West Germany without permission (October 1985). ... Injured wrist (February 25, 1987). ... Fractured nose (February 24, 1988). ... Injured shoulder (March 29, 1994); missed six games. ... Injured knee (March 8, 1995); missed 23 games. ... Suffered from the flu (March 9, 1996); missed two games. ... Injured hip (October 12, 1996); missed one game. ... Suffered from the flu (January 31, 1997); missed one game. ... Voluntarily entered NHL/NHLPA substance abuse and behavioral health program (November 6, 1997); missed 45 games. ... Suffered injury (October 16, 1999); missed one game.

HONORS: Won Bill Masterson Memorial Trophy (1999-2000).

MISCELLANEOUS: Member of Stanley Cup championship team (1995 and 2000). ... Holds New Jersey Devils franchise all-time records for most games played (1,070) and most penalty minutes (2,339).

Season Team	League	REGULAR SEASON								PLAYOFFS				
		Gms.	G	A	Pts.	PIM	+/-	PP	SH	Gms.	G	A	Pts.	PIM
80-81—Spokane Flyers	WHL	62	6	13	19	140	...	...	...	4	0	0	0	6
81-82—Spokane Flyers	WHL	26	1	11	12	147	...	...	...	—	—	—	—	—
—Seattle	WHL	38	1	22	23	151	...	...	...	14	1	9	10	49
82-83—Seattle	WHL	69	17	43	60	150	...	...	...	4	1	3	4	14

Season Team	League	REGULAR SEASON								PLAYOFFS				
		Gms.	G	A	Pts.	PIM	+/-	PP	SH	Gms.	G	A	Pts.	PIM
83-84—Kamloops	WHL	19	6	28	34	52	...			17	4	9	13	28
—New Jersey	NHL	11	1	4	5	17	-1	0	0	—	—	—	—	—
84-85—New Jersey	NHL	1	0	0	0	10	-1	0	0	—	—	—	—	—
—Maine	AHL	80	4	9	13	206	...	...	...	11	1	3	4	36
85-86—Maine	AHL	21	3	2	5	75	...	...	...	—	—	—	—	—
—New Jersey	NHL	44	0	10	10	100	1	0	0	—	—	—	—	—
86-87—New Jersey	NHL	79	2	12	14	183	-13	0	0	—	—	—	—	—
87-88—New Jersey	NHL	80	5	7	12	239	-3	1	0	20	1	6	7	83
88-89—New Jersey	NHL	80	5	5	10	283	-22	1	0	—	—	—	—	—
89-90—New Jersey	NHL	74	6	15	21	219	15	0	1	6	2	0	2	21
90-91—New Jersey	NHL	80	4	16	20	249	-10	1	2	7	0	1	1	10
91-92—New Jersey	NHL	80	1	7	8	170	7	0	0	7	0	3	3	16
92-93—New Jersey	NHL	84	2	11	13	236	4	0	0	5	0	0	0	8
93-94—New Jersey	NHL	78	1	9	10	176	27	0	0	20	0	1	1	45
94-95—New Jersey	NHL	25	1	2	3	54	4	0	0	20	1	0	1	22
95-96—New Jersey	NHL	80	2	4	6	115	-10	0	0	—	—	—	—	—
96-97—New Jersey	NHL	77	2	7	9	70	24	0	0	10	0	0	0	28
97-98—New Jersey	NHL	37	0	1	1	57	3	0	0	6	0	1	1	10
98-99—New Jersey	NHL	82	2	9	11	63	27	0	0	7	0	0	0	8
99-00—New Jersey	NHL	78	0	6	6	98	13	0	0	23	1	2	3	14
NHL Totals (17 years)		1070	34	125	159	2339	65	3	3	131	5	14	19	265

DANIELS, JEFF   LW

PERSONAL: Born June 24, 1968, in Oshawa, Ont. ... 6-1/200. ... Shoots left.
TRANSACTIONS/CAREER NOTES: Selected by Pittsburgh Penguins as underage junior in sixth round (sixth Penguins pick, 109th overall) of NHL entry draft (June 21, 1986). ... Traded by Penguins to Florida Panthers for D Greg Hawgood (March 19, 1994). ... Signed as free agent by Hartford Whalers (July 18, 1995). ... Tore knee ligament (December 20, 1996); missed 25 games. ... Whalers franchise moved to North Carolina and renamed Carolina Hurricanes for 1997-98 season; NHL approved move on June 25, 1997. ... Selected by Nashville Predators in NHL expansion draft (June 26, 1998). ... Signed as free agent by Carolina Hurricanes (August 31, 1999). ... Injured hip (October 29, 2000); missed one game. ... Suffered concussion (January 14, 2000); missed two games.
MISCELLANEOUS: Member of Stanley Cup championship team (1992).

D

Season Team	League	REGULAR SEASON								PLAYOFFS				
		Gms.	G	A	Pts.	PIM	+/-	PP	SH	Gms.	G	A	Pts.	PIM
84-85—Oshawa	OHL	59	7	11	18	16	...	...	...	—	—	—	—	—
85-86—Oshawa	OHL	62	13	19	32	23	...	...	...	6	0	1	1	0
86-87—Oshawa	OHL	54	14	9	23	22	...	...	...	15	3	2	5	5
87-88—Oshawa	OHL	64	29	39	68	59	...	...	...	4	2	3	5	0
88-89—Muskegon	IHL	58	21	21	42	58	...	...	...	11	3	5	8	11
89-90—Muskegon	IHL	80	30	47	77	39	...	...	...	6	1	1	2	7
90-91—Pittsburgh	NHL	11	0	2	2	2	0	0	0	—	—	—	—	—
—Muskegon	IHL	62	23	29	52	18	...	...	...	5	1	3	4	2
91-92—Pittsburgh	NHL	2	0	0	0	0	0	0	0	—	—	—	—	—
—Muskegon	IHL	44	19	16	35	38	...	...	...	10	5	4	9	9
92-93—Pittsburgh	NHL	58	5	4	9	14	-5	0	0	12	3	2	5	0
—Cleveland	IHL	3	2	1	3	0	...	...	...	—	—	—	—	—
93-94—Pittsburgh	NHL	63	3	5	8	20	-1	0	0	—	—	—	—	—
—Florida	NHL	7	0	0	0	0	0	0	0	—	—	—	—	—
94-95—Florida	NHL	3	0	0	0	0	0	0	0	—	—	—	—	—
—Detroit	IHL	25	8	12	20	6	...	...	...	5	1	0	1	0
95-96—Springfield	AHL	72	22	20	42	32	...	...	...	10	3	0	3	2
96-97—Springfield	AHL	38	18	14	32	19	...	...	...	16	7	3	10	4
—Hartford	NHL	10	0	2	2	0	2	0	0	—	—	—	—	—
97-98—New Haven	AHL	71	24	27	51	34	...	...	...	3	0	1	1	0
—Carolina	NHL	2	0	0	0	0	0	0	0	—	—	—	—	—
98-99—Milwaukee	IHL	62	12	31	43	19	...	...	...	2	1	1	2	0
—Nashville	NHL	9	1	3	4	2	-1	0	0	—	—	—	—	—
99-00—Carolina	NHL	69	3	4	7	10	-8	0	0	—	—	—	—	—
NHL Totals (9 years)		234	12	20	32	48	-13	0	0	12	3	2	5	0

DARBY, CRAIG   C   CANADIENS

PERSONAL: Born September 26, 1972, in Oneida, N.Y. ... 6-3/200. ... Shoots right.
HIGH SCHOOL: Albany (N.Y.) Academy.
COLLEGE: Providence.
TRANSACTIONS/CAREER NOTES: Selected by Montreal Canadiens in second round (third Canadiens pick, 43rd overall) of NHL entry draft (June 22, 1991). ... Traded by Canadiens with LW Kirk Muller and D Mathieu Schneider to New York Islanders for D Vladimir Malakhov and C Pierre Turgeon (April 5, 1995). ... Claimed on waivers by Philadelphia Flyers (June 4, 1996). ... Selected by Nashville Predators in NHL expansion draft (June 26, 1998). ... Signed as free agent by Canadiens (July 9, 1999).
HONORS: Named Hockey East co-Rookie of the Year with Ian Moran (1991-92). ... Named to Hockey East All-Rookie team (1991-92). ... Named to AHL All-Star first team (1997-98).

Season Team	League	REGULAR SEASON								PLAYOFFS				
		Gms.	G	A	Pts.	PIM	+/-	PP	SH	Gms.	G	A	Pts.	PIM
89-90—Albany Academy	N.Y. H.S.	29	32	53	85	...	...	...	...	—	—	—	—	—
90-91—Albany Academy	N.Y. H.S.	27	33	61	94	53	...	...	...	—	—	—	—	—
91-92—Providence College	Hockey East	35	17	24	41	47	...	...	...	—	—	—	—	—
92-93—Providence College	Hockey East	35	11	21	32	62	...	...	...	—	—	—	—	—

Season Team	League	REGULAR SEASON								PLAYOFFS				
		Gms.	G	A	Pts.	PIM	+/-	PP	SH	Gms.	G	A	Pts.	PIM
93-94—Fredericton	AHL	66	23	33	56	51	...	...	...	—	—	—	—	—
94-95—Fredericton	AHL	64	21	47	68	82	...	...	...	—	—	—	—	—
—Montreal	NHL	10	0	2	2	0	-5	0	0	—	—	—	—	—
—New York Islanders	NHL	3	0	0	0	0	-1	0	0	—	—	—	—	—
95-96—Worcester	AHL	68	22	28	50	47	...	...	...	4	1	1	2	2
—New York Islanders	NHL	10	0	2	2	0	-1	0	0	—	—	—	—	—
96-97—Philadelphia	AHL	59	26	33	59	24	...	...	...	10	3	6	9	0
—Philadelphia	NHL	9	1	4	5	2	2	0	1	—	—	—	—	—
97-98—Philadelphia	NHL	3	1	0	1	0	0	0	0	—	—	—	—	—
—Philadelphia	AHL	77	†42	45	87	34	...	...	...	20	5	9	14	4
98-99—Milwaukee	IHL	81	32	22	54	33	...	...	...	2	3	0	3	0
99-00—Montreal	NHL	76	7	10	17	14	-14	0	1	—	—	—	—	—
NHL Totals (5 years)		111	9	18	27	16	-19	0	2					

DARCHE, MATHIEU — LW — BLUE JACKETS

PERSONAL: Born November 26, 1976, in St. Laurent, Que. ... 6-1/225. ... Shoots left.
COLLEGE: McGill.
TRANSACTIONS/CAREER NOTES: Signed as non-drafted free agent by Columbus Blue Jackets (May 8, 2000).
HONORS: Named to OUA (East) All-Star first team (1998-99 and 1999-2000).

Season Team	League	REGULAR SEASON								PLAYOFFS				
		Gms.	G	A	Pts.	PIM	+/-	PP	SH	Gms.	G	A	Pts.	PIM
96-97—McGill University	CIAU	23	1	2	3	27	...	...	...	—	—	—	—	—
97-98—McGill University	CIAU	40	28	17	45	69	...	...	...	—	—	—	—	—
98-99—McGill University	CIAU	32	16	24	40	60	...	...	...	—	—	—	—	—
99-00—McGill University	CIAU	38	33	49	82	54	...	...	...	—	—	—	—	—

DAVIDSON, MATT — RW — BLUE JACKETS

PERSONAL: Born August 9, 1977, in Flin Flon, Man. ... 6-2/190. ... Shoots right.
HIGH SCHOOL: Beaverton (Ore.).
TRANSACTIONS/CAREER NOTES: Selected by Buffalo Sabres in fourth round (fifth Sabres pick, 94th overall) of NHL entry draft (July 8, 1995). ... Traded by Sabres with D Jean-Luc Grand-Pierre, fifth-round pick (C Tyler Kolarik) in 2000 draft and fifth-round pick in 2001 draft to Columbus Blue Jackets for future considerations (June 23, 2000).

Season Team	League	REGULAR SEASON								PLAYOFFS				
		Gms.	G	A	Pts.	PIM	+/-	PP	SH	Gms.	G	A	Pts.	PIM
93-94—Portland	WHL	59	4	12	16	18	...	...	...	10	0	0	0	4
94-95—Portland	WHL	72	17	20	37	51	...	...	...	9	1	3	4	0
95-96—Portland	WHL	70	24	26	50	96	...	...	...	7	2	2	4	2
96-97—Portland	WHL	72	44	27	71	47	...	...	...	6	0	1	1	2
97-98—Rochester	AHL	72	15	12	27	12	...	...	...	3	1	0	1	2
98-99—Rochester	AHL	80	26	15	41	42	...	...	...	18	2	1	3	6
99-00—Rochester	AHL	80	12	20	32	30	...	...	...	19	4	2	6	8

DAVIDSSON, JOHAN — C/RW

PERSONAL: Born January 6, 1976, in Jonkoping, Sweden. ... 6-1/181. ... Shoots left.
TRANSACTIONS/CAREER NOTES: Selected by Mighty Ducks of Anaheim in second round (second Mighty Ducks pick, 28th overall) of NHL entry draft (June 28, 1994). ... Sprained right ankle (January 1, 1999); missed five games. ... Traded by Mighty Ducks with future considerations to New York Islanders for LW Jorgen Jonsson (March 11, 2000).

Season Team	League	REGULAR SEASON								PLAYOFFS				
		Gms.	G	A	Pts.	PIM	+/-	PP	SH	Gms.	G	A	Pts.	PIM
92-93—HV 71 Jonkoping	Sweden	8	1	0	1	0	...	...	...	—	—	—	—	—
93-94—Swedish nat'l Jr. team	Sweden	6	1	4	5	6	...	...	...	—	—	—	—	—
—HV 71 Jonkoping	Sweden	38	2	5	7	4	...	...	...	—	—	—	—	—
94-95—HV 71 Jonkoping	Sweden	37	4	7	11	20	...	...	...	13	3	2	5	0
95-96—HV 71 Jonkoping	Sweden	39	7	11	18	20	...	...	...	4	0	2	2	0
96-97—HV 71 Jonkoping	Sweden	50	18	21	39	18	...	...	...	5	0	3	3	2
97-98—HIFK Helsinki	Finland	43	10	30	40	73	...	...	...	9	3	10	13	0
98-99—Anaheim	NHL	64	3	5	8	14	-9	1	0	1	0	0	0	0
—Cincinnati	AHL	9	1	6	7	2	...	...	...	—	—	—	—	—
99-00—Cincinnati	AHL	56	9	31	40	24	...	...	...	—	—	—	—	—
—Anaheim	NHL	5	1	0	1	2	0	0	0	—	—	—	—	—
—New York Islanders	NHL	14	2	4	6	0	0	0	0	—	—	—	—	—
NHL Totals (2 years)		83	6	9	15	16	-9	1	0	1	0	0	0	0

DAWE, JASON — LW — RANGERS

PERSONAL: Born May 29, 1973, in North York, Ont. ... 5-10/190. ... Shoots left. ... Name pronounced DAW.
TRANSACTIONS/CAREER NOTES: Selected by Buffalo Sabres in second round (second Sabres pick, 35th overall) of NHL entry draft (June 22, 1991). ... Sprained knee (February 11, 1995); missed three games. ... Fractured ribs (February 21, 1996); missed six games. ... Traded by Sabres to New York Islanders for LW Paul Kruse and LW Jason Holland (March 24, 1998). ... Claimed on waivers by Montreal Canadiens (December 15, 1998). ... Suffered concussion (February 17, 1999); missed two games. ... Signed as free agent by Nashville Predators (October 2, 1999). ... Traded by Predators to New York Rangers for D John Namestnikov (February 2, 2000).
HONORS: Won George Parsons Trophy (1992-93). ... Named to Can.HL All-Star second team (1992-93). ... Named to OHL All-Star first team (1992-93).
STATISTICAL PLATEAUS: Three-goal games: 1995-96 (1), 1997-98 (1). Total: 2.

Season Team	League	REGULAR SEASON								PLAYOFFS				
		Gms.	G	A	Pts.	PIM	+/-	PP	SH	Gms.	G	A	Pts.	PIM
89-90—Peterborough............	OHL	50	15	18	33	19	...	...	...	12	4	7	11	4
90-91—Peterborough............	OHL	66	43	27	70	43	...	...	...	4	3	1	4	0
91-92—Peterborough............	OHL	66	53	55	108	55	...	...	...	4	5	0	5	0
92-93—Peterborough............	OHL	59	58	68	126	80	...	...	...	21	18	33	51	18
—Rochester	AHL	0	0	0	0	0	—	—	—	3	1	0	1	0
93-94—Rochester	AHL	48	22	14	36	44	...	...	...	—	—	—	—	—
—Buffalo	NHL	32	6	7	13	12	1	3	0	6	0	1	1	6
94-95—Rochester	AHL	44	27	19	46	24	...	...	...	—	—	—	—	—
—Buffalo	NHL	42	7	4	11	19	-6	0	1	5	2	1	3	6
95-96—Buffalo	NHL	67	25	25	50	33	-8	8	1	—	—	—	—	—
—Rochester	AHL	7	5	4	9	2	...	...	...	—	—	—	—	—
96-97—Buffalo	NHL	81	22	26	48	32	14	4	1	11	2	1	3	6
97-98—Buffalo	NHL	68	19	17	36	36	10	4	1	—	—	—	—	—
—New York Islanders.....	NHL	13	1	2	3	6	-2	0	0	—	—	—	—	—
98-99—New York Islanders.....	NHL	22	2	3	5	8	0	0	0	—	—	—	—	—
—Montreal	NHL	37	4	5	9	14	0	1	0	—	—	—	—	—
99-00—Milwaukee..................	IHL	41	11	13	24	24	...	...	...	—	—	—	—	—
—Hartford	AHL	27	9	9	18	24	...	...	...	21	10	7	17	37
—New York Rangers......	NHL	3	0	1	1	2	0	0	0	—	—	—	—	—
NHL Totals (7 years)...........		365	86	90	176	162	9	20	4	22	4	3	7	18

DAZE, ERIC — RW — BLACKHAWKS

PERSONAL: Born July 2, 1975, in Montreal. ... 6-6/234. ... Shoots left. ... Name pronounced dah-ZAY.

TRANSACTIONS/CAREER NOTES: Selected by Chicago Blackhawks in fourth round (fifth Blackhawks pick, 90th overall) of NHL entry draft (June 26, 1993). ... Sprained left ankle prior to 1996-97 season; missed eight games. ... Suffered from the flu (January 20, 1997); missed one game. ... Injured back (March 27, 1998); missed two games. ... Bruised ankle (October 22, 1998); missed three games. ... Suffered back spasms (October 27, 1999); missed three games. ... Suffered from the flu (January 2, 2000); missed one game. ... Suffered from migraine headache (February 16, 2000); missed one game. ... Suffered back spasms (March 3, 2000) and underwent surgery; missed final 18 games of season.

HONORS: Named to QMJHL All-Star first team (1993-94 and 1994-95). ... Won Can.HL Most Sportsmanlike Player of the Year Award (1994-95). ... Won Frank J. Selke Trophy (1994-95). ... Named NHL Rookie of the Year by THE SPORTING NEWS (1995-96). ... Named to NHL All-Rookie team (1995-96).

STATISTICAL NOTES: Tied for NHL lead in game-tying goals with three (1998-99).

STATISTICAL PLATEAUS: Three-goal games: 1996-97 (1). ... Four-goal games: 1997-98 (1). ... Total hat tricks: 2.

D

Season Team	League	REGULAR SEASON								PLAYOFFS				
		Gms.	G	A	Pts.	PIM	+/-	PP	SH	Gms.	G	A	Pts.	PIM
92-93—Beauport	QMJHL	68	19	36	55	24	...	...	...	—	—	—	—	—
93-94—Beauport	QMJHL	66	59	48	107	31	...	...	...	15	16	8	24	2
94-95—Beauport	QMJHL	57	54	45	99	20	...	...	...	16	9	12	21	23
—Chicago......................	NHL	4	1	1	2	2	2	0	0	16	0	1	1	4
95-96—Chicago......................	NHL	80	30	23	53	18	16	2	0	10	3	5	8	0
96-97—Chicago......................	NHL	71	22	19	41	16	-4	11	0	6	2	1	3	2
97-98—Chicago......................	NHL	80	31	11	42	22	4	10	0	—	—	—	—	—
98-99—Chicago......................	NHL	72	22	20	42	22	-13	8	0	—	—	—	—	—
99-00—Chicago......................	NHL	59	23	13	36	28	-16	6	0	—	—	—	—	—
NHL Totals (6 years)...........		366	129	87	216	108	-11	37	0	32	5	7	12	6

DEADMARSH, ADAM — RW — AVALANCHE

PERSONAL: Born May 10, 1975, in Trail, B.C. ... 6-0/195. ... Shoots right. ... Cousin of Butch Deadmarsh, left winger with three NHL teams (1970-71 through 1974-75); and brother of Jake Deadmarsh, left winger, San Jose Sharks system.

HIGH SCHOOL: Lakeridge (Fruitvale, B.C.).

TRANSACTIONS/CAREER NOTES: Selected by Quebec Nordiques in first round (second Nordiques pick, 14th overall) of NHL entry draft (June 26, 1993). ... Nordiques franchise moved to Colorado and renamed Avalanche for 1995-96 season (June 21, 1995). ... Strained groin (April 3, 1996); missed four games. ... Strained shoulder (December 13, 1997); missed one game. ... Suffered from the flu (January 14, 1998); missed one game. ... Strained hip flexor (March 19, 1998); missed one game. ... Injured shoulder (April 1, 1998); missed two games. ... Bruised thigh (April 11, 1998); missed two games. ... Bruised ribs (October 9, 1998); missed first two games of season. ... Suffered infected left elbow (October 24, 1998); missed three games. ... Suffered back spasms (March 16, 1999); missed five games. ... Injured eye (April 3, 1999); missed final six games of regular season. ... Suffered hip pointer prior to start of 1999-2000 regular season; missed first two games of season. ... Bruised toe (December 12, 1999); missed one game. ... Sprained knee (January 13, 2000); missed three games. ... Injured rib (February 15, 2000); missed five games.

MISCELLANEOUS: Member of Stanley Cup championship team (1996). ... Scored on a penalty shot (vs. Jeff Hackett, March 1, 1997).

STATISTICAL NOTES: Tied for NHL lead with three game-tying goals (1997-98).

STATISTICAL PLATEAUS: Three-goal games: 1999-00 (1).

Season Team	League	REGULAR SEASON								PLAYOFFS				
		Gms.	G	A	Pts.	PIM	+/-	PP	SH	Gms.	G	A	Pts.	PIM
91-92—Portland	WHL	68	30	30	60	81	...	...	...	6	3	3	6	13
92-93—Portland	WHL	58	33	36	69	126	...	...	...	16	7	8	15	29
93-94—Portland	WHL	65	43	56	99	212	...	...	...	10	9	8	17	33
94-95—Portland	WHL	29	28	20	48	129	...	...	...	—	—	—	—	—
—Quebec	NHL	48	9	8	17	56	16	0	0	6	0	1	1	0
95-96—Colorado	NHL	78	21	27	48	142	20	3	0	22	5	12	17	25
96-97—Colorado	NHL	78	33	27	60	136	8	10	3	17	3	6	9	24
97-98—Colorado	NHL	73	22	21	43	125	0	10	0	7	2	0	2	4
—U.S. Olympic team.......	Int'l	4	1	0	1	2	...	...	...	—	—	—	—	—
98-99—Colorado	NHL	66	22	27	49	99	-2	10	0	19	8	4	12	20
99-00—Colorado	NHL	71	18	27	45	106	-10	5	0	17	4	11	15	21
NHL Totals (6 years)...........		414	125	137	262	664	32	38	3	88	22	34	56	94

DEAN, KEVIN — D — BLACKHAWKS

PERSONAL: Born April 1, 1969, in Madison, Wis. ... 6-3/210. ... Shoots left.
HIGH SCHOOL: Culver (Ind.) Military Academy.
COLLEGE: New Hampshire.
TRANSACTIONS/CAREER NOTES: Selected by New Jersey Devils in fourth round (fourth Devils pick, 86th overall) of NHL entry draft (June 13, 1987). ... Suffered rib injury (September 19, 1996); missed three games. ... Strained groin (November 25, 1998); missed three games. ... Reinjured groin (December 4, 1998); missed six games. ... Suffered from the flu (January 24, 1999); missed one game. ... Suffered from irregular heartbeat (February 1, 1999); missed two games. ... Strained right knee (February 9, 1999); missed five games. ... Selected by Atlanta Thrashers in NHL expansion draft (June 25, 1999). ... Traded by Thrashers to Dallas Stars for future considerations (December 15, 1999). ... Suffered irregular heartbeat (December 23, 1999); missed three games. ... Traded by Stars with C Derek Plante and second-round pick in 2001 draft to Chicago Blackhawks for D Sylvain Cote and D Dave Manson (February 8, 2000).
HONORS: Named to AHL All-Star first team (1994-95).
MISCELLANEOUS: Member of Stanley Cup championship team (1995).

Season Team	League	REGULAR SEASON								PLAYOFFS				
		Gms.	G	A	Pts.	PIM	+/-	PP	SH	Gms.	G	A	Pts.	PIM
85-86—Culver Military	Indiana H.S.	35	28	44	72	48	...	...	...	—	—	—	—	—
86-87—Culver Military	Indiana H.S.	25	19	25	44	30	...	...	...	—	—	—	—	—
87-88—Univ. of New Hamp.	Hockey East	27	1	6	7	34	...	...	...	—	—	—	—	—
88-89—Univ. of New Hamp.	Hockey East	34	1	12	13	28	...	...	...	—	—	—	—	—
89-90—Univ. of New Hamp.	Hockey East	39	2	6	8	42	...	...	...	—	—	—	—	—
90-91—Univ. of New Hamp.	Hockey East	31	10	12	22	22	...	...	...	—	—	—	—	—
—Utica	AHL	7	0	1	1	2	...	...	...	—	—	—	—	—
91-92—Utica	AHL	23	0	3	3	6	...	...	...	—	—	—	—	—
—Cincinnati	ECHL	30	3	22	25	43	...	...	...	9	1	6	7	8
92-93—Utica	AHL	57	2	16	18	76	...	...	...	5	1	0	1	8
—Cincinnati	IHL	13	2	1	3	15	...	...	...	—	—	—	—	—
93-94—Albany	AHL	70	9	33	42	92	...	...	...	5	0	2	2	7
94-95—Albany	AHL	68	5	37	42	66	...	...	...	8	0	4	4	4
—New Jersey	NHL	17	0	1	1	4	6	0	0	3	0	2	2	0
95-96—New Jersey	NHL	41	0	6	6	28	4	0	0	—	—	—	—	—
—Albany	AHL	1	1	0	1	2	...	...	...	—	—	—	—	—
96-97—New Jersey	NHL	28	2	4	6	6	2	0	0	1	1	0	1	0
—Albany	AHL	2	0	1	1	4	...	...	...	—	—	—	—	—
97-98—New Jersey	NHL	50	1	8	9	12	12	1	0	5	1	0	1	2
—Albany	AHL	2	0	1	1	2	...	...	...	—	—	—	—	—
98-99—New Jersey	NHL	62	1	10	11	22	4	1	0	7	0	0	0	0
99-00—Atlanta	NHL	23	1	0	1	14	-5	0	1	—	—	—	—	—
—Dallas	NHL	14	0	0	0	10	-1	0	0	—	—	—	—	—
—Chicago	NHL	27	2	8	10	12	9	0	0	—	—	—	—	—
NHL Totals (6 years)		262	7	37	44	108	31	2	1	16	2	2	4	2

DeBRUSK, LOUIE — LW — COYOTES

PERSONAL: Born March 19, 1971, in Cambridge, Ont. ... 6-2/238. ... Shoots left. ... Full Name: Dennis Louis DeBrusk. ... Name pronounced dee-BRUHSK.
HIGH SCHOOL: Saugeen (Port Elgin, Ont.).
TRANSACTIONS/CAREER NOTES: Selected by New York Rangers in third round (fourth Rangers pick, 49th overall) of NHL entry draft (June 17, 1989). ... Traded by Rangers with C Bernie Nicholls, RW Steven Rice and future considerations to Edmonton Oilers for C Mark Messier and future considerations (October 4, 1991); Rangers traded D David Shaw to Oilers for D Jeff Beukeboom to complete deal (November 12, 1991). ... Separated shoulder (January 28, 1992); missed four games. ... Strained groin (January 1993); missed five games. ... Strained abdominal muscle (January 1993); missed 11 games. ... Underwent blood tests (April 17, 1995); missed one game. ... Suspended two games by NHL for headbutting an opponent (October 6, 1995). ... Injured elbow (November 26, 1995); missed 14 games. ... Suspended four games and fined §1,000 by NHL for slashing (October 9, 1996). ... Signed as free agent by Tampa Bay Lightning (August 26, 1997). ... Traded by Lightning with fifth-round pick (D Jay Leach) in 1998 draft to Phoenix Coyotes for C Craig Janney (June 11, 1998). ... Suffered from the flu (April 17, 1999); missed final game of regular season.

Season Team	League	REGULAR SEASON								PLAYOFFS				
		Gms.	G	A	Pts.	PIM	+/-	PP	SH	Gms.	G	A	Pts.	PIM
87-88—Stratford Jr. B	OHA	43	13	14	27	205	...	...	...	—	—	—	—	—
88-89—London	OHL	59	11	11	22	149	...	...	...	19	1	1	2	43
89-90—London	OHL	61	21	19	40	198	...	...	...	6	2	2	4	24
90-91—London	OHL	61	31	33	64	*223	...	...	...	7	2	2	4	14
—Binghamton	AHL	2	0	0	0	7	...	...	...	2	0	0	0	9
91-92—Edmonton	NHL	25	2	1	3	124	4	0	0	—	—	—	—	—
—Cape Breton	AHL	28	2	2	4	73	...	...	...	—	—	—	—	—
92-93—Edmonton	NHL	51	8	2	10	205	-16	0	0	—	—	—	—	—
93-94—Edmonton	NHL	48	4	6	10	185	-9	0	0	—	—	—	—	—
—Cape Breton	AHL	5	3	1	4	58	...	...	...	—	—	—	—	—
94-95—Edmonton	NHL	34	2	0	2	93	-4	0	0	—	—	—	—	—
95-96—Edmonton	NHL	38	1	3	4	96	-7	0	0	—	—	—	—	—
96-97—Edmonton	NHL	32	0	2	2	94	-6	0	0	6	0	0	0	4
97-98—Tampa Bay	NHL	54	1	2	3	166	-2	0	0	—	—	—	—	—
—San Antonio	IHL	17	7	4	11	130	...	...	...	—	—	—	—	—
98-99—Las Vegas	IHL	26	3	6	9	160	...	...	...	—	—	—	—	—
—Phoenix	NHL	15	0	0	0	34	-2	0	0	6	2	0	2	6
—Springfield	AHL	3	1	0	1	0	...	...	...	—	—	—	—	—
—Long Beach	IHL	24	5	5	10	134	...	...	...	—	—	—	—	—
99-00—Phoenix	NHL	61	4	3	7	78	1	0	0	3	0	0	0	0
NHL Totals (9 years)		358	24	17	41	1075	-41	0	0	15	2	0	2	10

DELEEUW, ADAM — LW — RED WINGS

PERSONAL: Born February 29, 1980, in Brampton, Ont. ... 6-0/206. ... Shoots left.
TRANSACTIONS/CAREER NOTES: Selected by Detroit Red Wings in sixth round (seventh Red Wings pick, 151st overall) of NHL entry draft (June 27, 1998).

Season Team	League	REGULAR SEASON								PLAYOFFS				
		Gms.	G	A	Pts.	PIM	+/-	PP	SH	Gms.	G	A	Pts.	PIM
96-97—Brampton	Tier II Jr. A	45	11	17	28	97	...	...	...	—	—	—	—	—
97-98—Barrie	OHL	56	10	6	16	224	...	...	...	—	—	—	—	—
98-99—Barrie	OHL	39	15	16	31	146	...	...	...	—	—	—	—	—
—Toronto St. Michael's	OHL	29	10	5	15	55	...	...	...	—	—	—	—	—
99-00—Toronto St. Michael's	OHL	45	11	19	30	107	...	...	...	—	—	—	—	—
—Dayton	ECHL	2	0	0	0	2	...	...	...	3	0	0	0	2

DELMORE, ANDY — D — FLYERS

PERSONAL: Born December 26, 1976, in Windsor, Ont. ... 6-1/192. ... Shoots right.
TRANSACTIONS/CAREER NOTES: Signed as non-drafted free agent by Philadelphia Flyers (July 9, 1997). ... Sprained right knee (March 5, 2000); missed nine games.
HONORS: Named to OHL All-Star first team (1996-97).

Season Team	League	REGULAR SEASON								PLAYOFFS				
		Gms.	G	A	Pts.	PIM	+/-	PP	SH	Gms.	G	A	Pts.	PIM
92-93—Chatham Jr. B	OHA	47	4	21	25	38	...	...	...	—	—	—	—	—
93-94—North Bay	OHL	45	2	7	9	33	...	...	...	17	0	0	0	2
94-95—North Bay	OHL	40	2	14	16	21	...	...	...	—	—	—	—	—
—Sarnia	OHL	27	5	13	18	27	...	...	...	3	0	0	0	2
95-96—Sarnia	OHL	64	21	38	59	45	...	...	...	10	3	7	10	2
96-97—Sarnia	OHL	63	18	60	78	39	...	...	...	12	2	10	12	10
—Fredericton	AHL	4	0	1	1	0	...	...	...	—	—	—	—	—
97-98—Philadelphia	AHL	73	9	30	39	46	...	...	...	18	4	4	8	21
98-99—Philadelphia	AHL	70	5	18	23	51	...	...	...	15	1	4	5	6
—Philadelphia	NHL	2	0	1	1	0	-1	0	0	—	—	—	—	—
99-00—Philadelphia	AHL	39	12	14	26	31	...	...	...	—	—	—	—	—
—Philadelphia	NHL	27	2	5	7	8	-1	0	0	18	5	2	7	14
NHL Totals (2 years)		29	2	6	8	8	-2	0	0	18	5	2	7	14

DEMITRA, PAVOL — RW — BLUES

PERSONAL: Born November 29, 1974, in Dubnica, Czechoslovakia. ... 6-0/190. ... Shoots left. ... Name pronounced PA-vuhl dih-MEE-truh.
TRANSACTIONS/CAREER NOTES: Selected by Ottawa Senators in ninth round (ninth Senators pick, 227th overall) of NHL entry draft (June 26, 1993). ... Fractured ankle (October 14, 1993); missed 23 games. ... Traded by Senators to St. Louis Blues for D Christer Olsson (November 27, 1996). ... Suffered back spasms and bruised tailbone (December 8, 1997); missed 10 games. ... Fractured jaw (March 7, 1998); missed 11 games. ... Injured triceps (December 26, 1999); missed three games. ... Suffered concussion (March 24, 2000); missed remainder of season.
HONORS: Played in NHL All-Star Game (1999 and 2000). ... Won Lady Byng Memorial Trophy (1999-2000).
STATISTICAL PLATEAUS: Three-goal games: 1999-00 (1).

Season Team	League	REGULAR SEASON								PLAYOFFS				
		Gms.	G	A	Pts.	PIM	+/-	PP	SH	Gms.	G	A	Pts.	PIM
91-92—Sparta Dubnica	Czech Dv.II	28	13	10	23	12	...	...	...	—	—	—	—	—
92-93—Dukla Trencin	Czech.	46	11	17	28	0	...	...	...	—	—	—	—	—
—CAPEH Dubnica	Czech Dv.II	4	3	0	3		...	...	...	—	—	—	—	—
93-94—Ottawa	NHL	12	1	1	2	4	-7	1	0	—	—	—	—	—
—Prin. Edward Island	AHL	41	18	23	41	8	...	...	...	—	—	—	—	—
94-95—Prin. Edward Island	AHL	61	26	48	74	23	...	...	...	5	0	7	7	0
—Ottawa	NHL	16	4	3	7	0	-4	1	0	—	—	—	—	—
95-96—Prin. Edward Island	AHL	48	28	53	81	44	...	...	...	—	—	—	—	—
—Ottawa	NHL	31	7	10	17	6	-3	2	0	—	—	—	—	—
96-97—Las Vegas	IHL	22	8	13	21	10	...	...	...	—	—	—	—	—
—Grand Rapids	IHL	42	20	30	50	24	...	...	...	—	—	—	—	—
—St. Louis	NHL	8	3	0	3	2	0	2	0	6	1	3	4	6
97-98—St. Louis	NHL	61	22	30	52	22	11	4	4	10	3	3	6	2
98-99—St. Louis	NHL	82	37	52	89	16	13	14	0	13	5	4	9	4
99-00—St. Louis	NHL	71	28	47	75	8	34	8	0	—	—	—	—	—
NHL Totals (7 years)		281	102	143	245	58	44	32	4	29	9	10	19	12

DEMPSEY, NATHAN — D — MAPLE LEAFS

PERSONAL: Born July 14, 1974, in Spruce Grove, Alta. ... 6-0/190. ... Shoots left.
TRANSACTIONS/CAREER NOTES: Selected by Toronto Maple Leafs in 11th round (11th Leafs pick, 245th overall) of NHL entry draft (June 20, 1992).

Season Team	League	REGULAR SEASON								PLAYOFFS				
		Gms.	G	A	Pts.	PIM	+/-	PP	SH	Gms.	G	A	Pts.	PIM
91-92—Regina	WHL	70	4	22	26	72	...	...	...	—	—	—	—	—
92-93—Regina	WHL	72	12	29	41	95	...	...	...	13	3	8	11	14
—St. John's	AHL	—	—	—	—	—	...	...	...	2	0	0	0	0
93-94—Regina	WHL	56	14	36	50	100	...	...	...	4	0	0	0	4

D

Season Team	League	REGULAR SEASON								PLAYOFFS				
		Gms.	G	A	Pts.	PIM	+/-	PP	SH	Gms.	G	A	Pts.	PIM
94-95—St. John's	AHL	74	7	30	37	91	...	...	...	5	1	0	1	11
95-96—St. John's	AHL	73	5	15	20	103	...	...	...	4	1	0	1	9
96-97—St. John's	AHL	52	8	18	26	108	...	...	...	6	1	0	1	4
—Toronto	NHL	14	1	1	2	2	-2	0	0	—	—	—	—	—
97-98—St. John's	AHL	68	12	16	28	85	...	...	...	4	0	0	0	0
98-99—St. John's	AHL	67	2	29	31	70	...	...	...	5	0	1	1	2
99-00—St. John's	AHL	44	15	12	27	40	...	...	...	—	—	—	—	—
—Toronto	NHL	6	0	2	2	2	2	0	0	—	—	—	—	—
NHL Totals (2 years)		20	1	3	4	4	0	0	0					

DENIS, MARC — G — BLUE JACKETS

PERSONAL: Born August 1, 1977, in Montreal. ... 6-0/190. ... Catches left. ... Name pronounced deh-NEE.
TRANSACTIONS/CAREER NOTES: Selected by Colorado Avalanche in first round (first Avalanche pick, 25th overall) of NHL entry draft (July 8, 1995). ... Traded by Avalanche to Columbus Blue Jackets for second-round pick (traded to Carolina) in 2000 draft (June 7, 2000).
HONORS: Won Marcel Robert Trophy (1995-96). ... Won Can.HL Goaltender of the Year Award (1996-97). ... Won Jacques Plante Trophy (1996-97). ... Named to QMJHL All-Star first team (1996-97).

Season Team	League	REGULAR SEASON								PLAYOFFS						
		Gms.	Min	W	L	T	GA	SO	Avg.	Gms.	Min.	W	L	GA	SO	Avg.
94-95—Chicoutimi	QMJHL	32	1688	17	9	1	98	0	3.48	6	374	4	2	19	1	3.05
95-96—Chicoutimi	QMJHL	51	2895	23	21	4	157	2	3.25	16	917	8	†8	66	0	4.32
96-97—Chicoutimi	QMJHL	41	2317	22	15	2	104	4	*2.69	*21	*1226	*11	*10	*70	*1	3.43
—Colorado	NHL	1	60	0	1	0	3	0	3.00	—	—	—	—	—	—	—
—Hershey	AHL	—	—	—	—	—	—	—	—	4	56	1	0	1	0	*1.07
97-98—Hershey	AHL	47	2589	17	23	4	125	1	2.90	6	347	3	3	15	0	2.59
98-99—Hershey	AHL	52	2908	20	23	5	137	4	2.83	3	143	1	1	7	0	2.94
—Colorado	NHL	4	217	1	1	1	9	0	2.49	—	—	—	—	—	—	—
99-00—Colorado	NHL	23	1203	9	8	3	51	3	2.54	—	—	—	—	—	—	—
NHL Totals (3 years)		28	1480	10	10	4	63	3	2.55							

DESCOTEAUX, MATHIEU — D — CANADIENS

PERSONAL: Born September 23, 1977, in Pierreville, Que. ... 6-3/220. ... Shoots left. ... Name pronounced day-koh-TOH.
TRANSACTIONS/CAREER NOTES: Selected by Edmonton Oilers in first round (second Oilers pick, 19th overall) of NHL entry draft (June 22, 1996). ... Traded by Oilers with D Christian LaFlamme to Montreal Canadiens for D Igor Ulanov and D Alain Nasreddine (March 9, 2000).

Season Team	League	REGULAR SEASON								PLAYOFFS				
		Gms.	G	A	Pts.	PIM	+/-	PP	SH	Gms.	G	A	Pts.	PIM
94-95—Shawinigan	QMJHL	50	3	2	5	28	...	...	...	—	—	—	—	—
95-96—Shawinigan	QMJHL	69	2	13	15	129	...	...	...	6	0	0	0	6
96-97—Shawinigan	QMJHL	38	6	18	24	121	...	...	...	—	—	—	—	—
—Hull	QMJHL	32	6	19	25	34	...	...	...	14	2	5	7	20
97-98—Hamilton	AHL	67	2	8	10	70	...	...	...	2	0	0	0	0
98-99—Hamilton	AHL	74	6	12	18	49	...	...	...	4	0	0	0	0
99-00—Hamilton	AHL	49	5	7	12	29	...	...	...	—	—	—	—	—
—Quebec	AHL	12	0	6	6	6	...	...	...	2	0	1	1	0

DESJARDINS, ERIC — D — FLYERS

PERSONAL: Born June 14, 1969, in Rouyn, Que. ... 6-1/205. ... Shoots right. ... Name pronounced day-zhar-DAN.
TRANSACTIONS/CAREER NOTES: Selected by Montreal Canadiens as underage junior in second round (third Canadiens pick, 38th overall) of NHL entry draft (June 13, 1987). ... Suffered from the flu (January 1989). ... Pulled groin (November 2, 1989); missed seven games. ... Sprained left ankle (January 26, 1991); missed 16 games. ... Fractured right thumb (December 8, 1991); missed two games. ... Traded by Canadiens with LW Gilbert Dionne and C John LeClair to Philadelphia Flyers for RW Mark Recchi and third-round pick (C Martin Hohenberger) in 1995 draft (February 9, 1995). ... Slightly strained groin (March 28, 1995); missed one game. ... Reinjured groin (April 1, 1995); missed three games. ... Suffered from the flu (December 26, 1995); missed one game. ... Suffered inflamed pelvic bone (October 1, 1997); missed five games. ... Strained groin (October 27, 1998); missed four games. ... Suffered from stomach virus (March 6, 1999); missed three games. ... Sprained left knee (March 21, 1999); missed seven games. ... Suffered head injury prior to start of 1999-2000 season; missed first game of season.
HONORS: Named to QMJHL All-Star second team (1986-87). ... Won Emile (Butch) Bouchard Trophy (1987-88). ... Named to QMJHL All-Star first team (1987-88). ... Played in NHL All-Star Game (1992, 1996 and 2000). ... Named to NHL All-Star second team (1998-99 and 1999-2000).
RECORDS: Shares NHL single-game playoff record for most goals by defensemen—3 (June 3, 1993).
MISCELLANEOUS: Member of Stanley Cup championship team (1993). ... Captain of Philadelphia Flyers (March 27, 1999-remainder of season). ... Failed to score on a penalty shot (vs. Dominik Hasek, April 16, 2000 (playoffs)).

Season Team	League	REGULAR SEASON								PLAYOFFS				
		Gms.	G	A	Pts.	PIM	+/-	PP	SH	Gms.	G	A	Pts.	PIM
86-87—Granby	QMJHL	66	14	24	38	75	...	...	...	8	3	2	5	10
87-88—Granby	QMJHL	62	18	49	67	138	...	...	...	5	0	3	3	10
—Sherbrooke	AHL	3	0	0	0	6	...	...	...	4	0	2	2	2
88-89—Montreal	NHL	36	2	12	14	26	9	1	0	14	1	1	2	6
89-90—Montreal	NHL	55	3	13	16	51	1	1	0	6	0	0	0	10
90-91—Montreal	NHL	62	7	18	25	27	7	0	0	13	1	4	5	8
91-92—Montreal	NHL	77	6	32	38	50	17	4	0	11	3	3	6	4
92-93—Montreal	NHL	82	13	32	45	98	20	7	0	20	4	10	14	23
93-94—Montreal	NHL	84	12	23	35	97	-1	6	1	7	0	2	2	4
94-95—Montreal	NHL	9	0	6	6	2	2	0	0	—	—	—	—	—
—Philadelphia	NHL	34	5	18	23	12	10	1	0	15	4	4	8	10

Season Team	League	REGULAR SEASON								PLAYOFFS				
		Gms.	G	A	Pts.	PIM	+/-	PP	SH	Gms.	G	A	Pts.	PIM
95-96—Philadelphia	NHL	80	7	40	47	45	19	5	0	12	0	6	6	2
96-97—Philadelphia	NHL	82	12	34	46	50	25	5	1	19	2	8	10	12
97-98—Philadelphia	NHL	77	6	27	33	36	11	2	1	5	0	1	1	0
—Can. Olympic team	Int'l	6	0	0	0	2	...	...	...	—	—	—	—	—
98-99—Philadelphia	NHL	68	15	36	51	38	18	6	0	6	2	2	4	4
99-00—Philadelphia	NHL	81	14	41	55	32	20	8	0	18	2	10	12	2
NHL Totals (12 years).........		827	102	332	434	564	158	46	3	146	19	51	70	85

DEVEREAUX, BOYD   C

PERSONAL: Born April 16, 1978, in Seaforth, Ont. ... 6-2/195. ... Shoots left. ... Name pronounced DEH-vuh-roh.
TRANSACTIONS/CAREER NOTES: Selected by Edmonton Oilers in first round (first Oilers pick, sixth overall) of NHL entry draft (June 22, 1996). ... Suffered concussion (April 1, 2000); missed remainder of season.
HONORS: Won Can.HL Scholastic Player of the Year Award (1995-96). ... Named to OHL All-Rookie second team (1995-96). ... Won Bobby Smith Trophy (1995-96).
STATISTICAL PLATEAUS: Three-goal games: 1999-00 (1).

Season Team	League	REGULAR SEASON								PLAYOFFS				
		Gms.	G	A	Pts.	PIM	+/-	PP	SH	Gms.	G	A	Pts.	PIM
93-94—Stratford	OPJHL	46	12	27	39	8	...	...	...	—	—	—	—	—
94-95—Stratford	OPJHL	45	31	74	105	21	...	...	...	—	—	—	—	—
95-96—Kitchener	OHL	66	20	38	58	35	...	...	...	12	3	7	10	4
96-97—Kitchener	OHL	54	28	41	69	37	...	...	...	13	4	11	15	8
—Hamilton	AHL	—	—	—	—	—	...	...	...	1	0	1	1	0
97-98—Edmonton	NHL	38	1	4	5	6	-5	0	0	—	—	—	—	—
—Hamilton	AHL	14	5	6	11	6	...	...	...	9	1	1	2	8
98-99—Edmonton	NHL	61	6	8	14	23	2	0	1	1	0	0	0	0
—Hamilton	AHL	7	4	6	10	2	...	...	...	8	0	3	3	4
99-00—Edmonton	NHL	76	8	19	27	20	7	0	1	—	—	—	—	—
NHL Totals (3 years)..........		175	15	31	46	49	4	0	2	1	0	0	0	0

de VRIES, GREG   D   AVALANCHE

PERSONAL: Born January 4, 1973, in Sundridge, Ont. ... 6-3/215. ... Shoots left. ... Name pronounced duh-VREES.
COLLEGE: Bowling Green State.
TRANSACTIONS/CAREER NOTES: Signed as free agent by Edmonton Oilers (March 28, 1994). ... Sprained ankle (January 26, 1997); missed four games. ... Traded by Oilers with G Eric Fichaud and D Drake Berehowsky to Nashville Predators for F Jim Dowd and G Mikhail Shtalenkov (October 1, 1998). ... Traded by Predators to Colorado Avalanche for third-round pick (RW Branko Radivojevic) in 1999 draft (October 25, 1998). ... Suffered from the flu (December 27, 1999); missed two games.

Season Team	League	REGULAR SEASON								PLAYOFFS				
		Gms.	G	A	Pts.	PIM	+/-	PP	SH	Gms.	G	A	Pts.	PIM
91-92—Bowling Green	CCHA	24	0	3	3	20	...	...	...	—	—	—	—	—
92-93—Niagara Falls	OHL	62	3	23	26	86	...	...	...	4	0	1	1	6
93-94—Niagara Falls	OHL	64	5	40	45	135	...	...	...	—	—	—	—	—
—Cape Breton	AHL	9	0	0	0	11	...	...	...	1	0	0	0	0
94-95—Cape Breton	AHL	77	5	19	24	68	...	...	...	—	—	—	—	—
95-96—Edmonton	NHL	13	1	1	2	12	-2	0	0	—	—	—	—	—
—Cape Breton	AHL	58	9	30	39	174	...	...	...	—	—	—	—	—
96-97—Hamilton	AHL	34	4	14	18	26	...	...	...	—	—	—	—	—
—Edmonton	NHL	37	0	4	4	52	-2	0	0	12	0	1	1	8
97-98—Edmonton	NHL	65	7	4	11	80	-17	1	0	7	0	0	0	21
98-99—Nashville	NHL	6	0	0	0	4	-4	0	0	—	—	—	—	—
—Colorado	NHL	67	1	3	4	60	-3	0	0	19	0	2	2	22
99-00—Colorado	NHL	69	2	7	9	73	-7	0	0	5	0	0	0	4
NHL Totals (5 years)..........		257	11	19	30	281	-35	1	0	43	0	3	3	55

DeWOLF, JOSH   D   CANADIENS

PERSONAL: Born July 25, 1977, in Bloomington, Minn. ... 6-2/200. ... Shoots left. ... Full Name: Joshua DeWolf.
HIGH SCHOOL: Twin Cities (Bloomington, Minn.).
COLLEGE: St. Cloud (Minn.) State.
TRANSACTIONS/CAREER NOTES: Selected by New Jersey Devils in second round (third Devils pick, 41st overall) of NHL entry draft (June 22, 1996). ... Traded by Devils with D Sheldon Souray and second-round pick in 2001 draft to Montreal Canadiens for D Vladimir Malakhov (March 1, 2000).

Season Team	League	REGULAR SEASON								PLAYOFFS				
		Gms.	G	A	Pts.	PIM	+/-	PP	SH	Gms.	G	A	Pts.	PIM
93-94—Bloom. Jefferson	USHL	25	1	14	15	32	...	...	...	—	—	—	—	—
94-95—Bloom. Jefferson	USHL	28	6	22	28	52	...	...	...	—	—	—	—	—
95-96—Twin Cities	Minn. H.S.	40	11	15	26	38	...	...	...	—	—	—	—	—
96-97—St. Cloud State...........	WCHA	31	3	11	14	62	...	...	...	—	—	—	—	—
97-98—St. Cloud State...........	WCHA	37	9	9	18	78	...	...	...	—	—	—	—	—
—Albany	AHL	2	0	0	0	0	...	...	...	—	—	—	—	—
98-99—Albany.....................	AHL	75	1	17	18	111	...	...	...	5	0	0	0	2
99-00—Albany.....................	AHL	58	3	11	14	38	...	...	...	—	—	—	—	—
—Quebec	AHL	15	1	0	1	17	...	...	...	3	0	1	1	0

PERSONAL: Born April 6, 1965, in Edmonton. ... 6-2/220. ... Shoots right. ... Name pronounced DIH-dihk.

TRANSACTIONS/CAREER NOTES: Selected by New York Islanders as underage junior in first round (second Islanders pick, 16th overall) of NHL entry draft (June 8, 1983). ... Fractured left foot (November 1987). ... Fractured right hand (November 1988). ... Injured knee (January 1989). ... Traded by Islanders to Montreal Canadiens for D Craig Ludwig (September 4, 1990). ... Traded by Canadiens to Vancouver Canucks for fourth-round pick (LW Vladimir Vujtek) in 1991 draft (January 12, 1991). ... Bruised knee (March 16, 1991). ... Strained groin (January 4, 1993); missed three games. ... Suffered stress fracture in ankle (January 1, 1994); missed 14 games. ... Bruised foot (February 17, 1994); missed six games. ... Suffered eye contusion (March 31, 1994); missed five games. ... Traded by Canucks to Chicago Blackhawks for RW Bogdan Savenko and third-round pick (LW Larry Courville) in 1995 draft (April 7, 1995). ... Signed as free agent by Hartford Whalers (August 1, 1995). ... Strained hamstring (November 4, 1996); missed four games. ... Suffered hernia (December 16, 1996); missed nine games. ... Traded by Whalers to Phoenix Coyotes for RW Chris Murray (March 18, 1997). ... Suffered back spasms (December 3, 1997); missed two games. ... Injured hand (February 7, 1998); missed two games. ... Bruised shoulder (November 24, 1998); missed two games. ... Suffered charley horse (December 6, 1998); missed one game. ... Sprained knee (January 8, 1999); missed 14 games. ... Fractured foot (March 2, 1999); missed 21 games. ... Signed as free agent by Toronto Maple Leafs (January 28, 2000).

		REGULAR SEASON								PLAYOFFS				
Season Team	League	Gms.	G	A	Pts.	PIM	+/-	PP	SH	Gms.	G	A	Pts.	PIM
81-82—Lethbridge	WHL	71	1	15	16	81	...	...	...	12	0	3	3	27
82-83—Lethbridge	WHL	67	8	16	24	151	...	...	...	20	3	12	15	49
83-84—Lethbridge	WHL	65	10	24	34	133	...	...	...	5	1	4	5	27
—Indianapolis	IHL	—	—	—	—	—				10	1	6	7	19
84-85—New York Islanders	NHL	65	2	8	10	80	2	0	0	—	—	—	—	—
85-86—New York Islanders	NHL	10	1	2	3	2	5	0	0	—	—	—	—	—
—Springfield	AHL	61	6	14	20	175	...	...	...	—	—	—	—	—
86-87—Springfield	AHL	45	6	8	14	120	...	...	...	—	—	—	—	—
—New York Islanders	NHL	30	2	3	5	67	-3	0	0	14	0	1	1	35
87-88—New York Islanders	NHL	68	7	12	19	113	22	4	0	6	1	0	1	42
88-89—New York Islanders	NHL	65	11	21	32	155	9	6	0	—	—	—	—	—
89-90—New York Islanders	NHL	76	3	17	20	163	2	1	0	5	0	0	0	12
90-91—Montreal	NHL	32	1	2	3	39	3	0	0	—	—	—	—	—
—Vancouver	NHL	31	3	7	10	66	-8	0	0	6	1	0	1	11
91-92—Vancouver	NHL	77	6	21	27	229	-3	2	0	5	0	0	0	10
92-93—Vancouver	NHL	80	6	14	20	171	32	0	1	12	4	2	6	12
93-94—Vancouver	NHL	55	1	10	11	72	2	0	0	24	1	7	8	22
94-95—Vancouver	NHL	22	1	3	4	15	-8	1	0	—	—	—	—	—
—Chicago	NHL	13	1	0	1	48	3	0	0	16	1	3	4	22
95-96—Hartford	NHL	79	1	9	10	88	7	0	0	—	—	—	—	—
96-97—Hartford	NHL	56	1	10	11	40	-9	0	0	—	—	—	—	—
—Phoenix	NHL	11	1	2	3	23	2	1	0	7	0	0	0	10
97-98—Phoenix	NHL	78	8	10	18	118	14	1	0	6	0	2	2	20
98-99—Phoenix	NHL	44	0	2	2	72	9	0	0	3	0	0	0	2
99-00—Toronto	NHL	26	0	3	3	33	2	0	0	10	0	1	1	14
NHL Totals (16 years)		918	56	156	212	1594	83	16	1	114	8	16	24	212

PERSONAL: Born February 19, 1968, in Calgary. ... 5-10/190. ... Shoots right. ... Full Name: Robert DiMaio. ... Name pronounced duh-MIGH-oh.

TRANSACTIONS/CAREER NOTES: Selected by New York Islanders in sixth round (sixth Islanders pick, 118th overall) of NHL entry draft (June 13, 1987). ... Bruised left hand (February 1989). ... Sprained clavicle (November 1989). ... Sprained wrist (February 1992); missed four games. ... Reinjured wrist (February 29, 1992); missed remainder of season. ... Selected by Tampa Bay Lightning in NHL expansion draft (June 18, 1992). ... Bruised wrist (November 28, 1992); missed four games. ... Sprained ankle (February 14, 1993); missed nine games. ... Reinjured right ankle (March 20, 1993); missed three games. ... Reinjured right ankle (April 1, 1993); missed remainder of season. ... Fractured left leg (October 16, 1993); missed 27 games. ... Traded by Lightning to Philadelphia Flyers for RW Jim Cummins and fourth-round pick in 1995 draft (March 18, 1994). ... Bruised foot (February 28, 1995); missed two games. ... Suffered from the flu (April 16, 1995); missed one game. ... Suffered bone bruise in left leg (December 16, 1995); missed 14 games. ... Sprained right knee (March 29, 1996); missed final eight games of regular season. ... Selected by San Jose Sharks from Flyers in NHL waiver draft for cash (September 30, 1996). ... Traded by Sharks to Boston Bruins for fifth-round pick (RW Adam Nittel) in 1997 draft (September 30, 1996). ... Strained knee (November 6, 1996); missed five games. ... Suffered from the flu (December 17, 1996); missed one game. ... Sprained knee (March 8, 1997); missed two games. ... Injured hip (April 5, 1997); missed two games. ... Strained groin (January 12, 1998); missed one game. ... Suffered concussion (February 26, 1998); missed one game. ... Injured ankle (November 3, 1998); missed one game. ... Suffered viral meningitis (December 26, 1998); missed five games. ... Strained elbow (April 1, 1999); missed one game. ... Reinjured elbow (April 7, 1999); missed two games. ... Injured hip (October 20, 1999); missed one game. ... Bruised foot (November 10, 1999); missed two games. ... Fractured foot (November 17, 1999); missed eight games. ... Injured wrist (February 25, 2000); missed seven games. ... Traded by Bruins to New York Rangers for RW Mike Knuble (March 10, 2000). ... Suffered concussion (March 19, 2000); missed one game.

HONORS: Won Stafford Smythe Memorial Trophy (1987-88). ... Named to Memorial Cup All-Star team (1987-88).

MISCELLANEOUS: Failed to score on a penalty shot (vs. Andy Moog, October 4, 1997).

		REGULAR SEASON								PLAYOFFS				
Season Team	League	Gms.	G	A	Pts.	PIM	+/-	PP	SH	Gms.	G	A	Pts.	PIM
84-85—Kamloops	WHL	55	9	18	27	29	...	...	...	—	—	—	—	—
85-86—Kamloops	WHL	6	1	0	1	0	...	...	...	—	—	—	—	—
—Medicine Hat	WHL	55	20	30	50	82	...	...	...	—	—	—	—	—
86-87—Medicine Hat	WHL	70	27	43	70	130	...	...	...	20	7	11	18	46
87-88—Medicine Hat	WHL	54	47	43	90	120	...	...	...	14	12	19	†31	59
88-89—New York Islanders	NHL	16	1	0	1	30	-6	0	0	—	—	—	—	—
—Springfield	AHL	40	13	18	31	67	...	...	...	—	—	—	—	—
89-90—New York Islanders	NHL	7	0	0	0	2	0	0	0	1	1	0	1	4
—Springfield	AHL	54	25	27	52	69	...	...	...	16	4	7	11	45
90-91—New York Islanders	NHL	1	0	0	0	0	0	0	0	—	—	—	—	—
—Capital District	AHL	12	3	4	7	22	...	...	...	—	—	—	—	—

Season Team	League	Gms.	G	A	Pts.	PIM	+/-	PP	SH	Gms.	G	A	Pts.	PIM
91-92—New York Islanders.....	NHL	50	5	2	7	43	-23	0	2	—	—	—	—	—
92-93—Tampa Bay...............	NHL	54	9	15	24	62	0	2	0	—	—	—	—	—
93-94—Tampa Bay...............	NHL	39	8	7	15	40	-5	2	0	—	—	—	—	—
—Philadelphia...............	NHL	14	3	5	8	6	1	0	0	—	—	—	—	—
94-95—Philadelphia...........	NHL	36	3	1	4	53	8	0	0	15	2	4	6	4
95-96—Philadelphia...........	NHL	59	6	15	21	58	0	1	1	3	0	0	0	0
96-97—Boston.................	NHL	72	13	15	28	82	-21	0	3	—	—	—	—	—
97-98—Boston.................	NHL	79	10	17	27	82	-13	0	0	6	1	0	1	8
98-99—Boston.................	NHL	71	7	14	21	95	-14	1	0	12	2	0	2	8
99-00—Boston.................	NHL	50	5	16	21	42	-1	0	0	—	—	—	—	—
—New York Rangers.....	NHL	12	1	3	4	8	-8	0	0	—	—	—	—	—
NHL Totals (12 years).........		560	71	110	181	603	-82	6	6	37	6	4	10	24

DINEEN, KEVIN   RW   BLUE JACKETS

PERSONAL: Born October 28, 1963, in Quebec City. ... 5-11/189. ... Shoots right. ... Full Name: Kevin W. Dineen. ... Son of Bill Dineen, right winger with Detroit Red Wings (1953-54 through 1957-58) and Chicago Blackhawks (1957-58) and head coach with Philadelphia Flyers (1992-93); brother of Gord Dineen, defenseman with four NHL teams (1982-83 through 1994-95); and brother of Peter Dineen, defenseman with Los Angeles Kings (1986-87) and Red Wings (1989-90).

COLLEGE: University of Denver.

TRANSACTIONS/CAREER NOTES: Selected by Hartford Whalers as underage junior in third round (third Whalers pick, 56th overall) of NHL entry draft (June 9, 1982). ... Sprained left shoulder (October 24, 1985); missed nine games. ... Fractured knuckle (January 12, 1986); missed seven games. ... Sprained knee (February 14, 1986). ... Suffered shoulder tendinitis (September 1988). ... Underwent surgery to right knee cartilage (August 1, 1990). ... Suffered hip pointer (November 28, 1990). ... Hospitalized due to complications caused by Crohn's disease (January 1, 1991); missed eight games. ... Injured groin (March 1991). ... Traded by Whalers to Philadelphia Flyers for LW Murray Craven and fourth-round pick (LW Kevin Smyth) in 1992 draft (November 13, 1991). ... Sprained wrist (February 4, 1992); missed one game. ... Strained right rotator cuff (December 3, 1992); missed one game. ... Suffered injury (October 9, 1993); missed one game. ... Bruised right shoulder (November 13, 1993); missed two games. ... Suffered recurrence of Crohn's disease (February 10, 1994); missed five games. ... Separated shoulder (March 8, 1994); missed three games. ... Strained left shoulder (January 31, 1995); missed three games. ... Reinjured left shoulder (February 11, 1995); missed three games. ... Traded by Flyers to Whalers for third-round pick (D Kris Mallette) in 1997 draft (December 28, 1995). ... Fractured bone in wrist (February 9, 1996); missed 27 games. ... Strained abdominal muscle (March 13, 1997); missed one game. ... Whalers franchise moved to North Carolina and renamed Carolina Hurricanes for 1997-98 season; NHL approved move on June 25, 1997. ... Strained hamstring (October 4, 1997); missed five games. ... Reinjured hamstring (November 21, 1997); missed six games. ... Reinjured hamstring (December 26, 1997); missed seven games. ... Reinjured hamstring (January 10, 1998); missed two games. ... Suffered charley horse (February 7, 1998); missed one game. ... Injured groin (March 23, 1998); missed four games. ... Reinjured groin (April 8, 1998); missed one game. ... Strained groin (November 4, 1998); missed four games. ... Suffered back spasms (February 20, 1999); missed five games. ... Injured groin (March 6, 1999); missed six games. ... Signed as free agent by Ottawa Senators (September 2, 1999). ... Suspended one game by NHL for elbowing incident (November 1, 1999). ... Strained groin (December 11, 1999); missed three games. ... Reinjured groin (January 16, 2000); missed two games. ... Strained groin (March 25, 2000); missed three games. ... Separated left shoulder (April 6, 2000); missed final two games of season. ... Selected by Columbus Blue Jackets in NHL expansion draft (June 23, 2000).

HONORS: Named to THE SPORTING NEWS All-Star second team (1986-87). ... Played in NHL All-Star Game (1988 and 1989). ... Named Bud Light/NHL Man of the Year (1990-91).

MISCELLANEOUS: Captain of Philadelphia Flyers (1993-94). ... Captain of Hartford Whalers (1996-97). ... Captain of Carolina Hurricanes (1997-98). ... Holds Carolina Hurricanes franchise all-time record for most penalty minutes (1,441). ... Failed to score on a penalty shot (vs. Mike Richter, October 19, 1989).

STATISTICAL PLATEAUS: Three-goal games: 1985-86 (1), 1986-87 (1), 1988-89 (1), 1989-90 (2), 1992-93 (3), 1993-94 (1). Total: 9. ... Four-goal games: 1993-94 (1). ... Total hat tricks: 10.

		REGULAR SEASON								PLAYOFFS				
Season Team	League	Gms.	G	A	Pts.	PIM	+/-	PP	SH	Gms.	G	A	Pts.	PIM
80-81—St. Michael's Jr. B.......	ODHA	40	15	28	43	167	...	...	...	—	—	—	—	—
81-82—Univ. of Denver..........	WCHA	38	12	22	34	105	...	...	...	—	—	—	—	—
82-83—Univ. of Denver..........	WCHA	36	16	13	29	108	...	...	...	—	—	—	—	—
83-84—Canadian nat'l team	Int'l	52	5	11	16	2	...	...	...	—	—	—	—	—
—Can. Olympic team	Int'l	7	0	0	0	0	...	...	...	—	—	—	—	—
84-85—Binghamton...............	AHL	25	15	8	23	41	...	...	...	—	—	—	—	—
—Hartford....................	NHL	57	25	16	41	120	-6	8	4	—	—	—	—	—
85-86—Hartford............	NHL	57	33	35	68	124	16	6	0	10	6	7	13	18
86-87—Hartford............	NHL	78	40	39	79	110	7	11	0	6	2	1	3	31
87-88—Hartford............	NHL	74	25	25	50	217	-14	5	0	6	4	4	8	8
88-89—Hartford............	NHL	79	45	44	89	167	-6	20	1	4	1	0	1	10
89-90—Hartford............	NHL	67	25	41	66	164	7	8	2	6	3	2	5	18
90-91—Hartford............	NHL	61	17	30	47	104	-15	4	0	6	1	0	1	16
91-92—Hartford............	NHL	16	4	2	6	23	-6	1	0	—	—	—	—	—
—Philadelphia...............	NHL	64	26	30	56	130	1	5	3	—	—	—	—	—
92-93—Philadelphia...........	NHL	83	35	28	63	201	14	6	3	—	—	—	—	—
93-94—Philadelphia...........	NHL	71	19	23	42	113	-9	5	1	—	—	—	—	—
94-95—Houston................	IHL	17	6	4	10	42	...	...	...	—	—	—	—	—
—Philadelphia...............	NHL	40	8	5	13	39	-1	4	0	15	6	4	10	18
95-96—Philadelphia...........	NHL	26	0	2	2	50	-8	0	0	—	—	—	—	—
—Philadelphia...............	NHL	20	2	7	9	67	7	0	0	—	—	—	—	—
96-97—Hartford............	NHL	78	19	29	48	141	-6	8	0	—	—	—	—	—
97-98—Carolina...........	NHL	54	7	16	23	105	-7	0	0	—	—	—	—	—
98-99—Carolina...........	NHL	67	8	10	18	97	5	0	0	6	0	0	0	8
99-00—Ottawa.............	NHL	67	4	8	12	57	2	0	0	—	—	—	—	—
NHL Totals (16 years).........		1059	342	390	732	2029	-19	91	14	59	23	18	41	127

D

DINGMAN, CHRIS   LW   AVALANCHE

PERSONAL: Born July 6, 1976, in Edmonton. ... 6-4/245. ... Shoots left.
HIGH SCHOOL: Crocus Plains (Brandon, Man.).
TRANSACTIONS/CAREER NOTES: Selected by Calgary Flames in first round (first Flames pick, 19th overall) of NHL entry draft (June 28, 1994). ... Traded by Flames with RW Theo Fleury to Colorado Avalanche for LW Rene Corbet, D Wade Belak and future considerations (February 28, 1999); Flames acquired D Robyn Regehr to complete deal (March 27, 1999). ... Partially dislocated right shoulder (November 15, 1999); missed six games.

			REGULAR SEASON								PLAYOFFS			
Season Team	League	Gms.	G	A	Pts.	PIM	+/-	PP	SH		Gms.	G	A	Pts.	PIM
92-93—Brandon	WHL	50	10	17	27	64	...	...	...		4	0	0	0	0
93-94—Brandon	WHL	45	21	20	41	77	...	...	...		13	1	7	8	39
94-95—Brandon	WHL	66	40	43	83	201	...	...	...		3	1	0	1	9
95-96—Brandon	WHL	40	16	29	45	109	...	...	...		19	12	11	23	60
—Saint John	AHL	—	—	—	—	—	...	...	...		1	0	0	0	0
96-97—Saint John	AHL	71	5	6	11	195	...	...	...		—	—	—	—	—
97-98—Calgary	NHL	70	3	3	6	149	-11	1	0		—	—	—	—	—
98-99—Saint John	AHL	50	5	7	12	140	...	...	...		—	—	—	—	—
—Calgary	NHL	2	0	0	0	17	-2	0	0		—	—	—	—	—
—Hershey	AHL	17	1	3	4	102	...	...	...		5	0	2	2	6
—Colorado	NHL	1	0	0	0	7	0	0	0		—	—	—	—	—
99-00—Colorado	NHL	68	8	3	11	132	-2	2	0		—	—	—	—	—
NHL Totals (3 years)		141	11	6	17	305	-15	3	0						

DIVISEK, TOMAS   C   FLYERS

PERSONAL: Born July 17, 1979, in Most, Czechoslovakia. ... 6-2/194. ... Shoots left.
TRANSACTIONS/CAREER NOTES: Selected by Philadelphia Flyers in seventh round (ninth Flyers pick, 195th overall) of NHL entry draft (June 21, 1997).

			REGULAR SEASON								PLAYOFFS			
Season Team	League	Gms.	G	A	Pts.	PIM	+/-	PP	SH		Gms.	G	A	Pts.	PIM
95-96—Slavia Praha	Czech Jr.	36	20	27	47	12	...	...	...		—	—	—	—	—
96-97—Slavia Praha	Czech Jr.	41	17	25	42	18	...	...	...		—	—	—	—	—
—Slavia Praha	Czech Rep.	1	0	0	0	0	...	...	...		—	—	—	—	—
97-98—Slavia Praha	Czech Jr.	27	20	16	36	12	...	...	...		—	—	—	—	—
—Slavia Praha	Czech Rep.	22	2	0	2	8	...	...	...		—	—	—	—	—
98-99—Slavia Praha	Czech Rep.	45	8	4	12	26	...	...	...		—	—	—	—	—
99-00—Philadelphia	AHL	59	18	31	49	30	...	...	...		5	0	3	3	2

DOAN, SHANE   RW   COYOTES

PERSONAL: Born October 10, 1976, in Halkirk, Alta. ... 6-2/218. ... Shoots right. ... Name pronounced DOHN.
TRANSACTIONS/CAREER NOTES: Selected by Winnipeg Jets in first round (first Jets pick, seventh overall) of NHL entry draft (July 8, 1995). ... Suffered from the flu (January 8, 1996); missed one game. ... Bruised ribs (January 14, 1996); missed two games. ... Strained back (February 23, 1996); missed two games. ... Jets franchise moved to Phoenix and renamed Coyotes for 1996-97 season; NHL approved move on January 18, 1996. ... Sprained ankle (October 14, 1996); missed two games. ... Strained ligament in foot (November 8, 1996); missed eight games. ... Bruised hand (February 22, 1997); missed four games. ... Injured eye (February 20, 1999); missed one game. ... Injured forearm (March 15, 1999); missed one game.
HONORS: Won Stafford Smyth Memorial Trophy (1994-95). ... Named to Memorial Cup All-Star team (1994-95).

			REGULAR SEASON								PLAYOFFS			
Season Team	League	Gms.	G	A	Pts.	PIM	+/-	PP	SH		Gms.	G	A	Pts.	PIM
92-93—Kamloops	WHL	51	7	12	19	55	...	...	...		13	0	1	1	8
93-94—Kamloops	WHL	52	24	24	48	88	...	...	...		—	—	—	—	—
94-95—Kamloops	WHL	71	37	57	94	106	...	...	...		21	6	10	16	16
95-96—Winnipeg	NHL	74	7	10	17	101	-9	1	0		6	0	0	0	6
96-97—Phoenix	NHL	63	4	8	12	49	-3	0	0		4	0	0	0	2
97-98—Phoenix	NHL	33	5	6	11	35	-3	0	0		6	1	0	1	0
—Springfield	AHL	39	21	21	42	64	...	...	...		—	—	—	—	—
98-99—Phoenix	NHL	79	6	16	22	54	-5	0	0		7	2	2	4	6
99-00—Phoenix	NHL	81	26	25	51	66	6	1	1		4	1	2	3	8
NHL Totals (5 years)		330	48	65	113	305	-14	2	1		27	4	4	8	28

DOIG, JASON   D   RANGERS

PERSONAL: Born January 29, 1977, in Montreal. ... 6-3/228. ... Shoots right. ... Name pronounced DOYG.
TRANSACTIONS/CAREER NOTES: Selected by Winnipeg Jets in second round (third Jets pick, 34th overall) of NHL entry draft (July 8, 1995). ... Suffered irregular heart beat (November 17, 1995); missed four games. ... Jets franchise moved to Phoenix and renamed Coyotes for 1996-97 season; NHL approved move on January 18, 1996. ... Hyperextended elbow prior to 1996-97 season; missed first five games of season. ... Sprained knee (November 20, 1997); missed 26 games. ... Suffered torn pectoral muscle prior to the 1998-99 regular season; missed first 18 games of season. ... Traded by Coyotes with sixth-round pick (C Jay Dardis) in 1999 draft to New York Rangers for D Stan Neckar (March 23, 1999). ... Sprained knee (February 8, 2000); missed five games.
HONORS: Won Guy Lafleur Trophy (1995-96). ... Named to Memorial Cup All-Star team (1995-96).

Season Team	League	REGULAR SEASON								PLAYOFFS				
		Gms.	G	A	Pts.	PIM	+/-	PP	SH	Gms.	G	A	Pts.	PIM
93-94—St. Jean	QMJHL	63	8	17	25	65	...	...	...	5	0	2	2	2
94-95—Laval	QMJHL	55	13	42	55	259	...	...	...	20	4	13	17	39
95-96—Winnipeg	NHL	15	1	1	2	28	-2	0	0	—	—	—	—	—
—Springfield	AHL	5	0	0	0	28	...	...	...	—	—	—	—	—
—Laval	QMJHL	2	1	1	2	6	...	...	...	—	—	—	—	—
—Granby	QMJHL	27	6	35	41	*105	...	...	...	20	10	22	32	110
96-97—Las Vegas	IHL	6	0	1	1	19	...	...	...	—	—	—	—	—
—Granby	QMJHL	39	14	33	47	197	...	...	...	5	0	4	4	27
—Springfield	AHL	5	0	3	3	2	...	...	...	17	1	4	5	37
97-98—Springfield	AHL	46	2	25	27	153	...	...	...	3	0	0	0	2
—Phoenix	NHL	4	0	1	1	12	-4	0	0	—	—	—	—	—
98-99—Phoenix	NHL	9	0	1	1	10	2	0	0	—	—	—	—	—
—Springfield	AHL	32	3	5	8	67	...	...	...	—	—	—	—	—
—Hartford	AHL	8	1	4	5	40	...	...	...	7	1	1	2	39
99-00—New York Rangers	NHL	7	0	1	1	22	-2	0	0	—	—	—	—	—
—Hartford	AHL	27	3	11	14	70	...	...	...	21	1	5	6	20
NHL Totals (4 years)		35	1	4	5	72	-6	0	0					

DOLLAS, BOBBY — D

PERSONAL: Born January 31, 1965, in Montreal. ... 6-2/212. ... Shoots left. ... Name pronounced DAHL-ihz.

TRANSACTIONS/CAREER NOTES: Selected by Winnipeg Jets as underage junior in first round (second Jets pick, 14th overall) of NHL entry draft (June 8, 1983). ... Traded by Jets to Quebec Nordiques for RW Stu Kulak (December 17, 1987). ... Signed as free agent by Detroit Red Wings (October 18, 1990). ... Suffered from the flu (December 15, 1990); missed two games. ... Injured leg (January 9, 1991). ... Strained abdominal muscle (November 7, 1991); missed 15 games. ... Selected by Mighty Ducks of Anaheim in NHL expansion draft (June 24, 1993). ... Sprained left thumb (October 1, 1993); missed five games. ... Suffered from chicken pox (March 30, 1997); missed three games. ... Tore tendon in left wrist (October 30, 1997); missed 16 games. ... Traded by Mighty Ducks to Edmonton Oilers for D Drew Bannister (January 9, 1998). ... Partially dislocated shoulder (March 9, 1998); missed seven games. ... Traded by Oilers with C Tony Hrkac to Pittsburgh Penguins for LW Josef Beranek (June 16, 1998). ... Fractured toe (December 26, 1998); missed three games. ... Signed as free agent by Ottawa Senators (November 9, 1999). ... Claimed on waivers by Calgary Flames (November 11, 1999). ... Suffered back spasms (December 26, 1999); missed two games. ... Suffered concussion (February 18, 2000); missed four games. ... Suffered concussion (March 18, 2000); missed final 10 games of season.

HONORS: Won Raymond Lagace Trophy (1982-83). ... Named to QMJHL All-Star second team (1982-83). ... Won Eddie Shore Plaque (1992-93). ... Named to AHL All-Star first team (1992-93).

Season Team	League	REGULAR SEASON								PLAYOFFS				
		Gms.	G	A	Pts.	PIM	+/-	PP	SH	Gms.	G	A	Pts.	PIM
82-83—Laval	QMJHL	63	16	45	61	144	...	...	...	11	5	5	10	23
83-84—Laval	QMJHL	54	12	33	45	80	...	...	...	14	1	8	9	23
—Winnipeg	NHL	1	0	0	0	0	-2	0	0	—	—	—	—	—
84-85—Winnipeg	NHL	9	0	0	0	0	3	0	0	—	—	—	—	—
—Sherbrooke	AHL	8	1	3	4	4	...	...	...	17	3	6	9	17
85-86—Sherbrooke	AHL	25	4	7	11	29	...	...	...	—	—	—	—	—
—Winnipeg	NHL	46	0	5	5	66	-3	0	0	3	0	0	0	2
86-87—Sherbrooke	AHL	75	6	18	24	87	...	...	...	16	2	4	6	13
87-88—Quebec	NHL	9	0	0	0	2	-4	0	0	—	—	—	—	—
—Moncton	AHL	26	4	10	14	20	...	...	...	—	—	—	—	—
—Fredericton	AHL	33	4	8	12	27	...	...	...	15	2	2	4	24
88-89—Halifax	AHL	57	5	19	24	65	...	...	...	4	1	0	1	14
—Quebec	NHL	16	0	3	3	16	-11	0	0	—	—	—	—	—
89-90—Canadian nat'l team	Int'l	68	8	29	37	60	...	...	...	—	—	—	—	—
90-91—Detroit	NHL	56	3	5	8	20	6	0	0	7	1	0	1	13
91-92—Detroit	NHL	27	3	1	4	20	4	0	1	2	0	1	1	0
—Adirondack	AHL	19	1	6	7	33	...	...	...	18	7	4	11	22
92-93—Adirondack	AHL	64	7	36	43	54	...	...	...	11	3	8	11	8
—Detroit	NHL	6	0	0	0	2	-1	0	0	—	—	—	—	—
93-94—Anaheim	NHL	77	9	11	20	55	20	1	0	—	—	—	—	—
94-95—Anaheim	NHL	45	7	13	20	12	-3	3	1	—	—	—	—	—
95-96—Anaheim	NHL	82	8	22	30	64	9	0	1	—	—	—	—	—
96-97—Anaheim	NHL	79	4	14	18	55	17	1	0	11	0	0	0	4
97-98—Anaheim	NHL	22	0	1	1	27	-12	0	0	—	—	—	—	—
—Edmonton	NHL	30	2	5	7	22	6	0	0	11	0	0	0	16
98-99—Pittsburgh	NHL	70	2	8	10	60	-3	0	0	13	1	0	1	6
99-00—Long Beach	IHL	13	2	4	6	8	...	...	...	—	—	—	—	—
—Ottawa	NHL	1	0	0	0	0	2	0	0	—	—	—	—	—
—Calgary	NHL	49	3	7	10	28	4	1	0	—	—	—	—	—
NHL Totals (15 years)		625	41	95	136	449	32	6	3	47	2	1	3	41

DOME, ROBERT — C/LW — PENGUINS

PERSONAL: Born January 29, 1979, in Skalica, Czechoslovakia. ... 6-0/210. ... Shoots left. ... Name pronounced DEH-may.

TRANSACTIONS/CAREER NOTES: Selected by Pittsburgh Penguins in first round (first Penguins pick, 17th overall) of NHL entry draft (June 21, 1997).

Season Team	League	REGULAR SEASON								PLAYOFFS				
		Gms.	G	A	Pts.	PIM	+/-	PP	SH	Gms.	G	A	Pts.	PIM
94-95—Dukla Jrs.	Slov. Jr.	36	36	43	79	39	...	...	...	—	—	—	—	—
95-96—Utah	IHL	56	10	9	19	28	...	...	...	—	—	—	—	—
96-97—Long Beach	IHL	13	4	6	10	14	...	...	...	—	—	—	—	—
—Las Vegas	IHL	43	10	7	17	22	...	...	...	—	—	—	—	—

D

Season Team	League	REGULAR SEASON								PLAYOFFS				
		Gms.	G	A	Pts.	PIM	+/-	PP	SH	Gms.	G	A	Pts.	PIM
97-98—Pittsburgh	NHL	30	5	2	7	12	-1	1	0	—	—	—	—	—
—Syracuse	AHL	36	21	25	46	77	...	...	...	—	—	—	—	—
98-99—Syracuse	AHL	48	18	17	35	70	...	...	...	—	—	—	—	—
—Houston	IHL	20	2	4	6	24	...	...	...	—	—	—	—	—
99-00—Wilkes-Barre/Scranton	AHL	51	12	26	38	83	...	...	...	—	—	—	—	—
—Pittsburgh	NHL	22	2	5	7	0	1	0	0	—	—	—	—	—
NHL Totals (2 years)		52	7	7	14	12	0	1	0					

DOMENICHELLI, HNAT — LW — THRASHERS

PERSONAL: Born February 17, 1976, in Edmonton. ... 6-0/194. ... Shoots left. ... Name pronounced NAT dah-mih-nuh-KEHL-ee.

TRANSACTIONS/CAREER NOTES: Selected by Hartford Whalers in fourth round (second Whalers pick, 83rd overall) of NHL entry draft (June 29, 1994). ... Traded by Whalers with D Glen Featherstone, second-round pick (D Dimitri Kokorev) in 1997 draft and third-round pick (D Paul Manning) in 1998 draft to Calgary Flames for D Steve Chiasson and third-round pick (D Francis Lessard) in 1997 draft (March 5, 1997). ... Traded by Flames with LW Dmitri Vlasenkov to Atlanta Thrashers for D Darryl Shannon and LW Jason Botterill (February 11, 2000).

HONORS: Named to WHL (West) All-Star second team (1994-95). ... Won Brad Hornung Trophy (1995-96). ... Won Can.HL Most Sportsmanlike Player of the Year Award (1995-96). ... Named to Can.HL All-Star first team (1995-96). ... Named to WHL (West) All-Star first team (1995-96).

MISCELLANEOUS: Scored on a penalty shot (vs. Arturs Irbe, Febraury 27, 1998).

Season Team	League	REGULAR SEASON								PLAYOFFS				
		Gms.	G	A	Pts.	PIM	+/-	PP	SH	Gms.	G	A	Pts.	PIM
92-93—Kamloops	WHL	45	12	8	20	15	...	...	...	11	1	1	2	2
93-94—Kamloops	WHL	69	27	40	67	31	...	...	...	19	10	12	22	0
94-95—Kamloops	WHL	72	52	62	114	34	...	...	...	19	9	9	18	9
95-96—Kamloops	WHL	62	59	89	148	37	...	...	...	16	7	9	16	29
96-97—Hartford	NHL	13	2	1	3	7	-4	1	0	—	—	—	—	—
—Springfield	AHL	39	24	24	48	12	...	...	...	—	—	—	—	—
—Calgary	NHL	10	1	2	3	2	1	0	0	—	—	—	—	—
—Saint John	AHL	1	1	1	2	0	...	...	...	5	5	0	5	2
97-98—Saint John	AHL	48	33	13	46	24	...	...	...	19	7	8	15	14
—Calgary	NHL	31	9	7	16	6	4	1	0	—	—	—	—	—
98-99—Saint John	AHL	51	25	21	46	26	...	...	...	7	4	4	8	2
—Calgary	NHL	23	5	5	10	11	-4	3	0	—	—	—	—	—
99-00—Saint John	AHL	12	6	7	13	8	...	...	...	—	—	—	—	—
—Calgary	NHL	32	5	9	14	12	0	1	0	—	—	—	—	—
—Atlanta	NHL	27	6	9	15	4	-21	0	0	—	—	—	—	—
NHL Totals (4 years)		136	28	33	61	42	-24	6	0					

DOMI, TIE — RW — MAPLE LEAFS

PERSONAL: Born November 1, 1969, in Windsor, Ont. ... 5-10/200. ... Shoots right. ... Full Name: Tahir Domi. ... Name pronounced TIGH DOH-mee. ... Nickname: The Albanian Agressor.

TRANSACTIONS/CAREER NOTES: Selected by Toronto Maple Leafs in second round (second Maple Leafs pick, 27th overall) of NHL entry draft (June 11, 1988). ... Traded by Maple Leafs with G Mark Laforest to New York Rangers for RW Greg Johnston (June 28, 1990). ... Suspended six games by AHL for pre-game fighting (November 25, 1990). ... Sprained right knee (March 11, 1992); missed eight games. ... Traded by Rangers with LW Kris King to Winnipeg Jets for C Ed Olczyk (December 28, 1992). ... Fined $500 by NHL for premeditated fight (January 4, 1993). ... Sprained knee (January 25, 1994); missed three games. ... Traded by Jets to Maple Leafs for C Mike Eastwood and third-round pick (RW Brad Isbister) in 1995 draft (April 7, 1995). ... Strained groin (April 8, 1995); missed two games. ... Suffered from the flu (April 19, 1995); missed one game. ... Suspended eight games by NHL for fighting (October 17, 1995). ... Sprained knee (December 2, 1995); missed two games. ... Fined $1,000 by NHL for fighting (November 13, 1996). ... Sprained ankle (April 2, 1997); missed two games. ... Strained abdominal muscle (October 25, 1997); missed two games. ... Sprained knee (January 7, 1999); missed 10 games. ... Suffered injury (October 30, 1999); missed five games. ... Suffered injury (January 14, 2000); missed seven games.

Season Team	League	REGULAR SEASON								PLAYOFFS				
		Gms.	G	A	Pts.	PIM	+/-	PP	SH	Gms.	G	A	Pts.	PIM
85-86—Windsor Jr. B	OHA	32	8	17	25	346	...	...	...	—	—	—	—	—
86-87—Peterborough	OHL	18	1	1	2	79	...	...	...	—	—	—	—	—
87-88—Peterborough	OHL	60	22	21	43	*292	...	...	...	12	3	9	12	24
88-89—Peterborough	OHL	43	14	16	30	175	...	...	...	17	10	9	19	*70
89-90—Newmarket	AHL	57	14	11	25	285	...	...	...	—	—	—	—	—
—Toronto	NHL	2	0	0	0	42	0	0	0	—	—	—	—	—
90-91—New York Rangers	NHL	28	1	0	1	185	-5	0	0	—	—	—	—	—
—Binghamton	AHL	25	11	6	17	219	...	...	...	7	3	2	5	16
91-92—New York Rangers	NHL	42	2	4	6	246	-4	0	0	6	1	1	2	32
92-93—New York Rangers	NHL	12	2	0	2	95	-1	0	0	—	—	—	—	—
—Winnipeg	NHL	49	3	10	13	249	2	0	0	6	1	0	1	23
93-94—Winnipeg	NHL	81	8	11	19	*347	-8	0	0	—	—	—	—	—
94-95—Winnipeg	NHL	31	4	4	8	128	-6	0	0	—	—	—	—	—
—Toronto	NHL	9	0	1	1	31	1	0	0	7	1	0	1	0
95-96—Toronto	NHL	72	7	6	13	297	-3	0	0	6	0	2	2	4
96-97—Toronto	NHL	80	11	17	28	275	-17	2	0	—	—	—	—	—
97-98—Toronto	NHL	80	4	10	14	365	-5	0	0	—	—	—	—	—
98-99—Toronto	NHL	72	8	14	22	198	5	0	0	14	0	2	2	24
99-00—Toronto	NHL	70	5	9	14	198	-5	0	0	12	0	1	1	20
NHL Totals (11 years)		628	55	86	141	2656	-46	2	0	51	3	6	9	103

D

DONATO, TED   LW

PERSONAL: Born April 28, 1968, in Boston. ... 5-10/180. ... Shoots left. ... Full Name: Edward Paul Donato. ... Brother of Dan Donato, infielder, Tampa Bay Devil Rays organization. ... Name pronounced duh-NAH-toh.
HIGH SCHOOL: Catholic Memorial (Boston).
COLLEGE: Harvard (degree in history).
TRANSACTIONS/CAREER NOTES: Selected by Boston Bruins in sixth round (sixth Bruins pick, 98th overall) of NHL entry draft (June 13, 1987). ... Played in Europe during 1994-95 NHL lockout. ... Injured groin (November 21, 1996); missed two games. ... Fractured finger (March 9, 1997); missed 13 games. ... Suspended three games by NHL and fined $1,000 for high-sticking (December 22, 1997). ... Traded by Bruins to New York Islanders for LW Ken Belanger (November 7, 1998). ... Traded by Islanders to Ottawa Senators for fourth-round pick (traded to Phoenix) in 1999 draft (March 20, 1999). ... Traded by Senators with D Antti-Jussi Niemi to Mighty Ducks of Anaheim for G Patrick Lalime (June 18, 1999).
HONORS: Named NCAA Tournament Most Valuable Player (1988-89). ... Named to NCAA All-Tournament team (1988-89). ... Named to ECAC All-Star first team (1990-91).
MISCELLANEOUS: Failed to score on a penalty shot (vs. Kirk McLean, April 12, 1999).

Season Team	League	REGULAR SEASON								PLAYOFFS				
		Gms.	G	A	Pts.	PIM	+/-	PP	SH	Gms.	G	A	Pts.	PIM
86-87—Catholic Memorial.......	Mass. H.S.	22	29	34	63	30	...	...	...	—	—	—	—	—
87-88—Harvard University......	ECAC	28	12	14	26	24	...	...	...	—	—	—	—	—
88-89—Harvard University......	ECAC	34	14	37	51	30	...	...	...	—	—	—	—	—
89-90—Harvard University......	ECAC	16	5	6	11	34	...	...	...	—	—	—	—	—
90-91—Harvard University......	ECAC	28	19	37	56	26	...	...	...	—	—	—	—	—
91-92—U.S. national team......	Int'l	52	11	22	33	24	...	...	...	—	—	—	—	—
—U.S. Olympic team......	Int'l	8	4	3	7	8	...	...	...	—	—	—	—	—
—Boston	NHL	10	1	2	3	8	-1	0	0	15	3	4	7	4
92-93—Boston	NHL	82	15	20	35	61	2	3	2	4	0	1	1	0
93-94—Boston	NHL	84	22	32	54	59	0	9	2	13	4	2	6	10
94-95—TuTo Turku	Finland	14	5	5	10	47	...	...	...	—	—	—	—	—
—Boston	NHL	47	10	10	20	10	3	1	0	5	0	0	0	4
95-96—Boston	NHL	82	23	26	49	46	6	7	0	5	1	2	3	2
96-97—Boston	NHL	67	25	26	51	37	-9	6	2	—	—	—	—	—
97-98—Boston	NHL	79	16	23	39	54	6	3	0	5	0	0	0	2
98-99—Boston	NHL	14	1	3	4	4	0	0	0	—	—	—	—	—
—New York Islanders....	NHL	55	7	11	18	27	-10	2	0	—	—	—	—	—
—Ottawa	NHL	13	3	2	5	10	2	1	0	1	0	0	0	0
99-00—Anaheim	NHL	81	11	19	30	26	-3	2	0	—	—	—	—	—
NHL Totals (9 years)............		**614**	**134**	**174**	**308**	**342**	**-4**	**34**	**6**	**48**	**8**	**9**	**17**	**22**

DONOVAN, SHEAN   RW   THRASHERS

PERSONAL: Born January 22, 1975, in Timmins, Ont. ... 6-3/210. ... Shoots right. ... Name pronounced SHAWN DAHN-ih-vihn.
TRANSACTIONS/CAREER NOTES: Selected by San Jose Sharks in second round (second Sharks pick, 28th overall) of NHL entry draft (June 26, 1993). ... Suffered concussion (October 5, 1996); missed two games. ... Injured knee (December 21, 1996); missed two games. ... Traded by Sharks with first-round pick (C Alex Tanguay) in 1998 draft to Colorado Avalanche for C Mike Ricci and second-round pick (RW Jonathan Cheechoo) in 1998 draft (November 20, 1997). ... Bruised knee (January 3, 1998); missed one game. ... Bruised knee (January 21, 1998); missed three games. ... Suffered concussion (October 24, 1998); missed one game. ... Injured shoulder and jaw (February 5, 1999); missed one game. ... Injured hip (March 20, 1999); missed two games. ... Traded by Avalanche to Atlanta Thrashers for G Rick Tabaracci (December 8, 1999). ... Strained muscle in abdomen (January 1, 2000); missed three games. ... Fractured right foot (January 27, 2000); missed 20 games.

Season Team	League	REGULAR SEASON								PLAYOFFS				
		Gms.	G	A	Pts.	PIM	+/-	PP	SH	Gms.	G	A	Pts.	PIM
91-92—Ottawa	OHL	58	11	8	19	14	...	...	...	11	1	0	1	5
92-93—Ottawa	OHL	66	29	23	52	33	...	...	...	—	—	—	—	—
93-94—Ottawa	OHL	62	35	49	84	63	...	...	...	17	10	11	21	14
94-95—Ottawa	OHL	29	22	19	41	41	...	...	...	—	—	—	—	—
—San Jose....................	NHL	14	0	0	0	6	-6	0	0	7	0	1	1	6
—Kansas City..............	IHL	5	0	2	2	7	...	...	...	14	5	3	8	23
95-96—Kansas City..............	IHL	4	0	0	0	8	...	...	...	5	0	0	0	8
—San Jose....................	NHL	74	13	8	21	39	-17	0	1	—	—	—	—	—
96-97—San Jose....................	NHL	73	9	6	15	42	-18	0	1	—	—	—	—	—
—Kentucky...................	AHL	3	1	3	4	18	...	...	...	—	—	—	—	—
—Canadian nat'l team....	Int'l	10	0	1	1	31	...	...	...	—	—	—	—	—
97-98—San Jose....................	NHL	20	3	3	6	22	3	0	0	—	—	—	—	—
—Colorado..................	NHL	47	5	7	12	48	3	0	0	—	—	—	—	—
98-99—Colorado..................	NHL	68	7	12	19	37	4	1	0	5	0	0	0	2
99-00—Colorado..................	NHL	18	1	0	1	8	-4	0	0	—	—	—	—	—
—Atlanta.....................	NHL	33	4	7	11	18	-13	1	0	—	—	—	—	—
NHL Totals (6 years)............		**347**	**42**	**43**	**85**	**220**	**-48**	**2**	**2**	**12**	**0**	**1**	**1**	**8**

DOPITA, JIRI   C   PANTHERS

PERSONAL: Born December 2, 1968, in Sumperk, Czechoslovakia. ... 6-3/209. ... Shoots left.
TRANSACTIONS/CAREER NOTES: Selected by Boston Bruins in sixth round (fourth Bruins pick, 133rd overall) of NHL entry draft (June 20, 1992). ... Returned to draft pool by Bruins and selected by New York Islanders in fifth round (fourth Islanders pick, 123rd overall) of NHL entry draft (June 27, 1998). ... Rights traded by Islanders to Florida Panthers for fifth-round pick (D Adam Johnson) in 1999 draft (June 26, 1999).
MISCELLANEOUS: Member of gold-medal-winning Czech Republic Olympic team (1998).

Season Team	League	REGULAR SEASON Gms.	G	A	Pts.	PIM	+/-	PP	SH	PLAYOFFS Gms.	G	A	Pts.	PIM
88-89—DS Olomouc	Czech Dv.II					Statistics unavailable.								
89-90—Dukla Jihlava	Czech.	5	1	2	3	...	...	...	...	—	—	—	—	—
90-91—DS Olomouc	Czech.	42	11	13	24	...	...	...	...	—	—	—	—	—
91-92—DS Olomouc	Czech.	38	23	20	43	...	...	...	...	—	—	—	—	—
92-93—DS Olomouc	Czech.	28	12	17	29	...	...	...	...	—	—	—	—	—
—Eisbaren Berlin	Germany	11	7	8	15	49	...	...	...	4	3	5	8	5
94-95—Eisbaren Berlin	Germany	42	28	40	68	55	...	...	...	—	—	—	—	—
95-96—Petra Vsetin	Czech Rep.	38	19	20	39	20	...	...	...	13	9	11	20	10
96-97—Petra Vsetin	Czech Rep.	52	30	31	61	55	...	...	...	10	7	4	11	22
97-98—Petra Vsetin	Czech Rep.	50	21	34	55	64	...	...	...	10	*12	6	18	4
—Czech Rep. Oly. team..	Int'l	6	1	2	3	0	...	...	...	—	—	—	—	—
98-99—Vsetin	Czech Rep.	50	19	32	51	43	...	...	...	12	1	6	7	...
99-00—Vsetin	Czech Rep.	49	*30	29	59	83	...	...	...	9	0	4	4	6

DOWD, JIM — C — WILD

PERSONAL: Born December 25, 1968, in Brick, N.J. ... 6-1/190. ... Shoots right. ... Full Name: James Dowd.
HIGH SCHOOL: Brick (N.J.) Township.
COLLEGE: Lake Superior State (Mich.).
TRANSACTIONS/CAREER NOTES: Selected by New Jersey Devils in eighth round (seventh Devils pick, 149th overall) of NHL entry draft (June 13, 1987). ... Injured shoulder (February 2, 1995) and underwent shoulder surgery; missed 35 games. ... Traded by Devils with second-round pick (traded to Calgary) in 1997 draft to Hartford Whalers for RW Jocelyn Lemieux and second-round pick (traded to Dallas) in 1998 draft (December 19, 1995). ... Traded by Whalers with D Frantisek Kucera and second-round pick (D Ryan Bonni) in 1997 draft to Vancouver Canucks for D Jeff Brown and fifth-round pick (traded to Dallas) in 1998 draft (December 19, 1995). ... Selected by New York Islanders from Canucks in waiver draft for cash (September 30, 1996). ... Signed as free agent by Calgary Flames (July 10, 1997). ... Traded by Flames to Nashville Predators for future considerations (June 27, 1998). ... Traded by Predators with G Mikhail Shtalenkov to Edmonton Oilers for G Eric Fichaud, D Drake Berehowsky and D Greg de Vries (October 1, 1998). ... Selected by Minnesota Wild in NHL expansion draft (June 23, 2000).
HONORS: Named to NCAA All-America (West) second team (1989-90). ... Named to CCHA All-Star second team (1989-90). ... Named to NCAA All-America (West) first team (1990-91). ... Named CCHA Player of the Year (1990-91). ... Named to CCHA All-Star first team (1990-91).
MISCELLANEOUS: Member of Stanley Cup championship team (1995).

Season Team	League	REGULAR SEASON Gms.	G	A	Pts.	PIM	+/-	PP	SH	PLAYOFFS Gms.	G	A	Pts.	PIM
83-84—Brick Township	N.J. H.S.	...	19	30	49	...	...	...	...	—	—	—	—	—
84-85—Brick Township	N.J. H.S.	...	58	55	113	...	...	...	...	—	—	—	—	—
85-86—Brick Township	N.J. H.S.	...	47	51	98	...	...	...	...	—	—	—	—	—
86-87—Brick Township	N.J. H.S.	24	22	33	55	...	...	...	...	—	—	—	—	—
87-88—Lake Superior State	CCHA	45	18	27	45	16	...	...	...	—	—	—	—	—
88-89—Lake Superior State	CCHA	46	24	35	59	40	...	...	...	—	—	—	—	—
89-90—Lake Superior State	CCHA	46	25	67	92	30	...	...	...	—	—	—	—	—
90-91—Lake Superior State	CCHA	44	24	54	78	53	...	...	...	—	—	—	—	—
91-92—Utica	AHL	78	17	42	59	47	...	...	...	4	2	2	4	4
—New Jersey	NHL	1	0	0	0	0	0	0	0	—	—	—	—	—
92-93—Utica	AHL	78	27	45	72	62	...	...	...	5	1	7	8	10
—New Jersey	NHL	1	0	0	0	0	-1	0	0	—	—	—	—	—
93-94—Albany	AHL	58	26	37	63	76	...	...	...	—	—	—	—	—
—New Jersey	NHL	15	5	10	15	0	8	2	0	19	2	6	8	8
94-95—New Jersey	NHL	10	1	4	5	0	-5	1	0	11	2	1	3	8
95-96—New Jersey	NHL	28	4	9	13	17	-1	0	0	—	—	—	—	—
—Vancouver	NHL	38	1	6	7	6	-8	0	0	1	0	0	0	0
96-97—New York Islanders	NHL	3	0	0	0	0	-1	0	0	—	—	—	—	—
—Utah	IHL	48	10	21	31	27	...	...	...	—	—	—	—	—
—Saint John	AHL	24	5	11	16	18	...	...	...	5	1	2	3	0
97-98—Saint John	AHL	35	8	30	38	20	...	...	...	19	3	13	16	10
—Calgary	NHL	48	6	8	14	12	10	0	1	—	—	—	—	—
98-99—Hamilton	AHL	51	15	29	44	82	...	...	...	11	3	6	9	8
—Edmonton	NHL	1	0	0	0	0	0	0	0	—	—	—	—	—
99-00—Edmonton	NHL	69	5	18	23	45	10	2	0	5	2	1	3	4
NHL Totals (9 years)		214	22	55	77	80	12	5	1	36	6	8	14	20

DOWNEY, AARON — RW

PERSONAL: Born September 27, 1974, in Shelburne, Ontario. ... 6-0/210. ... Shoots right. ... Full Name: Aaron Douglas Downey.
TRANSACTIONS/CAREER NOTES: Signed as non-drafted free agent by Boston Bruins (January 20, 1998).

Season Team	League	REGULAR SEASON Gms.	G	A	Pts.	PIM	+/-	PP	SH	PLAYOFFS Gms.	G	A	Pts.	PIM
92-93—Guelph	OHL	53	3	3	6	88	...	...	...	5	1	0	1	0
93-94—Cole Harbor	MWJHL	35	8	20	28	210	...	...	...	—	—	—	—	—
94-95—Cole Harbor	MWJHL	40	10	31	41	320	...	...	...	—	—	—	—	—
95-96—Hampton	ECHL	65	12	11	23	354	...	...	...	—	—	—	—	—
96-97—Hampton	ECHL	64	8	8	16	338	...	...	...	9	0	3	3	26
—Portland	AHL	3	0	0	0	19	...	...	...	—	—	—	—	—
—Manitoba	IHL	2	0	0	0	19	...	...	...	—	—	—	—	—
97-98—Providence	AHL	78	5	10	15	*407	...	...	...	—	—	—	—	—
98-99—Providence	AHL	75	10	12	22	*401	...	...	...	19	1	1	2	46
99-00—Providence	AHL	47	6	4	10	221	...	...	...	14	1	0	1	24
—Boston	NHL	1	0	0	0	0	0	0	0	—	—	—	—	—
NHL Totals (1 year)		1	0	0	0	0	0	0	0					

PERSONAL: Born February 4, 1969, in Trail, B.C. ... 6-1/190. ... Shoots left. ... Full Name: Dallas James Drake.
COLLEGE: Northern Michigan.
TRANSACTIONS/CAREER NOTES: Selected by Detroit Red Wings in sixth round (sixth Red Wings pick, 116th overall) of NHL entry draft (June 17, 1989). ... Bruised left leg (November 27, 1992); missed three games. ... Suffered back spasms (December 28, 1992); missed one game. ... Bruised kneecap (January 23, 1993); missed three games. ... Suffered concussion (February 13, 1993); missed one game. ... Injured right wrist (October 16, 1993); missed three games. ... Injured tendon in right hand (December 14, 1993); missed 16 games. ... Traded by Detroit Red Wings with G Tim Cheveldae to Winnipeg Jets for G Bob Essensa and D Sergei Bautin (March 8, 1994). ... Suffered back spasms (March 17, 1995); missed four games. ... Bruised right shoulder (October 22, 1995); missed seven games. ... Suffered ear infection (November 21, 1995); missed two games. ... Strained Achilles' tendon (December 28, 1995); missed two games. ... Jets franchise moved to Phoenix and renamed Coyotes for 1996-97 season; NHL approved move on January 18, 1996. ... Sprained ankle (November 16, 1996); missed eight games. ... Sprained knee (January 29, 1997); missed 10 games. ... Suffered from the flu (October 19, 1997); missed one game. ... Injured knee (December 3, 1997); missed 12 games. ... Bruised knee (March 2, 1998); missed one game. ... Injured wrist (March 18, 1998); missed five games. ... Bruised ankle (October 21, 1998); missed one game. ... Suffered concussion (November 6, 1998); missed two games. ... Bruised elbow (December 28, 1998); missed one game. ... Suspended four games by NHL for illegal hit (December 29, 1998). ... Separated shoulder (January 29, 1999); missed 13 games. ... Strained shoulder (March 15, 1999); missed two games. ... Bruised shoulder (March 23, 1999); missed five games. ... Sprained shoulder (October 30, 1999); missed three games. ... Selected by Columbus Blue Jackets in NHL expansion draft (June 23, 2000). ... Signed as free agent by St. Louis Blues (July 1, 2000).
HONORS: Named to NCAA All-America (West) first team (1991-92). ... Won WCHA Player of the Year Award (1991-92). ... Named to WCHA All-Star first team (1991-92).

		REGULAR SEASON								PLAYOFFS				
Season Team	League	Gms.	G	A	Pts.	PIM	+/-	PP	SH	Gms.	G	A	Pts.	PIM
84-85—Rossland	KIJHL	30	13	37	50	...	...	...	...	—	—	—	—	—
85-86—Rossland	KIJHL	41	53	73	126	...	...	...	...	—	—	—	—	—
86-87—Rossland	KIJHL	40	55	80	135	...	...	...	...	—	—	—	—	—
87-88—Vernon	BCJHL	47	39	85	124	50	...	...	...	11	9	17	26	30
88-89—N. Michigan Univ.	WCHA	45	18	24	42	26	...	...	...	—	—	—	—	—
89-90—N. Michigan Univ.	WCHA	36	13	24	37	42	...	...	...	—	—	—	—	—
90-91—N. Michigan Univ.	WCHA	44	22	36	58	89	...	...	...	—	—	—	—	—
91-92—N. Michigan Univ.	WCHA	40	*39	44	83	58	...	...	...	—	—	—	—	—
92-93—Detroit	NHL	72	18	26	44	93	15	3	2	7	3	3	6	6
93-94—Detroit	NHL	47	10	22	32	37	5	0	1	—	—	—	—	—
—Adirondack	AHL	1	2	0	2	0	...	...	...	—	—	—	—	—
—Winnipeg	NHL	15	3	5	8	12	-6	1	1	—	—	—	—	—
94-95—Winnipeg	NHL	43	8	18	26	30	-6	0	0	—	—	—	—	—
95-96—Winnipeg	NHL	69	19	20	39	36	-7	4	4	3	0	0	0	0
96-97—Phoenix	NHL	63	17	19	36	52	-11	5	1	7	0	1	1	2
97-98—Phoenix	NHL	60	11	29	40	71	17	3	0	4	0	1	1	2
98-99—Phoenix	NHL	53	9	22	31	65	17	0	0	7	4	3	7	4
99-00—Phoenix	NHL	79	15	30	45	62	11	0	2	5	0	1	1	4
NHL Totals (8 years)		501	110	191	301	458	35	16	11	33	7	9	16	18

PERSONAL: Born May 24, 1971, in Toronto. ... 5-10/190. ... Shoots left. ... Full Name: Kris Bruce Draper. ... Related to Kevin Grimes, defenseman, Ottawa Senators system.
TRANSACTIONS/CAREER NOTES: Selected by Winnipeg Jets in third round (fourth Jets pick, 62nd overall) of NHL entry draft (June 17, 1989). ... Traded by Jets to Detroit Red Wings for future considerations (June 30, 1993). ... Sprained right knee ligament (February 4, 1995); missed eight games. ... Suffered from the flu (January 5, 1996); missed one game. ... Injured right knee (February 15, 1996); missed 12 games. ... Reinjured right knee (March 25, 1996); missed three games. ... Dislocated thumb (December 17, 1997) and underwent surgery; missed 18 games. ... Suspended two games by NHL for slashing incident (January 29, 1999). ... Suffered facial lacerations (November 15, 1999); missed three games. ... Fractured wrist (November 24, 1999); missed 25 games.
MISCELLANEOUS: Member of Stanley Cup championship team (1997 and 1998).

		REGULAR SEASON								PLAYOFFS				
Season Team	League	Gms.	G	A	Pts.	PIM	+/-	PP	SH	Gms.	G	A	Pts.	PIM
88-89—Canadian nat'l team	Int'l	60	11	15	26	16	...	...	...	—	—	—	—	—
89-90—Canadian nat'l team	Int'l	61	12	22	34	44	...	...	...	—	—	—	—	—
90-91—Winnipeg	NHL	3	1	0	1	5	0	0	0	—	—	—	—	—
—Moncton	AHL	7	2	1	3	2	...	...	...	—	—	—	—	—
—Ottawa	OHL	39	19	42	61	35	...	...	...	17	8	11	19	20
91-92—Moncton	AHL	61	11	18	29	113	...	...	...	4	0	1	1	6
—Winnipeg	NHL	10	2	0	2	2	0	0	0	2	0	0	0	0
92-93—Winnipeg	NHL	7	0	0	0	2	-6	0	0	—	—	—	—	—
—Moncton	AHL	67	12	23	35	40	...	...	...	5	2	2	4	18
93-94—Adirondack	AHL	46	20	23	43	49	...	...	...	—	—	—	—	—
—Detroit	NHL	39	5	8	13	31	11	0	1	7	2	2	4	4
94-95—Detroit	NHL	36	2	6	8	22	1	0	0	18	4	1	5	12
95-96—Detroit	NHL	52	7	9	16	32	2	0	1	18	4	2	6	18
96-97—Detroit	NHL	76	8	5	13	73	-11	1	0	20	2	4	6	12
97-98—Detroit	NHL	64	13	10	23	45	5	1	0	19	1	3	4	12
98-99—Detroit	NHL	80	4	14	18	79	2	0	1	10	0	1	1	6
99-00—Detroit	NHL	51	5	7	12	28	3	0	0	9	2	0	2	6
NHL Totals (10 years)		418	47	59	106	319	7	2	3	103	15	13	28	70

DRUKEN, HAROLD   C   CANUCKS

PERSONAL: Born January 26, 1979, in St. John's, Nfld. ... 6-0/200. ... Shoots left. ... Name pronounced DROO-kihn.
HIGH SCHOOL: Noble and Greenough (Dedham, Mass.).
TRANSACTIONS/CAREER NOTES: Selected by Vancouver Canucks in second round (third Canucks pick, 36th overall) of NHL entry draft (June 21, 1997).
HONORS: Named to OHL All-Rookie team (1996-97). ... Named to OHL All-Star second team (1998-99).

		REGULAR SEASON								PLAYOFFS				
Season Team	League	Gms.	G	A	Pts.	PIM	+/-	PP	SH	Gms.	G	A	Pts.	PIM
95-96—Noble ‡ Greenough.....	Mass. H.S.	30	37	28	65	28	...	...	...	—	—	—	—	—
96-97—Detroit..................	OHL	63	27	31	58	14	...	...	...	5	3	2	5	0
97-98—Plymouth..............	OHL	64	38	44	82	12	...	...	...	15	9	11	20	4
98-99—Plymouth..............	OHL	60	*58	45	103	34	...	...	...	11	9	12	21	14
99-00—Syracuse..............	AHL	47	20	25	45	32	...	...	...	4	1	2	3	6
—Vancouver..................	NHL	33	7	9	16	10	14	2	0	—	—	—	—	—
NHL Totals (1 year)............		33	7	9	16	10	14	2	0					

DRULIA, STAN   RW   LIGHTNING

PERSONAL: Born January 5, 1968, in Elmira, N.Y. ... 5-11/190. ... Shoots right. ... Name pronounced DROOL-yuh.
TRANSACTIONS/CAREER NOTES: Selected by Pittsburgh Penguins as underage junior in 11th round (11th Penguins pick, 214th overall) of NHL entry draft (June 21, 1986). ... Signed as free agent by Edmonton Oilers (May 1989). ... Signed as free agent by Tampa Bay Lightning (September 1, 1992). ... Signed as free agent by Lightning (September 29, 1999). ... Strained muscle in abdomen (December 10, 1999); missed one game. ... Suffered concussion (January 5, 2000); missed nine games. ... Bruised hand (March 1, 2000); missed two games. ... Strained wrist (March 17, 2000); missed three games.
HONORS: Won Jim Mahon Memorial Trophy (1988-89). ... Won Leo Lalonde Memorial Trophy (1988-89). ... Named to OHL All-Star first team (1988-89). ... Won ECHL Most Valuable Player Award (1990-91). ... Won ECHL Top Scorer Award (1990-91). ... Named to ECHL All-Star first team (1990-91). ... Named to AHL All-Star second team (1991-92). ... Named to IHL All-Star first team (1993-94 and 1994-95).
MISCELLANEOUS: Failed to score on a penalty shot (vs. Dominic Roussel, October 15, 1999).

		REGULAR SEASON								PLAYOFFS				
Season Team	League	Gms.	G	A	Pts.	PIM	+/-	PP	SH	Gms.	G	A	Pts.	PIM
84-85—Belleville	OHL	63	24	31	55	33	...	...	...	—	—	—	—	—
85-86—Belleville	OHL	66	43	37	80	73	...	...	...	—	—	—	—	—
86-87—Hamilton	OHL	55	27	51	78	26	...	...	...	—	—	—	—	—
87-88—Hamilton	OHL	65	52	69	121	44	...	...	...	14	8	16	24	12
88-89—Niagara Falls..............	OHL	47	52	93	145	59	...	...	...	17	11	*26	37	18
—Maine.........................	AHL	3	1	1	2	0	...	...	...	—	—	—	—	—
89-90—Cape Breton..............	AHL	31	5	7	12	2	...	...	...	—	—	—	—	—
—Phoenix......................	IHL	16	6	3	9	2	...	...	...	—	—	—	—	—
90-91—Knoxville.................	ECHL	64	*63	77	*140	39	...	...	...	3	3	2	5	4
91-92—New Haven................	AHL	77	49	53	102	46	...	...	...	5	2	4	6	4
92-93—Tampa Bay	NHL	24	2	1	3	10	1	0	0	—	—	—	—	—
—Atlanta.......................	IHL	47	28	26	54	38	...	...	...	3	2	3	5	4
93-94—Atlanta	IHL	79	54	60	114	70	...	...	...	14	13	12	25	8
94-95—Atlanta	IHL	66	41	49	90	60	...	...	...	5	1	5	6	2
95-96—Atlanta.....................	IHL	75	38	56	94	80	...	...	...	3	0	2	2	18
96-97—Detroit.....................	IHL	73	33	38	71	42	...	...	...	†21	5	*21	26	14
97-98—Detroit.....................	IHL	58	25	35	60	50	...	...	...	15	2	4	6	16
98-99—Detroit.....................	IHL	82	23	52	75	64	...	...	...	11	5	4	9	10
99-00—Tampa Bay	NHL	68	11	22	33	24	-18	1	2	—	—	—	—	—
NHL Totals (2 years)............		92	13	23	36	34	-17	1	2					

DRURY, CHRIS   C   AVALANCHE

PERSONAL: Born August 20, 1976, in Trumbull, Conn. ... 5-10/180. ... Shoots right. ... Brother of Ted Drury, center/left winger, Columbus Blue Jackets.
HIGH SCHOOL: Fairfield (Conn.) College Prep.
COLLEGE: Boston University.
TRANSACTIONS/CAREER NOTES: Selected by Quebec Nordiques in third round (fifth Nordiques pick, 72nd overall) of NHL entry draft (June 29, 1994). ... Nordiques franchise moved to Colorado and renamed Avalanche for 1995-96 season (June 21, 1995). ... Suffered hip pointer (October 29, 1998); missed two games.
HONORS: Named to NCAA All-America (East) second team (1995-96). ... Named to Hockey East All-Star team (1995-96 and 1996-97). ... Named to NCAA All-America (East) first team (1996-97 and 1997-98). ... Named Hockey East Player of the Year (1996-97 and 1997-98). ... Named to NCAA All-Tournament team (1996-97). ... Won Hobey Baker Memorial Award (1997-98). ... Named to Hockey East All-Star first team (1997-98). ... Named NHL Rookie of the Year by THE SPORTING NEWS (1998-99). ... Won Calder Memorial Trophy (1998-99). ... Named to NHL All-Rookie team (1998-99).
MISCELLANEOUS: Scored on a penalty shot (vs. Ken Wregget, March 18, 2000).

		REGULAR SEASON								PLAYOFFS				
Season Team	League	Gms.	G	A	Pts.	PIM	+/-	PP	SH	Gms.	G	A	Pts.	PIM
92-93—Fairfield College Prep..	Conn. H.S.	24	25	32	57	15	...	...	...	—	—	—	—	—
93-94—Fairfield College Prep..	Conn. H.S.	24	37	18	55		...	...	...	—	—	—	—	—
94-95—Boston University	Hockey East	39	12	15	27	38	...	...	...	—	—	—	—	—
95-96—Boston University	Hockey East	37	35	33	68	46	...	...	...	—	—	—	—	—
96-97—Boston University	Hockey East	41	38	24	62	64	...	...	...	—	—	—	—	—
97-98—Boston University	Hockey East	38	28	29	57	88	...	...	...	—	—	—	—	—
98-99—Colorado..................	NHL	79	20	24	44	62	9	6	0	19	6	2	8	4
99-00—Colorado..................	NHL	82	20	47	67	42	8	7	0	17	4	10	14	4
NHL Totals (2 years)............		161	40	71	111	104	17	13	0	36	10	12	22	8

PERSONAL: Born September 13, 1971, in Boston. ... 6-0/204. ... Shoots left. ... Full Name: Theodore Evans Drury. ... Brother of Chris Drury, center, Colorado Avalanche.

HIGH SCHOOL: Fairfield (Conn.) College Prep School.

COLLEGE: Harvard.

TRANSACTIONS/CAREER NOTES: Selected by Calgary Flames in second round (second Flames pick, 42nd overall) of NHL entry draft (June 17, 1989). ... Fractured kneecap (December 22, 1993); missed 15 games. ... Traded by Flames with D Gary Suter and LW Paul Ranheim to Hartford Whalers for C Mikael Nylander, D Zarley Zalapski and D James Patrick (March 10, 1994). ... Strained back (March 9, 1995); missed three games. ... Claimed by Ottawa Senators from Whalers in NHL waiver draft (October 2, 1995). ... Injured shoulder (November 4, 1995); missed three games. ... Suffered slight concussion (January 22, 1996); missed two games. ... Injured wrist (January 29, 1996). ... Traded by Senators with rights to D Marc Moro to Mighty Ducks of Anaheim for C Shaun Van Allen and D Jason York (October 1, 1996). ... Fractured wrist (January 31, 1997); missed five games. ... Traded by Mighty Ducks to New York Islanders for C Tony Hrkac and D Dean Malkoc (October 29, 1999). ... Injured back (February 15, 2000); missed one game. ... Selected by Columbus Blue Jackets in NHL expansion draft (June 23, 2000).

HONORS: Named to NCAA All-America (East) first team (1992-93). ... Named ECAC Player of the Year (1992-93). ... Named to ECAC All-Star first team (1992-93).

Season Team	League	REGULAR SEASON								PLAYOFFS				
		Gms.	G	A	Pts.	PIM	+/-	PP	SH	Gms.	G	A	Pts.	PIM
87-88—Fairfield College Prep..	Conn. H.S.	—	21	28	49	—	...	...	...	—	—	—	—	—
88-89—Fairfield College Prep..	Conn. H.S.	25	35	31	66	—	...	...	...	—	—	—	—	—
89-90—Harvard University	ECAC	17	9	13	22	10	...	...	...	—	—	—	—	—
90-91—Harvard University	ECAC	26	18	18	36	22	...	...	...	—	—	—	—	—
91-92—U.S. national team	Int'l	53	11	23	34	30	...	...	...	—	—	—	—	—
—U.S. Olympic team	Int'l	7	1	1	2	0	...	...	...	—	—	—	—	—
92-93—Harvard University	ECAC	31	22	41	*63	26	...	...	...	—	—	—	—	—
93-94—Calgary	NHL	34	5	7	12	26	-5	0	1	—	—	—	—	—
—U.S. national team	Int'l	11	1	4	5	11	...	...	...	—	—	—	—	—
—U.S. Olympic team	Int'l	7	1	2	3	2	...	...	...	—	—	—	—	—
—Hartford	NHL	16	1	5	6	10	-10	0	0	—	—	—	—	—
94-95—Hartford	NHL	34	3	6	9	21	-3	0	0	—	—	—	—	—
—Springfield	AHL	2	0	1	1	0	...	...	...	—	—	—	—	—
95-96—Ottawa	NHL	42	9	7	16	54	-19	1	0	—	—	—	—	—
96-97—Anaheim	NHL	73	9	9	18	54	-9	1	0	10	1	0	1	4
97-98—Anaheim	NHL	73	6	10	16	82	-10	0	1	—	—	—	—	—
98-99—Anaheim	NHL	75	5	6	11	83	2	0	0	4	0	0	0	0
99-00—Anaheim	NHL	11	1	1	2	6	-1	0	0	—	—	—	—	—
—New York Islanders	NHL	55	2	1	3	31	-8	1	0	—	—	—	—	—
NHL Totals (7 years)		413	41	52	93	367	-63	3	2	14	1	0	1	4

DUBINSKY, STEVE   RW

PERSONAL: Born July 9, 1970, in Montreal. ... 6-0/190. ... Shoots left. ... Name pronounced doo-BIHN-skee.

COLLEGE: Clarkson (N.Y.).

TRANSACTIONS/CAREER NOTES: Selected by Chicago Blackhawks in 11th round (11th Blackhawks pick, 226th overall) of NHL entry draft (June 16, 1990). ... Traded by Blackhawks with C Jeff Shantz to Calgary Flames for D Jamie Allison, C/LW Marty McInnis and RW Erik Andersson (October 27, 1998). ... Injured knee (March 13, 1999); missed eight games. ... Injured knee (December 12, 1999); missed final 52 games of season.

Season Team	League	REGULAR SEASON								PLAYOFFS				
		Gms.	G	A	Pts.	PIM	+/-	PP	SH	Gms.	G	A	Pts.	PIM
89-90—Clarkson	ECAC	35	7	10	17	24	...	...	...	—	—	—	—	—
90-91—Clarkson	ECAC	38	15	23	38	26	...	...	...	—	—	—	—	—
91-92—Clarkson	ECAC	33	21	34	55	40	...	...	...	—	—	—	—	—
92-93—Clarkson	ECAC	35	18	26	44	58	...	...	...	—	—	—	—	—
93-94—Chicago	NHL	27	2	6	8	16	1	0	0	6	0	0	0	10
—Indianapolis	IHL	54	15	25	40	63	...	...	...	—	—	—	—	—
94-95—Indianapolis	IHL	62	16	11	27	29	...	...	...	—	—	—	—	—
—Chicago	NHL	16	0	0	0	8	-5	0	0	—	—	—	—	—
95-96—Indianapolis	IHL	16	8	8	16	10	...	...	...	—	—	—	—	—
—Chicago	NHL	43	2	3	5	14	3	0	0	—	—	—	—	—
96-97—Indianapolis	IHL	77	32	40	72	53	...	...	...	1	3	1	4	0
—Chicago	NHL	5	0	0	0	0	2	0	0	4	1	0	1	4
97-98—Chicago	NHL	82	5	13	18	57	-6	0	1	—	—	—	—	—
98-99—Chicago	NHL	1	0	0	0	0	0	0	0	—	—	—	—	—
—Calgary	NHL	61	4	10	14	14	-7	0	2	—	—	—	—	—
99-00—Calgary	NHL	23	0	1	1	4	-12	0	0	—	—	—	—	—
NHL Totals (7 years)		258	13	33	46	113	-24	0	3	10	1	0	1	14

DUCHESNE, STEVE   D   RED WINGS

PERSONAL: Born June 30, 1965, in Sept-Iles, Que. ... 5-11/195. ... Shoots left. ... Name pronounced doo-SHAYN.

TRANSACTIONS/CAREER NOTES: Signed as non-drafted free agent by Los Angeles Kings (October 1, 1984). ... Strained left knee (January 26, 1988). ... Separated left shoulder (November 1988). ... Traded by Kings with C Steve Kasper and fourth-round pick (D Aris Brimanis) in 1991 draft to Philadelphia Flyers for D Jeff Chychrun and rights to RW Jari Kurri (May 30, 1991). ... Traded by Flyers with G Ron Hextall, C Mike Ricci, C Peter Forsberg, D Kerry Huffman, first-round pick (G Jocelyn Thibault) in 1993 draft, cash and future considerations to Quebec Nordiques for C Eric Lindros (June 20, 1992); Nordiques acquired LW Chris Simon and first-round pick (traded to Toronto) in 1994 draft to complete deal (July 21, 1992). ... Suffered concussion (January 2, 1993); missed one game. ... Suffered from the flu (March 20, 1993); missed one game. ... Refused to report to Nordiques in 1993-94 due to contract dispute. ... Traded by Nordiques with RW Denis Chasse to St. Louis

Blues for C Ron Sutter, C Bob Bassen and D Garth Butcher (January 23, 1994). ... Injured back (March 30, 1994); missed one game. ... Injured shoulder (March 31, 1995); missed one game. ... Traded by Blues to Ottawa Senators for second-round pick (traded to Buffalo) in 1996 draft (August 4, 1995). ... Sprained ankle (November 18, 1995); missed 20 games. ... Bruised hand (October 9, 1996); missed two games. ... Suffered sore back (March 4, 1997); missed two games. ... Traded by Senators to Blues for D Igor Kravchuk (August 25, 1997). ... Suffered sore knee (April 7, 1998); missed one game. ... Signed as free agent by Los Angeles Kings (July 2, 1998). ... Suffered back spasms (January 14, 1999); missed one game. ... Suffered an illness (February 13, 1999); missed one game. ... Traded by Kings to Flyers for D Dave Babych and fifth-round pick (G Nathan Marsters) in 2000 draft (March 23, 1999). ... Signed as free agent by Detroit Red Wings (September 3, 1999). ... Suspended two games by NHL for high-sticking incident (March 25, 2000).

HONORS: Named to QMJHL All-Star first team (1984-85). ... Named to NHL All-Rookie team (1986-87). ... Played in NHL All-Star Game (1989, 1990 and 1993).

STATISTICAL PLATEAUS: Three-goal games: 1988-89 (1), 1991-92 (1), 1993-94 (1). Total: 3.

Season Team	League	REGULAR SEASON								PLAYOFFS				
		Gms.	G	A	Pts.	PIM	+/-	PP	SH	Gms.	G	A	Pts.	PIM
83-84—Drummondville	QMJHL	67	1	34	35	79	...	...	...	—	—	—	—	—
84-85—Drummondville	QMJHL	65	22	54	76	94	...	...	...	5	4	7	11	8
85-86—New Haven	AHL	75	14	35	49	76	...	...	...	5	0	2	2	9
86-87—Los Angeles	NHL	75	13	25	38	74	8	5	0	5	2	2	4	4
87-88—Los Angeles	NHL	71	16	39	55	109	0	5	0	5	1	3	4	14
88-89—Los Angeles	NHL	79	25	50	75	92	31	8	5	11	4	4	8	12
89-90—Los Angeles	NHL	79	20	42	62	36	-3	6	0	10	2	9	11	6
90-91—Los Angeles	NHL	78	21	41	62	66	19	8	0	12	4	8	12	8
91-92—Philadelphia	NHL	78	18	38	56	86	-7	7	2	—	—	—	—	—
92-93—Quebec	NHL	82	20	62	82	57	15	8	0	6	0	5	5	6
93-94—St. Louis	NHL	36	12	19	31	14	1	8	0	4	0	2	2	2
94-95—St. Louis	NHL	47	12	26	38	36	29	1	0	7	0	4	4	2
95-96—Ottawa	NHL	62	12	24	36	42	-23	7	0	—	—	—	—	—
96-97—Ottawa	NHL	78	19	28	47	38	-9	10	2	7	1	4	5	0
97-98—St. Louis	NHL	80	14	42	56	32	9	5	1	10	0	4	4	6
98-99—Los Angeles	NHL	60	4	19	23	22	-6	1	0	—	—	—	—	—
—Philadelphia	NHL	11	2	5	7	2	0	1	0	6	0	2	2	2
99-00—Detroit	NHL	79	10	31	41	42	12	1	0	9	0	4	4	10
NHL Totals (14 years)		**995**	**218**	**491**	**709**	**748**	**76**	**81**	**10**	**92**	**14**	**51**	**65**	**72**

DUERDEN, DAVE — LW — PANTHERS

PERSONAL: Born April 11, 1977, in Oshawa, Ont. ... 6-2/200. ... Shoots left. ... Name pronounced DOOR-dihn.
HIGH SCHOOL: Thomas A. Stewart (Peterborough, Ont.).
TRANSACTIONS/CAREER NOTES: Selected by Florida Panthers in fourth round (fourth Panthers pick, 80th overall) of NHL entry draft (July 8, 1995).
HONORS: Named to OHL All-Star second team (1996-97).

Season Team	League	REGULAR SEASON								PLAYOFFS				
		Gms.	G	A	Pts.	PIM	+/-	PP	SH	Gms.	G	A	Pts.	PIM
93-94—Wexford	Tier II Jr. A	47	17	24	41	26	...	...	...	—	—	—	—	—
94-95—Peterborough	OHL	66	20	33	53	21	...	...	...	11	6	2	8	6
95-96—Peterborough	OHL	66	35	35	70	47	...	...	...	24	14	13	27	16
96-97—Peterborough	OHL	66	36	48	84	34	...	...	...	4	2	4	6	0
97-98—New Haven	AHL	36	6	7	13	10	...	...	...	—	—	—	—	—
—Fort Wayne	IHL	7	0	1	1	0	...	...	...	—	—	—	—	—
—Port Huron	UHL	7	0	4	4	10	...	...	...	—	—	—	—	—
98-99—Kentucky	AHL	36	8	9	17	9	...	...	...	6	0	2	2	0
—Miami	ECHL	13	10	7	17	0	...	...	...	—	—	—	—	—
99-00—Louisville	AHL	74	25	38	63	6	...	...	...	4	0	1	1	0
—Florida	NHL	2	0	0	0	0	0	0	0	—	—	—	—	—
NHL Totals (1 year)		**2**	**0**	**0**	**0**	**0**	**0**	**0**	**0**					

DUMONT, JEAN-PIERRE — RW — SABRES

PERSONAL: Born May 1, 1978, in Montreal. ... 6-1/187. ... Shoots left.
TRANSACTIONS/CAREER NOTES: Selected by New York Islanders in first round (first Islanders pick, third overall) of NHL entry draft (June 22, 1996). ... Traded by Islanders with fifth-round pick (traded to Philadelphia) in 1998 draft to Chicago Blackhawks for C/LW Dmitri Nabokov (May 30, 1998). ... Injured back (April 8, 1999); missed two games. ... Traded by Blackhawks with C Doug Gilmour to Buffalo Sabres for LW Michal Grosek (March 10, 2000).
HONORS: Won Michael Bossy Trophy (1995-96). ... Named to QMJHL All-Star second team (1996-97). ... Won Guy Lafleur Trophy (1997-98).
STATISTICAL PLATEAUS: Three-goal games: 1998-99 (1).

Season Team	League	REGULAR SEASON								PLAYOFFS				
		Gms.	G	A	Pts.	PIM	+/-	PP	SH	Gms.	G	A	Pts.	PIM
93-94—Val-d'Or	QMJHL	25	9	11	20	10	...	...	...	—	—	—	—	—
94-95—Val-d'Or	QMJHL	48	5	14	19	24	...	...	...	—	—	—	—	—
95-96—Val-d'Or	QMJHL	66	48	57	105	109	...	...	...	13	12	8	20	22
96-97—Val-d'Or	QMJHL	62	44	64	108	88	...	...	...	13	9	7	16	12
97-98—Val-d'Or	QMJHL	55	57	42	99	63	...	...	...	19	*31	15	*46	18
98-99—Portland	AHL	50	32	14	46	39	...	...	...	—	—	—	—	—
—Chicago	NHL	25	9	6	15	10	7	0	0	—	—	—	—	—
99-00—Chicago	NHL	47	10	8	18	18	-6	0	0	—	—	—	—	—
—Cleveland	IHL	7	5	2	7	8	...	...	...	—	—	—	—	—
—Rochester	AHL	13	7	10	17	18	...	...	...	21	*14	7	21	32
NHL Totals (2 years)		**72**	**19**	**14**	**33**	**28**	**1**	**0**	**0**					

DUNHAM, MIKE G PREDATORS

PERSONAL: Born June 1, 1972, in Johnson City, N.Y. ... 6-3/200. ... Catches left. ... Full Name: Michael Francis Dunham.
HIGH SCHOOL: Canterbury (New Milford, Conn.).
COLLEGE: Maine.
TRANSACTIONS/CAREER NOTES: Selected by New Jersey Devils in third round (fourth Devils pick, 53rd overall) of NHL entry draft (June 16, 1990). ... Injured hand (January 1, 1998); missed three games. ... Injured knee and underwent surgery (March 5, 1998); missed 18 games. ... Selected by Nashville Predators in NHL expansion draft (June 26, 1998). ... Strained right groin (November 29, 1998); missed seven games. ... Reinjured groin (December 19, 1998); missed 13 games. ... Strained groin (March 27, 1999); missed six games. ... Suffered from the flu (December 26, 1999); missed one game. ... Sprained right thumb (February 3, 2000); missed four games.
HONORS: Named to NCAA All-America (East) first team (1992-93). ... Named to Hockey East All-Star first team (1992-93). ... Shared Harry (Hap) Holmes Memorial Trophy with Corey Schwab (1994-95). ... Shared Jack Butterfield Trophy with Corey Schwab (1994-95). ... Named to AHL All-Star second team (1995-96). ... Shared William M. Jennings Trophy with Martin Brodeur (1996-97).
MISCELLANEOUS: Holds Nashville Predators all-time records for most games played by a goalie (96) and most wins (35). ... Stopped a penalty shot attempt (vs. John Madden, February 29, 2000). ... Allowed a penalty shot goal (vs. Markus Naslund, December 19, 1998).

			REGULAR SEASON								PLAYOFFS					
Season Team	League	Gms.	Min	W	L	T	GA	SO	Avg.	Gms.	Min.	W	L	GA	SO	Avg.
87-88—Canterbury School	Conn. H.S.	29	...	...	...	...	...	4	...	—	—	—	—	—	—	—
88-89—Canterbury School	Conn. H.S.	25	...	...	...	...	63	2	...	—	—	—	—	—	—	—
89-90—Canterbury School	Conn. H.S.	32	1558	...	...	...	55	...	2.12	—	—	—	—	—	—	—
90-91—Univ. of Maine	Hockey East	23	1275	14	5	2	63	2	*2.96	—	—	—	—	—	—	—
91-92—Univ. of Maine	Hockey East	7	382	6	0	0	14	1	2.20	—	—	—	—	—	—	—
—U.S. national team	Int'l	3	157	0	1	1	10	0	3.82	—	—	—	—	—	—	—
92-93—Univ. of Maine	Hockey East	25	1429	21	1	1	63	...	2.65	—	—	—	—	—	—	—
—U.S. national team	Int'l	1	60	0	0	1	1	0	1.00	—	—	—	—	—	—	—
93-94—U.S. national team	Int'l	33	1983	22	9	2	125	2	3.78	—	—	—	—	—	—	—
—U.S. Olympic team	Int'l	3	180	0	1	2	15	0	5.00	—	—	—	—	—	—	—
—Albany	AHL	5	305	2	2	1	26	0	5.11	—	—	—	—	—	—	—
94-95—Albany	AHL	35	2120	20	7	8	99	1	2.80	7	420	6	1	20	1	2.86
95-96—Albany	AHL	44	2591	30	10	2	109	1	2.52	3	181	1	2	5	1	1.66
96-97—Albany	AHL	3	184	1	1	1	12	0	3.91	—	—	—	—	—	—	—
—New Jersey	NHL	26	1013	8	7	1	43	2	2.55	—	—	—	—	—	—	—
97-98—New Jersey	NHL	15	773	5	5	3	29	1	2.25	—	—	—	—	—	—	—
98-99—Nashville	NHL	44	2472	16	23	3	127	1	3.08	—	—	—	—	—	—	—
99-00—Milwaukee	IHL	1	60	1	0	0	1	0	1.00	—	—	—	—	—	—	—
—Nashville	NHL	52	3077	19	27	6	146	0	2.85	—	—	—	—	—	—	—
NHL Totals (4 years)		137	7335	48	62	13	345	4	2.82							

DVORAK, RADEK RW RANGERS

PERSONAL: Born March 9, 1977, in Tabor, Czechoslovakia. ... 6-1/194. ... Shoots right. ... Name pronounced RA-dihk duh-VOHR-ak.
TRANSACTIONS/CAREER NOTES: Selected by Florida Panthers in first round (first Panthers pick, 10th overall) of NHL entry draft (July 8, 1995). ... Fractured left wrist (October 30, 1997); missed 15 games. ... Traded by Panthers to San Jose Sharks for G Mike Vernon and third-round pick (RW Sean O'Connor) in 2000 draft (December 30, 1999). ... Traded by Sharks to New York Rangers for RW Todd Harvey and fourth-round pick in 2001 draft (December 30, 1999).
MISCELLANEOUS: Failed to score on a penalty shot (vs. Manny Fernandez, March 13, 2000).
STATISTICAL PLATEAUS: Three-goal games: 1999-00 (1).

			REGULAR SEASON							PLAYOFFS				
Season Team	League	Gms.	G	A	Pts.	PIM	+/-	PP	SH	Gms.	G	A	Pts.	PIM
92-93—Motor-Ceske Bude.	Czech.	35	44	46	90	...	...	...	...	—	—	—	—	—
93-94—HC Ceske Budejovice	Czech Rep.	8	0	0	0	...	...	...	...	—	—	—	—	—
—Motor-Ceske Bude.	Czech Rep.	20	17	18	35	...	...	...	...	—	—	—	—	—
94-95—HC Ceske Budejovice	Czech Rep.	7	3	5	8	...	...	...	...	9	5	1	6	...
95-96—Florida	NHL	77	13	14	27	20	5	0	0	16	1	3	4	0
96-97—Florida	NHL	78	18	21	39	30	-2	2	0	3	0	0	0	0
97-98—Florida	NHL	64	12	24	36	33	-1	2	3	—	—	—	—	—
98-99—Florida	NHL	82	19	24	43	29	7	0	4	—	—	—	—	—
99-00—Florida	NHL	35	7	10	17	6	5	0	0	—	—	—	—	—
—New York Rangers	NHL	46	11	22	33	10	0	2	1	—	—	—	—	—
NHL Totals (5 years)		382	80	115	195	128	14	6	8	19	1	3	4	0

DWYER, GORDIE LW LIGHTNING

PERSONAL: Born January 25, 1978, in Dalhousie, N.B. ... 6-2/216. ... Shoots left.
TRANSACTIONS/CAREER NOTES: Selected by St. Louis Blues in third round (second Blues pick, 67th overall) of NHL entry draft (June 22, 1996). ... Returned to draft pool by Blues and selected by Montreal Canadiens in sixth round (fifth Canadiens pick, 152nd overall) of NHL entry draft (June 27, 1998). ... Traded by Canadiens to Tampa Bay Lightning for D Mike McBain (November 26, 1999). ... Injured finger (April 8, 2000); missed final game of season.

			REGULAR SEASON							PLAYOFFS				
Season Team	League	Gms.	G	A	Pts.	PIM	+/-	PP	SH	Gms.	G	A	Pts.	PIM
94-95—Hull	QMJHL	57	3	7	10	204	...	...	...	17	1	3	4	54
95-96—Hull	QMJHL	25	5	9	14	199	...	...	...	—	—	—	—	—
—Laval	QMJHL	22	5	17	22	72	...	...	...	—	—	—	—	—
—Beauport	QMJHL	22	4	9	13	87	...	...	...	20	3	5	8	104
96-97—Drummondville	QMJHL	66	21	48	69	391	...	...	...	8	6	1	7	39
97-98—Quebec	QMJHL	59	18	27	45	365	...	...	...	14	4	9	13	67
98-99—Fredericton	AHL	14	0	0	0	46	...	...	...	—	—	—	—	—
—New Orleans	ECHL	36	1	3	4	163	...	...	...	11	0	0	0	27
99-00—Quebec	AHL	7	0	0	0	37	...	...	...	—	—	—	—	—
—Detroit	IHL	27	0	2	2	147	...	...	...	—	—	—	—	—
—Tampa Bay	NHL	24	0	1	1	135	-6	0	0	—	—	—	—	—
NHL Totals (1 year)		24	0	1	1	135	-6	0	0					

PERSONAL: Born July 8, 1972, in Sept-Iles, Que. ... 6-3/214. ... Shoots left. ... Name pronounced DIGH-kowz.

TRANSACTIONS/CAREER NOTES: Selected by Chicago Blackhawks in first round (first Blackhawks pick, 16th overall) of NHL entry draft (June 16, 1990). ... Traded by Blackhawks to Philadelphia Flyers for D Bob Wilkie (February 16, 1995). ... Sprained knee (November 26, 1996); missed two games. ... Suffered facial lacerations (December 31, 1996); missed two games. ... Dislocated shoulder (January 28, 1997); missed 13 games. ... Traded by Flyers with RW Mikael Renberg to Tampa Bay Lightning for C Chris Gratton (August 20, 1997). ... Suffered from the flu (November 14, 1997); missed one game. ... Suffered from the flu (January 31, 1998); missed one game. ... Traded by Lightning to Flyers for D Petr Svoboda (December 28, 1998). ... Fractured cheekbone (December 29, 1998); missed one game. ... Traded by Flyers to Montreal Canadiens for future considerations (October 20, 1999). ... Injured knee (March 6, 2000); missed one game. ... Injured groin (March 18, 2000); missed five games.

HONORS: Won Raymond Lagace Trophy (1988-89). ... Won Michael Bossy Trophy (1989-90). ... Named to QMJHL All-Star first team (1989-90).

		REGULAR SEASON								PLAYOFFS				
Season Team	League	Gms.	G	A	Pts.	PIM	+/-	PP	SH	Gms.	G	A	Pts.	PIM
88-89—Hull	QMJHL	63	2	29	31	59	...	...	...	9	1	9	10	6
89-90—Hull	QMJHL	69	10	45	55	119	...	...	...	11	2	5	7	2
90-91—Longueuil	QMJHL	3	1	4	5	6	...	...	...	—	—	—	—	—
—Canadian nat'l team	Int'l	37	2	9	11	16	...	...	...	—	—	—	—	—
91-92—Longueuil	QMJHL	29	5	19	24	55	...	...	...	17	0	12	12	14
—Chicago	NHL	6	1	3	4	4	-1	1	0	—	—	—	—	—
92-93—Indianapolis	IHL	59	5	18	23	76	...	...	...	5	1	1	2	8
—Chicago	NHL	12	0	5	5	0	2	0	0	—	—	—	—	—
93-94—Indianapolis	IHL	73	7	25	32	132	...	...	...	—	—	—	—	—
94-95—Indianapolis	IHL	52	2	21	23	63	...	...	...	—	—	—	—	—
—Hershey	AHL	1	0	0	0	0	...	...	...	—	—	—	—	—
—Philadelphia	NHL	33	2	6	8	37	7	1	0	15	4	4	8	14
95-96—Philadelphia	NHL	82	5	15	20	101	12	1	0	12	2	2	4	22
96-97—Philadelphia	NHL	62	4	15	19	35	6	2	0	18	0	3	3	2
97-98—Tampa Bay	NHL	78	5	9	14	110	-8	0	1	—	—	—	—	—
98-99—Tampa Bay	NHL	33	2	1	3	18	-21	0	0	—	—	—	—	—
—Philadelphia	NHL	45	2	4	6	32	-2	1	0	5	1	0	1	4
99-00—Philadelphia	NHL	5	0	1	1	6	-2	0	0	—	—	—	—	—
—Montreal	NHL	67	7	12	19	40	-3	3	1	—	—	—	—	—
NHL Totals (8 years)		423	28	71	99	383	-10	9	2	50	7	9	16	42

D
E

PERSONAL: Born March 7, 1963, in Sussex, N.B. ... 5-10/195. ... Shoots left. ... Full Name: Michael Bryant Eagles.

TRANSACTIONS/CAREER NOTES: Selected by Quebec Nordiques as underage junior in sixth round (fifth Nordiques pick, 116th overall) of NHL entry draft (June 10, 1981). ... Fractured hand (October 1984). ... Injured ribs (February 21, 1986). ... Traded by Nordiques to Chicago Blackhawks for G Bob Mason (July 1988). ... Fractured left hand (February 1989). ... Bruised kidney (January 15, 1990); missed eight games. ... Traded by Blackhawks to Winnipeg Jets for fourth-round pick (D Igor Kravchuk) in 1991 draft (December 14, 1990). ... Fractured thumb (February 17, 1992); missed 14 games. ... Suffered concussion (November 30, 1993); missed one game. ... Strained shoulder (March 7, 1994); missed one game. ... Bruised kidneys (March 27, 1994); missed remainder of season. ... Traded by Jets with D Igor Ulanov to Washington Capitals for third-(traded to Dallas) and fifth-round (G Brian Elder) picks in 1995 draft (April 7, 1995). ... Fractured finger (January 1, 1996); missed 11 games. ... Fractured wrist (November 9, 1997); missed 17 games. ... Injured foot (February 1, 1998); missed six games. ... Reinjured foot (March 3, 1998); missed seven games.

MISCELLANEOUS: Scored on a penalty shot (vs. Doug Keans, November 9, 1987).

		REGULAR SEASON								PLAYOFFS				
Season Team	League	Gms.	G	A	Pts.	PIM	+/-	PP	SH	Gms.	G	A	Pts.	PIM
79-80—Melville	SJHL	55	46	30	76	77	...	...	...	—	—	—	—	—
80-81—Kitchener	OMJHL	56	11	27	38	64	...	...	...	18	4	2	6	36
81-82—Kitchener	OHL	62	26	40	66	148	...	...	...	15	3	11	14	27
82-83—Kitchener	OHL	58	26	36	62	133	...	...	...	12	5	7	12	27
—Quebec	NHL	2	0	0	0	2	-1	0	0	—	—	—	—	—
83-84—Fredericton	AHL	68	13	29	42	85	...	...	...	4	0	0	0	5
84-85—Fredericton	AHL	36	4	20	24	80	...	...	...	3	0	0	0	2
85-86—Quebec	NHL	73	11	12	23	49	3	1	0	3	0	0	0	2
86-87—Quebec	NHL	73	13	19	32	55	-15	0	2	4	1	0	1	10
87-88—Quebec	NHL	76	10	10	20	74	-18	1	2	—	—	—	—	—
88-89—Chicago	NHL	47	5	11	16	44	-8	0	0	—	—	—	—	—
89-90—Indianapolis	IHL	24	11	13	24	47	...	...	...	13	*10	10	20	34
—Chicago	NHL	23	1	2	3	34	-4	0	0	—	—	—	—	—
90-91—Indianapolis	IHL	25	15	14	29	47	...	...	...	—	—	—	—	—
—Winnipeg	NHL	44	0	9	9	79	-10	0	0	—	—	—	—	—
91-92—Winnipeg	NHL	65	7	10	17	118	-17	0	1	7	0	0	0	8
92-93—Winnipeg	NHL	84	8	18	26	131	-1	1	0	5	0	1	1	6
93-94—Winnipeg	NHL	73	4	8	12	96	-20	0	1	—	—	—	—	—
94-95—Winnipeg	NHL	27	2	1	3	40	-13	0	0	—	—	—	—	—
—Washington	NHL	13	1	3	4	8	2	0	0	7	0	2	2	4
95-96—Washington	NHL	70	4	7	11	75	-1	0	0	6	1	1	2	2
96-97—Washington	NHL	70	1	7	8	42	-4	0	0	—	—	—	—	—
97-98—Washington	NHL	36	1	3	4	16	-2	0	0	12	0	2	2	2
98-99—Washington	NHL	52	4	2	6	50	-5	0	0	—	—	—	—	—
99-00—Washington	NHL	25	2	0	2	15	-7	0	0	—	—	—	—	—
NHL Totals (16 years)		853	74	122	196	928	-121	3	6	44	2	6	8	34

PERSONAL: Born January 20, 1967, in Dade City, Fla. ... 6-1/198. ... Shoots left. ... Name pronounced AY-kihns.
TRANSACTIONS/CAREER NOTES: Selected by Washington Capitals as underage junior in 10th round (11th Capitals pick, 208th overall) of NHL entry draft (June 15, 1985). ... Injured back (October 1988). ... Signed as free agent by Winnipeg Jets (September 1989). ... Signed as free agent by Florida Panthers (July 14, 1993). ... Traded by Panthers to St. Louis Blues for fourth-round draft pick (RW Ivan Novoseltsev) in 1997 draft (September 28, 1995). ... Fractured wrist (December 8, 1995); missed 29 games. ... Claimed on waivers by Jets (March 20, 1996). ... Jets franchise moved to Phoenix and renamed Coyotes for 1996-97 season; NHL approved move on January 18, 1996. ... Suffered back spasms (November 26, 1996); missed three games. ... Traded by Coyotes with C Mike Eastwood to New York Rangers for D Jay More (February 6, 1997). ... Signed as free agent by Florida Panthers (July 7, 1997). ... Sprained left knee prior to 1997-98 season; missed first 11 games of season. ... Signed as free agent by Toronto Maple Leafs (July 14, 1998). ... Sprained shoulder (November 14, 1998); missed three games. ... Signed as free agent by New York Islanders (August 12, 1999). ... Traded by Islanders to Chicago Blackhawks for future considerations (March 3, 2000). ... Signed as free agent by Calgary Flames (July 27, 2000).
HONORS: Named to IHL All-Star second team (1999-2000).

		REGULAR SEASON								PLAYOFFS				
Season Team	League	Gms.	G	A	Pts.	PIM	+/-	PP	SH	Gms.	G	A	Pts.	PIM
84-85—Peterborough	OHL	48	0	8	8	96	...	...	...	7	0	0	0	18
85-86—Peterborough	OHL	60	6	16	22	134	...	...	...	16	0	1	1	30
86-87—Peterborough	OHL	54	3	11	14	145	...	...	...	12	1	4	5	37
87-88—Peterborough	OHL	64	11	27	38	129	...	...	...	12	3	12	15	16
88-89—Baltimore	AHL	62	0	10	10	139	...	...	...	—	—	—	—	—
89-90—Moncton	AHL	75	2	11	13	189	...	...	...	—	—	—	—	—
90-91—Moncton	AHL	75	1	12	13	132	...	...	...	9	0	1	1	44
91-92—Moncton	AHL	67	3	13	16	136	...	...	...	11	2	1	3	16
92-93—Moncton	AHL	55	4	6	10	132	...	...	...	—	—	—	—	—
—Winnipeg	NHL	14	0	2	2	38	2	0	0	—	—	—	—	—
93-94—Cincinnati	IHL	80	1	18	19	143	...	...	...	8	0	1	1	41
—Florida	NHL	1	0	0	0	0	0	0	0	—	—	—	—	—
94-95—Cincinnati	IHL	59	6	12	18	69	...	...	...	—	—	—	—	—
—Florida	NHL	17	0	1	1	35	2	0	0	—	—	—	—	—
95-96—St. Louis	NHL	16	0	1	1	34	-2	0	0	—	—	—	—	—
—Worcester	AHL	4	0	0	0	12	...	...	...	—	—	—	—	—
—Winnipeg	NHL	2	0	0	0	0	1	0	0	—	—	—	—	—
96-97—Springfield	AHL	38	6	7	13	63	...	...	...	—	—	—	—	—
—Phoenix	NHL	4	0	0	0	10	-3	0	0	—	—	—	—	—
—Binghamton	AHL	19	1	7	8	15	...	...	...	—	—	—	—	—
—New York Rangers	NHL	3	0	0	0	6	-1	0	0	4	0	0	0	4
97-98—Florida	NHL	23	0	1	1	44	1	0	0	—	—	—	—	—
—New Haven	AHL	4	0	1	1	7	...	...	...	—	—	—	—	—
98-99—Chicago	IHL	2	0	0	0	0	...	...	...	—	—	—	—	—
—Toronto	NHL	18	0	2	2	24	3	0	0	1	0	0	0	0
—St. John's	AHL	20	3	7	10	16	...	...	...	5	0	1	1	6
99-00—Chicago	IHL	68	5	26	31	99	...	...	...	16	1	4	5	16
—New York Islanders	NHL	2	0	1	1	2	3	0	0	—	—	—	—	—
NHL Totals (8 years)		100	0	8	8	193	6	0	0	5	0	0	0	4

E

PERSONAL: Born July 1, 1967, in Cornwall, Ont. ... 6-3/209. ... Shoots right. ... Full Name: Michael Barry Eastwood.
COLLEGE: Western Michigan.
TRANSACTIONS/CAREER NOTES: Selected by Toronto Maple Leafs in fifth round (fifth Maple Leafs pick, 91st overall) of NHL entry draft (June 13, 1987). ... Traded by Maple Leafs with third-round pick (RW Brad Isbister) in 1995 draft to Winnipeg Jets for RW Tie Domi (April 7, 1995). ... Jets franchise moved to Phoenix and renamed Coyotes for 1996-97 season; NHL approved move on January 18, 1996. ... Fractured wrist (October 28, 1996); missed eight games. ... Traded by Coyotes with D Dallas Eakins to New York Rangers for D Jay More (February 6, 1997). ... Traded by Rangers to St. Louis Blues for C Harry York (March 24, 1998). ... Suffered sore wrist (April 18, 1998); missed two games.
HONORS: Named to CCHA All-Star second team (1990-91).
STATISTICAL PLATEAUS: Three-goal games: 1999-00 (1).
STATISTICAL NOTES: Led NHL with 22.9 shooting percentage (1999-2000).

		REGULAR SEASON								PLAYOFFS				
Season Team	League	Gms.	G	A	Pts.	PIM	+/-	PP	SH	Gms.	G	A	Pts.	PIM
86-87—Pembroke	COJHL						Statistics unavailable.							
87-88—Western Michigan U.	CCHA	42	5	8	13	14	...	...	...	—	—	—	—	—
88-89—Western Michigan U.	CCHA	40	10	13	23	87	...	...	...	—	—	—	—	—
89-90—Western Michigan U.	CCHA	40	25	27	52	36	...	...	...	—	—	—	—	—
90-91—Western Michigan U.	CCHA	42	29	32	61	84	...	...	...	—	—	—	—	—
91-92—St. John's	AHL	61	18	25	43	28	...	...	...	16	9	10	19	16
—Toronto	NHL	9	0	2	2	4	-4	0	0	—	—	—	—	—
92-93—St. John's	AHL	60	24	35	59	32	...	...	...	—	—	—	—	—
—Toronto	NHL	12	1	6	7	21	-2	0	0	10	1	2	3	8
93-94—Toronto	NHL	54	8	10	18	28	2	1	0	18	3	2	5	12
94-95—Toronto	NHL	36	5	5	10	32	-12	0	0	—	—	—	—	—
—Winnipeg	NHL	13	3	6	9	4	3	0	0	—	—	—	—	—
95-96—Winnipeg	NHL	80	14	14	28	20	-14	2	0	6	0	1	1	2
96-97—Phoenix	NHL	33	1	3	4	4	-3	0	0	—	—	—	—	—
—New York Rangers	NHL	27	1	7	8	10	2	0	0	15	1	2	3	22
97-98—New York Rangers	NHL	48	5	5	10	16	-2	0	0	—	—	—	—	—
—St. Louis	NHL	10	1	0	1	6	0	0	0	3	1	0	1	0
98-99—St. Louis	NHL	82	9	21	30	36	6	0	0	13	1	1	2	6
99-00—St. Louis	NHL	79	19	15	34	32	5	1	3	7	1	1	2	6
NHL Totals (9 years)		483	67	94	161	213	-19	4	3	72	8	9	17	56

EATON, MARK   D   FLYERS

PERSONAL: Born May 6, 1977, in Wilmington, Del. ... 6-2/205. ... Shoots left. ... Full Name: Mark Andrew Eaton.
HIGH SCHOOL: Dickinson (Wilmington, Del.).
COLLEGE: Notre Dame.
TRANSACTIONS/CAREER NOTES: Signed as non-drafted free agent by Philadelphia Flyers (July 28, 1998). ... Suffered from stomach virus (March 26, 2000); missed one game.

		REGULAR SEASON								PLAYOFFS				
Season Team	League	Gms.	G	A	Pts.	PIM	+/-	PP	SH	Gms.	G	A	Pts.	PIM
97-98—Notre Dame	CCHA	41	12	17	29	32	...	...	...	—	—	—	—	—
98-99—Philadelphia	AHL	74	9	27	36	38	...	...	...	16	4	8	12	0
99-00—Philadelphia	NHL	27	1	1	2	8	1	0	0	7	0	0	0	0
—Philadelphia	AHL	47	9	17	26	6	...	...	...	—	—	—	—	—
NHL Totals (1 year)		27	1	1	2	8	1	0	0	7	0	0	0	0

EKMAN, NILS   LW   LIGHTNING

PERSONAL: Born March 11, 1976, in Stockholm, Sweden. ... 5-11/182. ... Shoots left.
TRANSACTIONS/CAREER NOTES: Selected by Calgary Flames in fifth round (sixth Flames pick, 107th overall) of NHL entry draft (June 29, 1994). ... Rights traded by Flames with fourth-round pick (traded to New York Islanders) in 2000 draft to Tampa Bay Lightning for C/LW Andreas Johansson (November 20, 1999). ... Injured hip (January 20, 2000); missed one game.
HONORS: Won Garry F. Longman Memorial Trophy (1999-2000).

		REGULAR SEASON								PLAYOFFS				
Season Team	League	Gms.	G	A	Pts.	PIM	+/-	PP	SH	Gms.	G	A	Pts.	PIM
93-94—Hammarby	Sweden Dv. 2	18	7	2	9	4	...	...	...	—	—	—	—	—
94-95—Hammarby	Sweden Dv. 2	29	10	7	17	18	...	...	...	—	—	—	—	—
95-96—Hammarby	Sweden Dv. 2	22	9	7	16	20	...	...	...	—	—	—	—	—
98-99—Blues Espoo	Finland	52	20	14	34	96	...	...	...	3	1	1	2	6
99-00—Tampa Bay	NHL	28	2	2	4	36	-8	1	0	—	—	—	—	—
—Detroit	IHL	10	7	2	9	8	...	...	...	—	—	—	—	—
—Long Beach	IHL	27	11	12	23	26	...	...	...	5	3	3	6	4
NHL Totals (1 year)		28	2	2	4	36	-8	1	0					

ELIAS, PATRIK   LW   DEVILS

PERSONAL: Born April 13, 1976, in Trebic, Czechoslovakia. ... 6-1/200. ... Shoots left. ... Name pronounced EH-lee-ahsh.
TRANSACTIONS/CAREER NOTES: Selected by New Jersey Devils in second round (second Devils pick, 51st overall) of NHL entry draft (June 28, 1994). ... Suffered from the flu (January 14, 1999); missed five games. ... Missed first nine games of 1999-2000 season due to contract dispute.
HONORS: Named to NHL All-Rookie team (1997-98). ... Played in NHL All-Star Game (2000).
MISCELLANEOUS: Member of Stanley Cup championship team (2000). ... Scored on a penalty shot (vs. Damian Rhodes, March 10, 2000).

		REGULAR SEASON								PLAYOFFS				
Season Team	League	Gms.	G	A	Pts.	PIM	+/-	PP	SH	Gms.	G	A	Pts.	PIM
92-93—HC Kladno	Czech.	2	0	0	0	0	...	...	...	—	—	—	—	—
93-94—HC Kladno	Czech Rep.	15	1	2	3	...	...	...	...	11	2	2	4	...
—Czech Rep. Oly. team..	Int'l	5	2	5	7	...	...	...	...	—	—	—	—	—
94-95—HC Kladno	Czech Rep.	28	4	3	7	...	...	...	...	7	1	2	3	...
95-96—Albany	AHL	74	27	36	63	83	...	...	...	4	1	1	2	2
—New Jersey	NHL	1	0	0	0	0	-1	0	0	—	—	—	—	—
96-97—Albany	AHL	57	24	43	67	76	...	...	...	6	1	2	3	8
—New Jersey	NHL	17	2	3	5	2	-4	0	0	8	2	3	5	4
97-98—New Jersey	NHL	74	18	19	37	28	18	5	0	4	0	1	1	0
—Albany	AHL	3	3	0	3	2	...	...	...	—	—	—	—	—
98-99—New Jersey	NHL	74	17	33	50	34	19	3	0	7	0	5	5	6
99-00—HC Pardubice	Czech Rep.	5	1	4	5	6	...	...	...	—	—	—	—	—
—New Jersey	NHL	72	35	37	72	58	16	9	0	23	7	†13	20	9
NHL Totals (5 years)		238	72	92	164	122	48	17	0	42	9	22	31	19

ELICH, MATT   RW   LIGHTNING

PERSONAL: Born September 22, 1979, in Detroit. ... 6-3/196. ... Shoots right. ... Name pronounced EE-lihch.
TRANSACTIONS/CAREER NOTES: Selected by Tampa Bay Lightning in third round (third Lightning pick, 61st overall) of NHL entry draft (June 21, 1997).

		REGULAR SEASON								PLAYOFFS				
Season Team	League	Gms.	G	A	Pts.	PIM	+/-	PP	SH	Gms.	G	A	Pts.	PIM
95-96—Windsor	OHL	52	10	2	12	17	...	...	...	5	1	0	1	2
96-97—Windsor	OHL	58	15	13	28	19	...	...	...	5	0	1	1	6
97-98—Windsor	OHL	20	9	12	21	8	...	...	...	—	—	—	—	—
—Kingston	OHL	34	14	4	18	2	...	...	...	12	2	4	6	2
98-99—Kingston	OHL	67	44	30	74	32	...	...	...	5	3	5	8	0
99-00—Detroit	IHL	48	12	4	16	12	...	...	...	—	—	—	—	—
—Tampa Bay	NHL	8	1	1	2	0	-1	0	0	—	—	—	—	—
NHL Totals (1 year)		8	1	1	2	0	-1	0	0					

ELLETT, DAVE   D

PERSONAL: Born March 30, 1964, in Cleveland. ... 6-2/205. ... Shoots left. ... Name pronounced EHL-iht.
COLLEGE: Bowling Green State.
TRANSACTIONS/CAREER NOTES: Selected by Winnipeg Jets as underage junior in fourth round (third Jets pick, 75th overall) of NHL entry draft (June 9, 1982). ... Bruised thigh (March 6, 1988); missed 10 games. ... Sprained ankle (November 16, 1988). ... Traded by Jets with C Paul Fenton to Toronto Maple Leafs for C Ed Olczyk and LW Mark Osborne (November 10, 1990). ... Separated shoulder (March 2, 1993); missed 14 games. ... Strained muscle in ribcage (December 11, 1993); missed 10 games. ... Separated shoulder (March 31, 1994); missed final six games of regular season. ... Cracked bone in foot (February 27, 1995); missed 15 games. ... Sprained knee (October 4, 1995); missed one game. ... Suffered from the flu (January 1, 1996). ... Scratched eye (December 27, 1996); missed one game. ... Bruised rib (January 31, 1997); missed four games. ... Traded by Maple Leafs with C Doug Gilmour and third-round pick (D Andre Lakos) in 1999 draft to New Jersey Devils for D Jason Smith, C Steve Sullivan and C Alyn McCauley (February 25, 1997). ... Signed as free agent by Boston Bruins (July 2, 1997). ... Suffered from the flu (December 21, 1998); missed one game. ... Injured elbow (December 31, 1998); missed nine games. ... Injured neck (April 26, 1999); missed remainder of playoffs. ... Signed as free agent by St. Louis Blues (October 20, 1999). ... Strained groin (February 21, 2000); missed three games.
HONORS: Named to NCAA All-Tournament team (1983-84). ... Named to CCHA All-Star second team (1983-84). ... Played in NHL All-Star Game (1989 and 1992).

Season Team	League	REGULAR SEASON								PLAYOFFS				
		Gms.	G	A	Pts.	PIM	+/-	PP	SH	Gms.	G	A	Pts.	PIM
81-82—Ottawa	COJHL	50	9	35	44	...	...	...	...	—	—	—	—	—
82-83—Bowling Green	CCHA	40	4	13	17	34	...	...	...	—	—	—	—	—
83-84—Bowling Green	CCHA	43	15	39	54	9	...	...	...	—	—	—	—	—
84-85—Winnipeg	NHL	80	11	27	38	85	20	3	0	8	1	5	6	4
85-86—Winnipeg	NHL	80	15	31	46	96	-38	2	0	3	0	1	1	0
86-87—Winnipeg	NHL	78	13	31	44	53	19	5	0	10	0	8	8	2
87-88—Winnipeg	NHL	68	13	45	58	106	-8	5	0	5	1	2	3	10
88-89—Winnipeg	NHL	75	22	34	56	62	-18	9	2	—	—	—	—	—
89-90—Winnipeg	NHL	77	17	29	46	96	-15	8	0	7	2	0	2	6
90-91—Winnipeg	NHL	17	4	7	11	6	-4	1	1	—	—	—	—	—
—Toronto	NHL	60	8	30	38	69	-4	5	0	—	—	—	—	—
91-92—Toronto	NHL	79	18	33	51	95	-13	9	1	—	—	—	—	—
92-93—Toronto	NHL	70	6	34	40	46	19	4	0	21	4	8	12	8
93-94—Toronto	NHL	68	7	36	43	42	6	5	0	18	3	15	18	31
94-95—Toronto	NHL	33	5	10	15	26	-6	3	0	7	0	2	2	0
95-96—Toronto	NHL	80	3	19	22	59	-10	1	1	6	0	0	0	4
96-97—Toronto	NHL	56	4	10	14	34	-8	0	0	—	—	—	—	—
—New Jersey	NHL	20	2	5	7	6	2	1	0	10	0	3	3	10
97-98—Boston	NHL	82	3	20	23	67	3	2	0	6	0	1	1	6
98-99—Boston	NHL	54	0	6	6	25	11	0	0	8	0	0	0	4
99-00—St. Louis	NHL	52	2	8	10	12	-4	0	0	7	0	1	1	2
NHL Totals (16 years)		1129	153	415	568	985	-48	63	5	116	11	46	57	87

ELLIOTT, JASON   G   RED WINGS

PERSONAL: Born October 11, 1975, in Chapman, Australia. ... 6-2/183. ... Catches left.
COLLEGE: Cornell.
TRANSACTIONS/CAREER NOTES: Selected by Detroit Red Wings in eighth round (eighth Red Wings pick, 205th overall) of NHL entry draft (June 29, 1994).

Season Team	League	REGULAR SEASON								PLAYOFFS						
		Gms.	Min	W	L	T	GA	SO	Avg.	Gms.	Min.	W	L	GA	SO	Avg.
94-95—Cornell University	ECAC	16	877	3	11	1	62	0	4.24	—	—	—	—	—	—	—
95-96—Cornell University	ECAC	19	971	12	2	1	38	2	2.35	—	—	—	—	—	—	—
96-97—Cornell University	ECAC	27	1475	16	7	2	67	0	2.73	—	—	—	—	—	—	—
97-98—Cornell University	ECAC	29	1683	14	12	2	74	2	2.64	—	—	—	—	—	—	—
98-99—Adirondack	AHL	51	2710	14	*27	5	146	2	3.23	1	59	0	1	2	0	2.03
99-00—Manitoba	IHL	43	2349	21	12	‡9	108	1	2.76	—	—	—	—	—	—	—

ELOMO, MIIKKA   LW   FLAMES

PERSONAL: Born April 21, 1977, in Turku, Finland. ... 6-0/198. ... Shoots left. ... Brother of Teemu Elomo, left winger, Dallas Stars system. ... Name pronounced EHL-ih-moh.
TRANSACTIONS/CAREER NOTES: Selected by Washington Capitals in first round (second Capitals pick, 23rd overall) of NHL entry draft (July 8, 1995). ... Traded by Capitals with fourth-round pick (G Levente Szuper) in 2000 draft to Calgary Flames for second-round pick (LW Matt Pettinger) in 2000 draft (June 24, 2000).

Season Team	League	REGULAR SEASON								PLAYOFFS				
		Gms.	G	A	Pts.	PIM	+/-	PP	SH	Gms.	G	A	Pts.	PIM
91-92—London	OHL	65	11	19	30	15	...	...	...	7	0	0	0	0
93-94—TPS Turku Jr.	Finland	30	8	5	13	24	...	...	...	5	1	1	2	2
94-95—Kiekko-67	Finland Div. 2	14	9	2	11	39	...	...	...	—	—	—	—	—
—TPS Turku Jr.	Finland	14	3	8	11	24	...	...	...	—	—	—	—	—
95-96—Kiekko-67	Finland Div. 2	21	9	6	15	100	...	...	...	—	—	—	—	—
—TPS Turku Jr.	Finland	6	0	2	2	18	...	...	...	—	—	—	—	—
—TPS Turku	Finland	10	1	1	2	8	...	...	...	3	0	0	0	2
96-97—Portland	AHL	52	8	9	17	37	...	...	...	—	—	—	—	—
97-98—Portland	AHL	33	1	1	2	54	...	...	...	—	—	—	—	—
—HIFK Helsinki	Finland	16	4	1	5	6	...	...	...	9	4	3	7	6
98-99—TPS Turku	Finland	36	5	10	15	76	...	...	...	10	3	5	8	6
99-00—Portland	AHL	59	21	14	35	50	...	...	...	—	—	—	—	—
—Washington	NHL	2	0	1	1	2	1	0	0	—	—	—	—	—
NHL Totals (1 year)		2	0	1	1	2	1	0	0					

ELORANTA, MIKKO — C/LW — BRUINS

PERSONAL: Born August 24, 1972, in Turku, Finland. ... 6-0/185. ... Shoots left.
TRANSACTIONS/CAREER NOTES: Selected by Boston Bruins in ninth round (ninth Bruins pick, 247th overall) of NHL entry draft (June 26, 1999). ... Fractured ankle (December 10, 1999); missed 26 games.

Season Team	League	Gms.	G	A	Pts.	PIM	+/-	PP	SH	Gms.	G	A	Pts.	PIM
				REGULAR SEASON								PLAYOFFS		
95-96—Ilves Tampere	Finland	43	18	15	33	86	...	...	...	3	0	2	2	2
96-97—TPS Turku	Finland	31	6	15	21	52	...	...	...	10	5	2	7	6
97-98—TPS Turku	Finland	46	23	14	37	82	...	...	...	2	0	0	0	8
98-99—TPS Turku	Finland	52	19	21	40	103	...	...	...	10	1	6	7	26
99-00—Boston	NHL	50	6	12	18	36	-10	1	0	—	—	—	—	—
NHL Totals (1 year)		50	6	12	18	36	-10	1	0					

EMERSON, NELSON — RW — KINGS

PERSONAL: Born August 17, 1967, in Hamilton, Ont. ... 5-10/180. ... Shoots right. ... Full Name: Nelson Donald Emerson.
COLLEGE: Bowling Green State.
TRANSACTIONS/CAREER NOTES: Selected by St. Louis Blues in third round (second Blues pick, 44th overall) of NHL entry draft (June 15, 1985). ... Fractured bone under eye (December 28, 1991). ... Injured leg (April 3, 1993); missed one game. ... Traded by Blues with D Stephane Quintal to Winnipeg Jets for D Phil Housley (September 24, 1993). ... Sprained neck (January 25, 1994); missed one game. ... Traded by Jets to Hartford Whalers for C Darren Turcotte (October 6, 1995). ... Suffered mild concussion (February 17, 1996); missed one game. ... Fractured ankle prior to 1996-97 season; missed five games. ... Fractured ankle (November 4, 1996); missed six games. ... Strained groin (January 1, 1997); missed three games. ... Whalers franchise moved to North Carolina and renamed Carolina Hurricanes for 1997-98 season; NHL approved move on June 25, 1997. ... Traded by Hurricanes to Chicago Blackhawks for D Paul Coffey (December 29, 1998). ... Separated shoulder (February 28, 1999); missed 18 games. ... Traded by Blackhawks to Ottawa Senators for RW Chris Murray (March 23, 1999). ... Signed as free agent by Atlanta Thrashers (July 20, 1999). ... Suspended one game by NHL for slashing incident (November 22, 1999). ... Suffered concussion (November 28, 1999); missed seven games. ... Traded by Thrashers with RW Kelly Buchberger to Los Angeles Kings for RW Donald Audette and D Frantisek Kaberle (March 13, 2000). ... Fractured finger (March 25, 2000); missed eight games.
HONORS: Named CCHA Rookie of the Year (1986-87). ... Named to NCAA All-America (West) second team (1987-88). ... Named to CCHA All-Star first team (1987-88 and 1989-90). ... Named to NCAA All-America (West) first team (1989-90). ... Named to CCHA All-Star second team (1988-89). ... Won Garry F. Longman Memorial Trophy (1990-91). ... Named to IHL All-Star first team (1990-91).
STATISTICAL PLATEAUS: Three-goal games: 1994-95 (1).

Season Team	League	Gms.	G	A	Pts.	PIM	+/-	PP	SH	Gms.	G	A	Pts.	PIM
				REGULAR SEASON								PLAYOFFS		
84-85—Stratford Jr. B	OHA	40	23	38	61	70	...	...	...	—	—	—	—	—
85-86—Stratford Jr. B	OHA	39	54	58	112	91	...	...	...	—	—	—	—	—
86-87—Bowling Green	CCHA	45	26	35	61	28	...	...	...	—	—	—	—	—
87-88—Bowling Green	CCHA	45	34	49	83	54	...	...	...	—	—	—	—	—
88-89—Bowling Green	CCHA	44	22	46	68	46	...	...	...	—	—	—	—	—
89-90—Bowling Green	CCHA	44	30	52	82	42	...	...	...	—	—	—	—	—
—Peoria	IHL	3	1	1	2	0	...	...	...	—	—	—	—	—
90-91—St. Louis	NHL	4	0	3	3	2	-2	0	0	—	—	—	—	—
—Peoria	IHL	73	36	79	115	91	...	...	...	17	9	12	21	16
91-92—St. Louis	NHL	79	23	36	59	66	-5	3	0	6	3	3	6	21
92-93—St. Louis	NHL	82	22	51	73	62	2	5	2	11	1	6	7	6
93-94—Winnipeg	NHL	83	33	41	74	80	-38	4	5	—	—	—	—	—
94-95—Winnipeg	NHL	48	14	23	37	26	-12	4	1	—	—	—	—	—
95-96—Hartford	NHL	81	29	29	58	78	-7	12	2	—	—	—	—	—
96-97—Hartford	NHL	66	9	29	38	34	-21	2	1	—	—	—	—	—
97-98—Carolina	NHL	81	21	24	45	50	-17	6	0	—	—	—	—	—
98-99—Carolina	NHL	35	8	13	21	36	1	3	0	—	—	—	—	—
—Chicago	NHL	27	4	10	14	13	8	0	0	—	—	—	—	—
—Ottawa	NHL	3	1	1	2	2	-1	0	0	4	1	3	4	0
99-00—Atlanta	NHL	58	14	19	33	47	-24	4	0	—	—	—	—	—
—Los Angeles	NHL	5	1	1	2	0	1	0	0	1	0	0	0	0
NHL Totals (10 years)		652	179	280	459	496	-115	43	11	22	5	12	17	27

EMMONS, JOHN — C — SENATORS

PERSONAL: Born August 17, 1974, in San Jose, Calif. ... 6-0/185. ... Shoots left. ... Full Name: John T. Emmons.
HIGH SCHOOL: New Canaan (Conn.).
COLLEGE: Yale.
TRANSACTIONS/CAREER NOTES: Selected by Calgary Flames in fifth round (seventh Flames pick, 122nd overall) of NHL entry draft (June 26, 1993). ... Signed as free agent by Ottawa Senators (July 28, 1998).

Season Team	League	Gms.	G	A	Pts.	PIM	+/-	PP	SH	Gms.	G	A	Pts.	PIM
				REGULAR SEASON								PLAYOFFS		
90-91—New Canaan H.S.	Conn. H.S.	20	19	37	56	20	...	...	...	—	—	—	—	—
91-92—New Canaan H.S.	Conn. H.S.	22	24	49	73	24	...	...	...	—	—	—	—	—
92-93—Yale University	ECAC	28	3	5	8	66	...	...	...	—	—	—	—	—
93-94—Yale University	ECAC	25	5	12	17	66	...	...	...	—	—	—	—	—
94-95—Yale University	ECAC	28	4	16	20	57	...	...	...	—	—	—	—	—
95-96—Yale University	ECAC	31	8	20	28	124	...	...	...	—	—	—	—	—
96-97—Dayton	ECHL	69	20	37	57	62	...	...	...	4	0	1	1	2
—Fort Wayne	IHL	1	0	0	0	0	...	...	...	—	—	—	—	—
97-98—Michigan	IHL	81	9	25	34	85	...	...	...	4	1	1	2	10
98-99—Detroit	IHL	75	13	22	35	172	...	...	...	11	4	5	9	22
99-00—Grand Rapids	IHL	64	10	16	26	78	...	...	...	16	1	4	5	28
—Ottawa	NHL	10	0	0	0	6	-2	0	0	—	—	—	—	—
NHL Totals (1 year)		10	0	0	0	6	-2	0	0					

E

ERIKSSON, ANDERS　　　　D　　　　BLACKHAWKS

PERSONAL: Born January 9, 1975, in Bollnas, Sweden. ... 6-2/220. ... Shoots left.
TRANSACTIONS/CAREER NOTES: Selected by Detroit Red Wings in first round (first Red Wings pick, 22nd overall) of NHL entry draft (June 26, 1993). ... Traded by Red Wings with first-round pick (D Steve McCarthy) in 1999 draft and first-round pick in 2001 draft to Chicago Blackhawks for D Chris Chelios (March 23, 1999).
MISCELLANEOUS: Member of Stanley Cup championship team (1998).

Season Team	League	Gms.	G	A	Pts.	PIM	+/-	PP	SH	Gms.	G	A	Pts.	PIM
				REGULAR SEASON								PLAYOFFS		
92-93—MoDo Ornskoldsvik	Sweden	20	0	2	2	2	...	...	...	—	—	—	—	—
93-94—MoDo Ornskoldsvik	Sweden	38	2	8	10	42	...	...	...	11	0	0	0	8
94-95—MoDo Ornskoldsvik	Sweden	39	3	6	9	54	...	...	...	—	—	—	—	—
95-96—Adirondack	AHL	75	6	36	42	64	...	...	...	3	0	0	0	0
—Detroit.........................	NHL	1	0	0	0	2	1	0	0	3	0	0	0	0
96-97—Detroit........................	NHL	23	0	6	6	10	5	0	0	—	—	—	—	—
—Adirondack.................	AHL	44	3	25	28	36	...	...	...	4	0	1	1	4
97-98—Detroit........................	NHL	66	7	14	21	32	21	1	0	18	0	5	5	16
98-99—Detroit........................	NHL	61	2	10	12	34	5	0	0	—	—	—	—	—
—Chicago....................	NHL	11	0	8	8	0	6	0	0	—	—	—	—	—
99-00—Chicago....................	NHL	73	3	25	28	20	4	0	0	—	—	—	—	—
NHL Totals (5 years)............		**235**	**12**	**63**	**75**	**98**	**42**	**1**	**0**	**21**	**0**	**5**	**5**	**16**

ERSKINE, JOHN　　　　D　　　　STARS

PERSONAL: Born June 26, 1980, in Kingston, Ont. ... 6-4/197. ... Shoots left.
TRANSACTIONS/CAREER NOTES: Selected by Dallas Stars in second round (first Stars pick, 39th overall) of NHL entry draft (June 27, 1998).
HONORS: Named to OHL All-Rookie second team (1997-98). ... Won Max Kaminsky Trophy (1999-2000). ... Named to OHL All-Star first team (1999-2000). ... Named to Can.HL All-Star second team (1999-2000).

Season Team	League	Gms.	G	A	Pts.	PIM	+/-	PP	SH	Gms.	G	A	Pts.	PIM
				REGULAR SEASON								PLAYOFFS		
96-97—Quinte	Tier II Jr. A	48	4	16	20	241	...	...	...	—	—	—	—	—
97-98—London	OHL	55	0	9	9	205	...	...	...	16	0	5	5	25
98-99—London	OHL	57	8	12	20	208	...	...	...	25	5	10	15	38
99-00—London	OHL	58	12	31	43	177	...	...	...	—	—	—	—	—

ESCHE, ROBERT　　　　G　　　　COYOTES

PERSONAL: Born January 22, 1978, in Utica, N.Y. ... 6-0/188. ... Catches left. ... Name pronounced EHSH.
TRANSACTIONS/CAREER NOTES: Selected by Phoenix Coyotes in sixth round (fifth Coyotes pick, 139th overall) of NHL entry draft (June 22, 1996).
HONORS: Named to OHL All-Star second team (1997-98).

Season Team	League	Gms.	Min	W	L	T	GA	SO	Avg.	Gms.	Min.	W	L	GA	SO	Avg.
					REGULAR SEASON								PLAYOFFS			
95-96—Det. Jr. Red Wings........	OHL	23	1219	13	6	0	76	1	3.74	3	105	0	2	4	0	2.29
96-97—Det. Jr. Red Wings........	OHL	58	3241	24	28	2	206	2	3.81	5	317	1	4	19	0	3.60
97-98—Plymouth	OHL	48	2810	29	13	4	135	3	2.88	15	869	8	†7	45	0	3.11
98-99—Springfield	AHL	55	2957	24	20	6	138	1	2.80	1	60	0	1	4	0	4.00
—Phoenix......................	NHL	3	130	0	1	0	7	0	3.23	—	—	—	—	—	—	—
99-00—Houston	IHL	7	419	4	2	‡1	16	2	2.29	—	—	—	—	—	—	—
—Phoenix......................	NHL	8	408	2	5	0	23	0	3.38	—	—	—	—	—	—	—
—Springfield..................	AHL	21	1207	9	9	2	61	2	3.03	3	180	1	2	12	0	4.00
NHL Totals (2 years)............		**11**	**538**	**2**	**6**	**0**	**30**	**0**	**3.35**							

ESSENSA, BOB　　　　G　　　　CANUCKS

PERSONAL: Born January 14, 1965, in Toronto. ... 6-0/188. ... Catches left. ... Full Name: Robert Earle Essensa. ... Name pronounced EH-sihn-zuh.
HIGH SCHOOL: Henry Carr (Rexdale, Ont.).
COLLEGE: Michigan State.
TRANSACTIONS/CAREER NOTES: Selected by Winnipeg Jets in fourth round (fifth Jets pick, 69th overall) of NHL entry draft (June 8, 1983). ... Injured groin (September 1990); missed three weeks. ... Sprained knee (October 12, 1991); missed four games. ... Injured left hamstring (December 8, 1991); missed four games. ... Sprained knee (March 6, 1992); missed seven games. ... Strained knee (March 6, 1993); missed two games. ... Traded by Jets with D Sergei Bautin to Detroit Red Wings for G Tim Cheveldae and LW Dallas Drake (March 8, 1994). ... Traded by Red Wings to Edmonton Oilers for future considerations (June 14, 1996). ... Signed as free agent by Phoenix Coyotes (September 5, 1999). ... Strained hamstring (January 4, 2000); missed seven games. ... Signed as free agent by Vancouver Canucks (July 26, 2000).
HONORS: Named to CCHA All-Star first team (1984-85). ... Named to CCHA All-Star second team (1985-86). ... Named to NHL All-Rookie team (1989-90).
MISCELLANEOUS: Stopped a penalty shot attempt (vs. Philippe Bozon, November 3, 1993; vs. Keith Tkachuk, January 24, 1998). ... Allowed a penalty shot goal (vs. Steve Yzerman, February 13, 1989; vs. Mike Craig, January 21, 1991; vs. Paul Ranheim, October 31, 1993). ... Holds Phoenix Coyotes franchise all-time records for games played by a goaltender (311) and wins (129). ... Holds Edmonton Oilers record for goals-against average (2.73).

Season Team	League	REGULAR SEASON								PLAYOFFS						
		Gms.	Min	W	L	T	GA	SO	Avg.	Gms.	Min.	W	L	GA	SO	Avg.
81-82—Henry Carr H.S.	MTHL	17	948	...	...	...	79		5.00	—	—	—	—	—	—	—
82-83—Henry Carr H.S.	MTHL	31	1840	...	...	...	98	2	3.20	—	—	—	—	—	—	—
83-84—Michigan State	CCHA	17	947	11	4	0	44	2	2.79	—	—	—	—	—	—	—
84-85—Michigan State	CCHA	18	1059	15	2	0	29	2	1.64	—	—	—	—	—	—	—
85-86—Michigan State	CCHA	23	1333	17	4	1	74	1	3.33	—	—	—	—	—	—	—
86-87—Michigan State	CCHA	25	1383	19	3	1	64	*2	*2.78	—	—	—	—	—	—	—
87-88—Moncton	AHL	27	1287	7	11	1	100	1	4.66	—	—	—	—	—	—	—
88-89—Winnipeg	NHL	20	1102	6	8	3	68	1	3.70	—	—	—	—	—	—	—
—Fort Wayne	IHL	22	1287	14	7	0	70	0	3.26	—	—	—	—	—	—	—
89-90—Moncton	AHL	6	358	3	3	0	15	0	2.51	—	—	—	—	—	—	—
—Winnipeg	NHL	36	2035	18	9	5	107	1	3.15	4	206	2	1	12	0	3.50
90-91—Moncton	AHL	2	125	1	0	1	6	0	2.88	—	—	—	—	—	—	—
—Winnipeg	NHL	55	2916	19	24	6	153	4	3.15	—	—	—	—	—	—	—
91-92—Winnipeg	NHL	47	2627	21	17	6	126	†5	2.88	1	33	0	0	3	0	5.45
92-93—Winnipeg	NHL	67	3855	33	26	6	227	2	3.53	6	367	2	4	20	0	3.27
93-94—Winnipeg	NHL	56	3136	19	30	6	201	1	3.85	—	—	—	—	—	—	—
—Detroit	NHL	13	778	4	7	2	34	1	2.62	2	109	0	2	9	0	4.95
94-95—San Diego	IHL	16	919	6	8	‡1	52	0	3.39	1	59	0	1	3	0	3.05
95-96—Adirondack	AHL	3	178	1	2	0	11	0	3.71	—	—	—	—	—	—	—
—Fort Wayne	IHL	45	2529	24	14	‡5	122	1	2.89	5	298	2	3	12	0	2.42
96-97—Edmonton	NHL	19	868	4	8	0	41	1	2.83	—	—	—	—	—	—	—
97-98—Edmonton	NHL	16	825	6	6	1	35	0	2.55	1	27	0	0	1	0	2.22
98-99—Edmonton	NHL	39	2091	12	14	6	96	0	2.75	—	—	—	—	—	—	—
99-00—Phoenix	NHL	30	1573	13	10	3	73	1	2.78	—	—	—	—	—	—	—
NHL Totals (10 years)		398	21806	155	159	44	1161	17	3.19	14	742	4	7	45	0	3.64

FALLOON, PAT RW

PERSONAL: Born September 22, 1972, in Foxwarren, Man. ... 5-11/200. ... Shoots right. ... Full Name: Patrick Falloon. ... Name pronounced fuh-LOON.

TRANSACTIONS/CAREER NOTES: Selected by San Jose Sharks in first round (first Sharks pick, second overall) of NHL entry draft (June 22, 1991). ... Bruised shoulder (November 19, 1992); missed one game. ... Dislocated right shoulder (January 10, 1993) and underwent surgery; missed remainder of season. ... Injured hamstring (March 2, 1995); missed one game. ... Traded by Sharks to Philadelphia Flyers for LW Martin Spanhel and first-(traded to Winnipeg) and fourth-round (traded to Buffalo) picks in 1996 draft (November 16, 1995). ... Strained left groin (December 21, 1996); missed seven games. ... Reinjured left groin (January 13, 1997); missed three games. ... Strained muscle in abdomen (January 9, 1998); missed four games. ... Traded by Flyers with C Vaclav Prospal and second-round pick (LW Chris Bala) in 1998 draft to Ottawa Senators for RW Alexandre Daigle (January 17, 1998). ... Signed as free agent by Edmonton Oilers (August 21, 1998). ... Claimed on waivers by Pittsburgh Penguins (February 4, 2000).

HONORS: Named WHL (West) Division Rookie of the Year (1988-89). ... Named to WHL All-Star second team (1988-89). ... Won WHL (West) Division Most Sportsmanlike Player Award (1989-90). ... Named to WHL (West) All-Star first team (1989-90 and 1990-91). ... Won Can.HL Most Sportsmanlike Player of the Year Award (1990-91). ... Won Brad Hornung Trophy (1990-91). ... Won Stafford Smythe Memorial Trophy (1990-91). ... Named to Memorial Cup All-Star team (1990-91).

Season Team	League	REGULAR SEASON							PLAYOFFS				
		Gms.	G	A	Pts.	PIM	+/-	PP	SH	Gms.	G	A	Pts.	PIM
87-88—Yellowbeard	TIER II	52	74	69	143	50	...	...	...	—	—	—	—	—
88-89—Spokane	WHL	72	22	56	78	41	...	...	...	5	5	8	13	4
89-90—Spokane	WHL	71	60	64	124	48	...	...	...	6	5	8	13	4
90-91—Spokane	WHL	61	64	74	138	33	...	...	...	15	10	14	24	10
91-92—San Jose	NHL	79	25	34	59	16	-32	5	0	—	—	—	—	—
92-93—San Jose	NHL	41	14	14	28	12	-25	5	1	—	—	—	—	—
93-94—San Jose	NHL	83	22	31	53	18	-3	6	0	14	1	2	3	6
94-95—San Jose	NHL	46	12	7	19	25	-4	0	0	11	3	1	4	0
95-96—San Jose	NHL	9	3	0	3	4	-1	0	0	—	—	—	—	—
—Philadelphia	NHL	62	22	26	48	6	15	9	0	12	3	2	5	2
96-97—Philadelphia	NHL	52	11	12	23	10	-8	2	0	14	3	1	4	2
97-98—Philadelphia	NHL	30	5	7	12	8	3	1	0	—	—	—	—	—
—Ottawa	NHL	28	3	3	6	8	-11	2	0	1	0	0	0	0
98-99—Edmonton	NHL	82	17	23	40	20	-4	8	0	4	0	1	1	4
99-00—Edmonton	NHL	33	5	13	18	4	6	1	0	—	—	—	—	—
—Pittsburgh	NHL	30	4	9	13	10	-2	0	0	10	1	0	1	2
NHL Totals (9 years)		575	143	179	322	141	-66	39	1	66	11	7	18	16

FANKHOUSER, SCOTT G THRASHERS

PERSONAL: Born July 1, 1975, in Bismark, N.D. ... 6-2/206. ... Catches left.

COLLEGE: Massachusetts-Lowell.

TRANSACTIONS/CAREER NOTES: Selected by St. Louis Blues in 11th round (eighth Blues pick, 276th overall) of NHL entry draft (June 29, 1994). ... Signed as free agent by Atlanta Thrashers (August 24, 1999). ... Injured hand (January 31, 2000); missed two games.

Season Team	League	REGULAR SEASON								PLAYOFFS						
		Gms.	Min	W	L	T	GA	SO	Avg.	Gms.	Min.	W	L	GA	SO	Avg.
95-96—Mass.-Lowell	Hockey East	11	499	4	4	1	37	...	4.45	—	—	—	—	—	—	—
96-97—Mass.-Lowell	Hockey East	11	518	2	4	1	38	...	4.40	—	—	—	—	—	—	—
97-98—Mass.-Lowell	Hockey East	16	798	4	7	2	48	...	3.61	—	—	—	—	—	—	—
98-99—Mass.-Lowell	Hockey East	32	1729	16	14	0	80	1	2.78	—	—	—	—	—	—	—
99-00—Greenville	ECHL	8	419	7	1	0	18	0	2.58	—	—	—	—	—	—	—
—Orlando	IHL	6	320	3	2	1	14	0	2.63	—	—	—	—	—	—	—
—Atlanta	NHL	16	920	2	11	2	49	0	3.20	—	—	—	—	—	—	—
—Louisville	AHL	1	59	0	1	0	3	0	3.05	—	—	—	—	—	—	—
NHL Totals (1 year)		16	920	2	11	2	49	0	3.20	—	—	—	—	—	—	—

E
F

FARKAS, JEFF   C   MAPLE LEAFS

PERSONAL: Born January 24, 1978, in Amherst, Mass. ... 6-0/185. ... Shoots left.
COLLEGE: Boston College.
TRANSACTIONS/CAREER NOTES: Selected by Toronto Maple Leafs in third round (first Maple Leafs pick, 57th overall) of NHL entry draft (June 21, 1997).
HONORS: Named to Hockey East All-Star first team (1999-2000). ... Named to NCAA All-America (East) first team (1999-2000). ... Named to NCAA All-Tournament team (1999-2000).

				REGULAR SEASON							PLAYOFFS			
Season Team	League	Gms.	G	A	Pts.	PIM	+/-	PP	SH	Gms.	G	A	Pts.	PIM
94-95—Niagara	NAJHL	53	54	58	112	34	...	...	...	—	—	—	—	—
95-96—Niagara	NAJHL	74	64	107	171	95	...	...	...	—	—	—	—	—
96-97—Boston College	Hockey East	35	13	23	36	34	...	...	...	—	—	—	—	—
97-98—Boston College	Hockey East	40	11	28	39	42	...	...	...	—	—	—	—	—
98-99—Boston College	Hockey East	43	32	25	57	56	...	...	...	—	—	—	—	—
99-00—Boston College	Hockey East	41	32	26	*58	59	...	...	...	—	—	—	—	—
—Toronto	NHL	—	—	—	—	—				3	1	0	1	2
NHL Totals (1 year)		0	0	0	0	0	0	0	0	3	1	0	1	2

FATA, RICO   RW   FLAMES

PERSONAL: Born February 12, 1980, in Sault Ste. Marie, Ont. ... 5-11/197. ... Shoots left.
TRANSACTIONS/CAREER NOTES: Selected by Calgary Flames in first round (first Flames pick, sixth overall) of NHL entry draft (June 27, 1998).

				REGULAR SEASON							PLAYOFFS			
Season Team	League	Gms.	G	A	Pts.	PIM	+/-	PP	SH	Gms.	G	A	Pts.	PIM
95-96—Sault Ste. Marie	OMJHL	62	11	15	26	52	...	...	...	—	—	—	—	—
96-97—London	OHL	59	19	34	53	76	...	...	...	—	—	—	—	—
97-98—London	OHL	64	43	33	76	110	...	...	...	16	9	5	14	*49
98-99—Calgary	NHL	20	0	1	1	4	0	0	0	—	—	—	—	—
—London	OHL	23	15	18	33	41	...	...	...	25	10	12	22	42
99-00—Calgary	NHL	2	0	0	0	0	-1	0	0	—	—	—	—	—
—Saint John	AHL	76	29	29	58	65	...	...	...	3	0	0	0	4
NHL Totals (2 years)		22	0	1	1	4	-1	0	0					

FEDOROV, SERGEI   C   RED WINGS

PERSONAL: Born December 13, 1969, in Pskov, U.S.S.R. ... 6-2/200. ... Shoots left. ... Brother of Fedor Fedorov, center, Tampa Bay Lightning system. ... Name pronounced SAIR-gay FEH-duh-rahf.
TRANSACTIONS/CAREER NOTES: Selected by Detroit Red Wings in fourth round (fourth Red Wings pick, 74th overall) of NHL entry draft (June 17, 1989). ... Bruised left shoulder (October 1990). ... Reinjured left shoulder (January 16, 1991). ... Sprained left shoulder (November 27, 1992); missed seven games. ... Suffered from the flu (January 30, 1993); missed two games. ... Suffered charley horse (February 11, 1993); missed one game. ... Suffered concussion (April 5, 1994); missed two games. ... Suspended four games without pay and fined $500 by NHL for high-sticking incident in playoff game (May 17, 1994); suspension reduced to three games due to abbreviated 1994-95 season. ... Suffered from the flu (February 7, 1995); missed one game. ... Bruised right hamstring (April 9, 1995); missed one game. ... Suffered from tonsillitis (October 6, 1995); missed three games. ... Sprained left wrist (December 15, 1995); missed one game. ... Strained groin (January 9, 1997); missed two games. ... Reinjured groin (January 20, 1997); missed six games. ... Missed first 59 games of 1997-98 season due to contract dispute. ... Tendered offer sheet by Carolina Hurricanes (February 19, 1998). ... Offer matched by Red Wings (February 26, 1998). ... Suspended two games and fined $1,000 by NHL for illegal check (March 31, 1998). ... Suspended five games by NHL for slashing incident (March 3, 1999). ... Suffered head injury (November 20, 1999); missed six games. ... Injured neck (January 16, 2000); missed three games. ... Injured wrist (February 18, 2000); missed five games.
HONORS: Named to NHL All-Rookie team (1990-91). ... Played in NHL All-Star Game (1992, 1994 and 1996). ... Named NHL Player of the Year by THE SPORTING NEWS (1993-94). ... Named to THE SPORTING NEWS All-Star first team (1993-94). ... Won Hart Memorial Trophy (1993-94). ... Won Frank J. Selke Trophy (1993-94 and 1995-96). ... Won Lester B. Pearson Award (1993-94). ... Named to NHL All-Star first team (1993-94).
MISCELLANEOUS: Member of Stanley Cup championship team (1997 and 1998). ... Member of silver-medal-winning Russian Olympic team (1998). ... Scored on a penalty shot (vs. Andy Moog, December 27, 1993). ... Failed to score on a penalty shot (vs. Kelly Hrudey, February 12, 1995).
STATISTICAL PLATEAUS: Three-goal games: 1993-94 (1). ... Four-goal games: 1994-95 (1). ... Five-goal games: 1996-97 (1). ... Total hat tricks: 3.

				REGULAR SEASON							PLAYOFFS			
Season Team	League	Gms.	G	A	Pts.	PIM	+/-	PP	SH	Gms.	G	A	Pts.	PIM
85-86—Dynamo Minsk	USSR	15	6	1	7	10	...	...	...	—	—	—	—	—
86-87—CSKA Moscow	USSR	29	6	6	12	12	...	...	...	—	—	—	—	—
87-88—CSKA Moscow	USSR	48	7	9	16	20	...	...	...	—	—	—	—	—
88-89—CSKA Moscow	USSR	44	9	8	17	35	...	...	...	—	—	—	—	—
89-90—CSKA Moscow	USSR	48	19	10	29	20	...	...	...	—	—	—	—	—
90-91—Detroit	NHL	77	31	48	79	66	11	11	3	7	1	5	6	4
91-92—Detroit	NHL	80	32	54	86	72	7	7	2	11	5	5	10	8
92-93—Detroit	NHL	73	34	53	87	72	33	13	4	7	3	6	9	23
93-94—Detroit	NHL	82	56	64	120	34	48	13	4	7	1	7	8	6
94-95—Detroit	NHL	42	20	30	50	24	6	7	3	17	7	*17	*24	6
95-96—Detroit	NHL	78	39	68	107	48	49	11	3	19	2	*18	20	10
96-97—Detroit	NHL	74	30	33	63	30	29	9	2	20	8	12	20	12
97-98—Russian Oly. team	Int'l	6	1	5	6	8	...	...	...	—	—	—	—	—
—Detroit	NHL	21	6	11	17	25	10	2	0	22	10	10	20	12
98-99—Detroit	NHL	77	26	37	63	66	9	6	0	10	1	8	9	8
99-00—Detroit	NHL	68	27	35	62	22	8	4	4	—	—	—	—	—
NHL Totals (10 years)		672	301	433	734	459	229	83	27	120	38	88	126	89

F

FEDOTENKO, RUSLAN　　　RW　　　FLYERS

PERSONAL: Born January 18, 1979, in Kiev, U.S.S.R. ... 6-2/190.
TRANSACTIONS/CAREER NOTES: Signed as non-drafted free agent by Philadelphia Flyers (August 3, 1999).

		REGULAR SEASON								PLAYOFFS				
Season Team	League	Gms.	G	A	Pts.	PIM	+/-	PP	SH	Gms.	G	A	Pts.	PIM
97-98—Melfort	SJHL	68	35	31	66	...	...	...	...	—	—	—	—	—
98-99—Sioux City	USHL	55	43	34	77	139	...	...	...	5	5	1	6	9
99-00—Philadelphia	AHL	67	16	34	50	42	...	...	...	2	0	0	0	0
—Trenton	ECHL	8	5	3	8	9	...	...	...	—	—	—	—	—

FERENCE, ANDREW　　　D　　　PENGUINS

PERSONAL: Born March 17, 1979, in Edmonton. ... 5-10/190. ... Shoots left.
TRANSACTIONS/CAREER NOTES: Selected by Pittsburgh Penguins in eighth round (eighth Penguins pick, 208th overall) of 1997 NHL entry draft. ... Suffered from the flu (December 9, 1999); missed four games.
HONORS: Named to WHL (West) All-Star first team (1997-98). ... Won Can.HL Plus/Minus Award (1997-98). ... Named to WHL (West) All-Star second team (1998-99).

		REGULAR SEASON								PLAYOFFS				
Season Team	League	Gms.	G	A	Pts.	PIM	+/-	PP	SH	Gms.	G	A	Pts.	PIM
95-96—Portland	WHL	72	9	31	40	159	...	...	...	7	1	3	4	12
96-97—Portland	WHL	72	12	32	44	163	...	...	...	—	—	—	—	—
97-98—Portland	WHL	72	11	57	68	142	...	...	...	16	2	18	20	28
98-99—Portland	WHL	40	11	21	32	104	...	...	...	4	1	4	5	10
—Kansas City	IHL	5	1	2	3	4	...	...	...	3	0	0	0	9
99-00—Pittsburgh	NHL	30	2	4	6	20	3	0	0	—	—	—	—	—
—Wilkes-Barre/Scranton	AHL	44	8	20	28	58	...	...	...	—	—	—	—	—
NHL Totals (1 year)		30	2	4	6	20	3	0	0					

FERENCE, BRAD　　　D　　　PANTHERS

PERSONAL: Born April 2, 1979, in Calgary. ... 6-3/196. ... Shoots right. ... Name pronounced FAIR-intz.
TRANSACTIONS/CAREER NOTES: Selected by Vancouver Canucks in first round (first Canucks pick, 10th overall) of NHL entry draft (June 21, 1997). ... Traded by Canucks with RW Pavel Bure, D Bret Hedican and third-round pick (RW Robert Fried) in 2000 draft to Florida Panthers for D Ed Jovanovski, G Kevin Weekes, C Dave Gagner, C Mike Brown and first-round pick (C Nathan Smith) in 2000 draft (January 17, 1999).
HONORS: Named to Can.HL All-Rookie team (1996-97).

		REGULAR SEASON								PLAYOFFS				
Season Team	League	Gms.	G	A	Pts.	PIM	+/-	PP	SH	Gms.	G	A	Pts.	PIM
95-96—Spokane	WHL	5	0	2	2	18	...	...	...	—	—	—	—	—
96-97—Spokane	WHL	67	6	20	26	324	...	...	...	9	0	4	4	21
97-98—Spokane	WHL	54	9	29	38	213	...	...	...	18	0	7	7	59
98-99—Spokane	WHL	31	3	22	25	125	...	...	...	—	—	—	—	—
—Tri-City	WHL	20	6	15	21	116	...	...	...	12	1	9	10	63
99-00—Louisville	AHL	58	2	7	9	231	...	...	...	2	0	0	0	2
—Florida	NHL	13	0	2	2	46	2	0	0	—	—	—	—	—
NHL Totals (1 year)		13	0	2	2	46	2	0	0					

FERGUSON, CRAIG　　　RW

PERSONAL: Born April 8, 1970, in Castro Valley, Calif. ... 5-11/190. ... Shoots left.
COLLEGE: Yale.
TRANSACTIONS/CAREER NOTES: Selected by Montreal Canadiens in seventh round (seventh Canadiens pick, 146th overall) of NHL entry draft (June 22, 1991). ... Traded by Canadiens with LW Yves Sarault to Calgary Flames for eighth-round pick (D Petr Kubos) in 1997 draft (November 25, 1995). ... Traded by Flames to Los Angeles Kings for LW Pat Conacher (February 10, 1996). ... Signed as free agent by Florida Panthers (August 6, 1996). ... Released by Panthers (June 30, 2000).

		REGULAR SEASON								PLAYOFFS				
Season Team	League	Gms.	G	A	Pts.	PIM	+/-	PP	SH	Gms.	G	A	Pts.	PIM
88-89—Yale University	ECAC	24	11	6	17	20	...	...	...	—	—	—	—	—
89-90—Yale University	ECAC	35	6	15	21	38	...	...	...	—	—	—	—	—
90-91—Yale University	ECAC	29	11	10	21	34	...	...	...	—	—	—	—	—
91-92—Yale University	ECAC	27	9	16	25	28	...	...	...	—	—	—	—	—
92-93—Wheeling	ECHL	9	6	5	11	24	...	...	...	—	—	—	—	—
—Fredericton	AHL	55	15	13	28	20	...	...	...	5	0	1	1	2
93-94—Fredericton	AHL	57	29	32	61	60	...	...	...	17	6	2	8	6
—Montreal	NHL	2	0	1	1	0	1	0	0	—	—	—	—	—
94-95—Fredericton	AHL	80	27	35	62	62	...	...	...	17	6	2	8	6
—Montreal	NHL	1	0	0	0	0	0	0	0	—	—	—	—	—
95-96—Montreal	NHL	10	1	0	1	2	-5	0	0	—	—	—	—	—
—Calgary	NHL	8	0	0	0	4	-4	0	0	—	—	—	—	—
—Saint John	AHL	18	5	13	18	8	...	...	...	—	—	—	—	—
—Phoenix	IHL	31	6	9	15	25	...	...	...	4	0	2	2	6
96-97—Carolina	AHL	74	29	41	70	57	...	...	...	—	—	—	—	—
—Florida	NHL	3	0	0	0	0	-1	0	0	—	—	—	—	—
97-98—New Haven	AHL	64	24	28	52	41	...	...	...	3	2	1	3	2
98-99—New Haven	AHL	61	18	27	45	76	...	...	...	—	—	—	—	—
99-00—Louisville	AHL	61	29	27	56	28	...	...	...	4	1	3	4	2
—Florida	NHL	3	0	0	0	0	-2	0	0	—	—	—	—	—
NHL Totals (5 years)		27	1	1	2	6	-11	0	0					

FERNANDEZ, MANNY   G   WILD

PERSONAL: Born August 27, 1974, in Etobicoke, Ont. ... 6-0/185. ... Catches left. ... Full Name: Emmanuel Fernandez. ... Nephew of Jacques Lemaire, head coach, Minnesota Wild; and Hall of Fame center with Montreal Canadiens (1967-68 through 1978-79).

TRANSACTIONS/CAREER NOTES: Selected by Quebec Nordiques in third round (fourth Nordiques pick, 52nd overall) of NHL entry draft (June 20, 1992). ... Traded by Nordiques to Dallas Stars for D Tommy Sjodin and third-round pick (C Chris Drury) in 1994 draft (February 13, 1994). ... Traded by Stars with D Brad Lukowich to Minnesota Wild for third-round pick (C Joel Lundqvist) in 2000 draft and fourth-round pick in 2002 draft (June 12, 2000).

HONORS: Won Guy Lafleur Trophy (1992-93). ... Won Michel Briere Trophy (1993-94). ... Named to QMJHL All-Star first team (1993-94). ... Named to Can.HL All-Star second team (1993-94). ... Named to IHL All-Star second team (1994-95).

MISCELLANEOUS: Stopped a penalty shot attempt (vs. Radek Dvorak, March 13, 2000).

| | | REGULAR SEASON | | | | | | | | PLAYOFFS | | | | | | |
Season Team	League	Gms.	Min	W	L	T	GA	SO	Avg.	Gms.	Min.	W	L	GA	SO	Avg.
91-92—Laval	QMJHL	31	1593	14	13	2	99	1	3.73	9	468	3	5	†39	0	5.00
92-93—Laval	QMJHL	43	2348	26	14	2	141	1	3.60	13	818	12	1	42	0	3.08
93-94—Laval	QMJHL	51	2776	29	14	1	143	*5	3.09	19	1116	14	5	49	†1	*2.63
94-95—Kalamazoo	IHL	46	2470	21	10	‡9	115	2	2.79	12	655	9	1	†30	1	2.75
—Dallas	NHL	1	59	0	1	0	3	0	3.05	—	—	—	—	—	—	—
95-96—Michigan	IHL	47	2663	22	15	‡9	133	†4	3.00	6	372	5	1	14	0	*2.26
—Dallas	NHL	5	249	0	1	1	19	0	4.58	—	—	—	—	—	—	—
96-97—Michigan	IHL	48	2721	20	24	‡2	142	2	3.13	4	277	1	3	15	0	3.25
97-98—Michigan	IHL	55	3023	27	17	5	139	5	2.76	2	89	0	2	7	0	4.72
—Dallas	NHL	2	69	1	0	0	2	0	1.74	1	2	0	0	0	0	...
98-99—Houston	IHL	50	2949	34	6	‡9	116	2	2.36	*19	*1126	*11	*8	49	1	2.61
—Dallas	NHL	1	60	0	1	0	2	0	2.00	—	—	—	—	—	—	—
99-00—Dallas	NHL	24	1353	11	8	3	48	1	2.13	1	17	0	0	1	0	3.53
NHL Totals (5 years)		33	1790	12	11	4	74	1	2.48	2	19	0	0	1	0	3.16

FERRARO, CHRIS   RW/C   ISLANDERS

PERSONAL: Born January 24, 1973, in Port Jefferson, N.Y. ... 5-10/185. ... Shoots right. ... Twin brother of Peter Ferraro, center, Boston Bruins. ... Name pronounced fuh-RAH-roh.

COLLEGE: Maine.

TRANSACTIONS/CAREER NOTES: Selected by New York Rangers in fourth round (fourth Rangers pick, 85th overall) of NHL entry draft (June 20, 1992). ... Claimed on waivers by Pittsburgh Penguins (October 1, 1997). ... Signed as free agent by Edmonton Oilers (August 13, 1998). ... Signed as free agent by New York Islanders (July 7, 1999). ... Suffered concussion (March 21, 2000); missed eight games.

HONORS: Named to Hockey East Rookie All-Star team (1992-93).

| | | REGULAR SEASON | | | | | | | | PLAYOFFS | | | | |
Season Team	League	Gms.	G	A	Pts.	PIM	+/-	PP	SH	Gms.	G	A	Pts.	PIM
90-91—Dubuque	USHL	45	53	44	97	—	...	...	...	—	—	—	—	—
91-92—Waterloo	USHL	38	49	50	99	106	...	...	...	—	—	—	—	—
92-93—Univ. of Maine	Hockey East	39	25	26	51	46	...	...	...	—	—	—	—	—
93-94—U.S. national team	Int'l	48	8	34	42	58	...	...	...	—	—	—	—	—
—Univ. of Maine	Hockey East	4	0	1	1	8	...	...	...	—	—	—	—	—
94-95—Atlanta	IHL	54	13	14	27	72	...	...	...	—	—	—	—	—
—Binghamton	AHL	13	6	4	10	38	...	...	...	10	2	3	5	16
95-96—Binghamton	AHL	77	32	67	99	208	...	...	...	4	4	2	6	13
—New York Rangers	NHL	2	1	0	1	0	-3	1	0	—	—	—	—	—
96-97—Binghamton	AHL	53	29	34	63	94	...	...	...	—	—	—	—	—
—New York Rangers	NHL	12	1	1	2	6	1	0	0	—	—	—	—	—
97-98—Pittsburgh	NHL	46	3	4	7	43	-2	0	0	—	—	—	—	—
98-99—Hamilton	AHL	72	35	41	76	104	...	...	...	11	8	5	13	20
—Edmonton	NHL	2	1	0	1	0	1	0	0	—	—	—	—	—
99-00—New York Islanders	NHL	11	1	3	4	8	1	0	0	—	—	—	—	—
—Providence	AHL	21	9	9	18	32	...	...	...	—	—	—	—	—
NHL Totals (5 years)		73	7	8	15	57	-2	1	0	—	—	—	—	—

FERRARO, PETER   C   BRUINS

PERSONAL: Born January 24, 1973, in Port Jefferson, N.Y. ... 5-10/180. ... Shoots right. ... Twin brother of Chris Ferraro, right wing/center, New York Islanders. ... Name pronounced fuh-RAH-roh.

COLLEGE: Maine.

TRANSACTIONS/CAREER NOTES: Selected by New York Rangers in first round (first Rangers pick, 24th overall) of NHL entry draft (June 20, 1992). ... Claimed on waivers by Pittsburgh Penguins (October 1, 1997). ... Claimed on waivers by Rangers (January 14, 1998). ... Signed as free agent by Boston Bruins (July 21, 1998). ... Sprained muscle in chest (November 27, 1998); missed nine games. ... Suffered concussion (January 4, 1999); missed three games. ... Injured foot (February 9, 1999); missed one game. ... Selected by Atlanta Thrashers in NHL expansion draft (June 25, 1999). ... Traded by Thrashers to Bruins for C Randy Robitaille (June 25, 1999).

HONORS: Named to AHL All-Star first team (1995-96). ... Won Jack Butterfield Trophy (1998-99).

| | | REGULAR SEASON | | | | | | | | PLAYOFFS | | | | |
Season Team	League	Gms.	G	A	Pts.	PIM	+/-	PP	SH	Gms.	G	A	Pts.	PIM
90-91—Dubuque	USHL	29	21	31	52	83	...	...	...	—	—	—	—	—
91-92—Waterloo	USHL	42	48	53	101	168	...	...	...	—	—	—	—	—
92-93—Univ. of Maine	Hockey East	36	18	32	50	106	...	...	...	—	—	—	—	—
93-94—U.S. national team	Int'l	59	28	39	67	48	...	...	...	—	—	—	—	—
—U.S. Olympic team	Int'l	8	6	0	6	6	...	...	...	—	—	—	—	—
—Univ. of Maine	Hockey East	4	3	6	9	16	...	...	...	—	—	—	—	—

Season Team	League	REGULAR SEASON								PLAYOFFS				
		Gms.	G	A	Pts.	PIM	+/-	PP	SH	Gms.	G	A	Pts.	PIM
94-95—Atlanta	IHL	61	15	24	39	118	...	...	...	—	—	—	—	—
—Binghamton	AHL	12	2	6	8	67	...	...	...	11	4	3	7	51
95-96—Binghamton	AHL	68	48	53	101	157	...	...	...	4	1	6	7	22
—New York Rangers	NHL	5	0	1	1	0	-5	0	0	—	—	—	—	—
96-97—Binghamton	AHL	75	38	39	77	171	...	...	...	4	3	1	4	18
—New York Rangers	NHL	2	0	0	0	0	0	0	0	2	0	0	0	0
97-98—Pittsburgh	NHL	29	3	4	7	12	-2	0	0	—	—	—	—	—
—Hartford	AHL	36	17	23	40	54	...	...	...	15	8	6	14	59
—New York Rangers	NHL	1	0	0	0	2	-2	0	0	—	—	—	—	—
98-99—Boston	NHL	46	6	8	14	44	10	1	0	—	—	—	—	—
—Providence	AHL	16	15	10	25	14	...	...	...	19	9	12	21	38
99-00—Providence	AHL	48	21	25	46	98	...	...	...	13	5	7	12	14
—Boston	NHL	5	0	1	1	0	-1	0	0	—	—	—	—	—
NHL Totals (5 years)		88	9	14	23	58	0	1	0	2	0	0	0	0

FERRARO, RAY C THRASHERS

PERSONAL: Born August 23, 1964, in Trail, B.C. ... 5-9/200. ... Shoots left. ... Name pronounced fuh-RAH-roh.

TRANSACTIONS/CAREER NOTES: Selected by Hartford Whalers as underage junior in fifth round (fifth Whalers pick, 88th overall) of NHL entry draft (June 9, 1982). ... Traded by Whalers to New York Islanders for D Doug Crossman (November 13, 1990). ... Fractured right fibula (December 10, 1992); missed 36 games. ... Suffered from the flu (March 25, 1993); missed one game. ... Injured knee (March 9, 1995); missed one game. ... Signed as free agent by New York Rangers (July 19, 1995). ... Traded by Rangers with C Nathan Lafayette, C Ian Laperriere, D Mattias Norstrom and fourth-round pick (D Sean Blanchard) in 1997 draft to Los Angeles Kings for RW Shane Churla, LW Jari Kurri and D Marty McSorley (March 14, 1996). ... Strained neck (February 1, 1997); missed one game. ... Tore cartilage in left knee (October 5, 1997); missed 17 games. ... Underwent knee surgery (December 9, 1997); missed eight games. ... Strained lower back (January 20, 1998); missed two games. ... Suffered from the flu (March 2, 1998); missed one game. ... Strained left knee (March 21, 1998); missed three games. ... Reinjured left knee (April 11, 1998); missed three games. ... Tore lateral meniscus in right knee (January 5, 1999); missed eight games. ... Signed as free agent by Atlanta Thrashers (August 2, 1999).

HONORS: Won WHL Most Valuable Player Trophy (1983-84). ... Won Bob Brownridge Memorial Trophy (1983-84). ... Won WHL Player of the Year Award (1983-84). ... Named to WHL (East) All-Star first team (1983-84). ... Played in NHL All-Star Game (1992).

MISCELLANEOUS: Shares Atlanta Thrashers all-time record for most games played (81).

STATISTICAL PLATEAUS: Three-goal games: 1984-85 (2), 1986-87 (1), 1988-89 (1), 1989-90 (1), 1991-92 (1), 1995-96 (1). Total: 7. ... Four-goal games: 1991-92 (1). ... Total hat tricks: 8.

Season Team	League	REGULAR SEASON								PLAYOFFS				
		Gms.	G	A	Pts.	PIM	+/-	PP	SH	Gms.	G	A	Pts.	PIM
81-82—Penticton	BCJHL	48	65	70	135	50	...	...	...	—	—	—	—	—
82-83—Portland	WHL	50	41	49	90	39	...	...	...	14	14	10	24	13
83-84—Brandon	WHL	72	*108	84	*192	84	...	...	...	11	13	15	28	20
84-85—Binghamton	AHL	37	20	13	33	29	...	...	...	—	—	—	—	—
—Hartford	NHL	44	11	17	28	40	-1	6	0	—	—	—	—	—
85-86—Hartford	NHL	76	30	47	77	57	12	14	0	10	3	6	9	4
86-87—Hartford	NHL	80	27	32	59	42	-9	14	0	6	1	1	2	8
87-88—Hartford	NHL	68	21	29	50	81	1	6	0	6	1	1	2	6
88-89—Hartford	NHL	80	41	35	76	86	1	11	0	4	2	0	2	4
89-90—Hartford	NHL	79	25	29	54	109	-15	7	0	7	0	3	3	2
90-91—Hartford	NHL	15	2	5	7	18	-1	1	0	—	—	—	—	—
—New York Islanders	NHL	61	19	16	35	52	-11	5	0	—	—	—	—	—
91-92—New York Islanders	NHL	80	40	40	80	92	25	7	0	—	—	—	—	—
92-93—New York Islanders	NHL	46	14	13	27	40	0	3	0	18	13	7	20	18
—Capital District	AHL	1	0	2	2	2	...	...	...	—	—	—	—	—
93-94—New York Islanders	NHL	82	21	32	53	83	1	5	0	4	1	0	1	6
94-95—New York Islanders	NHL	47	22	21	43	30	1	2	0	—	—	—	—	—
95-96—New York Rangers	NHL	65	25	29	54	82	13	8	0	—	—	—	—	—
—Los Angeles	NHL	11	4	2	6	10	-13	1	0	—	—	—	—	—
96-97—Los Angeles	NHL	81	25	21	46	112	-22	11	0	—	—	—	—	—
97-98—Los Angeles	NHL	40	6	9	15	42	-10	0	0	3	0	1	1	2
98-99—Los Angeles	NHL	65	13	18	31	59	0	4	0	—	—	—	—	—
99-00—Atlanta	NHL	81	19	25	44	88	-33	10	0	—	—	—	—	—
NHL Totals (16 years)		1101	365	420	785	1123	-61	115	0	58	21	19	40	50

FICHAUD, ERIC G CANADIENS

PERSONAL: Born November 4, 1975, in Anjou, Que. ... 5-11/171. ... Catches left. ... Name pronounced FEE-shoh.

HIGH SCHOOL: CEGEP de Chicoutimi (Que.).

TRANSACTIONS/CAREER NOTES: Selected by Toronto Maple Leafs in first round (first Maple Leafs pick, 16th overall) of NHL entry draft (June 28, 1994). ... Traded by Maple Leafs to New York Islanders for C Benoit Hogue, third-round pick (RW Ryan Pepperall) in 1995 draft and fifth-round pick (D Brandon Sugden) in 1996 draft (April 6, 1995). ... Strained abdominal muscle (October 12, 1996); missed two games. ... Partially dislocated left shoulder (December 2, 1997); missed seven games. ... Underwent shoulder surgery while assigned to Utah Grizzlies of IHL (January 20, 1998); missed remainder of season. ... Traded by Islanders to Edmonton Oilers for LW Mike Watt (June 18, 1998). ... Traded by Oilers with D Drake Berehowsky and D Greg de Vries to Nashville Predators for F Jim Dowd and G Mikhail Shtalenkov (October 1, 1998). ... Partially dislocated left shoulder (December 8, 1998); missed five games. ... Reinjured shoulder (January 4, 1999) and underwent surgery; missed remainder of season. ... Traded by Predators to Carolina Hurricanes for fourth-round pick (C/RW Yevgeny Pavlov) in 1999 draft and future considerations (June 26, 1999). ... Claimed on waivers by Montreal Canadiens (February 11, 2000). ... Injured shoulder (February 11, 2000); missed 14 games.

HONORS: Named to Memorial Cup All-Star team (1993-94). ... Won Hap Emms Memorial Trophy (1993-94). ... Won QMJHL Top Draft Prospect Award (1993-94). ... Won Guy Lafleur Award (1993-94). ... Named to QMJHL All-Star first team (1994-95).

MISCELLANEOUS: Stopped a penalty shot attempt (vs. Shaun Van Allen, December 1, 1998).

			REGULAR SEASON							PLAYOFFS						
Season Team	League	Gms.	Min	W	L	T	GA	SO	Avg.	Gms.	Min.	W	L	GA	SO	Avg.
92-93 —Chicoutimi..................	QMJHL	43	2040	18	13	1	149	0	4.38	—	—	—	—	—	—	—
93-94 —Chicoutimi..................	QMJHL	63	3493	37	21	3	192	4	3.30	26	1560	16	10	86	†1	3.31
94-95 —Chicoutimi..................	QMJHL	46	2637	21	19	4	151	4	3.44	7	430	2	5	20	0	2.79
95-96 —Worcester	AHL	34	1988	13	15	6	97	1	2.93	2	127	1	1	7	0	3.31
—New York Islanders.......	NHL	24	1234	7	12	2	68	1	3.31	—	—	—	—	—	—	—
96-97 —New York Islanders.......	NHL	34	1759	9	14	4	91	0	3.10	—	—	—	—	—	—	—
97-98 —New York Islanders.......	NHL	17	807	3	8	3	40	0	2.97	—	—	—	—	—	—	—
—Utah	IHL	1	40	0	0	0	3	0	4.50	—	—	—	—	—	—	—
98-99 —Milwaukee..................	IHL	8	480	5	2	‡1	25	0	3.13	—	—	—	—	—	—	—
—Nashville	NHL	9	447	0	6	0	24	0	3.22	—	—	—	—	—	—	—
99-00 —Carolina.....................	NHL	9	490	3	5	1	24	1	2.94	—	—	—	—	—	—	—
—Quebec	AHL	6	368	4	1	1	17	0	2.77	3	177	0	3	10	0	3.39
NHL Totals (5 years).............		93	4737	22	45	10	247	2	3.13							

FILIPOWICZ, JAYME — D — PREDATORS

PERSONAL: Born June 15, 1976, in Arlington Heights, Ill. ... 6-2/222. ... Shoots left.
COLLEGE: New Hampshire.
TRANSACTIONS/CAREER NOTES: Signed as non-drafted free agent by Nashville Predators (June 17, 1999).
HONORS: Named to NCAA All-America (East) second team (1998-99). ... Named to Hockey East All-Star first team (1998-99). ... Named to NCAA All-Tournament team (1998-99).

			REGULAR SEASON							PLAYOFFS				
Season Team	League	Gms.	G	A	Pts.	PIM	+/-	PP	SH	Gms.	G	A	Pts.	PIM
95-96 —Dubuque	USHL	45	7	29	36	106	...	...	...	—	—	—	—	—
96-97 —Univ. of New Hamp.....	Hockey East	35	3	16	19	43	...	...	...	—	—	—	—	—
97-98 —Univ. of New Hamp.....	Hockey East	38	3	28	31	47	...	...	...	—	—	—	—	—
98-99 —Univ. of New Hamp.....	Hockey East	41	8	30	38	56	...	...	...	—	—	—	—	—
99-00 —Milwaukee..................	IHL	76	9	23	32	118	...	...	...	3	0	1	1	0

FINLEY, BRIAN — G — PREDATORS

PERSONAL: Born July 3, 1981, in Sault Ste. Marie, Ont. ... 6-2/180. ... Catches right.
TRANSACTIONS/CAREER NOTES: Selected by Nashville Predators in first round (first Predators pick, sixth overall) of NHL entry draft (June 26, 1999).
HONORS: Named to OHL All-Rookie first team (1997-98). ... Named to Can.HL All-Star second team (1998-99). ... Named to OHL All-Star first team (1998-99).

			REGULAR SEASON							PLAYOFFS						
Season Team	League	Gms.	Min	W	L	T	GA	SO	Avg.	Gms.	Min.	W	L	GA	SO	Avg.
97-98 —Barrie	OHL	41	2154	23	14	1	105	3	2.92	5	260	1	3	13	0	3.00
98-99 —Barrie	OHL	52	3063	*36	10	4	136	3	2.66	5	323	4	1	15	0	2.79
99-00 —Barrie	OHL	47	2540	24	12	6	130	2	3.07	*23	1353	14	†8	*58	1	2.57

FINLEY, JEFF — D — BLUES

PERSONAL: Born April 14, 1967, in Edmonton. ... 6-2/205. ... Shoots left. ... Full Name: John Jeffrey Finley.
HIGH SCHOOL: Vernon Senior Secondary (B.C.).
TRANSACTIONS/CAREER NOTES: Selected by New York Islanders as underage junior in third round (fourth Islanders pick, 55th overall) of NHL entry draft (June 15, 1985). ... Suffered swollen left knee (September 1988). ... Traded by Islanders to Ottawa Senators for D Chris Luongo (June 30, 1993). ... Signed as free agent by Philadelphia Flyers (August 2, 1993). ... Traded by Flyers to Winnipeg Jets for LW Russ Romaniuk (June 26, 1995). ... Separated shoulder (December 10, 1995); missed one game. ... Jets franchise moved to Phoenix and renamed Coyotes for 1996-97 season; NHL approved move on January 18, 1996. ... Suffered from the flu (December 7, 1996); missed two games. ... Strained hip flexor (December 30, 1996); missed one game. ... Sprained ankle (March 27, 1997); missed remainder of regular season and first six games of playoffs. ... Signed as free agent by New York Rangers (July 16, 1997). ... Traded by Rangers with D Geoff Smith to St. Louis Blues for future considerations (February 13, 1999); Rangers acquired RW Chris Kenady to complete deal (February 22, 1999). ... Injured back (December 21, 1999); missed two games. ... Injured groin (March 12, 2000); missed one game. ... Suffered back spasms (March 30, 2000); missed final five games of regular season.

			REGULAR SEASON							PLAYOFFS				
Season Team	League	Gms.	G	A	Pts.	PIM	+/-	PP	SH	Gms.	G	A	Pts.	PIM
83-84 —Portland	WHL	5	0	0	0	0	...	...	...	5	0	1	1	4
—Summerland	BCJHL	49	0	21	21	14	...	...	...	—	—	—	—	—
84-85 —Portland	WHL	69	6	44	50	57	...	...	...	6	1	2	3	2
85-86 —Portland	WHL	70	11	59	70	83	...	...	...	15	1	7	8	16
86-87 —Portland	WHL	72	13	53	66	113	...	...	...	20	1	†21	22	27
87-88 —Springfield	AHL	52	5	18	23	50	...	...	...	—	—	—	—	—
—New York Islanders.....	NHL	10	0	5	5	15	5	0	0	1	0	0	0	2
88-89 —New York Islanders.....	NHL	4	0	0	0	6	1	0	0	—	—	—	—	—
—Springfield	AHL	65	3	16	19	55	...	...	...	—	—	—	—	—
89-90 —New York Islanders.....	NHL	11	0	1	1	0	0	0	0	5	0	2	2	2
—Springfield	AHL	57	1	15	16	41	...	...	...	13	1	4	5	23
90-91 —Capital District	AHL	67	10	34	44	34	...	...	...	—	—	—	—	—
—New York Islanders.....	NHL	11	0	0	0	4	-1	0	0	—	—	—	—	—
91-92 —Capital District	AHL	20	1	9	10	6	...	...	...	—	—	—	—	—
—New York Islanders.....	NHL	51	1	10	11	26	-6	0	0	—	—	—	—	—
92-93 —Capital District	AHL	61	6	29	35	34	...	...	...	4	0	1	1	0
93-94 —Philadelphia	NHL	55	1	8	9	24	16	0	0					

F

Season Team	League	REGULAR SEASON								PLAYOFFS				
		Gms.	G	A	Pts.	PIM	+/-	PP	SH	Gms.	G	A	Pts.	PIM
94-95—Hershey	AHL	36	2	9	11	33	...	...	...	6	0	1	1	8
95-96—Springfield	AHL	14	3	12	15	22	...	...	...	—	—	—	—	—
—Winnipeg	NHL	65	1	5	6	81	-2	0	0	6	0	0	0	4
96-97—Phoenix	NHL	65	3	7	10	40	-8	1	0	1	0	0	0	2
97-98—New York Rangers	NHL	63	1	6	7	55	-3	0	0	—	—	—	—	—
98-99—Hartford	AHL	42	2	10	12	28	...	...	...	—	—	—	—	—
—New York Rangers	NHL	2	0	0	0	0	-1	0	0	—	—	—	—	—
—St. Louis	NHL	30	1	2	3	20	12	0	0	13	1	2	3	8
99-00—St. Louis	NHL	74	2	8	10	38	26	0	0	7	0	2	2	4
NHL Totals (11 years)		441	10	52	62	309	39	1	0	33	1	6	7	22

FISCHER, JIRI   D   RED WINGS

PERSONAL: Born July 31, 1980, in Horovice, Czechoslovakia. ... 6-5/210. ... Shoots left.
TRANSACTIONS/CAREER NOTES: Selected by Detroit Red Wings in first round (first Red Wings pick, 25th overall) of NHL entry draft (June 27, 1998).
HONORS: Named to QMJHL All-Star first team (1998-99). ... Won Emile "Butch" Bouchard Trophy (1998-99). ... Named to Can.HL All-Star second team (1998-99).

Season Team	League	REGULAR SEASON								PLAYOFFS				
		Gms.	G	A	Pts.	PIM	+/-	PP	SH	Gms.	G	A	Pts.	PIM
95-96—Poldi Kladno	Czech Rep.	39	6	10	16	...	...	...	...	—	—	—	—	—
96-97—Poldi Kladno	Czech Rep.	38	11	16	27	...	...	...	...	—	—	—	—	—
97-98—Hull	QMJHL	70	3	19	22	112	...	...	...	11	1	4	5	16
98-99—Hull	QMJHL	65	22	56	78	141	...	...	...	23	6	17	23	44
99-00—Detroit	NHL	52	0	8	8	45	1	0	0	—	—	—	—	—
—Cincinnati	AHL	7	0	2	2	10	...	...	...	—	—	—	—	—
NHL Totals (1 year)		52	0	8	8	45	1	0	0	—	—	—	—	—

FISET, STEPHANE   G   KINGS

PERSONAL: Born June 17, 1970, in Montreal. ... 6-1/198. ... Catches left. ... Name pronounced fih-SAY.
TRANSACTIONS/CAREER NOTES: Selected by Quebec Nordiques in second round (third Nordiques pick, 24th overall) of NHL entry draft (June 13, 1987). ... Twisted knee (December 9, 1990). ... Sprained left knee (January 14, 1992); missed 12 games. ... Suffered slipped disc (November 4, 1993); missed 18 games. ... Injured groin (February 28, 1995); missed two games. ... Nordiques franchise moved to Colorado and renamed Avalanche for 1995-96 season (June 21, 1995). ... Traded by Avalanche with first-round pick (D Mathieu Biron) in 1998 draft to Los Angeles Kings for LW Eric Lacroix and first-round pick (D Martin Skoula) in 1998 draft (June 20, 1996). ... Strained abdominal muscle (December 3, 1996); missed one game. ... Strained groin and abdominal muscles (March 5, 1997); missed 13 games. ... Bruised thigh (January 24, 1998); missed one game. ... Strained groin (February 28, 1998); missed two games. ... Strained right groin (October 18, 1998); missed four games. ... Strained left groin (October 28, 1998); missed 12 games. ... Strained right groin (December 16, 1998); missed seven games. ... Bruised right hand (November 9, 1999); missed 14 games. ... Strained left groin (March 4, 2000); missed six games.
HONORS: Won Can.HL Goaltender of the Year Award (1988-89). ... Won Jacques Plante Trophy (1988-89). ... Named to QMJHL All-Star first team (1988-89).
MISCELLANEOUS: Member of Stanley Cup championship team (1996). ... Holds Los Angeles Kings all-time record for goals-against average (2.80). ... Stopped a penalty shot attempt (vs. Craig Janney, January 9, 1992; vs. Chris Dahlquist, March 21, 1992; vs. Peter Bondra, April 4, 1998; vs. Paul Kariya, March 18, 1999; vs. Mike Ricci, October 24, 1999). ... Allowed a penalty shot goal (vs. Kevin Miller, December 5, 1995; vs. Peter Bondra, January 29, 1999; vs. Tomas Sandstrom, February 15, 1999).

F

Season Team	League	REGULAR SEASON								PLAYOFFS						
		Gms.	Min	W	L	T	GA	SO	Avg.	Gms.	Min.	W	L	GA	SO	Avg.
87-88—Victoriaville	QMJHL	40	2221	14	17	4	146	1	3.94	2	163	0	2	10	0	3.68
88-89—Victoriaville	QMJHL	43	2401	25	14	0	138	1	*3.45	12	711	9	2	33	0	*2.78
89-90—Victoriaville	QMJHL	24	1383	14	6	3	63	1	2.73	*14	*790	7	6	*49	0	3.72
—Quebec	NHL	6	342	0	5	1	34	0	5.96	—	—	—	—	—	—	—
90-91—Quebec	NHL	3	186	0	2	1	12	0	3.87	—	—	—	—	—	—	—
—Halifax	AHL	36	1902	10	15	8	131	0	4.13	—	—	—	—	—	—	—
91-92—Halifax	AHL	29	1675	8	14	6	110	†3	3.94	—	—	—	—	—	—	—
—Quebec	NHL	23	1133	7	10	2	71	1	3.76	—	—	—	—	—	—	—
92-93—Quebec	NHL	37	1939	18	9	4	110	0	3.40	1	21	0	0	1	0	2.86
—Halifax	AHL	3	180	2	1	0	11	0	3.67	—	—	—	—	—	—	—
93-94—Quebec	NHL	50	2798	20	25	4	158	2	3.39	—	—	—	—	—	—	—
94-95—Quebec	NHL	32	1879	17	10	3	87	2	2.78	4	209	1	2	16	0	4.59
95-96—Colorado	NHL	37	2107	22	6	7	103	1	2.93	1	1	0	0	0	0	...
96-97—Los Angeles	NHL	44	2482	13	24	5	132	4	3.19	—	—	—	—	—	—	—
97-98—Los Angeles	NHL	60	3497	26	25	8	158	2	2.71	2	93	0	2	7	0	4.52
98-99—Los Angeles	NHL	42	2403	18	21	1	104	3	2.60	—	—	—	—	—	—	—
99-00—Los Angeles	NHL	47	2592	20	15	7	119	1	2.75	4	200	0	3	10	0	3.00
NHL Totals (11 years)		381	21358	161	152	43	1088	16	3.06	12	524	1	7	34	0	3.89

FISHER, MIKE   C   SENATORS

PERSONAL: Born June 5, 1980, in Peterborough, Ont. ... 6-1/193. ... Shoots right.
TRANSACTIONS/CAREER NOTES: Selected by Ottawa Senators in second round (second Senators pick, 44th overall) of NHL entry draft (June 27, 1998). ... Suffered hip pointer (October 5, 1999); missed three games. ... Tore anterior cruciate ligament in right knee (December 30, 1999); missed remainder of season.

Season Team	League	REGULAR SEASON								PLAYOFFS				
		Gms.	G	A	Pts.	PIM	+/-	PP	SH	Gms.	G	A	Pts.	PIM
96-97—Peterborough	Tier II Jr. A	51	26	30	56	33	...	...	...	—	—	—	—	—
97-98—Sudbury	OHL	66	24	25	49	65	...	...	...	9	2	2	4	13
98-99—Sudbury	OHL	68	41	65	106	55	...	...	...	4	2	1	3	4
99-00—Ottawa	NHL	32	4	5	9	15	-6	0	0	—	—	—	—	—
NHL Totals (1 year)		32	4	5	9	15	-6	0	0					

FITZGERALD, TOM RW PREDATORS

PERSONAL: Born August 28, 1968, in Billerica, Mass. ... 6-0/196. ... Shoots right. ... Full Name: Thomas James Fitzgerald.
HIGH SCHOOL: Austin Prep (Reading, Mass.).
COLLEGE: Providence.
TRANSACTIONS/CAREER NOTES: Selected by New York Islanders in first round (first Islanders pick, 17th overall) of NHL entry draft (June 21, 1986). ... Bruised left knee (November 7, 1990). ... Strained abdominal muscle (October 22, 1991); missed 16 games. ... Tore rib cage muscle (October 24, 1992); missed four games. ... Selected by Florida Panthers in NHL expansion draft (June 24, 1993). ... Suffered sore hip (March 18, 1994); missed one game. ... Bruised eye (November 13, 1996); missed one game. ... Suffered from the flu (December 29, 1996); missed one game. ... Strained abdominal muscle (January 25, 1997); missed three games. ... Reinjured abdominal muscle (February 22, 1997); missed five games. ... Traded by Panthers to Colorado Avalanche for rights to LW Mark Parrish and third-round pick (D Lance Ward) in 1998 draft (March 24, 1998). ... Signed as free agent by Nashville Predators (July 6, 1998). ... Strained neck (December 8, 1998); missed one game.
RECORDS: Shares NHL single-game playoff record for most shorthanded goals—2 (May 8, 1993).
MISCELLANEOUS: Captain of Nashville Predators (1998-99 and 1999-2000). ... Holds Nashville Predators all-time record for most games played (162). ... Failed to score on a penalty shot (vs. Mark Fitzpatrick, January 31, 1998).

Season Team	League	REGULAR SEASON								PLAYOFFS				
		Gms.	G	A	Pts.	PIM	+/-	PP	SH	Gms.	G	A	Pts.	PIM
84-85—Austin Prep	Mass. H.S.	18	20	21	41	...	...	...	...	—	—	—	—	—
85-86—Austin Prep	Mass. H.S.	24	35	38	73	...	...	...	...	—	—	—	—	—
86-87—Providence College	Hockey East	27	8	14	22	22	...	...	...	—	—	—	—	—
87-88—Providence College	Hockey East	36	19	15	34	50	...	...	...	—	—	—	—	—
88-89—Springfield	AHL	61	24	18	42	43	...	...	...	—	—	—	—	—
—New York Islanders	NHL	23	3	5	8	10	1	0	0	—	—	—	—	—
89-90—Springfield	AHL	53	30	23	53	32	...	...	...	14	2	9	11	13
—New York Islanders	NHL	19	2	5	7	4	-3	0	0	4	1	0	1	4
90-91—New York Islanders	NHL	41	5	5	10	24	-9	0	0	—	—	—	—	—
—Capital District	AHL	27	7	7	14	50	...	...	...	—	—	—	—	—
91-92—New York Islanders	NHL	45	6	11	17	28	-3	0	2	—	—	—	—	—
—Capital District	AHL	4	1	1	2	4	...	...	...	—	—	—	—	—
92-93—New York Islanders	NHL	77	9	18	27	34	-2	0	3	18	2	5	7	18
93-94—Florida	NHL	83	18	14	32	54	-3	0	3	—	—	—	—	—
94-95—Florida	NHL	48	3	13	16	31	-3	0	0	—	—	—	—	—
95-96—Florida	NHL	82	13	21	34	75	-3	1	6	22	4	4	8	34
96-97—Florida	NHL	71	10	14	24	64	7	0	2	5	0	1	1	0
97-98—Florida	NHL	69	10	5	15	57	-4	0	1	—	—	—	—	—
—Colorado	NHL	11	2	1	3	22	0	0	1	7	0	1	1	20
98-99—Nashville	NHL	80	13	19	32	48	-18	0	0	—	—	—	—	—
99-00—Nashville	NHL	82	13	9	22	66	-18	0	3	—	—	—	—	—
NHL Totals (12 years)		731	107	140	247	517	-58	1	21	56	7	11	18	76

FITZPATRICK, MARK G

PERSONAL: Born November 13, 1968, in Toronto. ... 6-2/198. ... Catches left.
TRANSACTIONS/CAREER NOTES: Selected by Los Angeles Kings as underage junior in second round (second Kings pick, 27th overall) of NHL entry draft (June 13, 1987). ... Traded by Kings with D Wayne McBean and future considerations to New York Islanders for G Kelly Hrudey (February 22, 1989); Islanders acquired D Doug Crossman to complete deal (May 23, 1989). ... Developed Eosinophilic Myalgia Syndrome (EMS) after a reaction to L-Trytophan, an ingredient in a vitamin supplement (September 1990); returned to play March 1991. ... Suffered recurrence of EMS and underwent biopsy on right thigh (October 22, 1991); missed 10 games. ... Strained abdominal muscle (December 15, 1992); missed five games. ... Traded by Islanders with first-round pick (C Adam Deadmarsh) in 1993 draft to Quebec Nordiques for G Ron Hextall and first-round pick (C/RW Todd Bertuzzi) in 1993 draft (June 20, 1993). ... Selected by Florida Panthers in NHL expansion draft (June 24, 1993). ... Suspended two games without pay and fined $500 by NHL for high-sticking incident (February 16, 1994). ... Sprained lower back (April 22, 1995); missed one game. ... Suffered recurring back spasms (April 26, 1995); missed remainder of season. ... Traded by Panthers with RW Jody Hull to Tampa Bay Lightning for RW Dino Ciccarelli and D Jeff Norton (January 15, 1998). ... Traded by Lightning with fourth-round pick (traded to Montreal) in 1999 draft to Chicago Blackhawks for D Michal Sykora (July 17, 1998). ... Signed as free agent by Carolina Hurricanes (August 7, 1999).
HONORS: Won Top Goaltender Trophy (1985-86). ... Named to WHL All-Star second team (1985-86 and 1987-88). ... Named to Memorial Cup All-Star team (1986-87 and 1987-88). ... Won Bill Masterton Memorial Trophy (1991-92).
MISCELLANEOUS: Stopped a penalty shot attempt (vs. Doug Gilmour, October 7, 1989; vs. Dean McAmmond, January 5, 1996; vs. Jaromir Jagr, November 9, 1996; vs. Tom Fitzgerald, January 31, 1998). ... Allowed a penalty shot goal (vs. Mike Sillinger, January 14, 1997).

Season Team	League	REGULAR SEASON								PLAYOFFS						
		Gms.	Min	W	L	T	GA	SO	Avg.	Gms.	Min.	W	L	GA	SO	Avg.
83-84—Revelstoke	BCJHL	21	1019	...	...	...	90	0	5.30	—	—	—	—	—	—	—
84-85—Medicine Hat	WHL	3	180	...	...	...	9	0	3.00	—	—	—	—	—	—	—
85-86—Medicine Hat	WHL	41	2074	26	6	1	99	1	*2.86	*19	986	12	5	*58	0	3.53
86-87—Medicine Hat	WHL	50	2844	31	11	4	159	*4	3.35	*20	*1224	12	8	71	†1	3.48
87-88—Medicine Hat	WHL	63	3600	36	15	6	194	†2	*3.23	16	959	12	4	52	†1	*3.25
88-89—New Haven	AHL	18	980	10	5	1	54	1	3.31	—	—	—	—	—	—	—
—Los Angeles	NHL	17	957	6	7	3	64	0	4.01	—	—	—	—	—	—	—
—New York Islanders	NHL	11	627	3	5	2	41	0	3.92	—	—	—	—	—	—	—

Season Team	League	REGULAR SEASON								PLAYOFFS						
		Gms.	Min	W	L	T	GA	SO	Avg.	Gms.	Min.	W	L	GA	SO	Avg.
89-90 —New York Islanders	NHL	47	2653	19	19	5	150	3	3.39	4	152	0	2	13	0	5.13
90-91 —Capital District	AHL	12	734	3	7	2	47	0	3.84	—	—	—	—	—	—	—
—New York Islanders	NHL	2	120	1	1	0	6	0	3.00	—	—	—	—	—	—	—
91-92 —Capital District	AHL	14	782	6	5	1	39	0	2.99	—	—	—	—	—	—	—
—New York Islanders	NHL	30	1743	11	13	5	93	0	3.20	—	—	—	—	—	—	—
92-93 —New York Islanders	NHL	39	2253	17	15	5	130	0	3.46	3	77	0	1	4	0	3.12
—Capital District	AHL	5	284	1	3	1	18	0	3.80	—	—	—	—	—	—	—
93-94 —Florida	NHL	28	1603	12	8	6	73	1	2.73	—	—	—	—	—	—	—
94-95 —Florida	NHL	15	819	6	7	2	36	2	2.64	—	—	—	—	—	—	—
95-96 —Florida	NHL	34	1786	15	11	3	88	0	2.96	2	60	0	0	6	0	6.00
96-97 —Florida	NHL	30	1680	8	9	9	66	0	2.36	—	—	—	—	—	—	—
97-98 —Florida	NHL	12	640	2	7	2	32	1	3.00	—	—	—	—	—	—	—
—Fort Wayne	IHL	2	119	1	1	0	8	0	4.03	—	—	—	—	—	—	—
—Tampa Bay	NHL	34	1938	7	24	1	102	1	3.16	—	—	—	—	—	—	—
98-99 —Chicago	NHL	27	1403	6	8	6	64	0	2.74	—	—	—	—	—	—	—
99-00 —Cincinnati	IHL	24	1379	11	11	‡1	59	4	2.57	—	—	—	—	—	—	—
—Carolina	NHL	3	107	0	2	0	8	0	4.49	—	—	—	—	—	—	—
NHL Totals (12 years)		329	18329	113	136	49	953	8	3.12	9	289	0	3	23	0	4.78

FITZPATRICK, RORY — D — PREDATORS

PERSONAL: Born January 11, 1975, in Rochester, N.Y. ... 6-2/205. ... Shoots right.

TRANSACTIONS/CAREER NOTES: Selected by Montreal Canadiens in second round (second Canadiens pick, 47th overall) of NHL entry draft (June 26, 1993). ... Traded by Canadiens with C Pierre Turgeon and C Craig Conroy to St. Louis Blues for LW Shayne Corson, D Murray Baron and fifth-round pick (D Gennady Razin) in 1997 draft (October 29, 1996). ... Selected by Boston Bruins from Blues in NHL waiver draft (October 5, 1998). ... Claimed on waivers by Blues (October 7, 1998). ... Traded by Blues to Nashville Predators for D Dan Keczmer (February 9, 2000).

HONORS: Named to OHL All-Rookie team (1992-93).

Season Team	League	REGULAR SEASON								PLAYOFFS				
		Gms.	G	A	Pts.	PIM	+/-	PP	SH	Gms.	G	A	Pts.	PIM
90-91 —Rochester Jr. B	OHA	40	0	5	5	...	...	...	...	—	—	—	—	—
91-92 —Rochester Jr. B	OHA	28	8	28	36	141	...	...	...	—	—	—	—	—
92-93 —Sudbury	OHL	58	4	20	24	68	...	...	...	14	0	0	0	17
93-94 —Sudbury	OHL	65	12	34	46	112	...	...	...	10	2	5	7	10
94-95 —Sudbury	OHL	56	12	36	48	72	...	...	...	18	3	15	18	21
—Fredericton	AHL	—	—	—	—	—	...	...	...	10	1	2	3	5
95-96 —Fredericton	AHL	18	4	6	10	36	...	...	...	—	—	—	—	—
—Montreal	NHL	42	0	2	2	18	-7	0	0	6	1	1	2	0
96-97 —Montreal	NHL	6	0	1	1	6	-2	0	0	—	—	—	—	—
—Worcester	AHL	49	4	13	17	78	...	...	...	5	1	2	3	0
—St. Louis	NHL	2	0	0	0	2	-2	0	0	—	—	—	—	—
97-98 —Worcester	AHL	62	8	22	30	111	...	...	...	11	0	3	3	26
98-99 —Worcester	AHL	53	5	16	21	82	...	...	...	4	0	1	1	17
—St. Louis	NHL	1	0	0	0	2	-3	0	0	—	—	—	—	—
99-00 —Worcester	AHL	28	0	5	5	48	...	...	...	—	—	—	—	—
—Milwaukee	IHL	27	2	1	3	27	...	...	...	3	0	2	2	2
NHL Totals (3 years)		51	0	3	3	28	-14	0	0	6	1	1	2	0

FLAHERTY, WADE — G — ISLANDERS

F

PERSONAL: Born January 11, 1968, in Terrace, B.C. ... 6-0/187. ... Catches left.

TRANSACTIONS/CAREER NOTES: Selected by Buffalo Sabres in ninth round (10th Sabres pick, 181st overall) of NHL entry draft (June 11, 1988). ... Signed as free agent by San Jose Sharks (September 3, 1991). ... Injured ribs (February 28, 1995); missed three games. ... Strained groin (February 1, 1996); missed two games. ... Suffered back spasms (March 8, 1996); missed six games. ... Suffered back spasms (March 31, 1996); missed seven games. ... Fractured collarbone (September 12, 1996); missed 23 games. ... Signed as free agent by New York Islanders (July 1, 1997). ... Sprained shoulder (November 21, 1999) and underwent surgery; missed remainder of season.

HONORS: Named to WHL All-Star second team (1987-88). ... Won ECHL Playoff Most Valuable Player Award (1989-90). ... Shared James Norris Memorial Trophy with Arturs Irbe (1991-92). ... Named to IHL All-Star second team (1992-93 and 1993-94).

Season Team	League	REGULAR SEASON								PLAYOFFS						
		Gms.	Min	W	L	T	GA	SO	Avg.	Gms.	Min.	W	L	GA	SO	Avg.
84-85 —Kelowna	WHL	1	55	0	0	0	5	0	5.45	—	—	—	—	—	—	—
85-86 —Seattle	WHL	9	271	1	3	0	36	0	7.97	—	—	—	—	—	—	—
—Spokane	WHL	5	161	0	3	0	21	0	7.83	—	—	—	—	—	—	—
86-87 —Nanaimo	BCJHL	15	830	...	...	...	53	0	3.83	—	—	—	—	—	—	—
—Victoria	WHL	3	127	0	2	0	16	0	7.56	—	—	—	—	—	—	—
87-88 —Victoria	WHL	36	2052	20	15	0	135	0	3.95	5	300	2	3	18	0	3.60
88-89 —Victoria	WHL	42	2408	21	19	0	180	0	4.49	8	480	3	5	35	0	4.38
89-90 —Kalamazoo	IHL	1	13	0	0	0	0	0		—	—	—	—	—	—	—
—Greensboro	ECHL	27	1308	12	10	0	96	...	4.40	†9	567	*8	1	21	0	*2.22
90-91 —Kansas City	IHL	†56	2990	16	31	‡4	*224	0	4.49	1	1	0	0	0	0	...
91-92 —Kansas City	IHL	43	2603	26	14	‡3	140	1	3.23	1	1	0	0	0	0	...
—San Jose	NHL	3	178	0	3	0	13	0	4.38	—	—	—	—	—	—	—
92-93 —Kansas City	IHL	61	*3642	*34	19	0	*195	2	3.21	12	*733	6	*5	†34	*1	2.78
—San Jose	NHL	1	60	0	1	0	5	0	5.00	—	—	—	—	—	—	—
93-94 —Kansas City	IHL	60	*3564	32	19	‡9	202	0	3.40	—	—	—	—	—	—	—
94-95 —San Jose	NHL	18	852	5	6	1	44	1	3.10	7	377	2	3	31	0	4.93
95-96 —San Jose	NHL	24	1137	3	12	1	92	0	4.85	—	—	—	—	—	—	—

		REGULAR SEASON								PLAYOFFS						
Season Team	League	Gms.	Min	W	L	T	GA	SO	Avg.	Gms.	Min.	W	L	GA	SO	Avg.
96-97—Kentucky	AHL	19	1032	8	6	2	54	1	3.14	3	200	1	2	11	0	3.30
—San Jose	NHL	7	359	2	4	0	31	0	5.18	—	—	—	—	—	—	—
97-98—Utah	IHL	24	1341	16	5	‡3	40	3	1.79	—	—	—	—	—	—	—
—New York Islanders	NHL	16	694	4	4	3	23	3	1.99	—	—	—	—	—	—	—
98-99—New York Islanders	NHL	20	1048	5	11	2	53	0	3.03	—	—	—	—	—	—	—
—Lowell	AHL	5	305	1	3	1	16	0	3.15	—	—	—	—	—	—	—
99-00—New York Islanders	NHL	4	182	0	1	1	7	0	2.31	—	—	—	—	—	—	—
NHL Totals (8 years)		93	4510	19	42	8	268	4	3.57	7	377	2	3	31	0	4.93

FLEURY, THEO   RW   RANGERS

PERSONAL: Born June 29, 1968, in Oxbow, Sask. ... 5-6/180. ... Shoots right. ... Full Name: Theoren Fleury. ... Name pronounced THAIR-ihn FLUH-ree.

TRANSACTIONS/CAREER NOTES: Selected by Calgary Flames in eighth round (ninth Flames pick, 166th overall) of NHL entry draft (June 13, 1987). ... Played in Europe during 1994-95 NHL lockout. ... Injured eye (April 6, 1996); missed two games. ... Injured knee (April 6, 1997); missed one game. ... Traded by Flames with LW Chris Dingman to Colorado Avalanche for LW Rene Corbet, D Wade Belak and future considerations (February 28, 1999); Flames acquired D Robyn Regehr to complete deal (March 27, 1999). ... Sprained knee (March 1, 1999); missed seven games. ... Signed as free agent by New York Rangers (July 8, 1999). ... Suffered back spasms (February 8, 2000); missed one game. ... Strained right knee (April 8, 2000); missed final game of season.

HONORS: Named to WHL (East) All-Star first team (1986-87). ... Shared Bob Clarke Trophy with Joe Sakic (1987-88). ... Named to WHL All-Star second team (1987-88). ... Shared Alka-Seltzer Plus Award with Marty McSorley (1990-91). ... Played in NHL All-Star Game (1991, 1992 and 1996-1999). ... Named to NHL All-Star second team (1994-95).

RECORDS: Holds NHL single-game record for highest plus-minus rating—9 (February 10, 1993).

STATISTICAL PLATEAUS: Three-goal games: 1990-91 (5), 1992-93 (1), 1993-94 (1), 1995-96 (3), 1996-97 (1), 1998-99 (3). Total: 14.

MISCELLANEOUS: Member of Stanley Cup championship team (1989). ... Captain of Calgary Flames (1995-96 and 1996-97). ... Holds Calgary Flames all-time records for most goals (364) and most points (830). ... Scored on a penalty shot (vs. Jacques Cloutier, February 23, 1991; vs. Rick Wamsley, December 11, 1992; vs. Patrick Roy, October 22, 1996).

		REGULAR SEASON							PLAYOFFS				
Season Team	League	Gms.	G	A	Pts.	PIM	+/-	PP	SH	Gms.	G	A	Pts.	PIM
84-85—Moose Jaw	WHL	71	29	46	75	82	...	...	...	—	—	—	—	—
85-86—Moose Jaw	WHL	72	43	65	108	124	...	...	...	—	—	—	—	—
86-87—Moose Jaw	WHL	66	61	68	129	110	...	...	...	9	7	9	16	34
87-88—Moose Jaw	WHL	65	68	92	†160	235	...	...	...	—	—	—	—	—
—Salt Lake City	IHL	2	3	4	7	7	...	...	...	8	11	5	16	16
88-89—Salt Lake City	IHL	40	37	37	74	81	...	...	...	—	—	—	—	—
—Calgary	NHL	36	14	20	34	46	5	5	0	22	5	6	11	24
89-90—Calgary	NHL	80	31	35	66	157	22	9	3	6	2	3	5	10
90-91—Calgary	NHL	79	51	53	104	136	†48	9	7	7	2	5	7	14
91-92—Calgary	NHL	80	33	40	73	133	0	11	1	—	—	—	—	—
92-93—Calgary	NHL	83	34	66	100	88	14	12	2	6	5	7	12	27
93-94—Calgary	NHL	83	40	45	85	186	30	16	1	7	6	4	10	5
94-95—Tappara	Finland	10	8	9	17	22	...	...	...	—	—	—	—	—
—Calgary	NHL	47	29	29	58	112	6	9	2	7	7	7	14	2
95-96—Calgary	NHL	80	46	50	96	112	17	17	5	4	2	1	3	14
96-97—Calgary	NHL	81	29	38	67	104	-12	9	2	—	—	—	—	—
97-98—Calgary	NHL	82	27	51	78	197	0	3	2	—	—	—	—	—
—Can. Olympic team	Int'l	6	1	3	4	2	...	...	...	—	—	—	—	—
98-99—Calgary	NHL	60	30	39	69	68	18	7	3	—	—	—	—	—
—Colorado	NHL	15	10	14	24	18	8	1	0	18	5	12	17	20
99-00—New York Rangers	NHL	80	15	49	64	68	-4	1	0	—	—	—	—	—
NHL Totals (12 years)		886	389	529	918	1425	152	109	28	77	34	45	79	116

FOMITCHEV, ALEX   G   OILERS

PERSONAL: Born February 19, 1979, in Moscow, U.S.S.R. ... 5-10/180. ... Catches left. ... Full Name: Alexandre Fomitchev.

TRANSACTIONS/CAREER NOTES: Selected by Edmonton Oilers in ninth round (10th Oilers pick, 231st overall) of NHL entry draft (June 21, 1997).

HONORS: Named to WHL (East) All-Star first team (1998-99).

		REGULAR SEASON								PLAYOFFS						
Season Team	League	Gms.	Min	W	L	T	GA	SO	Avg.	Gms.	Min.	W	L	GA	SO	Avg.
96-97—St. Albert	AJHL	41	2063	...	...	...	99	4	2.88	—	—	—	—	—	—	—
97-98—Calgary	WHL	60	3381	32	23	2	168	1	2.98	*18	*1075	9	*9	*50	*2	2.79
98-99—Calgary	WHL	57	3317	*39	10	7	142	4	2.57	*21	*1299	*16	5	*61	1	2.82
99-00—Calgary	WHL	1	60	1	0	0	5	0	5.00	—	—	—	—	—	—	—
—Seattle	WHL	46	2685	20	21	4	126	3	2.82	7	420	4	3	24	0	3.43

FOOTE, ADAM   D   AVALANCHE

PERSONAL: Born July 10, 1971, in Toronto. ... 6-1/202. ... Shoots right. ... Full Name: Adam David Vernon Foote. ... Name pronounced FUT.

TRANSACTIONS/CAREER NOTES: Selected by Quebec Nordiques in second round (second Nordiques pick, 22nd overall) of NHL entry draft (June 17, 1989). ... Fractured right thumb (February 1992); missed remainder of season. ... Injured knee (October 21, 1992); missed one game. ... Suffered from the flu (January 28, 1993); missed two games. ... Injured groin (January 18, 1994); missed eight games. ... Suffered herniated disc (February 11, 1994) and underwent surgery; missed remainder of season. ... Injured back (February 9, 1995); missed two games. ... Injured groin (February 28, 1995); missed two games. ... Injured groin (March 26, 1995); missed four games. ... Reinjured groin (April 6, 1995); missed five games. ... Nordiques franchise moved to Colorado and renamed Avalanche for 1995-96 season (June 21, 1995).

F

... Fractured wrist prior to 1995-96 season; missed first two games of season. ... Separated left shoulder (January 6, 1996); missed five games. ... Bruised left knee (February 8, 1997); missed two games. ... Bruised knee (January 2, 1998); missed one game. ... Bruised knee (January 10, 1998); missed three games. ... Injured elbow (October 24, 1998); missed 15 games. ... Suffered concussion (December 4, 1998); missed three games. ... Injured shoulder (October 10, 1999); missed one game. ...Reinjured shoulder (October 21, 1999); missed six games. ... Reinjured shoulder (November 17, 1999); missed eight games. ... Injured groin (January 9, 2000); missed one game. ... Injured groin (February 10, 2000); missed six games.

HONORS: Named to OHL All-Star first team (1990-91).

MISCELLANEOUS: Member of Stanley Cup championship team (1996).

Season Team	League	REGULAR SEASON								PLAYOFFS				
		Gms.	G	A	Pts.	PIM	+/-	PP	SH	Gms.	G	A	Pts.	PIM
88-89—Sault Ste. Marie	OHL	66	7	32	39	120	...	...	...	—	—	—	—	—
89-90—Sault Ste. Marie	OHL	61	12	43	55	199	...	...	...	—	—	—	—	—
90-91—Sault Ste. Marie	OHL	59	18	51	69	93	...	...	...	14	5	12	17	28
91-92—Quebec	NHL	46	2	5	7	44	-4	0	0	—	—	—	—	—
—Halifax	AHL	6	0	1	1	2	...			—	—	—	—	—
92-93—Quebec	NHL	81	4	12	16	168	6	0	1	6	0	1	1	2
93-94—Quebec	NHL	45	2	6	8	67	3	0	0	—	—	—	—	—
94-95—Quebec	NHL	35	0	7	7	52	17	0	0	6	0	1	1	14
95-96—Colorado	NHL	73	5	11	16	88	27	1	0	22	1	3	4	36
96-97—Colorado	NHL	78	2	19	21	135	16	0	0	17	0	4	4	62
97-98—Colorado	NHL	77	3	14	17	124	-3	0	0	7	0	0	0	23
—Can. Olympic team	Int'l	6	0	1	1	4	...			—	—	—	—	—
98-99—Colorado	NHL	64	5	16	21	92	20	3	0	19	2	3	5	24
99-00—Colorado	NHL	59	5	13	18	98	5	1	0	16	0	7	7	28
NHL Totals (9 years)		558	28	103	131	868	87	5	1	93	3	19	22	189

FORBES, COLIN LW SENATORS

PERSONAL: Born February 16, 1976, in New Westminister, B.C. ... 6-3/205. ... Shoots left.

TRANSACTIONS/CAREER NOTES: Selected by Philadelphia Flyers in seventh round (fifth Flyers pick, 166th overall) of NHL entry draft (June 29, 1994). ... Bruised thumb (November 7, 1998); missed one game. ... Suffered from stomach virus (January 7, 1999); missed one game. ... Traded by Flyers with fifth-round pick (G Michal Lanicek) in 1999 draft to Tampa Bay Lightning for RW Mikael Andersson and RW Sandy McCarthy (March 20, 1999). ... Traded by Lightning to Ottawa Senators for C Bruce Gardiner (November 11, 1999).

Season Team	League	REGULAR SEASON								PLAYOFFS				
		Gms.	G	A	Pts.	PIM	+/-	PP	SH	Gms.	G	A	Pts.	PIM
93-94—Sherwood Park	AJHL	47	18	22	40	76	...	...	...	—	—	—	—	—
94-95—Portland	WHL	72	24	31	55	108	...	...	...	9	1	3	4	10
95-96—Portland	WHL	72	33	44	77	137	...	...	...	7	2	5	7	14
—Hershey	AHL	2	1	0	1	2	...			4	0	2	2	2
96-97—Philadelphia	AHL	74	21	28	49	108	...			10	5	5	10	33
—Philadelphia	NHL	3	1	0	1	0	0	0	0	3	0	0	0	0
97-98—Philadelphia	AHL	13	7	4	11	22	...			—	—	—	—	—
—Philadelphia	NHL	63	12	7	19	59	2	2	0	5	0	0	0	2
98-99—Philadelphia	NHL	66	9	7	16	51	0	0	0	—	—	—	—	—
—Tampa Bay	NHL	14	3	1	4	10	-5	0	1	—	—	—	—	—
99-00—Tampa Bay	NHL	8	0	0	0	18	-4	0	0	—	—	—	—	—
—Ottawa	NHL	45	2	5	7	12	-1	0	0	5	1	0	1	14
NHL Totals (4 years)		199	27	20	47	150	-8	2	1	13	1	0	1	16

FORSBERG, PETER C AVALANCHE

F

PERSONAL: Born July 20, 1973, in Ornskoldsvik, Sweden. ... 6-0/190. ... Shoots left. ... Son of Kent Forsberg, head coach, Swedish Olympic team.

TRANSACTIONS/CAREER NOTES: Selected by Philadelphia Flyers in first round (first Flyers pick, sixth overall) of NHL entry draft (June 22, 1991). ... Traded by Flyers with G Ron Hextall, C Mike Ricci, D Steve Duchesne, D Kerry Huffman, first-round pick (G Jocelyn Thibault) in 1993 draft, cash and future considerations to Quebec Nordiques for C Eric Lindros (June 20, 1992); Nordiques acquired LW Chris Simon and first-round pick (traded to Toronto) in 1994 draft to complete deal (July 21, 1992). ... Played in Europe during 1994-95 NHL lockout. ... Suffered from the flu (March 1, 1995); missed one game. ... Nordiques franchise moved to Colorado and renamed Avalanche for 1995-96 season (June 21, 1995). ... Bruised thigh (December 14, 1996); missed 17 games. ... Bruised shoulder (November 8, 1997); missed three games. ... Pulled groin (March 26, 1998); missed seven games. ... Suffered concussion (May 7, 1998); missed two playoff games. ... Suffered charley horse (May 22, 1998); missed one playoff game. ... Injured groin (December 14, 1998); missed one game. ... Injured elbow (March 4, 1999); missed three games. ... Underwent shoulder surgery prior to start of 1999-2000 season; missed first 23 games of season. ... Suffered hip pointer (November 30, 1999); missed two games. ... Suffered concussion (February 1, 2000); missed five games. ... Bruised shoulder (March 26, 2000); missed two games. ... Separated shoulder (April 7, 2000); missed final game of season.

HONORS: Named to Swedish League All-Star team (1991-92). ... Named Swedish League Player of the Year (1993-94). ... Named NHL Rookie of the Year by THE SPORTING NEWS (1994-95). ... Won Calder Memorial Trophy (1994-95). ... Named to NHL All-Rookie team (1994-95). ... Played in NHL All-Star Game (1996, 1998 and 1999). ... Named to play in NHL All-Star Game (1997); replaced by LW Brendan Shanahan due to injury. ... Named to THE SPORTING NEWS All-Star team (1997-98). ... Named to NHL All-Star first team (1997-98 and 1998-99). ... Named to play in NHL All-Star Game (2000); replaced by LW Patrik Elias due to injury.

MISCELLANEOUS: Member of Stanley Cup championship team (1996). ... Member of gold-medal-winning Swedish Olympic team (1994). ... Holds Colorado Avalanche record for most assists (277) and points (390). ... Failed to score on a penalty shot (vs. Tim Cheveldae, February 1, 1996; vs. Grant Fuhr, December 6, 1996).

STATISTICAL PLATEAUS: Three-goal games: 1995-96 (2), 1996-97 (1), 1998-99 (1). Total: 4.

Season Team	League	REGULAR SEASON								PLAYOFFS				
		Gms.	G	A	Pts.	PIM	+/-	PP	SH	Gms.	G	A	Pts.	PIM
89-90—MoDo Hockey Jrs.	Sweden Jr.	30	15	12	27	42	...	...	...	—	—	—	—	—
90-91—MoDo Ornskoldsvik	Sweden	23	7	10	17	22	...	...	...	—	—	—	—	—
91-92—MoDo Ornskoldsvik	Sweden	39	9	19	28	78	...	...	...	—	—	—	—	—
92-93—MoDo Ornskoldsvik	Sweden	39	23	24	47	92	...	...	...	3	4	1	5	0

Season Team	League	REGULAR SEASON								PLAYOFFS				
		Gms.	G	A	Pts.	PIM	+/-	PP	SH	Gms.	G	A	Pts.	PIM
93-94—MoDo Ornskoldsvik ...	Sweden	39	18	26	44	82	...	...	...	11	9	7	16	14
—Swedish Oly. team	Int'l	8	2	6	8	6	...	...	...	—	—	—	—	—
94-95—MoDo Ornskoldsvik ...	Sweden	11	5	9	14	20	...	...	...	—	—	—	—	—
—Quebec	NHL	47	15	35	50	16	17	3	0	6	2	4	6	4
95-96—Colorado	NHL	82	30	86	116	47	26	7	3	22	10	11	21	18
96-97—Colorado	NHL	65	28	58	86	73	31	5	4	14	5	12	17	10
97-98—Colorado	NHL	72	25	66	91	94	6	7	3	7	6	5	11	12
—Swedish Oly. team	Int'l	4	1	4	5	6	...	...	...	—	—	—	—	—
98-99—Colorado	NHL	78	30	67	97	108	27	9	2	19	8	16	*24	31
99-00—Colorado	NHL	49	14	37	51	52	9	3	0	16	7	8	15	12
NHL Totals (6 years)...........		393	142	349	491	390	116	34	12	84	38	56	94	87

FOUNTAIN, MIKE   G   SENATORS

PERSONAL: Born January 26, 1972, in North York, Ont. ... 6-1/180. ... Catches left. ... Full Name: Michael Fountain. ... Name pronounced FOWN-tihn.
COLLEGE: Trent (Ont.).
TRANSACTIONS/CAREER NOTES: Selected by Vancouver Canucks in second round (third Canucks pick, 45th overall) of NHL entry draft (June 20, 1992). ... Signed as free agent by Carolina Hurricanes (August 14, 1997). ... Signed as free agent by Ottawa Senators (July 12, 1999).
HONORS: Named to Can.HL All-Star second team (1991-92). ... Named to OHL All-Star first team (1991-92). ... Named to AHL All-Star second team (1993-94).

Season Team	League	REGULAR SEASON								PLAYOFFS						
		Gms.	Min	W	L	T	GA	SO	Avg.	Gms.	Min.	W	L	GA	SO	Avg.
88-89—Huntsville Jr. C	OHA	22	1306	...	...	...	82	0	3.77	—	—	—	—	—	—	—
89-90—Chatham Jr. B	OHA	21	1249	...	...	...	76	0	3.65	—	—	—	—	—	—	—
90-91—Sault Ste. Marie	OHL	7	380	5	2	0	19	0	3.00	—	—	—	—	—	—	—
—Oshawa	OHL	30	1483	17	5	1	84	0	3.40	8	292	1	4	26	0	5.34
91-92—Oshawa	OHL	40	2260	18	13	6	149	1	3.96	7	428	3	4	26	0	3.64
92-93—Canadian nat'l team	Int'l	13	...	7	5	1	37	1	—	—	—	—	—	—	—	—
—Hamilton	AHL	12	618	2	8	0	46	0	4.47	—	—	—	—	—	—	—
93-94—Hamilton	AHL	70	*4005	*34	28	6	241	*4	3.61	3	146	0	2	12	0	4.93
94-95—Syracuse	AHL	61	*3618	25	*29	7	225	2	3.73	—	—	—	—	—	—	—
95-96—Syracuse	AHL	54	3060	21	27	3	184	1	3.61	15	915	8	*7	57	†2	3.74
96-97—Vancouver	NHL	6	245	2	2	0	14	1	3.43	—	—	—	—	—	—	—
—Syracuse	AHL	25	1462	8	14	2	78	1	3.20	2	120	0	2	12	0	6.00
97-98—New Haven	AHL	50	2923	25	19	5	139	3	2.85	—	—	—	—	—	—	—
—Carolina	NHL	3	163	0	3	0	10	0	3.68	—	—	—	—	—	—	—
98-99—New Haven	AHL	51	2989	23	24	3	150	2	3.01	—	—	—	—	—	—	—
99-00—Grand Rapids	IHL	36	1851	25	7	‡4	77	3	2.50	1	20	0	0	4	0	12.00
—Ottawa	NHL	1	16	0	0	0	1	0	3.75	—	—	—	—	—	—	—
NHL Totals (3 years).............		10	424	2	5	0	25	1	3.54							

FRANCIS, RON   C   HURRICANES

PERSONAL: Born March 1, 1963, in Sault Ste. Marie, Ont. ... 6-3/200. ... Shoots left. ... Full Name: Ronald Francis. ... Cousin of Mike Liut, goaltender with three NHL teams (1979-80 through 1991-92) and Cincinnati Stingers of WHA (1977-78 and 1978-79).
TRANSACTIONS/CAREER NOTES: Selected by Hartford Whalers as underage junior in first round (first Whalers pick, fourth overall) of NHL entry draft (June 10, 1981). ... Injured eye (January 27, 1982); missed three weeks. ... Strained ligaments in right knee (November 30, 1983). ... Fractured left ankle (January 18, 1986); missed 27 games. ... Fractured left index finger (January 28, 1989); missed 11 games. ... Fractured nose (November 24, 1990). ... Traded by Whalers with D Ulf Samuelsson and D Grant Jennings to Pittsburgh Penguins for C John Cullen, D Zarley Zalapski and RW Jeff Parker (March 4, 1991). ... Suffered from the flu (February 19, 1995); missed one game. ... Suffered back spasms (February 21, 1995); missed three games. ... Strained hip flexor (January 5, 1996); missed two games. ... Suspended two games and fined §1000 by NHL for checking player from behind (February 27, 1996). ... Fractured left foot (May 11, 1996); missed remainder of playoffs. ... Injured groin (February 22, 1997); missed one game. ... Pulled hamstring (April 16, 1998); missed one game. ... Signed as free agent by Carolina Hurricanes (July 13, 1998). ... Suffered from vertigo (November 26, 1999); missed two games. ... Injured back (January 27, 2000); missed two games.
HONORS: Played in NHL All-Star Game (1983, 1985, 1990 and 1996). ... Won Lady Byng Memorial Trophy (1994-95 and 1997-98). ... Won Frank J. Selke Trophy (1994-95). ... Won NHL Alka-Seltzer Plus award (1994-95).
MISCELLANEOUS: Member of Stanley Cup championship teams (1991 and 1992). ... Captain of Hartford Whalers (1984-85 through 1990-1991). ... Captain of Pittsburgh Penguins (1994-95, 1995-96 and 1997-98). ... Captain of Carolina Hurricanes (1999-2000). ... Holds Carolina Hurricanes franchise all-time records for most games played (874), most goals (308), most assists (638) and most points (946). ... Scored on a penalty shot (vs. Richard Sevigny, January 17, 1986).
STATISTICAL PLATEAUS: Three-goal games: 1982-83 (1), 1984-85 (1), 1985-86 (2), 1987-88 (1), 1988-89 (1), 1989-90 (1), 1990-91 (1), 1995-96 (1), 1997-98 (1). Total: 10. ... Four-goal games: 1983-84 (1). ... Total hat tricks: 11.

Season Team	League	REGULAR SEASON								PLAYOFFS				
		Gms.	G	A	Pts.	PIM	+/-	PP	SH	Gms.	G	A	Pts.	PIM
80-81—Sault Ste. Marie	OMJHL	64	26	43	69	33	...	...	...	19	7	8	15	34
81-82—Sault Ste. Marie	OHL	25	18	30	48	46	...	...	...	—	—	—	—	—
—Hartford	NHL	59	25	43	68	51	-13	12	0	—	—	—	—	—
82-83—Hartford	NHL	79	31	59	90	60	-25	4	2	—	—	—	—	—
83-84—Hartford	NHL	72	23	60	83	45	-10	5	0	—	—	—	—	—
84-85—Hartford	NHL	80	24	57	81	66	-23	4	0	—	—	—	—	—
85-86—Hartford	NHL	53	24	53	77	24	8	7	1	10	1	2	3	4
86-87—Hartford	NHL	75	30	63	93	45	10	7	0	6	2	2	4	6
87-88—Hartford	NHL	80	25	50	75	87	-8	11	1	6	2	5	7	2
88-89—Hartford	NHL	69	29	48	77	36	4	8	0	4	0	2	2	0
89-90—Hartford	NHL	80	32	69	101	73	13	15	1	7	3	3	6	8

F

Season Team	League	REGULAR SEASON								PLAYOFFS				
		Gms.	G	A	Pts.	PIM	+/-	PP	SH	Gms.	G	A	Pts.	PIM
90-91—Hartford	NHL	67	21	55	76	51	-2	10	1	—	—	—	—	—
—Pittsburgh	NHL	14	2	9	11	21	0	0	0	24	7	10	17	24
91-92—Pittsburgh	NHL	70	21	33	54	30	-7	5	1	21	8	*19	27	6
92-93—Pittsburgh	NHL	84	24	76	100	68	6	9	2	12	6	11	17	19
93-94—Pittsburgh	NHL	82	27	66	93	62	-3	8	0	6	0	2	2	6
94-95—Pittsburgh	NHL	44	11	*48	59	18	*30	3	0	12	6	13	19	4
95-96—Pittsburgh	NHL	77	27	92	119	56	25	12	1	11	3	6	9	4
96-97—Pittsburgh	NHL	81	27	63	90	20	7	10	1	5	1	2	3	2
97-98—Pittsburgh	NHL	81	25	62	87	20	12	7	0	6	1	5	6	2
98-99—Carolina	NHL	82	21	31	52	34	-2	8	0	3	0	1	1	0
99-00—Carolina	NHL	78	23	50	73	18	10	7	0	—	—	—	—	—
NHL Totals (19 years)		1407	472	1087	1559	885	32	152	11	133	40	83	123	87

FREADRICH, KYLE   LW   LIGHTNING

PERSONAL: Born December 28, 1978, in Edmonton. ... 6-5/231. ... Shoots left. ... Name pronounced FREED-rihk.

TRANSACTIONS/CAREER NOTES: Selected by Vancouver Canucks in third round (fourth Canucks pick, 64th overall) of NHL entry draft (June 21, 1997). ... Signed as free agent by Tampa Bay Lightning (July 16, 1999). ... Suffered back spasms (March 3, 2000); missed three games.

Season Team	League	REGULAR SEASON								PLAYOFFS				
		Gms.	G	A	Pts.	PIM	+/-	PP	SH	Gms.	G	A	Pts.	PIM
96-97—Prince George	WHL	12	0	0	0	12	...	...	...	—	—	—	—	—
—Regina	WHL	50	1	3	4	152	...	...	...	4	0	0	0	8
97-98—Regina	WHL	62	6	5	11	259	...	...	...	9	0	1	1	25
98-99—Regina	WHL	52	2	2	4	215	...	...	...	—	—	—	—	—
—Syracuse	AHL	5	0	0	0	20	...	...	...	—	—	—	—	—
—Louisiana	ECHL	5	0	0	0	17	...	...	...	4	0	0	0	2
99-00—Detroit	IHL	45	0	1	1	203	...	...	...	—	—	—	—	—
—Louisiana	ECHL	3	0	0	0	17	...	...	...	—	—	—	—	—
—Tampa Bay	NHL	10	0	0	0	39	-1	0	0	—	—	—	—	—
NHL Totals (1 year)		10	0	0	0	39	-1	0	0					

FRIESEN, JEFF   LW   SHARKS

PERSONAL: Born August 5, 1976, in Meadow Lake, Sask. ... 6-0/205. ... Shoots left. ... Name pronounced FREE-sihn.

HIGH SCHOOL: Robert Usher (Regina, Sask.).

TRANSACTIONS/CAREER NOTES: Selected by San Jose Sharks in first round (first Sharks pick, 11th overall) of NHL entry draft (June 28, 1994). ... Injured hand (October 18, 1996); missed two games. ... Missed first two games of 1997-98 season due to contract dispute. ... Injured shoulder (December 26, 1998); missed two games.

HONORS: Won Can.HL Rookie of the Year Award (1992-93). ... Won Jim Piggott Memorial Trophy (1992-93). ... Named to NHL All-Rookie team (1994-95).

MISCELLANEOUS: Holds San Jose Sharks all-time records for most games played (448), most assists (177) and most points (314). ... Shares San Jose Sharks all-time record for most goals (137). ... Scored on a penalty shot (vs. Jim Carey, December 2, 1995). ... Failed to score on a penalty shot (vs. Roman Turek, December 30, 1999).

STATISTICAL PLATEAUS: Three-goal games: 1995-96 (1), 1999-00 (1). Total: 2.

Season Team	League	REGULAR SEASON								PLAYOFFS				
		Gms.	G	A	Pts.	PIM	+/-	PP	SH	Gms.	G	A	Pts.	PIM
91-92—Regina	WHL	4	3	1	4	2	...	...	...	—	—	—	—	—
92-93—Regina	WHL	70	45	38	83	23	...	...	...	13	7	10	17	8
93-94—Regina	WHL	66	51	67	118	48	...	...	...	4	3	2	5	2
94-95—Regina	WHL	25	21	23	44	22	...	...	...	—	—	—	—	—
—San Jose	NHL	48	15	10	25	14	-8	5	1	11	1	5	6	4
95-96—San Jose	NHL	79	15	31	46	42	-19	2	0	—	—	—	—	—
96-97—San Jose	NHL	82	28	34	62	75	-8	6	2	—	—	—	—	—
97-98—San Jose	NHL	79	31	32	63	40	8	7	†6	6	0	1	1	2
98-99—San Jose	NHL	78	22	35	57	42	3	10	1	6	2	2	4	14
99-00—San Jose	NHL	82	26	35	61	47	-2	11	3	11	2	2	4	10
NHL Totals (6 years)		448	137	177	314	260	-26	41	13	34	5	10	15	30

FUHR, GRANT   G

PERSONAL: Born September 28, 1962, in Spruce Grove, Alta. ... 5-10/201. ... Catches right. ... Name pronounced FYOOR.

TRANSACTIONS/CAREER NOTES: Selected by Edmonton Oilers in first round (first Oilers pick, eighth overall) of NHL entry draft (June 10, 1981). ... Suffered partial separation of right shoulder (December 1981). ... Strained left knee ligaments (December 13, 1983) and underwent surgery. ... Separated shoulder (February 1985). ... Bruised left shoulder (November 3, 1985); missed 10 games. ... Bruised left shoulder (November 1987). ... Injured right knee (November 1987). ... Suffered cervical neck strain (January 18, 1989). ... Underwent appendectomy (September 14, 1989); missed first six games of season. ... Underwent reconstructive surgery to left shoulder (December 27, 1989). ... Tore adhesions in left shoulder (March 13, 1990). ... Suspended six months by NHL for admitting to using drugs earlier in career (September 27, 1990). ... Traded by Oilers with RW/LW Glenn Anderson and LW Craig Berube to Toronto Maple Leafs for LW Vincent Damphousse, D Luke Richardson, G Peter Ing, C Scott Thornton and future considerations (September 19, 1991). ... Sprained thumb (October 17, 1991); missed two games. ... Pulled groin (November 12, 1991); missed three games. ... Sprained knee (February 11, 1992); missed four games. ... Sprained knee (October 20, 1992); missed 10 games. ... Strained shoulder (December 5, 1992); missed three games. ... Bruised shoulder muscle (January 17, 1993); missed four games. ... Traded by Maple Leafs with fifth-round pick (D Kevin Popp) in 1995 draft to Buffalo Sabres for LW Dave Andreychuk, G Daren Puppa and first-round pick (D Kenny Jonsson) in 1993 draft (February 2, 1993). ... Injured knee (November 24, 1993); missed 24 games. ... Traded by Sabres with D Philippe Boucher and D Denis Tsygurov to Los Angeles Kings for D Alexei Zhitnik, D

Charlie Huddy, G Robb Stauber and fifth-round pick (D Marian Menhart) in 1995 draft (February 14, 1995). ... Signed as free agent by St. Louis Blues (July 11, 1995). ... Injured knee (March 31, 1996); missed three games. ... Underwent knee surgery due to injury suffered in playoffs (April 27, 1996); missed remainder of playoffs. ... Suffered sore arm (November 6, 1997); missed two games. ... Strained ligament and tore cartilage in right knee (February 26, 1998); missed eight games. ... Bruised knee (April 12, 1998); missed one game. ... Strained right knee (October 16, 1998); missed two games. ... Strained groin (November 7, 1998); missed 11 games. ... Underwent arthroscopic knee surgery (February 6, 1999); missed 16 games. ... Traded by Blues to Calgary Flames for third-round pick (C Justin Papineau) in 2000 draft (September 5, 1999). ... Injured knee (December 20, 1999); missed 16 games. ... Reinjured knee (February 2, 2000); missed nine games.

HONORS: Won Stewart (Butch) Paul Memorial Trophy (1979-80). ... Named to WHL All-Star first team (1979-80 and 1980-81). ... Won WHL Top Goaltender Trophy (1980-81). ... Named to THE SPORTING NEWS All-Star second team (1981-82 and 1985-86). ... Named to NHL All-Star second team (1981-82). ... Played in NHL All-Star Game (1982, 1984-1986, 1988 and 1989). ... Named All-Star Game Most Valuable Player (1986). ... Won Vezina Trophy (1987-88). ... Named to THE SPORTING NEWS All-Star first team (1987-88). ... Named to NHL All-Star first team (1987-88). ... Shared William M. Jennings Trophy with Dominik Hasek (1993-94).

RECORDS: Holds NHL single-season records for most points by a goaltender—14 (1983-84); most games by a goaltender—79 (1995-96); and most consecutive appearances—76 (1995-96). ... Shares NHL single-season playoff record for most wins by a goaltender—16 (1987-88).

MISCELLANEOUS: Member of Stanley Cup championship teams (1984, 1985, 1987, 1988 and 1990). ... Holds Edmonton Oilers all-time record for most wins (226). ... Stopped penalty shot attempt (vs. Ron Duguay, January 9, 1984; vs. Brent Peterson, January 13, 1984; vs. Ron Sutter, May 28, 1985 (playoffs); vs. Dave Poulin, May 30, 1985 (playoffs); vs. Brendan Shanahan, December 27, 1992; vs. Dave Hannan, October 22, 1995; vs. Peter Forsberg, December 6, 1996). ... Allowed penalty shot goal (vs. Steve Yzerman, January 3, 1992; vs. Alexei Gusarov, March 10, 1993).

			REGULAR SEASON								PLAYOFFS					
Season Team	League	Gms.	Min	W	L	T	GA	SO	Avg.	Gms.	Min.	W	L	GA	SO	Avg.
79-80—Victoria	WHL	43	2488	30	12	0	130	2	3.14	8	465	5	3	22	0	2.84
80-81—Victoria	WHL	59	*3448	48	9	1	160	†4	*2.78	15	899	12	3	45	1	3.00
81-82—Edmonton	NHL	48	2847	28	5	14	157	0	3.31	5	309	2	3	26	0	5.05
82-83—Moncton	AHL	10	604	4	5	1	40	0	3.97	—	—	—	—	—	—	—
—Edmonton	NHL	32	1803	13	12	5	129	0	4.29	1	11	0	0	0	0	...
83-84—Edmonton	NHL	45	2625	30	10	4	171	1	3.91	16	883	11	4	44	1	2.99
84-85—Edmonton	NHL	46	2559	26	8	7	165	1	3.87	†18	*1064	*15	3	55	0	3.10
85-86—Edmonton	NHL	40	2184	29	8	0	143	0	3.93	9	541	5	4	28	0	3.11
86-87—Edmonton	NHL	44	2388	22	13	3	137	0	3.44	19	1148	14	5	47	0	2.46
87-88—Edmonton	NHL	*75	*4304	40	24	9	*246	†4	3.43	*19	*1136	*16	2	55	0	2.90
88-89—Edmonton	NHL	59	3341	23	26	6	213	1	3.83	7	417	3	4	24	1	3.45
89-90—Cape Breton	AHL	2	120	2	0	0	6	0	3.00	—	—	—	—	—	—	—
—Edmonton	NHL	21	1081	9	7	3	70	1	3.89	—	—	—	—	—	—	—
90-91—Cape Breton	AHL	4	240	2	2	0	17	0	4.25	—	—	—	—	—	—	—
—Edmonton	NHL	13	778	6	4	3	39	1	3.01	17	1019	8	7	51	0	3.00
91-92—Toronto	NHL	66	3774	25	*33	5	*230	2	3.66	—	—	—	—	—	—	—
92-93—Toronto	NHL	29	1665	13	9	4	87	1	3.14	—	—	—	—	—	—	—
—Buffalo	NHL	29	1694	11	15	2	98	0	3.47	8	474	3	4	27	1	3.42
93-94—Buffalo	NHL	32	1726	13	12	3	106	2	3.68	—	—	—	—	—	—	—
—Rochester	AHL	5	310	3	0	2	10	0	1.94	—	—	—	—	—	—	—
94-95—Buffalo	NHL	3	180	1	2	0	12	0	4.00	—	—	—	—	—	—	—
—Los Angeles	NHL	14	698	1	7	3	47	0	4.04	—	—	—	—	—	—	—
95-96—St. Louis	NHL	*79	4365	30	28	*16	*209	3	2.87	2	69	1	0	1	0	0.87
96-97—St. Louis	NHL	73	4261	33	27	11	193	3	2.72	6	357	2	4	13	2	2.18
97-98—St. Louis	NHL	58	3274	29	21	6	138	3	2.53	10	616	6	4	28	0	2.73
98-99—St. Louis	NHL	39	2193	16	11	8	89	2	2.44	13	790	6	6	31	1	2.35
99-00—Calgary	NHL	23	1205	5	13	2	77	0	3.83	—	—	—	—	—	—	—
—Saint John	AHL	2	99	0	2	0	10	0	6.06	—	—	—	—	—	—	—
NHL Totals (19 years)		868	48945	403	295	114	2756	25	3.38	150	8834	92	50	430	6	2.92

GAGNE, SIMON   C   FLYERS

PERSONAL: Born February 29, 1980, in Ste. Foy, Que. ... 6-0/175. ... Shoots left.

TRANSACTIONS/CAREER NOTES: Selected by Philadelphia Flyers in first round (first Flyers pick, 22nd overall) of NHL entry draft (June 27, 1998). ... Suffered from the flu (January 2, 2000); missed one game. ... Suffered from the flu (March 23, 2000); missed one game.

HONORS: Named to QMJHL All-Star second team (1998-99). ... Named to NHL All-Rookie team (1999-2000).

			REGULAR SEASON						PLAYOFFS				
Season Team	League	Gms.	G	A	Pts.	PIM	+/-	PP	SH	Gms.	G	A	Pts.	PIM
96-97—Beauport	QMJHL	51	9	22	31	39	...	...	...	—	—	—	—	—
97-98—Quebec	QMJHL	53	30	39	69	26	...	...	...	12	11	5	16	23
98-99—Quebec	QMJHL	61	50	70	120	42	...	...	...	13	9	8	17	4
99-00—Philadelphia	NHL	80	20	28	48	22	11	8	1	17	5	5	10	2
NHL Totals (1 year)		80	20	28	48	22	11	8	1	17	5	5	10	2

F
G

GALANOV, MAXIM   D

PERSONAL: Born March 13, 1974, in Krasnoyarsk, U.S.S.R. ... 6-1/210. ... Shoots left. ... Name pronounced guh-LAH-nahf.

TRANSACTIONS/CAREER NOTES: Selected by New York Rangers in third round (third Rangers pick, 61st overall) of NHL entry draft (June 26, 1993). ... Selected by Pittsburgh Penguins from Rangers in NHL waiver draft (October 5, 1998). ... Injured shoulder (January 26, 1999); missed seven games. ... Separated shoulder (March 13, 1999); missed 17 games. ... Selected by Atlanta Thrashers in NHL expansion draft (June 25, 1999). ... Injured wrist prior to start of 1999-2000 season and underwent surgery; missed first 36 games of season. ... Bruised foot (February 15, 2000); missed one game.

Season Team	League	REGULAR SEASON								PLAYOFFS				
		Gms.	G	A	Pts.	PIM	+/-	PP	SH	Gms.	G	A	Pts.	PIM
92-93—Lada Togliatti	CIS	41	4	2	6	12	...	...	...	10	1	1	2	12
93-94—Lada Togliatti	CIS	7	1	0	1	4	...	...	...	12	1	0	1	8
94-95—Lada Togliatti	CIS	45	5	6	11	54	...	...	...	9	0	1	1	12
95-96—Binghamton	AHL	72	17	36	53	24	...	...	...	4	1	1	2	0
96-97—Binghamton	AHL	73	13	30	43	30	...	...	...	3	0	0	0	2
97-98—Hartford	AHL	61	6	24	30	22	...	...	...	13	3	6	9	2
—New York Rangers	NHL	6	0	1	1	2	1	0	0	—	—	—	—	—
98-99—Pittsburgh	NHL	51	4	3	7	14	-8	2	0	1	0	0	0	0
99-00—Atlanta	NHL	40	4	3	7	20	-12	0	0	—	—	—	—	—
NHL Totals (3 years)		97	8	7	15	36	-19	2	0	1	0	0	0	0

GALLEY, GARRY   D

PERSONAL: Born April 16, 1963, in Ottawa. ... 6-0/207. ... Shoots left.

COLLEGE: Bowling Green State.

TRANSACTIONS/CAREER NOTES: Selected by Los Angeles Kings in fifth round (fourth Kings pick, 100th overall) of NHL entry draft (June 8, 1983). ... Injured knee (December 8, 1985). ... Traded by Kings to Washington Capitals for G Al Jensen (February 14, 1987). ... Signed as free agent by Boston Bruins; third-round pick in 1989 draft awarded to Capitals as compensation (July 8, 1988). ... Sprained left shoulder (September 30, 1989); missed first nine games of season. ... Suffered lacerations to cheek, both lips and part of neck (October 6, 1990). ... Dislocated right shoulder (December 22, 1990). ... Bruised left kneecap (March 23, 1991); missed two games. ... Pulled hamstring (April 17, 1991); missed three playoff games. ... Traded by Bruins with C Wes Walz and third-round pick (D Milos Holan) in 1993 draft to Philadelphia Flyers for D Gord Murphy, RW Brian Dobbin, third-round pick (LW Sergei Zholtok) in 1992 draft and fourth-round pick (D Charles Paquette) in 1993 draft (January 2, 1992). ... Bruised ribs (January 9, 1992); missed one game. ... Fractured foot (March 3, 1992); missed two games. ... Bruised jaw (February 24, 1993); missed one game. ... Strained shoulder (March 6, 1994); missed three games. ... Sprained wrist (February 13, 1995); missed three games. ... Traded by Flyers to Buffalo Sabres for D Petr Svoboda (April 7, 1995). ... Injured shoulder (November 12, 1995); missed three games. ... Injured knee (February 14, 1996); missed one game. ... Strained right shoulder (November 7, 1996); missed four games. ... Suffered concussion (December 4, 1996); missed two games. ... Tore abdominal muscle (February 9, 1997); missed one game. ... Fractured jaw (February 23, 1997); missed two games. ... Signed as free agent by Kings (July 5, 1997). ... Bruised left knee (February 24, 1998); missed three games. ... Strained abdominal muscle (April 5, 1999); missed six games. ... Suffered concussion (December 19, 1999); missed nine games.

HONORS: Named to CCHA All-Star first team (1982-83 and 1983-84). ... Named to NCAA All-Tournament team (1983-84). ... Played in NHL All-Star Game (1991 and 1994).

Season Team	League	REGULAR SEASON								PLAYOFFS				
		Gms.	G	A	Pts.	PIM	+/-	PP	SH	Gms.	G	A	Pts.	PIM
81-82—Bowling Green	CCHA	42	3	36	39	48	...	...	...	—	—	—	—	—
82-83—Bowling Green	CCHA	40	17	29	46	40	...	...	...	—	—	—	—	—
83-84—Bowling Green	CCHA	44	15	52	67	61	...	...	...	—	—	—	—	—
84-85—Los Angeles	NHL	78	8	30	38	82	3	1	1	3	1	0	1	2
85-86—Los Angeles	NHL	49	9	13	22	46	-9	1	0	—	—	—	—	—
—New Haven	AHL	4	2	6	8	6	...	...	...	—	—	—	—	—
86-87—Los Angeles	NHL	30	5	11	16	57	-9	2	0	—	—	—	—	—
—Washington	NHL	18	1	10	11	10	3	1	0	2	0	0	0	0
87-88—Washington	NHL	58	7	23	30	44	11	3	0	13	2	4	6	13
88-89—Boston	NHL	78	8	21	29	80	-7	2	1	9	0	1	1	33
89-90—Boston	NHL	71	8	27	35	75	2	1	0	21	3	3	6	34
90-91—Boston	NHL	70	6	21	27	84	0	1	0	16	1	5	6	17
91-92—Boston	NHL	38	2	12	14	83	-3	1	0	—	—	—	—	—
—Philadelphia	NHL	39	3	15	18	34	1	2	0	—	—	—	—	—
92-93—Philadelphia	NHL	83	13	49	62	115	18	4	1	—	—	—	—	—
93-94—Philadelphia	NHL	81	10	60	70	91	-11	5	1	—	—	—	—	—
94-95—Philadelphia	NHL	33	2	20	22	20	0	1	0	—	—	—	—	—
—Buffalo	NHL	14	1	9	10	10	4	1	0	5	0	3	3	4
95-96—Buffalo	NHL	78	10	44	54	81	-2	7	1	—	—	—	—	—
96-97—Buffalo	NHL	71	4	34	38	102	10	1	1	12	0	6	6	14
97-98—Los Angeles	NHL	74	9	28	37	63	-5	7	0	4	0	1	1	2
98-99—Los Angeles	NHL	60	4	12	16	30	-9	3	0	—	—	—	—	—
99-00—Los Angeles	NHL	70	9	21	30	52	9	2	0	4	0	0	0	0
NHL Totals (16 years)		1093	119	460	579	1159	6	46	6	89	7	23	30	119

G

GARDINER, BRUCE   C   BLUE JACKETS

PERSONAL: Born February 11, 1972, in North York, Ont. ... 6-1/193. ... Shoots right.

COLLEGE: Colgate.

TRANSACTIONS/CAREER NOTES: Selected by St. Louis Blues in sixth round (sixth Blues pick, 131st overall) of NHL entry draft (June 22, 1991). ... Signed as free agent by Ottawa Senators (June 14, 1994). ... Fractured leg (September 23, 1995). ... Bruised left foot (November 27, 1996); missed two games. ... Separated left shoulder (February 1, 1997); missed 10 games. ... Bruised thigh (November 6, 1997); missed two games. ... Bruised thigh (November 15, 1997); missed three games. ... Tore medial collateral ligament in knee (December 13, 1997); missed 21 games. ... Sprained thumb (October 23, 1998); missed six games. ... Bruised foot (January 1, 1999); missed one game. ... Reinjured foot (January 30, 1999); missed two games. ... Reinjured foot (February 6, 1999); missed seven games. ... Reinjured foot (March 6, 1999); missed seven games. ... Sprained medial collateral ligament in left knee (October 14, 1999); missed three games. ... Traded by Senators to Tampa Bay Lightning for LW Colin Forbes (November 11, 1999). ... Sprained knee (November 17, 1999); missed 13 games. ... Injured abdomen (February 27, 2000); missed four games. ... Selected by Columbus Blue Jackets in NHL expansion draft (June 23, 2000).

HONORS: Named to ECAC All-Star second team (1993-94).

Season Team	League	Gms.	G	A	Pts.	PIM	+/-	PP	SH	Gms.	G	A	Pts.	PIM
90-91—Colgate University.......	ECAC	27	4	9	13	72	...	...	...	—	—	—	—	—
91-92—Colgate University.......	ECAC	23	7	8	15	77	...	...	...	—	—	—	—	—
92-93—Colgate University.......	ECAC	33	17	12	29	64	...	...	...	—	—	—	—	—
93-94—Colgate University.......	ECAC	33	23	23	46	68	...	...	...	—	—	—	—	—
—Peoria	IHL	3	0	0	0	0	...	...	...	—	—	—	—	—
94-95—Prin. Edward Island	AHL	72	17	20	37	132	...	...	...	7	4	1	5	4
95-96—Prin. Edward Island	AHL	38	11	13	24	87	...	...	...	5	2	4	6	4
96-97—Ottawa	NHL	67	11	10	21	49	4	0	1	7	0	1	1	2
97-98—Ottawa	NHL	55	7	11	18	50	2	0	0	11	1	3	4	2
98-99—Ottawa	NHL	59	4	8	12	43	6	0	0	3	0	0	0	4
99-00—Ottawa	NHL	10	0	3	3	4	1	0	0	—	—	—	—	—
—Tampa Bay	NHL	41	3	6	9	37	-21	0	0	—	—	—	—	—
NHL Totals (4 years)...........		**232**	**25**	**38**	**63**	**183**	**-8**	**0**	**1**	**21**	**1**	**4**	**5**	**8**

GARDNER, GREG   G   BLUE JACKETS

PERSONAL: Born November 21, 1975, in Mississuaga, Ont. ... 6-0/190. ... Catches left.
COLLEGE: Niagara.
TRANSACTIONS/CAREER NOTES: Signed as non-drafted free agent by Columbus Blue Jackets (May 4, 2000).

			REGULAR SEASON							PLAYOFFS					
Season Team	League	Gms.	Min	W	L	T	GA	SO	Avg.	Gms.	Min.	W	L	GA	SO	Avg.
96-97—Niagara.........................	Indep.	17	939	8	5	2	54	0	3.45	—	—	—	—	—	—	—
97-98—Niagara.........................	Indep.	25	1454	12	10	3	74	0	3.05	—	—	—	—	—	—	—
98-99—Niagara.........................	Indep.	30	1742	15	10	3	78	4	2.69	—	—	—	—	—	—	—
99-00—Niagara.........................	Indep.	*41	*2503	*29	8	*4	64	*12	*1.53	—	—	—	—	—	—	—

GARNER, TYRONE   G   FLAMES

PERSONAL: Born July 27, 1978, in Stoney Creek, Ont. ... 6-1/200. ... Catches left.
TRANSACTIONS/CAREER NOTES: Selected by New York Islanders in fourth round (fourth Islanders pick, 83rd overall) of NHL entry draft (June 22, 1996). ... Traded by Islanders with LW Marty McInnis and sixth-round pick (D Ilja Demidov) in 1997 draft to Calgary Flames for C Robert Reichel (March 18, 1997).
HONORS: Named to OHL All-Star second team (1998-99).

			REGULAR SEASON							PLAYOFFS					
Season Team	League	Gms.	Min	W	L	T	GA	SO	Avg.	Gms.	Min.	W	L	GA	SO	Avg.
95-96—Oshawa	OHL	32	1697	11	15	4	112	0	3.96	—	—	—	—	—	—	—
96-97—Oshawa	OHL	9	434	6	1	0	20	0	2.76	3	88	1	0	6	0	4.09
97-98—Oshawa	OHL	54	2946	23	17	*8	162	1	3.30	7	450	3	4	25	0	3.33
98-99—Oshawa	OHL	44	2496	24	15	3	124	4	2.98	17	1021	9	8	70	0	4.11
—Calgary	NHL	3	139	0	2	0	12	0	5.18	—	—	—	—	—	—	—
99-00—Saint John..................	AHL	19	940	4	8	4	70	0	4.47	—	—	—	—	—	—	—
—Dayton	ECHL	3	113	0	2	0	11	0	5.84	—	—	—	—	—	—	—
—Johnstown	ECHL	17	971	8	6	‡3	48	0	2.97	1	59	0	1	2	0	2.03
NHL Totals (1 year)..............		**3**	**139**	**0**	**2**	**0**	**12**	**0**	**5.18**							

GARON, MATHIEU   G   CANADIENS

PERSONAL: Born January 9, 1978, in Chandler, Que. ... 6-2/182. ... Catches right.
TRANSACTIONS/CAREER NOTES: Selected by Montreal Canadiens in second round (second Canadiens pick, 44th overall) of NHL entry draft (June 22, 1996).
HONORS: Won Raymond Lagace Trophy (1995-96). ... Named to QMJHL All-Rookie team (1995-96). ... Named to Can.HL All-Star first team (1997-98). ... Won Jacques Plante Trophy (1997-98). ... Named to QMJHL All-Star first team (1997-98). ... Won Can.HL Goaltender of the Year Award (1997-98).

			REGULAR SEASON							PLAYOFFS					
Season Team	League	Gms.	Min	W	L	T	GA	SO	Avg.	Gms.	Min.	W	L	GA	SO	Avg.
95-96—Victoriaville	QMJHL	51	2709	18	27	0	189	1	4.19	12	676	7	4	38	1	3.37
96-97—Victoriaville	QMJHL	53	3026	29	18	3	148	*6	2.93	6	330	2	4	23	0	4.18
97-98—Victoriaville	QMJHL	47	2802	27	18	2	125	5	2.68	6	345	2	4	22	0	3.83
98-99—Fredericton	AHL	40	2222	14	22	2	114	3	3.08	6	208	1	1	12	0	3.46
99-00—Quebec.........................	AHL	53	2884	17	28	3	149	2	3.10	1	20	0	0	3	0	9.00

GARPENLOV, JOHAN   LW

PERSONAL: Born March 21, 1968, in Stockholm, Sweden. ... 6-0/186. ... Shoots left. ... Name pronounced YO-hahn GAHR-pihn-lahf.
TRANSACTIONS/CAREER NOTES: Selected by Detroit Red Wings in fifth round (fifth Red Wings pick, 85th overall) of NHL entry draft (June 9, 1984). ... Traded by Red Wings to San Jose Sharks for D Bob McGill and eighth-round pick (G C.J. Denomme) in 1992 draft (March 10, 1992). ... Strained back (October 20, 1992); missed three games. ... Suffered from the flu (March 25, 1993); missed one game. ... Injured thigh (October 10, 1993); missed one game. ... Sprained groin (January 30, 1995); missed six games. ... Traded by Sharks to Florida Panthers for fifth-round pick (traded back to Florida) in 1998 draft (March 3, 1995). ... Sprained knee ligament (November 18, 1996); missed 13 games. ... Sprained knee ligament (February 22, 1997); missed 16 games. ... Strained groin (December 5, 1997); missed 10 games. ... Selected by Atlanta Thrashers in NHL expansion draft (June 25, 1999). ... Injured wrist (January 1, 2000); missed seven games.
STATISTICAL PLATEAUS: Three-goal games: 1990-91 (1), 1992-93 (1), 1995-96 (1). Total: 3. ... Four-goal games: 1990-91 (1). ... Total hat tricks: 4.

G

Season Team	League	Gms.	G	A	Pts.	PIM	+/-	PP	SH		Gms.	G	A	Pts.	PIM
REGULAR SEASON											**PLAYOFFS**				
86-87—Djurgarden Stockholm	Sweden	29	5	8	13	20	...	...	...		—	—	—	—	—
87-88—Djurgarden Stockholm	Sweden	30	7	10	17	12	...	...	...		—	—	—	—	—
88-89—Djurgarden Stockholm	Sweden	36	12	19	31	20	...	...	...		—	—	—	—	—
89-90—Djurgarden Stockholm	Sweden	39	20	13	33	36	...	...	...		8	2	4	6	4
90-91—Detroit	NHL	71	18	22	40	18	-4	2	0		6	0	1	1	4
91-92—Detroit	NHL	16	1	1	2	4	2	0	0		—	—	—	—	—
—Adirondack	AHL	9	3	3	6	6	...	...	...		—	—	—	—	—
—San Jose	NHL	12	5	6	11	4	-2	1	0		—	—	—	—	—
92-93—San Jose	NHL	79	22	44	66	56	-26	14	0		—	—	—	—	—
93-94—San Jose	NHL	80	18	35	53	28	9	7	0		14	4	6	10	6
94-95—San Jose	NHL	13	1	1	2	2	-3	0	0		—	—	—	—	—
—Florida	NHL	27	3	9	12	0	4	0	0		—	—	—	—	—
95-96—Florida	NHL	82	23	28	51	36	-10	8	0		20	4	2	6	8
96-97—Florida	NHL	53	11	25	36	47	10	1	0		4	2	0	2	4
97-98—Florida	NHL	39	2	3	5	8	-6	0	0		—	—	—	—	—
98-99—Florida	NHL	64	8	9	17	42	-9	0	1		—	—	—	—	—
99-00—Atlanta	NHL	73	2	14	16	31	-30	0	0		—	—	—	—	—
NHL Totals (10 years)		609	114	197	311	276	-65	33	1		44	10	9	19	22

GAUTHIER, DENIS   D   FLAMES

PERSONAL: Born October 1, 1976, in Montreal. ... 6-2/210. ... Shoots left. ... Full Name: Denis Gauthier Jr.. ... Name pronounced GO-tee-ay.
TRANSACTIONS/CAREER NOTES: Selected by Calgary Flames in first round (first Flames pick, 20th overall) of NHL entry draft (July 8, 1995). ... Suffered concussion (September 27, 1997); missed two games. ... Suffered concussion (January 10, 1999); missed two games. ... Injured groin (March 25, 1999); missed two games. ... Injured shoulder (October 26, 1999); missed 11 games. ... Suspended two games by NHL for elbowing incident (December 7, 1999). ... Suffered hip pointer (February 1, 2000); missed remainder of season.
HONORS: Named to Can.HL All-Star first team (1995-96). ... Won Emile Bouchard Trophy (1995-96). ... Named to QMJHL All-Star first team (1995-96).

Season Team	League	Gms.	G	A	Pts.	PIM	+/-	PP	SH		Gms.	G	A	Pts.	PIM
REGULAR SEASON											**PLAYOFFS**				
92-93—Drummondville	QMJHL	61	1	7	8	136	...	...	...		10	0	5	5	40
93-94—Drummondville	QMJHL	60	0	7	7	176	...	...	...		9	2	0	2	41
94-95—Drummondville	QMJHL	64	9	31	40	190	...	...	...		4	0	5	5	12
95-96—Drummondville	QMJHL	53	25	49	74	140	...	...	...		6	4	4	8	32
—Saint John	AHL	5	2	0	2	8	...	...	...		16	1	6	7	20
96-97—Saint John	AHL	73	3	28	31	74	...	...	...		5	0	0	0	6
97-98—Calgary	NHL	10	0	0	0	16	-5	0	0		—	—	—	—	—
—Saint John	AHL	68	4	20	24	154	...	...	...		21	0	4	4	83
98-99—Saint John	AHL	16	0	3	3	31	...	...	...		—	—	—	—	—
—Calgary	NHL	55	3	4	7	68	3	0	0		—	—	—	—	—
99-00—Calgary	NHL	39	1	1	2	50	-4	0	0		—	—	—	—	—
NHL Totals (3 years)		104	4	5	9	134	-6	0	0						

GAVEY, AARON   LW   WILD

PERSONAL: Born February 22, 1974, in Sudbury, Ont. ... 6-2/200. ... Shoots left. ... Name pronounced GAY-vee.
TRANSACTIONS/CAREER NOTES: Selected by Tampa Bay Lightning in fourth round (fourth Lightning pick, 74th overall) of NHL entry draft (June 20, 1992). ... Suffered facial laceration (February 4, 1996); missed eight games. ... Traded by Lightning to Calgary Flames for G Rick Tabaracci (November 19, 1996). ... Strained neck (February 28, 1997); missed 14 games. ... Strained abdominal muscle (January 11, 1997); missed 37 games. ... Sprained thumb (April 15, 1998); missed two games. ... Traded by Flames to Dallas Stars for C Bob Bassen (July 14, 1998). ... Fractured hand (September 22, 1998); missed first three games of 1998-99 season. ... Sprained knee (February 2, 2000); missed one game. ... Traded by Stars with C Pavel Patera, eighth-round pick (C Eric Johansson) in 2000 draft and fourth-round pick in 2002 draft to Minnesota Wild for D Brad Lukowich, third- and ninth-round picks in 2001 draft (June 25, 2000).

Season Team	League	Gms.	G	A	Pts.	PIM	+/-	PP	SH		Gms.	G	A	Pts.	PIM
REGULAR SEASON											**PLAYOFFS**				
90-91—Peterborough Jr. B	OHA	42	26	30	56	68	...	...	...		—	—	—	—	—
91-92—Sault Ste. Marie	OHL	48	7	11	18	27	...	...	...		19	5	1	6	10
92-93—Sault Ste. Marie	OHL	62	45	39	84	114	...	...	...		18	5	9	14	36
93-94—Sault Ste. Marie	OHL	60	42	60	102	116	...	...	...		14	11	10	21	22
94-95—Atlanta	IHL	66	18	17	35	85	...	...	...		5	0	1	1	9
95-96—Tampa Bay	NHL	73	8	4	12	56	-6	1	1		6	0	0	0	4
96-97—Tampa Bay	NHL	16	1	2	3	12	-1	0	0		—	—	—	—	—
—Calgary	NHL	41	7	9	16	34	-11	3	0		—	—	—	—	—
97-98—Calgary	NHL	26	2	3	5	24	-5	0	0		—	—	—	—	—
—Saint John	AHL	8	4	3	7	28	...	...	...		—	—	—	—	—
98-99—Dallas	NHL	7	0	0	0	10	-1	0	0		—	—	—	—	—
—Michigan	IHL	67	24	33	57	128	...	...	...		5	2	3	5	4
99-00—Michigan	IHL	28	14	15	29	73	...	...	...		—	—	—	—	—
—Dallas	NHL	41	7	6	13	44	0	1	0		13	1	2	3	10
NHL Totals (5 years)		204	25	24	49	180	-24	5	1		19	1	2	3	14

GELINAS, MARTIN   LW   HURRICANES

PERSONAL: Born June 5, 1970, in Shawinigan, Que. ... 5-11/195. ... Shoots left. ... Name pronounced MAHR-tahn ZHEHL-ih-nuh.
HIGH SCHOOL: Polyvalente Val- Maurice (Shawinigan, Que.).

G

TRANSACTIONS/CAREER NOTES: Fractured left clavicle (November 1983). ... Suffered hairline fracture of clavicle (July 1986). ... Selected by Los Angeles Kings in first round (first Kings pick, seventh overall) of NHL entry draft (June 11, 1988). ... Traded by Kings with C Jimmy Carson, first-round picks in 1989 (traded to New Jersey), 1991 (LW Martin Rucinsky) and 1993 (D Nick Stajduhar) drafts and cash to Edmonton Oilers for C Wayne Gretzky, RW/D Marty McSorley and LW/C Mike Krushelnyski (August 9, 1988). ... Suspended five games by NHL (March 9, 1990). ... Underwent shoulder surgery (June 1990). ... Traded by Oilers with sixth-round pick (C Nicholas Checco) in 1993 draft to Quebec Nordiques for LW Scott Pearson (June 20, 1993). ... Injured thigh (October 20, 1993); missed one game. ... Separated left shoulder (November 25, 1993); missed 10 games. ... Claimed on waivers by Vancouver Canucks (January 15, 1994). ... Suffered charley horse (March 27, 1994); missed six games. ... Injured knee (April 30, 1995); missed last game of season and eight playoff games. ... Fractured rib (November 2, 1996); missed eight games. ... Sprained knee (October 13, 1997); missed 16 games. ... Traded by Canucks with G Kirk McLean to Carolina Hurricanes for LW Geoff Sanderson, D Enrico Ciccone and G Sean Burke (January 3, 1998). ... Strained quadriceps (October 27, 1998); missed two games. ... Bruised thigh (April 3, 1999); missed four games.

HONORS: Won Can.HL Rookie of the Year Award (1987-88). ... Won Michel Bergeron Trophy (1987-88). ... Named to QMJHL All-Star first team (1987-88).

MISCELLANEOUS: Member of Stanley Cup championship team (1990).

STATISTICAL PLATEAUS: Three-goal games: 1989-90 (1), 1996-97 (1). Total: 2. ... Four-goal games: 1996-97 (1). ... Total hat tricks: 3.

		REGULAR SEASON								PLAYOFFS				
Season Team	League	Gms.	G	A	Pts.	PIM	+/-	PP	SH	Gms.	G	A	Pts.	PIM
87-88—Hull	QMJHL	65	63	68	131	74	...	...	...	17	15	18	33	32
88-89—Edmonton	NHL	6	1	2	3	0	-1	0	0	—				
—Hull	QMJHL	41	38	39	77	31	...	...	...	9	5	4	9	14
89-90—Edmonton	NHL	46	17	8	25	30	0	5	0	20	2	3	5	6
90-91—Edmonton	NHL	73	20	20	40	34	-7	4	0	18	3	6	9	25
91-92—Edmonton	NHL	68	11	18	29	62	14	1	0	15	1	3	4	10
92-93—Edmonton	NHL	65	11	12	23	30	3	0	0	—				
93-94—Quebec	NHL	31	6	6	12	8	-2	0	0	—				
—Vancouver	NHL	33	8	8	16	26	-6	3	0	24	5	4	9	14
94-95—Vancouver	NHL	46	13	10	23	36	8	1	0	3	0	1	1	0
95-96—Vancouver	NHL	81	30	26	56	59	8	3	4	6	1	1	2	12
96-97—Vancouver	NHL	74	35	33	68	42	6	6	1	—				
97-98—Vancouver	NHL	24	4	4	8	10	-6	1	1	—				
—Carolina	NHL	40	12	14	26	30	1	2	1	—				
98-99—Carolina	NHL	76	13	15	28	67	3	0	0	6	0	3	3	2
99-00—Carolina	NHL	81	14	16	30	40	-10	3	0	—				
NHL Totals (12 years)		744	195	192	387	474	11	29	7	92	12	21	33	69

GIGUERE, JEAN-SEBASTIEN   G   MIGHTY DUCKS

PERSONAL: Born June 16, 1977, in Montreal. ... 6-0/185. ... Catches left. ... Name pronounced zhee-GAIR.

TRANSACTIONS/CAREER NOTES: Selected by Hartford Whalers in first round (first Whalers pick, 13th overall) of NHL entry draft (July 8, 1995). ... Whalers franchise moved to North Carolina and renamed Carolina Hurricanes for 1997-98 season; NHL approved move on June 25, 1997. ... Traded by Hurricanes with C Andrew Cassels to Calgary Flames for LW Gary Roberts and G Trevor Kidd (August 25, 1997). ... Strained hamstring (December 27, 1998); missed seven games. ... Traded by Flames to Mighty Ducks of Anaheim for second-round pick (traded to Washington) in 2000 draft (June 10, 2000).

HONORS: Named to QMJHL All-Star second team (1996-97). ... Shared Harry (Hap) Holmes Trophy with Tyler Moss (1997-98).

		REGULAR SEASON							PLAYOFFS					
Season Team	League	Gms.	Min	W	L	T	GA	SO	Avg.	Gms.	Min.	W	L	GA	SO	Avg.
93-94—Verdun	QMJHL	25	1234	13	5	2	66	0	3.21	—						
94-95—Halifax	QMJHL	47	2755	14	27	5	181	2	3.94	7	417	3	4	17	1	2.45
95-96—Verdun	QMJHL	55	3228	26	23	2	185	1	3.44	6	356	1	5	24	0	4.04
96-97—Halifax	QMJHL	50	3009	28	19	3	169	2	3.37	16	954	9	7	58	0	3.65
—Hartford	NHL	8	394	1	4	0	24	0	3.65	—						
97-98—Saint John	AHL	31	1758	16	10	3	72	2	2.46	10	537	5	3	27	0	3.02
98-99—Saint John	AHL	39	2145	18	16	3	123	3	3.44	7	304	3	2	21	0	4.14
—Calgary	NHL	15	860	6	7	1	46	0	3.21	—						
99-00—Saint John	AHL	41	2243	17	17	3	114	0	3.05	3	178	0	3	9	0	3.03
—Calgary	NHL	7	330	1	3	1	15	0	2.73	—						
NHL Totals (3 years)		30	1584	8	14	2	85	0	3.22							

GILCHRIST, BRENT   LW   RED WINGS

PERSONAL: Born April 3, 1967, in Moose Jaw, Sask. ... 5-11/180. ... Shoots left.

TRANSACTIONS/CAREER NOTES: Selected by Montreal Canadiens as underage junior in sixth round (sixth Canadiens pick, 79th overall) of NHL entry draft (June 15, 1985). ... Injured knee (January 1987). ... Fractured right index finger (November 17, 1990); missed 19 games. ... Separated left shoulder (February 6, 1991); missed two games. ... Reinjured left shoulder (February 13, 1991); missed five games. ... Traded by Canadiens with LW Shayne Corson and LW Vladimir Vujtek to Edmonton Oilers for LW Vincent Damphousse and fourth-round pick (D Adam Wiesel) in 1993 draft (August 27, 1992). ... Suffered concussion (October 1992); missed two games. ... Fractured nose (December 21, 1992); missed two games. ... Traded by Oilers to Minnesota North Stars for C Todd Elik (March 5, 1993). ... Separated shoulder (March 18, 1993); missed remainder of season. ... North Stars franchise moved from Minnesota to Dallas and renamed Stars for 1993-94 season. ... Strained shoulder (October 27, 1993); missed four games. ... Pulled groin (November 21, 1993); missed four games. ... Strained groin (February 20, 1995); missed two games. ... Strained groin and sprained wrist (February 26, 1995); missed 13 games. ... Suffered from sore wrist (April 11, 1995); missed one game. ... Injured groin (October 14, 1995); missed four games. ... Strained hip flexor (November 6, 1996); missed two games. ... Strained groin (December 21, 1996); missed three games. ... Strained groin (March 5, 1997); missed two games. ... Strained groin (March 16, 1997); missed seven games. ... Signed as free agent by Detroit Red Wings (July 8, 1997). ... Injured groin (March 4, 1998); missed 20 games. ... Selected by Tampa Bay Lightning from Red Wings in NHL waiver draft (October 5, 1998). ... Traded by Lightning to Red Wings for sixth-round pick (traded back to Detroit) in 1999 draft (October 5, 1998). ... Underwent surgery for hernia (September 21, 1998); missed first 68 games of season. ... Strained lower abdominal muscle (March 21, 1999); missed eight games. ... Suffered hernia prior to start of 1999-2000 season; missed first 56 games of season.

MISCELLANEOUS: Member of Stanley Cup championship team (1998). ... Failed to score on a penalty shot (vs. Kirk McLean, January 27, 1994).

STATISTICAL PLATEAUS: Three-goal games: 1991-92 (1).

G

Season Team	League	Gms.	G	A	Pts.	PIM	+/-	PP	SH	Gms.	G	A	Pts.	PIM
83-84—Kelowna	WHL	69	16	11	27	16	...	...	...	—	—	—	—	—
84-85—Kelowna	WHL	51	35	38	73	58	...	...	...	6	5	2	7	8
85-86—Spokane	WHL	52	45	45	90	57	...	...	...	9	6	7	13	19
86-87—Spokane	WHL	46	45	55	100	71	...	...	...	5	2	7	9	6
—Sherbrooke	AHL	—	—	—	—	—	...	...	...	10	2	7	9	2
87-88—Sherbrooke	AHL	77	26	48	74	83	...	...	...	6	1	3	4	6
88-89—Montreal	NHL	49	8	16	24	16	9	0	0	9	1	1	2	10
—Sherbrooke	AHL	7	6	5	11	7	...	...	...	—	—	—	—	—
89-90—Montreal	NHL	57	9	15	24	28	3	1	0	8	2	0	2	2
90-91—Montreal	NHL	51	6	9	15	10	-3	1	0	13	5	3	8	6
91-92—Montreal	NHL	79	23	27	50	57	29	2	0	11	2	4	6	6
92-93—Edmonton	NHL	60	10	10	20	47	-10	2	0	—	—	—	—	—
—Minnesota	NHL	8	0	1	1	2	-2	0	0	—	—	—	—	—
93-94—Dallas	NHL	76	17	14	31	31	0	3	1	9	3	1	4	2
94-95—Dallas	NHL	32	9	4	13	16	-3	1	3	5	0	1	1	2
95-96—Dallas	NHL	77	20	22	42	36	-11	6	1	—	—	—	—	—
96-97—Dallas	NHL	67	10	20	30	24	6	2	0	6	2	2	4	2
97-98—Detroit	NHL	61	13	14	27	40	4	5	0	15	2	1	3	12
98-99—Detroit	NHL	5	1	0	1	0	-1	0	0	3	0	0	0	0
99-00—Detroit	NHL	24	4	2	6	24	1	0	0	6	0	0	0	6
NHL Totals (12 years)		646	130	154	284	331	22	23	5	85	17	13	30	48

GILL, HAL — D — BRUINS

PERSONAL: Born April 6, 1975, in Concord, Mass. ... 6-7/240. ... Shoots left.
HIGH SCHOOL: Nashoba Regional (Bolton, Mass.).
COLLEGE: Providence.
TRANSACTIONS/CAREER NOTES: Selected by Boston Bruins in eighth round (eighth Bruins pick, 207th overall) of NHL entry draft (June 26, 1993). ... Suffered from the flu (January 21, 1998); missed one game. ... Strained hip flexor (April 7, 1999); missed two games. ... Suffered from the flu (January 11, 2000); missed one game.

Season Team	League	Gms.	G	A	Pts.	PIM	+/-	PP	SH	Gms.	G	A	Pts.	PIM
93-94—Providence College	Hockey East	31	1	2	3	26	...	...	...	—	—	—	—	—
94-95—Providence College	Hockey East	26	1	3	4	22	...	...	...	—	—	—	—	—
95-96—Providence College	Hockey East	39	5	12	17	54	...	...	...	—	—	—	—	—
96-97—Providence College	Hockey East	35	5	16	21	52	...	...	...	—	—	—	—	—
97-98—Boston	NHL	68	2	4	6	47	4	0	0	6	0	0	0	4
—Providence	AHL	4	1	0	1	23	...	...	...	—	—	—	—	—
98-99—Boston	NHL	80	3	7	10	63	-10	0	0	12	0	0	0	14
99-00—Boston	NHL	81	3	9	12	51	0	0	0	—	—	—	—	—
NHL Totals (3 years)		229	8	20	28	161	-6	0	0	18	0	0	0	18

GILL, TODD — D — RED WINGS

PERSONAL: Born November 9, 1965, in Brockville, Ont. ... 6-2/179. ... Shoots left.
TRANSACTIONS/CAREER NOTES: Selected by Toronto Maple Leafs as underage junior in second round (second Maple Leafs pick, 25th overall) of NHL entry draft (June 9, 1984). ... Fractured right foot (October 1987). ... Bruised shoulder (March 1989). ... Fractured finger (October 15, 1991); missed three games. ... Strained back (February 8, 1992); missed three games. ... Injured back prior to 1992-93 season; missed first two games of season. ... Bruised foot (November 14, 1992); missed 11 games. ... Strained groin (November 1, 1993); missed 26 games. ... Suffered back spasms (February 24, 1994); missed 13 games. ... Injured shoulder (March 17, 1995); missed one game. ... Pulled hamstring (November 10, 1995); missed four games. ... Suffered back spasms (February 7, 1996); missed four games. ... Traded by Maple Leafs to San Jose Sharks for C Jamie Baker and fifth-round pick (C Peter Cava) in 1996 draft (June 14, 1996). ... Suffered sore knee (April 9, 1997); missed three games. ... Traded by Sharks to St. Louis Blues for RW Joe Murphy (March 24, 1998). ... Bruised foot (November 23, 1998); missed three games. ... Claimed on waivers by Detroit Red Wings (December 30, 1998). ... Fractured forearm (February 1, 1999); missed 24 games. ... Signed as free agent by Phoenix Coyotes (July 15, 1999). ... Strained muscle in abdomen (November 23, 1999); missed seven games. ... Lacerated face (December 22, 1999); missed one game. ... Strained muscle in abdomen (January 8, 2000); missed 13 games. ... Traded by Coyotes to Red Wings for LW Philippe Audet (March 13, 2000).
MISCELLANEOUS: Captain of San Jose Sharks (1996-97 through March 2, 1998).

Season Team	League	Gms.	G	A	Pts.	PIM	+/-	PP	SH	Gms.	G	A	Pts.	PIM
82-83—Windsor	OHL	70	12	24	36	108	...	...	...	3	0	0	0	11
83-84—Windsor	OHL	68	9	48	57	184	...	...	...	3	1	1	2	10
84-85—Toronto	NHL	10	1	0	1	13	-1	0	0	—	—	—	—	—
—Windsor	OHL	53	17	40	57	148	...	...	...	4	0	1	1	14
85-86—St. Catharines	AHL	58	8	25	33	90	...	...	...	10	1	6	7	17
—Toronto	NHL	15	1	2	3	28	0	0	0	1	0	0	0	0
86-87—Newmarket	AHL	11	1	8	9	33	...	...	...	—	—	—	—	—
—Toronto	NHL	61	4	27	31	92	-3	1	0	13	2	2	4	42
87-88—Newmarket	AHL	2	0	1	1	2	...	...	...	—	—	—	—	—
—Toronto	NHL	65	8	17	25	131	-20	1	0	6	1	3	4	20
88-89—Toronto	NHL	59	11	14	25	72	-3	0	0	—	—	—	—	—
89-90—Toronto	NHL	48	1	14	15	92	-8	0	0	5	0	3	3	16
90-91—Toronto	NHL	72	2	22	24	113	-4	0	0	—	—	—	—	—
91-92—Toronto	NHL	74	2	15	17	91	-22	1	0	—	—	—	—	—
92-93—Toronto	NHL	69	11	32	43	66	4	5	0	21	1	10	11	26
93-94—Toronto	NHL	45	4	24	28	44	8	2	0	18	1	5	6	37
94-95—Toronto	NHL	47	7	25	32	64	-8	3	1	7	0	3	3	6

G

Season Team	League	REGULAR SEASON								PLAYOFFS				
		Gms.	G	A	Pts.	PIM	+/-	PP	SH	Gms.	G	A	Pts.	PIM
95-96—Toronto	NHL	74	7	18	25	116	-15	1	0	6	0	0	0	24
96-97—San Jose	NHL	79	0	21	21	101	-20	0	0	—	—	—	—	—
97-98—San Jose	NHL	64	8	13	21	31	-13	4	0	—	—	—	—	—
—St. Louis	NHL	11	5	4	9	10	2	3	0	10	2	2	4	10
98-99—St. Louis	NHL	28	2	3	5	16	-6	1	0	—	—	—	—	—
—Detroit	NHL	23	2	2	4	11	-4	0	0	2	0	1	1	0
99-00—Phoenix	NHL	41	1	6	7	30	-10	0	0	—	—	—	—	—
—Detroit	NHL	13	2	0	2	15	2	0	0	9	0	1	1	4
NHL Totals (16 years)		898	79	259	338	1136	-121	22	1	98	7	30	37	185

GILMOUR, DOUG   LW/C   SABRES

PERSONAL: Born June 25, 1963, in Kingston, Ont. ... 5-11/185. ... Shoots left. ... Full Name: Douglas Gilmour.
TRANSACTIONS/CAREER NOTES: Selected by St. Louis Blues as underage junior in seventh round (fourth Blues pick, 134th overall) of NHL entry draft (June 9, 1982). ... Sprained ankle (October 7, 1985); missed four games. ... Suffered concussion (January 1988). ... Bruised shoulder (March 1988). ... Traded by Blues with RW Mark Hunter, LW Steve Bozek and D/RW Michael Dark to Calgary Flames for C Mike Bullard, C Craig Coxe and D Tim Corkery (September 5, 1988). ... Suffered abscessed jaw (March 1989); missed six games. ... Fractured bone in right foot (August 12, 1989). ... Traded by Flames with D Ric Nattress, D Jamie Macoun, LW Kent Manderville and G Rick Wamsley to Toronto Maple Leafs for LW Craig Berube, D Alexander Godynyuk, LW Gary Leeman, D Michel Petit and G Jeff Reese (January 2, 1992). ... Suspended eight off-days and fined $500 by NHL for slashing (November 27, 1992). ... Suspended one preseason game and fined $500 by NHL for headbutting (September 26, 1993). ... Played in Europe during 1994-95 NHL lockout. ... Suffered pinched nerve in neck (February 8, 1995); missed one game. ... Fractured nose (April 7, 1995); missed three games. ... Bruised ribs (March 19, 1996); missed one game. ... Traded by Maple Leafs with D Dave Ellett and third-round pick (D Andre Lakos) in 1999 draft to New Jersey Devils for D Jason Smith, C Steve Sullivan and C Alyn McCauley (February 25, 1997). ... Bruised eye (March 5, 1997); missed three games. ... Injured knee (March 5, 1998) and underwent surgery; missed 18 games. ... Signed as free agent by Chicago Blackhawks (July 3, 1998). ... Injured back (March 27, 1999) and underwent surgery; missed final 10 games of season. ... Bruised ribs (March 1, 2000); missed five games. ... Traded by Blackhawks with RW Jean-Pierre Dumont to Buffalo Sabres for LW Michal Grosek (March 10, 2000). ... Suffered from the flu (April 7, 2000); missed final two games of season.
HONORS: Won Red Tilson Trophy (1982-83). ... Won Eddie Powers Memorial Trophy (1982-83). ... Named to OHL All-Star first team (1982-83). ... Won Frank J. Selke Trophy (1992-93). ... Named to THE SPORTING NEWS All-Star second team (1992-93). ... Played in NHL All-Star Game (1993 and 1994).
MISCELLANEOUS: Member of Stanley Cup championship team (1989). ... Captain of Toronto Maple Leafs (1994-95 through February 25, 1997). ... Captain of Chicago Blackhawks (1999-March 10, 2000). ... Failed to score on a penalty shot (vs. Gilles Meloche, February 3, 1985; vs. Pat Riggin, March 1, 1987; vs. Mark Fitzpatrick, October 7, 1989; vs. Peter Skudra, October 16, 1999).
STATISTICAL PLATEAUS: Three-goal games: 1985-86 (1), 1987-88 (1), 1993-94 (1). Total: 3.

Season Team	League	REGULAR SEASON								PLAYOFFS				
		Gms.	G	A	Pts.	PIM	+/-	PP	SH	Gms.	G	A	Pts.	PIM
80-81—Cornwall	QMJHL	51	12	23	35	35	...	...	...	—	—	—	—	—
81-82—Cornwall	OHL	67	46	73	119	42	...	...	...	5	6	9	15	2
82-83—Cornwall	OHL	68	*70	*107	*177	62	...	...	...	8	8	10	18	16
83-84—St. Louis	NHL	80	25	28	53	57	6	3	1	11	2	9	11	10
84-85—St. Louis	NHL	78	21	36	57	49	3	3	1	3	1	1	2	2
85-86—St. Louis	NHL	74	25	28	53	41	-3	2	1	19	9	12	†21	25
86-87—St. Louis	NHL	80	42	63	105	58	-2	17	1	6	2	2	4	16
87-88—St. Louis	NHL	72	36	50	86	59	-13	19	2	10	3	14	17	18
88-89—Calgary	NHL	72	26	59	85	44	45	11	0	22	11	11	22	20
89-90—Calgary	NHL	78	24	67	91	54	20	12	1	6	3	1	4	8
90-91—Calgary	NHL	78	20	61	81	144	27	2	2	7	1	1	2	0
91-92—Calgary	NHL	38	11	27	38	46	12	4	1	—	—	—	—	—
—Toronto	NHL	40	15	34	49	32	13	6	0	—	—	—	—	—
92-93—Toronto	NHL	83	32	95	127	100	32	15	3	21	10	†25	35	30
93-94—Toronto	NHL	83	27	84	111	105	25	10	1	18	6	22	28	42
94-95—Rapperswil	Switz. Div. 2	9	2	13	15	16	...	...	...	—	—	—	—	—
—Toronto	NHL	44	10	23	33	26	-5	3	0	7	0	6	6	6
95-96—Toronto	NHL	81	32	40	72	77	-5	10	2	6	1	7	8	12
96-97—Toronto	NHL	61	15	45	60	46	-5	2	1	—	—	—	—	—
—New Jersey	NHL	20	7	15	22	22	7	2	0	10	0	4	4	14
97-98—New Jersey	NHL	63	13	40	53	68	10	3	0	6	5	2	7	4
98-99—Chicago	NHL	72	16	40	56	56	-16	7	1	—	—	—	—	—
99-00—Chicago	NHL	63	22	34	56	51	-12	8	0	—	—	—	—	—
—Buffalo	NHL	11	3	14	17	12	3	2	0	5	0	1	1	0
NHL Totals (17 years)		1271	422	883	1305	1147	142	141	18	157	54	118	172	207

GIONTA, BRIAN   RW   DEVILS

G

PERSONAL: Born January 18, 1979, in Rochester, N.Y. ... 5-7/160. ... Shoots right.
COLLEGE: Boston College.
TRANSACTIONS/CAREER NOTES: Selected by New Jersey Devils in third round (fourth Devils pick, 82nd overall) of NHL entry draft (June 27, 1998).
HONORS: Named to NCAA All-America East second team (1997-98). ... Named to Hockey East All-Star second team (1997-98). ... Named Hockey East Rookie of the Year (1997-98). ... Named to NCAA All-America (East) first team (1998-99 and 1999-2000). ... Named to Hockey East All-Star first team (1998-99 and 1999-2000).

Season Team	League	REGULAR SEASON								PLAYOFFS				
		Gms.	G	A	Pts.	PIM	+/-	PP	SH	Gms.	G	A	Pts.	PIM
97-98—Boston College	Hockey East	40	30	32	62	44	...	...	...	—	—	—	—	—
98-99—Boston College	Hockey East	39	27	33	60	46	...	...	...	—	—	—	—	—
99-00—Boston College	Hockey East	42	*33	23	56	66	...	...	...	—	—	—	—	—

GIRARD, JONATHAN · D · BRUINS

PERSONAL: Born May 27, 1980, in Joliette, Que. ... 5-11/192. ... Shoots right.
TRANSACTIONS/CAREER NOTES: Selected by Boston Bruins in second round (first Bruins pick, 48th overall) of NHL entry draft (June 27, 1998).
HONORS: Named to QMJHL All-Rookie team (1996-97). ... Named to QMJHL All-Star second team (1997-98). ... Named to QMJHL All-Star first team (1998-99 and 1999-2000).

		REGULAR SEASON								PLAYOFFS				
Season Team	League	Gms.	G	A	Pts.	PIM	+/-	PP	SH	Gms.	G	A	Pts.	PIM
96-97—Laval	QMJHL	38	11	21	32	23	...	...	...	3	0	3	3	0
97-98—Laval	QMJHL	64	20	47	67	44	...	...	...	16	2	16	18	13
98-99—Acadie-Bathurst	QMJHL	50	9	58	67	60	...	...	...	23	13	18	31	22
—Boston	NHL	3	0	0	0	0	1	0	0	—	—	—	—	—
99-00—Boston	NHL	23	1	2	3	2	-1	0	0	—	—	—	—	—
—Providence	AHL	5	0	1	1	0	...	...	...	—	—	—	—	—
—Moncton	QMJHL	26	10	25	35	36	...	...	...	16	3	15	18	36
NHL Totals (2 years)		26	1	2	3	2	0	0	0					

GIROUX, RAY · D · ISLANDERS

PERSONAL: Born July 20, 1976, in North Bay, Ont. ... 5-11/185. ... Shoots left. ... Full Name: Raymond Giroux.
COLLEGE: Yale.
TRANSACTIONS/CAREER NOTES: Selected by Philadelphia Flyers in eighth round (seventh Flyers pick, 202nd overall) of NHL entry draft (June 29, 1994). ... Rights traded by Flyers to New York Islanders for sixth-round pick (traded to Montreal) in 2000 draft (August 25, 1998). ... Fractured finger (February 10, 2000); missed 12 games.
HONORS: Named to ECAC All-Star second team (1996-97). ... Named to NCAA All-America (East) first team (1997-98). ... Named ECAC Player of the Year (1997-98). ... Named to ECAC All-Star first team (1997-98).

		REGULAR SEASON								PLAYOFFS				
Season Team	League	Gms.	G	A	Pts.	PIM	+/-	PP	SH	Gms.	G	A	Pts.	PIM
94-95—Yale University	ECAC	31	1	9	10	20	...	...	...	—	—	—	—	—
95-96—Yale University	ECAC	30	3	17	20	36	...	...	...	—	—	—	—	—
96-97—Yale University	ECAC	32	9	12	21	38	...	...	...	—	—	—	—	—
97-98—Yale University	ECAC	35	9	30	39	62	...	...	...	—	—	—	—	—
98-99—Lowell	AHL	59	13	19	32	92	...	...	...	3	1	1	2	0
99-00—Lowell	AHL	49	12	21	33	34	...	...	...	7	0	0	0	2
—New York Islanders	NHL	14	0	9	9	10	0	0	0	—	—	—	—	—
NHL Totals (1 year)		14	0	9	9	10	0	0	0					

GOLDMANN, ERICH · D

PERSONAL: Born April 7, 1976, in Dingolfing, West Germany. ... 6-3/212. ... Shoots left. ... Name pronounced GOHLD-mahn.
TRANSACTIONS/CAREER NOTES: Selected by Ottawa Senators in eighth round (fifth Senators pick, 212th overall) of NHL entry draft (June 22, 1996). ... Sprained right ankle (November 11, 1999); missed 22 games.

		REGULAR SEASON								PLAYOFFS				
Season Team	League	Gms.	G	A	Pts.	PIM	+/-	PP	SH	Gms.	G	A	Pts.	PIM
92-93—Landshut Jrs.	Germany	32	7	7	14	32	...	...	...	—	—	—	—	—
93-94—Landshut	Germany	33	0	0	0	4	...	...	...	—	—	—	—	—
94-95—Mannheim	Germany	31	0	0	0	22	...	...	...	10	1	0	1	2
95-96—Mannheim	Germany	47	0	3	3	40	...	...	...	8	0	0	0	2
96-97—Kaufbeuren	Germany	44	2	4	6	58	...	...	...	6	1	0	1	2
97-98—Worcester	AHL	31	0	2	2	40	...	...	...	—	—	—	—	—
—German Oly. team	Int'l	4	0	1	1	27	...	...	...	—	—	—	—	—
—Detroit	IHL	3	0	0	0	2	...	...	...	—	—	—	—	—
—Dayton	ECHL	3	0	2	2	5	...	...	...	5	0	0	0	8
98-99—Cincinnati	IHL	5	0	1	1	7	...	...	...	—	—	—	—	—
—Hershey	AHL	21	1	1	2	23	...	...	...	—	—	—	—	—
—Cincinnati	AHL	32	0	2	2	18	...	...	...	3	0	0	0	2
99-00—Detroit	IHL	11	1	0	1	13	...	...	...	—	—	—	—	—
—Grand Rapids	IHL	26	1	1	2	15	...	...	...	—	—	—	—	—
—Ottawa	NHL	1	0	0	0	0	0	0	0	—	—	—	—	—
NHL Totals (1 year)		1	0	0	0	0	0	0	0					

G

GOLUBOVSKY, YAN · D · RED WINGS

PERSONAL: Born March 9, 1976, in Novosibirsk, U.S.S.R. ... 6-3/183. ... Shoots right. ... Name pronounced goh-loo-BAHV-skee.
TRANSACTIONS/CAREER NOTES: Selected by Detroit Red Wings in first round (first Red Wings pick, 23rd overall) of NHL entry draft (June 28, 1994). ... Injured rib (November 20, 1999); missed six games. ... Injured hand (February 8, 2000); missed 12 games.

		REGULAR SEASON								PLAYOFFS				
Season Team	League	Gms.	G	A	Pts.	PIM	+/-	PP	SH	Gms.	G	A	Pts.	PIM
93-94—Dynamo-2 Moscow	CIS Div. III	10	0	1	1	...	...	...	...	—	—	—	—	—
—Russian Penguins	IHL	8	0	0	0	23	...	...	...	—	—	—	—	—
94-95—Adirondack	AHL	57	4	2	6	39	...	...	...	—	—	—	—	—
95-96—Adirondack	AHL	71	5	16	21	97	...	...	...	3	0	0	0	2
96-97—Adirondack	AHL	62	2	11	13	67	...	...	...	4	0	0	0	0

Season Team	League	REGULAR SEASON								PLAYOFFS				
		Gms.	G	A	Pts.	PIM	+/-	PP	SH	Gms.	G	A	Pts.	PIM
97-98—Adirondack	AHL	52	1	15	16	57	...	...	...	3	0	0	0	2
—Detroit	NHL	12	0	2	2	6	1	0	0	—	—	—	—	—
98-99—Detroit	NHL	17	0	1	1	16	4	0	0	—	—	—	—	—
—Adirondack	AHL	43	2	2	4	32	...	...	...	2	0	0	0	4
99-00—Detroit	NHL	21	1	2	3	8	3	0	0	—	—	—	—	—
NHL Totals (3 years)		50	1	5	6	30	8	0	0					

GOMEZ, SCOTT — C — DEVILS

PERSONAL: Born December 23, 1979, in Anchorage, Alaska. ... 5-11/200. ... Shoots left.
TRANSACTIONS/CAREER NOTES: Selected by New Jersey Devils in first round (second Devils pick, 27th overall) of NHL entry draft (June 27, 1998).
HONORS: Named to WHL All-Rookie Team (1997-98). ... Named to WHL (West) All-Star first team (1998-99). ... Named NHL Rookie of the Year by THE SPORTING NEWS (1999-2000). ... Won Calder Memorial Trophy (1999-2000). ... Named to NHL All-Rookie Team (1999-2000). ... Played in NHL All-Star Game (2000).
MISCELLANEOUS: Member of Stanley Cup championship team (2000).
STATISTICAL PLATEAUS: Three-goal games: 1999-00 (1).

Season Team	League	REGULAR SEASON								PLAYOFFS				
		Gms.	G	A	Pts.	PIM	+/-	PP	SH	Gms.	G	A	Pts.	PIM
96-97—Surrey Jr. A	BCJHL	56	48	76	124	94	...	...	...	—	—	—	—	—
97-98—Tri-City	WHL	45	12	37	49	57	...	...	...	—	—	—	—	—
98-99—Tri-City	WHL	58	30	*78	108	55	...	...	...	10	6	13	19	31
99-00—New Jersey	NHL	82	19	51	70	78	14	7	0	23	4	6	10	4
NHL Totals (1 year)		82	19	51	70	78	14	7	0	23	4	6	10	4

GONCHAR, SERGEI — D — CAPITALS

PERSONAL: Born April 13, 1974, in Chelyabinsk, U.S.S.R. ... 6-2/208. ... Shoots left. ... Name pronounced GAHN-shahr.
TRANSACTIONS/CAREER NOTES: Selected by Washington Capitals in first round (first Capitals pick, 14th overall) of NHL entry draft (June 20, 1992). ... Injured groin (November 30, 1995); missed two games. ... Suffered from the flu (December 13, 1995); missed one game. ... Suffered from the flu (November 7, 1996); missed one game. ... Hyperextended elbow (November 18, 1996); missed one game. ... Suffered back spasms (December 28, 1996); missed eight games. ... Bruised knee (January 29, 1997); missed two games. ... Sprained knee (February 26, 1997); missed 12 games. ... Sprained knee (October 23, 1998); missed 10 games. ... Strained groin (January 1, 1999); missed one game. ... Sprained wrist (January 30, 1999); missed eight games. ... Sprained ankle (March 13, 1999); missed two games. ... Reinjured ankle (April 7, 1999); missed remainder of season. ... Suffered injury (November 11, 1999); missed five games. ... Injured neck (February 28, 2000); missed two games. ... Reinjured neck (March 5, 2000); missed two games.
STATISTICAL PLATEAUS: Three-goal games: 1999-00 (1).

Season Team	League	REGULAR SEASON								PLAYOFFS				
		Gms.	G	A	Pts.	PIM	+/-	PP	SH	Gms.	G	A	Pts.	PIM
90-91—Mechel Chelyabinsk	USSR	2	0	0	0	0	...	...	...	—	—	—	—	—
91-92—Traktor Chelyabinsk	CIS	31	1	0	1	6	...	...	...	—	—	—	—	—
92-93—Dynamo Moscow	CIS	31	1	3	4	70	...	...	...	10	0	0	0	12
93-94—Dynamo Moscow	CIS	44	4	5	9	36	...	...	...	10	0	3	3	14
—Portland	AHL	—	—	—	—	—				2	0	0	0	0
94-95—Portland	AHL	61	10	32	42	67	...	...	...	—	—	—	—	—
—Washington	NHL	31	2	5	7	22	4	0	0	7	2	2	4	2
95-96—Washington	NHL	78	15	26	41	60	25	4	0	6	2	4	6	4
96-97—Washington	NHL	57	13	17	30	36	-11	3	0	—	—	—	—	—
97-98—Washington	NHL	72	5	16	21	66	2	2	0	21	7	4	11	30
—Russian Oly. team	Int'l	6	0	2	2	0	...	...	...	—	—	—	—	—
98-99—Washington	NHL	53	21	10	31	57	1	13	1	—	—	—	—	—
99-00—Washington	NHL	73	18	36	54	52	26	5	0	5	1	0	1	6
NHL Totals (6 years)		364	74	110	184	293	47	27	1	39	12	10	22	42

GONEAU, DANIEL — RW — RANGERS

PERSONAL: Born January 16, 1976, in Lachine, Que. ... 6-0/195. ... Shoots left. ... Name pronounced guh-NOH.
TRANSACTIONS/CAREER NOTES: Selected by Boston Bruins in second round (second Bruins pick, 48th overall) of NHL entry draft (June 28, 1994). ... Returned to draft pool by Bruins and selected by New York Rangers in second round (second Rangers pick, 48th overall) of NHL entry draft (June 22, 1996).
HONORS: Won Can.HL Plus/Minus Award (1995-96). ... Named to QMJHL All-Star first team (1995-96).

G

Season Team	League	REGULAR SEASON								PLAYOFFS				
		Gms.	G	A	Pts.	PIM	+/-	PP	SH	Gms.	G	A	Pts.	PIM
92-93—Laval	QMJHL	62	16	25	41	44	...	...	...	13	0	4	4	4
93-94—Laval	QMJHL	68	29	57	86	81	...	...	...	19	8	21	29	45
94-95—Laval	QMJHL	56	16	31	47	78	...	...	...	20	5	10	15	33
95-96—Granby	QMJHL	67	54	51	105	115	...	...	...	21	11	22	33	40
96-97—New York Rangers	NHL	41	10	3	13	10	-5	3	0	—	—	—	—	—
—Binghamton	AHL	39	15	15	30	10	...	...	...	—	—	—	—	—
97-98—New York Rangers	NHL	11	2	0	2	4	-4	0	0	—	—	—	—	—
—Hartford	AHL	66	21	26	47	44	...	...	...	13	1	4	5	18
98-99—Hartford	AHL	72	20	19	39	56	...	...	...	2	1	0	1	0
99-00—Hartford	AHL	51	15	17	32	48	...	...	...	22	1	2	3	6
—New York Rangers	NHL	1	0	0	0	0	-1	0	0	—	—	—	—	—
NHL Totals (3 years)		53	12	3	15	14	-10	3	0					

GOREN, LEE — RW — BRUINS

PERSONAL: Born December 26, 1977, in Winnipeg. ... 6-3/190. ... Shoots right.
COLLEGE: North Dakota.
TRANSACTIONS/CAREER NOTES: Selected by Boston Bruins in third round (fifth Bruins pick, 63rd overall) of NHL entry draft (June 21, 1997).
HONORS: Named to WCHA All-Star first team (1999-2000). ... Named to NCAA All-America (West) second team (1999-2000). ... Named to NCAA All-Tournament team (1999-2000). ... Named NCAA Tournament Most Valuable Player (1999-2000).

		REGULAR SEASON								PLAYOFFS				
Season Team	League	Gms.	G	A	Pts.	PIM	+/-	PP	SH	Gms.	G	A	Pts.	PIM
95-96—Minote	Jr. A	64	31	55	86	...				—	—	—	—	—
96-97—Univ. of North Dakota.	WCHA					Did not play.				—	—	—	—	—
97-98—Univ. of North Dakota.	WCHA	29	3	13	16	26	...	...	...	—	—	—	—	—
98-99—Univ. of North Dakota.	WCHA	38	26	19	45	20	...	...	...	—	—	—	—	—
99-00—Univ. of North Dakota.	WCHA	44	*34	29	63	42	...	...	...	—	—	—	—	—

GOSSELIN, DAVID — C — PREDATORS

PERSONAL: Born June 22, 1977, in Levis, Que. ... 6-1/197. ... Shoots right.
TRANSACTIONS/CAREER NOTES: Selected by New Jersey Devils in third round (fourth Devils pick, 78th overall) of NHL entry draft (July 8, 1995). ... Signed as free agent by Nashville Predators (July 9, 1998).

		REGULAR SEASON								PLAYOFFS				
Season Team	League	Gms.	G	A	Pts.	PIM	+/-	PP	SH	Gms.	G	A	Pts.	PIM
94-95—Sherbrooke	QMJHL	58	8	8	16	36	...	...	...	7	0	0	0	2
95-96—Sherbrooke	QMJHL	55	24	24	48	147	...	...	...	7	2	2	4	4
96-97—Sherbrooke	QMJHL	23	11	15	26	52	...	...	...	—	—	—	—	—
—Chicoutimi	QMJHL	28	17	35	52	60	...	...	...	12	9	7	16	16
97-98—Chicoutimi	QMJHL	69	46	64	110	139	...	...	...	6	1	4	5	8
98-99—Milwaukee	IHL	74	17	11	28	78	...	...	...	2	0	2	2	2
99-00—Milwaukee	IHL	70	21	20	41	118	...	...	...	3	0	0	0	10
—Nashville	NHL	10	2	1	3	6	-4	0	0	—	—	—	—	—
NHL Totals (1 year)		10	2	1	3	6	-4	0	0					

GRAHAME, JOHN — G — BRUINS

PERSONAL: Born August 31, 1975, in Denver. ... 6-2/210. ... Catches left. ... Full Name: John Gillies Mark Grahame. ... Son of Ron Grahame, goaltender with three NHL teams (1977-78 through 1980-81). ... Name pronounced GRAY-ihm.
COLLEGE: Lake Superior State (Mich.).
TRANSACTIONS/CAREER NOTES: Selected by Boston Bruins in ninth round (seventh Bruins pick, 229th overall) of NHL entry draft (June 29, 1994).

		REGULAR SEASON								PLAYOFFS						
Season Team	League	Gms.	Min	W	L	T	GA	SO	Avg.	Gms.	Min.	W	L	GA	SO	Avg.
93-94—Sioux City	USHL	20	1136				72	0	3.80	—	—	—	—	—	—	—
94-95—Lake Superior State	CCHA	28	1616	16	7	3	75	1	2.78	—	—	—	—	—	—	—
95-96—Lake Superior State	CCHA	29	1658	21	4	2	67	2	2.42	—	—	—	—	—	—	—
96-97—Lake Superior State	CCHA	37	2197	19	13	4	134	3	3.66	—	—	—	—	—	—	—
97-98—Providence	AHL	55	3054	15	*31	4	164	3	3.22	—	—	—	—	—	—	—
98-99—Providence	AHL	48	2771	*37	9	1	134	3	2.90	19	*1209	*15	4	*48	†1	2.38
99-00—Boston	NHL	24	1344	7	10	5	55	2	2.46	—	—	—	—	—	—	—
—Providence	AHL	27	1528	11	13	2	86	1	3.38	13	839	10	3	35	0	2.50
NHL Totals (1 year)		24	1344	7	10	5	55	2	2.46							

GRANATO, TONY — RW — SHARKS

PERSONAL: Born June 25, 1964, in Downers Grove, Ill. ... 5-10/185. ... Shoots right. ... Full Name: Anthony Lewis Granato. ... Name pronounced gruh-NAH-toh.
HIGH SCHOOL: Northwood School (Lake Placid, N.Y.).
COLLEGE: Wisconsin.
TRANSACTIONS/CAREER NOTES: Selected by New York Rangers in sixth round (fifth Rangers pick, 120th overall) of NHL entry draft (June 9, 1982). ... Bruised foot (February 1989). ... Traded by Rangers with RW Tomas Sandstrom to Los Angeles Kings for C Bernie Nicholls (January 20, 1990). ... Strained groin (January 25, 1990); missed 12 games. ... Injured knee (March 20, 1990). ... Tore rib cartilage (December 18, 1990); missed 10 games. ... Strained back (October 6, 1992); missed three games. ... Strained back (December 4, 1993); missed one game. ... Strained lower back (December 13, 1993); missed nine games. ... Suspended 15 games without pay and fined $500 by NHL for slashing incident (February 16, 1994). ... Strained back (April 3, 1994); missed remainder of season. ... Strained hip flexor (March 13, 1995); missed one game. ... Fractured bone in foot (April 6, 1995); missed 13 games. ... Underwent brain surgery (February 14, 1996); missed remainder of season. ... Signed as free agent by San Jose Sharks (August 15, 1996). ... Injured back (December 21, 1996); missed one game. ... Reinjured back (January 29, 1997); missed two games. ... Suspended three games and fined $1,000 by NHL for cross-checking incident (February 5, 1997). ... Injured jaw (November 1, 1997); missed 19 games. ... Suspended two games and fined $1,000 by NHL for high-sticking incident (January 24, 1998). ... Suffered injury (November 21, 1998); missed two games. ... Injured back (December 10, 1998); missed six games. ... Tore anterior cruciate ligament in knee (January 11, 1999); missed 36 games.
HONORS: Named to NCAA All-America (West) second team (1984-85 and 1986-87). ... Named to WCHA All-Star second team (1986-87). ... Named to NHL All-Rookie team (1988-89). ... Played in NHL All-Star Game (1997). ... Won Bill Masterton Memorial Trophy (1996-97).
MISCELLANEOUS: Failed to score on a penalty shot (vs. Jocelyn Thibault, November 25, 1993).
STATISTICAL PLATEAUS: Three-goal games: 1988-89 (2), 1991-92 (1), 1994-95 (1), 1996-97 (2). Total: 6. ... Four-goal games: 1988-89 (1). ... Total hat tricks: 7.

G

Season Team	League	REGULAR SEASON								PLAYOFFS				
		Gms.	G	A	Pts.	PIM	+/-	PP	SH	Gms.	G	A	Pts.	PIM
81-82—Northwood School	N.Y. H.S.						Statistics unavailable.							
82-83—Northwood School	N.Y. H.S.						Statistics unavailable.							
83-84—Univ. of Wisconsin.....	WCHA	35	14	17	31	48	...	...	...	—	—	—	—	—
84-85—Univ. of Wisconsin.....	WCHA	42	33	34	67	94	...	...	...	—	—	—	—	—
85-86—Univ. of Wisconsin.....	WCHA	32	25	24	49	36	...	...	...	—	—	—	—	—
86-87—Univ. of Wisconsin.....	WCHA	42	28	45	73	64	...	...	...	—	—	—	—	—
87-88—U.S. national team.....	Int'l	49	40	31	71	55	...	...	...	—	—	—	—	—
—U.S. Olympic team.....	Int'l	6	1	7	8	4	...	...	...	—	—	—	—	—
—Denver.....	IHL	22	13	14	27	36	...	...	...	8	9	4	13	16
88-89—New York Rangers.....	NHL	78	36	27	63	140	17	4	4	4	1	1	2	21
89-90—New York Rangers.....	NHL	37	7	18	25	77	1	1	0	—	—	—	—	—
—Los Angeles................	NHL	19	5	6	11	45	-2	1	0	10	5	4	9	12
90-91—Los Angeles.....	NHL	68	30	34	64	154	22	11	1	12	1	4	5	28
91-92—Los Angeles.....	NHL	80	39	29	68	187	4	7	2	6	1	5	6	10
92-93—Los Angeles.....	NHL	81	37	45	82	171	-1	14	2	24	6	11	17	50
93-94—Los Angeles.....	NHL	50	7	14	21	150	-2	2	0	—	—	—	—	—
94-95—Los Angeles.....	NHL	33	13	11	24	68	9	2	0	—	—	—	—	—
95-96—Los Angeles.....	NHL	49	17	18	35	46	-5	5	0	—	—	—	—	—
96-97—San Jose.....	NHL	76	25	15	40	159	-7	5	1	—	—	—	—	—
97-98—San Jose.....	NHL	59	16	9	25	70	3	3	0	1	0	0	0	0
98-99—San Jose.....	NHL	35	6	6	12	54	4	0	1	6	1	1	2	2
99-00—San Jose.....	NHL	48	6	7	13	39	2	1	0	12	0	1	1	14
NHL Totals (12 years).........		**713**	**244**	**239**	**483**	**1360**	**45**	**56**	**11**	**75**	**15**	**27**	**42**	**137**

GRAND-PIERRE, JEAN-LUC   D   BLUE JACKETS

PERSONAL: Born February 2, 1977, in Montreal. ... 6-3/207. ... Shoots right. ... Name pronounced zhah-LOOK GRAHN-pee-AIR.
HIGH SCHOOL: CEGEP de Val d'Or (Que.).
TRANSACTIONS/CAREER NOTES: Selected by St. Louis Blues in seventh round (sixth Blues pick, 179th overall) of NHL entry draft (July 8, 1995). ... Traded by Blues with second-round pick (D Cory Sarich) in 1996 draft and third-round pick (RW Maxim Afinogenov) in 1997 draft to Buffalo Sabres for LW Yuri Khmylev and eighth-round pick (C Andrei Podkonicky) in 1996 draft (March 20, 1996). ... Suspended one game by NHL for tripping incident (April 10, 1999). ... Suffered from the flu (March 12, 2000); missed one game. ... Traded by Sabres with RW Matt Davidson, fifth-round pick (C Tyler Kolarik) in 2000 draft and fifth-round pick in 2001 draft to Columbus Blue Jackets for future considerations (June 23, 2000).

Season Team	League	REGULAR SEASON								PLAYOFFS				
		Gms.	G	A	Pts.	PIM	+/-	PP	SH	Gms.	G	A	Pts.	PIM
93-94—Beauport......................	QMJHL	46	1	4	5	27	...	...	...	1	0	0	0	0
94-95—Val-d'Or.....................	QMJHL	59	10	13	23	126	...	...	...	—	—	—	—	—
95-96—Val-d'Or.....................	QMJHL	67	13	21	34	209	...	...	...	13	1	4	5	47
96-97—Val-d'Or.....................	QMJHL	58	9	24	33	196	...	...	...	13	5	8	13	46
97-98—Rochester	AHL	75	4	6	10	211	...	...	...	4	0	0	0	2
98-99—Rochester	AHL	56	5	4	9	90	...	...	...	—	—	—	—	—
—Buffalo	NHL	16	0	1	1	17	0	0	0	—	—	—	—	—
99-00—Buffalo	NHL	11	0	0	0	15	-1	0	0	4	0	0	0	4
—Rochester	AHL	62	5	8	13	124	...	...	...	17	0	1	1	40
NHL Totals (2 years)...........		**27**	**0**	**1**	**1**	**32**	**-1**	**0**	**0**	**4**	**0**	**0**	**0**	**4**

GRATTON, BENOIT   LW   FLAMES

PERSONAL: Born December 28, 1976, in Montreal. ... 5-11/194. ... Shoots left. ... Name pronounced gruh-TAH.
TRANSACTIONS/CAREER NOTES: Selected by Washington Capitals in fifth round (sixth Capitals pick, 105th overall) of NHL entry draft (July 8, 1995). ... Injured groin (December 20, 1997); missed one game. ... Traded by Capitals to Calgary Flames for D Steve Shirreffs (August 18, 1999).

Season Team	League	REGULAR SEASON								PLAYOFFS				
		Gms.	G	A	Pts.	PIM	+/-	PP	SH	Gms.	G	A	Pts.	PIM
93-94—Laval........................	QMJHL	51	9	14	23	70	...	...	...	20	2	1	3	19
94-95—Laval........................	QMJHL	71	30	58	88	199	...	...	...	20	8	21	29	42
95-96—Laval........................	QMJHL	38	21	39	60	130	...	...	...	—	—	—	—	—
—Granby......................	QMJHL	27	12	46	58	97	...	...	...	21	13	26	39	68
96-97—Portland	AHL	76	6	40	46	140	...	...	...	5	2	1	3	14
97-98—Portland	AHL	58	19	31	50	137	...	...	...	8	4	2	6	24
—Washington	NHL	6	0	1	1	6	1	0	0	—	—	—	—	—
98-99—Portland	AHL	64	18	42	60	135	...	...	...	—	—	—	—	—
—Washington	NHL	16	4	3	7	16	-1	0	0	—	—	—	—	—
99-00—Saint John	AHL	65	17	49	66	137	...	...	...	3	0	1	1	4
—Calgary	NHL	10	0	2	2	10	1	0	0	—	—	—	—	—
NHL Totals (3 years)...........		**32**	**4**	**6**	**10**	**32**	**1**	**0**	**0**					

GRATTON, CHRIS   C   SABRES

PERSONAL: Born July 5, 1975, in Brantford, Ont. ... 6-4/219. ... Shoots left. ... Name pronounced GRA-tuhn.
HIGH SCHOOL: Loyalist Collegiate (Brantford, Ont.).
TRANSACTIONS/CAREER NOTES: Selected by Tampa Bay Lightning in first round (first Lightning pick, third overall) of NHL entry draft (June 26, 1993). ... Bruised shoulder (April 2, 1995); missed two games. ... Traded by Lightning to Philadelphia Flyers for RW Mikael Renberg and D Karl Dykhuis (August 29, 1997). ... Traded by Flyers with C/RW Mike Sillinger to Lightning for RW Mikael Renberg and C Daymond Langkow (December 12, 1998). ... Suspended three games by NHL for spitting at referee (December 25, 1998). ... Bruised right foot (February 17, 2000); missed seven games. ... Traded by Lightning with second-round pick in 2001 draft to Buffalo Sabres for C/RW Brian Holzinger, C Wayne Primeau, D Cory Sarich and third-round pick (RW Alexandre Kharitonov) in 2000 draft (March 9, 2000).

G

HONORS: Won Emms Family Award (1991-92). ... Named to OHL Rookie All-Star team (1991-92). ... Won OHL Top Draft Prospect Award (1992-93).
MISCELLANEOUS: Captain of Tampa Bay Lightning (November 10, 1999-March 9, 2000).
STATISTICAL PLATEAUS: Three-goal games: 1996-97 (1).

			REGULAR SEASON							PLAYOFFS				
Season Team	League	Gms.	G	A	Pts.	PIM	+/-	PP	SH	Gms.	G	A	Pts.	PIM
90-91—Brantford Jr. B	OHA	31	30	30	60	28	...	...	...	—	—	—	—	—
91-92—Kingston	OHL	62	27	39	66	35	...	...	...	—	—	—	—	—
92-93—Kingston	OHL	58	55	54	109	125	...	...	...	16	11	18	29	42
93-94—Tampa Bay	NHL	84	13	29	42	123	-25	5	1	—	—	—	—	—
94-95—Tampa Bay	NHL	46	7	20	27	89	-2	2	0	—	—	—	—	—
95-96—Tampa Bay	NHL	82	17	21	38	105	-13	7	0	6	0	2	2	27
96-97—Tampa Bay	NHL	82	30	32	62	201	-28	9	0	—	—	—	—	—
97-98—Philadelphia	NHL	82	22	40	62	159	11	5	0	5	2	0	2	10
98-99—Philadelphia	NHL	26	1	7	8	41	-8	0	0	—	—	—	—	—
—Tampa Bay	NHL	52	7	19	26	102	-20	1	0	—	—	—	—	—
99-00—Tampa Bay	NHL	58	14	27	41	121	-24	4	0	—	—	—	—	—
—Buffalo	NHL	14	1	7	8	15	1	0	0	5	0	1	1	4
NHL Totals (7 years)		526	112	202	314	956	-108	33	1	16	2	3	5	41

GRAVES, ADAM   LW   RANGERS

PERSONAL: Born April 12, 1968, in Tecumseh, Ont. ... 6-0/200. ... Shoots left.
TRANSACTIONS/CAREER NOTES: Bruised shoulder (February 1986). ... Selected by Detroit Red Wings as underage junior in second round (second Red Wings pick, 22nd overall) of NHL entry draft (June 21, 1986). ... Traded by Red Wings with C/RW Joe Murphy, LW Petr Klima and D Jeff Sharples to Edmonton Oilers for C Jimmy Carson, C Kevin McClelland and fifth-round pick (traded to Montreal Canadiens) in 1991 draft (November 2, 1989). ... Signed as free agent by New York Rangers (September 2, 1991); Oilers received C/LW Troy Mallette as compensation (September 9, 1991). ... Suffered from infected elbow (February 11, 1995); missed one game. ... Sprained right knee (October 26, 1997); missed 10 games.
HONORS: Won King Clancy Memorial Trophy (1993-94). ... Named to THE SPORTING NEWS All-Star first team (1993-94). ... Named to NHL All-Star second team (1993-94). ... Played in NHL All-Star Game (1994).
MISCELLANEOUS: Member of Stanley Cup championship team (1990 and 1994). ... Captain of New York Rangers (1995-96 and November 26, 1999-February 9, 2000).
STATISTICAL PLATEAUS: Three-goal games: 1989-90 (1), 1991-92 (1), 1992-93 (1), 1993-94 (1), 1994-95 (1), 1996-97 (1). Total: 6.

			REGULAR SEASON							PLAYOFFS				
Season Team	League	Gms.	G	A	Pts.	PIM	+/-	PP	SH	Gms.	G	A	Pts.	PIM
84-85—King City Jr. B	OHA	25	23	33	56	29	...	...	...	—	—	—	—	—
85-86—Windsor	OHL	62	27	37	64	35	...	...	...	16	5	11	16	10
86-87—Windsor	OHL	66	45	55	100	70	...	...	...	14	9	8	17	32
—Adirondack	AHL	—	—	—	—	—	...	...	...	5	0	1	1	0
87-88—Detroit	NHL	9	0	1	1	8	-2	0	0	—	—	—	—	—
—Windsor	OHL	37	28	32	60	107	...	...	...	12	14	18	†32	16
88-89—Detroit	NHL	56	7	5	12	60	-5	0	0	5	0	0	0	4
—Adirondack	AHL	14	10	11	21	28	...	...	...	14	11	7	18	17
89-90—Detroit	NHL	13	0	1	1	13	-5	0	0	—	—	—	—	—
—Edmonton	NHL	63	9	12	21	123	5	1	0	22	5	6	11	17
90-91—Edmonton	NHL	76	7	18	25	127	-21	2	0	18	2	4	6	22
91-92—New York Rangers	NHL	80	26	33	59	139	19	4	4	10	5	3	8	22
92-93—New York Rangers	NHL	84	36	29	65	148	-4	12	1	—	—	—	—	—
93-94—New York Rangers	NHL	84	52	27	79	127	27	20	4	23	10	7	17	24
94-95—New York Rangers	NHL	47	17	14	31	51	9	9	0	10	4	4	8	8
95-96—New York Rangers	NHL	82	22	36	58	100	18	9	1	10	7	1	8	4
96-97—New York Rangers	NHL	82	33	28	61	66	10	10	4	15	2	1	3	12
97-98—New York Rangers	NHL	72	23	12	35	41	-30	10	0	—	—	—	—	—
98-99—New York Rangers	NHL	82	38	15	53	47	-12	14	2	—	—	—	—	—
99-00—New York Rangers	NHL	77	23	17	40	14	-15	11	0	—	—	—	—	—
NHL Totals (13 years)		907	293	248	541	1064	-6	102	16	113	35	26	61	113

GREEN, JOSH   LW   OILERS

PERSONAL: Born November 16, 1977, in Camrose, Alta. ... 6-4/213. ... Shoots left.
TRANSACTIONS/CAREER NOTES: Selected by Los Angeles Kings in second round (first Kings pick, 30th overall) of NHL entry draft (June 22, 1996). ... Strained shoulder (October 18, 1998); missed three games. ... Traded by Kings with C Olli Jokinen, D Mathieu Biron and first-round pick (LW Taylor Pyatt) in 1999 draft to New York Islanders for RW Zigmund Palffy, C Bryan Smolinski, G Marcel Cousineau and fourth-round pick (C Daniel Johansson) in 1999 draft (June 20, 1999). ... Injured shoulder (March 21, 2000); missed remainder of season. ... Traded by Islanders with D Eric Brewer and second-round pick (LW Brad Winchester) in 2000 draft to Edmonton Oilers for D Roman Hamrlik (June 24, 2000).

			REGULAR SEASON							PLAYOFFS				
Season Team	League	Gms.	G	A	Pts.	PIM	+/-	PP	SH	Gms.	G	A	Pts.	PIM
93-94—Medicine Hat	WHL	63	22	22	44	43	...	...	...	3	0	0	0	4
94-95—Medicine Hat	WHL	68	32	23	55	64	...	...	...	5	5	1	6	2
95-96—Medicine Hat	WHL	46	18	25	43	55	...	...	...	5	2	2	4	4
96-97—Medicine Hat	WHL	51	25	32	57	61	...	...	...	—	—	—	—	—
—Swift Current	WHL	23	10	15	25	33	...	...	...	10	9	7	16	19
97-98—Portland	WHL	31	35	19	54	36	...	...	...	—	—	—	—	—
—Fredericton	AHL	43	16	15	31	14	...	...	...	4	1	3	4	6
98-99—Los Angeles	NHL	27	1	3	4	8	-5	1	0	—	—	—	—	—
—Springfield	AHL	41	15	15	30	29	...	...	...	—	—	—	—	—
99-00—Lowell	AHL	17	6	2	8	19	...	...	...	—	—	—	—	—
—New York Islanders	NHL	49	12	14	26	41	-7	2	0	—	—	—	—	—
NHL Totals (2 years)		76	13	17	30	49	-12	3	0					

G

GREEN, TRAVIS   C   COYOTES

PERSONAL: Born December 20, 1970, in Castlegar, B.C. ... 6-2/200. ... Shoots right.

TRANSACTIONS/CAREER NOTES: Selected by New York Islanders in second round (second Islanders pick, 23rd overall) of NHL entry draft (June 17, 1989). ... Suffered sore groin (November 30, 1995); missed two games. ... Sprained knee (February 8, 1996); missed nine games. ... Traded by Islanders with D Doug Houda and RW Tony Tuzzolino to Mighty Ducks of Anaheim for D J.J. Daigneault, C Mark Janssens and RW Joe Sacco (February 6, 1998). ... Strained groin (February 7, 1998); missed five games. ... Sprained right knee (November 20, 1998); missed three games. ... Traded by Mighty Ducks with first-round pick (C Scott Kelman) in 1999 draft to Phoenix Coyotes for D Oleg Tverdovsky (June 26, 1999). ... Suffered knee infection (November 25, 1999); missed three games. ... Suffered concussion (March 21, 2000); missed one game.

STATISTICAL PLATEAUS: Three-goal games: 1993-94 (1).

		REGULAR SEASON							PLAYOFFS				
Season Team	League	Gms.	G	A	Pts.	PIM	+/-	PP	SH	Gms.	G	A	Pts.	PIM
85-86—Castlegar	KIJHL	35	30	40	70	41	...	...	...	—	—	—	—	—
86-87—Spokane	WHL	64	8	17	25	27	...	...	...	3	0	0	0	0
87-88—Spokane	WHL	72	33	53	86	42	...	...	...	15	10	10	20	13
88-89—Spokane	WHL	72	51	51	102	79	...	...	...	—	—	—	—	—
89-90—Spokane	WHL	50	45	44	89	80	...	...	...	—	—	—	—	—
—Medicine Hat	WHL	25	15	24	39	19	...	...	...	3	0	0	0	2
90-91—Capital District	AHL	73	21	34	55	26	...	...	...	—	—	—	—	—
91-92—Capital District	AHL	71	23	27	50	10	...	...	...	7	0	4	4	21
92-93—Capital District	AHL	20	12	11	23	39	...	...	...	—	—	—	—	—
—New York Islanders	NHL	61	7	18	25	43	4	1	0	12	3	1	4	6
93-94—New York Islanders	NHL	83	18	22	40	44	16	1	0	4	0	0	0	2
94-95—New York Islanders	NHL	42	5	7	12	25	-10	0	0	—	—	—	—	—
95-96—New York Islanders	NHL	69	25	45	70	42	-20	14	1	—	—	—	—	—
96-97—New York Islanders	NHL	79	23	41	64	38	-5	10	0	—	—	—	—	—
97-98—New York Islanders	NHL	54	14	12	26	66	-19	8	0	—	—	—	—	—
—Anaheim	NHL	22	5	11	16	16	-10	1	0	—	—	—	—	—
98-99—Anaheim	NHL	79	13	17	30	81	-7	3	1	4	0	1	1	4
99-00—Phoenix	NHL	78	25	21	46	45	-4	6	0	5	2	1	3	2
NHL Totals (8 years)		567	135	194	329	400	-55	44	2	25	5	3	8	14

GREIG, MARK   RW   FLYERS

PERSONAL: Born January 25, 1970, in High River, Alta. ... 5-11/190. ... Shoots right. ... Name pronounced GRAYG.

TRANSACTIONS/CAREER NOTES: Selected by Hartford Whalers in first round (first Whalers pick, 15th overall) of NHL entry draft (June 16, 1990). ... Injured right knee (April 11, 1993); missed final three games of regular season. ... Traded by Whalers with sixth-round pick (G Doug Bonner) in 1995 draft to Toronto Maple Leafs for D Ted Crowley (January 25, 1994). ... Strained hip flexor (February 21, 1994); missed one game. ... Signed as free agent by Calgary Flames (August 9, 1994). ... Signed as free agent by Philadelphia Flyers (August 4, 1998).

HONORS: Named to WHL (East) All-Star first team (1989-90).

		REGULAR SEASON							PLAYOFFS				
Season Team	League	Gms.	G	A	Pts.	PIM	+/-	PP	SH	Gms.	G	A	Pts.	PIM
86-87—Calgary	WHL	5	0	0	0	0	...	...	...	—	—	—	—	—
87-88—Lethbridge	WHL	65	9	18	27	38	...	...	...	—	—	—	—	—
88-89—Lethbridge	WHL	71	36	72	108	113	...	...	...	8	5	5	10	16
89-90—Lethbridge	WHL	65	55	80	135	149	...	...	...	18	11	21	32	35
90-91—Hartford	NHL	4	0	0	0	0	-1	0	0	—	—	—	—	—
—Springfield	AHL	73	32	55	87	73	...	...	...	17	2	6	8	22
91-92—Hartford	NHL	17	0	5	5	6	7	0	0	—	—	—	—	—
—Springfield	AHL	50	20	27	47	38	...	...	...	9	1	1	2	20
92-93—Hartford	NHL	22	1	7	8	27	-11	0	0	—	—	—	—	—
—Springfield	AHL	55	20	38	58	86	...	...	...	—	—	—	—	—
93-94—Hartford	NHL	31	4	5	9	31	-6	0	0	—	—	—	—	—
—Springfield	AHL	4	0	4	4	21	...	...	...	—	—	—	—	—
—Toronto	NHL	13	2	2	4	10	1	0	0	—	—	—	—	—
—St. John's	AHL	9	4	6	10	0	...	...	...	11	4	2	6	26
94-95—Saint John	AHL	67	31	50	81	82	...	...	...	2	0	1	1	0
—Calgary	NHL	8	1	1	2	2	1	0	0	—	—	—	—	—
95-96—Atlanta	IHL	71	25	48	73	104	...	...	...	3	2	1	3	4
96-97—Quebec	IHL	5	1	2	3	0	...	...	...	—	—	—	—	—
—Houston	IHL	59	12	30	42	59	...	...	...	13	5	8	13	2
97-98—Grand Rapids	IHL	69	26	36	62	103	...	...	...	3	0	4	4	4
98-99—Philadelphia	AHL	67	23	46	69	102	...	...	...	7	1	5	6	14
—Philadelphia	NHL	7	1	3	4	2	1	0	0	2	0	1	1	0
99-00—Philadelphia	AHL	68	34	48	82	116	...	...	...	5	3	2	5	6
—Philadelphia	NHL	11	3	2	5	6	0	0	0	3	0	0	0	0
NHL Totals (7 years)		113	12	25	37	84	-8	0	0	5	0	1	1	0

GRENIER, MARTIN   D   BRUINS

PERSONAL: Born November 2, 1980, in Laval, Que. ... 6-5/230. ... Shoots left.

TRANSACTIONS/CAREER NOTES: Selected by Colorado Avalanche in second round (second Avalanche pick, 45th overall) of NHL entry draft (June 26, 1999). ... Traded by Avalanche with LW Brian Rolston, C Samual Pahlsson and first-round pick (LW Martin Samuelsson) in 2000 draft to Boston Bruins for D Ray Bourque and LW Dave Andreychuk (March 6, 2000).

		REGULAR SEASON							PLAYOFFS				
Season Team	League	Gms.	G	A	Pts.	PIM	+/-	PP	SH	Gms.	G	A	Pts.	PIM
97-98—Quebec	QMJHL	61	4	11	15	202	...	...	...	14	0	2	2	36
98-99—Quebec	QMJHL	60	7	18	25	*479	...	...	...	13	0	4	4	29
99-00—Quebec	QMJHL	67	11	35	46	302	...	...	...	7	1	4	5	27

G

PERSONAL: Born January 5, 1975, in Detroit. ... 6-1/227. ... Shoots right.
HIGH SCHOOL: St. Sebastian's Country Day (Needham, Mass.).
COLLEGE: Boston University.
TRANSACTIONS/CAREER NOTES: Selected by St. Louis Blues in ninth round (seventh Blues pick, 219th overall) of NHL entry draft (June 26, 1993). ... Rights traded by Blues with rights to G Curtis Joseph to Edmonton Oilers for first-round picks in 1996 (C Marty Reasoner) and 1997 (traded to Los Angeles) drafts (August 4, 1995); picks had been awarded earlier to Oilers as compensation for Blues signing free agent LW Shayne Corson (July 28, 1995). ... Strained medial collateral ligament in left knee (November 19, 1997); missed 14 games. ... Fractured clavicle (November 24, 1999); missed four games. ... Suffered torn triceps (March 13, 2000) and underwent surgery; missed remainder of season.
HONORS: Named to NCAA All-America (East) first team (1994-95). ... Named to Hockey East All-Star first team (1994-95).
STATISTICAL PLATEAUS: Three-goal games: 1998-99 (1).

		REGULAR SEASON								PLAYOFFS				
Season Team	League	Gms.	G	A	Pts.	PIM	+/-	PP	SH	Gms.	G	A	Pts.	PIM
92-93—St. Sebastian's	USHS (East)	22	16	27	43	32	...	...	...	—	—	—	—	—
93-94—Boston University	Hockey East	39	9	9	18	56	...	...	...	—	—	—	—	—
94-95—Boston University	Hockey East	37	29	26	55	85	...	...	...	—	—	—	—	—
95-96—Boston University	Hockey East	38	21	25	46	82	...	...	...	—	—	—	—	—
96-97—Edmonton	NHL	79	15	17	32	45	7	4	0	12	3	1	4	4
97-98—Edmonton	NHL	66	9	6	15	73	-3	1	0	12	2	2	4	13
98-99—Edmonton	NHL	82	20	24	44	54	5	3	2	4	1	1	2	6
99-00—Edmonton	NHL	65	9	22	31	68	9	0	3	—	—	—	—	—
NHL Totals (4 years)		292	53	69	122	240	18	8	5	28	6	4	10	23

PERSONAL: Born May 20, 1965, in Kamloops, B.C. ... 6-5/239. ... Shoots left. ... Full Name: Stuart Grimson. ... Nickname: The Grim Reaper.
COLLEGE: Manitoba.
TRANSACTIONS/CAREER NOTES: Selected by Detroit Red Wings in 10th round (11th Red Wings pick, 186th overall) of NHL entry draft (June 8, 1983). ... Returned to draft pool and selected by Calgary Flames in seventh round (eighth Flames pick, 143rd overall) of NHL entry draft (June 15, 1985). ... Fractured cheekbone (January 9, 1990). ... Claimed on waivers by Chicago Blackhawks (October 1, 1990). ... Injured eye (February 3, 1993). ... Selected by Mighty Ducks of Anaheim in NHL expansion draft (June 24, 1993). ... Lacerated hand (January 16, 1994); missed one game. ... Lacerated hand (March 9, 1994); missed one game. ... Lacerated hand (March 26, 1994); missed five games. ... Traded by Mighty Ducks with D Mark Ferner and sixth-round pick (LW Magnus Nilsson) in 1996 draft to Red Wings for C/RW Mike Sillinger and D Jason York (April 4, 1995). ... Signed by New York Rangers to offer sheet (August 18, 1995); Red Wings matched offer (August 24, 1995). ... Suffered from the flu (December 12, 1995); missed two games. ... Suspended two games and fined $1,000 by NHL for striking another player with a gloved hand (January 12, 1996). ... Claimed on waivers by Hartford Whalers (October 12, 1996). ... Whalers franchise moved to North Carolina and renamed Carolina Hurricanes for 1997-98 season; NHL approved move on June 25, 1997. ... Traded by Hurricanes with D Kevin Haller to Mighty Ducks of Anaheim for D Dave Karpa and fourth-round pick (traded to Atlanta) in 2000 draft (August 11, 1998). ... Suspended one playoff game by NHL for cross-checking incident (April 26, 1999). ... Strained neck (October 2, 1999); missed one game. ... Fractured left hand (January 18, 2000); missed 14 games. ... Signed as free agent by Los Angeles Kings (July 6, 2000).

		REGULAR SEASON								PLAYOFFS				
Season Team	League	Gms.	G	A	Pts.	PIM	+/-	PP	SH	Gms.	G	A	Pts.	PIM
82-83—Regina	WHL	48	0	1	1	144	...	...	...	5	0	0	0	14
83-84—Regina	WHL	63	8	8	16	131	...	...	...	21	0	1	1	29
84-85—Regina	WHL	71	24	32	56	248	...	...	...	8	1	2	3	14
85-86—Univ. of Manitoba	CWUAA	12	7	4	11	113	...	...	...	3	1	1	2	20
86-87—Univ. of Manitoba	CWUAA	29	8	8	16	67	...	...	...	14	4	2	6	28
87-88—Salt Lake City	IHL	38	9	5	14	268	...	...	...	—	—	—	—	—
88-89—Calgary	NHL	1	0	0	0	5	0	0	0	—	—	—	—	—
—Salt Lake City	IHL	72	9	18	27	*397	...	...	...	15	2	3	5	*86
89-90—Salt Lake City	IHL	62	8	16		319	...	...	...	4	0	0	0	8
—Calgary	NHL	3	0	0	0	17	-1	0	0	—	—	—	—	—
90-91—Chicago	NHL	35	0	1	1	183	-3	0	0	5	0	0	0	46
91-92—Chicago	NHL	54	2	2	4	234	-2	0	0	14	0	1	1	10
—Indianapolis	IHL	5	1	1	2	17	...	...	...	—	—	—	—	—
92-93—Chicago	NHL	78	1	1	2	193	2	1	0	2	0	0	0	4
93-94—Anaheim	NHL	77	1	5	6	199	-6	0	0	—	—	—	—	—
94-95—Anaheim	NHL	31	0	1	1	110	-7	0	0	—	—	—	—	—
—Detroit	NHL	11	0	0	0	37	-4	0	0	11	1	0	1	26
95-96—Detroit	NHL	56	0	1	1	128	-10	0	0	2	0	0	0	0
96-97—Detroit	NHL	1	0	0	0	0	-1	0	0	—	—	—	—	—
—Hartford	NHL	75	2	2	4	218	-7	0	0	—	—	—	—	—
97-98—Carolina	NHL	82	3	4	7	204	0	1	0	—	—	—	—	—
98-99—Anaheim	NHL	73	3	0	3	158	0	0	0	3	0	0	0	30
99-00—Anaheim	NHL	50	1	2	3	116	0	0	0	—	—	—	—	—
NHL Totals (12 years)		627	13	19	32	1802	-39	1	0	37	1	1	2	116

G

PERSONAL: Born June 1, 1975, in Vyskov, Czechoslovakia. ... 6-2/216. ... Shoots right. ... Name pronounced GROH-shek.
TRANSACTIONS/CAREER NOTES: Selected by Winnipeg Jets in sixth round (seventh Jets pick, 145th overall) of NHL entry draft (June 26, 1993). ... Sprained knee ligaments (February 15, 1995); missed four games. ... Fractured foot (April 5, 1995); missed remainder of season. ... Traded by Jets with D Darryl Shannon to Buffalo Sabres for D Craig Muni (February 15, 1996). ... Suffered back spasms (April 9, 1999); missed five games. ... Traded by Sabres to Chicago Blackhawks for C Doug Gilmour and RW Jean-Pierre Dumont (March 10, 2000).
STATISTICAL PLATEAUS: Three-goal games: 1996-97 (1).

Season Team	League	REGULAR SEASON								PLAYOFFS				
		Gms.	G	A	Pts.	PIM	+/-	PP	SH	Gms.	G	A	Pts.	PIM
92-93—ZPS Zlin	Czech.	17	1	3	4	0	...	...	...	—	—	—	—	—
93-94—Moncton	AHL	20	1	2	3	47	...	...	...	2	0	0	0	0
—Tacoma	WHL	30	25	20	45	106	...	...	...	7	2	2	4	30
—Winnipeg	NHL	3	1	0	1	0	-1	0	0	—	—	—	—	—
94-95—Springfield	AHL	45	10	22	32	98	...	...	...	—	—	—	—	—
—Winnipeg	NHL	24	2	2	4	21	-3	0	0	—	—	—	—	—
95-96—Springfield	AHL	39	16	19	35	68	...	...	...	—	—	—	—	—
—Winnipeg	NHL	1	0	0	0	0	-1	0	0	—	—	—	—	—
—Buffalo	NHL	22	6	4	10	31	0	2	0	—	—	—	—	—
96-97—Buffalo	NHL	82	15	21	36	71	25	1	0	12	3	3	6	8
97-98—Buffalo	NHL	67	10	20	30	60	9	2	0	15	6	4	10	28
98-99—Buffalo	NHL	76	20	30	50	102	21	4	0	13	0	4	4	28
99-00—Buffalo	NHL	61	11	23	34	35	12	2	0	—	—	—	—	—
—Chicago	NHL	14	2	4	6	12	-1	1	0	—	—	—	—	—
NHL Totals (7 years)		350	67	104	171	332	61	12	0	40	9	11	20	64

GRUDEN, JOHN — D — SENATORS

PERSONAL: Born June 4, 1970, in Virginia, Minn. ... 6-0/203. ... Shoots left. ... Name pronounced GROO-dihn.
COLLEGE: Ferris State (Mich.).
TRANSACTIONS/CAREER NOTES: Selected by Boston Bruins in seventh round (seventh Bruins pick, 168th overall) of NHL entry draft (June 16, 1990). ... Suffered back spasms (March 15, 1995); missed two games. ... Signed as free agent by Ottawa Senators (July 22, 1998).
HONORS: Named to NCAA All-America (West) first team (1993-94). ... Named to CCHA All-Star first team (1993-94). ... Named to IHL All-Star second team (1997-98).

Season Team	League	REGULAR SEASON								PLAYOFFS				
		Gms.	G	A	Pts.	PIM	+/-	PP	SH	Gms.	G	A	Pts.	PIM
90-91—Ferris State	CCHA	37	4	11	15	27	...	...	...	—	—	—	—	—
91-92—Ferris State	CCHA	37	9	14	23	24	...	...	...	—	—	—	—	—
92-93—Ferris State	CCHA	41	16	14	30	58	...	...	...	—	—	—	—	—
93-94—Ferris State	CCHA	38	11	25	36	52	...	...	...	—	—	—	—	—
—Boston	NHL	7	0	1	1	2	-3	0	0	—	—	—	—	—
94-95—Boston	NHL	38	0	6	6	22	3	0	0	—	—	—	—	—
—Providence	AHL	1	0	1	1	0	...	...	...	—	—	—	—	—
95-96—Boston	NHL	14	0	0	0	4	-3	0	0	3	0	1	1	0
—Providence	AHL	39	5	19	24	29	...	...	...	—	—	—	—	—
96-97—Providence	AHL	78	18	27	45	52	...	...	...	10	3	6	9	4
97-98—Detroit	IHL	76	13	42	55	74	...	...	...	23	1	8	9	16
98-99—Detroit	IHL	59	10	28	38	52	...	...	...	10	0	1	1	6
—Detroit	NHL	13	0	1	1	8	0	0	0	—	—	—	—	—
99-00—Grand Rapids	IHL	50	5	17	22	24	...	...	...	12	1	4	5	8
—Ottawa	NHL	9	0	0	0	4	0	0	0	—	—	—	—	—
NHL Totals (5 years)		81	0	8	8	40	-3	0	0	3	0	1	1	0

GUERIN, BILL — RW — OILERS

PERSONAL: Born November 9, 1970, in Wilbraham, Mass. ... 6-2/210. ... Shoots right. ... Full Name: William Robert Guerin. ... Name pronounced GAIR-ihn.
COLLEGE: Boston College.
TRANSACTIONS/CAREER NOTES: Selected by New Jersey Devils in first round (first Devils pick, fifth overall) of NHL entry draft (June 17, 1989). ... Suffered from the flu (February 1992); missed three games. ... Suffered from sore leg (March 19, 1994); missed two games. ... Suffered from the flu (December 6, 1995); missed two games. ... Missed first 21 games of 1997-98 season due to contract dispute. ... Traded by Devils with RW Valeri Zelepukin to Edmonton Oilers for C Jason Arnott and D Bryan Muir (January 4, 1998). ... Sprained medial collateral ligament in left knee (April 12, 1999); missed final two games of regular season and one playoff game. ... Suffered from the flu (December 9, 1999); missed one game.
MISCELLANEOUS: Member of Stanley Cup championship team (1995).
STATISTICAL PLATEAUS: Three-goal games: 1996-97 (1).

Season Team	League	REGULAR SEASON								PLAYOFFS				
		Gms.	G	A	Pts.	PIM	+/-	PP	SH	Gms.	G	A	Pts.	PIM
85-86—Springfield Jr. B	NEJHL	48	26	19	45	71	...	...	...	—	—	—	—	—
86-87—Springfield Jr. B	NEJHL	32	34	20	54	40	...	...	...	—	—	—	—	—
87-88—Springfield Jr. B	NEJHL	38	31	44	75	146	...	...	...	—	—	—	—	—
88-89—Springfield Jr. B	NEJHL	31	32	37	69	90	...	...	...	—	—	—	—	—
89-90—Boston College	Hockey East	39	14	11	25	64	...	...	...	—	—	—	—	—
90-91—Boston College	Hockey East	38	26	19	45	102	...	...	...	—	—	—	—	—
91-92—U.S. national team	Int'l	46	12	15	27	67	...	...	...	—	—	—	—	—
—Utica	AHL	22	13	10	23	6	...	...	...	4	1	3	4	14
—New Jersey	NHL	5	0	1	1	9	1	0	0	6	3	0	3	4
92-93—New Jersey	NHL	65	14	20	34	63	14	0	0	5	1	1	2	4
—Utica	AHL	18	10	7	17	47	...	...	...	—	—	—	—	—
93-94—New Jersey	NHL	81	25	19	44	101	14	2	0	17	2	1	3	35
94-95—New Jersey	NHL	48	12	13	25	72	6	4	0	20	3	8	11	30
95-96—New Jersey	NHL	80	23	30	53	116	7	8	0	—	—	—	—	—
96-97—New Jersey	NHL	82	29	18	47	95	-2	7	0	8	2	1	3	18
97-98—New Jersey	NHL	19	5	5	10	13	0	1	0	—	—	—	—	—
—Edmonton	NHL	40	13	16	29	80	1	8	0	12	7	1	8	17
—U.S. Olympic team	Int'l	4	0	3	3	2	...	...	...	—	—	—	—	—
98-99—Edmonton	NHL	80	30	34	64	133	7	13	0	3	0	2	2	2
99-00—Edmonton	NHL	70	24	22	46	123	4	11	0	5	3	2	5	9
NHL Totals (9 years)		570	175	178	353	805	52	54	0	76	21	16	37	119

G

GUOLLA, STEVE   C   THRASHERS

PERSONAL: Born March 15, 1973, in Scarborough, Ont. ... 6-0/191. ... Shoots left. ... Full Name: Stephen Guolla. ... Name pronounced GWAH-luh.
HIGH SCHOOL: Stephen Leacock (Agincourt, Ont.).
COLLEGE: Michigan State.
TRANSACTIONS/CAREER NOTES: Selected by Ottawa Senators (first Senators pick, third overall) in NHL supplemental draft (June 28, 1994). ... Signed as free agent by San Jose Sharks (August 26, 1996). ... Traded by Sharks with D Andrei Zyuzin, D Bill Houlder and LW Shawn Burr to Tampa Bay Lightning for LW Niklas Sundstrom and third-round pick (traded to Chicago) in 2000 draft (August 4, 1999). ... Injured ankle (October 23, 1999); missed four games. ... Strained groin (January 7, 2000); missed four games. ... Claimed on waivers by Atlanta Thrashers (March 1, 2000).
HONORS: Named to NCCA All-America (West) second team (1993-94). ... Named to CCHA All-Star second team (1993-94). ... Named to AHL All-Star second team (1997-98 and 1998-99). ... Won Les Cunningham Plaque (1997-98 and 1998-99).

		REGULAR SEASON									PLAYOFFS				
Season Team	League	Gms.	G	A	Pts.	PIM	+/-	PP	SH		Gms.	G	A	Pts.	PIM
90-91—Wexford Jr. B	MTHL	...	37	42	79	...	...	...	...		—	—	—	—	—
91-92—Michigan State	CCHA	33	4	9	13	8	...	...	...		—	—	—	—	—
92-93—Michigan State	CCHA	39	19	35	54	6	...	...	...		—	—	—	—	—
93-94—Michigan State	CCHA	41	23	46	69	16	...	...	...		—	—	—	—	—
94-95—Michigan State	CCHA	40	16	35	51	16	...	...	...		—	—	—	—	—
95-96—Prin. Edward Island	AHL	72	32	48	80	28	...	...	...		3	0	0	0	0
96-97—Kentucky	AHL	34	22	22	44	10	...	...	...		4	2	1	3	0
—San Jose	NHL	43	13	8	21	14	-10	2	0		—	—	—	—	—
97-98—Kentucky	AHL	69	37	63	100	45	...	...	...		3	0	0	0	0
—San Jose	NHL	7	1	1	2	0	-2	0	0		—	—	—	—	—
98-99—Kentucky	AHL	53	29	47	76	33	...	...	...		—	—	—	—	—
—San Jose	NHL	14	2	2	4	6	3	0	0		—	—	—	—	—
99-00—Tampa Bay	NHL	46	6	10	16	11	2	2	0		—	—	—	—	—
—Atlanta	NHL	20	4	9	13	4	-13	2	0		—	—	—	—	—
NHL Totals (4 years)		130	26	30	56	35	-20	6	0						

GUREN, MIROSLAV   D   CANADIENS

PERSONAL: Born September 24, 1976, in Uherske Hradiste, Czechoslovakia. ... 6-2/213. ... Shoots left.
TRANSACTIONS/CAREER NOTES: Selected by Montreal Canadiens in third round (second Canadiens pick, 60th overall) of NHL entry draft (July 8, 1995).

		REGULAR SEASON									PLAYOFFS				
Season Team	League	Gms.	G	A	Pts.	PIM	+/-	PP	SH		Gms.	G	A	Pts.	PIM
93-94—ZPS Zlin	Czech Rep.	22	1	5	6	...	...	...	...		3	0	0	0	...
94-95—ZPS Zlin	Czech Rep.	32	3	7	10	...	...	...	...		12	1	0	1	...
95-96—ZPS Zlin	Czech Rep.	27	1	2	3	...	...	...	...		7	1	0	1	...
96-97—Fredericton	AHL	79	6	26	32	26	...	...	...		—	—	—	—	—
97-98—Fredericton	AHL	78	15	36	51	36	...	...	...		4	1	2	3	0
98-99—Montreal	NHL	12	0	1	1	4	-1	0	0		—	—	—	—	—
—Fredericton	AHL	63	5	16	21	24	...	...	...		15	4	7	11	10
99-00—Montreal	NHL	24	1	2	3	12	-5	1	0		—	—	—	—	—
—Quebec	AHL	29	5	12	17	16	...	...	...		3	0	0	0	2
NHL Totals (2 years)		36	1	3	4	16	-6	1	0						

GUSAROV, ALEXEI   D   AVALANCHE

PERSONAL: Born July 8, 1964, in Leningrad, U.S.S.R. ... 6-3/185. ... Shoots left. ... Name pronounced GOO-sah-rahf.
TRANSACTIONS/CAREER NOTES: Selected by Quebec Nordiques in 11th round (11th Nordiques pick, 213th overall) in the NHL entry draft (June 11, 1988). ... Suffered hairline fracture of left ankle (December 15, 1990); missed seven games. ... Hyperextended right knee (February 28, 1991). ... Fractured finger (October 13, 1991); missed four games. ... Suffered from the flu (February 9, 1993); missed two games. ... Suffered concussion (March 31, 1993); missed two games. ... Bruised left thumb (November 13, 1993); missed one game. ... Suffered from the flu (January 11, 1994); missed two games. ... Suffered from inflammation of sinuses (March 30, 1994); missed two games. ... Injured foot (January 21, 1995); missed nine games. ... Reinjured foot (February 11, 1995); missed six games. ... Injured knee (March 26, 1995); missed last 17 games of season and entire playoffs. ... Nordiques franchise moved to Colorado and renamed Avalanche for 1995-96 season (June 21, 1995). ... Suffered concussion (December 13, 1995); missed two games. ... Suffered from the flu (November 11, 1996); missed three games. ... Scratched cornea (November 30, 1996); missed three games. ... Suffered concussion (December 17, 1996); missed 13 games. ... Suffered from the flu (January 28, 1998); missed one game. ... Injured finger (April 2, 1998); missed one game. ... Fractured finger (November 17, 1998); missed 25 games. ... Sprained knee (April 24, 1999); missed 14 playoff games. ... Injured shoulder (October 16, 1999) and underwent surgery; missed 12 games. ... Fractured finger (November 19, 1999); missed 11 games. ... Suffered from the flu (January 6, 2000); missed two games. ... Suspended two games by NHL for cross-checking incident (January 14, 2000). ... Suffered concussion (January 25, 2000); missed four games. ... Fractured leg (February 27, 2000); missed remainder of season.
MISCELLANEOUS: Member of Stanley Cup championship team (1996). ... Member of gold-medal-winning U.S.S.R. Olympic team (1988). ... Member of silver-medal-winning Russian Olympic team (1998). ... Scored on a penalty shot (vs. Grant Fuhr, March 10, 1993).

		REGULAR SEASON									PLAYOFFS				
Season Team	League	Gms.	G	A	Pts.	PIM	+/-	PP	SH		Gms.	G	A	Pts.	PIM
81-82—SKA Leningrad	USSR	20	1	2	3	16	...	...	...		—	—	—	—	—
82-83—SKA Leningrad	USSR	42	2	1	3	32	...	...	...		—	—	—	—	—
83-84—SKA Leningrad	USSR	43	2	3	5	32	...	...	...		—	—	—	—	—
84-85—CSKA Moscow	USSR	36	3	2	5	26	...	...	...		—	—	—	—	—
85-86—CSKA Moscow	USSR	40	3	5	8	30	...	...	...		—	—	—	—	—
86-87—CSKA Moscow	USSR	38	4	7	11	24	...	...	...		—	—	—	—	—
87-88—CSKA Moscow	USSR	39	3	2	5	28	...	...	...		—	—	—	—	—

G

Season Team	League	REGULAR SEASON								PLAYOFFS				
		Gms.	G	A	Pts.	PIM	+/-	PP	SH	Gms.	G	A	Pts.	PIM
88-89—CSKA Moscow	USSR	42	5	4	9	37	...	...	...	—	—	—	—	—
89-90—CSKA Moscow	USSR	42	4	7	11	42	...	...	...	—	—	—	—	—
90-91—CSKA Moscow	USSR	15	0	0	0	12	...	...	...	—	—	—	—	—
—Quebec	NHL	36	3	9	12	12	-4	1	0	—	—	—	—	—
—Halifax	AHL	2	0	3	3	2	...	...	...	—	—	—	—	—
91-92—Quebec	NHL	68	5	18	23	22	-9	3	0	—	—	—	—	—
—Halifax	AHL	3	0	0	0	0	...	...	...	—	—	—	—	—
92-93—Quebec	NHL	79	8	22	30	57	18	0	2	5	0	1	1	0
93-94—Quebec	NHL	76	5	20	25	38	3	0	1	—	—	—	—	—
94-95—Quebec	NHL	14	1	2	3	6	-1	0	0	—	—	—	—	—
95-96—Colorado	NHL	65	5	15	20	29		0	0	21	0	9	9	12
96-97—Colorado	NHL	58	2	12	14	28	4	0	0	17	0	3	3	14
97-98—Colorado	NHL	72	4	10	14	42	9	0	1	7	0	1	1	6
—Russian Oly. team	Int'l	6	0	1	1	8	...	...	...	—	—	—	—	—
98-99—Colorado	NHL	54	3	10	13	24	12	1	0	5	0	0	0	2
99-00—Colorado	NHL	33	2	2	4	10	-8	0	0	—	—	—	—	—
NHL Totals (10 years)		556	38	120	158	295	53	5	4	55	0	14	14	34

GUSEV, SERGEY — D — LIGHTNING

PERSONAL: Born July 31, 1975, in Nizhny Tagil, U.S.S.R. ... 6-1/205. ... Shoots left. ... Name pronounced GOO-sehf.

TRANSACTIONS/CAREER NOTES: Selected by Dallas Stars in third round (fourth Stars pick, 69th overall) of NHL entry draft (July 8, 1995). ... Bruised thigh (October 18, 1997); missed two games. ... Traded by Stars to Tampa Bay Lightning for LW Benoit Hogue and conditional pick in 2001 draft (March 21, 1999). ... Tore anterior cruciate ligament in knee (December 19, 1999); missed remainder of season.

Season Team	League	REGULAR SEASON								PLAYOFFS				
		Gms.	G	A	Pts.	PIM	+/-	PP	SH	Gms.	G	A	Pts.	PIM
94-95—CSK VVS Samara	CIS	50	3	5	8	58	...	...	...	—	—	—	—	—
95-96—Michigan	IHL	73	11	17	28	76	...	...	...	—	—	—	—	—
96-97—Michigan	IHL	51	7	8	15	44	...	...	...	4	0	4	4	6
97-98—Dallas	NHL	9	0	0	0	2	-5	0	0	—	—	—	—	—
—Michigan	IHL	36	3	6	9	36	...	...	...	4	0	2	2	6
98-99—Dallas	NHL	22	1	4	5	6	5	0	0	—	—	—	—	—
—Michigan	IHL	12	0	6	6	14	...	...	...	—	—	—	—	—
—Tampa Bay	NHL	14	0	3	3	10	-8	0	0	—	—	—	—	—
99-00—Tampa Bay	NHL	28	2	3	5	6	-9	1	0	—	—	—	—	—
NHL Totals (3 years)		73	3	10	13	24	-17	1	0					

HACKETT, JEFF — G — CANADIENS

PERSONAL: Born June 1, 1968, in London, Ont. ... 6-1/198. ... Catches left.

TRANSACTIONS/CAREER NOTES: Selected by New York Islanders as underage junior in second round (second Islanders pick, 34th overall) of NHL entry draft (June 13, 1987). ... Strained groin (May 13, 1990). ... Selected by San Jose Sharks in NHL expansion draft (May 30, 1991). ... Injured groin and hamstring (December 3, 1991); missed nine games. ... Injured knee (March 23, 1992). ... Injured groin (October 30, 1992); missed 12 games. ... Suffered the flu (February 20, 1993); missed five games. ... Traded by Sharks to Chicago Blackhawks for third-round pick (C Alexei Yegorov) in 1994 draft (July 13, 1993). ... Pulled groin (October 17, 1995); missed three games. ... Fractured finger (March 22, 1996); missed three games. ... Fractured finger (October 6, 1996); missed 12 games. ... Pulled groin (March 18, 1997); missed two games. ... Sprained ankle (October 9, 1997); missed 11 games. ... Traded by Blackhawks with D Eric Weinrich, D Alain Nasreddine and fourth-round pick (D Chris Dyment) in 1999 draft to Montreal Canadiens for G Jocelyn Thibault, D Dave Manson and D Brad Brown (November 16, 1998). ... Injured knee (March 27, 1999); missed one game. ... Injured hip flexor (April 1, 1999); missed five games. ... Suffered back spasms and bruised shoulder (October 18, 1999); missed one game.

HONORS: Won F.W. (Dinty) Moore Trophy (1986-87). ... Shared Dave Pinkney Trophy with Sean Evoy (1986-87). ... Won Jack Butterfield Trophy (1989-90).

MISCELLANEOUS: Stopped a penalty shot attempt (vs. Brett Hull, January 4, 1996). ... Allowed a penalty shot goal (vs. Randy Wood, January 11, 1994; vs. Geoff Courtnall, December 13, 1996; vs. Adam Deadmarsh, March 1, 1997; vs. Kimmo Timonen, November 18, 1999).

Season Team	League	REGULAR SEASON								PLAYOFFS						
		Gms.	Min.	W	L	T	GA	SO	Avg.	Gms.	Min.	W	L	GA	SO	Avg.
85-86—London Jr. B	OHA	19	1150	...	...	...	66	0	3.44	—	—	—	—	—	—	—
86-87—Oshawa	OHL	31	1672	18	9	2	85	2	3.05	15	895	8	7	40	0	2.68
87-88—Oshawa	OHL	53	3165	30	21	2	205	0	3.89	7	438	3	4	31	0	4.25
88-89—New York Islanders	NHL	13	662	4	7	0	39	0	3.53	—	—	—	—	—	—	—
—Springfield	AHL	29	1677	12	14	2	116	0	4.15	—	—	—	—	—	—	—
89-90—Springfield	AHL	54	3045	24	25	3	187	1	3.68	†17	934	10	5	*60	0	3.85
90-91—New York Islanders	NHL	30	1508	5	18	1	91	0	3.62	—	—	—	—	—	—	—
91-92—San Jose	NHL	42	2314	11	27	1	148	0	3.84	—	—	—	—	—	—	—
92-93—San Jose	NHL	36	2000	2	30	1	176	0	5.28	—	—	—	—	—	—	—
93-94—Chicago	NHL	22	1084	2	12	3	62	0	3.43	—	—	—	—	—	—	—
94-95—Chicago	NHL	7	328	1	3	2	13	0	2.38	2	26	0	0	1	0	2.31
95-96—Chicago	NHL	35	2000	18	11	4	80	4	2.40	1	60	0	1	5	0	5.00
96-97—Chicago	NHL	41	2473	19	18	4	89	2	2.16	6	345	2	4	25	0	4.35
97-98—Chicago	NHL	58	3441	21	25	11	126	8	2.20	—	—	—	—	—	—	—
98-99—Chicago	NHL	10	524	2	6	1	33	0	3.78	—	—	—	—	—	—	—
—Montreal	NHL	53	3091	24	20	9	117	5	2.27	—	—	—	—	—	—	—
99-00—Montreal	NHL	56	3301	23	25	7	132	3	2.40	—	—	—	—	—	—	—
NHL Totals (11 years)		403	22726	132	202	44	1106	22	2.92	9	431	2	5	31	0	4.32

G
H

HAGGERTY, SEAN LW PREDATORS

PERSONAL: Born February 11, 1976, in Rye, N.Y. ... 6-1/186. ... Shoots left. ... Brother of Ryan Haggerty, center in Edmonton Oilers system (1991-92 through 1995-96).
HIGH SCHOOL: Westminster School (Simsbury, Conn.).
TRANSACTIONS/CAREER NOTES: Selected by Toronto Maple Leafs in second round (second Maple Leafs pick, 48th overall) of NHL entry draft (June 28, 1994). ... Traded by Maple Leafs with C Darby Hendrickson, D Kenny Jonsson and first-round pick (G Roberto Luongo) in 1997 draft to New York Islanders for LW Wendel Clark, D Mathieu Schneider and D D.J. Smith (March 13, 1996). ... Claimed on waivers by Nashville Predators (May 23, 2000).
HONORS: Named to OHL All-Rookie team (1993-94). ... Named to Memorial Cup All-Star team (1994-95). ... Named to OHL All-Star second team (1995-96). ... Named to AHL All-Star second team (1997-98).

		REGULAR SEASON								PLAYOFFS				
Season Team	League	Gms.	G	A	Pts.	PIM	+/-	PP	SH	Gms.	G	A	Pts.	PIM
90-91—Westminster Prep	USHS (East)	25	20	22	42	...	...	...	...	—	—	—	—	—
91-92—Westminster Prep	USHS (East)	25	24	36	60	...	...	...	...	—	—	—	—	—
92-93—Boston	NEJHL	72	70	111	181	80	...	...	...	—	—	—	—	—
93-94—Det. Jr. Red Wings	OHL	60	31	32	63	21	...	...	...	17	9	10	19	11
94-95—Det. Jr. Red Wings	OHL	61	40	49	89	37	...	...	...	21	13	24	37	18
95-96—Det. Jr. Red Wings	OHL	66	*60	51	111	78	...	...	...	17	15	9	24	30
—Toronto	NHL	1	0	0	0	0	0	0	0	—	—	—	—	—
—Worcester	AHL	—	—	—	—	—				1	0	0	0	2
96-97—Kentucky	AHL	77	13	22	35	60	...	...	...	4	1	0	1	4
97-98—Kentucky	AHL	63	33	20	53	64	...	...	...	3	0	2	2	4
—New York Islanders	NHL	5	0	0	0	0	-3	0	0	—	—	—	—	—
98-99—Lowell	AHL	77	19	27	46	40	...	...	...	3	0	1	1	0
99-00—Kansas City	IHL	76	27	33	60	94	...	...	...	—	—	—	—	—
—New York Islanders	NHL	5	1	1	2	4	3	0	0	—	—	—	—	—
NHL Totals (3 years)		11	1	1	2	4	0	0	0					

HAJT, CHRIS D OILERS

PERSONAL: Born July 5, 1978, in Amherst, N.Y. ... 6-3/206. ... Shoots left. ... Son of Bill Hajt, defenseman with Buffalo Sabres (1973-74 through 1986-87). ... Name pronounced HIGHT.
TRANSACTIONS/CAREER NOTES: Selected by Edmonton Oilers in second round (third Oilers pick, 32nd overall) of NHL entry draft (June 22, 1996).
HONORS: Named to OHL All-Star second team (1997-98).

		REGULAR SEASON								PLAYOFFS				
Season Team	League	Gms.	G	A	Pts.	PIM	+/-	PP	SH	Gms.	G	A	Pts.	PIM
94-95—Guelph	OHL	57	1	7	8	35	...	...	...	14	0	2	2	9
95-96—Guelph	OHL	63	8	27	35	69	...	...	...	16	0	6	6	13
96-97—Guelph	OHL	58	11	15	26	62	...	...	...	18	0	8	8	25
97-98—Guelph	OHL	44	2	21	23	42	...	...	...	12	1	5	6	11
98-99—Hamilton	AHL	64	0	4	4	36	...	...	...	—	—	—	—	—
99-00—Hamilton	AHL	54	0	8	8	30	...	...	...	10	0	2	2	0

HALKO, STEVE D HURRICANES

PERSONAL: Born March 8, 1974, in Etobicoke, Ont. ... 6-1/190. ... Shoots right. ... Full Name: Steven Halko. ... Name pronounced HAHL-koh.
HIGH SCHOOL: Notre Dame Secondary School (Brampton, Ont.).
COLLEGE: Michigan.
TRANSACTIONS/CAREER NOTES: Selected by Hartford Whalers in 10th round (10th Whalers pick, 225th overall) of NHL entry draft (June 20, 1992). ... Whalers franchise moved to North Carolina and renamed Carolina Hurricanes for 1997-98 season; NHL approved move on June 25, 1997.
HONORS: Named to CCHA All-Star second team (1994-95 and 1995-96). ... Named to NCAA All-Tournament team (1995-96).

		REGULAR SEASON								PLAYOFFS				
Season Team	League	Gms.	G	A	Pts.	PIM	+/-	PP	SH	Gms.	G	A	Pts.	PIM
91-92—Thornhill	OHA Jr. A	44	15	46	61	43	...	...	...	—	—	—	—	—
92-93—Univ. of Michigan	CCHA	39	1	12	13	12	...	...	...	—	—	—	—	—
93-94—Univ. of Michigan	CCHA	41	2	13	15	32	...	...	...	—	—	—	—	—
94-95—Univ. of Michigan	CCHA	39	2	14	16	20	...	...	...	—	—	—	—	—
95-96—Univ. of Michigan	CCHA	43	4	16	20	32	...	...	...	—	—	—	—	—
96-97—Springfield	AHL	70	1	5	6	37	...	...	...	11	0	2	2	8
97-98—Carolina	NHL	18	0	2	2	10	-1	0	0	—	—	—	—	—
—New Haven	AHL	65	1	19	20	44	...	...	...	1	0	0	0	0
98-99—New Haven	AHL	42	2	7	9	58	...	...	...	—	—	—	—	—
—Carolina	NHL	20	0	3	3	24	5	0	0	4	0	0	0	2
99-00—Carolina	NHL	58	0	8	8	25	0	0	0	—	—	—	—	—
NHL Totals (3 years)		96	0	13	13	59	4	0	0	4	0	0	0	2

HALLER, KEVIN D ISLANDERS

H

PERSONAL: Born December 5, 1970, in Trochu, Alta. ... 6-2/199. ... Shoots left. ... Name pronounced HAW-luhr.
TRANSACTIONS/CAREER NOTES: Fractured leg (October 1986). ... Fractured leg (May 1987). ... Selected by Buffalo Sabres in first round (first Sabres pick, 14th overall) of NHL entry draft (June 17, 1989). ... Separated shoulder (May 7, 1991); missed seven games. ... Traded by Sabres to Montreal Canadiens for D Petr Svoboda (March 10, 1992). ... Suspended four games and fined $500 by NHL for slashing (November 2, 1993). ... Traded by Canadiens to Philadelphia Flyers for D Yves Racine (June 29, 1994). ... Pulled right groin (January 26, 1995); missed four games. ... Suffered from the flu (March 2, 1995); missed two games. ... Strained groin (March 15, 1995); missed six games. ... Suffered sprained muscle in chest (December 16, 1995); missed 13 games. ... Fractured thumb (April 27, 1996); missed remainder of playoffs. ...

Traded by Flyers with first- (traded to San Jose) and seventh-round (C Andrew Merrick) picks in 1997 draft to Hartford Whalers for D Paul Coffey and third-round pick (D Kris Mallette) in 1997 draft (December 15, 1996). ... Suffered from the flu (December 20, 1996); missed one game. ... Strained groin (January 1, 1997); missed 13 games. ... Sprained shoulder (March 5, 1997); missed six games. ... Whalers franchise moved to North Carolina and renamed Carolina Hurricanes for 1997-98 season; NHL approved move on June 25, 1997. ... Suffered infected ankle (March 15, 1998); missed one game. ... Injured groin (March 28, 1998); missed 11 games. ... Traded by Hurricanes with LW Stu Grimson to Mighty Ducks of Anaheim for D Dave Karpa and fourth-round pick (traded to Atlanta) in 2000 draft (August 11, 1998). ... Underwent knee surgery prior to start of 1999-2000 season; missed first game of season. ... Sprained knee (November 15, 1999); missed 12 games. ... Signed as free agent by New York Islanders (July 3, 2000).

HONORS: Won Bill Hunter Trophy (1989-90). ... Named to WHL (East) All-Star first team (1989-90).
MISCELLANEOUS: Member of Stanley Cup championship team (1993).

		REGULAR SEASON								PLAYOFFS				
Season Team	League	Gms.	G	A	Pts.	PIM	+/-	PP	SH	Gms.	G	A	Pts.	PIM
87-88—Olds	AJHL	54	13	31	44	58	...	...	...	—	—	—	—	—
88-89—Regina	WHL	72	10	31	41	99	...	...	...	—	—	—	—	—
89-90—Regina	WHL	58	16	37	53	93	...	...	...	11	2	9	11	16
—Buffalo	NHL	2	0	0	0	0	0	0	0	—	—	—	—	—
90-91—Rochester	AHL	52	2	8	10	53	...	...	...	10	2	1	3	6
—Buffalo	NHL	21	1	8	9	20	9	1	0	6	1	4	5	10
91-92—Buffalo	NHL	58	6	15	21	75	-13	2	0	—	—	—	—	—
—Rochester	AHL	4	0	0	0	18	...	...	...	—	—	—	—	—
—Montreal	NHL	8	2	2	4	17	4	1	0	9	0	0	0	6
92-93—Montreal	NHL	73	11	14	25	117	7	6	0	17	1	6	7	16
93-94—Montreal	NHL	68	4	9	13	118	3	0	0	7	1	1	2	19
94-95—Philadelphia	NHL	36	2	8	10	48	16	0	0	15	4	4	8	10
95-96—Philadelphia	NHL	69	5	9	14	92	18	0	2	6	0	1	1	8
96-97—Philadelphia	NHL	27	0	5	5	37	-1	0	0	—	—	—	—	—
—Hartford	NHL	35	2	6	8	48	-11	0	0	—	—	—	—	—
97-98—Carolina	NHL	65	3	5	8	94	-5	0	0	—	—	—	—	—
98-99—Anaheim	NHL	82	1	6	7	122	-1	0	0	4	0	0	0	2
99-00—Anaheim	NHL	67	3	5	8	61	-8	0	0	—	—	—	—	—
NHL Totals (11 years)		611	40	92	132	849	18	10	2	64	7	16	23	71

HALPERN, JEFF — C — CAPITALS

PERSONAL: Born May 3, 1976, in Potomac, Md. ... 5-11/198. ... Shoots right.
COLLEGE: Princeton.
TRANSACTIONS/CAREER NOTES: Signed as non-drafted free agent by Washington Capitals (March 29, 1999). ... Suffered back spasms (February 19, 2000); missed three games.
HONORS: Named to ECAC All-Star second team (1997-98 and 1998-99).

		REGULAR SEASON								PLAYOFFS				
Season Team	League	Gms.	G	A	Pts.	PIM	+/-	PP	SH	Gms.	G	A	Pts.	PIM
95-96—Princeton University	ECAC	29	3	11	14	30	...	...	...	—	—	—	—	—
96-97—Princeton University	ECAC	33	7	24	31	35	...	...	...	—	—	—	—	—
97-98—Princeton University	ECAC	36	*28	25	*53	46	...	...	...	—	—	—	—	—
98-99—Princeton University	ECAC	33	†22	22	44	32	...	...	...	—	—	—	—	—
—Portland	AHL	6	2	1	3	4	...	...	...	—	—	—	—	—
99-00—Washington	NHL	79	18	11	29	39	21	4	4	5	2	1	3	0
NHL Totals (1 year)		79	18	11	29	39	21	4	4	5	2	1	3	0

HAMEL, DENIS — RW — SABRES

PERSONAL: Born May 10, 1977, in Lachute, Que. ... 6-2/200. ... Shoots left. ... Name pronounced uh-MEHL.
TRANSACTIONS/CAREER NOTES: Selected by St. Louis Blues in sixth round (fifth Blues pick, 153rd overall) of NHL entry draft (July 8, 1995). ... Rights traded by Blues to Buffalo Sabres for D Charlie Huddy (March 19, 1996).

		REGULAR SEASON								PLAYOFFS				
Season Team	League	Gms.	G	A	Pts.	PIM	+/-	PP	SH	Gms.	G	A	Pts.	PIM
94-95—Chicoutimi	QMJHL	66	15	12	27	155	...	...	...	13	2	0	2	29
95-96—Chicoutimi	QMJHL	65	40	49	89	199	...	...	...	17	10	14	24	64
96-97—Chicoutimi	QMJHL	70	50	50	100	339	...	...	...	20	15	10	25	65
97-98—Rochester	AHL	74	10	15	25	98	...	...	...	4	1	2	3	0
98-99—Rochester	AHL	74	16	17	33	121	...	...	...	20	3	4	7	10
99-00—Rochester	AHL	76	34	24	58	122	...	...	...	21	6	7	13	49
—Buffalo	NHL	3	1	0	1	0	-1	0	0	—	—	—	—	—
NHL Totals (1 year)		3	1	0	1	0	-1	0	0	—	—	—	—	—

HAMRLIK, ROMAN — D — ISLANDERS

PERSONAL: Born April 12, 1974, in Gottwaldov, Czechoslovakia. ... 6-2/215. ... Shoots left. ... Brother of Martin Hamrlik, defenseman with Hartford Whalers (1991-92 through 1993-94) and St. Louis Blues (1993-94 and 1994-95) organizations. ... Name pronounced ROH-muhn HAM-uhr-lihk.
TRANSACTIONS/CAREER NOTES: Selected by Tampa Bay Lightning in first round (first Lightning pick, first overall) of NHL entry draft (June 20, 1992). ... Bruised shoulder (November 3, 1993); missed six games. ... Bruised shoulder (March 1, 1994); missed seven games. ... Played in Europe during 1994-95 NHL lockout. ... Suffered back spasms (January 9, 1997); missed two games. ... Traded by Lightning with C Paul Comrie to Edmonton Oilers for C Steve Kelly, D Bryan Marchment and C Jason Bonsignore (December 30, 1997). ... Fractured toe (January 5, 1999); missed six games. ... Bruised finger (December 1, 1999); missed two games. ... Traded by Oilers to Islanders for D Eric Brewer, LW Josh Green and second-round pick (LW Brad Winchester) in 2000 draft (June 24, 2000).
HONORS: Played in NHL All-Star Game (1996 and 1999).
MISCELLANEOUS: Member of gold-medal-winning Czech Republic Olympic team (1998).

H

Season Team	League	REGULAR SEASON								PLAYOFFS				
		Gms.	G	A	Pts.	PIM	+/-	PP	SH	Gms.	G	A	Pts.	PIM
90-91—TJ Zlin..................	Czech.	14	2	2	4	18	...	...	...	—	—	—	—	—
91-92—ZPS Zlin..................	Czech.	34	5	5	10	34	...	...	...	—	—	—	—	—
92-93—Tampa Bay................	NHL	67	6	15	21	71	-21	1	0	—	—	—	—	—
—Atlanta	IHL	2	1	1	2	2	...	...	...	—	—	—	—	—
93-94—Tampa Bay................	NHL	64	3	18	21	135	-14	0	0	—	—	—	—	—
94-95—ZPS Zlin..................	Czech Rep.	2	1	0	1	10	...	...	...	—	—	—	—	—
—Tampa Bay................	NHL	48	12	11	23	86	-18	7	1	—	—	—	—	—
95-96—Tampa Bay................	NHL	82	16	49	65	103	-24	12	0	5	0	1	1	4
96-97—Tampa Bay................	NHL	79	12	28	40	57	-29	6	0	—	—	—	—	—
97-98—Tampa Bay................	NHL	37	3	12	15	22	-18	1	0	—	—	—	—	—
—Edmonton................	NHL	41	6	20	26	48	3	4	1	12	0	6	6	12
—Czech Rep. Oly. team..	Int'l	6	1	0	1	2	...	...	...	—	—	—	—	—
98-99—Edmonton................	NHL	75	8	24	32	70	9	3	0	3	0	0	0	2
99-00—Edmonton................	NHL	80	8	37	45	68	1	5	0	5	0	1	1	4
NHL Totals (8 years)...........		573	74	214	288	660	-111	39	2	25	0	8	8	22

HANDZUS, MICHAL — C — BLUES

PERSONAL: Born March 11, 1977, in Banska Bystrica, Czechoslovakia. ... 6-5/210. ... Shoots left. ... Name pronounced han-ZOOZ.
TRANSACTIONS/CAREER NOTES: Selected by St. Louis Blues in fourth round (third Blues pick, 101st overall) of NHL entry draft (July 8, 1995). ... Bruised shoulder (February 26, 1999); missed five games. ... Bruised shoulder (March 25, 1999); missed final 11 games of regular season and two playoffs games.

Season Team	League	REGULAR SEASON								PLAYOFFS				
		Gms.	G	A	Pts.	PIM	+/-	PP	SH	Gms.	G	A	Pts.	PIM
93-94—IS Banska Byst. Jrs. ...	Slovakia	40	23	36	59	...	...	...	...	—	—	—	—	—
94-95—IS Banska Bystrica......	Slov. Div. II	22	15	14	29	10	...	...	...	—	—	—	—	—
95-96—IS Banska Bystrica......	Slov. Div. II	19	3	1	4	8	...	...	...	—	—	—	—	—
96-97—Poprad......................	Slovakia	44	15	18	33	...	...	...	...	—	—	—	—	—
97-98—Worcester	AHL	69	27	36	63	54	...	...	...	11	2	6	8	10
98-99—St. Louis	NHL	66	4	12	16	30	-9	0	0	11	0	2	2	8
99-00—St. Louis	NHL	81	25	28	53	44	19	3	4	7	0	3	3	6
NHL Totals (2 years)...........		147	29	40	69	74	10	3	4	18	0	5	5	14

HANNAN, SCOTT — D — SHARKS

PERSONAL: Born January 23, 1979, in Richmond, B.C. ... 6-2/220. ... Shoots left.
TRANSACTIONS/CAREER NOTES: Selected by San Jose Sharks in first round (second Sharks pick, 23rd overall) of NHL entry draft (June 21, 1997).
HONORS: Name to WHL (West) All-Star first team (1998-99).

Season Team	League	REGULAR SEASON								PLAYOFFS				
		Gms.	G	A	Pts.	PIM	+/-	PP	SH	Gms.	G	A	Pts.	PIM
94-95—Tacoma	WHL	2	0	0	0	0	...	...	...	—	—	—	—	—
95-96—Kelowna....................	WHL	69	4	5	9	76	...	...	...	6	0	1	1	4
96-97—Kelowna....................	WHL	70	17	26	43	101	...	...	...	6	0	0	0	8
97-98—Kelowna....................	WHL	47	10	30	40	70	...	...	...	—	—	—	—	—
98-99—San Jose..................	NHL	5	0	2	2	6	0	0	0	—	—	—	—	—
—Kelowna....................	WHL	47	15	30	45	92	...	...	...	6	1	2	3	14
—Kentucky...................	AHL	2	0	0	0	2	...	...	...	12	0	2	2	10
99-00—Kentucky...................	AHL	41	5	12	17	40	...	...	...	—	—	—	—	—
—San Jose..................	NHL	30	1	2	3	10	7	0	0	1	0	1	1	0
NHL Totals (2 years)...........		35	1	4	5	16	7	0	0	1	0	1	1	0

HANSEN, TAVIS — C/RW — COYOTES

PERSONAL: Born June 17, 1975, in Prince Albert, Sask. ... 6-1/180. ... Shoots right.
TRANSACTIONS/CAREER NOTES: Selected by Winnipeg Jets in third round (third Jets pick, 58th overall) of NHL entry draft (June 29, 1994). ... Jets franchise moved to Phoenix and renamed Coyotes for 1996-97 season; NHL approved move on January 18, 1996.

Season Team	League	REGULAR SEASON								PLAYOFFS				
		Gms.	G	A	Pts.	PIM	+/-	PP	SH	Gms.	G	A	Pts.	PIM
93-94—Tacoma	WHL	71	23	31	54	122	...	...	...	8	1	3	4	17
94-95—Tacoma	WHL	71	32	41	73	142	...	...	...	4	1	1	2	8
—Winnipeg	NHL	1	0	0	0	0	0	0	0	—	—	—	—	—
95-96—Springfield	AHL	67	6	16	22	85	...	...	...	5	1	2	3	2
96-97—Springfield	AHL	12	3	1	4	23	...	...	...	—	—	—	—	—
—Phoenix....................	NHL	1	0	0	0	0	0	0	0	—	—	—	—	—
97-98—Springfield	AHL	73	20	14	34	70	...	...	...	4	1	2	3	18
98-99—Springfield	AHL	63	23	11	34	85	...	...	...	3	0	1	1	5
—Phoenix....................	NHL	20	2	1	3	12	-4	0	0	2	0	0	0	0
99-00—Springfield	AHL	59	21	27	48	164	...	...	...	5	2	1	3	4
—Phoenix....................	NHL	5	0	0	0	0	0	0	0	—	—	—	—	—
NHL Totals (4 years)...........		27	2	1	3	12	-4	0	0	2	0	0	0	0

HARLOCK, DAVID   D   THRASHERS

PERSONAL: Born March 16, 1971, in Toronto. ... 6-2/220. ... Shoots left. ... Full Name: David Alan Harlock.
COLLEGE: Michigan.
TRANSACTIONS/CAREER NOTES: Selected by New Jersey Devils in second round (second Devils pick, 24th overall) of NHL entry draft (June 16, 1990). ... Signed as free agent by Toronto Maple Leafs (August 20, 1993). ... Loaned by Maple Leafs to Canadian national team (October 3, 1993). ... Signed as free agent by Washington Capitals (August 31, 1997). ... Signed as free agent by New York Islanders (August 19, 1998). ... Bruised foot (October 29, 1998); missed one game. ... Selected by Atlanta Thrashers in NHL expansion draft (June 25, 1999). ... Strained shoulder (December 23, 1999) and underwent surgery; missed 36 games.
MISCELLANEOUS: Member of silver-medal-winning Canadian Olympic team (1994).

		REGULAR SEASON								PLAYOFFS				
Season Team	League	Gms.	G	A	Pts.	PIM	+/-	PP	SH	Gms.	G	A	Pts.	PIM
86-87—Toronto Red Wings....	MTHL	86	17	55	72	60	...	...	...	—	—	—	—	—
87-88—Toronto Red Wings....	MTHL	70	16	56	72	100	...	...	...	—	—	—	—	—
88-89—St. Michael's Jr. B......	ODHA	25	4	15	19	34	...	...	...	—	—	—	—	—
89-90—Univ. of Michigan.......	CCHA	42	2	13	15	44	...	...	...	—	—	—	—	—
90-91—Univ. of Michigan.......	CCHA	39	2	8	10	70	...	...	...	—	—	—	—	—
91-92—Univ. of Michigan.......	CCHA	44	1	6	7	80	...	...	...	—	—	—	—	—
92-93—Univ. of Michigan.......	CCHA	38	3	9	12	58	...	...	...	—	—	—	—	—
—Canadian nat'l team	Int'l	4	0	0	0	2	...	...	...	—	—	—	—	—
93-94—Canadian nat'l team	Int'l	41	0	3	3	28	...	...	...	—	—	—	—	—
—Can. Olympic team	Int'l	8	0	0	0	8	...	...	...	—	—	—	—	—
—Toronto..................	NHL	6	0	0	0	0	-2	0	0	—	—	—	—	—
—St. John's..................	AHL	10	0	3	3	2	...	...	...	9	0	0	0	6
94-95—St. John's..................	AHL	58	0	6	6	44	...	...	...	5	0	0	0	0
—Toronto..................	NHL	1	0	0	0	0	-1	0	0	—	—	—	—	—
95-96—St. John's..................	AHL	77	0	12	12	92	...	...	...	4	0	1	1	2
—Toronto..................	NHL	1	0	0	0	0	0	0	0	—	—	—	—	—
—Portland..................	AHL	1	0	0	0	0	...	...	...	—	—	—	—	—
96-97—San Antonio................	IHL	69	3	10	13	82	...	...	...	9	0	0	0	10
97-98—Portland..................	AHL	71	3	15	18	66	...	...	...	10	2	2	4	6
—Washington	NHL	6	0	0	0	4	2	0	0	—	—	—	—	—
98-99—New York Islanders.....	NHL	70	2	6	8	68	-16	0	0	—	—	—	—	—
99-00—Atlanta	NHL	44	0	6	6	36	-8	0	0	—	—	—	—	—
NHL Totals (6 years)...........		128	2	12	14	108	-25	0	0					

HARVEY, TODD   RW   SHARKS

PERSONAL: Born February 17, 1975, in Hamilton, Ont. ... 6-0/205. ... Shoots right.
TRANSACTIONS/CAREER NOTES: Selected by Dallas Stars in first round (first Stars pick, ninth overall) of NHL entry draft (June 26, 1993). ... Strained back (March 13, 1995); missed one game. ... Sprained knee (October 30, 1995); missed two games. ... Strained groin (November 3, 1996); missed one game. ... Sprained knee (November 19, 1996); missed five games. ... Suffered from the flu (December 29, 1996); missed one game. ... Suspended two games and fined $1,000 by NHL for elbowing incident (February 2, 1997). ... Bruised hand (April 4, 1997); missed one game. ... Suffered concussion (November 16, 1997); missed one game. ... Strained hip flexor (December 20, 1997); missed one game. ... Sprained knee (January 7, 1998); missed five games. ... Injured hand (February 4, 1998); missed one game. ... Strained lower back (March 13, 1998); missed one game. ... Underwent right knee surgery (March 22, 1998); missed 12 games. ... Traded by Stars with LW Bob Errey and fourth-round pick (LW Boyd Kane) in 1998 draft to New York Rangers for RW Mike Keane, C Brian Skrudland and sixth-round pick (RW Pavel Patera) in 1998 draft (March 24, 1998). ... Strained hip flexor (October 9, 1998); missed first two games of season. ... Suspended one game and fined $1,000 by NHL for roughing incident (December 13, 1998). ... Bruised right thumb (December 11, 1998); missed two games. ... Sprained medial collateral ligament in knee (January 13, 1999); missed 10 games. ... Fractured thumb (February 17, 1999); missed remainder of season. ... Sprained knee (November 18, 1999); missed three games. ... Traded by Rangers with fourth-round pick in 2001 draft to San Jose Sharks for RW Radek Dvorak (December 30, 1999).
HONORS: Named to Can.HL All-Rookie team (1991-92). ... Named to OHL Rookie All-Star team (1991-92).
STATISTICAL PLATEAUS: Three-goal games: 1994-95 (1).

		REGULAR SEASON								PLAYOFFS				
Season Team	League	Gms.	G	A	Pts.	PIM	+/-	PP	SH	Gms.	G	A	Pts.	PIM
89-90—Cambridge Jr. B..........	OHA	41	35	27	62	213	...	...	...	—	—	—	—	—
90-91—Cambridge Jr. B..........	OHA	35	32	39	71	174	...	...	...	—	—	—	—	—
91-92—Det. Jr. Red Wings......	OHL	58	21	43	64	141	...	...	...	7	3	5	8	32
92-93—Det. Jr. Red Wings......	OHL	55	50	50	100	83	...	...	...	15	9	12	21	39
93-94—Det. Jr. Red Wings......	OHL	49	34	51	85	75	...	...	...	17	10	12	22	26
94-95—Det. Jr. Red Wings......	OHL	11	8	14	22	12	...	...	...	—	—	—	—	—
—Dallas......................	NHL	40	11	9	20	67	-3	2	0	5	0	0	0	8
95-96—Dallas......................	NHL	69	9	20	29	136	-13	3	0	—	—	—	—	—
—Michigan....................	IHL	5	1	3	4	8	...	...	...	—	—	—	—	—
96-97—Dallas......................	NHL	71	9	22	31	142	19	1	0	7	0	1	1	10
97-98—Dallas......................	NHL	59	9	10	19	104	5	0	0	—	—	—	—	—
98-99—New York Rangers......	NHL	37	11	17	28	72	-1	6	0	—	—	—	—	—
99-00—New York Rangers......	NHL	31	3	3	6	62	-9	0	0	—	—	—	—	—
—San Jose....................	NHL	40	8	4	12	78	-2	2	0	12	1	0	1	8
NHL Totals (6 years)..........		347	60	85	145	661	-4	14	0	24	1	1	2	26

HASEK, DOMINIK   G   SABRES

PERSONAL: Born January 29, 1965, in Pardubice, Czechoslovakia. ... 5-11/168. ... Catches left. ... Name pronounced HA-shehk.
TRANSACTIONS/CAREER NOTES: Selected by Chicago Blackhawks in 10th round (11th Blackhawks pick, 199th overall) of NHL entry draft (June 8, 1983). ... Traded by Blackhawks to Buffalo Sabres for G Stephane Beauregard and fourth-round pick (LW Eric Daze) in 1993 draft (August 7, 1992). ... Injured groin (November 25, 1992); missed three games. ... Strained abdominal muscle (January 6, 1993); missed six games. ... Played in Europe during 1994-95 NHL lockout. ... Strained rotator cuff (March 16, 1995); missed three games. ... Injured abdominal

muscle (December 15, 1995); missed 10 games. ... Sprained left knee (April 6, 1996); missed last two games of season. ... Fractured rib (March 19, 1997); missed five games. ... Sprained knee ligament (April 21, 1997); missed six playoff games. ... Suspended three playoff games and fined $10,000 by NHL for grabbing a reporter who had written a critical column (May 1, 1997). ... Suffered ear infection (April 15, 1998); missed one game. ... Strained groin (February 17, 1999); missed 12 games. ... Strained back (March 23, 1999); missed one game. ... Announced retirement to follow 1999-2000 season (July 29, 1999). ... Tore groin muscle (October 29, 1999); missed 40 games.

HONORS: Named Czechoslovakian League Player of the Year (1986-87, 1988-89 and 1989-90). ... Named to Czechoslovakian League All-Star team (1988-89 and 1989-90). ... Named to IHL All-Star first team (1990-91). ... Named to NHL All-Rookie team (1991-92). ... Won Vezina Trophy (1993-94, 1994-95 and 1996-97 through 1998-99). ... Shared William M. Jennings Trophy with Grant Fuhr (1993-94). ... Named to The Sporting News All-Star second team (1993-94). ... Named to NHL All-Star first team (1993-94, 1994-95 and 1996-97 through 1998-99). ... Named to The Sporting News All-Star team (1994-95 and 1996-97 through 1998-99). ... Played in NHL All-Star Game (1996-1999). ... Named NHL Player of the Year by The Sporting News (1996-97 and 1997-98). ... Won Lester B. Pearson Award (1996-97 and 1997-98). ... Won Hart Memorial Trophy (1996-97 and 1997-98). ... Named to play in NHL All-Star Game (2000); replaced by G Roman Turek due to injury.

MISCELLANEOUS: Mermber of gold-medal-winning Czech Republic Olympic team (1998). ... Holds Buffalo Sabres all-time records for most games played in by a goalie (424), most wins (197), most shutouts (44) and goals-against average (2.24). ... Stopped a penalty shot attempt (vs. Mark Recchi, March 8, 1995; vs. Mario Lemieux, March 23, 1996; vs. Vincent Damphousse, March 8, 1997; vs. Jason Allison, April 10, 1997; vs. Eric Desjardins, April 16, 2000 (playoffs)). ... Allowed a penalty shot goal (vs. John MacLean, February 27, 1997; vs. Jere Lehtinen, October 7, 1997; vs. Mats Sundin, May 29, 1999 (playoffs); vs Olli Jokinen, March 4, 2000).

STATISTICAL NOTES: Led NHL in save percentage with .930 in 1993-94, .930 in 1994-95, .920 in 1995-96, .930 in 1996-97, .932 in 1997-98 and .937 in 1998-99. ... Tied for NHL lead with .919 save percentage (1999-2000).

			REGULAR SEASON								PLAYOFFS						
Season Team	League	Gms.	Min	W	L	T	GA	SO	Avg.	Gms.	Min.	W	L	GA	SO	Avg.
81-82—Pardubice............	Czech Rep.	12	661	...	...	...	34	0	3.09	—	—	—	—	—	—	—
82-83—Pardubice............	Czech Rep.	42	2358	...	...	...	105	0	2.67	—	—	—	—	—	—	—
83-84—Pardubice............	Czech Rep.	40	2304	...	...	...	108	0	2.81	—	—	—	—	—	—	—
84-85—Pardubice............	Czech Rep.	42	2419	...	...	...	131	0	3.25	—	—	—	—	—	—	—
85-86—Pardubice............	Czech Rep.	45	2689	...	...	...	138	0	3.08	—	—	—	—	—	—	—
86-87—Pardubice............	Czech Rep.	23	2515	...	...	...	103	0	2.46	—	—	—	—	—	—	—
87-88—Pardubice............	Czech Rep.	31	2265	...	...	...	98	0	2.60	—	—	—	—	—	—	—
—Czech. Olympic Team....	Int'l	8	217	...	...	...	18		4.98	—	—	—	—	—	—	—
88-89—Pardubice............	Czech Rep.	42	2507	...	...	...	114	0	2.73	—	—	—	—	—	—	—
89-90—Dukla Jihlava........	Czech.	40	2251	...	...	...	80	0	2.13	—	—	—	—	—	—	—
90-91—Chicago................	NHL	5	195	3	0	1	8	0	2.46	3	69	0	0	3	0	2.61
—Indianapolis............	IHL	33	1903	20	11	‡4	80	*5	*2.52	1	60	1	0	3	0	3.00
91-92—Indianapolis........	IHL	20	1162	7	10	‡3	69	1	3.56	—	—	—	—	—	—	—
—Chicago..................	NHL	20	1014	10	4	1	44	1	2.60	3	158	0	2	8	0	3.04
92-93—Buffalo................	NHL	28	1429	11	10	4	75	0	3.15	1	45	1	0	1	0	1.33
93-94—Buffalo................	NHL	58	3358	30	20	6	109	†7	*1.95	7	484	3	4	13	2	*1.61
94-95—HC Pardubice........	Czech Rep.	2	125	...	...	...	6		2.88	—	—	—	—	—	—	—
—Buffalo..................	NHL	41	2416	19	14	7	85	†5	*2.11	5	309	1	4	18	0	3.50
95-96—Buffalo................	NHL	59	3417	22	†30	6	161	2	2.83	—	—	—	—	—	—	—
96-97—Buffalo................	NHL	67	4037	37	20	10	153	5	2.27	3	153	1	1	5	0	1.96
97-98—Buffalo................	NHL	*72	*4220	33	23	13	147	*13	2.09	15	948	10	5	32	1	2.03
—Czech Rep. Oly. team....	Int'l	6	369	5	1	0	6	2	.98	—	—	—	—	—	—	—
98-99—Buffalo................	NHL	64	3817	30	18	14	119	9	1.87	19	1217	13	6	36	2	1.77
99-00—Buffalo................	NHL	35	2066	15	11	6	76	3	2.21	5	301	1	4	12	0	2.39
NHL Totals (10 years)...........		449	25969	210	150	68	977	45	2.26	61	3684	30	26	128	5	2.08

HATCHER, DERIAN   D   STARS

PERSONAL: Born June 4, 1972, in Sterling Heights, Mich. ... 6-5/230. ... Shoots left. ... Brother of Kevin Hatcher, defenseman, Carolina Hurricanes.

TRANSACTIONS/CAREER NOTES: Underwent knee surgery (January 1989). ... Selected by Minnesota North Stars in first round (first North Stars pick, eighth overall) of NHL entry draft (June 16, 1990). ... Suspended 10 games by NHL (December 1991). ... Fractured ankle in off-ice incident (January 19, 1992); missed 21 games. ... Sprained knee (January 6, 1993); missed 14 games. ... Suspended one game by NHL for game misconduct penalty (March 9, 1993). ... North Stars franchise moved from Minnesota to Dallas and renamed Stars for 1993-94 season. ... Sprained ankle (February 2, 1995); missed one game. ... Suffered staph infection on little finger (February 14, 1995); missed four games. ... Injured right knee ligament (May 1, 1995); missed entire playoffs. ... Injured shoulder (November 14, 1995); missed three games. ... Strained knee (December 8, 1996); missed 14 games. ... Underwent knee surgery (March 19, 1997); missed five games. ... Injured knee (March 8, 1998); missed seven games. ... Suspended four pre-season games and fined $1,000 by NHL for injuring another player (September 23, 1998). ... Suspended seven games by NHL for illegal check (April 17, 1999); missed final two games of regular season and first five play-off games. ... Suffered lacerated calf (December 17, 1999); missed 24 games. ... Strained Achilles' tendon (March 8, 2000); missed one game.

HONORS: Played in NHL All-Star Game (1997).

MISCELLANEOUS: Member of Stanley Cup championship team (1999). ... Captain of Dallas Stars (1995-96 through 1999-2000). ... Holds Dallas Stars record for most penalty minutes (776).

			REGULAR SEASON							PLAYOFFS				
Season Team	League	Gms.	G	A	Pts.	PIM	+/-	PP	SH	Gms.	G	A	Pts.	PIM
88-89—Detroit G.P.D..............	MNHL	51	19	35	54	100	...	...	...	—	—	—	—	—
89-90—North Bay..............	OHL	64	14	38	52	81	...	...	...	5	2	3	5	8
90-91—North Bay..............	OHL	64	13	50	63	163	...	...	...	10	2	10	12	28
91-92—Minnesota..............	NHL	43	8	4	12	88	7	0	0	5	0	2	2	8
92-93—Minnesota..............	NHL	67	4	15	19	178	-27	0	0	—	—	—	—	—
—Kalamazoo..............	IHL	2	1	2	3	21	...	...	...	—	—	—	—	—
93-94—Dallas..............	NHL	83	12	19	31	211	19	2	1	9	0	2	2	14
94-95—Dallas..............	NHL	43	5	11	16	105	3	2	0	—	—	—	—	—
95-96—Dallas..............	NHL	79	8	23	31	129	-12	2	0	—	—	—	—	—
96-97—Dallas..............	NHL	63	3	19	22	97	8	0	0	7	0	2	2	20
97-98—Dallas..............	NHL	70	6	25	31	132	9	3	0	17	3	3	6	39
—U.S. Olympic team......	Int'l	4	0	0	0	0	...	...	...	—	—	—	—	—
98-99—Dallas..............	NHL	80	9	21	30	102	21	3	0	18	1	6	7	24
99-00—Dallas..............	NHL	57	2	22	24	68	6	0	0	23	1	3	4	29
NHL Totals (9 years)...........		585	57	159	216	1110	34	12	1	79	5	18	23	134

H

HATCHER, KEVIN — D — HURRICANES

PERSONAL: Born September 9, 1966, in Detroit. ... 6-3/220. ... Shoots right. ... Full Name: Kevin John Hatcher. ... Brother of Derian Hatcher, defenseman, Dallas Stars.

TRANSACTIONS/CAREER NOTES: Selected by Washington Capitals as underage junior in first round (first Capitals pick, 17th overall) of NHL entry draft (June 9, 1984). ... Tore left knee cartilage (October 1987). ... Strained groin (January 1989). ... Fractured two metatarsal bones in left foot (February 5, 1989); missed 15 games. ... Sprained left knee (April 27, 1990). ... Did not attend Capitals training camp due to contract dispute (September 1990). ... Injured right knee (November 10, 1990). ... Suspended one game by NHL for game misconduct penalties (February 2, 1993). ... Fractured right hand (December 23, 1993); missed 10 games. ... Suffered from the flu (March 29, 1994); missed one game. ... Pulled thigh (April 9, 1994); missed one game. ... Traded by Capitals to Dallas Stars for D Mark Tinordi and rights to D Rick Mrozik (January 18, 1995). ... Injured shoulder (October 17, 1995); missed three games. ... Suspended four games and fined $1,000 by NHL for slashing (December 5, 1995). ... Traded by Stars to Pittsburgh Penguins for D Sergei Zubov (June 22, 1996). ... Suffered stiff neck (February 5, 1997); missed two games. ... Bruised lower leg (November 8, 1997); missed six games. ... Suffered from the flu (April 16, 1998); missed one game. ... Fractured foot (March 4, 1999); missed 16 games. ... Traded by Penguins to New York Rangers for D Peter Popovic (September 30, 1999). ... Signed as free agent by Carolina Hurricanes (July 31, 2000).

HONORS: Named to OHL All-Star second team (1984-85). ... Played in NHL All-Star Game (1990-1992, 1996 and 1997).

STATISTICAL PLATEAUS: Three-goal games: 1992-93 (1), 1995-96 (1). Total: 2.

		REGULAR SEASON								PLAYOFFS				
Season Team	League	Gms.	G	A	Pts.	PIM	+/-	PP	SH	Gms.	G	A	Pts.	PIM
83-84—North Bay	OHL	67	10	39	49	61	...	...	...	4	2	2	4	11
84-85—North Bay	OHL	58	26	37	63	75	...	...	...	8	5	8	13	9
—Washington	NHL	2	1	0	1	0	1	0	1	1	0	0	0	0
85-86—Washington	NHL	79	9	10	19	119	6	1	0	9	1	1	2	19
86-87—Washington	NHL	78	8	16	24	144	-29	1	0	7	1	0	1	20
87-88—Washington	NHL	71	14	27	41	137	1	5	0	14	5	7	12	55
88-89—Washington	NHL	62	13	27	40	101	19	3	0	6	1	4	5	20
89-90—Washington	NHL	80	13	41	54	102	4	4	0	11	0	8	8	32
90-91—Washington	NHL	79	24	50	74	69	-10	9	2	11	3	3	6	8
91-92—Washington	NHL	79	17	37	54	105	18	8	1	7	2	4	6	19
92-93—Washington	NHL	83	34	45	79	114	-7	13	1	6	0	1	1	14
93-94—Washington	NHL	72	16	24	40	108	-13	6	0	11	3	4	7	37
94-95—Dallas	NHL	47	10	19	29	66	-4	3	0	5	2	1	3	2
95-96—Dallas	NHL	74	15	26	41	58	-24	7	0	—	—	—	—	—
96-97—Pittsburgh	NHL	80	15	39	54	103	11	9	0	5	1	1	2	4
97-98—Pittsburgh	NHL	74	19	29	48	66	-3	13	1	6	1	0	1	12
—U.S. Olympic team	Int'l	3	0	2	2	0	...	...	...	—	—	—	—	—
98-99—Pittsburgh	NHL	66	11	27	38	24	11	4	2	13	2	3	5	4
99-00—New York Rangers	NHL	74	4	19	23	38	-10	2	0	—	—	—	—	—
NHL Totals (16 years)		1100	223	436	659	1354	-29	88	8	112	22	37	59	246

HAUER, BRETT — D

PERSONAL: Born July 11, 1971, in Richfield, Minn. ... 6-2/180. ... Shoots right. ... Full Name: Brett Timothy Hauer. ... Cousin of Don Jackson, defenseman with three NHL teams (1977-78 through 1986-87). ... Name pronounced HOW-uhr.

HIGH SCHOOL: Richfield (Minn.).

COLLEGE: Minnesota-Duluth.

TRANSACTIONS/CAREER NOTES: Selected by Vancouver Canucks in fourth round (third Canucks pick, 71st overall) of NHL entry draft (June 17, 1989). ... Traded by Canucks to Edmonton Oilers for sixth-round pick (D Larry Shapley) in 1997 draft (August 24, 1995).

HONORS: Named WCHA Student-Athlete of the Year (1992-93). ... Named to NCAA All-America West first team (1992-93). ... Named to WCHA All-Star first team (1992-93). ... Named to IHL All-Star first team (1998-99 and 1999-2000). ... Won Larry D. Gordon Trophy (1999-2000).

		REGULAR SEASON								PLAYOFFS				
Season Team	League	Gms.	G	A	Pts.	PIM	+/-	PP	SH	Gms.	G	A	Pts.	PIM
87-88—Richfield H.S.	Minn. H.S.	24	3	3	6		...	...	...	—	—	—	—	—
88-89—Richfield H.S.	Minn. H.S.	24	8	15	23	70	...	...	...	—	—	—	—	—
89-90—Minnesota-Duluth	WCHA	37	2	6	8	44	...	...	...	—	—	—	—	—
90-91—Minnesota-Duluth	WCHA	30	1	7	8	54	...	...	...	—	—	—	—	—
91-92—Minnesota-Duluth	WCHA	33	8	14	22	40	...	...	...	—	—	—	—	—
92-93—Minnesota-Duluth	WCHA	40	10	46	56	54	...	...	...	—	—	—	—	—
93-94—U.S. national team	Int'l	57	6	14	20	88	...	...	...	—	—	—	—	—
—U.S. Olympic team	Int'l	8	0	0	0	10	...	...	...	—	—	—	—	—
—Las Vegas	IHL	21	0	7	7	8	...	...	...	1	0	0	0	0
94-95—AIK	Sweden	37	1	3	4	38	...	...	...	—	—	—	—	—
95-96—Cape Breton	AHL	17	3	5	8	29	...	...	...	—	—	—	—	—
—Edmonton	NHL	29	4	2	6	30	-11	2	0	—	—	—	—	—
96-97—Chicago	IHL	81	10	30	40	50	...	...	...	4	2	0	2	4
97-98—Manitoba	IHL	82	13	48	61	58	...	...	...	3	0	0	0	2
98-99—Manitoba	IHL	81	15	56	71	66	...	...	...	5	0	5	5	4
99-00—Manitoba	IHL	77	13	47	60	92	...	...	...	2	0	1	1	2
—Edmonton	NHL	5	0	2	2	2	-2	0	0	—	—	—	—	—
NHL Totals (2 years)		34	4	4	8	32	-13	2	0					

HAVELID, NICLAS — D — MIGHTY DUCKS

PERSONAL: Born April 12, 1973, in Enkoping, Sweden. ... 5-11/200. ... Shoots left.

TRANSACTIONS/CAREER NOTES: Selected by Mighty Ducks of Anaheim in third round (second Mighty Ducks pick, 83rd overall) of NHL entry draft (June 26, 1999). ... Fractured finger (January 15, 2000); missed 23 games.

Season Team	League	REGULAR SEASON Gms.	G	A	Pts.	PIM	+/-	PP	SH	PLAYOFFS Gms.	G	A	Pts.	PIM
91-92—AIK Solna	Sweden	10	0	0	0	2	...	...	...	—	—	—	—	—
92-93—AIK Solna	Sweden	22	1	0	1	16	...	...	...	—	—	—	—	—
93-94—AIK Solna	Sweden Dv. 2				Statistics unavailable.									
94-95—AIK Solna	Sweden	40	3	7	10	38	...	...	...	—	—	—	—	—
95-96—AIK Solna	Sweden	40	5	6	11	30	...	...	...	—	—	—	—	—
96-97—AIK Solna	Sweden	49	3	6	9	42	...	...	...	7	1	2	3	8
97-98—AIK Solna	Sweden	43	8	4	12	42	...	...	...	—	—	—	—	—
98-99—Malmo	Sweden	50	10	12	22	42	...	...	...	8	0	4	4	10
99-00—Anaheim	NHL	50	2	7	9	20	0	0	0	—	—	—	—	—
—Cincinnati	AHL	2	0	0	0	0				—	—	—	—	—
NHL Totals (1 year)		50	2	7	9	20	0	0	0					

HAVLAT, MARTIN — C/LW — SENATORS

PERSONAL: Born April 19, 1981, in Brno, Czechoslovakia. ... 6-1/178. ... Shoots left.

TRANSACTIONS/CAREER NOTES: Selected by Ottawa Senators in first round (first Senators pick, 26th pick overall) of NHL entry draft (June 26, 1999).

Season Team	League	REGULAR SEASON Gms.	G	A	Pts.	PIM	+/-	PP	SH	PLAYOFFS Gms.	G	A	Pts.	PIM
96-97—Ytong Brno Jrs.	Czech. Jrs.	34	43	27	70		...	...	...	—	—	—	—	—
97-98—Ytong Brno Jrs.	Czech. Jrs.	32	38	29	67		...	...	...	—	—	—	—	—
98-99—Zelezarny Trinec Jrs.	Czech. Jrs.	31	28	23	51		...	...	...	—	—	—	—	—
—Zelezarny Trinec	Czech Rep.	24	2	3	5	4	...	...	...	8	0	0	0	...
99-00—Zelezarny Trinec	Czech Rep.	46	13	29	42	42	...	...	...	4	0	2	2	8

HAWGOOD, GREG — D — CANUCKS

PERSONAL: Born August 10, 1968, in St. Albert, Alta. ... 5-10/190. ... Shoots left. ... Full Name: Gregory William Hawgood.

TRANSACTIONS/CAREER NOTES: Selected by Boston Bruins as underage junior in 10th round (ninth Bruins pick, 202nd overall) of NHL entry draft (June 21, 1986). ... Announced that he would play in Italy for 1990-91 season (July 1990). ... Traded by Bruins to Edmonton Oilers for C Vladimir Ruzicka (October 22, 1990). ... Traded by Oilers with C Josef Beranek to Philadelphia Flyers for D Brian Benning (January 16, 1993). ... Traded by Flyers to Florida Panthers for future considerations (November 28, 1993). ... Bruised left thumb (January 13, 1994); missed seven games. ... Traded by Panthers to Pittsburgh Penguins for LW Jeff Daniels (March 19, 1994). ... Dislocated left shoulder (February 14, 1995); missed eight games. ... Signed as free agent by San Jose Sharks (September 8, 1996). ... Suspended two games and fined $1,000 by NHL for slashing incident (December 31, 1996). ... Signed as free agent by Vancouver Canucks (September 30, 1999). ... Sprained knee (November 15, 1999); missed one game.

HONORS: Named to WHL (West) All-Star first team (1985-86 through 1987-88). ... Won Can.HL Defenseman of the Year Award (1987-88). ... Won Bill Hunter Trophy (1987-88). ... Won Eddie Shore Plaque (1991-92). ... Named to AHL All-Star first team (1991-92). ... Named to IHL All-Star first team (1995-96, 1997-98 and 1998-99). ... Won James Norris Memorial Trophy (1995-96). ... Won Governors Trophy (1995-96 and 1998-99).

Season Team	League	REGULAR SEASON Gms.	G	A	Pts.	PIM	+/-	PP	SH	PLAYOFFS Gms.	G	A	Pts.	PIM
83-84—Kamloops	WHL	49	10	23	33	39	...	...	...	—	—	—	—	—
84-85—Kamloops	WHL	66	25	40	65	72	...	...	...	—	—	—	—	—
85-86—Kamloops	WHL	71	34	85	119	86	...	...	...	16	9	22	31	16
86-87—Kamloops	WHL	61	30	93	123	139	...	...	...	—	—	—	—	—
87-88—Boston	NHL	1	0	0	0	0	-1	0	0	3	1	0	1	0
—Kamloops	WHL	63	48	85	133	142	...	...	...	16	10	16	26	33
88-89—Boston	NHL	56	16	24	40	84	4	5	0	10	0	2	2	2
—Maine	AHL	21	2	9	11	41	...	...	...	—	—	—	—	—
89-90—Boston	NHL	77	11	27	38	76	12	2	0	15	1	3	4	12
90-91—Asiago	Italy	2	3	0	3	9	...	...	...	—	—	—	—	—
—Maine	AHL	5	0	1	1	13	...	...	...	—	—	—	—	—
—Cape Breton	AHL	55	10	32	42	73	...	...	...	4	0	3	3	23
—Edmonton	NHL	6	0	1	1	6	-2	0	0	—	—	—	—	—
91-92—Cape Breton	AHL	56	20	55	75	26	...	...	...	3	2	2	4	0
—Edmonton	NHL	20	2	11	13	22	19	0	0	13	0	3	3	23
92-93—Edmonton	NHL	29	5	13	18	35	-1	2	0	—	—	—	—	—
—Philadelphia	NHL	40	6	22	28	39	-7	5	0	—	—	—	—	—
93-94—Philadelphia	NHL	19	3	12	15	19	2	3	0	—	—	—	—	—
—Florida	NHL	33	2	14	16	9	8	0	0	—	—	—	—	—
—Pittsburgh	NHL	12	1	2	3	8	-1	1	0	1	0	0	0	0
94-95—Cleveland	IHL	—	—	—	—	—	...	...	...	3	1	0	1	4
—Pittsburgh	NHL	21	1	4	5	25	2	1	0	—	—	—	—	—
95-96—Las Vegas	IHL	78	20	65	85	101	...	...	...	15	5	11	16	24
96-97—San Jose	NHL	63	6	12	18	69	-22	3	0	—	—	—	—	—
97-98—Houston	IHL	81	19	52	71	75	...	...	...	4	0	4	4	0
98-99—Houston	IHL	76	17	57	74	90	...	...	...	19	4	8	12	24
99-00—Vancouver	NHL	79	5	17	22	26	5	2	0	—	—	—	—	—
NHL Totals (10 years)		456	58	159	217	418	18	24	0	42	2	8	10	37

HAY, DWAYNE — LW — LIGHTNING

PERSONAL: Born February 11, 1977, in London, Ont. ... 6-1/183. ... Shoots left.

HIGH SCHOOL: Bishop MacDonnell (Guelph, Ont.).

TRANSACTIONS/CAREER NOTES: Selected by Washington Capitals in second round (third Capitals pick, 43rd overall) of NHL entry draft (July 8, 1995). ... Traded by Capitals with fourth-round pick (RW Morgan McCormick) in 1999 draft to Florida Panthers for F Esa Tikkanen (March 9, 1998). ... Traded by Panthers with C Ryan Johnson to Tampa Bay Lightning for C/RW Mike Sillinger (March 14, 2000).

Season Team	League	REGULAR SEASON								PLAYOFFS				
		Gms.	G	A	Pts.	PIM	+/-	PP	SH	Gms.	G	A	Pts.	PIM
93-94—Listowel Jr. B	OHA	48	10	24	34	56	...	...	...	—	—	—	—	—
94-95—Guelph	OHL	65	26	28	54	37	...	...	...	14	5	7	12	6
95-96—Guelph	OHL	60	28	30	58	49	...	...	...	16	4	9	13	18
96-97—Guelph	OHL	32	17	17	34	21	...	...	...	11	4	6	10	0
97-98—Portland	AHL	58	6	7	13	35	...	...	...	—	—	—	—	—
—Washington	NHL	2	0	0	0	2	0	0	0	—	—	—	—	—
—New Haven	AHL	10	3	2	5	4	...	...	...	2	0	0	0	0
98-99—Florida	NHL	9	0	0	0	0	-1	0	0	—	—	—	—	—
—New Haven	AHL	46	18	17	35	22	...	...	...	—	—	—	—	—
99-00—Louisville	AHL	41	11	20	31	18	...	...	...	—	—	—	—	—
—Florida	NHL	6	0	0	0	2	-2	0	0	—	—	—	—	—
—Tampa Bay	NHL	13	1	1	2	2	0	0	0	—	—	—	—	—
NHL Totals (3 years)		30	1	1	2	6	-3	0	0					

HEALY, GLENN   G

PERSONAL: Born August 23, 1962, in Pickering, Ont. ... 5-9/190. ... Catches left. ... Full Name: Glenn M. Healy.
COLLEGE: Western Michigan.
TRANSACTIONS/CAREER NOTES: Signed as free agent by Los Angeles Kings (June 13, 1985). ... Signed as free agent by New York Islanders (August 16, 1989); Kings received fourth-round pick (traded to Minnesota) in 1990 draft as compensation. ... Strained left ankle ligaments (October 13, 1990); missed eight games. ... Fractured right index finger (November 10, 1991); missed five games. ... Fractured right thumb (January 3, 1992); missed 10 games. ... Severed tip of finger in practice (March 2, 1992) and underwent reconstructive surgery; missed 13 games. ... Suffered from tendinitis in right wrist (January 9, 1993); missed four games. ... Selected by Mighty Ducks of Anaheim in NHL expansion draft (June 24, 1993). ... Selected by Tampa Bay Lightning in Phase II of NHL expansion draft (June 25, 1993). ... Traded by Lightning to New York Rangers for third-round pick (traded back to Tampa Bay) in 1993 draft (June 25, 1993). ... Signed as free agent by Toronto Maple Leafs (July 8, 1997). ... Strained groin (December 4, 1997); missed 10 games. ... Sprained knee (January 10, 1999); missed 11 games.
HONORS: Named to NCAA All-America (West) second team (1984-85). ... Named to CCHA All-Star second team (1984-85).
MISCELLANEOUS: Member of Stanley Cup championship team (1994).

Season Team	League	REGULAR SEASON								PLAYOFFS						
		Gms.	Min	W	L	T	GA	SO	Avg.	Gms.	Min.	W	L	GA	SO	Avg.
81-82—Western Michigan U.	CCHA	27	1569	7	19	1	116	0	4.44	—	—	—	—	—	—	—
82-83—Western Michigan U.	CCHA	30	1733	8	19	2	116	0	4.02	—	—	—	—	—	—	—
83-84—Western Michigan U.	CCHA	38	2242	19	16	3	146	0	3.91	—	—	—	—	—	—	—
84-85—Western Michigan U.	CCHA	37	2172	21	14	2	118	0	3.26	—	—	—	—	—	—	—
85-86—Toledo	IHL	7	402	...	...	...	28	0	4.18	—	—	—	—	—	—	—
—New Haven	AHL	43	2410	21	15	4	160	0	3.98	2	119	0	2	11	0	5.55
—Los Angeles	NHL	1	51	0	0	0	6	0	7.06	—	—	—	—	—	—	—
86-87—New Haven	AHL	47	2828	21	15	0	173	1	3.67	7	427	3	4	19	0	2.67
87-88—Los Angeles	NHL	34	1869	12	18	1	135	1	4.33	4	240	1	3	20	0	5.00
88-89—Los Angeles	NHL	48	2699	25	19	2	192	0	4.27	3	97	0	1	6	0	3.71
89-90—New York Islanders	NHL	39	2197	12	19	6	128	2	3.50	4	166	1	2	9	0	3.25
90-91—New York Islanders	NHL	53	2999	18	24	9	166	0	3.32	—	—	—	—	—	—	—
91-92—New York Islanders	NHL	37	1960	14	16	4	124	1	3.80	—	—	—	—	—	—	—
92-93—New York Islanders	NHL	47	2655	22	20	2	146	1	3.30	18	1109	9	8	59	0	3.19
93-94—New York Rangers	NHL	29	1368	10	12	2	69	2	3.03	2	68	0	0	1	0	.88
94-95—New York Rangers	NHL	17	888	8	6	1	35	1	2.36	5	230	2	1	13	0	3.39
95-96—New York Rangers	NHL	44	2564	17	14	11	124	2	2.90	—	—	—	—	—	—	—
96-97—New York Rangers	NHL	23	1357	5	12	4	59	1	2.61	—	—	—	—	—	—	—
97-98—Toronto	NHL	21	1068	4	10	2	53	0	2.98	—	—	—	—	—	—	—
98-99—Chicago	IHL	10	597	6	3	‡1	33	0	3.32	—	—	—	—	—	—	—
—Toronto	NHL	9	546	6	3	0	27	0	2.97	1	20	0	0	0	0	...
99-00—Toronto	NHL	20	1164	9	10	0	59	2	3.04	—	—	—	—	—	—	—
NHL Totals (14 years)		422	23385	162	183	44	1323	13	3.39	37	1930	13	15	108	0	3.36

HEBERT, GUY   G   MIGHTY DUCKS

PERSONAL: Born January 7, 1967, in Troy, N.Y. ... 5-11/185. ... Catches left. ... Full Name: Guy Andrew Hebert. ... Name pronounced GEE ay-BAIR.
HIGH SCHOOL: LaSalle Institute (Troy, N.Y.).
COLLEGE: Hamilton College (N.Y.).
TRANSACTIONS/CAREER NOTES: Selected by St. Louis Blues in eighth round (eighth Blues pick, 159th overall) of NHL entry draft (June 13, 1987). ... Selected by Mighty Ducks of Anaheim in NHL expansion draft (June 24, 1993). ... Suffered concussion (April 30, 1995); missed one game. ... Suffered concussion (December 9, 1996); missed two games. ... Strained right shoulder (March 8, 1998); missed remainder of season. ... Separated shoulder (October 9, 1998); missed first game of season. ... Suffered neck spasms (December 26, 1999); missed two games.
HONORS: Shared James Norris Memorial Trophy with Pat Jablonski (1990-91). ... Named to IHL All-Star second team (1990-91). ... Played in NHL All-Star Game (1997).
MISCELLANEOUS: Holds Mighty Ducks of Anaheim all-time records for most games played by a goaltender (400), most wins (161), most shutouts (25) and goals-against average (2.71). ... Stopped a penalty shot attempt (vs. Alexandre Daigle, December 30, 1996; vs. Tony Amonte, February 1, 1998; vs. Glen Murray, February 7, 1998). ... Allowed a penalty shot goal (vs. Ray Whitney, March 21, 1999).

Season Team	League	REGULAR SEASON								PLAYOFFS						
		Gms.	Min	W	L	T	GA	SO	Avg.	Gms.	Min.	W	L	GA	SO	Avg.
85-86—Hamilton College	Div. II	18	1011	4	12	2	69	2	4.09	—	—	—	—	—	—	—
86-87—Hamilton College	Div. II	18	1070	12	5	0	40	0	2.24	—	—	—	—	—	—	—
87-88—Hamilton College	Div. II	8	450	5	3	0	19	0	2.53	—	—	—	—	—	—	—
88-89—Hamilton College	Div. II	25	1453	18	7	0	62	0	2.56	—	—	—	—	—	—	—
89-90—Peoria	IHL	30	1706	7	13	‡7	124	1	4.36	2	76	0	1	5	0	3.95
90-91—Peoria	IHL	36	2093	24	10	‡1	100	2	*2.87	8	458	3	4	32	0	4.19

H

Season Team	League	REGULAR SEASON								PLAYOFFS						
		Gms.	Min.	W	L	T	GA	SO	Avg.	Gms.	Min.	W	L	GA	SO	Avg.
91-92—Peoria	IHL	29	1731	20	9	0	98	0	3.40	4	239	3	1	9	0	*2.26
—St. Louis	NHL	13	738	5	5	1	36	0	2.93	—	—	—	—	—	—	...
92-93—St. Louis	NHL	24	1210	8	8	2	74	1	3.67	1	2	0	0	0	0	...
93-94—Anaheim	NHL	52	2991	20	27	3	141	2	2.83	—	—	—	—	—	—	—
94-95—Anaheim	NHL	39	2092	12	20	4	109	2	3.13	—	—	—	—	—	—	—
95-96—Anaheim	NHL	59	3326	28	23	5	157	4	2.83	—	—	—	—	—	—	—
96-97—Anaheim	NHL	67	3863	29	25	12	172	4	2.67	9	534	4	4	18	1	2.02
97-98—Anaheim	NHL	46	2660	13	24	6	130	3	2.93	—	—	—	—	—	—	—
98-99—Anaheim	NHL	69	4083	31	29	9	165	6	2.42	4	208	0	3	15	0	4.33
99-00—Anaheim	NHL	68	3976	28	†31	9	166	4	2.51	—	—	—	—	—	—	—
NHL Totals (9 years)		437	24939	174	192	51	1150	26	2.77	14	744	4	7	33	1	2.66

HECHT, JOCHEN   C   BLUES

PERSONAL: Born June 21, 1977, in Mannheim, West Germany. ... 6-3/196. ... Shoots left. ... Full Name: Jochen Thomas Hecht.
TRANSACTIONS/CAREER NOTES: Selected by St. Louis Blues in second round (first Blues pick, 49th overall) of NHL entry draft (July 8, 1995). ... Sprained ankle (January 13, 2000); missed 13 games. ... Reinjured ankle (February 23, 2000); missed six games.

Season Team	League	REGULAR SEASON							PLAYOFFS				
		Gms.	G	A	Pts.	PIM	+/-	PP	SH	Gms.	G	A	Pts.	PIM
94-95—Mannheim	Germany	43	11	12	23	68	...	...	...	10	5	4	9	12
95-96—Mannheim	Germany	44	12	16	28	68	...	...	...	8	3	2	5	6
96-97—Mannheim	Germany	46	21	21	42	36	...	...	...	—	—	—	—	—
97-98—Mannheim	Germany	44	7	19	26	42	...	...	...	10	1	1	2	14
—German Oly. team	Int'l	4	1	0	1	6	...	...	...	—	—	—	—	—
98-99—Worcester	AHL	74	21	35	56	48	...	...	...	4	1	1	2	2
—St. Louis	NHL	3	0	0	0	0	-2	0	0	5	2	0	2	0
99-00—St. Louis	NHL	63	13	21	34	28	20	5	0	7	4	6	10	2
NHL Totals (2 years)		66	13	21	34	28	18	5	0	12	6	6	12	2

HEDBERG, JOHAN   G   SHARKS

PERSONAL: Born May 5, 1973, in Leksand, Sweden. ... 5-11/185. ... Catches left.
TRANSACTIONS/CAREER NOTES: Selected by Philadelphia Flyers in ninth round (eighth Flyers pick, 218th overall) of NHL entry draft (June 29, 1994). ... Traded by Flyers to San Jose Sharks for seventh-round pick (C Pavel Kasparik) in 1999 draft (July 6, 1998).

Season Team	League	REGULAR SEASON								PLAYOFFS						
		Gms.	Min	W	L	T	GA	SO	Avg.	Gms.	Min.	W	L	GA	SO	Avg.
92-93—Leksand	Sweden	10	600	...	...	...	24	0	2.40	—	—	—	—	—	—	—
93-94—Leksand	Sweden	17	1020	...	...	...	48	0	2.82	—	—	—	—	—	—	—
94-95—Leksand	Sweden	17	986	...	...	...	58	1	3.53	—	—	—	—	—	—	—
95-96—Leksand	Sweden	34	2013	...	...	...	95	0	2.83	4	240	...	...	13	...	3.25
96-97—Leksand	Sweden	38	2260	...	...	...	95	3	2.52	4	581	...	...	18	1	1.86
97-98—Baton Rouge	ECHL	2	100	1	1	0	7	0	4.20	—	—	—	—	—	—	—
—Detroit	IHL	16	726	7	2	‡2	32	1	2.64	—	—	—	—	—	—	—
—Manitoba	IHL	14	745	8	4	‡1	32	1	2.58	2	106	0	2	6	0	3.40
98-99—Leksand	Sweden	48	2940	...	...	...	140	0	2.86	4	255	...	...	15	0	3.53
99-00—Kentucky	AHL	33	1973	18	9	5	88	3	2.68	5	311	3	2	10	1	1.93

HEDICAN, BRET   D   PANTHERS

PERSONAL: Born August 10, 1970, in St. Paul, Minn. ... 6-2/205. ... Shoots left. ... Full Name: Bret Michael Hedican. ... Name pronounced HEHD-ih-kihn.
HIGH SCHOOL: North St. Paul (Minn.).
COLLEGE: St. Cloud (Minn.) State.
TRANSACTIONS/CAREER NOTES: Selected by St. Louis Blues in 10th round (10th Blues pick, 198th overall) of NHL entry draft (June 11, 1988). ... Strained knee ligaments (September 27, 1992); missed first 15 games of season. ... Injured shoulder (October 24, 1993); missed three games. ... Injured groin (January 18, 1994); missed six games. ... Traded by Blues with D Jeff Brown and C Nathan LaFayette to Vancouver Canucks for C Craig Janney (March 21, 1994). ... Strained groin (March 27, 1994); missed three games. ... Injured back (February 1, 1996); missed three games. ... Strained back (October 5, 1996); missed six games. ... Strained groin (December 4, 1996); missed five games. ... Strained groin (December 26, 1996); missed four games. ... Missed one game for personal reasons (December 13, 1997). ... Strained back (January 21, 1998); missed one game. ... Strained abdominal muscle (February 17, 1998); missed six games. ... Sprained ankle (September 23, 1998); missed first game of season. ... Traded by Canucks with RW Pavel Bure, D Brad Ference and third-round pick (RW Robert Fried) in 2000 draft to Florida Panthers for D Ed Jovanovski, G Kevin Weekes, C Dave Gagner, C Mike Brown and first-round pick (C Nathan Smith) in 2000 draft (January 17, 1999). ... Injured eye (February 11, 1999); missed eight games. ... Strained groin (March 31, 1999); missed eight games. ... Suspended three games by NHL for slashing incident (November 3, 1999). ... Strained groin (October 22, 1999); missed two games. ... Strained groin (February 26, 2000); missed one game.
HONORS: Named to WCHA All-Star first team (1990-91).

Season Team	League	REGULAR SEASON							PLAYOFFS				
		Gms.	G	A	Pts.	PIM	+/-	PP	SH	Gms.	G	A	Pts.	PIM
88-89—St. Cloud State	WCHA	28	5	3	8	28	...	...	...	—	—	—	—	—
89-90—St. Cloud State	WCHA	36	4	17	21	37	...	...	...	—	—	—	—	—
90-91—St. Cloud State	WCHA	41	18	30	48	52	...	...	...	—	—	—	—	—
91-92—U.S. national team	Int'l	54	1	8	9	59	...	...	...	—	—	—	—	—
—U.S. Olympic team	Int'l	8	0	0	0	4	...	...	...	—	—	—	—	—
—St. Louis	NHL	4	1	0	1	0	1	0	0	5	0	0	0	0
92-93—Peoria	IHL	19	0	8	8	10	...	...	...	—	—	—	—	—
—St. Louis	NHL	42	0	8	8	30	-2	0	0	10	0	0	0	14

Season Team	League	REGULAR SEASON								PLAYOFFS				
		Gms.	G	A	Pts.	PIM	+/-	PP	SH	Gms.	G	A	Pts.	PIM
93-94—St. Louis	NHL	61	0	11	11	64	-8	0	0	—	—	—	—	—
—Vancouver	NHL	8	0	1	1	0	1	0	0	24	1	6	7	16
94-95—Vancouver	NHL	45	2	11	13	34	-3	0	0	11	0	2	2	6
95-96—Vancouver	NHL	77	6	23	29	83	8	1	0	6	0	1	1	10
96-97—Vancouver	NHL	67	4	15	19	51	-3	2	0	—	—	—	—	—
97-98—Vancouver	NHL	71	3	24	27	79	3	1	0	—	—	—	—	—
98-99—Vancouver	NHL	42	2	11	13	34	7	0	2	—	—	—	—	—
—Florida	NHL	25	3	7	10	17	-2	0	0	—	—	—	—	—
99-00—Florida	NHL	76	6	19	25	68	4	2	0	4	0	0	0	0
NHL Totals (9 years)		518	27	130	157	460	6	6	2	60	1	9	10	46

HEEREMA, JEFF   RW   HURRICANES

PERSONAL: Born January 17, 1980, in Thunder Bay, Ont. ... 6-1/184. ... Shoots right.
TRANSACTIONS/CAREER NOTES: Selected by Carolina Hurricanes in first round (first Hurricanes pick, 11th overall) of NHL entry draft (June 27, 1998).
HONORS: Named to OHL All-Rookie Second Team (1997-98).

Season Team	League	REGULAR SEASON								PLAYOFFS				
		Gms.	G	A	Pts.	PIM	+/-	PP	SH	Gms.	G	A	Pts.	PIM
97-98—Sarnia	OHL	63	32	40	72	88	...	...	...	5	4	1	5	10
98-99—Sarnia	OHL	62	31	39	70	113	...	...	...	6	5	1	6	0
99-00—Sarnia	OHL	67	36	41	77	62	...	...	...	7	4	2	6	10

HEFFLER, ERIC   G   OILERS

PERSONAL: Born February 29, 1976, in Williamsville, N.Y. ... 6-3/190. ... Catches left.
COLLEGE: St. Lawrence (N.Y.).
TRANSACTIONS/CAREER NOTES: Signed as a non-drafted free agent by Edmonton Oilers (May 10, 1999).
HONORS: Named to NCAA All-America (East) first team (1998-99). ... Named to ECAC All-Star first team (1998-99).

Season Team	League	REGULAR SEASON								PLAYOFFS					
		Gms.	Min	W	L	T	GA	SO	Avg.	Gms.	Min.	W	L	GA	SO	Avg.
95-96—St. Lawrence Univ.	ECAC	4	55	0	0	0	3	0	3.27	—	—	—	—	—	—	—
96-97—St. Lawrence Univ.	ECAC	12	458	2	3	1	31	0	4.06	—	—	—	—	—	—	—
97-98—St. Lawrence Univ.	ECAC	26	1529	8	14	0	73	2	2.86	—	—	—	—	—	—	—
98-99—St. Lawrence Univ.	ECAC	*37	*2206	22	12	3	88	3	2.39	—	—	—	—	—	—	—
—Hamilton	AHL	2	119	1	1	0	5	0	2.52	—	—	—	—	—	—	—
99-00—Hamilton	AHL	47	2643	11	25	†7	138	5	3.13	—	—	—	—	—	—	—

HEINS, SHAWN   D   SHARKS

PERSONAL: Born December 24, 1973, in Eganville, Ont. ... 6-4/210. ... Shoots left.
TRANSACTIONS/CAREER NOTES: Signed as non-drafted free agent by San Jose Sharks (January 5, 1998). ... Injured finger (February 29, 2000); missed five games.
HONORS: Named to AHL All-Star first team (1999-2000).

Season Team	League	REGULAR SEASON								PLAYOFFS				
		Gms.	G	A	Pts.	PIM	+/-	PP	SH	Gms.	G	A	Pts.	PIM
91-92—Peterborough	OHL	49	1	1	2	73	...	...	...	—	—	—	—	—
92-93—Peterborough	OHL	5	0	0	0	10	...	...	...	—	—	—	—	—
—Windsor	OHL	53	7	10	17	107	...	...	...	—	—	—	—	—
93-94—Renfrew	EOGHL	32	16	34	50	250	...	...	...	—	—	—	—	—
94-95—Renfrew	EOGHL	49	40	90	130	175	...	...	...	—	—	—	—	—
95-96—Cape Breton	AHL	1	0	0	0	0	...	...	...	—	—	—	—	—
—Mobile	ECHL	62	7	20	27	152	...	...	...	—	—	—	—	—
96-97—Mobile	ECHL	56	6	17	23	253	...	...	...	3	0	2	2	2
—Kansas City	IHL	6	0	0	0	9	...	...	...	11	1	0	1	49
97-98—Kansas City	IHL	82	22	28	50	303	...	...	...	—	—	—	—	—
98-99—Canadian nat'l team	Int'l	36	5	16	21	66	...	...	...	—	—	—	—	—
—San Jose	NHL	5	0	0	0	13	0	0	0	—	—	—	—	—
—Kentucky	AHL	18	2	2	4	108	...	...	...	12	2	7	9	10
99-00—Kentucky	AHL	69	11	52	63	238	...	...	...	9	3	3	6	44
—San Jose	NHL	1	0	0	0	2	-1	0	0	—	—	—	—	—
NHL Totals (2 years)		6	0	0	0	15	-1	0	0					

HEINZE, STEVE   RW   BLUE JACKETS

PERSONAL: Born January 30, 1970, in Lawrence, Mass. ... 5-11/193. ... Shoots right. ... Full Name: Stephen Herbert Heinze. ... Name pronounced HIGHNS.
HIGH SCHOOL: Lawrence Academy (Groton, Mass.).
COLLEGE: Boston College.
TRANSACTIONS/CAREER NOTES: Selected by Boston Bruins in second round (second Bruins pick, 60th overall) of NHL entry draft (June 11, 1988). ... Injured shoulder (May 1, 1992). ... Injured shoulder (March 20, 1993); missed 11 games. ... Injured knee (February 18, 1994); missed five games. ... Reinjured knee (March 26, 1994); missed two games. ... Strained abdominal muscle (December 5, 1996); missed one game. ... Strained hip and groin and tore knee ligament (December 17, 1996); missed remainder of season. ... Sprained ankle (October 7,

H

1997); missed seven games. ... Fractured foot (October 23, 1997); missed 14 games. ... Injured finger (October 24, 1998); missed one game. ... Strained hip flexor (February 9, 1999); missed five games. ... Suffered from the flu (March 1, 1999); missed three games. ... Suffered from the flu (February 3, 2000); missed one game. ... Strained muscle in ribs (March 10, 2000); missed six games. ... Selected by Columbus Blue Jackets in NHL expansion draft (June 23, 2000).

HONORS: Named to Hockey East All-Rookie team (1988-89). ... Named to NCAA All-America (East) first team (1989-90). ... Named to Hockey East All-Star first team (1989-90).

MISCELLANEOUS: Failed to score on a penalty shot (vs. Corey Schwab, December 17, 1997).

STATISTICAL PLATEAUS: Three-goal games: 1992-93 (1), 1995-96 (1), 1997-98 (2). Total: 4.

Season Team	League	REGULAR SEASON								PLAYOFFS				
		Gms.	G	A	Pts.	PIM	+/-	PP	SH	Gms.	G	A	Pts.	PIM
86-87—Lawrence Academy.....	Mass. H.S.	23	26	24	50	...	...	...	...	—	—	—	—	—
87-88—Lawrence Academy.....	Mass. H.S.	23	30	25	55	...	...	...	...	—	—	—	—	—
88-89—Boston College	Hockey East	36	26	23	49	26	...	...	...	—	—	—	—	—
89-90—Boston College	Hockey East	40	27	36	63	41	...	...	...	—	—	—	—	—
90-91—Boston College	Hockey East	35	21	26	47	35	...	...	...	—	—	—	—	—
91-92—U.S. national team	Int'l	49	18	15	33	38	...	...	...	—	—	—	—	—
—U.S. Olympic team......	Int'l	8	1	3	4	8	...	...	...	—	—	—	—	—
—Boston	NHL	14	3	4	7	6	-1	0	0	7	0	3	3	17
92-93—Boston	NHL	73	18	13	31	24	20	0	2	4	1	1	2	2
93-94—Boston	NHL	77	10	11	21	32	-2	0	2	13	2	3	5	7
94-95—Boston	NHL	36	7	9	16	23	0	0	1	5	0	0	0	0
95-96—Boston	NHL	76	16	12	28	43	-3	0	1	5	1	1	2	4
96-97—Boston	NHL	30	17	8	25	27	-8	4	2	—	—	—	—	—
97-98—Boston	NHL	61	26	20	46	54	8	9	0	6	0	0	0	6
98-99—Boston	NHL	73	22	18	40	30	7	9	0	12	4	3	7	0
99-00—Boston	NHL	75	12	13	25	36	-8	2	0	—	—	—	—	—
NHL Totals (9 years)..........		**515**	**131**	**108**	**239**	**275**	**13**	**24**	**8**	**52**	**8**	**11**	**19**	**36**

HEJDUK, MILAN · RW · AVALANCHE

PERSONAL: Born February 14, 1976, in Sstnad-Laberm, Czechoslovakia. ... 5-11/185. ... Shoots right.

TRANSACTIONS/CAREER NOTES: Selected by Quebec Nordiques in fourth round (sixth Nordiques pick, 72nd overall) of NHL entry draft (June 29, 1994). ... Nordiques franchise moved to Colorado and renamed Avalanche for 1995-96 season (June 21, 1995).

HONORS: Named Czech Republic League Rookie of the Year (1993-94). ... Named to NHL All-Rookie team (1998-99). ... Played in NHL All-Star Game (2000).

MISCELLANEOUS: Member of gold-medal-winning Czech Republic Olympic Team (1998).

Season Team	League	REGULAR SEASON								PLAYOFFS				
		Gms.	G	A	Pts.	PIM	+/-	PP	SH	Gms.	G	A	Pts.	PIM
93-94—HC Pardubice..............	Czech Rep.	22	6	3	9	...	...	...	...	10	5	1	6	...
94-95—HC Pardubice	Czech Rep.					Did not play.								
95-96—HC Pardubice..............	Czech Rep.	37	13	7	20	...	...	...	...	—	—	—	—	—
96-97—HC Pardubice..............	Czech Rep.	51	27	11	38	10	...	...	...	10	6	0	6	27
97-98—Pojistovna Pardubice..	Czech Rep.	48	26	19	45	20	...	...	...	3	0	0	0	2
—Czech Rep. Oly. team..	Int'l	4	0	0	0	2	...	...	...	—	—	—	—	—
98-99—Colorado	NHL	82	14	34	48	26	8	4	0	16	6	6	12	4
99-00—Colorado	NHL	82	36	36	72	16	14	13	0	17	5	4	9	6
NHL Totals (2 years)...........		**164**	**50**	**70**	**120**	**42**	**22**	**17**	**0**	**33**	**11**	**10**	**21**	**10**

HELENIUS, SAMI · D · STARS

PERSONAL: Born January 22, 1974, in Helsinki, Finland. ... 6-5/225. ... Shoots left. ... Name pronounced huh-LEH-nuhz.

TRANSACTIONS/CAREER NOTES: Selected by Calgary Flames in fifth round (fifth Flames pick, 102nd overall) of NHL entry draft (June 20, 1992). ... Traded by Flames to Tampa Bay Lightning for future considerations (January 29, 1999). ... Traded by Lightning to Colorado Avalanche for future considerations (March 23, 1999). ... Signed as free agent by Dallas Stars (July 12, 2000).

Season Team	League	REGULAR SEASON								PLAYOFFS				
		Gms.	G	A	Pts.	PIM	+/-	PP	SH	Gms.	G	A	Pts.	PIM
91-92—Jokerit Helsinki..........	Finland Jr.					Statistics unavailable.								
92-93—Vantaa HT	Finland Div. 2	21	3	2	5	60	...	...	...	—	—	—	—	—
—Jokerit Helsinki	Finland Jr.	1	0	0	0	0	...	...	...	—	—	—	—	—
93-94—Reipas Lahti................	Finland	37	2	3	5	46	...	...	...	—	—	—	—	—
94-95—Saint John	AHL	69	2	5	7	217	...	...	...	—	—	—	—	—
95-96—Saint John	AHL	68	0	3	3	231	...	...	...	10	0	0	0	9
96-97—Saint John	AHL	72	5	10	15	218	...	...	...	2	0	0	0	0
—Calgary	NHL	3	0	1	1	0	1	0	0	—	—	—	—	—
97-98—Saint John	AHL	63	1	2	3	185	...	...	...	—	—	—	—	—
—Las Vegas	IHL	10	0	1	1	19	...	...	...	4	0	0	0	25
98-99—Calgary	NHL	4	0	0	0	8	-2	0	0	—	—	—	—	—
—Chicago......................	IHL	4	0	0	0	11	...	...	...	—	—	—	—	—
—Tampa Bay	NHL	4	1	0	1	15	-3	0	1	—	—	—	—	—
—Las Vegas	IHL	42	2	3	5	193	...	...	...	—	—	—	—	—
—Hershey	AHL	8	0	0	0	29	...	...	...	5	0	0	0	16
99-00—Hershey	AHL	12	0	1	1	31	...	...	...	9	0	0	0	40
—Colorado	NHL	33	0	0	0	46	-5	0	0	—	—	—	—	—
NHL Totals (3 years)...........		**44**	**1**	**1**	**2**	**69**	**-9**	**0**	**1**					

H

HELMER, BRYAN   D

PERSONAL: Born July 15, 1972, in Sault Ste. Marie, Ont. ... 6-1/190. ... Shoots right.
TRANSACTIONS/CAREER NOTES: Signed as non-drafted free agent by New Jersey Devils (October 1, 1993). ... Signed as free agent by Phoenix Coyotes (July 22, 1998). ... Claimed on waivers by St. Louis Blues (December 19, 1998).
HONORS: Named to AHL All-Star first team (1997-98).

| | | REGULAR SEASON | | | | | | | | PLAYOFFS | | | | |
Season Team	League	Gms.	G	A	Pts.	PIM	+/-	PP	SH	Gms.	G	A	Pts.	PIM
89-90—Wellington	OJHL	51	6	22	28	204	...	...	...	—	—	—	—	—
—Belleville	OHL	6	0	1	1	0	...	...	...	—	—	—	—	—
90-91—Wellington	OJHL	50	11	14	25	109	...	...	...	—	—	—	—	—
91-92—Wellington	OJHL	45	19	32	51	66	...	...	...	—	—	—	—	—
92-93—Wellington	OJHL	57	25	62	87	62	...	...	...	—	—	—	—	—
93-94—Albany	AHL	65	4	19	23	79	...	...	...	5	0	0	0	9
94-95—Albany	AHL	77	7	36	43	101	...	...	...	7	1	0	1	0
95-96—Albany	AHL	80	14	30	44	107	...	...	...	4	2	0	2	6
96-97—Albany	AHL	77	12	27	39	113	...	...	...	16	1	7	8	10
97-98—Albany	AHL	80	14	49	63	101	...	...	...	13	4	9	13	18
98-99—Phoenix	NHL	11	0	0	0	23	2	0	0	—	—	—	—	—
—Las Vegas	IHL	8	1	3	4	28	...	...	...	—	—	—	—	—
—St. Louis	NHL	29	0	4	4	19	3	0	0	—	—	—	—	—
—Worcester	AHL	16	7	8	15	18	...	...	...	4	0	0	0	12
99-00—Worcester	AHL	54	10	25	35	124	...	...	...	9	1	4	5	10
—St. Louis	NHL	15	1	1	2	10	-3	1	0	—	—	—	—	—
NHL Totals (2 years)		55	1	5	6	52	2	1	0					

HENDERSON, JAY   LW   BRUINS

PERSONAL: Born September 17, 1978, in Edmonton. ... 5-11/188. ... Shoots left. ... Full Name: Jay Elliot Henderson. ... Nickname: Hendy.
TRANSACTIONS/CAREER NOTES: Selected by Boston Bruins in 12th round (12th Bruins pick, 246th overall) of NHL entry draft (June 21, 1997). ... Injured knee (April 4, 2000); missed final three games of season.

| | | REGULAR SEASON | | | | | | | | PLAYOFFS | | | | |
Season Team	League	Gms.	G	A	Pts.	PIM	+/-	PP	SH	Gms.	G	A	Pts.	PIM
94-95—Red Deer	WHL	54	3	9	12	80	...	...	...	—	—	—	—	—
95-96—Red Deer	WHL	71	15	13	28	139	...	...	...	10	1	1	2	11
96-97—Edmonton	WHL	66	28	32	60	127	...	...	...	—	—	—	—	—
97-98—Edmonton	WHL	72	49	45	94	132	...	...	...	—	—	—	—	—
—Providence	AHL	11	3	1	4	11	...	...	...	—	—	—	—	—
98-99—Providence	AHL	55	7	9	16	172	...	...	...	2	0	0	0	2
—Boston	NHL	4	0	0	0	2	-1	0	0	—	—	—	—	—
99-00—Providence	AHL	60	18	27	45	200	...	...	...	14	1	2	3	16
—Boston	NHL	16	1	3	4	9	1	0	0	—	—	—	—	—
NHL Totals (2 years)		20	1	3	4	11	0	0	0					

HENDRICKSON, DARBY   LW   WILD

PERSONAL: Born August 28, 1972, in Richfield, Minn. ... 6-1/195. ... Shoots left.
HIGH SCHOOL: Richfield (Minn.).
COLLEGE: Minnesota.
TRANSACTIONS/CAREER NOTES: Selected by Toronto Maple Leafs in fourth round (third Maple Leafs pick, 73rd overall) of NHL entry draft (June 16, 1990). ... Suspended three games by NHL for kneeing incident (October 26, 1995). ... Suffered from the flu (December 30, 1995); missed one game. ... Traded by Maple Leafs with LW Sean Haggerty, D Kenny Jonsson and first-round pick (G Roberto Luongo) in 1997 draft to New York Islanders for LW Wendel Clark, D Mathieu Schneider and D D.J. Smith (March 13, 1996). ... Traded by Islanders to Maple Leafs for fifth-round pick (C Jiri Dopita) in 1998 draft (October 11, 1996). ... Strained back (January 27, 1997); missed five games. ... Suffered back spasms (November 4, 1997); missed two games. ... Suffered back spasms (November 3, 1998); missed six games. ... Traded by Maple Leafs to Vancouver Canucks for D/LW Chris McAllister (February 16, 1999). ... Injured ankle (September 11, 1999); missed four games. ... Selected by Minnesota Wild in NHL expansion draft (June 23, 2000).
HONORS: Won WCHA Rookie of the Year Award (1991-92). ... Named to WCHA All-Rookie team (1991-92).

| | | REGULAR SEASON | | | | | | | | PLAYOFFS | | | | |
Season Team	League	Gms.	G	A	Pts.	PIM	+/-	PP	SH	Gms.	G	A	Pts.	PIM
87-88—Richfield H.S.	Minn. H.S.	22	12	9	21	10	...	...	...	—	—	—	—	—
88-89—Richfield H.S.	Minn. H.S.	22	22	20	42	12	...	...	...	—	—	—	—	—
89-90—Richfield H.S.	Minn. H.S.	24	23	27	50	49	...	...	...	—	—	—	—	—
90-91—Richfield H.S.	Minn. H.S.	27	32	29	61		...	...	...	—	—	—	—	—
91-92—Univ. of Minnesota	WCHA	41	25	28	53	61	...	...	...	—	—	—	—	—
92-93—Univ. of Minnesota	WCHA	31	12	15	27	35	...	...	...	—	—	—	—	—
93-94—U.S. national team	Int'l	59	12	16	28	30	...	...	...	—	—	—	—	—
—U.S. Olympic team	Int'l	8	0	0	0	6	...	...	...	—	—	—	—	—
—St. John's	AHL	6	4	1	5	4	...	...	...	3	1	1	2	0
—Toronto	NHL	—	—	—	—	—	...	...	...	2	0	0	0	0
94-95—St. John's	AHL	59	16	20	36	48	...	...	...	—	—	—	—	—
—Toronto	NHL	8	0	1	1	4	0	0	0	—	—	—	—	—
95-96—Toronto	NHL	46	6	6	12	47	-2	0	0	—	—	—	—	—
—New York Islanders	NHL	16	1	4	5	33	-6	0	0	—	—	—	—	—
96-97—St. John's	AHL	12	5	4	9	21	...	...	...	—	—	—	—	—
—Toronto	NHL	64	11	6	17	47	-20	0	1	—	—	—	—	—
—U.S. national team	Int'l	8	0	1	1	8	...	...	...	—	—	—	—	—

H

Season Team	League	REGULAR SEASON								PLAYOFFS				
		Gms.	G	A	Pts.	PIM	+/-	PP	SH	Gms.	G	A	Pts.	PIM
97-98—Toronto	NHL	80	8	4	12	67	-20	0	0	—	—	—	—	—
98-99—Toronto	NHL	35	2	3	5	30	-4	0	0	—	—	—	—	—
—Vancouver	NHL	27	2	2	4	22	-15	1	0	—	—	—	—	—
99-00—Vancouver	NHL	40	5	4	9	14	-3	0	1	—	—	—	—	—
—Syracuse	AHL	20	5	8	13	16	...	...	...	—	—	—	—	—
NHL Totals (7 years)		316	35	30	65	264	-70	1	2	2	0	0	0	0

HENRICH, MICHAEL   RW   OILERS

PERSONAL: Born March 3, 1980, in Thornhill, Ont. ... 6-2/206. ... Shoots right.
TRANSACTIONS/CAREER NOTES: Selected by Edmonton Oilers in first round (first Oilers pick, 13th overall) of NHL entry draft (June 27, 1998).

Season Team	League	REGULAR SEASON								PLAYOFFS				
		Gms.	G	A	Pts.	PIM	+/-	PP	SH	Gms.	G	A	Pts.	PIM
96-97—Barrie	OHL	52	9	15	24	19	...	...	...	9	0	5	5	0
97-98—Barrie	OHL	66	41	22	63	75	...	...	...	5	1	3	4	4
98-99—Barrie	OHL	62	38	33	71	42	...	...	...	12	0	2	2	4
99-00—Barrie	OHL	66	38	48	86	69	...	...	...	25	10	18	28	30

HENRY, ALEX   D   OILERS

PERSONAL: Born October 18, 1979, in Elliot Lake, Ont. ... 6-5/220. ... Shoots left.
TRANSACTIONS/CAREER NOTES: Selected by Edmonton Oilers in third round (second Oilers pick, 67th overall) of NHL entry draft (June 27, 1998).

Season Team	League	REGULAR SEASON								PLAYOFFS				
		Gms.	G	A	Pts.	PIM	+/-	PP	SH	Gms.	G	A	Pts.	PIM
96-97—London	OHL	61	1	10	11	65	...	...	...	—	—	—	—	—
97-98—London	OHL	62	5	9	14	97	...	...	...	16	0	3	3	14
98-99—London	OHL	68	5	23	28	105	...	...	...	25	3	10	13	22
99-00—Hamilton	AHL	60	1	0	1	69	...	...	...	—	—	—	—	—

HERBERS, IAN   D   WILD

PERSONAL: Born July 18, 1967, in Jasper, Alta. ... 6-4/225. ... Shoots left.
COLLEGE: University of Alberta.
TRANSACTIONS/CAREER NOTES: Signed as non-drafted free agent by Edmonton Oilers (September 9, 1992). ... Signed as free agent by Tampa Bay Lightning (September 29, 1999). ... Injured hand (November 24, 1999); missed eight games. ... Traded by Lightning to New York Islanders for seventh-round pick (traded back to New York Islanders) in 2000 draft (March 9, 2000). ... Sprained ankle (March 19, 2000); missed seven games. ... Selected by Minnesota Wild in NHL expansion draft (June 23, 2000).
HONORS: Named to CWUAA All-Star second team (1989-90). ... Named to CIAU All-Canadian team (1990-91 and 1991-92). ... Named to CWUAA All-Star first team (1990-91 and 1991-92). ... Won Spectrum-Randy Gregg Award (1991-92). ... Won Mervyn "Red" Dutton Trophy (1991-92).

Season Team	League	REGULAR SEASON								PLAYOFFS				
		Gms.	G	A	Pts.	PIM	+/-	PP	SH	Gms.	G	A	Pts.	PIM
84-85—Kelowna	BCJHL	68	3	14	17	120	...	...	...	6	0	1	1	9
85-86—Spokane	WHL	29	1	6	7	85	...	...	...	—	—	—	—	—
—Univ. of Alberta	CWUAA	32	1	4	5	109	...	...	...	10	1	0	1	37
86-87—Swift Current	WHL	72	5	8	13	230	...	...	...	4	1	1	2	12
87-88—Univ. of Alberta	CWUAA	56	5	14	19	238	...	...	...	4	0	2	2	4
88-89—Univ. of Alberta	CWUAA	47	4	22	26	137	...	...	...	—	—	—	—	—
89-90—Univ. of Alberta	CWUAA	45	5	31	36	83	...	...	...	—	—	—	—	—
90-91—Univ. of Alberta	CWUAA	45	6	24	30	87	...	...	...	—	—	—	—	—
91-92—Univ. of Alberta	CWUAA	43	14	34	48	86	...	...	...	—	—	—	—	—
92-93—Cape Breton	AHL	77	7	15	22	129	...	...	...	10	0	1	1	16
93-94—Edmonton	NHL	22	0	2	2	32	-6	0	0	—	—	—	—	—
—Cape Breton	AHL	53	7	16	23	122	...	...	...	5	0	3	3	12
94-95—Cape Breton	AHL	36	1	11	12	104	...	...	...	—	—	—	—	—
—Detroit	IHL	37	1	5	6	46	...	...	...	5	1	1	2	6
95-96—Detroit	IHL	73	3	11	14	140	...	...	...	12	3	5	8	29
96-97—Detroit	IHL	67	3	16	19	129	...	...	...	†21	0	4	4	34
97-98—Detroit	IHL	70	6	6	12	100	...	...	...	23	0	3	3	54
98-99—Detroit	IHL	82	8	16	24	142	...	...	...	11	1	3	4	18
99-00—Detroit	IHL	13	1	4	5	22	...	...	...	—	—	—	—	—
—Tampa Bay	NHL	37	0	0	0	45	-12	0	0	—	—	—	—	—
—New York Islanders	NHL	6	0	3	3	2	6	0	0	—	—	—	—	—
NHL Totals (2 years)		65	0	5	5	79	-12	0	0					

HERPERGER, CHRIS   LW   BLACKHAWKS

PERSONAL: Born February 24, 1974, in Esterhazy, Sask. ... 6-0/190. ... Shoots left. ... Name pronounced HUHR-puhr-guhr.
TRANSACTIONS/CAREER NOTES: Signed by Philadelphia Flyers in 10th round (10th Flyers pick, 223rd overall) of NHL entry draft (June 20, 1992). ... Traded by Flyers with seventh-round pick (LW Tony Mohagen) in 1997 draft to Mighty Ducks of Anaheim for C Bob Corkum (February 6, 1996). ... Signed as free agent by Chicago Blackhawks (September 2, 1998).
HONORS: Named to WHL (West) All-Star second team (1994-95).

H

Season Team	League	REGULAR SEASON								PLAYOFFS				
		Gms.	G	A	Pts.	PIM	+/-	PP	SH	Gms.	G	A	Pts.	PIM
90-91—Swift Current	WHL	10	0	1	1	5	...	...	...	—	—	—	—	—
91-92—Swift Current	WHL	72	14	19	33	44	...	...	...	8	0	1	1	9
92-93—Seattle	WHL	66	29	18	47	61	...	...	...	5	1	1	2	6
93-94—Seattle	WHL	71	44	51	95	110	...	...	...	9	12	10	22	12
94-95—Seattle	WHL	59	49	52	101	106	...	...	...	4	4	0	4	6
—Hershey	AHL	4	0	0	0	0	...	...	...	—	—	—	—	—
95-96—Hershey	AHL	46	8	12	20	36	...	...	...	—	—	—	—	—
—Baltimore	AHL	21	2	3	5	17	...	...	...	9	2	3	5	6
96-97—Baltimore	AHL	67	19	22	41	88	...	...	...	3	0	0	0	0
97-98—Canadian nat'l team	Int'l	62	20	30	50	102	...	...	...	—	—	—	—	—
98-99—Indianapolis	IHL	79	19	29	48	81	...	...	...	7	0	4	4	4
99-00—Chicago	NHL	9	0	0	0	5	-2	0	0	—	—	—	—	—
—Cleveland	IHL	73	22	26	48	122	...	...	...	9	3	3	6	8
NHL Totals (1 year)		9	0	0	0	5	-2	0	0					

HERR, MATT — LW — CAPITALS

PERSONAL: Born May 26, 1976, in Hackensack, N.J. ... 6-2/203. ... Shoots left. ... Full Name: Matthew Herr.
HIGH SCHOOL: Hotchkiss (Lakeville, Conn.).
COLLEGE: Michigan.
TRANSACTIONS/CAREER NOTES: Selected by Washington Capitals in fourth round (fourth Capitals pick, 93rd overall) of NHL entry draft (June 29, 1994).
MISCELLANEOUS: Selected by Atlanta Braves organization in 29th round of free-agent draft (June 2, 1994); did not sign.

Season Team	League	REGULAR SEASON								PLAYOFFS				
		Gms.	G	A	Pts.	PIM	+/-	PP	SH	Gms.	G	A	Pts.	PIM
90-91—Hotchkiss	Conn. H.S.	26	9	5	14	...	...	...	...	—	—	—	—	—
91-92—Hotchkiss	Conn. H.S.	25	17	16	33	...	...	...	...	—	—	—	—	—
92-93—Hotchkiss	Conn. H.S.	24	48	30	78	...	...	...	...	—	—	—	—	—
93-94—Hotchkiss	Conn. H.S.	20	28	19	47	...	...	...	...	—	—	—	—	—
94-95—Univ. of Michigan	CCHA	37	11	8	19	51	...	...	...	—	—	—	—	—
95-96—Univ. of Michigan	CCHA	40	18	13	31	55	...	...	...	—	—	—	—	—
96-97—Univ. of Michigan	CCHA	43	29	23	52	67	...	...	...	—	—	—	—	—
97-98—Univ. of Michigan	CCHA	29	13	17	30	60	...	...	...	—	—	—	—	—
98-99—Washington	NHL	30	2	2	4	8	-7	1	0	—	—	—	—	—
—Portland	AHL	46	15	14	29	29	...	...	...	—	—	—	—	—
99-00—Portland	AHL	77	22	21	43	51	...	...	...	4	1	1	2	4
NHL Totals (1 year)		30	2	2	4	8	-7	1	0					

HEWARD, JAMIE — D — BLUE JACKETS

PERSONAL: Born March 30, 1971, in Regina, Sask. ... 6-2/207. ... Shoots right. ... Name pronounced HYOO-uhrd.
TRANSACTIONS/CAREER NOTES: Selected by Pittsburgh Penguins in first round (first Penguins pick, 16th overall) of NHL entry draft (June 17, 1989). ... Signed as free agent by Toronto Maple Leafs (May 4, 1995). ... Signed as free agent by Philadelphia Flyers (July 10, 1997). ... Signed as free agent by Nashville Predators (August 6, 1998). ... Sprained ankle (December 8, 1998); missed five games. ... Injured heel (March 14, 1999); missed five games. ... Signed as free agent by New York Islanders (July 7, 1999). ... Suffered concussion (October 23, 1999); missed two games. ... Strained lower back (December 9, 1999); missed two games. ... Fractured right ankle (February 17, 2000); missed remainder of season. ... Claimed on waivers by Columbus Blue Jackets (May 26, 2000).
HONORS: Named to WHL (East) All-Star first team (1990-91). ... Named to AHL All-Star first team (1995-96 and 1997-98). ... Won Eddie Shore Plaque (1997-98).

Season Team	League	REGULAR SEASON								PLAYOFFS				
		Gms.	G	A	Pts.	PIM	+/-	PP	SH	Gms.	G	A	Pts.	PIM
87-88—Regina	WHL	68	10	17	27	17	...	...	...	4	1	1	2	2
88-89—Regina	WHL	52	31	28	59	29	...	...	...	—	—	—	—	—
89-90—Regina	WHL	72	14	44	58	42	...	...	...	11	2	2	4	10
90-91—Regina	WHL	71	23	61	84	41	...	...	...	8	2	9	11	6
91-92—Muskegon	IHL	54	6	21	27	37	...	...	...	14	1	4	5	4
92-93—Cleveland	IHL	58	9	18	27	64	...	...	...	—	—	—	—	—
93-94—Cleveland	IHL	73	8	16	24	72	...	...	...	—	—	—	—	—
94-95—Canadian nat'l team	Int'l	51	11	35	46	32	...	...	...	—	—	—	—	—
95-96—St. John's	AHL	73	22	34	56	33	...	...	...	3	1	1	2	6
—Toronto	NHL	5	0	0	0	0	-1	0	0	—	—	—	—	—
96-97—Toronto	NHL	20	1	4	5	6	-6	0	0	—	—	—	—	—
—St. John's	AHL	27	8	19	27	26	...	...	...	9	1	3	4	6
97-98—Philadelphia	AHL	72	17	48	65	54	...	...	...	20	3	16	19	10
98-99—Nashville	NHL	63	6	12	18	44	-24	4	0	—	—	—	—	—
99-00—New York Islanders	NHL	54	6	11	17	26	-9	2	0	—	—	—	—	—
NHL Totals (4 years)		142	13	27	40	76	-40	6	0					

HICKS, ALEX — LW

PERSONAL: Born September 4, 1969, in Calgary. ... 6-0/190. ... Shoots left.
COLLEGE: Wisconsin-Eau Claire.
TRANSACTIONS/CAREER NOTES: Signed as non-drafted free agent by Mighty Ducks of Anaheim (August 23, 1995). ... Traded by Mighty Ducks with D Fredrik Olausson to Pittsburgh Penguins for LW Shawn Antoski and D Dmitri Mironov (November 19, 1996). ... Suffered hip pointer (December 15, 1996); missed four games. ... Bruised leg (February 5, 1997); missed one game. ... Strained groin (February 18, 1997);

H

missed two games. ... Strained groin (March 24, 1997); missed one game. ... Injured foot (October 15, 1997); missed one game. ... Fractured foot (December 1, 1997); missed 13 games. ... Separated shoulder (March 2, 1998); missed nine games. ... Suffered concussion (April 16, 1998); missed one game. ... Signed as free agent by San Jose Sharks (September 12, 1998). ... Traded by Sharks with fifth-round pick (traded to New York Islanders) in 1999 draft to Florida Panthers for D Jeff Norton (November 11, 1998). ... Sprained knee and ankle (November 28, 1998); missed three games. ... Suffered concussion (January 2, 1999); missed seven games.

Season Team	League	REGULAR SEASON								PLAYOFFS				
		Gms.	G	A	Pts.	PIM	+/-	PP	SH	Gms.	G	A	Pts.	PIM
88-89—Wisconsin-Eau Claire..	NCAA	30	21	26	47	42	...	...	...	—	—	—	—	—
89-90—Wisconsin-Eau Claire..	NCAA	34	31	48	79	30	...	...	...	—	—	—	—	—
90-91—Wisconsin-Eau Claire..	NCAA	26	22	35	57	43	...	...	...	—	—	—	—	—
91-92—Wisconsin-Eau Claire..	NCAA	26	24	42	66	63	...	...	...	—	—	—	—	—
92-93—Adirondack	AHL	3	0	0	0	0	...	...	...	—	—	—	—	—
—Toledo	ECHL	50	26	34	60	100	...	...	...	16	6	10	16	79
93-94—Toledo	ECHL	60	31	49	80	240	...	...	...	14	10	10	20	56
—Adirondack	AHL	8	1	3	4	2	...	...	...	—	—	—	—	—
94-95—Las Vegas	IHL	78	24	42	66	212	...	...	...	9	2	4	6	47
95-96—Baltimore	AHL	13	2	10	12	23	...	...	...	—	—	—	—	—
—Anaheim	NHL	64	10	11	21	37	11	0	0	—	—	—	—	—
96-97—Anaheim	NHL	18	2	6	8	14	1	0	0	—	—	—	—	—
—Pittsburgh	NHL	55	5	15	20	76	-6	0	0	5	0	1	1	2
97-98—Pittsburgh	NHL	58	7	13	20	54	4	0	0	6	0	0	0	2
98-99—San Jose	NHL	4	0	1	1	4	-1	0	0	—	—	—	—	—
—Florida	NHL	51	0	6	6	58	-4	0	0	—	—	—	—	—
99-00—Florida	NHL	8	1	2	3	4	3	0	0	4	0	1	1	4
—Louisville	AHL	17	6	5	11	23	...	...	...	—	—	—	—	—
NHL Totals (5 years)		258	25	54	79	247	8	0	0	15	0	2	2	8

HIGGINS, MATT　　　　　C　　　　　CANADIENS

PERSONAL: Born October 29, 1977, in Vernon, B.C. ... 6-2/190. ... Shoots left.
TRANSACTIONS/CAREER NOTES: Selected by Montreal Canadiens in first round (first Canadiens pick, 18th overall) of NHL entry draft (June 22, 1996). ... Suffered concussion (November 21, 1998); missed three games.

Season Team	League	REGULAR SEASON								PLAYOFFS				
		Gms.	G	A	Pts.	PIM	+/-	PP	SH	Gms.	G	A	Pts.	PIM
93-94—Moose Jaw	WHL	64	6	10	16	10	...	...	...	—	—	—	—	—
94-95—Moose Jaw	WHL	72	36	34	70	26	...	...	...	10	1	2	3	2
95-96—Moose Jaw	WHL	67	30	33	63	43	...	...	...	13	3	5	8	2
96-97—Moose Jaw	WHL	71	33	57	90	51	...	...	...	12	3	5	8	2
97-98—Fredericton	AHL	50	5	22	27	12	...	...	...	4	1	2	3	2
—Montreal	NHL	1	0	0	0	0	-1	0	0	—	—	—	—	—
98-99—Montreal	NHL	25	1	0	1	0	-2	0	0	—	—	—	—	—
—Fredericton	AHL	11	3	4	7	6	...	...	...	5	0	2	2	0
99-00—Montreal	NHL	25	0	2	2	4	-6	0	0	—	—	—	—	—
—Quebec	AHL	29	1	15	16	21	...	...	...	—	—	—	—	—
NHL Totals (3 years)		51	1	2	3	4	-9	0	0					

HILL, SEAN　　　　　D　　　　　BLUES

PERSONAL: Born February 14, 1970, in Duluth, Minn. ... 6-0/203. ... Shoots right. ... Full Name: Sean Ronald Hill.
COLLEGE: Wisconsin.
TRANSACTIONS/CAREER NOTES: Selected by Montreal Canadiens in eighth round (ninth Canadiens pick, 167th overall) of NHL entry draft (June 11, 1988). ... Strained abdominal muscle (October 13, 1992); missed 14 games. ... Selected by Mighty Ducks of Anaheim in NHL expansion draft (June 24, 1993). ... Sprained shoulder (January 6, 1994); missed nine games. ... Traded by Mighty Ducks with ninth-round pick (G Frederic Cassivi) in 1994 draft to Ottawa Senators for third-round pick (traded to Tampa Bay) in 1994 draft (June 29, 1994). ... Strained abdominal muscle during 1995-96 season; missed two games. ... Tore left knee ligament (October 18, 1996); missed remainder of season. ... Traded by Senators to Carolina Hurricanes for RW Chris Murray (November 18, 1997). ... Strained hip flexor (December 1, 1997); missed three games. ... Fractured fibula (March 26, 1998); missed final 11 games of season. ... Fractured ankle and strained abdominal muscle (December 21, 1998); missed 20 games. ... Strained abdominal muscle (February 13, 1999); missed one game. ... Sprained ankle (March 21, 1999); missed four games. ... Fractured cheekbone (April 14, 1999); missed final two games of season. ... Strained groin (December 22, 1999); missed 18 games. ... Reinjured groin (April 3, 2000); missed final two games of season. ... Signed as free agent by St. Louis Blues (July 1, 2000).
HONORS: Named to WCHA All-Star second team (1989-90 and 1990-91). ... Named to NCAA All-America (West) second team (1990-91).
MISCELLANEOUS: Member of Stanley Cup championship team (1993).

Season Team	League	REGULAR SEASON								PLAYOFFS				
		Gms.	G	A	Pts.	PIM	+/-	PP	SH	Gms.	G	A	Pts.	PIM
88-89—Univ. of Wisconsin	WCHA	45	2	23	25	69	...	...	...	—	—	—	—	—
89-90—Univ. of Wisconsin	WCHA	42	14	39	53	78	...	...	...	—	—	—	—	—
90-91—Univ. of Wisconsin	WCHA	37	19	32	51	122	...	...	...	—	—	—	—	—
—Fredericton	AHL	—					...	...	...	3	0	2	2	2
—Montreal	NHL	—					...	...	...	1	0	0	0	0
91-92—Fredericton	AHL	42	7	20	27	65	...	...	...	7	1	3	4	6
—U.S. national team	Int'l	12	4	3	7	16	...	...	...	—	—	—	—	—
—U.S. Olympic team	Int'l	8	2	0	2	6	...	...	...	—	—	—	—	—
—Montreal	NHL	—					...	...	...	4	1	0	1	2
92-93—Montreal	NHL	31	2	6	8	54	-5	1	0	3	0	0	0	4
—Fredericton	AHL	6	1	3	4	10	...	...	...	—	—	—	—	—
93-94—Anaheim	NHL	68	7	20	27	78	-12	2	1	—	—	—	—	—
94-95—Ottawa	NHL	45	1	14	15	30	-11	0	0	—	—	—	—	—

H

Season Team	League	REGULAR SEASON								PLAYOFFS				
		Gms.	G	A	Pts.	PIM	+/-	PP	SH	Gms.	G	A	Pts.	PIM
95-96—Ottawa	NHL	80	7	14	21	94	-26	2	0	—	—	—	—	—
96-97—Ottawa	NHL	5	0	0	0	4	1	0	0	—	—	—	—	—
97-98—Ottawa	NHL	13	1	1	2	6	-3	0	0	—	—	—	—	—
—Carolina	NHL	42	0	5	5	48	-2	0	0	—	—	—	—	—
98-99—Carolina	NHL	54	0	10	10	48	9	0	0	—	—	—	—	—
99-00—Carolina	NHL	62	13	31	44	59	3	8	0	—	—	—	—	—
NHL Totals (10 years).........		400	31	101	132	421	-46	13	1	8	1	0	1	6

HILLIER, CRAIG   G   PENGUINS

PERSONAL: Born February 28, 1978, in Cole Harbour, Nova Scotia. ... 6-1/183. ... Catches left.
TRANSACTIONS/CAREER NOTES: Selected by Pittsburgh Penguins in first round (first Penguins pick, 23rd overall) of NHL entry draft (June 22, 1996).
HONORS: Named to OHL All-Star first team (1995-96). ... Shared Dave Pinkney Trophy with Seamus Kotyk (1997-98).

Season Team	League	REGULAR SEASON								PLAYOFFS					
		Gms.	Min	W	L	T	GA	SO	Avg.	Gms.	Min.	W	L	GA	SO	Avg.
94-95—Ottawa..........................	OHL	24	1078	6	7	2	69	1	3.84	—	—	—	—	—	—	—
95-96—Ottawa..........................	OHL	44	2439	24	14	3	117	2	2.88	3	130	0	2	12	0	5.54
96-97—Ottawa..........................	OHL	36	2007	23	6	4	89	2	2.66	10	540	4	5	33	0	3.67
97-98—Ottawa..........................	OHL	46	2587	27	12	4	108	*6	*2.50	9	447	6	2	20	1	2.68
98-99—Syracuse	AHL	36	1919	9	18	6	126	1	3.94	—	—	—	—	—	—	—
99-00—Wilkes-Barre/Scranton ..	AHL	11	520	1	6	2	36	0	4.15	—	—	—	—	—	—	—
—Johnstown	ECHL	5	212	2	2	0	15	0	4.25	—	—	—	—	—	—	—
—Toledo	ECHL	9	375	2	6	0	41	0	6.56	—	—	—	—	—	—	—
—Charlotte	ECHL	3	121	0	2	0	10	0	4.96	—	—	—	—	—	—	—

HINOTE, DAN   RW   AVALANCHE

PERSONAL: Born January 30, 1977, in Leesburg, Fla. ... 6-0/190. ... Shoots right.
COLLEGE: Army.
TRANSACTIONS/CAREER NOTES: Selected by Colorado Avalanche in seventh round (ninth Avalanche pick, 167th overall) of NHL entry draft (June 22, 1996).

Season Team	League	REGULAR SEASON								PLAYOFFS				
		Gms.	G	A	Pts.	PIM	+/-	PP	SH	Gms.	G	A	Pts.	PIM
95-96—Army..........................	Indep.	33	20	24	44	20	...	...	...	—	—	—	—	—
96-97—Oshawa......................	OHL	60	15	13	28	58	...	...	...	18	4	5	9	8
97-98—Hershey	AHL	24	1	4	5	25	...	...	...	—	—	—	—	—
—Oshawa......................	OHL	35	12	15	27	39	...	...	...	5	2	2	4	7
98-99—Hershey	AHL	65	4	16	20	95	...	...	...	5	3	1	4	6
99-00—Colorado	NHL	27	1	3	4	10	0	0	0	—	—	—	—	—
—Hershey	AHL	55	28	31	59	96	...	...	...	14	4	5	9	19
NHL Totals (1 year).............		27	1	3	4	10	0	0	0					

HLAVAC, JAN   LW   RANGERS

PERSONAL: Born September 20, 1976, in Prague, Czechoslovakia. ... 6-0/183. ... Shoots left. ... Name pronounced YAHN luh-VAHCH.
TRANSACTIONS/CAREER NOTES: Selected by New York Islanders in second round (second Islanders pick, 28th overall) of NHL entry draft (July 8, 1995). ... Rights traded by Islanders to Calgary Flames for LW Jorgen Jonsson (July 14, 1998). ... Rights traded by Flames with first-(C Jamie Lundmark) and third-round (D Pat Aufiero) picks in 1999 draft to New York Rangers for C Marc Savard and first-round pick (C/LW Oleg Saprykin) in 1999 draft (June 26, 1999). ... Strained hip flexor (March 15, 2000); missed two games. ... Bruised foot (April 4, 2000); missed one game.
STATISTICAL PLATEAUS: Three-goal games: 1999-00 (1).

Season Team	League	REGULAR SEASON								PLAYOFFS				
		Gms.	G	A	Pts.	PIM	+/-	PP	SH	Gms.	G	A	Pts.	PIM
93-94—Sparta Prague Jr.	Czech Rep.	27	12	15	27	...	...	...	...	—	—	—	—	—
—Sparta Prague............	Czech Rep.	9	1	1	2	...	...	...	...	—	—	—	—	—
94-95—Sparta Prague............	Czech Rep.	38	7	6	13	...	...	...	...	5	0	2	2	...
95-96—Sparta Prague............	Czech Rep.	34	8	5	13	...	...	...	...	12	1	2	3	...
96-97—Sparta Praha..............	Czech Rep.	38	8	13	21	24	...	...	...	10	5	2	7	2
97-98—Sparta Praha..............	Czech Rep.	48	17	30	47	40	...	...	...	5	1	0	1	2
98-99—Sparta Praha..............	Czech Rep.	49	*33	20	53	52	...	...	...	6	1	3	4	...
99-00—New York Rangers	NHL	67	19	23	42	16	3	6	0	—	—	—	—	—
—Hartford	AHL	3	1	0	1	0	...	...	...	—	—	—	—	—
NHL Totals (1 year).............		67	19	23	42	16	3	6	0					

HNILICKA, MILAN   G   THRASHERS

PERSONAL: Born June 24, 1973, in Kladno, Czechoslovakia. ... 6-0/180. ... Catches left. ... Name pronounced MEE-lahn nun-LEECH-kuh.
TRANSACTIONS/CAREER NOTES: Selected by New York Islanders in fourth round (fourth Islanders pick, 70th overall) of NHL entry draft (June 22, 1991). ... Signed as free agent by New York Rangers (July 22, 1999). ... Signed as free agent by Atlanta Thrashers (July 28, 2000).
HONORS: Shared Harry (Hap) Holmes Memorial Trophy with Jean-Francois Labbe (1999-2000).

H

Season Team	League	REGULAR SEASON								PLAYOFFS						
Season Team	League	Gms.	Min	W	L	T	GA	SO	Avg.	Gms.	Min.	W	L	GA	SO	Avg.
89-90—Poldi Kladno	Czech Rep.	24	1113	...	...	...	70	...	3.77	—	—	—	—	—	—	—
90-91—Poldi Kladno	Czech Rep.	35	2122	...	...	...	98	...	2.77	—	—	—	—	—	—	—
91-92—Poldi Kladno	Czech Rep.	30	1788	...	...	...	107	...	3.59	—	—	—	—	—	—	—
92-93—Swift Current	WHL	65	3679	*46	12	2	206	2	3.36	17	1017	12	5	54	*2	3.19
93-94—Salt Lake City	IHL	9	381	5	1	‡0	25	0	3.94	—	—	—	—	—	—	—
—Richmond	ECHL	43	2299	18	16	‡5	155	0	4.05	—	—	—	—	—	—	—
94-95—Denver	IHL	15	798	9	4	‡1	47	1	3.53	—	—	—	—	—	—	—
95-96—Poldi Kladno	Czech Rep.	33	1959	...	...	...	93	1	2.84	8	493	...	...	24	...	2.92
96-97—Poldi Kladno	Czech Rep.	48	2736	...	...	...	120	4	2.63	3	151	...	...	14	0	5.56
97-98—Sparta Praha	Czech Rep.	49	2847	...	...	...	99	...	2.09	11	632	...	...	31	...	3.00
98-99—Sparta Praha	Czech Rep.	50	2877	...	...	...	109	...	2.27	8	507	...	...	13	...	1.54
99-00—New York Rangers	NHL	2	86	0	1	0	5	0	3.49	—	—	—	—	—	—	—
—Hartford	AHL	36	1979	22	11	0	71	5	2.15	3	99	0	1	6	0	3.64
NHL Totals (1 year)		2	86	0	1	0	5	0	3.49							

HODSON, KEVIN G CANADIENS

PERSONAL: Born March 27, 1972, in Winnipeg. ... 6-0/182. ... Catches left.
TRANSACTIONS/CAREER NOTES: Signed as non-drafted free agent by Chicago Blackhawks (August 27, 1992). ... Signed as free agent by Detroit Red Wings (May 3, 1993). ... Strained hip flexor (March 10, 1998); missed two games. ... Reinjured hip (March 17, 1998); missed one game. ... Traded by Red Wings with second-round pick (RW Sheldon Keefe) in 1999 draft to Tampa Bay Lightning for LW Wendel Clark, G Bill Ranford and sixth-round pick (RW Kent McDonell) in 1999 draft (March 23, 1999). ... Injured groin (April 8, 1999); missed final five games of season. ... Traded by Lightning to Montreal Canadiens for seventh-round pick (traded to Philadelphia) in 2000 draft (June 2, 2000).
HONORS: Won Hap Emms Memorial Trophy (1992-93).
MISCELLANEOUS: Member of Stanley Cup championship team (1998).

Season Team	League	REGULAR SEASON								PLAYOFFS						
Season Team	League	Gms.	Min	W	L	T	GA	SO	Avg.	Gms.	Min.	W	L	GA	SO	Avg.
90-91—S.S. Marie	OHL	30	1638	18	11	0	88	2	*3.22	10	600	*9	1	28	0	2.80
91-92—S.S. Marie	OHL	50	2722	28	12	4	151	0	3.33	18	1116	12	6	59	1	3.17
92-93—S.S. Marie	OHL	26	1470	18	5	2	76	1	*3.10	8	448	8	0	17	0	2.28
—Indianapolis	IHL	14	777	5	9	0	53	0	4.09	—	—	—	—	—	—	—
93-94—Adirondack	AHL	37	2083	20	10	5	102	2	2.94	3	89	0	2	10	0	6.74
94-95—Adirondack	AHL	51	2731	19	22	8	161	1	3.54	4	238	0	4	14	0	3.53
95-96—Adirondack	AHL	32	1654	13	13	2	87	0	3.16	3	149	0	2	8	0	3.22
—Detroit	NHL	4	163	2	0	0	3	1	1.10	—	—	—	—	—	—	—
96-97—Detroit	NHL	6	294	2	2	1	8	1	1.63	—	—	—	—	—	—	—
—Quebec	IHL	2	118	1	1	0	7	0	3.56	—	—	—	—	—	—	—
97-98—Detroit	NHL	21	988	9	3	3	44	2	2.67	1	0	0	0	0	0	...
98-99—Detroit	NHL	4	175	0	2	0	9	0	3.09	—	—	—	—	—	—	—
—Adirondack	AHL	6	349	1	3	2	19	0	3.27	—	—	—	—	—	—	—
—Tampa Bay	NHL	5	238	2	1	1	11	0	2.77	—	—	—	—	—	—	—
99-00—Tampa Bay	NHL	24	769	2	7	4	47	0	3.67	—	—	—	—	—	—	—
—Detroit	IHL	9	505	4	6	0	22	0	2.61	—	—	—	—	—	—	—
NHL Totals (5 years)		64	2627	17	15	9	122	4	2.79	1	0	0	0	0	0	...

HOGLUND, JONAS LW MAPLE LEAFS

PERSONAL: Born August 29, 1972, in Karlstad, Sweden. ... 6-3/215. ... Shoots right. ... Name pronounced YOH-nuhz HOHG-luhnd.
TRANSACTIONS/CAREER NOTES: Selected by Calgary Flames in 10th round (11th Flames pick, 222nd overall) of NHL entry draft (June 20, 1992). ... Traded by Flames with D Zarley Zalapski to Montreal Canadiens for RW Valeri Bure and fourth-round pick (C Shaun Sutter) in 1998 draft (February 1, 1998). ... Signed as free agent by Toronto Maple Leafs (July 7, 1999).

Season Team	League	REGULAR SEASON							PLAYOFFS				
Season Team	League	Gms.	G	A	Pts.	PIM	+/-	PP	SH	Gms.	G	A	Pts.	PIM
88-89—Farjestad Karlstad	Sweden	1	0	0	0	0	...	...	...	—	—	—	—	—
89-90—Farjestad Karlstad	Sweden	1	0	0	0	0	...	...	...	—	—	—	—	—
90-91—Farjestad Karlstad	Sweden	40	5	5	10	4	...	...	...	8	1	0	1	0
91-92—Farjestad Karlstad	Sweden	40	14	11	25	6	...	...	...	6	2	4	6	2
92-93—Farjestad Karlstad	Sweden	40	13	13	26	14	...	...	...	3	1	0	1	0
93-94—Farjestad Karlstad	Sweden	22	7	2	9	10	...	...	...	—	—	—	—	—
94-95—Farjestad Karlstad	Sweden	40	14	12	26	16	...	...	...	4	3	2	5	0
95-96—Farjestad Karlstad	Sweden	40	32	11	43	18	...	...	...	8	2	1	3	6
96-97—Calgary	NHL	68	19	16	35	12	-4	3	0	—	—	—	—	—
97-98—Calgary	NHL	50	6	8	14	16	-9	0	0	—	—	—	—	—
—Montreal	NHL	28	6	5	11	6	2	4	0	10	2	0	2	0
98-99—Montreal	NHL	74	8	10	18	16	-5	1	0	—	—	—	—	—
99-00—Toronto	NHL	82	29	27	56	10	-2	9	1	12	2	4	6	2
NHL Totals (4 years)		302	68	66	134	60	-18	17	1	22	4	4	8	2

HOGUE, BENOIT C

PERSONAL: Born October 28, 1966, in Repentigny, Que. ... 5-10/194. ... Shoots left. ... Name pronounced BEHN-wah HOHG.
TRANSACTIONS/CAREER NOTES: Selected by Buffalo Sabres as underage junior in second round (second Sabres pick, 35th overall) of NHL entry draft (June 15, 1985). ... Suspended six games by AHL for fighting (October 1987). ... Suffered sore back (March 1988). ... Fractured left cheekbone (October 11, 1989); missed 20 games. ... Sprained left ankle (March 14, 1990). ... Traded by Sabres with C Pierre Turgeon, D Uwe Krupp and C Dave McLlwain to New York Islanders for C Pat LaFontaine, LW Randy Wood, D Randy Hillier and future considerations; Sabres later received fourth-round pick (D Dean Melanson) in 1992 draft (October 25, 1991). ... Suffered stiff neck (December 7, 1992);

H

missed five games. ... Suffered sore hand and foot (January 14, 1993); missed three games. ... Sprained knee ligament (March 14, 1993); missed six games. ... Injured shoulder (February 4, 1995); missed one game. ... Traded by Islanders with third-round pick (RW Ryan Pepperall) in 1995 draft and fifth-round pick (D Brandon Sugden) in 1996 draft to Toronto Maple Leafs for G Eric Fichaud (April 6, 1995). ... Sprained wrist (December 27, 1995); missed four games. ... Traded by Maple Leafs with LW Randy Wood to Dallas Stars for C Dave Gagner (January 28, 1996). ... Sprained neck (November 27, 1996); missed one game. ... Injured elbow (February 2, 1997); missed two games. ... Reinjured elbow (February 23, 1997); missed four games. ... Fractured ankle (December 3, 1997); missed 12 games. ... Suffered facial fracture (March 8, 1998); missed 13 games. ... Signed as free agent by Tampa Bay Lightning (July 29, 1998). ... Traded by Lightning with conditional pick in 2001 draft to Stars for D Sergey Gusev (March 21, 1999). ... Signed as free agent by Phoenix Coyotes (February 3, 2000). ... Strained neck (March 23, 2000); missed one game.

MISCELLANEOUS: Member of Stanley Cup championship team (1999). ... Scored on a penalty shot (vs. Ron Tugnutt, February, 16, 1993; vs. Ron Hextall, January 24, 1995).

STATISTICAL PLATEAUS: Three-goal games: 1992-93 (1).

			REGULAR SEASON							PLAYOFFS				
Season Team	League	Gms.	G	A	Pts.	PIM	+/-	PP	SH	Gms.	G	A	Pts.	PIM
83-84—St. Jean	QMJHL	59	14	11	25	42	...	...	...	—	—	—	—	—
84-85—St. Jean	QMJHL	63	46	44	90	92	...	...	...	—	—	—	—	—
85-86—St. Jean	QMJHL	65	54	54	108	115	...	...	...	9	6	4	10	26
86-87—Rochester	AHL	52	14	20	34	52	...	...	...	12	5	4	9	8
87-88—Buffalo	NHL	3	1	1	2	0	3	0	0	—	—	—	—	—
—Rochester	AHL	62	24	31	55	141	...	...	...	7	6	1	7	46
88-89—Buffalo	NHL	69	14	30	44	120	-5	1	2	5	0	0	0	17
89-90—Buffalo	NHL	45	11	7	18	79	0	1	0	3	0	0	0	10
90-91—Buffalo	NHL	76	19	28	47	76	-8	1	0	5	3	1	4	10
91-92—Buffalo	NHL	3	0	1	1	0	0	0	0	—	—	—	—	—
—New York Islanders	NHL	72	30	45	75	67	30	8	0	—	—	—	—	—
92-93—New York Islanders	NHL	70	33	42	75	108	13	5	3	18	6	6	12	31
93-94—New York Islanders	NHL	83	36	33	69	73	-7	9	5	4	0	1	1	4
94-95—New York Islanders	NHL	33	6	4	10	34	0	1	0	—	—	—	—	—
—Toronto	NHL	12	3	3	6	0	0	1	0	7	0	0	0	6
95-96—Toronto	NHL	44	12	25	37	68	6	3	0	—	—	—	—	—
—Dallas	NHL	34	7	20	27	36	4	2	0	—	—	—	—	—
96-97—Dallas	NHL	73	19	24	43	54	8	5	0	7	2	2	4	6
97-98—Dallas	NHL	53	6	16	22	35	7	3	0	17	4	2	6	16
98-99—Tampa Bay	NHL	62	11	14	25	50	-12	2	0	—	—	—	—	—
—Dallas	NHL	12	1	3	4	4	2	0	0	14	0	2	2	16
99-00—Phoenix	NHL	27	3	10	13	10	-1	0	0	5	1	2	3	2
NHL Totals (13 years)		771	212	306	518	814	40	42	10	85	16	16	32	118

HOLDEN, JOSH   C   CANUCKS

PERSONAL: Born January 18, 1978, in Calgary. ... 6-1/190. ... Shoots left.
TRANSACTIONS/CAREER NOTES: Selected by Vancouver Canucks in first round (first Canucks pick, 12th overall) of NHL entry draft (June 22, 1996). ... Suffered hernia prior to start of 1999-2000 season; missed first 22 games of season.
HONORS: Named to WHL (East) All-Star second team (1997-98).

			REGULAR SEASON							PLAYOFFS				
Season Team	League	Gms.	G	A	Pts.	PIM	+/-	PP	SH	Gms.	G	A	Pts.	PIM
94-95—Regina	WHL	62	20	23	43	45	...	...	...	4	3	1	4	0
95-96—Regina	WHL	70	57	55	112	105	...	...	...	11	4	5	9	23
96-97—Regina	WHL	58	49	49	98	148	...	...	...	5	3	2	5	10
97-98—Regina	WHL	56	41	58	99	134	...	...	...	2	2	2	4	10
98-99—Syracuse	AHL	38	14	15	29	48	...	...	...	—	—	—	—	—
—Vancouver	NHL	30	2	4	6	10	-10	1	0	—	—	—	—	—
99-00—Syracuse	AHL	45	19	32	51	113	...	...	...	4	1	0	1	10
—Vancouver	NHL	6	1	5	6	2	2	0	0	—	—	—	—	—
NHL Totals (2 years)		36	3	9	12	12	-8	1	0					

HOLIK, BOBBY   C   DEVILS

PERSONAL: Born January 1, 1971, in Jihlava, Czechoslovakia. ... 6-4/230. ... Shoots right. ... Full Name: Robert Holik. ... Name pronounced hoh-LEEK.
TRANSACTIONS/CAREER NOTES: Selected by Hartford Whalers in first round (first Whalers pick, 10th overall) of NHL entry draft (June 17, 1989). ... Traded by Whalers with second-round pick (LW Jay Pandolfo) in 1993 draft and future considerations to New Jersey Devils for G Sean Burke and D Eric Weinrich (August 28, 1992). ... Fractured right thumb (January 22, 1993); missed 22 games. ... Bruised left shoulder (December 8, 1993); missed 11 games. ... Fractured left index finger (October 7, 1995); missed 13 games. ... Sprained left ankle (February 28, 1996); missed six games. ... Suspended two games and fined $1,000 by NHL for tripping incident (November 8, 1998). ... Suspended two games by NHL for slashing incident (March 23, 1999). ... Suspended three games by NHL for slashing incident (November 25, 1999).
HONORS: Played in NHL All-Star Game (1998 and 1999).
MISCELLANEOUS: Member of Stanley Cup championship team (1995 and 2000).
STATISTICAL PLATEAUS: Three-goal games: 1992-93 (2), 1998-99 (1). Total: 3.

			REGULAR SEASON							PLAYOFFS				
Season Team	League	Gms.	G	A	Pts.	PIM	+/-	PP	SH	Gms.	G	A	Pts.	PIM
87-88—Dukla Jihlava	Czech.	31	5	9	14	...	...	...	...	—	—	—	—	—
88-89—Dukla Jihlava	Czech.	24	7	10	17	...	...	...	...	—	—	—	—	—
89-90—Dukla Jihlava	Czech.	42	15	26	41	...	...	...	...	—	—	—	—	—
—Czech. national team	Int'l	10	1	5	6	0	...	...	...	—	—	—	—	—
90-91—Hartford	NHL	78	21	22	43	113	-3	8	0	6	0	0	0	7
91-92—Hartford	NHL	76	21	24	45	44	4	1	0	7	0	1	1	6

H

Season Team	League	REGULAR SEASON								PLAYOFFS				
		Gms.	G	A	Pts.	PIM	+/-	PP	SH	Gms.	G	A	Pts.	PIM
92-93—Utica	AHL	1	0	0	0	2	...	...	...	—	—	—	—	—
—New Jersey	NHL	61	20	19	39	76	-6	7	0	5	1	1	2	6
93-94—New Jersey	NHL	70	13	20	33	72	28	2	0	20	0	3	3	6
94-95—New Jersey	NHL	48	10	10	20	18	9	0	0	20	4	4	8	22
95-96—New Jersey	NHL	63	13	17	30	58	9	1	0	—	—	—	—	—
96-97—New Jersey	NHL	82	23	39	62	54	24	5	0	10	2	3	5	4
97-98—New Jersey	NHL	82	29	36	65	100	23	8	0	5	0	0	0	8
98-99—New Jersey	NHL	78	27	37	64	119	16	5	0	7	0	7	7	6
99-00—New Jersey	NHL	79	23	23	46	106	7	7	0	23	3	7	10	14
NHL Totals (10 years)		717	200	247	447	760	111	44	0	103	10	26	36	79

HOLLAND, JASON — D — SABRES

PERSONAL: Born April 30, 1976, in Morinville, Alta. ... 6-2/193. ... Shoots right.
HIGH SCHOOL: Norkam (Kamloops, B.C.).
TRANSACTIONS/CAREER NOTES: Selected by New York Islanders in second round (second Islanders pick, 38th overall) of NHL entry draft (June 28, 1994). ... Traded by Islanders with LW Paul Kruse to Buffalo Sabres for RW Jason Dawe (March 24, 1998). ... Injured shoulder (October 2, 1999); missed two games.
HONORS: Named to Can.HL All-Star second team (1995-96). ... Named to WHL (West) All-Star first team (1995-96). ... Named to AHL All-Rookie team (1996-97).

Season Team	League	REGULAR SEASON								PLAYOFFS				
		Gms.	G	A	Pts.	PIM	+/-	PP	SH	Gms.	G	A	Pts.	PIM
92-93—Kamloops	WHL	4	0	0	0	2	...	...	...					
93-94—Kamloops	WHL	59	14	15	29	80	...	...	...	18	2	3	5	4
94-95—Kamloops	WHL	71	9	32	41	65	...	...	...	21	2	7	9	9
95-96—Kamloops	WHL	63	24	33	57	98	...	...	...	16	4	9	13	22
96-97—Kentucky	AHL	72	14	25	39	46	...	...	...	4	0	2	2	0
—New York Islanders	NHL	4	1	0	1	0	1	0	0	—	—	—	—	—
97-98—Kentucky	AHL	50	10	16	26	29	...	...	...	—	—	—	—	—
—New York Islanders	NHL	8	0	0	0	4	-4	0	0	—	—	—	—	—
—Rochester	AHL	9	0	4	4	10	...	...	...	4	0	3	3	4
98-99—Buffalo	NHL	3	0	0	0	8	-1	0	0	—	—	—	—	—
—Rochester	AHL	74	4	25	29	36	...	...	...	20	2	5	7	8
99-00—Buffalo	NHL	9	0	1	1	0	0	0	0	1	0	0	0	0
—Rochester	AHL	54	3	15	18	24	...	...	...	12	1	0	1	2
NHL Totals (4 years)		24	1	1	2	12	-4	0	0	1	0	0	0	0

HOLMSTROM, TOMAS — LW — RED WINGS

PERSONAL: Born January 23, 1973, in Pieta, Sweden. ... 6-0/198. ... Shoots left.
TRANSACTIONS/CAREER NOTES: Selected by Detroit Red Wings in 10th round (ninth Red Wings pick, 257th overall) of NHL entry draft (June 29, 1994). ... Sprained knee (October 30, 1996); missed seven games. ... Bruised shoulder (March 28, 1997); missed one game. ... Sprained knee (November 17, 1999); missed five games. ... Suffered injury (March 3, 2000); missed one game. ... Suffered facial lacerations (March 29, 2000); missed two games.
MISCELLANEOUS: Member of Stanley Cup championship team (1997 and 1998).

Season Team	League	REGULAR SEASON								PLAYOFFS				
		Gms.	G	A	Pts.	PIM	+/-	PP	SH	Gms.	G	A	Pts.	PIM
94-95—Lulea	Sweden	40	14	14	28	56	...	...	...	8	1	2	3	20
95-96—Lulea	Sweden	34	12	11	23	78	...	...	...	11	6	2	8	22
96-97—Detroit	NHL	47	6	3	9	33	-10	3	0	1	0	0	0	0
—Adirondack	AHL	6	3	1	4	7	...	...	...	—	—	—	—	—
97-98—Detroit	NHL	57	5	17	22	44	6	1	0	22	7	12	19	16
98-99—Detroit	NHL	82	13	21	34	69	-11	5	0	10	4	3	7	4
99-00—Detroit	NHL	72	13	22	35	43	4	4	0	9	3	1	4	16
NHL Totals (4 years)		258	37	63	100	189	-11	13	0	42	14	16	30	36

HOLZINGER, BRIAN — C/RW — LIGHTNING

PERSONAL: Born October 10, 1972, in Parma, Ohio. ... 5-11/190. ... Shoots right. ... Full Name: Brian Alan Holzinger. ... Name pronounced HOHL-zihng-uhr.
HIGH SCHOOL: Parma (Ohio).
COLLEGE: Bowling Green State.
TRANSACTIONS/CAREER NOTES: Selected by Buffalo Sabres in sixth round (seventh Sabres pick, 124th overall) of NHL entry draft (June 22, 1991). ... Bruised heel (November 10, 1997); missed three games. ... Sprained ankle (March 1, 1998); missed seven games. ... Suffered from the flu (January 7, 1999); missed one game. ... Injured shoulder (October 17, 1999); missed three games. ... Injured shoulder (January 6, 2000); missed three games. ... Traded by Sabres with C Wayne Primeau, D Cory Sarich and third-round pick (RW Alexandre Kharitonov) in 2000 draft to Tampa Bay Lightning for C Chris Gratton and second-round pick in 2001 draft (March 9, 2000). ... Strained muscle in abdomen (March 12, 2000); missed three games.
HONORS: Named to CCHA All-Star second team (1993-94). ... Won Hobey Baker Memorial Award (1994-95). ... Named to NCAA All-America (West) first team (1994-95). ... Named CCHA Player of the Year (1994-95). ... Named to CCHA All-Star first team (1994-95).

H

Season Team	League	REGULAR SEASON								PLAYOFFS				
		Gms.	G	A	Pts.	PIM	+/-	PP	SH	Gms.	G	A	Pts.	PIM
90-91—Det. Jr. Red Wings......	NAJHL	37	45	41	86	16	...	...	...	—	—	—	—	—
91-92—Bowling Green............	CCHA	30	14	8	22	36	...	...	...	—	—	—	—	—
92-93—Bowling Green............	CCHA	41	31	26	57	44	...	...	...	—	—	—	—	—
93-94—Bowling Green............	CCHA	38	22	15	37	24	...	...	...	—	—	—	—	—
94-95—Bowling Green............	CCHA	38	35	34	69	42	...	...	...	—	—	—	—	—
—Buffalo....................	NHL	4	0	3	3	0	2	0	0	4	2	1	3	2
95-96—Buffalo....................	NHL	58	10	10	20	37	-21	5	0	—	—	—	—	—
—Rochester	AHL	17	10	11	21	14	...	...	...	19	10	14	24	10
96-97—Buffalo....................	NHL	81	22	29	51	54	9	2	2	12	2	5	7	8
97-98—Buffalo....................	NHL	69	14	21	35	36	-2	4	2	15	4	7	11	18
98-99—Buffalo....................	NHL	81	17	17	34	45	2	5	0	21	3	5	8	33
99-00—Buffalo....................	NHL	59	7	17	24	30	4	0	1	—	—	—	—	—
—Tampa Bay..................	NHL	14	3	3	6	21	-7	1	1	—	—	—	—	—
NHL Totals (6 years)............		366	73	100	173	223	-13	17	6	52	11	18	29	61

HORACEK, JAN   D   BLUES

PERSONAL: Born May 22, 1979, in Benesov, Czechoslovakia. ... 6-4/206. ... Shoots right. ... Name pronounced HOHR-ih-chehk.
TRANSACTIONS/CAREER NOTES: Selected by St. Louis Blues in fourth round (third Blues pick, 98th overall) of NHL entry draft (June 21, 1997).

Season Team	League	REGULAR SEASON								PLAYOFFS				
		Gms.	G	A	Pts.	PIM	+/-	PP	SH	Gms.	G	A	Pts.	PIM
95-96—Slavia Praha................	Czech Rep.	8	0	1	1	4	...	...	...	—	—	—	—	—
—Slavia Praha Jrs.........	Czech Rep.	18	1	5	6	...	...	...	...	—	—	—	—	—
—HC Kralupy...............	Czech II	11	0	0	0	...	...	...	...	—	—	—	—	—
96-97—Slavia Praha Jrs.........	Czech Rep.	25	4	14	18	...	...	...	...	—	—	—	—	—
—Slavia Praha............	Czech Rep.	9	0	0	0	6	...	...	...	3	0	0	0	...
—HC Beroun	Czech II	2	0	0	0	...	...	...	...	—	—	—	—	—
97-98—Moncton	QMJHL	54	3	18	21	146	...	...	...	10	1	5	6	20
98-99—Slavia Praha............	Czech Rep.	1	0	0	0	2	...	...	...	—	—	—	—	—
—Worcester	AHL	53	1	13	14	119	...	...	...	4	0	0	0	6
99-00—Worcester	AHL	68	1	8	9	145	...	...	...	9	0	0	0	2

HORCOFF, SHAWN   C   OILERS

PERSONAL: Born September 17, 1978, in Trail, B.C. ... 6-1/194. ... Shoots left.
HIGH SCHOOL: Stanley Humphres Secondary (Castlegar, B.C.).
COLLEGE: Michigan State.
TRANSACTIONS/CAREER NOTES: Selected by Edmonton Oilers in fourth round (third Oilers pick, 99th overall) of NHL entry draft (June 27, 1998).
HONORS: Named to CCHA All-Star first team (1999-2000). ... Named to NCAA All-America (West) All-Star first team (1999-2000).

Season Team	League	REGULAR SEASON								PLAYOFFS				
		Gms.	G	A	Pts.	PIM	+/-	PP	SH	Gms.	G	A	Pts.	PIM
96-97—Michigan State............	CCHA	40	10	13	23	20	...	...	...	—	—	—	—	—
97-98—Michigan State............	CCHA	34	14	13	27	50	...	...	...	—	—	—	—	—
98-99—Michigan State............	CCHA	39	12	25	37	70	...	...	...	—	—	—	—	—
99-00—Michigan State............	CCHA	41	14	*48	*62	46	...	...	...	—	—	—	—	—

HOSSA, MARIAN   LW   SENATORS

PERSONAL: Born January 12, 1979, in Stara Lubovna, Czechoslovakia. ... 6-1/199. ... Shoots left. ... Brother of Marcel Hossa, center, Montreal Canadiens system. ... Name pronounced HOH-suh.
TRANSACTIONS/CAREER NOTES: Selected by Ottawa Senators in first round (first Senators pick, 12th overall) of NHL entry draft (June 21, 1997). ... Tore anterior cruciate and medial collateral ligaments in knee (May 21, 1998); missed first 22 games of season. ... Suffered concussion (November 18, 1999); missed one game. ... Bruised left wrist (January 6, 2000); missed two games. ... Suffered illness (February 1, 2000); missed one game.
HONORS: Won Jim Piggott Memorial Trophy (1997-98). ... Named to WHL (West) All-Star first team (1997-98). ... Named to Can.HL All-Star first team (1997-98). ... Named to NHL All-Rookie team (1998-99).

Season Team	League	REGULAR SEASON								PLAYOFFS				
		Gms.	G	A	Pts.	PIM	+/-	PP	SH	Gms.	G	A	Pts.	PIM
95-96—Dukla Trencin Jrs........	Slovakia Jrs.	53	42	49	91	26	...	...	...	—	—	—	—	—
96-97—Dukla Trencin.............	Slovakia	46	25	19	44	33	...	...	...	7	5	5	10	...
97-98—Ottawa	NHL	7	0	1	1	0	-1	0	0	—	—	—	—	—
—Portland....................	WHL	53	45	40	85	50	...	...	...	16	13	6	19	6
98-99—Ottawa	NHL	60	15	15	30	37	18	1	0	4	0	2	2	4
99-00—Ottawa	NHL	78	29	27	56	32	5	5	0	6	0	0	0	2
NHL Totals (3 years)............		145	44	43	87	69	22	6	0	10	0	2	2	6

HOUDA, DOUG   D   SABRES

PERSONAL: Born June 3, 1966, in Blairmore, Alta. ... 6-2/190. ... Shoots right. ... Name pronounced HOO-duh.
TRANSACTIONS/CAREER NOTES: Selected by Detroit Red Wings as underage junior in second round (second Red Wings pick, 28th overall) of NHL entry draft (June 9, 1984). ... Fractured left cheekbone (September 23, 1988). ... Injured knee and underwent surgery (November 21, 1989). ... Traded by Red Wings to Hartford Whalers for D Doug Crossman (February 20, 1991). ... Separated shoulder (February 28, 1994); missed three games. ... Strained shoulder (March 15, 1994); missed two games. ... Traded by Whalers to Los Angeles Kings for RW Marc Potvin (November 3, 1993). ... Traded by Kings to Buffalo Sabres for D Sean O'Donnell (July 26, 1994). ... Severed tendon in hand (February 11, 1995); missed 12 games. ... Signed as free agent by New York Islanders (October 23, 1996). ... Traded by Islanders with C Travis Green

H

and RW Tony Tuzzolino to Mighty Ducks of Anaheim for D J.J. Daigneault, C Mark Janssens and RW Joe Sacco (February 6, 1998). ... Traded by Mighty Ducks to Red Wings for future considerations (October 8, 1998). ... Signed as free agent by Sabres (July 13, 1999).
HONORS: Named to WHL All-Star second team (1984-85). ... Named to AHL All-Star first team (1987-88).

		REGULAR SEASON								PLAYOFFS				
Season Team	League	Gms.	G	A	Pts.	PIM	+/-	PP	SH	Gms.	G	A	Pts.	PIM
81-82—Calgary	WHL	3	0	0	0	0	...	...	...	—	—	—	—	—
82-83—Calgary	WHL	71	5	23	28	99	...	...	...	16	1	3	4	44
83-84—Calgary	WHL	69	6	30	36	195	...	...	...	4	0	0	0	7
84-85—Calgary	WHL	65	20	54	74	182	...	...	...	8	3	4	7	29
—Kalamazoo	IHL	—	—	—	—	—	...	...	...	7	0	2	2	10
85-86—Calgary	WHL	16	4	10	14	60	...	...	...	—	—	—	—	—
—Medicine Hat	WHL	35	9	23	32	80	...	...	...	25	4	19	23	64
—Detroit	NHL	6	0	0	0	4	-7	0	0	—	—	—	—	—
86-87—Adirondack	AHL	77	6	23	29	142	...	...	...	11	1	8	9	50
87-88—Detroit	NHL	11	1	1	2	10	0	0	0	—	—	—	—	—
—Adirondack	AHL	71	10	32	42	169	...	...	...	11	0	3	3	44
88-89—Adirondack	AHL	7	0	3	3	8	...	...	...	—	—	—	—	—
—Detroit	NHL	57	2	11	13	67	17	0	0	6	0	1	1	0
89-90—Detroit	NHL	73	2	9	11	127	-5	0	0	—	—	—	—	—
90-91—Adirondack	AHL	38	9	17	26	67	...	...	...	—	—	—	—	—
—Detroit	NHL	22	0	4	4	43	-2	0	0	—	—	—	—	—
—Hartford	NHL	19	1	2	3	41	-3	0	0	6	0	0	0	8
91-92—Hartford	NHL	56	3	6	9	125	-2	1	0	6	0	2	2	13
92-93—Hartford	NHL	60	2	6	8	167	-19	0	0	—	—	—	—	—
93-94—Hartford	NHL	7	0	0	0	23	-4	0	0	—	—	—	—	—
—Los Angeles	NHL	54	2	6	8	165	-15	0	0	—	—	—	—	—
94-95—Buffalo	NHL	28	1	2	3	68	1	0	0	—	—	—	—	—
95-96—Buffalo	NHL	38	1	3	4	52	3	0	0	—	—	—	—	—
—Rochester	AHL	21	1	6	7	41	...	...	...	19	3	5	8	30
96-97—Utah	IHL	3	0	0	0	7	...	...	...	—	—	—	—	—
—New York Islanders	NHL	70	2	8	10	99	1	0	0	—	—	—	—	—
97-98—New York Islanders	NHL	31	1	2	3	47	-6	0	0	—	—	—	—	—
—Anaheim	NHL	24	1	2	3	52	-5	0	1	—	—	—	—	—
98-99—Adirondack	AHL	73	7	21	28	122	...	...	...	3	0	1	1	4
—Detroit	NHL	3	0	1	1	0	-2	0	0	—	—	—	—	—
99-00—Rochester	AHL	79	7	17	24	175	...	...	...	21	1	8	9	39
—Buffalo	NHL	1	0	0	0	12	0	0	0	—	—	—	—	—
NHL Totals (14 years)		560	19	63	82	1102	-48	1	1	18	0	3	3	21

HOULDER, BILL   D   PREDATORS

PERSONAL: Born March 11, 1967, in Thunder Bay, Ont. ... 6-2/211. ... Shoots left. ... Full Name: William Houlder.
TRANSACTIONS/CAREER NOTES: Selected by Washington Capitals as underage junior in fourth round (fourth Capitals pick, 82nd overall) of NHL entry draft (June 15, 1985). ... Pulled groin (January 1989). ... Traded by Capitals to Buffalo Sabres for D Shawn Anderson (September 30, 1990). ... Selected by Mighty Ducks of Anaheim in NHL expansion draft (June 24, 1993). ... Traded by Mighty Ducks to St. Louis Blues for D Jason Marshall (August 29, 1994). ... Signed as free agent by Tampa Bay Lightning (August 1, 1995). ... Strained groin (October 7, 1995); missed two games. ... Injured ribs (November 8, 1995); missed four games. ... Strained groin (February 3, 1996); missed three games. ... Reinjured groin (March 5, 1996); missed six games ... Reinjured groin (March 26, 1996); missed five games. ... Bruised wrist (November 4, 1996); missed three games. ... Signed as free agent by San Jose Sharks (July 9, 1997). ... Injured knee (March 6, 1999); missed five games. ... Traded by Sharks with D Andrei Zyuzin, LW Shawn Burr and C Steve Guolla to Lightning for LW Niklas Sundstrom and third-round pick (traded to Chicago) in 2000 draft (August 4, 1999). ... Claimed on waivers by Nashville Predators (November 10, 1999). ... Suffered concussion (November 11, 1999); missed 11 games.
HONORS: Named to AHL All-Star first team (1990-91). ... Won Governors Trophy (1992-93). ... Named to IHL All-Star first team (1992-93).
MISCELLANEOUS: Captain of Tampa Bay Lightning (October 2, 1999-November 9, 1999).

		REGULAR SEASON								PLAYOFFS				
Season Team	League	Gms.	G	A	Pts.	PIM	+/-	PP	SH	Gms.	G	A	Pts.	PIM
83-84—Thunder Bay Beavers	TBAHA	23	4	18	22	37	...	...	...	—	—	—	—	—
84-85—North Bay	OHL	66	4	20	24	37	...	...	...	8	0	0	0	2
85-86—North Bay	OHL	59	5	30	35	97	...	...	...	10	1	6	7	12
86-87—North Bay	OHL	62	17	51	68	68	...	...	...	22	4	19	23	20
87-88—Washington	NHL	30	1	2	3	10	-2	0	0	—	—	—	—	—
—Fort Wayne	IHL	43	10	14	24	32	...	...	...	—	—	—	—	—
88-89—Baltimore	AHL	65	10	36	46	50	...	...	...	—	—	—	—	—
—Washington	NHL	8	0	3	3	4	7	0	0	—	—	—	—	—
89-90—Baltimore	AHL	26	3	7	10	12	...	...	...	7	0	2	2	2
—Washington	NHL	41	1	11	12	28	8	0	0	—	—	—	—	—
90-91—Rochester	AHL	69	13	53	66	28	...	...	...	15	5	13	18	4
—Buffalo	NHL	7	0	2	2	4	-2	0	0	—	—	—	—	—
91-92—Rochester	AHL	42	8	26	34	16	...	...	...	16	5	6	11	4
—Buffalo	NHL	10	1	0	1	8	-2	0	0	—	—	—	—	—
92-93—San Diego	IHL	64	24	48	72	39	...	...	...	—	—	—	—	—
—Buffalo	NHL	15	3	5	8	6	5	0	0	8	0	2	2	4
93-94—Anaheim	NHL	80	14	25	39	40	-18	3	0	—	—	—	—	—
94-95—St. Louis	NHL	41	5	13	18	20	16	1	0	4	1	1	2	0
95-96—Tampa Bay	NHL	61	5	23	28	22	1	3	0	6	0	1	1	4
96-97—Tampa Bay	NHL	79	4	21	25	30	16	0	0	—	—	—	—	—
97-98—San Jose	NHL	82	7	25	32	48	13	4	0	6	1	2	3	2
98-99—San Jose	NHL	76	9	23	32	40	8	7	0	6	3	0	3	4
99-00—Tampa Bay	NHL	14	1	2	3	2	-3	1	0	—	—	—	—	—
—Nashville	NHL	57	2	12	14	24	-6	1	0	—	—	—	—	—
NHL Totals (13 years)		601	53	167	220	286	41	20	0	30	5	6	11	14

H

HOUSLEY, PHIL   D   FLAMES

PERSONAL: Born March 9, 1964, in St. Paul, Minn. ... 5-10/185. ... Shoots left. ... Full Name: Phil F. Housley.
HIGH SCHOOL: South St. Paul (Minn.).
TRANSACTIONS/CAREER NOTES: Selected by Buffalo Sabres as underage player in first round (first Sabres pick, sixth overall) of NHL entry draft (June 9, 1982). ... Bruised shoulder (January 1984). ... Suspended three games by NHL (October 1984). ... Injured back (November 1987). ... Bruised back (January 12, 1989). ... Suffered hip pointer and bruised back (March 18, 1989). ... Pulled shoulder ligaments while playing at World Cup Tournament (April 1989). ... Traded by Sabres with LW Scott Arniel, RW Jeff Parker and first-round pick (C Keith Tkachuk) in 1990 draft to Winnipeg Jets for C Dale Hawerchuk and first-round pick (LW Brad May) in 1990 draft (June 16, 1990). ... Strained abdominal muscle (February 26, 1992); missed five games. ... Strained groin (October 31, 1992); missed two games. ... Sprained wrist (January 19, 1993); missed two games. ... Traded by Jets to St. Louis Blues for RW Nelson Emerson and D Stephane Quintal (September 24, 1993). ... Suffered back spasms (October 26, 1993); missed five games. ... Suffered sore back (November 18, 1993). ... Underwent back surgery (January 4, 1994); missed 53 games. ... Traded by Blues with second-round picks in 1996 (C Steve Begin) and 1997 (RW John Tripp) drafts to Calgary Flames for free-agent rights to D Al MacInnis and fourth-round pick (D Didier Tremblay) in 1997 draft (July 4, 1994). ... Played in Europe during 1994-95 NHL lockout. ... Injured right pinky (February 9, 1995); missed five games. ... Suffered from the flu (January 10, 1996); missed two games. ... Suffered from the flu (January 17, 1996); missed one game. ... Traded by Flames with D Dan Keczmer to New Jersey Devils for D Tommy Albelin, D Cale Hulse and LW Jocelyn Lemieux (February 26, 1996). ... Signed as free agent by Washington Capitals (July 22, 1996). ... Strained groin (March 16, 1997); missed five games. ... Fractured finger (March 7, 1998); missed 10 games. ... Claimed on waivers by Flames (July 21, 1998). ... Injured abdomen (February 19, 1999); missed one game.
HONORS: Named to NHL All-Rookie team (1982-83). ... Played in NHL All-Star Game (1984, 1989-1993 and 2000). ... Named to THE SPORTING NEWS All-Star second team (1991-92). ... Named to NHL All-Star second team (1991-92).
MISCELLANEOUS: Failed to score on a penalty shot (vs. Curtis Joseph, December 19, 1992). ... Member of Team U.S.A. at World Junior Championships and World Cup Tournament (1982).
STATISTICAL PLATEAUS: Three-goal games: 1982-83 (1), 1987-88 (1). Total: 2.

			REGULAR SEASON							PLAYOFFS				
Season Team	League	Gms.	G	A	Pts.	PIM	+/-	PP	SH	Gms.	G	A	Pts.	PIM
80-81—St. Paul's	USHL	6	7	7	14	6	...	...	...	—	—	—	—	—
81-82—South St. Paul H.S......	Minn. H.S.	22	31	34	65	18	...	...	...	—	—	—	—	—
82-83—Buffalo	NHL	77	19	47	66	39	-4	11	0	10	3	4	7	2
83-84—Buffalo	NHL	75	31	46	77	33	4	13	2	3	0	0	0	6
84-85—Buffalo	NHL	73	16	53	69	28	15	3	0	5	3	2	5	2
85-86—Buffalo	NHL	79	15	47	62	54	-9	7	0	—	—	—	—	—
86-87—Buffalo	NHL	78	21	46	67	57	-2	8	1	—	—	—	—	—
87-88—Buffalo	NHL	74	29	37	66	96	-17	6	0	6	2	4	6	6
88-89—Buffalo	NHL	72	26	44	70	47	6	5	0	5	1	3	4	2
89-90—Buffalo	NHL	80	21	60	81	32	11	8	1	6	1	4	5	4
90-91—Winnipeg	NHL	78	23	53	76	24	-13	12	1	—	—	—	—	—
91-92—Winnipeg	NHL	74	23	63	86	92	-5	11	0	7	1	4	5	0
92-93—Winnipeg	NHL	80	18	79	97	52	-14	6	0	6	0	7	7	2
93-94—St. Louis	NHL	26	7	15	22	12	-5	4	0	4	2	1	3	4
94-95—Grasshoppers	Switz. Div. 2	10	6	8	14	34	...	...	...	—	—	—	—	—
—Calgary	NHL	43	8	35	43	18	17	3	0	7	0	9	9	0
95-96—Calgary	NHL	59	16	36	52	22	-2	6	0	—	—	—	—	—
—New Jersey	NHL	22	1	15	16	8	-4	0	0	—	—	—	—	—
96-97—Washington	NHL	77	11	29	40	24	-10	3	1	—	—	—	—	—
97-98—Washington	NHL	64	6	25	31	24	-10	4	1	18	0	4	4	4
98-99—Calgary	NHL	79	11	43	54	52	14	4	0	—	—	—	—	—
99-00—Calgary	NHL	78	11	44	55	24	-12	5	0	—	—	—	—	—
NHL Totals (18 years)........		1288	313	817	1130	738	-40	119	7	77	13	42	55	32

HRDINA, JAN   C   PENGUINS

PERSONAL: Born February 5, 1976, in Hradec Kralove, Czechoslovakia. ... 6-0/200. ... Shoots right. ... Name pronounced YAHN huhr-DEE-nuh.
TRANSACTIONS/CAREER NOTES: Selected by Pittsburgh Penguins in fifth round (fourth Penguins pick, 128th overall) of NHL entry draft (July 8, 1995). ... Sprained ankle (October 14, 1999); missed 12 games.

			REGULAR SEASON							PLAYOFFS				
Season Team	League	Gms.	G	A	Pts.	PIM	+/-	PP	SH	Gms.	G	A	Pts.	PIM
93-94—Std.Hradec Kralove	Czech Rep.	21	1	5	6	...	...	...	...	—	—	—	—	—
94-95—Seattle..................	WHL	69	41	59	100	79	...	...	...	4	0	1	1	8
95-96—Seattle..................	WHL	30	19	28	47	37	...	...	...	—	—	—	—	—
—Spokane..................	WHL	18	10	16	26	25	...	...	...	18	5	14	19	49
96-97—Cleveland	IHL	68	23	31	54	82	...	...	...	13	1	2	3	8
97-98—Syracuse	AHL	72	20	24	44	82	...	...	...	5	1	3	4	10
98-99—Pittsburgh..................	NHL	82	13	29	42	40	-2	3	0	13	4	1	5	12
99-00—Pittsburgh..................	NHL	70	13	33	46	43	13	3	0	9	4	8	12	2
NHL Totals (2 years)...........		152	26	62	88	83	11	6	0	22	8	9	17	14

HRKAC, TONY   C   MIGHTY DUCKS

PERSONAL: Born July 7, 1966, in Thunder Bay, Ont. ... 5-11/170. ... Shoots left. ... Full Name: Anthony J. Hrkac. ... Name pronounced HUHR-kuhz.
COLLEGE: North Dakota.
TRANSACTIONS/CAREER NOTES: Selected by St. Louis Blues as underage junior in second round (second Blues pick, 32nd overall) of NHL entry draft (June 9, 1984). ... Bruised left leg (January 1987). ... Sprained shoulder (January 12, 1988). ... Lacerated ankle (March 1988). ... Bruised left shoulder (November 28, 1989). ... Traded by Blues with G Greg Millen to Quebec Nordiques for D Jeff Brown (December 13, 1989). ... Traded by Nordiques to San Jose Sharks for RW Greg Paslawski (May 30, 1991). ... Injured wrist during preseason (September 1991); missed first 27 games of season. ... Traded by Sharks to Chicago Blackhawks for future considerations (February 7, 1992). ... Signed as free

H

agent by Blues (July 30, 1993). ... Signed as free agent by Dallas Stars (July 25, 1997). ... Claimed on waivers by Edmonton Oilers (January 6, 1998). ... Traded by Oilers with D Bobby Dollas to Pittsburgh Penguins for LW Josef Beranek (June 16, 1998). ... Selected by Nashville Predators in NHL expansion draft (June 26, 1998). ... Traded by Predators to Stars for future considerations (July 9, 1998). ... Signed as free agent by New York Islanders (July 29, 1999). ... Traded by Islanders with D Dean Malkoc to Mighty Ducks of Anaheim for C/LW Ted Drury (October 29, 1999).

HONORS: Won Hobey Baker Memorial Award (1986-87). ... Won WCHA Most Valuable Player Award (1986-87). ... Named NCAA Tournament Most Valuable Player (1986-87). ... Named to NCAA All-America (West) first team (1986-87). ... Named to WCHA All-Star first team (1986-87). ... Named to NCAA All-Tournament team (1986-87). ... Won James Gatschene Memorial Trophy (1992-93). ... Won Leo P. Lamoureux Memorial Trophy (1992-93). ... Named to IHL All-Star first team (1992-93).

MISCELLANEOUS: Member of Stanley Cup championship team (1999).

Season Team	League	REGULAR SEASON								PLAYOFFS				
		Gms.	G	A	Pts.	PIM	+/-	PP	SH	Gms.	G	A	Pts.	PIM
83-84—Orillia	OHA	42	*52	54	*106	20	...	...	...	—	—	—	—	—
84-85—Univ. of North Dakota	WCHA	36	18	36	54	16	...	...	...	—	—	—	—	—
85-86—Canadian nat'l team	Int'l	62	19	30	49	36	...	...	...	—	—	—	—	—
86-87—Univ. of North Dakota	WCHA	48	46	*70	*116	48	...	...	...	—	—	—	—	—
—St. Louis	NHL	—	—	—	—	—	—	—	—	3	0	0	0	0
87-88—St. Louis	NHL	67	11	37	48	22	5	2	1	10	6	1	7	4
88-89—St. Louis	NHL	70	17	28	45	8	-10	5	0	4	1	1	2	0
89-90—St. Louis	NHL	28	5	12	17	8	1	1	0	—	—	—	—	—
—Quebec	NHL	22	4	8	12	2	-5	2	0	—	—	—	—	—
—Halifax	AHL	20	12	21	33	4	...	...	...	6	5	9	14	4
90-91—Halifax	AHL	3	4	1	5	2	...	...	...	—	—	—	—	—
—Quebec	NHL	70	16	32	48	16	-22	6	0	—	—	—	—	—
91-92—San Jose	NHL	22	2	10	12	4	-2	0	0	—	—	—	—	—
—Chicago	NHL	18	1	2	3	6	4	0	0	3	0	0	0	2
92-93—Indianapolis	IHL	80	45	*87	*132	70	...	...	...	5	0	2	2	2
93-94—St. Louis	NHL	36	6	5	11	8	-11	1	1	4	0	0	0	0
—Peoria	IHL	45	30	51	81	25	...	...	...	1	1	2	3	0
94-95—Milwaukee	IHL	71	24	67	91	26	...	...	...	15	4	9	13	16
95-96—Milwaukee	IHL	43	14	28	42	18	...	...	...	5	1	3	4	4
96-97—Milwaukee	IHL	81	27	61	88	20	...	...	...	3	1	1	2	2
97-98—Michigan	IHL	20	7	15	22	6	...	...	...	—	—	—	—	—
—Dallas	NHL	13	5	3	8	0	0	3	0	—	—	—	—	—
—Edmonton	NHL	36	8	11	19	10	3	4	0	12	0	3	3	2
98-99—Dallas	NHL	69	13	14	27	26	2	2	0	5	0	2	2	4
99-00—New York Islanders	NHL	7	0	2	2	0	-1	0	0	—	—	—	—	—
—Anaheim	NHL	60	4	7	11	8	-2	1	0	—	—	—	—	—
NHL Totals (10 years)		518	92	171	263	118	-38	27	2	41	7	7	14	12

HUARD, BILL   LW

PERSONAL: Born June 24, 1967, in Welland, Ont. ... 6-1/215. ... Shoots left. ... Name pronounced HYOO-uhrd.

TRANSACTIONS/CAREER NOTES: Signed as free agent by New Jersey Devils (October 1, 1989). ... Signed as free agent by Boston Bruins (December 4, 1992). ... Signed as free agent by Ottawa Senators (July 20, 1993). ... Injured hip (December 9, 1993); missed three games. ... Strained back (February 23, 1994); missed nine games. ... Strained groin (March 29, 1995); missed five games. ... Traded by Senators to Quebec Nordiques for rights to D Mika Stromberg and fourth-round pick (LW Kevin Boyd) in 1995 draft (April 7, 1995). ... Nordiques franchise moved to Colorado and renamed Avalanche for 1995-96 season (June 21, 1995). ... Claimed by Dallas Stars from Avalanche in NHL waiver draft (October 2, 1995). ... Separated shoulder (October 10, 1996); missed 11 games. ... Strained shoulder (November 20, 1996); missed three games. ... Signed as free agent by Edmonton Oilers (July 3, 1997). ... Sprained medial collateral ligament in knee (October 13, 1997); missed nine games. ... Fractured left hand (November 22, 1997); missed 24 games. ... Fractured right wrist (February 2, 1998); missed seven games. ... Sprained medial collateral ligament in left knee (December 18, 1998); missed 13 games. ... Signed as free agent by Los Angeles Kings (July 21, 1999). ... Traded by Kings to Atlanta Thrashers for future considerations (January 25, 2000).

Season Team	League	REGULAR SEASON								PLAYOFFS				
		Gms.	G	A	Pts.	PIM	+/-	PP	SH	Gms.	G	A	Pts.	PIM
86-87—Peterborough	OHL	61	14	11	25	61	...	...	...	12	5	2	7	19
87-88—Peterborough	OHL	66	28	33	61	132	...	...	...	12	7	8	15	33
88-89—Carolina	ECHL	40	27	21	48	177	...	...	...	10	7	2	9	70
89-90—Utica	AHL	27	1	7	8	67	...	...	...	5	0	1	1	33
—Nashville	ECHL	34	24	27	51	212	...	...	...	—	—	—	—	—
90-91—Utica	AHL	72	11	16	27	359	...	...	...	—	—	—	—	—
91-92—Utica	AHL	62	9	11	20	233	...	...	...	4	1	1	2	4
92-93—Providence	AHL	72	18	19	37	302	...	...	...	6	3	0	3	9
—Boston	NHL	2	0	0	0	0	0	0	0	—	—	—	—	—
93-94—Ottawa	NHL	63	2	2	4	162	-19	0	0	—	—	—	—	—
94-95—Ottawa	NHL	26	1	1	2	64	-2	0	0	—	—	—	—	—
—Quebec	NHL	7	2	2	4	13	2	0	0	1	0	0	0	0
95-96—Dallas	NHL	51	6	6	12	176	3	0	0	—	—	—	—	—
—Michigan	IHL	12	1	1	2	74	...	...	...	—	—	—	—	—
96-97—Dallas	NHL	40	5	6	11	105	5	0	0	—	—	—	—	—
97-98—Edmonton	NHL	30	0	1	1	72	-5	0	0	4	0	0	0	2
98-99—Edmonton	NHL	3	0	0	0	0	0	0	0	—	—	—	—	—
—Houston	IHL	38	9	5	14	201	...	...	...	10	0	0	0	8
99-00—Lowell	AHL	13	2	2	4	65	...	...	...	—	—	—	—	—
—Los Angeles	NHL	1	0	0	0	2	0	0	0	—	—	—	—	—
—Orlando	IHL	19	4	2	6	85	...	...	...	3	0	0	0	10
NHL Totals (8 years)		223	16	18	34	594	-16	0	0	5	0	0	0	2

H

HULBIG, JOE   LW

PERSONAL: Born September 29, 1973, in Norwood, Mass. ... 6-3/215. ... Shoots left. ... Name pronounced HUHL-bihg.
HIGH SCHOOL: St. Sebastian's Country Day (Needham, Mass.).
COLLEGE: Providence.
TRANSACTIONS/CAREER NOTES: Selected by Edmonton Oilers in first round (first Oilers pick, 13th overall) of NHL entry draft (June 20, 1992). ... Signed as free agent by Boston Bruins (July 19, 1999). ... Strained groin (January 4, 2000); missed remainder of season.

Season Team	League	REGULAR SEASON								PLAYOFFS				
		Gms.	G	A	Pts.	PIM	+/-	PP	SH	Gms.	G	A	Pts.	PIM
89-90—St. Sebastian's	USHS (East)	30	13	12	25	...	...	...	...	—	—	—	—	—
90-91—St. Sebastian's	USHS (East)	...	23	19	42	...	...	...	...	—	—	—	—	—
91-92—St. Sebastian's	USHS (East)	17	19	24	43	30	...	...	...	—	—	—	—	—
92-93—Providence College	Hockey East	26	3	13	16	22	...	...	...	—	—	—	—	—
93-94—Providence College	Hockey East	28	6	4	10	36	...	...	...	—	—	—	—	—
94-95—Providence College	Hockey East	37	14	21	35	36	...	...	...	—	—	—	—	—
95-96—Providence College	Hockey East	31	14	22	36	56	...	...	...	—	—	—	—	—
96-97—Hamilton	AHL	73	18	28	46	59	...	...	...	16	6	10	16	6
—Edmonton	NHL	6	0	0	0	0	-1	0	0	6	0	1	1	2
97-98—Edmonton	NHL	17	2	2	4	2	-1	0	0	—	—	—	—	—
—Hamilton	AHL	46	15	16	31	52	...	...	...	3	0	1	1	2
98-99—Hamilton	AHL	76	22	24	46	68	...	...	...	11	4	2	6	18
—Edmonton	NHL	1	0	0	0	2	1	0	0	—	—	—	—	—
99-00—Providence	AHL	15	4	5	9	17	...	...	...	—	—	—	—	—
—Boston	NHL	24	2	2	4	8	-8	0	0	—	—	—	—	—
NHL Totals (4 years)		**48**	**4**	**4**	**8**	**12**	**-9**	**0**	**0**	**6**	**0**	**1**	**1**	**2**

HULL, BRETT   RW   STARS

PERSONAL: Born August 9, 1964, in Belleville, Ont. ... 5-11/203. ... Shoots right. ... Full Name: Brett A. Hull. ... Son of Bobby Hull, Hall of Fame left winger with three NHL teams (1957-58 through 1971-72 and 1979-80) and Winnipeg Jets of WHA (1972-73 through 1978-79); and nephew of Dennis Hull, left winger with Chicago Blackhawks (1964-65 through 1976-77) and Detroit Red Wings (1977-78).
COLLEGE: Minnesota-Duluth.
TRANSACTIONS/CAREER NOTES: Selected by Calgary Flames in sixth round (sixth Flames pick, 117th overall) of NHL entry draft (June 9, 1984). ... Traded by Flames with LW Steve Bozek to St. Louis Blues for D Rob Ramage and G Rick Wamsley (March 7, 1988). ... Sprained left ankle (January 15, 1991); missed two regular-season games and All-Star Game. ... Suffered back spasms (March 12, 1992); missed seven games. ... Suffered sore wrist (March 20, 1993); missed four games. ... Injured abdominal muscle (October 7, 1993); missed three games. ... Strained groin (November 1, 1995); missed two games. ... Reinjured groin (November 10, 1995); missed five games. ... Injured hamstring (March 28, 1996); missed four games. ... Strained groin (March 30, 1997); missed four games. ... Strained buttocks (December 8, 1997); missed two games. ... Fractured left hand (December 27, 1997); missed 13 games. ... Signed as free agent by Dallas Stars (July 3, 1998). ... Bruised kidney (November 20, 1998); missed two games. ... Strained groin (November 25, 1998); missed one game. ... Reinjured groin (December 2, 1998); missed six games. ... Strained back (January 10, 1999); missed one game. ... Strained hamstring (February 24, 1999); missed 11 games. ... Injured groin (January 12, 2000); missed one game. ... Fractured nose (February 9, 2000); missed one game. ... Strained hip flexor (March 8, 2000); missed one game.
HONORS: Won WCHA Freshman of the Year Award (1984-85). ... Named to WCHA All-Star first team (1985-86). ... Won Dudley (Red) Garrett Memorial Trophy (1986-87). ... Named to AHL All-Star first team (1986-87). ... Won Lady Byng Memorial Trophy (1989-90). ... Won Dodge Ram Tough Award (1989-90 and 1990-91). ... Named to THE SPORTING NEWS All-Star first team (1989-90 through 1991-92). ... Named to NHL All-Star first team (1989-90 through 1991-92). ... Played in NHL All-Star Game (1989, 1990, 1992-1994, 1996 and 1997). ... Named NHL Player of the Year by THE SPORTING NEWS (1990-91). ... Won Hart Memorial Trophy (1990-91). ... Won Lester B. Pearson Award (1990-91). ... Won Pro Set NHL Player of the Year Award (1990-91). ... Named All-Star Game Most Valuable Player (1992).
RECORDS: Holds NHL single-season record for most goals by a right winger—86 (1990-91).
STATISTICAL PLATEAUS: Three-goal games: 1987-88 (1), 1989-90 (5), 1990-91 (4), 1991-92 (8), 1993-94 (3), 1994-95 (1), 1996-97 (2), 1997-98 (1). Total: 26. ... Four-goal games: 1994-95 (1), 1995-96 (1). Total: 2. ... Total hat tricks: 28.
MISCELLANEOUS: Member of Stanley Cup championship team (1999). ... Captain of St. Louis Blues (1992-93 through October 22, 1995). ... Holds St. Louis Blues all-time record for most goals (527). ... Failed to score on a penalty shot (vs. Glen Healy, December 31, 1992; vs. Bill Ranford, March 26, 1995; vs. Jeff Hackett, January 4, 1996). ... Shares distinction with Bobby Hull of being the first father-son duo to win the same NHL trophy (both the Lady Byng Memorial and Hart Memorial trophies).
STATISTICAL NOTES: Became the first son of an NHL 50-goal scorer to score 50 goals in one season (1989-90). ... Tied for NHL lead with 12 game-winning goals (1989-90). ... Led NHL in game-winning goals with 11 (1990-91) and 11 (1998-99).

Season Team	League	REGULAR SEASON								PLAYOFFS				
		Gms.	G	A	Pts.	PIM	+/-	PP	SH	Gms.	G	A	Pts.	PIM
82-83—Penticton	BCJHL	50	48	56	104	27	...	...	...	—	—	—	—	—
83-84—Penticton	BCJHL	56	*105	83	*188	20	...	...	...	—	—	—	—	—
84-85—Minnesota-Duluth	WCHA	48	32	28	60	24	...	...	...	—	—	—	—	—
85-86—Minnesota-Duluth	WCHA	42	*52	32	84	46	...	...	...	—	—	—	—	—
—Calgary	NHL	—	—	—	—	—	...	...	...	2	0	0	0	0
86-87—Moncton	AHL	67	50	42	92	16	...	...	...	3	2	2	4	2
—Calgary	NHL	5	1	0	1	0	-1	0	0	4	2	1	3	0
87-88—Calgary	NHL	52	26	24	50	12	10	4	0	—	—	—	—	—
—St. Louis	NHL	13	6	8	14	4	4	2	0	10	7	2	9	4
88-89—St. Louis	NHL	78	41	43	84	33	-17	16	0	10	5	5	10	6
89-90—St. Louis	NHL	80	*72	41	113	24	-1	*27	0	12	13	8	21	17
90-91—St. Louis	NHL	78	*86	45	131	22	23	*29	0	13	11	8	19	4
91-92—St. Louis	NHL	73	*70	39	109	48	-2	20	5	6	4	4	8	4
92-93—St. Louis	NHL	80	54	47	101	41	-27	29	0	11	8	5	13	2
93-94—St. Louis	NHL	81	57	40	97	38	-3	†25	3	4	2	1	3	0
94-95—St. Louis	NHL	48	29	21	50	10	13	9	3	7	6	2	8	0
95-96—St. Louis	NHL	70	43	40	83	30	4	16	5	13	6	5	11	10
96-97—St. Louis	NHL	77	42	40	82	10	-9	12	2	6	2	7	9	2
97-98—St. Louis	NHL	66	27	45	72	26	-1	10	0	10	3	3	6	2
—U.S. Olympic team	Int'l	4	2	1	3	0	...	...	...	—	—	—	—	—
98-99—Dallas	NHL	60	32	26	58	30	19	15	0	22	8	7	15	4
99-00—Dallas	NHL	79	24	35	59	43	-21	11	0	23	*11	†13	*24	4
NHL Totals (15 years)		**940**	**610**	**494**	**1104**	**371**	**-9**	**225**	**18**	**153**	**88**	**71**	**159**	**59**

H

PERSONAL: Born February 2, 1969, in Cambridge, Ont. ... 6-2/195. ... Shoots right.

HIGH SCHOOL: Thomas A. Stewart (Peterborough, Ont.).

TRANSACTIONS/CAREER NOTES: Pulled groin (February 1987). ... Selected by Hartford Whalers as underage junior in first round (first Whalers pick, 18th overall) of NHL entry draft (June 13, 1987). ... Injured hamstring (March 1989). ... Traded by Whalers to New York Rangers for C Carey Wilson and third-round pick (C Mikael Nylander) in 1991 draft (July 9, 1990). ... Sprained muscle in right hand (October 6, 1990). ... Bruised left big toe (November 19, 1990); missed six games. ... Injured knee (March 13, 1991). ... Traded by Rangers to Ottawa Senators for future considerations (July 28, 1992). ... Injured groin (December 7, 1992); missed three games. ... Suffered concussion (January 10, 1993); missed one game. ... Sprained ankle (January 19, 1993); missed eight games. ... Sprained left ankle (April 1, 1993); missed two games. ... Signed as free agent by Florida Panthers (August 10, 1993). ... Bruised right shoulder (February 1, 1994); missed one game. ... Separated right shoulder (March 4, 1994); missed three games. ... Separated right shoulder (March 18, 1994); missed six games. ... Suffered viral illness (February 1, 1995); missed two games. ... Fractured rib (October 28, 1995); missed four games. ... Suffered back spasms (May 5, 1996); missed four playoff games. ... Fractured left wrist (December 20, 1997); missed 13 games. ... Traded by Panthers with G Mark Fitzpatrick to Tampa Bay Lightning for RW Dino Ciccarelli and D Jeff Norton (January 15, 1998). ... Injured ankle (February 2, 1998); missed two games. ... Injured knee (April 2, 1998); missed three games. ... Signed as free agent by Philadelphia Flyers (October 7, 1998). ... Strained groin (October 31, 1998); missed two games. ... Suffered concussion (December 20, 1998); missed one game. ... Suffered post-concussion syndrome (December 26, 1998); missed four games. ... Sprained left ankle (April 8, 1999); missed two games. ... Selected by Atlanta Thrashers in NHL expansion draft (June 25, 1999). ... Traded by Thrashers to Flyers for future considerations (October 15, 1999). ... Sprained medial collateral ligament in left knee (January 27, 2000); missed 10 games.

HONORS: Named to OHL All-Star second team (1987-88).

STATISTICAL PLATEAUS: Three-goal games: 1988-89 (1).

			REGULAR SEASON								PLAYOFFS				
Season Team	League	Gms.	G	A	Pts.	PIM	+/-	PP	SH	Gms.	G	A	Pts.	PIM
84-85—Cambridge Jr. B	OHA	38	13	17	30	39	...	...	...	—	—	—	—	—
85-86—Peterborough	OHL	61	20	22	42	29	...	...	...	16	1	5	6	4
86-87—Peterborough	OHL	49	18	34	52	22	...	...	...	12	4	9	13	14
87-88—Peterborough	OHL	60	50	44	94	33	...	...	...	12	10	8	18	8
88-89—Hartford	NHL	60	16	18	34	10	6	6	0	1	0	0	0	2
89-90—Binghamton	AHL	21	7	10	17	6	...	...	...	—	—	—	—	—
—Hartford	NHL	38	7	10	17	21	-6	2	0	5	0	1	1	2
90-91—New York Rangers	NHL	47	5	8	13	10	2	0	0	—	—	—	—	—
91-92—New York Rangers	NHL	3	0	0	0	2	-4	0	0	—	—	—	—	—
—Binghamton	AHL	69	34	31	65	28	...	...	...	11	5	2	7	4
92-93—Ottawa	NHL	69	13	21	34	14	-24	5	1	—	—	—	—	—
93-94—Florida	NHL	69	13	13	26	8	6	0	1	—	—	—	—	—
94-95—Florida	NHL	46	11	8	19	8	-1	0	0	—	—	—	—	—
95-96—Florida	NHL	78	20	17	37	25	5	2	0	14	3	2	5	0
96-97—Florida	NHL	67	10	6	16	4	1	0	1	5	0	0	0	0
97-98—Florida	NHL	21	2	0	2	4	1	0	1	—	—	—	—	—
—Tampa Bay	NHL	28	2	4	6	4	2	0	0	—	—	—	—	—
98-99—Philadelphia	NHL	72	3	11	14	12	-2	0	0	6	0	0	0	4
99-00—Orlando	IHL	1	0	0	0	0	...	...	...	—	—	—	—	—
—Philadelphia	NHL	67	10	3	13	4	8	0	2	18	0	1	1	0
NHL Totals (12 years)		665	112	119	231	126	-6	15	6	49	3	4	7	8

HULSE, CALE D PREDATORS

PERSONAL: Born November 10, 1973, in Edmonton. ... 6-3/215. ... Shoots right. ... Name pronounced HUHLZ.

COLLEGE: Portland.

TRANSACTIONS/CAREER NOTES: Selected by New Jersey Devils in third round (third Devils pick, 66th overall) of NHL entry draft (June 20, 1992). ... Traded by Devils with D Tommy Albelin and RW Jocelyn Lemieux to Calgary Flames for D Phil Housley and D Dan Keczmer (February 26, 1996). ... Bruised ankle (February 28, 1997); missed four games. ... Reinjured ankle (March 7, 1997); missed one game. ... Reinjured ankle (March 21, 1997); missed one game. ... Suffered bruised ribs (April 1, 1999); missed six games. ... Fractured hand (September 18, 1999); missed first four games of season. ... Sprained ankle (February 23, 2000); missed nine games. ... Traded by Flames with third-round pick in 2001 draft to Nashville Predators for RW Sergei Krivokrasov (March 14, 2000); missed Predators final 12 games due to sprained ankle.

			REGULAR SEASON								PLAYOFFS				
Season Team	League	Gms.	G	A	Pts.	PIM	+/-	PP	SH	Gms.	G	A	Pts.	PIM
90-91—Calgary Royals	AJHL	49	3	23	26	220	...	...	...	—	—	—	—	—
91-92—Portland	WHL	70	4	18	22	250	...	...	...	6	0	2	2	27
92-93—Portland	WHL	72	10	26	36	284	...	...	...	16	4	4	8	*65
93-94—Albany	AHL	79	7	14	21	186	...	...	...	5	0	3	3	11
94-95—Albany	AHL	77	5	13	18	215	...	...	...	12	1	1	2	17
95-96—Albany	AHL	42	4	23	27	107	...	...	...	—	—	—	—	—
—New Jersey	NHL	8	0	0	0	15	-2	0	0	—	—	—	—	—
—Saint John	AHL	13	2	7	9	39	...	...	...	—	—	—	—	—
—Calgary	NHL	3	0	0	0	5	3	0	0	1	0	0	0	0
96-97—Calgary	NHL	63	1	6	7	91	-2	0	1	—	—	—	—	—
97-98—Calgary	NHL	79	5	22	27	169	1	1	1	—	—	—	—	—
98-99—Calgary	NHL	73	3	9	12	117	-8	0	0	—	—	—	—	—
99-00—Calgary	NHL	47	1	6	7	47	-11	0	0	—	—	—	—	—
NHL Totals (5 years)		273	10	43	53	444	-19	1	2	1	0	0	0	0

H

HURLBUT, MIKE D SABRES

PERSONAL: Born July 10, 1966, in Massena, N.Y. ... 6-2/200. ... Shoots left. ... Full Name: Michael Ray Hurlbut.

HIGH SCHOOL: Northwood (Lake Placid, N.Y.).

COLLEGE: St. Lawrence (N.Y.).

TRANSACTIONS/CAREER NOTES: Selected by New York Rangers in NHL supplemental draft (June 10, 1988). ... Sprained left knee (January 25, 1993); missed 13 games. ... Traded by Rangers to Quebec Nordiques for D Alexander Karpovtsev (September 9, 1993). ... Nordiques franchise moved to Colorado and renamed Avalanche for 1995-96 season (June 21, 1995). ... Signed as free agent by Buffalo Sabres (August 11, 1997).

HONORS: Named to NCAA All-America (East) first team (1988-89). ... Named to ECAC All-Star first team (1988-89). ... Named to AHL All-Star second team (1994-95).

		REGULAR SEASON								PLAYOFFS				
Season Team	League	Gms.	G	A	Pts.	PIM	+/-	PP	SH	Gms.	G	A	Pts.	PIM
84-85—Northwood School......	N.Y. H.S.	34	20	27	47	30	...	...	...	—	—	—	—	—
85-86—St. Lawrence Univ.......	ECAC	25	2	10	12	40	...	...	...	—	—	—	—	—
86-87—St. Lawrence Univ......	ECAC	35	8	15	23	44	...	...	...	—	—	—	—	—
87-88—St. Lawrence Univ......	ECAC	38	6	12	18	18	...	...	...	—	—	—	—	—
88-89—St. Lawrence Univ......	ECAC	36	8	25	33	30	...	...	...	—	—	—	—	—
—Denver....................	IHL	8	0	2	2	13	...	...	...	4	1	2	3	2
89-90—Flint....................	IHL	74	3	34	37	38	...	...	...	3	0	1	1	2
90-91—Binghamton...............	AHL	33	2	11	13	27	...	...	...	3	0	1	1	0
—San Diego................	IHL	2	1	0	1	0	...	...	...	—	—	—	—	—
91-92—Binghamton...............	AHL	79	16	39	55	64	...	...	...	11	2	7	9	8
92-93—Binghamton...............	AHL	46	11	25	36	46	...	...	...	14	2	5	7	12
—New York Rangers......	NHL	23	1	8	9	16	4	1	0	—	—	—	—	—
93-94—Cornwall................	AHL	77	13	33	46	100	...	...	...	13	3	7	10	12
—Quebec	NHL	1	0	0	0	0	-1	0	0	—	—	—	—	—
94-95—Cornwall................	AHL	74	11	49	60	69	...	...	...	3	1	0	1	15
95-96—Houston.................	IHL	38	3	12	15	33	...	...	...	—	—	—	—	—
—Minnesota................	IHL	22	1	4	5	22	...	...	...	—	—	—	—	—
96-97—Houston.................	IHL	70	11	24	35	62	...	...	...	13	5	8	13	12
97-98—Buffalo.................	NHL	3	0	0	0	2	-1	0	0	—	—	—	—	—
—Rochester..............	AHL	45	10	20	30	48	...	...	...	4	1	1	2	2
98-99—Rochester..............	AHL	72	15	39	54	46	...	...	...	20	4	5	9	12
—Buffalo.................	NHL	1	0	0	0	0	2	0	0	—	—	—	—	—
99-00—Rochester..............	AHL	74	10	29	39	83	...	...	...	21	5	6	11	14
—Buffalo.................	NHL	1	0	0	0	2	1	0	0	—	—	—	—	—
NHL Totals (5 years)..........		29	1	8	9	20	5	1	0					

HURME, JANI   G   SENATORS

PERSONAL: Born January 7, 1975, in Turku, Finland. ... 6-0/187. ... Catches left. ... Name pronounced hoor-MAY.

TRANSACTIONS/CAREER NOTES: Selected by Ottawa Senators in third round (second Senators pick, 58th overall) of NHL entry draft (June 21, 1997).

HONORS: Named to IHL All-Star second team (1999-2000).

		REGULAR SEASON								PLAYOFFS						
Season Team	League	Gms.	Min	W	L	T	GA	SO	Avg.	Gms.	Min.	W	L	GA	SO	Avg.
92-93—TPS Turku Jr.	Finland	12	669	...	...	...	47	0	4.22	1	60	...	...	...	11	...
93-94—TPS Turku	Finland	1	2	...	...	...	0	0	...	—	—	—	—	—	—	—
—Kiekko-67 Turku	Fin. Div. 2	3	190	...	...	...	7	0	2.21	—	—	—	—	—	—	—
—Kiekko-67 Turku Jrs....	Finland	18	...	...	...	...	...	...	...	—	—	—	—	—	—	—
94-95—Kiekko-67 Turku	Fin. Div. 2	19	1049	...	...	...	53	...	3.03	3	180	...	...	6	...	2.00
—TPS Turku Jr.	Finland	2	125	...	...	...	5	0	2.40	—	—	—	—	—	—	—
—Kiekko-67 Turku Jrs....	Finland	9	540	...	...	...	47	...	5.22	—	—	—	—	—	—	—
95-96—TPS Turku	Finland	16	945	...	...	...	34	2	2.16	10	545	...	...	22	2	2.42
—Kiekko-67 Turku	Fin. Div. 2	16	968	...	...	...	39	1	2.42	—	—	—	—	—	—	—
—TPS Turku Jr.	Finland	13	777	...	...	...	34	1	2.63	—	—	—	—	—	—	—
96-97—TPS Turku	Finland	48	2917	31	11	6	101	6	2.08	12	722	...	...	39	0	3.24
97-98—Detroit.......................	IHL	6	290	2	2	‡2	20	0	4.14	—	—	—	—	—	—	—
—Indianapolis	IHL	29	1506	11	11	‡3	83	...	3.31	3	130	1	0	10	0	4.62
98-99—Detroit.......................	IHL	12	643	7	3	‡1	26	1	2.43	—	—	—	—	—	—	—
—Cincinnati	IHL	26	1428	14	9	‡2	81	0	3.40	—	—	—	—	—	—	—
99-00—Grand Rapids...............	IHL	52	2948	35	15	‡4	107	4	2.18	*17	*1028	*10	*7	*37	1	2.16
—Ottawa.........................	NHL	1	60	1	0	0	2	0	2.00	—	—	—	—	—	—	—
NHL Totals (1 year)...............		1	60	1	0	0	2	0	2.00							

HUSCROFT, JAMIE   D   CAPITALS

PERSONAL: Born January 9, 1967, in Creston, B.C. ... 6-3/206. ... Shoots right. ... Full Name: James Huscroft. ... Name pronounced HUZ-krawft.

TRANSACTIONS/CAREER NOTES: Selected by New Jersey Devils as underage junior in ninth round (ninth Devils pick, 171st overall) of NHL entry draft (June 15, 1985). ... Fractured right wrist (October 1988). ... Injured groin (December 1988). ... Fractured foot (January 1989); missed 19 games. ... Signed as free agent by Boston Bruins (July 16, 1992). ... Signed as free agent by Calgary Flames (July 27, 1995). ... Strained back prior to 1995-96 season; missed one game. ... Bruised foot (October 27, 1995); missed one game. ... Suffered from the flu (December 11, 1995); missed three games. ... Injured groin (April 1, 1996); missed three games. ... Cut forearm (March 4, 1997); missed three games. ... Traded by Flames to Tampa Bay Lightning for G Tyler Moss (March 18, 1997). ... Traded by Lightning to Vancouver Canucks for D Enrico Ciccone (March 14, 1998). ... Traded by Canucks to Phoenix Coyotes for future considerations (March 8, 1999). ... Bruised ribs (March 23, 1999); missed five games. ... Signed as free agent by Washington Capitals (August 9, 1999). ... Injured ribs (November 13, 1999); missed five games.

		REGULAR SEASON								PLAYOFFS				
Season Team	League	Gms.	G	A	Pts.	PIM	+/-	PP	SH	Gms.	G	A	Pts.	PIM
83-84—Seattle........................	WHL	63	0	12	12	77	...	...	...	5	0	0	0	15
84-85—Seattle........................	WHL	69	3	13	16	273	...	...	...	—	—	—	—	—
85-86—Seattle........................	WHL	66	6	20	26	394	...	...	...	5	0	1	1	18

H

Season Team	League	REGULAR SEASON								PLAYOFFS				
		Gms.	G	A	Pts.	PIM	+/-	PP	SH	Gms.	G	A	Pts.	PIM
86-87—Seattle	WHL	21	1	18	19	99	...	...	...	20	0	3	3	0
—Medicine Hat	WHL	35	4	21	25	170	...	...	...	20	0	3	3	*125
87-88—Flint	IHL	3	1	0	1	2	...	...	...	16	0	1	1	110
—Utica	AHL	71	5	7	12	316	...	...	...	—	—	—	—	—
88-89—Utica	AHL	41	2	10	12	215	...	...	...	5	0	0	0	40
—New Jersey	NHL	15	0	2	2	51	-3	0	0	—	—	—	—	—
89-90—New Jersey	NHL	42	2	3	5	149	-2	0	0	5	0	0	0	16
—Utica	AHL	22	3	6	9	122	...	...	...	—	—	—	—	—
90-91—New Jersey	NHL	8	0	1	1	27	1	0	0	3	0	0	0	6
—Utica	AHL	59	3	15	18	339	...	...	...	—	—	—	—	—
91-92—Utica	AHL	50	4	7	11	224	...	...	...	—	—	—	—	—
92-93—Providence	AHL	69	2	15	17	257	...	...	...	2	0	1	1	6
93-94—Providence	AHL	32	1	10	11	157	...	...	...	—	—	—	—	—
—Boston	NHL	36	0	1	1	144	-2	0	0	4	0	0	0	9
94-95—Boston	NHL	34	0	6	6	103	-3	0	0	5	0	0	0	11
95-96—Calgary	NHL	70	3	9	12	162	14	0	0	4	0	1	1	4
96-97—Calgary	NHL	39	0	4	4	117	2	0	0	—	—	—	—	—
—Tampa Bay	NHL	13	0	1	1	34	-4	0	0	—	—	—	—	—
97-98—Tampa Bay	NHL	44	0	3	3	122	-4	0	0	—	—	—	—	—
—Vancouver	NHL	7	0	1	1	55	2	0	0	—	—	—	—	—
98-99—Vancouver	NHL	26	0	1	1	63	-3	0	0	—	—	—	—	—
—Phoenix	NHL	11	0	1	1	27	-1	0	0	—	—	—	—	—
99-00—Portland	AHL	56	0	12	12	154	...	...	...	4	0	0	0	14
—Washington	NHL	7	0	0	0	11	-5	0	0	—	—	—	—	—
NHL Totals (10 years)		352	5	33	38	1065	-8	0	0	21	0	1	1	46

HUSELIUS, KRISTIAN — LW — PANTHERS

PERSONAL: Born November 10, 1978, in Stockholm, Sweden. ... 6-1/183. ... Shoots left.
TRANSACTIONS/CAREER NOTES: Selected by Florida Panthers in second round (second Panthers pick, 47th overall) of NHL entry draft (June 21, 1997).

Season Team	League	REGULAR SEASON								PLAYOFFS				
		Gms.	G	A	Pts.	PIM	+/-	PP	SH	Gms.	G	A	Pts.	PIM
94-95—Hammarby	Sweden Jr.	17	6	2	8	2	...	...	...	—	—	—	—	—
95-96—Hammarby	Sweden Jr.	25	13	8	21	14	...	...	...	—	—	—	—	—
—Hammarby	Sweden Dv. 2	6	1	0	1	0	...	...	...	—	—	—	—	—
96-97—Farjestad Karlstad	Sweden	13	2	0	2	4	...	...	...	5	1	0	1	0
97-98—Farjestad Karlstad	Sweden	34	2	1	3	2	...	...	...	11	0	0	0	0
98-99—Farjestad Karlstad	Sweden	28	4	4	8	4	...	...	...	—	—	—	—	—
—V. Frolunda Goteborg	Sweden	20	2	2	4	2	...	...	...	4	1	0	1	0
99-00—V. Frolunda Goteborg	Sweden	50	21	23	44	20	...	...	...	5	2	2	4	8

IGINLA, JAROME — RW — FLAMES

PERSONAL: Born July 1, 1977, in Edmonton. ... 6-1/202. ... Shoots right. ... Name pronounced ih-GIHN-luh.
TRANSACTIONS/CAREER NOTES: Selected by Dallas Stars in first round (first Stars pick, 11th overall) of NHL entry draft (July 8, 1995). ... Traded by Stars with C Corey Millen to Calgary Flames for C Joe Nieuwendyk (December 19, 1995). ... Fractured bone in right hand (January 21, 1997); missed 10 games. ... Missed first three games of 1999-2000 season due to contract dispute. ... Bruised knee (March 22, 2000); missed two games.
HONORS: Won George Parsons Trophy (1994-95). ... Won Four Broncos Memorial Trophy (1995-96). ... Named to Can.HL All-Star first team (1995-96). ... Named to WHL (West) All-Star first team (1995-96). ... Named to NHL All-Rookie team (1996-97).

Season Team	League	REGULAR SEASON								PLAYOFFS				
		Gms.	G	A	Pts.	PIM	+/-	PP	SH	Gms.	G	A	Pts.	PIM
93-94—Kamloops	WHL	48	6	23	29	33	...	...	...	19	3	6	9	10
94-95—Kamloops	WHL	72	33	38	71	111	...	...	...	21	7	11	18	34
95-96—Kamloops	WHL	63	63	73	136	120	...	...	...	16	16	13	29	44
—Calgary	NHL	—	—	—	—	—	...	...	...	2	1	1	2	0
96-97—Calgary	NHL	82	21	29	50	37	-4	8	1	—	—	—	—	—
97-98—Calgary	NHL	70	13	19	32	29	-10	0	2	—	—	—	—	—
98-99—Calgary	NHL	82	28	23	51	58	1	7	0	—	—	—	—	—
99-00—Calgary	NHL	77	29	34	63	26	0	12	0	—	—	—	—	—
NHL Totals (5 years)		311	91	105	196	150	-13	27	3	2	1	1	2	0

IRBE, ARTURS — G — HURRICANES

PERSONAL: Born February 2, 1967, in Riga, U.S.S.R. ... 5-8/190. ... Catches left. ... Name pronounced AHR-tuhrs UHR-bay.
TRANSACTIONS/CAREER NOTES: Selected by Minnesota North Stars in 10th round (11th North Stars pick, 196th overall) of NHL entry draft (June 17, 1989). ... Selected by San Jose Sharks in NHL dispersal draft (May 30, 1991). ... Sprained knee (November 27, 1992); missed 19 games. ... Injured foot (February 15, 1995); missed one game. ... Injured knee (January 17, 1996); remainder of season. ... Signed as free agent by Dallas Stars (July 22, 1996). ... Strained groin (November 8, 1996); missed six games. ... Signed as free agent by Vancouver Canucks (August 5, 1997). ... Signed as free agent by Carolina Hurricanes (September 10, 1998).
HONORS: Named Soviet League Rookie of the Year (1987-88). ... Shared James Norris Memorial Trophy with Wade Flaherty (1991-92). ... Named to IHL All-Star first team (1991-92). ... Played in NHL All-Star Game (1994 and 1999).
MISCELLANEOUS: Holds San Jose Sharks all-time records for most games played by goalie (183) and most wins (57). ... Holds Carolina Hurricanes franchise all-time records for goals-against average (2.33). ... Stopped a penalty shot attempt (vs. Kevyn Adams, February 14, 2000). ... Allowed a penalty shot goal (vs. Mats Sundin, March 15, 1995; vs. Igor Larionov, November 22, 1995; vs. Hnat Domenichelli, February 27, 1998).

			REGULAR SEASON								PLAYOFFS						
Season Team	League	Gms.	Min	W	L	T	GA	SO	Avg.	Gms.	Min.	W	L	GA	SO	Avg.
86-87—Dynamo Riga	USSR	2	27	...	...	...	1	0	2.22	—	—	—	—	—	—	—
87-88—Dynamo Riga	USSR	34	1870	...	...	...	84	0	2.70	—	—	—	—	—	—	—
88-89—Dynamo Riga	USSR	41	2460	...	...	...	117	0	2.85	—	—	—	—	—	—	—
89-90—Dynamo Riga	USSR	48	2880	...	...	...	116	0	2.42	—	—	—	—	—	—	—
90-91—Dynamo Riga	USSR	46	2713	...	...	...	133	0	2.94	—	—	—	—	—	—	—
91-92—Kansas City	IHL	32	1955	24	7	‡1	80	0	*2.46	15	914	12	3	44	0	2.89
—San Jose	NHL	13	645	2	6	3	48	0	4.47	—	—	—	—	—	—	—
92-93—Kansas City	IHL	6	364	3	3	0	20	0	3.30	—	—	—	—	—	—	—
—San Jose	NHL	36	2074	7	26	0	142	1	4.11	—	—	—	—	—	—	—
93-94—San Jose	NHL	*74	*4412	30	28	*16	209	3	2.84	14	806	7	7	50	0	3.72
94-95—San Jose	NHL	38	2043	14	19	3	111	4	3.26	6	316	2	4	27	0	5.13
95-96—San Jose	NHL	22	1112	4	12	4	85	0	4.59	—	—	—	—	—	—	—
—Kansas City	IHL	4	226	1	2	1	16	0	4.25	—	—	—	—	—	—	—
96-97—Dallas	NHL	35	1965	17	12	3	88	3	2.69	1	13	0	0	0	0	...
97-98—Vancouver	NHL	41	1999	14	11	6	91	2	2.73	—	—	—	—	—	—	—
98-99—Carolina	NHL	62	3663	27	20	12	135	6	2.22	6	408	2	4	15	0	2.21
99-00—Carolina	NHL	*75	4345	34	28	9	*175	5	2.42	—	—	—	—	—	—	—
NHL Totals (9 years)		396	22238	149	162	56	1084	24	2.92	27	1543	11	15	92	0	3.58

ISBISTER, BRAD — RW — ISLANDERS

PERSONAL: Born May 7, 1977, in Edmonton. ... 6-4/228. ... Shoots right. ... Name pronounced ihs-BIH-stuhr.
HIGH SCHOOL: Milwaukie (Ore.).
TRANSACTIONS/CAREER NOTES: Selected by Winnipeg Jets in third round (fourth Jets pick, 67th overall) of NHL entry draft (July 8, 1995). ... Jets franchise moved to Phoenix and renamed Coyotes for 1996-97 season; NHL approved move on January 18, 1996. ... Strained muscle in abdomen (November 22, 1997); missed six games. ... Strained groin (January 8, 1999); missed six games. ... Suffered from hernia (January 27, 1999); missed 19 games. ... Strained groin (March 11, 1999); missed remainder of season. ... Traded by Coyotes with third-round pick (C Brian Collins) in 1999 draft to New York Islanders for C Robert Reichel and third- (C/LW Jason Jaspers) and fourth-round (C Preston Mizzi) picks in 1999 draft (March 20, 1999). ... Sprained ankle (January 26, 2000); missed 18 games.
HONORS: Named to WHL (West) All-Star second team (1996-97).
MISCELLANEOUS: Scored on a penalty shot (vs. Sean Burke, January 10, 2000). ... Failed to score on a penalty shot (vs. Damian Rhodes, March 16, 2000).

			REGULAR SEASON							PLAYOFFS				
Season Team	League	Gms.	G	A	Pts.	PIM	+/-	PP	SH	Gms.	G	A	Pts.	PIM
93-94—Portland	WHL	64	7	10	17	45	...	...	...	10	0	2	2	0
94-95—Portland	WHL	67	16	20	36	123	...	...	...	—	—	—	—	—
95-96—Portland	WHL	71	45	44	89	184	...	...	...	7	2	4	6	20
96-97—Springfield	AHL	7	3	1	4	14	...	...	...	9	1	2	3	10
—Portland	WHL	24	15	18	33	45	...	...	...	6	2	1	3	16
97-98—Phoenix	NHL	66	9	8	17	102	4	1	0	5	0	0	0	2
—Springfield	AHL	9	8	2	10	36	...	...	...	—	—	—	—	—
98-99—Las Vegas	IHL	2	0	0	0	9	...	...	...	—	—	—	—	—
—Springfield	AHL	4	1	1	2	12	...	...	...	—	—	—	—	—
—Phoenix	NHL	32	4	4	8	46	1	0	0	—	—	—	—	—
99-00—New York Islanders	NHL	64	22	20	42	100	-18	9	0	—	—	—	—	—
NHL Totals (3 years)		162	35	32	67	248	-13	10	0	5	0	0	0	2

JACKMAN, BARRET — D — BLUES

PERSONAL: Born March 5, 1981, in Trail, B.C. ... 6-1/200. ... Shoots left.
TRANSACTIONS/CAREER NOTES: Selected by St. Louis Blues in first round (first Blues pick, 17th overall) of NHL entry draft (June 26, 1999).
HONORS: Named to WHL (East) All-Star second team (1999-2000).

			REGULAR SEASON							PLAYOFFS				
Season Team	League	Gms.	G	A	Pts.	PIM	+/-	PP	SH	Gms.	G	A	Pts.	PIM
97-98—Regina	WHL	68	2	11	13	224	...	...	...	9	0	3	3	32
98-99—Regina	WHL	70	8	36	44	259	...	...	...	—	—	—	—	—
99-00—Regina	WHL	53	9	37	46	175	...	...	...	6	1	1	2	19
—Worcester	AHL	—	—	—	—	—	...	...	...	2	0	0	0	13

JACKMAN, RICHARD — D — STARS

PERSONAL: Born June 28, 1978, in Toronto. ... 6-2/192. ... Shoots right.
TRANSACTIONS/CAREER NOTES: Selected by Dallas Stars in first round (first Stars pick, fifth overall) of NHL entry draft (June 22, 1996).
HONORS: Named to Can.HL All-Rookie team (1995-96). ... Named to OHL All-Rookie first team (1995-96). ... Named to OHL All-Star second team (1997-98).

			REGULAR SEASON							PLAYOFFS				
Season Team	League	Gms.	G	A	Pts.	PIM	+/-	PP	SH	Gms.	G	A	Pts.	PIM
95-96—Sault Ste. Marie	OHL	66	13	29	42	97	...	...	...	4	1	0	1	15
96-97—Sault Ste. Marie	OHL	53	13	34	47	116	...	...	...	10	2	6	8	24
97-98—Sault Ste. Marie	OHL	60	33	40	73	111	...	...	...	—	—	—	—	—
—Michigan	IHL	14	1	5	6	10	...	...	...	4	0	0	0	10
98-99—Michigan	IHL	71	13	17	30	106	...	...	...	5	0	4	4	6
99-00—Michigan	IHL	50	3	16	19	51	...	...	...	—	—	—	—	—
—Dallas	NHL	22	1	2	3	6	-1	1	0	—	—	—	—	—
NHL Totals (1 year)		22	1	2	3	6	-1	1	0					

JAGR, JAROMIR RW PENGUINS

PERSONAL: Born February 15, 1972, in Kladno, Czechoslovakia. ... 6-2/235. ... Shoots left. ... Name pronounced YAHR-oh-meer YAH-gihr.

TRANSACTIONS/CAREER NOTES: Selected by Pittsburgh Penguins in first round (first Penguins pick, fifth overall) of NHL entry draft (June 16, 1990). ... Separated shoulder (February 23, 1993); missed three games. ... Strained groin (January 21, 1994); missed four games. ... Played in Europe during 1994-95 NHL lockout. ... Suffered from the flu (January 11, 1997); missed one game. ... Strained groin (February 16, 1997); missed three games. ... Pulled groin (February 27, 1997); missed 13 games. ... Strained groin (April 10, 1997); missed two games. ... Strained hip flexor and groin (November 14, 1997); missed four games. ... Injured groin (April 16, 1998); missed one game. ... Injured groin (April 5, 1999); missed one game. ... Bruised thigh (November 18, 1999); missed one game. ... Strained muscle in abdomen (January 15, 2000); missed four games. ... Injured hamstring (February 21, 2000); missed 12 games. ... Bruised upper back (March 26, 2000); missed two games.

HONORS: Named to Czechoslovakian League All-Star team (1989-90). ... Named to NHL All-Rookie team (1990-91). ... Won Art Ross Trophy (1994-95, 1997-98 through 1999-2000). ... Named to THE SPORTING NEWS All-Star team (1994-95, 1995-96, 1998-99 and 1999-2000). ... Named to NHL All-Star first team (1994-95, 1995-96, 1997-98 through 1999-2000). ... Played in NHL All-Star Game (1988, 1990-1994 and 1998-2000). ... Named to play in NHL All-Star Game (1997); replaced by C Adam Oates due to injury. ... Named to NHL All-Star second team (1996-97). ... Named NHL Player of the Year by THE SPORTING NEWS (1998-99 and 1999-2000). ... Won Lester B. Pearson Award (1998-99 and 1999-2000). ... Won Hart Memorial Trophy (1998-99).

RECORDS: Holds NHL single-season records for most points by a right winger—149 (1995-96); and most assists by a right winger—87 (1995-96).

STATISTICAL PLATEAUS: Three-goal games: 1990-91 (1), 1994-95 (1), 1996-97 (2), 1999-00 (2). Total: 6.

MISCELLANEOUS: Member of Stanley Cup championship teams (1991 and 1992). ... Member of gold-medal-winning Czech Republic Olympic team (1998). ... Captain of Pittsburgh Penguins (1998-99 and 1999-2000). ... Failed to score on a penalty shot (vs. Don Beaupre, January 26, 1993; vs. Mark Fitzpatrick, November 9, 1996).

STATISTICAL NOTES: Led NHL with 12 game-winning goals (1995-96).

Season Team	League	REGULAR SEASON								PLAYOFFS				
		Gms.	G	A	Pts.	PIM	+/-	PP	SH	Gms.	G	A	Pts.	PIM
88-89—Poldi Kladno	Czech.	39	8	10	18	...	...	...	...	—	—	—	—	—
89-90—Poldi Kladno	Czech.	51	30	30	60	...	...	...	...	—	—	—	—	—
90-91—Pittsburgh	NHL	80	27	30	57	42	-4	7	0	24	3	10	13	6
91-92—Pittsburgh	NHL	70	32	37	69	34	12	4	0	†21	11	13	24	6
92-93—Pittsburgh	NHL	81	34	60	94	61	30	10	1	12	5	4	9	23
93-94—Pittsburgh	NHL	80	32	67	99	61	15	9	0	6	2	4	6	16
94-95—HC Kladno	Czech Rep.	11	8	14	22	10	...	...	...	—	—	—	—	—
—HC Bolzano	Euro	5	8	8	16	4	...	...	...	—	—	—	—	—
—HC Bolzano	Italy	1	0	0	0	0	...	...	...	—	—	—	—	—
—Schalker Haie	Ger. Div. II	1	1	10	11	0	...	...	...	—	—	—	—	—
—Pittsburgh	NHL	48	32	38	†70	37	23	8	3	12	10	5	15	6
95-96—Pittsburgh	NHL	82	62	87	149	96	31	20	1	18	11	12	23	18
96-97—Pittsburgh	NHL	63	47	48	95	40	22	11	2	5	4	4	8	4
97-98—Pittsburgh	NHL	77	35	†67	102	64	17	7	0	6	4	5	9	2
—Czech Rep. Oly. team..	Int'l	6	1	4	5	2	...	...	...	—	—	—	—	—
98-99—Pittsburgh	NHL	81	44	*83	*127	66	17	10	1	9	5	7	12	16
99-00—Pittsburgh	NHL	63	42	54	*96	50	25	10	0	11	8	8	16	6
NHL Totals (10 years)		725	387	571	958	551	188	96	8	124	63	72	135	103

JAKOPIN, JOHN D PANTHERS

PERSONAL: Born May 16, 1975, in Toronto. ... 6-5/239. ... Shoots left. ... Name pronounced JAK-oh-pihn.

COLLEGE: Merrimack College (Mass.).

TRANSACTIONS/CAREER NOTES: Selected by Detroit Red Wings in fourth round (fourth Red Wings pick, 97th overall) of NHL entry draft (June 26, 1993). ... Signed as free agent by Florida Panthers (June 4, 1997). ... Strained neck (November 5, 1999); missed five games. ... Injured groin (February 1, 2000); missed remainder of season.

HONORS: Named to Hockey East All-Rookie team (1993-94).

Season Team	League	REGULAR SEASON								PLAYOFFS				
		Gms.	G	A	Pts.	PIM	+/-	PP	SH	Gms.	G	A	Pts.	PIM
92-93—St. Michael's	Tier II Jr. A	45	9	21	30	42	...	...	...	—	—	—	—	—
93-94—Merrimack College	Hockey East	36	2	8	10	64	...	...	...	—	—	—	—	—
94-95—Merrimack College	Hockey East	37	4	10	14	42	...	...	...	—	—	—	—	—
95-96—Merrimack College	Hockey East	32	10	15	25	68	...	...	...	—	—	—	—	—
96-97—Merrimack College	Hockey East	31	4	12	16	68	...	...	...	—	—	—	—	—
—Adirondack	AHL	3	0	0	0	9	...	...	...	—	—	—	—	—
97-98—New Haven	AHL	60	2	18	20	151	...	...	...	3	0	0	0	0
—Florida	NHL	2	0	0	0	4	-3	0	0	—	—	—	—	—
98-99—New Haven	AHL	60	2	7	9	154	...	...	...	—	—	—	—	—
—Florida	NHL	3	0	0	0	0	-1	0	0	—	—	—	—	—
99-00—Florida	NHL	17	0	0	0	26	-2	0	0	—	—	—	—	—
—Louisville	AHL	23	4	6	10	47	...	...	...	—	—	—	—	—
NHL Totals (3 years)		22	0	0	0	30	-6	0	0					

JANSSENS, MARK C BLACKHAWKS

PERSONAL: Born May 19, 1968, in Surrey, B.C. ... 6-3/216. ... Shoots left.

TRANSACTIONS/CAREER NOTES: Selected by New York Rangers as underage junior in fourth round (fourth Rangers pick, 72nd overall) of NHL entry draft (June 21, 1986). ... Fractured skull and suffered cerebral concussion (December 10, 1988). ... Traded by Rangers to Minnesota North Stars for C Mario Thyer and third-round pick (D Maxim Galanov) in 1993 draft (March 10, 1992). ... Traded by North Stars to Hartford Whalers for C James Black (September 3, 1992). ... Separated shoulder (December 26, 1992); missed five games. ... Suffered slight concussion (February 4, 1995); missed two games. ... Sprained knee (January 22, 1997); missed 14 games. ... Traded by Whalers to Mighty Ducks of Anaheim for LW Bates Battaglia and fourth-round pick (C Josef Vasicek) in 1998 draft (March 18, 1997). ... Traded by Mighty Ducks with D J.J. Daigneault and RW Joe Sacco to New York Islanders for C Travis Green, D Doug Houda and RW Tony Tuzzolino (February 6, 1998). ... Traded by Islanders to Phoenix Coyotes for ninth-round pick (RW Jason Doyle) in 1998 draft (March 24, 1998). ... Signed as free agent by Chicago Blackhawks (July 3, 1998). ... Lacerated leg (November 10, 1998); missed four games. ... Injured back (March 6, 1999); missed 11 games. ... Reinjured back (April 2, 1999); missed two games. ... Suffered sore back (December 9, 1999) and underwent surgery; missed 33 games. ... Traded by Blackhawks to Philadelphia Flyers for ninth-round pick (D Arne Ramholt) in 2000 draft (June 12, 2000). ... Claimed on waivers by Blackhawks (July 6, 2000).

		REGULAR SEASON								PLAYOFFS				
Season Team	League	Gms.	G	A	Pts.	PIM	+/-	PP	SH	Gms.	G	A	Pts.	PIM
84-85—Regina	WHL	70	8	22	30	51	...	...	...	5	1	1	2	0
85-86—Regina	WHL	71	25	38	63	146	...	...	...	9	0	2	2	17
86-87—Regina	WHL	68	24	38	62	209	...	...	...	3	0	1	1	14
87-88—Regina	WHL	71	39	51	90	202	...	...	...	4	3	4	7	6
—New York Rangers	NHL	1	0	0	0	0	0	0	0	—	—	—	—	—
—Colorado	IHL	6	2	2	4	24	...	...	...	12	3	2	5	20
88-89—New York Rangers	NHL	5	0	0	0	0	-4	0	0	—	—	—	—	—
—Denver	IHL	38	19	19	38	104	...	...	...	4	3	0	3	18
89-90—New York Rangers	NHL	80	5	8	13	161	-26	0	0	9	2	1	3	10
90-91—New York Rangers	NHL	67	9	7	16	172	-1	0	0	6	3	0	3	6
91-92—New York Rangers	NHL	4	0	0	0	5	-1	0	0	—	—	—	—	—
—Binghamton	AHL	55	10	23	33	109	...	...	...	—	—	—	—	—
—Minnesota	NHL	3	0	0	0	0	-1	0	0	—	—	—	—	—
—Kalamazoo	IHL	2	0	0	0	2	...	...	...	11	1	2	3	22
92-93—Hartford	NHL	76	12	17	29	237	-15	0	0	—	—	—	—	—
93-94—Hartford	NHL	84	2	10	12	137	-13	0	0	—	—	—	—	—
94-95—Hartford	NHL	46	2	5	7	93	-8	0	0	—	—	—	—	—
95-96—Hartford	NHL	81	2	7	9	155	-13	0	0	—	—	—	—	—
96-97—Hartford	NHL	54	2	4	6	90	-10	0	0	—	—	—	—	—
—Anaheim	NHL	12	0	2	2	47	-3	0	0	11	0	0	0	15
97-98—Anaheim	NHL	55	4	5	9	116	-22	0	0	—	—	—	—	—
—New York Islanders	NHL	12	0	0	0	34	-3	0	0	—	—	—	—	—
—Phoenix	NHL	7	1	2	3	4	4	0	0	1	0	0	0	2
98-99—Chicago	NHL	60	1	0	1	65	-11	0	0	—	—	—	—	—
99-00—Chicago	NHL	36	0	6	6	73	-2	0	0	—	—	—	—	—
NHL Totals (13 years)		683	40	73	113	1389	-129	0	0	27	5	1	6	33

JILLSON, JEFF   D   SHARKS

PERSONAL: Born July 24, 1980, in North Smithfield, R.I. ... 6-3/219. ... Shoots right.
HIGH SCHOOL: Mount St. Charles (Woonsocket, R.I.).
COLLEGE: Michigan.
TRANSACTIONS/CAREER NOTES: Selected by San Jose Sharks in first round (first Sharks pick, 14th overall) of NHL entry draft (June 26, 1999).
HONORS: Named to CCHA All-Star first team (1999-2000). ... Named to NCAA All-America (West) first team (1999-2000).

		REGULAR SEASON								PLAYOFFS				
Season Team	League	Gms.	G	A	Pts.	PIM	+/-	PP	SH	Gms.	G	A	Pts.	PIM
96-97—Mount St. Charles	USHS (East)	15	16	14	30	20	...	...	...	—	—	—	—	—
97-98—Mount St. Charles	USHS (East)	15	10	13	23	32	...	...	...	—	—	—	—	—
98-99—Univ. of Michigan	CCHA	38	5	19	24	71	...	...	...	—	—	—	—	—
99-00—Univ. of Michigan	CCHA	36	8	26	34	111	...	...	...	—	—	—	—	—

JINDRICH, ROBERT   D   SHARKS

PERSONAL: Born November 14, 1976, in Plzen, Czechoslovakia. ... 5-11/190. ... Shoots left.
TRANSACTIONS/CAREER NOTES: Selected by San Jose Sharks in seventh round (10th Sharks pick, 168th overall) of NHL entry draft (July 8, 1995).

		REGULAR SEASON								PLAYOFFS				
Season Team	League	Gms.	G	A	Pts.	PIM	+/-	PP	SH	Gms.	G	A	Pts.	PIM
94-95—HC Keramika Plzen	Czech Rep.	11	1	0	1	...	...	...	...	—	—	—	—	—
—Sokolov	Czech Rep.					Statistics unavailable.				—	—	—	—	—
95-96—HC Keramika Plzen	Czech Rep.	37	1	3	4	...	...	...	...	—	—	—	—	—
96-97—HC Keramika Plzen	Czech Rep.	49	7	9	16	44	...	...	...	—	—	—	—	—
97-98—HC Keramika Plzen	Czech Rep.	39	2	5	7	...	...	...	...	—	—	—	—	—
—Beroun	Czech Rep.	13	4	2	6	...	...	...	...	—	—	—	—	—
98-99—HC Keramika Plzen	Czech Rep.	52	6	12	18	24	...	...	...	5	1	0	1	...
99-00—Kentucky	AHL	78	2	21	23	51	...	...	...	9	0	4	4	6

JOHANSSON, ANDREAS   C/LW   FLAMES

PERSONAL: Born May 19, 1973, in Hofors, Sweden. ... 6-2/202. ... Shoots left. ... Name pronounced yoh-HAN-suhn.
TRANSACTIONS/CAREER NOTES: Selected by New York Islanders in seventh round (seventh Islanders pick, 136th overall) of NHL entry draft (June 22, 1991). ... Injured back (April 5, 1996); missed three games. ... Traded by Islanders with D Darius Kasparaitis to Pittsburgh Penguins for C Bryan Smolinski (November 17, 1996). ... Bruised shoulder (December 10, 1996); missed 12 games. ... Suffered from the flu (January 26, 1997); missed one game. ... Suffered back spasms (February 15, 1997); missed one game. ... Bruised ribs (November 15, 1997); missed six games. ... Sprained medial collateral ligament in knee (March 8, 1998); missed 10 games. ... Signed as free agent by Ottawa Senators (September 29, 1998). ... Injured left knee (January 18, 1999); missed two games. ... Reinjured left knee (February 25, 1999); missed three games. ... Strained hamstring (March 8, 1999); missed two games. ... Injured knee (April 5, 1999); missed two games. ... Suffered back

spasms (April 15, 1999); missed one game. ... Traded by Senators to Tampa Bay Lightning for LW Rob Zamuner and second-round pick in 2000, 2001 or 2002 draft to complete deal that allowed Tampa Bay to sign general manager Rick Dudley (June 30, 1999). ... Suffered concussion (October 7, 1999); missed one game. ... Bruised foot (November 2, 1999); missed four games. ... Traded by Lightning to Calgary Flames for rights to LW Nils Ekman and fourth-round pick (traded to New York Islanders) in 2000 draft (November 20, 1999). ... Suffered injury (December 21, 1999); missed three games. ... Suffered from the flu (January 5, 2000); missed three games. ... Suffered back spasms (January 12, 2000); missed 15 games. ... Injured back (March 11, 2000); missed remainder of season.

				REGULAR SEASON							PLAYOFFS			
Season Team	League	Gms.	G	A	Pts.	PIM	+/-	PP	SH	Gms.	G	A	Pts.	PIM
90-91—Falun	Sweden	31	12	10	22	38	...	...	...	—	—	—	—	—
91-92—Farjestad Karlstad	Sweden	30	3	1	4	4	...	...	...	6	0	0	0	4
92-93—Farjestad Karlstad	Sweden	38	4	7	11	38	...	...	...	2	0	0	0	0
93-94—Farjestad Karlstad	Sweden	20	3	6	9	6	...	...	...	—	—	—	—	—
94-95—Farjestad Karlstad	Sweden	36	9	10	19	42	...	...	...	4	0	0	0	10
95-96—Worcester	AHL	29	5	5	10	32	...	...	...	—	—	—	—	—
—Utah	IHL	22	4	13	17	28	...	...	...	12	0	5	5	6
—New York Islanders	NHL	3	0	1	1	0	1	0	0	—	—	—	—	—
96-97—New York Islanders	NHL	15	2	2	4	0	-6	1	0	—	—	—	—	—
—Pittsburgh	NHL	27	2	7	9	20	-6	0	0	—	—	—	—	—
—Cleveland	IHL	10	2	4	6	42	...	...	...	11	1	5	6	8
97-98—Pittsburgh	NHL	50	5	10	15	20	4	0	1	1	0	0	0	0
—Swedish Oly. team	Int'l	3	0	0	0	2	...	...	...	—	—	—	—	—
98-99—Ottawa	NHL	69	21	16	37	34	1	7	0	2	0	0	0	0
99-00—Tampa Bay	NHL	12	2	3	5	8	1	0	0	—	—	—	—	—
—Calgary	NHL	28	3	7	10	14	-3	1	0	—	—	—	—	—
NHL Totals (5 years)		204	35	46	81	96	-8	9	1	3	0	0	0	0

JOHANSSON, CALLE — D — CAPITALS

PERSONAL: Born February 14, 1967, in Goteborg, Sweden. ... 5-11/203. ... Shoots left. ... Name pronounced KAL-ee yoh-HAHN-suhn.
TRANSACTIONS/CAREER NOTES: Selected by Buffalo Sabres in first round (first Sabres pick, 14th overall) of NHL entry draft (June 15, 1985). ... Dislocated thumb (October 9, 1988). ... Traded by Sabres with second-round pick (G Byron Dafoe) in 1989 draft to Washington Capitals for D Grant Ledyard, G Clint Malarchuk and sixth-round pick (C Brian Holzinger) in 1991 draft (March 6, 1989). ... Injured back (October 7, 1989); missed 10 games. ... Bruised ribs (January 9, 1993); missed seven games. ... Played in Europe during 1994-95 NHL lockout. ... Suffered from the flu (March 25, 1995); missed two games. ... Fractured hand (April 4, 1996); missed remainder of season. ... Fractured jaw (November 12, 1996); missed 16 games. ... Bruised foot (February 14, 1997); missed one game. ... Sprained knee (January 13, 1998); missed nine games. ... Sprained knee (March 15, 1999); missed remainder of season.
HONORS: Named to NHL All-Rookie team (1987-88).

				REGULAR SEASON							PLAYOFFS			
Season Team	League	Gms.	G	A	Pts.	PIM	+/-	PP	SH	Gms.	G	A	Pts.	PIM
83-84—Vastra Frolunda	Sweden	34	5	10	15	20	...	...	...	—	—	—	—	—
84-85—Vastra Frolunda	Sweden	36	14	15	29	20	...	...	...	6	1	2	3	4
85-86—Bjorkloven	Sweden	17	1	1	2	14	...	...	...	—	—	—	—	—
86-87—Bjorkloven	Sweden	30	2	13	15	18	...	...	...	6	1	3	4	6
87-88—Buffalo	NHL	71	4	38	42	37	12	2	0	6	0	1	1	0
88-89—Buffalo	NHL	47	2	11	13	33	-7	0	0	—	—	—	—	—
—Washington	NHL	12	1	7	8	4	1	1	0	6	1	2	3	0
89-90—Washington	NHL	70	8	31	39	25	7	4	0	15	1	6	7	4
90-91—Washington	NHL	80	11	41	52	23	-2	2	1	10	2	7	9	8
91-92—Washington	NHL	80	14	42	56	49	2	5	2	7	0	5	5	4
92-93—Washington	NHL	77	7	38	45	56	3	6	0	6	0	5	5	4
93-94—Washington	NHL	84	9	33	42	59	3	4	0	6	1	3	4	4
94-95—Kloten	Switzerland	5	1	2	3	8	...	...	...	—	—	—	—	—
—Washington	NHL	46	5	26	31	35	-6	4	0	7	3	1	4	0
95-96—Washington	NHL	78	10	25	35	50	13	4	0	—	—	—	—	—
96-97—Washington	NHL	65	6	11	17	16	-2	2	0	—	—	—	—	—
97-98—Washington	NHL	73	15	20	35	30	-11	10	1	21	2	8	10	16
—Swedish Oly. team	Int'l	4	0	0	0	2	...	...	...	—	—	—	—	—
98-99—Washington	NHL	67	8	21	29	22	10	2	0	—	—	—	—	—
99-00—Washington	NHL	82	7	25	32	24	13	1	0	5	1	2	3	0
NHL Totals (13 years)		932	107	369	476	463	36	47	4	89	11	40	51	40

JOHNSON, BRENT — G — BLUES

PERSONAL: Born March 12, 1977, in Farmington, Mich. ... 6-2/200. ... Catches left. ... Full Name: Brent Spencer Johnson. ... Nickname: Johnny.
HIGH SCHOOL: Farmington (Mich.).
TRANSACTIONS/CAREER NOTES: Selected by Colorado Avalanche in fifth round (fifth Avalanche pick, 129th overall) of NHL entry draft (July 8, 1995). ... Rights traded by Avalanche to St. Louis Blues for third-round pick (RW Ville Nieminen) in 1997 draft and conditional third-round pick in 2000 draft (May 30, 1997).

				REGULAR SEASON							PLAYOFFS				
Season Team	League	Gms.	Min	W	L	T	GA	SO	Avg.	Gms.	Min.	W	L	GA	SO	Avg.
94-95—Owen Sound	OHL	18	904	3	9	1	75	0	4.98	4	253	0	4	24	0	5.69
95-96—Owen Sound	OHL	58	3211	24	28	1	243	1	4.54	6	371	2	4	29	0	4.69
96-97—Owen Sound	OHL	50	2798	20	28	1	201	1	4.31	4	253	0	4	24	0	5.69
97-98—Worcester	AHL	42	2241	14	15	7	119	0	3.19	6	332	3	2	19	0	3.43
98-99—Worcester	AHL	49	2925	22	22	4	146	2	2.99	4	238	1	3	12	0	3.03
—St. Louis	NHL	6	286	3	2	0	10	0	2.10	—	—	—	—	—	—	—
99-00—Worcester	AHL	58	3319	24	27	5	161	3	2.91	9	561	4	5	23	1	2.46
NHL Totals (1 year)		6	286	3	2	0	10	0	2.10							

JOHNSON, CRAIG   LW   KINGS

PERSONAL: Born March 8, 1972, in St. Paul, Minn. ... 6-2/197. ... Shoots left.
HIGH SCHOOL: Hill-Murray (St. Paul, Minn.).
COLLEGE: Minnesota.
TRANSACTIONS/CAREER NOTES: Selected by St. Louis Blues in second round (first Blues pick, 33rd overall) of NHL entry draft (June 16, 1990). ... Separated shoulder (December 1990). ... Traded by Blues with C Patrice Tardiff, C Roman Vopat, fifth-round pick (D Peter Hogan) in 1996 draft and first-round pick (LW Matt Zultek) in 1997 draft to Los Angeles Kings for C Wayne Gretzky (February 27, 1996). ... Sprained left shoulder (March 13, 1996); missed seven games. ... Strained abdominal muscle prior to 1996-97 season; missed first seven games of season. ... Strained groin (November 2, 1996); missed one game. ... Strained abdominal muscle (November 30, 1996); missed 36 games. ... Strained groin (March 29, 1997); missed six games. ... Suffered from the flu (December 18, 1997); missed two games. ... Bruised abdomen (February 2, 1998); missed three games. ... Injured ribs (January 14, 1999); missed four games. ... Lacerated finger (February 16, 2000); missed three games.
HONORS: Named to WCHA All-Rookie Team (1990-91).

J

		REGULAR SEASON								PLAYOFFS				
Season Team	League	Gms.	G	A	Pts.	PIM	+/-	PP	SH	Gms.	G	A	Pts.	PIM
87-88—Hill-Murray H.S.	Minn. H.S.	28	14	20	34	4	...	...	...	—	—	—	—	—
88-89—Hill-Murray H.S.	Minn. H.S.	24	22	30	52	10	...	...	...	—	—	—	—	—
89-90—Hill-Murray H.S.	Minn. H.S.	23	15	36	51	...	...	...	...	—	—	—	—	—
90-91—Univ. of Minnesota	WCHA	33	13	18	31	34	...	...	...	—	—	—	—	—
91-92—Univ. of Minnesota	WCHA	44	19	39	58	70	...	...	...	—	—	—	—	—
92-93—Univ. of Minnesota	WCHA	42	22	24	46	70	...	...	...	—	—	—	—	—
93-94—U.S. national team	Int'l	54	25	26	51	64	...	...	...	—	—	—	—	—
—U.S. Olympic team	Int'l	8	0	4	4	4	...	...	...	—	—	—	—	—
94-95—Peoria	IHL	16	2	6	8	25	...	...	...	9	0	4	4	10
—St. Louis	NHL	15	3	3	6	6	4	0	0	1	0	0	0	2
95-96—Worcester	AHL	5	3	0	3	2	...	...	...	—	—	—	—	—
—St. Louis	NHL	49	8	7	15	30	-4	1	0	—	—	—	—	—
—Los Angeles	NHL	11	5	4	9	6	-4	3	0	—	—	—	—	—
96-97—Mobile	ECHL	4	0	0	0	74	...	...	...	—	—	—	—	—
—Los Angeles	NHL	31	4	3	7	26	-7	1	0	—	—	—	—	—
—Oklahoma City	CHL	36	6	11	17	134	...	...	...	—	—	—	—	—
—Michigan	IHL	2	0	0	0	2	...	...	...	—	—	—	—	—
—Manitoba	IHL	16	2	2	4	38	...	...	...	—	—	—	—	—
97-98—Los Angeles	NHL	74	17	21	38	42	9	6	0	4	1	0	1	4
98-99—Los Angeles	NHL	69	7	12	19	32	-12	2	0	—	—	—	—	—
—Houston	IHL	1	0	0	0	0	...	...	...	—	—	—	—	—
99-00—Los Angeles	NHL	76	9	14	23	28	-10	1	0	4	1	0	1	2
NHL Totals (6 years)		325	53	64	117	170	-24	14	0	9	2	0	2	8

JOHNSON, GREG   C   PREDATORS

PERSONAL: Born March 16, 1971, in Thunder Bay, Ont. ... 5-10/202. ... Shoots left. ... Full Name: Gregory Johnson. ... Brother of Ryan Johnson, center, Tampa Bay Lightning.
COLLEGE: North Dakota.
TRANSACTIONS/CAREER NOTES: Selected by Philadelphia Flyers in second round (first Flyers pick, 33rd overall) of NHL entry draft (June 17, 1989). ... Separated right shoulder (November 24, 1990). ... Rights traded by Flyers with fifth-round pick (G Frederic Deschenes) in 1994 draft to Detroit Red Wings for RW Jim Cummins and fourth-round pick (traded to Boston) in 1993 draft (June 20, 1993). ... Loaned to Canadian Olympic Team (January 19, 1994). ... Returned to Red Wings (March 1, 1994). ... Sprained left ankle (April 14, 1995); missed final nine games of season. ... Injured left hand (October 8, 1995); missed two games. ... Injured knee (March 19, 1996); missed 12 games. ... Traded by Red Wings to Pittsburgh Penguins for RW Tomas Sandstrom (January 27, 1997). ... Bruised shoulder (April 3, 1997); missed one game. ... Strained groin (October 3, 1997); missed five games. ... Traded by Penguins to Chicago Blackhawks for D Tuomas Gronman (October 27, 1997). ... Strained groin (October 31, 1997); missed three games. ... Selected by Nashville Predators in NHL expansion draft (June 26, 1998). ... Suffered concussion (December 10, 1998); missed four games. ... Strained groin (February 20, 1999); missed five games. ... Suffered stress fracture in ankle (April 7, 1999); missed final five games of season.
HONORS: Named to USHL All-Star first team (1988-89). ... Named Canadian Junior A Player of the Year (1989). ... Named to Centennial Cup All-Star first team (1989). ... Named to NCAA All-America (West) first team (1990-91 and 1992-93). ... Named to WCHA All-Star first team (1990-91 through 1992-93). ... Named to NCAA All-America (West) second team (1991-92).
MISCELLANEOUS: Member of silver-medal-winning Canadian Olympic team (1994).

		REGULAR SEASON								PLAYOFFS				
Season Team	League	Gms.	G	A	Pts.	PIM	+/-	PP	SH	Gms.	G	A	Pts.	PIM
88-89—Thunder Bay Jrs.	USHL	47	32	64	96	4	...	...	...	12	5	13	18	...
89-90—Univ. of North Dakota	WCHA	44	17	38	55	11	...	...	...	—	—	—	—	—
90-91—Univ. of North Dakota	WCHA	38	18	*61	79	6	...	...	...	—	—	—	—	—
91-92—Univ. of North Dakota	WCHA	39	20	54	74	8	...	...	...	—	—	—	—	—
92-93—Canadian nat'l team	Int'l	23	6	14	20	2	...	...	...	—	—	—	—	—
—Univ. of North Dakota	WCHA	34	19	45	64	18	...	...	...	—	—	—	—	—
93-94—Detroit	NHL	52	6	11	17	22	-7	1	1	7	2	2	4	2
—Canadian nat'l team	Int'l	6	2	6	8	4	...	...	...	—	—	—	—	—
—Can. Olympic team	Int'l	8	0	3	3	0	...	...	...	—	—	—	—	—
—Adirondack	AHL	3	2	4	6	0	...	...	...	4	0	4	4	2
94-95—Detroit	NHL	22	3	5	8	14	1	2	0	1	0	0	0	0
95-96—Detroit	NHL	60	18	22	40	30	6	5	0	13	3	1	4	8
96-97—Detroit	NHL	43	6	10	16	12	-5	0	0	—	—	—	—	—
—Pittsburgh	NHL	32	7	9	16	14	-13	1	0	5	1	0	1	2
97-98—Pittsburgh	NHL	5	1	0	1	2	0	0	0	—	—	—	—	—
—Chicago	NHL	69	11	22	33	38	-2	4	0	—	—	—	—	—
98-99—Nashville	NHL	68	16	34	50	24	-8	2	3	—	—	—	—	—
99-00—Nashville	NHL	82	11	33	44	40	-15	2	0	—	—	—	—	—
NHL Totals (7 years)		433	79	146	225	196	-43	17	4	26	6	3	9	12

JOHNSON, MATT   LW   THRASHERS

PERSONAL: Born November 23, 1975, in Welland, Ont. ... 6-5/235. ... Shoots left.
TRANSACTIONS/CAREER NOTES: Selected by Los Angeles Kings in second round (second Kings pick, 33rd overall) of NHL entry draft (June 28, 1994). ... Suffered from the flu (February 25, 1995); missed one game. ... Bruised right hand (April 3, 1995); missed four games. ... Strained shoulder (December 18, 1996); missed six games. ... Suffered concussion (February 1, 1997); missed one game. ... Suspended four games and fined $1,000 by NHL for elbowing incident (February 5, 1997). ... Strained back (March 10, 1997); missed final 13 games of season. ... Suspended four games and fined $1,000 by NHL for slashing incident (September 29, 1997). ... Strained groin (December 23, 1997); missed one game. ... Strained left biceps (March 21, 1998); missed three games. ... Suspended 12 games by NHL for deliberately injuring another player (November 23, 1998). ... Selected by Atlanta Thrashers in NHL expansion draft (June 25, 1999). ... Injured groin (October 7, 1999); missed two games. ... Strained hip flexor (November 25, 1999); missed two games. ... Suffered eye injury (December 13, 1999); missed nine games. ... Sprained medial collateral ligament in knee (March 28, 2000); missed two games.

			REGULAR SEASON							PLAYOFFS				
Season Team	League	Gms.	G	A	Pts.	PIM	+/-	PP	SH	Gms.	G	A	Pts.	PIM
91-92—Welland	Jr. B	38	6	19	25	214	...	...	...	—	—	—	—	—
92-93—Peterborough	OHL	66	8	17	25	211	...	...	...	16	1	1	2	54
93-94—Peterborough	OHL	50	13	24	37	233	...	...	...	—	—	—	—	—
94-95—Peterborough	OHL	14	1	2	3	43	...	...	...	—	—	—	—	—
—Los Angeles	NHL	14	1	0	1	102	0	0	0	—	—	—	—	—
95-96—Los Angeles	NHL	1	0	0	0	5	0	0	0	—	—	—	—	—
—Phoenix	IHL	29	4	4	8	87	...	...	...	—	—	—	—	—
96-97—Los Angeles	NHL	52	1	3	4	194	-4	0	0	—	—	—	—	—
97-98—Los Angeles	NHL	66	2	4	6	249	-8	0	0	4	0	0	0	6
98-99—Los Angeles	NHL	49	2	1	3	131	-5	0	0	—	—	—	—	—
99-00—Atlanta	NHL	64	2	5	7	144	-11	0	0	—	—	—	—	—
NHL Totals (6 years)		246	8	13	21	825	-28	0	0	4	0	0	0	6

JOHNSON, MIKE   RW   LIGHTNING

PERSONAL: Born October 3, 1974, in Scarborough, Ont. ... 6-2/200. ... Shoots right. ... Full Name: Michael Johnson.
HIGH SCHOOL: Sir John A. MacDonald (Toronto).
COLLEGE: Bowling Green State.
TRANSACTIONS/CAREER NOTES: Signed as non-drafted free agent by Toronto Maple Leafs (March 16, 1997). ... Suspended two games by NHL for elbowing incident (April 8, 1999). ... Traded by Maple Leafs with D Marek Posmyk and fifth-(RW Pavel Sedov) and sixth-round (D Aaron Gionet) picks in 2000 draft to Tampa Bay Lightning for C Darcy Tucker and fourth-round pick (RW Miguel Delisle) in 2000 draft (February 9, 2000). ... Suffered injury (November 27, 1999); missed two games. ... Suffered facial fracture (March 17, 2000); missed one game.
HONORS: Named to NHL All-Rookie team (1997-98).

			REGULAR SEASON							PLAYOFFS				
Season Team	League	Gms.	G	A	Pts.	PIM	+/-	PP	SH	Gms.	G	A	Pts.	PIM
93-94—Bowling Green	CCHA	38	6	14	20	18	...	...	...	—	—	—	—	—
94-95—Bowling Green	CCHA	37	16	33	49	35	...	...	...	—	—	—	—	—
95-96—Bowling Green	CCHA	30	12	19	31	22	...	...	...	—	—	—	—	—
96-97—Bowling Green	CCHA	38	30	32	62	46	...	...	...	—	—	—	—	—
—Toronto	NHL	13	2	2	4	4	-2	0	1	—	—	—	—	—
97-98—Toronto	NHL	82	15	32	47	24	-4	5	0	—	—	—	—	—
98-99—Toronto	NHL	79	20	24	44	35	13	5	3	17	3	2	5	4
99-00—Toronto	NHL	52	11	14	25	23	8	2	1	—	—	—	—	—
—Tampa Bay	NHL	28	10	12	22	4	-2	4	0	—	—	—	—	—
NHL Totals (4 years)		254	58	84	142	90	13	16	5	17	3	2	5	4

JOHNSON, RYAN   C   LIGHTNING

PERSONAL: Born June 14, 1976, in Thunder Bay, Ont. ... 6-1/200. ... Shoots left. ... Brother of Greg Johnson, center, Nashville Predators.
COLLEGE: North Dakota.
TRANSACTIONS/CAREER NOTES: Selected by Florida Panthers in second round (fourth Panthers pick, 36th overall) of NHL entry draft (June 28, 1994). ... Loaned to Canadian national team prior to 1995-96 season. ... Bruised left ankle (October 16, 1999); missed two games. ... Suffered from the flu (January 6, 2000); missed one game. ... Traded by Panthers with LW Dwayne Hay to Tampa Bay Lightning for C/RW Mike Sillinger (March 14, 2000).

			REGULAR SEASON							PLAYOFFS				
Season Team	League	Gms.	G	A	Pts.	PIM	+/-	PP	SH	Gms.	G	A	Pts.	PIM
93-94—Thunder Bay Jrs.	USHL	48	14	36	50	28	...	...	...	—	—	—	—	—
94-95—Univ. of North Dakota	WCHA	38	6	22	28	39	...	...	...	—	—	—	—	—
95-96—Canadian nat'l team	Int'l	28	5	12	17	14	...	...	...	—	—	—	—	—
—Univ. of North Dakota	WCHA	21	2	17	19	14	...	...	...	—	—	—	—	—
96-97—Carolina	AHL	79	18	24	42	28	...	...	...	—	—	—	—	—
97-98—New Haven	AHL	64	19	48	67	12	...	...	...	3	0	1	1	0
—Florida	NHL	10	0	2	2	0	-4	0	0	—	—	—	—	—
98-99—New Haven	AHL	37	8	19	27	18	...	...	...	—	—	—	—	—
—Florida	NHL	1	1	0	1	0	0	0	0	—	—	—	—	—
99-00—Florida	NHL	66	4	12	16	14	1	0	0	—	—	—	—	—
—Tampa Bay	NHL	14	0	2	2	2	-9	0	0	—	—	—	—	—
NHL Totals (3 years)		91	5	16	21	16	-12	0	0	—	—	—	—	—

JOHNSSON, KIM   D   RANGERS

PERSONAL: Born March 16, 1976, in Malmo, Sweden. ... 6-2/189. ... Shoots left. ... Full Name: Kimmo Johnsson.
TRANSACTIONS/CAREER NOTES: Selected by New York Rangers in 11th round (15th Rangers pick, 286th overall) of NHL entry draft (June 29, 1994). ... Suffered eye injury (February 8, 2000); missed one game.

Season Team	League	REGULAR SEASON								PLAYOFFS				
		Gms.	G	A	Pts.	PIM	+/-	PP	SH	Gms.	G	A	Pts.	PIM
							Statistics unavailable.								
93-94—Malmo	Sweden									1	0	0	0	0
94-95—Malmo	Sweden	13	0	0	0	4	...	...	...					
95-96—Malmo	Sweden	38	2	0	2	30	...	...	...	4	0	1	1	8
96-97—Malmo	Sweden	49	4	9	13	42	...	...	...	4	0	0	0	2
97-98—Malmo	Sweden	45	5	9	14	29	...	...	...	—	—	—	—	—
98-99—Malmo	Sweden	49	9	8	17	76	...	...	...	8	2	3	5	12
99-00—New York Rangers	NHL	76	6	15	21	46	-13	1	0	—	—	—	—	—
NHL Totals (1 year)		76	6	15	21	46	-13	1	0					

JOKINEN, OLLI   C   PANTHERS

PERSONAL: Born December 5, 1978, in Kuopio, Finland. ... 6-3/218. ... Shoots left. ... Name pronounced OH-lee YOH-kih-nehn.
TRANSACTIONS/CAREER NOTES: Selected by Los Angeles Kings in first round (first Kings pick, third overall) of NHL entry draft (June 21, 1997). ... Traded by Kings with LW Josh Green, D Mathieu Biron and first-round pick (LW Taylor Pyatt) in 1999 draft to New York Islanders for RW Zigmund Palffy, C Bryan Smolinski, G Marcel Cousineau and fourth-round pick (C Daniel Johansson) in 1999 draft (June 20, 1999). ... Traded by Islanders with G Roberto Luongo to Florida Panthers for RW Mark Parrish and LW Oleg Kvasha (June 24, 2000).
MISCELLANEOUS: Scored on a penalty shot (vs. Dominik Hasek, March 4, 2000).

Season Team	League	REGULAR SEASON								PLAYOFFS				
		Gms.	G	A	Pts.	PIM	+/-	PP	SH	Gms.	G	A	Pts.	PIM
94-95—KalPa Kuopio	Finland Jr.	6	0	1	1	6	...	...	...	—	—	—	—	—
95-96—KalPa Kuopio	Finland Jr.	15	1	1	2	2	...	...	...	—	—	—	—	—
—KalPa Kuopio	Finland	15	1	1	2	2	...	...	...	—	—	—	—	—
96-97—HIFK Helsinki	Finland	50	14	27	41	88	...	...	...	—	—	—	—	—
97-98—Los Angeles	NHL	8	0	0	0	6	-5	0	0	—	—	—	—	—
—HIFK Helsinki	Finland	30	11	28	39	8	...	...	...	9	7	2	9	2
98-99—Springfield	AHL	9	3	6	9	6	...	...	...	—	—	—	—	—
—Los Angeles	NHL	66	9	12	21	44	-10	3	1	—	—	—	—	—
99-00—New York Islanders	NHL	82	11	10	21	80	0	1	2	—	—	—	—	—
NHL Totals (3 years)		156	20	22	42	130	-15	4	3					

JONES, KEITH   RW   FLYERS

PERSONAL: Born November 8, 1968, in Brantford, Ont. ... 6-2/200. ... Shoots left.
COLLEGE: Western Michigan.
TRANSACTIONS/CAREER NOTES: Selected by Washington Capitals in seventh round (seventh Capitals pick, 141st overall) of NHL entry draft (June 11, 1988). ... Suffered from the flu (January 21, 1993); missed two games. ... Sprained wrist (January 25, 1994); missed six games. ... Injured foot (March 16, 1995); missed one game. ... Separated ribs and bruised foot (March 29, 1995); missed six games. ... Injured groin (March 12, 1996); missed seven games. ... Reinjured groin (March 29, 1996); missed seven games. ... Traded by Capitals with first- (D Scott Parker) and fourth-round (traded back to Washington) picks in 1998 draft to Colorado Avalanche for D Curtis Leschyshyn and LW Chris Simon (November 2, 1996). ... Injured knee (April 26, 1997); missed remainder of playoffs. ... Injured knee (October 1, 1997) and underwent surgery; missed 58 games. ... Suspended two games and fined $1,000 by NHL for illegal check to the head (October 15, 1998). ... Traded by Avalanche to Philadelphia Flyers for LW Shjon Podein (November 12, 1998). ... Bruised left knee (November 22, 1998); missed one game. ... Underwent knee surgery (September 29, 1999); missed first 25 games of season.
HONORS: Named to CCHA All-Star first team (1991-92).
MISCELLANEOUS: Failed to score on a penalty shot (vs. Patrick Labrecque, November 1, 1995).

Season Team	League	REGULAR SEASON								PLAYOFFS				
		Gms.	G	A	Pts.	PIM	+/-	PP	SH	Gms.	G	A	Pts.	PIM
87-88—Niagara Falls	OHA	40	50	80	130	...	...	...	...	—	—	—	—	—
88-89—Western Michigan U.	CCHA	37	9	12	21	51	...	...	...	—	—	—	—	—
89-90—Western Michigan U.	CCHA	40	19	18	37	82	...	...	...	—	—	—	—	—
90-91—Western Michigan U.	CCHA	41	30	19	49	106	...	...	...	—	—	—	—	—
91-92—Western Michigan U.	CCHA	35	25	31	56	77	...	...	...	—	—	—	—	—
—Baltimore	AHL	6	2	4	6	0	...	...	...	—	—	—	—	—
92-93—Baltimore	AHL	8	7	3	10	4	...	...	...	—	—	—	—	—
—Washington	NHL	71	12	14	26	124	18	0	0	6	0	0	0	10
93-94—Washington	NHL	68	16	19	35	149	4	5	0	11	0	1	1	36
—Portland	AHL	6	5	7	12	4	...	...	...	—	—	—	—	—
94-95—Washington	NHL	40	14	6	20	65	-2	1	0	7	4	4	8	22
95-96—Washington	NHL	68	18	23	41	103	8	5	0	2	0	0	0	7
96-97—Washington	NHL	11	2	3	5	13	-2	1	0	—	—	—	—	—
—Colorado	NHL	67	23	20	43	105	5	13	1	6	3	3	6	4
97-98—Colorado	NHL	23	3	7	10	22	-4	1	0	7	0	0	0	13
—Hershey	AHL	4	2	1	3	2	...	...	...	—	—	—	—	—
98-99—Colorado	NHL	12	2	2	4	20	-6	1	0	—	—	—	—	—
—Philadelphia	NHL	66	18	31	49	78	29	2	0	6	2	1	3	14
99-00—Philadelphia	NHL	57	9	16	25	82	8	1	0	18	3	3	6	14
NHL Totals (8 years)		483	117	141	258	761	58	30	1	63	12	12	24	120

JONES, TY   RW   BLACKHAWKS

PERSONAL: Born February 22, 1979, in Richland, Wash. ... 6-3/218. ... Shoots right.
TRANSACTIONS/CAREER NOTES: Selected by Chicago Blackhawks in first round (second Blackhawks pick, 16th overall) of NHL entry draft (June 21, 1997).

Season Team	League	REGULAR SEASON								PLAYOFFS				
		Gms.	G	A	Pts.	PIM	+/-	PP	SH	Gms.	G	A	Pts.	PIM
95-96—Spokane	WHL	34	1	0	1	77	...	...	...	3	0	0	0	6
96-97—Spokane	WHL	67	20	34	54	202	...	...	...	9	2	4	6	—
97-98—Spokane	WHL	60	36	48	84	161	...	...	...	18	2	14	16	35
98-99—Spokane	WHL	26	15	12	27	98	...	...	...	—	—	—	—	—
—Kamloops	WHL	20	3	16	19	84	...	...	...	14	5	3	8	22
—Chicago	NHL	8	0	0	0	12	-1	0	0	—	—	—	—	—
99-00—Cleveland	IHL	10	1	1	2	34	...	...	...	—	—	—	—	—
—Florida	ECHL	48	11	26	37	81	...	...	...	5	1	1	2	7
NHL Totals (1 year)		8	0	0	0	12	-1	0	0					

JONSSON, HANS — D — PENGUINS

PERSONAL: Born August 2, 1973, in Jarved, Sweden. ... 6-1/202. ... Shoots left. ... Name pronounced YOOHN-suhn.

TRANSACTIONS/CAREER NOTES: Selected by Pittsburgh Penguins in 11th round (11th Penguins pick, 286th overall) of NHL entry draft (June 29, 1993). ... Bruised hip (February 1, 2000); missed two games. ... Suffered lacerated elbow (March 19, 2000); missed one game.

Season Team	League	REGULAR SEASON								PLAYOFFS				
		Gms.	G	A	Pts.	PIM	+/-	PP	SH	Gms.	G	A	Pts.	PIM
91-92—MoDo Ornskoldsvik	Sweden	6	0	1	1	4	...	...	...	—	—	—	—	—
92-93—MoDo Ornskoldsvik	Sweden	40	2	2	4	24	...	...	...	3	0	1	1	2
93-94—MoDo Ornskoldsvik	Sweden	23	4	1	5	18	...	...	...	10	0	1	1	12
94-95—MoDo Ornskoldsvik	Sweden	39	4	6	10	30	...	...	...	—	—	—	—	—
95-96—MoDo Ornskoldsvik	Sweden	36	10	6	16	30	...	...	...	8	2	1	3	24
96-97—MoDo Ornskoldsvik	Sweden	27	7	5	12	18	...	...	...	—	—	—	—	—
97-98—MoDo Ornskoldsvik	Sweden	40	8	6	14	40	...	...	...	8	1	1	2	12
98-99—MoDo Ornskoldsvik	Sweden	41	3	4	7	40	...	...	...	13	2	4	6	22
99-00—Pittsburgh	NHL	68	3	11	14	12	-5	0	1	11	0	1	1	6
NHL Totals (1 year)		68	3	11	14	12	-5	0	1	11	0	1	1	6

JONSSON, JORGEN — LW — MIGHTY DUCKS

PERSONAL: Born September 29, 1972, in Angelholm, Sweden. ... 6-0/195. ... Shoots left. ... Brother of Kenny Jonsson, defenseman, New York Islanders. ... Name pronounced YOHR-guhn YAHN-suhn.

TRANSACTIONS/CAREER NOTES: Selected by Calgary Flames in ninth round (11th Flames pick, 227th overall) of NHL entry draft (June 29, 1994). ... Rights traded by Flames to New York Islanders for LW Jan Hlavac (July 14, 1998). ... Traded by Islanders to Mighty Ducks of Anaheim for C/RW Johan Davidsson and future considerations (March 11, 2000).

Season Team	League	REGULAR SEASON								PLAYOFFS				
		Gms.	G	A	Pts.	PIM	+/-	PP	SH	Gms.	G	A	Pts.	PIM
92-93—Rogle Angelholm	Sweden	40	17	11	28	28	...	...	...	—	—	—	—	—
93-94—Rogle Angelholm	Sweden	40	17	14	31	46	...	...	...	—	—	—	—	—
94-95—Rogle Angelholm	Sweden	22	4	6	10	18	...	...	...	—	—	—	—	—
95-96—Farjestad Karlstad	Sweden	39	11	15	26	36	...	...	...	8	0	4	4	6
96-97—Farjestad Karlstad	Sweden	49	12	21	33	58	...	...	...	14	9	5	14	14
97-98—Farjestad Karlstad	Sweden	45	22	25	47	53	...	...	...	12	2	9	11	12
—Swedish Oly. team	Int'l	1	0	0	0	0	...	...	...	—	—	—	—	—
98-99—Farjestad Karlstad	Sweden	48	17	24	41	44	...	...	...	4	0	2	2	4
99-00—New York Islanders	NHL	68	11	17	28	16	-6	1	2	—	—	—	—	—
—Anaheim	NHL	13	1	2	3	0	-2	0	0	—	—	—	—	—
NHL Totals (1 year)		81	12	19	31	16	-8	1	2					

JONSSON, KENNY — D — ISLANDERS

PERSONAL: Born October 6, 1974, in Angelholm, Sweden. ... 6-3/211. ... Shoots left. ... Brother of Jorgen Jonsson, left winger, Mighty Ducks of Anaheim. ... Name pronounced YAHN-suhn.

TRANSACTIONS/CAREER NOTES: Selected by Toronto Maple Leafs in first round (first Maple Leafs pick, 12th overall) of NHL entry draft (June 26, 1993). ... Played in Europe during 1994-95 NHL lockout. ... Suffered from the flu (February 13, 1995); missed two games. ... Strained hip flexor (February 27, 1995); missed one game. ... Suffered hip pointer (April 7, 1995); missed one game. ... Suffered from the flu (April 19, 1995); missed one game. ... Strained back (December 9, 1995); missed one game. ... Separated shoulder (January 30, 1996); missed 17 games. ... Traded by Maple Leafs with C Darby Hendrickson, LW Sean Haggerty and first-round pick (G Robert Luongo) in 1997 draft to New York Islanders for LW Wendel Clark, D Mathieu Schneider and D D.J. Smith (March 13, 1996). ... Suffered from the flu (December 23, 1996); missed one game. ... Sprained knee (February 4, 1998); missed one game. ... Suffered concussion (November 17, 1998); missed eight games. ... Sprained knee (January 16, 1999); missed nine games. ... Fractured finger (April 17, 1999); missed final game of season. ... Suffered illness (December 30, 1999); missed four games. ... Suffered concussion (January 19, 2000); missed 11 games. ... Sprained left wrist (March 26, 2000); missed one game. ... Suffered headaches (April 1, 2000); missed final five games of regular season.

HONORS: Named Swedish League Rookie of the Year (1992-93). ... Named to NHL All-Rookie team (1994-95). ... Named to play in NHL All-Star Game (1999); replaced by D Mattias Norstrom due to injury.

MISCELLANEOUS: Captain of New York Islanders (1999-2000).

Season Team	League	REGULAR SEASON								PLAYOFFS				
		Gms.	G	A	Pts.	PIM	+/-	PP	SH	Gms.	G	A	Pts.	PIM
91-92—Rogle Angelholm	Sweden	30	4	11	15	24	...	...	...	—	—	—	—	—
92-93—Rogle Angelholm	Sweden	39	3	10	13	42	...	...	...	—	—	—	—	—
93-94—Rogle Angelholm	Sweden	36	4	13	17	40	...	...	...	3	1	1	2	...
—Swedish Oly. team	Int'l	3	1	0	1	0	...	...	...	—	—	—	—	—
94-95—Rogle Angelholm	Sweden	8	3	1	4	20	...	...	...	—	—	—	—	—
—St. John's	AHL	10	2	5	7	2	...	...	...	—	—	—	—	—
—Toronto	NHL	39	2	7	9	16	-8	0	0	4	0	0	0	0

Season Team	League	Gms.	G	A	Pts.	PIM	+/-	PP	SH	Gms.	G	A	Pts.	PIM
95-96—Toronto	NHL	50	4	22	26	22	12	3	0	—	—	—	—	—
—New York Islanders	NHL	16	0	4	4	10	-5	0	0	—	—	—	—	—
96-97—New York Islanders	NHL	81	3	18	21	24	10	1	0	—	—	—	—	—
97-98—New York Islanders	NHL	81	14	26	40	58	-2	6	0	—	—	—	—	—
98-99—New York Islanders	NHL	63	8	18	26	34	-18	6	0	—	—	—	—	—
99-00—New York Islanders	NHL	65	1	24	25	32	-15	1	0	—	—	—	—	—
NHL Totals (6 years)		395	32	119	151	196	-26	17	0	4	0	0	0	0

JOSEPH, CHRIS   D   COYOTES

PERSONAL: Born September 10, 1969, in Burnaby, B.C. ... 6-3/212. ... Shoots left. ... Full Name: Robin Christopher Joseph.
HIGH SCHOOL: Alpha (Burnaby, B.C.).
TRANSACTIONS/CAREER NOTES: Selected by Pittsburgh Penguins in first round (first Penguins pick, fifth overall) of NHL entry draft (June 13, 1987). ... Traded by Penguins with C Craig Simpson, C Dave Hannan and D Moe Mantha to Edmonton Oilers for D Paul Coffey, LW Dave Hunter and RW Wayne Van Dorp (November 24, 1987). ... Strained knee ligaments (January 1989). ... Traded by Oilers to Tampa Bay Lightning for D Bob Beers (November 12, 1993). ... Selected by Pittsburgh Penguins from Oilers in NHL waiver draft for cash (January 18, 1995). ... Injured knee (March 2, 1995); missed 14 games. ... Injured knee (March 7, 1996); missed four games. ... Selected by Vancouver Canucks in NHL waiver draft for cash (September 30, 1996). ... Injured groin (December 18, 1996); missed seven games. ... Suffered from the flu (February 27, 1997); missed two games. ... Signed as free agent by Philadelphia Flyers (September 4, 1997). ... Signed as free agent by Ottawa Senators (July 29, 1999). ... Claimed by Canucks from Senators in NHL waiver draft (September 27, 1999). ... Injured groin (February 16, 2000); missed 11 games. ... Claimed on waivers by Phoenix Coyotes (March 14, 2000).

Season Team	League	Gms.	G	A	Pts.	PIM	+/-	PP	SH	Gms.	G	A	Pts.	PIM
85-86—Seattle	WHL	72	4	8	12	50	...	...	...	5	0	3	3	12
86-87—Seattle	WHL	67	13	45	58	155	...	...	...	—	—	—	—	—
87-88—Pittsburgh	NHL	17	0	4	4	12	2	0	0	—	—	—	—	—
—Edmonton	NHL	7	0	4	4	6	-3	0	0	—	—	—	—	—
—Nova Scotia	AHL	8	0	2	2	8	...	...	...	4	0	0	0	9
—Seattle	WHL	23	5	14	19	49	...	...	...	—	—	—	—	—
88-89—Cape Breton	AHL	5	1	1	2	18	...	...	...	—	—	—	—	—
—Edmonton	NHL	44	4	5	9	54	-9	0	0	—	—	—	—	—
89-90—Edmonton	NHL	4	0	2	2	2	-2	0	0	—	—	—	—	—
—Cape Breton	AHL	61	10	20	30	69	...	...	...	6	2	1	3	4
90-91—Edmonton	NHL	49	5	17	22	59	3	2	0	—	—	—	—	—
91-92—Edmonton	NHL	7	0	0	0	8	-1	0	0	5	1	3	4	2
—Cape Breton	AHL	63	14	29	43	72	...	...	...	5	0	2	2	8
92-93—Edmonton	NHL	33	2	10	12	48	-9	1	0	—	—	—	—	—
93-94—Edmonton	NHL	10	1	1	2	28	-8	1	0	—	—	—	—	—
—Tampa Bay	NHL	66	10	19	29	108	-13	7	0	—	—	—	—	—
94-95—Pittsburgh	NHL	33	5	10	15	46	3	3	0	10	1	1	2	12
95-96—Pittsburgh	NHL	70	5	14	19	71	6	0	0	15	1	0	1	8
96-97—Vancouver	NHL	63	3	13	16	62	-21	2	0	—	—	—	—	—
97-98—Philadelphia	NHL	15	1	0	1	19	1	0	0	1	0	0	0	2
—Philadelphia	AHL	6	2	3	5	2	...	...	...	—	—	—	—	—
98-99—Cincinnati	IHL	27	11	19	30	38	...	...	...	—	—	—	—	—
—Philadelphia	NHL	2	0	0	0	2	0	0	0	—	—	—	—	—
—Philadelphia	AHL	51	9	29	38	26	...	...	...	16	3	10	13	8
99-00—Vancouver	NHL	38	2	9	11	6	-4	1	0	—	—	—	—	—
—Phoenix	NHL	9	0	0	0	0	-5	0	0	—	—	—	—	—
NHL Totals (13 years)		467	38	108	146	531	-60	17	0	31	3	4	7	24

JOSEPH, CURTIS   G   MAPLE LEAFS

PERSONAL: Born April 29, 1967, in Keswick, Ont. ... 5-11/190. ... Catches left. ... Full Name: Curtis Shayne Joseph. ... Nickname: Cujo.
HIGH SCHOOL: Huron Heights (Newmarket, Ont.).
COLLEGE: Wisconsin.
TRANSACTIONS/CAREER NOTES: Signed as non-drafted free agent by St. Louis Blues (June 16, 1989). ... Dislocated left shoulder (April 11, 1990). ... Underwent surgery to left shoulder (May 10, 1990). ... Sprained right knee (February 26, 1991); missed remainder of season. ... Injured ankle (March 12, 1992); missed seven games. ... Suffered sore knee (January 2, 1993); missed three games. ... Suffered from the flu (February 9, 1993); missed one game. ... Slightly strained groin (January 26, 1995); missed three games. ... Pulled hamstring (April 16, 1995); missed four games. ... Traded by Blues with rights to RW Michael Grier to Edmonton Oilers for first-round picks in 1996 (C Marty Reasoner) and 1997 (traded to Los Angeles) drafts (August 4, 1995); picks had been awarded to Oilers as compensation for Blues signing free agent LW Shayne Corson (July 28, 1995). ... Injured right knee (March 30, 1996); missed three games. ... Strained groin (December 18, 1996); missed seven games. ... Signed as free agent by Toronto Maple Leafs (July 15, 1998). ... Strained groin (January 21, 1999); missed one game.
HONORS: Named OHA Most Valuable Player (1986-87). ... Won WCHA Most Valuable Player Award (1988-89). ... Won WCHA Rookie of the Year Award (1988-89). ... Named to NCAA All-America (West) second team (1988-89). ... Named to WCHA All-Star first team (1988-89). ... Played in NHL All-Star Game (1994 and 2000). ... Named to play in NHL All-Star Game (1999); replaced by G Ron Tugnutt due to injury. ... Won King Clancy Memorial Trophy (1999-2000).
MISCELLANEOUS: Holds Edmonton Oilers all-time record for most shutouts (14). ... Stopped a penalty shot attempt (vs. Greg Adams, January 25, 1992; vs. Todd Elik, April 16, 1992; vs. Phil Housley, December 19, 1992; vs. Mike Donnelly, April 7, 1994; vs. J.F. Jomphe, April 15, 1998; vs. Landon Wilson, March 17, 1999; vs. Ulf Dahlen, April 1, 2000). ... Allowed a penalty shot goal (vs. Valeri Kamensky, October 26, 1996; vs. Adam Oates, November 18, 1998).
STATISTICAL NOTES: Led NHL with .911 save percentage (1992-93).

Season Team	League	REGULAR SEASON								PLAYOFFS						
		Gms.	Min	W	L	T	GA	SO	Avg.	Gms.	Min.	W	L	GA	SO	Avg.
86-87—Richmond Hill	OHA						Statistics unavailable.									
87-88—Notre Dame................	SCMHL	36	2174	25	4	7	94	1	2.59	—	—	—	—	—	—	—
88-89—Univ. of Wisconsin.......	WCHA	38	2267	21	11	5	94	1	2.49	—	—	—	—	—	—	—
89-90—Peoria....................	IHL	23	1241	10	8	‡2	80	0	3.87	—	—	—	—	—	—	—
—St. Louis	NHL	15	852	9	5	1	48	0	3.38	6	327	4	1	18	0	3.30
90-91—St. Louis	NHL	30	1710	16	10	2	89	0	3.12	—	—	—	—	—	—	—
91-92—St. Louis	NHL	60	3494	27	20	10	175	2	3.01	6	379	2	4	23	0	3.64
92-93—St. Louis	NHL	68	3890	29	28	9	196	1	3.02	11	715	7	4	27	2	2.27
93-94—St. Louis	NHL	71	4127	36	23	11	213	1	3.10	4	246	0	4	15	0	3.66
94-95—St. Louis	NHL	36	1914	20	10	1	89	1	2.79	7	392	3	3	24	0	3.67
95-96—Las Vegas	IHL	15	873	12	2	1	29	1	1.99	—	—	—	—	—	—	—
—Edmonton	NHL	34	1936	15	16	2	111	0	3.44	—	—	—	—	—	—	—
96-97—Edmonton	NHL	72	4100	32	29	9	200	6	2.93	12	767	5	7	36	2	2.82
97-98—Edmonton	NHL	71	4132	29	31	9	181	8	2.63	12	716	5	7	23	1	1.93
98-99—Toronto	NHL	67	4001	35	24	7	†171	3	2.56	17	1011	9	†8	41	1	2.43
99-00—Toronto	NHL	63	3801	36	20	7	158	4	2.49	12	729	6	6	25	1	2.06
NHL Totals (11 years)............		587	33957	284	216	68	1631	26	2.88	87	5282	41	44	232	9	2.64

JOVANOVSKI, ED — D — CANUCKS

PERSONAL: Born June 26, 1976, in Windsor, Ont. ... 6-2/210. ... Shoots left. ... Name pronounced joh-vuh-NAHV-skee.

HIGH SCHOOL: Riverside Secondary (Windsor, Ont.).

TRANSACTIONS/CAREER NOTES: Selected by Florida Panthers in first round (first Panthers pick, first overall) of NHL entry draft (June 28, 1994). ... Fractured right index finger (September 29, 1995); missed first 11 games of season. ... Sprained knee (January 15, 1997); missed 16 games. ... Traded by Panthers with G Kevin Weekes, C Dave Gagner, C Mike Brown and first-round pick (C Nathan Smith) in 2000 draft to Vancouver Canucks for RW Pavel Bure, D Bret Hedican, D Brad Ference and third-round pick (RW Robert Fried) in 2000 draft (January 17, 1999). ... Fractured foot (February 9, 1999); missed eight games. ... Injured groin (January 12, 2000); missed six games. ... Injured hip (March 13, 2000); missed one game.

HONORS: Named to Can.HL All-Rookie team (1993-94). ... Named to OHL All-Star second team (1993-94). ... Named to OHL All-Rookie team (1993-94). ... Named to Can.HL All-Star second team (1994-95). ... Named to OHL All-Star first team (1994-95). ... Named to NHL All-Rookie team (1995-96).

Season Team	League	REGULAR SEASON								PLAYOFFS				
		Gms.	G	A	Pts.	PIM	+/-	PP	SH	Gms.	G	A	Pts.	PIM
92-93—Windsor	OHL Jr. B	48	7	46	53	88	...	...	...	—	—	—	—	—
93-94—Windsor	OHL	62	15	35	50	221	...	...	...	4	0	0	0	15
94-95—Windsor	OHL	50	23	42	65	198	...	...	...	9	2	7	9	39
95-96—Florida	NHL	70	10	11	21	137	-3	2	0	22	1	8	9	52
96-97—Florida	NHL	61	7	16	23	172	-1	3	0	5	0	0	0	4
97-98—Florida	NHL	81	9	14	23	158	-12	2	1	—	—	—	—	—
98-99—Florida	NHL	41	3	13	16	82	-4	1	0	—	—	—	—	—
—Vancouver	NHL	31	2	9	11	44	-5	0	0	—	—	—	—	—
99-00—Vancouver	NHL	75	5	21	26	54	-3	1	0	—	—	—	—	—
NHL Totals (5 years)............		359	36	84	120	647	-28	9	1	27	1	8	9	56

JUNEAU, JOE — LW — COYOTES

PERSONAL: Born January 5, 1968, in Pont-Rouge, Que. ... 6-0/199. ... Shoots left. ... Name pronounced zhoh-AY ZHOO-noh.

COLLEGE: Rensselaer Polytechnic Institute (N.Y.).

TRANSACTIONS/CAREER NOTES: Selected by Boston Bruins in fourth round (third Bruins pick, 81st overall) of NHL entry draft (June 11, 1988). ... Suffered ligament problem in back (November 1990). ... Fractured jaw (November 7, 1993); missed seven games. ... Reinjured jaw (February 18, 1994); missed two games. ... Traded by Bruins to Washington Capitals for D Al Iafrate (March 21, 1994). ... Strained hip flexor (January 29, 1995); missed one game. ... Strained back (February 15, 1995); missed one game. ... Bruised arm (April 11, 1995); missed one game. ... Injured leg (April 30, 1995); missed one game. ... Suffered from the flu (January 17, 1996); missed two games. ... Pulled hamstring (November 19, 1996); missed eight games. ... Bruised back and shoulder (January 1, 1997); missed two games. ... Sprained shoulder (February 7, 1997); missed four games. ... Sprained shoulder (February 18, 1997); missed five games. ... Strained hip (March 26, 1997); missed four games. ... Strained hip (April 12, 1997); missed one game. ... Strained groin (October 29, 1997); missed eight games. ... Strained posterior cruciate ligament in knee (December 13, 1997); missed 16 games. ... Suffered from the flu (December 17, 1998); missed one game. ... Bruised foot (February 28, 1999); missed one game. ... Suffered from headaches (March 9, 1999); missed five games. ... Traded by Capitals with third-round pick (LW Tim Preston) in 1999 draft to Buffalo Sabres for D Alexei Tezikov and future considerations (March 23, 1999). ... Suffered from the flu (March 27, 1999); missed two games. ... Suffered concussion (April 13, 1999); missed final three games of regular season. ... Signed as free agent by Ottawa Senators (October 25, 1999). ... Strained hip flexor (February 19, 2000); missed five games. ... Strained hip flexor (April 4, 2000); missed two games. ... Selected by Minnesota Wild in NHL expansion draft (June 23, 2000). ... Traded by Wild to Phoenix Coyotes for C Rickard Wallin (June 23, 2000).

HONORS: Named to NCAA All-America (East) first team (1989-90). ... Named to ECAC All-Star first team (1989-90). ... Named to NCAA All-America (East) second team (1990-91). ... Named to ECAC All-Star second team (1990-91). ... Named to NHL All-Rookie team (1992-93).

RECORDS: Holds NHL single-season record for most assists by a left winger—70 (1992-93). ... Holds NHL single-season record for most assists by a rookie—70 (1992-93).

STATISTICAL PLATEAUS: Three-goal games: 1992-93 (1), 1996-97 (1). Total: 2.

MISCELLANEOUS: Member of silver-medal-winning Canadian Olympic team (1992).

Season Team	League	REGULAR SEASON								PLAYOFFS				
		Gms.	G	A	Pts.	PIM	+/-	PP	SH	Gms.	G	A	Pts.	PIM
87-88—R.P.I.	ECAC	31	16	29	45	18	...	...	...	—	—	—	—	—
88-89—R.P.I.	ECAC	30	12	23	35	40	...	...	...	—	—	—	—	—
89-90—R.P.I.	ECAC	34	18	*52	*70	31	...	...	...	—	—	—	—	—
—Canadian nat'l team	Int'l	3	0	2	2	4	...	...	...	—	—	—	—	—

Season Team	League	REGULAR SEASON								PLAYOFFS				
		Gms.	G	A	Pts.	PIM	+/-	PP	SH	Gms.	G	A	Pts.	PIM
90-91—R.P.I.	ECAC	29	23	40	63	70	...	...	...	—	—	—	—	—
—Canadian nat'l team	Int'l	7	2	3	5	0	...	...	...	—	—	—	—	—
91-92—Canadian nat'l team	Int'l	60	20	49	69	35	...	...	...	—	—	—	—	—
—Can. Olympic team	Int'l	8	6	9	15	4	...	...	...	—	—	—	—	—
—Boston	NHL	14	5	14	19	4	6	2	0	15	4	8	12	21
92-93—Boston	NHL	84	32	70	102	33	23	9	0	4	2	4	6	6
93-94—Boston	NHL	63	14	58	72	35	11	4	0	—	—	—	—	—
—Washington	NHL	11	5	8	13	6	0	2	0	11	4	5	9	6
94-95—Washington	NHL	44	5	38	43	8	-1	3	0	7	2	6	8	2
95-96—Washington	NHL	80	14	50	64	30	-3	7	2	5	0	7	7	6
96-97—Washington	NHL	58	15	27	42	8	-11	9	1	—	—	—	—	—
97-98—Washington	NHL	56	9	22	31	26	-8	4	1	21	7	10	17	8
98-99—Washington	NHL	63	14	27	41	20	-3	2	1	—	—	—	—	—
—Buffalo	NHL	9	1	1	2	2	-1	0	0	20	3	8	11	10
99-00—Ottawa	NHL	65	13	24	37	22	3	2	0	6	2	1	3	0
NHL Totals (9 years)		547	127	339	466	194	16	44	5	89	24	49	73	59

KABERLE, FRANTISEK　　　　D　　　　THRASHERS

PERSONAL: Born November 8, 1973, in Kladno, Czechoslovakia. ... 6-0/185. ... Shoots left. ... Brother of Tomas Kaberle, defenseman, Toronto Maple Leafs.

TRANSACTIONS/CAREER NOTES: Selected by Los Angeles Kings in third round (third Kings pick, 76th overall) of NHL entry draft (June 26, 1999). ... Traded by Kings with RW Donald Audette to Atlanta Thrashers for RW Kelly Buchberger and RW Nelson Emerson (March 13, 2000).

Season Team	League	REGULAR SEASON								PLAYOFFS				
		Gms.	G	A	Pts.	PIM	+/-	PP	SH	Gms.	G	A	Pts.	PIM
91-92—Poldi Kladno	Czech.	37	1	4	5	8	...	...	...	8	0	1	1	0
92-93—Poldi Kladno	Czech.	49	6	9	15		...	...	...	—	—	—	—	—
93-94—HC Kladno	Czech Rep.	40	4	15	19		...	...	...	9	1	2	3	...
94-95—HC Kladno	Czech Rep.	40	7	17	24		...	...	...	8	0	3	3	...
95-96—MoDo Ornskoldsvik	Sweden	40	5	7	12	34	...	...	...	8	0	1	1	0
96-97—MoDo Ornskoldsvik	Sweden	50	3	11	14	28	...	...	...	—	—	—	—	—
97-98—MoDo Ornskoldsvik	Sweden	46	5	4	9	22	...	...	...	9	1	1	2	4
98-99—MoDo Ornskoldsvik	Sweden	45	15	18	33	4	...	...	...	13	2	5	7	8
99-00—Los Angeles	NHL	37	0	9	9	4	3	0	0	—	—	—	—	—
—Long Beach	IHL	18	2	8	10	8	...	...	...	—	—	—	—	—
—Lowell	AHL	4	0	2	2	0	...	...	...	—	—	—	—	—
—Atlanta	NHL	14	1	6	7	6	-13	0	1	—	—	—	—	—
NHL Totals (1 year)		51	1	15	16	10	-10	0	1					

KABERLE, TOMAS　　　　D　　　　MAPLE LEAFS

PERSONAL: Born March 2, 1978, in Rakovnik, Czechoslovakia. ... 6-2/200. ... Shoots left. ... Brother of Frantisek Kaberle, defenseman, Atlanta Thrashers.

TRANSACTIONS/CAREER NOTES: Selected by Toronto Maple Leafs in eighth round (13th Maple Leafs pick, 204th overall) of NHL entry draft (June 22, 1996).

Season Team	League	REGULAR SEASON								PLAYOFFS				
		Gms.	G	A	Pts.	PIM	+/-	PP	SH	Gms.	G	A	Pts.	PIM
95-96—Poldi Kladno Jrs.	Czech Rep.	23	6	13	19	19	...	...	...	—	—	—	—	—
—Poldi Kladno	Czech Rep.	23	0	1	1	2	...	...	...	2	0	0	0	0
96-97—Poldi Kladno	Czech Rep.	49	0	5	5	26	...	...	...	3	0	0	0	0
97-98—Poldi Kladno	Czech Rep.	47	4	19	23	12	...	...	...	—	—	—	—	—
—St. John's	AHL	2	0	0	0	0	...	...	...	—	—	—	—	—
98-99—Toronto	NHL	57	4	18	22	12	3	0	0	14	0	3	3	2
99-00—Toronto	NHL	82	7	33	40	24	3	2	0	12	1	4	5	0
NHL Totals (2 years)		139	11	51	62	36	6	2	0	26	1	7	8	2

KALININ, DMITRI　　　　D　　　　SABRES

PERSONAL: Born July 22, 1980, in Chelyabinsk, U.S.S.R. ... 6-2/198. ... Shoots left.

TRANSACTIONS/CAREER NOTES: Selected by Buffalo Sabres in first round (first Sabres pick, 18th overall) of NHL entry draft (June 27, 1998).

Season Team	League	REGULAR SEASON								PLAYOFFS				
		Gms.	G	A	Pts.	PIM	+/-	PP	SH	Gms.	G	A	Pts.	PIM
95-96—Traktor Chelyabinsk	CIS Jr.	30	10	10	20	60	...	...	...	—	—	—	—	—
—Nadezhda Chelyabinsk	CIS Div. II	20	0	3	3	10	...	...	...	—	—	—	—	—
96-97—Traktor Chelyabinsk	Russian	2	0	0	0	0	...	...	...	0	—	—	—	—
—Traktor-2 Chelyabinsk .	Rus. Div. III	20	0	0	0	10	...	...	...	—	—	—	—	—
97-98—Traktor Chelyabinsk	Russian	26	0	2	2	24	...	...	...	—	—	—	—	—
98-99—Moncton	QMJHL	39	7	18	25	44	...	...	...	4	1	1	2	0
—Rochester	AHL	3	0	1	1	14	...	...	...	7	0	0	0	6
99-00—Rochester	AHL	75	2	19	21	52	...	...	...	21	2	9	11	8
—Buffalo	NHL	4	0	0	0	4	0	0	0	—	—	—	—	—
NHL Totals (1 year)		4	0	0	0	4	0	0	0					

J

K

KAMENSKY, VALERI — LW — RANGERS

PERSONAL: Born April 18, 1966, in Voskresensk, U.S.S.R. ... 6-2/202. ... Shoots right. ... Name pronounced kuh-MEHN-skee.
TRANSACTIONS/CAREER NOTES: Selected by Quebec Nordiques in seventh round (eighth Nordiques pick, 129th overall) of NHL entry draft (June 11, 1988). ... Fractured leg (October 1991); missed 57 games. ... Fractured left thumb (October 17, 1992); missed three games. ... Fractured right ankle (October 27, 1992); missed 47 games. ... Bruised left foot (October 21, 1993); missed two games. ... Bruised right foot (December 21, 1993); missed one game. ... Played in Europe during 1994-95 NHL lockout. ... Suffered kidney infection (February 26, 1995); missed eight games. ... Nordiques franchise moved to Colorado and renamed Avalanche for 1995-96 season (June 21, 1995). ... Bruised ribs (January 3, 1996); missed one game. ... Separated shoulder (December 31, 1996); missed six games. ... Injured shoulder (February 25, 1997); missed three games. ... Bruised shoulder (December 13, 1997); missed three games. ... Suffered from the flu (December 31, 1997); missed two games. ... Bruised foot (November 8, 1998); missed two games. ... Fractured arm (March 14, 1999); missed final 15 games of regular season and first eight playoff games. ... Signed as free agent by New York Rangers (July 6, 1999). ... Suffered stress fracture in arm (October 1, 1999); missed six games. ... Fractured arm (October 24, 1999); missed ten games. ... Bruised forearm (December 3, 1999); missed seven games. ... Bruised ankle (April 4, 2000); missed one game.
HONORS: Won Soviet Player of the Year Award (1990-91). ... Played in NHL All-Star Game (1998).
MISCELLANEOUS: Member of Stanley Cup championship team (1996). ... Member of gold-medal-winning U.S.S.R. Olympic team (1988). ... Member of silver-medal-winning Russian Olympic team (1998). ... Scored on penalty shot (vs. Curtis Joseph, October 26, 1996).
STATISTICAL PLATEAUS: Three-goal games: 1995-96 (2), 1996-97 (1), 1997-98 (1), 1998-99 (1). Total: 5.

Season Team	League	REGULAR SEASON								PLAYOFFS				
		Gms.	G	A	Pts.	PIM	+/-	PP	SH	Gms.	G	A	Pts.	PIM
82-83—Khimik	USSR	5	0	0	0	0	...	...	...	—	—	—	—	—
83-84—Khimik	USSR	20	2	2	4	6	...	...	...	—	—	—	—	—
84-85—Khimik	USSR	45	9	3	12	24	...	...	...	—	—	—	—	—
85-86—CSKA Moscow	USSR	40	15	9	24	8	...	...	...	—	—	—	—	—
86-87—CSKA Moscow	USSR	37	13	8	21	16	...	...	...	—	—	—	—	—
87-88—CSKA Moscow	USSR	51	26	20	46	40	...	...	...	—	—	—	—	—
—Soviet Olympic Team	Int'l	8	4	2	6	4	...	...	...	—	—	—	—	—
88-89—CSKA Moscow	USSR	40	18	10	28	30	...	...	...	—	—	—	—	—
89-90—CSKA Moscow	USSR	45	19	18	37	38	...	...	...	—	—	—	—	—
90-91—CSKA Moscow	USSR	46	20	26	46	66	...	...	...	—	—	—	—	—
91-92—Quebec	NHL	23	7	14	21	14	-1	2	0	—	—	—	—	—
92-93—Quebec	NHL	32	15	22	37	14	13	2	3	6	0	1	1	6
93-94—Quebec	NHL	76	28	37	65	42	12	6	0	—	—	—	—	—
94-95—Ambri Piotta	Switzerland	12	13	6	19	2	...	...	...	—	—	—	—	—
—Quebec	NHL	40	10	20	30	22	3	5	1	2	1	0	1	0
95-96—Colorado	NHL	81	38	47	85	85	14	18	1	22	10	12	22	28
96-97—Colorado	NHL	68	28	38	66	38	5	8	0	17	8	14	22	16
97-98—Colorado	NHL	75	26	40	66	60	-2	8	0	7	2	3	5	18
—Russian Oly. team	Int'l	6	1	2	3	0	...	...	...	—	—	—	—	—
98-99—Colorado	NHL	65	14	30	44	28	1	2	0	10	4	5	9	4
99-00—New York Rangers	NHL	58	13	19	32	24	-13	3	0					
NHL Totals (9 years)		518	179	267	446	327	32	54	5	64	25	35	60	72

KAPANEN, SAMI — RW — HURRICANES

PERSONAL: Born June 14, 1973, in Helsinki, Finland. ... 5-10/175. ... Shoots left. ... Name pronounced KAP-ih-nehn.
TRANSACTIONS/CAREER NOTES: Selected by Hartford Whalers in fourth round (fourth Whalers pick, 87th overall) of NHL entry draft (July 8, 1995). ... Suffered from the flu (October 20, 1996); missed two games. ... Sprained knee (November 30, 1996); missed 16 games. ... Sprained knee (January 10, 1997); missed nine games. ... Sprained knee (February 26, 1997); missed three games. ... Sprained knee (March 15, 1997); missed six games. ... Suffered from the flu (April 5, 1997); missed one game. ... Whalers franchise moved to North Carolina and renamed Carolina Hurricanes for 1997-98 season; NHL approved move on June 25, 1997. ... Suffered from the flu (March 12, 1998); missed one game. ... Bruised knee (October 24, 1998); missed one game. ... Bruised shoulder (February 19, 2000); missed two games. ... Suffered concussion (March 29, 2000); missed four games.
HONORS: Played in NHL All-Star Game (2000).
MISCELLANEOUS: Member of bronze-medal-winning Finnish Olympic team (1998). ... Scored on a penalty shot (vs. Jim Carey, March 12, 1997). ... Failed to score on a penalty shot (vs. Tom Barrasso, January 7, 1999).
STATISTICAL PLATEAUS: Three-goal games: 1997-98 (2).

Season Team	League	REGULAR SEASON								PLAYOFFS				
		Gms.	G	A	Pts.	PIM	+/-	PP	SH	Gms.	G	A	Pts.	PIM
90-91—KalPa Kuopio	Finland	14	1	2	3	2	...	...	...	8	2	1	3	2
91-92—KalPa Kuopio	Finland	42	15	10	25	8	...	...	...	—	—	—	—	—
92-93—KalPa Kuopio	Finland	37	4	17	21	12	...	...	...	—	—	—	—	—
93-94—KalPa Kuopio	Finland	48	23	32	55	16	...	...	...	—	—	—	—	—
94-95—HIFK Helsinki	Finland	49	14	28	42	42	...	...	...	3	0	0	0	0
95-96—Springfield	AHL	28	14	17	31	4	...	...	...	3	1	2	3	0
—Hartford	NHL	35	5	4	9	6	0	0	0	—	—	—	—	—
96-97—Hartford	NHL	45	13	12	25	2	6	3	0	—	—	—	—	—
97-98—Carolina	NHL	81	26	37	63	16	9	4	0	—	—	—	—	—
—Fin. Olympic team	Int'l	6	0	1	1	0	...	...	...	—	—	—	—	—
98-99—Carolina	NHL	81	24	35	59	10	-1	5	0	5	1	1	2	0
99-00—Carolina	NHL	76	24	24	48	12	10	7	0	—	—	—	—	—
NHL Totals (5 years)		318	92	112	204	46	24	19	0	5	1	1	2	0

KARALAHTI, JERE — D — KINGS

PERSONAL: Born March 25, 1975, in Helsinki, Finland. ... 6-2/210. ... Shoots right. ... Name pronounced YAIR-ee KAIR-uh-LAH-tee.
TRANSACTIONS/CAREER NOTES: Selected by Los Angeles Kings in sixth round (seventh Kings pick, 146th overall) of NHL entry draft (June 26, 1993).

Season Team	League	Gms.	G	A	Pts.	PIM	+/-	PP	SH	Gms.	G	A	Pts.	PIM
91-92—HIFK Juniors	Finland Jr.	30	12	5	17	36	...	...	...	—	—	—	—	—
92-93—HIFK Juniors	Finland Jr.	30	2	13	15	49	...	...	...	—	—	—	—	—
93-94—HIFK Helsinki	Finland	46	1	10	11	36	...	...	...	3	0	0	0	6
94-95—HIFK Helsinki	Finland	37	1	7	8	42	...	...	...	3	0	0	0	0
95-96—HIFK Helsinki	Finland	36	4	6	10	102	...	...	...	3	0	0	0	4
96-97—HIFK Helsinki	Finland	18	3	5	8	20	...	...	...	—	—	—	—	—
97-98—HIFK Helsinki	Finland	43	14	16	30	32	...	...	...	9	2	0	2	8
98-99—HIFK Helsinki	Finland	49	11	22	33	65	...	...	...	11	1	1	2	10
99-00—HIFK Helsinki	Finland	13	2	2	4	55	...	...	...	—	—	—	—	—
—Long Beach	IHL	10	0	3	3	4	...	...	...	—	—	—	—	—
—Los Angeles	NHL	48	6	10	16	18	3	4	0	4	0	1	1	2
NHL Totals (1 year)		48	6	10	16	18	3	4	0	4	0	1	1	2

KARIYA, PAUL   LW   MIGHTY DUCKS

PERSONAL: Born October 16, 1974, in Vancouver. ... 5-10/180. ... Shoots left. ... Brother of Steve Kariya, left winger, Vancouver Canucks. ... Name pronounced kuh-REE-uh.
COLLEGE: Maine.
TRANSACTIONS/CAREER NOTES: Selected by Mighty Ducks of Anaheim in first round (first Mighty Ducks pick, fourth overall) of NHL entry draft (June 26, 1993). ... Suffered lower back spasms (February 12, 1995); missed one game. ... Strained abdominal muscle prior to 1996-97 season; missed first 11 games of season. ... Suffered mild concussion (November 13, 1996); missed two games. ... Missed first 32 games of 1997-98 season due to contract dispute. ... Suffered concussion (February 1, 1998); missed remainder of season. ... Injured hip prior to start of 1999-2000 season; missed first game of season. ... Fractured right foot (February 18, 2000); missed seven games.
HONORS: Won Hobey Baker Memorial Award (1992-93). ... Named Hockey East Player of the Year (1992-93). ... Named Hockey East Rookie of the Year (1992-93). ... Named to NCAA All-America (East) All-Star first team (1992-93). ... Named to NCAA All-Tournament team (1992-93). ... Named to Hockey East All-Star first team (1992-93). ... Named to Hockey East All-Rookie team (1992-93). ... Named to Hockey East All-Decade team (1994). ... Named to NHL All-Rookie team (1994-95). ... Played in NHL All-Star Game (1996, 1997, 1999 and 2000). ... Won Lady Byng Memorial Trophy (1995-96 and 1996-97). ... Named to NHL All-Star first team (1995-96, 1996-97 and 1998-99). ... Named to THE SPORTING NEWS All-Star team (1998-99 and 1999-2000). ... Named to NHL All-Star second team (1999-2000).
MISCELLANEOUS: Member of silver-medal-winning Canadian Olympic team (1994). ... Captain of Mighty Ducks of Anaheim (1996-97, December 11, 1997 through February 4, 1998, 1998-99 and 1999-2000). ... Holds Mighty Ducks of Anaheim all-time records for most goals (210), most assists (254) and most points (464). ... Scored on a penalty shot (vs. Kevin Weekes, January 21, 1998; vs. Corey Hirsch, February 20, 1999). ... Failed to score on a penalty shot (vs. Stephane Fiset, March 18, 1999).
STATISTICAL NOTES: Led NHL with 10 game-winning goals (1996-97). ... Led NHL in shots with 429 (1998-99).
STATISTICAL PLATEAUS: Three-goal games: 1996-97 (2), 1997-98 (1). Total: 3.

Season Team	League	Gms.	G	A	Pts.	PIM	+/-	PP	SH	Gms.	G	A	Pts.	PIM
90-91—Penticton	BCJHL	54	45	67	112	8	...	...	...	—	—	—	—	—
91-92—Penticton	BCJHL	40	46	86	132	16	...	...	...	—	—	—	—	—
92-93—Univ. of Maine	Hockey East	39	25	*75	*100	12	...	...	...	—	—	—	—	—
93-94—Canadian nat'l team	Int'l	23	7	34	41	2	...	...	...	—	—	—	—	—
—Can. Olympic team	Int'l	8	3	4	7	2	...	...	...	—	—	—	—	—
—Univ. of Maine	Hockey East	12	8	16	24	4	...	...	...	—	—	—	—	—
94-95—Anaheim	NHL	47	18	21	39	4	-17	7	1	—	—	—	—	—
95-96—Anaheim	NHL	82	50	58	108	20	9	20	3	—	—	—	—	—
96-97—Anaheim	NHL	69	44	55	99	6	36	15	3	11	7	6	13	4
97-98—Anaheim	NHL	22	17	14	31	23	12	3	0	—	—	—	—	—
98-99—Anaheim	NHL	82	39	62	101	40	17	11	2	3	1	3	4	0
99-00—Anaheim	NHL	74	42	44	86	24	22	11	3	—	—	—	—	—
NHL Totals (6 years)		376	210	254	464	117	79	67	12	14	8	9	17	4

KARIYA, STEVE   LW   CANUCKS

PERSONAL: Born December 22, 1977, in Vancouver. ... 5-7/170. ... Shoots left. ... Brother of Paul Kariya, left winger, Mighty Ducks of Anaheim.
COLLEGE: Maine.
TRANSACTIONS/CAREER NOTES: Signed as non-drafted free agent by Vancouver Canucks (April 16, 1999).
HONORS: Named to NCAA All-America (East) first team (1998-99). ... Named to Hockey East All-Star first team (1998-99).

Season Team	League	Gms.	G	A	Pts.	PIM	+/-	PP	SH	Gms.	G	A	Pts.	PIM
94-95—Nanaimo	BCJHL	60	39	60	99	...	...	...	...	—	—	—	—	—
95-96—Univ. of Maine	Hockey East	39	7	15	22	38	...	...	...	—	—	—	—	—
96-97—Univ. of Maine	Hockey East	35	19	31	50	10	...	...	...	—	—	—	—	—
97-98—Univ. of Maine	Hockey East	35	25	25	50	10	...	...	...	—	—	—	—	—
98-99—Univ. of Maine	Hockey East	41	27	38	65	24	...	...	...	—	—	—	—	—
99-00—Vancouver	NHL	45	8	11	19	22	9	0	0	—	—	—	—	—
—Syracuse	AHL	29	18	23	41	22	...	...	...	4	2	1	3	0
NHL Totals (1 year)		45	8	11	19	22	9	0	0	—	—	—	—	—

KARLSSON, ANDREAS   C   THRASHERS

PERSONAL: Born August 19, 1975, in Leksand, Sweden. ... 6-3/195. ... Shoots left.
TRANSACTIONS/CAREER NOTES: Selected by Calgary Flames in sixth round (eighth Flames pick, 148th overall) of NHL entry draft (June 26, 1993). ... Traded by Flames to Atlanta Thrashers for future considerations (June 25, 1999). ... Strained shoulder (February 3, 2000); missed 11 games.

Season Team	League	REGULAR SEASON								PLAYOFFS				
		Gms.	G	A	Pts.	PIM	+/-	PP	SH	Gms.	G	A	Pts.	PIM
92-93—Leksand	Sweden	13	0	0	0	6	...	...	...	—	—	—	—	—
93-94—Leksand	Sweden	21	0	0	0	10	...	...	...	—	—	—	—	—
94-95—Leksand	Sweden	24	7	8	15	4	...	...	...	4	0	1	1	0
95-96—Leksand	Sweden	40	10	13	23	10	...	...	...	5	2	1	3	4
96-97—Leksand	Sweden	49	13	11	24	39	...	...	...	9	2	0	2	2
97-98—Leksand	Sweden	33	9	14	23	20	...	...	...	4	1	0	1	0
98-99—Leksand	Sweden	49	18	15	33	18	...	...	...	4	1	0	1	6
99-00—Orlando	IHL	18	5	5	10	6	...	...	...	—	—	—	—	—
—Atlanta	NHL	51	5	9	14	14	-17	1	0	—	—	—	—	—
NHL Totals (1 year)		51	5	9	14	14	-17	1	0					

KARPA, DAVE   D   HURRICANES

PERSONAL: Born May 7, 1971, in Regina, Sask. ... 6-1/210. ... Shoots right. ... Full Name: David James Karpa.
COLLEGE: Ferris State (Mich.).
TRANSACTIONS/CAREER NOTES: Selected by Quebec Nordiques in fourth round (fourth Nordiques pick, 68th overall) of NHL entry draft (June 22, 1991). ... Fractured right wrist (January 26, 1994); missed 18 games. ... Traded by Nordiques to Los Angeles Kings for fourth-round pick in 1995 or 1996 draft (February 28, 1995); trade invalidated by NHL because Karpa failed his physical examination (March 3, 1995). ... Traded by Nordiques to Mighty Ducks of Anaheim for fourth-round pick (traded to St. Louis) in 1997 draft (March 8, 1995). ... Underwent right wrist surgery (May 9, 1995). ... Bruised right knee (November 24, 1995); missed eight games. ... Fractured right hand (February 4, 1997); missed 13 games. ... Traded by Mighty Ducks with fourth-round pick (traded to Atlanta) in 2000 draft to Carolina Hurricanes for LW Stu Grimson and D Kevin Haller (August 11, 1998). ... Injured hamstring (December 6, 1997); missed two games. ... Suffered torn anterior cruciate ligament and medial collateral ligament in knee (November 22, 1998); missed 41 games. ... Bruised shoulder (March 10, 1999); missed five games. ... Reinjured shoulder (March 26, 1999); missed three games. ... Injured foot (March 29, 2000); missed final five games of season.
MISCELLANEOUS: Holds Mighty Ducks of Anaheim all-time record for most penalty minutes (788).

Season Team	League	REGULAR SEASON								PLAYOFFS				
		Gms.	G	A	Pts.	PIM	+/-	PP	SH	Gms.	G	A	Pts.	PIM
88-89—Notre Dame	SCMHL	...	16	37	53	...	...	...	...	—	—	—	—	—
89-90—Notre Dame	SCMHL	43	9	19	28	271	...	...	...	—	—	—	—	—
90-91—Ferris State	CCHA	41	6	19	25	109	...	...	...	—	—	—	—	—
91-92—Ferris State	CCHA	34	7	12	19	124	...	...	...	—	—	—	—	—
—Halifax	AHL	2	0	0	0	4	...	...	...	—	—	—	—	—
—Quebec	NHL	4	0	0	0	14	2	0	0	—	—	—	—	—
92-93—Halifax	AHL	71	4	27	31	167	...	...	...	—	—	—	—	—
—Quebec	NHL	12	0	1	1	13	-6	0	0	3	0	0	0	0
93-94—Quebec	NHL	60	5	12	17	148	0	2	0	—	—	—	—	—
—Cornwall	AHL	1	0	0	0	0	...	...	...	12	2	2	4	27
94-95—Cornwall	AHL	6	0	2	2	19	...	...	...	—	—	—	—	—
—Quebec	NHL	2	0	0	0	0	-1	0	0	—	—	—	—	—
—Anaheim	NHL	26	1	5	6	91	0	0	0	—	—	—	—	—
95-96—Anaheim	NHL	72	3	16	19	270	-3	0	1	—	—	—	—	—
96-97—Anaheim	NHL	69	2	11	13	210	11	0	0	8	1	1	2	20
97-98—Anaheim	NHL	78	1	11	12	217	-3	0	0	—	—	—	—	—
98-99—Carolina	NHL	33	0	2	2	55	1	0	0	2	0	0	0	2
99-00—Cincinnati	IHL	39	1	8	9	147	...	...	...	—	—	—	—	—
—Carolina	NHL	27	1	4	5	52	9	0	0	—	—	—	—	—
NHL Totals (9 years)		383	13	62	75	1070	10	2	1	13	1	1	2	22

KARPOVTSEV, ALEXANDER   D   MAPLE LEAFS

PERSONAL: Born April 7, 1970, in Moscow, U.S.S.R. ... 6-3/215. ... Shoots right. ... Name pronounced KAHR-puht-sehf.
TRANSACTIONS/CAREER NOTES: Selected by Quebec Nordiques in seventh round (seventh Nordiques pick, 158th overall) of NHL entry draft (June 16, 1990). ... Traded by Nordiques to New York Rangers for D Mike Hurlbut (September 9, 1993). ... Bruised buttocks (October 9, 1993); missed one game. ... Bruised hip (November 3, 1993); missed six games. ... Reinjured hip (November 23, 1993); missed one game. ... Injured face (February 28, 1994); missed two games. ... Suffered injury (March 14, 1994); missed two games. ... Played in Europe during 1994-95 NHL lockout. ... Suffered sore ankle (April 14, 1995); missed one game. ... Hyperextended elbow (October 29, 1995); missed one game. ... Suffered back spasms (February 10, 1996); missed one game. ... Suffered back spasms (February 18, 1996); missed two games. ... Bruised thumb (March 13, 1996); missed two games. ... Suffered back spasms (March 27, 1996); missed six games. ... Bruised toe (April 3, 1997); missed one game. ... Hyperextended elbow (April 10, 1997); missed one game. ... Suffered throat infection (October 10, 1997); missed one game. ... Sprained right wrist (January 19, 1998); missed one game. ... Underwent wrist surgery (February 2, 1998); missed 28 games. ... Bruised knee (October 13, 1998); missed two games. ... Traded by Rangers with fourth-round pick (LW Mirko Murovic) in 1999 draft to Toronto Maple Leafs for D Mathieu Schneider (October 14, 1998). ... Fractured thumb (November 14, 1998); missed 12 games. ... Sprained wrist (January 2, 1999); missed three games ... Strained wrist (February 2, 1999); missed three games. ... Fractured finger (March 17, 1999); missed three games. ... Strained shoulder (April 26, 1999); missed three playoff games. ... Suffered injury (November 5, 1999); missed one game. ... Sprained shoulder (November 26, 1999); missed five games. ... Fractured hand (January 11, 2000); missed four games. ... Suffered injury (March 16, 2000); missed one game. ... Suffered injury (March 23, 2000); missed one game.
MISCELLANEOUS: Member of Stanley Cup championship team (1994). ... Member of silver-medal-winning Russian Olympic team (1998).
STATISTICAL NOTES: Led NHL in plus/minus with 39 in 1998-99.

Season Team	League	REGULAR SEASON								PLAYOFFS				
		Gms.	G	A	Pts.	PIM	+/-	PP	SH	Gms.	G	A	Pts.	PIM
89-90—Dynamo Moscow	USSR	35	1	1	2	27	...	...	...	—	—	—	—	—
90-91—Dynamo Moscow	USSR	40	0	5	5	15	...	...	...	—	—	—	—	—
91-92—Dynamo Moscow	CIS	28	3	2	5	22	...	...	...	—	—	—	—	—
92-93—Dynamo Moscow	CIS	40	3	11	14	100	...	...	...	—	—	—	—	—
93-94—New York Rangers	NHL	67	3	15	18	58	12	1	0	17	0	4	4	12
94-95—Dynamo Moscow	CIS	13	0	2	2	10	...	...	...	—	—	—	—	—
—New York Rangers	NHL	47	4	8	12	30	-4	1	0	8	1	0	1	0

K

Season Team	League	REGULAR SEASON								PLAYOFFS				
		Gms.	G	A	Pts.	PIM	+/-	PP	SH	Gms.	G	A	Pts.	PIM
95-96—New York Rangers......	NHL	40	2	16	18	26	12	1	0	6	0	1	1	4
96-97—New York Rangers......	NHL	77	9	29	38	59	1	6	1	13	1	3	4	20
97-98—New York Rangers......	NHL	47	3	7	10	38	-1	1	0	—	—	—	—	—
98-99—New York Rangers......	NHL	2	1	0	1	0	§1	0	0	—	—	—	—	—
—Toronto	NHL	56	2	25	27	52	§38	1	0	14	1	3	4	12
99-00—Toronto	NHL	69	3	14	17	54	9	3	0	11	0	3	3	4
NHL Totals (7 years)..........		405	27	114	141	317	68	14	1	69	3	14	17	52

KASPARAITIS, DARIUS   D   PENGUINS

PERSONAL: Born October 16, 1972, in Elektrenai, U.S.S.R. ... 5-11/212. ... Shoots left. ... Name pronounced kas-puhr-IGH-tihz.

TRANSACTIONS/CAREER NOTES: Selected by New York Islanders in first round (first Islanders pick, fifth overall) of NHL entry draft (June 20, 1992). ... Suffered back spasms (February 12, 1993); missed two games. ... Strained back (April 15, 1993); missed one game. ... Strained lower back (November 10, 1993); missed two games. ... Jammed wrist (March 5, 1994); missed four games. ... Tore knee ligament (February 20, 1995); missed remainder of season and first 15 games of 1995-96 season. ... Suffered from the flu (December 2, 1995); missed two games. ... Suffered back spasms (December 9, 1995); missed 16 games. ... Injured groin (February 8, 1996); missed two games. ... Traded by Islanders with C Andreas Johansson to Pittsburgh Penguins for C Bryan Smolinski (November 17, 1996). ... Suffered concussion (December 23, 1996); missed two games. ... Suffered facial laceration (January 2, 1997); missed one game. ... Twisted ankle (January 23, 1997); missed one game. ... Suffered concussion (March 18, 1997); missed three games. ... Suffered from the flu (March 29, 1998); missed one game. ... Injured knee (September 20, 1998); missed first eight games of season. ... Strained knee (December 21, 1998); missed one game. ... Strained groin (February 24, 1999); missed two games. ... Strained knee (March 5, 1999) and underwent surgery; missed remainder of season. ... Injured knee prior to start of 1999-2000 season; missed first four games of season. ... Suspended two games by NHL for elbowing incident (October 20, 1999). ... Suffered from headaches (December 30, 1999); missed two games. ... Suspended one game by NHL for second major penalty and game misconduct in season (January 19, 2000).

MISCELLANEOUS: Member of gold-medal-winning Unified Olympic team (1992). ... Member of silver-medal-winning Russian Olympic team (1998).

Season Team	League	REGULAR SEASON								PLAYOFFS				
		Gms.	G	A	Pts.	PIM	+/-	PP	SH	Gms.	G	A	Pts.	PIM
88-89—Dynamo Moscow........	USSR	3	0	0	0	0	...	...	...	—	—	—	—	—
89-90—Dynamo Moscow........	USSR	1	0	0	0	0	...	...	...	—	—	—	—	—
90-91—Dynamo Moscow........	USSR	17	0	1	1	10	...	...	...	—	—	—	—	—
91-92—Dynamo Moscow........	CIS	31	2	10	12	14	...	...	...	—	—	—	—	—
—Unif. Olympic team....	Int'l	8	0	2	2	2	...	...	...	—	—	—	—	—
92-93—Dynamo Moscow........	CIS	7	1	3	4	8	...	...	...	—	—	—	—	—
—New York Islanders.....	NHL	79	4	17	21	166	15	0	0	18	0	5	5	31
93-94—New York Islanders.....	NHL	76	1	10	11	142	-6	0	0	4	0	0	0	8
94-95—New York Islanders.....	NHL	13	0	1	1	22	-11	0	0	—	—	—	—	—
95-96—New York Islanders.....	NHL	46	1	7	8	93	-12	0	0	—	—	—	—	—
96-97—New York Islanders.....	NHL	18	0	5	5	16	-7	0	0	—	—	—	—	—
—Pittsburgh...............	NHL	57	2	16	18	84	24	0	0	5	0	0	0	6
97-98—Pittsburgh...............	NHL	81	4	8	12	127	3	0	2	5	0	0	0	8
—Russian Oly. team......	Int'l	6	0	2	2	6	...	...	...	—	—	—	—	—
98-99—Pittsburgh...............	NHL	48	1	4	5	70	12	0	0	—	—	—	—	—
99-00—Pittsburgh...............	NHL	73	3	12	15	146	-12	1	0	11	1	1	2	10
NHL Totals (8 years)..........		491	16	80	96	866	6	1	2	43	1	6	7	63

KEANE, MIKE   RW   STARS

PERSONAL: Born May 29, 1967, in Winnipeg. ... 6-0/185. ... Shoots right. ... Name pronounced KEEN.

TRANSACTIONS/CAREER NOTES: Signed as non-drafted free agent by Montreal Canadiens (September 25, 1985). ... Cut left kneecap (December 21, 1988). ... Cut left kneecap (October 31, 1990); missed seven games. ... Injured neck (March 1991). ... Sprained ankle (January 16, 1992); missed four games. ... Reinjured ankle (February 1, 1992); missed 10 games. ... Bruised ankle (March 11, 1992); missed one game. ... Suspended four off-days and fined $500 by NHL for swinging stick in preseason game (October 13, 1992). ... Suffered wrist tendinitis (January 26, 1993); missed three games. ... Suffered back spasms (February 12, 1993); missed two games. ... Fractured toe (February 27, 1993); missed two games. ... Suffered back spasms (October 16, 1993); missed one game. ... Suffered back spasms (January 12, 1994); missed three games. ... Injured groin (November 1, 1995); missed one game. ... Injured neck (November 18, 1995); missed three games. ... Injured groin (November 25, 1995); missed two games. ... Traded by Canadiens with G Patrick Roy to Colorado Avalanche for G Jocelyn Thibault, LW Martin Rucinsky and RW Andrei Kovalenko (December 6, 1995). ... Signed as free agent by New York Rangers (July 7, 1997). ... Traded by Rangers with C Brian Skrudland and sixth-round pick (RW Pavel Patera) in 1998 draft to Dallas Stars for LW Bob Errey, RW Todd Harvey and fourth-round pick (LW Boyd Kane) in 1998 draft (March 24, 1998). ... Strained back (March 5, 2000); missed one game.

MISCELLANEOUS: Member of Stanley Cup championship team (1993, 1996 and 1999). ... Captain of Montreal Canadiens (1994-95 through December 6, 1995). ... Scored on a penalty shot (vs. Corey Schwab, October 24, 1997).

Season Team	League	REGULAR SEASON								PLAYOFFS				
		Gms.	G	A	Pts.	PIM	+/-	PP	SH	Gms.	G	A	Pts.	PIM
83-84—Winnipeg	WHL	1	0	0	0	0	...	...	...	—	—	—	—	—
84-85—Moose Jaw	WHL	65	17	26	43	141	...	...	...	—	—	—	—	—
85-86—Moose Jaw	WHL	67	34	49	83	162	...	...	...	13	6	8	14	9
86-87—Moose Jaw	WHL	53	25	45	70	107	...	...	...	9	3	9	12	11
—Sherbrooke	AHL	—	—	—	—	—	...	...	...	9	2	2	4	16
87-88—Sherbrooke	AHL	78	25	43	68	70	...	...	...	6	1	1	2	18
88-89—Montreal	NHL	69	16	19	35	69	9	5	0	21	4	3	7	17
89-90—Montreal	NHL	74	9	15	24	78	0	1	0	11	0	1	1	8
90-91—Montreal	NHL	73	13	23	36	50	6	2	1	12	3	2	5	6
91-92—Montreal	NHL	67	11	30	41	64	16	2	0	8	1	1	2	16
92-93—Montreal	NHL	77	15	45	60	95	29	0	0	19	2	13	15	6
93-94—Montreal	NHL	80	16	30	46	119	6	6	2	6	3	1	4	4
94-95—Montreal	NHL	48	10	10	20	15	5	1	0	—	—	—	—	—

Season Team	League	Gms.	G	A	Pts.	PIM	+/-	PP	SH	Gms.	G	A	Pts.	PIM
95-96—Montreal	NHL	18	0	7	7	6	-6	0	0	—	—	—	—	—
—Colorado	NHL	55	10	10	20	40	1	0	2	22	3	2	5	16
96-97—Colorado	NHL	81	10	17	27	63	2	0	1	17	3	1	4	24
97-98—New York Rangers	NHL	70	8	10	18	47	-12	2	0	—	—	—	—	—
—Dallas	NHL	13	2	3	5	5	0	0	0	17	4	4	8	0
98-99—Dallas	NHL	81	6	23	29	62	-2	1	1	23	5	2	7	6
99-00—Dallas	NHL	81	13	21	34	41	9	0	4	23	2	4	6	14
NHL Totals (12 years)		887	139	263	402	754	63	20	11	179	30	34	64	117

KECZMER, DAN   D

PERSONAL: Born May 25, 1968, in Mount Clemens, Mich. ... 6-1/205. ... Shoots left. ... Full Name: Daniel Leonard Keczmer. ... Name pronounced KEHZ-muhr.
COLLEGE: Lake Superior State (Mich.).
TRANSACTIONS/CAREER NOTES: Selected by Minnesota North Stars in 10th round (11th North Stars pick, 201st overall) of NHL entry draft (June 21, 1986). ... Injured shoulder (February 2, 1990). ... Claimed by San Jose Sharks as part of ownership change with North Stars (October 1990). ... Traded by Sharks to Hartford Whalers for C Dean Evason (October 2, 1991). ... Bruised right leg (February 8, 1993); missed three games. ... Traded by Whalers to Calgary Flames for G Jeff Reese (November 19, 1993). ... Separated right shoulder (February 16, 1995); missed 10 games. ... Traded by Flames with D Phil Housley to New Jersey Devils for D Tommy Albelin, D Cale Hulse and RW Jocelyn Lemieux (February 26, 1996). ... Signed as free agent by Dallas Stars (August 7, 1996). ... Suffered from meningitis (October 4, 1998); missed first four games of season. ... Claimed on waivers by Nashville Predators (March 11, 1999). ... Traded by Predators to St. Louis Blues for D Rory Fitzpatrick (February 9, 2000).
HONORS: Named to CCHA All-Star second team (1989-90).

Season Team	League	Gms.	G	A	Pts.	PIM	+/-	PP	SH	Gms.	G	A	Pts.	PIM
86-87—Lake Superior State	CCHA	38	3	5	8	28	...	...	...	—	—	—	—	—
87-88—Lake Superior State	CCHA	41	2	15	17	34	...	...	...	—	—	—	—	—
88-89—Lake Superior State	CCHA	46	3	26	29	70	...	...	...	—	—	—	—	—
89-90—Lake Superior State	CCHA	43	13	23	36	48	...	...	...	—	—	—	—	—
90-91—Minnesota	NHL	9	0	1	1	6	0	0	0	—	—	—	—	—
—Kalamazoo	IHL	60	4	20	24	60	...	...	...	9	1	2	3	10
91-92—U.S. national team	Int'l	51	3	11	14	56	...	...	...	—	—	—	—	—
—Springfield	AHL	18	3	4	7	10	...	...	...	4	0	0	0	6
—Hartford	NHL	1	0	0	0	0	-1	0	0	—	—	—	—	—
92-93—Springfield	AHL	37	1	13	14	38	...	...	...	12	0	4	4	14
—Hartford	NHL	23	4	4	8	28	-3	2	0	—	—	—	—	—
93-94—Hartford	NHL	12	0	1	1	12	-6	0	0	—	—	—	—	—
—Springfield	AHL	7	0	1	1	4	...	...	...	—	—	—	—	—
—Calgary	NHL	57	1	20	21	48	-2	0	0	3	0	0	0	4
94-95—Calgary	NHL	28	2	3	5	10	7	0	0	7	0	1	1	2
95-96—Saint John	AHL	22	3	11	14	14	...	...	...	—	—	—	—	—
—Calgary	NHL	13	0	0	0	14	-6	0	0	—	—	—	—	—
—Albany	AHL	17	0	4	4	4	...	...	...	1	0	0	0	0
96-97—Michigan	IHL	42	3	17	20	24	...	...	...	—	—	—	—	—
—Dallas	NHL	13	0	1	1	6	3	0	0	—	—	—	—	—
97-98—Dallas	NHL	17	1	2	3	26	5	0	0	2	0	0	0	2
—Michigan	IHL	44	1	11	12	29	...	...	...	—	—	—	—	—
98-99—Dallas	NHL	22	0	1	1	22	-2	0	0	—	—	—	—	—
—Michigan	IHL	5	0	1	1	2	...	...	...	—	—	—	—	—
—Nashville	NHL	16	0	0	0	12	-3	0	0	—	—	—	—	—
99-00—Nashville	NHL	24	0	5	5	28	-2	0	0	—	—	—	—	—
—Milwaukee	IHL	18	1	3	4	10	...	...	...	—	—	—	—	—
—Worcester	AHL	25	1	9	10	12	...	...	...	9	0	1	1	10
NHL Totals (10 years)		235	8	38	46	212	-10	2	0	12	0	1	1	8

KEEFE, SHELDON   RW   LIGHTNING

PERSONAL: Born September 17, 1980, in Brampton, Ont. ... 5-11/185. ... Shoots right.
TRANSACTIONS/CAREER NOTES: Selected by Tampa Bay Lightning in second round (first Lightning pick, 47th overall) of NHL entry draft (June 26, 1999).
HONORS: Won Emms Family Award (1998-99). ... Won Eddie Powers Memorial Trophy (1999-2000). ... Won Jim Mahon Memorial Trophy (1999-2000). ... Named to OHL All-Star second team (1999-2000). ... Named to Can.HL All-Star second team (1999-2000).

Season Team	League	Gms.	G	A	Pts.	PIM	+/-	PP	SH	Gms.	G	A	Pts.	PIM
96-97—Quinte	Tier II Jr. A	44	21	23	44		...	...	...	—	—	—	—	—
97-98—Caledon	Jr. A	51	52	51	103	117	...	...	...	—	—	—	—	—
98-99—Toronto St. Michael's	OHL	38	37	37	74	80	...	...	...	—	—	—	—	—
—Barrie	OHL	28	14	28	42	60	...	...	...	10	5	5	10	31
99-00—Barrie	OHL	66	48	*73	*121	95	...	...	...	25	10	13	23	41

KELLEHER, CHRIS   D   PENGUINS

PERSONAL: Born March 23, 1975, in Cambridge, Mass. ... 6-1/210. ... Shoots left.
HIGH SCHOOL: Belmont (Mass.) Hill, then St. Sebastian's Country Day (Needham, Mass.).
COLLEGE: Boston University.

TRANSACTIONS/CAREER NOTES: Selected by Pittsburgh Penguins in fifth round (fifth Penguins pick, 130th overall) of NHL entry draft (June 26, 1993).
HONORS: Named to NCAA All-America (East) second team (1996-97 and 1997-98). ... Named to Hockey East All-Star second team (1997-98).

		REGULAR SEASON								PLAYOFFS				
Season Team	League	Gms.	G	A	Pts.	PIM	+/-	PP	SH	Gms.	G	A	Pts.	PIM
90-91—Belmont Hill	Mass. H.S.	20	4	23	27	14	...	...	...	—	—	—	—	—
91-92—St. Sebastian's	USHS (East)	28	7	27	34	12	...	...	...	—	—	—	—	—
92-93—St. Sebastian's	USHS (East)	25	8	30	38	16	...	...	...	—	—	—	—	—
93-94—St. Sebastian's	USHS (East)	24	10	21	31	...	...	...	...	—	—	—	—	—
94-95—Boston University	Hockey East	35	3	17	20	62	...	...	...	—	—	—	—	—
95-96—Boston University	Hockey East	37	7	18	25	43	...	...	...	—	—	—	—	—
96-97—Boston University	Hockey East	39	10	24	34	54	...	...	...	—	—	—	—	—
97-98—Boston University	Hockey East	37	4	26	30	40	...	...	...	—	—	—	—	—
98-99—Syracuse	AHL	45	1	4	5	43	...	...	...	—	—	—	—	—
99-00—Wilkes-Barre/Scranton	AHL	67	0	12	12	40	...	...	...	—	—	—	—	—

KELLY, STEVE   C   DEVILS

PERSONAL: Born October 26, 1976, in Vancouver. ... 6-2/211. ... Shoots left.
TRANSACTIONS/CAREER NOTES: Selected by Edmonton Oilers in first round (first Oilers pick, sixth overall) of NHL entry draft (July 8, 1995). ... Traded by Oilers to Tampa Bay Lightning with C Jason Bonsignore and D Bryan Marchment for D Roman Hamrlik and C Paul Comrie (December 30, 1997). ... Suffered from the flu (January 21, 1998); missed two games. ... Suffered from the flu (January 31, 1998); missed one game. ... Suffered concussion (October 10, 1998); missed eight games. ... Traded by Lightning to New Jersey Devils for seventh-round pick (G Brian Eklund) in 2000 draft (October 7, 1999).
MISCELLANEOUS: Member of Stanley Cup championship team (2000).

		REGULAR SEASON								PLAYOFFS				
Season Team	League	Gms.	G	A	Pts.	PIM	+/-	PP	SH	Gms.	G	A	Pts.	PIM
92-93—Prince Albert	WHL	65	11	9	20	75	...	...	...	—	—	—	—	—
93-94—Prince Albert	WHL	65	19	42	61	106	...	...	...	—	—	—	—	—
94-95—Prince Albert	WHL	68	31	41	72	153	...	...	...	15	7	9	16	35
95-96—Prince Albert	WHL	70	27	74	101	203	...	...	...	18	13	18	31	47
96-97—Hamilton	AHL	48	9	29	38	111	...	...	...	11	3	3	6	24
—Edmonton	NHL	8	1	0	1	6	-1	0	0	6	0	0	0	2
97-98—Edmonton	NHL	19	0	2	2	8	-4	0	0	—	—	—	—	—
—Hamilton	AHL	11	2	8	10	18	...	...	...	—	—	—	—	—
—Tampa Bay	NHL	24	2	1	3	15	-9	1	0	—	—	—	—	—
—Milwaukee	IHL	5	0	1	1	19	...	...	...	—	—	—	—	—
—Cleveland	IHL	5	1	1	2	29	...	...	...	1	0	1	1	0
98-99—Tampa Bay	NHL	34	1	3	4	27	-15	0	0	—	—	—	—	—
—Cleveland	IHL	18	6	7	13	36	...	...	...	—	—	—	—	—
99-00—Detroit	IHL	1	0	0	0	4	...	...	...	—	—	—	—	—
—Albany	AHL	76	21	36	57	131	...	...	...	3	1	1	2	2
—New Jersey	NHL	1	0	0	0	0	0	0	0	10	0	0	0	4
NHL Totals (4 years)		86	4	6	10	56	-29	1	0	16	0	0	0	6

KENADY, CHRIS   RW

PERSONAL: Born April 10, 1973, in Mound, Minn. ... 6-2/208. ... Shoots left. ... Name pronounced KEHN-ih-dee.
HIGH SCHOOL: Mound (Minn.) Westonka.
COLLEGE: University of Denver.
TRANSACTIONS/CAREER NOTES: Selected by St. Louis Blues in eighth round (eighth Blues pick, 175th overall) of NHL entry draft (June 22, 1991). ... Traded by Blues to New York Rangers (February 22, 1999), completing deal in which Rangers traded D Jeff Finley and D Geoff Smith to Blues for future considerations (February 13, 1999).

		REGULAR SEASON								PLAYOFFS				
Season Team	League	Gms.	G	A	Pts.	PIM	+/-	PP	SH	Gms.	G	A	Pts.	PIM
90-91—St. Paul's	USHL	45	16	20	36	57	...	...	...	—	—	—	—	—
91-92—Univ. of Denver	WCHA	36	8	5	13	56	...	...	...	—	—	—	—	—
92-93—Univ. of Denver	WCHA	38	8	16	24	95	...	...	...	—	—	—	—	—
93-94—Univ. of Denver	WCHA	37	14	11	25	125	...	...	...	—	—	—	—	—
94-95—Univ. of Denver	WCHA	39	21	17	38	113	...	...	...	—	—	—	—	—
95-96—Worcester	AHL	43	9	10	19	58	...	...	...	2	0	0	0	0
96-97—Worcester	AHL	73	23	26	49	131	...	...	...	5	0	1	1	2
97-98—Worcester	AHL	63	23	22	45	84	...	...	...	11	1	5	6	26
—St. Louis	NHL	5	0	2	2	0	1	0	0	—	—	—	—	—
98-99—Utah	IHL	35	7	6	13	68	...	...	...	—	—	—	—	—
—Long Beach	IHL	19	1	6	7	47	...	...	...	—	—	—	—	—
—Hartford	AHL	22	2	6	8	52	...	...	...	2	0	1	1	6
99-00—Hartford	AHL	71	15	16	31	196	...	...	...	21	8	3	11	40
—New York Rangers	NHL	2	0	0	0	0	-1	0	0	—	—	—	—	—
NHL Totals (2 years)		7	0	2	2	0	0	0	0					

KESA, DAN   RW   LIGHTNING

PERSONAL: Born November 23, 1971, in Vancouver. ... 6-0/215. ... Shoots right. ... Name pronounced KEH-suh.
TRANSACTIONS/CAREER NOTES: Selected by Vancouver Canucks in fifth round (fifth Canucks pick, 95th overall) of NHL entry draft (June 22, 1991). ... Traded by Canucks with LW Greg Adams and fifth-round pick (traded to Los Angeles) in 1995 draft to Dallas Stars for RW Russ Courtnall (April 7, 1995). ... Traded by Stars to Hartford Whalers for C Robert Petrovicky (November 29, 1995). ... Whalers franchise moved

to North Carolina and renamed Carolina Hurricanes for 1997-98 season; NHL approved move on June 25, 1997. ... Suffered from the flu (February 2, 1999); missed two games. ... Strained quadricep (April 13, 1999); missed three games. ... Signed as free agent by Pittsburgh Penguins (August 20, 1998). ... Signed as free agent by Tampa Bay Lightning (September 5, 1999). ... Strained groin (January 24, 2000); missed six games.

MISCELLANEOUS: Failed to score on a penalty shot (vs. Roberto Luongo, January 13, 2000).

Season Team	League	REGULAR SEASON								PLAYOFFS				
		Gms.	G	A	Pts.	PIM	+/-	PP	SH	Gms.	G	A	Pts.	PIM
88-89—Richmond	BCJHL	44	21	21	42	71	...	...	...	—	—	—	—	—
89-90—Richmond	BCJHL	54	39	38	77	103	...	...	...	—	—	—	—	—
90-91—Prince Albert	WHL	69	30	23	53	116	...	...	...	3	1	1	2	0
91-92—Prince Albert	WHL	62	46	51	97	201	...	...	...	10	9	10	19	27
92-93—Hamilton	AHL	62	16	24	40	76	...	...	...	—	—	—	—	—
93-94—Hamilton	AHL	53	37	33	70	33	...	...	...	4	1	4	5	4
—Vancouver	NHL	19	2	4	6	18	-3	1	0	—	—	—	—	—
94-95—Syracuse	AHL	70	34	44	78	81	...	...	...	—	—	—	—	—
95-96—Detroit	IHL	27	9	6	15	22	...	...	...	12	6	4	10	4
—Springfield	AHL	22	10	5	15	13	...	...	...	—	—	—	—	—
—Michigan	IHL	15	4	11	15	33	...	...	...	—	—	—	—	—
—Dallas	NHL	3	0	0	0	0	-1	0	0	—	—	—	—	—
96-97—Detroit	IHL	60	22	21	43	19	...	...	...	20	7	5	12	20
97-98—Detroit	IHL	76	40	37	77	40	...	...	...	20	*13	5	18	14
98-99—Pittsburgh	NHL	67	2	8	10	27	-9	0	0	13	1	0	1	0
—Detroit	IHL	8	3	5	8	12	...	...	...	—	—	—	—	—
99-00—Tampa Bay	NHL	50	4	10	14	21	-11	0	1	—	—	—	—	—
—Detroit	IHL	5	3	0	3	2	...	...	...	—	—	—	—	—
—Manitoba	IHL	1	0	0	0	0	...	...	...	—	—	—	—	—
NHL Totals (4 years)		139	8	22	30	66	-24	1	1	13	1	0	1	0

KHABIBULIN, NIKOLAI — G — COYOTES

PERSONAL: Born January 13, 1973, in Sverdlovsk, U.S.S.R. ... 6-1/195. ... Catches left. ... Name pronounced hah-bee-BOO-lihn.
TRANSACTIONS/CAREER NOTES: Selected by Winnipeg Jets in ninth round (eighth Jets pick, 204th overall) of NHL entry draft (June 20, 1992). ... Sprained knee (November 30, 1995); missed 20 games. ... Jets franchise moved to Phoenix and renamed Coyotes for 1996-97 season; NHL approved move on January 18, 1996. ... Bruised hand (November 6, 1998); missed two games. ... Strained groin (March 2, 1999); missed one game. ... Sat out entire 1999-2000 season due to contract dispute; played with Long Beach of IHL.
HONORS: Played in NHL All-Star Game (1998 and 1999).
MISCELLANEOUS: Holds Phoenix Coyotes franchise all-time records for most shutouts (21) and goals-against average (2.75). ... Stopped a penalty shot attempt (vs. Bob Errey, March 22, 1995; vs. Kevin Stevens, February 26, 1996; vs. Dino Ciccarelli, December 3, 1997). ... Allowed a penalty shot goal (vs. Pavel Bure, January 26, 1998).

Season Team	League	REGULAR SEASON								PLAYOFFS						
		Gms.	Min	W	L	T	GA	SO	Avg.	Gms.	Min.	W	L	GA	SO	Avg.
88-89—Avtomo. Sverdlovsk	USSR	1	3	0	0	0	0	0	...	—	—	—	—	—	—	—
89-90—Avtomo. Sverd. Jr.	USSR						Statistics unavailable.			—	—	—	—	—	—	—
90-91—Sputnik Nizhny Tagil	USSR Dv.III						Statistics unavailable.			—	—	—	—	—	—	—
91-92—CSKA Moscow	CIS	2	34	...	...	...	2		3.53	—	—	—	—	—	—	—
92-93—CSKA Moscow	CIS	13	491	...	...	...	27		3.30	—	—	—	—	—	—	—
93-94—Russian Penguins	IHL	12	639	2	7	‡2	47	0	4.41	—	—	—	—	—	—	—
—CSKA Moscow	CIS	46	2625	...	...	...	116	5	2.65	3	193	1	2	11	0	3.42
94-95—Springfield	AHL	23	1240	9	9	3	80	0	3.87	—	—	—	—	—	—	—
—Winnipeg	NHL	26	1339	8	9	4	76	0	3.41	—	—	—	—	—	—	—
95-96—Winnipeg	NHL	53	2914	26	20	3	152	2	3.13	6	359	2	4	19	0	3.18
96-97—Phoenix	NHL	72	4091	30	33	6	193	7	2.83	7	426	3	4	15	1	2.11
97-98—Phoenix	NHL	70	4026	30	28	10	†184	4	2.74	4	185	2	1	13	0	4.22
98-99—Phoenix	NHL	63	3657	32	23	7	130	8	2.13	7	449	3	4	18	0	2.41
99-00—Long Beach	IHL	33	1936	26	11	‡1	59	5	*1.83	5	321	2	3	15	0	2.80
NHL Totals (5 years)		284	16027	126	113	30	735	21	2.75	24	1419	10	13	65	1	2.75

KHRISTICH, DMITRI — RW — MAPLE LEAFS

PERSONAL: Born July 23, 1969, in Kiev, U.S.S.R. ... 6-2/195. ... Shoots right. ... Name pronounced KHRIHZ-tihch.
TRANSACTIONS/CAREER NOTES: Selected by Washington Capitals in sixth round (sixth Capitals pick, 120th overall) of NHL entry draft (June 11, 1988). ... Injured hip (February 16, 1990); missed six games. ... Fractured foot (October 3, 1992); missed 20 games. ... Traded by Capitals with G Byron Dafoe to Los Angeles Kings for first- (C Alexander Volchkov) and fourth-round (RW Justin Davis) picks in 1996 draft (July 8, 1995). ... Suffered concussion (December 22, 1995); missed three games. ... Sprained right knee (February 23, 1996); missed three games. ... Suffered laceration near right eye (February 7, 1997); missed seven games. ... Traded by Kings with G Byron Dafoe to Boston Bruins for C Jozef Stumpel, RW Sandy Moger and fourth-round pick (traded to New Jersey) in 1998 draft (August 29, 1997). ... Strained shoulder (September 30, 1998); missed first game of season. ... Injured shoulder (March 24, 1999); missed two games. ... Rights traded by Bruins to Toronto Maple Leafs for second-round pick (RW Ivan Huml) in 2000 draft (October 21, 1999). ... Suffered injury (February 12, 2000); missed one game. ... Injured groin (February 16, 2000); missed 12 games. ... Suffered injury (March 23, 2000); missed seven games.
HONORS: Played in NHL All-Star Game (1997 and 1999).
MISCELLANEOUS: Scored on a penalty shot (vs. Darcy Wakaluk, January 7, 1992).
STATISTICAL NOTES: Led NHL with 20.1 shooting percentage (1998-99).
STATISTICAL PLATEAUS: Three-goal games: 1992-93 (2), 1998-99 (1). Total: 3.

Season Team	League	REGULAR SEASON								PLAYOFFS				
		Gms.	G	A	Pts.	PIM	+/-	PP	SH	Gms.	G	A	Pts.	PIM
88-89—Sokol Kiev	USSR	42	17	8	25	15	...	...	...	—	—	—	—	—
89-90—Sokol Kiev	USSR	47	14	22	36	32	...	...	...	—	—	—	—	—
90-91—Sokol Kiev	USSR	28	10	12	22	20	...	...	...	—	—	—	—	—
—Baltimore	AHL	3	0	0	0	0	...	...	...	—	—	—	—	—
—Washington	NHL	40	13	14	27	21	-1	1	0	11	1	3	4	6

K

Season Team	League	Gms.	G	A	Pts.	PIM	+/-	PP	SH	Gms.	G	A	Pts.	PIM
91-92—Washington	NHL	80	36	37	73	35	24	14	1	7	3	2	5	15
92-93—Washington	NHL	64	31	35	66	28	29	9	1	6	2	5	7	2
93-94—Washington	NHL	83	29	29	58	73	-2	10	0	11	2	3	5	10
94-95—Washington	NHL	48	12	14	26	41	0	8	0	7	1	4	5	0
95-96—Los Angeles	NHL	76	27	37	64	44	0	12	0	—	—	—	—	—
96-97—Los Angeles	NHL	75	19	37	56	38	8	3	0	—	—	—	—	—
97-98—Boston	NHL	82	29	37	66	42	25	13	2	6	2	2	4	2
98-99—Boston	NHL	79	29	42	71	48	11	13	1	12	3	4	7	6
99-00—Toronto	NHL	53	12	18	30	24	8	3	0	12	1	2	3	0
NHL Totals (10 years)..........		680	237	300	537	394	102	86	5	72	15	25	40	41

KIDD, TREVOR   G   PANTHERS

PERSONAL: Born March 29, 1972, in Dugald, Man. ... 6-2/190. ... Catches left.

TRANSACTIONS/CAREER NOTES: Selected by Calgary Flames in first round (first Flames pick, 11th overall) of NHL entry draft (June 16, 1990). ... Sprained left ankle (October 18, 1993); missed one game. ... Traded by Flames with LW Gary Roberts to Carolina Hurricanes for G Jean-Sebastien Giguere and C Andrew Cassels (August 25, 1997). ... Strained groin (November 9, 1997); missed seven games. ... Fractured finger on right hand (December 20, 1997); missed seven games. ... Injured groin (April 16, 1998); missed three games. ... Selected by Atlanta Thrashers in NHL expansion draft (June 25, 1999). ... Traded by Thrashers to Florida Panthers for D Gord Murphy, C Herbert Vasiljevs, D Daniel Tjarnqvist and sixth-round pick (traded to Dallas) in 1999 draft (June 25, 1999). ... Separated shoulder (December 13, 1999); missed 29 games.

HONORS: Won Del Wilson Trophy (1989-90). ... Named to WHL (West) All-Star first team (1989-90).

MISCELLANEOUS: Member of silver-medal-winning Canadian Olympic team (1992). ... Holds Calgary Flames all-time record for most shutouts (10). ... Holds Carolina Hurricanes records for most games played by a goaltender (72) and wins (28). ... Stopped a penalty shot attempt (vs. Teemu Selanne, February 6, 1995; vs. Brendan Shanahan, November 5, 1997). ... Allowed a penalty shot goal (vs. Wendel Clark, November 24, 1993; vs. Joe Sakic, January 14, 1996).

Season Team	League	Gms.	Min.	W	L	T	GA	SO	Avg.	Gms.	Min.	W	L	GA	SO	Avg.
88-89—Brandon	WHL	32	1509	11	13	1	102	0	4.06	—	—	—	—	—	—	—
89-90—Brandon	WHL	*63	*3676	24	32	2	254	2	4.15	—	—	—	—	—	—	—
90-91—Brandon	WHL	30	1730	10	19	1	117	0	4.06	—	—	—	—	—	—	—
—Spokane	WHL	14	749	8	3	0	44	0	3.52	15	926	*14	1	32	*2	*2.07
91-92—Canadian nat'l team	Int'l	28	1349	18	4	4	79	2	3.51	—	—	—	—	—	—	—
—Can. Olympic team........	Int'l	1	60	1	0	0	0	1	...	—	—	—	—	—	—	—
—Calgary	NHL	2	120	1	1	0	8	0	4.00	—	—	—	—	—	—	—
92-93—Salt Lake City	IHL	30	1696	10	16	0	111	1	3.93	—	—	—	—	—	—	—
93-94—Calgary	NHL	31	1614	13	7	6	85	0	3.16	—	—	—	—	—	—	—
94-95—Calgary	NHL	†43	2463	22	14	6	107	3	2.61	7	434	3	4	26	1	3.59
95-96—Calgary	NHL	47	2570	15	21	8	119	3	2.78	2	83	0	1	9	0	6.51
96-97—Calgary	NHL	55	2979	21	23	6	141	4	2.84	—	—	—	—	—	—	—
97-98—Carolina	NHL	47	2685	21	21	3	97	3	2.17	—	—	—	—	—	—	—
98-99—Carolina	NHL	25	1358	7	10	6	61	2	2.70	—	—	—	—	—	—	—
99-00—Florida	NHL	28	1574	14	11	2	69	1	2.63	—	—	—	—	—	—	—
—Louisville......................	AHL	1	60	0	1	0	5	0	5.00	—	—	—	—	—	—	—
NHL Totals (8 years)............		278	15363	114	108	37	687	16	2.68	9	517	3	5	35	1	4.06

KILGER, CHAD   C   OILERS

PERSONAL: Born November 27, 1976, in Cornwall, Ont. ... 6-4/215. ... Shoots left. ... Son of Bob Kilger, former NHL referee (1970-71 through 1979-80) and current deputy speaker in House of Commons in Canadian Parliament.

TRANSACTIONS/CAREER NOTES: Selected by Mighty Ducks of Anaheim in first round (first Mighty Ducks pick, fourth overall) of NHL entry draft (July 8, 1995). ... Traded by Mighty Ducks with D Oleg Tverdovsky and third-round pick (D Per-Anton Lundstrom) to Winnipeg Jets for C Marc Chouinard, RW Teemu Selanne and fourth-round pick (traded to Toronto) in 1996 draft (February 7, 1996). ... Suffered from the flu (February 21, 1996); missed one game. ... Jets franchise moved to Phoenix and renamed Coyotes for 1996-97 season; NHL approved move on January 18, 1996. ... Bruised thigh (October 7, 1996); missed one game. ... Traded by Coyotes with D Jayson More to Chicago Blackhawks for D Keith Carney and RW Jim Cummins (March 4, 1998). ... Suffered concussion (February 19, 1999); missed three games. ... Traded by Blackhawks with LW Daniel Cleary, LW Ethan Moreau and D Christian Laflamme to Edmonton Oilers for D Boris Mironov, LW Dean McAmmond and D Jonas Elofsson (March 20, 1999). ... Suffered hip pointer (December 30, 1999); missed five games. ... Suffered hip pointer (February 23, 2000); missed two games.

Season Team	League	Gms.	G	A	Pts.	PIM	+/-	PP	SH	Gms.	G	A	Pts.	PIM
92-93—Cornwall	CJHL	55	30	36	66	26	...	...	...	6	0	0	0	0
93-94—Kingston	OHL	66	17	35	52	23	...	...	...	6	7	2	9	8
94-95—Kingston	OHL	65	42	53	95	95	...	...	...	6	5	2	7	10
95-96—Anaheim	NHL	45	5	7	12	22	-2	0	0	—	—	—	—	—
—Winnipeg	NHL	29	2	3	5	12	-2	0	0	4	1	0	1	0
96-97—Phoenix......................	NHL	24	4	3	7	13	-5	1	0	—	—	—	—	—
—Springfield	AHL	52	17	28	45	36	...	...	...	16	5	7	12	56
97-98—Springfield	AHL	35	14	14	28	33	...	...	...	—	—	—	—	—
—Phoenix......................	NHL	10	0	1	1	4	-2	0	0	—	—	—	—	—
—Chicago.......................	NHL	22	3	8	11	6	2	2	0	—	—	—	—	—
98-99—Chicago......................	NHL	64	14	11	25	30	-1	2	1	—	—	—	—	—
—Edmonton	NHL	13	1	1	2	4	-3	0	0	4	0	0	0	4
99-00—Edmonton	NHL	40	3	2	5	18	-6	0	0	3	0	0	0	0
—Hamilton	AHL	3	3	3	6	0	...	...	...	—	—	—	—	—
NHL Totals (5 years)...........		247	32	36	68	109	-19	5	1	11	1	0	1	4

K

KINCH, MATT   D   SABRES

PERSONAL: Born February 17, 1980, in Red Deer, Alta. ... 5-11/189. ... Shoots left. ... Full Name: Matthew Kinch.
TRANSACTIONS/CAREER NOTES: Selected by Buffalo Sabres in fifth round (eighth Sabres pick, 146th overall) of NHL entry draft (June 26, 1999).
HONORS: Won Brad Hornung Trophy (1998-99). ... Won Can.HL Most Sportsmanlike Player of the Year Award (1998-99). ... Named to WHL (East) All-Star first team (1998-99). ... Named to Can.HL All-Star second team (1998-99). ... Named to WHL (East) All-Star second team (1999-2000).

Season Team	League		REGULAR SEASON								PLAYOFFS			
		Gms.	G	A	Pts.	PIM	+/-	PP	SH	Gms.	G	A	Pts.	PIM
97-98—Calgary	WHL	55	7	24	31	13	...	...	...	18	3	2	5	4
98-99—Calgary	WHL	68	14	69	83	16	...	...	...	21	7	23	30	8
99-00—Calgary	WHL	62	14	61	75	24	...	...	...	13	2	12	14	8

KING, DEREK   LW

PERSONAL: Born February 11, 1967, in Hamilton, Ont. ... 5-11/212. ... Shoots left.
TRANSACTIONS/CAREER NOTES: Selected by New York Islanders as underage junior in first round (second Islanders pick, 13th overall) of NHL entry draft (June 15, 1985). ... Fractured left wrist (December 12, 1987). ... Separated shoulder (November 23, 1988). ... Suffered concussion (November 2, 1990). ... Separated right shoulder (February 14, 1991). ... Bruised hip (November 27, 1992); missed two games. ... Suffered hip pointer (December 26, 1992); missed four games. ... Fractured finger on left hand (April 3, 1993); missed one game. ... Suffered hip pointer (January 8, 1994); missed two games. ... Injured knee (March 9, 1995); missed one game. ... Injured elbow (April 28, 1995); missed two games. ... Injured foot (November 24, 1995); missed one game. ... Fractured jaw and suffered concussion (March 3, 1996); missed remainder of season. ... Traded by Islanders to Hartford Whalers for fifth-round pick (C Adam Edinger) in 1997 draft (March 18, 1997). ... Signed as free agent by Toronto Maple Leafs (July 3, 1997). ... Sprained ankle (October 7, 1997); missed five games. ... Traded by Maple Leafs with conditional eighth-round pick in 2000 draft to St. Louis Blues for D Tyler Harlton and conditional eighth-round pick in 2000 draft (October 20, 1999).
HONORS: Won Emms Family Award (1984-85). ... Named to OHL All-Star first team (1986-87).
MISCELLANEOUS: Scored on a penalty shot (vs. John Vanbiesbrouck, February 7, 1998).
STATISTICAL PLATEAUS: Three-goal games: 1989-90 (1), 1991-92 (2), 1993-94 (1), 1996-97 (1), 1997-98 (1). Total: 6. ... Four-goal games: 1990-91 (1). ... Total hat tricks: 7.

Season Team	League		REGULAR SEASON								PLAYOFFS			
		Gms.	G	A	Pts.	PIM	+/-	PP	SH	Gms.	G	A	Pts.	PIM
83-84—Hamilton Jr. A	OHA	37	10	14	24	142	...	...	...	—	—	—	—	—
84-85—Sault Ste. Marie	OHL	63	35	38	73	106	...	...	...	16	3	13	16	11
85-86—Sault Ste. Marie	OHL	25	12	17	29	33	...	...	...	—	—	—	—	—
—Oshawa	OHL	19	8	13	21	15	...	...	...	6	3	2	5	13
86-87—Oshawa	OHL	57	53	53	106	74	...	...	...	17	14	10	24	40
—New York Islanders	NHL	2	0	0	0	0	0	0	0	—	—	—	—	—
87-88—New York Islanders	NHL	55	12	24	36	30	7	1	0	5	0	2	2	2
—Springfield	AHL	10	7	6	13	6	...	...	...	—	—	—	—	—
88-89—Springfield	AHL	4	4	0	4	0	...	...	...	—	—	—	—	—
—New York Islanders	NHL	60	14	29	43	14	10	4	0	—	—	—	—	—
89-90—Springfield	AHL	21	11	12	23	33	...	...	...	—	—	—	—	—
—New York Islanders	NHL	46	13	27	40	20	2	5	0	4	0	0	0	4
90-91—New York Islanders	NHL	66	19	26	45	44	1	2	0	—	—	—	—	—
91-92—New York Islanders	NHL	80	40	38	78	46	-10	21	0	—	—	—	—	—
92-93—New York Islanders	NHL	77	38	38	76	47	-4	21	0	18	3	11	14	14
93-94—New York Islanders	NHL	78	30	40	70	59	18	10	0	4	0	1	1	0
94-95—New York Islanders	NHL	43	10	16	26	41	-5	7	0	—	—	—	—	—
95-96—New York Islanders	NHL	61	12	20	32	23	-10	5	1	—	—	—	—	—
96-97—New York Islanders	NHL	70	23	30	53	20	-6	5	0	—	—	—	—	—
—Hartford	NHL	12	3	3	6	2	0	1	0	—	—	—	—	—
97-98—Toronto	NHL	77	21	25	46	43	-7	4	0	—	—	—	—	—
98-99—Toronto	NHL	81	24	28	52	20	15	8	0	16	1	3	4	4
99-00—Toronto	NHL	3	0	0	0	2	-2	0	0	—	—	—	—	—
—St. Louis	NHL	19	2	7	9	6	0	1	0	—	—	—	—	—
—Grand Rapids	IHL	52	19	30	49	25	...	...	...	17	7	8	15	8
NHL Totals (14 years)		830	261	351	612	417	9	95	1	47	4	17	21	24

KING, KRIS   LW

PERSONAL: Born February 18, 1966, in Bracebridge, Ont. ... 5-11/205. ... Shoots left.
TRANSACTIONS/CAREER NOTES: Selected by Washington Capitals as underage junior in fourth round (fourth Capitals pick, 80th overall) of NHL entry draft (June 9, 1984). ... Signed as free agent by Detroit Red Wings (June 1987). ... Traded by Red Wings to New York Rangers for LW Chris McRae and fifth-round pick (D Tony Burns) in 1990 draft (September 7, 1989). ... Sprained knee (January 7, 1991); missed six games. ... Traded by Rangers with RW Tie Domi to Winnipeg Jets for C Ed Olczyk (December 28, 1992). ... Suffered abdominal injury (February 13, 1996); missed one game. ... Jets franchise moved to Phoenix and renamed Coyotes for 1996-97 season; NHL approved move on January 18, 1996. ... Signed as free agent by Toronto Maple Leafs (July 7, 1997). ... Fractured hand (December 7, 1998); missed eight games. ... Released by Maple Leafs (June 28, 2000).
HONORS: Won King Clancy Trophy (1995-96).

Season Team	League		REGULAR SEASON								PLAYOFFS			
		Gms.	G	A	Pts.	PIM	+/-	PP	SH	Gms.	G	A	Pts.	PIM
82-83—Gravenhurst	SOJHL	32	72	53	125	115	...	...	...	—	—	—	—	—
83-84—Peterborough	OHL	62	13	18	31	168	...	...	...	8	3	3	6	14
84-85—Peterborough	OHL	61	18	35	53	222	...	...	...	16	2	8	10	28
85-86—Peterborough	OHL	58	19	40	59	254	...	...	...	8	4	0	4	21

K

Season Team	League	REGULAR SEASON								PLAYOFFS				
		Gms.	G	A	Pts.	PIM	+/-	PP	SH	Gms.	G	A	Pts.	PIM
86-87—Peterborough..............	OHL	46	23	33	56	160	...	...	...	12	5	8	13	41
—Binghamton	AHL	7	0	0	0	18	...	...	...	—	—	—	—	—
87-88—Adirondack	AHL	78	21	32	53	337	...	...	...	10	4	4	8	53
—Detroit.........................	NHL	3	1	0	1	2	1	0	0	—	—	—	—	—
88-89—Detroit.....................	NHL	55	2	3	5	168	-7	0	0	2	0	0	0	2
89-90—New York Rangers	NHL	68	6	7	13	286	2	0	0	10	0	1	1	38
90-91—New York Rangers	NHL	72	11	14	25	154	-1	0	0	6	2	0	2	36
91-92—New York Rangers	NHL	79	10	9	19	224	13	0	0	13	4	1	5	14
92-93—New York Rangers	NHL	30	0	3	3	67	-1	0	0	—	—	—	—	—
—Winnipeg	NHL	48	8	8	16	136	5	0	0	6	1	1	2	4
93-94—Winnipeg	NHL	83	4	8	12	205	-22	0	0	—	—	—	—	—
94-95—Winnipeg	NHL	48	4	2	6	85	0	0	0	—	—	—	—	—
95-96—Winnipeg	NHL	81	9	11	20	151	-7	0	1	5	0	1	1	4
96-97—Phoenix....................	NHL	81	3	11	14	185	-7	0	0	7	0	0	0	17
97-98—Toronto....................	NHL	82	3	3	6	199	-13	0	0	—	—	—	—	—
98-99—Toronto....................	NHL	67	2	2	4	105	-16	0	1	17	1	1	2	25
99-00—Toronto....................	NHL	39	2	4	6	55	4	0	0	1	0	0	0	2
—Chicago......................	IHL	15	2	4	6	19	...	...	...	—	—	—	—	—
NHL Totals (13 years)..........		836	65	85	150	2022	-49	0	2	67	8	5	13	142

KINNEAR, GEORDIE — D — THRASHERS

PERSONAL: Born July 9, 1973, in Simcoe, Ont. ... 6-1/195. ... Shoots left. ... Name pronounced JOHR-dee kuh-NEER.
TRANSACTIONS/CAREER NOTES: Selected by New Jersey Devils in seventh round (seventh Devils pick, 162nd overall) of NHL entry draft (June 20, 1992). ... Signed as free agent by Atlanta Thrashers (August 12, 1999).

Season Team	League	REGULAR SEASON								PLAYOFFS				
		Gms.	G	A	Pts.	PIM	+/-	PP	SH	Gms.	G	A	Pts.	PIM
90-91—Peterborough..............	Jr. B	6	0	6	6	51	...	...	...	—	—	—	—	—
—Peterborough..............	OHL	37	1	0	1	76	...	...	...	2	0	0	0	10
91-92—Peterborough..............	OHL	63	5	16	21	195	...	...	...	10	0	2	2	36
92-93—Peterborough..............	OHL	58	6	22	28	161	...	...	...	19	1	5	6	43
93-94—Albany........................	AHL	59	3	12	15	197	...	...	...	5	0	0	0	21
94-95—Albany........................	AHL	68	5	11	16	136	...	...	...	9	1	1	2	7
95-96—Albany........................	AHL	73	4	7	11	170	...	...	...	4	0	1	1	2
96-97—Albany........................	AHL	59	2	9	11	175	...	...	...	10	0	1	1	15
97-98—Albany........................	AHL	78	1	15	16	206	...	...	...	13	1	1	2	68
98-99—Albany........................	AHL	55	1	13	14	162	...	...	...	5	0	1	1	0
99-00—Orlando......................	IHL	69	1	5	6	231	...	...	...	6	0	0	0	9
—Atlanta	NHL	4	0	0	0	13	-1	0	0	—	—	—	—	—
NHL Totals (1 year)............		4	0	0	0	13	-1	0	0	—	—	—	—	—

KIPRUSOFF, MIIKKA — G — SHARKS

PERSONAL: Born October 26, 1976, in Turku, Finland. ... 6-2/190. ... Catches left. ... Brother of Marko Kiprusoff, defenseman, Montreal Canadiens system.
TRANSACTIONS/CAREER NOTES: Selected by San Jose Sharks in fifth round (fifth Sharks pick, 115th overall) of NHL entry draft (July 8, 1995).

Season Team	League	REGULAR SEASON								PLAYOFFS						
		Gms.	Min	W	L	T	GA	SO	Avg.	Gms.	Min.	W	L	GA	SO	Avg.
93-94—TPS Turku Jr.	Finland	35	...	...	...	...	...	...	...	6	...	...	...	...	...	...
94-95—TPS Turku Jr.	Finland	31	1880	...	...	...	93	...	2.97	—	—	—	—	—	—	—
—TPS Turku	Finland	4	240	...	...	...	12	0	3.00	2	120	...	...	7	...	3.50
95-96—TPS Turku	Finland	12	550	...	...	...	38	...	4.15	—	—	—	—	—	—	—
—Kiekko	Finland	5	300	...	...	...	7	...	1.40	—	—	—	—	—	—	—
96-97—AIK	Sweden	42	2466	...	...	...	104	3	2.53	7	420	...	...	23	0	3.29
97-98—AIK Solna	Sweden	42	2457	...	...	...	110	...	2.69	—	—	—	—	—	—	—
98-99—TPS Turku	Finland	39	2259	*26	6	6	70	4	1.86	10	580	*9	1	15	*3	*1.55
99-00—Kentucky	AHL	47	2759	23	19	4	114	3	2.48	5	239	1	3	13	0	3.26

KJELLBERG, PATRIC — LW — PREDATORS

PERSONAL: Born June 17, 1969, in Trelleborg, Sweden. ... 6-2/208. ... Shoots left.
TRANSACTIONS/CAREER NOTES: Selected by Montreal Canadiens in fourth round (fourth Canadiens pick, 83rd overall) of NHL entry draft (June 11, 1988). ... Signed as free agent by Nashville Predators (June 26, 1998). ... Bruised hip (March 28, 1999); missed final nine games of season.
MISCELLANEOUS: Member of gold-medal-winning Swedish Olympic team (1994).

Season Team	League	REGULAR SEASON								PLAYOFFS				
		Gms.	G	A	Pts.	PIM	+/-	PP	SH	Gms.	G	A	Pts.	PIM
86-87—Falun.........................	Sweden	27	11	13	24	14	...	...	...	—	—	—	—	—
87-88—Falun.........................	Sweden	29	15	10	25	18	...	...	...	—	—	—	—	—
88-89—AIK Solna...................	Sweden	25	7	9	16	8	...	...	...	—	—	—	—	—
89-90—AIK Solna...................	Sweden	33	8	16	24	6	...	...	...	3	1	0	1	0
90-91—AIK Solna...................	Sweden	38	4	11	15	18	...	...	...	—	—	—	—	—
91-92—AIK Solna...................	Sweden	40	20	13	33	16	...	...	...	—	—	—	—	—
—Swedish Oly. team	Int'l	8	1	3	4	0	...	...	...	—	—	—	—	—

K

		REGULAR SEASON								PLAYOFFS				
Season Team	League	Gms.	G	A	Pts.	PIM	+/-	PP	SH	Gms.	G	A	Pts.	PIM
92-93—Montreal	NHL	7	0	0	0	2	-3	0	0	—	—	—	—	—
—Fredericton	AHL	41	10	27	37	14	...	...	...	5	2	2	4	0
93-94—HV 71 Jonkoping	Sweden	40	11	17	28	18	...	...	...	—	—	—	—	—
—Swedish Oly. team	Int'l	8	0	1	1	2	...	...	...	—	—	—	—	—
94-95—HV 71 Jonkoping	Sweden	29	5	15	20	12	...	...	...	—	—	—	—	—
95-96—Djurgarden Stockholm	Sweden	40	9	7	16	10	...	...	...	4	0	2	2	2
96-97—Djurgarden Stockholm	Sweden	49	29	11	40	18	...	...	...	4	2	3	5	2
97-98—Swedish Oly. team	Int'l	4	1	0	1	0	...	...	...	—	—	—	—	—
—Djurgarden Stockholm	Sweden	46	30	18	48	16	...	...	...	15	7	3	10	12
98-99—Nashville	NHL	71	11	20	31	24	-13	2	0	—	—	—	—	—
99-00—Nashville	NHL	82	23	23	46	14	-11	9	0	—	—	—	—	—
NHL Totals (3 years)		160	34	43	77	40	-27	11	0					

KLATT, TRENT — RW — CANUCKS

PERSONAL: Born January 30, 1971, in Minneapolis. ... 6-1/210. ... Shoots right. ... Full Name: Trent Thomas Klatt. ... Name pronounced KLAT.
HIGH SCHOOL: Osseo (Minn.).
COLLEGE: Minnesota.
TRANSACTIONS/CAREER NOTES: Selected by Washington Capitals in fourth round (fifth Capitals pick, 82nd overall) of NHL entry draft (June 17, 1989). ... Rights traded by Capitals with LW Steve Maltais to Minnesota North Stars for D Sean Chambers (June 21, 1991). ... Injured finger (January 7, 1993); missed three games. ... North Stars franchise moved from Minnesota to Dallas and renamed Stars for 1993-94 season. ... Strained back (November 7, 1993); missed one game. ... Sprained knee (November 11, 1993); missed two games. ... Sprained knee (February 6, 1994); missed three games. ... Traded by Stars to Philadelphia Flyers for LW Brent Fedyk (December 13, 1995). ... Suffered concussion (March 9, 1997); missed two games. ... Traded by Flyers to Vancouver Canucks for sixth-round pick (traded to Atlanta) in 2000 draft (October 19, 1998).
MISCELLANEOUS: Failed to score on a penalty shot (vs. John Vanbiesbrouck, October 1, 1997).
STATISTICAL PLATEAUS: Three-goal games: 1996-97 (1).

		REGULAR SEASON								PLAYOFFS				
Season Team	League	Gms.	G	A	Pts.	PIM	+/-	PP	SH	Gms.	G	A	Pts.	PIM
87-88—Osseo H.S.	Minn. H.S.	22	19	17	36	...	...	...	...	—	—	—	—	—
88-89—Osseo H.S.	Minn. H.S.	22	24	39	63	...	...	...	...	—	—	—	—	—
89-90—Univ. of Minnesota	WCHA	38	22	14	36	16	...	...	...	—	—	—	—	—
90-91—Univ. of Minnesota	WCHA	39	16	28	44	58	...	...	...	—	—	—	—	—
91-92—Univ. of Minnesota	WCHA	44	30	36	66	78	...	...	...	—	—	—	—	—
—Minnesota	NHL	1	0	0	0	0	0	0	0	6	0	0	0	2
92-93—Kalamazoo	IHL	31	8	11	19	18	...	...	...	—	—	—	—	—
—Minnesota	NHL	47	4	19	23	38	2	1	0	—	—	—	—	—
93-94—Dallas	NHL	61	14	24	38	30	13	3	0	9	2	1	3	4
—Kalamazoo	IHL	6	3	2	5	4	...	...	...	—	—	—	—	—
94-95—Dallas	NHL	47	12	10	22	26	-2	5	0	5	1	0	1	0
95-96—Dallas	NHL	22	4	4	8	23	0	0	0	—	—	—	—	—
—Michigan	IHL	2	1	2	3	5	...	...	...	—	—	—	—	—
—Philadelphia	NHL	49	3	8	11	21	2	0	0	12	4	1	5	0
96-97—Philadelphia	NHL	76	24	21	45	20	9	5	5	19	4	3	7	12
97-98—Philadelphia	NHL	82	14	28	42	16	2	5	0	5	0	0	0	0
98-99—Philadelphia	NHL	2	0	0	0	0	0	0	0	—	—	—	—	—
—Vancouver	NHL	73	4	10	14	12	-3	0	0	—	—	—	—	—
99-00—Syracuse	AHL	24	13	10	23	6	...	...	...	—	—	—	—	—
—Vancouver	NHL	47	10	10	20	26	-8	8	0	—	—	—	—	—
NHL Totals (9 years)		507	89	134	223	212	15	27	5	56	11	5	16	18

KLEE, KEN — D/RW — CAPITALS

PERSONAL: Born April 24, 1971, in Indianapolis. ... 6-1/211. ... Shoots right. ... Full Name: Kenneth William Klee.
HIGH SCHOOL: Rockhurst (Kansas City, Mo.).
COLLEGE: St. Michael's College (Vt.), then Bowling Green State.
TRANSACTIONS/CAREER NOTES: Selected by Washington Capitals in ninth round (11th Capitals pick, 177th overall) of NHL entry draft (June 16, 1990). ... Injured foot (January 27, 1995); missed six games. ... Pulled groin (March 12, 1996); missed 13 games. ... Sprained knee (April 10, 1996); missed two games. ... Fractured facial bone (March 28, 1998); missed eight games. ... Bruised foot (February 12, 2000); missed one game.
MISCELLANEOUS: Failed to score on penalty shot (vs. Mike Richter, March 12, 1997).

		REGULAR SEASON								PLAYOFFS				
Season Team	League	Gms.	G	A	Pts.	PIM	+/-	PP	SH	Gms.	G	A	Pts.	PIM
89-90—Bowling Green	CCHA	39	0	5	5	52	...	...	...	—	—	—	—	—
90-91—Bowling Green	CCHA	37	7	28	35	50	...	...	...	—	—	—	—	—
91-92—Bowling Green	CCHA	10	0	1	1	14	...	...	...	—	—	—	—	—
92-93—Baltimore	AHL	77	4	14	18	68	...	...	...	7	0	1	1	15
93-94—Portland	AHL	65	2	9	11	87	...	...	...	17	1	2	3	14
94-95—Portland	AHL	49	5	7	12	89	...	...	...	—	—	—	—	—
—Washington	NHL	23	3	1	4	41	2	0	0	7	0	0	0	4
95-96—Washington	NHL	66	8	3	11	60	-1	0	1	1	0	0	0	0
96-97—Washington	NHL	80	3	8	11	115	-5	0	0	—	—	—	—	—
97-98—Washington	NHL	51	4	2	6	46	-3	0	0	9	1	0	1	10
98-99—Washington	NHL	78	7	13	20	80	-9	0	0	—	—	—	—	—
99-00—Washington	NHL	80	7	13	20	79	8	0	0	5	0	1	1	10
NHL Totals (6 years)		378	32	40	72	421	-8	0	1	22	1	1	2	24

K

KLEMM, JON   D   AVALANCHE

PERSONAL: Born January 8, 1970, in Cranbrook, B.C. ... 6-3/200. ... Shoots right. ... Full Name: Jonathan Darryl Klemm.
TRANSACTIONS/CAREER NOTES: Signed as non-drafted free agent by Quebec Nordiques (May 14, 1991). ... Injured abdomen (March 28, 1995); missed five games. ... Reinjured abdomen (April 8, 1995); missed remainder of season. ... Nordiques franchise moved to Colorado and renamed Avalanche for 1995-96 season (June 21, 1995). ... Injured groin (January 27, 1996); missed one game. ... Sprained left thumb (October 30, 1997) and underwent surgery; missed 11 games. ... Strained groin (December 27, 1997); missed one game. ... Tore patella tendon in knee (November 15, 1998); missed 29 games. ... Suffered from appendicitis (March 25, 1999); missed six games. ... Injured groin (October 20, 1999); missed seven games. ... Suffered back spasms (February 25, 2000); missed one game.
HONORS: Named to WHL (West) All-Star second team (1990-91).
MISCELLANEOUS: Member of Stanley Cup championship team (1996).

Season Team	League	REGULAR SEASON Gms.	G	A	Pts.	PIM	+/-	PP	SH	PLAYOFFS Gms.	G	A	Pts.	PIM
87-88—Seattle	WHL	68	6	7	13	24	...	...	...	—	—	—	—	—
88-89—Seattle	WHL	2	1	1	2	0	...	...	...	—	—	—	—	—
—Spokane	WHL	66	6	34	40	42	...	...	...	—	—	—	—	—
89-90—Spokane	WHL	66	3	28	31	100	...	...	...	6	1	1	2	5
90-91—Spokane	WHL	72	7	58	65	65	...	...	...	15	3	6	9	8
91-92—Halifax	AHL	70	6	13	19	40	...	...	...	—	—	—	—	—
—Quebec	NHL	4	0	1	1	0	2	0	0	—	—	—	—	—
92-93—Halifax	AHL	80	3	20	23	32	...	...	...	—	—	—	—	—
93-94—Cornwall	AHL	66	4	26	30	78	...	...	...	13	1	2	3	6
—Quebec	NHL	7	0	0	0	4	-1	0	0	—	—	—	—	—
94-95—Cornwall	AHL	65	6	13	19	84	...	...	...	—	—	—	—	—
—Quebec	NHL	4	1	0	1	2	3	0	0	—	—	—	—	—
95-96—Colorado	NHL	56	3	12	15	20	12	0	1	15	2	1	3	0
96-97—Colorado	NHL	80	9	15	24	37	12	1	2	17	1	1	2	6
97-98—Colorado	NHL	67	6	8	14	30	-3	0	0	4	0	0	0	0
98-99—Colorado	NHL	39	1	2	3	31	4	0	0	19	0	1	1	10
99-00—Colorado	NHL	73	5	7	12	34	26	0	0	17	2	1	3	9
NHL Totals (8 years)		330	25	45	70	158	55	1	3	72	5	4	9	25

KLOUCEK, TOMAS   D   RANGERS

PERSONAL: Born March 7, 1980, in Prague, Czechoslovakia. ... 6-3/203. ... Shoots left.
TRANSACTIONS/CAREER NOTES: Selected by New York Rangers in fifth round (sixth Rangers pick, 131st overall) of NHL entry draft (June 27, 1998).

Season Team	League	REGULAR SEASON Gms.	G	A	Pts.	PIM	+/-	PP	SH	PLAYOFFS Gms.	G	A	Pts.	PIM
95-96—Slavia Praha Jrs.	Czech Rep.	40	2	8	10	...	...	...	...	—	—	—	—	—
96-97—Slavia Praha Jrs.	Czech Rep.	43	4	14	18	44	...	...	...	—	—	—	—	—
97-98—Slavia Praha Jrs.	Czech Rep.	43	1	9	10	...	...	...	...	—	—	—	—	—
98-99—Cape Breton	QMJHL	59	4	17	21	162	...	...	...	2	0	0	0	4
99-00—Hartford	AHL	73	2	8	10	113	...	...	...	23	0	4	4	18

KNUBLE, MIKE   LW   BRUINS

PERSONAL: Born July 4, 1972, in Toronto. ... 6-3/222. ... Shoots right. ... Full Name: Michael Knuble. ... Name pronounced kuh-NOO-buhl.
HIGH SCHOOL: East Kentwood (Mich.).
COLLEGE: Michigan.
TRANSACTIONS/CAREER NOTES: Selected by Detroit Red Wings in fourth round (fourth Red Wings pick, 76th overall) of NHL entry draft (June 22, 1991). ... Traded by Red Wings to New York Rangers for third-round pick (traded back to New York Rangers) in 2000 draft (October 1, 1998). ... Traded by Rangers to Boston Bruins for LW Rob DiMaio (March 10, 2000).
HONORS: Named to CCHA All-Star second team (1993-94 and 1994-95). ... Named to NCAA All-America (West) second team (1994-95).
MISCELLANEOUS: Member of Stanley Cup championship team (1998).

Season Team	League	REGULAR SEASON Gms.	G	A	Pts.	PIM	+/-	PP	SH	PLAYOFFS Gms.	G	A	Pts.	PIM
88-89—East Kentwood H.S.	Mich. H.S.	28	52	37	89	60	...	...	...	—	—	—	—	—
89-90—East Kentwood H.S.	Mich. H.S.	29	63	40	103	40	...	...	...	—	—	—	—	—
90-91—Kalamazoo	NAJHL	36	18	24	42	30	...	...	...	—	—	—	—	—
91-92—Univ. of Michigan	CCHA	43	7	8	15	48	...	...	...	—	—	—	—	—
92-93—Univ. of Michigan	CCHA	39	26	16	42	57	...	...	...	—	—	—	—	—
93-94—Univ. of Michigan	CCHA	41	32	26	58	71	...	...	...	—	—	—	—	—
94-95—Univ. of Michigan	CCHA	34	38	22	60	62	...	...	...	—	—	—	—	—
95-96—Adirondack	AHL	80	22	23	45	59	...	...	...	3	1	0	1	0
96-97—Adirondack	AHL	68	28	35	63	54	...	...	...	—	—	—	—	—
—Detroit	NHL	9	1	0	1	0	-1	0	0	—	—	—	—	—
97-98—Detroit	NHL	53	7	6	13	16	2	0	0	3	0	1	1	0
98-99—New York Rangers	NHL	82	15	20	35	26	-7	3	0	—	—	—	—	—
99-00—New York Rangers	NHL	59	9	5	14	18	-5	1	0	—	—	—	—	—
—Boston	NHL	14	3	3	6	8	-2	1	0	—	—	—	—	—
NHL Totals (4 years)		217	35	34	69	68	-13	5	0	3	0	1	1	0

K

KNUTSEN, ESPEN   C   BLUE JACKETS

PERSONAL: Born January 12, 1972, in Oslo, Norway. ... 5-11/180. ... Shoots left. ... Name pronounced kuh-NOOT-sihn.
TRANSACTIONS/CAREER NOTES: Selected by Hartford Whalers in 10th round (ninth Whalers pick, 204th overall) of NHL entry draft (June 16, 1990). ... Rights traded by Whalers to Mighty Ducks of Anaheim for RW Kevin Brown (October 1, 1996). ... Traded by Mighty Ducks to Columbus Blue Jackets for fourth-round pick in 2001 draft (May 25, 2000).

			REGULAR SEASON							**PLAYOFFS**				
Season Team	League	Gms.	G	A	Pts.	PIM	+/-	PP	SH	Gms.	G	A	Pts.	PIM
89-90—Valerengen	Knutsen	34	22	26	48	...	...	...	...	—	—	—	—	—
90-91—Valerengen	Knutsen	31	30	24	54	42	...	...	...	5	3	4	7	...
91-92—Valerengen	Knutsen	30	28	26	54	37	...	...	...	8	7	8	15	15
92-93—Valerengen	Knutsen	13	11	13	24	4	...	...	...	—	—	—	—	—
93-94—Valerengen	Knutsen	38	32	26	58	20	...	...	...	—	—	—	—	—
94-95—Djurgarden Stockholm	Sweden	30	6	14	20	18	...	...	...	3	0	1	1	0
95-96—Djurgarden Stockholm	Sweden	32	10	23	33	50	...	...	...	4	1	0	1	2
96-97—Djurgarden Stockholm	Sweden	39	16	33	49	20	...	...	...	4	2	4	6	6
97-98—Anaheim	NHL	19	3	0	3	6	-10	1	0	—	—	—	—	—
—Cincinnati	AHL	41	4	13	17	18	...	...	...	—	—	—	—	—
98-99—Djurgarden Stockholm	Sweden	39	18	24	42	32	...	...	...	4	0	1	1	2
99-00—Djurgarden Stockholm	Sweden	48	18	35	53	65	...	...	...	13	5	*16	*21	2
NHL Totals (1 year)		19	3	0	3	6	-10	1	0					

K

KOCHAN, DIETER   G   LIGHTNING

PERSONAL: Born November 5, 1974, in Saskatoon, Sask. ... 6-1/165. ... Catches left.
HIGH SCHOOL: North (Sioux City, Iowa).
COLLEGE: Northern Michigan.
TRANSACTIONS/CAREER NOTES: Selected by Vancouver Canucks in fourth round (third Canucks pick, 98th overall) of NHL entry draft (June 26, 1993). ... Signed as free agent by Tampa Bay Lightning (March 27, 2000).
HONORS: Named to UHL All-Star second team (1999-2000).

			REGULAR SEASON								**PLAYOFFS**					
Season Team	League	Gms.	Min	W	L	T	GA	SO	Avg.	Gms.	Min.	W	L	GA	SO	Avg.
91-92—Sioux City	USHL	23	1131	7	10	0	100	...	5.31	—	—	—	—	—	—	—
92-93—Kelowna	BCJHL	44	2582	34	8	0	137	1	*3.18	—	—	—	—	—	—	—
93-94—N. Michigan U.	WCHA	16	984	9	7	0	57	2	3.48	—	—	—	—	—	—	—
94-95—N. Michigan U.	WCHA	29	1512	8	17	3	107	0	4.25	—	—	—	—	—	—	—
95-96—N. Michigan U.	WCHA	31	1627	7	21	2	123	0	4.54	—	—	—	—	—	—	—
96-97—N. Michigan U.	WCHA	26	1528	8	15	2	99	0	3.89	—	—	—	—	—	—	—
97-98—Louisville Riverfrogs	ECHL	18	980	7	9	‡2	61	1	3.73	—	—	—	—	—	—	—
98-99—Binghamton	UHL	40	2321	18	16	‡5	115	2	2.97	4	207	1	2	9	0	2.61
99-00—Binghamton	UHL	43	2544	29	11	‡3	110	4	2.59	—	—	—	—	—	—	—
—Orlando	IHL	4	240	4	0	0	4	1	1.00	—	—	—	—	—	—	—
—Grand Rapids	IHL	2	93	1	0	‡1	1	0	.65	—	—	—	—	—	—	—
—Springfield	AHL	2	120	1	1	0	5	1	2.50	—	—	—	—	—	—	—
—Tampa Bay	NHL	5	238	1	4	0	17	0	4.29	—	—	—	—	—	—	—
NHL Totals (1 year)		5	238	1	4	0	17	0	4.29							

KOHN, LADISLAV   RW   MIGHTY DUCKS

PERSONAL: Born March 4, 1975, in Uherske Hrada, Czechoslovakia. ... 5-10/172. ... Shoots left. ... Name pronounced KOHN.
TRANSACTIONS/CAREER NOTES: Selected by Calgary Flames in seventh round (ninth Flames pick, 175th overall) in NHL entry draft (June 29, 1994). ... Suffered concussion (November 26, 1997); missed 12 games. ... Traded by Flames to Toronto Maple Leafs for D David Cooper (July 2, 1998). ... Claimed by Atlanta Thrashers from Maple Leafs in NHL waiver draft (September 27, 1999). ... Traded by Thrashers to Mighty Ducks of Anaheim for eighth-round pick (D Evan Nielsen) in 2000 draft (September 27, 1999). ... Strained groin (November 26, 1999); missed five games.

			REGULAR SEASON							**PLAYOFFS**				
Season Team	League	Gms.	G	A	Pts.	PIM	+/-	PP	SH	Gms.	G	A	Pts.	PIM
93-94—Brandon	WHL	2	0	0	0	0	...	...	...	—	—	—	—	—
—Swift Current	WHL	69	33	35	68	68	...	...	...	7	5	4	9	8
94-95—Swift Current	WHL	65	32	60	92	122	...	...	...	6	2	6	8	14
—Saint John	AHL	1	0	0	0	0	...	...	...	—	—	—	—	—
95-96—Saint John	AHL	73	28	45	73	97	...	...	...	16	6	5	11	12
—Calgary	NHL	5	1	0	1	2	-1	0	0	—	—	—	—	—
96-97—Saint John	AHL	76	28	29	57	81	...	...	...	5	0	0	0	0
97-98—Saint John	AHL	65	25	31	56	90	...	...	...	21	*14	6	20	20
—Calgary	NHL	4	0	1	1	0	2	0	0	—	—	—	—	—
98-99—St. John's	AHL	61	27	42	69	90	...	...	...	—	—	—	—	—
—Toronto	NHL	16	1	3	4	4	1	0	0	2	0	0	0	5
99-00—Anaheim	NHL	77	5	16	21	27	-17	1	0	—	—	—	—	—
NHL Totals (4 years)		102	7	20	27	33	-15	1	0	2	0	0	0	5

KOIVU, SAKU   C   CANADIENS

PERSONAL: Born November 23, 1974, in Turku, Finland. ... 5-10/181. ... Shoots left. ... Name pronounced SAK-oo KOY-voo.
TRANSACTIONS/CAREER NOTES: Selected by Montreal Canadiens in first round (first Canadiens pick, 21st overall) of NHL entry draft (June 26, 1993). ... Tore knee ligament (December 7, 1996); missed 26 games. ... Sprained shoulder (March 10, 1997); missed five games. ...

Suffered from tonsillitis (March 29, 1997); missed one game. ... Strained ribcage (January 8, 1998); missed seven games. ... Fractured hand (April 7, 1998); missed six games. ... Strained abdominal muscle (October 24, 1998); missed 12 games. ... Suffered from elbow infection (January 18, 1999); missed three games. ... Injured knee (March 24, 1999); missed two games. ... Suffered injury (October 30, 1999); missed five games. ... Separated shoulder (November 2, 1999); missed 40 games. ... Tore medial collateral ligament in knee (March 11, 2000); missed remainder of season.

HONORS: Played in NHL All-Star Game (1998).

MISCELLANEOUS: Captain of Montreal Canadiens (1999-2000). ... Member of bronze-medal-winning Finnish Olympic team (1994 and 1998).

Season Team	League	REGULAR SEASON								PLAYOFFS				
		Gms.	G	A	Pts.	PIM	+/-	PP	SH	Gms.	G	A	Pts.	PIM
91-92—TPS Turku Jr.	Finland	42	30	37	67	63	...	...	...	—	—	—	—	—
92-93—TPS Turku	Finland	46	3	7	10	28	...	...	...	—	—	—	—	—
93-94—TPS Turku	Finland	47	23	30	53	42	...	...	...	11	4	8	12	16
—Fin. Olympic team	Int'l	8	4	3	7	12	...	...	...	—	—	—	—	—
94-95—TPS Turku	Finland	45	27	47	74	73	...	...	...	13	7	10	17	16
95-96—Montreal	NHL	82	20	25	45	40	-7	8	3	6	3	1	4	8
96-97—Montreal	NHL	50	17	39	56	38	7	5	0	5	1	3	4	10
97-98—Montreal	NHL	69	14	43	57	48	8	2	2	6	2	3	5	2
—Fin. Olympic team	Int'l	6	2	8	10	4	...	...	...	—	—	—	—	—
98-99—Montreal	NHL	65	14	30	44	38	-7	4	2	—	—	—	—	—
99-00—Montreal	NHL	24	3	18	21	14	7	1	0	—	—	—	—	—
NHL Totals (5 years)		290	68	155	223	178	8	20	7	17	6	7	13	20

KOLKUNOV, ALEXEI   C   PENGUINS

PERSONAL: Born February 3, 1977, in Belgorod, U.S.S.R. ... 6-0/201. ... Shoots left.

TRANSACTIONS/CAREER NOTES: Selected by Pittsburgh Penguins in sixth round (fifth Penguins pick, 154th overall) of NHL entry draft (July 8, 1995).

Season Team	League	REGULAR SEASON								PLAYOFFS				
		Gms.	G	A	Pts.	PIM	+/-	PP	SH	Gms.	G	A	Pts.	PIM
94-95—Krylja Sov. Moscow	CIS	44	9	16	25	36	...	...	...	2	0	0	0	4
—Soviet Wings	CIS	7	0	0	0	0	...	...	...	4	1	0	1	0
95-96—Soviet Wings	CIS	43	9	3	12	35	...	...	...	—	—	—	—	—
96-97—Kryla Sov. Moscow	Russian	44	9	16	25	36	...	...	...	2	0	0	0	4
97-98—Kryla Sov. Moscow	Russian	20	6	4	10	22	...	...	...	—	—	—	—	—
98-99—Syracuse	AHL	55	5	13	18	20	...	...	...	—	—	—	—	—
99-00—Wilkes-Barre/Scranton	AHL	75	12	25	37	33	...	...	...	—	—	—	—	—

KOLNIK, JURAJ   RW   ISLANDERS

PERSONAL: Born November 13, 1980, in Nitra, Czechoslovakia. ... 5-10/182. ... Shoots right.

TRANSACTIONS/CAREER NOTES: Selected by New York Islanders in fourth round (seventh Islanders pick, 101st overall) of NHL entry draft (June 26, 1999).

Season Team	League	REGULAR SEASON								PLAYOFFS				
		Gms.	G	A	Pts.	PIM	+/-	PP	SH	Gms.	G	A	Pts.	PIM
97-98—Plastika Nitra	Slovakia	28	1	3	4	6	...	...	...	—	—	—	—	—
98-99—Quebec	QMJHL	12	6	5	11	6	...	...	...	—	—	—	—	—
—Rimouski	QMJHL	50	36	37	73	34	...	...	...	11	9	6	15	6
99-00—Rimouski	QMJHL	47	53	53	106	53	...	...	...	14	10	17	27	16

KOLZIG, OLAF   G   CAPITALS

PERSONAL: Born April 6, 1970, in Johannesburg, South Africa. ... 6-3/226. ... Catches left. ... Name pronounced OH-lahf KOHL-zihg.

TRANSACTIONS/CAREER NOTES: Selected by Washington Capitals in first round (first Capitals pick, 19th overall) of NHL entry draft (June 17, 1989). ... Dislocated kneecap (October 13, 1993); missed 14 games. ... Suffered from mononucleosis (October 8, 1996); missed three games.

HONORS: Shared Harry (Hap) Holmes Memorial Trophy with Byron Dafoe (1993-94). ... Won Jack Butterfield Trophy (1993-94). ... Played in NHL All-Star Game (1998 and 2000). ... Named to NHL All-Star first team (1999-2000). ... Won Vezina Trophy (1999-2000).

RECORDS: Shares NHL single-season playoff record for most shutouts—4 (1998).

MISCELLANEOUS: Stopped a penalty shot attempt (vs. Mike Hough, February 29, 1996; vs. Todd Marchant, January 26, 1997; vs. Sergei Nemchinov, March 11, 2000). ... Allowed a penalty shot goal (vs. Viktor Kozlov, February 23, 2000).

Season Team	League	REGULAR SEASON							PLAYOFFS					
		Gms.	Min	W	L	T	GA	SO	Avg.	Gms.	Min.	W	L	GA	SO	Avg.
87-88—New Westminster	WHL	15	650	6	5	0	48	1	4.43	3	149	0	0	11	0	4.43
88-89—Tri-City	WHL	30	1671	16	10	2	97	1	*3.48	—	—	—	—	—	—	—
89-90—Washington	NHL	2	120	0	2	0	12	0	6.00	—	—	—	—	—	—	—
—Tri-City	WHL	48	2504	27	27	3	187	1	4.48	6	318	4	0	27	0	5.09
90-91—Baltimore	AHL	26	1367	10	12	1	72	0	3.16	—	—	—	—	—	—	—
—Hampton Roads	ECHL	21	1248	11	9	‡1	71	2	3.41	3	180	1	2	14	0	4.67
91-92—Baltimore	AHL	28	1503	5	17	2	105	1	4.19	—	—	—	—	—	—	—
—Hampton Roads	ECHL	14	847	11	3	0	41	0	2.90	—	—	—	—	—	—	—
92-93—Rochester	AHL	49	2737	25	16	4	168	0	3.68	17	*1040	9	*8	61	0	3.52
—Washington	NHL	1	20	0	0	0	2	0	6.00	—	—	—	—	—	—	—
93-94—Portland	AHL	29	1726	16	8	5	88	3	3.06	17	1035	†12	5	44	0	*2.55
—Washington	NHL	7	224	0	3	0	20	0	5.36	—	—	—	—	—	—	—
94-95—Washington	NHL	14	724	2	8	2	30	0	2.49	2	44	1	0	1	0	1.36
—Portland	AHL	2	125	1	0	1	3	0	1.44	—	—	—	—	—	—	—

K

Season Team	League	REGULAR SEASON								PLAYOFFS						
		Gms.	Min	W	L	T	GA	SO	Avg.	Gms.	Min.	W	L	GA	SO	Avg.
95-96—Washington	NHL	18	897	4	8	2	46	0	3.08	5	341	2	3	11	0	1.94
—Portland	AHL	5	300	5	0	0	7	1	1.40	—	—	—	—	—	—	—
96-97—Washington	NHL	29	1644	8	15	4	71	2	2.59	—	—	—	—	—	—	—
97-98—Washington	NHL	64	3788	33	18	10	139	5	2.20	21	1351	12	9	44	4	1.95
—German Oly. team	Int'l	2	120	2	0	0	2	1	1.00	—	—	—	—	—	—	—
98-99—Washington	NHL	64	3586	26	†31	3	154	4	2.58	—	—	—	—	—	—	—
99-00—Washington	NHL	73	*4371	41	20	11	163	5	2.24	5	284	1	4	16	0	3.38
NHL Totals (9 years)		272	15374	114	105	32	637	16	2.49	33	2020	16	16	72	4	2.14

KOMARNISKI, ZENITH   D   CANUCKS

PERSONAL: Born August 13, 1978, in Edmonton. ... 6-0/200. ... Shoots left. ... Name pronounced ZEH-nihth koh-mahr-NIH-skee.
TRANSACTIONS/CAREER NOTES: Selected by Vancouver Canucks in third round (second Canucks pick, 75th overall) of NHL entry draft (June 22, 1996). ... Injured shoulder (November 26, 1999); missed four games.
HONORS: Named to WHL (West) All-Star first team (1996-97).

Season Team	League	REGULAR SEASON							PLAYOFFS				
		Gms.	G	A	Pts.	PIM	+/-	PP	SH	Gms.	G	A	Pts.	PIM
94-95—Tri-City	WHL	66	5	19	24	110	...	...	...	17	1	2	3	47
95-96—Tri-City	WHL	42	5	21	26	85	...	...	...	—	—	—	—	—
96-97—Tri-City	WHL	58	12	44	56	112	...	...	...	—	—	—	—	—
97-98—Tri-City	WHL	3	0	4	4	18	...	...	...	—	—	—	—	—
—Spokane	WHL	43	7	20	27	90	...	...	...	18	4	6	10	49
98-99—Syracuse	AHL	58	9	19	28	89	...	...	...	—	—	—	—	—
99-00—Syracuse	AHL	42	4	12	16	130	...	...	...	4	2	0	2	6
—Vancouver	NHL	18	1	1	2	8	-1	0	0	—	—	—	—	—
NHL Totals (1 year)		18	1	1	2	8	-1	0	0					

KONOWALCHUK, STEVE   RW   CAPITALS

PERSONAL: Born November 11, 1972, in Salt Lake City. ... 6-2/210. ... Shoots left. ... Full Name: Steven Reed Konowalchuk. ... Name pronounced kah-nah-WAHL-chuhk.
TRANSACTIONS/CAREER NOTES: Selected by Washington Capitals in third round (fifth Capitals pick, 58th overall) of NHL entry draft (June 22, 1991). ... Separated shoulder (October 13, 1995); missed four games. ... Injured left hand (March 26, 1996); missed eight games. ... Separated rib cartilage prior to 1996-97 season; missed four games. ... Strained groin (January 28, 1998); missed two games. ... Sprained ankle (October 10, 1998); missed 15 games. ... Suffered concussion (March 2, 1999); missed remainder of season.
HONORS: Won Four Broncos Memorial Trophy (1991-92). ... Named to Can.HL All-Star second team (1991-92). ... Named to WHL (West) All-Star first team (1991-92).
MISCELLANEOUS: Failed to score on a penalty shot (vs. Mike Richter, March 5, 1995).
STATISTICAL PLATEAUS: Three-goal games: 1995-96 (2).

Season Team	League	REGULAR SEASON							PLAYOFFS				
		Gms.	G	A	Pts.	PIM	+/-	PP	SH	Gms.	G	A	Pts.	PIM
90-91—Portland	WHL	72	43	49	92	78	...	...	...	—	—	—	—	—
91-92—Portland	WHL	64	51	53	104	95	...	...	...	6	3	6	9	12
—Baltimore	AHL	3	1	1	2	0	...	...	...	—	—	—	—	—
—Washington	NHL	1	0	0	0	0	0	0	0	—	—	—	—	—
92-93—Baltimore	AHL	37	18	28	46	74	...	...	...	—	—	—	—	—
—Washington	NHL	36	4	7	11	16	4	1	0	2	0	1	1	0
93-94—Portland	AHL	8	11	4	15	4	...	...	...	—	—	—	—	—
—Washington	NHL	62	12	14	26	33	9	0	0	11	0	1	1	10
94-95—Washington	NHL	46	11	14	25	44	7	3	3	7	2	5	7	12
95-96—Washington	NHL	70	23	22	45	92	13	7	1	2	0	2	2	0
96-97—Washington	NHL	78	17	25	42	67	-3	2	1	—	—	—	—	—
97-98—Washington	NHL	80	10	24	34	80	9	2	0	—	—	—	—	—
98-99—Washington	NHL	45	12	12	24	26	0	4	1	—	—	—	—	—
99-00—Washington	NHL	82	16	27	43	80	19	3	0	5	1	0	1	2
NHL Totals (9 years)		500	105	145	250	438	58	22	6	27	3	9	12	24

KOROLEV, EVGENY   D   ISLANDERS

PERSONAL: Born July 24, 1978, in Moscow, U.S.S.R. ... 6-1/186. ... Shoots left.
TRANSACTIONS/CAREER NOTES: Selected by New York Islanders in sixth round (seventh Islanders pick, 138th overall) of NHL entry draft (June 22, 1996).

Season Team	League	REGULAR SEASON							PLAYOFFS				
		Gms.	G	A	Pts.	PIM	+/-	PP	SH	Gms.	G	A	Pts.	PIM
95-96—Peterborough	OHL	60	2	12	14	60	...	...	...	6	0	0	0	2
96-97—Peterborough	OHL	64	5	17	22	60	...	...	...	11	1	1	2	8
97-98—Peterborough	OHL	37	5	21	26	39	...	...	...	—	—	—	—	—
—London	OHL	27	4	10	14	36	...	...	...	15	2	7	9	29
98-99—Lowell	AHL	54	2	6	8	48	...	...	...	2	0	1	1	0
—Roanoke	ECHL	2	0	1	1	0	...	...	...	—	—	—	—	—
99-00—Lowell	AHL	57	1	10	11	61	...	...	...	6	0	0	0	4
—New York Islanders	NHL	17	1	2	3	8	-10	0	0	—	—	—	—	—
NHL Totals (1 year)		17	1	2	3	8	-10	0	0					

KOROLEV, IGOR   C   MAPLE LEAFS

PERSONAL: Born September 6, 1970, in Moscow, U.S.S.R. ... 6-1/190. ... Shoots left. ... Name pronounced EE-gohr KOHR-ih-lehv.
TRANSACTIONS/CAREER NOTES: Selected by St. Louis Blues in second round (first Blues pick, 38th overall) of NHL entry draft (June 20, 1992). ... Suffered from the flu (March 3, 1994); missed one game. ... Injured hip (March 12, 1994); missed three games. ... Selected by Winnipeg Jets from Blues in NHL waiver draft for cash (January 18, 1995). ... Played in Europe during 1994-95 NHL lockout. ... Fractured wrist (December 10, 1995); missed two games. ... Suffered hip pointer (February 1, 1996); missed three games. ... Jets franchise moved to Phoenix and renamed Coyotes for 1996-97 season; NHL approved move on January 18, 1996. ... Signed as free agent by Toronto Maple Leafs (September 28, 1997). ... Sprained shoulder (October 28, 1997); missed one game. ... Strained back (January 6, 1998); missed one game. ... Suffered back spasms (January 9, 1999); missed three games. ... Fractured finger (March 20, 1999); missed 13 games. ... Fractured fibula (April 22, 1999); missed remainder of playoffs. ... Suffered injury (October 13, 1999); missed two games.
STATISTICAL PLATEAUS: Three-goal games: 1995-96 (1).

		REGULAR SEASON								PLAYOFFS				
Season Team	League	Gms.	G	A	Pts.	PIM	+/-	PP	SH	Gms.	G	A	Pts.	PIM
88-89—Dynamo Moscow........	USSR	1	0	0	0	2	...	...	...	—	—	—	—	—
89-90—Dynamo Moscow........	USSR	17	3	2	5	2	...	...	...	—	—	—	—	—
90-91—Dynamo Moscow........	USSR	38	12	4	16	12	...	...	...	—	—	—	—	—
91-92—Dynamo Moscow.......	CIS	39	15	12	27	16	...	...	...	—	—	—	—	—
92-93—Dynamo Moscow.......	CIS	5	1	2	3	4	...	...	...	—	—	—	—	—
—St. Louis	NHL	74	4	23	27	20	-1	2	0	3	0	0	0	0
93-94—St. Louis	NHL	73	6	10	16	40	-12	0	0	2	0	0	0	0
94-95—Dynamo Moscow.......	CIS	13	4	6	10	18	...	...	...	—	—	—	—	—
—Winnipeg	NHL	45	8	22	30	10	1	1	0	—	—	—	—	—
95-96—Winnipeg	NHL	73	22	29	51	42	1	8	0	6	0	3	3	0
96-97—Michigan	IHL	4	2	2	4	0	...	...	...	—	—	—	—	—
—Phoenix...................	IHL	4	2	6	8	4	...	...	...	—	—	—	—	—
—Phoenix...................	NHL	41	3	7	10	28	-5	2	0	1	0	0	0	0
97-98—Toronto	NHL	78	17	22	39	22	-18	6	3	—	—	—	—	—
98-99—Toronto	NHL	66	13	34	47	46	11	1	0	1	0	0	0	0
99-00—Toronto	NHL	80	20	26	46	22	12	5	3	12	0	4	4	6
NHL Totals (8 years)...........		530	93	173	266	230	-11	25	6	25	0	7	7	6

KOROLYUK, ALEX   RW   SHARKS

PERSONAL: Born January 15, 1976, in Moscow, U.S.S.R. ... 5-9/195. ... Shoots left. ... Full Name: Alexander Korolyuk. ... Name pronounced KOH-rohl-yook.
TRANSACTIONS/CAREER NOTES: Selected by San Jose Sharks in sixth round (sixth Sharks pick, 141st overall) of NHL entry draft (June 29, 1994). ... Suffered eye injury (December 2, 1999); missed three games. ... Injured back (January 19, 2000); missed eight games. ... Reinjured back (February 11, 2000); missed four games.
MISCELLANEOUS: Scored on a penalty shot (vs. Roman Turek, January 11, 2000).

		REGULAR SEASON								PLAYOFFS				
Season Team	League	Gms.	G	A	Pts.	PIM	+/-	PP	SH	Gms.	G	A	Pts.	PIM
93-94—Soviet Wings	CIS	22	4	4	8	20	...	...	...	3	1	0	1	4
94-95—Soviet Wings	CIS	52	16	13	29	62	...	...	...	4	1	2	3	4
95-96—Soviet Wings	CIS	50	30	19	49	77	...	...	...	—	—	—	—	—
96-97—Soviet Wings	CIS	17	8	5	13	46	...	...	...	—	—	—	—	—
—Manitoba..................	IHL	42	20	16	36	71	...	...	...	—	—	—	—	—
97-98—San Jose....................	NHL	19	2	3	5	6	-5	1	0	—	—	—	—	—
—Kentucky...................	AHL	44	16	23	39	96	...	...	...	3	0	0	0	0
98-99—Kentucky...................	AHL	23	9	13	22	16	...	...	...	—	—	—	—	—
—San Jose..................	NHL	55	12	18	30	26	3	2	0	6	1	3	4	2
99-00—San Jose..................	NHL	57	14	21	35	35	4	3	0	9	0	3	3	6
NHL Totals (3 years)...........		131	28	42	70	67	2	6	0	15	1	6	7	8

KOVALENKO, ANDREI   RW   BRUINS

PERSONAL: Born July 7, 1970, in Gorky, U.S.S.R. ... 5-10/215. ... Shoots right. ... Name pronounced koh-vuh-LEHN-koh.
TRANSACTIONS/CAREER NOTES: Selected by Quebec Nordiques in eighth round (sixth Nordiques pick, 148th overall) of NHL entry draft (June 16, 1990). ... Suffered from tonsillitis (December 22, 1992); missed two games. ... Suffered from the flu (March 15, 1993); missed one game. ... Suffered concussion (November 4, 1993); missed five games. ... Bruised ribs (January 11, 1994); missed two games. ... Injured shoulder (January 25, 1994); missed 14 games. ... Suffered from tonsillitis (April 3, 1994); missed two games. ... Played in Europe during 1994-95 NHL lockout. ... Pulled groin (March 9, 1995); missed one game. ... Injured neck (April 5, 1995); missed one game. ... Injured thumb (April 20, 1995); missed one game. ... Nordiques franchise moved to Colorado and renamed Avalanche for 1995-96 season (June 21, 1995). ... Traded by Avalanche with G Jocelyn Thibault and LW Martin Rucinsky to Montreal Canadiens for G Patrick Roy and RW Mike Keane (December 6, 1995). ... Fractured nose (December 16, 1995); missed five games. ... Strained left rotator cuff (February 15, 1996); missed two games. ... Traded by Canadiens to Edmonton Oilers for C Scott Thornton (September 6, 1996). ... Suffered back spasms (February 17, 1997); missed two games. ... Suffered hip pointer (March 1, 1997); missed five games. ... Suffered back spasms (October 13, 1997); missed one game. ... Suffered rib injury (December 30, 1997); missed one game. ... Suffered from the flu (March 4, 1998); missed one game. ... Suffered back spasms (March 11, 1998); missed three games. ... Suffered back spasms (March 30, 1998); missed final eight games of regular season and 11 playoff games. ... Traded by Oilers to Philadelphia Flyers for C/RW Alexandre Daigle (January 29, 1999). ... Traded by Flyers to Carolina Hurricanes for D Adam Burt (March 6, 1999). ... Suffered back spasms (November 17, 1999); missed three games. ... Injured knee (April 8, 2000); missed final game of season. ... Signed as free agent by Boston Bruins (July 25, 2000).
MISCELLANEOUS: Member of gold-medal-winning Unified Olympic team (1992). ... Member of silver-medal-winning Russian Olympic team (1998). ... Scored on a penalty shot (vs. Kirk McLean, December 4, 1993).
STATISTICAL PLATEAUS: Three-goal games: 1992-93 (1).

K

– 189 –

Season Team	League	REGULAR SEASON								PLAYOFFS				
		Gms.	G	A	Pts.	PIM	+/-	PP	SH	Gms.	G	A	Pts.	PIM
88-89—CSKA Moscow............	USSR	10	1	0	1	0	...	...	...	—	—	—	—	—
89-90—CSKA Moscow............	USSR	48	8	5	13	18	...	...	...	—	—	—	—	—
90-91—CSKA Moscow............	USSR	45	13	8	21	26	...	...	...	—	—	—	—	—
91-92—CSKA Moscow............	CIS	44	19	13	32	32	...	...	...	—	—	—	—	—
—Unif. Olympic team......	Int'l	8	1	1	2	2	...	...	...	—	—	—	—	—
92-93—CSKA Moscow............	CIS	3	3	1	4	4	...	...	...	—	—	—	—	—
—Quebec....................	NHL	81	27	41	68	57	13	8	1	4	1	0	1	2
93-94—Quebec....................	NHL	58	16	17	33	46	-5	5	0	—	—	—	—	—
94-95—Lada Togliatti..............	CIS	11	9	2	11	14	...	...	...	—	—	—	—	—
—Quebec....................	NHL	45	14	10	24	31	-4	1	0	6	0	1	1	2
95-96—Colorado..................	NHL	26	11	11	22	16	11	3	0	—	—	—	—	—
—Montreal..................	NHL	51	17	17	34	33	9	3	0	6	0	0	0	6
96-97—Edmonton.................	NHL	74	32	27	59	81	-5	14	0	12	4	3	7	6
97-98—Edmonton.................	NHL	59	6	17	23	28	-14	1	0	1	0	0	0	2
—Russian Oly. team.......	Int'l	6	4	1	5	14	...	...	...	—	—	—	—	—
98-99—Edmonton.................	NHL	43	13	14	27	30	-4	2	0	—	—	—	—	—
—Philadelphia..............	NHL	13	0	1	1	2	-5	0	0	—	—	—	—	—
—Carolina..................	NHL	18	6	6	12	0	3	1	0	4	0	2	2	2
99-00—Carolina..................	NHL	76	15	24	39	38	-13	2	0	—	—	—	—	—
NHL Totals (8 years)...........		544	157	185	342	362	-14	40	1	33	5	6	11	20

KOVALEV, ALEXEI   C   PENGUINS

PERSONAL: Born February 24, 1973, in Moscow, U.S.S.R. ... 6-1/215. ... Shoots left. ... Name pronounced KOH-vuh-lahf.

TRANSACTIONS/CAREER NOTES: Selected by New York Rangers in first round (first Rangers pick, 15th overall) of NHL entry draft (June 22, 1991). ... Suffered back spasms (January 16, 1993); missed one game. ... Suspended one game by NHL (November 10, 1993). ... Suspended five games by NHL for tripping (November 30, 1993). ... Suspended two games by NHL (February 12, 1994). ... Played in Europe during 1994-95 NHL lockout. ... Suffered from the flu (December 2, 1995); missed one game. ... Tore knee ligament (January 8, 1997); missed remainder of season. ... Sprained knee and underwent athroscopic surgery (January 22, 1998); missed eight games. ... Separated shoulder (October 27, 1998); missed five games. ... Bruised shoulder (November 21, 1998); missed one game. ... Traded by Rangers with C Harry York and future considerations to Pittsburgh Penguins for C Petr Nedved, C Sean Pronger and D Chris Tamer (November 25, 1998). ... Bruised shoulder (November 21, 1998); missed one game.

MISCELLANEOUS: Member of Stanley Cup championship team (1994). ... Member of gold-medal-winning Unified Olympic team (1992). ... Member of silver-medal-winning Russian Olympic team (1998). ... Failed to score on a penalty shot (vs. Jon Casey, October 5, 1993).

STATISTICAL PLATEAUS: Three-goal games: 1992-93 (1), 1996-97 (1). Total: 2.

Season Team	League	REGULAR SEASON								PLAYOFFS				
		Gms.	G	A	Pts.	PIM	+/-	PP	SH	Gms.	G	A	Pts.	PIM
89-90—Dynamo Moscow........	USSR	1	0	0	0	0	...	...	...	—	—	—	—	—
90-91—Dynamo Moscow........	USSR	18	1	2	3	4	...	...	...	—	—	—	—	—
91-92—Dynamo Moscow........	CIS	33	16	9	25	20	...	...	...	—	—	—	—	—
—Unif. Olympic team.....	Int'l	8	1	2	3	14	...	...	...	—	—	—	—	—
92-93—New York Rangers......	NHL	65	20	18	38	79	-10	3	0	—	—	—	—	—
—Binghamton.............	AHL	13	13	11	24	35	...	...	...	9	3	5	8	14
93-94—New York Rangers......	NHL	76	23	33	56	154	18	7	0	23	9	12	21	18
94-95—Lada Togliatti..............	CIS	12	8	8	16	49	...	...	...	—	—	—	—	—
—New York Rangers......	NHL	48	13	15	28	30	-6	1	1	10	4	7	11	10
95-96—New York Rangers......	NHL	81	24	34	58	98	5	8	1	11	3	4	7	14
96-97—New York Rangers......	NHL	45	13	22	35	42	11	1	0	—	—	—	—	—
97-98—New York Rangers......	NHL	73	23	30	53	44	-22	8	0	—	—	—	—	—
98-99—New York Rangers......	NHL	14	3	4	7	12	-6	1	0	—	—	—	—	—
—Pittsburgh................	NHL	63	20	26	46	37	8	5	1	10	5	7	12	14
99-00—Pittsburgh................	NHL	82	26	40	66	94	-3	9	2	11	1	5	6	10
NHL Totals (8 years)...........		547	165	222	387	590	-5	43	5	65	22	35	57	66

KOZLOV, SLAVA   LW   RED WINGS

PERSONAL: Born May 3, 1972, in Voskresensk, U.S.S.R. ... 5-10/195. ... Shoots left. ... Full Name: Vyacheslav Kozlov. ... Name pronounced VYACH-ih-slav KAHS-lahf.

TRANSACTIONS/CAREER NOTES: Selected by Detroit Red Wings in third round (second Red Wings pick, 45th overall) of NHL entry draft (June 16, 1990). ... Played in Europe during 1994-95 NHL lockout. ... Bruised left foot (April 16, 1995); missed one game. ... Sprained knee (April 15, 1998); missed two games. ... Suspended three games by NHL for elbowing incident (December 18, 1998). ... Injured ankle (December 22, 1999); missed three games. ... Reinjured ankle (January 4, 2000); missed four games. ... Suffered concussion (March 29, 2000); missed two games.

HONORS: Named Soviet League Rookie of the Year (1989-90).

MISCELLANEOUS: Member of Stanley Cup championship team (1997 and 1998).

STATISTICAL PLATEAUS: Three-goal games: 1993-94 (1), 1998-99 (1). Total: 2. ... Four-goal games: 1995-96 (1). ... Total hat tricks: 3.

Season Team	League	REGULAR SEASON								PLAYOFFS				
		Gms.	G	A	Pts.	PIM	+/-	PP	SH	Gms.	G	A	Pts.	PIM
87-88—Khimik	USSR	2	0	1	1	0	...	...	...	—	—	—	—	—
88-89—Khimik	USSR	13	0	1	1	2	...	...	...	—	—	—	—	—
89-90—Khimik	USSR	45	14	12	26	38	...	...	...	—	—	—	—	—
90-91—Khimik	USSR	45	11	13	24	46	...	...	...	—	—	—	—	—
91-92—Khimik	USSR	11	6	5	11	12	...	...	...	—	—	—	—	—
—Detroit............	NHL	7	0	2	2	2	-2	0	0	—	—	—	—	—
92-93—Detroit............	NHL	17	4	1	5	14	-1	0	0	4	0	2	2	2
—Adirondack........	AHL	45	23	36	59	54	...	...	...	4	1	1	2	4

Season Team	League	REGULAR SEASON								PLAYOFFS				
		Gms.	G	A	Pts.	PIM	+/-	PP	SH	Gms.	G	A	Pts.	PIM
93-94—Detroit	NHL	77	34	39	73	50	27	8	2	7	2	5	7	12
—Adirondack	AHL	3	0	1	1	15	...	...	...	—	—	—	—	—
94-95—CSKA Moscow	CIS	10	3	4	7	14	...	...	...	—	—	—	—	—
—Detroit	NHL	46	13	20	33	45	12	5	0	18	9	7	16	10
95-96—Detroit	NHL	82	36	37	73	70	33	9	0	19	5	7	12	10
96-97—Detroit	NHL	75	23	22	45	46	21	3	0	20	8	5	13	14
97-98—Detroit	NHL	80	25	27	52	46	14	6	0	22	6	8	14	10
98-99—Detroit	NHL	79	29	29	58	45	10	6	1	10	6	1	7	4
99-00—Detroit	NHL	72	18	18	36	28	11	4	0	8	2	1	3	12
NHL Totals (9 years)		535	182	195	377	346	125	41	3	108	38	36	74	74

KOZLOV, VIKTOR   C   PANTHERS

PERSONAL: Born February 14, 1975, in Togliatti, U.S.S.R. ... 6-5/232. ... Shoots right. ... Name pronounced KAHZ-lahf.
TRANSACTIONS/CAREER NOTES: Selected by San Jose Sharks in first round (first Sharks pick, sixth overall) of NHL entry draft (June 26, 1993). ... Suffered displaced ankle fracture (November 27, 1994); missed 13 games. ... Played in Europe during 1994-95 NHL lockout. ... Bruised ankle (March 26, 1997); missed four games. ... Traded by Sharks with fifth-round pick (D Jaroslav Spacek) in 1998 draft to Florida Panthers for LW Dave Lowry and first-round pick (traded to Tampa Bay) in 1998 draft (November 13, 1997). ... Separated right shoulder (November 18, 1997); missed 16 games. ... Suffered concussion (April 1, 1998); missed three games. ... Separated shoulder (October 30, 1998); missed six games. ... Reinjured shoulder (January 8, 1999); missed one game. ... Strained shoulder (January 20, 1999); missed three games. ... Fractured finger (April 3, 1999); missed final seven games of season. ... Sprained shoulder (March 8, 2000); missed two games.
HONORS: Named to play in NHL All-Star Game (1999); missed game due to injury. ... Played in NHL All-Star Game (2000).
MISCELLANEOUS: Scored on a penalty shot (vs. Olaf Kolzig, February 23, 2000).
STATISTICAL PLATEAUS: Three-goal games: 1999-00 (1).

Season Team	League	REGULAR SEASON								PLAYOFFS				
		Gms.	G	A	Pts.	PIM	+/-	PP	SH	Gms.	G	A	Pts.	PIM
90-91—Lada Togliatti	USSR Div. II	2	2	0	2	0	...	...	...	—	—	—	—	—
91-92—Lada Togliatti	CIS	3	0	0	0	0	...	...	...	—	—	—	—	—
92-93—Dynamo Moscow	CIS	30	6	5	11	4	...	...	...	10	3	0	3	0
93-94—Dynamo Moscow	CIS	42	16	9	25	14	...	...	...	7	3	2	5	0
94-95—Dynamo Moscow	CIS	3	1	1	2	2	...	...	...	—	—	—	—	—
—San Jose	NHL	16	2	0	2	2	-5	0	0	—	—	—	—	—
—Kansas City	IHL	—	—	—	—	—				13	4	5	9	12
95-96—Kansas City	IHL	15	4	7	11	12	...	...	...	—	—	—	—	—
—San Jose	NHL	62	6	13	19	6	-15	1	0	—	—	—	—	—
96-97—San Jose	NHL	78	16	25	41	40	-16	4	0	—	—	—	—	—
97-98—San Jose	NHL	18	5	2	7	2	-2	2	0	—	—	—	—	—
—Florida	NHL	46	12	11	23	14	-1	3	2	—	—	—	—	—
98-99—Florida	NHL	65	16	35	51	24	13	5	1	—	—	—	—	—
99-00—Florida	NHL	80	17	53	70	16	24	6	0	4	0	1	1	0
NHL Totals (6 years)		365	74	139	213	104	-2	21	3	4	0	1	1	0

KRAFT, MILAN   C   PENGUINS

PERSONAL: Born January 17, 1980, in Plzen, Czechoslovakia. ... 6-3/191. ... Shoots right.
TRANSACTIONS/CAREER NOTES: Selected by Pittsburgh Penguins in first round (first Penguins pick, 23rd overall) of NHL entry draft (June 27, 1998).

Season Team	League	REGULAR SEASON								PLAYOFFS				
		Gms.	G	A	Pts.	PIM	+/-	PP	SH	Gms.	G	A	Pts.	PIM
96-97—Plzen Jrs.	Czech Rep.	36	26	17	43	...	...	...	...	—	—	—	—	—
—ZKZ Plzen	Czech Rep.	9	0	1	1	2	...	...	...	—	—	—	—	—
97-98—Plzen Jrs.	Czech Rep.	24	22	23	45	12	...	...	...	—	—	—	—	—
—ZKZ Plzen	Czech Rep.	16	0	5	5	0	...	...	...	—	—	—	—	—
98-99—Prince Albert	WHL	68	40	46	86	32	...	...	...	14	7	13	20	6
99-00—Prince Albert	WHL	56	34	35	69	42	...	...	...	6	4	1	5	4

KRAVCHUK, IGOR   D   SENATORS

PERSONAL: Born September 13, 1966, in Ufa, U.S.S.R. ... 6-1/218. ... Shoots left. ... Name pronounced EE-gohr KRAV-chuhk.
TRANSACTIONS/CAREER NOTES: Selected by Chicago Blackhawks in fourth round (fifth Blackhawks pick, 71st overall) of NHL entry draft (June 22, 1991). ... Sprained knee (October 25, 1992); missed four games. ... Sprained left ankle (December 29, 1992); missed 18 games. ... Traded by Blackhawks with C Dean McAmmond to Edmonton Oilers for RW Joe Murphy (February 25, 1993). ... Sprained left knee (April 6, 1993); missed remainder of season. ... Strained groin (November 15, 1993); missed three games. ... Injured left knee (January 30, 1995) and underwent surgery (February 6, 1995); missed 12 games. ... Suffered deep bone bruise to left leg (October 21, 1995); missed six games. ... Injured knee (November 20, 1995); missed four games. ... Traded by Oilers with D Ken Sutton to St. Louis Blues for D Donald Dufresne and D Jeff Norton (January 4, 1996). ... Traded by Blues to Ottawa Senators for D Steve Duchesne (August 25, 1997). ... Bruised hip (March 20, 1998); missed one game. ... Strained hip flexor (November 26, 1998); missed one game. ... Suffered from the flu (March 30, 1999); missed one game. ... Bruised leg (April 10, 1999); missed one game. ... Suffered partially torn medial collateral ligament in left knee (October 30, 1999); missed 15 games. ... Sprained left knee (December 11, 1999); missed one game. ... Bruised right foot (January 11, 2000); missed one game.
HONORS: Played in NHL All-Star Game (1998).
MISCELLANEOUS: Member of gold-medal-winning U.S.S.R. Olympic team (1988) and gold-medal-winning Unified Olympic team (1992). ... Member of silver-medal-winning Russian Olympic team (1998).

Season Team	League	REGULAR SEASON Gms.	G	A	Pts.	PIM	+/-	PP	SH	PLAYOFFS Gms.	G	A	Pts.	PIM
87-88—CSKA Moscow	USSR	47	1	8	9	12	...	...	...	—	—	—	—	—
—Unif. Olympic team	Int'l	6	1	0	1	0	...	...	...	—	—	—	—	—
88-89—CSKA Moscow	USSR	27	3	4	7	2	...	...	...	—	—	—	—	—
89-90—CSKA Moscow	USSR	48	1	3	4	16	...	...	...	—	—	—	—	—
90-91—CSKA Moscow	USSR	41	6	5	11	16	...	...	...	—	—	—	—	—
91-92—CSKA Moscow	CIS	30	3	7	10	2	...	...	...	—	—	—	—	—
—Unif. Olympic team	Int'l	8	3	2	5	6	...	...	...	—	—	—	—	—
—Chicago	NHL	18	1	8	9	4	-3	0	0	18	2	6	8	8
92-93—Chicago	NHL	38	6	9	15	30	11	3	0	—	—	—	—	—
—Edmonton	NHL	17	4	8	12	2	-8	1	0	—	—	—	—	—
93-94—Edmonton	NHL	81	12	38	50	16	-12	5	0	—	—	—	—	—
94-95—Edmonton	NHL	36	7	11	18	29	-15	3	1	—	—	—	—	—
95-96—Edmonton	NHL	26	4	4	8	10	-13	3	0	—	—	—	—	—
—St. Louis	NHL	40	3	12	15	24	-6	0	0	10	1	5	6	4
96-97—St. Louis	NHL	82	4	24	28	35	7	1	0	2	0	0	0	2
97-98—Ottawa	NHL	81	8	27	35	8	-19	3	1	11	2	3	5	4
—Russian Oly. team	Int'l	6	0	2	2	2	...	...	...	—	—	—	—	—
98-99—Ottawa	NHL	79	4	21	25	32	14	3	0	4	0	0	0	0
99-00—Ottawa	NHL	64	6	12	18	20	-5	5	0	6	1	1	2	0
NHL Totals (9 years)		562	59	174	233	210	-49	27	2	51	6	15	21	18

KRISTEK, JAROSLOV   RW   SABRES

K

PERSONAL: Born March 16, 1980, in Zlin, Czechoslovakia. ... 6-0/183. ... Shoots left.
TRANSACTIONS/CAREER NOTES: Selected by Buffalo Sabres in second round (fourth Sabres pick, 50th overall) of NHL entry draft (June 27, 1998).

Season Team	League	REGULAR SEASON Gms.	G	A	Pts.	PIM	+/-	PP	SH	PLAYOFFS Gms.	G	A	Pts.	PIM
95-96—ZPS Zlin Jrs.	Czech Rep.	34	33	20	53	...	...	...	...	—	—	—	—	—
96-97—ZPS Zlin Jrs.	Czech Rep.	44	28	27	55	...	...	...	...	—	—	—	—	—
97-98—ZPS Zlin Jrs.	Czech Rep.	7	8	5	13	...	...	...	...	—	—	—	—	—
—ZPS Zlin	Czech Rep.	37	2	8	10	20	...	...	...	—	—	—	—	—
—Prostejov	Czech Rp. Dv. 2	4	0	0	0	0	...	...	...	—	—	—	—	—
98-99—Tri-City	WHL	70	38	48	86	55	...	...	...	12	4	3	7	2
99-00—Tri-City	WHL	45	26	25	51	16	...	...	...	2	0	0	0	0

KRIVOKRASOV, SERGEI   RW   WILD

PERSONAL: Born April 15, 1974, in Angarsk, U.S.S.R. ... 5-11/185. ... Shoots left. ... Name pronounced SAIR-gay KREE-voh-KRAS-ahf.
TRANSACTIONS/CAREER NOTES: Selected by Chicago Blackhawks in first round (first Blackhawks pick, 12th overall) of NHL entry draft (June 20, 1992). ... Sprained knee (January 31, 1996); missed 14 games. ... Sprained knee (March 14, 1996); missed 13 games. ... Sprained left knee (December 17, 1997); missed 16 games. ... Lacerated elbow (March 9, 1998); missed five games. ... Traded by Blackhawks to Nashville Predators for future considerations (June 27, 1998). ... Suspended three pre-season games and fined $1,000 by NHL for high-sticking incident (October 1, 1998). ... Injured leg (December 19, 1998); missed 10 games. ... Sprained ankle (January 28, 1999); missed two games. ... Bruised hand (November 11, 1999); missed one game. ... Traded by Predators to Calgary Flames for D Cale Hulse and third-round pick in 2001 draft (March 14, 2000). ... Selected by Minnesota Wild in NHL expansion draft (June 23, 2000).
HONORS: Played in NHL All-Star Game (1999).
MISCELLANEOUS: Member of silver-medal-winning Russian Olympic team (1998).

Season Team	League	REGULAR SEASON Gms.	G	A	Pts.	PIM	+/-	PP	SH	PLAYOFFS Gms.	G	A	Pts.	PIM
90-91—CSKA Moscow	USSR	41	4	0	4	8	...	...	...	—	—	—	—	—
91-92—CSKA Moscow	CIS	42	10	8	18	35	...	...	...	—	—	—	—	—
92-93—Chicago	NHL	4	0	0	0	2	-2	0	0	—	—	—	—	—
—Indianapolis	IHL	78	36	33	69	157	...	...	...	5	3	1	4	2
93-94—Indianapolis	IHL	53	19	26	45	145	...	...	...	—	—	—	—	—
—Chicago	NHL	9	1	0	1	4	-2	0	0	—	—	—	—	—
94-95—Indianapolis	IHL	29	12	15	27	41	...	...	...	—	—	—	—	—
—Chicago	NHL	41	12	7	19	33	9	6	0	10	0	0	0	8
95-96—Indianapolis	IHL	9	4	5	9	28	...	...	...	—	—	—	—	—
—Chicago	NHL	46	6	10	16	32	10	0	0	5	1	0	1	2
96-97—Chicago	NHL	67	13	11	24	42	-1	2	0	6	1	0	1	4
97-98—Chicago	NHL	58	10	13	23	33	-1	1	0	—	—	—	—	—
—Russian Oly. team	Int'l	6	0	0	0	4	...	...	...	—	—	—	—	—
98-99—Nashville	NHL	70	25	23	48	42	-5	10	0	—	—	—	—	—
99-00—Nashville	NHL	63	9	17	26	40	-7	3	0	—	—	—	—	—
—Calgary	NHL	12	1	10	11	4	2	0	0	—	—	—	—	—
NHL Totals (8 years)		370	77	91	168	232	3	22	0	21	2	0	2	14

KROG, JASON   C   ISLANDERS

PERSONAL: Born October 9, 1975, in Fernie, B.C. ... 5-11/191.
COLLEGE: New Hampshire.
TRANSACTIONS/CAREER NOTES: Signed as non-drafted free agent by New York Islanders (April 10, 1999). ... Sprained right ankle (March 27, 2000); missed final six games of season.
HONORS: Named to NCAA All-America (East) second team (1996-97). ... Named to Hockey East All-Star first team (1996-97 through 1998-99). ... Won Hobey Baker Memorial Award (1998-99). ... Named to NCAA All-America (East) first team (1998-99). ... Named to NCAA All-Tournament team (1998-99).

Season Team	League	REGULAR SEASON Gms.	G	A	Pts.	PIM	+/-	PP	SH	PLAYOFFS Gms.	G	A	Pts.	PIM
95-96—Univ. of New Hamp.....	Hockey East	34	4	16	20	20	...	...	...	—	—	—	—	—
96-97—Univ. of New Hamp.....	Hockey East	39	23	44	67	28	...	...	...	—	—	—	—	—
97-98—Univ. of New Hamp.....	Hockey East	38	†33	33	66	44	...	...	...	—	—	—	—	—
98-99—Univ. of New Hamp.....	Hockey East	41	*34	*51	*85	38	...	...	...	—	—	—	—	—
99-00—Lowell	AHL	45	6	21	27	22	...	...	...	—	—	—	—	—
—New York Islanders.....	NHL	17	2	4	6	6	-1	1	0	—	—	—	—	—
—Providence	AHL	11	9	8	17	4	...	...	...	6	2	2	4	0
NHL Totals (1 year)..............		17	2	4	6	6	-1	1	0					

KRON, ROBERT   C   BLUE JACKETS

PERSONAL: Born February 27, 1967, in Brno, Czechoslovakia. ... 5-11/182. ... Shoots left. ... Name pronounced KRAHN.
TRANSACTIONS/CAREER NOTES: Selected by Vancouver Canucks in fourth round (fifth Canucks pick, 88th overall) of NHL entry draft (June 15, 1985). ... Underwent surgery to repair torn knee ligaments and wrist fracture (March 22, 1991). ... Fractured ankle (January 28, 1992); missed 22 games. ... Traded by Canucks with third-round pick (D Marek Malik) in 1993 draft and future considerations to Hartford Whalers for C/LW Murray Craven and fifth-round pick (D Scott Walker) in 1993 draft (March 22, 1993); Whalers aquired RW Jim Sandlak to complete deal (May 17, 1993). ... Sprained shoulder (February 26, 1994); missed seven games. ... Fractured thumb (March 29, 1995); missed 11 games. ... Injured groin (March 27, 1996); missed one game. ... Strained abdominal muscle (April 8, 1996); missed three games. ... Sprained knee (January 25, 1997); missed 12 games. ... Whalers franchise moved to North Carolina and renamed Carolina Hurricanes for 1997-98 season; NHL approved move on June 25, 1997. ... Strained groin (November 11, 1998); missed one game. ... Strained groin (February 26, 1999); missed five games. ... Selected by Columbus Blue Jackets in NHL expansion draft (June 23, 2000).

Season Team	League	REGULAR SEASON Gms.	G	A	Pts.	PIM	+/-	PP	SH	PLAYOFFS Gms.	G	A	Pts.	PIM
84-85—Zetor Brno	Czech.	40	6	8	14	6	...	...	...	—	—	—	—	—
85-86—Zetor Brno	Czech.	44	5	6	11		...	...	...	—	—	—	—	—
86-87—Zetor Brno	Czech.	28	14	11	25		...	...	...	—	—	—	—	—
87-88—Zetor Brno	Czech.	32	12	6	18		...	...	...	—	—	—	—	—
88-89—Zetor Brno	Czech.	43	28	19	47		...	...	...	—	—	—	—	—
89-90—Dukla Trencin..............	Czech.	39	22	22	44		...	...	...	—	—	—	—	—
90-91—Vancouver.................	NHL	76	12	20	32	21	-11	2	3	—	—	—	—	—
91-92—Vancouver.................	NHL	36	2	2	4	2	-9	0	0	11	1	2	3	2
92-93—Vancouver.................	NHL	32	10	11	21	14	10	2	2	—	—	—	—	—
—Hartford	NHL	13	4	2	6	4	-5	2	0	—	—	—	—	—
93-94—Hartford	NHL	77	24	26	50	8	0	2	1	—	—	—	—	—
94-95—Hartford	NHL	37	10	8	18	10	-3	3	1	—	—	—	—	—
95-96—Hartford	NHL	77	22	28	50	6	-1	8	1	—	—	—	—	—
96-97—Hartford	NHL	68	10	12	22	10	-18	2	0	—	—	—	—	—
97-98—Carolina	NHL	81	16	20	36	12	-8	4	0	—	—	—	—	—
98-99—Carolina	NHL	75	9	16	25	10	-13	3	1	5	2	0	2	0
99-00—Carolina	NHL	81	13	27	40	8	-4	2	1	—	—	—	—	—
NHL Totals (10 years).........		653	132	172	304	105	-62	30	10	16	3	2	5	2

KRUSE, PAUL   LW

PERSONAL: Born March 15, 1970, in Merritt, B.C. ... 6-0/214. ... Shoots left. ... Name pronounced KROOS.
TRANSACTIONS/CAREER NOTES: Selected by Calgary Flames in fourth round (sixth Flames pick, 83rd overall) of NHL entry draft (June 16, 1990). ... Injured eye (March 8, 1992); missed four games. ... Suffered hip pointer (March 21, 1993); missed one game. ... Broke toe on right foot (September 27, 1993); missed 12 games. ... Bruised left foot (March 2, 1995); missed one game. ... Bruised left knee (April 29, 1995); missed one game. ... Bruised ribs (February 13, 1996); missed three games. ... Cut wrist (April 9, 1996); missed two games. ... Traded by Flames to New York Islanders for third-round pick (traded to Hartford) in 1997 draft (November 27, 1996). ... Strained abdominal muscle (March 16, 1997); missed 12 games. ... Traded by Islanders with LW Jason Holland to Buffalo Sabres for RW Jason Dawe (March 24, 1998). ... Strained hip flexor (February 4, 1998); missed one game. ... Bruised hand (March 6, 1998); missed one game. ... Sprained knee (April 15, 1998); missed final two games of regular season and nine playoff games. ... Strained hip flexor (November 3, 1998); missed three games. ... Reinjured hip flexor (November 14, 1998); missed three games. ... Reinjured hip flexor and strained groin (November 28, 1998); missed 12 games. ... Injured groin (November 13, 1999); missed three games.

Season Team	League	REGULAR SEASON Gms.	G	A	Pts.	PIM	+/-	PP	SH	PLAYOFFS Gms.	G	A	Pts.	PIM
86-87—Merritt........................	BCJHL	35	8	15	23	120	...	...	...	—	—	—	—	—
87-88—Merritt........................	BCJHL	44	12	32	44	227	...	...	...	4	1	4	5	18
—Moose Jaw	WHL	1	0	0	0	0	...	...	...	—	—	—	—	—
88-89—Kamloops	WHL	68	8	15	23	209	...	...	...	—	—	—	—	—
89-90—Kamloops	WHL	67	22	23	45	291	...	...	...	17	3	5	8	†79
90-91—Salt Lake City.............	IHL	83	24	20	44	313	...	...	...	4	1	1	2	4
—Calgary	NHL	1	0	0	0	7	-1	0	0	—	—	—	—	—
91-92—Salt Lake City.............	IHL	57	14	15	29	267	...	...	...	5	1	2	3	19
—Calgary	NHL	16	3	1	4	65	1	0	0	—	—	—	—	—
92-93—Salt Lake City.............	IHL	35	1	4	5	206	...	...	...	—	—	—	—	—
—Calgary	NHL	27	2	3	5	41	2	0	0	—	—	—	—	—
93-94—Calgary	NHL	68	3	8	11	185	-6	0	0	7	0	0	0	14
94-95—Calgary	NHL	45	11	5	16	141	13	0	0	7	4	2	6	10
95-96—Calgary	NHL	75	3	12	15	145	-5	0	0	3	0	0	0	4
96-97—Calgary	NHL	14	2	0	2	30	-4	0	0	—	—	—	—	—
—New York Islanders.....	NHL	48	4	2	6	111	-5	0	0	—	—	—	—	—
97-98—New York Islanders.....	NHL	62	6	1	7	138	-12	0	0	—	—	—	—	—
—Buffalo	NHL	12	1	1	2	49	1	0	0	1	1	0	1	4
98-99—Buffalo	NHL	43	3	0	3	114	0	0	0	10	0	0	0	4
99-00—Buffalo	NHL	11	0	0	0	43	-2	0	0	—	—	—	—	—
—Utah	IHL	44	10	13	23	71	...	...	...	5	0	3	3	28
NHL Totals (10 years).........		422	38	33	71	1069	-18	0	0	28	5	2	7	36

KUBA, FILIP   D   WILD

PERSONAL: Born December 29, 1976, in Ostrava, Czechoslovakia. ... 6-3/205. ... Shoots left. ... Name pronounced KOO-buh.
TRANSACTIONS/CAREER NOTES: Selected by Florida Panthers in eighth round (eighth Panthers pick, 192nd overall) of NHL entry draft (July 8, 1995). ... Traded by Panthers to Calgary Flames for RW Rocky Thompson (March 16, 2000). ... Selected by Minnesota Wild in NHL expansion draft (June 23, 2000).

Season Team	League	REGULAR SEASON Gms.	G	A	Pts.	PIM	+/-	PP	SH	PLAYOFFS Gms.	G	A	Pts.	PIM
94-95—Vitkovice Jrs.	Czech Rep.	35	10	15	25	...	...	...	...	—	—	—	—	—
—Vitkovice	Czech Rep.	—	—	—	—	—	...	...	...	4	0	0	0	2
95-96—Vitkovice	Czech Rep.	19	0	1	1	...	...	...	...	—	—	—	—	—
96-97—Carolina	AHL	51	0	12	12	38	...	...	...	—	—	—	—	—
97-98—New Haven	AHL	77	4	13	17	58	...	...	...	3	1	1	2	0
98-99—Kentucky	AHL	45	2	8	10	33	...	...	...	10	0	1	1	4
—Florida	NHL	5	0	1	1	0	2	0	0	—	—	—	—	—
99-00—Florida	NHL	13	1	5	6	2	-3	1	0	—	—	—	—	—
—Houston	IHL	27	3	6	9	13	...	...	...	11	1	2	3	4
NHL Totals (2 years)		18	1	6	7	2	-1	1	0					

KUBINA, PAVEL   D   LIGHTNING

PERSONAL: Born April 15, 1977, in Caledna, Czechoslovakia. ... 6-4/230. ... Shoots left. ... Name pronounced koo-BEE-nuh.
TRANSACTIONS/CAREER NOTES: Selected by Tampa Bay Lightning in seventh round (sixth Lightning pick, 179th overall) of NHL entry draft (June 22, 1996). ... Injured knee (November 8, 1998); missed two games. ... Injured shoulder (November 29, 1998); missed three games. ... Bruised rib (January 5, 2000); missed two games. ... Bruised hand (March 1, 2000); missed one game. ... Injured ankle (March 21, 2000); missed final nine games of season.

Season Team	League	REGULAR SEASON Gms.	G	A	Pts.	PIM	+/-	PP	SH	PLAYOFFS Gms.	G	A	Pts.	PIM
93-94—HC Vitkovice	Czech Rep.	1	0	0	0	0	...	...	...	—	—	—	—	—
94-95—HC Vitkovice	Czech Rep.	8	2	0	2	0	...	...	...	4	0	0	0	0
95-96—HC Vitkovice	Czech Rep.	32	3	4	7	0	...	...	...	4	0	0	0	0
96-97—Moose Jaw	WHL	61	12	32	44	116	...	...	...	11	2	5	7	27
—HC Vitkovice	Czech Rep.	1	0	0	0	0	...	...	...	—	—	—	—	—
97-98—Adirondack	AHL	55	4	8	12	86	...	...	...	1	1	0	1	14
—Tampa Bay	NHL	10	1	2	3	22	-1	0	0	—	—	—	—	—
98-99—Tampa Bay	NHL	68	9	12	21	80	-33	3	1	—	—	—	—	—
—Cleveland	IHL	6	2	2	4	16	...	...	...	—	—	—	—	—
99-00—Tampa Bay	NHL	69	8	18	26	93	-19	6	0	—	—	—	—	—
NHL Totals (3 years)		147	18	32	50	195	-53	9	1					

KVASHA, OLEG   C   ISLANDERS

PERSONAL: Born July 26, 1978, in Moscow, U.S.S.R. ... 6-5/216. ... Shoots right. ... Name pronounced kuh-VA-shuh.
TRANSACTIONS/CAREER NOTES: Selected by Florida Panthers in third round (third Panthers pick, 65th overall) of NHL entry draft (June 22, 1996). ... Bruised right ankle (December 16, 1998); missed one game. ... Bruised shoulder (February 27, 1999); missed one game. ... Separated left shoulder (March 31, 1999); missed final nine games of season. ... Sprained knee (March 7, 2000); missed two games. ... Traded by Panthers with RW Mark Parrish to New York Islanders for C Olli Jokinen and G Roberto Luongo (June 24, 2000).

Season Team	League	REGULAR SEASON Gms.	G	A	Pts.	PIM	+/-	PP	SH	PLAYOFFS Gms.	G	A	Pts.	PIM
94-95—CSKA	CIS Jr.					Statistics unavailable.								
95-96—CSKA Moscow	CIS	38	2	3	5	14	...	...	...	2	0	0	0	0
96-97—CSKA Moscow	USSR	44	20	22	42	115	...	...	...	—	—	—	—	—
97-98—New Haven	AHL	57	13	16	29	46	...	...	...	3	2	1	3	0
98-99—Florida	NHL	68	12	13	25	45	5	4	0	—	—	—	—	—
99-00—Florida	NHL	78	5	20	25	34	3	2	0	4	0	0	0	0
NHL Totals (2 years)		146	17	33	50	79	8	6	0	4	0	0	0	0

LAAKSONEN, ANTTI   LW   WILD

PERSONAL: Born October 3, 1973, in Tammela, Finland. ... 6-0/180. ... Shoots left. ... Full Name: Antti Akseli Laaksonen.
COLLEGE: University of Denver.
TRANSACTIONS/CAREER NOTES: Selected by Boston Bruins in eighth round (10th Bruins pick, 191st overall) of NHL entry draft (July 21, 1997). ... Signed as free agent by Minnesota Wild (July 20, 2000).

Season Team	League	REGULAR SEASON Gms.	G	A	Pts.	PIM	+/-	PP	SH	PLAYOFFS Gms.	G	A	Pts.	PIM
93-94—Univ. of Denver	WCHA	36	12	9	21	38	...	...	...	—	—	—	—	—
94-95—Univ. of Denver	WCHA	40	17	18	35	42	...	...	...	—	—	—	—	—
95-96—Univ. of Denver	WCHA	39	25	28	53	71	...	...	...	—	—	—	—	—
96-97—Univ. of Denver	WCHA	39	21	17	38	63	...	...	...	—	—	—	—	—
97-98—Providence	AHL	38	3	2	5	14	...	...	...	—	—	—	—	—
—Charlotte	ECHL	15	4	3	7	12	...	...	...	6	0	3	3	0
98-99—Boston	NHL	11	1	2	3	2	-1	0	0	—	—	—	—	—
—Providence	AHL	66	25	33	58	52	...	...	...	19	7	2	9	28
99-00—Providence	AHL	40	10	12	22	57	...	...	...	14	5	4	9	4
—Boston	NHL	27	6	3	9	2	3	0	0	—	—	—	—	—
NHL Totals (2 years)		38	7	5	12	4	2	0	0					

LABBE, JEAN-FRANCOIS   G   RANGERS

PERSONAL: Born June 15, 1972, in Sherbrooke, Que. ... 5-10/172. ... Catches left. ... Name pronounced lah-BAY.
TRANSACTIONS/CAREER NOTES: Signed as non-drafted free agent by Ottawa Senators (May 12, 1994). ... Traded by Senators to Colorado Avalanche for conditional draft pick (September 20, 1995). ... Signed as free agent by Edmonton Oilers (August 8, 1997). ... Signed as free agent by New York Rangers (July 16, 1998).
HONORS: Won Jacques Plante Trophy (1991-92). ... Named to QMJHL All-Star first team (1991-92). ... Named Col.HL Rookie of the Year (1993-94). ... Named Col.HL Playoff Most Valuable Player (1993-94). ... Named to Col.HL All-Star first team (1993-94). ... Won Les Cunningham Award (1996-97). ... Won Baz Batien Trophy (1996-97). ... Won Harry (Hap) Holmes Memorial Trophy (1996-97). ... Named to AHL All-Star first team (1996-97). ... Shared Harry (Hap) Holmes Memorial Trophy with Milan Hnilicka (1999-2000).

			REGULAR SEASON							PLAYOFFS						
Season Team	League	Gms.	Min	W	L	T	GA	SO	Avg.	Gms.	Min.	W	L	GA	SO	Avg.
89-90 —Trois-Rivieres	QMJHL	28	1499	13	10	0	106	1	4.24	3	132	1	1	8	0	3.64
90-91 —Trois-Rivieres	QMJHL	54	2870	35	14	0	158	5	3.30	5	230	1	4	19	0	4.96
91-92 —Trois-Rivieres	QMJHL	48	2749	31	13	3	142	3	*3.10	15	791	10	3	33	†1	*2.50
92-93 —Hull	QMJHL	46	2701	25	16	2	155	2	3.44	10	518	6	3	24	†1	*2.78
93-94 —Prin. Edward Island	AHL	7	390	4	3	0	22	0	3.38	—	—	—	—	—	—	—
—Thunder Bay	Col.HL	52	*2900	*35	11	4	150	*2	*3.10	8	493	7	1	18	*2	*2.19
94-95 —Prin. Edward Island	AHL	32	1817	13	14	3	94	2	3.10	—	—	—	—	—	—	—
—Thunder Bay	Col.HL	2		2	0	0	...	...	...	—	—	—	—	—	—	—
95-96 —Cornwall	AHL	55	2971	25	21	5	144	3	2.91	8	470	3	5	21	1	2.68
96-97 —Hershey	AHL	66	3811	†34	22	9	160	*6	*2.52	*23	*1364	*14	8	59	1	2.60
97-98 —Hamilton	AHL	52	3139	24	17	11	149	2	2.85	7	414	3	4	20	0	2.90
98-99 —Hartford	AHL	*59	*3392	28	26	3	*182	2	3.22	7	447	3	4	22	0	2.95
99-00 —Hartford	AHL	49	2853	27	13	†7	120	1	2.52	*22	*1320	*15	7	*48	3	2.18
—New York Rangers	NHL	1	60	0	1	0	3	0	3.00							
NHL Totals (1 year)		1	60	0	1	0	3	0	3.00							

LACHANCE, SCOTT   D

PERSONAL: Born October 22, 1972, in Charlottesville, Va. ... 6-1/212. ... Shoots left. ... Full Name: Scott Joseph Lachance. ... Brother of Bob Lachance, right winger with St. Louis Blues system (1992-93 through 1997-98) and Atlanta Thrashers system (1999-2000).
COLLEGE: Boston University.
TRANSACTIONS/CAREER NOTES: Selected by New York Islanders in first round (first Islanders pick, fourth overall) of NHL entry draft (June 22, 1991). ... Sprained wrist (April 13, 1993); missed remainder of season. ... Underwent wrist surgery (April 30, 1993). ... Suffered mild separation of right shoulder (October 8, 1993); missed four games. ... Fractured ankle (February 25, 1995); missed 22 games. ... Injured groin (October 31, 1995); missed 27 games. ... Suffered broken finger (November 1, 1997); missed two games. ... Strained abdominal muscle (March 14, 1998); missed five games. ... Reinjured abdomen (March 28, 1998); missed 11 games. ... Suffered charley horse (November 21, 1998); missed one game. ... Suffered from the flu (December 22, 1998); missed one game. ... Sprained knee (January 5, 1999); missed one game. ... Traded by Islanders to Montreal Canadiens for third-round pick (RW Mattias Weinhandl) in 1999 draft (March 9, 1999). ... Injured back (November 23, 1999); missed 12 games.
HONORS: Named to Hockey East All-Rookie team (1990-91). ... Played in NHL All-Star Game (1997).

			REGULAR SEASON							PLAYOFFS				
Season Team	League	Gms.	G	A	Pts.	PIM	+/-	PP	SH	Gms.	G	A	Pts.	PIM
88-89 —Springfield Jr. B	NEJHL	36	8	28	36	20	...	...	...	—	—	—	—	—
89-90 —Springfield Jr. B	NEJHL	34	25	41	66	62	...	...	...	—	—	—	—	—
90-91 —Boston University	Hockey East	31	5	19	24	48	...	...	...	—	—	—	—	—
91-92 —U.S. national team	Int'l	36	1	10	11	34	...	...	...	—	—	—	—	—
—U.S. Olympic team	Int'l	8	0	1	1	6	...	...	...	—	—	—	—	—
—New York Islanders	NHL	17	1	4	5	9	13	0	0	—	—	—	—	—
92-93 —New York Islanders	NHL	75	7	17	24	67	-1	0	1	—	—	—	—	—
93-94 —New York Islanders	NHL	74	3	11	14	70	-5	0	0	3	0	0	0	0
94-95 —New York Islanders	NHL	26	6	7	13	26	2	3	0	—	—	—	—	—
95-96 —New York Islanders	NHL	55	3	10	13	54	-19	1	0	—	—	—	—	—
96-97 —New York Islanders	NHL	81	3	11	14	47	-7	1	0	—	—	—	—	—
97-98 —New York Islanders	NHL	63	2	11	13	45	-11	1	0	—	—	—	—	—
98-99 —New York Islanders	NHL	59	1	8	9	30	-19	1	0	—	—	—	—	—
—Montreal	NHL	17	1	1	2	11	-2	0	0	—	—	—	—	—
99-00 —Montreal	NHL	57	0	6	6	22	-4	0	0	—	—	—	—	—
NHL Totals (9 years)		524	27	86	113	381	-53	7	1	3	0	0	0	0

LaCOUTURE, DAN   LW   OILERS

PERSONAL: Born April 13, 1977, in Hyannis, Mass. ... 6-1/201. ... Shoots left. ... Name pronounced LA-kuh-toor.
COLLEGE: Boston University.
TRANSACTIONS/CAREER NOTES: Selected by New York Islanders in second round (second Islanders pick, 29th overall) of NHL entry draft (June 22, 1996). ... Traded by Islanders to Edmonton Oilers for RW Mariusz Czerkawski (August 25, 1997).

			REGULAR SEASON							PLAYOFFS				
Season Team	League	Gms.	G	A	Pts.	PIM	+/-	PP	SH	Gms.	G	A	Pts.	PIM
94-95 —Springfield Jr. B	EJHL	49	37	39	76	100	...	...	...	—	—	—	—	—
95-96 —Jr. Whalers	EJHL	42	36	48	84	102	...	...	...	—	—	—	—	—
96-97 —Boston University	Hockey East	31	13	12	25	18	...	...	...	—	—	—	—	—
97-98 —Hamilton	AHL	77	15	10	25	31	...	...	...	5	1	0	1	0
98-99 —Hamilton	AHL	72	17	14	31	73	...	...	...	9	2	1	3	2
—Edmonton	NHL	3	0	0	0	0	1	0	0	—	—	—	—	—
99-00 —Hamilton	AHL	70	23	17	40	85	...	...	...	6	2	1	3	0
—Edmonton	NHL	5	0	0	0	10	0	0	0	1	0	0	0	0
NHL Totals (2 years)		8	0	0	0	10	1	0	0	1	0	0	0	0

LACROIX, DAN   C   ISLANDERS

PERSONAL: Born March 11, 1969, in Montreal. ... 6-2/205. ... Shoots left. ... Full Name: Daniel Lacroix. ... Name pronounced luh-KWAH.
TRANSACTIONS/CAREER NOTES: Selected as underage junior by New York Rangers in second round (second Rangers pick, 31st overall) of NHL entry draft (June 13, 1987). ... Traded by Rangers to Boston Bruins for D Glen Featherstone (August 19, 1994). ... Claimed on waivers by Rangers (March 23, 1995). ... Signed as free agent by Philadelphia Flyers (July 15, 1996). ... Bruised ribs (September 25, 1996); missed first five games of season. ... Suspended two games and fined $1,000 by NHL for throwing flagrant elbow (October 17, 1996). ... Suspended three games and fined $1,000 by NHL for cross-checking incident (March 5, 1998). ... Sprained left knee (March 26, 1998); missed four games. ... Suffered laceration around left eye (April 9, 1998); missed four games. ... Traded by Flyers to Edmonton Oilers for LW Valeri Zelepukin (October 5, 1998). ... Signed as free agent by New York Islanders (August 12, 1999).
HONORS: Won Marcel Robert Trophy (1988-89).

Season Team	League	REGULAR SEASON								PLAYOFFS				
		Gms.	G	A	Pts.	PIM	+/-	PP	SH	Gms.	G	A	Pts.	PIM
86-87—Granby	QMJHL	54	9	16	25	311	...	...	...	8	1	2	3	22
87-88—Granby	QMJHL	58	24	50	74	468	...	...	...	5	0	4	4	12
88-89—Granby	QMJHL	70	45	49	94	320	...	...	...	4	1	1	2	57
—Denver	IHL	2	0	1	1	0	...	...	...	2	0	1	1	0
89-90—Flint	IHL	61	12	16	28	128	...	...	...	4	2	0	2	24
90-91—Binghamton	AHL	54	7	12	19	237	...	...	...	5	1	0	1	24
91-92—Binghamton	AHL	52	12	20	32	149	...	...	...	11	2	4	6	28
92-93—Binghamton	AHL	73	21	22	43	255	...	...	...	—	—	—	—	—
93-94—New York Rangers	NHL	4	0	0	0	0	0	0	0	—	—	—	—	—
—Binghamton	AHL	59	20	23	43	278	...	...	...	—	—	—	—	—
94-95—Providence	AHL	40	15	11	26	266	...	...	...	—	—	—	—	—
—Boston	NHL	23	1	0	1	38	-2	0	0	—	—	—	—	—
—New York Rangers	NHL	1	0	0	0	0	0	0	0	—	—	—	—	—
95-96—Binghamton	AHL	26	12	15	27	155	...	...	...	—	—	—	—	—
—New York Rangers	NHL	25	2	2	4	30	-1	0	0	—	—	—	—	—
96-97—Philadelphia	NHL	74	7	1	8	163	-1	1	0	12	0	1	1	22
97-98—Philadelphia	NHL	56	1	4	5	135	0	0	0	4	0	0	0	4
98-99—Edmonton	NHL	4	0	0	0	13	0	0	0	—	—	—	—	—
—Hamilton	AHL	46	13	9	22	260	...	...	...	11	3	1	4	65
99-00—Chicago	IHL	61	3	10	13	194	...	...	...	7	0	0	0	28
—New York Islanders	NHL	1	0	0	0	0	-1	0	0	—	—	—	—	—
NHL Totals (7 years)		188	11	7	18	379	-5	1	0	16	0	1	1	26

LACROIX, ERIC   LW   RANGERS

PERSONAL: Born July 15, 1971, in Montreal. ... 6-1/207. ... Shoots left. ... Name pronounced luh-KWAH.
HIGH SCHOOL: Governor Dummer (Byfield, Mass.).
COLLEGE: St. Lawrence (N.Y.).
TRANSACTIONS/CAREER NOTES: Selected by Toronto Maple Leafs in seventh round (sixth Maple Leafs pick, 136th overall) of NHL entry draft (June 16, 1990). ... Separated shoulder (November 27, 1993); missed eight games. ... Traded by Maple Leafs with D Chris Snell and fourth-round pick (C Eric Belanger) in 1996 draft to Los Angeles Kings for RW Dixon Ward, C Guy Leveque, RW Shayne Toporowski and C Kelly Fairchild (October 3, 1994). ... Sprained knee (February 4, 1995); missed one game. ... Sprained knee (February 23, 1995); missed two games. ... Suspended three games by NHL for unnecessary contact with an official (October 16, 1995). ... Suspended five games by NHL for checking from behind (November 22, 1995). ... Traded by Kings with first-round pick (D Martin Skoula) in 1998 draft to Colorado Avalanche for G Stephane Fiset and first-round pick (D Mathieu Biron) in 1998 draft (June 20, 1996). ... Traded by Avalanche to Kings for C Roman Vopat and sixth-round pick (traded to Chicago) in 1999 draft (October 29, 1998). ... Fractured right clavicle (December 12, 1998); missed nine games. ... Traded by Kings to New York Rangers for C Sean Pronger (February 12, 1999). ... Fractured hand (October 11, 1999); missed eight games. ... Sprained knee (November 11, 1999); missed one game.
STATISTICAL PLATEAUS: Three-goal games: 1996-97 (1).

Season Team	League	REGULAR SEASON								PLAYOFFS				
		Gms.	G	A	Pts.	PIM	+/-	PP	SH	Gms.	G	A	Pts.	PIM
89-90—Governor Dummer	Mass. H.S.	...	23	18	41	...				—	—	—	—	—
90-91—St. Lawrence Univ.	ECAC	35	13	11	24	35	...	...	...	—	—	—	—	—
91-92—St. Lawrence Univ.	ECAC	34	11	20	31	40	...	...	...	—	—	—	—	—
92-93—St. John's	AHL	76	15	19	34	59	...	...	...	9	5	3	8	4
93-94—St. John's	AHL	59	17	22	39	69	...	...	...	11	5	3	8	6
—Toronto	NHL	3	0	0	0	2	0	0	0	2	0	0	0	0
94-95—St. John's	AHL	1	0	0	0	2	...	...	...	—	—	—	—	—
—Phoenix	IHL	25	7	1	8	31	...	...	...	—	—	—	—	—
—Los Angeles	NHL	45	9	7	16	54	2	2	1	—	—	—	—	—
95-96—Los Angeles	NHL	72	16	16	32	110	-11	3	0	—	—	—	—	—
96-97—Colorado	NHL	81	18	18	36	26	16	2	0	17	1	4	5	19
97-98—Colorado	NHL	82	16	15	31	84	0	5	0	7	0	0	0	6
98-99—Colorado	NHL	7	0	0	0	2	-2	0	0	—	—	—	—	—
—Los Angeles	NHL	27	0	1	1	12	-5	0	0	—	—	—	—	—
—New York Rangers	NHL	30	2	1	3	4	-5	0	0	—	—	—	—	—
99-00—New York Rangers	NHL	70	4	8	12	24	-12	0	0	—	—	—	—	—
NHL Totals (7 years)		417	65	66	131	318	-17	12	1	26	1	4	5	25

LAFLAMME, CHRISTIAN   D   CANADIENS

PERSONAL: Born November 24, 1976, in St. Charles, Que. ... 6-1/210. ... Shoots right. ... Name pronounced lah-FLAHM.
TRANSACTIONS/CAREER NOTES: Selected by Chicago Blackhawks in second round (second Blackhawks pick, 45th overall) of NHL entry draft (July 8, 1995). ... Fractured left foot (October 1, 1997); missed six games. ... Fractured right cheekbone (January 24, 1998); missed four games. ... Traded by Blackhawks with C Chad Kilger, LW Daniel Cleary and LW Ethan Moreau to Edmonton Oilers for D Boris Mironov, LW

Dean McAmmond and D Jonas Elofsson (March 20, 1999). ... Suffered concussion (March 28, 1999); missed one game. ... Bruised shoulder (January 11, 2000); missed one game. ... Traded by Oilers with D Mathieu Descoteaux to Montreal Canadiens for D Igor Ulanov and D Alain Nasreddine (March 9, 2000).

HONORS: Named to QMJHL All-Rookie team (1992-93). ... Named to QMJHL All-Star second team (1994-95).

		REGULAR SEASON								PLAYOFFS				
Season Team	League	Gms.	G	A	Pts.	PIM	+/-	PP	SH	Gms.	G	A	Pts.	PIM
92-93—Verdun	QMJHL	69	2	17	19	70	...	...	...	3	0	2	2	6
93-94—Verdun	QMJHL	72	4	34	38	85	...	...	...	4	0	3	3	4
94-95—Beauport	QMJHL	67	6	41	47	82	...	...	...	8	1	4	5	6
95-96—Beauport	QMJHL	41	13	23	36	63	...	...	...	20	7	17	24	32
96-97—Indianapolis	IHL	62	5	15	20	60	...	...	...	4	1	1	2	16
—Chicago	NHL	4	0	1	1	2	3	0	0	—				
97-98—Chicago	NHL	72	0	11	11	59	14	0	0	—				
98-99—Chicago	NHL	62	2	11	13	70	0	0	0	—				
—Portland	AHL	2	0	1	1	2	...	...	...	—				
—Edmonton	NHL	11	0	1	1	0	-3	0	0	4	0	1	1	2
99-00—Edmonton	NHL	50	0	5	5	32	-4	0	0	—				
—Montreal	NHL	15	0	2	2	8	-5	0	0	—				
NHL Totals (4 years)		214	2	31	33	171	5	0	0	4	0	1	1	2

LALIME, PATRICK   G   SENATORS

PERSONAL: Born July 7, 1974, in St. Bonaventure, Que. ... 6-3/185. ... Catches left. ... Name pronounced luh-LEEM.
TRANSACTIONS/CAREER NOTES: Selected by Pittsburgh Penguins in sixth round (sixth Penguins pick, 156th overall) of NHL entry draft (June 26, 1993). ... Rights traded by Penguins to Mighty Ducks of Anaheim for C Sean Pronger (March 24, 1998). ... Traded by Mighty Ducks to Ottawa Senators for LW Ted Donato and D Antti-Jussi Niemi (June 18, 1999). ... Suffered from the flu (February 1, 2000); missed one game.
HONORS: Named to NHL All-Rookie team (1996-97). ... Named to IHL All-Star first team (1998-99).

		REGULAR SEASON								PLAYOFFS						
Season Team	League	Gms.	Min.	W	L	T	GA	SO	Avg.	Gms.	Min.	W	L	GA	SO	Avg.
92-93—Shawinigan	QMJHL	44	2467	10	24	4	192	0	4.67	—						
93-94—Shawinigan	QMJHL	48	2733	22	20	2	192	1	4.22	5	223	1	3	25	0	6.73
94-95—Hampton Roads	ECHL	26	1471	15	7	‡3	82	2	3.34	—						
—Cleveland	IHL	23	1230	7	10	‡4	91	0	4.44	—						
95-96—Cleveland	IHL	41	2314	20	12	‡7	149	0	3.86	—						
96-97—Cleveland	IHL	14	834	6	6	‡2	45	1	3.24	—						
—Pittsburgh	NHL	39	2058	21	12	3	101	3	2.94	—						
97-98—Grand Rapids	IHL	31	1749	10	10	‡9	76	2	2.61	1	77	0	1	4	0	3.12
98-99—Kansas City	IHL	*66	*3789	*39	20	‡4	*190	2	3.01	3	179	1	2	6	1	2.01
99-00—Ottawa	NHL	38	2038	19	14	3	79	3	2.33	—						
NHL Totals (2 years)		77	4096	40	26	6	180	6	2.64							

LAMBERT, DENNY   LW   THRASHERS

PERSONAL: Born January 7, 1970, in Wawa, Ont. ... 5-10/215. ... Shoots left. ... Name pronounced lam-BAIR.
TRANSACTIONS/CAREER NOTES: Signed as non-drafted free agent by Mighty Ducks of Anaheim (August 16, 1993). ... Signed as free agent by Ottawa Senators (July 8, 1996). ... Selected by Nashville Predators in NHL expansion draft (June 26, 1998). ... Suspended four games and fined $1,000 by NHL for slashing incident (October 23, 1998). ... Suffered illness (February 4, 1999); missed two games. ... Traded by Predators to Atlanta Thrashers for C Randy Robitaille (August 16, 1999). ... Injured thumb (March 31, 2000); missed four games.
MISCELLANEOUS: Holds Atlanta Thrashers all-time record for most penalty minutes (219).

		REGULAR SEASON								PLAYOFFS				
Season Team	League	Gms.	G	A	Pts.	PIM	+/-	PP	SH	Gms.	G	A	Pts.	PIM
88-89—Sault Ste. Marie	OHL	61	14	15	29	203	...	...	...	—				
89-90—Sault Ste. Marie	OHL	61	23	29	52	*276	...	...	...	—				
90-91—Sault Ste. Marie	OHL	59	28	39	67	169	...	...	...	14	7	9	16	48
91-92—San Diego	IHL	71	17	14	31	229	...	...	...	3	0	0	0	10
—St. Thomas	Col.HL	5	2	6	8	9	...	...	...	—				
92-93—San Diego	IHL	56	18	12	30	277	...	...	...	14	1	1	2	44
93-94—San Diego	IHL	79	13	14	27	314	...	...	...	6	1	0	1	45
94-95—San Diego	IHL	75	25	35	60	222	...	...	...	—				
—Anaheim	NHL	13	1	3	4	4	3	0	0	—				
95-96—Anaheim	NHL	33	0	8	8	55	-2	0	0	—				
—Baltimore	AHL	44	14	28	42	126	...	...	...	12	3	9	12	39
96-97—Ottawa	NHL	80	4	16	20	217	-4	0	0	6	0	1	1	9
97-98—Ottawa	NHL	72	9	10	19	250	4	0	0	11	0	0	0	19
98-99—Nashville	NHL	76	5	11	16	218	-3	1	0	—				
99-00—Atlanta	NHL	73	5	6	11	*219	-17	2	0	—				
NHL Totals (6 years)		347	24	54	78	963	-19	3	0	17	0	1	1	28

LAMOTHE, MARC   G

PERSONAL: Born February 27, 1974, in New Liskeard, Ont. ... 6-2/210. ... Catches left. ... Name pronounced luh-MAHTH.
TRANSACTIONS/CAREER NOTES: Selected by Montreal Canadiens in fourth round (sixth Canadiens pick, 92nd overall) of NHL entry draft (June 20, 1992). ... Signed as free agent by Chicago Blackhawks (August 21, 1996).

Season Team	League	Gms.	Min	W	L	T	GA	SO	Avg.	Gms.	Min.	W	L	GA	SO	Avg.
				REGULAR SEASON								**PLAYOFFS**				
90-91—Ottawa	OHA Mj. Jr.	25	1220	...	...	...	82	1	4.03	—	—	—	—	—	—	—
91-92—Kingston	OHL	42	2378	10	25	2	189	1	4.77	—	—	—	—	—	—	—
92-93—Kingston	OHL	45	2489	23	12	6	162	†1	3.91	15	733	8	5	46	†1	3.77
93-94—Kingston	OHL	48	2828	23	20	5	177	†2	3.76	6	224	2	2	12	0	3.21
94-95—Fredericton	AHL	9	428	2	5	0	32	0	4.49	—	—	—	—	—	—	—
—Wheeling	ECHL	13	737	9	2	‡1	38	0	3.09	—	—	—	—	—	—	—
95-96—Fredericton	AHL	23	1165	5	9	3	73	1	3.76	3	160	1	2	9	0	3.38
96-97—Indianapolis	IHL	38	2271	20	14	‡4	100	1	2.64	1	20	0	1	3	0	3.00
97-98—Indianapolis	IHL	31	1773	18	10	‡2	72	3	2.44	4	178	1	3	10	0	3.37
98-99—Indianapolis	IHL	32	1823	9	16	‡6	115	1	3.78	6	338	3	3	10	*2	1.78
—Detroit	IHL	—	—	—	—	—	—	—	—	1	80	0	1	5	0	3.75
99-00—Cleveland	IHL	44	2455	23	18	‡4	112	2	2.74	4	325	2	2	12	0	2.22
—Chicago	NHL	2	116	1	1	0	10	0	5.17	—	—	—	—	—	—	—
NHL Totals (1 year)		2	116	1	1	0	10	0	5.17							

LANG, ROBERT — C — PENGUINS

PERSONAL: Born December 19, 1970, in Teplice, Czechoslovakia. ... 6-2/216. ... Shoots right.

TRANSACTIONS/CAREER NOTES: Selected by Los Angeles Kings in seventh round (sixth Kings pick, 133rd overall) of NHL entry draft (June 16, 1990). ... Dislocated shoulder (April 3, 1994); missed remainder of season. ... Played in Europe during 1994-95 NHL lockout. ... Strained left shoulder (March 26, 1995); missed one game. ... Strained back (November 20, 1995); missed seven games. ... Signed as free agent by Edmonton Oilers (October 19, 1996). ... Loaned by Oilers to Sparta Praha of Czech Republic League (October 19, 1996). ... Signed as free agent by Pittsburgh Penguins (September 2, 1997). ... Claimed by Boston Bruins from Penguins in NHL waiver draft (September 28, 1997). ... Claimed on waivers by Penguins (October 25, 1997). ... Fractured thumb (March 21, 1998); missed nine games. ... Bruised ankle (March 23, 1999); missed 10 games. ... Suffered back spasms (October 16, 1999); missed one game. ... Injured thumb (December 14, 1999); missed one game. ... Suffered facial injury (March 9, 2000); missed two games.

MISCELLANEOUS: Member of gold-medal-winning Czech Republic Olympic team (1998).

STATISTICAL NOTES: Tied for NHL lead in game-tying goals with three (1998-99).

Season Team	League	Gms.	G	A	Pts.	PIM	+/-	PP	SH	Gms.	G	A	Pts.	PIM
						REGULAR SEASON						**PLAYOFFS**		
88-89—Litvinov	Czech.	7	3	2	5	0	...	...	...	—	—	—	—	—
89-90—Litvinov	Czech.	39	11	10	21	20	...	...	...	—	—	—	—	—
90-91—Litvinov	Czech.	56	26	26	52	38	...	...	...	—	—	—	—	—
91-92—Litvinov	Czech.	43	12	31	43	34	...	...	...	—	—	—	—	—
—Czech. national team	Int'l	8	5	8	13	8	...	...	...	—	—	—	—	—
—Czech. Olympic Team	Int'l	8	5	8	13	8	...	...	...	—	—	—	—	—
92-93—Los Angeles	NHL	11	0	5	5	2	-3	0	0	—	—	—	—	—
—Phoenix	IHL	38	9	21	30	20	...	...	...	—	—	—	—	—
93-94—Phoenix	IHL	44	11	24	35	34	...	...	...	—	—	—	—	—
—Los Angeles	NHL	32	9	10	19	10	7	0	0	—	—	—	—	—
94-95—Chem. Litvinov	Czech Rep.	16	4	19	23	28	...	...	...	—	—	—	—	—
—Los Angeles	NHL	36	4	8	12	4	-7	0	0	—	—	—	—	—
95-96—Los Angeles	NHL	68	6	16	22	10	-15	0	2	—	—	—	—	—
96-97—Sparta Praha	Czech Rep.	38	14	27	41	30	...	...	...	5	1	2	3	4
97-98—Boston	NHL	3	0	0	0	2	1	0	0	—	—	—	—	—
—Houston	IHL	9	1	7	8	4	...	...	...	—	—	—	—	—
—Pittsburgh	NHL	51	9	13	22	14	6	1	1	6	0	3	3	2
—Czech Rep. Oly. team	Int'l	6	0	3	3	0	...	...	...	—	—	—	—	—
98-99—Pittsburgh	NHL	72	21	23	44	24	-10	7	0	12	0	2	2	0
99-00—Pittsburgh	NHL	78	23	42	65	14	-9	13	0	11	3	3	6	0
NHL Totals (7 years)		351	72	117	189	80	-30	21	3	29	3	8	11	2

LANGDON, DARREN — LW — RANGERS

PERSONAL: Born January 8, 1971, in Deer Lake, Nfld. ... 6-1/210. ... Shoots left.

TRANSACTIONS/CAREER NOTES: Signed as non-drafted free agent by New York Rangers (August 16, 1993). ... Suspended three games by NHL for abuse of an official in preseason game (September 23, 1995). ... Sprained right knee (December 13, 1996); missed 13 games. ... Suspended two games by NHL for initiating an altercation (March 7, 1997). ... Sprained knee (November 21, 1997); missed six games. ... Bruised sternum (March 4, 1998); missed three games. ... Strained groin (January 2, 2000); missed remainder of season.

Season Team	League	Gms.	G	A	Pts.	PIM	+/-	PP	SH	Gms.	G	A	Pts.	PIM
						REGULAR SEASON						**PLAYOFFS**		
91-92—Summerside	MJHL	44	34	49	83	441	...	...	...	—	—	—	—	—
92-93—Binghamton	AHL	18	3	4	7	115	...	...	...	8	0	1	1	14
—Dayton	ECHL	54	23	22	45	429	...	...	...	3	0	1	1	40
93-94—Binghamton	AHL	54	2	7	9	327	...	...	...	—	—	—	—	—
94-95—Binghamton	AHL	55	6	14	20	296	...	...	...	11	1	3	4	84
—New York Rangers	NHL	18	1	1	2	62	0	0	0	—	—	—	—	—
95-96—New York Rangers	NHL	64	7	4	11	175	2	0	0	2	0	0	0	0
—Binghamton	AHL	1	0	0	0	12	...	...	...	—	—	—	—	—
96-97—New York Rangers	NHL	60	3	6	9	195	-1	0	0	10	0	0	0	2
97-98—New York Rangers	NHL	70	3	3	6	197	0	0	0	—	—	—	—	—
98-99—New York Rangers	NHL	44	0	0	0	80	-3	0	0	—	—	—	—	—
99-00—New York Rangers	NHL	21	0	1	1	26	-2	0	0	—	—	—	—	—
NHL Totals (6 years)		277	14	15	29	735	-4	0	0	12	0	0	0	2

LANGENBRUNNER, JAMIE — RW — STARS

PERSONAL: Born July 24, 1975, in Duluth, Minn. ... 6-1/200. ... Shoots right. ... Name pronounced LANG-ihn-BRUH-nuhr.
HIGH SCHOOL: Cloquet (Minn.).
TRANSACTIONS/CAREER NOTES: Selected by Dallas Stars in second round (second Stars pick, 35th overall) of NHL entry draft (June 26, 1993). ... Suffered back spasms (February 21, 1997); missed one game. ... Suffered whiplash (January 12, 1998); missed one game. ... Injured shoulder (January 6, 1999); missed five games. ... Strained abdominal muscle (March 26, 1999); missed one game. ... Suffered concussion (November 30, 1999); missed one game. ... Sprained shoulder (December 17, 1999); missed one game. ... Suffered pinched nerve in neck (January 7, 2000); missed 11 games. ... Strained neck (February 16, 2000); missed three games.
MISCELLANEOUS: Member of Stanley Cup championship team (1999).

		REGULAR SEASON								PLAYOFFS				
Season Team	League	Gms.	G	A	Pts.	PIM	+/-	PP	SH	Gms.	G	A	Pts.	PIM
90-91—Cloquet H.S.	Minn. H.S.	20	6	16	22	8	...	...	...	—	—	—	—	—
91-92—Cloquet H.S.	Minn. H.S.	23	16	23	39	24	...	...	...	—	—	—	—	—
92-93—Cloquet H.S.	Minn. H.S.	27	27	62	89	18	...	...	...	—	—	—	—	—
93-94—Peterborough	OHL	62	33	58	91	53	...	...	...	7	4	6	10	2
94-95—Peterborough	OHL	62	42	57	99	84	...	...	...	11	8	14	22	12
—Dallas	NHL	2	0	0	0	2	0	0	0	—	—	—	—	—
—Kalamazoo	IHL	—	—	—	—	—	...	...	...	11	1	3	4	2
95-96—Michigan	IHL	59	25	40	65	129	...	...	...	10	3	10	13	8
—Dallas	NHL	12	2	2	4	6	-2	1	0	—	—	—	—	—
96-97—Dallas	NHL	76	13	26	39	51	-2	3	0	5	1	1	2	14
97-98—Dallas	NHL	81	23	29	52	61	9	8	0	16	1	4	5	14
—U.S. Olympic team	Int'l	3	0	0	0	4	...	...	...	—	—	—	—	—
98-99—Dallas	NHL	75	12	33	45	62	10	4	0	23	10	7	17	16
99-00—Dallas	NHL	65	18	21	39	68	16	4	2	15	1	7	8	18
NHL Totals (6 years)		**311**	**68**	**111**	**179**	**250**	**31**	**20**	**2**	**59**	**13**	**19**	**32**	**62**

LANGKOW, DAYMOND — C — FLYERS

PERSONAL: Born September 27, 1976, in Edmonton. ... 5-11/180. ... Shoots left.
TRANSACTIONS/CAREER NOTES: Selected by Tampa Bay Lightning in first round (first Lightning pick, fifth overall) of NHL entry draft (July 8, 1995). ... Suffered from the flu (October 1, 1997); missed one game. ... Suffered from concussion (January 7, 1998); missed two games. ... Suffered from the flu (January 31, 1998); missed three games ... Traded by Lightning with RW Mikael Renberg to Philadelphia Flyers for C Chris Gratton and C/RW Mike Sillinger (December 12, 1998).
HONORS: Won Bob Clarke Trophy (1994-95). ... Named to Can.HL All-Star first team (1994-95). ... Named to WHL (West) All-Star first team (1994-95). ... Named to WHL (West) All-Star second team (1995-96).
MISCELLANEOUS: Failed to score on a penalty shot (vs. Robbie Tallas, November 24, 1998).

		REGULAR SEASON								PLAYOFFS				
Season Team	League	Gms.	G	A	Pts.	PIM	+/-	PP	SH	Gms.	G	A	Pts.	PIM
91-92—Tri-City	WHL	1	0	0	0	0	...	...	...	4	2	2	4	15
92-93—Tri-City	WHL	65	22	42	64	96	...	...	...	4	1	0	1	4
93-94—Tri-City	WHL	61	40	43	83	174	...	...	...	4	2	2	4	15
94-95—Tri-City	WHL	72	67	73	140	142	...	...	...	17	12	15	27	52
95-96—Tampa Bay	NHL	4	0	1	1	0	-1	0	0	—	—	—	—	—
—Tri-City	WHL	48	30	61	91	103	...	...	...	11	14	13	27	20
96-97—Adirondack	AHL	2	1	1	2	0	...	...	...	—	—	—	—	—
—Tampa Bay	NHL	79	15	13	28	35	1	3	1	—	—	—	—	—
97-98—Tampa Bay	NHL	68	8	14	22	62	-9	2	0	—	—	—	—	—
98-99—Cleveland	IHL	4	1	1	2	18	...	...	...	—	—	—	—	—
—Tampa Bay	NHL	22	4	6	10	15	0	1	0	—	—	—	—	—
—Philadelphia	NHL	56	10	13	23	24	-8	3	1	6	0	2	2	2
99-00—Philadelphia	NHL	82	18	32	50	56	1	5	0	16	5	5	10	23
NHL Totals (5 years)		**311**	**55**	**79**	**134**	**192**	**-16**	**14**	**2**	**22**	**5**	**7**	**12**	**25**

LANGKOW, SCOTT — G — THRASHERS

PERSONAL: Born April 21, 1975, in Sherwood Park, Alta. ... 5-11/190. ... Catches left.
HIGH SCHOOL: Aloha (Beaverton, Ore.).
TRANSACTIONS/CAREER NOTES: Selected by Winnipeg Jets in second round (second Jets pick, 31st overall) of NHL entry draft (June 26, 1993). ... Jets franchise moved to Phoenix and renamed Coyotes for 1996-97 season; NHL approved move on January 18, 1996. ... Traded by Coyotes to Atlanta Thrashers for future considerations (June 25, 1999).
HONORS: Named to WHL (West) All-Star second team (1993-94 and 1994-95). ... Won Harry (Hap) Holmes Memorial Trophy (1995-96). ... Named to AHL All-Star first team (1997-98). ... Won Baz Bastien Trophy (1997-98).
MISCELLANEOUS: Allowed a penalty shot goal (vs. Daniel Alfredsson, March 4, 2000).

		REGULAR SEASON							PLAYOFFS					
Season Team	League	Gms.	Min	W	L	T	GA	SO	Avg.	Gms.	Min.	W	L	GA	SO	Avg.
91-92—Portland	WHL	1	33	0	0	0	2	0	3.64	—	—	—	—	—	—	—
92-93—Portland	WHL	34	2064	24	8	2	119	2	3.46	9	535	6	3	31	0	3.48
93-94—Portland	WHL	39	2302	27	9	1	121	2	3.15	10	600	6	4	34	0	3.40
94-95—Portland	WHL	63	3638	20	36	5	240	1	3.96	8	510	3	5	30	0	3.53
95-96—Springfield	AHL	39	2329	18	15	6	116	3	2.99	7	392	4	2	23	0	3.52
—Winnipeg	NHL	1	6	0	0	0	0	0	...	—	—	—	—	—	—	—
96-97—Springfield	AHL	33	1929	15	9	7	85	0	2.64	—	—	—	—	—	—	—
97-98—Springfield	AHL	51	2875	30	13	5	128	3	2.67	4	216	1	3	14	0	3.89
—Phoenix	NHL	3	137	0	1	1	10	0	4.38	—	—	—	—	—	—	—

Season Team	League	REGULAR SEASON								PLAYOFFS					
		Gms.	Min	W	L	T	GA	SO	Avg.	Gms.	Min.	W	L	GA	SO	Avg.
98-99—Las Vegas	IHL	27	1402	7	14	‡2	97	1	4.15	—	—	—	—	—	—	—
—Utah	IHL	21	1227	10	9	‡2	59	1	2.89	—	—	—	—	—	—	—
—Phoenix	NHL	1	35	0	0	0	3	0	5.14	—	—	—	—	—	—	—
99-00—Orlando	IHL	27	1487	16	8	‡2	57	4	2.30	6	381	2	3	16	0	2.52
—Atlanta	NHL	15	765	3	11	0	55	0	4.31	—	—	—	—	—	—	—
NHL Totals (4 years)		20	943	3	12	1	68	0	4.33							

LANK, JEFF　　　　　　　　　　D

PERSONAL: Born March 1, 1975, in Indianhead, Sask. ... 6-3/185. ... Shoots left.
HIGH SCHOOL: Carlton Comprehensive (Prince Albert, Sask.).
TRANSACTIONS/CAREER NOTES: Selected by Montreal Canadiens in fifth round (sixth Canadiens pick, 113th overall) of NHL entry draft (June 26, 1993). ... Returned to draft pool by Canadiens and selected by Philadelphia Flyers in ninth round (ninth Flyers pick, 230th overall) of NHL entry draft (July 8, 1995).

Season Team	League	REGULAR SEASON								PLAYOFFS				
		Gms.	G	A	Pts.	PIM	+/-	PP	SH	Gms.	G	A	Pts.	PIM
90-91—Columbia Valley	KIJHL	36	4	28	32	40	...	...	...	—	—	—	—	—
91-92—Prince Albert	WHL	56	2	8	10	26	...	...	...	9	0	0	0	2
92-93—Prince Albert	WHL	63	1	11	12	60	...	...	...	—	—	—	—	—
93-94—Prince Albert	WHL	72	9	38	47	62	...	...	...	—	—	—	—	—
94-95—Prince Albert	WHL	68	12	25	37	60	...	...	...	13	2	10	12	8
95-96—Hershey	AHL	72	7	13	20	70	...	...	...	5	0	0	0	8
96-97—Philadelphia	AHL	44	2	12	14	49	...	...	...	7	2	1	3	4
97-98—Philadelphia	AHL	69	7	9	16	59	...	...	...	20	1	4	5	22
98-99—Philadelphia	AHL	51	5	10	15	36	...	...	...	2	0	0	0	2
99-00—Philadelphia	AHL	26	1	4	5	16	...	...	...	3	0	0	0	2
—Philadelphia	NHL	2	0	0	0	2	0	0	0	—	—	—	—	—
NHL Totals (1 year)		2	0	0	0	2	0	0	0					

LAPERRIERE, IAN　　　　C/RW　　　　KINGS

PERSONAL: Born January 19, 1974, in Montreal. ... 6-1/197. ... Shoots left. ... Name pronounced EE-ihn luh-PAIR-ee-AIR.
TRANSACTIONS/CAREER NOTES: Selected by St. Louis Blues in seventh round (sixth Blues pick, 158th overall) of NHL entry draft (June 20, 1992). ... Suffered concussion (March 26, 1995); missed three games. ... Traded by Blues to New York Rangers for LW Stephane Matteau (December 28, 1995). ... Traded by Rangers with C Ray Ferraro, C Nathan Lafayette, D Matis Norstrom and fourth-round pick (D Sean Blanchard) in 1997 draft to Los Angeles Kings for RW Shane Churla, LW Jari Kurri and D/RW Marty McSorley (March 14, 1996). ... Sprained left shoulder (March 16, 1996); missed two games. ... Strained shoulder (October 29, 1996); missed three games. ... Strained hip flexor (February 1, 1997); missed three games. ... Suffered concussion (February 25, 1997); missed two games. ... Underwent shoulder surgery (March 17, 1997); missed final 11 games of regular season. ... Suffered blurred vision (December 31, 1997); missed three games. ... Suffered partial tear of anterior cruciate ligament in knee (October 12, 1998); missed nine games. ... Suffered inflammation of left knee (January 2, 1999); missed one game. ... Sprained knee (December 30, 1999); missed three games.
HONORS: Named to QMJHL All-Star second team (1992-93).

Season Team	League	REGULAR SEASON								PLAYOFFS				
		Gms.	G	A	Pts.	PIM	+/-	PP	SH	Gms.	G	A	Pts.	PIM
90-91—Drummondville	QMJHL	65	19	29	48	117	...	...	...	—	—	—	—	—
91-92—Drummondville	QMJHL	70	28	49	77	160	...	...	...	—	—	—	—	—
92-93—Drummondville	QMJHL	60	44	†96	140	188	...	...	...	10	6	13	19	20
93-94—Drummondville	QMJHL	62	41	72	113	150	...	...	...	9	4	6	10	35
—St. Louis	NHL	1	0	0	0	0	0	0	0	—	—	—	—	—
—Peoria	IHL	—	—	—	—	—				5	1	3	4	2
94-95—Peoria	IHL	51	16	32	48	111	...	...	...	—	—	—	—	—
—St. Louis	NHL	37	13	14	27	85	12	1	0	7	0	4	4	21
95-96—St. Louis	NHL	33	3	6	9	87	-4	1	0	—	—	—	—	—
—Worcester	AHL	3	2	1	3	22	...			—	—	—	—	—
—New York Rangers	NHL	28	1	2	3	53	-5	0	0	—	—	—	—	—
—Los Angeles	NHL	10	2	3	5	15	-2	0	0	—	—	—	—	—
96-97—Los Angeles	NHL	62	8	15	23	102	-25	0	1	—	—	—	—	—
97-98—Los Angeles	NHL	77	6	15	21	131	0	0	1	4	1	0	1	6
98-99—Los Angeles	NHL	72	3	10	13	138	-5	0	0	—	—	—	—	—
99-00—Los Angeles	NHL	79	9	13	22	185	-14	0	0	4	0	0	0	2
NHL Totals (7 years)		399	45	78	123	796	-43	2	2	15	1	4	5	29

LAPLANTE, DARRYL　　　　LW　　　　WILD

PERSONAL: Born March 28, 1977, in Calgary. ... 6-0/198. ... Shoots right. ... Name pronounced luh-PLANT.
COLLEGE: Vanier (Edson, Alta.).
TRANSACTIONS/CAREER NOTES: Selected by Detroit Red Wings in third round (third Red Wings pick, 58th overall) of NHL entry draft (July 8, 1995). ... Fractured cheekbone (February 14, 2000); missed eight games. ... Selected by Minnesota Wild in NHL expansion draft (June 23, 2000).

Season Team	League	REGULAR SEASON								PLAYOFFS				
		Gms.	G	A	Pts.	PIM	+/-	PP	SH	Gms.	G	A	Pts.	PIM
94-95—Moose Jaw	WHL	71	22	24	46	66	...	...	...	10	2	2	4	7
95-96—Moose Jaw	WHL	72	42	40	82	76	...	...	...	12	2	4	6	15
96-97—Moose Jaw	WHL	69	38	42	80	79	...	...	...	3	0	1	1	4
97-98—Adirondack	AHL	77	15	10	25	51	...	...	...	3	0	1	1	4
—Detroit	NHL	2	0	0	0	0	0	0	0	—	—	—	—	—
98-99—Adirondack	AHL	71	17	15	32	96	...	...	...	3	0	1	1	0
—Detroit	NHL	3	0	0	0	0	0	0	0	—	—	—	—	—

Season Team	League	REGULAR SEASON								PLAYOFFS				
		Gms.	G	A	Pts.	PIM	+/-	PP	SH	Gms.	G	A	Pts.	PIM
99-00—Cincinnati	AHL	35	13	9	22	47	...	...	...	—	—	—	—	—
—Detroit	NHL	30	0	6	6	10	-2	0	0	—	—	—	—	—
NHL Totals (3 years)		35	0	6	6	10	-2	0	0	—	—	—	—	—

LAPOINTE, CLAUDE   C   ISLANDERS

PERSONAL: Born October 11, 1968, in Lachine, Que. ... 5-9/183. ... Shoots left. ... Name pronounced KLOHD luh-pwah.

TRANSACTIONS/CAREER NOTES: Selected by Quebec Nordiques in 12th round (12th Nordiques pick, 234th overall) of NHL entry draft (June 11, 1988). ... Tore groin muscle (February 9, 1991). ... Injured groin (October 23, 1991); missed one game. ... Injured back in training camp (September 1992); missed first five games of season. ... Bruised hip (April 6, 1993); missed two games. ... Sprained left knee (October 18, 1993); missed 13 games. ... Sprained back (February 1, 1994); missed nine games. ... Injured back (March 19, 1994); missed three games. ... Suffered lower back pain (January 21, 1995); missed 16 games. ... Suffered from the flu (April 16, 1995); missed one game. ... Injured hip (April 30, 1995); missed one game. ... Nordiques franchise moved to Colorado and renamed Avalanche for 1995-96 season (June 21, 1995). ... Traded by Avalanche to Calgary Flames for seventh-round pick (C Samuel Pahlsson) in 1996 draft (November 1, 1995). ... Injured groin (December 20, 1995); missed one game. ... Reinjured groin (December 27, 1995); missed three games. ... Reinjured groin (January 5, 1996); missed three games. ... Injured hip (January 26, 1996); missed 17 games. ... Signed as free agent by New York Islanders (August 22, 1996). ... Hyperextended ankle (January 2, 1997); missed one game. ... Suffered sore ankle (January 25, 1997); missed one game. ... Bruised foot (January 22, 1998); missed three games. ... Fractured toe (February 1, 1998); missed three games. ... Injured foot (October 16, 1999); missed one game. ... Sprained medial collateral ligament in knee (October 30, 1999); missed two games. ... Suffered facial lacerations (December 29, 1999); missed one game. ... Suffered from the flu (April 6, 2000); missed two games.

MISCELLANEOUS: Failed to score on a penalty shot (vs. Mike Richter, October 22, 1998; vs. Mike Vernon, January 12, 2000).

Season Team	League	REGULAR SEASON								PLAYOFFS				
		Gms.	G	A	Pts.	PIM	+/-	PP	SH	Gms.	G	A	Pts.	PIM
85-86—Trois-Rivieres	QMJHL	72	19	38	57	74	...	...	...	—	—	—	—	—
86-87—Trois-Rivieres	QMJHL	70	47	57	104	123	...	...	...	—	—	—	—	—
87-88—Laval	QMJHL	69	37	83	120	143	...	...	...	13	2	17	19	53
88-89—Laval	QMJHL	63	32	72	104	158	...	...	...	17	5	14	19	66
89-90—Halifax	AHL	63	18	19	37	51	...	...	...	6	1	1	2	34
90-91—Quebec	NHL	13	2	2	4	4	3	0	0	—	—	—	—	—
—Halifax	AHL	43	17	17	34	46	...	...	...	—	—	—	—	—
91-92—Quebec	NHL	78	13	20	33	86	-8	0	2	—	—	—	—	—
92-93—Quebec	NHL	74	10	26	36	98	5	0	0	6	2	4	6	8
93-94—Quebec	NHL	59	11	17	28	70	2	1	1	—	—	—	—	—
94-95—Quebec	NHL	29	4	8	12	41	5	0	0	5	0	0	0	8
95-96—Colorado	NHL	3	0	0	0	0	-1	0	0	—	—	—	—	—
—Calgary	NHL	32	4	5	9	20	2	0	2	2	0	0	0	0
—Saint John	AHL	12	5	3	8	10	...	...	...	—	—	—	—	—
96-97—Utah	IHL	9	7	6	13	14	...	...	...	—	—	—	—	—
—New York Islanders	NHL	73	13	5	18	49	-12	0	3	—	—	—	—	—
97-98—New York Islanders	NHL	78	10	10	20	47	-9	0	1	—	—	—	—	—
98-99—New York Islanders	NHL	82	14	23	37	62	-19	2	2	—	—	—	—	—
99-00—New York Islanders	NHL	76	15	16	31	60	-22	2	1	—	—	—	—	—
NHL Totals (10 years)		597	96	132	228	537	-54	5	12	13	2	4	6	16

L

LAPOINTE, MARTIN   RW   RED WINGS

PERSONAL: Born September 12, 1973, in Lachine, Que. ... 5-11/215. ... Shoots right. ... Name pronounced MAHR-tahn luh-POYNT.

TRANSACTIONS/CAREER NOTES: Selected by Detroit Red Wings in first round (first Red Wings pick, 10th overall) of NHL entry draft (June 22, 1991). ... Fractured wrist (October 9, 1991); missed 22 games. ... Injured left knee (February 29, 1996); missed eight games. ... Injured leg (April 10, 1996); missed two games. ... Fractured finger (December 1, 1996); missed four games. ... Strained hamstring (February 25, 1998); missed one game. ... Suspended two games and fined $1,000 by NHL for cross-checking incident (March 18, 1998). ... Suffered back spasms (December 22, 1998); missed one game. ... Bruised knee (February 12, 1999); missed three games.

HONORS: Won Michel Bergeron Trophy (1989-90). ... Named to QMJHL All-Star first team (1989-90 and 1992-93). ... Named to QMJHL All-Star second team (1990-91).

MISCELLANEOUS: Member of Stanley Cup championship team (1997 and 1998).

STATISTICAL PLATEAUS: Three-goal games: 1999-00 (1).

Season Team	League	REGULAR SEASON								PLAYOFFS				
		Gms.	G	A	Pts.	PIM	+/-	PP	SH	Gms.	G	A	Pts.	PIM
89-90—Laval	QMJHL	65	42	54	96	77	...	...	...	14	8	17	25	54
90-91—Laval	QMJHL	64	44	54	98	66	...	...	...	13	7	14	21	26
91-92—Detroit	NHL	4	0	1	1	5	2	0	0	3	0	1	1	4
—Laval	QMJHL	31	25	30	55	84	...	...	...	10	4	10	14	32
—Adirondack	AHL	—	—	—	—	—	...	...	...	8	2	2	4	4
92-93—Adirondack	AHL	8	1	2	3	9	...	...	...	—	—	—	—	—
—Detroit	NHL	3	0	0	0	0	-2	0	0	—	—	—	—	—
—Laval	QMJHL	35	38	51	89	41	...	...	...	13	*13	*17	*30	22
93-94—Adirondack	AHL	28	25	21	46	47	...	...	...	4	1	1	2	8
—Detroit	NHL	50	8	8	16	55	7	2	0	4	0	0	0	6
94-95—Adirondack	AHL	39	29	16	45	80	...	...	...	—	—	—	—	—
—Detroit	NHL	39	4	6	10	73	1	0	0	2	0	1	1	8
95-96—Detroit	NHL	58	6	3	9	93	0	1	0	11	1	2	3	12
96-97—Detroit	NHL	78	16	17	33	167	-14	5	1	20	4	8	12	60
97-98—Detroit	NHL	79	15	19	34	106	0	4	0	21	9	6	15	20
98-99—Detroit	NHL	77	16	13	29	141	7	7	1	10	0	2	2	20
99-00—Detroit	NHL	82	16	25	41	121	17	1	1	9	3	1	4	20
NHL Totals (9 years)		470	81	92	173	761	18	20	3	80	17	21	38	150

PERSONAL: Born December 7, 1976, in Montreal. ... 6-3/240. ... Shoots right. ... Name pronounced la-RAHK.

TRANSACTIONS/CAREER NOTES: Selected by Edmonton Oilers in second round (second Oilers pick, 31st overall) of NHL entry draft (July 8, 1995). ... Fractured left foot (November 17, 1997); missed five games. ... Tore cartilage in right knee (December 5, 1997); missed seven games. ... Suspended two games by AHL for checking from behind (October 21, 1998). ... Bruised sternum (January 17, 1999); missed two games. ... Sprained ankle (March 24, 1999); missed three games. ... Suffered concussion (April 1, 1999); missed three games. ... Suffered eye injury (December 19, 1999); missed two games. ... Sprained knee (March 27, 2000); missed one game.

STATISTICAL PLATEAUS: Three-goal games: 1999-00 (1).

			REGULAR SEASON								PLAYOFFS				
Season Team	League	Gms.	G	A	Pts.	PIM	+/-	PP	SH		Gms.	G	A	Pts.	PIM
93-94—St. Jean	QMJHL	70	11	11	22	142	...	...	...		4	0	0	0	7
94-95—St. Jean	QMJHL	62	19	22	41	259	...	...	...		7	1	1	2	42
95-96—Laval	QMJHL	11	8	13	21	76	...	...	...		—	—	—	—	—
—St. Hyacinthe	QMJHL	8	3	4	7	59	...	...	...		—	—	—	—	—
—Granby	QMJHL	22	9	7	16	125	...	...	...		18	7	6	13	104
96-97—Hamilton	AHL	73	14	20	34	179	...	...	...		15	1	3	4	12
97-98—Hamilton	AHL	46	10	20	30	154	...	...	...		3	0	0	0	11
—Edmonton	NHL	11	0	0	0	59	-4	0	0		—	—	—	—	—
98-99—Hamilton	AHL	25	6	8	14	93	...	...	...		—	—	—	—	—
—Edmonton	NHL	39	3	2	5	57	-1	0	0		4	0	0	0	2
99-00—Edmonton	NHL	76	8	8	16	123	5	0	0		5	0	1	1	6
NHL Totals (3 years)		126	11	10	21	239	0	0	0		9	0	1	1	8

PERSONAL: Born December 3, 1960, in Voskresensk, U.S.S.R. ... 5-10/170. ... Shoots left. ... Name pronounced EE-gohr LAIR-ee-AH-nahf.

TRANSACTIONS/CAREER NOTES: Selected by Vancouver Canucks in 11th round (11th Canucks pick, 214th overall) of NHL entry draft (June 15, 1985). ... Injured groin (October 25, 1990); missed four games. ... Sprained ankle (January 8, 1991). ... Reinjured ankle (January 30, 1991); missed seven games. ... Signed to play with Lugano of Switzerland (July 14, 1992). ... Selected by San Jose Sharks in NHL waiver draft (October 4, 1992). ... Injured shoulder (September 30, 1993); missed four games. ... Reinjured shoulder (October 16, 1993); missed four games. ... Suffered from the flu (November 7, 1993); missed two games. ... Sprained knee (December 12, 1993); missed 10 games. ... Suffered from respiratory infection (February 11, 1994); missed one game. ... Suffered from the flu (February 26, 1994); missed two games. ... Injured groin (February 15, 1995); missed three games. ... Injured foot (February 26, 1995); missed 12 games. ... Traded by Sharks with second-round pick (traded to St. Louis) in 1998 draft to Detroit Red Wings for RW Ray Sheppard (October 25, 1995). ... Suffered from the flu (December 29, 1995); missed two games. ... Pulled groin (October 15, 1996); missed four games. ... Bruised wrist (October 30, 1996); missed seven games. ... Suffered from the flu (March 21, 1997); missed one game. ... Bruised back (April 8, 1997); missed three games. ... Injured groin (December 5, 1997); missed two games. ... Strained groin (December 26, 1997); missed one game. ... Reinjured groin (December 29, 1997); missed one game. ... Strained groin (March 18, 1998); missed two games. ... Reinjured groin (March 26, 1998); missed three games. ... Injured elbow (April 9, 1998); missed four games. ... Injured groin (March 17, 1999); missed three games. ... Signed as free agent by Florida Panthers (July 1, 2000).

HONORS: Named to Soviet League All-Star team (1982-83 and 1985-86 through 1987-88). ... Won Soviet Player of the Year Award (1987-88). ... Played in NHL All-Star Game (1998).

MISCELLANEOUS: Member of Stanley Cup championship team (1997 and 1998). ... Member of gold-medal-winning U.S.S.R. Olympic teams (1984 and 1988). ... Scored on a penalty shot (vs. Arturs Irbe, November 22, 1995).

STATISTICAL PLATEAUS: Three-goal games: 1991-92 (2), 1993-94 (2). Total: 4.

			REGULAR SEASON								PLAYOFFS				
Season Team	League	Gms.	G	A	Pts.	PIM	+/-	PP	SH		Gms.	G	A	Pts.	PIM
77-78—Khimik Voskresensk ...	USSR	6	3	0	3	4	...	...	...		—	—	—	—	—
78-79—Khimik Voskresensk ...	USSR	25	3	4	7	12	...	...	...		—	—	—	—	—
79-80—Khimik Voskresensk ...	USSR	42	11	7	18	24	...	...	...		—	—	—	—	—
80-81—Khimik Voskresensk ...	USSR	56	22	23	45	36	...	...	...		—	—	—	—	—
81-82—CSKA Moscow	USSR	46	31	22	53	6	...	...	...		—	—	—	—	—
82-83—CSKA Moscow	USSR	44	20	19	39	20	...	...	...		—	—	—	—	—
83-84—CSKA Moscow	USSR	43	15	26	41	30	...	...	...		—	—	—	—	—
—Soviet Olympic Team	Int'l	7	1	4	5	6	...	...	...		—	—	—	—	—
84-85—CSKA Moscow	USSR	40	18	28	46	20	...	...	...		—	—	—	—	—
85-86—CSKA Moscow	USSR	40	21	31	52	33	...	...	...		—	—	—	—	—
86-87—CSKA Moscow	USSR	39	20	26	46	34	...	...	...		—	—	—	—	—
87-88—CSKA Moscow	USSR	51	25	32	57	54	...	...	...		—	—	—	—	—
—Soviet Olympic Team ..	Int'l	8	4	9	13	4	...	...	...		—	—	—	—	—
88-89—CSKA Moscow	USSR	31	15	12	27	22	...	...	...		—	—	—	—	—
89-90—Vancouver	NHL	74	17	27	44	20	-5	8	0		—	—	—	—	—
90-91—Vancouver	NHL	64	13	21	34	14	-3	1	1		6	1	0	1	6
91-92—Vancouver	NHL	72	21	44	65	54	7	10	3		13	3	7	10	4
92-93—Lugano	Switzerland	24	10	19	29	44	...	...	...		—	—	—	—	—
93-94—San Jose	NHL	60	18	38	56	40	20	3	2		14	5	13	18	10
94-95—San Jose	NHL	33	4	20	24	14	-3	0	0		11	1	8	9	2
95-96—San Jose	NHL	4	1	1	2	0	-6	1	0		—	—	—	—	—
—Detroit	NHL	69	21	50	71	34	37	9	1		19	6	7	13	6
96-97—Detroit	NHL	64	12	42	54	26	31	2	1		20	4	8	12	8
97-98—Detroit	NHL	69	8	39	47	40	14	3	0		22	3	10	13	12
98-99—Detroit	NHL	75	14	49	63	48	13	4	2		7	0	2	2	4
99-00—Detroit	NHL	79	9	38	47	28	13	3	0		9	1	2	3	6
NHL Totals (10 years)		663	138	369	507	318	118	44	10		121	24	57	81	54

LARSEN, BRAD — LW — AVALANCHE

PERSONAL: Born June 28, 1977, in Nakusp, B.C. ... 6-0/210. ... Shoots left.
TRANSACTIONS/CAREER NOTES: Selected by Ottawa Senators in third round (third Senators pick, 53rd overall) of NHL entry draft (July 8, 1995). ... Rights traded by Senators to Colorado Avalanche for D Janne Laukkanen (January 25, 1996); did not sign. ... Returned to draft pool by Avalanche and selected by Avalanche in fourth round (fifth Avalanche pick, 87th overall) of NHL entry draft (June 21, 1997).
HONORS: Named to WHL (East) All-Star second team (1996-97).

		REGULAR SEASON								PLAYOFFS				
Season Team	League	Gms.	G	A	Pts.	PIM	+/-	PP	SH	Gms.	G	A	Pts.	PIM
92-93—Nelson	Tier II Jr. A	42	31	37	68	164	...	...	...	—	—	—	—	—
93-94—Swift Current	WHL	64	15	18	33	37	...	...	...	7	1	2	3	4
94-95—Swift Current	WHL	62	24	33	57	73	...	...	...	6	0	1	1	2
95-96—Swift Current	WHL	51	30	47	77	67	...	...	...	6	3	2	5	13
96-97—Swift Current	WHL	61	36	46	82	61	...	...	...	—	—	—	—	—
97-98—Hershey	AHL	65	12	10	22	80	...	...	...	7	3	2	5	2
—Colorado	NHL	1	0	0	0	0	0	0	0	—	—	—	—	—
98-99—Hershey	AHL	18	3	4	7	11	...	...	...	5	1	0	1	6
99-00—Hershey	AHL	52	13	26	39	66	...	...	...	14	5	2	7	29
NHL Totals (1 year)		1	0	0	0	0	0	0	0					

LAUKKANEN, JANNE — D — PENGUINS

PERSONAL: Born March 19, 1970, in Lahti, Finland. ... 6-1/194. ... Shoots left. ... Name pronounced YAH-nee LOW-kih-nihn.
TRANSACTIONS/CAREER NOTES: Selected by Quebec Nordiques in eighth round (eighth Nordiques pick, 156th overall) of NHL entry draft (June 22, 1991). ... Injured groin (April 14, 1995); missed two games. ... Reinjured groin (April 30, 1995); missed last game of season. ... Nordiques franchise moved to Colorado and renamed Avalanche for 1995-96 season (June 21, 1995). ... Traded by Avalanche to Ottawa Senators for LW Brad Larsen (January 25, 1996). ... Suffered hip flexor during 1995-96 season; missed five games. ... Sprained left knee (March 25, 1996); missed two games. ... Bruised finger (November 15, 1996); missed one game. ... Suffered from the flu (December 10, 1996); missed two games. ... Suffered from the flu (March 17, 1997); missed one game. ... Injured knee (March 25, 1997); missed two games. ... Suffered concussion (October 19, 1997); missed two games. ... Strained groin (November 20, 1997); missed five games. ... Suffered from the flu (February 2, 1998); missed one game. ... Bruised foot (March 1, 1998); missed one game. ... Strained groin (March 13, 1998); missed five games. ... Reinjured groin (March 25, 1998); missed eight games. ... Underwent offseason abdominal surgery; missed first 19 games of 1998-99 season. ... Injured groin (November 23, 1998); missed four games. ... Suffered back spasms (January 26, 1999); missed three games. ... Strained back (April 3, 1999); missed one game. ... Suffered concussion (April 7, 1999); missed five games. ... Injured left shoulder (November 30, 1999); missed three games. ... Injured right ankle (December 29, 1999); missed one game. ... Suffered from the flu (January 20, 2000); missed one game. ... Suffered illness (January 26, 2000); missed three game. ... Traded by Senators with G Ron Tugnutt to Pittsburgh Penguins for G Tom Barrasso (March 14, 2000). ... Bruised ribs (March 24, 2000); missed one game. ... Reinjured ribs (April 5, 2000); missed one game.
MISCELLANEOUS: Member of bronze-medal-winning Finnish Olympic team (1994 and 1998).

		REGULAR SEASON								PLAYOFFS				
Season Team	League	Gms.	G	A	Pts.	PIM	+/-	PP	SH	Gms.	G	A	Pts.	PIM
89-90—Ilves Tampere	Finland	39	5	6	11	10	...	...	...	—	—	—	—	—
90-91—Reipas	Finland	44	8	14	22	56	...	...	...	—	—	—	—	—
91-92—Helsinki HPK	Finland	43	5	14	19	62	...	...	...	—	—	—	—	—
—Fin. Olympic team	Int'l	8	0	1	1	6	...	...	...	—	—	—	—	—
92-93—HPK Hameenlinna	Finland	47	8	21	29	76	...	...	...	12	1	4	5	10
93-94—HPK Hameenlinna	Finland	48	5	24	29	46	...	...	...	—	—	—	—	—
—Fin. Olympic team	Int'l	8	0	2	2	12	...	...	...	—	—	—	—	—
94-95—Cornwall	AHL	55	8	26	34	41	...	...	...	—	—	—	—	—
—Quebec	NHL	11	0	3	3	4	3	0	0	6	1	0	1	2
95-96—Cornwall	AHL	35	7	20	27	60	...	...	...	—	—	—	—	—
—Colorado	NHL	3	1	0	1	0	-1	1	0	—	—	—	—	—
—Ottawa	NHL	20	0	2	2	14	0	0	0	—	—	—	—	—
96-97—Ottawa	NHL	76	3	18	21	76	-14	2	0	7	0	1	1	6
97-98—Ottawa	NHL	60	4	17	21	64	-15	2	0	11	2	2	4	8
—Fin. Olympic team	Int'l	6	0	0	0	4	...	...	...	—	—	—	—	—
98-99—Ottawa	NHL	50	1	11	12	40	18	0	0	4	0	0	0	4
99-00—Ottawa	NHL	60	1	11	12	55	14	0	0	—	—	—	—	—
—Pittsburgh	NHL	11	1	7	8	12	3	1	0	11	2	4	6	10
NHL Totals (6 years)		291	11	69	80	265	8	6	0	39	5	7	12	30

LAUS, PAUL — RW — PANTHERS

PERSONAL: Born September 26, 1970, in Beamsville, Ont. ... 6-1/212. ... Shoots right. ... Name pronounced LAWS.
TRANSACTIONS/CAREER NOTES: Selected by Pittsburgh Penguins in second round (second Penguins pick, 37th overall) of NHL entry draft (June 17, 1989). ... Selected by Florida Panthers in NHL expansion draft (June 24, 1993). ... Strained groin (February 19, 1995); missed six games. ... Separated left shoulder (April 16, 1995); missed two games. ... Bruised left ankle (October 16, 1996); missed two games. ... Sprained ankle (March 5, 1997); missed one game. ... Bruised hand (March 19, 1997); missed two games. ... Suffered back spasms (March 11, 1998); missed four games. ... Suffered torn right hamstring (April 7, 1999); missed final five games of season. ... Fractured hand (March 29, 2000); missed five games.
MISCELLANEOUS: Holds Florida Panthers all-time record for most penalty minutes (1,479). ... Played defense (1986-87 through 1998-99).

		REGULAR SEASON								PLAYOFFS				
Season Team	League	Gms.	G	A	Pts.	PIM	+/-	PP	SH	Gms.	G	A	Pts.	PIM
86-87—St. Catharines Jr. B	OHA	40	1	8	9	56	...	...	...	—	—	—	—	—
87-88—Hamilton	OHL	56	1	9	10	171	...	...	...	14	0	0	0	28
88-89—Niagara Falls	OHL	49	1	10	11	225	...	...	...	15	0	5	5	56
89-90—Niagara Falls	OHL	60	13	35	48	231	...	...	...	16	6	16	22	71

Season Team	League	REGULAR SEASON								PLAYOFFS				
		Gms.	G	A	Pts.	PIM	+/-	PP	SH	Gms.	G	A	Pts.	PIM
90-91—Muskegon	IHL	35	3	4	7	103	...	...	...	4	0	0	0	13
—Albany	IHL	7	0	0	0	7	...	...	...	—	—	—	—	—
—Knoxville	ECHL	20	6	12	18	83	...	...	...	—	—	—	—	—
91-92—Muskegon	IHL	75	0	21	21	248	...	...	...	14	2	5	7	70
92-93—Cleveland	IHL	76	8	18	26	427	...	...	...	4	1	0	1	27
93-94—Florida	NHL	39	2	0	2	109	9	0	0	—	—	—	—	—
94-95—Florida	NHL	37	0	7	7	138	12	0	0	—	—	—	—	—
95-96—Florida	NHL	78	3	6	9	236	-2	0	0	21	2	6	8	*62
96-97—Florida	NHL	77	0	12	12	313	13	0	0	5	0	1	1	4
97-98—Florida	NHL	77	0	11	11	293	-5	0	0	—	—	—	—	—
98-99—Florida	NHL	75	1	9	10	218	-1	0	0	—	—	—	—	—
99-00—Florida	NHL	77	3	8	11	172	-1	0	0	4	0	0	0	8
NHL Totals (7 years)		460	9	53	62	1479	25	0	0	30	2	7	9	74

LAWRENCE, MARK　　　　RW　　　　ISLANDERS

PERSONAL: Born January 27, 1972, in Burlington, Ont. ... 6-4/219. ... Shoots right.
TRANSACTIONS/CAREER NOTES: Selected by Dallas Stars in sixth round (fourth Stars pick, 118th overall) of NHL entry draft (June 22, 1991). ... Signed as free agent by New York Islanders (July 29, 1997).

Season Team	League	REGULAR SEASON								PLAYOFFS				
		Gms.	G	A	Pts.	PIM	+/-	PP	SH	Gms.	G	A	Pts.	PIM
87-88—Burlington Jr. B	OHA	40	11	12	23	90	...	...	...	—	—	—	—	—
88-89—Niagara Falls	OHL	63	9	27	36	142	...	...	...	—	—	—	—	—
89-90—Niagara Falls	OHL	54	15	18	33	123	...	...	...	16	2	5	7	42
90-91—Det. Jr. Red Wings	OHL	66	27	38	65	53	...	...	...	—	—	—	—	—
91-92—Det. Jr. Red Wings	OHL	28	19	26	45	54	...	...	...	—	—	—	—	—
—North Bay	OHL	24	13	14	27	21	...	...	...	21	*23	12	35	36
92-93—Dayton	ECHL	20	8	14	22	46	...	...	...	—	—	—	—	—
—Kalamazoo	IHL	57	22	13	35	47	...	...	...	—	—	—	—	—
93-94—Kalamazoo	IHL	64	17	20	37	90	...	...	...	—	—	—	—	—
94-95—Kalamazoo	IHL	77	21	29	50	92	...	...	...	16	3	7	10	28
—Dallas	NHL	2	0	0	0	0	0	0	0	—	—	—	—	—
95-96—Michigan	IHL	55	15	14	29	92	...	...	...	10	3	4	7	30
—Dallas	NHL	13	0	1	1	17	0	0	0	—	—	—	—	—
96-97—Michigan	IHL	68	15	21	36	141	...	...	...	4	0	0	0	18
97-98—Utah	IHL	80	36	28	64	102	...	...	...	4	1	1	2	4
—New York Islanders	NHL	2	0	0	0	2	0	0	0	—	—	—	—	—
98-99—Lowell	AHL	21	10	6	16	28	...	...	...	—	—	—	—	—
—New York Islanders	NHL	60	14	16	30	38	-8	4	0	—	—	—	—	—
99-00—New York Islanders	NHL	29	1	5	6	26	-13	0	0	—	—	—	—	—
—Lowell	AHL	18	4	4	8	8	...	...	...	7	2	2	4	10
—Chicago	IHL	16	4	6	10	32	...	...	...	—	—	—	—	—
NHL Totals (5 years)		106	15	22	37	83	-21	4	0	—	—	—	—	—

LEACH, STEVE　　　　RW

PERSONAL: Born January 16, 1966, in Cambridge, Mass. ... 5-11/199. ... Shoots right. ... Full Name: Stephen Morgan Leach. ... Uncle of Jay Leach, defenseman, Phoenix Coyotes system.
HIGH SCHOOL: Matignon (Cambridge, Mass.).
COLLEGE: New Hampshire.
TRANSACTIONS/CAREER NOTES: Selected by Washington Capitals in second round (second Capitals pick, 34th overall) of NHL entry draft (June 9, 1984). ... Strained left knee (February 1989). ... Injured thumb (March 1990). ... Suffered concussion (October 10, 1990). ... Separated right shoulder (February 2, 1991); missed four games. ... Traded by Capitals to Boston Bruins for LW Randy Burridge (June 21, 1991). ... Injured thigh (October 1992); missed one game. ... Injured ribs (January 1993); missed four games. ... Injured knee (January 8, 1994); missed 25 games. ... Reinjured knee (March 7, 1994); missed 15 games. ... Broke foot (April 8, 1995). ... Traded by Bruins to St. Louis Blues for F Kevin Sawyer and D Steve Staois (March 7, 1996). ... Injured ankle (November 3, 1996); missed 59 games. ... Traded by Blues to Carolina Hurricanes for D Alexander Godynyuk and sixth-round pick (D Brad Voth) in 1998 draft (June 27, 1997). ... Strained neck (December 12, 1998); missed two games. ... Reinjured neck (January 24, 1998); missed remainder of season. ... Signed as free agent by Phoenix Coyotes (December 3, 1998). ... Strained shoulder (January 8, 1999); missed six games. ... Signed as free agent by Pittsburgh Penguins (October 19, 1999). ... Injured back (December 21, 1999); missed three games. ... Injured shoulder (February 24, 2000); missed eight games.
HONORS: Named to Hockey East All-Freshman team (1984-85).

Season Team	League	REGULAR SEASON								PLAYOFFS				
		Gms.	G	A	Pts.	PIM	+/-	PP	SH	Gms.	G	A	Pts.	PIM
83-84—Matignon	Mass. H.S.	21	27	22	49	49	...	...	...	—	—	—	—	—
84-85—Univ. of New Hamp.	Hockey East	41	12	25	37	53	...	...	...	—	—	—	—	—
85-86—Univ. of New Hamp.	Hockey East	25	22	6	28	30	...	...	...	—	—	—	—	—
—Washington	NHL	11	1	1	2	2	0	0	0	6	0	1	1	0
86-87—Binghamton	AHL	54	18	21	39	39	...	...	...	13	3	1	4	6
—Washington	NHL	15	1	0	1	6	-4	0	0	—	—	—	—	—
87-88—U.S. national team	Int'l	53	26	20	46		...	...	...	—	—	—	—	—
—U.S. Olympic team	Int'l	6	1	2	3	0	...	...	...	—	—	—	—	—
—Washington	NHL	8	1	1	2	17	2	0	0	9	2	1	3	0
88-89—Washington	NHL	74	11	19	30	94	-4	4	0	6	1	0	1	12
89-90—Washington	NHL	70	18	14	32	104	10	0	0	14	2	2	4	6
90-91—Washington	NHL	68	11	19	30	99	-9	4	0	9	1	2	3	8
91-92—Boston	NHL	78	31	29	60	147	-8	12	0	15	4	4	8	10
92-93—Boston	NHL	79	26	25	51	126	-6	9	0	4	1	1	2	2

		REGULAR SEASON								PLAYOFFS				
Season Team	League	Gms.	G	A	Pts.	PIM	+/-	PP	SH	Gms.	G	A	Pts.	PIM
93-94—Boston	NHL	42	5	10	15	74	-10	1	0	5	0	1	1	2
94-95—Boston	NHL	35	5	6	11	68	-3	1	0	—	—	—	—	—
95-96—Boston	NHL	59	9	13	22	86	-4	1	0	—	—	—	—	—
—St. Louis	NHL	14	2	4	6	22	-3	0	0	11	3	2	5	10
96-97—St. Louis	NHL	17	2	1	3	24	-2	0	0	6	0	0	0	33
97-98—Carolina	NHL	45	4	5	9	42	-19	1	1	—	—	—	—	—
98-99—Ottawa	NHL	9	0	2	2	6	-1	0	0	—	—	—	—	—
—Springfield	AHL	13	5	3	8	10	...	...	...	—	—	—	—	—
—Phoenix	NHL	22	1	1	2	37	-6	0	0	7	1	1	2	2
99-00—Pittsburgh	NHL	56	2	3	5	24	-11	0	0	—	—	—	—	—
—Wilkes-Barre/Scranton	AHL	4	2	3	5	4	...	...	...	—	—	—	—	—
NHL Totals (15 years)		702	130	153	283	978	-78	33	1	92	15	11	26	85

LECAVALIER, VINCENT — C — LIGHTNING

PERSONAL: Born April 21, 1980, in Ile-Bizard, Que. ... 6-4/205. ... Shoots left.

TRANSACTIONS/CAREER NOTES: Selected by Tampa Bay Lightning in first round (first Lightning pick, first overall) of NHL entry draft (June 27, 1998). ... Injured ankle (April 6, 2000); missed final two games of season.

HONORS: Won Can.HL Rookie of the Year Award (1996-97). ... Won Michel Bergeron Trophy (1996-97). ... Named to Can.HL All-Rookie team (1996-97). ... Named to QMJHL All-Rookie team (1996-97). ... Won Michael Bossy Trophy (1997-98). ... Won Can.HL Top Draft Prospect Award (1997-98). ... Named to Can.HL All-Star first team (1997-98). ... Named to QMJHL All-Star first team (1997-98).

MISCELLANEOUS: Captain of Tampa Bay Lightning (March 11, 2000-remainder of season).

		REGULAR SEASON								PLAYOFFS				
Season Team	League	Gms.	G	A	Pts.	PIM	+/-	PP	SH	Gms.	G	A	Pts.	PIM
96-97—Rimouski	QMJHL	64	42	60	102	36	...	...	...	4	4	3	7	2
97-98—Rimouski	QMJHL	58	44	71	115	117	...	...	...	18	15	†26	41	46
98-99—Tampa Bay	NHL	82	13	15	28	23	-19	2	0	—	—	—	—	—
99-00—Tampa Bay	NHL	80	25	42	67	43	-25	6	0	—	—	—	—	—
NHL Totals (2 years)		162	38	57	95	66	-44	8	0					

LeCLAIR, JOHN — LW — FLYERS

PERSONAL: Born July 5, 1969, in St. Albans, Vt. ... 6-3/226. ... Shoots left. ... Full Name: John Clark LeClair.

HIGH SCHOOL: Bellows Free Academy (St. Albans, Vt.).

COLLEGE: Vermont.

TRANSACTIONS/CAREER NOTES: Selected by Montreal Canadiens in second round (second Canadiens pick, 33rd overall) of NHL entry draft (June 13, 1987). ... Injured thigh; missed 16 games during 1988-89 season. ... Injured knee and underwent surgery (January 20, 1990); missed remainder of season. ... Injured shoulder (January 15, 1992); missed four games. ... Suffered charley horse (January 20, 1993); missed four games. ... Sprained knee (October 2, 1993); missed eight games. ... Bruised sternum (March 28, 1994); missed two games. ... Traded by Canadiens with LW Gilbert Dionne and D Eric Desjardins to Philadelphia Flyers for RW Mark Recchi and third-round pick (C Martin Hohenberger) in 1995 draft (February 9, 1995). ... Strained right hip (April 18, 1995); missed one playoff game. ... Strained hip flexor (March 9, 1999); missed four games. ... Suffered back spasms (April 1, 1999); missed two games.

HONORS: Named to ECAC All-Star second team (1990-91). ... Named to NHL All-Star first team (1994-95 and 1997-98). ... Played in NHL All-Star Game (1996-2000). ... Named to NHL All-Star second team (1995-96, 1996-97 and 1998-99). ... Named to THE SPORTING NEWS All-Star team (1994-95, 1996-97 and 1997-98).

MISCELLANEOUS: Member of Stanley Cup championship team (1993).

STATISTICAL NOTES: Tied for NHL lead with three game-tying goals (1998-99).

STATISTICAL PLATEAUS: Three-goal games: 1994-95 (2), 1995-96 (2), 1996-97 (1), 1997-98 (1), 1998-99 (1). Total: 7. ... Four-goal games: 1996-97 (1), 1998-99 (1). Total: 2. ... Total hat tricks: 9.

		REGULAR SEASON								PLAYOFFS				
Season Team	League	Gms.	G	A	Pts.	PIM	+/-	PP	SH	Gms.	G	A	Pts.	PIM
85-86—Bellows Free Acad.	VT. H.S.	22	41	28	69	14	...	...	...	—	—	—	—	—
86-87—Bellows Free Acad.	VT. H.S.	23	44	40	84	25	...	...	...	—	—	—	—	—
87-88—Univ. of Vermont	ECAC	31	12	22	34	62	...	...	...	—	—	—	—	—
88-89—Univ. of Vermont	ECAC	19	9	12	21	40	...	...	...	—	—	—	—	—
89-90—Univ. of Vermont	ECAC	10	10	6	16	38	...	...	...	—	—	—	—	—
90-91—Univ. of Vermont	ECAC	33	25	20	45	58	...	...	...	—	—	—	—	—
—Montreal	NHL	10	2	5	7	2	1	0	0	3	0	0	0	0
91-92—Montreal	NHL	59	8	11	19	14	5	3	0	8	1	1	2	4
—Fredericton	AHL	8	7	7	14	10	...	...	...	2	0	0	0	4
92-93—Montreal	NHL	72	19	25	44	33	11	2	0	20	4	6	10	14
93-94—Montreal	NHL	74	19	24	43	32	17	1	0	7	2	1	3	8
94-95—Montreal	NHL	9	1	4	5	10	-1	1	0	—	—	—	—	—
—Philadelphia	NHL	37	25	24	49	20	21	5	0	15	5	7	12	4
95-96—Philadelphia	NHL	82	51	46	97	64	21	19	0	11	6	5	11	6
96-97—Philadelphia	NHL	82	50	47	97	58	*44	10	0	19	9	12	21	10
97-98—Philadelphia	NHL	82	51	36	87	32	30	16	0	5	1	1	2	8
—U.S. Olympic team	Int'l	4	0	1	1	0	...	...	...	—	—	—	—	—
98-99—Philadelphia	NHL	76	43	47	90	30	36	16	0	6	3	0	3	12
99-00—Philadelphia	NHL	82	40	37	77	36	8	13	0	18	6	7	13	6
NHL Totals (10 years)		665	309	306	615	331	193	86	0	112	37	40	77	72

LECLERC, MIKE   LW   MIGHTY DUCKS

PERSONAL: Born November 10, 1976, in Winnipeg. ... 6-1/205. ... Shoots left. ... Name pronounced luh-KLAIR.
TRANSACTIONS/CAREER NOTES: Selected by Mighty Ducks of Anaheim in third round (third Mighty Ducks pick, 55th overall) of NHL entry draft (July 8, 1995). ... Underwent elbow surgery (October 29, 1999); missed 11 games. ... Injured elbow (December 17, 1999); missed two games.
HONORS: Named to WHL (Central/East) All-Star second team (1995-96). ... Named to AHL All-Rookie team (1996-97).

		REGULAR SEASON								PLAYOFFS				
Season Team	League	Gms.	G	A	Pts.	PIM	+/-	PP	SH	Gms.	G	A	Pts.	PIM
91-92—St. Boniface	Tier II Jr. A	43	16	12	28	25	...	...	...	—	—	—	—	—
—Victoria	WHL	2	0	0	0	0	...	...	...	—	—	—	—	—
92-93—Victoria	WHL	70	4	11	15	118	...	...	...	—	—	—	—	—
93-94—Victoria	WHL	68	29	11	40	112	...	...	...	—	—	—	—	—
94-95—Prince George	WHL	43	20	36	56	78	...	...	...	—	—	—	—	—
—Brandon	WHL	23	5	8	13	50	...	...	...	18	10	6	16	33
95-96—Brandon	WHL	71	58	53	111	161	...	...	...	19	6	19	25	25
96-97—Baltimore	AHL	71	29	27	56	134	...	...	...	—	—	—	—	—
—Anaheim	NHL	5	1	1	2	0	2	0	0	1	0	0	0	0
97-98—Cincinnati	AHL	48	18	22	40	83	...	...	...	—	—	—	—	—
—Anaheim	NHL	7	0	0	0	6	-6	0	0	—	—	—	—	—
98-99—Cincinnati	AHL	65	25	28	53	153	...	...	...	3	0	1	1	19
—Anaheim	NHL	7	0	0	0	4	-2	0	0	1	0	0	0	0
99-00—Anaheim	NHL	69	8	11	19	70	-15	0	0	—	—	—	—	—
NHL Totals (4 years)		88	9	12	21	80	-21	0	0	2	0	0	0	0

LEDYARD, GRANT   D

PERSONAL: Born November 19, 1961, in Winnipeg. ... 6-2/195. ... Shoots left.
TRANSACTIONS/CAREER NOTES: Signed as non-drafted free agent by New York Rangers (July 7, 1982). ... Injured hip (October 1984). ... Traded by Rangers to Los Angeles Kings for LW Brian MacLellan and fourth-round pick (C Michael Sullivan) in 1987 draft; Rangers also sent second-round pick (D Neil Wilkinson) in 1986 draft and fourth-round pick (RW John Weisbrod) in 1987 draft to Minnesota North Stars and the North Stars sent G Roland Melanson to the Kings as part of the same deal (December 1986). ... Sprained ankle (October 1987). ... Traded by Kings to Washington Capitals for RW Craig Laughlin (February 9, 1988). ... Traded by Capitals with G Clint Malarchuk and sixth-round pick (C Brian Holzinger) in 1991 draft to Buffalo Sabres for D Calle Johansson and second-round pick (G Byron Dafoe) in 1989 draft (March 6, 1989). ... Injured knee (February 12, 1991). ... Injured shoulder (March 2, 1991). ... Bruised ankle (March 14, 1992); missed four games. ... Fractured finger (October 28, 1992); missed 25 games. ... Injured eye (March 7, 1993); missed three games. ... Signed as free agent by Dallas Stars (August 13, 1993). ... Sprained ankle (February 13, 1995); missed two games. ... Fractured ankle (April 16, 1995); missed last eight games of season and first game of playoffs. ... Suffered from the flu (May 14, 1995); missed one game. ... Fractured orbital bone prior to 1996-97 season; missed first game of season. ... Suspended two games and fined $1,000 by NHL for kneeing incident (November 26, 1996). ... Suffered from the flu (February 2, 1997); missed two games. ... Signed as free agent by Vancouver Canucks (July 14, 1997). ... Suffered concussion (October 30, 1997); missed one game. ... Traded by Canucks to Boston Bruins for eighth-round pick (LW Curtis Valentine) in 1998 draft (March 3, 1998). ... Sprained knee (November 7, 1998); missed one game. ... Sprained knee (December 21, 1998); missed 13 games. ... Injured knee (February 26, 1999); missed three games. ... Signed as free agent by Ottawa Senators (November 17, 1999).
HONORS: Named MJHL Most Valuable Player (1981-82). ... Named to MJHL All-Star first team (1981-82). ... Won Bob Gassoff Award (1983-84). ... Won Max McNab Trophy (1983-84).

		REGULAR SEASON								PLAYOFFS				
Season Team	League	Gms.	G	A	Pts.	PIM	+/-	PP	SH	Gms.	G	A	Pts.	PIM
79-80—Fort Garry	MJHL	49	13	24	37	90	...	...	...	—	—	—	—	—
80-81—Saskatoon	WHL	71	9	28	37	148	...	...	...	—	—	—	—	—
81-82—Fort Garry	MJHL	63	25	45	70	150	...	...	...	—	—	—	—	—
82-83—Tulsa	CHL	80	13	29	42	115	...	...	...	—	—	—	—	—
83-84—Tulsa	CHL	58	9	17	26	71	...	...	...	9	5	4	9	10
84-85—New Haven	AHL	36	6	20	26	18	...	...	...	—	—	—	—	—
—New York Rangers	NHL	42	8	12	20	53	8	1	0	3	0	2	2	4
85-86—New York Rangers	NHL	27	2	9	11	20	-7	0	0	—	—	—	—	—
—Los Angeles	NHL	52	7	18	25	78	-22	4	0	—	—	—	—	—
86-87—Los Angeles	NHL	67	14	23	37	93	-40	5	0	5	0	0	0	10
87-88—New Haven	AHL	3	2	1	3	4	...	...	...	—	—	—	—	—
—Los Angeles	NHL	23	1	7	8	52	-7	1	0	—	—	—	—	—
—Washington	NHL	21	4	3	7	14	-4	1	0	14	1	0	1	30
88-89—Washington	NHL	61	3	11	14	43	1	1	0	—	—	—	—	—
—Buffalo	NHL	13	1	5	6	8	1	0	0	5	1	2	3	2
89-90—Buffalo	NHL	67	2	13	15	37	2	0	0	—	—	—	—	—
90-91—Buffalo	NHL	60	8	23	31	46	13	2	1	6	3	3	6	10
91-92—Buffalo	NHL	50	5	16	21	45	-4	0	0	—	—	—	—	—
92-93—Buffalo	NHL	50	2	14	16	45	-2	1	0	8	0	0	0	8
—Rochester	AHL	5	0	2	2	8	...	...	...	—	—	—	—	—
93-94—Dallas	NHL	84	9	37	46	42	7	6	0	9	1	2	3	6
94-95—Dallas	NHL	38	5	13	18	20	6	4	0	3	0	0	0	2
95-96—Dallas	NHL	73	5	19	24	20	-15	2	0	—	—	—	—	—
96-97—Dallas	NHL	67	1	15	16	61	31	0	0	7	0	2	2	0
97-98—Vancouver	NHL	49	2	13	15	14	-2	1	0	—	—	—	—	—
—Boston	NHL	22	2	7	9	6	-2	1	0	6	0	0	0	2
98-99—Boston	NHL	47	4	8	12	33	-8	1	0	2	0	0	0	2
99-00—Ottawa	NHL	40	2	4	6	8	-3	0	0	6	0	0	0	16
NHL Totals (16 years)		953	87	270	357	738	-47	31	1	74	6	11	17	92

L

LEEB, BRAD — LW — CANUCKS

PERSONAL: Born August 27, 1979, in Red Deer, Alta. ... 5-11/180. ... Shoots right.
TRANSACTIONS/CAREER NOTES: Signed as non-drafted free agent by Vancouver Canucks (October 8, 1999).
HONORS: Named to WHL (East) All-Star second team (1998-99).

		REGULAR SEASON								PLAYOFFS				
Season Team	League	Gms.	G	A	Pts.	PIM	+/-	PP	SH	Gms.	G	A	Pts.	PIM
94-95—Red Deer	WHL	3	0	0	0	4	...	...	...	—	—	—	—	—
95-96—Red Deer	WHL	38	3	6	9	30	...	...	...	10	2	0	2	11
96-97—Red Deer	WHL	70	15	20	35	76	...	...	...	16	3	3	6	6
97-98—Red Deer	WHL	63	23	23	46	88	...	...	...	3	2	0	2	2
99-00—Syracuse	AHL	61	19	18	37	50	...	...	...	4	0	0	0	6
—Vancouver	NHL	2	0	0	0	2	-2	0	0	—	—	—	—	—
NHL Totals (1 year)		2	0	0	0	2	-2	0	0					

LEETCH, BRIAN — D — RANGERS

PERSONAL: Born March 3, 1968, in Corpus Christi, Texas. ... 6-0/185. ... Shoots left. ... Full Name: Brian Joseph Leetch.
HIGH SCHOOL: Avon (Conn.) Old Farms School for Boys.
COLLEGE: Boston College.
TRANSACTIONS/CAREER NOTES: Selected by New York Rangers in first round (first Rangers pick, ninth overall) of NHL entry draft (June 21, 1986). ... Fractured bone in left foot (December 1988). ... Suffered hip pointer (March 15, 1989). ... Fractured left ankle (March 14, 1990). ... Injured ankle (November 21, 1992); missed one game. ... Suffered stretched nerve in neck (December 17, 1992); missed 34 games. ... Fractured ankle (March 19, 1993) and underwent ankle surgery; missed remainder of season. ... Suffered nerve compression in right leg (January 4, 1998); missed two games. ... Suffered head injury (April 5, 1998); missed four games. ... Fractured arm (November 24, 1999); missed 32 games.
HONORS: Named Hockey East Player of the Year (1986-87). ... Named Hockey East Rookie of the Year (1986-87). ... Named Hockey East Tournament Most Valuable Player (1986-87). ... Named to NCAA All-America (East) first team (1986-87). ... Named to Hockey East All-Star first team (1986-87). ... Named to Hockey East All-Freshman team (1986-87). ... Named NHL Rookie of the Year by THE SPORTING NEWS (1988-89). ... Won Calder Memorial Trophy (1988-89). ... Named to NHL All-Rookie team (1988-89). ... Named to THE SPORTING NEWS All-Star second team (1990-91 and 1993-94). ... Named to NHL All-Star second team (1990-91, 1993-94 and 1995-96). ... Played in NHL All-Star Game (1990-1992, 1994 and 1996-1998). ... Won James Norris Memorial Trophy (1991-92 and 1996-97). ... Named to THE SPORTING NEWS All-Star first team (1991-92). ... Named to NHL All-Star first team (1991-92 and 1996-97). ... Won Conn Smythe Trophy (1993-94). ... Named to Hockey East All-Decade team (1994). ... Named to THE SPORTING NEWS All-Star team (1996-97).
RECORDS: Holds NHL single-season record for most goals by a rookie defenseman—23 (1988-89).
MISCELLANEOUS: Member of Stanley Cup championship team (1994). ... Captain of New York Rangers (1997-98 through November 26, 1999 and Febraury 9, 2000-remainder of season).

		REGULAR SEASON								PLAYOFFS				
Season Team	League	Gms.	G	A	Pts.	PIM	+/-	PP	SH	Gms.	G	A	Pts.	PIM
84-85—Avon Old Farms H.S.	Conn. H.S.	26	30	46	76	15	...	...	...	—	—	—	—	—
85-86—Avon Old Farms H.S.	Conn. H.S.	28	40	44	84	18	...	...	...	—	—	—	—	—
86-87—Boston College	Hockey East	37	9	38	47	10	...	...	...	—	—	—	—	—
87-88—U.S. national team	Int'l	60	13	61	74	38	...	...	...	—	—	—	—	—
—U.S. Olympic team	Int'l	6	1	5	6	4	...	...	...	—	—	—	—	—
—New York Rangers	NHL	17	2	12	14	0	5	1	0	—	—	—	—	—
88-89—New York Rangers	NHL	68	23	48	71	50	8	8	3	4	3	2	5	2
89-90—New York Rangers	NHL	72	11	45	56	26	-18	5	0	—	—	—	—	—
90-91—New York Rangers	NHL	80	16	72	88	42	2	6	0	6	1	3	4	0
91-92—New York Rangers	NHL	80	22	80	102	26	25	10	1	13	4	11	15	4
92-93—New York Rangers	NHL	36	6	30	36	26	2	2	1	—	—	—	—	—
93-94—New York Rangers	NHL	84	23	56	79	67	28	17	1	23	11	*23	*34	6
94-95—New York Rangers	NHL	48	9	32	41	18	0	3	0	10	6	8	14	8
95-96—New York Rangers	NHL	82	15	70	85	30	12	7	0	11	1	6	7	4
96-97—New York Rangers	NHL	82	20	58	78	40	31	9	0	15	2	8	10	6
97-98—New York Rangers	NHL	76	17	33	50	32	-36	11	0	—	—	—	—	—
—U.S. Olympic team	Int'l	4	1	1	2	0	...	...	...	—	—	—	—	—
98-99—New York Rangers	NHL	82	13	42	55	42	-7	4	0	—	—	—	—	—
99-00—New York Rangers	NHL	50	7	19	26	20	-16	3	0	—	—	—	—	—
NHL Totals (13 years)		857	184	597	781	419	36	86	6	82	28	61	89	30

LEFEBVRE, SYLVAIN — D — RANGERS

PERSONAL: Born October 14, 1967, in Richmond, Que. ... 6-3/205. ... Shoots left. ... Name pronounced luh-FAYV.
TRANSACTIONS/CAREER NOTES: Signed as non-drafted free agent by Montreal Canadiens (September 24, 1986). ... Traded by Canadiens to Toronto Maple Leafs for third-round pick (D Martin Belanger) in 1994 draft (August 20, 1992). ... Traded by Maple Leafs with LW Wendel Clark, RW Landon Wilson and first-round pick (D Jeffrey Kealty) in 1994 draft to Quebec Nordiques for C Mats Sundin, D Garth Butcher, LW Todd Warriner and first-round pick (traded to Washington) in 1994 draft (June 28, 1994). ... Nordiques franchise moved to Colorado and renamed Avalanche for 1995-96 season (June 21, 1995). ... Sprained right ankle (November 29, 1995); missed six games. ... Fractured forearm (December 18, 1996); missed 10 games. ... Suffered sore hip (December 12, 1997); missed one game. ... Injured eye (November 8, 1998); missed six games. ... Signed as free agent by New York Rangers (July 16, 1999).
HONORS: Named to AHL All-Star second team (1988-89).
MISCELLANEOUS: Member of Stanley Cup championship team (1996).

		REGULAR SEASON								PLAYOFFS				
Season Team	League	Gms.	G	A	Pts.	PIM	+/-	PP	SH	Gms.	G	A	Pts.	PIM
84-85—Laval	QMJHL	66	7	5	12	31	...	...	...	—	—	—	—	—
85-86—Laval	QMJHL	71	8	17	25	48	...	...	...	14	1	0	1	25
86-87—Laval	QMJHL	70	10	36	46	44	...	...	...	15	1	6	7	12

L

Season Team	League	REGULAR SEASON								PLAYOFFS				
		Gms.	G	A	Pts.	PIM	+/-	PP	SH	Gms.	G	A	Pts.	PIM
87-88—Sherbrooke	AHL	79	3	24	27	73	...	...	...	6	2	3	5	4
88-89—Sherbrooke	AHL	77	15	32	47	119	...	...	...	6	1	3	4	4
89-90—Montreal	NHL	68	3	10	13	61	18	0	0	6	0	0	0	2
90-91—Montreal	NHL	63	5	18	23	30	-11	1	0	11	0	0	1	6
91-92—Montreal	NHL	69	3	14	17	91	9	0	0	2	0	0	0	2
92-93—Toronto	NHL	81	2	12	14	90	8	0	0	21	3	3	6	20
93-94—Toronto	NHL	84	2	9	11	79	33	0	0	18	0	3	3	16
94-95—Quebec	NHL	48	2	11	13	17	13	0	0	6	0	2	2	2
95-96—Colorado	NHL	75	5	11	16	49	26	2	0	22	0	5	5	12
96-97—Colorado	NHL	71	2	11	13	30	12	1	0	17	0	0	0	25
97-98—Colorado	NHL	81	0	10	10	48	2	0	0	7	0	0	0	4
98-99—Colorado	NHL	76	2	18	20	48	18	0	0	19	0	1	1	12
99-00—New York Rangers	NHL	82	2	10	12	43	-13	0	0	—	—	—	—	—
NHL Totals (11 years)		798	28	134	162	586	115	4	0	129	4	14	18	101

LEGACE, MANNY   G   RED WINGS

PERSONAL: Born February 4, 1973, in Toronto. ... 5-9/165. ... Catches left. ... Name pronounced LEH-guh-see.
HIGH SCHOOL: Stamford Collegiate (Niagara Falls, Ont.).
TRANSACTIONS/CAREER NOTES: Selected by Hartford Whalers in eighth round (fifth Whalers pick, 188th overall) of NHL entry draft (June 26, 1993). ... Whalers franchise moved to North Carolina and renamed Carolina Hurricanes for 1997-98 season; NHL approved move on June 25, 1997. ... Traded by Hurricanes to Los Angeles Kings for conditional pick in 1999 draft (July 31, 1998); Legace did not meet conditions for the pick and the draft choice was forfeited. ... Signed as free agent by Detroit Red Wings (July 15, 1999). ... Claimed on waivers by Vancouver Canucks (September 30, 1999). ... Claimed on waivers by Detroit Red Wings (October 13, 1999).
HONORS: Named to Can.HL All-Star second team (1992-93). ... Named to OHL All-Star first team (1992-93). ... Won Harry (Hap) Holmes Memorial Trophy (1995-96). ... Won Baz Bastien Trophy (1995-96). ... Named to AHL All-Star first team (1995-96).
MISCELLANEOUS: Member of silver-medal-winning Canadian Olympic team (1994).

Season Team	League	REGULAR SEASON								PLAYOFFS					
		Gms.	Min	W	L	T	GA	SO	Avg.	Gms.	Min.	W	L	GA	SO	Avg.
89-90—Vaughan-Thornhill Jr. B	OHA	29	1660	...	...	...	119	1	4.30	—						—
90-91—Niagara Falls	OHL	30	1515	...	...	...	107	0	4.24	4	119	...	...	10	0	5.04
91-92—Niagara Falls	OHL	43	2384	...	...	...	143	0	3.60	14	791	...	...	56	0	4.25
92-93—Niagara Falls	OHL	†48	*2630	22	19	3	*170	0	3.88	4	240	0	4	18	0	4.50
93-94—Canadian nat'l team	Int'l	16	859	8	6	0	36	2	2.51	—						—
94-95—Springfield	AHL	39	2169	12	17	6	128	2	3.54	—						—
95-96—Springfield	AHL	37	2196	20	12	4	83	*5	*2.27	4	220	1	3	18	0	4.91
96-97—Springfield	AHL	36	2119	17	14	5	107	1	3.03	12	746	9	3	25	†2	2.01
—Richmond	ECHL	3	157	2	1	0	8	0	3.06	—						—
97-98—Las Vegas	IHL	41	2107	18	16	‡4	111	1	3.16	4	237	1	3	16	0	4.05
—Springfield	AHL	6	345	4	2	0	16	0	2.78	—						—
98-99—Long Beach	IHL	33	1796	22	8	‡1	67	2	2.24	6	338	4	2	9	0	1.60
—Los Angeles	NHL	17	899	2	9	2	39	0	2.60	—						—
99-00—Manitoba	IHL	42	2409	20	18	‡5	104	2	2.59	2	141	0	2	7	0	2.98
—Detroit	NHL	4	240	4	0	0	11	0	2.75	—						—
NHL Totals (2 years)		21	1139	6	9	2	50	0	2.63							

LEGAULT, JAY   LW   MIGHTY DUCKS

PERSONAL: Born May 15, 1979, in Peterborough, Ont. ... 6-4/217. ... Shoots left.
TRANSACTIONS/CAREER NOTES: Selected by Mighty Ducks of Anaheim in third round (third Mighty Ducks pick, 72nd overall) of NHL entry draft (June 21, 1997).

Season Team	League	REGULAR SEASON								PLAYOFFS				
		Gms.	G	A	Pts.	PIM	+/-	PP	SH	Gms.	G	A	Pts.	PIM
95-96—Oshawa	OHL	61	2	11	13	37	...	...	...	—	—	—	—	—
96-97—Oshawa	OHL	39	13	26	39	50	...	...	...	—	—	—	—	—
—London	OHL	67	19	39	58	87	...	...	...	—	—	—	—	—
97-98—London	OHL	61	39	56	95	87	...	...	...	16	1	8	9	34
98-99—London	OHL	65	43	51	94	99	...	...	...	25	8	18	26	40
99-00—Cincinnati	AHL	70	15	19	34	75	...	...	...	—	—	—	—	—
—Dayton	ECHL	2	0	0	0	2	...	...	...	—	—	—	—	—

LEGWAND, DAVID   C   PREDATORS

PERSONAL: Born August 17, 1980, in Detroit. ... 6-2/185. ... Shoots left.
TRANSACTIONS/CAREER NOTES: Selected by Nashville Predators in first round (first Predators pick, second overall) of NHL entry draft (June 27, 1998). ... Fractured left foot (January 13, 2000); missed 11 games.
HONORS: Named to Can.HL All-Star second team (1997-98). ... Won Red Tilson Trophy (1997-98). ... Won Emms Family Award (1997-98). ... Won Can.HL Rookie of the Year Award (1997-98). ... Named to OHL All-Star first team (1997-98). ... Named to OHL All-Rookie first team (1997-98).

Season Team	League	REGULAR SEASON								PLAYOFFS				
		Gms.	G	A	Pts.	PIM	+/-	PP	SH	Gms.	G	A	Pts.	PIM
96-97—Detroit	Jr. A	44	21	41	62	58	...	...	...	—	—	—	—	—
97-98—Plymouth	OHL	59	54	51	105	56	...	...	...	15	8	12	20	24
98-99—Plymouth	OHL	55	31	49	80	65	...	...	...	11	3	8	11	8
—Nashville	NHL	1	0	0	0	0	0	0	0	—	—	—	—	—
99-00—Nashville	NHL	71	13	15	28	30	-6	4	0	—	—	—	—	—
NHL Totals (2 years)		72	13	15	28	30	-6	4	0					

LEHTINEN, JERE   LW   STARS

PERSONAL: Born June 24, 1973, in Espoo, Finland. ... 6-0/192. ... Shoots right. ... Name pronounced YAIR-ee LEH-tih-nehn.
TRANSACTIONS/CAREER NOTES: Selected by Minnesota North Stars in fourth round (third North Stars pick, 88th overall) of NHL entry draft (June 20, 1992). ... North Stars franchise moved from Minnesota to Dallas and renamed Stars for 1993-94 season. ... Strained groin (December 21, 1995); missed six games. ... Reinjured groin (January 10, 1996); missed one game. ... Sprained ankle (March 20, 1996); missed remainder of season. ... Sprained knee (January 31, 1997); missed 13 games. ... Sprained knee (March 5, 1997); missed five games. ... Separated shoulder (October 19, 1997); missed 10 games. ... Fractured thumb (November 14, 1998); missed five games. ... Sprained ankle (March 25, 1999); missed two games. ... Fractured ankle (October 16, 1999); missed 30 games. ... Reinjured ankle (January 19, 2000); missed 35 games.
HONORS: Played in NHL All-Star Game (1998). ... Won Frank J. Selke Trophy (1997-98 and 1998-99).
MISCELLANEOUS: Member of Stanley Cup championship team (1999). ... Member of bronze-medal-winning Finnish Olympic team (1994 and 1998). ... Scored on a penalty shot (vs. Dominik Hasek, October 7, 1997).

Season Team	League	REGULAR SEASON								PLAYOFFS				
		Gms.	G	A	Pts.	PIM	+/-	PP	SH	Gms.	G	A	Pts.	PIM
90-91—Kiekko-Espoo	Finland	32	15	9	24	12	...	...	...	—	—	—	—	—
91-92—Kiekko-Espoo	Finland	43	32	17	49	6	...	...	...	—	—	—	—	—
92-93—Kiekko-Espoo	Finland	45	13	14	27	6	...	...	...	—	—	—	—	—
93-94—TPS Turku	Finland	42	19	20	39	6	...	...	...	11	11	2	13	2
—Fin. Olympic team	Int'l	8	3	0	3	11	...	...	...	—	—	—	—	—
94-95—TPS Turku	Finland	39	19	23	42	33	...	...	...	13	8	6	14	4
95-96—Dallas	NHL	57	6	22	28	16	5	0	0	—	—	—	—	—
—Michigan	IHL	1	1	0	1	0	...	...	...	—	—	—	—	—
96-97—Dallas	NHL	63	16	27	43	2	26	3	1	7	2	2	4	0
97-98—Dallas	NHL	72	23	19	42	20	19	7	2	12	3	5	8	2
—Fin. Olympic team	Int'l	6	4	2	6	2	...	...	...	—	—	—	—	—
98-99—Dallas	NHL	74	20	32	52	18	29	7	1	23	10	3	13	2
99-00—Dallas	NHL	17	3	5	8	0	1	0	0	13	1	5	6	2
NHL Totals (5 years)		283	68	105	173	56	80	17	4	55	16	15	31	6

LEMIEUX, CLAUDE   RW

PERSONAL: Born July 16, 1965, in Buckingham, Que. ... 6-1/215. ... Shoots right. ... Brother of Jocelyn Lemieux, right winger with seven NHL teams (1986-87 through 1997-98). ... Name pronounced luh-MYOO.
TRANSACTIONS/CAREER NOTES: Selected by Montreal Canadiens as underage junior in second round (second Canadiens pick, 26th overall) of NHL entry draft (June 8, 1983). ... Tore ankle ligaments (October 1987). ... Fractured orbital bone above right eye (January 14, 1988). ... Pulled groin (March 1989). ... Underwent surgery to repair torn stomach muscle (November 1, 1989); missed 41 games. ... Traded by Canadiens to New Jersey Devils for LW Sylvain Turgeon (September 4, 1990). ... Bruised right eye retina (February 25, 1991). ... Suffered sore back (November 27, 1991); missed four games. ... Injured ankle (March 11, 1992); missed two games. ... Suffered back spasms (October 24, 1992); missed three games. ... Injured right elbow (March 21, 1993); missed one game. ... Suspended three games and fined $500 by NHL for altercation with opponent's bench (March 28, 1995). ... Traded by Devils to New York Islanders for RW Steve Thomas (October 3, 1995). ... Traded by Islanders to Colorado Avalanche for LW Wendel Clark (October 3, 1995). ... Fractured finger (December 3, 1995); missed two games. ... Suspended one playoff game and fined $1,000 by NHL for punching another player (May 24, 1996). ... Suspended two games in Stanley Cup finals and fined $1,000 by NHL for checking from behind (June 2, 1996). ... Tore abdominal muscle (October 5, 1996); missed 37 games. ... Injured back (March 2, 1998); missed two games. ... Traded by Avalanche with second-round pick (D Matt DeMarchi) in 2000 draft and swap of first-round picks in 2000 draft to Devils for LW Brian Rolston and a conditional third-round pick in the 2001 draft (November 3, 1999).
HONORS: Named to QMJHL All-Star second team (1983-84). ... Won Guy Lafleur Trophy (1984-85). ... Named to QMJHL All-Star first team (1984-85). ... Won Conn Smythe Trophy (1994-95).
MISCELLANEOUS: Member of Stanley Cup championship teams (1986, 1995, 1996 and 2000).
STATISTICAL PLATEAUS: Three-goal games: 1988-89 (1), 1990-91 (2), 1992-93 (1), 1995-96 (2), 1997-98 (1). Total: 7.
STATISTICAL NOTES: Led NHL in games played with 83 (1999-2000).

Season Team	League	REGULAR SEASON								PLAYOFFS				
		Gms.	G	A	Pts.	PIM	+/-	PP	SH	Gms.	G	A	Pts.	PIM
82-83—Trois-Rivieres	QMJHL	62	28	38	66	187	...	...	...	4	1	0	1	30
83-84—Verdun	QMJHL	51	41	45	86	225	...	...	...	9	8	12	20	63
—Montreal	NHL	8	1	1	2	12	-2	0	0	—	—	—	—	—
—Nova Scotia	AHL	—	—	—	—	—	...	...	...	2	1	0	1	0
84-85—Verdun	QMJHL	52	58	66	124	152	...	...	...	14	*23	17	*40	38
—Montreal	NHL	1	0	1	1	7	1	0	0	—	—	—	—	—
85-86—Sherbrooke	AHL	58	21	32	53	145	...	...	...	—	—	—	—	—
—Montreal	NHL	10	1	2	3	22	-6	1	0	20	10	6	16	68
86-87—Montreal	NHL	76	27	26	53	156	0	5	0	17	4	9	13	41
87-88—Montreal	NHL	78	31	30	61	137	16	6	0	11	3	2	5	20
88-89—Montreal	NHL	69	29	22	51	136	14	7	0	18	4	3	7	58
89-90—Montreal	NHL	39	8	10	18	106	-8	3	0	11	1	3	4	38
90-91—New Jersey	NHL	78	30	17	47	105	-8	10	0	7	4	0	4	34
91-92—New Jersey	NHL	74	41	27	68	109	9	13	1	7	4	3	7	26
92-93—New Jersey	NHL	77	30	51	81	155	3	13	0	5	2	0	2	19
93-94—New Jersey	NHL	79	18	26	44	86	13	5	0	20	7	11	18	44
94-95—New Jersey	NHL	45	6	13	19	86	2	1	0	20	*13	3	16	20
95-96—Colorado	NHL	79	39	32	71	117	14	9	2	19	5	7	12	55
96-97—Colorado	NHL	45	11	17	28	43	-4	5	0	17	13	10	23	32
97-98—Colorado	NHL	78	26	27	53	115	-7	11	1	7	3	3	6	8
98-99—Colorado	NHL	82	27	24	51	102	0	11	0	19	3	11	14	26
99-00—Colorado	NHL	§13	3	6	9	4	0	0	0	—	—	—	—	—
—New Jersey	NHL	§70	17	21	38	86	-3	7	0	23	4	6	10	28
NHL Totals (17 years)		1001	345	353	698	1584	34	107	4	221	80	77	157	517

LEROUX, JEAN-YVES   LW   BLACKHAWKS

PERSONAL: Born June 24, 1976, in Montreal. ... 6-2/211. ... Shoots left. ... Name pronounced zhahn-eev luh-ROO.
TRANSACTIONS/CAREER NOTES: Selected by Chicago Blackhawks in second round (second Blackhawks pick, 40th overall) of NHL entry draft (June 28, 1994). ... Pulled abdominal muscle (October 29, 1997); missed two games. ... Injured shoulder (November 20, 1997); missed one game. ... Injured shoulder (December 4, 1997); missed one game. ... Injured back (February 3, 1998); missed three games. ... Suffered concussion (March 29, 1998); missed four games. ... Tore abdominal muscle (September 19, 1998) and underwent surgery; missed first 42 games of season. ... Suffered from strept throat (November 27, 1999); missed one game. ... Strained groin (December 6, 1999); missed 18 games. ... Fractured finger (March 3, 2000); missed seven games.

		REGULAR SEASON								PLAYOFFS				
Season Team	League	Gms.	G	A	Pts.	PIM	+/-	PP	SH	Gms.	G	A	Pts.	PIM
92-93—Beauport	QMJHL	62	20	25	45	33	...	...	...	—	—	—	—	—
93-94—Beauport	QMJHL	45	14	25	39	43	...	...	...	15	7	6	13	33
94-95—Beauport	QMJHL	59	19	33	52	125	...	...	...	17	4	6	10	39
95-96—Beauport	QMJHL	54	41	41	82	176	...	...	...	20	5	18	23	20
96-97—Indianapolis	IHL	69	14	17	31	112	...	...	...	4	1	0	1	2
—Chicago	NHL	1	0	1	1	5	1	0	0	—	—	—	—	—
97-98—Chicago	NHL	66	6	7	13	55	-2	0	0	—	—	—	—	—
98-99—Chicago	NHL	40	3	5	8	21	-7	0	0	—	—	—	—	—
99-00—Chicago	NHL	54	3	5	8	43	-10	0	0	—	—	—	—	—
NHL Totals (4 years)		161	12	18	30	124	-18	0	0					

LESCHYSHYN, CURTIS   D   WILD

PERSONAL: Born September 21, 1969, in Thompson, Man. ... 6-1/205. ... Shoots left. ... Full Name: Curtis Michael Leschyshyn. ... Name pronounced luh-SIH-shihn.
TRANSACTIONS/CAREER NOTES: Selected by Quebec Nordiques in first round (first Nordiques pick, third overall) of NHL entry draft (June 11, 1988). ... Separated shoulder (January 10, 1989). ... Sprained left knee (November 1989). ... Injured knee ligaments (February 18, 1991) and underwent surgery; missed final 19 games of 1990-91 season and first 30 games of 1991-92 season. ... Strained back (October 13, 1992); missed two games. ... Injured right collarbone (December 30, 1994); missed two games. ... Pulled thigh muscle (March 19, 1994); missed two games. ... Injured groin (March 31, 1994); missed remainder of season. ... Lacerated groin (April 22, 1995); missed last four games of season. ... Nordiques franchise moved to Colorado and renamed Avalanche for 1995-96 season (June 21, 1995). ... Injured hip flexor (January 17, 1996); missed three games. ... Traded by Avalanche with LW Chris Simon to Washington Capitals for RW Keith Jones and first- (D Scott Parker) and fourth-round (traded back to Washington) picks in 1998 draft (November 2, 1996). ... Traded by Capitals to Hartford Whalers for C Andrei Nikolishin (November 9, 1996). ... Injured abdominal muscle (March 7, 1997); missed five games. ... Whalers franchise moved to North Carolina and renamed Carolina Hurricanes for 1997-98 season; NHL approved move on June 25, 1997. ... Strained groin (September 25, 1997); missed four games. ... Strained groin (November 13, 1997); missed one game. ... Suffered back spasms (February 28, 1998); missed one game. ... Suffered back spasms (December 5, 1998); missed three games. ... Bruised sternum (December 19, 1998); missed one game. ... Strained groin (January 4, 1999); missed six games. ... Strained groin (March 24, 1999); missed six games. ... Strained groin (January 27, 2000); missed 20 games. ... Reinjured groin (March 17, 2000); missed nine games. ... Selected by Minnesota Wild in NHL expansion draft (June 23, 2000).
HONORS: Named to WHL (East) All-Star first team (1987-88).
MISCELLANEOUS: Member of Stanley Cup championship team (1996).

		REGULAR SEASON								PLAYOFFS				
Season Team	League	Gms.	G	A	Pts.	PIM	+/-	PP	SH	Gms.	G	A	Pts.	PIM
85-86—Saskatoon	WHL	1	0	0	0	0	...	...	...	—	—	—	—	—
86-87—Saskatoon	WHL	70	14	26	40	107	...	...	...	11	1	5	6	14
87-88—Saskatoon	WHL	56	14	41	55	86	...	...	...	10	2	5	7	16
88-89—Quebec	NHL	71	4	9	13	71	-32	1	1	—	—	—	—	—
89-90—Quebec	NHL	68	2	6	8	44	-41	1	0	—	—	—	—	—
90-91—Quebec	NHL	55	3	7	10	49	-19	2	0	—	—	—	—	—
91-92—Quebec	NHL	42	5	12	17	42	-28	3	0	—	—	—	—	—
—Halifax	AHL	6	0	2	2	4	...	...	...	—	—	—	—	—
92-93—Quebec	NHL	82	9	23	32	61	25	4	0	6	1	1	2	6
93-94—Quebec	NHL	72	5	17	22	65	-2	3	0	—	—	—	—	—
94-95—Quebec	NHL	44	2	13	15	20	29	0	0	3	0	1	1	4
95-96—Colorado	NHL	77	4	15	19	73	32	0	0	17	1	2	3	8
96-97—Colorado	NHL	11	0	5	5	6	1	0	0	—	—	—	—	—
—Washington	NHL	2	0	0	0	2	0	0	0	—	—	—	—	—
—Hartford	NHL	64	4	13	17	30	-19	1	1	—	—	—	—	—
97-98—Carolina	NHL	73	2	10	12	45	-2	1	0	—	—	—	—	—
98-99—Carolina	NHL	65	2	7	9	50	-1	0	0	6	0	0	0	6
99-00—Carolina	NHL	53	0	2	2	14	-19	0	0	—	—	—	—	—
NHL Totals (12 years)		779	42	139	181	572	-76	16	2	32	2	4	6	24

LESSARD, FRANCIS   D   FLYERS

PERSONAL: Born May 30, 1979, in Montreal. ... 6-2/184. ... Shoots right. ... Name pronounced luh-SAHRD.
TRANSACTIONS/CAREER NOTES: Selected by Carolina Hurricanes in third round (third Hurricanes pick, 80th overall) of NHL entry draft (June 21, 1997). ... Traded by Hurricanes to Philadelphia Flyers for eighth-round pick (G Antti Jokela) in 1999 draft (May 25, 1999).

		REGULAR SEASON								PLAYOFFS				
Season Team	League	Gms.	G	A	Pts.	PIM	+/-	PP	SH	Gms.	G	A	Pts.	PIM
96-97—Val-d'Or	QMJHL	66	1	9	10	287	...	...	...	—	—	—	—	—
97-98—Val-d'Or	QMJHL	63	3	20	23	338	...	...	...	19	1	6	7	*101
98-99—Drummondville	QMJHL	53	12	36	48	295	...	...	...	—	—	—	—	—
99-00—Philadelphia	AHL	78	4	8	12	416	...	...	...	5	0	1	1	7

LETANG, ALAN   D   STARS

PERSONAL: Born September 4, 1975, in Renfrew, Ont. ... 6-0/205. ... Shoots left. ... Name pronounced luh-TANG.
HIGH SCHOOL: Huron Heights Secondary School (Newmarket, Ont.).
TRANSACTIONS/CAREER NOTES: Signed as non-drafted free agent by Dallas Stars (March 22, 1999). ... Separated shoulder (November 17, 1999); missed five games.

		REGULAR SEASON								PLAYOFFS				
Season Team	League	Gms.	G	A	Pts.	PIM	+/-	PP	SH	Gms.	G	A	Pts.	PIM
91-92—Cornwall	OHL	47	1	4	5	45	...	...	...	6	0	0	0	2
92-93—Newmarket	OHL	66	1	25	26	14	...	...	...	6	0	3	3	2
93-94—Newmarket	OHL	58	3	21	24	30	...	...	...	—	—	—	—	—
94-95—Sarnia	OHL	62	5	36	41	35	...	...	...	4	2	2	4	6
95-96—Fredericton	AHL	71	0	26	26	40	...	...	...	10	0	3	3	4
96-97—Fredericton	AHL	60	2	9	11	8	...	...	...	—	—	—	—	—
97-98—Kaufbeuren	Germany	15	1	5	6	8	...	...	...	—	—	—	—	—
—SC Langnau	Switzerland	11	4	3	7	6	...	...	...	—	—	—	—	—
—Augsburger Panther	Germany	17	0	1	1	4	...	...	...	—	—	—	—	—
98-99—Canadian nat'l team	Int'l	42	3	9	12	20	...	...	...	—	—	—	—	—
—Michigan	IHL	12	3	3	6	0	...	...	...	5	0	2	2	0
99-00—Dallas	NHL	8	0	0	0	2	-5	0	0	—	—	—	—	—
—Michigan	IHL	51	1	12	13	30	...	...	...	—	—	—	—	—
NHL Totals (1 year)		8	0	0	0	2	-5	0	0	—	—	—	—	—

LETOWSKI, TREVOR   C   COYOTES

PERSONAL: Born April 5, 1977, in Thunder Bay, Ont. ... 5-10/176. ... Shoots right.
TRANSACTIONS/CAREER NOTES: Selected by Phoenix Coyotes in seventh round (sixth Coyotes pick, 174th overall) of NHL entry draft (June 22, 1996).

		REGULAR SEASON								PLAYOFFS				
Season Team	League	Gms.	G	A	Pts.	PIM	+/-	PP	SH	Gms.	G	A	Pts.	PIM
94-95—Sarnia	OHL	66	22	19	41	33	...	...	...	4	0	1	1	9
95-96—Sarnia	OHL	66	36	63	99	66	...	...	...	10	9	5	14	10
96-97—Sarnia	OHL	55	35	73	108	51	...	...	...	12	9	12	21	20
97-98—Springfield	AHL	75	11	20	31	26	...	...	...	4	1	2	3	18
98-99—Springfield	AHL	67	32	35	67	46	...	...	...	3	1	0	1	2
—Phoenix	NHL	14	2	2	4	2	1	0	0	—	—	—	—	—
99-00—Phoenix	NHL	82	19	20	39	20	2	3	4	5	1	1	2	4
NHL Totals (2 years)		96	21	22	43	22	3	3	4	5	1	1	2	4

LIDSTROM, NICKLAS   D   RED WINGS

PERSONAL: Born April 28, 1970, in Vasteras, Sweden. ... 6-2/190. ... Shoots left. ... Name pronounced NIHK-luhs LIHD-struhm.
TRANSACTIONS/CAREER NOTES: Selected by Detroit Red Wings in third round (third Red Wings pick, 53rd overall) of NHL entry draft (June 17, 1989). ... Played in Europe during 1994-95 NHL lockout. ... Suffered back spasms (April 9, 1995); missed five games. ... Suffered from the flu (April 14, 1996); missed one game. ... Suffered from the flu (January 20, 1997); missed one game.
HONORS: Named to Swedish League All-Star team (1990-91). ... Named to NHL All-Rookie team (1991-92). ... Played in NHL All-Star Game (1996 and 1998-2000). ... Named to THE SPORTING NEWS All-Star team (1997-98 through 1999-2000). ... Named to NHL All-Star first team (1997-98 through 1999-2000).
MISCELLANEOUS: Member of Stanley Cup championship team (1997 and 1998).

		REGULAR SEASON								PLAYOFFS				
Season Team	League	Gms.	G	A	Pts.	PIM	+/-	PP	SH	Gms.	G	A	Pts.	PIM
87-88—Vasteras	Sweden	3	0	0	0	0	...	...	...	—	—	—	—	—
88-89—Vasteras	Sweden	19	0	2	2	4	...	...	...	—	—	—	—	—
89-90—Vasteras	Sweden	39	8	8	16	14	...	...	...	—	—	—	—	—
90-91—Vasteras	Sweden	20	2	12	14	14	...	...	...	—	—	—	—	—
91-92—Detroit	NHL	80	11	49	60	22	36	5	0	11	1	2	3	0
92-93—Detroit	NHL	84	7	34	41	28	7	3	0	7	1	0	1	0
93-94—Detroit	NHL	84	10	46	56	26	43	4	0	7	3	2	5	0
94-95—Vasteras	Sweden	13	2	10	12	4	...	...	...	—	—	—	—	—
—Detroit	NHL	43	10	16	26	6	15	7	0	18	4	12	16	8
95-96—Vasteras	Sweden	13	2	10	12	4	...	...	...	—	—	—	—	—
—Detroit	NHL	81	17	50	67	20	29	8	1	19	5	9	14	10
96-97—Detroit	NHL	79	15	42	57	30	11	8	0	20	2	6	8	2
97-98—Detroit	NHL	80	17	42	59	18	22	7	1	22	6	13	19	8
—Swedish Oly. team	Int'l	4	1	1	2	2	...	...	...	—	—	—	—	—
98-99—Detroit	NHL	81	14	43	57	14	14	6	2	10	2	9	11	4
99-00—Detroit	NHL	81	20	53	73	18	19	9	4	9	2	4	6	4
NHL Totals (9 years)		693	121	375	496	182	196	57	8	123	26	57	83	36

LIND, JUHA   C/LW   CANADIENS

PERSONAL: Born January 2, 1974, in Helsinki, Finland. ... 5-11/185. ... Shoots left. ... Name pronounced YOO-hah LIHND.
TRANSACTIONS/CAREER NOTES: Selected by Minnesota North Stars in eighth round (sixth North Stars pick, 178th overall) of NHL entry draft (June 26, 1992). ... North Stars franchise moved from Minnesota to Dallas and renamed Stars for 1993-94 season. ... Bruised thigh (March 29, 1998); missed nine games. ... Strained lower back (October 26, 1999); missed five games. ... Traded by Stars to Montreal Canadiens for C Scott Thornton (January 22, 2000). ... Injured foot (February 2, 2000); missed one game. ... Strained hip flexor (February 12, 2000); missed 17 games.
MISCELLANEOUS: Member of bronze-medal-winning Finnish Olympic team (1998).

Season Team	League	Gms.	G	A	Pts.	PIM	+/-	PP	SH		Gms.	G	A	Pts.	PIM
91-92—Jokerit Helsinki	Finland Jr.	28	16	24	40	10	...	...	...		—	—	—	—	—
92-93—Vantaa HT	Finland Div. 2	25	8	12	20	8	...	...	...		—	—	—	—	—
—Jokerit Helsinki	Finland	6	0	0	0	2	...	...	...		1	0	0	0	0
93-94—Jokerit Helsinki	Finland	47	17	11	28	37	...	...	...		11	2	5	7	4
94-95—Jokerit Helsinki	Finland	50	10	8	18	12	...	...	...		11	1	2	3	6
95-96—Jokerit Helsinki	Finland	50	15	22	37	32	...	...	...		11	4	5	9	4
96-97—Jokerit	Finland	50	16	22	38	28	...	...	...		9	5	3	8	0
97-98—Michigan	IHL	8	2	2	4	2	...	...	...		—	—	—	—	—
—Dallas	NHL	39	2	3	5	6	4	0	0		15	2	2	4	8
—Fin. Olympic team	Int'l	6	0	1	1	6	...	...	...		—	—	—	—	—
98-99—Jokerit	Finland	50	20	19	39	22	...	...	...		3	3	1	4	2
99-00—Dallas	NHL	34	3	4	7	6	-1	0	0		—	—	—	—	—
—Montreal	NHL	13	1	2	3	4	-2	0	0		—	—	—	—	—
NHL Totals (2 years)		86	6	9	15	16	1	0	0		15	2	2	4	8

LINDEN, TREVOR   C   CANADIENS

PERSONAL: Born April 11, 1970, in Medicine Hat, Alta. ... 6-4/211. ... Shoots right. ... Brother of Jamie Linden, right winger with Florida Panthers organization (1993-94 through 1996-97).

TRANSACTIONS/CAREER NOTES: Selected by Vancouver Canucks in first round (first Canucks pick, second overall) of NHL entry draft (June 11, 1988). ... Hyperextended elbow (October 1989). ... Separated shoulder (March 17, 1990). ... Sprained knee ligament (December 1, 1996); missed 24 games. ... Bruised ribs (March 8, 1997); missed eight games. ... Injured knee (April 5, 1997); missed one game. ... Strained groin (November 16, 1997); missed eight games. ... Sprained medial collateral ligament in knee (January 26, 1998); missed six games. ... Traded by Canucks to New York Islanders for D Bryan McCabe, LW Todd Bertuzzi and third-round pick (LW Jarkko Ruutu) in 1998 draft (February 6, 1998). ... Traded by Islanders to Montreal Canadiens for first-round pick (D Branislav Mezei) in 1999 draft (May 29, 1999). ... Sprained ankle (December 1, 1999); missed 14 games. ... Reinjured ankle (January 6, 2000); missed six games. ... Fractured ribs (March 14, 2000); missed final 12 games of regular season.

HONORS: Named to WHL All-Star second team (1987-88). ... Named to Memorial Cup All-Star team (1987-88). ... Named to NHL All-Rookie team (1988-89). ... Played in NHL All-Star Game (1991 and 1992). ... Won King Clancy Memorial Trophy (1996-97).

MISCELLANEOUS: Captain of Vancouver Canucks (1990-91 through 1996-97). ... Captain of New York Islanders (March 3, 1998 through 1998-99).

STATISTICAL PLATEAUS: Three-goal games: 1988-89 (2), 1990-91 (1), 1995-96 (1), 1999-00 (1). Total: 5.

Season Team	League	Gms.	G	A	Pts.	PIM	+/-	PP	SH		Gms.	G	A	Pts.	PIM
85-86—Medicine Hat	WHL	5	2	0	2	0	...	...	...		—	—	—	—	—
86-87—Medicine Hat	WHL	72	14	22	36	59	...	...	...		20	5	4	9	17
87-88—Medicine Hat	WHL	67	46	64	110	76	...	...	...		16	†13	12	25	19
88-89—Vancouver	NHL	80	30	29	59	41	-10	10	1		7	3	4	7	8
89-90—Vancouver	NHL	73	21	30	51	43	-17	6	2		—	—	—	—	—
90-91—Vancouver	NHL	80	33	37	70	65	-25	16	2		6	0	7	7	2
91-92—Vancouver	NHL	80	31	44	75	101	3	6	1		13	4	8	12	6
92-93—Vancouver	NHL	84	33	39	72	64	19	8	0		12	5	8	13	16
93-94—Vancouver	NHL	84	32	29	61	73	6	10	2		24	12	13	25	18
94-95—Vancouver	NHL	48	18	22	40	40	-5	9	0		11	2	6	8	12
95-96—Vancouver	NHL	82	33	47	80	42	6	12	1		6	4	4	8	6
96-97—Vancouver	NHL	49	9	31	40	27	5	2	2		—	—	—	—	—
97-98—Vancouver	NHL	42	7	14	21	49	-13	2	0		—	—	—	—	—
—New York Islanders	NHL	25	10	7	17	33	-1	3	2		—	—	—	—	—
—Can. Olympic team	Int'l	6	1	0	1	10	...	...	...		—	—	—	—	—
98-99—New York Islanders	NHL	82	18	29	47	32	-14	8	1		—	—	—	—	—
99-00—Montreal	NHL	50	13	17	30	34	-3	4	0		—	—	—	—	—
NHL Totals (12 years)		859	288	375	663	644	-49	96	14		79	30	50	80	68

LINDGREN, MATS   C   ISLANDERS

PERSONAL: Born October 1, 1974, in Skelleftea, Sweden. ... 6-2/202. ... Shoots left.

HIGH SCHOOL: Lindsay Thurber (Red Deer, Alta.).

TRANSACTIONS/CAREER NOTES: Selected by Winnipeg Jets in first round (first Jets pick, 15th overall) of NHL entry draft (June 26, 1993). ... Traded by Jets with D Boris Mironov and first-(C Jason Bonsignore) and fourth-round (RW Adam Copeland) picks in 1994 draft to Edmonton Oilers for D Dave Manson and sixth-round pick (traded to New Jersey) in 1994 draft (March 15, 1994). ... Strained lower back (March 17, 1995); missed 23 games. ... Suffered dislocated shoulder (September 23, 1998); missed first seven games of season. ... Suffered from the flu (November 14, 1998); missed one game. ... Traded by Oilers with eighth-round pick (F Radek Martinek) in 1999 draft to New York Islanders for G Tommy Salo (March 20, 1999). ... Injured shoulder (January 17, 2000) and underwent surgery; missed remainder of season.

HONORS: Named Swedish League Rookie of the Year (1993-94).

Season Team	League	Gms.	G	A	Pts.	PIM	+/-	PP	SH		Gms.	G	A	Pts.	PIM
90-91—Skelleftea	Sweden Dv. 2	1	0	0	0	0	...	...	...		—	—	—	—	—
91-92—Skelleftea	Sweden Dv. 2	29	14	8	22	14	...	...	...		—	—	—	—	—
92-93—Skelleftea	Sweden Dv. 2	32	20	14	34	18	...	...	...		—	—	—	—	—
93-94—Farjestad Karlstad	Sweden	22	11	6	17	26	...	...	...		—	—	—	—	—
94-95—Farjestad Karlstad	Sweden	37	17	15	32	20	...	...	...		3	0	0	0	4
95-96—Cape Breton	AHL	13	7	5	12	6	...	...	...		—	—	—	—	—
96-97—Hamilton	AHL	9	6	7	13	6	...	...	...		—	—	—	—	—
—Edmonton	NHL	69	11	14	25	12	-7	2	3		12	0	4	4	0
97-98—Edmonton	NHL	82	13	13	26	42	0	1	3		12	1	1	2	10
—Swedish Oly. team	Int'l	4	0	0	0	2	...	...	...		—	—	—	—	—
98-99—Edmonton	NHL	48	5	12	17	22	4	0	1		—	—	—	—	—
—New York Islanders	NHL	12	5	3	8	2	2	3	0		—	—	—	—	—
99-00—New York Islanders	NHL	43	9	7	16	24	0	1	0		—	—	—	—	—
NHL Totals (4 years)		254	43	49	92	102	-1	7	7		24	1	5	6	10

PERSONAL: Born February 28, 1973, in London, Ont. ... 6-4/236. ... Shoots right. ... Brother of Brett Lindros, right winger with New York Islanders (1994-95 and 1995-96). ... Name pronounced LIHND-rahz.

TRANSACTIONS/CAREER NOTES: Selected by Quebec Nordiques in first round (first Nordiques pick, first overall) of NHL entry draft (June 22, 1991); refused to report. ... Traded by Nordiques to Philadelphia Flyers for G Ron Hextall, C Mike Ricci, C Peter Forsberg, D Steve Duchesne, D Kerry Huffman, first-round pick (G Jocelyn Thibault) in 1993 draft, cash and future considerations (June 20, 1992); Nordiques aquired LW Chris Simon and first-round pick (traded to Toronto Maple Leafs) in 1994 draft to complete deal (July 21, 1992). ... Sprained knee ligament (November 22, 1992); missed nine games. ... Injured knee (December 29, 1992); missed two games. ... Reinjured knee (January 10, 1993); missed 12 games. ... Tore ligament in right knee (November 12, 1993); missed 14 games. ... Suffered back spasms (March 6, 1994); missed one game. ... Sprained shoulder (April 4, 1994); missed remainder of season. ... Suffered from the flu (January 29, 1995); missed one game. ... Bruised eye (April 30, 1995); missed last game of season and first three playoff games. ... Bruised left knee (November 2, 1995); missed seven games. ... Injured knee (April 5, 1996); missed two games. ... Pulled right groin (October 1, 1996); missed 23 games. ... Bruised bone in back (February 13, 1997); missed two games. ... Suffered charley horse (March 2, 1997); missed one game. ... Bruised calf (March 22, 1997); missed two games. ... Suspended two games and fined $2,000 by NHL for two high-sticking incidents (April 9, 1997). ... Bruised ribs (November 6, 1997); missed one game. ... Suffered concussion (March 8, 1998); missed 18 games. ... Fined $1,000 by NHL for slashing incident (December 5, 1998). ... Suffered concussion (December 29, 1998); missed two games. ... Suspended two games by NHL for high-sticking incident (March 28, 1999). ... Suffered collapsed lung (April 1, 1999); missed remainder of season. ... Suffered illness (October 28, 1999); missed two games. ... Bruised left hand (December 11, 1999); missed two games. ... Suffered concussion (January 14, 2000); missed four games. ... Suffered back spasms (February 20, 2000); missed five games. ... Suffered concussion (March 13, 2000); missed final 14 games of regular season and missed 16 playoff games.

HONORS: Named to Memorial Cup All-Star Team (1989-90). ... Won Can.HL Player of the Year Award (1990-91). ... Won Can.HL Plus/Minus Award (1990-91). ... Won Can.HL Top Draft Prospect Award (1990-91). ... Won Red Tilson Trophy (1990-91). ... Won Eddie Powers Memorial Trophy (1990-91). ... Named to OHL All-Star first team (1990-91). ... Named to NHL All-Rookie team (1992-93). ... Played in NHL All-Star Game (1994 and 1996-2000). ... Named NHL Player of the Year by THE SPORTING NEWS (1994-95). ... Won Hart Memorial Trophy (1994-95). ... Won Lester B. Pearson Award (1994-95). ... Named to THE SPORTING NEWS All-Star first team (1994-95). ... Named to NHL All-Star first team (1994-95). ... Named to NHL All-Star second team (1995-96).

MISCELLANEOUS: Member of silver-medal-winning Canadian Olympic team (1992). ... Captain of Philadelphia Flyers (1994-95 through March 27, 1999). ... Scored on a penalty shot (vs. Don Beaupre, December 26, 1992; vs. Steve Shields, May 11, 1997 (playoffs)).

STATISTICAL NOTES: Tied for NHL lead with three game-tying goals (1998-99).

STATISTICAL PLATEAUS: Three-goal games: 1992-93 (3), 1993-94 (1), 1994-95 (3), 1995-96 (1), 1997-98 (1), 1999-00 (1). Total: 10. ... Four-goal games: 1996-97 (1). ... Total hat tricks: 11.

Season Team	League	REGULAR SEASON								PLAYOFFS				
		Gms.	G	A	Pts.	PIM	+/-	PP	SH	Gms.	G	A	Pts.	PIM
88-89—St. Michaels	MTHL	37	24	43	67	193	...	...	...	—	—	—	—	—
89-90—Detroit Compuware	NAJHL	14	23	29	52	123	...	...	...	—	—	—	—	—
—Oshawa	OHL	25	17	19	36	61	...	...	...	17	*18	18	36	*76
90-91—Oshawa	OHL	57	*71	78	*149	189	...	...	...	16	*18	20	*38	*93
91-92—Oshawa	OHL	13	9	22	31	54	...	...	...	—	—	—	—	—
—Canadian nat'l team	Int'l	24	19	16	35	34	...	...	...	—	—	—	—	—
—Can. Olympic team	Int'l	8	5	6	11	6	...	...	...	—	—	—	—	—
92-93—Philadelphia	NHL	61	41	34	75	147	28	8	1	—	—	—	—	—
93-94—Philadelphia	NHL	65	44	53	97	103	16	13	2	—	—	—	—	—
94-95—Philadelphia	NHL	46	29	41	†70	60	27	7	0	12	4	11	15	18
95-96—Philadelphia	NHL	73	47	68	115	163	26	15	0	12	6	6	12	43
96-97—Philadelphia	NHL	52	32	47	79	136	31	9	0	19	12	14	26	40
97-98—Philadelphia	NHL	63	30	41	71	134	14	10	1	5	1	2	3	17
—Can. Olympic team	Int'l	6	2	3	5	2	...	...	...	—	—	—	—	—
98-99—Philadelphia	NHL	71	40	53	93	120	35	10	1	—	—	—	—	—
99-00—Philadelphia	NHL	55	27	32	59	83	11	10	1	2	1	0	1	0
NHL Totals (8 years)		486	290	369	659	946	188	82	6	50	24	33	57	118

PERSONAL: Born May 17, 1971, in Big Fork, Mont. ... 6-0/195. ... Shoots left. ... Full Name: William Hamilton Lindsay.

TRANSACTIONS/CAREER NOTES: Selected by Quebec Nordiques in fifth round (sixth Nordiques pick, 103rd overall) of NHL entry draft (June 22, 1991). ... Separated right shoulder (December 26, 1992); missed four games. ... Selected by Florida Panthers in NHL expansion draft (June 24, 1993). ... Lacerated left hand (February 22, 1996); missed seven games. ... Strained hip flexor (April 1, 1996); missed three games. ... Sprained knee (March 26, 1999); missed one game. ... Reinjured knee (April 7, 1999); missed final six games of season. ... Traded by Panthers to Calgary Flames for D Todd Simpson (September 30, 1999). ... Suffered injury (March 7, 2000); missed one game. ... Suffered injury (March 15, 2000); missed one game.

HONORS: Named to WHL (West) All-Star second team (1991-92).

MISCELLANEOUS: Holds Florida Panthers all-time record for most games played (443).

Season Team	League	REGULAR SEASON								PLAYOFFS				
		Gms.	G	A	Pts.	PIM	+/-	PP	SH	Gms.	G	A	Pts.	PIM
89-90—Tri-City	WHL	72	40	45	85	84	...	...	...	—	—	—	—	—
90-91—Tri-City	WHL	63	46	47	93	151	...	...	...	—	—	—	—	—
91-92—Tri-City	WHL	42	34	59	93	111	...	...	...	3	2	3	5	16
—Quebec	NHL	23	2	4	6	14	-6	0	0	—	—	—	—	—
92-93—Quebec	NHL	44	4	9	13	16	0	0	0	—	—	—	—	—
—Halifax	AHL	20	11	13	24	18	...	...	...	—	—	—	—	—
93-94—Florida	NHL	84	6	6	12	97	-2	0	0	—	—	—	—	—
94-95—Florida	NHL	48	10	9	19	46	1	0	1	—	—	—	—	—
95-96—Florida	NHL	73	12	22	34	57	13	0	3	22	5	5	10	18
96-97—Florida	NHL	81	11	23	34	120	1	0	1	3	0	1	1	8
97-98—Florida	NHL	82	12	16	28	80	-2	0	2	—	—	—	—	—
98-99—Florida	NHL	75	12	15	27	92	-1	0	1	—	—	—	—	—
99-00—Calgary	NHL	80	8	12	20	86	-7	0	0	—	—	—	—	—
NHL Totals (9 years)		590	77	116	193	608	-3	0	8	25	5	6	11	26

LINTNER, RICHARD   D   PREDATORS

PERSONAL: Born November 15, 1977, in Trencin, Czechoslovakia. ... 6-3/214. ... Shoots right.
TRANSACTIONS/CAREER NOTES: Selected by Phoenix Coyotes in fifth round (fourth Coyotes pick, 119th overall) of NHL entry draft (June 22, 1996). ... Traded by Coyotes with C Cliff Ronning to Nashville Predators for future considerations (October 31, 1998). ... Injured shoulder (April 3, 2000); missed final two games of season.

		REGULAR SEASON								PLAYOFFS				
Season Team	League	Gms.	G	A	Pts.	PIM	+/-	PP	SH	Gms.	G	A	Pts.	PIM
94-95—Dukla Trencin Jrs........	Slovakia	42	12	13	25	25	...	...	...	—	—	—	—	—
95-96—Dukla Trencin Jrs........	Slovakia	30	15	17	32	210	...	...	...	—	—	—	—	—
—Dukla Trencin..............	Slovakia	2	0	0	0	0	...	...	...	—	—	—	—	—
96-97—Spisska Nova Ves	Slovakia	35	2	1	3	...	...	...	...	—	—	—	—	—
97-98—Springfield	AHL	71	6	9	15	61	...	...	...	3	1	1	2	4
98-99—Springfield	AHL	8	0	1	1	16	...	...	...	—	—	—	—	—
—Milwaukee...................	IHL	66	9	16	25	75	...	...	...	—	—	—	—	—
99-00—Nashville....................	NHL	33	1	5	6	22	-6	0	0	—	—	—	—	—
—Milwaukee...................	IHL	31	13	8	21	37	...	...	...	—	—	—	—	—
NHL Totals (1 year)............		33	1	5	6	22	-6	0	0					

LITTLE, NEIL   G   FLYERS

PERSONAL: Born December 18, 1971, in Medicine Hat, Alta. ... 6-1/193. ... Catches left.
COLLEGE: Rensselaer Polytechnic Institute (N.Y.).
TRANSACTIONS/CAREER NOTES: Selected by Philadelphia Flyers in 11th round (10th Flyers pick, 226th overall) of NHL entry draft (June 22, 1991).
HONORS: Named SJHL Rookie of the Year (1989-90). ... Named to SJHL All-Star first team (1989-90). ... Named NCAA All-America East second team (1992-93). ... Named to ECAC All-Star first team (1992-93).

		REGULAR SEASON								PLAYOFFS						
Season Team	League	Gms.	Min	W	L	T	GA	SO	Avg.	Gms.	Min.	W	L	GA	SO	Avg.
89-90 —Estevan	SJHL	46	2707	21	19	4	150	1	3.32	—	—	—	—	—	—	—
90-91—R.P.I.	ECAC	18	1032	9	8	0	71	0	4.13	—	—	—	—	—	—	—
91-92—R.P.I.	ECAC	28	1532	11	11	3	96	0	3.76	—	—	—	—	—	—	—
92-93—R.P.I.	ECAC	31	1801	19	9	3	88	0	2.93	—	—	—	—	—	—	—
93-94—R.P.I.	ECAC	27	1570	16	7	4	88	0	3.36	—	—	—	—	—	—	—
—Hershey	AHL	1	18	0	0	0	1	0	3.33	—	—	—	—	—	—	—
94-95—Hershey........	AHL	19	919	5	7	3	60	0	3.92	—	—	—	—	—	—	—
—Johnstown	ECHL	16	897	7	6	‡1	55	0	3.68	3	145	0	2	11	0	4.55
95-96—Hershey........	AHL	48	2679	21	18	6	149	0	3.34	1	59	0	1	4	0	4.07
96-97—Philadelphia ..	AHL	54	3007	31	12	7	145	0	2.89	10	620	6	4	20	1	1.94
97-98—Philadelphia ..	AHL	51	2961	*31	11	7	145	0	2.94	*20	*1193	*15	†5	*48	*3	2.41
98-99—Grand Rapids..	IHL	50	2740	18	21	‡5	144	3	3.15	—	—	—	—	—	—	—
99-00—Philadelphia ..	AHL	51	2830	26	18	2	143	1	3.03	5	298	2	3	15	0	3.02

LOW, REED   RW   BLUES

PERSONAL: Born June 26, 1976, in Moose Jaw, Sask. ... 6-5/228. ... Shoots right. ... Name pronounced LOH.
TRANSACTIONS/CAREER NOTES: Selected by St. Louis Blues in seventh round (seventh Blues pick, 177th overall) of NHL entry draft (June 22, 1996).

		REGULAR SEASON								PLAYOFFS				
Season Team	League	Gms.	G	A	Pts.	PIM	+/-	PP	SH	Gms.	G	A	Pts.	PIM
94-95—Regina	WHL	2	0	0	0	5	...	...	...	—	—	—	—	—
95-96—Moose Jaw	WHL	61	12	7	19	221	...	...	...	—	—	—	—	—
96-97—Moose Jaw	WHL	62	16	11	27	228	...	...	...	12	2	1	3	50
97-98—Baton Rouge.........	ECHL	39	4	2	6	145	...	...	...	—	—	—	—	—
—Worcester	AHL	17	1	1	2	75	...	...	...	3	0	0	0	0
98-99—Worcester	AHL	77	5	6	11	239	...	...	...	4	0	0	0	2
99-00—Worcester	AHL	80	12	16	28	203	...	...	...	9	1	3	4	16

LOWRY, DAVE   LW   FLAMES

PERSONAL: Born February 14, 1965, in Sudbury, Ont. ... 6-1/200. ... Shoots left. ... Name pronounced LOW-ree.
HIGH SCHOOL: Sir Wilfrid Laurier (London, Ont.).
TRANSACTIONS/CAREER NOTES: Selected as underage junior by Vancouver Canucks in sixth round (fourth Canucks pick, 110th overall) of NHL entry draft (June 8, 1983). ... Traded by Canucks to St. Louis Blues for C Ernie Vargas (September 29, 1988). ... Injured groin (March 1990). ... Sprained shoulder (October 1991); missed two games. ... Injured knee (October 26, 1992); missed 26 games. ... Selected by Florida Panthers in NHL expansion draft (June 24, 1993). ... Fractured cheekbone (November 26, 1993); missed three games. ... Injured knee (December 12, 1993); missed one game. ... Suffered abrasion to right cornea (April 28, 1995); missed three games. ... Sprained left knee (October 24, 1995); missed 18 games. ... Sprained knee ligament (February 9, 1997); missed three games. ... Traded by Panthers with first-round pick (traded to Tampa Bay) in 1998 draft to San Jose Sharks for LW Viktor Kozlov and fifth-round pick (D Jaroslav Spacek) in 1998 draft (November 13, 1997). ... Signed as free agent by San Jose Sharks (October 5, 1998). ... Injured shoulder (October 24, 1999); missed five games. ... Reinjured shoulder (November 27, 1999); missed 12 games. ... Injured back (January 29, 2000); missed six games. ... Signed as free agent by Calgary Flames (July 25, 2000).

HONORS: Named to OHL All-Star first team (1984-85).

Season Team	League	Gms.	G	A	Pts.	PIM	+/-	PP	SH	Gms.	G	A	Pts.	PIM
					REGULAR SEASON							PLAYOFFS		
82-83—London	OHL	42	11	16	27	48	...	...	...	3	0	0	0	14
83-84—London	OHL	66	29	47	76	125	...	...	...	8	6	6	12	41
84-85—London	OHL	61	60	60	120	94	...	...	...	8	6	5	11	10
85-86—Vancouver	NHL	73	10	8	18	143	-21	1	0	3	0	0	0	0
86-87—Vancouver	NHL	70	8	10	18	176	-23	0	0	—	—	—	—	—
87-88—Fredericton	AHL	46	18	27	45	59	...	...	...	14	7	3	10	72
—Vancouver	NHL	22	1	3	4	38	-2	0	0	—	—	—	—	—
88-89—Peoria	IHL	58	31	35	66	45	...	...	...	—	—	—	—	—
—St. Louis	NHL	21	3	3	6	11	1	0	1	10	0	5	5	4
89-90—St. Louis	NHL	78	19	6	25	75	1	0	2	12	2	1	3	39
90-91—St. Louis	NHL	79	19	21	40	168	19	0	2	13	1	4	5	35
91-92—St. Louis	NHL	75	7	13	20	77	-11	0	0	6	0	1	1	20
92-93—St. Louis	NHL	58	5	8	13	101	-18	0	0	11	2	0	2	14
93-94—Florida	NHL	80	15	22	37	64	-4	3	0	—	—	—	—	—
94-95—Florida	NHL	45	10	10	20	25	-3	2	0	—	—	—	—	—
95-96—Florida	NHL	63	10	14	24	36	-2	0	0	22	10	7	17	39
96-97—Florida	NHL	77	15	14	29	51	2	2	0	5	0	0	0	0
97-98—Florida	NHL	7	0	0	0	2	-1	0	0	—	—	—	—	—
—San Jose	NHL	50	4	4	8	51	0	0	0	6	0	0	0	18
98-99—San Jose	NHL	61	6	9	15	24	-5	2	0	1	0	0	0	0
99-00—San Jose	NHL	32	1	4	5	18	1	0	0	12	1	2	3	6
NHL Totals (15 years)		891	133	149	282	1060	-66	10	5	101	16	20	36	175

LUCHINKIN, SERGEI   RW   BLUE JACKETS

PERSONAL: Born October 16, 1976, in Dmitrov, U.S.S.R. ... 5-11/172. ... Shoots left. ... Name pronounced loo-CHIHN-kihn.
TRANSACTIONS/CAREER NOTES: Selected by Dallas Stars in eighth round (ninth Stars pick, 202nd overall) of NHL entry draft (July 8, 1995). ... Selected by Columbus Blue Jackets in NHL expansion draft (June 23, 2000).

Season Team	League	Gms.	G	A	Pts.	PIM	+/-	PP	SH	Gms.	G	A	Pts.	PIM
					REGULAR SEASON							PLAYOFFS		
94-95—Dynamo Moscow	CIS	6	1	0	1	4	...	...	...	—	—	—	—	—
96-97—Dynamo Moscow	Russian	18	1	5	6	4	...	...	...	—	—	—	—	—
97-98—Dynamo Moscow	Russian	6	0	1	1	0	...	...	...	—	—	—	—	—
—Spartak Moscow	Russian	10	0	1	1	4	...	...	...	—	—	—	—	—
98-99—Spartak Moscow	Russian	33	4	5	9	18	...	...	...	—	—	—	—	—
99-00—						Statistics unavailable.								

LUHNING, WARREN   RW   STARS

PERSONAL: Born July 3, 1975, in Edmonton. ... 6-2/205. ... Shoots right. ... Name pronounced LOO-nihng.
COLLEGE: Michigan.
TRANSACTIONS/CAREER NOTES: Selected by New York Islanders in fourth round (fourth Islanders pick, 92nd overall) of NHL entry draft (June 26, 1993). ... Signed as free agent by Dallas Stars (September 1, 1999).

Season Team	League	Gms.	G	A	Pts.	PIM	+/-	PP	SH	Gms.	G	A	Pts.	PIM
					REGULAR SEASON							PLAYOFFS		
92-93—Calgary Royals	AJHL	46	18	25	43	287	...	...	...	—	—	—	—	—
93-94—Univ. of Michigan	CCHA	38	13	6	19	83	...	...	...	—	—	—	—	—
94-95—Univ. of Michigan	CCHA	36	17	24	41	80	...	...	...	—	—	—	—	—
95-96—Univ. of Michigan	CCHA	40	20	32	52	123	...	...	...	—	—	—	—	—
96-97—Univ. of Michigan	CCHA	43	22	23	45	106	...	...	...	—	—	—	—	—
97-98—Kentucky	AHL	51	6	7	13	82	...	...	...	—	—	—	—	—
—New York Islanders	NHL	8	0	0	0	0	-4	0	0	—	—	—	—	—
98-99—Lowell	AHL	56	20	20	40	67	...	...	...	3	0	3	3	16
—New York Islanders	NHL	11	0	0	0	8	-4	0	0	—	—	—	—	—
99-00—Dallas	NHL	10	0	1	1	13	-2	0	0	—	—	—	—	—
—Michigan	IHL	3	1	1	2	4	...	...	...	—	—	—	—	—
NHL Totals (3 years)		29	0	1	1	21	-10	0	0					

LUKOWICH, BRAD   D   STARS

PERSONAL: Born August 12, 1976, in Cranbrook, B.C. ... 6-1/200. ... Shoots left. ... Name pronounced LOO-kih-wihch.
HIGH SCHOOL: Norkam Secondary (Kamloops, B.C.).
TRANSACTIONS/CAREER NOTES: Selected by New York Islanders in fourth round (fourth Islanders pick, 90th overall) of NHL entry draft (June 29, 1994). ... Traded by Islanders to Dallas Stars for third-round pick (D Robert Schnabel) in 1997 draft (June 1, 1996). ... Suffered back spasms (December 6, 1999); missed one game. ... Traded by Stars with G Manny Fernandez to Minnesota Wild for third-round pick (C Joel Lundqvist) in 2000 draft and fourth-round pick in 2002 draft (June 12, 2000). ... Traded by Wild with third- and ninth-round picks in 2001 draft to Stars for C Aaron Gavey, C Pavel Patera, eighth-round pick (C Eric Johansson) in 2000 draft and fourth-round pick in 2002 draft (June 25, 2000).

Season Team	League	Gms.	G	A	Pts.	PIM	+/-	PP	SH	Gms.	G	A	Pts.	PIM
					REGULAR SEASON							PLAYOFFS		
92-93—Cranbook	Tier II Jr. A	54	21	41	62	162	...	...	...	—	—	—	—	—
—Kamloops	WHL	1	0	0	0	0	...	...	...	—	—	—	—	—
93-94—Kamloops	WHL	42	5	11	16	166	...	...	...	16	0	1	1	35
94-95—Kamloops	WHL	63	10	35	45	125	...	...	...	18	0	7	7	21
95-96—Kamloops	WHL	65	14	55	69	114	...	...	...	13	2	10	12	29

L

Season Team	League	REGULAR SEASON								PLAYOFFS				
		Gms.	G	A	Pts.	PIM	+/-	PP	SH	Gms.	G	A	Pts.	PIM
96-97—Michigan	IHL	69	2	6	8	77	...	...	...	4	0	1	1	2
97-98—Michigan	IHL	60	6	27	33	104	...	...	...	4	0	4	4	14
—Dallas	NHL	4	0	1	1	2	-2	0	0	—	—	—	—	—
98-99—Michigan	IHL	67	8	21	29	95	...	...	...	—	—	—	—	—
—Dallas	NHL	14	1	2	3	19	3	0	0	8	0	1	1	4
99-00—Dallas	NHL	60	3	1	4	50	-14	0	0	—	—	—	—	—
NHL Totals (3 years)		78	4	4	8	71	-13	0	0	8	0	1	1	4

LUMME, JYRKI D COYOTES

PERSONAL: Born July 16, 1966, in Tampere, Finland. ... 6-1/209. ... Shoots left. ... Name pronounced YUHR-kee LOO-mee.

TRANSACTIONS/CAREER NOTES: Selected by Montreal Canadiens in third round (third Canadiens pick, 57th overall) of NHL entry draft (June 21, 1986). ... Strained left knee ligaments (December 1988). ... Stretched knee ligaments (February 21, 1989). ... Bruised right foot (November 1989). ... Traded by Canadiens to Vancouver Canucks for second-round pick (C Craig Darby) in 1991 draft (March 6, 1990). ... Cut eye (November 19, 1991); missed three games. ... Sprained knee (January 19, 1993); missed nine games. ... Played in Europe during 1994-95 NHL lockout. ... Injured knee (February 15, 1995); missed six games. ... Bruised ribs (March 1, 1995); missed five games. ... Sprained ankle (November 13, 1996); missed two games. ... Strained shoulder (December 23, 1996); missed 11 games. ... Suffered charley horse (March 13, 1997); missed three games. ... Injured groin (October 11, 1997); missed two games. ... Strained groin (October 26, 1997); missed five games. ... Signed as free agent by Phoenix Coyotes (July 3, 1998). ... Strained groin (February 8, 1999); missed four games. ... Strained shoulder (March 2, 1999); missed 16 games. ... Suffered sore shoulder (April 14, 1999); missed two games. ... Bruised shoulder (November 14, 1999); missed three games. ... Bruised hand (March 5, 2000); missed four games.

MISCELLANEOUS: Member of silver-medal-winning Finnish Olympic team (1988). ... Member of bronze-medal-winning Finnish Olympic team (1998).

Season Team	League	REGULAR SEASON								PLAYOFFS				
		Gms.	G	A	Pts.	PIM	+/-	PP	SH	Gms.	G	A	Pts.	PIM
84-85—Koo Vee	Finland	30	6	4	10	44	...	...	...	—	—	—	—	—
85-86—Ilves Tampere	Finland	31	1	5	6	4	...	...	...	—	—	—	—	—
86-87—Ilves Tampere	Finland	43	12	12	24	52	...	...	...	4	0	1	1	0
87-88—Ilves Tampere	Finland	43	8	22	30	75	...	...	...	—	—	—	—	—
—Fin. Olympic team	Int'l	6	0	1	1	2	...	...	...	—	—	—	—	—
88-89—Montreal	NHL	21	1	3	4	10	3	1	0	—	—	—	—	—
—Sherbrooke	AHL	26	4	11	15	10	...	...	...	6	1	3	4	4
89-90—Montreal	NHL	54	1	19	20	41	17	0	0	—	—	—	—	—
—Vancouver	NHL	11	3	7	10	8	0	0	0	—	—	—	—	—
90-91—Vancouver	NHL	80	5	27	32	59	-15	1	0	6	2	3	5	0
91-92—Vancouver	NHL	75	12	32	44	65	25	3	1	13	2	3	5	4
92-93—Vancouver	NHL	74	8	36	44	55	30	3	2	12	0	5	5	6
93-94—Vancouver	NHL	83	13	42	55	50	3	1	3	24	2	11	13	16
94-95—Ilves Tampere	Finland	12	4	4	8	24	...	...	...	—	—	—	—	—
—Vancouver	NHL	36	5	12	17	26	4	3	0	11	2	6	8	8
95-96—Vancouver	NHL	80	17	37	54	50	-9	8	0	6	1	3	4	2
96-97—Vancouver	NHL	66	11	24	35	32	8	5	0	—	—	—	—	—
97-98—Vancouver	NHL	74	9	21	30	34	-25	4	0	—	—	—	—	—
—Fin. Olympic team	Int'l	6	1	0	1	16	...	...	...	—	—	—	—	—
98-99—Phoenix	NHL	60	7	21	28	34	5	1	0	7	0	1	1	6
99-00—Phoenix	NHL	74	8	32	40	44	9	4	0	5	0	1	1	2
NHL Totals (12 years)		788	100	313	413	508	55	34	6	84	9	33	42	44

LUNDMARK, JAMIE C RANGERS

PERSONAL: Born January 16, 1981, in Edmonton. ... 6-0/174. ... Shoots right.

TRANSACTIONS/CAREER NOTES: Selected by New York Rangers in first round (second Rangers pick, ninth overall) of NHL entry draft (June 26, 1999).

HONORS: Named to WHL (East) All-Star second team (1998-99).

Season Team	League	REGULAR SEASON								PLAYOFFS				
		Gms.	G	A	Pts.	PIM	+/-	PP	SH	Gms.	G	A	Pts.	PIM
97-98—St. Albert	Jr. A	53	33	58	91	176	...	...	...	—	—	—	—	—
98-99—Moose Jaw	WHL	70	40	51	91	121	...	...	...	11	5	4	9	24
99-00—Moose Jaw	WHL	37	21	27	48	33	...	...	...	—	—	—	—	—

LUONGO, ROBERTO G PANTHERS

PERSONAL: Born April 4, 1979, in St. Leonard, Que. ... 6-3/175. ... Catches left. ... Name pronounced luh-WAHN-goh.

TRANSACTIONS/CAREER NOTES: Selected by New York Islanders in first round (first Islanders pick, fourth overall) of NHL entry draft (June 21, 1997). ... Traded by Islanders with C Olli Jokinen to Florida Panthers for RW Mark Parrish and LW Oleg Kvasha (June 24, 2000).

HONORS: Won Michael Bossy Trophy (1996-97).

MISCELLANEOUS: Stopped a penalty shot attempt (vs. Dan Kesa, January 13, 2000).

Season Team	League	REGULAR SEASON								PLAYOFFS						
		Gms.	Min	W	L	T	GA	SO	Avg.	Gms.	Min.	W	L	GA	SO	Avg.
95-96—Val-d'Or	QMJHL	23	1199	6	11	4	74	0	3.70	3	68	0	1	5	0	4.41
96-97—Val-d'Or	QMJHL	60	3305	32	21	2	171	2	3.10	13	777	8	5	44	0	3.40
97-98—Val-d'Or	QMJHL	54	3046	27	20	5	157	*7	3.09	*17	*1019	*14	3	37	*2	*2.18
98-99—Val-d'Or	QMJHL	21	1177	6	10	2	77	1	3.93	—	—	—	—	—	—	—
—Acadie-Bathurst	QMJHL	22	1341	14	7	1	74	0	3.31	*23	*1400	*16	6	64	0	2.74
99-00—Lowell	AHL	26	1517	10	12	4	74	1	2.93	6	359	3	3	18	0	3.01
—New York Islanders	NHL	24	1292	7	14	1	70	1	3.25	—	—	—	—	—	—	—
NHL Totals (1 year)		24	1292	7	14	1	70	1	3.25							

LYASHENKO, ROMAN　　　　C　　　　STARS

PERSONAL: Born May 2, 1979, in Murmansk, U.S.S.R. ... 6-0/188. ... Shoots right.
TRANSACTIONS/CAREER NOTES: Selected by Dallas Stars in second round (second Stars pick, 52nd overall) of NHL entry draft (June 21, 1997). ... Separated shoulder (November 17, 1999); missed five games. ... Sprained shoulder (December 21, 1999); missed one game. ... Sprained shoulder (December 31, 1999); missed two games.

		REGULAR SEASON								PLAYOFFS				
Season Team	League	Gms.	G	A	Pts.	PIM	+/-	PP	SH	Gms.	G	A	Pts.	PIM
95-96—Torpedo-2 Yaroslavl....	CIS Div. II	60	7	10	17	12	...	...	...	—	—	—	—	—
96-97—Torpedo Yaroslavl	Russian	42	5	7	12	16	...	...	...	9	3	0	3	6
—Torpedo-2 Yaroslavl....	Rus. Div. III	2	1	1	2	8	...	...	...	—	—	—	—	—
97-98—Torpedo Yaroslavl	Russian	46	7	6	13	28	...	...	...	—	—	—	—	—
98-99—Torpedo Yaroslavl	Russian	42	10	9	19	51	...	...	...	9	0	4	4	8
99-00—Michigan....................	IHL	9	3	2	5	8	...	...	...	—	—	—	—	—
—Dallas....................	NHL	58	6	6	12	10	-2	0	0	16	2	1	3	0
NHL Totals (1 year).............		58	6	6	12	10	-2	0	0	16	2	1	3	0

LYDMAN, TONI　　　　D　　　　FLAMES

PERSONAL: Born September 25, 1977, in Lahti, Finland. ... 6-1/183. ... Shoots left.
TRANSACTIONS/CAREER NOTES: Selected by Calgary Flames in fourth round (fifth Flames pick, 89th overall) of NHL entry draft (June 22, 1996).

		REGULAR SEASON								PLAYOFFS				
Season Team	League	Gms.	G	A	Pts.	PIM	+/-	PP	SH	Gms.	G	A	Pts.	PIM
93-94—Reipas Jrs..................	Finland	1	0	0	0	0	...	...	...	—	—	—	—	—
94-95—Reipas Jrs..................	Finland	26	6	4	10	10	...	...	...	—	—	—	—	—
95-96—Reipas Jrs..................	Finland	1	0	0	0	0	...	...	...	—	—	—	—	—
—Reipas Lahti...............	Finland	39	5	2	7	30	...	...	...	—	—	—	—	—
96-97—Tappara...................	Finland	49	1	2	3	65	...	...	...	3	0	0	0	6
97-98—Tappara Tampere	Finland	48	4	10	14	48	...	...	...	4	0	2	2	0
98-99—HIFK Helsinki	Finland	42	4	7	11	36	...	...	...	11	0	3	3	2
99-00—HIFK Helsinki	Finland	46	4	18	22	36	...	...	...	9	0	4	4	6

MacINNIS, AL　　　　D　　　　BLUES

PERSONAL: Born July 11, 1963, in Inverness, Nova Scotia ... 6-2/208. ... Shoots right. ... Full Name: Allan MacInnis. ... Name pronounced muh-KIHN-ihz.
HIGH SCHOOL: KCI (Kitchener, Ont.).
TRANSACTIONS/CAREER NOTES: Selected by Calgary Flames as underage junior in first round (first Flames pick, 15th overall) of NHL entry draft (June 10, 1981). ... Twisted knee (February 1985). ... Lacerated hand (March 23, 1986). ... Stretched ligaments of knee (April 8, 1990). ... Separated shoulder (November 22, 1991); missed eight games. ... Dislocated left hip (November 12, 1992); missed 34 games. ... Strained shoulder (December 22, 1993); missed one game. ... Strained shoulder (January 2, 1994); missed four games. ... Bruised knee (February 24, 1994); missed four games. ... Traded by Flames with fourth-round pick (D Didier Tremblay) in 1997 draft to St. Louis Blues for D Phil Housley and second-round pick in 1996 (C Steve Begin) and 1997 (RW John Tripp) drafts (July 4, 1994). ... Injured shoulder (January 31, 1995); missed eight games. ... Suffered from the flu (April 9, 1995); missed three games. ... Injured shoulder (April 25, 1995); missed final five games of season. ... Dislocated shoulder (February 4, 1997); missed nine games. ... Dislocated shoulder (December 13, 1997); missed nine games. ... Suffered laceration around left eye (April 12, 1998); missed one game. ... Fractured fibula (October 9, 1999); missed 11 games. ... Suffered rib injury (January 14, 2000); missed one game. ... Suffered collapsed lung (January 21, 2000); missed five games. ... Suffered back spasms (February 10, 2000); missed three games.
HONORS: Named to OHL All-Star first team (1981-82 and 1982-83). ... Named to Memorial Cup All-Star team (1981-82). ... Won Max Kaminsky Trophy (1982-83). ... Played in NHL All-Star Game (1985, 1988, 1990-1992, 1994 and 1996-2000). ... Named to NHL All-Star second team (1986-87, 1988-89 and 1993-94). ... Won Conn Smythe Trophy (1988-89). ... Named to THE SPORTING NEWS All-Star first team (1989-90 and 1990-91). ... Named to THE SPORTING NEWS All-Star second team (1993-94). ... Named to NHL All-Star first team (1989-90, 1990-91 and 1998-99). ... Named to THE SPORTING NEWS All-Star team (1998-99). ... Won James Norris Memorial Trophy (1998-99).
MISCELLANEOUS: Member of Stanley Cup championship team (1989). ... Holds Calgary Flames franchise all-time records for most games played (803) and most assists (609). ... Scored on a penalty shot (vs. Kelly Hrudey, April 4, 1990 (playoffs)).
STATISTICAL PLATEAUS: Three-goal games: 1991-92 (1), 1996-97 (1), 1998-99 (1). Total: 3.

		REGULAR SEASON								PLAYOFFS				
Season Team	League	Gms.	G	A	Pts.	PIM	+/-	PP	SH	Gms.	G	A	Pts.	PIM
79-80—Regina Blues............	SJHL	59	20	28	48	110	...	...	...	—	—	—	—	—
80-81—Kitchener	OMJHL	47	11	28	39	59	...	...	...	18	4	12	16	20
81-82—Kitchener	OHL	59	25	50	75	145	...	...	...	15	5	10	15	44
—Calgary	NHL	2	0	0	0	0	0	0	0	—	—	—	—	—
82-83—Kitchener	OHL	51	38	46	84	67	...	...	...	8	3	8	11	9
—Calgary	NHL	14	1	3	4	9	0	0	0	—	—	—	—	—
83-84—Colorado	CHL	19	5	14	19	22	...	...	...	—	—	—	—	—
—Calgary	NHL	51	11	34	45	42	0	7	0	11	2	12	14	13
84-85—Calgary	NHL	67	14	52	66	75	7	8	0	4	1	2	3	8
85-86—Calgary	NHL	77	11	57	68	76	39	4	0	21	4	*15	19	30
86-87—Calgary	NHL	79	20	56	76	97	20	7	0	4	1	0	1	0
87-88—Calgary	NHL	80	25	58	83	114	13	7	2	7	3	6	9	18
88-89—Calgary	NHL	79	16	58	74	126	38	8	0	22	7	*24	*31	46
89-90—Calgary	NHL	79	28	62	90	82	20	14	0	6	2	3	5	8
90-91—Calgary	NHL	78	28	75	103	90	42	17	0	7	2	3	5	8
91-92—Calgary	NHL	72	20	57	77	83	13	11	0	—	—	—	—	—
92-93—Calgary	NHL	50	11	43	54	61	15	7	0	6	1	6	7	10
93-94—Calgary	NHL	75	28	54	82	95	35	12	1	7	2	6	8	12

L

M

Season Team	League	REGULAR SEASON								PLAYOFFS				
		Gms.	G	A	Pts.	PIM	+/-	PP	SH	Gms.	G	A	Pts.	PIM
94-95—St. Louis	NHL	32	8	20	28	43	19	2	0	7	1	5	6	10
95-96—St. Louis	NHL	82	17	44	61	88	5	9	1	13	3	4	7	6
96-97—St. Louis	NHL	72	13	30	43	65	2	6	1	6	1	2	3	4
97-98—St. Louis	NHL	71	19	30	49	80	6	9	1	8	2	6	8	12
—Can. Olympic team	Int'l	6	2	0	2	2	...	...	...	—	—	—	—	—
98-99—St. Louis	NHL	82	20	42	62	70	33	11	1	13	4	8	12	20
99-00—St. Louis	NHL	61	11	28	39	34	20	6	0	7	1	3	4	14
NHL Totals (19 years)		1203	301	803	1104	1330	327	145	...	149	37	105	142	233

MacLEAN, DONALD   C   MAPLE LEAFS

PERSONAL: Born January 14, 1977, in Sydney, Nova Scotia. ... 6-2/199. ... Shoots left.

TRANSACTIONS/CAREER NOTES: Selected by Los Angeles Kings in second round (second Kings pick, 33rd overall) of NHL entry draft (July 8, 1995). ... Traded by Kings to Toronto Maple Leafs for C Craig Charron (February 23, 2000).

Season Team	League	REGULAR SEASON								PLAYOFFS				
		Gms.	G	A	Pts.	PIM	+/-	PP	SH	Gms.	G	A	Pts.	PIM
94-95—Beauport	QMJHL	64	15	27	42	37	...	...	...	17	4	4	8	6
95-96—Beauport	QMJHL	1	0	1	1	0	...	...	...	—	—	—	—	—
—Laval	QMJHL	21	17	11	28	29	...	...	...	—	—	—	—	—
—Hull	QMJHL	39	26	34	60	44	...	...	...	17	6	7	13	14
96-97—Hull	QMJHL	69	34	47	81	67	...	...	...	14	11	10	21	29
97-98—Los Angeles	NHL	22	5	2	7	4	-1	2	0	—	—	—	—	—
—Fredericton	AHL	39	9	5	14	32	...	...	...	4	1	3	4	2
98-99—Springfield	AHL	41	5	14	19	31	...	...	...	—	—	—	—	—
—Grand Rapids	IHL	28	6	13	19	8	...	...	...	—	—	—	—	—
99-00—Lowell	AHL	40	11	17	28	18	...	...	...	—	—	—	—	—
—St. John's	AHL	21	14	12	26	8	...	...	...	—	—	—	—	—
NHL Totals (1 year)		22	5	2	7	4	-1	2	0					

MacLEAN, JOHN   RW   RANGERS

PERSONAL: Born November 20, 1964, in Oshawa, Ont. ... 6-0/205. ... Shoots right. ... Name pronounced muh-KLAYN.

TRANSACTIONS/CAREER NOTES: Selected by New Jersey Devils as underage junior in first round (first Devils pick, sixth overall) of NHL entry draft (June 8, 1983). ... Bruised shoulder (November 1984). ... Injured right knee (January 25, 1985). ... Reinjured knee and underwent surgery (January 31, 1985). ... Bruised ankle (November 2, 1986). ... Sprained right elbow (December 1988). ... Bruised ribs (March 1, 1989). ... Suffered concussion and stomach contusions (October 1990). ... Suffered concussion (December 11, 1990). ... Tore ligament in right knee (September 3, 1991); missed entire 1991-92 season. ... Underwent surgery to right knee (November 23, 1991). ... Injured forearm (November 3, 1993); missed two games. ... Lacerated eye (February 24, 1994); missed one game. ... Bruised foot (April 9, 1995); missed one game. ... Injured knee (March 10, 1996); missed six games. ... Traded by Devils with D Ken Sutton to San Jose Sharks for D Doug Bodger and LW Dody Wood (December 7, 1997). ... Signed as free agent by New York Rangers (July 9, 1998). ... Suffered eye injury (March 6, 2000); missed four games.

HONORS: Named to Memorial Cup All-Star team (1982-83). ... Played in NHL All-Star Game (1989 and 1991).

MISCELLANEOUS: Member of Stanley Cup championship team (1995). ... Holds New Jersey Devils franchise all-time records for most goals (347), assists (354) and points (701). ... Scored on a penalty shot (vs. Dominik Hasek, February 27, 1997; vs. Bill Ranford, January 10, 1999).

STATISTICAL PLATEAUS: Three-goal games: 1987-88 (1), 1988-89 (3), 1990-91 (2). Total: 6.

Season Team	League	REGULAR SEASON								PLAYOFFS				
		Gms.	G	A	Pts.	PIM	+/-	PP	SH	Gms.	G	A	Pts.	PIM
81-82—Oshawa	OHL	67	17	22	39	197	...	...	...	12	3	6	9	63
82-83—Oshawa	OHL	66	47	51	98	138	...	...	...	17	*18	20	†38	35
83-84—New Jersey	NHL	23	1	0	1	10	-7	0	0	—	—	—	—	—
—Oshawa	OHL	30	23	36	59	58	...	...	...	7	2	5	7	18
84-85—New Jersey	NHL	61	13	20	33	44	-11	1	0	—	—	—	—	—
85-86—New Jersey	NHL	74	21	36	57	112	-2	1	0	—	—	—	—	—
86-87—New Jersey	NHL	80	31	36	67	120	-23	9	0	—	—	—	—	—
87-88—New Jersey	NHL	76	23	16	39	147	-10	12	0	20	7	11	18	60
88-89—New Jersey	NHL	74	42	45	87	122	26	14	0	—	—	—	—	—
89-90—New Jersey	NHL	80	41	38	79	80	17	10	3	6	4	1	5	12
90-91—New Jersey	NHL	78	45	33	78	150	8	19	2	7	5	3	8	20
91-92—New Jersey	NHL				Did not play.									
92-93—New Jersey	NHL	80	24	24	48	102	-6	7	1	5	0	1	1	10
93-94—New Jersey	NHL	80	37	33	70	95	30	8	0	20	6	10	16	22
94-95—New Jersey	NHL	46	17	12	29	32	13	2	1	20	5	13	18	14
95-96—New Jersey	NHL	76	20	28	48	91	3	3	3	—	—	—	—	—
96-97—New Jersey	NHL	80	29	25	54	49	11	5	0	10	4	5	9	4
97-98—New Jersey	NHL	26	3	8	11	14	-6	1	0	—	—	—	—	—
—San Jose	NHL	51	13	19	32	28	0	5	0	6	2	3	5	4
98-99—New York Rangers	NHL	82	28	27	55	46	5	11	1	—	—	—	—	—
99-00—New York Rangers	NHL	77	18	24	42	52	-2	6	2	—	—	—	—	—
NHL Totals (17 years)		1144	406	424	830	1294	46	114	13	94	33	47	80	146

MADDEN, JOHN   C   DEVILS

PERSONAL: Born May 4, 1973, in Barrie, Ont. ... 5-11/195. ... Shoots left.

COLLEGE: Michigan.

TRANSACTIONS/CAREER NOTES: Signed as non-drafted free agent by New Jersey Devils (June 26, 1997).

HONORS: Named CCHA Tournament Most Valuable Player (1995-96). ... Named to NCAA All-America (West) first team (1996-97). ... Named to CCHA All-Star first team (1996-97).
MISCELLANEOUS: Member of Stanley Cup championship team (2000). ... Failed to score on a penalty shot (vs. Mike Dunham, February 29, 2000).

		REGULAR SEASON							PLAYOFFS				
Season Team	League	Gms.	G	A	Pts.	PIM	+/-	PP	SH	Gms.	G	A	Pts.	PIM
92-93—Barrie	COJHL	62	...	...	163	...	...	...	...	18	...	...	36	...
93-94—Univ. of Michigan	CCHA	36	6	11	17	14	...	...	...	—	—	—	—	—
94-95—Univ. of Michigan	CCHA	39	21	22	43	8	...	...	...	—	—	—	—	—
95-96—Univ. of Michigan	CCHA	43	27	30	57	45	...	...	...	—	—	—	—	—
96-97—Univ. of Michigan	CCHA	42	26	37	63	56	...	...	...	—	—	—	—	—
97-98—Albany	AHL	74	20	36	56	40	...	...	...	13	3	13	16	14
98-99—Albany	AHL	75	38	60	98	44	...	...	...	5	2	2	4	6
—New Jersey	NHL	4	0	1	1	0	-2	0	0	—	—	—	—	—
99-00—New Jersey	NHL	74	16	9	25	6	7	0	*6	20	3	4	7	0
NHL Totals (2 years)		78	16	10	26	6	5	0	6	20	3	4	7	0

MAIR, ADAM — C — MAPLE LEAFS

PERSONAL: Born February 15, 1979, in Hamilton, Ont. ... 6-2/194. ... Shoots right.
TRANSACTIONS/CAREER NOTES: Selected by Toronto Maple Leafs in fourth round (second Maple Leafs pick, 84th overall) of NHL entry draft (June 21, 1997).

		REGULAR SEASON							PLAYOFFS				
Season Team	League	Gms.	G	A	Pts.	PIM	+/-	PP	SH	Gms.	G	A	Pts.	PIM
94-95—Ohsweken	Jr. B	39	21	23	44	91	...	...	...	—	—	—	—	—
95-96—Owen Sound	OHL	62	12	15	27	63	...	...	...	6	0	0	0	2
96-97—Owen Sound	OHL	65	16	35	51	113	...	...	...	4	1	0	1	2
97-98—Owen Sound	OHL	56	25	27	52	179	...	...	...	11	6	3	9	31
98-99—Owen Sound	OHL	43	23	41	64	109	...	...	...	16	10	10	20	47
—Toronto	NHL	—	—	—	—	—	—	—	—	5	1	0	1	14
99-00—St. John's	AHL	66	22	27	49	124	...	...	...	—	—	—	—	—
—Toronto	NHL	8	1	0	1	6	-1	0	0	5	0	0	0	8
NHL Totals (2 years)		8	1	0	1	6	-1	0	0	10	1	0	1	22

MALAKHOV, VLADIMIR — D — RANGERS

PERSONAL: Born August 30, 1968, in Sverdlovsk, U.S.S.R. ... 6-4/230. ... Shoots left. ... Name pronounced MAL-uh-kahf.
TRANSACTIONS/CAREER NOTES: Selected by New York Islanders in 10th round (12th Islanders pick, 191st overall) of NHL entry draft (June 17, 1989). ... Suffered sore groin prior to 1992-93 season; missed first two games of season. ... Injured right shoulder (January 16, 1993); missed eight games. ... Sprained shoulder (March 14, 1993); missed five games. ... Suffered concussion (December 7, 1993); missed one game. ... Strained lower back (December 28, 1993); missed six games. ... Strained hip flexor (February 9, 1995); missed five games. ... Suffered charley horse (March 14, 1995); missed two games. ... Traded by Islanders with C Pierre Turgeon to Montreal Canadiens for LW Kirk Muller, D Mathieu Schneider and C Craig Darby (April 5, 1995). ... Strained hip flexor (April 24, 1995); missed one game. ... Suffered from stomach flu (October 25, 1995); missed two games. ... Bruised right leg (December 12, 1995); missed two games. ... Bruised ribs (October 24, 1996); missed one game. ... Fractured thumb (December 23, 1996); missed 16 games. ... Bruised lower back (October 29, 1997); missed one game. ... Sprained knee (December 10, 1997); missed four games. ... Suffered shoulder tendinitis (February 28, 1998); missed three games. ... Suffered back spasms (November 9, 1998); missed two games. ... Suffered back spasms (December 5, 1998); missed six games. ... Suffered back spasms (January 31, 1999); missed two games. ... Sprained knee (March 28, 1999); missed six games. ... Reinjured knee (April 10, 1999); missed final three games of season. ... Torn anterior cruciate ligament in knee (September 17, 1999); missed first 53 games of 1999-2000 season. ... Injured knee (February 14, 2000); missed two games. ... Traded by Canadiens to New Jersey Devils for D Sheldon Souray, D Josh DeWolf and second-round draft pick in 2001 draft (March 1, 2000). ... Signed as free agent by New York Rangers (July 10, 2000).
HONORS: Named to NHL All-Rookie team (1992-93).
MISCELLANEOUS: Member of Stanley Cup championship team (2000). ... Member of gold-medal-winning Unified Olympic team (1992).
STATISTICAL PLATEAUS: Three-goal games: 1997-98 (1).

		REGULAR SEASON							PLAYOFFS				
Season Team	League	Gms.	G	A	Pts.	PIM	+/-	PP	SH	Gms.	G	A	Pts.	PIM
86-87—Spartak Moscow	USSR	22	0	1	1	12	...	...	...	—	—	—	—	—
87-88—Spartak Moscow	USSR	28	2	2	4	26	...	...	...	—	—	—	—	—
88-89—CSKA Moscow	USSR	34	6	2	8	16	...	...	...	—	—	—	—	—
89-90—CSKA Moscow	USSR	48	2	10	12	34	...	...	...	—	—	—	—	—
90-91—CSKA Moscow	USSR	46	5	13	18	22	...	...	...	—	—	—	—	—
91-92—CSKA Moscow	CIS	40	1	9	10	12	...	...	...	—	—	—	—	—
—Unif. Olympic team	Int'l	8	3	0	3	4	...	...	...	—	—	—	—	—
92-93—Capital District	AHL	3	2	1	3	11	...	...	...	—	—	—	—	—
—New York Islanders	NHL	64	14	38	52	59	14	7	0	17	3	6	9	12
93-94—New York Islanders	NHL	76	10	47	57	80	29	4	0	4	0	0	0	6
94-95—New York Islanders	NHL	26	3	13	16	32	-1	1	0	—	—	—	—	—
—Montreal	NHL	14	1	4	5	14	-2	0	0	—	—	—	—	—
95-96—Montreal	NHL	61	5	23	28	79	7	2	0	—	—	—	—	—
96-97—Montreal	NHL	65	10	20	30	43	3	5	0	5	0	0	0	6
97-98—Montreal	NHL	74	13	31	44	70	16	8	0	9	3	4	7	10
98-99—Montreal	NHL	62	13	21	34	77	-7	8	0	—	—	—	—	—
99-00—Montreal	NHL	7	0	0	0	4	0	0	0	—	—	—	—	—
—New Jersey	NHL	17	1	4	5	19	1	1	0	23	1	4	5	18
NHL Totals (8 years)		466	70	201	271	477	60	36	0	58	7	14	21	52

M

PERSONAL: Born April 21, 1970, in Prince George, B.C. ... 6-0/211. ... Shoots left. ... Name pronounced mal-GOO-nuhz.
TRANSACTIONS/CAREER NOTES: Selected by Detroit Red Wings in fourth round (third Red Wings pick, 66th overall) of NHL entry draft (June 16, 1990). ... Injured knee (September 26, 1992); missed first 10 games of season. ... Traded by Red Wings to Philadelphia Flyers for fifth-round pick (G David Arsenault) in 1995 draft (September 8, 1993). ... Sprained medial collateral ligament in left knee (February 5, 1994); missed 12 games. ... Signed as free agent by Winnipeg Jets (August 5, 1995). ... Traded by Jets to Washington Capitals for RW Denis Chasse (February 15, 1996). ... Injured shoulder (April 6, 1996); missed three games. ... Strained hip flexor (November 6, 1998); missed four games. ... Traded by Capitals to Nashville Predators for conditional pick in 2001 draft (February 3, 2000). ... Claimed on waivers by Calgary Flames (February 6, 2000). ... Suffered concussion (February 14, 2000); missed remainder of season.
HONORS: Named to WHL (West) All-Star first team (1989-90).

		REGULAR SEASON								PLAYOFFS				
Season Team	League	Gms.	G	A	Pts.	PIM	+/-	PP	SH	Gms.	G	A	Pts.	PIM
87-88—Prince George	BCJHL	54	12	34	46	99	...	...	...	—	—	—	—	—
—New Westminster	WHL	6	0	0	0	0	...	...	...	—	—	—	—	—
88-89—Seattle	WHL	72	11	41	52	51	...	...	...	—	—	—	—	—
89-90—Seattle	WHL	63	15	48	63	116	...	...	...	13	2	9	11	32
90-91—Adirondack	AHL	78	5	19	24	70	...	...	...	2	0	0	0	4
91-92—Adirondack	AHL	69	4	28	32	82	...	...	...	18	2	6	8	28
92-93—Adirondack	AHL	45	3	12	15	39	...	...	...	11	3	3	6	8
93-94—Philadelphia	NHL	67	1	3	4	86	2	0	0	—	—	—	—	—
94-95—Hershey	AHL	32	3	5	8	28	...	...	...	6	2	1	3	31
—Philadelphia	NHL	4	0	0	0	4	-1	0	0	—	—	—	—	—
95-96—Winnipeg	NHL	29	0	1	1	32	-10	0	0	—	—	—	—	—
—Portland	AHL	16	2	5	7	18	...	...	...	13	1	3	4	19
—Washington	NHL	1	0	0	0	0	0	0	0	—	—	—	—	—
96-97—Portland	AHL	68	6	12	18	59	...	...	...	5	0	0	0	8
—Washington	NHL	6	0	0	0	2	2	0	0	—	—	—	—	—
97-98—Portland	AHL	69	14	25	39	73	...	...	...	9	1	1	2	19
—Washington	NHL	8	0	0	0	12	1	0	0	—	—	—	—	—
98-99—Portland	AHL	33	2	10	12	49	...	...	...	—	—	—	—	—
—Washington	NHL	10	0	0	0	6	-5	0	0	—	—	—	—	—
—Detroit	IHL	9	0	2	2	10	...	...	...	11	0	1	1	21
99-00—Utah	IHL	34	4	9	13	55	...	...	...	—	—	—	—	—
—Calgary	NHL	4	0	1	1	2	1	0	0	—	—	—	—	—
NHL Totals (7 years)		129	1	5	6	144	-10	0	0					

PERSONAL: Born May 18, 1980, in Mississauga, Ont. ... 6-2/210. ... Shoots left.
TRANSACTIONS/CAREER NOTES: Selected by New York Rangers in first round (first Rangers pick, seventh overall) of NHL entry draft (June 27, 1998). ... Sprained ankle (November 18, 1999); missed four games.

		REGULAR SEASON								PLAYOFFS				
Season Team	League	Gms.	G	A	Pts.	PIM	+/-	PP	SH	Gms.	G	A	Pts.	PIM
96-97—Guelph	OHL	61	16	28	44	26	...	...	...	18	7	7	14	11
97-98—Guelph	OHL	57	16	35	51	29	...	...	...	12	7	6	13	8
98-99—New York Rangers	NHL	73	8	8	16	13	-2	1	0	—	—	—	—	—
99-00—New York Rangers	NHL	27	0	0	0	4	-6	0	0	—	—	—	—	—
—Hartford	AHL	12	1	5	6	2	...	...	...	23	1	2	3	10
—Guelph	OHL	5	2	2	4	4	...	...	...	6	0	2	2	4
NHL Totals (2 years)		100	8	8	16	17	-8	1	0					

PERSONAL: Born June 24, 1975, in Ostrava, Czechoslovakia. ... 6-5/210. ... Shoots left. ... Name pronounced muh-REHK muh-LEEK.
TRANSACTIONS/CAREER NOTES: Selected by Hartford Whalers in third round (second Whalers pick, 72nd overall) of NHL entry draft (June 26, 1993). ... Suffered from the flu (January 20, 1997); missed three games. ... Bruised shin (March 20, 1997); missed four games. ... Whalers franchise moved to North Carolina and renamed Carolina Hurricanes for 1997-98 season; NHL approved move on June 25, 1997. ... Injured knee (April 7, 1999); missed one game.

		REGULAR SEASON								PLAYOFFS				
Season Team	League	Gms.	G	A	Pts.	PIM	+/-	PP	SH	Gms.	G	A	Pts.	PIM
91-92—TJ Vitkovice Jrs	Czech. Jrs.				Statistics unavailable.									
92-93—TJ Vitkovice	Czech.	20	5	10	15	16	...	...	...	—	—	—	—	—
93-94—HC Vitkovice	Czech Rep.	38	3	3	6	...	...	...	...	3	0	1	1	...
94-95—Springfield	AHL	58	11	30	41	91	...	...	...	—	—	—	—	—
—Hartford	NHL	1	0	1	1	0	1	0	0	—	—	—	—	—
95-96—Springfield	AHL	68	8	14	22	135	...	...	...	8	1	3	4	20
—Hartford	NHL	7	0	0	0	4	-3	0	0	—	—	—	—	—
96-97—Springfield	AHL	3	0	3	3	4	...	...	...	—	—	—	—	—
—Hartford	NHL	47	1	5	6	50	5	0	0	—	—	—	—	—
97-98—Malmoif	Sweden	37	1	5	6	21	...	...	...	—	—	—	—	—
98-99—HC Vitkovice	Czech Rep.	1	1	0	1	6	...	...	...	—	—	—	—	—
—New Haven	AHL	21	2	8	10	28	...	...	...	—	—	—	—	—
—Carolina	NHL	52	2	9	11	36	-6	1	0	4	0	0	0	4
99-00—Carolina	NHL	57	4	10	14	63	13	0	0	—	—	—	—	—
NHL Totals (5 years)		164	7	25	32	153	10	1	0	4	0	0	0	4

M

MALTBY, KIRK RW RED WINGS

PERSONAL: Born December 22, 1972, in Guelph, Ont. ... 6-0/190. ... Shoots right.
COLLEGE: Georgian (Ont.).
TRANSACTIONS/CAREER NOTES: Selected by Edmonton Oilers in third round (fourth Oilers pick, 65th overall) of NHL entry draft (June 20, 1992). ... Suffered chip fracture of ankle bone (February 2, 1994); missed 13 games. ... Lacerated right eye (March 1, 1995); missed last game of season. ... Scratched left cornea (February 1, 1996); missed 16 games. ... Traded by Oilers to Detroit Red Wings for D Dan McGillis (March 20, 1996). ... Separated shoulder (September 24, 1997); missed 16 games. ... Suffered from lower abdminal pain (November 14, 1998); missed 19 games. ... Sprained knee (December 31, 1998); missed five games. ... Injured ankle (March 31, 1999); missed one game. ... Suspended four games by NHL for slashing incident (March 17, 1999). ... Suffered hernia (October 5, 1999); missed 41 games.
MISCELLANEOUS: Member of Stanley Cup championship team (1997 and 1998).

		REGULAR SEASON								PLAYOFFS				
Season Team	League	Gms.	G	A	Pts.	PIM	+/-	PP	SH	Gms.	G	A	Pts.	PIM
88-89—Cambridge Jr. B	OHA	48	28	18	46	138	...	...	...	—	—	—	—	—
89-90—Owen Sound	OHL	61	12	15	27	90	...	...	...	12	1	6	7	15
90-91—Owen Sound	OHL	66	34	32	66	100	...	...	...	—	—	—	—	—
91-92—Owen Sound	OHL	64	50	41	91	99	...	...	...	5	3	3	6	18
92-93—Cape Breton	AHL	73	22	23	45	130	...	...	...	16	3	3	6	45
93-94—Edmonton	NHL	68	11	8	19	74	-2	0	1	—	—	—	—	—
94-95—Edmonton	NHL	47	8	3	11	49	-11	0	2	—	—	—	—	—
95-96—Edmonton	NHL	49	2	6	8	61	-16	0	0	—	—	—	—	—
—Cape Breton	AHL	4	1	2	3	6	...	...	...	—	—	—	—	—
—Detroit	NHL	6	1	0	1	6	0	0	0	8	0	1	1	4
96-97—Detroit	NHL	66	3	5	8	75	3	0	0	20	5	2	7	24
97-98—Detroit	NHL	65	14	9	23	89	11	2	1	22	3	1	4	30
98-99—Detroit	NHL	53	8	6	14	34	-6	0	1	10	1	0	1	8
99-00—Detroit	NHL	41	6	8	14	24	1	0	2	8	0	1	1	4
NHL Totals (7 years)		395	53	45	98	412	-20	2	7	68	9	5	14	70

MANDERVILLE, KENT C FLYERS

PERSONAL: Born April 12, 1971, in Edmonton. ... 6-3/200. ... Shoots left. ... Full Name: Kent Stephen Manderville.
COLLEGE: Cornell.
TRANSACTIONS/CAREER NOTES: Selected by Calgary Flames in second round (first Flames pick, 24th overall) of NHL entry draft (June 17, 1989). ... Traded by Flames with C Doug Gilmour, D Jamie Macoun, D Ric Nattress and G Rick Wamsley to Toronto Maple Leafs for LW Craig Berube, D Alexander Godynyuk, RW Gary Leeman, D Michel Petit and G Jeff Reese (January 2, 1992). ... Bruised hand (October 5, 1993); missed one game. ... Suffered from the flu (December 17, 1993); missed two games. ... Sprained ankle (January 30, 1995); missed one game. ... Traded by Maple Leafs to Edmonton Oilers for C Peter White and fourth-round pick (RW Jason Sessa) in 1996 draft (December 4, 1995). ... Sprained left wrist (February 18, 1996); missed nine games. ... Signed as free agent by Hartford Whalers (October 1, 1996). ... Whalers franchise moved to North Carolina and renamed Carolina Hurricanes for 1997-98 season; NHL approved move on June 25, 1997. ... Strained abdominal muscle (March 12, 1998); missed four games. ... Suffered concussion (December 15, 1999); missed 10 games. ... Traded by Hurricanes to Philadelphia Flyers for RW Sandy McCarthy (March 14, 2000).
HONORS: Named ECAC Rookie of the Year (1989-90). ... Named to ECAC All-Rookie team (1989-90).
MISCELLANEOUS: Member of silver-medal-winning Canadian Olympic team (1992).
STATISTICAL PLATEAUS: Three-goal games: 1996-97 (1).

		REGULAR SEASON								PLAYOFFS				
Season Team	League	Gms.	G	A	Pts.	PIM	+/-	PP	SH	Gms.	G	A	Pts.	PIM
88-89—Notre Dame	SJHL	58	39	36	75	165	...	...	...	—	—	—	—	—
89-90—Cornell University	ECAC	26	11	15	26	28	...	...	...	—	—	—	—	—
90-91—Cornell University	ECAC	28	17	14	31	60	...	...	...	—	—	—	—	—
—Canadian nat'l team	Int'l	3	1	2	3	0	...	...	...	—	—	—	—	—
91-92—Canadian nat'l team	Int'l	63	16	23	39	75	...	...	...	—	—	—	—	—
—Can. Olympic team	Int'l	8	1	2	3	0	...	...	...	—	—	—	—	—
—Toronto	NHL	15	0	4	4	0	1	0	0	—	—	—	—	—
—St. John's	AHL	—	—	—	—	—	...	...	...	12	5	9	14	14
92-93—Toronto	NHL	18	1	1	2	17	-9	0	0	18	1	0	1	8
—St. John's	AHL	56	19	28	47	86	...	...	...	2	0	2	2	0
93-94—Toronto	NHL	67	7	9	16	63	5	0	0	12	1	0	1	4
94-95—Toronto	NHL	36	0	1	1	22	-2	0	0	7	0	0	0	6
95-96—St. John's	AHL	27	16	12	28	26	...	...	...	—	—	—	—	—
—Edmonton	NHL	37	3	5	8	38	-5	0	2	—	—	—	—	—
96-97—Springfield	AHL	23	5	20	25	18	...	...	...	—	—	—	—	—
—Hartford	NHL	44	6	5	11	18	3	0	0	—	—	—	—	—
97-98—Carolina	NHL	77	4	4	8	31	-6	0	0	—	—	—	—	—
98-99—Carolina	NHL	81	5	11	16	38	9	0	0	6	0	0	0	2
99-00—Carolina	NHL	56	1	4	5	12	-8	0	0	—	—	—	—	—
—Philadelphia	NHL	13	0	3	3	4	2	0	0	18	0	1	1	22
NHL Totals (9 years)		444	27	47	74	243	-10	0	2	61	2	1	3	42

MANELUK, MIKE RW

PERSONAL: Born October 1, 1973, in Winnipeg. ... 5-11/190. ... Shoots right. ... Name pronounced MAN-ih-luhk.
TRANSACTIONS/CAREER NOTES: Signed as non-drafted free agent by Mighty Ducks of Anaheim (January 28, 1994). ... Traded by Mighty Ducks to Ottawa Senators for RW Kevin Brown (July 1, 1996). ... Traded by Senators to Philadelphia Flyers for cash (October 21, 1997). ... Traded by Flyers to Chicago Blackhawks for C Roman Vopat (November 17, 1998). ... Bruised ribs (December 8, 1998); missed two games. ... Claimed on waivers by New York Rangers (March 4, 1999). ... Signed as free agent by Flyers (August 2, 1999).
HONORS: Won Jack Butterfield Trophy (1997-98). ... Named to AHL All-Star first team (1999-2000).

Season Team	League	Gms.	G	A	Pts.	PIM	+/-	PP	SH	Gms.	G	A	Pts.	PIM
90-91—St. Boniface	MJHL	45	29	41	70	199	...	...	...	—	—	—	—	—
91-92—Brandon	WHL	68	23	30	53	102	...	...	...	—	—	—	—	—
92-93—Brandon	WHL	72	36	51	87	75	...	...	...	4	2	1	3	2
93-94—Brandon	WHL	63	50	47	97	112	...	...	...	13	11	3	14	23
—San Diego	IHL	—	—	—	—	—	...	...	...	1	0	0	0	0
94-95—San Diego	IHL	10	0	1	1	4	...	...	...	—	—	—	—	—
—Canadian nat'l team	Int'l	44	36	24	60	34	...	...	...	—	—	—	—	—
95-96—Baltimore	AHL	74	33	38	71	73	...	...	...	6	4	3	7	14
96-97—Worcester	AHL	70	27	27	54	89	...	...	...	5	1	2	3	14
97-98—Worcester	AHL	5	3	3	6	4	...	...	...	—	—	—	—	—
—Philadelphia	AHL	66	27	35	62	62	...	...	...	20	13	*21	*34	30
98-99—Philadelphia	NHL	13	2	6	8	8	4	0	0	—	—	—	—	—
—Chicago	NHL	28	4	3	7	8	2	1	0	—	—	—	—	—
—New York Rangers	NHL	4	0	0	0	4	-1	0	0	—	—	—	—	—
99-00—Philadelphia	AHL	73	*47	40	87	158	...	...	...	4	1	2	3	4
—Philadelphia	NHL	1	0	0	0	4	0	0	0	—	—	—	—	—
NHL Totals (2 years)		46	6	9	15	24	5	1	0					

MANN, CAMERON RW BRUINS

PERSONAL: Born April 20, 1977, in Thompson, Man. ... 6-0/194. ... Shoots right.
HIGH SCHOOL: Thomas A. Stewart (Peterborough, Ont.).
TRANSACTIONS/CAREER NOTES: Selected by Boston Bruins in fourth round (fifth Bruins pick, 99th overall) of NHL entry draft (July 8, 1995). ... Suffered from the flu (March 21, 1999); missed one game.
HONORS: Named to OHL All-Star first team (1995-96 and 1996-97). ... Won Jim Mahon Memorial Trophy (1995-96). ... Won Stafford Smythe Memorial Trophy (May 1996). ... Named to Memorial Cup All-Star team (1995-96).

Season Team	League	Gms.	G	A	Pts.	PIM	+/-	PP	SH	Gms.	G	A	Pts.	PIM
93-94—Peterborough	Tier II Jr. A	16	3	14	17	23	...	...	...	—	—	—	—	—
—Peterborough	OHL	49	8	17	25	18	...	...	...	7	1	1	2	2
94-95—Peterborough	OHL	64	18	25	43	40	...	...	...	11	3	8	11	4
95-96—Peterborough	OHL	66	42	60	102	108	...	...	...	24	*27	16	*43	33
96-97—Peterborough	OHL	51	33	50	83	91	...	...	...	11	10	18	28	16
97-98—Providence	AHL	71	21	26	47	99	...	...	...	—	—	—	—	—
—Boston	NHL	9	0	1	1	4	1	0	0	—	—	—	—	—
98-99—Providence	AHL	43	21	25	46	65	...	...	...	11	7	7	14	4
—Boston	NHL	33	5	2	7	17	0	1	0	1	0	0	0	0
99-00—Boston	NHL	32	8	4	12	13	-6	1	0	—	—	—	—	—
—Providence	AHL	29	7	12	19	45	...	...	...	11	6	7	13	0
NHL Totals (3 years)		74	13	7	20	34	-5	2	0	1	0	0	0	0

M

MANSON, DAVE D

PERSONAL: Born January 27, 1967, in Prince Albert, Sask. ... 6-2/220. ... Shoots left. ... Full Name: David Manson.
HIGH SCHOOL: Carleton (Prince Albert, Sask.).
TRANSACTIONS/CAREER NOTES: Selected by Chicago Blackhawks as underage junior in first round (first Blackhawks pick, 11th overall) of NHL entry draft (June 15, 1985). ... Suspended three games by NHL for pushing linesman (October 8, 1989). ... Bruised right thigh (December 8, 1989). ... Suspended 13 games by NHL for abusing linesman and returning to ice to fight (December 23, 1989). ... Suspended three games by NHL for biting (February 27, 1990). ... Suspended four games by NHL for attempting to injure another player (October 20, 1990). ... Traded by Blackhawks with third-round pick (RW Kirk Maltby) in 1992 draft to Edmonton Oilers for D Steve Smith (October 2, 1991). ... Suspended five off-days and fined $500 by NHL for spearing (October 19, 1992). ... Strained ligaments in left knee (December 7, 1992); missed one game. ... Separated shoulder (October 22, 1993); missed 13 games. ... Traded by Oilers with sixth-round pick (D Chris Kibermanis) in 1994 draft to Winnipeg Jets for C Mats Lindgren, D Boris Mironov and first- (C Jason Bonsignore) and fourth-round (RW Adam Copeland) picks in 1994 draft (March 15, 1994). ... Bruised kidneys (January 21, 1995); missed one game. ... Bruised hand (April 19, 1995); missed two games. ... Jets franchise moved to Phoenix and renamed Coyotes for 1996-97 season; NHL approved move on January 18, 1996. ... Fractured toe (November 8, 1996); missed five games. ... Traded by Coyotes to Montreal Canadiens for D Murray Baron and RW Chris Murray (March 18, 1997). ... Fined $1,000 by NHL for criticizing a referee (April 21, 1997). ... Strained hip flexor (February 7, 1998); missed one game. ... Suffered hip pointer (October 17, 1998); missed two games. ... Suspended three games and fined $1,000 by NHL for elbowing incident (October 29, 1998). ... Traded by Canadiens with G Jocelyn Thibault and D Brad Brown to Blackhawks for G Jeff Hackett, D Eric Weinrich, D Alain Nasreddine and fourth-round pick (D Chris Dyment) in 1999 draft (November 16, 1998). ... Suspended three games by NHL for fighting incident (October 6, 1999). ... Bruised foot (October 30, 1999); missed four games. ... Traded by Blackhawks with D Sylvain Cote to Dallas Stars for C Derek Plante, D Kevin Dean and second-round pick in 2001 draft (February 8, 2000).
HONORS: Named to WHL All-Star second team (1985-86). ... Played in NHL All-Star Game (1989 and 1993).
MISCELLANEOUS: Failed to score on a penalty shot (vs. Darcy Wakaluk, January 24, 1991).

Season Team	League	Gms.	G	A	Pts.	PIM	+/-	PP	SH	Gms.	G	A	Pts.	PIM
83-84—Prince Albert	WHL	70	2	7	9	233	...	...	...	5	0	0	0	4
84-85—Prince Albert	WHL	72	8	30	38	247	...	...	...	13	1	0	1	34
85-86—Prince Albert	WHL	70	14	34	48	177	...	...	...	20	1	8	9	63
86-87—Chicago	NHL	63	1	8	9	146	-2	0	0	3	0	0	0	10
87-88—Saginaw	IHL	6	0	3	3	37	...	...	...	—	—	—	—	—
—Chicago	NHL	54	1	6	7	185	-12	0	0	5	0	0	0	27
88-89—Chicago	NHL	79	18	36	54	352	5	8	1	16	0	8	8	*84
89-90—Chicago	NHL	59	5	23	28	301	4	1	0	20	2	4	6	46
90-91—Chicago	NHL	75	14	15	29	191	20	6	1	6	0	1	1	36
91-92—Edmonton	NHL	79	15	32	47	220	9	7	0	16	3	9	12	44

Season Team	League	REGULAR SEASON								PLAYOFFS				
		Gms.	G	A	Pts.	PIM	+/-	PP	SH	Gms.	G	A	Pts.	PIM
92-93—Edmonton	NHL	83	15	30	45	210	-28	9	1	—	—	—	—	—
93-94—Edmonton	NHL	57	3	13	16	140	-4	0	0	—	—	—	—	—
—Winnipeg	NHL	13	1	4	5	51	-10	1	0	—	—	—	—	—
94-95—Winnipeg	NHL	44	3	15	18	139	-20	2	0	—	—	—	—	—
95-96—Winnipeg	NHL	82	7	23	30	205	8	3	0	6	2	1	3	30
96-97—Phoenix	NHL	66	3	17	20	164	-25	2	0	—	—	—	—	—
—Montreal	NHL	9	1	1	2	23	-1	0	0	—	—	—	—	—
97-98—Montreal	NHL	81	4	30	34	122	22	2	0	10	0	1	1	14
98-99—Montreal	NHL	11	0	2	2	48	-3	0	0	—	—	—	—	—
—Chicago	NHL	64	6	15	21	107	4	2	0	—	—	—	—	—
99-00—Chicago	NHL	37	0	7	7	40	2	0	0	—	—	—	—	—
—Dallas	NHL	26	1	2	3	22	10	0	0	23	0	0	0	33
NHL Totals (14 years)		982	98	279	377	2666	-21	43	3	105	7	24	31	324

MAPLETOFT, JUSTIN   C   ISLANDERS

PERSONAL: Born June 11, 1981, in Lloydminster, Sask. ... 6-1/180. ... Shoots left.
TRANSACTIONS/CAREER NOTES: Selected by New York Islanders in fifth round (ninth Islanders pick, 130th overall) of NHL entry draft (June 26, 1999).
HONORS: Named to WHL (East) All-Star first team (1999-2000).

Season Team	League	REGULAR SEASON								PLAYOFFS				
		Gms.	G	A	Pts.	PIM	+/-	PP	SH	Gms.	G	A	Pts.	PIM
97-98—Red Deer	WHL	65	9	4	13	41	...	...	...	5	1	0	1	0
98-99—Red Deer	WHL	72	24	22	46	81	...	...	...	9	2	3	5	12
99-00—Red Deer	WHL	72	39	57	96	135	...	...	...	4	2	1	3	28

MARA, PAUL   D   LIGHTNING

PERSONAL: Born September 7, 1979, in Ridgewood, N.J. ... 6-4/210. ... Shoots left.
HIGH SCHOOL: Belmont Hill (Mass.).
TRANSACTIONS/CAREER NOTES: Selected by Tampa Bay Lightning in first round (first Lightning pick, seventh overall) of NHL entry draft (June 21, 1997). ... Fractured jaw (November 9, 1999); missed 13 games.
HONORS: Named to OHL All-Rookie team (1996-97).

Season Team	League	REGULAR SEASON								PLAYOFFS				
		Gms.	G	A	Pts.	PIM	+/-	PP	SH	Gms.	G	A	Pts.	PIM
94-95—Belmont Hill	Mass. H.S.	29	19	24	43	24	...	...	...	—	—	—	—	—
95-96—Belmont Hill	Mass. H.S.	28	18	20	38	40	...	...	...	—	—	—	—	—
96-97—Sudbury	OHL	44	9	34	43	61	...	...	...	—	—	—	—	—
97-98—Sudbury	OHL	25	8	18	26	79	...	...	...	—	—	—	—	—
—Plymouth	OHL	25	8	15	23	30	...	...	...	15	3	14	17	30
98-99—Plymouth	OHL	52	13	41	54	95	...	...	...	11	5	7	12	28
—Tampa Bay	NHL	1	1	1	2	0	-3	1	0	—	—	—	—	—
99-00—Detroit	IHL	15	3	5	8	22	...	...	...	—	—	—	—	—
—Tampa Bay	NHL	54	7	11	18	73	-27	4	0	—	—	—	—	—
NHL Totals (2 years)		55	8	12	20	73	-30	5	0					

MARACLE, NORM   G   THRASHERS

PERSONAL: Born October 2, 1974, in Belleville, Ont. ... 5-9/195. ... Catches left. ... Name pronounced MAIR-ih-kuhl.
HIGH SCHOOL: Marion Graham (Regina, Sask.).
TRANSACTIONS/CAREER NOTES: Selected by Detroit Red Wings in fifth round (sixth Red Wings pick, 126th overall) of NHL entry draft (June 26, 1993). ... Selected by Atlanta Thrashers in NHL expansion draft (June 25, 1999). ... Sprained ankle (November 1, 1999); missed 12 games.
HONORS: Named to Can.HL All-Rookie team (1991-92). ... Named to WHL (East) All-Star second team (1992-93). ... Won Can.HL Goaltender-of-the-Year Award (1993-94). ... Won Del Wilson Trophy (1993-94). ... Named to Can.HL All-Star first team (1993-94). ... Named to WHL (East) All-Star first team (1993-94). ... Named to AHL All-Star second team (1996-97 and 1997-98).
MISCELLANEOUS: Holds Atlanta Thrashers all-time record for most games played by a goaltender (32). ... Shares Atlanta Thrashers all-time record for most shutouts (1).

Season Team	League	REGULAR SEASON							PLAYOFFS					
		Gms.	Min	W	L	T	GA	SO	Avg.	Gms.	Min.	W	L	GA	SO	Avg.
91-92—Saskatoon	WHL	29	1529	13	6	3	87	1	3.41	15	860	9	5	37	0	2.58
92-93—Saskatoon	WHL	53	2939	27	18	3	160	1	3.27	9	569	4	5	33	0	3.48
93-94—Saskatoon	WHL	56	3219	*41	13	1	148	2	2.76	16	939	†11	5	48	†1	3.07
94-95—Adirondack	AHL	39	1997	12	15	2	119	0	3.58	—	—	—	—	—	—	—
95-96—Adirondack	AHL	54	2949	24	18	6	135	2	2.75	1	29	0	1	4	0	8.28
96-97—Adirondack	AHL	*68	*3843	†34	22	9	*173	5	2.70	4	192	1	3	10	1	3.13
97-98—Adirondack	AHL	*66	*3710	27	29	8	*190	1	3.07	3	180	0	3	10	0	3.33
—Detroit	NHL	4	178	2	0	1	6	0	2.02	—	—	—	—	—	—	—
98-99—Adirondack	AHL	6	359	3	3	0	18	0	3.01	—	—	—	—	—	—	—
—Detroit	NHL	16	821	6	5	2	31	0	2.27	2	58	0	0	3	0	3.10
99-00—Atlanta	NHL	32	1618	4	19	2	94	1	3.49	—	—	—	—	—	—	—
NHL Totals (3 years)		52	2617	12	24	5	131	1	3.00	2	58	0	0	3	0	3.10

PERSONAL: Born August 12, 1973, in Buffalo. ... 5-10/178. ... Shoots left. ... Brother of Terry Marchant, left winger, Edmonton Oilers system (1994-95 through 1998-99). ... Name pronounced MAHR-shahnt.

COLLEGE: Clarkson (N.Y.).

TRANSACTIONS/CAREER NOTES: Selected by New York Rangers in seventh round (eighth Rangers pick, 164th overall) of NHL entry draft (June 26, 1993). ... Traded by Rangers to Edmonton Oilers for C Craig MacTavish (March 21, 1994). ... Suffered concussion (March 9, 1997); missed three games. ... Strained groin (November 10, 1997); missed four games. ... Scratched left eye (February 4, 1998); missed two games.

MISCELLANEOUS: Failed to score on a penalty shot (vs. Damian Rhodes, November 13, 1996; vs. Olaf Kolzig, January 26, 1997).

		REGULAR SEASON							**PLAYOFFS**				
Season Team	League	Gms.	G	A	Pts.	PIM	+/-	PP	SH	Gms.	G	A	Pts.	PIM
91-92—Clarkson	ECAC	33	20	12	32	32	...	...	...	—	—	—	—	—
92-93—Clarkson	ECAC	33	18	28	46	38	...	...	...	—	—	—	—	—
93-94—U.S. national team	Int'l	59	28	39	67	48	...	...	...	—	—	—	—	—
—U.S. Olympic team	Int'l	8	1	1	2	6	...	...	...	—	—	—	—	—
—Binghamton	AHL	8	2	7	9	6	...	...	...	—	—	—	—	—
—New York Rangers	NHL	1	0	0	0	0	-1	0	0	—	—	—	—	—
—Edmonton	NHL	3	0	1	1	2	-1	0	0	—	—	—	—	—
—Cape Breton	AHL	3	1	4	5	2	...	...	...	5	1	1	2	0
94-95—Cape Breton	AHL	38	22	25	47	25	...	...	...	—	—	—	—	—
—Edmonton	NHL	45	13	14	27	32	-3	3	2	—	—	—	—	—
95-96—Edmonton	NHL	81	19	19	38	66	-19	2	3	—	—	—	—	—
96-97—Edmonton	NHL	79	14	19	33	44	11	0	4	12	4	2	6	12
97-98—Edmonton	NHL	76	14	21	35	71	9	2	1	12	1	1	2	10
98-99—Edmonton	NHL	82	14	22	36	65	3	3	1	4	1	1	2	12
99-00—Edmonton	NHL	82	17	23	40	70	7	0	1	3	1	0	1	2
NHL Totals (7 years)		449	91	119	210	350	6	10	12	31	7	4	11	36

PERSONAL: Born May 1, 1969, in Scarborough, Ont. ... 6-1/185. ... Shoots left.

TRANSACTIONS/CAREER NOTES: Selected by Winnipeg Jets as underage junior in first round (first Jets pick, 16th overall) of NHL entry draft (June 13, 1987). ... Suspended six games by AHL for fighting (December 10, 1989). ... Sprained shoulder (March 1990). ... Suffered back spasms (March 13, 1991). ... Traded by Jets with D Chris Norton to Chicago Blackhawks for C Troy Murray and LW Warren Rychel (July 22, 1991). ... Fractured cheekbone (December 12, 1991); missed 12 games. ... Suspended one preseason game and fined $500 by NHL for head-butting (September 30, 1993). ... Traded by Blackhawks with RW Steve Larmer to Hartford Whalers for LW Patrick Poulin and D Eric Weinrich (November 2, 1993). ... Suspended two games and fined $500 by NHL for illegal check (December 21, 1993). ... Sprained ankle (January 14, 1994); missed three games. ... Sprained ankle (February 19, 1994); missed remainder of season. ... Awarded to Edmonton Oilers as compensation for Whalers signing free agent RW Steven Rice (August 30, 1994). ... Suspended one game by NHL for game misconduct penalties (March 22, 1995). ... Suspended two games by NHL for game misconduct penalties (March 27, 1995). ... Strained lower back (April 15, 1995); missed two games. ... Suspended three games and fined $500 by NHL for leaving bench to fight (April 29, 1995). ... Suspended five games by NHL for kneeing player in preseason game (September 25, 1995). ... Injured ribs (October 22, 1996); missed two games. ... Suffered from the flu (January 28, 1997); missed one game. ... Cracked ribs (February 13, 1997); missed eight games. ... Suffered concussion (April 18, 1997); missed remainder of season. ... Suspended three games and fined $1,000 by NHL for hitting another player (December 5, 1997). ... Traded by Oilers to Tampa Bay Lightning with C Steve Kelly and C Jason Bonsignore for D Roman Hamrlik and C Paul Comrie (December 30, 1997). ... Suspended three games by NHL for kneeing incident (February 6, 1998). ... Suspended eight games and fined $1,000 by NHL for kneeing incident (February 25, 1998). ... Traded by Lightning with D David Shaw and first-round pick (traded to Nashville) in 1998 draft to San Jose Sharks for LW Andrei Nazarov, first-round pick (C Vincent Lecavalier) in 1998 draft and future considerations (March 24, 1998). ... Injured shoulder (January 7, 1999); missed 20 games. ... Suspended one game by NHL for unsportsmanlike conduct (April 6, 1999). ... Injured knee (October 2, 1999); missed nine games. ... Suffered from the flu (December 8, 1999); missed one game. ... Injured ankle (January 5, 2000); missed 14 games. ... Injured groin (March 2, 2000); missed five games. ... Suspended three games by NHL for spearing incident (March 19, 2000). ... Injured neck (April 3, 2000); missed one game.

HONORS: Named to OHL All-Star second team (1988-89).

MISCELLANEOUS: Failed to score on a penalty shot (vs. Pat Jablonski, December 31, 1992).

		REGULAR SEASON							**PLAYOFFS**				
Season Team	League	Gms.	G	A	Pts.	PIM	+/-	PP	SH	Gms.	G	A	Pts.	PIM
84-85—Toronto Nationals	MTHL	...	14	35	49	229	...	...	...	—	—	—	—	—
85-86—Belleville	OHL	57	5	15	20	225	...	...	...	21	0	7	7	*83
86-87—Belleville	OHL	52	6	38	44	238	...	...	...	6	0	4	4	17
87-88—Belleville	OHL	56	7	51	58	200	...	...	...	6	1	3	4	19
88-89—Belleville	OHL	43	14	36	50	198	...	...	...	5	0	1	1	12
—Winnipeg	NHL	2	0	0	0	2	0	0	0	—	—	—	—	—
89-90—Winnipeg	NHL	7	0	2	2	28	0	0	0	—	—	—	—	—
—Moncton	AHL	56	4	19	23	217	...	...	...	—	—	—	—	—
90-91—Winnipeg	NHL	28	2	2	4	91	-5	0	0	—	—	—	—	—
—Moncton	AHL	33	2	11	13	101	...	...	...	—	—	—	—	—
91-92—Chicago	NHL	58	5	10	15	168	-4	2	0	16	1	0	1	36
92-93—Chicago	NHL	78	5	15	20	313	15	1	0	4	0	0	0	12
93-94—Chicago	NHL	13	1	4	5	42	-2	0	0	—	—	—	—	—
—Hartford	NHL	42	3	7	10	124	-12	0	1	—	—	—	—	—
94-95—Edmonton	NHL	40	1	5	6	184	-11	0	0	—	—	—	—	—
95-96—Edmonton	NHL	78	3	15	18	202	-7	0	0	—	—	—	—	—
96-97—Edmonton	NHL	71	3	13	16	132	13	1	0	3	0	0	0	4
97-98—Edmonton	NHL	27	0	4	4	58	-2	0	0	—	—	—	—	—
—Tampa Bay	NHL	22	2	4	6	43	-3	0	0	—	—	—	—	—
—San Jose	NHL	12	0	3	3	43	2	0	0	6	0	0	0	10
98-99—San Jose	NHL	59	2	6	8	101	-7	0	0	6	0	0	0	4
99-00—San Jose	NHL	49	0	4	4	72	3	0	0	11	2	1	3	12
NHL Totals (12 years)		586	27	94	121	1603	-20	4	1	46	3	1	4	78

M

MARHA, JOSEF　　　　　　　C　　　　　　　BLACKHAWKS

PERSONAL: Born June 2, 1976, in Havlickov Brod, Czechoslovakia. ... 6-0/176. ... Shoots left. ... Name pronounced MAHR-hah.
TRANSACTIONS/CAREER NOTES: Selected by Quebec Nordiques in second round (third Nordiques pick, 35th overall) of NHL entry draft (June 28, 1994). ... Nordiques franchise moved to Colorado and renamed Avalanche for 1995-96 season (June 21, 1995). ... Traded by Avalanche to Mighty Ducks of Anaheim for LW Warren Rychel and fourth-round pick (D Sanny Lindstrom) in 1999 draft (March 24, 1998). ... Sprained ankle (October 10, 1998); missed nine games. ... Traded by Mighty Ducks to Chicago Blackhawks for fourth-round pick (C Alexander Chagodayev) in 1999 draft (January 28, 1999).

		REGULAR SEASON								PLAYOFFS				
Season Team	League	Gms.	G	A	Pts.	PIM	+/-	PP	SH	Gms.	G	A	Pts.	PIM
91-92—Jihlava	Czech	25	12	13	25	0	...	...	...	—	—	—	—	—
92-93—Dukla Jihlava	Czech.	7	2	2	4	4	...	...	...	—	—	—	—	—
93-94—Dukla Jihlava	Czech Rep.	41	7	2	9	...	...	...	...	3	0	1	1	...
94-95—Dukla Jihlava	Czech Rep.	35	3	7	10	...	...	...	...	—	—	—	—	—
95-96—Cornwall	AHL	74	18	30	48	30	...	...	...	8	1	2	3	10
—Colorado	NHL	2	0	1	1	0	1	0	0	—	—	—	—	—
96-97—Hershey	AHL	67	23	49	72	44	...	...	...	19	6	†16	*22	10
—Colorado	NHL	6	0	1	1	0	0	0	0	—	—	—	—	—
97-98—Hershey	AHL	55	6	46	52	30	...	...	...	—	—	—	—	—
—Colorado	NHL	11	2	5	7	4	0	0	0	—	—	—	—	—
—Anaheim	NHL	12	7	4	11	0	4	3	0	—	—	—	—	—
98-99—Anaheim	NHL	10	0	1	1	0	-4	0	0	—	—	—	—	—
—Cincinnati	AHL	3	1	0	1	4	...	...	...	—	—	—	—	—
—Chicago	NHL	22	2	5	7	4	5	1	0	—	—	—	—	—
—Portland	AHL	8	0	8	8	2	...	...	...	—	—	—	—	—
99-00—Chicago	NHL	81	10	12	22	18	-10	2	1	—	—	—	—	—
NHL Totals (5 years)		144	21	29	50	26	-4	6	1					

MARKOV, ANDREI　　　　　　　D　　　　　　　CANADIENS

PERSONAL: Born December 20, 1978, in Voskresensk, U.S.S.R. ... 6-0/185. ... Shoots left.
TRANSACTIONS/CAREER NOTES: Selected by Montreal Canadiens in sixth round (sixth Canadiens pick, 162nd overall) of NHL entry draft (June 27, 1998).

		REGULAR SEASON								PLAYOFFS				
Season Team	League	Gms.	G	A	Pts.	PIM	+/-	PP	SH	Gms.	G	A	Pts.	PIM
95-96—Khimik Voskresensk	CIS	36	0	0	0	14	...	...	...	—	—	—	—	—
96-97—Khimik Voskresensk	Russian	43	8	4	12	32	...	...	...	2	1	1	2	0
97-98—Khimik Voskresensk	Russian	43	10	5	15	83	...	...	...	—	—	—	—	—
98-99—Dynamo Moscow	Russian	38	10	11	21	32	...	...	...	16	3	6	9	6
99-00—Dynamo Moscow	Russian	29	11	12	23	28	...	...	...	17	4	3	7	8

MARKOV, DANNY　　　　　　　D　　　　　　　MAPLE LEAFS

M

PERSONAL: Born July 11, 1976, in Moscow, U.S.S.R. ... 6-1/190. ... Shoots left. ... Full Name: Daniil Markov.
TRANSACTIONS/CAREER NOTES: Selected by Toronto Maple Leafs in ninth round (seventh Maple Leafs pick, 223rd overall) of NHL entry draft (July 8, 1995). ... Suffered concussion (October 16, 1998); missed one game. ... Fractured foot (November 11, 1998); missed two games. ... Suffered throat injury (November 23, 1998); missed two games. ... Suffered back spasms (December 7, 1998); missed two games. ... Separated shoulder (December 16, 1998); missed 11 games. ... Suffered injury (December 15, 1999); missed three games. ... Injured ankle (January 5, 2000); missed 10 games. ... Suffered injury (March 15, 2000); missed one game. ... Injured foot (March 23, 2000); missed final eight games of season.

		REGULAR SEASON								PLAYOFFS				
Season Team	League	Gms.	G	A	Pts.	PIM	+/-	PP	SH	Gms.	G	A	Pts.	PIM
93-94—Spartak Moscow	CIS	13	1	0	1	6	...	...	...	1	0	0	0	0
94-95—Spartak Moscow	CIS	39	0	1	1	36	...	...	...	—	—	—	—	—
95-96—Spartak Moscow	CIS	38	2	0	2	12	...	...	...	2	0	0	0	2
96-97—Spartak Moscow	Russian	36	3	6	9	41	...	...	...	—	—	—	—	—
—St. John's	AHL	10	2	4	6	18	...	...	...	11	2	6	8	14
97-98—St. John's	AHL	52	3	23	26	124	...	...	...	2	0	1	1	0
—Toronto	NHL	25	2	5	7	28	0	1	0	—	—	—	—	—
98-99—Toronto	NHL	57	4	8	12	47	5	0	0	17	0	6	6	18
99-00—Toronto	NHL	59	0	10	10	28	13	0	0	12	0	3	3	10
NHL Totals (3 years)		141	6	23	29	103	18	1	0	29	0	9	9	28

MARLEAU, PATRICK　　　　　　　C　　　　　　　SHARKS

PERSONAL: Born September 15, 1979, in Swift Current, Sask. ... 6-2/210. ... Shoots left. ... Name pronounced MAHR-loh.
TRANSACTIONS/CAREER NOTES: Selected by San Jose Sharks in first round (first Sharks pick, second overall) of NHL entry draft (June 21, 1997).
HONORS: Named to Can.HL All-Star second team (1996-97). ... Named to WHL (West) All-Star first team (1996-97).

		REGULAR SEASON								PLAYOFFS				
Season Team	League	Gms.	G	A	Pts.	PIM	+/-	PP	SH	Gms.	G	A	Pts.	PIM
94-95—Swift Current	Jr. A	30	30	22	52	20	...	...	...	—	—	—	—	—
95-96—Seattle	WHL	72	32	42	74	22	...	...	...	5	3	4	7	4
96-97—Seattle	WHL	71	51	74	125	37	...	...	...	15	7	16	23	12
97-98—San Jose	NHL	74	13	19	32	14	5	1	0	5	0	1	1	0
98-99—San Jose	NHL	81	21	24	45	24	10	4	0	6	2	1	3	4
99-00—San Jose	NHL	81	17	23	40	36	-9	3	0	5	1	1	2	2
NHL Totals (3 years)		236	51	66	117	74	6	8	0	16	3	3	6	6

MARSHALL, GRANT   RW   STARS

PERSONAL: Born June 9, 1973, in Mississauga, Ont. ... 6-1/193. ... Shoots right.
HIGH SCHOOL: Hillcrest (Thunder Bay, Ont.).
TRANSACTIONS/CAREER NOTES: Selected by Toronto Maple Leafs in first round (second Maple Leafs pick, 23rd overall) of NHL entry draft (June 20, 1992). ... Awarded to Dallas Stars with C Peter Zezel as compensation for Maple Leafs signing free-agent RW Mike Craig (August 10, 1994). ... Strained muscle (November 15, 1996); missed four games. ... Sprained shoulder (December 8, 1996); missed four games. ... Suffered concussion (January 4, 1997); missed two games. ... Strained groin (November 21, 1997); missed five games. ... Strained groin (April 16, 1998); missed one game. ... Fined $1,000 by NHL for elbowing incident (May 8, 1998). ... Injured groin prior to start of 1999-2000 season; missed first four games of season. ... Reinjured groin (October 13, 1999); missed 22 games. ... Reinjured groin (December 15, 1999); missed two games. ... Reinjured groin (December 27, 1999); missed five games. ... Reinjured groin (March 13, 2000); missed three games.
MISCELLANEOUS: Member of Stanley Cup championship team (1999).

			REGULAR SEASON								PLAYOFFS				
Season Team	League	Gms.	G	A	Pts.	PIM	+/-	PP	SH		Gms.	G	A	Pts.	PIM
90-91—Ottawa	OHL	26	6	11	17	25	...	...	...		1	0	0	0	0
91-92—Ottawa	OHL	61	32	51	83	132	...	...	...		11	6	11	17	11
92-93—Newmarket	OHL	31	12	25	37	85	...	...	...		7	4	7	11	20
—Ottawa	OHL	30	14	28	42	83	...	...	...		—	—	—	—	—
—St. John's	AHL	2	0	0	0	0	...	...	...		2	0	0	0	2
93-94—St. John's	AHL	67	11	29	40	155	...	...	...		11	1	5	6	17
94-95—Kalamazoo	IHL	61	17	29	46	96	...	...	...		16	9	3	12	27
—Dallas	NHL	2	0	1	1	0	1	0	0		—	—	—	—	—
95-96—Dallas	NHL	70	9	19	28	111	0	0	0		—	—	—	—	—
96-97—Dallas	NHL	56	6	4	10	98	5	0	0		5	0	2	2	8
97-98—Dallas	NHL	72	9	10	19	96	-2	3	0		17	0	2	2	47
98-99—Dallas	NHL	82	13	18	31	85	1	2	0		14	0	3	3	20
99-00—Dallas	NHL	45	2	6	8	38	-5	1	0		14	0	1	1	4
NHL Totals (6 years)		327	39	58	97	428	0	6	0		50	0	8	8	79

MARSHALL, JASON   D   MIGHTY DUCKS

PERSONAL: Born February 22, 1971, in Cranbrook, B.C. ... 6-2/200. ... Shoots right.
TRANSACTIONS/CAREER NOTES: Selected by St. Louis Blues in first round (first Blues pick, ninth overall) of NHL entry draft (June 17, 1989). ... Traded by Blues to Mighty Ducks of Anaheim for D Bill Houlder (August 29, 1994). ... Lacerated finger (November 24, 1996); missed two games. ... Bruised hand (March 19, 1997); missed five games. ... Separated right shoulder (December 19, 1997); missed eight games. ... Strained left hamstring (December 18, 1998); missed six games. ... Suffered illness (March 17, 1999); missed one game.

			REGULAR SEASON								PLAYOFFS				
Season Team	League	Gms.	G	A	Pts.	PIM	+/-	PP	SH		Gms.	G	A	Pts.	PIM
87-88—Columbia Valley	KIJHL	40	4	28	32	150	...	...	...		—	—	—	—	—
88-89—Vernon	BCJHL	48	10	30	40	197	...	...	...		31	6	6	12	141
—Canadian nat'l team	Int'l	2	0	1	1	0	...	...	...		—	—	—	—	—
89-90—Canadian nat'l team	Int'l	72	1	11	12	57	...	...	...		—	—	—	—	—
90-91—Tri-City	WHL	59	10	34	44	236	...	...	...		7	1	2	3	20
—Peoria	IHL	—	—	—	—	—	...	...	...		18	0	1	1	48
91-92—Peoria	IHL	78	4	18	22	178	...	...	...		10	0	1	1	16
—St. Louis	NHL	2	0	1	1	4	0	0	0		—	—	—	—	—
92-93—Peoria	IHL	77	4	16	20	229	...	...	...		4	0	0	0	20
93-94—Peoria	IHL	20	1	1	2	72	...	...	...		3	2	0	2	2
—Canadian nat'l team	Int'l	41	3	10	13	60	...	...	...		—	—	—	—	—
94-95—San Diego	IHL	80	7	18	25	218	...	...	...		5	0	1	1	8
—Anaheim	NHL	1	0	0	0	0	-2	0	0		—	—	—	—	—
95-96—Baltimore	AHL	57	1	13	14	150	...	...	...		—	—	—	—	—
—Anaheim	NHL	24	0	1	1	42	3	0	0		—	—	—	—	—
96-97—Anaheim	NHL	73	1	9	10	140	6	0	0		7	0	1	1	4
97-98—Anaheim	NHL	72	3	6	9	189	-8	1	0		—	—	—	—	—
98-99—Anaheim	NHL	72	1	7	8	142	-5	0	0		4	1	0	1	10
99-00—Anaheim	NHL	55	0	3	3	88	-10	0	0		—	—	—	—	—
NHL Totals (7 years)		299	6	26	32	605	-16	1	0		11	1	1	2	14

MARTINS, STEVE   C   LIGHTNING

PERSONAL: Born April 13, 1972, in Gatineau, Que. ... 5-9/175. ... Shoots left.
HIGH SCHOOL: Choate Rosemary Hall (Wallingford, Conn.).
COLLEGE: Harvard (Psychology).
TRANSACTIONS/CAREER NOTES: Injured ankle; missed first 11 games of 1992-93 season. ... Selected by Hartford Whalers in first round (first Whalers pick, fifth overall) of NHL supplemental draft (June 24, 1994). ... Whalers franchise moved to North Carolina and renamed Carolina Hurricanes for 1997-98 season; NHL approved move on June 25, 1997. ... Signed as free agent by Ottawa Senators (July 22, 1998). ... Suffered back spasms (December 4, 1998); missed four games. ... Injured hip flexor (February 13, 1999); missed three games. ... Reinjured hip flexor (February 23, 1999); missed four games. ... Suffered from the flu (March 24, 1999); missed four games. ... Claimed on waivers by Tampa Bay Lightning (October 29, 1999). ... Strained groin (November 13, 1999); missed one game. ... Sprained ankle (December 4, 1999); missed 12 games.
HONORS: Named to NCAA All-America (East) first team (1993-94). ... Named ECAC Player of the Year (1993-94). ... Named to NCAA All-Tournament team (1993-94). ... Named to ECAC All-Star first team (1993-94).

			REGULAR SEASON								PLAYOFFS			
Season Team	League	Gms.	G	A	Pts.	PIM	+/-	PP	SH		Gms.	G	A	Pts.	PIM
91-92—Harvard University	ECAC	20	13	14	27	26	...	...	...		—	—	—	—	—
92-93—Harvard University	ECAC	18	6	8	14	40	...	...	...		—	—	—	—	—
93-94—Harvard University	ECAC	32	25	35	60	93	...	...	...		—	—	—	—	—

Season Team	League	Gms.	G	A	Pts.	PIM	+/-	PP	SH	Gms.	G	A	Pts.	PIM
94-95—Harvard University	ECAC	28	15	23	38	93	...	...	...	—	—	—	—	—
95-96—Springfield	AHL	30	9	20	29	10	...	...	...	—	—	—	—	—
—Hartford	NHL	23	1	3	4	8	-3	0	0	—	—	—	—	—
96-97—Springfield	AHL	63	12	31	43	78	...	...	...	17	1	3	4	26
—Hartford	NHL	2	0	1	1	0	0	0	0	—	—	—	—	—
97-98—Chicago	IHL	78	20	41	61	122	...	...	...	21	6	14	20	28
—Carolina	NHL	3	0	0	0	0	0	0	0	—	—	—	—	—
98-99—Detroit	IHL	4	1	6	7	16	...	...	...	—	—	—	—	—
—Ottawa	NHL	36	4	3	7	10	4	1	0	—	—	—	—	—
99-00—Ottawa	NHL	2	1	0	1	0	-1	0	0	—	—	—	—	—
—Tampa Bay	NHL	57	5	7	12	37	-11	0	1	—	—	—	—	—
NHL Totals (5 years)		123	11	14	25	55	-11	1	1					

MATHIEU, ALEXANDRE   C   PENGUINS

PERSONAL: Born February 12, 1979, in Repentigny, Que. ... 6-2/177. ... Shoots left.
TRANSACTIONS/CAREER NOTES: Selected by Pittsburgh Penguins in fourth round (fourth Penguins pick, 97th overall) of NHL entry draft (June 21, 1997).

			REGULAR SEASON							PLAYOFFS				
Season Team	League	Gms.	G	A	Pts.	PIM	+/-	PP	SH	Gms.	G	A	Pts.	PIM
96-97—Halifax	QMJHL	70	12	22	34	18	...	...	...	18	2	5	7	2
97-98—Halifax	QMJHL	68	35	41	76	52	...	...	...	5	1	1	2	4
98-99—Halifax	QMJHL	69	21	27	48	90	...	...	...	5	0	1	1	4
99-00—Wilkes-Barre/Scranton	AHL	52	4	4	8	18	...	...	...					

MATHIEU, MARQUIS   C

PERSONAL: Born May 31, 1973, in Hartford, Conn. ... 5-11/190. ... Shoots right. ... Full Name: Marquis Johnny Mathieu.
TRANSACTIONS/CAREER NOTES: Signed as non-drafted free agent by Boston Bruins (October 27, 1998).

			REGULAR SEASON							PLAYOFFS				
Season Team	League	Gms.	G	A	Pts.	PIM	+/-	PP	SH	Gms.	G	A	Pts.	PIM
91-92—St. Jean	QMJHL	70	20	36	56	166	...	...	...	—	—	—	—	—
92-93—St. Jean	QMJHL	70	31	36	67	115	...	...	...	2	1	0	1	33
93-94—Fredericton	AHL	22	4	6	10	28	...	...	...	—	—	—	—	—
—Wheeling	ECHL	42	12	11	23	75	...	...	...	9	1	3	4	23
94-95—Worcester	AHL	2	0	0	0	0	...	...	...	—	—	—	—	—
—Toledo	ECHL	33	13	22	35	168	...	...	...	—	—	—	—	—
—Raleigh	ECHL	33	15	17	32	181	...	...	...	—	—	—	—	—
95-96—Worcester	AHL	17	3	10	13	26	...	...	...	—	—	—	—	—
—Houston	IHL	2	1	0	1	9	...	...	...	—	—	—	—	—
—Birmingham	ECHL	18	5	7	12	87	...	...	...	—	—	—	—	—
—Johnstown	ECHL	25	4	17	21	89	...	...	...	—	—	—	—	—
96-97—Worcester	AHL	30	8	16	24	88	...	...	...	1	0	0	0	0
97-98—Wheeling	ECHL	58	26	29	55	276	...	...	...	15	1	10	11	38
98-99—Providence	AHL	64	15	15	30	166	...	...	...	19	4	7	11	30
—Boston	NHL	9	0	0	0	8	-1	0	0	—	—	—	—	—
99-00—Boston	NHL	6	0	2	2	4	-2	0	0	—	—	—	—	—
—Providence	AHL	18	3	3	6	45	...	...	...					
NHL Totals (2 years)		15	0	2	2	12	-3	0	0					

MATTE, CHRISTIAN   RW   WILD

PERSONAL: Born January 20, 1975, in Hull, Que. ... 5-11/170. ... Shoots right. ... Name pronounced MAT.
TRANSACTIONS/CAREER NOTES: Selected by Quebec Nordiques in sixth round (eighth Nordiques pick, 153rd overall) of NHL entry draft (June 26, 1993). ... Nordiques franchise moved to Colorado and renamed Avalanche for 1995-96 season (June 21, 1995). ... Fractured hand (January 2, 1997); missed six games. ... Signed as free agent by Minnesota Wild (July 10, 2000).
HONORS: Named to QMJHL All-Star second team (1993-94). ... Won John B. Sollenberger Trophy (1999-2000). ... Named to AHL All-Star first team (1999-2000).

			REGULAR SEASON							PLAYOFFS				
Season Team	League	Gms.	G	A	Pts.	PIM	+/-	PP	SH	Gms.	G	A	Pts.	PIM
92-93—Granby	QMJHL	68	17	36	53	56	...	...	...	—	—	—	—	—
93-94—Granby	QMJHL	59	50	47	97	103	...	...	...	7	5	5	10	12
—Cornwall	AHL	1	0	0	0	0	...	...	...	—	—	—	—	—
94-95—Granby	QMJHL	66	50	66	116	86	...	...	...	13	11	7	18	12
—Cornwall	AHL	—	—	—	—	—	...	...	...	3	0	1	1	2
95-96—Cornwall	AHL	64	20	32	52	51	...	...	...	7	1	1	2	6
96-97—Hershey	AHL	49	18	18	36	78	...	...	...	22	8	3	11	25
—Colorado	NHL	5	1	1	2	0	1	0	0	—	—	—	—	—
97-98—Hershey	AHL	71	33	40	73	109	...	...	...	7	3	2	5	4
—Colorado	NHL	5	0	0	0	6	0	0	0	—	—	—	—	—
98-99—Hershey	AHL	60	31	47	78	48	...	...	...	5	2	1	3	8
—Colorado	NHL	7	1	1	2	0	-2	0	0	—	—	—	—	—
99-00—Hershey	AHL	73	43	*61	*104	85	...	...	...	14	8	6	14	10
—Colorado	NHL	5	0	1	1	4	-2	0	0	—	—	—	—	—
NHL Totals (4 years)		22	2	3	5	10	-3	0	0					

MATTEAU, STEPHANE   LW   SHARKS

PERSONAL: Born September 2, 1969, in Rouyn-Noranda, Que. ... 6-4/220. ... Shoots left. ... Name pronounced muh-TOH.

TRANSACTIONS/CAREER NOTES: Selected by Calgary Flames as underage junior in second round (second Flames pick, 25th overall) of NHL entry draft (June 13, 1987). ... Bruised thigh (October 10, 1991); missed 43 games. ... Traded by Flames to Chicago Blackhawks for D Trent Yawney (December 16, 1991). ... Fractured left foot (January 27, 1992); missed 12 games. ... Suffered tonsillitis (September 1992); missed first three games of 1992-93 season. ... Pulled groin (December 17, 1993); missed three games. ... Traded by Blackhawks with RW Brian Noonan to New York Rangers for RW Tony Amonte and rights to LW Matt Oates (March 21, 1994). ... Suffered from the flu (February 1, 1995); missed one game. ... Suffered back spasms (April 24, 1995); missed two games. ... Fractured hand (September 24, 1995); missed six games. ... Traded by Rangers to St. Louis Blues for C Ian Laperriere (December 28, 1995). ... Traded by Blues to San Jose Sharks for C Darren Turcotte (July 25, 1997). ... Injured back (October 9, 1997); missed three games. ... Injured back (December 16, 1997); missed two games. ... Injured hand (March 12, 1998); missed four games. ... Injured back (October 9, 1998); missed first game of season. ... Injured neck (November 7, 1998); missed two games. ... Injured thumb (November 27, 1998); missed three games. ... Injured back (January 5, 1999); missed three games. ... Injured back (March 9, 1999); missed three games. ... Reinjured back (April 8, 1999); missed one game. ... Injured back (March 6, 2000); missed four games.

MISCELLANEOUS: Member of Stanley Cup championship team (1994).

			REGULAR SEASON								PLAYOFFS				
Season Team	League	Gms.	G	A	Pts.	PIM	+/-	PP	SH		Gms.	G	A	Pts.	PIM
85-86—Hull	QMJHL	60	6	8	14	19	...	...	...		4	0	0	0	0
86-87—Hull	QMJHL	69	27	48	75	113	...	...	...		8	3	7	10	8
87-88—Hull	QMJHL	57	17	40	57	179	...	...	...		18	5	14	19	84
88-89—Hull	QMJHL	59	44	45	89	202	...	...	...		9	8	6	14	30
—Salt Lake City	IHL	—	—	—	—	—					9	0	4	4	13
89-90—Salt Lake City	IHL	81	23	35	58	130	...	...	...		10	6	3	9	38
90-91—Calgary	NHL	78	15	19	34	93	17	0	1		5	0	1	1	0
91-92—Calgary	NHL	4	1	0	1	19	2	0	0		—	—	—	—	—
—Chicago	NHL	20	5	8	13	45	3	1	0		18	4	6	10	24
92-93—Chicago	NHL	79	15	18	33	98	6	2	0		3	0	1	1	2
93-94—Chicago	NHL	65	15	16	31	55	10	2	0		—	—	—	—	—
—New York Rangers	NHL	12	4	3	7	2	5	1	0		23	6	3	9	20
94-95—New York Rangers	NHL	41	3	5	8	25	-8	0	0		9	0	1	1	10
95-96—New York Rangers	NHL	32	4	2	6	22	-4	1	0		—	—	—	—	—
—St. Louis	NHL	46	7	13	20	65	-4	3	0		11	0	2	2	8
96-97—St. Louis	NHL	74	16	20	36	50	11	1	2		5	0	0	0	0
97-98—San Jose	NHL	73	15	14	29	60	4	1	0		4	0	1	1	0
98-99—San Jose	NHL	68	8	15	23	73	2	0	0		5	0	0	0	6
99-00—San Jose	NHL	69	12	12	24	61	-3	0	0		10	0	2	2	8
NHL Totals (10 years)		661	120	145	265	668	41	12	3		93	10	17	27	78

MATTSSON, JESPER   C   FLAMES

PERSONAL: Born May 13, 1975, in Malmo, Sweden. ... 6-0/185. ... Shoots right. ... Name pronounced YEHZ-puhr MATT-suhn.

TRANSACTIONS/CAREER NOTES: Selected by Calgary Flames in first round (first Flames pick, 18th overall) of NHL entry draft (June 26, 1993).

			REGULAR SEASON								PLAYOFFS				
Season Team	League	Gms.	G	A	Pts.	PIM	+/-	PP	SH		Gms.	G	A	Pts.	PIM
91-92—Malmo	Sweden	24	0	1	1	2	...	...	...		5	0	0	0	0
92-93—Malmo	Sweden	40	9	8	17	14	...	...	...		5	0	0	0	0
93-94—Malmo	Sweden	40	3	6	9	14	...	...	...		9	1	2	3	2
94-95—Malmo	Sweden	37	9	6	15	18	...	...	...		9	2	0	2	18
95-96—Saint John	AHL	73	12	26	38	18	...	...	...		9	1	1	2	2
96-97—Saint John	AHL	72	22	18	40	32	...	...	...		3	1	1	2	0
97-98—Saint John	AHL	29	7	11	18	30	...	...	...		—	—	—	—	—
98-99—Malmo	Sweden	48	14	16	30	49	...	...	...		8	2	2	4	4
99-00—Malmo	Sweden	50	17	19	36	40	...	...	...		6	0	0	0	6

MATVICHUK, RICHARD   D   STARS

PERSONAL: Born February 5, 1973, in Edmonton. ... 6-2/215. ... Shoots left. ... Name pronounced MAT-vih-chuhk.

TRANSACTIONS/CAREER NOTES: Selected by Minnesota North Stars in first round (first North Stars pick, eighth overall) of 1991 NHL entry draft (June 22, 1991). ... Strained lower back (November 9, 1992); missed two games. ... Sprained ankle (December 27, 1992); missed 10 games. ... North Stars franchise moved from Minnesota to Dallas and renamed Stars for 1993-94 season. ... Bruised shoulder (April 5, 1994); missed one game. ... Tore knee ligaments (September 20, 1994) and underwent surgery; missed first 16 games of season. ... Suffered concussion (March 13, 1996); missed five games. ... Bruised shoulder (October 26, 1996); missed two games. ... Strained groin (February 18, 1997); missed 19 games. ... Tore anterior cruciate ligament in knee (January 21, 1998); missed eight games. ... Bruised thigh (December 31, 1998); missed one game. ... Suffered from headaches (January 8, 1999); missed one game. ... Strained groin (March 14, 1999); missed two games. ... Reinjured groin (March 19, 1999); missed final 14 games of regular season and one playoff game. ... Injured knee (October 16, 1999); missed three games. ... Injured knee (November 10, 1999); missed three games. ... Suffered from the flu (January 23, 2000); missed one game. ... Sprained thumb (February 2, 2000); missed one game. ... Sprained knee (March 1, 2000); missed one game.

HONORS: Won Bill Hunter Trophy (1991-92). ... Named to Can.HL All-Star second team (1991-92). ... Named to WHL (East) All-Star first team (1991-92).

MISCELLANEOUS: Member of Stanley Cup championship team (1999).

			REGULAR SEASON								PLAYOFFS				
Season Team	League	Gms.	G	A	Pts.	PIM	+/-	PP	SH		Gms.	G	A	Pts.	PIM
88-89—Fort Saskatchewan	AJHL	58	7	36	43	147	...	...	...		—	—	—	—	—
89-90—Saskatoon	WHL	56	8	24	32	126	...	...	...		10	2	8	10	16
90-91—Saskatoon	WHL	68	13	36	49	117	...	...	...		—	—	—	—	—
91-92—Saskatoon	WHL	58	14	40	54	126	...	...	...		22	1	9	10	61
92-93—Minnesota	NHL	53	2	3	5	26	-8	1	0		—	—	—	—	—
—Kalamazoo	IHL	3	0	1	1	6	...	...	...		—	—	—	—	—

M

Season Team	League	REGULAR SEASON								PLAYOFFS				
		Gms.	G	A	Pts.	PIM	+/-	PP	SH	Gms.	G	A	Pts.	PIM
93-94—Kalamazoo	IHL	43	8	17	25	84	...	...	...	—	—	—	—	—
—Dallas	NHL	25	0	3	3	22	1	0	0	7	1	1	2	12
94-95—Dallas	NHL	14	0	2	2	14	-7	0	0	5	0	2	2	4
—Kalamazoo	IHL	17	0	6	6	16	...	...	...	—	—	—	—	—
95-96—Dallas	NHL	73	6	16	22	71	4	0	0	—	—	—	—	—
96-97—Dallas	NHL	57	5	7	12	87	1	0	2	7	0	1	1	20
97-98—Dallas	NHL	74	3	15	18	63	7	0	0	16	1	1	2	14
98-99—Dallas	NHL	64	3	9	12	51	23	1	0	22	1	5	6	20
99-00—Dallas	NHL	70	4	21	25	42	7	0	0	23	2	5	7	14
NHL Totals (8 years)		430	23	76	99	376	28	2	2	80	5	15	20	84

MAY, BRAD   LW   COYOTES

PERSONAL: Born November 29, 1971, in Toronto. ... 6-1/210. ... Shoots left.

TRANSACTIONS/CAREER NOTES: Selected by Buffalo Sabres in first round (first Sabres pick, 14th overall) of NHL entry draft (June 16, 1990). ... Injured knee (August 1990). ... Injured left knee ligaments (November 1990). ... Fractured bone in hand (March 11, 1995); missed 15 games. ... Injured left arm (March 3, 1996); missed one game. ... Suspended one game for accumulating three game misconduct penalties (March 31, 1996). ... Underwent right shoulder surgery (October 14, 1996); missed 27 games. ... Broken right hand (December 20, 1996); missed nine games. ... Fractured thumb (March 1, 1997); missed four games. ... Strained shoulder (September 27, 1997); missed first six games of season. ... Injured knee (December 29, 1997); missed 11 games. ... Traded by Sabres with third-round pick (traded to Tampa Bay) in 1999 draft to Vancouver Canucks for LW Geoff Sanderson (February 4, 1998). ... Strained groin (October 30, 1998); missed five games. ... Fractured hand (March 26, 1999); missed final 10 games of season. ... Sprained medial collateral ligament in knee (December 10, 1999); missed 13 games. ... Traded by Canucks to Phoenix Coyotes for future considerations (June 25, 2000).

HONORS: Named to OHL All-Star second team (1989-90 and 1990-91).

MISCELLANEOUS: Scored on a penalty shot (vs. Andy Moog, November, 11, 1992).

Season Team	League	REGULAR SEASON								PLAYOFFS				
		Gms.	G	A	Pts.	PIM	+/-	PP	SH	Gms.	G	A	Pts.	PIM
87-88—Markham Jr. B	OHA	6	1	1	2	21	...	...	...	—	—	—	—	—
88-89—Niagara Falls	OHL	65	8	14	22	304	...	...	...	17	0	1	1	55
89-90—Niagara Falls	OHL	61	33	58	91	223	...	...	...	16	9	13	22	64
90-91—Niagara Falls	OHL	34	37	32	69	93	...	...	...	14	11	14	25	53
91-92—Buffalo	NHL	69	11	6	17	309	-12	1	0	7	1	4	5	2
92-93—Buffalo	NHL	82	13	13	26	242	3	0	0	8	1	1	2	14
93-94—Buffalo	NHL	84	18	27	45	171	-6	3	0	7	0	2	2	9
94-95—Buffalo	NHL	33	3	3	6	87	5	1	0	4	0	0	0	2
95-96—Buffalo	NHL	79	15	29	44	295	6	3	0	—	—	—	—	—
96-97—Buffalo	NHL	42	3	4	7	106	-8	1	0	10	1	1	2	32
97-98—Buffalo	NHL	36	4	7	11	113	2	0	0	—	—	—	—	—
—Vancouver	NHL	27	9	3	12	41	0	4	0	—	—	—	—	—
98-99—Vancouver	NHL	66	6	11	17	102	-14	1	0	—	—	—	—	—
99-00—Vancouver	NHL	59	9	7	16	90	-2	0	0	—	—	—	—	—
NHL Totals (9 years)		577	91	110	201	1556	-26	14	0	36	3	8	11	59

MAYERS, JAMAL   RW   BLUES

PERSONAL: Born October 24, 1974, in Toronto. ... 6-2/212. ... Shoots right. ... Full Name: Jamal David Mayers. ... Nickname: Jammer.

HIGH SCHOOL: Erindale Secondary (Mississauga, Ont.).

COLLEGE: Western Michigan (Marketing).

TRANSACTIONS/CAREER NOTES: Selected by St. Louis Blues in fourth round (third Blues pick, 89th overall) of NHL entry draft (June 26, 1993). ... Suspended one playoff game by NHL for slashing incident (May 7, 1999).

Season Team	League	REGULAR SEASON								PLAYOFFS				
		Gms.	G	A	Pts.	PIM	+/-	PP	SH	Gms.	G	A	Pts.	PIM
90-91—Thornhill	Jr. A	44	12	24	36	78	...	...	...	—	—	—	—	—
91-92—Thornhill	Jr. A	56	38	69	107	36	...	...	...	—	—	—	—	—
92-93—Western Michigan U.	CCHA	38	8	17	25	26	...	...	...	—	—	—	—	—
93-94—Western Michigan U.	CCHA	40	17	32	49	40	...	...	...	—	—	—	—	—
94-95—Western Michigan U.	CCHA	39	13	33	46	40	...	...	...	—	—	—	—	—
95-96—Western Michigan U.	CCHA	38	17	22	39	75	...	...	...	—	—	—	—	—
96-97—Worcester	AHL	62	12	14	26	104	...	...	...	5	4	4	8	4
—St. Louis	NHL	6	0	1	1	2	-3	0	0	—	—	—	—	—
97-98—Worcester	AHL	61	19	24	43	117	...	...	...	11	3	4	7	10
98-99—Worcester	AHL	20	9	7	16	34	...	...	...	—	—	—	—	—
—St. Louis	NHL	34	4	5	9	40	-3	0	0	11	0	1	1	8
99-00—St. Louis	NHL	79	7	10	17	90	0	0	0	7	0	4	4	2
NHL Totals (3 years)		119	11	16	27	132	-6	0	0	18	0	5	5	10

McALLISTER, CHRIS   D   MAPLE LEAFS

PERSONAL: Born June 16, 1975, in Saskatoon, Sask. ... 6-8/225. ... Shoots left.

TRANSACTIONS/CAREER NOTES: Selected by Vancouver Canucks in second round (first Canucks pick, 40th overall) of NHL entry draft (July 8, 1995). ... Suffered from heel spur (December 13, 1997); missed three games. ... Traded by Canucks to Toronto Maple Leafs for C Darby Hendrickson (February 16, 1999). ... Suspended two games by NHL for leaving the bench during an altercation (February 26, 1999). ... Suffered injury (October 20, 1999); missed six games. ... Suffered injury (January 22, 2000); missed one game. ... Injured foot (March 30, 2000); missed final five games of season.

Season Team	League	Gms.	G	A	Pts.	PIM	+/-	PP	SH	Gms.	G	A	Pts.	PIM
93-94—Humboldt	SJHL	50	3	5	8	150	...	...	...	—	—	—	—	—
—Saskatoon	WHL	2	0	0	0	5	...	...	...	—	—	—	—	—
94-95—Saskatoon	WHL	65	2	8	10	134	...	...	...	10	0	0	0	28
95-96—Syracuse	AHL	68	0	2	2	142	...	...	...	16	0	0	0	34
96-97—Syracuse	AHL	43	3	1	4	108	...	...	...	3	0	0	0	6
97-98—Syracuse	AHL	23	0	1	1	71	...	...	...	5	0	0	0	21
—Vancouver	NHL	36	1	2	3	106	-12	0	0	—	—	—	—	—
98-99—Vancouver	NHL	28	1	1	2	63	-7	0	0	—	—	—	—	—
—Syracuse	AHL	5	0	0	0	24	...	...	...	—	—	—	—	—
—Toronto	NHL	20	0	2	2	39	4	0	0	6	0	1	1	4
99-00—Toronto	NHL	36	0	3	3	68	-4	0	0	—	—	—	—	—
NHL Totals (3 years)		120	2	8	10	276	-19	0	0	6	0	1	1	4

McALPINE, CHRIS   D   BLACKHAWKS

PERSONAL: Born December 1, 1971, in Roseville, Minn. ... 6-0/210. ... Shoots right. ... Full Name: Christopher McAlpine. ... Name pronounced muh-KAL-pighn.
HIGH SCHOOL: Roseville (Minn.).
COLLEGE: Minnesota.
TRANSACTIONS/CAREER NOTES: Selected by New Jersey Devils in seventh round (seventh Devils pick, 137th overall) of NHL entry draft (June 16, 1990). ... Injured thumb (March 26, 1995); missed four games. ... Traded by Devils with ninth-round pick (C James Desmarais) in 1999 draft to St. Louis Blues for C Peter Zezel (February 11, 1997). ... Suffered from the flu (March 14, 1998); missed one game. ... Bruised thigh (December 17, 1998); missed nine games. ... Traded by Blues with G Rich Parent to Tampa Bay Lightning for RW Stephane Richer (January 13, 2000). ... Suffered concussion (January 29, 2000); missed two games. ... Traded by Lightning to Atlanta Thrashers for D Mikko Kuparinen (March 11, 2000). ... Strained groin (March 23, 2000); missed six games. ... Signed as free agent by Chicago Blackhawks (July 27, 2000).
HONORS: Named to NCCA All-America (West) second team (1993-94). ... Named to WCHA All-Star first team (1993-94).
MISCELLANEOUS: Member of Stanley Cup championship team (1995).

Season Team	League	Gms.	G	A	Pts.	PIM	+/-	PP	SH	Gms.	G	A	Pts.	PIM
89-90—Roseville H.S.	Minn. H.S.	25	15	13	28	...	...	...	...	—	—	—	—	—
90-91—Univ. of Minnesota	WCHA	38	7	9	16	112	...	...	...	—	—	—	—	—
91-92—Univ. of Minnesota	WCHA	39	3	9	12	126	...	...	...	—	—	—	—	—
92-93—Univ. of Minnesota	WCHA	41	14	9	23	82	...	...	...	—	—	—	—	—
93-94—Univ. of Minnesota	WCHA	36	12	18	30	121	...	...	...	—	—	—	—	—
94-95—Albany	AHL	48	4	18	22	49	...	...	...	—	—	—	—	—
—New Jersey	NHL	24	0	3	3	17	4	0	0	—	—	—	—	—
95-96—Albany	AHL	57	5	14	19	72	...	...	...	4	0	0	0	13
96-97—Albany	AHL	44	1	9	10	48	...	...	...	—	—	—	—	—
—St. Louis	NHL	15	0	0	0	24	-2	0	0	4	0	1	1	0
97-98—St. Louis	NHL	54	3	7	10	36	14	0	0	10	0	0	0	16
98-99—St. Louis	NHL	51	1	1	2	50	-10	0	0	13	0	0	0	2
99-00—St. Louis	NHL	21	1	1	2	14	1	0	0	—	—	—	—	—
—Worcester	AHL	10	1	4	5	4	...	...	...	—	—	—	—	—
—Tampa Bay	NHL	10	1	1	2	10	-5	0	0	—	—	—	—	—
—Detroit	IHL	8	0	0	0	6	...	...	...	—	—	—	—	—
—Atlanta	NHL	3	0	0	0	2	-4	0	0	—	—	—	—	—
NHL Totals (5 years)		178	6	13	19	153	-2	0	0	27	0	1	1	18

McAMMOND, DEAN   LW   BLACKHAWKS

PERSONAL: Born June 15, 1973, in Grand Cache, Alta. ... 5-11/195. ... Shoots left.
TRANSACTIONS/CAREER NOTES: Selected by Chicago Blackhawks in first round (first Blackhawks pick, 22nd overall) of NHL entry draft (June 22, 1991). ... Traded by Blackhawks with D Igor Kravchuk to Edmonton Oilers for RW Joe Murphy (February 25, 1993). ... Severed left Achilles' tendon (February 1, 1995); missed final 41 games of season. ... Fractured nose (November 11, 1996); missed two games. ... Suffered from the flu (January 21, 1997); missed two games. ... Suffered back spasms (March 1, 1997); missed remainder of season. ... Traded by Oilers with D Boris Mironov and D Jonas Elofsson to Blackhawks for C Chad Kilger, LW Daniel Cleary, LW Ethan Moreau and D Christian Laflamme (March 20, 1999). ... Bruised ribs (October 4, 1999); missed five games. ... Suffered sore wrist (December 9, 1999); missed one game.
HONORS: Won Can.HL Plus/Minus Award (1991-92).
MISCELLANEOUS: Failed to score on a penalty shot (vs. Mark Fitzpatrick, January 5, 1996).

Season Team	League	Gms.	G	A	Pts.	PIM	+/-	PP	SH	Gms.	G	A	Pts.	PIM
89-90—Prince Albert	WHL	53	11	11	22	49	...	...	...	14	2	3	5	18
90-91—Prince Albert	WHL	71	33	35	68	108	...	...	...	2	0	1	1	6
91-92—Prince Albert	WHL	63	37	54	91	189	...	...	...	10	12	11	23	26
—Chicago	NHL	5	0	2	2	0	-2	0	0	3	0	0	0	2
92-93—Prince Albert	WHL	30	19	29	48	44	...	...	...	—	—	—	—	—
—Swift Current	WHL	18	10	13	23	29	...	...	...	17	*16	19	35	20
93-94—Edmonton	NHL	45	6	21	27	16	12	2	0	—	—	—	—	—
—Cape Breton	AHL	28	9	12	21	38	...	...	...	—	—	—	—	—
94-95—Edmonton	NHL	6	0	0	0	0	-1	0	0	—	—	—	—	—
95-96—Edmonton	NHL	53	15	15	30	23	6	4	0	—	—	—	—	—
—Cape Breton	AHL	22	9	15	24	55	...	...	...	—	—	—	—	—
96-97—Edmonton	NHL	57	12	17	29	28	-15	4	0	—	—	—	—	—
97-98—Edmonton	NHL	77	19	31	50	46	9	8	0	12	1	4	5	12
98-99—Edmonton	NHL	65	9	16	25	36	5	1	0	—	—	—	—	—
—Chicago	NHL	12	1	4	5	2	3	0	0	—	—	—	—	—
99-00—Chicago	NHL	76	14	18	32	72	11	1	0	—	—	—	—	—
NHL Totals (8 years)		396	76	124	200	223	28	20	0	15	1	4	5	14

M

McCABE, BRYAN   D   BLACKHAWKS

PERSONAL: Born June 8, 1975, in Toronto. ... 6-1/210. ... Shoots left.
HIGH SCHOOL: Joel E. Ferris (Spokane, Wash.).
TRANSACTIONS/CAREER NOTES: Selected by New York Islanders in second round (second Islanders pick, 40th overall) of NHL entry draft (June 26, 1993). ... Traded by Islanders with LW Todd Bertuzzi and third-round pick (LW Jarkko Ruutu) in 1998 draft to Vancouver Canucks for C Trevor Linden (February 6, 1998). ... Missed first 13 games of 1998-99 season due to contract dispute. ... Traded by Canucks with first-round pick (RW Pavel Vorobiev) in 2000 draft to Chicago Blackhawks for first-round pick (traded to Tampa Bay) in 1999 draft (June 26, 1999). ... Fractured orbital bone (March 11, 2000); missed two games.
HONORS: Named to WHL (West) All-Star second team (1992-93). ... Named to WHL (West) All-Star first team (1993-94). ... Named to WHL (East) All-Star first team (1994-95). ... Named to Memorial Cup All-Star team (1994-95).
MISCELLANEOUS: Captain of New York Islanders (1997 through February 7, 1998).

		REGULAR SEASON								PLAYOFFS				
Season Team	League	Gms.	G	A	Pts.	PIM	+/-	PP	SH	Gms.	G	A	Pts.	PIM
91-92—Medicine Hat..............	WHL	68	6	24	30	157	...	...	...	4	0	0	0	6
92-93—Medicine Hat..............	WHL	14	0	13	13	83	...	...	...	—	—	—	—	—
—Spokane......................	WHL	46	3	44	47	134	...	...	...	10	1	5	6	28
93-94—Spokane......................	WHL	64	22	62	84	218	...	...	...	3	0	4	4	4
94-95—Spokane......................	WHL	42	14	39	53	115	...	...	...	—	—	—	—	—
—Brandon......................	WHL	20	6	10	16	38	...	...	...	18	4	13	17	59
95-96—New York Islanders.....	NHL	82	7	16	23	156	-24	3	0	—	—	—	—	—
96-97—New York Islanders.....	NHL	82	8	20	28	165	-2	2	1	—	—	—	—	—
97-98—New York Islanders.....	NHL	56	3	9	12	145	9	1	0	—	—	—	—	—
—Vancouver..................	NHL	26	1	11	12	64	10	0	1	—	—	—	—	—
98-99—Vancouver..................	NHL	69	7	14	21	120	-11	1	2	—	—	—	—	—
99-00—Chicago......................	NHL	79	6	19	25	139	-8	2	0	—	—	—	—	—
NHL Totals (5 years)............		394	32	89	121	789	-26	9	4					

McCARTHY, SANDY   RW   HURRICANES

PERSONAL: Born June 15, 1972, in Toronto. ... 6-3/225. ... Shoots right.
TRANSACTIONS/CAREER NOTES: Selected by Calgary Flames in third round (third Flames pick, 52nd overall) of NHL entry draft (June 22, 1991). ... Strained right shoulder (December 18, 1993); missed two games. ... Strained shoulder (December 27, 1993); missed one game. ... Strained right knee (January 20, 1995); missed five games. ... Suffered hernia (February 3, 1995); missed six games. ... Injured ribs (December 16, 1995); missed seven games. ... Fractured ankle (October 9, 1996); missed 25 games. ... Reinjured left ankle (January 9, 1997) and underwent surgery; missed 23 games. ... Bruised shoulder (November 13, 1997); missed six games. ... Injured groin (December 9, 1997); missed two games. ... Suffered hip pointer (December 22, 1997); missed four games. ... Suffered charley horse (January 24, 1998); missed one game. ... Traded by Flames with third- (LW Brad Richards) and fifth-round (D Curtis Rich) picks in 1998 draft to Tampa Bay Lightning for C Jason Wiemer (March 24, 1998). ... Traded by Lightning with RW Mikael Andersson to Philadelphia Flyers for LW Colin Forbes and fifth-round pick (G Michal Lanicek) in 1999 draft (March 20, 1999). ... Sprained right knee (November 5, 1999); missed one game. ... Injured groin (February 19, 2000); missed four games. ... Traded by Flyers to Carolina Hurricanes for C Kent Manderville (March 14, 2000).

		REGULAR SEASON								PLAYOFFS				
Season Team	League	Gms.	G	A	Pts.	PIM	+/-	PP	SH	Gms.	G	A	Pts.	PIM
89-90—Laval	QMJHL	65	10	11	21	269	...	...	...	—	—	—	—	—
90-91—Laval	QMJHL	68	21	19	40	297	...	...	...	—	—	—	—	—
91-92—Laval	QMJHL	62	39	51	90	326	...	...	...	8	4	5	9	81
92-93—Salt Lake City..............	IHL	77	18	20	38	220	...	...	...	—	—	—	—	—
93-94—Calgary	NHL	79	5	5	10	173	-3	0	0	7	0	0	0	34
94-95—Calgary	NHL	37	5	3	8	101	1	0	0	6	0	1	1	17
95-96—Calgary	NHL	75	9	7	16	173	-8	3	0	4	0	0	0	10
96-97—Calgary	NHL	33	3	5	8	113	-8	1	0	—	—	—	—	—
97-98—Calgary	NHL	52	8	5	13	170	-18	1	0	—	—	—	—	—
—Tampa Bay	NHL	14	0	5	5	71	-1	0	0	—	—	—	—	—
98-99—Tampa Bay	NHL	67	5	7	12	135	-22	1	0	—	—	—	—	—
—Philadelphia	NHL	13	0	1	1	25	-2	0	0	6	0	1	1	0
99-00—Philadelphia	NHL	58	6	5	11	111	-5	1	0	—	—	—	—	—
—Carolina	NHL	13	0	0	0	9	2	0	0	—	—	—	—	—
NHL Totals (7 years)............		441	41	43	84	1081	-64	7	0	23	0	2	2	61

McCARTHY, STEVE   D   BLACKHAWKS

PERSONAL: Born February 3, 1981, in Trail, B.C. ... 6-0/197. ... Shoots left.
TRANSACTIONS/CAREER NOTES: Selected by Chicago Blackhawks in first round (first Blackhawks pick, 23rd overall) of NHL entry draft (June 26, 1999).
HONORS: Named to WHL (East) All-Star first team (1999-2000).

		REGULAR SEASON								PLAYOFFS				
Season Team	League	Gms.	G	A	Pts.	PIM	+/-	PP	SH	Gms.	G	A	Pts.	PIM
96-97—Edmonton	WHL	2	0	0	0	0	...	...	...	—	—	—	—	—
97-98—Edmonton	WHL	58	11	29	40	59	...	...	...	—	—	—	—	—
98-99—Kootenay	WHL	57	19	33	52	79	...	...	...	6	0	5	5	8
99-00—Chicago......................	NHL	5	1	1	2	4	0	1	0	—	—	—	—	—
—Kootenay	WHL	37	13	23	36	36	...	...	...	—	—	—	—	—
NHL Totals (1 year).............		5	1	1	2	4	0	1	0					

McCARTY, DARREN   RW   RED WINGS

PERSONAL: Born April 1, 1972, in Burnaby, B.C. ... 6-1/215. ... Shoots right.
HIGH SCHOOL: Quinte Secondary School (Belleville, Ont.).
TRANSACTIONS/CAREER NOTES: Selected by Detroit Red Wings in second round (second Red Wings pick, 46th overall) of NHL entry draft (June 20, 1992). ... Injured groin (January 29, 1994); missed five games. ... Injured shoulder (March 23, 1994); missed five games. ... Separated right shoulder (February 7, 1995); missed eight games. ... Injured right hand (March 30, 1995); missed two games. ... Injured left knee (April 9, 1995); missed five games. ... Injured right heel (November 7, 1995); missed one game ... Separated shoulder (December 2, 1995); missed six games. ... Lacerated right forearm (January 12, 1996); missed three games. ... Injured left hand (February 15, 1996); missed seven games. ... Injured hand (January 3, 1997); missed seven games. ... Bruised thigh (January 29, 1997); missed four games. ... Injured groin (April 5, 1997); missed two games. ... Fractured foot (January 11, 1998); missed eight games. ... Suffered from vertigo (April 4, 1998); missed three games. ... Strained groin (March 12, 1999); missed three games. ... Reinjured groin (April 5, 1999); missed three games. ... Strained groin (November 12, 1999); missed 39 games. ... Injured leg (March 5, 2000); missed final 17 games of regular season.
HONORS: Won Jim Mahon Memorial Trophy (1991-92). ... Named to Can.HL All-Star first team (1991-92). ... Named to OHL All-Star first team (1991-92).
MISCELLANEOUS: Member of Stanley Cup championship team (1997 and 1998).

		REGULAR SEASON								PLAYOFFS				
Season Team	League	Gms.	G	A	Pts.	PIM	+/-	PP	SH	Gms.	G	A	Pts.	PIM
88-89—Peterborough Jr. B	OHA	34	18	17	35	135	...	...	...	—	—	—	—	—
89-90—Belleville	OHL	63	12	15	27	142	...	...	...	11	1	1	2	21
90-91—Belleville	OHL	60	30	37	67	151	...	...	...	6	2	2	4	13
91-92—Belleville	OHL	65	*55	72	127	177	...	...	...	5	1	4	5	13
92-93—Adirondack	AHL	73	17	19	36	278	...	...	...	11	0	1	1	33
93-94—Detroit	NHL	67	9	17	26	181	12	0	0	7	2	2	4	8
94-95—Detroit	NHL	31	5	8	13	88	5	1	0	18	3	2	5	14
95-96—Detroit	NHL	63	15	14	29	158	14	8	0	19	3	2	5	20
96-97—Detroit	NHL	68	19	30	49	126	14	5	0	20	3	4	7	34
97-98—Detroit	NHL	71	15	22	37	157	0	5	1	22	3	8	11	34
98-99—Detroit	NHL	69	14	26	40	108	10	6	0	10	1	2	3	23
99-00—Detroit	NHL	24	6	6	12	48	1	0	0	9	0	1	1	12
NHL Totals (7 years)............		**393**	**83**	**123**	**206**	**866**	**56**	**25**	**1**	**105**	**15**	**20**	**35**	**145**

McCAULEY, ALYN   C   MAPLE LEAFS

PERSONAL: Born May 29, 1977, in Brockville, Ont. ... 5-11/190. ... Shoots left.
HIGH SCHOOL: Canterbury (Ottawa, Ont.).
TRANSACTIONS/CAREER NOTES: Selected by New Jersey Devils in fourth round (fifth Devils pick, 79th overall) of NHL entry draft (July 8, 1995). ... Traded by Devils with D Jason Smith and C Steve Sullivan to Toronto Maple Leafs for C Doug Gilmour, D Dave Ellett and third-round pick (D Andre Lakos) in 1999 draft (February 25, 1997). ... Fractured ankle (December 31, 1997); missed 17 games. ... Strained shoulder (February 26, 1998); missed three games. ... Sprained left knee (December 30, 1998); missed 22 games. ... Suffered concussion (March 3, 1999); missed remainder of season. ... Suffered injury (October 9, 1999); missed one game. ... Suffered from flu (December 4, 1999); missed six games. ... Suffered illness (January 11, 2000); missed one game.
HONORS: Named to OHL All-Star first team (1995-96 and 1996-97). ... Won Red Tilson Trophy (1995-96 and 1996-97). ... Won Can.HL Player of the Year Award (1996-97). ... Won William Hanley Trophy (1996-97). ... Named to Can.HL All-Star first team (1996-97).

		REGULAR SEASON								PLAYOFFS				
Season Team	League	Gms.	G	A	Pts.	PIM	+/-	PP	SH	Gms.	G	A	Pts.	PIM
92-93—Kingston Jr. A	MTHL	38	31	29	60	18	...	...	...	—	—	—	—	—
93-94—Ottawa	OHL	38	13	23	36	10	...	...	...	13	5	14	19	4
94-95—Ottawa	OHL	65	16	38	54	20	...	...	...	—	—	—	—	—
95-96—Ottawa	OHL	55	34	48	82	24	...	...	...	2	0	0	0	0
96-97—Ottawa	OHL	50	†56	56	112	16	...	...	...	22	14	22	36	14
—St. John's..................	AHL	—	—	—	—	—	...	...	...	3	0	1	1	0
97-98—Toronto	NHL	60	6	10	16	6	-7	0	0	—	—	—	—	—
98-99—Toronto	NHL	39	9	15	24	2	7	1	0	—	—	—	—	—
99-00—Toronto	NHL	45	5	5	10	10	-6	1	0	5	0	0	0	6
—St. John's..................	AHL	5	1	1	2	0	...	...	...	—	—	—	—	—
NHL Totals (3 years)............		**144**	**20**	**30**	**50**	**18**	**-6**	**2**	**0**	**5**	**0**	**0**	**0**	**6**

McCLEARY, TRENT   RW   CANADIENS

PERSONAL: Born September 8, 1972, in Swift Current, Sask. ... 6-0/180. ... Shoots right.
TRANSACTIONS/CAREER NOTES: Signed as non-drafted free agent by Ottawa Senators (October 9, 1992). ... Bruised foot during 1995-96 season; missed two games. ... Injured right thumb (April 1, 1996); missed two games. ... Traded by Senators with third-round pick (LW Eric Naud) in 1996 draft to Boston Bruins for C Shawn McEachern (June 22, 1996). ... Strained abdominal muscle (January 4, 1997); missed one game. ... Sprained knee (February 11, 1997); missed 18 games. ... Signed as free agent by Montreal Canadiens (October 9, 1998). ... Fractured larynx (January 29, 2000); missed remainder of season.

		REGULAR SEASON								PLAYOFFS				
Season Team	League	Gms.	G	A	Pts.	PIM	+/-	PP	SH	Gms.	G	A	Pts.	PIM
89-90—Swift Current	WHL	70	3	15	18	43	...	...	...	4	1	0	1	0
90-91—Swift Current	WHL	70	16	24	40	53	...	...	...	3	0	0	0	2
91-92—Swift Current	WHL	72	23	22	45	240	...	...	...	8	1	2	3	16
92-93—Swift Current	WHL	63	17	33	50	138	...	...	...	17	5	4	9	16
—New Haven	AHL	2	1	0	1	6	...	...	...	—	—	—	—	—
93-94—Prin. Edward Island	AHL	4	0	0	0	6	...	...	...	—	—	—	—	—
—Thunder Bay	Col.HL	51	23	17	40	123	...	...	...	9	2	11	13	15
94-95—Prin. Edward Island	AHL	51	9	20	29	60	...	...	...	9	2	3	5	26
95-96—Ottawa	NHL	75	4	10	14	68	-15	0	1	—	—	—	—	—

M

Season Team	League	REGULAR SEASON								PLAYOFFS				
		Gms.	G	A	Pts.	PIM	+/-	PP	SH	Gms.	G	A	Pts.	PIM
96-97—Boston	NHL	59	3	5	8	33	-16	0	0	—	—	—	—	—
97-98—Detroit	IHL	21	1	1	2	45	...	...	...	—	—	—	—	—
—Las Vegas	IHL	54	7	6	13	120	...	...	...	3	1	0	1	2
98-99—Montreal	NHL	46	0	0	0	29	-1	0	0	—	—	—	—	—
99-00—Montreal	NHL	12	1	0	1	4	2	0	0	—	—	—	—	—
—Quebec	AHL	27	7	9	16	56	...	...	...	—	—	—	—	—
NHL Totals (4 years)		192	8	15	23	134	-30	0	1					

McDONELL, KENT — RW — RED WINGS

PERSONAL: Born March 1, 1979, in Cornwall, Ont. ... 6-2/198. ... Shoots right.
TRANSACTIONS/CAREER NOTES: Selected by Carolina Hurricanes in ninth round (ninth Hurricanes pick, 225th overall) of NHL entry draft (June 21, 1997). ... Returned to draft pool by Hurricanes and selected by Detroit Red Wings in sixth round (third Red Wings pick, 181st overall) of NHL entry draft (June 26, 1999).

Season Team	League	REGULAR SEASON								PLAYOFFS				
		Gms.	G	A	Pts.	PIM	+/-	PP	SH	Gms.	G	A	Pts.	PIM
96-97—Guelph	OHL	56	7	5	12	57	...	...	...	16	0	2	2	4
97-98—Guelph	OHL	57	28	23	51	76	...	...	...	12	7	4	11	18
98-99—Guelph	OHL	60	31	38	69	110	...	...	...	11	4	3	7	36
99-00—Guelph	OHL	56	35	35	70	100	...	...	...	6	1	4	5	6

McEACHERN, SHAWN — LW — SENATORS

PERSONAL: Born February 28, 1969, in Waltham, Mass. ... 5-11/193. ... Shoots left. ... Full Name: Shawn K. McEachern. ... Name pronounced muh-KEH-kuhrn.
HIGH SCHOOL: Matignon (Cambridge, Mass.).
COLLEGE: Boston University.
TRANSACTIONS/CAREER NOTES: Selected by Pittsburgh Penguins in sixth round (sixth Penguins pick, 110th overall) of NHL entry draft (June 13, 1987). ... Traded by Penguins to Los Angeles Kings for D Marty McSorley (August 27, 1993). ... Traded by Kings to Penguins for D Marty McSorley and D Jim Paek (February 15, 1994). ... Played in Europe during 1994-95 NHL lockout. ... Suspended for first three games of 1994-95 season and fined $500 by NHL for slashing incident (September 21, 1994); suspension reduced to two games due to abbreviated 1994-95 season. ... Traded by Penguins with LW Kevin Stevens to Boston Bruins for C Bryan Smolinski and RW Glen Murray (August 2, 1995). ... Traded by Bruins to Ottawa Senators for RW Trent McCleary and third-round pick (LW Eric Naud) in 1996 draft (June 22, 1996). ... Fractured jaw (December 6, 1996); missed 17 games. ... Suffered back spasms (February 7, 1998); missed one game. ... Injured wrist (April 3, 1999); missed one game. ... Injured groin (April 8, 1999); missed four games. ... Suffered illness (February 1, 2000); missed one game. ... Bruised shoulder (February 26, 2000); missed four games. ... Fractured left thumb (March 25, 2000); missed first eight games of season.
HONORS: Named to Hockey East All-Star second team (1989-90). ... Named Hockey East Tournament Most Valuable Player (1990-91). ... Named to NCAA All-America (East) first team (1990-91). ... Named to Hockey East All-Star first team (1990-91).
MISCELLANEOUS: Member of Stanley Cup championship team (1992).
STATISTICAL PLATEAUS: Three-goal games: 1997-98 (1).

M

Season Team	League	REGULAR SEASON								PLAYOFFS				
		Gms.	G	A	Pts.	PIM	+/-	PP	SH	Gms.	G	A	Pts.	PIM
85-86—Matignon	Mass. H.S.	20	32	20	52	...	...	...	...	—	—	—	—	—
86-87—Matignon	Mass. H.S.	16	29	28	57	...	...	...	...	—	—	—	—	—
87-88—Matignon	Mass. H.S.	22	52	40	92	...	...	...	...	—	—	—	—	—
88-89—Boston University	Hockey East	36	20	28	48	32	...	...	...	—	—	—	—	—
89-90—Boston University	Hockey East	43	25	31	56	78	...	...	...	—	—	—	—	—
90-91—Boston University	Hockey East	41	34	48	82	43	...	...	...	—	—	—	—	—
91-92—U.S. national team	Int'l	57	26	23	49	38	...	...	...	—	—	—	—	—
—U.S. Olympic team	Int'l	8	1	0	1	10	...	...	...	—	—	—	—	—
—Pittsburgh	NHL	15	0	4	4	0	1	0	0	19	2	7	9	4
92-93—Pittsburgh	NHL	84	28	33	61	46	21	7	0	12	3	2	5	10
93-94—Los Angeles	NHL	49	8	13	21	24	1	0	3	—	—	—	—	—
—Pittsburgh	NHL	27	12	9	21	10	13	0	2	6	1	0	1	2
94-95—Kiekko-Espoo	Finland	8	1	3	4	6	...	...	...	—	—	—	—	—
—Pittsburgh	NHL	44	13	13	26	22	4	1	2	11	0	2	2	8
95-96—Boston	NHL	82	24	29	53	34	-5	3	2	5	2	1	3	8
96-97—Ottawa	NHL	65	11	20	31	18	-5	0	1	7	2	0	2	8
97-98—Ottawa	NHL	81	24	24	48	42	1	8	2	11	0	4	4	8
98-99—Ottawa	NHL	77	31	25	56	46	8	7	0	4	2	0	2	6
99-00—Ottawa	NHL	69	29	22	51	24	2	10	0	6	0	3	3	4
NHL Totals (9 years)		593	180	192	372	266	41	36	12	81	12	19	31	58

McGILLIS, DAN — D — FLYERS

PERSONAL: Born July 1, 1972, in Hawkesbury, Ont. ... 6-2/225. ... Shoots left. ... Full Name: Daniel McGillis.
COLLEGE: Northeastern.
TRANSACTIONS/CAREER NOTES: Selected by Detroit Red Wings in 10th round (10th Red Wings pick, 238th overall) of NHL entry draft (June 20, 1992). ... Signed as free agent by Edmonton Oilers (September 6, 1996). ... Traded by Oilers with second-round pick (D Jason Beckett) in 1998 draft to Philadelphia Flyers for D Janne Niinimaa (March 24, 1998). ... Suffered neck spasms (February 21, 1999); missed two games. ... Injured left knee (March 30, 1999); missed one game. ... Fractured right foot (November 28, 1999); missed four games. ... Strained groin (February 22, 2000); missed 10 games.
HONORS: Named to Hockey East All-Star first team (1994-95). ... Named to NCAA All-America (East) first team (1995-96). ... Named to Hockey East All-Star team (1995-96).

Season Team	League	REGULAR SEASON								PLAYOFFS				
		Gms.	G	A	Pts.	PIM	+/-	PP	SH	Gms.	G	A	Pts.	PIM
91-92—Hawkesbury	Tier II Jr. A	36	5	19	24	106	...	...	...	—	—	—	—	—
92-93—Northeastern Univ.	Hockey East	35	5	12	17	42	...	...	...	—	—	—	—	—
93-94—Northeastern Univ.	Hockey East	38	4	25	29	82	...	...	...	—	—	—	—	—
94-95—Northeastern Univ.	Hockey East	34	9	22	31	70	...	...	...	—	—	—	—	—
95-96—Northeastern Univ.	Hockey East	34	12	24	36	50	...	...	...	—	—	—	—	—
96-97—Edmonton	NHL	73	6	16	22	52	2	2	1	12	0	5	5	24
97-98—Edmonton	NHL	67	10	15	25	74	-17	5	0	—	—	—	—	—
—Philadelphia	NHL	13	1	5	6	35	-4	1	0	5	1	2	3	10
98-99—Philadelphia	NHL	78	8	37	45	61	16	6	0	6	0	1	1	12
99-00—Philadelphia	NHL	68	4	14	18	55	16	3	0	18	2	6	8	12
NHL Totals (4 years)		299	29	87	116	277	13	17	1	41	3	14	17	58

McINNIS, MARTY   LW   MIGHTY DUCKS

PERSONAL: Born June 2, 1970, in Weymouth, Mass. ... 5-11/190. ... Shoots right. ... Full Name: Martin Edward McInnis. ... Name pronounced muh-KIH-nihz.

HIGH SCHOOL: Milton (Mass.) Academy.

COLLEGE: Boston College.

TRANSACTIONS/CAREER NOTES: Selected by New York Islanders in eighth round (10th Islanders pick, 163rd overall) of NHL entry draft (June 11, 1988). ... Injured eye (March 9, 1993); missed two games. ... Fractured patella (March 27, 1993); missed remainder of regular season and 14 playoff games. ... Sprained wrist (April 18, 1995); missed one game. ... Injured ribs (March 7, 1996); missed one game. ... Injured ribs (March 16, 1996); missed six games. ... Traded by Islanders with G Tyrone Garner and sixth-round pick (D Ilja Demidov) in 1997 draft to Calgary Flames for C Robert Reichel (March 18, 1997). ... Injured shoulder (December 23, 1997); missed six games. ... Traded by Flames with D Jamie Allison and RW Erik Andersson to Chicago Blackhawks for C Jeff Shantz and C/LW Steve Dubinsky (October 27, 1998). ... Traded by Blackhawks to Mighty Ducks of Anaheim for fourth-round pick (traded to Washington) in 2000 draft (October 27, 1998). ... Strained groin (January 28, 2000); missed 11 games. ... Reinjured groin (March 8, 2000); missed nine games.

MISCELLANEOUS: Failed to score on a penalty shot (vs. Tom Draper, March 8, 1992).

STATISTICAL PLATEAUS: Three-goal games: 1997-98 (1).

Season Team	League	REGULAR SEASON								PLAYOFFS				
		Gms.	G	A	Pts.	PIM	+/-	PP	SH	Gms.	G	A	Pts.	PIM
86-87—Milton Academy	Mass. H.S.	...	21	19	40	...	...	...	...	—	—	—	—	—
87-88—Milton Academy	Mass. H.S.	25	26	25	51	...	...	...	...	—	—	—	—	—
88-89—Boston College	Hockey East	39	13	19	32	8	...	...	...	—	—	—	—	—
89-90—Boston College	Hockey East	41	24	29	53	43	...	...	...	—	—	—	—	—
90-91—Boston College	Hockey East	38	21	36	57	40	...	...	...	—	—	—	—	—
91-92—U.S. national team	Int'l	54	15	19	34	20	...	...	...	—	—	—	—	—
—U.S. Olympic team	Int'l	8	5	2	7	4	...	...	...	—	—	—	—	—
—New York Islanders	NHL	15	3	5	8	0	6	0	0	—	—	—	—	—
92-93—New York Islanders	NHL	56	10	20	30	24	7	0	1	3	0	1	1	0
—Capital District	AHL	10	4	12	16	2	...	...	...	—	—	—	—	—
93-94—New York Islanders	NHL	81	25	31	56	24	31	3	5	4	0	0	0	0
94-95—New York Islanders	NHL	41	9	7	16	8	-1	0	0	—	—	—	—	—
95-96—New York Islanders	NHL	74	12	34	46	39	-11	2	0	—	—	—	—	—
96-97—New York Islanders	NHL	70	20	22	42	20	-7	4	1	—	—	—	—	—
—Calgary	NHL	10	3	4	7	2	-1	1	0	—	—	—	—	—
97-98—Calgary	NHL	75	19	25	44	34	1	5	4	—	—	—	—	—
98-99—Calgary	NHL	6	1	1	2	6	-1	0	0	—	—	—	—	—
—Anaheim	NHL	75	18	34	52	36	-14	11	1	4	2	0	2	2
99-00—Anaheim	NHL	62	10	18	28	26	-4	2	1	—	—	—	—	—
NHL Totals (9 years)		565	130	201	331	219	6	28	13	11	2	1	3	2

McKAY, RANDY   RW   DEVILS

PERSONAL: Born January 25, 1967, in Montreal. ... 6-2/210. ... Shoots right. ... Full Name: Hugh Randall McKay.

COLLEGE: Michigan Tech.

TRANSACTIONS/CAREER NOTES: Selected by Detroit Red Wings in sixth round (sixth Red Wings pick, 113th overall) of NHL entry draft (June 15, 1987). ... Injured knee (February 1989). ... Lacerated forearm (February 23, 1991). ... Sent by Red Wings with C Dave Barr to New Jersey Devils as compensation for Red Wings signing free agent RW Troy Crowder (September 9, 1991). ... Sprained knee (January 16, 1993); missed nine games. ... Injured groin (February 24, 1995); missed nine games. ... Reinjured groin (March 18, 1995); missed six games. ... Suffered charley horse (May 26, 1995); missed one playoff game. ... Suffered concussion (December 31, 1995); missed five games. ... Bruised eye (February 27, 1997); missed five games. ... Sprained left knee (March 26, 1998); missed eight games. ... Strained groin (September 23, 1998); missed first four games of season. ... Suffered infected elbow (December 19, 1998); missed one game. ... Suffered from the flu (December 26, 1998); missed four games. ... Suffered sore back (January 20, 1999); missed one game. ... Bruised knee (April 3, 1999); missed one game. ... Suspended three games by NHL for slashing incident (November 1, 1999). ... Suffered injury (January 3, 2000); missed one game. ... Strained hip flexor (January 17, 2000); missed two games. ... Suffered injury (January 29, 2000); missed one game. ... Suffered injury (February 3, 2000); missed one game. ... Injured ankle (March 2, 2000); missed seven games.

MISCELLANEOUS: Member of Stanley Cup championship team (1995 and 2000).

STATISTICAL PLATEAUS: Three-goal games: 1996-97 (1), 1997-98 (1). Total: 2.

Season Team	League	REGULAR SEASON								PLAYOFFS				
		Gms.	G	A	Pts.	PIM	+/-	PP	SH	Gms.	G	A	Pts.	PIM
84-85—Michigan Tech	WCHA	25	4	5	9	32	...	...	...	—	—	—	—	—
85-86—Michigan Tech	WCHA	40	12	22	34	46	...	...	...	—	—	—	—	—
86-87—Michigan Tech	WCHA	39	5	11	16	46	...	...	...	—	—	—	—	—
87-88—Michigan Tech	WCHA	41	17	24	41	70	...	...	...	—	—	—	—	—
—Adirondack	AHL	10	0	3	3	12	...	...	...	6	0	4	4	0
88-89—Adirondack	AHL	58	29	34	63	170	...	...	...	14	4	7	11	60
—Detroit	NHL	3	0	0	0	0	-1	0	0	2	0	0	0	2

Season Team	League	REGULAR SEASON								PLAYOFFS				
		Gms.	G	A	Pts.	PIM	+/-	PP	SH	Gms.	G	A	Pts.	PIM
89-90—Detroit	NHL	33	3	6	9	51	1	0	0	—	—	—	—	—
—Adirondack	AHL	36	16	23	39	99	...	...	...	6	3	0	3	35
90-91—Detroit	NHL	47	1	7	8	183	-15	0	0	5	0	1	1	41
91-92—New Jersey	NHL	80	17	16	33	246	6	2	0	7	1	3	4	10
92-93—New Jersey	NHL	73	11	11	22	206	0	1	0	5	0	0	0	16
93-94—New Jersey	NHL	78	12	15	27	244	24	0	0	20	1	2	3	24
94-95—New Jersey	NHL	33	5	7	12	44	10	0	0	19	8	4	12	11
95-96—New Jersey	NHL	76	11	10	21	145	7	3	0	—	—	—	—	—
96-97—New Jersey	NHL	77	9	18	27	109	15	0	0	10	1	1	2	0
97-98—New Jersey	NHL	74	24	24	48	86	30	8	0	6	0	1	1	0
98-99—New Jersey	NHL	70	17	20	37	143	10	3	0	7	3	2	5	2
99-00—New Jersey	NHL	67	16	23	39	80	8	3	0	23	0	6	6	9
NHL Totals (12 years)		711	126	157	283	1537	95	20	0	104	14	20	34	115

McKEE, JAY   D   SABRES

PERSONAL: Born September 8, 1977, in Kingston, Ont. ... 6-3/205. ... Shoots left.
HIGH SCHOOL: Stamford (Niagara Falls, Ont.).
TRANSACTIONS/CAREER NOTES: Selected by Buffalo Sabres in first round (first Sabres pick, 14th overall) of NHL entry draft (July 8, 1995). ... Bruised stomach (March 29, 1998); missed two games. ... Bruised hand (October 30, 1998); missed one game. ... Bruised foot (February 13, 1999); missed six games. ... Suffered from the flu (March 13, 1999); missed two games.
HONORS: Named to OHL All-Star second team (1995-96).

Season Team	League	REGULAR SEASON								PLAYOFFS				
		Gms.	G	A	Pts.	PIM	+/-	PP	SH	Gms.	G	A	Pts.	PIM
92-93—Ernestown	Jr. C	36	0	17	17	37	...	...	...	—	—	—	—	—
93-94—Sudbury	OHL	51	0	1	1	51	...	...	...	3	0	0	0	0
94-95—Sudbury	OHL	39	6	6	12	91	...	...	...	—	—	—	—	—
—Niagara Falls	OHL	26	3	13	16	60	...	...	...	6	2	3	5	10
95-96—Niagara Falls	OHL	64	5	41	46	129	...	...	...	10	1	5	6	16
—Rochester	AHL	4	0	1	1	15	...	...	...	—	—	—	—	—
—Buffalo	NHL	1	0	1	1	2	1	0	0	—	—	—	—	—
96-97—Buffalo	NHL	43	1	9	10	35	3	0	0	3	0	0	0	0
—Rochester	AHL	7	2	5	7	4	...	...	...	—	—	—	—	—
97-98—Buffalo	NHL	56	1	13	14	42	-1	0	0	1	0	0	0	0
—Rochester	AHL	13	1	7	8	11	...	...	...	—	—	—	—	—
98-99—Buffalo	NHL	72	0	6	6	75	20	0	0	21	0	3	3	24
99-00—Buffalo	NHL	78	5	12	17	50	5	1	0	1	0	0	0	0
NHL Totals (5 years)		250	7	41	48	204	28	1	0	26	0	3	3	24

McKENNA, STEVE   LW   WILD

PERSONAL: Born August 21, 1973, in Toronto. ... 6-8/255. ... Shoots left.
COLLEGE: Merrimack College (Mass.).
TRANSACTIONS/CAREER NOTES: Signed as non-drafted free agent by Los Angeles Kings (May 17, 1996). ... Strained abdominal muscle (November 9, 1998); missed 14 games. ... Reinjured abdominal muscle (December 9, 1998); missed 42 games. ... Lacerated eye (October 4, 1999); missed six games. ... Selected by Minnesota Wild in NHL expansion draft (June 23, 2000).

Season Team	League	REGULAR SEASON								PLAYOFFS				
		Gms.	G	A	Pts.	PIM	+/-	PP	SH	Gms.	G	A	Pts.	PIM
93-94—Merrimack College	Hockey East	37	1	2	3	74	...	...	...	—	—	—	—	—
94-95—Merrimack College	Hockey East	37	1	9	10	74	...	...	...	—	—	—	—	—
95-96—Merrimack College	Hockey East	33	3	11	14	67	...	...	...	—	—	—	—	—
96-97—Phoenix	IHL	66	6	5	11	187	...	...	...	—	—	—	—	—
—Los Angeles	NHL	9	0	0	0	37	1	0	0	—	—	—	—	—
97-98—Fredericton	AHL	6	2	1	3	48	...	...	...	—	—	—	—	—
—Los Angeles	NHL	62	4	4	8	150	-9	1	0	3	0	1	1	8
98-99—Los Angeles	NHL	20	1	0	1	36	-3	0	0	—	—	—	—	—
99-00—Los Angeles	NHL	46	0	5	5	125	3	0	0	—	—	—	—	—
NHL Totals (4 years)		137	5	9	14	348	-8	1	0	3	0	1	1	8

McKENZIE, JIM   RW   DEVILS

PERSONAL: Born November 3, 1969, in Gull Lake, Sask. ... 6-4/227. ... Shoots left.
TRANSACTIONS/CAREER NOTES: Selected by Hartford Whalers in fourth round (third Whalers pick, 73rd overall) of NHL entry draft (June 17, 1989). ... Injured elbow (January 31, 1992); missed two games. ... Suffered hip flexor (November 11, 1992); missed three games. ... Suffered hip flexor (December 5, 1992); missed four games. ... Suffered back spasms (January 24, 1993); missed three games. ... Suspended two games by NHL for game misconduct penalties (April 3, 1993). ... Suspended three games by NHL for game misconduct penalties (April 10, 1993). ... Traded by Whalers to Florida Panthers for D Alexander Godynyuk (December 16, 1993). ... Traded by Panthers to Dallas Stars for fourth-round pick (LW Jamie Wright) in 1994 draft (December 16, 1993). ... Traded by Stars to Pittsburgh Penguins for RW Mike Needham (March 21, 1994). ... Fractured toe (November 24, 1993); missed four games. ... Bruised hand (March 11, 1995); missed one game. ... Sprained wrist (April 5, 1995); missed seven games. ... Signed as free agent by New York Islanders (July 31, 1995). ... Claimed by Winnipeg Jets in NHL waiver draft (October 2, 1995). ... Jets franchise moved to Phoenix and renamed Coyotes for 1996-97 season; NHL approved move on January 18, 1996. ... Fractured leg (November 8, 1996); missed five games. ... Suffered from the flu (January 27, 1997); missed one game. ... Fractured leg (December 23, 1997); missed 11 games. ... Traded by Coyotes to Mighty Ducks of Anaheim for C J.F. Jomphe (June 18, 1998). ... Suffered laceration below right eye (January 10, 1999); missed five games. ... Injured ankle (February 3, 1999); missed two games. ... Suspended four games by NHL for fighting incident (October 5, 1999). ... Fractured right hand (November 9, 1999); missed 10 games. ... Claimed on waivers by Washington Capitals (January 18, 2000). ... Signed as free agent by New Jersey Devils (July 3, 2000).
STATISTICAL PLATEAUS: Three-goal games: 1996-97 (1).

M

Season Team	League	REGULAR SEASON								PLAYOFFS				
		Gms.	G	A	Pts.	PIM	+/-	PP	SH	Gms.	G	A	Pts.	PIM
85-86—Moose Jaw	WHL	3	0	2	2	0	...	...	...	—	—	—	—	—
86-87—Moose Jaw	WHL	65	5	3	8	125	...	...	...	9	0	0	0	7
87-88—Moose Jaw	WHL	62	1	17	18	134	...	...	...	—	—	—	—	—
88-89—Victoria	WHL	67	15	27	42	176	...	...	...	8	1	4	5	30
89-90—Binghamton	AHL	56	4	12	16	149	...	...	...	—	—	—	—	—
—Hartford	NHL	5	0	0	0	4	0	0	0	—	—	—	—	—
90-91—Springfield	AHL	24	3	4	7	102	...	...	...	—	—	—	—	—
—Hartford	NHL	41	4	3	7	108	-7	0	0	6	0	0	0	8
91-92—Hartford	NHL	67	5	1	6	87	-6	0	0	—	—	—	—	—
92-93—Hartford	NHL	64	3	6	9	202	-10	0	0	—	—	—	—	—
93-94—Hartford	NHL	26	1	2	3	67	-6	0	0	—	—	—	—	—
—Dallas	NHL	34	2	3	5	63	4	0	0	—	—	—	—	—
—Pittsburgh	NHL	11	0	0	0	16	-5	0	0	3	0	0	0	0
94-95—Pittsburgh	NHL	39	2	1	3	63	-7	0	0	5	0	0	0	4
95-96—Winnipeg	NHL	73	4	2	6	202	-4	0	0	1	0	0	0	2
96-97—Phoenix	NHL	65	5	3	8	200	-5	0	0	7	0	0	0	2
97-98—Phoenix	NHL	64	3	4	7	146	-7	0	0	1	0	0	0	0
98-99—Anaheim	NHL	73	5	4	9	99	-18	1	0	4	0	0	0	4
99-00—Anaheim	NHL	31	3	3	6	48	-5	0	0	—	—	—	—	—
—Washington	NHL	30	1	2	3	16	0	0	0	1	0	0	0	0
NHL Totals (11 years)		623	38	34	72	1321	-76	1	0	28	0	0	0	20

McLAREN, KYLE   D   BRUINS

PERSONAL: Born June 18, 1977, in Humboldt, Sask. ... 6-4/219. ... Shoots left.

TRANSACTIONS/CAREER NOTES: Selected by Boston Bruins in first round (first Bruins pick, ninth overall) of NHL entry draft (July 8, 1995). ... Injured back (November 21, 1995); missed one game. ... Injured knee (November 25, 1995); missed five games. ... Suffered from the flu (January 3, 1996); missed one game. ... Suffered concussion (March 10, 1996); missed one game. ... Suffered charley horse (October 26, 1996); missed two games. ... Strained shoulder (February 2, 1997); missed 13 games. ... Injured foot (March 15, 1997); missed one game. ... Sprained thumb (March 27, 1997); missed remainder of season. ... Suffered hip pointer (November 1, 1997); missed five games. ... Injured knee (December 17, 1997); missed one game. ... Fractured foot (March 19, 1998); missed seven games. ... Strained groin (April 7, 1998); missed three games. ... Missed first 15 games of 1998-99 season due to contract dispute. ... Separated shoulder (January 15, 1999); missed 14 games. ... Injured foot (April 10, 1999); missed one game. ... Strained thumb (November 18, 1999); missed seven games. ... Tore knee cartilage (April 1, 2000); missed final four games of season.

HONORS: Named to NHL All-Rookie team (1995-96).

Season Team	League	REGULAR SEASON								PLAYOFFS				
		Gms.	G	A	Pts.	PIM	+/-	PP	SH	Gms.	G	A	Pts.	PIM
93-94—Tacoma	WHL	62	1	9	10	53	...	...	...	6	1	4	5	6
94-95—Tacoma	WHL	47	13	19	32	68	...	...	...	4	1	1	2	4
95-96—Boston	NHL	74	5	12	17	73	16	0	0	5	0	0	0	14
96-97—Boston	NHL	58	5	9	14	54	-9	0	0	—	—	—	—	—
97-98—Boston	NHL	66	5	20	25	56	13	2	0	6	1	0	1	4
98-99—Boston	NHL	52	6	18	24	48	1	3	0	12	0	3	3	10
99-00—Boston	NHL	71	8	11	19	67	-4	2	0	—	—	—	—	—
NHL Totals (5 years)		321	29	70	99	298	17	7	0	23	1	3	4	28

McLEAN, KIRK   G   RANGERS

PERSONAL: Born June 26, 1966, in Willowdale, Ont. ... 6-1/180. ... Catches left. ... Name pronounced muh-KLAYN.

TRANSACTIONS/CAREER NOTES: Selected by New Jersey Devils as underage junior in sixth round (sixth Devils pick, 107th overall) of NHL entry draft (June 9, 1984). ... Traded by Devils with C Greg Adams and second-round pick (D Leif Rohlin) in 1988 draft to Vancouver Canucks for C Patrik Sundstrom, second- (LW Jeff Christian) and fourth-round (LW Matt Ruchty) picks in 1988 draft (September 15, 1987). ... Suffered tendinitis in left wrist (February 25, 1991). ... Injured knee (January 13, 1996); missed 18 games. ... Injured knee (November 11, 1996); missed 19 games. ... Injured finger (March 5, 1997); missed nine games. ... Traded by Canucks to Hurricanes with LW Martin Gelinas for LW Geoff Sanderson, D Enrico Ciccone and G Sean Burke (January 3, 1998). ... Traded by Hurricanes to Florida Panthers for RW Ray Sheppard (March 24, 1998). ... Bruised ribs (February 14, 1999); missed three games. ... Signed as free agent by New York Rangers (July 13, 1999). ... Suffered from the flu (February 26, 2000); missed one game.

HONORS: Played in NHL All-Star Game (1990 and 1992). ... Named to THE SPORTING NEWS All-Star second team (1991-92). ... Named to NHL All-Star second team (1991-92).

RECORDS: Shares NHL single-season playoff record for most minutes played by a goaltender—1,544 (1994); and most shutouts—4 (1994).

MISCELLANEOUS: Holds Vancouver Canucks all-time record for most games played by goalie (516), most wins (211) and most shutouts (20). ... Stopped penalty shot attempt (vs. Brent Gilchrist, January 27, 1994; vs. Ted Donato, April 12, 1999). ... Allowed penalty shot goal (vs. Brent Ashton, December 11, 1988; vs. Mike Donnelly, November 12, 1992; vs. Andrei Kovalenko, December 4, 1993).

Season Team	League	REGULAR SEASON							PLAYOFFS						
		Gms.	Min.	W	L	T	GA	SO	Avg.	Gms.	Min.	W	L	GA	SO	Avg.
83-84—Oshawa	OHL	17	940	5	9	0	67	0	4.28	—	—	—	—	—	—	—
84-85—Oshawa	OHL	47	2581	23	17	2	143	1	*3.32	5	271	1	3	21	0	4.65
85-86—Oshawa	OHL	51	2830	24	21	2	169	1	3.58	4	201	1	2	18	0	5.37
—New Jersey	NHL	2	111	1	1	0	11	0	5.95	—	—	—	—	—	—	—
86-87—New Jersey	NHL	4	160	1	1	0	10	0	3.75	—	—	—	—	—	—	—
—Maine	AHL	45	2606	15	23	4	140	1	3.22	—	—	—	—	—	—	—
87-88—Vancouver	NHL	41	2380	11	27	3	147	1	3.71	—	—	—	—	—	—	—
88-89—Vancouver	NHL	42	2477	20	17	3	127	4	3.08	5	302	2	3	18	0	3.58
89-90—Vancouver	NHL	*63	*3739	21	30	10	*216	0	3.47	—	—	—	—	—	—	—
90-91—Vancouver	NHL	41	1969	10	22	3	131	0	3.99	2	123	1	1	7	0	3.41

Season Team	League	REGULAR SEASON								PLAYOFFS						
		Gms.	Min	W	L	T	GA	SO	Avg.	Gms.	Min.	W	L	GA	SO	Avg.
91-92 —Vancouver...................	NHL	65	3852	†38	17	9	176	†5	2.74	13	785	6	7	33	†2	2.52
92-93 —Vancouver...................	NHL	54	3261	28	21	5	184	3	3.39	12	754	6	6	42	0	3.34
93-94 —Vancouver...................	NHL	52	3128	23	26	3	156	3	2.99	24	*1544	15	†9	59	†4	2.29
94-95 —Vancouver...................	NHL	40	2374	18	12	10	109	1	2.75	11	660	4	†7	36	0	3.27
95-96 —Vancouver...................	NHL	45	2645	15	21	9	156	2	3.54	1	21	0	1	3	0	8.57
96-97 —Vancouver...................	NHL	44	2581	21	18	3	138	0	3.21	—	—	—	—	—	—	—
97-98 —Vancouver...................	NHL	29	1583	6	17	4	97	1	3.68	—	—	—	—	—	—	—
—Carolina.....................	NHL	8	401	4	2	0	22	0	3.29	—	—	—	—	—	—	—
—Florida......................	NHL	7	406	4	2	1	22	0	3.25	—	—	—	—	—	—	—
98-99 —Florida......................	NHL	30	1597	9	10	4	73	2	2.74	—	—	—	—	—	—	—
99-00 —New York Rangers	NHL	22	1206	7	8	4	58	0	2.89	—	—	—	—	—	—	—
NHL Totals (15 years)...........		589	33870	237	252	71	1833	22	3.25	68	4189	34	34	198	6	2.84

McLENNAN, JAMIE   G   WILD

PERSONAL: Born June 30, 1971, in Edmonton. ... 6-0/190. ... Catches left.
HIGH SCHOOL: St. Albert (Edmonton).
TRANSACTIONS/CAREER NOTES: Selected by New York Islanders in third round (third Islanders pick, 48th overall) of NHL entry draft (June 22, 1991). ... Signed as free agent by St. Louis Blues (July 3, 1996). ... Strained groin (October 29, 1997); missed two games. ... Strained groin (March 22, 1998); missed one game. ... Strained hip flexor (January 19, 1999); missed one game. ... Suffered from the flu (March 11, 1999); missed two games. ... Selected by Minnesota Wild in NHL expansion draft (June 23, 2000).
HONORS: Won Del Wilson Trophy (1990-91). ... Named to WHL (East) All-Star first team (1990-91). ... Won Bill Masterton Memorial Trophy (1997-98).

Season Team	League	REGULAR SEASON								PLAYOFFS						
		Gms.	Min	W	L	T	GA	SO	Avg.	Gms.	Min.	W	L	GA	SO	Avg.
88-89 —Spokane....................	WHL	11	578	...	...	...	63	0	6.54	—	—	—	—	—	—	—
—Lethbridge.................	WHL	7	368	...	...	...	22	0	3.59	—	—	—	—	—	—	—
89-90 —Lethbridge.................	WHL	34	1690	20	4	2	110	1	3.91	13	677	6	5	44	0	3.90
90-91 —Lethbridge.................	WHL	56	3230	32	18	4	205	0	3.81	*16	*970	8	8	*56	0	3.46
91-92 —Capital District	AHL	18	952	4	10	2	60	1	3.78	—	—	—	—	—	—	—
—Richmond	ECHL	32	1837	16	12	‡2	114	0	3.72	—	—	—	—	—	—	—
92-93 —Capital District	AHL	38	2171	17	14	6	117	1	3.23	1	20	0	1	5	0	15.00
93-94 —Salt Lake City	IHL	24	1320	8	12	‡2	80	0	3.64	—	—	—	—	—	—	—
—New York Islanders.......	NHL	22	1287	8	7	6	61	0	2.84	2	82	0	1	6	0	4.39
94-95 —New York Islanders.......	NHL	21	1185	6	11	2	67	0	3.39	—	—	—	—	—	—	—
—Denver	IHL	4	240	3	0	‡1	12	0	3.00	11	641	8	2	23	1	*2.15
95-96 —Utah	IHL	14	728	9	2	‡2	29	0	2.39	—	—	—	—	—	—	—
—New York Islanders.......	NHL	13	636	3	9	1	39	0	3.68	—	—	—	—	—	—	—
—Worcester	AHL	22	1215	14	7	1	57	0	2.81	2	118	0	2	8	0	4.07
96-97 —Worcester	AHL	39	2152	18	13	4	100	2	2.79	4	262	2	2	16	0	3.66
97-98 —St. Louis	NHL	30	1658	16	8	2	60	2	2.17	1	14	0	1	1	0	4.29
98-99 —St. Louis	NHL	33	1763	13	14	4	70	3	2.38	1	37	0	1	0	0	...
99-00 —St. Louis	NHL	19	1009	9	5	2	33	2	1.96	—	—	—	—	—	—	—
NHL Totals (6 years)............		138	7538	55	54	17	330	7	2.63	4	133	0	2	7	0	3.16

McSORLEY, MARTY   D

PERSONAL: Born May 18, 1963, in Hamilton, Ont. ... 6-1/235. ... Shoots right. ... Full Name: Martin James McSorley.
TRANSACTIONS/CAREER NOTES: Signed as non-drafted free agent by Pittsburgh Penguins (April 1983). ... Traded by Penguins with C Tim Hrynewich to Edmonton Oilers for G Gilles Meloche (August 1985). ... Suspended by NHL for AHL incident (March 1987). ... Sprained knee (November 1987). ... Suspended three playoff games by NHL for spearing (April 23, 1988). ... Traded by Oilers with C Wayne Gretzky and LW/C Mike Krushelnyski to Los Angeles Kings for C Jimmy Carson, LW Martin Gelinas, first-round picks in 1989 (traded to New Jersey), 1991 (LW Martin Rucinsky) and 1993 (D Nick Stajduhar) drafts and cash (August 9, 1988). ... Injured shoulder (December 31, 1988). ... Sprained knee (February 1989). ... Suspended four games by NHL for game-misconduct penalties (1989-90). ... Twisted right knee (October 14, 1990); missed four games. ... Twisted ankle (February 9, 1991). ... Suspended three games by NHL for striking another player with a gloved hand (March 2, 1991). ... Suffered from throat virus (November 23, 1991); missed six games. ... Sprained shoulder (February 19, 1992); missed three games. ... Suspended six off-days and fined $500 by NHL for cross-checking (October 31, 1992). ... Suspended one game by NHL for game misconduct penalties (November 27, 1992). ... Traded by Kings to Pittsburgh Penguins for LW Shawn McEachern (August 27, 1993). ... Sprained ankle (November 16, 1993); missed eight games. ... Traded by Penguins with D Jim Paek to Los Angeles Kings for RW Tomas Sandstrom and C Shawn McEachern (February 15, 1993). ... Suspended four games without pay and fined $500 for eye-gouging incident (February 23, 1994). ... Injured abdomen (April 7, 1994); missed remainder of season. ... Strained groin (February 12, 1995); missed seven games. ... Strained groin (January 5, 1996); missed six games. ... Bruised left thigh (February 28, 1996); missed 11 games. ... Traded by Kings with RW Shane Churla and LW Jari Kurri to New York Rangers for C Ray Ferraro, C Nathan Lafayette, C Ian Laperriere, D Mattias Norstrom and fourth-round pick (D Sean Blanchard) in 1997 draft (March 14, 1996). ... Injured groin (April 4, 1996); missed four games. ... Injured groin (April 12, 1996); missed one game. ... Traded by Rangers to San Jose Sharks for D Jayson More, C Brian Swanson and fourth-round pick (D Tomi Kallarsson) in 1997 draft (August 20, 1996). ... Underwent hip surgery (September 10, 1996); missed first 17 games of season. ... Injured groin (November 16, 1996); missed five games. ... Reinjured groin (January 2, 1997); missed three games. ... Strained knee (October 9, 1997); missed three games. ... Strained groin (October 29, 1997); missed three games. ... Signed as free agent by Oilers (October 1, 1998). ... Separated left shoulder (October 24, 1998); missed 21 games. ... Strained groin (January 17, 1999); missed four games. ... Signed as free agent by Boston Bruins (December 7, 1999). ... Injured shoulder (February 1, 2000); missed four games. ... Suspended final 23 games of season by NHL for slashing incident (February 23, 2000).
HONORS: Shared Alka-Seltzer Plus Award with Theoren Fleury (1990-91).
MISCELLANEOUS: Member of Stanley Cup championship team (1987 and 1988). ... Holds Los Angeles Kings all-time record for most penalty minutes (1,846).

M

Season Team	League	REGULAR SEASON								PLAYOFFS				
		Gms.	G	A	Pts.	PIM	+/-	PP	SH	Gms.	G	A	Pts.	PIM
81-82—Belleville	OHL	58	6	13	19	234	...	...	...	—	—	—	—	—
82-83—Belleville	OHL	70	10	41	51	183	...	...	...	4	0	0	0	7
—Baltimore	AHL	2	0	0	0	22	...	...	...	—	—	—	—	—
83-84—Pittsburgh	NHL	72	2	7	9	224	-39	0	0	—	—	—	—	—
84-85—Baltimore	AHL	58	6	24	30	154	...	...	...	14	0	7	7	47
—Pittsburgh	NHL	15	0	0	0	15	-3	0	0	—	—	—	—	—
85-86—Edmonton	NHL	59	11	12	23	265	9	0	0	8	0	2	2	50
—Nova Scotia	AHL	9	2	4	6	34	...	...	...	—	—	—	—	—
86-87—Edmonton	NHL	41	2	4	6	159	-4	0	0	21	4	3	7	65
—Nova Scotia	AHL	7	2	2	4	48	...	...	...	—	—	—	—	—
87-88—Edmonton	NHL	60	9	17	26	223	23	0	0	16	0	3	3	67
88-89—Los Angeles	NHL	66	10	17	27	350	3	2	0	11	0	2	2	33
89-90—Los Angeles	NHL	75	15	21	36	322	2	2	1	10	1	3	4	18
90-91—Los Angeles	NHL	61	7	32	39	221	†48	1	1	12	0	0	0	58
91-92—Los Angeles	NHL	71	7	22	29	268	-13	2	1	6	1	0	1	21
92-93—Los Angeles	NHL	81	15	26	41	*399	1	3	3	24	4	6	10	60
93-94—Pittsburgh	NHL	47	3	18	21	139	-9	0	0	—	—	—	—	—
—Los Angeles	NHL	18	4	6	10	55	-3	1	0	—	—	—	—	—
94-95—Los Angeles	NHL	41	3	18	21	83	-14	1	0	—	—	—	—	—
95-96—Los Angeles	NHL	59	10	21	31	148	-14	1	1	—	—	—	—	—
—New York Rangers	NHL	9	0	2	2	21	-6	0	0	4	0	0	0	0
96-97—San Jose	NHL	57	4	12	16	186	-6	0	1	—	—	—	—	—
97-98—San Jose	NHL	56	2	10	12	140	10	0	0	—	—	—	—	—
98-99—Edmonton	NHL	46	2	3	5	101	-5	0	0	3	0	0	0	2
99-00—Boston	NHL	27	2	3	5	62	2	0	0	—	—	—	—	—
NHL Totals (17 years)		961	108	251	359	3381	-18	13	8	115	10	19	29	374

MELANSON, DEAN D FLYERS

PERSONAL: Born November 19, 1973, in Antigonish, Nova Scotia ... 5-11/211. ... Shoots right. ... Name pronounced muh-LAHN-suhn.
TRANSACTIONS/CAREER NOTES: Selected by Buffalo Sabres in fourth round (fourth Sabres pick, 80th overall) of NHL entry draft (June 20, 1992). ... Signed as free agent by Philadelphia Flyers (July 13, 1999).

Season Team	League	REGULAR SEASON								PLAYOFFS				
		Gms.	G	A	Pts.	PIM	+/-	PP	SH	Gms.	G	A	Pts.	PIM
90-91—St. Hyacinthe	QMJHL	69	10	17	27	110	...	...	...	4	0	1	1	2
91-92—St. Hyacinthe	QMJHL	42	8	19	27	158	...	...	...	6	1	2	3	25
92-93—St. Hyacinthe	QMJHL	57	13	29	42	253	...	...	...	—	—	—	—	—
—Rochester	AHL	8	0	1	1	6	...	...	...	14	1	6	7	18
93-94—Rochester	AHL	80	1	21	22	138	...	...	...	4	0	1	1	2
94-95—Rochester	AHL	43	4	7	11	84	...	...	...	—	—	—	—	—
—Buffalo	NHL	5	0	0	0	4	-1	0	0	—	—	—	—	—
95-96—Rochester	AHL	70	3	13	16	204	...	...	...	14	3	3	6	22
96-97—Quebec	IHL	72	3	21	24	95	...	...	...	7	0	2	2	12
97-98—Rochester	AHL	73	7	9	16	228	...	...	...	4	0	2	2	0
98-99—Rochester	AHL	79	7	27	34	192	...	...	...	17	3	2	5	32
99-00—Philadelphia	AHL	58	11	25	36	178	...	...	...	4	2	3	5	10
NHL Totals (1 year)		5	0	0	0	4	-1	0	0					

MELICHAR, JOSEF D PENGUINS

PERSONAL: Born January 20, 1979, in Ceske Budejovice, Czechoslovakia. ... 6-2/214. ... Shoots left.
TRANSACTIONS/CAREER NOTES: Selected by Pittsburgh Penguins in third round (third Penguins pick, 71st overall) of NHL entry draft (June 21, 1997).

Season Team	League	REGULAR SEASON								PLAYOFFS				
		Gms.	G	A	Pts.	PIM	+/-	PP	SH	Gms.	G	A	Pts.	PIM
95-96—HC Ceske Bude. Jrs.	Czech Rep.	38	3	4	7	...	...	...	...	—	—	—	—	—
96-97—HC Ceske Bude. Jrs.	Czech Rep.	41	2	3	5	10	...	...	...	—	—	—	—	—
97-98—Tri-City	WHL	67	9	24	33	152	...	...	...	—	—	—	—	—
98-99—Tri-City	WHL	65	8	28	36	125	...	...	...	11	1	0	1	15
99-00—Wilkes-Barre/Scranton	AHL	80	3	9	12	126	...	...	...	—	—	—	—	—

MELLANBY, SCOTT RW PANTHERS

PERSONAL: Born June 11, 1966, in Montreal. ... 6-1/205. ... Shoots right. ... Full Name: Scott Edgar Mellanby.
HIGH SCHOOL: Henry Carr (Rexdale, Ont.).
COLLEGE: Wisconsin.
TRANSACTIONS/CAREER NOTES: Selected by Philadelphia Flyers as underage junior in second round (first Flyers pick, 27th overall) of NHL entry draft (June 9, 1984). ... Lacerated right index finger (October 1987). ... Severed nerve and damaged tendon in left forearm (August 1989); missed first 20 games of season. ... Suffered viral infection (November 1989). ... Traded by Flyers with LW Craig Berube and C Craig Fisher to Edmonton Oilers for RW Dave Brown, D Corey Foster and rights to RW Jari Kurri (May 30, 1991). ... Injured shoulder (February 14, 1993); missed 15 games. ... Selected by Florida Panthers in NHL expansion draft (June 24, 1993). ... Fractured nose and lacerated face (February 1, 1994); missed four games. ... Fractured finger (March 7, 1996); missed three games. ... Sprained left knee (January 9, 1998); missed three games. ... Strained groin (September 29, 1998); missed first nine games of season. ... Injured neck (January 16, 1999); missed one game. ... Reinjured neck (January 21, 1999); missed three games. ... Suspended one game by NHL for cross-checking incident (March 21, 1999). ... Suffered slight concussion (April 5, 1999); missed one game. ... Suffered concussion (October 12, 1999); missed three games. ... Suffered from the flu (March 3, 2000); missed one game.

MISCELLANEOUS: Captain of Florida Panthers (1997-98 through 1999-2000). ... Holds Florida Panthers all-time records for most goals (153), assists (188) and points (341).
STATISTICAL NOTES: Tied for NHL lead with 3 game-tying goals (1998-99).

		REGULAR SEASON								PLAYOFFS				
Season Team	League	Gms.	G	A	Pts.	PIM	+/-	PP	SH	Gms.	G	A	Pts.	PIM
83-84—Henry Carr H.S.	MTHL	39	37	37	74	97	...	...	...	—	—	—	—	—
84-85—Univ. of Wisconsin......	WCHA	40	14	24	38	60	...	...	...	—	—	—	—	—
85-86—Univ. of Wisconsin......	WCHA	32	21	23	44	89	...	...	...	—	—	—	—	—
—Philadelphia	NHL	2	0	0	0	0	-1	0	0	—	—	—	—	—
86-87—Philadelphia	NHL	71	11	21	32	94	8	1	0	24	5	5	10	46
87-88—Philadelphia	NHL	75	25	26	51	185	-7	7	0	7	0	1	1	16
88-89—Philadelphia	NHL	76	21	29	50	183	-13	11	0	19	4	5	9	28
89-90—Philadelphia	NHL	57	6	17	23	77	-4	0	0	—	—	—	—	—
90-91—Philadelphia	NHL	74	20	21	41	155	8	5	0	—	—	—	—	—
91-92—Edmonton	NHL	80	23	27	50	197	5	7	0	16	2	1	3	29
92-93—Edmonton	NHL	69	15	17	32	147	-4	6	0	—	—	—	—	—
93-94—Florida.......................	NHL	80	30	30	60	149	0	17	0	—	—	—	—	—
94-95—Florida.......................	NHL	48	13	12	25	90	-16	4	0	—	—	—	—	—
95-96—Florida.......................	NHL	79	32	38	70	160	4	19	0	22	3	6	9	44
96-97—Florida.......................	NHL	82	27	29	56	170	7	9	1	5	0	2	2	4
97-98—Florida.......................	NHL	79	15	24	39	127	-14	6	0	—	—	—	—	—
98-99—Florida.......................	NHL	67	18	27	45	85	5	4	0	—	—	—	—	—
99-00—Florida.......................	NHL	77	18	28	46	126	14	6	0	4	0	1	1	2
NHL Totals (15 years)..........		1016	274	346	620	1945	-8	102	1	97	14	21	35	169

MESSIER, ERIC   D   AVALANCHE

PERSONAL: Born October 29, 1973, in Drummondville, Que. ... 6-2/200. ... Shoots left. ... Name pronounced MEHZ-yay.
COLLEGE: University of Quebec.
TRANSACTIONS/CAREER NOTES: Signed as free agent by Colorado Avalanche (June 14, 1995). ... Sprained ankle (October 28, 1997); missed three games. ... Fractured left elbow (October 10, 1998); missed 27 games. ... Injured eye (December 19, 1998); missed two games. ... Suffered injury (November 26, 1999); missed one game.

		REGULAR SEASON								PLAYOFFS				
Season Team	League	Gms.	G	A	Pts.	PIM	+/-	PP	SH	Gms.	G	A	Pts.	PIM
91-92—Trois-Rivieres..............	QMJHL	58	2	10	12	28	...	...	...	15	2	2	4	13
92-93—Sherbrooke	QMJHL	51	4	17	21	82	...	...	...	15	0	4	4	18
93-94—Sherbrooke	QMJHL	67	4	24	28	69	...	...	...	12	1	7	8	14
94-95—Univ. of Quebec	OUAA	13	8	5	13	20	...	...	...	4	0	3	3	8
95-96—Cornwall	AHL	72	5	9	14	111	...	...	...	8	1	1	2	20
96-97—Hershey	AHL	55	16	26	42	69	...	...	...	9	3	8	11	14
—Colorado	NHL	21	0	0	0	4	7	0	0	—	—	—	—	—
97-98—Colorado	NHL	62	4	12	16	20	4	0	0	—	—	—	—	—
98-99—Colorado	NHL	31	4	2	6	14	0	1	0	3	0	0	0	0
—Hershey	AHL	6	1	3	4	4	...	...	...	—	—	—	—	—
99-00—Colorado	NHL	61	3	6	9	24	0	1	0	—	—	—	—	—
NHL Totals (4 years)..........		175	11	20	31	62	11	2	0	3	0	0	0	0

M

MESSIER, MARK   C   RANGERS

PERSONAL: Born January 18, 1961, in Edmonton. ... 6-1/205. ... Shoots left. ... Full Name: Mark Douglas Messier. ... Brother of Paul Messier, center with Colorado Rockies (1978-79); cousin of Mitch Messier, center/right winger with Minnesota North Stars (1987-88 through 1990-91); cousin of Joby Messier, defenseman with New York Rangers (1992-93 through 1994-95); and brother-in-law of John Blum, defenseman with four NHL teams (1982-83 through 1989-90). ... Name pronounced MEHZ-yay.
TRANSACTIONS/CAREER NOTES: Given five-game trial by Indianapolis Racers (November 1978). ... Signed as free agent by Cincinnati Stingers of WHA (January 1979). ... Selected by Edmonton Oilers in third round (second Oilers pick, 48th overall) of NHL entry draft (August 9, 1979). ... Injured ankle (November 7, 1981). ... Fractured wrist (March 1983). ... Suspended six games by NHL for hitting another player with stick (January 18, 1984). ... Sprained knee ligaments (November 1984). ... Suspended 10 games by NHL for injuring another player (December 26, 1984). ... Bruised left foot (December 3, 1985); missed 17 games. ... Suspended six games by NHL for injuring another player with his stick (October 23, 1988). ... Twisted left knee (January 28, 1989). ... Strained right knee (February 3, 1989). ... Bruised left knee (February 12, 1989). ... Sprained left knee ligaments (October 16, 1990); missed 10 games. ... Reinjured left knee (December 12, 1990); missed three games. ... Reinjured knee (December 22, 1990); missed nine games. ... Fractured left thumb (February 11, 1991); missed eight games. ... Missed one game due to contract dispute (October 1991). ... Traded by Oilers with future considerations to New York Rangers for C Bernie Nicholls, LW Louie DeBrusk, RW Steven Rice and future considerations (October 4, 1991); Oilers traded D Jeff Beukeboom to Rangers for D David Shaw to complete deal (November 12, 1991). ... Sprained ligament in wrist (January 19, 1993); missed six games. ... Strained rib cage muscle (February 27, 1993); missed two games. ... Strained rib cage muscle (March 11, 1993); missed one game. ... Suspended three off-days and fined $500 by NHL for stick-swinging incident (March 18, 1993). ... Sprained wrist (December 22, 1993); missed six games. ... Bruised thigh (March 16, 1994); missed two games. ... Suffered back spasms (April 30, 1995); missed two games. ... Bruised shoulder (February 27, 1996); missed two games. ... Bruised ribs (April 4, 1996); missed six games. ... Suspended two games and fined $1,000 by NHL for checking opponent from behind (October 8, 1996). ... Hyperextended elbow (December 7, 1996); missed four games. ... Suffered back spasms (February 23, 1997); missed two games. ... Suffered charley horse (March 27, 1997); missed two games. ... Signed as free agent by Vancouver Canucks (July 28, 1997). ... Suffered concussion (December 22, 1998); missed one game. ... Sprained medial collateral ligament in knee (February 11, 1999); missed 18 games. ... Injured groin (March 31, 1999); missed four games. ... Sprained medial collateral ligament in knee (November 9, 1999); missed 15 games. ... Injured knee (December 29, 2000); missed one game. ... Signed as free agent by Rangers (July 13, 2000).
HONORS: Named to THE SPORTING NEWS All-Star first team (1981-82, 1982-83, 1989-90 and 1991-92). ... Named to NHL All-Star first team (1981-82, 1982-83, 1989-90 and 1991-92). ... Played in NHL All-Star Game (1982-1984, 1986, 1988-1992, 1994, 1996-1998 and 2000). ... Won Conn Smythe Trophy (1983-84). ... Named to THE SPORTING NEWS All-Star second team (1983-84). ... Named to THE SPORTING NEWS All-Star second team (1986-87). ... Named NHL Player of the Year by THE SPORTING NEWS (1989-90 and 1991-92). ... Won Hart Memorial Trophy (1989-90 and 1991-92). ... Won Lester B. Pearson Award (1989-90 and 1991-92).

RECORDS: Holds NHL career playoff record for most shorthanded goals—11; and most games—236. ... Shares NHL single-game playoff record for most shorthanded goals—2 (April 21, 1992). ... Shares NHL career All-Star Game record for most assists—13.
STATISTICAL PLATEAUS: Three-goal games: 1980-81 (1), 1981-82 (2), 1982-83 (2), 1983-84 (2), 1985-86 (1), 1987-88 (1), 1989-90 (2), 1991-92 (2), 1995-96 (1), 1996-97 (2). Total: 15. ... Four-goal games: 1982-83 (1), 1988-89 (1), 1989-90 (1), 1991-92 (1). Total: 4. ... Total hat tricks: 19.
MISCELLANEOUS: Member of Stanley Cup championship teams (1984, 1985, 1987, 1988, 1990 and 1994). ... Captain of Edmonton Oilers (1988-89 through 1990-91). ... Captain of New York Rangers (1991-92 through 1996-97). ... Captain of Vancouver Canucks (1997-98 through 1999-2000).

Season Team	League	REGULAR SEASON								PLAYOFFS				
		Gms.	G	A	Pts.	PIM	+/-	PP	SH	Gms.	G	A	Pts.	PIM
76-77—Spruce Grove	AJHL	57	27	39	66	91	...	...	...	—	—	—	—	—
77-78—St. Albert	AJHL							Statistics unavailable.						
—Portland	WHL	—	—	—	—	—	...	...	...	7	4	1	5	2
78-79—Indianapolis	WHA	5	0	0	0	0	...	...	...	—	—	—	—	—
—Cincinnati	WHA	47	1	10	11	58	...	...	...	—	—	—	—	—
79-80—Houston	CHL	4	0	3	3	4	...	...	...	—	—	—	—	—
—Edmonton	NHL	75	12	21	33	120	-10	1	1	3	1	2	3	2
80-81—Edmonton	NHL	72	23	40	63	102	-12	4	0	9	2	5	7	13
81-82—Edmonton	NHL	78	50	38	88	119	21	10	0	5	1	2	3	8
82-83—Edmonton	NHL	77	48	58	106	72	19	12	1	15	15	6	21	14
83-84—Edmonton	NHL	73	37	64	101	165	40	7	4	19	8	18	26	19
84-85—Edmonton	NHL	55	23	31	54	57	8	4	5	18	12	13	25	12
85-86—Edmonton	NHL	63	35	49	84	68	36	10	5	10	4	6	10	18
86-87—Edmonton	NHL	77	37	70	107	73	21	7	4	21	12	16	28	16
87-88—Edmonton	NHL	77	37	74	111	103	21	12	3	19	11	23	34	29
88-89—Edmonton	NHL	72	33	61	94	130	-5	6	6	7	1	11	12	8
89-90—Edmonton	NHL	79	45	84	129	79	19	13	6	22	9	*22	†31	20
90-91—Edmonton	NHL	53	12	52	64	34	15	3	1	18	4	11	15	16
91-92—New York Rangers	NHL	79	35	72	107	76	31	12	4	11	7	7	14	6
92-93—New York Rangers	NHL	75	25	66	91	72	-6	7	2	—	—	—	—	—
93-94—New York Rangers	NHL	76	26	58	84	76	25	6	2	23	12	18	30	33
94-95—New York Rangers	NHL	46	14	39	53	40	8	3	3	10	3	10	13	8
95-96—New York Rangers	NHL	74	47	52	99	122	29	14	1	11	4	7	11	16
96-97—New York Rangers	NHL	71	36	48	84	88	12	7	5	15	3	9	12	6
97-98—Vancouver	NHL	82	22	38	60	58	-10	8	2	—	—	—	—	—
98-99—Vancouver	NHL	59	13	35	48	33	-12	4	2	—	—	—	—	—
99-00—Vancouver	NHL	66	17	37	54	30	-15	6	0	—	—	—	—	—
WHA Totals (1 year)		52	1	10	11	58	...	...	...					
NHL Totals (21 years)		1479	627	1087	1714	1717	235	156	57	236	109	186	295	244

METROPOLIT, GLEN   C   CAPITALS

PERSONAL: Born June 25, 1974, in Toronto. ... 5-11/196. ... Shoots right.
TRANSACTIONS/CAREER NOTES: Signed as non-drafted free agent by Washington Capitals (July 20, 1999).

Season Team	League	REGULAR SEASON								PLAYOFFS				
		Gms.	G	A	Pts.	PIM	+/-	PP	SH	Gms.	G	A	Pts.	PIM
95-96—Nashville	ECHL	58	30	31	61	62	...	...	...	5	3	8	11	2
—Atlanta	IHL	1	0	0	0	0	...	...	...	—	—	—	—	—
96-97—Pensacola	ECHL	54	35	47	82	45	...	...	...	12	9	16	25	28
—Quebec	IHL	22	5	4	9	14	...	...	...	5	0	0	0	2
97-98—Grand Rapids	IHL	79	20	35	55	90	...	...	...	3	1	1	2	0
98-99—Grand Rapids	IHL	77	28	53	81	92	...	...	...	—	—	—	—	—
99-00—Washington	NHL	30	6	13	19	4	5	1	0	2	0	0	0	2
—Portland	AHL	48	18	42	60	73	...	...	...	1	1	0	1	0
NHL Totals (1 year)		30	6	13	19	4	5	1	0	2	0	0	0	2

MEZEI, BRANISLAV   D   ISLANDERS

PERSONAL: Born October 8, 1980, in Nitra, Czechoslovakia. ... 6-5/221. ... Shoots left.
TRANSACTIONS/CAREER NOTES: Selected by New York Islanders in first round (third Islanders pick, 10th overall) of NHL entry draft (June 26, 1999).
HONORS: Named to OHL All-Star first team (1999-2000).

Season Team	League	REGULAR SEASON								PLAYOFFS				
		Gms.	G	A	Pts.	PIM	+/-	PP	SH	Gms.	G	A	Pts.	PIM
96-97—Plastika Nitra Jrs.	Slovakia Jrs.	40	8	17	25	42	...	...	...	—	—	—	—	—
97-98—Belleville	OHL	53	3	5	8	58	...	...	...	8	0	2	2	8
98-99—Belleville	OHL	60	5	18	23	90	...	...	...	18	0	4	4	29
99-00—Belleville	OHL	58	7	21	28	99	...	...	...	6	0	3	3	10

MICHAUD, ALFIE   G   CANUCKS

PERSONAL: Born November 6, 1976, in Selkirk, Man. ... 5-10/177. ... Catches left.
COLLEGE: Maine.
TRANSACTIONS/CAREER NOTES: Signed as non-drafted free agent by Vancouver Canucks (June 17, 1999).
HONORS: Named to NCAA All-Tournament team (1998-99). ... Named NCAA Tournament Most Valuable Player (1998-99).

Season Team	League	Gms.	Min	W	L	T	GA	SO	Avg.	Gms.	Min.	W	L	GA	SO	Avg.
96-97—Univ. of Maine...............	Hockey East	29	1515	17	8	1	78	1	3.09	—	—	—	—	—	—	—
97-98—Univ. of Maine...............	Hockey East	32	1794	15	12	†4	94	2	3.14	—	—	—	—	—	—	—
98-99—Univ. of Maine...............	Hockey East	37	2147	*28	6	3	83	3	2.32	—	—	—	—	—	—	—
99-00—Syracuse...................	AHL	38	2052	10	17	5	132	0	3.86	—	—	—	—	—	—	—
—Vancouver.....................	NHL	2	69	0	1	0	5	0	4.35	—	—	—	—	—	—	—
NHL Totals (1 year)...............		2	69	0	1	0	5	0	4.35							

MIKA, PETR   C   ISLANDERS

PERSONAL: Born February 12, 1979, in Prague, Czechoslovakia. ... 6-4/195. ... Shoots right. ... Name pronounced MEE-kuh.
TRANSACTIONS/CAREER NOTES: Selected by New York Islanders in fourth round (sixth Islanders pick, 85th overall) of NHL entry draft (June 21, 1997).

		REGULAR SEASON								PLAYOFFS				
Season Team	League	Gms.	G	A	Pts.	PIM	+/-	PP	SH	Gms.	G	A	Pts.	PIM
95-96—Slavia Praha Jrs..........	Czech Rep.	26	5	12	17	...	...	...	...	—	—	—	—	—
—Slavia Praha..................	Czech Rep.	1	0	0	0	...	...	...	...	—	—	—	—	—
96-97—Slavia Praha Jrs..........	Czech Rep.	15	8	0	8	...	...	...	...	—	—	—	—	—
—HC Beroun...................	Czech II	9	1	0	1	...	...	...	...	—	—	—	—	—
—Slavia Praha..................	Czech Rep.	20	1	2	3	6	...	...	...	—	—	—	—	—
97-98—Ottawa	OHL	41	10	8	18	28	...	...	...	—	—	—	—	—
98-99—Slavia Praha..............	Czech Rep.	49	6	5	11	57	...	...	...	—	—	—	—	—
99-00—Lowell......................	AHL	50	8	9	17	20	...	...	...	6	0	0	0	0
—New York Islanders.....	NHL	3	0	0	0	0	-1	0	0	—	—	—	—	—
NHL Totals (1 year).............		3	0	0	0	0	-1	0	0					

MILLAR, CRAIG   D   PREDATORS

PERSONAL: Born July 12, 1976, in Winnipeg. ... 6-2/206. ... Shoots left.
TRANSACTIONS/CAREER NOTES: Selected by Buffalo Sabres in ninth round (10th Sabres pick, 225th overall) of NHL entry draft (June 29, 1994). ... Traded by Sabres with LW Barrie Moore to Edmonton Oilers for LW/RW Miroslav Satan (March 18, 1997). ... Traded by Oilers to Nashville Predators for third-round pick (C Mike Comrie) in 1999 draft (June 26, 1999).
HONORS: Named to WHL (Central/East) All-Star first team (1995-96). ... Named to AHL All-Rookie team (1996-97).

		REGULAR SEASON								PLAYOFFS				
Season Team	League	Gms.	G	A	Pts.	PIM	+/-	PP	SH	Gms.	G	A	Pts.	PIM
92-93—Swift Current	WHL	43	2	1	3	8	...	...	...	—	—	—	—	—
93-94—Swift Current	WHL	66	2	9	11	53	...	...	...	—	—	—	—	—
94-95—Swift Current	WHL	72	8	42	50	80	...	...	...	6	1	1	2	10
95-96—Swift Current	WHL	72	31	46	77	151	...	...	...	6	1	0	1	22
96-97—Rochester	AHL	64	7	18	25	65	...	...	...	—	—	—	—	—
—Edmonton....................	NHL	1	0	0	0	2	0	0	0	—	—	—	—	—
—Hamilton......................	AHL	10	1	3	4	10	...	...	...	22	4	4	8	21
97-98—Hamilton...................	AHL	60	10	22	32	113	...	...	...	9	3	1	4	22
—Edmonton....................	NHL	11	4	0	4	8	-3	1	0	—	—	—	—	—
98-99—Edmonton.................	NHL	24	0	2	2	19	-6	0	0	—	—	—	—	—
—Hamilton......................	AHL	43	3	17	20	38	...	...	...	11	1	5	6	18
99-00—Nashville..................	NHL	57	3	11	14	28	-6	0	0	—	—	—	—	—
—Milwaukee...................	IHL	8	1	5	6	6	...	...	...	—	—	—	—	—
NHL Totals (4 years)...........		93	7	13	20	57	-15	1	0					

MILLER, AARON   D   AVALANCHE

PERSONAL: Born August 11, 1971, in Buffalo. ... 6-3/205. ... Shoots right. ... Full Name: Aaron Michael Miller.
COLLEGE: Vermont.
TRANSACTIONS/CAREER NOTES: Selected by New York Rangers in fifth round (sixth Rangers pick, 88th overall) of NHL entry draft (June 17, 1989). ... Traded by Rangers with fifth-round pick (LW Bill Lindsay) in 1991 draft to Quebec Nordiques for D Joe Cirella (January 17, 1991). ... Nordiques franchise moved to Colorado and renamed Avalanche for 1995-96 season (June 21, 1995). ... Suffered concussion (October 24, 1998); missed one game. ... Bruised knee (November 8, 1998); missed one game. ... Suffered back spasms (March 17, 1999); missed three games. ... Bruised sternum (November 17, 1999); missed 27 games.
HONORS: Named to ECAC All-Rookie team (1989-90). ... Named to NCAA All-America (East) second team (1992-93). ... Named to ECAC All-Star first team (1992-93).

		REGULAR SEASON								PLAYOFFS				
Season Team	League	Gms.	G	A	Pts.	PIM	+/-	PP	SH	Gms.	G	A	Pts.	PIM
87-88—Niagara	NAJHL	30	4	9	13	2	...	...	...	—	—	—	—	—
88-89—Niagara	NAJHL	59	24	38	62	60	...	...	...	—	—	—	—	—
89-90—Univ. of Vermont........	ECAC	31	1	15	16	24	...	...	...	—	—	—	—	—
90-91—Univ. of Vermont........	ECAC	30	3	7	10	22	...	...	...	—	—	—	—	—
91-92—Univ. of Vermont........	ECAC	31	3	16	19	36	...	...	...	—	—	—	—	—
92-93—Univ. of Vermont........	ECAC	30	4	13	17	16	...	...	...	—	—	—	—	—
93-94—Cornwall	AHL	64	4	10	14	49	...	...	...	13	0	2	2	10
—Quebec	NHL	1	0	0	0	0	-1	0	0	—	—	—	—	—
94-95—Cornwall	AHL	76	4	18	22	69	...	...	...	—	—	—	—	—
—Quebec	NHL	9	0	3	3	6	2	0	0	—	—	—	—	—
95-96—Cornwall	AHL	62	4	23	27	77	...	...	...	8	0	1	1	6
—Colorado	NHL	5	0	0	0	0	0	0	0	—	—	—	—	—
96-97—Colorado	NHL	56	5	12	17	15	15	0	0	17	1	2	3	10
97-98—Colorado	NHL	55	2	2	4	51	0	0	0	7	0	0	0	8
98-99—Colorado	NHL	76	5	13	18	42	3	1	0	19	1	5	6	10
99-00—Colorado	NHL	53	1	7	8	36	3	0	0	17	1	1	2	6
NHL Totals (7 years)...........		255	13	37	50	150	22	1	0	60	3	8	11	34

M

MILLER, KEVIN   C

PERSONAL: Born September 9, 1965, in Lansing, Mich. ... 5-11/190. ... Shoots right. ... Full Name: Kevin Bradley Miller. ... Brother of Kelly Miller, right winger with New York Rangers (1984-85 through 1986-87) and Washington Capitals (1986-87 through 1998-99); and brother of Kip Miller, center with six NHL teams (1988-89 through 1999-2000).

HIGH SCHOOL: Eastern (Lansing, Mich.).

COLLEGE: Michigan State.

TRANSACTIONS/CAREER NOTES: Selected by New York Rangers in 10th round (10th Rangers pick, 202nd overall) of NHL entry draft (June 9, 1984). ... Injured groin (September 1990). ... Sprained shoulder (December 1990). ... Traded by Rangers with D Dennis Vial and RW Jim Cummings to Detroit Red Wings for RW Joe Kocur and D Per Djoos (March 5, 1991). ... Traded by Red Wings to Washington Capitals for RW Dino Ciccarelli (June 20, 1992). ... Traded by Capitals to St. Louis Blues for D Paul Cavallini (November 1, 1992). ... Suffered sore knee (November 3, 1993). ... Injured knee (November 24, 1993); missed two games. ... Injured hip (March 30, 1994); missed one game. ... Suffered sore groin (April 8, 1994); missed three games. ... Traded by Blues to San Jose Sharks for C Todd Elik (March 23, 1995). ... Injured knee (March 15, 1996); missed two games. ... Traded by Sharks to Pittsburgh Penguins for fifth-round pick in 1996 draft (March 20, 1996). ... Signed as free agent by Chicago Blackhawks (July 17, 1996). ... Suffered from the flu (November 22, 1996); missed one game. ... Pulled groin (January 10, 1997); missed two games. ... Strained groin (December 20, 1997); missed one game. ... Signed as free agent by New York Islanders (October 9, 1998). ... Signed as free agent by Ottawa Senators (August 24, 1999). ... Separated right shoulder (March 30, 2000); missed four games.

MISCELLANEOUS: Scored on a penalty shot (vs. Patrick Roy, October 30, 1991; vs. Stephane Fiset, December 5, 1995). ... Failed to score on a penalty shot (vs. Mike Vernon, December 17, 1993).

STATISTICAL PLATEAUS: Three-goal games: 1991-92 (1), 1992-93 (1), 1993-94 (1), 1995-96 (1). Total: 4.

Season Team	League	REGULAR SEASON								PLAYOFFS				
		Gms.	G	A	Pts.	PIM	+/-	PP	SH	Gms.	G	A	Pts.	PIM
84-85—Michigan State	CCHA	44	11	29	40	84	...	...	...	—	—	—	—	—
85-86—Michigan State	CCHA	45	19	52	71	112	...	...	...	—	—	—	—	—
86-87—Michigan State	CCHA	42	25	56	81	63	...	...	...	—	—	—	—	—
87-88—Michigan State	CCHA	9	6	3	9	18	...	...	...	—	—	—	—	—
—U.S. Olympic team	Int'l	50	32	34	66	...	...	...	...	—	—	—	—	—
88-89—New York Rangers	NHL	24	3	5	8	2	-1	0	0	—	—	—	—	—
—Denver	IHL	55	29	47	76	19	...	...	...	4	2	1	3	2
89-90—New York Rangers	NHL	16	0	5	5	2	-1	0	0	1	0	0	0	0
—Flint	IHL	48	19	23	42	41	...	...	...	—	—	—	—	—
90-91—New York Rangers	NHL	63	17	27	44	63	1	1	2	—	—	—	—	—
—Detroit	NHL	11	5	2	7	4	-4	0	1	7	3	2	5	20
91-92—Detroit	NHL	80	20	26	46	53	6	3	1	9	0	2	2	4
92-93—Washington	NHL	10	0	3	3	35	-4	0	0	—	—	—	—	—
—St. Louis	NHL	72	24	22	46	65	6	8	3	10	0	3	3	11
93-94—St. Louis	NHL	75	23	25	48	83	6	6	3	3	1	0	1	4
94-95—St. Louis	NHL	15	2	5	7	0	4	0	0	—	—	—	—	—
—San Jose	NHL	21	6	7	13	13	0	1	1	6	0	0	0	2
95-96—San Jose	NHL	68	22	20	42	41	-8	2	2	—	—	—	—	—
—Pittsburgh	NHL	13	6	5	11	4	4	1	0	18	3	2	5	8
96-97—Chicago	NHL	69	14	17	31	41	-10	5	1	6	0	1	1	0
97-98—Indianapolis	IHL	26	11	11	22	41	...	...	...	2	1	1	2	0
—Chicago	NHL	37	4	7	11	8	-4	0	0	—	—	—	—	—
98-99—New York Islanders	NHL	33	1	5	6	13	-5	0	0	—	—	—	—	—
—Chicago	IHL	30	11	20	31	8	...	...	...	10	2	7	9	22
99-00—Grand Rapids	IHL	63	20	34	54	51	...	...	...	17	*11	7	†18	30
—Ottawa	NHL	9	3	2	5	2	1	1	0	1	0	0	0	0
NHL Totals (12 years)		616	150	183	333	429	-9	28	14	61	7	10	17	49

MILLER, KIP   C

PERSONAL: Born June 11, 1969, in Lansing, Mich. ... 5-10/190. ... Shoots left. ... Full Name: Kip Charles Miller. ... Brother of Kelly Miller, right winger with New York Rangers (1984-85 through 1986-87) and Washington Capitals (1986-87 through 1998-99); and brother of Kevin Miller, left winger with nine NHL teams (1988-89 through 1999-2000).

HIGH SCHOOL: Eastern (Lansing, Mich.).

COLLEGE: Michigan State.

TRANSACTIONS/CAREER NOTES: Selected by Quebec Nordiques in fourth round (fourth Nordiques pick, 72nd overall) of NHL entry draft (June 13, 1987). ... Injured hand and forearm in off-ice accident (November 1987). ... Traded by Nordiques to Minnesota North Stars for LW Steve Maltais (March 8, 1992). ... North Stars franchise moved from Minnesota to Dallas and renamed Stars for 1993-94 season. ... Signed as free agent by San Jose Sharks (August 10, 1993). ... Signed as free agent by New York Islanders (August 2, 1994). ... Signed as free agent by Chicago Blackhawks (August 10, 1995). ... Signed as free agent by Islanders (November 26, 1997). ... Selected by Pittsburgh Penguins from Islanders in NHL waiver draft (October 5, 1998). ... Injured eye (March 20, 1999); missed one game. ... Sprained knee (October 30, 1999); missed one game. ... Traded by Penguins to Mighty Ducks of Anaheim for future considerations (January 30, 2000).

HONORS: Named to NCAA All-America (West) first team (1988-89 and 1989-90). ... Named to CCHA All-Star first team (1988-89 and 1989-90). ... Won Hobey Baker Memorial Award (1989-90). ... Named CCHA Player of the Year (1989-90). ... Won N.R. (Bud) Poile Trophy (1994-95).

Season Team	League	REGULAR SEASON								PLAYOFFS				
		Gms.	G	A	Pts.	PIM	+/-	PP	SH	Gms.	G	A	Pts.	PIM
86-87—Michigan State	CCHA	41	20	19	39	92	...	...	...	—	—	—	—	—
87-88—Michigan State	CCHA	39	16	25	41	51	...	...	...	—	—	—	—	—
88-89—Michigan State	CCHA	47	32	45	77	94	...	...	...	—	—	—	—	—
89-90—Michigan State	CCHA	45	*48	53	*101	60	...	...	...	—	—	—	—	—
90-91—Quebec	NHL	13	4	3	7	7	-1	0	0	—	—	—	—	—
—Halifax	AHL	66	36	33	69	40	...	...	...	—	—	—	—	—
91-92—Quebec	NHL	36	5	10	15	12	-21	1	0	—	—	—	—	—
—Halifax	AHL	24	9	17	26	8	...	...	...	—	—	—	—	—
—Minnesota	NHL	3	1	2	3	2	-1	1	0	—	—	—	—	—
—Kalamazoo	IHL	6	1	8	9	4	...	...	...	12	3	9	12	12

			REGULAR SEASON							PLAYOFFS				
Season Team	League	Gms.	G	A	Pts.	PIM	+/-	PP	SH	Gms.	G	A	Pts.	PIM
92-93—Kalamazoo	IHL	61	17	39	56	59	...	...	...	—	—	—	—	—
93-94—San Jose....................	NHL	11	2	2	4	6	-1	0	0	—	—	—	—	—
—Kansas City................	IHL	71	38	54	92	51	...	...	...	—	—	—	—	—
94-95—Denver.....................	IHL	71	46	60	106	54	...	...	...	17	*15	14	29	8
—New York Islanders.....	NHL	8	0	1	1	0	1	0	0	—	—	—	—	—
95-96—Indianapolis	IHL	73	32	59	91	46	...	...	...	5	2	6	8	2
—Chicago...................	NHL	10	1	4	5	2	1	0	0	—	—	—	—	—
96-97—Chicago...................	IHL	43	11	41	52	32	...	...	...	—	—	—	—	—
—Indianapolis	IHL	37	17	24	41	18	...	...	...	4	2	2	4	2
97-98—Utah	IHL	72	38	59	97	30	...	...	...	4	3	2	5	10
—New York Islanders.....	NHL	9	1	3	4	2	-2	0	0	—	—	—	—	—
98-99—Pittsburgh.................	NHL	77	19	23	42	22	1	1	0	13	2	7	9	19
99-00—Pittsburgh.................	NHL	44	4	15	19	10	-1	0	0	—	—	—	—	—
—Anaheim	NHL	30	6	17	23	4	1	2	0	—	—	—	—	—
NHL Totals (8 years)...........		241	43	80	123	67	-23	5	0	13	2	7	9	19

MILLEY, NORM — RW — SABRES

PERSONAL: Born February 14, 1980, in Toronto. ... 5-11/175. ... Shoots right. ... Full Name: Norman Milley.
TRANSACTIONS/CAREER NOTES: Selected by Buffalo Sabres in second round (third Sabres pick, 47th overall) of NHL entry draft (June 27, 1998).
HONORS: Named to Can.HL All-Rookie team (1996-97). ... Named to OHL All-Rookie first team (1996-97). ... Named to OHL All-Star second team (1998-99). ... Won Jim Mahon Award (1998-99). ... Named to OHL All-Star first team (1999-2000). ... Named to Can.HL All-Star first team (1999-2000).

			REGULAR SEASON							PLAYOFFS				
Season Team	League	Gms.	G	A	Pts.	PIM	+/-	PP	SH	Gms.	G	A	Pts.	PIM
95-96—Toronto Red Wings.....	MTHL	42	42	36	78	109	...	...	...	—	—	—	—	—
96-97—Sudbury....................	OHL	61	30	32	62	15	...	...	...	—	—	—	—	—
97-98—Sudbury....................	OHL	62	33	41	74	48	...	...	...	10	0	1	1	4
98-99—Sudbury....................	OHL	68	52	68	120	47	...	...	...	4	2	3	5	4
99-00—Sudbury....................	OHL	68	*52	60	112	47	...	...	...	12	8	11	19	6

MINARD, MIKE — G

PERSONAL: Born November 1, 1976, in Owen Sound, Ont. ... 6-3/205. ... Catches left. ... Name pronounced mih-NAHRD.
TRANSACTIONS/CAREER NOTES: Selected by Edmonton Oilers in fourth round (fourth Oilers pick, 83rd overall) of NHL entry draft (July 8, 1995).

			REGULAR SEASON							PLAYOFFS					
Season Team	League	Gms.	Min	W	L	T	GA	SO	Avg.	Gms.	Min.	W	L	GA	SO	Avg.
94-95—Chilliwack...................	BCJHL	40	2330	...	...	...	136	0	3.50	—	—	—	—	—	—	—
95-96—Barrie	OHL	1	52	0	1	0	8	0	9.23	—	—	—	—	—	—	—
—Det. Jr. Red Wings........	OHL	42	2314	25	10	4	128	2	3.32	17	922	9	6	55	1	3.58
96-97—Hamilton	AHL	3	100	1	1	0	7	0	4.20	—	—	—	—	—	—	—
—Wheeling..................	ECHL	23	899	3	7	‡1	69	0	4.61	3	148	0	2	16	0	6.49
97-98—Hamilton	AHL	2	80	1	0	0	2	0	1.50	—	—	—	—	—	—	—
—New Orleans..............	ECHL	11	429	6	2	0	30	0	4.20	—	—	—	—	—	—	—
—Milwaukee................	IHL	8	362	2	2	0	19	0	3.15	—	—	—	—	—	—	—
98-99—Dayton	ECHL	15	788	8	5	‡2	42	1	3.20	—	—	—	—	—	—	—
—Milwaukee................	IHL	10	531	3	5	0	27	0	3.05	—	—	—	—	—	—	—
—Hamilton	AHL	11	645	8	3	0	30	1	2.79	1	20	0	0	0	0	...
99-00—Edmonton	NHL	1	60	1	0	0	3	0	3.00	—	—	—	—	—	—	—
—Hamilton	AHL	38	1987	16	12	5	102	0	3.08	1	23	0	0	0	0	...
NHL Totals (1 year)...............		1	60	1	0	0	3	0	3.00							

MIRONOV, BORIS — D — BLACKHAWKS

PERSONAL: Born March 21, 1972, in Moscow, U.S.S.R. ... 6-3/223. ... Shoots right. ... Brother of Dmitri Mironov, defenseman, Washington Capitals. ... Name pronounced MEER-ih-nahf.
TRANSACTIONS/CAREER NOTES: Selected by Winnipeg Jets in second round (second Jets pick, 27th overall) of NHL entry draft (June 20, 1992). ... Bruised back (February 2, 1994); missed three games. ... Traded by Jets with C Mats Lindgren and first- (C Jason Bonsignore) and fourth-round (RW Adam Copeland) picks in 1994 draft to Edmonton Oilers for D Dave Manson and sixth-round pick (D Chris Kibermanis) in 1994 draft (March 15, 1994). ... Bruised ankle (April 3, 1995); missed one game. ... Strained lower back (April 13, 1995); missed 10 games. ... Strained abdominal muscle (January 21, 1997); missed 12 games. ... Strained groin (February 19, 1997); missed five games. ... Strained groin (March 7, 1997); missed five games. ... Bruised right shoulder (February 3, 1999); missed two games. ... Traded by Oilers with LW Dean McAmmond and D Jonas Elofsson to Chicago Blackhawks for C Chad Kilger, LW Daniel Cleary, LW Ethan Moreau and D Christian Laflamme (March 20, 1999). ... Suffered charley horse (March 25, 1999); missed one game. ... Suffered hip pointer (December 4, 1999); missed one game. ... Sprained knee (March 26, 2000); missed final seven games of season.
HONORS: Named to NHL All-Rookie team (1993-94).
MISCELLANEOUS: Member of silver-medal-winning Russian Olympic team (1998).

			REGULAR SEASON							PLAYOFFS				
Season Team	League	Gms.	G	A	Pts.	PIM	+/-	PP	SH	Gms.	G	A	Pts.	PIM
88-89—CSKA Moscow...........	USSR	1	0	0	0	0	...	...	...	—	—	—	—	—
89-90—CSKA Moscow...........	USSR	7	0	0	0	0	...	...	...	—	—	—	—	—
90-91—CSKA Moscow...........	USSR	36	1	5	6	16	...	...	...	—	—	—	—	—
91-92—CSKA Moscow...........	CIS	36	2	1	3	22	...	...	...	—	—	—	—	—

M

Season Team	League	REGULAR SEASON								PLAYOFFS				
		Gms.	G	A	Pts.	PIM	+/-	PP	SH	Gms.	G	A	Pts.	PIM
92-93—CSKA Moscow............	CIS	19	0	5	5	20	...	...	...	—	—	—	—	—
93-94—Winnipeg................	NHL	65	7	22	29	96	-29	5	0	—	—	—	—	—
—Edmonton..................	NHL	14	0	2	2	14	-4	0	0	—	—	—	—	—
94-95—Cape Breton............	AHL	4	2	5	7	23	...	...	...	—	—	—	—	—
—Edmonton..................	NHL	29	1	7	8	40	-9	0	0	—	—	—	—	—
95-96—Edmonton...............	NHL	78	8	24	32	101	-23	7	0	—	—	—	—	—
96-97—Edmonton...............	NHL	55	6	26	32	85	2	2	0	12	2	8	10	16
97-98—Edmonton...............	NHL	81	16	30	46	100	-8	10	1	12	3	3	6	27
—Russian Oly. team.......	Int'l	6	0	2	2	2	...	...	...	—	—	—	—	—
98-99—Edmonton...............	NHL	63	11	29	40	104	6	5	0	—	—	—	—	—
—Chicago...................	NHL	12	0	9	9	27	7	0	0	—	—	—	—	—
99-00—Chicago................	NHL	58	9	28	37	72	-3	4	2	—	—	—	—	—
NHL Totals (7 years)...........		455	58	177	235	639	-61	33	3	24	5	11	16	43

MIRONOV, DMITRI D CAPITALS

PERSONAL: Born December 25, 1965, in Moscow, U.S.S.R. ... 6-4/229. ... Shoots right. ... Brother of Boris Mironov, defenseman, Chicago Blackhawks. ... Name pronounced MIHR-ih-nahf.

TRANSACTIONS/CAREER NOTES: Selected by Toronto Maple Leafs in eighth round (seventh Maple Leafs pick, 160th overall) of NHL entry draft (June 22, 1991). ... Fractured nose (March 23, 1992). ... Suffered infected tooth (March 18, 1993); missed 10 games. ... Bruised quadricep (December 28, 1993); missed one game. ... Lacerated lip (March 7, 1994); missed two games. ... Suffered rib muscle strain (April 2, 1994); missed remainder of season. ... Bruised thigh (February 18, 1995); missed one game. ... Separated shoulder (March 27, 1995); missed 14 games. ... Traded by Maple Leafs with second-round pick (traded to New Jersey) in 1996 draft to Pittsburgh Penguins for D Larry Murphy (July 8, 1995). ... Bruised shoulder (March 14, 1996); missed eight games. ... Traded by Penguins with LW Shawn Antoski to Mighty Ducks of Anaheim for C Alex Hicks and D Fredrik Olausson (November 19, 1996). ... Traded by Mighty Ducks to Detroit Red Wings for D Jamie Pushor and fourth-round pick (C Viktor Wallin) in 1998 draft (March 24, 1998). ... Signed as free agent by Washington Capitals (July 14, 1998). ... Strained back (February 7, 1999); missed remainder of season. ... Bruised tailbone (February 23, 2000); missed four games. ... Suffered from the flu (April 1, 2000); missed one game.

HONORS: Played in NHL All-Star Game (1998).

MISCELLANEOUS: Member of Stanley Cup championship team (1998). ... Member of gold-medal-winning Unified Olympic team (1992). ... Member of silver-medal-winning Russian Olympic team (1998).

Season Team	League	REGULAR SEASON								PLAYOFFS				
		Gms.	G	A	Pts.	PIM	+/-	PP	SH	Gms.	G	A	Pts.	PIM
85-86—CSKA Moscow............	USSR	9	0	1	1	8	...	...	...	—	—	—	—	—
86-87—CSKA Moscow............	USSR	20	1	3	4	10	...	...	...	—	—	—	—	—
87-88—Soviet Wings	USSR	44	12	6	18	30	...	...	...	—	—	—	—	—
88-89—Soviet Wings	USSR	44	5	6	11	44	...	...	...	—	—	—	—	—
89-90—Soviet Wings	USSR	45	4	11	15	34	...	...	...	—	—	—	—	—
90-91—Soviet Wings	USSR	45	16	12	28	22	...	...	...	—	—	—	—	—
91-92—Soviet Wings	USSR	35	15	16	31	62	...	...	...	—	—	—	—	—
—Unif. Olympic team......	Int'l	8	3	1	4	4	...	...	...	—	—	—	—	—
—Toronto	NHL	7	1	0	1	0	-4	0	0	—	—	—	—	—
92-93—Toronto	NHL	59	7	24	31	40	-1	4	0	14	1	2	3	2
93-94—Toronto	NHL	76	9	27	36	78	5	3	0	18	6	9	15	6
94-95—Toronto	NHL	33	5	12	17	28	6	2	0	6	2	1	3	2
95-96—Pittsburgh.................	NHL	72	3	31	34	88	19	1	0	15	0	1	1	10
96-97—Pittsburgh.................	NHL	15	1	5	6	24	-4	0	0	—	—	—	—	—
—Anaheim	NHL	62	12	34	46	77	20	3	1	11	1	10	11	10
97-98—Anaheim	NHL	66	6	30	36	115	-7	2	0	—	—	—	—	—
—Russian Oly. team.......	Int'l	6	0	3	3	0	...	...	...	—	—	—	—	—
—Detroit....................	NHL	11	2	5	7	4	0	1	0	7	0	3	3	14
98-99—Washington	NHL	46	2	14	16	80	-5	2	0	—	—	—	—	—
99-00—Washington	NHL	73	3	19	22	28	7	1	0	4	0	0	0	4
NHL Totals (9 years)...........		520	51	201	252	562	36	19	1	75	10	26	36	48

MITCHELL, WILLIE D DEVILS

PERSONAL: Born April 23, 1977, in Port McNeill, B.C. ... 6-3/205. ... Shoots left. ... Full Name: Willis Mitchell.

COLLEGE: Clarkson (N.Y.).

TRANSACTIONS/CAREER NOTES: Selected by New Jersey Devils in eighth round (12th Devils pick, 199th overall) of NHL entry draft (June 22, 1996).

HONORS: Named to NCAA All-America (East) second team (1998-99). ... Named to ECAC All-Star first team (1998-99).

Season Team	League	REGULAR SEASON								PLAYOFFS				
		Gms.	G	A	Pts.	PIM	+/-	PP	SH	Gms.	G	A	Pts.	PIM
95-96—Melfort......................	Jr. A	19	2	6	8	0	...	...	...	14	0	2	2	12
96-97—Melfort......................	Jr. A	64	14	42	56	227	...	...	...	4	0	1	1	23
97-98—Clarkson	ECAC	34	9	17	26	105	...	...	...	—	—	—	—	—
98-99—Clarkson	ECAC	34	10	19	29	40	...	...	...	—	—	—	—	—
—Albany......................	AHL	6	1	3	4	29	...	...	...	—	—	—	—	—
99-00—Albany......................	AHL	63	5	14	19	71	...	...	...	5	1	2	3	4
—New Jersey................	NHL	2	0	0	0	0	1	0	0	—	—	—	—	—
NHL Totals (1 year).............		2	0	0	0	0	1	0	0					

M

MODANO, MIKE   C   STARS

PERSONAL: Born June 7, 1970, in Livonia, Mich. ... 6-3/205. ... Shoots left. ... Full Name: Michael Modano. ... Name pronounced muh-DAH-noh.
TRANSACTIONS/CAREER NOTES: Selected by Minnesota North Stars in first round (first North Stars pick, first overall) of NHL entry draft (June 11, 1988). ... Fractured left wrist (January 24, 1989). ... Fractured nose (March 4, 1990). ... Pulled groin (November 30, 1992); missed two games. ... North Stars franchise moved from Minnesota to Dallas and renamed Stars for 1993-94 season. ... Strained medial collateral ligament in knee (January 6, 1994); missed six games. ... Suffered concussion (February 26, 1994); missed two games. ... Bruised ankle (March 12, 1995); missed four games. ... Ruptured tendons in ankle (April 4, 1995) and underwent surgery; missed remainder of season. ... Injured stomach muscle (November 9, 1995); missed four games. ... Suffered from the flu (February 9, 1997); missed one game. ... Bruised ankle (November 12, 1997); missed one game. ... Tore medial collateral ligament in knee (December 5, 1997); missed 10 games. ... Reinjured knee (January 2, 1998); missed two games. ... Separated shoulder (March 13, 1998); missed 17 games. ... Strained groin (March 31, 1999); missed four games. ... Strained ligaments in neck, suffered concussion and fractured nose (October 2, 1999); missed three games. ... Suffered concussion (January 12, 2000); missed one game. ... Strained hip flexor (March 28, 2000); missed one game.
HONORS: Named to WHL (East) All-Star first team (1988-89). ... Named to NHL All-Rookie team (1989-90). ... Played in NHL All-Star Game (1993 and 1998-2000). ... Named to play in NHL All-Star Game (1997); replaced by LW Keith Tkachuk due to injury. ... Named to NHL All-Star second team (1999-2000).
MISCELLANEOUS: Member of Stanley Cup championship team (1999). ... Holds Dallas Stars franchise all-time record for most goals (349). ... Failed to score on a penalty shot (vs. Tyler Moss, December 7, 1998).
STATISTICAL PLATEAUS: Three-goal games: 1989-90 (1), 1993-94 (1), 1997-98 (1), 1998-99 (3). Total: 6. ... Four-goal games: 1995-96 (1). ... Total hat tricks: 7.
STATISTICAL NOTES: Tied for NHL lead with three game-tying goals (1999-2000).

Season Team	League	REGULAR SEASON								PLAYOFFS				
		Gms.	G	A	Pts.	PIM	+/-	PP	SH	Gms.	G	A	Pts.	PIM
86-87—Prince Albert	WHL	70	32	30	62	96	...	...	...	8	1	4	5	4
87-88—Prince Albert	WHL	65	47	80	127	80	...	...	...	9	7	11	18	18
88-89—Prince Albert	WHL	41	39	66	105	74	...	...	...	—	—	—	—	—
—Minnesota	NHL	—	—	—	—	—	—	—	—	2	0	0	0	0
89-90—Minnesota	NHL	80	29	46	75	63	-7	12	0	7	1	1	2	12
90-91—Minnesota	NHL	79	28	36	64	61	2	9	0	23	8	12	20	16
91-92—Minnesota	NHL	76	33	44	77	46	-9	5	0	7	3	2	5	4
92-93—Minnesota	NHL	82	33	60	93	83	-7	9	0	—	—	—	—	—
93-94—Dallas	NHL	76	50	43	93	54	-8	18	0	9	7	3	10	16
94-95—Dallas	NHL	30	12	17	29	8	7	4	1	—	—	—	—	—
95-96—Dallas	NHL	78	36	45	81	63	-12	8	4	—	—	—	—	—
96-97—Dallas	NHL	80	35	48	83	42	43	9	5	7	4	1	5	0
97-98—Dallas	NHL	52	21	38	59	32	25	7	5	17	4	10	14	12
—U.S. Olympic team	Int'l	4	2	0	2	0	...	...	...	—	—	—	—	—
98-99—Dallas	NHL	77	34	47	81	44	29	6	4	23	5	*18	23	16
99-00—Dallas	NHL	77	38	43	81	48	0	11	1	23	10	†13	23	10
NHL Totals (12 years)		787	349	467	816	544	63	98	20	118	42	60	102	86

MODIN, FREDRIK   LW   LIGHTNING

PERSONAL: Born October 8, 1974, in Sundsvall, Sweden. ... 6-4/220. ... Shoots left. ... Name pronounced moh-DEEN.
TRANSACTIONS/CAREER NOTES: Selected by Toronto Maple Leafs in third round (third Maple Leafs pick, 64th overall) of NHL entry draft (June 29, 1994). ... Suffered concussion (October 22, 1996); missed three games. ... Suffered from the flu (March 10, 1997); missed one game. ... Strained groin (December 2, 1997); missed two games. ... Fractured collar bone (February 13, 1999); missed 15 games. ... Traded by Maple Leafs to Tampa Bay Lightning for D Cory Cross and seventh-round pick in 2001 draft (October 1, 1999).

Season Team	League	REGULAR SEASON								PLAYOFFS				
		Gms.	G	A	Pts.	PIM	+/-	PP	SH	Gms.	G	A	Pts.	PIM
91-92—Sundsvall Timra	Sweden Dv. 2	11	1	0	1	0	...	...	...	—	—	—	—	—
92-93—Sundsvall Timra	Sweden Dv. 2	30	5	7	12	12	...	...	...	—	—	—	—	—
93-94—Sundsvall Timra	Sweden Dv. 2	30	16	15	31	36	...	...	...	—	—	—	—	—
94-95—Brynas Gavle	Sweden	38	9	10	19	33	...	...	...	14	4	4	8	6
95-96—Brynas Gavle	Sweden	22	4	8	12	22	...	...	...	—	—	—	—	—
96-97—Toronto	NHL	76	6	7	13	24	-14	0	0	—	—	—	—	—
97-98—Toronto	NHL	74	16	16	32	32	-5	1	0	—	—	—	—	—
98-99—Toronto	NHL	67	16	15	31	35	14	1	0	8	0	0	0	6
99-00—Tampa Bay	NHL	80	22	26	48	18	-26	3	0	—	—	—	—	—
NHL Totals (4 years)		297	60	64	124	109	-31	5	0	8	0	0	0	6

MODRY, JAROSLAV   D   KINGS

PERSONAL: Born February 27, 1971, in Ceske-Budejovice, Czechoslovakia. ... 6-2/219. ... Shoots left. ... Name pronounced MOH-dree.
TRANSACTIONS/CAREER NOTES: Selected by New Jersey Devils in ninth round (10th Devils pick, 179th overall) of NHL entry draft (June 16, 1990). ... Played in Europe during 1994-95 NHL lockout. ... Injured ankle (January 31, 1995); missed two games. ... Reinjured ankle (February 18, 1995); missed three games. ... Traded by Devils to Ottawa Senators for fourth-round pick (C Alyn McCauley) in 1995 draft (July 8, 1995). ... Ruptured eardrum (December 27, 1995). ... Traded by Senators to Los Angeles Kings for RW Kevin Brown (March 20, 1996). ... Sprained left knee (January 14, 1997); missed one game.

Season Team	League	REGULAR SEASON								PLAYOFFS				
		Gms.	G	A	Pts.	PIM	+/-	PP	SH	Gms.	G	A	Pts.	PIM
88-89—Budejovice	Czech.	28	0	1	1	...	...	...	...	—	—	—	—	—
89-90—Budejovice	Czech.	41	2	2	4	...	...	...	...	—	—	—	—	—
90-91—Dukla Trencin	Czech.	33	1	9	10	6	...	...	...	—	—	—	—	—
91-92—Dukla Trencin	Czech.	18	0	4	4	...	...	...	...	—	—	—	—	—
—Budejovice	Czech Dv.II	14	4	10	14	...	...	...	...	—	—	—	—	—
92-93—Utica	AHL	80	7	35	42	62	...	...	...	5	0	2	2	2

M

Season Team	League	REGULAR SEASON								PLAYOFFS				
		Gms.	G	A	Pts.	PIM	+/-	PP	SH	Gms.	G	A	Pts.	PIM
93-94—New Jersey	NHL	41	2	15	17	18	10	2	0	—	—	—	—	—
—Albany	AHL	19	1	5	6	25	...	...	...	—	—	—	—	—
94-95—HC Ceske Budejovice..	Czech Rep.	19	1	3	4	30	...	...	...	—	—	—	—	—
—New Jersey	NHL	11	0	0	0	0	-1	0	0	—	—	—	—	—
—Albany	AHL	18	5	6	11	14	...	...	...	14	3	3	6	4
95-96—Ottawa	NHL	64	4	14	18	38	-17	1	0	—	—	—	—	—
—Los Angeles	NHL	9	0	3	3	6	-4	0	0	—	—	—	—	—
96-97—Los Angeles	NHL	30	3	3	6	25	-13	1	1	—	—	—	—	—
—Phoenix	IHL	23	3	12	15	17	...	...	...	—	—	—	—	—
—Utah	IHL	11	1	4	5	20	...	...	...	7	0	1	1	6
97-98—Utah	IHL	74	12	21	33	72	...	...	...	4	0	2	2	6
98-99—Long Beach	IHL	64	6	29	35	44	...	...	...	8	4	2	6	4
—Los Angeles	NHL	5	0	1	1	0	1	0	0	—	—	—	—	—
99-00—Los Angeles	NHL	26	5	4	9	18	-2	5	0	2	0	0	0	2
—Long Beach	IHL	11	2	4	6	8	...	...	...	—	—	—	—	—
NHL Totals (6 years)		186	14	40	54	105	-26	9	1	2	0	0	0	2

MOGILNY, ALEXANDER — RW — DEVILS

PERSONAL: Born February 18, 1969, in Khabarovsk, U.S.S.R. ... 5-11/200. ... Shoots left. ... Name pronounced moh-GIHL-nee.

TRANSACTIONS/CAREER NOTES: Selected by Buffalo Sabres in fifth round (fourth Sabres pick, 89th overall) of NHL entry draft (June 11, 1988). ... Suffered from the flu (November 26, 1989). ... Missed games due to fear of flying (January 22, 1990); spent remainder of season traveling on ground. ... Separated shoulder (February 8, 1991); missed six games. ... Suffered from the flu (November 1991); missed two games. ... Suffered from the flu (December 18, 1991); missed one game. ... Bruised shoulder (October 10, 1992); missed six games. ... Fractured fibula and tore ankle ligaments (May 6, 1993); missed remainder of 1992-93 playoffs and first nine games of 1993-94 season. ... Suffered sore ankle (February 2, 1994); missed four games. ... Suffered inflamed tendon in ankle (February 15, 1994); missed four games. ... Played in Europe during 1994-95 NHL lockout. ... Pinched nerve in neck (April 9, 1995); missed three games. ... Traded by Sabres with fifth-round pick (LW Todd Norman) in 1995 draft to Vancouver Canucks for RW Mike Peca, D Mike Wilson and first-round pick (D Jay McKee) in 1995 draft (July 8, 1995). ... Pulled hamstring (October 28, 1995); missed three games. ... Suffered from the flu (December 3, 1996); missed two games. ... Strained groin (April 4, 1997); missed remainder of season. ... Missed first 16 games of 1997-98 season due to contract dispute. ... Injured groin (December 15, 1997); missed 11 games. ... Strained back (February 24, 1998); missed four games. ... Sprained medial collateral ligament in knee (November 21, 1998); missed 17 games. ... Bruised kidney (January 4, 1999); missed two games. ... Strained abdominal muscle (February 20, 1999); missed four games. ... Injured back (November 26, 1999); missed eight games. ... Injured hip (January 12, 2000); missed seven games. ... Injured shoulder (February 12, 2000); missed eight games. ... Traded by Canucks to New Jersey Devils for C Brendan Morrison and C Denis Pederson (March 14, 2000).

HONORS: Played in NHL All-Star Game (1992-1994 and 1996). ... Named to THE SPORTING NEWS All-Star second team (1992-93). ... Named to NHL All-Star second team (1992-93 and 1995-96).

RECORDS: Shares NHL record for fastest goal from start of a game—5 seconds (December 21, 1991).

STATISTICAL PLATEAUS: Three-goal games: 1990-91 (1), 1991-92 (1), 1992-93 (5), 1993-94 (1), 1995-96 (3), 1996-97 (1). Total: 12. ... Four-goal games: 1992-93 (2). ... Total hat tricks: 14.

MISCELLANEOUS: Member of Stanley Cup championship team (2000). ... Member of gold-medal-winning U.S.S.R. Olympic team (1988). ... Captain of Buffalo Sabres (1993-94 and 1994-95). ... Scored on a penalty shot (vs. Chris Osgood, December 1, 1997). ... Failed to score on a penalty shot (vs. Bill Ranford, January 10, 1992; vs. Robb Stauber, December 17, 1993).

STATISTICAL NOTES: Led NHL with 11 game-winning goals (1992-93).

Season Team	League	REGULAR SEASON								PLAYOFFS				
		Gms.	G	A	Pts.	PIM	+/-	PP	SH	Gms.	G	A	Pts.	PIM
86-87—CSKA Moscow	USSR	28	15	1	16	4	...	...	...	—	—	—	—	—
87-88—CSKA Moscow	USSR	39	12	8	20	20	...	...	...	—	—	—	—	—
88-89—CSKA Moscow	USSR	31	11	11	22	24	...	...	...	—	—	—	—	—
89-90—Buffalo	NHL	65	15	28	43	16	8	4	0	4	0	1	1	2
90-91—Buffalo	NHL	62	30	34	64	16	14	3	3	6	0	6	6	2
91-92—Buffalo	NHL	67	39	45	84	73	7	15	0	2	0	2	2	0
92-93—Buffalo	NHL	77	†76	51	127	40	7	27	0	7	7	3	10	6
93-94—Buffalo	NHL	66	32	47	79	22	8	17	0	7	4	2	6	6
94-95—Spartak Moscow	CIS	1	0	1	1	0	...	...	...	—	—	—	—	—
—Buffalo	NHL	44	19	28	47	36	0	12	0	5	3	2	5	2
95-96—Vancouver	NHL	79	55	52	107	16	14	10	5	6	1	8	9	8
96-97—Vancouver	NHL	76	31	42	73	18	9	7	1	—	—	—	—	—
97-98—Vancouver	NHL	51	18	27	45	36	-6	5	4	—	—	—	—	—
98-99—Vancouver	NHL	59	14	31	45	58	0	3	2	—	—	—	—	—
99-00—Vancouver	NHL	47	21	17	38	16	7	3	1	—	—	—	—	—
—New Jersey	NHL	12	3	3	6	4	-4	2	0	23	4	3	7	4
NHL Totals (11 years)		705	353	405	758	351	64	108	16	60	19	27	46	30

MOORE, BARRIE — LW

PERSONAL: Born May 22, 1975, in London, Ont. ... 5-11/198. ... Shoots left.

HIGH SCHOOL: Lo-Ellen Park Secondary School (Sudbury, Ont.).

TRANSACTIONS/CAREER NOTES: Selected by Buffalo Sabres in eighth round (sixth Sabres pick, 194th overall) of NHL entry draft (June 26, 1993). ... Traded by Sabres with D Craig Millar to Edmonton Oilers for F Miroslav Satan (March 18, 1997). ... Traded by Oilers to Wahington Capitals for LW Brad Church (February 3, 1999). ... Selected by Columbus Blue Jackets in NHL expansion draft (June 23, 2000).

Season Team	League	REGULAR SEASON								PLAYOFFS				
		Gms.	G	A	Pts.	PIM	+/-	PP	SH	Gms.	G	A	Pts.	PIM
90-91—Strathroy Jr. B	OHA	19	9	10	19	30	...	...	...	—	—	—	—	—
91-92—Sudbury	OHL	62	15	38	53	57	...	...	...	11	0	7	7	12
92-93—Sudbury	OHL	57	13	26	39	71	...	...	...	14	4	3	7	19
93-94—Sudbury	OHL	65	36	49	85	69	...	...	...	10	3	5	8	14
94-95—Sudbury	OHL	60	47	42	89	67	...	...	...	18	15	14	29	24

Season Team	League	REGULAR SEASON								PLAYOFFS				
		Gms.	G	A	Pts.	PIM	+/-	PP	SH	Gms.	G	A	Pts.	PIM
95-96—Rochester	AHL	64	26	29	55	40	...	...	...	18	3	6	9	18
—Buffalo	NHL	3	0	0	0	0	0	0	0	—	—	—	—	—
96-97—Rochester	AHL	32	14	15	29	14	...	...	...	—	—	—	—	—
—Buffalo	NHL	31	2	6	8	18	1	1	0	—	—	—	—	—
—Hamilton	AHL	9	5	2	7	0	...	...	...	22	2	6	8	15
—Edmonton	NHL	4	0	0	0	0	0	0	0	—	—	—	—	—
97-98—Hamilton	AHL	70	22	29	51	64	...	...	...	8	0	1	1	4
98-99—Indianapolis	IHL	43	9	10	19	18	...	...	...	—	—	—	—	—
—Portland	AHL	23	3	7	10	4	...	...	...	—	—	—	—	—
99-00—Portland	AHL	80	18	33	51	50	...	...	...	4	0	0	0	6
—Washington	NHL	1	0	0	0	0	0	0	0	—	—	—	—	—
NHL Totals (3 years)		39	2	6	8	18	1	1	0					

MORAN, BRAD   C   BLUE JACKETS

PERSONAL: Born March 20, 1979, in Abbotsford, B.C. ... 5-11/180. ... Shoots left.
TRANSACTIONS/CAREER NOTES: Selected by Buffalo Sabres in seventh round (eighth Sabres pick, 191st pick overall) of NHL entry draft (June 27, 1998). ... Signed as free agent by Columbus Blue Jackets (June 5, 2000).
HONORS: Named to WHL (East) All-Star first team (1998-99 and 1999-2000). ... Won Four Broncos Memorial Trophy (1999-2000). ... Won Bob Clarke Trophy (1999-2000). ... Named to Can.HL All-Star second team (1999-2000).

Season Team	League	REGULAR SEASON								PLAYOFFS				
		Gms.	G	A	Pts.	PIM	+/-	PP	SH	Gms.	G	A	Pts.	PIM
96-97—Calgary	WHL	72	30	36	66	61	...	...	...	—	—	—	—	—
97-98—Calgary	WHL	72	53	49	102	64	...	...	...	18	10	8	18	20
98-99—Calgary	WHL	71	60	58	118	96	...	...	...	21	17	†25	42	26
99-00—Calgary	WHL	72	48	*72	*120	84	...	...	...	13	7	15	22	18

MORAN, IAN   RW/D   PENGUINS

PERSONAL: Born August 24, 1972, in Cleveland. ... 6-0/206. ... Shoots right. ... Name pronounced muh-RAN.
HIGH SCHOOL: Belmont Hill (Mass.).
COLLEGE: Boston College.
TRANSACTIONS/CAREER NOTES: Underwent knee surgery (June 1988). ... Separated shoulder (March 1989). ... Selected by Pittsburgh Penguins in sixth round (fifth Penguins pick, 107th overall) of NHL entry draft (June 16, 1990). ... Bruised shoulder (November 22, 1995); missed nine games. ... Injured shoulder (February 21, 1996); missed one game. ... Underwent shoulder surgery (March 21, 1996); missed remainder of season. ... Injured back and neck (April 10, 1997); missed two games. ... Bruised kneecap and underwent surgery (September 30, 1997); missed 34 games. ... Suffered concussion (February 2, 1998); missed four games. ... Injured knee (March 21, 1998); missed five games. ... Injured ankle (October 26, 1998); missed five games. ... Reinjured ankle (November 7, 1998); missed nine games. ... Bruised ankle (January 5, 1999); missed two games. ... Bruised right testicle (February 5, 1999); missed three games. ... Injured ankle (April 3, 1999); missed one game. ... Fractured foot (December 2, 1999); missed two games. ... Suffered from the flu (January 2, 2000); missed one game. ... Bruised ankle (April 7, 2000); missed final game of season.
HONORS: Named Hockey East co-Rookie of the Year with Craig Darby (1991-92). ... Named to Hockey East All-Rookie team (1991-92).

Season Team	League	REGULAR SEASON								PLAYOFFS				
		Gms.	G	A	Pts.	PIM	+/-	PP	SH	Gms.	G	A	Pts.	PIM
87-88—Belmont Hill	Mass. H.S.	25	3	13	16	15	...	...	...	—	—	—	—	—
88-89—Belmont Hill	Mass. H.S.	23	7	25	32	8	...	...	...	—	—	—	—	—
89-90—Belmont Hill	Mass. H.S.	...	10	36	46	0	...	...	...	—	—	—	—	—
90-91—Belmont Hill	Mass. H.S.	23	7	44	51	12	...	...	...	—	—	—	—	—
91-92—Boston College	Hockey East	30	2	16	18	44	...	...	...	—	—	—	—	—
92-93—Boston College	Hockey East	31	8	12	20	32	...	...	...	—	—	—	—	—
93-94—U.S. national team	Int'l	50	8	15	23	69	...	...	...	—	—	—	—	—
—Cleveland	IHL	33	5	13	18	39	...	...	...	—	—	—	—	—
94-95—Cleveland	IHL	64	7	31	38	94	...	...	...	4	0	1	1	2
—Pittsburgh	NHL	—								8	0	0	0	0
95-96—Pittsburgh	NHL	51	1	1	2	47	-1	0	0	—	—	—	—	—
96-97—Cleveland	IHL	36	6	23	29	26	...	...	...	—	—	—	—	—
—Pittsburgh	NHL	36	4	5	9	22	-11	0	0	5	1	2	3	4
97-98—Pittsburgh	NHL	37	1	6	7	19	0	0	0	6	0	0	0	2
98-99—Pittsburgh	NHL	62	4	5	9	37	1	0	1	13	0	2	2	8
99-00—Pittsburgh	NHL	73	4	8	12	28	-10	0	0	11	0	1	1	2
NHL Totals (6 years)		259	14	25	39	153	-21	0	1	43	1	5	6	16

MORAVEC, DAVID   RW   SABRES

PERSONAL: Born March 24, 1973, in Czech Republic. ... 6-0/180. ... Shoots left.
TRANSACTIONS/CAREER NOTES: Selected by Buffalo Sabres in eighth round (ninth Sabres pick, 218th overall) of NHL entry draft (June 27, 1998).

Season Team	League	REGULAR SEASON								PLAYOFFS				
		Gms.	G	A	Pts.	PIM	+/-	PP	SH	Gms.	G	A	Pts.	PIM
96-97—HC Vitkovice	Czech Rep.	52	18	22	40	30	...	...	...	9	6	3	9	0
97-98—HC Vitkovice	Czech Rep.	51	38	26	64	28	...	...	...	11	6	9	15	8
98-99—HC Vitkovice	Czech Rep.	50	21	22	43	44	...	...	...	4	1	1	2	...
99-00—Buffalo	NHL	1	0	0	0	0	-1	0	0	—	—	—	—	—
—HC Vitkovice	Czech Rep.	38	11	18	29	34	...	...	...	—	—	—	—	—
NHL Totals (1 year)		1	0	0	0	0	-1	0	0					

MOREAU, ETHAN   LW   OILERS

PERSONAL: Born September 22, 1975, in Orillia, Ont. ... 6-2/205. ... Shoots left. ... Name pronounced MOHR-oh.
TRANSACTIONS/CAREER NOTES: Selected by Chicago Blackhawks in first round (first Blackhawks pick, 14th overall) of NHL entry draft (June 28, 1994). ... Fractured knuckle (November 16, 1997); missed seven games. ... Fractured ankle (December 14, 1997); missed 20 games. ... Traded by Blackhawks with LW Daniel Cleary, C Chad Kilger and D Christian Laflamme to Edmonton Oilers for D Boris Mironov, LW Dean McAmmond and D Jonas Elofsson (March 20, 1999). ... Injured ribs (November 24, 1999); missed eight games. ... Suffered from the flu (December 27, 1999); missed one game.
HONORS: Won Bobby Smith Trophy (1993-94).

		REGULAR SEASON								PLAYOFFS				
Season Team	League	Gms.	G	A	Pts.	PIM	+/-	PP	SH	Gms.	G	A	Pts.	PIM
90-91—Orillia	OHA	42	17	22	39	26	...	...	...	—	—	—	—	—
91-92—Niagara Falls	OHL	62	20	35	55	39	...	...	...	17	4	6	10	4
92-93—Niagara Falls	OHL	65	32	41	73	69	...	...	...	4	0	3	3	4
93-94—Niagara Falls	OHL	59	44	54	98	100	...	...	...	—	—	—	—	—
94-95—Niagara Falls	OHL	39	25	41	66	69	...	...	...	—	—	—	—	—
—Sudbury	OHL	23	13	17	30	22	...	...	...	18	6	12	18	26
95-96—Indianapolis	IHL	71	21	20	41	126	...	...	...	5	4	0	4	8
—Chicago	NHL	8	0	1	1	4	1	0	0	—	—	—	—	—
96-97—Chicago	NHL	82	15	16	31	123	13	0	0	6	1	0	1	9
97-98—Chicago	NHL	54	9	9	18	73	0	2	0	—	—	—	—	—
98-99—Chicago	NHL	66	9	6	15	84	-5	0	0	—	—	—	—	—
—Edmonton	NHL	14	1	5	6	8	2	0	0	4	0	3	3	6
99-00—Edmonton	NHL	73	17	10	27	62	8	1	0	5	0	1	1	0
NHL Totals (5 years)		297	51	47	98	354	19	3	0	15	1	4	5	15

MORISSETTE, DAVE   LW

PERSONAL: Born December 24, 1971, in Baie Comeau, Que. ... 6-1/218. ... Shoots left.
TRANSACTIONS/CAREER NOTES: Selected by Washington Capitals in seventh round (seventh Capitals pick, 146th overall) of NHL entry draft (June 21, 1991). ... Signed as free agent by Montreal Canadiens (October 6, 1998). ... Injured eye (October 19, 1998); missed two games.

		REGULAR SEASON								PLAYOFFS				
Season Team	League	Gms.	G	A	Pts.	PIM	+/-	PP	SH	Gms.	G	A	Pts.	PIM
88-89—Shawinigan	QMJHL	66	4	11	15	298	...	...	...	9	0	1	1	43
89-90—Shawinigan	QMJHL	66	2	9	11	269	...	...	...	—	—	—	—	—
90-91—Shawinigan	QMJHL	64	20	26	46	224	...	...	...	6	1	1	2	17
91-92—Hampton Roads	ECHL	47	6	10	16	293	...	...	...	13	1	3	4	74
—Baltimore	AHL	2	0	0	0	6	...	...	...	—	—	—	—	—
92-93—Hampton Roads	ECHL	54	9	13	22	226	...	...	...	2	0	0	0	2
93-94—Roanoke	ECHL	45	8	10	18	278	...	...	...	2	0	1	1	4
94-95—Minnesota	IHL	50	1	4	5	174	...	...	...	—	—	—	—	—
95-96—Minnesota	IHL	33	3	2	5	104	...	...	...	—	—	—	—	—
96-97—Houston	IHL	59	2	1	3	214	...	...	...	2	0	0	0	0
97-98—Houston	IHL	67	4	4	8	254	...	...	...	2	0	0	0	2
98-99—Montreal	NHL	10	0	0	0	52	1	0	0	—	—	—	—	—
—Fredericton	AHL	39	4	4	8	152	...	...	...	12	1	0	1	31
99-00—Quebec	AHL	47	2	4	6	231	...	...	...	2	0	0	0	0
—Montreal	NHL	1	0	0	0	5	0	0	0	—	—	—	—	—
NHL Totals (2 years)		11	0	0	0	57	1	0	0					

MORO, MARC   D   PREDATORS

PERSONAL: Born July 17, 1977, in Toronto. ... 6-1/215. ... Shoots left. ... Name pronounced muh-ROH.
HIGH SCHOOL: Loyalist C & VI (Kingston, Ont.).
TRANSACTIONS/CAREER NOTES: Selected by Ottawa Senators in second round (second Senators pick, 27th overall) of NHL entry draft (July 8, 1995). ... Rights traded by Senators with C Ted Drury to Mighty Ducks of Anaheim for C Shaun Van Allen and D Jason York (October 1, 1996). ... Traded by Mighty Ducks with G Chris Mason to Nashville Predators for G Dominic Roussel (October 5, 1998). ... Suffered injury (March 29, 2000); missed final four games of season.

		REGULAR SEASON								PLAYOFFS				
Season Team	League	Gms.	G	A	Pts.	PIM	+/-	PP	SH	Gms.	G	A	Pts.	PIM
92-93—Mississauga	Jr. A	2	0	0	0	0	...	...	...	—	—	—	—	—
93-94—Kingston	Tier II Jr. A	12	0	2	2	20	...	...	...	—	—	—	—	—
—Kingston	OHL	43	0	3	3	81	...	...	...	—	—	—	—	—
94-95—Kingston	OHL	64	4	12	16	255	...	...	...	6	0	0	0	23
95-96—Kingston	OHL	66	4	17	21	261	...	...	...	6	0	0	0	12
—Prin. Edward Island	AHL	2	0	0	0	7	...	...	...	2	0	0	0	4
96-97—Kingston	OHL	37	4	8	12	97	...	...	...	—	—	—	—	—
—Sault Ste. Marie	OHL	63	4	13	17	171	...	...	...	11	1	6	7	38
97-98—Cincinnati	AHL	74	1	6	7	181	...	...	...	—	—	—	—	—
—Anaheim	NHL	1	0	0	0	0	0	0	0	—	—	—	—	—
98-99—Milwaukee	IHL	80	0	5	5	264	...	...	,	2	0	0	0	4
99-00—Milwaukee	IHL	64	5	5	10	203	...	...	...	—	—	—	—	—
—Nashville	NHL	8	0	0	0	40	-3	0	0	—	—	—	—	—
NHL Totals (2 years)		9	0	0	0	40	-3	0	0					

MOROZOV, ALEXEI — RW — PENGUINS

PERSONAL: Born February 16, 1977, in Moscow, U.S.S.R. ... 6-1/196. ... Shoots left. ... Name pronounced muh-ROH-sahf.
TRANSACTIONS/CAREER NOTES: Selected by Pittsburgh Penguins in first round (first Penguins pick, 24th overall) of NHL entry draft (July 8, 1995). ... Fractured toe (December 27, 1997); missed one game. ... Suffered concussion (November 14, 1998); missed three games. ... Suffered concussion (December 21, 1998); missed 12 games. ... Suffered charley horse (October 30, 1999); missed eight games. ... Bruised back (January 25, 2000); missed two games. ... Suffered charley horse (March 16, 2000); missed four games.
MISCELLANEOUS: Member of silver-medal-winning Russian Olympic team (1998).
STATISTICAL PLATEAUS: Three-goal games: 1999-00 (1).

		REGULAR SEASON							PLAYOFFS				
Season Team	League	Gms.	G	A	Pts.	PIM	+/-	PP	SH	Gms.	G	A	Pts.	PIM
93-94—Soviet Wings	CIS	7	0	0	0	0	...	...	...	3	0	0	0	2
94-95—Soviet Wings	CIS	48	15	12	27	53	...	...	...	4	0	3	3	0
95-96—Soviet Wings	CIS	47	12	9	21	26	...	...	...	—	—	—	—	—
96-97—Kryla Sov. Moscow	Russian	44	21	11	32	32	...	...	...	2	0	1	1	2
97-98—Pittsburgh	NHL	76	13	13	26	8	-4	2	0	6	0	1	1	2
—Russian Oly. team	Int'l	6	2	2	4	0	...	...	...	—	—	—	—	—
98-99—Pittsburgh	NHL	67	9	10	19	14	5	0	0	10	1	1	2	0
99-00—Pittsburgh	NHL	68	12	19	31	14	12	0	1	5	0	0	0	0
NHL Totals (3 years)		211	34	42	76	36	13	2	1	21	1	2	3	2

MORRIS, DEREK — D — FLAMES

PERSONAL: Born August 24, 1978, in Edmonton. ... 5-11/200. ... Shoots right.
TRANSACTIONS/CAREER NOTES: Selected by Calgary Flames in first round (first Flames pick, 13th overall) of NHL entry draft (June 22, 1996). ... Separated shoulder (February 22, 1999); missed 10 games. ... Suffered concussion (December 14, 1999); missed three games.
HONORS: Named to Can.HL All-Star second team (1996-97). ... Named to WHL (East) All-Star first team (1996-97). ... Named to NHL All-Rookie team (1997-98).

		REGULAR SEASON							PLAYOFFS				
Season Team	League	Gms.	G	A	Pts.	PIM	+/-	PP	SH	Gms.	G	A	Pts.	PIM
95-96—Regina	WHL	67	8	44	52	70	...	...	...	11	1	7	8	26
96-97—Regina	WHL	67	18	57	75	180	...	...	...	5	0	3	3	9
—Saint John	AHL	7	0	3	3	7	...	...	...	5	0	3	3	7
97-98—Calgary	NHL	82	9	20	29	88	1	5	1	—	—	—	—	—
98-99—Calgary	NHL	71	7	27	34	73	4	3	0	—	—	—	—	—
99-00—Calgary	NHL	78	9	29	38	80	2	3	0	—	—	—	—	—
NHL Totals (3 years)		231	25	76	101	241	7	11	1					

MORRISON, BRENDAN — C — CANUCKS

PERSONAL: Born August 12, 1975, in Pitt Meadows, B.C. ... 5-11/190. ... Shoots left.
HIGH SCHOOL: Pitt Meadows (B.C.) Secondary.
COLLEGE: Michigan.
TRANSACTIONS/CAREER NOTES: Selected by New Jersey Devils in second round (third Devils pick, 39th overall) of NHL entry draft (June 26, 1993). ... Missed first nine games of 1999-2000 season due to contract dispute. ... Suffered injury (October 29, 1999); missed two games. ... Traded by Devils with C Denis Pederson to Vancouver Canucks for RW Alexander Mogilny (March 14, 2000).
HONORS: Won CCHA Rookie of the Year Award (1993-94). ... Named to CCHA All-Rookie team (1993-94). ... Named to NCAA All-America (West) first team (1994-95, 1995-96 and 1996-97). ... Named to CCHA All-Star first team (1994-95, 1995-96 and 1996-97). ... Named CCHA Player of the Year (1995-96 and 1996-97). ... Named NCAA Tournament Most Valuable Player (1995-96). ... Named to NCAA All-Tournament team (1995-96). ... Won Hobey Baker Memorial Award (1996-97). ... Named CCHA Tournament Most Valuable Player (1996-97).

		REGULAR SEASON							PLAYOFFS				
Season Team	League	Gms.	G	A	Pts.	PIM	+/-	PP	SH	Gms.	G	A	Pts.	PIM
92-93—Penticton	BCJHL	56	35	59	94	45	...	...	...	—	—	—	—	—
93-94—Univ. of Michigan	CCHA	38	20	28	48	24	...	...	...	—	—	—	—	—
94-95—Univ. of Michigan	CCHA	39	23	53	76	42	...	...	...	—	—	—	—	—
95-96—Univ. of Michigan	CCHA	35	28	44	72	41	...	...	...	—	—	—	—	—
96-97—Univ. of Michigan	CCHA	43	31	57	88	52	...	...	...	—	—	—	—	—
97-98—Albany	AHL	72	35	49	84	44	...	...	...	8	3	4	7	19
—New Jersey	NHL	11	5	4	9	0	3	0	0	3	0	1	1	0
98-99—New Jersey	NHL	76	13	33	46	18	-4	5	0	7	0	2	2	0
99-00—HC Pardubice	Czech Rep.	6	5	2	7	2	...	...	...	—	—	—	—	—
—New Jersey	NHL	44	5	21	26	8	8	2	0	—	—	—	—	—
—Vancouver	NHL	12	2	7	9	10	4	0	0	—	—	—	—	—
NHL Totals (3 years)		143	25	65	90	36	11	7	0	10	0	3	3	0

MORROW, BRENDEN — LW — STARS

PERSONAL: Born January 16, 1979, in Carlisle, Sask. ... 5-11/200. ... Shoots left.
TRANSACTIONS/CAREER NOTES: Selected by Dallas Stars in first round (first Stars pick, 25th overall) of NHL entry draft (June 21, 1997).
HONORS: Named to WHL (West) All-Star first team (1998-99).

		REGULAR SEASON							PLAYOFFS				
Season Team	League	Gms.	G	A	Pts.	PIM	+/-	PP	SH	Gms.	G	A	Pts.	PIM
95-96—Portland	WHL	65	13	12	25	61	...	...	...	7	0	0	0	8
96-97—Portland	WHL	71	39	49	88	178	...	...	...	6	2	1	3	4
97-98—Portland	WHL	68	34	52	86	184	...	...	...	16	10	8	18	65
98-99—Portland	WHL	61	41	44	85	248	...	...	...	4	0	4	4	18
99-00—Michigan	IHL	9	2	0	2	18	...	...	...	—	—	—	—	—
—Dallas	NHL	64	14	19	33	81	8	3	0	21	2	4	6	22
NHL Totals (1 year)		64	14	19	33	81	8	3	0	21	2	4	6	22

M

MOTTAU, MIKE — D — RANGERS

PERSONAL: Born March 19, 1978, in Quincy, Mass. ... 6-0/192. ... Shoots left.
COLLEGE: Boston College.
TRANSACTIONS/CAREER NOTES: Selected by New York Rangers in seventh round (10th pick, 182nd overall) of 1997 NHL entry draft.
HONORS: Named to NCAA All-America East second team (1997-98). ... Named to NCAA All-Tournament team (1997-98 and 1999-2000). ... Named to Hockey East All-Star first team (1997-98 and 1999-2000). ... Named to NCAA All-America (East) first team (1998-99 and 1999-2000). ... Named to Hockey East All-Star second team (1998-99). ... Won Hobey Baker Memorial Award (1999-2000).

| | | | REGULAR SEASON | | | | | | | | PLAYOFFS | | | |
Season Team	League	Gms.	G	A	Pts.	PIM	+/-	PP	SH		Gms.	G	A	Pts.	PIM
96-97—Boston College	Hockey Easta	38	5	18	23	77	...	...	...		—	—	—	—	—
97-98—Boston College	Hockey East	40	13	36	49	50	...	...	...		—	—	—	—	—
98-99—Boston College	Hockey East	43	3	39	42	44	...	...	...		—	—	—	—	—
99-00—Boston College	Hockey East	42	6	*37	43	57	...	...	...		—	—	—	—	—

MOWERS, MARK — C — PREDATORS

PERSONAL: Born February 16, 1974, in Whitesboro, N.Y. ... 5-11/184. ... Shoots right.
COLLEGE: New Hampshire.
TRANSACTIONS/CAREER NOTES: Signed as non-drafted free agent by Nashville (June 11, 1998). ... Injured knee (March 19, 2000); missed final nine games of season.
HONORS: Named to NCAA All-America (East) first team (1997-98). ... Named to Hockey East All-Star second team (1997-98). ... Won Ken McKenzie Trophy (1998-99).

| | | | REGULAR SEASON | | | | | | | | PLAYOFFS | | | |
Season Team	League	Gms.	G	A	Pts.	PIM	+/-	PP	SH		Gms.	G	A	Pts.	PIM
94-95 —Univ. of New Hamp.	Hockey East	36	13	23	36	16	...	...	...		—	—	—	—	—
95-96 —Univ. of New Hamp.	Hockey East	34	21	26	47	18	...	...	...		—	—	—	—	—
96-97 —Univ. of New Hamp.	Hockey East	39	26	32	58	52	...	...	...		—	—	—	—	—
97-98 —Univ. of New Hamp.	Hockey East	35	25	31	56	32	...	...	...		—	—	—	—	—
98-99 —Milwaukee	IHL	51	14	22	36	24	...	...	...		1	0	0	0	0
—Nashville	NHL	30	0	6	6	4	-4	0	0		—	—	—	—	—
99-00 —Milwaukee	IHL	23	11	15	26	34	...	...	...		—	—	—	—	—
—Nashville	NHL	41	4	5	9	10	0	0	0		—	—	—	—	—
NHL Totals (2 years)		71	4	11	15	14	-4	0	0						

MUCKALT, BILL — RW — ISLANDERS

PERSONAL: Born July 15, 1974, in Surrey, B.C. ... 6-1/200. ... Shoots right.
HIGH SCHOOL: Kelowna (B.C.) Christian.
COLLEGE: Michigan.
TRANSACTIONS/CAREER NOTES: Selected by Vancouver Canucks in ninth round (seventh Canucks pick, 221st overall) of NHL entry draft (June 29, 1994). ... Sprained ankle (March 27, 1999); missed final nine games of season. ... Traded by Canucks with G Kevin Weekes and C Dave Scatchard to New York Islanders for G Felix Potvin, second-(traded to Atlanta) and third-round (C Thatcher Bell) picks in 2000 draft (December 19, 1999). ... Separated left shoulder (January 13, 2000) and underwent surgery; missed remainder of season.
HONORS: Named to NCAA All-America (West) first team (1997-98). ... Named to CCHA All-Star first team (1997-98).

| | | | REGULAR SEASON | | | | | | | | PLAYOFFS | | | |
Season Team	League	Gms.	G	A	Pts.	PIM	+/-	PP	SH		Gms.	G	A	Pts.	PIM
91-92 —Merritt	BCJHL	55	14	11	25	75	...	...	...		—	—	—	—	—
92-93 —Merritt	BCJHL	59	31	43	74	80	...	...	...		5	5	2	7	11
93-94 —Merritt	BCJHL	43	58	51	109	99	...	...	...		—	—	—	—	—
—Kelowna	BCJHL	15	12	10	22	20	...	...	...		28	19	19	38	25
94-95 —Univ. of Michigan	CCHA	39	19	18	37	42	...	...	...		—	—	—	—	—
95-96 —Univ. of Michigan	CCHA	41	28	30	58	34	...	...	...		—	—	—	—	—
96-97 —Univ. of Michigan	CCHA	36	26	38	64	69	...	...	...		—	—	—	—	—
97-98 —Univ. of Michigan	CCHA	44	32	*33	*65	94	...	...	...		—	—	—	—	—
98-99 —Vancouver	NHL	73	16	20	36	98	-9	4	2		—	—	—	—	—
99-00 —Vancouver	NHL	33	4	8	12	17	6	1	0		—	—	—	—	—
—New York Islanders	NHL	12	4	3	7	4	5	0	0		—	—	—	—	—
NHL Totals (2 years)		118	24	31	55	119	2	5	2						

MUIR, BRYAN — D — LIGHTNING

PERSONAL: Born June 8, 1973, in Winnipeg. ... 6-4/220. ... Shoots left. ... Name pronounced MYOOR.
COLLEGE: New Hampshire.
TRANSACTIONS/CAREER NOTES: Signed as non-drafted free agent by Edmonton Oilers (April 30, 1996). ... Traded by Oilers with C Jason Arnott to New Jersey Devils for RW Bill Guerin and RW Valeri Zelepukin (January 4, 1998). ... Traded by Devils to Chicago Blackhawks for future considerations (November 13, 1998). ... Injured back (April 5, 1999); missed three games. ... Traded by Blackhawks with LW Reid Simpson to Tampa Bay Lightning for C Michael Nylander (November 12, 1999). ... Fractured ankle (November 17, 1999); missed 18 games. ... Injured ankle (March 12, 2000); missed 11 games.

| | | | REGULAR SEASON | | | | | | | | PLAYOFFS | | | |
Season Team	League	Gms.	G	A	Pts.	PIM	+/-	PP	SH		Gms.	G	A	Pts.	PIM
92-93 —Univ. of New Hamp.	Hockey East	26	1	2	3	24	...	...	...		—	—	—	—	—
93-94 —Univ. of New Hamp.	Hockey East	36	0	4	4	48	...	...	...		—	—	—	—	—
94-95 —Univ. of New Hamp.	Hockey East	28	9	9	18	48	...	...	...		—	—	—	—	—
95-96 —Canadian nat'l team	Int'l	42	6	12	18	36	...	...	...		—	—	—	—	—
—Edmonton	NHL	5	0	0	0	6	-4	0	0		—	—	—	—	—
96-97 —Hamilton	AHL	75	8	16	24	80	...	...	...		14	0	5	5	12
—Edmonton	NHL	—									5	0	0	0	4

M

Season Team	League	REGULAR SEASON								PLAYOFFS				
		Gms.	G	A	Pts.	PIM	+/-	PP	SH	Gms.	G	A	Pts.	PIM
97-98—Hamilton	AHL	28	3	10	13	62	...	...	...	—	—	—	—	—
—Edmonton	NHL	7	0	0	0	17	0	0	0	—	—	—	—	—
—Albany	AHL	41	3	10	13	67	...	...	...	13	3	0	3	12
98-99—New Jersey	NHL	1	0	0	0	0	0	0	0	—	—	—	—	—
—Albany	AHL	10	0	0	0	29	...	...	...	—	—	—	—	—
—Chicago	NHL	53	1	4	5	50	1	0	0	—	—	—	—	—
—Portland	AHL	2	1	1	2	2	...	...	...	—	—	—	—	—
99-00—Chicago	NHL	11	2	3	5	13	-1	0	1	—	—	—	—	—
—Tampa Bay	NHL	30	1	1	2	32	-8	0	0	—	—	—	—	—
NHL Totals (5 years)		107	4	8	12	118	-12	0	1	5	0	0	0	4

MULHERN, RYAN   RW   CAPITALS

PERSONAL: Born January 11, 1973, in Philadelphia, Pa. ... 6-1/202. ... Shoots right. ... Full Name: Ryan Patrick Mulhern.
HIGH SCHOOL: Malvern Prep (Pa.), then St. George's School (Newport, R.I.), then Canterbury (New Milford, Conn.).
COLLEGE: Brown.
TRANSACTIONS/CAREER NOTES: Selected by Calgary Flames in eighth round (eighth Flames pick, 174th overall) in NHL entry draft (June 6, 1994). ... Signed as free agent by Washington Capitals (March 17, 1997).
HONORS: Named to AHL All-Star first team (1997-98).

Season Team	League	REGULAR SEASON								PLAYOFFS				
		Gms.	G	A	Pts.	PIM	+/-	PP	SH	Gms.	G	A	Pts.	PIM
91-92—Canterbury School	Conn. H.S.	37	51	27	78	50	...	...	...	—	—	—	—	—
92-93—Brown University	ECAC	31	15	9	24	46	...	...	...	—	—	—	—	—
93-94—Brown University	ECAC	27	18	17	35	48	...	...	...	—	—	—	—	—
94-95—Brown University	ECAC	30	18	16	34	108	...	...	...	—	—	—	—	—
95-96—Brown University	ECAC	32	10	15	25	78	...	...	...	—	—	—	—	—
96-97—Hampton Roads	ECHL	40	22	16	38	52	...	...	...	—	—	—	—	—
—Portland	AHL	38	19	15	34	16	...	...	...	5	1	1	2	2
97-98—Portland	AHL	71	25	40	65	85	...	...	...	6	1	0	1	12
—Washington	NHL	3	0	0	0	0	0	0	0	—	—	—	—	—
98-99—Kansas City	IHL	59	7	11	18	82	...	...	...	—	—	—	—	—
—Las Vegas	IHL	23	9	6	15	8	...	...	...	—	—	—	—	—
99-00—Portland	AHL	73	20	16	36	61	...	...	...	3	0	0	0	6
NHL Totals (1 year)		3	0	0	0	0	0	0	0					

MULLER, KIRK   C   STARS

PERSONAL: Born February 8, 1966, in Kingston, Ont. ... 6-0/205. ... Shoots left. ... Name pronounced MUH-luhr.
TRANSACTIONS/CAREER NOTES: Selected by New Jersey Devils as underage junior in first round (first Devils pick, second overall) of NHL entry draft (June 9, 1984). ... Strained knee (January 13, 1986). ... Fractured ribs (April 1986). ... Traded by Devils with G Roland Melanson to Montreal Canadiens for RW Stephane Richer and RW Tom Chorske (September 1991). ... Injured eye (January 21, 1992); missed one game. ... Bruised ribs (November 7, 1992); missed one game. ... Sprained wrist (March 6, 1993); missed two games. ... Injured shoulder (October 11, 1993); missed eight games. ... Traded by Canadiens with D Mathieu Schneider and C Craig Darby to New York Islanders for C Pierre Turgeon and D Vladimir Malakhov (April 5, 1995). ... Traded by Islanders to Toronto Maple Leafs for LW Ken Belanger and G Damian Rhodes (January 23, 1996). ... Separated shoulder (January 3, 1997); missed two games. ... Bruised ankle (March 8, 1997); missed two games. ... Traded by Maple Leafs to Florida Panthers for RW Jason Podollan (March 18, 1997). ... Suspended two games and fined $1,000 by NHL for high-sticking incident (December 1, 1997). ... Sprained left knee (December 20, 1997); missed eight games. ... Signed as free agent by Dallas Stars (December 15, 1999). ... Suffered back spasms (March 28, 2000); missed one game.
HONORS: Won William Hanley Trophy (1982-83). ... Played in NHL All-Star Game (1985, 1986, 1988, 1990, 1992 and 1993).
MISCELLANEOUS: Member of Stanley Cup championship team (1993). ... Captain of New Jersey Devils (1987-88 through 1990-91). ... Captain of Montreal Canadiens (1994-95). ... Scored on a penalty shot (vs. Greg Millen, March 21, 1987). ... Failed to score on a penalty shot (vs. Mike Vernon, March 14, 1989).
STATISTICAL PLATEAUS: Three-goal games: 1986-87 (1), 1987-88 (3), 1991-92 (2), 1995-96 (1). Total: 7.

Season Team	League	REGULAR SEASON								PLAYOFFS				
		Gms.	G	A	Pts.	PIM	+/-	PP	SH	Gms.	G	A	Pts.	PIM
80-81—Kingston	OMJHL	2	0	0	0	0	...	...	...	—	—	—	—	—
81-82—Kingston	OHL	67	12	39	51	27	...	...	...	4	5	1	6	4
82-83—Guelph	OHL	66	52	60	112	41	...	...	...	—	—	—	—	—
83-84—Can. Olympic team	Int'l	15	2	2	4	6	...	...	...	—	—	—	—	—
—Canadian nat'l team	Int'l	15	2	2	4	6	...	...	...	—	—	—	—	—
—Guelph	OHL	49	31	63	94	27	...	...	...	—	—	—	—	—
84-85—New Jersey	NHL	80	17	37	54	69	-31	9	1	—	—	—	—	—
85-86—New Jersey	NHL	77	25	41	66	45	-19	5	1	—	—	—	—	—
86-87—New Jersey	NHL	79	26	50	76	75	-7	10	1	—	—	—	—	—
87-88—New Jersey	NHL	80	37	57	94	114	19	17	2	20	4	8	12	37
88-89—New Jersey	NHL	80	31	43	74	119	-23	12	1	—	—	—	—	—
89-90—New Jersey	NHL	80	30	56	86	74	-1	9	0	6	1	3	4	11
90-91—New Jersey	NHL	80	19	51	70	76	1	7	0	7	0	2	2	10
91-92—Montreal	NHL	78	36	41	77	86	15	15	1	11	4	3	7	31
92-93—Montreal	NHL	80	37	57	94	77	8	12	0	20	10	7	17	18
93-94—Montreal	NHL	76	23	34	57	96	-1	9	2	7	6	2	8	4
94-95—Montreal	NHL	33	8	11	19	33	-21	3	1	—	—	—	—	—
—New York Islanders	NHL	12	3	5	8	14	3	1	1	—	—	—	—	—
95-96—New York Islanders	NHL	15	4	3	7	15	-10	0	0	—	—	—	—	—
—Toronto	NHL	36	9	16	25	42	-3	7	0	6	3	2	5	0
96-97—Toronto	NHL	66	20	17	37	85	-23	9	1	—	—	—	—	—
—Florida	NHL	10	1	2	3	4	-2	1	0	5	1	2	3	4
97-98—Florida	NHL	70	8	21	29	54	-14	1	0	—	—	—	—	—
98-99—Florida	NHL	82	4	11	15	49	-11	0	0	—	—	—	—	—
99-00—Dallas	NHL	47	7	15	22	24	-3	3	0	23	2	3	5	18
NHL Totals (16 years)		1161	345	568	913	1151	-123	130	11	105	31	32	63	133

M

PERSONAL: Born March 23, 1967, in Willowdale, Ont. ... 6-3/195. ... Shoots right. ... Full Name: Gordon Murphy.

TRANSACTIONS/CAREER NOTES: Selected by Philadelphia Flyers as underage junior in ninth round (10th Flyers pick, 189th overall) of NHL entry draft (June 15, 1985). ... Injured left foot and suffered hip pointer (March 24, 1990). ... Traded with RW Brian Dobbin, third-round pick (LW Sergei Zholtok) in 1992 draft and fourth-round pick (D Charles Paquette) in 1993 draft to Boston Bruins for D Garry Galley, C Wes Walz and third-round pick (D Milos Holan) in 1993 draft (January 2, 1992). ... Injured ankle (January 1993); missed 16 games. ... Traded by Bruins to Dallas Stars for future considerations (June 20, 1993); Stars acquired G Andy Moog for G Jon Casey to complete deal (June 25, 1993). ... Selected by Florida Panthers in NHL expansion draft (June 24, 1993). ... Suffered illness (March 26, 1995); missed one game. ... Sprained left ankle (April 5, 1995); missed one game. ... Sprained right ankle (January 29, 1996); missed nine games. ... Injured toe (April 8, 1996); missed three games. ... Suffered from the flu (January 27, 1998); missed three games. ... Sprained neck (February 20, 1999); missed final 25 games of season. ... Traded by Panthers with C Herbert Vasiljevs, D Daniel Tjarnqvist and sixth-round pick (traded to Dallas) in 1999 draft to Atlanta Thrashers for G Trevor Kidd (June 25, 1999). ... Strained hip flexor (November 28, 1999); missed two games. ... Injured hip (February 7, 2000); missed four games. ... Dislocated shoulder (March 4, 2000); missed remainder of season.

HONORS: Named to Memorial Cup All-Star team (1986-87).

			REGULAR SEASON							PLAYOFFS				
Season Team	League	Gms.	G	A	Pts.	PIM	+/-	PP	SH		Gms.	G	A	Pts.	PIM
83-84—Don Mills Flyers	MTHL	65	24	42	66	130	...	...	...		—	—	—	—	—
84-85—Oshawa	OHL	59	3	12	15	25	...	...	...		—	—	—	—	—
85-86—Oshawa	OHL	64	7	15	22	56	...	...	...		6	1	1	2	6
86-87—Oshawa	OHL	56	7	30	37	95	...	...	...		24	6	16	22	22
87-88—Hershey	AHL	62	8	20	28	44	...	...	...		12	0	8	8	12
88-89—Philadelphia	NHL	75	4	31	35	68	-3	3	0		19	2	7	9	13
89-90—Philadelphia	NHL	75	14	27	41	95	-7	4	0		—	—	—	—	—
90-91—Philadelphia	NHL	80	11	31	42	58	-7	6	0		—	—	—	—	—
91-92—Philadelphia	NHL	31	2	8	10	33	-4	0	0		—	—	—	—	—
—Boston	NHL	42	3	6	9	51	2	0	0		15	1	0	1	12
92-93—Boston	NHL	49	5	12	17	62	-13	3	0		—	—	—	—	—
—Providence	AHL	2	1	3	4	2	...	...	...		—	—	—	—	—
93-94—Florida	NHL	84	14	29	43	71	-11	9	0		—	—	—	—	—
94-95—Florida	NHL	46	6	16	22	24	-14	5	0		—	—	—	—	—
95-96—Florida	NHL	70	8	22	30	30	5	4	0		14	0	4	4	6
96-97—Florida	NHL	80	8	15	23	51	3	2	0		5	0	5	5	4
97-98—Florida	NHL	79	6	11	17	46	-3	3	0		—	—	—	—	—
98-99—Florida	NHL	51	0	7	7	16	4	0	0		—	—	—	—	—
99-00—Atlanta	NHL	58	1	10	11	38	-26	0	0		—	—	—	—	—
NHL Totals (12 years)		**820**	**82**	**225**	**307**	**643**	**-74**	**39**	**0**		**53**	**3**	**16**	**19**	**35**

PERSONAL: Born October 17, 1967, in London, Ont. ... 6-0/190. ... Shoots left. ... Full Name: Joseph Patrick Murphy.

COLLEGE: Michigan State.

M

TRANSACTIONS/CAREER NOTES: Selected by Detroit Red Wings in first round (first Red Wings pick, first overall) of NHL entry draft (June 21, 1986). ... Sprained right ankle (January 1988). ... Traded by Red Wings with C/LW Adam Graves, LW Petr Klima and D Jeff Sharples to Edmonton Oilers for C Jimmy Carson, C Kevin McClelland and fifth-round pick (traded to Montreal Canadiens) in 1991 draft (November 2, 1989). ... Bruised both thighs (March 1990). ... Did not report to Oilers in 1992-93 season because of contract dispute; missed 63 games. ... Traded by Oilers to Chicago Blackhawks for D Igor Kravchuk and C Dean McAmmond (February 25, 1993). ... Pulled groin (February 3, 1995); missed three games. ... Reinjured groin (March 6, 1995); missed four games. ... Sprained knee (March 21, 1995); missed one game. ... Suspended 10 games by NHL for being third man in fight (September 20, 1995). ... Strained back (December 28, 1995); missed four games. ... Strained back (January 6, 1996). ... Signed as free agent by St. Louis Blues (July 3, 1996). ... Suffered from a virus (October 31, 1996); missed five games. ... Strained groin (January 30, 1997); missed one game. ... Tore ligament in left wrist (November 6, 1997); missed 42 games. ... Strained back (March 3, 1998); missed one game. ... Traded by Blues to San Jose Sharks for D Todd Gill (March 24, 1998). ... Suspended two games and fined $1,000 by NHL for slashing incident (March 31, 1998). ... Strained hamstring (October 22, 1998); missed three games. ... Reinjured hamstring (October 31, 1998); missed one game. ... Injured groin (January 15, 1999); missed two games. ... Signed as free agent by Boston Bruins (November 12, 1999). ... Injured knee (November 17, 1999); missed eight games. ... Strained abdominal muscle (January 19, 2000); missed one game. ... Claimed on waivers by Washington Capitals (February 10, 2000).

HONORS: Named BCJHL Rookie of the Year (1984-85). ... Named CCHA Rookie of the Year (1985-86).

MISCELLANEOUS: Member of Stanley Cup championship team (1990).

			REGULAR SEASON							PLAYOFFS				
Season Team	League	Gms.	G	A	Pts.	PIM	+/-	PP	SH		Gms.	G	A	Pts.	PIM
84-85—Penticton	BCJHL	51	68	84	*152	92	...	...	...		—	—	—	—	—
85-86—Michigan State	CCHA	35	24	37	61	50	...	...	...		—	—	—	—	—
—Canadian nat'l team	Int'l	8	3	3	6	2	...	...	...		—	—	—	—	—
86-87—Adirondack	AHL	71	21	38	59	61	...	...	...		10	2	1	3	33
—Detroit	NHL	5	0	1	1	2	0	0	0		—	—	—	—	—
87-88—Adirondack	AHL	6	5	6	11	4	...	...	...		—	—	—	—	—
—Detroit	NHL	50	10	9	19	37	-4	1	0		8	0	1	1	6
88-89—Detroit	NHL	26	1	7	8	28	-7	0	0		—	—	—	—	—
—Adirondack	AHL	47	31	35	66	66	...	...	...		16	6	11	17	17
89-90—Detroit	NHL	9	3	1	4	4	4	0	0		—	—	—	—	—
—Edmonton	NHL	62	7	18	25	56	1	2	0		22	6	8	14	16
90-91—Edmonton	NHL	80	27	35	62	35	2	4	1		15	2	5	7	14
91-92—Edmonton	NHL	80	35	47	82	52	17	10	2		16	8	16	24	12
92-93—Chicago	NHL	19	7	10	17	18	-3	5	0		4	0	0	0	8
93-94—Chicago	NHL	81	31	39	70	111	1	7	4		6	1	3	4	25
94-95—Chicago	NHL	40	23	18	41	89	7	7	0		16	9	3	12	29
95-96—Chicago	NHL	70	22	29	51	86	-3	8	0		10	6	3	8	33
96-97—St. Louis	NHL	75	20	25	45	69	-1	4	1		6	1	1	2	10
97-98—St. Louis	NHL	27	4	9	13	22	8	2	0		—	—	—	—	—
—San Jose	NHL	10	5	4	9	14	1	2	0		6	1	1	2	20
98-99—San Jose	NHL	76	25	23	48	73	10	7	0		6	0	3	3	4
99-00—Boston	NHL	26	7	7	14	41	-7	3	0		—	—	—	—	—
—Washington	NHL	29	5	8	13	53	8	1	0		5	0	0	0	8
NHL Totals (14 years)		**765**	**232**	**290**	**522**	**790**	**34**	**63**	**8**		**120**	**34**	**43**	**77**	**185**

MURPHY, LARRY   D   RED WINGS

PERSONAL: Born March 8, 1961, in Scarborough, Ont. ... 6-2/215. ... Shoots right. ... Full Name: Lawrence Thomas Murphy.
TRANSACTIONS/CAREER NOTES: Selected by Los Angeles Kings as underage junior in first round (first Kings pick, fourth overall) of NHL entry draft (June 11, 1980). ... Traded by Kings to Washington Capitals for D Brian Engblom and RW Ken Houston (October 18, 1983). ... Injured foot (October 29, 1985). ... Fractured ankle (May 1988). ... Traded by Capitals with RW Mike Gartner to Minnesota North Stars for RW Dino Ciccarelli and D Bob Rouse (March 7, 1989). ... Traded by North Stars with D Peter Taglianetti to Pittsburgh Penguins for D Jim Johnson and D Chris Dahlquist (December 11, 1990). ... Fractured right foot (February 22, 1991); played until March 5 then missed five games. ... Suffered back spasms (March 28, 1993); missed one game. ... Traded by Penguins to Toronto Maple Leafs for D Dmitri Mironov and second-round pick (traded to New Jersey) in 1996 draft (July 8, 1995). ... Traded by Maple Leafs to Detroit Red Wings for future considerations (March 18, 1997). ... Suffered concussion (February 1, 1999); missed one game.
HONORS: Won Max Kaminsky Trophy (1979-80). ... Named to OMJHL All-Star first team (1979-80). ... Named to Memorial Cup All-Star team (1979-80). ... Named to THE SPORTING NEWS All-Star second team (1986-87 and 1992-93). ... Named to NHL All-Star second team (1986-87, 1992-93 and 1994-95). ... Played in NHL All-Star Game (1994, 1996 and 1999).
RECORDS: Holds NHL rookie-season records for most points by a defenseman—76; and most assists by a defenseman—60 (1980-81).
MISCELLANEOUS: Member of Stanley Cup championship team (1991, 1992, 1997 and 1998).

		REGULAR SEASON								PLAYOFFS				
Season Team	League	Gms.	G	A	Pts.	PIM	+/-	PP	SH	Gms.	G	A	Pts.	PIM
78-79—Peterborough	OMJHL	66	6	21	27	82	...	...	...	19	1	9	10	42
79-80—Peterborough	OMJHL	68	21	68	89	88	...	...	...	14	4	13	17	20
80-81—Los Angeles	NHL	80	16	60	76	79	17	5	1	4	3	0	3	2
81-82—Los Angeles	NHL	79	22	44	66	95	-13	8	1	10	2	8	10	12
82-83—Los Angeles	NHL	77	14	48	62	81	2	9	0	—	—	—	—	—
83-84—Los Angeles	NHL	6	0	3	3	0	-4	0	0	—	—	—	—	—
—Washington	NHL	72	13	33	46	50	12	2	0	8	0	3	3	6
84-85—Washington	NHL	79	13	42	55	51	21	3	0	5	2	3	5	0
85-86—Washington	NHL	78	21	44	65	50	3	8	1	9	1	5	6	6
86-87—Washington	NHL	80	23	58	81	39	25	8	0	7	2	2	4	6
87-88—Washington	NHL	79	8	53	61	72	2	7	0	13	4	4	8	33
88-89—Washington	NHL	65	7	29	36	70	-5	3	0	—	—	—	—	—
—Minnesota	NHL	13	4	6	10	12	5	3	0	5	0	2	2	8
89-90—Minnesota	NHL	77	10	58	68	44	-13	4	0	7	1	2	3	31
90-91—Minnesota	NHL	31	4	11	15	38	-8	1	0	—	—	—	—	—
—Pittsburgh	NHL	44	5	23	28	30	2	2	0	23	5	18	23	44
91-92—Pittsburgh	NHL	77	21	56	77	48	33	7	2	21	6	10	16	19
92-93—Pittsburgh	NHL	83	22	63	85	73	45	6	2	12	2	11	13	10
93-94—Pittsburgh	NHL	84	17	56	73	44	10	7	0	6	0	5	5	0
94-95—Pittsburgh	NHL	48	13	25	38	18	12	4	0	12	2	13	15	0
95-96—Toronto	NHL	82	12	49	61	34	-2	8	0	6	0	2	2	4
96-97—Toronto	NHL	69	7	32	39	20	1	4	0	—	—	—	—	—
—Detroit	NHL	12	2	4	6	0	2	1	0	20	2	9	11	8
97-98—Detroit	NHL	82	11	41	52	37	35	2	1	22	3	12	15	2
98-99—Detroit	NHL	80	10	42	52	42	21	5	1	10	0	2	2	8
99-00—Detroit	NHL	81	10	30	40	45	4	7	0	9	2	3	5	2
NHL Totals (20 years)		1558	285	910	1195	1072	207	114	9	209	37	114	151	201

MURRAY, CHRIS   RW   BLUES

PERSONAL: Born October 25, 1974, in Port Hardy, B.C. ... 6-2/209. ... Shoots right.
TRANSACTIONS/CAREER NOTES: Selected by Montreal Canadiens in third round (third Canadiens pick, 54th overall) of NHL entry draft (June 29, 1994). ... Suspended three games without pay and fined $1,000 by NHL for cross-checking incident (April 3, 1996). ... Fractured hand (October 3, 1996); missed 10 games. ... Traded by Canadiens with D Murray Baron to Phoenix Coyotes for D Dave Manson (March 18, 1997). ... Traded by Coyotes to Hartford Whalers for D Gerald Diduck (March 18, 1997). ... Suffered from the flu (March 27, 1997); missed two games. ... Whalers franchise moved to North Carolina and renamed Carolina Hurricanes for 1997-98 season; NHL approved move on June 25, 1997. ... Sprained knee (October 18, 1997); missed 11 games. ... Traded by Hurricanes to Ottawa Senators for D Sean Hill (November 18, 1997). ... Injured shoulder (November 27, 1997); missed nine games. ... Tore medial collateral ligament in left knee (January 16, 1999); missed 21 games. ... Traded by Senators to Chicago Blackhawks for RW Nelson Emerson (March 23, 1999). ... Missed three games for personal reasons (March 25-28, 1999). ... Dislocated shoulder (April 5, 1999); missed final four games of season. ... Claimed on waivers by Dallas Stars (September 30, 1999). ... Signed as free agent by St. Louis Blues (July 27, 2000).

		REGULAR SEASON								PLAYOFFS				
Season Team	League	Gms.	G	A	Pts.	PIM	+/-	PP	SH	Gms.	G	A	Pts.	PIM
90-91—Bellingham Jr. A	BCJHL	54	5	8	13	150	...	...	...	—	—	—	—	—
91-92—Kamloops	WHL	33	1	1	2	168	...	...	...	5	0	0	0	10
92-93—Kamloops	WHL	62	6	10	16	217	...	...	...	13	0	4	4	34
93-94—Kamloops	WHL	59	14	16	30	260	...	...	...	15	4	2	6	107
94-95—Fredericton	AHL	55	6	12	18	234	...	...	...	12	1	1	2	50
—Montreal	NHL	3	0	0	0	4	0	0	0	—	—	—	—	—
95-96—Fredericton	AHL	30	13	13	26	217	...	...	...	—	—	—	—	—
—Montreal	NHL	48	3	4	7	163	5	0	0	4	0	0	0	4
96-97—Montreal	NHL	56	4	2	6	114	-8	0	0	—	—	—	—	—
—Hartford	NHL	8	1	1	2	10	1	0	0	—	—	—	—	—
97-98—Carolina	NHL	7	0	1	1	22	2	0	0	—	—	—	—	—
—Ottawa	NHL	46	5	3	8	96	1	0	0	11	1	0	1	8
98-99—Ottawa	NHL	38	1	6	7	65	-2	0	0	—	—	—	—	—
—Chicago	NHL	4	0	0	0	14	0	0	0	—	—	—	—	—
99-00—Dallas	NHL	32	2	1	3	62	-7	0	0	—	—	—	—	—
—Michigan	IHL	31	5	2	7	78	...	...	...	—	—	—	—	—
NHL Totals (6 years)		242	16	18	34	550	-8	0	0	15	1	0	1	12

M

MURRAY, GLEN   RW   KINGS

PERSONAL: Born November 1, 1972, in Halifax, Nova Scotia. ... 6-3/222. ... Shoots right.

TRANSACTIONS/CAREER NOTES: Selected by Boston Bruins in first round (first Bruins pick, 18th overall) of NHL entry draft (June 22, 1991). ... Injured elbow (December 15, 1993); missed two games. ... Traded by Bruins with C Bryan Smolinski to Pittsburgh Penguins for LW Kevin Stevens and LW Shawn McEachern (August 2, 1995). ... Separated shoulder (January 1, 1996); missed 10 games. ... Suffered concussion (April 11, 1996); missed one game. ... Traded by Penguins to Los Angeles Kings for C Ed Olczyk (March 18, 1997). ... Suffered from the flu (November 13, 1997); missed one game. ... Tore medial collateral ligament in right knee (January 2, 1999); missed 19 games. ... Strained groin (March 28, 1999); missed two games. ... Bruised chest (January 13, 2000); missed three games.

MISCELLANEOUS: Failed to score on a penalty shot (vs. Guy Hebert, February 7, 1998).

STATISTICAL PLATEAUS: Three-goal games: 1997-98 (1), 1999-00 (1). Total: 2.

		REGULAR SEASON								PLAYOFFS				
Season Team	League	Gms.	G	A	Pts.	PIM	+/-	PP	SH	Gms.	G	A	Pts.	PIM
89-90—Sudbury	OHL	62	8	28	36	17	...	...	...	7	0	0	0	4
90-91—Sudbury	OHL	66	27	38	65	82	...	...	...	5	8	4	12	10
91-92—Sudbury	OHL	54	37	47	84	93	...	...	...	11	7	4	11	18
—Boston	NHL	5	3	1	4	0	2	1	0	15	4	2	6	10
92-93—Providence	AHL	48	30	26	56	42	...	...	...	6	1	4	5	4
—Boston	NHL	27	3	4	7	8	-6	2	0	—	—	—	—	—
93-94—Boston	NHL	81	18	13	31	48	-1	0	0	13	4	5	9	14
94-95—Boston	NHL	35	5	2	7	46	-11	0	0	2	0	0	0	2
95-96—Pittsburgh	NHL	69	14	15	29	57	4	0	0	18	2	6	8	10
96-97—Pittsburgh	NHL	66	11	11	22	24	-19	3	0	—	—	—	—	—
—Los Angeles	NHL	11	5	3	8	8	-2	0	0	—	—	—	—	—
97-98—Los Angeles	NHL	81	29	31	60	54	6	7	3	4	2	0	2	6
98-99—Los Angeles	NHL	61	16	15	31	36	-14	3	3	—	—	—	—	—
99-00—Los Angeles	NHL	78	29	33	62	60	13	10	1	4	0	0	0	2
NHL Totals (9 years)		514	133	128	261	341	-28	26	7	56	12	13	25	44

MURRAY, REM   LW   OILERS

PERSONAL: Born October 9, 1972, in Stratford, Ont. ... 6-2/195. ... Shoots left. ... Full Name: Raymond Murray.

COLLEGE: Michigan State.

TRANSACTIONS/CAREER NOTES: Selected by Los Angeles Kings in sixth round (fifth Kings pick, 135th overall) of NHL entry draft (June 20, 1992). ... Signed as free agent by Edmonton Oilers (August 17, 1995). ... Missed first five games of 1997-98 season recovering from wrist injury and off-season appendectomy. ... Strained neck (March 17, 1998); missed one game. ... Suffered from the flu (April 6, 1998); missed three games. ... Separated shoulder (October 7, 1999); missed seven games. ... Sprained medial collateral ligament in knee (November 3, 1999); missed 28 games.

HONORS: Named to CCHA All-Star second team (1994-95).

STATISTICAL PLATEAUS: Three-goal games: 1996-97 (1).

		REGULAR SEASON								PLAYOFFS				
Season Team	League	Gms.	G	A	Pts.	PIM	+/-	PP	SH	Gms.	G	A	Pts.	PIM
90-91—Stratford Jr. B	OHA	48	39	59	98	22	...	...	...	—	—	—	—	—
91-92—Michigan State	CCHA	44	12	36	48	16	...	...	...	—	—	—	—	—
92-93—Michigan State	CCHA	40	22	35	57	24	...	...	...	—	—	—	—	—
93-94—Michigan State	CCHA	41	16	38	54	18	...	...	...	—	—	—	—	—
94-95—Michigan State	CCHA	40	20	36	56	21	...	...	...	—	—	—	—	—
95-96—Cape Breton	AHL	79	31	59	90	40	...	...	...	—	—	—	—	—
96-97—Edmonton	NHL	82	11	20	31	16	9	1	0	12	1	2	3	4
97-98—Edmonton	NHL	61	9	9	18	39	-9	2	2	11	1	4	5	2
98-99—Edmonton	NHL	78	21	18	39	20	4	4	1	4	1	1	2	2
99-00—Edmonton	NHL	44	9	5	14	8	-2	2	0	5	0	1	1	2
NHL Totals (4 years)		265	50	52	102	83	2	9	3	32	3	8	11	10

MYERS, SCOTT   G   PENGUINS

PERSONAL: Born June 11, 1979, in Winnipeg. ... 5-11/172. ... Catches right.

TRANSACTIONS/CAREER NOTES: Selected by Pittsburgh Penguins in fourth round (fourth Penguins pick, 110th overall) of NHL entry draft (June 27, 1998).

		REGULAR SEASON							PLAYOFFS					
Season Team	League	Gms.	Min	W	L	T	GA	SO	Avg.	Gms.	Min.	W	L	GA	SO	Avg.
96-97—Prince George	WHL	25	1284	6	14	1	94	0	4.39	—	—	—	—	—	—	—
97-98—Prince George	WHL	48	2822	29	13	4	139	2	2.96	11	665	5	6	25	2	2.26
98-99—Prince George	WHL	*66	*3771	30	†28	6	*214	0	3.40	7	418	3	4	23	0	3.30
99-00—Prince George	WHL	49	2693	30	15	3	128	1	2.85	13	796	8	5	28	*3	2.11

MYHRES, BRANTT   RW

PERSONAL: Born March 18, 1974, in Edmonton. ... 6-4/215. ... Shoots right. ... Name pronounced MIGH-urhs.

HIGH SCHOOL: Sir Winston Churchill (Calgary).

TRANSACTIONS/CAREER NOTES: Selected by Tampa Bay Lightning in fifth round (fifth Lightning pick, 97th overall) of NHL entry draft (June 20, 1992). ... Injured shoulder (April 11, 1995); missed one game. ... Injured hip (February 1, 1997); missed one game. ... Sprained ankle (February 23, 1997); missed three games. ... Suffered from the flu (April 4, 1997); missed three games. ... Traded by Lightning with third-round pick (D Alex Henry) in 1998 draft to Edmonton Oilers for C Vladimir Vujtek (July 16, 1997). ... Traded by Oilers to Philadelphia Flyers for F Jason Bowen (October 15, 1997). ... Bruised left hand (November 26, 1997); missed two games. ... Signed as free agent by San Jose Sharks (September 11, 1998). ... Suspended 12 games by NHL for leaving the bench to start a fight (February 12, 1999). ... Injured hand (October 28, 1999); missed seven games. ... Injured back (February 15, 2000); missed eight games.

Season Team	League	Gms.	G	A	Pts.	PIM	+/-	PP	SH	Gms.	G	A	Pts.	PIM
90-91—Portland	WHL	59	2	7	9	125	...	...	...	—	—	—	—	—
91-92—Portland	WHL	4	0	2	2	22	...	...	...	—	—	—	—	—
—Lethbridge	WHL	53	4	11	15	359	...	...	...	5	0	0	0	36
92-93—Lethbridge	WHL	64	13	35	48	277	...	...	...	3	0	0	0	11
93-94—Atlanta	IHL	2	0	0	0	17	...	...	...	—	—	—	—	—
—Lethbridge	WHL	34	10	21	31	103	...	...	...	—	—	—	—	—
—Spokane	WHL	27	10	22	32	139	...	...	...	3	1	4	5	7
94-95—Atlanta	IHL	40	5	5	10	213	...	...	...	—	—	—	—	—
—Tampa Bay	NHL	15	2	0	2	81	-2	0	0	—	—	—	—	—
95-96—Atlanta	IHL	12	0	2	2	58	...	...	...	—	—	—	—	—
96-97—San Antonio	IHL	12	0	0	0	98	...	...	...	—	—	—	—	—
—Tampa Bay	NHL	47	3	1	4	136	1	0	0	—	—	—	—	—
97-98—Philadelphia	AHL	18	4	4	8	67	...	...	...	—	—	—	—	—
—Philadelphia	NHL	23	0	0	0	169	-1	0	0	—	—	—	—	—
98-99—San Jose	NHL	30	1	0	1	116	-2	0	0	—	—	—	—	—
—Kentucky	AHL	4	0	0	0	16	...	...	...	—	—	—	—	—
99-00—San Jose	NHL	13	0	1	1	97	0	0	0	—	—	—	—	—
—Kentucky	AHL	10	1	5	6	18	...	...	...	7	0	1	1	21
NHL Totals (5 years)		128	6	2	8	599	-4	0	0					

NABOKOV, DIMITRI   C/LW   ISLANDERS

PERSONAL: Born January 4, 1977, in Novosibirsk, U.S.S.R. ... 6-2/209. ... Shoots right.
TRANSACTIONS/CAREER NOTES: Selected by Chicago Blackhawks in first round (first Blackhawks pick, 19th overall) of NHL entry draft (July 8, 1995). ... Traded by Blackhawks to New York Islanders for LW Jean-Pierre Dumont and fifth-round pick (traded to Philadelphia) in 1998 draft (May 30, 1998).
HONORS: Named to WHL (East) All-Star second team (1996-97).

Season Team	League	Gms.	G	A	Pts.	PIM	+/-	PP	SH	Gms.	G	A	Pts.	PIM
93-94—Soviet Wings	CIS	17	0	2	2	6	...	...	...	3	0	0	0	0
94-95—Soviet Wings	CIS	49	15	12	27	32	...	...	...	4	5	0	5	6
95-96—Soviet Wings	CIS	50	12	14	26	51	...	...	...	—	—	—	—	—
96-97—Soviet Wings	Russia	1	0	0	0	0	...	...	...	—	—	—	—	—
—Regina	WHL	50	39	56	95	61	...	...	...	5	2	3	5	2
—Indianapolis	IHL	2	0	0	0	0	...	...	...	—	—	—	—	—
97-98—Indianapolis	IHL	46	6	15	21	16	...	...	...	5	2	1	3	0
—Chicago	NHL	25	7	4	11	10	-1	3	0	—	—	—	—	—
98-99—Lowell	AHL	73	17	25	42	46	...	...	...	3	0	1	1	0
—New York Islanders	NHL	4	0	2	2	2	4	0	0	—	—	—	—	—
99-00—Lowell	AHL	51	8	26	34	42	...	...	...	6	1	2	3	2
—New York Islanders	NHL	26	4	7	11	16	-8	0	0	—	—	—	—	—
NHL Totals (3 years)		55	11	13	24	28	-5	3	0					

NABOKOV, EVGENI   G   SHARKS

PERSONAL: Born July 25, 1975, in Ust-Kamenogorsk, U.S.S.R. ... 6-0/200. ... Catches left. ... Name pronounced nuh-BAH-kahf.
TRANSACTIONS/CAREER NOTES: Selected by San Jose Sharks in ninth round (ninth Sharks pick, 219th overall) of NHL entry draft (June 29, 1994).

Season Team	League	Gms.	Min	W	L	T	GA	SO	Avg.	Gms.	Min.	W	L	GA	SO	Avg.
92-93—Torpedo Ust-Kam.	CIS	4	109	...	...	...	5	...	2.75	—	—	—	—	—	—	—
93-94—Torpedo Ust-Kam.	CIS	11	539	...	...	...	29	0	3.23	—	—	—	—	—	—	—
94-95—Dynamo Moscow	CIS	37	2075	...	...	...	70	...	2.02	—	—	—	—	—	—	—
95-96—Dynamo Moscow	CIS	37	1948	...	...	...	70	...	2.16	6	298	...	...	7	...	1.41
96-97—Dynamo Moscow	Russian	27	1588	...	...	...	56	2	2.12	4	255	...	...	12	0	2.82
97-98—Kentucky	AHL	33	1867	10	21	2	122	0	3.92	1	23	0	0	1	0	2.61
98-99—Kentucky	AHL	43	2429	26	14	1	106	5	2.62	11	599	6	5	30	2	3.01
99-00—Cleveland	IHL	20	1164	16	4	3	52	0	2.68	—	—	—	—	—	—	—
—San Jose	NHL	11	414	2	2	1	15	1	2.17	1	20	0	0	0	0	...
—Kentucky	AHL	2	120	1	1	0	3	1	1.50	—	—	—	—	—	—	—
NHL Totals (1 year)		11	414	2	2	1	15	1	2.17	1	20	0	0	0	0	...

M
N

NAGY, LADISLAV   C   BLUES

PERSONAL: Born June 1, 1979, in Presov, Yugoslavia. ... 5-11/183. ... Shoots left.
TRANSACTIONS/CAREER NOTES: Selected by St. Louis Blues in seventh round (sixth Blues pick, 177th overall) of NHL entry draft (June 21, 1997).
HONORS: Won Michel Bergeron Trophy (1998-99).

Season Team	League	Gms.	G	A	Pts.	PIM	+/-	PP	SH	Gms.	G	A	Pts.	PIM
96-97—Dragon Presov	Slov. Div. II	11	6	5	11	...	...	...	...	—	—	—	—	—
97-98—HC Kosice	Slovakia	29	19	15	34	41	...	...	...	—	—	—	—	—
98-99—Halifax	QMJHL	63	*71	55	126	148	...	...	...	5	3	3	6	18
—Worcester	AHL	—	—	—	—	—	...	...	...	3	2	2	4	0
99-00—Worcester	AHL	69	23	28	51	67	...	...	...	2	1	0	1	0
—St. Louis	NHL	11	2	4	6	2	2	1	0	6	1	1	2	0
NHL Totals (1 year)		11	2	4	6	2	2	1	0	6	1	1	2	0

NAMESTNIKOV, JOHN — D — PREDATORS

PERSONAL: Born October 9, 1971, in Norvgrood, U.S.S.R. ... 5-11/190. ... Shoots right. ... Full Name: Yevgeny Namestnikov. ... Name pronounced ehv-GEH-nee nuh-MEHST-nih-kahf.

TRANSACTIONS/CAREER NOTES: Selected by Vancouver Canucks in sixth round (fifth Canucks pick, 117th overall) of NHL entry draft (June 22, 1991). ... Sprained ankle (May 7, 1995); missed 10 playoff games. ... Signed as free agent by New York Islanders (July 16, 1997). ... Signed as free agent by New York Rangers (August 25, 1999). ... Claimed by Canucks from Rangers in NHL waiver draft (September 27, 1999). ... Claimed on waivers by Rangers (October 1, 1999). ... Traded by Rangers to Nashville Predators for LW Jason Dawe (February 2, 2000).

			REGULAR SEASON								PLAYOFFS				
Season Team	League	Gms.	G	A	Pts.	PIM	+/-	PP	SH		Gms.	G	A	Pts.	PIM
88-89—Torpedo Gorky	Russian	2	0	0	0	2	...	...	...		—	—	—	—	—
89-90—Torpedo Gorky	Russian	23	0	0	0	25	...	...	...		—	—	—	—	—
90-91—Tor. Nizhny-Nov.	USSR	45	1	2	3	49	...	...	...		—	—	—	—	—
91-92—CSKA Moscow	CIS	42	1	1	2	47	...	...	...		—	—	—	—	—
92-93—CSKA Moscow	CIS	42	5	5	10	68	...	...	...		—	—	—	—	—
93-94—Hamilton	AHL	59	7	27	34	97	...	...	...		4	0	2	2	19
—Vancouver	NHL	17	0	5	5	10	-2	0	0		—	—	—	—	—
94-95—Syracuse	AHL	59	11	22	33	59	...	...	...		—	—	—	—	—
—Vancouver	NHL	16	0	3	3	4	2	0	0		1	0	0	0	2
95-96—Syracuse	AHL	59	13	34	47	85	...	...	...		15	1	8	9	16
—Vancouver	NHL	—	—	—	—	—	—	—	—		1	0	0	0	0
96-97—Syracuse	AHL	55	9	37	46	73	...	...	...		3	2	0	2	0
—Vancouver	NHL	2	0	0	0	4	-1	0	0		—	—	—	—	—
97-98—Utah	IHL	62	6	19	25	48	...	...	...		4	1	0	1	2
—New York Islanders	NHL	6	0	1	1	4	-1	0	0		—	—	—	—	—
98-99—Lowell	AHL	42	12	14	26	42	...	...	...		—	—	—	—	—
99-00—Hartford	AHL	33	1	9	10	14	...	...	...		—	—	—	—	—
—Milwaukee	IHL	12	2	3	5	17	...	...	...		3	0	0	0	0
—Nashville	NHL	2	0	0	0	2	0	0	0		—	—	—	—	—
NHL Totals (6 years)		43	0	9	9	24	-2	0	0		2	0	0	0	2

NASH, TYSON — LW — BLUES

PERSONAL: Born March 11, 1975, in Edmonton. ... 5-11/195. ... Shoots left.

TRANSACTIONS/CAREER NOTES: Selected by Vancouver Canucks in 10th round (eighth Canucks pick, 247th overall) of NHL entry draft (June 29, 1994). ... Signed as free agent by St. Louis Blues (July 24, 1998). ... Suffered concussion (December 5, 1999); missed three games. ... Injured shoulder (March 11, 2000); missed final 13 games of regular season.

			REGULAR SEASON								PLAYOFFS				
Season Team	League	Gms.	G	A	Pts.	PIM	+/-	PP	SH		Gms.	G	A	Pts.	PIM
90-91—Kamloops	WHL	3	0	0	0	0	...	...	...		—	—	—	—	—
91-92—Kamloops	WHL	33	1	6	7	32	...	...	...		4	0	0	0	0
92-93—Kamloops	WHL	61	10	16	26	78	...	...	...		13	3	2	5	32
93-94—Kamloops	WHL	65	20	36	56	137	...	...	...		16	3	3	6	12
94-95—Kamloops	WHL	63	34	41	75	70	...	...	...		21	10	7	17	30
95-96—Syracuse	AHL	50	4	7	11	58	...	...	...		4	0	0	0	11
—Raleigh	ECHL	6	1	1	2	8	...	...	...		—	—	—	—	—
96-97—Syracuse	AHL	77	17	17	34	105	...	...	...		3	0	2	2	0
97-98—Syracuse	AHL	74	20	20	40	184	...	...	...		5	0	2	2	28
98-99—Worcester	AHL	55	14	22	36	143	...	...	...		4	4	1	5	27
—St. Louis	NHL	2	0	0	0	5	-1	0	0		1	0	0	0	2
99-00—St. Louis	NHL	66	4	9	13	150	6	0	1		6	1	0	1	24
NHL Totals (2 years)		68	4	9	13	155	5	0	1		7	1	0	1	26

NASLUND, MARKUS — LW — CANUCKS

PERSONAL: Born July 30, 1973, in Ornskoldsvik, Sweden. ... 6-0/186. ... Shoots left. ... Name pronounced NAZ-luhnd.

TRANSACTIONS/CAREER NOTES: Selected by Pittsburgh Penguins in first round (first Penguins pick, 16th overall) of NHL entry draft (June 22, 1991). ... Traded by Penguins to Vancouver Canucks for LW Alex Stojanov (March 20, 1996). ... Suffered from flu (November 26, 1996); missed one game.

HONORS: Played in NHL All-Star Game (1999).

MISCELLANEOUS: Scored on a penalty shot (vs. Mike Dunham, December 19, 1998).

STATISTICAL PLATEAUS: Three-goal games: 1995-96 (1), 1995-96 (1), 1998-99 (1). Total: 3.

			REGULAR SEASON								PLAYOFFS				
Season Team	League	Gms.	G	A	Pts.	PIM	+/-	PP	SH		Gms.	G	A	Pts.	PIM
89-90—MoDo Hockey Jrs.	Sweden Jr.	33	43	35	78	20	...	...	...		—	—	—	—	—
90-91—MoDo Ornskoldsvik	Sweden	32	10	9	19	14	...	...	...		—	—	—	—	—
91-92—MoDo Ornskoldsvik	Sweden	39	22	18	40	54	...	...	...		—	—	—	—	—
92-93—MoDo Ornskoldsvik	Sweden	39	22	17	39	67	...	...	...		3	3	2	5	...
93-94—Pittsburgh	NHL	71	4	7	11	27	-3	1	0		—	—	—	—	—
—Cleveland	IHL	5	1	6	7	4	...	...	...		—	—	—	—	—
94-95—Pittsburgh	NHL	14	2	2	4	2	0	0	0		—	—	—	—	—
—Cleveland	IHL	7	3	4	7	6	...	...	...		4	1	3	4	8
95-96—Pittsburgh	NHL	66	19	33	52	36	17	3	0		—	—	—	—	—
—Vancouver	NHL	10	3	0	3	6	3	1	0		6	1	2	3	8
96-97—Vancouver	NHL	78	21	20	41	30	-15	4	0		—	—	—	—	—
97-98—Vancouver	NHL	76	14	20	34	56	5	2	1		—	—	—	—	—
98-99—Vancouver	NHL	80	36	30	66	74	-13	15	2		—	—	—	—	—
99-00—Vancouver	NHL	82	27	38	65	64	-5	6	2		—	—	—	—	—
NHL Totals (7 years)		477	126	150	276	295	-11	32	5		6	1	2	3	8

PERSONAL: Born July 7, 1974, in Chicago. ... 5-11/185. ... Shoots right. ... Name pronounced nah-MEHN-koh.
COLLEGE: North Dakota.
TRANSACTIONS/CAREER NOTES: Selected by St. Louis Blues in eighth round (ninth Blues pick, 182nd overall) of NHL entry draft (June 20, 1992). ... Signed as free agent by Minnesota Wild (June 13, 2000).
HONORS: Named to WCHA All-Star first team (1994-95). ... Named to WCHA All-Star first team (1995-96).

		REGULAR SEASON								PLAYOFFS				
Season Team	League	Gms.	G	A	Pts.	PIM	+/-	PP	SH	Gms.	G	A	Pts.	PIM
91-92—Dubuque	USHL	24	6	19	25	4	...	...	...	—	—	—	—	—
92-93—Univ. of North Dakota	WCHA	38	10	24	34	26	...	...	...	—	—	—	—	—
93-94—Univ. of North Dakota	WCHA	32	4	22	26	22	...	...	...	—	—	—	—	—
94-95—Univ. of North Dakota	WCHA	39	13	26	39	78	...	...	...	—	—	—	—	—
95-96—Univ. of North Dakota	WCHA	37	11	30	41	52	...	...	...	—	—	—	—	—
96-97—Worcester	AHL	54	6	22	28	72	...	...	...	1	0	0	0	0
97-98—Worcester	AHL	71	12	34	46	63	...	...	...	11	1	7	8	8
98-99—Utah	IHL	20	4	3	7	20	...	...	...	—	—	—	—	—
—Las Vegas	IHL	34	5	16	21	37	...	...	...	—	—	—	—	—
—Kansas City	IHL	21	3	8	11	4	...	...	...	3	1	2	3	4
99-00—Kansas City	IHL	54	9	27	36	79	...	...	...	—	—	—	—	—

PERSONAL: Born April 22, 1974, in Chelyabinsk, U.S.S.R. ... 6-5/234. ... Shoots right. ... Name pronounced nuh-ZAH-rahf.
TRANSACTIONS/CAREER NOTES: Selected by San Jose Sharks in first round (second Sharks pick, 10th overall) of NHL entry draft (June 20, 1992). ... Suspended four games and fined $500 by NHL for head-butting (March 8, 1995). ... Suffered facial fracture (February 5, 1997); missed 14 games. ... Suspended 13 games by NHL for physical abuse of officials (March 25, 1997). ... Injured knee (October 13, 1997); missed seven games. ... Traded by Sharks with first-round pick (C Vincent Lecavalier) in 1998 draft and future considerations to Tampa Bay Lightning for D Bryan Marchment, D David Shaw and first-round pick (traded to Nashville) in 1998 draft (March 24, 1998). ... Injured finger (November 8, 1998); missed one game. ... Suspended seven games and fined $1,000 by NHL for cross-checking incident (November 19, 1998). ... Traded by Lightning to Calgary Flames for C Michael Nylander (January 19, 1999).

		REGULAR SEASON								PLAYOFFS				
Season Team	League	Gms.	G	A	Pts.	PIM	+/-	PP	SH	Gms.	G	A	Pts.	PIM
90-91—Mechel Chelyabinsk	USSR	2	0	0	0	0	...	...	...	—	—	—	—	—
91-92—Dynamo Moscow	CIS	2	1	0	1	2	...	...	...	—	—	—	—	—
92-93—Dynamo Moscow	CIS	42	8	2	10	79	...	...	...	10	1	1	2	8
93-94—Kansas City	IHL	71	15	18	33	64	...	...	...	—	—	—	—	—
—San Jose	NHL	1	0	0	0	0	0	0	0	—	—	—	—	—
94-95—Kansas City	IHL	43	15	10	25	55	...	...	...	—	—	—	—	—
—San Jose	NHL	26	3	5	8	94	-1	0	0	6	0	0	0	9
95-96—San Jose	NHL	42	7	7	14	62	-15	2	0	—	—	—	—	—
—Kansas City	IHL	27	4	6	10	118	...	...	...	2	0	0	0	2
96-97—San Jose	NHL	60	12	15	27	222	-4	1	0	—	—	—	—	—
—Kentucky	AHL	3	1	2	3	4	...	...	...	—	—	—	—	—
97-98—San Jose	NHL	40	1	1	2	112	-4	0	0	—	—	—	—	—
—Tampa Bay	NHL	14	1	1	2	58	-9	0	0	—	—	—	—	—
98-99—Tampa Bay	NHL	26	2	0	2	43	-5	0	0	—	—	—	—	—
—Calgary	NHL	36	5	9	14	30	1	0	0	—	—	—	—	—
99-00—Calgary	NHL	76	10	22	32	78	3	1	0	—	—	—	—	—
NHL Totals (7 years)		321	41	60	101	699	-34	4	0	6	0	0	0	9

PERSONAL: Born July 7, 1975, in Zaria, Nigeria. ... 6-2/222. ... Shoots left. ... Name pronounced ruh-MOHN EHN-duhr.
HIGH SCHOOL: Bishop MacDonnell (Guelph, Ont.).
TRANSACTIONS/CAREER NOTES: Selected by Buffalo Sabres in third round (third Sabres pick, 69th overall) of NHL entry draft (June 29, 1994). ... Strained hip flexor (December 1, 1998); missed six games. ... Claimed on waivers by New York Rangers (December 18, 1998). ... Sprained knee (January 2, 1999); missed four games. ... Claimed on waivers by Atlanta Thrashers (December 11, 1999). ... Suffered eye injury (March 10, 2000); missed seven games. ... Injured thumb (March 31, 2000); missed final five games of season.

		REGULAR SEASON								PLAYOFFS				
Season Team	League	Gms.	G	A	Pts.	PIM	+/-	PP	SH	Gms.	G	A	Pts.	PIM
91-92—Clearwater	Jr. C	4	0	4	4	4	...	...	...	—	—	—	—	—
—Sarnia	Jr. B	30	2	5	7	46	...	...	...	—	—	—	—	—
92-93—Guelph	Jr. B	24	7	8	15	202	...	...	...	—	—	—	—	—
—Guelph	OHL	22	1	3	4	30	...	...	...	4	0	1	1	4
93-94—Guelph	OHL	61	6	33	39	176	...	...	...	9	4	1	5	24
94-95—Guelph	OHL	63	10	21	31	187	...	...	...	14	0	4	4	28
95-96—Rochester	AHL	73	2	12	14	306	...	...	...	17	1	2	3	33
96-97—Rochester	AHL	68	5	11	16	282	...	...	...	10	3	1	4	21
—Buffalo	NHL	2	0	0	0	2	1	0	0	—	—	—	—	—
97-98—Rochester	AHL	50	1	12	13	207	...	...	...	4	0	2	2	16
—Buffalo	NHL	1	0	0	0	2	-1	0	0	—	—	—	—	—
98-99—Buffalo	NHL	8	0	0	0	16	1	0	0	—	—	—	—	—
—New York Rangers	NHL	31	1	3	4	46	-2	0	0	—	—	—	—	—
—Hartford	AHL	6	0	1	1	4	...	...	...	—	—	—	—	—
99-00—Hartford	AHL	2	0	0	0	0	...	...	...	—	—	—	—	—
—Atlanta	NHL	27	1	0	1	71	-17	0	0	—	—	—	—	—
NHL Totals (4 years)		69	2	3	5	137	-18	0	0					

N

PERSONAL: Born December 22, 1975, in Ceske-Budejovice, Czechoslovakia. ... 6-1/207. ... Shoots left. ... Full Name: Stanislav Neckar. ... Name pronounced NEHTS-kash.

TRANSACTIONS/CAREER NOTES: Selected by Ottawa Senators in second round (second Senators pick, 29th overall) of NHL entry draft (June 28, 1994). ... Suffered partially torn knee ligament (October 18, 1996); missed remainder of the season. ... Injured right knee (January 24, 1998); missed two games. ... Reinjured knee (April 3, 1998) and underwent surgery; missed final nine games of season. ... Fractured right foot (October 22, 1998); missed 16 games. ... Traded by Senators to New York Rangers for LW Bill Berg and second-round pick (traded to Anaheim) in 1999 draft (November 27, 1998). ... Traded by Rangers to Phoenix Coyotes for D Jason Doig and sixth-round pick (C Jay Dardis) in 1999 draft (March 23, 1999). ... Strained knee (October 18, 1999); missed 13 games.

		REGULAR SEASON								PLAYOFFS				
Season Team	League	Gms.	G	A	Pts.	PIM	+/-	PP	SH	Gms.	G	A	Pts.	PIM
91-92—Budejovice	Czech Dv.II	18	1	3	4	...	...	...	...	—	—	—	—	—
92-93—Motor-Ceske Bude.	Czech.	42	2	9	11	12	...	...	...	—	—	—	—	—
93-94—HC Ceske Budejovice	Czech Rep.	12	3	2	5	2	...	...	...	3	0	0	0	0
94-95—Detroit	IHL	15	2	2	4	15	...	...	...	—	—	—	—	—
—Ottawa	NHL	48	1	3	4	37	-20	0	0	—	—	—	—	—
95-96—Ottawa	NHL	82	3	9	12	54	-16	1	0	—	—	—	—	—
96-97—Ottawa	NHL	5	0	0	0	2	2	0	0	—	—	—	—	—
97-98—Ottawa	NHL	60	2	2	4	31	-14	0	0	9	0	0	0	2
98-99—Ottawa	NHL	3	0	2	2	0	-1	0	0	—	—	—	—	—
—New York Rangers	NHL	18	0	0	0	8	-1	0	0	—	—	—	—	—
—Phoenix	NHL	11	0	1	1	10	3	0	0	6	0	1	1	4
99-00—Phoenix	NHL	66	2	8	10	36	1	0	0	5	0	0	0	0
NHL Totals (6 years)		293	8	25	33	178	-46	1	0	20	0	1	1	6

PERSONAL: Born December 9, 1971, in Liberec, Czechoslovakia. ... 6-3/195. ... Shoots left. ... Name pronounced NEHD-VEHD.

TRANSACTIONS/CAREER NOTES: Selected by Vancouver Canucks in first round (first Canucks pick, second overall) of NHL entry draft (June 16, 1990). ... Signed to offer sheet by St. Louis Blues (March 4, 1994); C Craig Janney and second-round pick (C Dave Scatchard) in 1994 draft awarded to Canucks as compensation (March 14, 1994). ... Traded by Blues to New York Rangers for LW Esa Tikkanen and D Doug Lidster (July 24, 1994); trade arranged as compensation for Blues signing coach Mike Keenan. ... Strained abdomen (February 27, 1995); missed two games. ... Traded by Rangers with D Sergei Zubov to Pittsburgh Penguins for LW Luc Robitaille and D Ulf Samuelsson (August 31, 1995). ... Bruised thigh (November 18, 1995); missed two games. ... Bruised tailbone (December 19, 1996); missed two games. ... Sprained wrist (January 14, 1997); missed two games. ... Suffered charley horse (February 8, 1997); missed one game. ... Sprained wrist (March 20, 1997); missed three games. ... Missed all of 1997-98 season and first 18 games of 1998-99 season due to contract dispute; played for Las Vegas of IHL. ... Traded by Penguins with D Sean Pronger and D Chris Tamer to Rangers for RW Alexei Kovalev, C Harry York and future considerations (November 25, 1998). ... Strained muscle in ribcage (April 2, 1999); missed final seven games of season. ... Strained groin (December 2, 1999); missed four games. ... Bruised ribs (March 15, 2000); missed two games.

HONORS: Won Can.HL Rookie of the Year Award (1989-90). ... Won Jim Piggott Memorial Trophy (1989-90).

MISCELLANEOUS: Member of silver-medal-winning Canadian Olympic team (1994).

STATISTICAL PLATEAUS: Three-goal games: 1998-99 (1), 1999-00 (3). Total: 4. ... Four-goal games: 1995-96 (1). ... Total hat tricks: 5.

		REGULAR SEASON								PLAYOFFS				
Season Team	League	Gms.	G	A	Pts.	PIM	+/-	PP	SH	Gms.	G	A	Pts.	PIM
88-89—Litvinov Jrs.	Czech Rep.	20	32	19	51	12	...	...	...	—	—	—	—	—
89-90—Seattle	WHL	71	65	80	145	80	...	...	...	11	4	9	13	2
90-91—Vancouver	NHL	61	10	6	16	20	-21	1	0	6	0	1	1	0
91-92—Vancouver	NHL	77	15	22	37	36	-3	5	0	10	1	4	5	16
92-93—Vancouver	NHL	84	38	33	71	96	20	2	1	12	2	3	5	2
93-94—Canadian nat'l team	Int'l	17	19	12	31	16	...	...	...	—	—	—	—	—
—Can. Olympic team	Int'l	8	5	1	6	6	...	...	...	—	—	—	—	—
—St. Louis	NHL	19	6	14	20	8	2	2	0	4	0	1	1	4
94-95—New York Rangers	NHL	46	11	12	23	26	-1	1	0	10	3	2	5	6
95-96—Pittsburgh	NHL	80	45	54	99	68	37	8	1	18	10	10	20	16
96-97—Pittsburgh	NHL	74	33	38	71	66	-2	12	3	5	1	2	3	12
97-98—Sparta Praha	Czech Rep.	5	2	3	5	8	...	...	...	6	0	2	2	52
—Las Vegas	IHL	3	3	3	6	4	...	...	...	—	—	—	—	—
98-99—Las Vegas	IHL	13	8	10	18	32	...	...	...	—	—	—	—	—
—New York Rangers	NHL	56	20	27	47	50	-6	9	1	—	—	—	—	—
99-00—New York Rangers	NHL	76	24	44	68	40	2	6	2	—	—	—	—	—
NHL Totals (9 years)		573	202	250	452	410	28	46	8	65	17	23	40	56

PERSONAL: Born January 14, 1964, in Moscow, U.S.S.R. ... 6-0/205. ... Shoots left. ... Name pronounced SAIR-gay nehm-CHEE-nahf.

TRANSACTIONS/CAREER NOTES: Selected by New York Rangers in 12th round (14th Rangers pick, 244th overall) of NHL entry draft (June 16, 1990). ... Sprained knee (November 4, 1991); missed seven games. ... Strained buttocks (April 4, 1993); missed three games. ... Suspended eight games and fined $500 by NHL for hitting another player (March 16, 1994). ... Bruised Achilles' tendon (January 30, 1995); missed one game. ... Suffered mild concussion (December 13, 1995); missed one game. ... Bruised elbow (April 7, 1996); missed two games. ... Traded by Rangers with RW Brian Noonan to Vancouver Canucks for LW Esa Tikkanen and RW Russ Courtnall (March 8, 1997). ... Strained rib muscle (February 28, 1997); missed 11 games. ... Injured foot (April 4, 1997); missed three games. ... Signed as free agent by New York Islanders (July 2, 1997). ... Suffered back spasms (November 28, 1997); missed two games. ... Suffered back spasms (December 17, 1997); missed one game. ... Injured back (April 6, 1998); missed one game. ... Suffered concussion (April 11, 1998); missed two games. ... Strained neck (April 16, 1998); missed final two games of season. ... Bruised hip (December 22, 1998); missed two games. ... Injured knee (February 7, 1999); missed one game. ... Reinjured knee (February 12, 1999); missed one game. ... Traded by Islanders to New Jersey Devils for fourth-

N

round pick (traded to Los Angeles) in 1999 draft (March 22, 1999). ... Injured hip (April 8, 1999); missed two games ... Reinjured hip (April 14, 1999); missed final two games of regular season and three playoff games. ... Strained muscle in abdomen (December 26, 1999); missed 16 games. ... Suffered stiff neck (March 2, 2000); missed one game. ... Suffered pinched nerve in neck (March 19, 2000); missed one game.
MISCELLANEOUS: Member of Stanley Cup championship team (1994 and 2000). ... Member of silver-medal-winning Russian Olympic team (1998). ... Failed to score on a penalty shot (vs. Olaf Kolzig, March 11, 2000).
STATISTICAL PLATEAUS: Three-goal games: 1992-93 (1).

				REGULAR SEASON							PLAYOFFS			
Season Team	League	Gms.	G	A	Pts.	PIM	+/-	PP	SH	Gms.	G	A	Pts.	PIM
81-82—Soviet Wings	USSR	15	1	0	1	0	...	...	...	—	—	—	—	—
82-83—CSKA Moscow	USSR	11	0	0	0	2	...	...	...	—	—	—	—	—
83-84—CSKA Moscow	USSR	20	6	5	11	4	...	...	...	—	—	—	—	—
84-85—CSKA Moscow	USSR	31	2	4	6	4	...	...	...	—	—	—	—	—
85-86—Soviet Wings	USSR	39	7	12	19	28	...	...	...	—	—	—	—	—
86-87—Soviet Wings	USSR	40	13	9	22	24	...	...	...	—	—	—	—	—
87-88—Soviet Wings	USSR	48	17	11	28	26	...	...	...	—	—	—	—	—
88-89—Soviet Wings	USSR	43	15	14	29	28	...	...	...	—	—	—	—	—
89-90—Soviet Wings	USSR	48	17	16	33	34	...	...	...	—	—	—	—	—
90-91—Soviet Wings	USSR	46	21	24	45	30	...	...	...	—	—	—	—	—
91-92—New York Rangers	NHL	73	30	28	58	15	19	2	0	13	1	4	5	8
92-93—New York Rangers	NHL	81	23	31	54	34	15	0	1	—	—	—	—	—
93-94—New York Rangers	NHL	76	22	27	49	36	13	4	0	23	2	5	7	6
94-95—New York Rangers	NHL	47	7	6	13	16	-6	0	0	10	4	5	9	2
95-96—New York Rangers	NHL	78	17	15	32	38	9	0	0	6	0	1	1	2
96-97—New York Rangers	NHL	63	6	13	19	12	5	1	0	—	—	—	—	—
—Vancouver	NHL	6	2	3	5	4	4	0	0	—	—	—	—	—
97-98—New York Islanders	NHL	74	10	19	29	24	3	2	1	—	—	—	—	—
—Russian Oly. team	Int'l	6	1	0	1	0	...	...	...	—	—	—	—	—
98-99—New York Islanders	NHL	67	8	8	16	22	-17	1	0	—	—	—	—	—
—New Jersey	NHL	10	4	0	4	6	4	1	0	4	0	0	0	0
99-00—New Jersey	NHL	53	10	16	26	18	1	0	1	21	3	2	5	2
NHL Totals (9 years)		628	139	166	305	225	50	11	3	77	10	17	27	20

NEMECEK, JAN   D   KINGS

PERSONAL: Born February 14, 1976, in Pisek, Czechoslovakia. ... 6-1/215. ... Shoots right. ... Name pronounced YAHN NEHM-ih-chehk.
TRANSACTIONS/CAREER NOTES: Selected by Los Angeles Kings in ninth round (seventh Kings pick, 215th overall) of NHL entry draft (June 29, 1994). ... Bruised left knee (April 15, 1999); missed final two games of season.
HONORS: Named to QMJHL All-Star second team (1995-96).

				REGULAR SEASON							PLAYOFFS			
Season Team	League	Gms.	G	A	Pts.	PIM	+/-	PP	SH	Gms.	G	A	Pts.	PIM
92-93—Budejovice	Czech.	15	0	0	0		...	...	...	—	—	—	—	—
93-94—Budejovice	Czech Rep.	16	0	1	1	16	...	...	...	—	—	—	—	—
94-95—Hull	QMJHL	49	10	16	26	48	...	...	...	21	5	9	14	10
95-96—Hull	QMJHL	57	17	49	66	58	...	...	...	17	2	13	15	10
96-97—Phoenix	IHL	24	1	1	2	2	...	...	...	—	—	—	—	—
—Mississippi	ECHL	20	3	9	12	16	...	...	...	3	0	0	0	4
97-98—Fredericton	AHL	65	7	24	31	43	...	...	...	2	0	0	0	0
98-99—Long Beach	IHL	66	5	16	21	42	...	...	...	—	—	—	—	—
—Los Angeles	NHL	6	1	0	1	4	-1	0	0	—	—	—	—	—
99-00—Long Beach	IHL	71	9	15	24	22	...	...	...	6	1	0	1	4
—Los Angeles	NHL	1	0	0	0	0	0	0	0	—	—	—	—	—
NHL Totals (2 years)		7	1	0	1	4	-1	0	0					

NEMIROVSKY, DAVID   RW   MAPLE LEAFS   N

PERSONAL: Born August 1, 1976, in Toronto. ... 6-2/200. ... Shoots right. ... Name pronounced nehm-uh-RAHV-skee.
TRANSACTIONS/CAREER NOTES: Selected by Florida Panthers in fourth round (fifth Panthers pick, 84th overall) of NHL entry draft (June 29, 1994). ... Bruised knee (November 9, 1997); missed one game. ... Traded by Panthers to Toronto Maple Leafs for D Jeff Ware (February 17, 1999).

				REGULAR SEASON							PLAYOFFS			
Season Team	League	Gms.	G	A	Pts.	PIM	+/-	PP	SH	Gms.	G	A	Pts.	PIM
91-92—Pickering-Weston	Jr. A	38	27	23	50	70	...	...	...	—	—	—	—	—
92-93—Weston-North York	MTHL	40	19	23	42	27	...	...	...	—	—	—	—	—
93-94—Ottawa	OHL	64	21	31	52	18	...	...	...	17	10	10	20	2
94-95—Ottawa	OHL	59	27	29	56	25	...	...	...	—	—	—	—	—
95-96—Florida	NHL	9	0	2	2	2	-1	0	0	—	—	—	—	—
—Sarnia	OHL	26	18	27	45	14	...	...	...	10	8	8	16	6
—Carolina	AHL	5	1	2	3	0	...	...	...	—	—	—	—	—
96-97—Carolina	AHL	34	21	21	42	18	...	...	...	—	—	—	—	—
—Florida	NHL	39	7	7	14	32	1	1	0	3	1	0	1	0
97-98—Florida	NHL	41	9	12	21	8	-3	2	0	—	—	—	—	—
—New Haven	AHL	29	10	15	25	10	...	...	...	1	1	0	1	0
98-99—Fort Wayne	IHL	44	22	13	35	24	...	...	...	—	—	—	—	—
—Florida	NHL	2	0	1	1	0	1	0	0	—	—	—	—	—
—St. John's	AHL	22	3	9	12	18	...	...	...	5	4	1	5	0
99-00—St. John's	AHL	57	18	25	43	69	...	...	...	—	—	—	—	—
NHL Totals (4 years)		91	16	22	38	42	-2	3	0	3	1	0	1	0

NICKULAS, ERIC   RW   BRUINS

PERSONAL: Born March 25, 1975, in Cape Cod, Mass. ... 5-11/190. ... Shoots right.
HIGH SCHOOL: Barnstable (Hyannis, Mass.), then Tabor (Marion, Mass.), then Cushing Academy (Ashburnham, Mass.).
COLLEGE: New Hampshire.
TRANSACTIONS/CAREER NOTES: Selected by Boston Bruins in fourth round (third Bruins pick, 99th overall) of NHL entry draft (June 29, 1994).
HONORS: Won Ken McKenzie Trophy (1997-98).
STATISTICAL PLATEAUS: Three-goal games: 1996-97 (1).

		REGULAR SEASON								PLAYOFFS				
Season Team	League	Gms.	G	A	Pts.	PIM	+/-	PP	SH	Gms.	G	A	Pts.	PIM
91-92—Barnstable H.S.	Mass. Jr. A	24	30	25	55	...				—	—	—	—	—
92-93—Tabor Academy	Mass. H.S.	28	25	25	50	...				—	—	—	—	—
93-94—Cushing Academy	Mass. H.S.	25	46	36	82	...				—	—	—	—	—
94-95—Univ. of New Hamp.	Hockey East	33	15	9	24	32	...			—	—	—	—	—
95-96—Univ. of New Hamp.	Hockey East	34	26	12	38	66	...			—	—	—	—	—
96-97—Univ. of New Hamp.	Hockey East	39	29	22	51	80	...			—	—	—	—	—
97-98—Orlando	IHL	76	22	9	31	77	...			6	0	0	0	10
98-99—Providence	AHL	75	31	27	58	83	...			18	8	12	20	33
—Boston	NHL	2	0	0	0	0	0	0	0	1	0	0	0	2
99-00—Providence	AHL	40	6	6	12	37	...			12	2	3	5	20
—Boston	NHL	20	5	6	11	12	-1	1	0	—	—	—	—	—
NHL Totals (2 years)		22	5	6	11	12	-1	1	0	1	0	0	0	2

NIEDERMAYER, ROB   C   PANTHERS

PERSONAL: Born December 28, 1974, in Cassiar, B.C. ... 6-2/204. ... Shoots left. ... Brother of Scott Niedermayer, defenseman, New Jersey Devils. ... Name pronounced NEE-duhr-MIGH-uhr.
COLLEGE: Medicine Hat (Alta.).
TRANSACTIONS/CAREER NOTES: Selected by Florida Panthers in first round (first Panthers pick, fifth overall) of NHL entry draft (June 26, 1993). ... Separated right shoulder (November 18, 1993); missed 17 games. ... Sprained knee ligament (November 22, 1996); missed 17 games. ... Strained groin (March 5, 1997); missed two games. ... Sprained wrist (March 20, 1997); missed three games. ... Suffered concussion (October 1, 1997); missed 10 games. ... Dislocated right thumb (November 18, 1997); missed 15 games. ... Underwent knee surgery during 1997-98 All-Star break; missed eight games. ... Suffered post-concussion syndrome (March 19, 1998); missed remainder of season. ... Suffered head injury (March 3, 2000); missed one game.
HONORS: Won WHL Top Draft Prospect Award (1992-93). ... Named to WHL (East) All-Star first team (1992-93).
MISCELLANEOUS: Failed to score on a penalty shot (vs. Corey Hirsch, March 13, 1997).

		REGULAR SEASON								PLAYOFFS				
Season Team	League	Gms.	G	A	Pts.	PIM	+/-	PP	SH	Gms.	G	A	Pts.	PIM
90-91—Medicine Hat	WHL	71	24	26	50	8	...	...	...	12	3	7	10	2
91-92—Medicine Hat	WHL	71	32	46	78	77	...	...	...	4	2	3	5	2
92-93—Medicine Hat	WHL	52	43	34	77	67	...	...	...	—	—	—	—	—
93-94—Florida	NHL	65	9	17	26	51	-11	3	0	—	—	—	—	—
94-95—Medicine Hat	WHL	13	9	15	24	14	...			—	—	—	—	—
—Florida	NHL	48	4	6	10	36	-13	1	0	—	—	—	—	—
95-96—Florida	NHL	82	26	35	61	107	1	11	0	22	5	3	8	12
96-97—Florida	NHL	60	14	24	38	54	4	3	0	5	2	1	3	6
97-98—Florida	NHL	33	8	7	15	41	-9	5	0	—	—	—	—	—
98-99—Florida	NHL	82	18	33	51	50	-13	6	1	—	—	—	—	—
99-00—Florida	NHL	81	10	23	33	46	-5	1	0	4	1	0	1	6
NHL Totals (7 years)		451	89	145	234	385	-46	30	1	31	8	4	12	24

NIEDERMAYER, SCOTT   D   DEVILS

PERSONAL: Born August 31, 1973, in Edmonton. ... 6-1/200. ... Shoots left. ... Brother of Rob Niedermayer, center, Florida Panthers. ... Name pronounced NEE-duhr-MIGH-uhr.
TRANSACTIONS/CAREER NOTES: Stretched left knee ligaments (March 12, 1991); missed nine games. ... Selected by New Jersey Devils in first round (first Devils pick, third overall) of NHL entry draft (June 22, 1991). ... Suffered sore back (December 9, 1992); missed four games. ... Injured knee (December 19, 1995); missed three games. ... Strained groin (February 12, 1997); missed one game. ... Suffered from the flu (February 4, 1998); missed one game. ... Missed first nine games of 1998-99 season due to contact dispute; played for Utah of IHL. ... Strained hip flexor (January 15, 2000); missed one game. ... Suffered illness (January 26, 2000); missed one game. ... Suspended final nine games of regular season and one playoff game by NHL for high-sticking incident (March 21, 2000).
HONORS: Won Can.HL Scholastic Player of the Year Award (1990-91). ... Named WHL Scholastic Player of the Year (1990-91). ... Named to WHL (West) All-Star first team (1990-91 and 1991-92). ... Won Stafford Smythe Memorial Trophy (1991-92). ... Named to Can.HL All-Star first team (1991-92). ... Named to Memorial Cup All-Star team (1991-92). ... Named to NHL All-Rookie team (1992-93). ... Played in NHL All-Star Game (1998). ... Named to NHL All-Star second team (1997-98).
MISCELLANEOUS: Member of Stanley Cup championship team (1995 and 2000). ... Scored on a penalty shot (vs. Jose Theodore, November 11, 1998). ... Failed to score on a penalty shot (vs. Ken Wregget, February 7, 1996).

		REGULAR SEASON								PLAYOFFS				
Season Team	League	Gms.	G	A	Pts.	PIM	+/-	PP	SH	Gms.	G	A	Pts.	PIM
89-90—Kamloops	WHL	64	14	55	69	64	...	...	...	17	2	14	16	35
90-91—Kamloops	WHL	57	26	56	82	52	...	...	...	—	—	—	—	—
91-92—New Jersey	NHL	4	0	1	1	2	1	0	0	—	—	—	—	—
—Kamloops	WHL	35	7	32	39	61	...	...	...	17	9	14	23	28
92-93—New Jersey	NHL	80	11	29	40	47	8	5	0	5	0	3	3	2
93-94—New Jersey	NHL	81	10	36	46	42	34	5	0	20	2	2	4	8

			REGULAR SEASON							PLAYOFFS				
Season Team	League	Gms.	G	A	Pts.	PIM	+/-	PP	SH	Gms.	G	A	Pts.	PIM
94-95—New Jersey	NHL	48	4	15	19	18	19	4	0	20	4	7	11	10
95-96—New Jersey	NHL	79	8	25	33	46	5	6	0	—	—	—	—	—
96-97—New Jersey	NHL	81	5	30	35	64	-4	3	0	10	2	4	6	6
97-98—New Jersey	NHL	81	14	43	57	27	5	11	0	6	0	2	2	4
98-99—Utah	IHL	5	0	2	2	0	...	...	...	—	—	—	—	—
—New Jersey	NHL	72	11	35	46	26	16	1	1	7	1	3	4	18
99-00—New Jersey	NHL	71	7	31	38	48	19	1	0	22	5	2	7	10
NHL Totals (9 years)		597	70	245	315	320	103	36	1	90	14	23	37	58

NIELSEN, CHRIS   RW   BLUE JACKETS

PERSONAL: Born February 16, 1980, in Moshi, Tanzania. ... 6-1/190. ... Shoots right.
TRANSACTIONS/CAREER NOTES: Selected by New York Islanders in second round (second Islanders pick, 36th overall) of NHL entry draft (June 27, 1998). ... Traded by Islanders to Columbus Blue Jackets for fourth-(traded to Anaheim) and ninth-round (F Dmitri Altarev) picks in 2000 draft (May 11, 2000).

			REGULAR SEASON							PLAYOFFS				
Season Team	League	Gms.	G	A	Pts.	PIM	+/-	PP	SH	Gms.	G	A	Pts.	PIM
96-97—Calgary	WHL	62	11	19	30	39	...	...	...	18	2	4	6	10
97-98—Calgary	WHL	68	22	29	51	31	...	...	...	—	—	—	—	—
98-99—Calgary	WHL	70	22	24	46	45	...	...	...	21	11	5	16	28
99-00—Calgary	WHL	62	38	31	69	86	...	...	...	13	14	9	23	20

NIELSEN, JEFF   RW   WILD

PERSONAL: Born September 20, 1971, in Grand Rapids, Minn. ... 6-0/200. ... Shoots left. ... Full Name: Jeffrey Michael Nielsen.
HIGH SCHOOL: Grand Rapids (Minn.).
COLLEGE: Minnesota.
TRANSACTIONS/CAREER NOTES: Selected by New York Rangers in fourth round (fourth Rangers pick, 69th overall) of NHL entry draft (June 16, 1990). ... Signed as free agent by Mighty Ducks of Anaheim (August 11, 1997). ... Fractured left fibula (January 27, 1998); missed 15 games. ... Suffered injury (January 31, 2000); missed one game. ... Selected by Minnesota Wild in NHL expansion draft (June 23, 2000).
HONORS: Named to WCHA All-Star second team (1993-94).

			REGULAR SEASON							PLAYOFFS				
Season Team	League	Gms.	G	A	Pts.	PIM	+/-	PP	SH	Gms.	G	A	Pts.	PIM
87-88—Grand Rapids H.S.	Minn. H.S.	21	9	11	20	14	...	...	...	—	—	—	—	—
88-89—Grand Rapids H.S.	Minn. H.S.	25	13	17	30	26	...	...	...	—	—	—	—	—
89-90—Grand Rapids H.S.	Minn. H.S.	28	32	25	57	...	...	...	...	—	—	—	—	—
90-91—Univ. of Minnesota	WCHA	45	11	14	25	50	...	...	...	—	—	—	—	—
91-92—Univ. of Minnesota	WCHA	41	14	14	28	70	...	...	...	—	—	—	—	—
92-93—Univ. of Minnesota	WCHA	42	21	20	41	80	...	...	...	—	—	—	—	—
93-94—Univ. of Minnesota	WCHA	41	29	16	45	94	...	...	...	—	—	—	—	—
94-95—Binghamton	AHL	76	24	13	37	139	...	...	...	7	0	0	0	22
95-96—Binghamton	AHL	64	22	20	42	56	...	...	...	4	1	1	2	4
96-97—Binghamton	AHL	76	27	26	53	71	...	...	...	4	0	0	0	7
—New York Rangers	NHL	2	0	0	0	2	-1	0	0	—	—	—	—	—
97-98—Cincinnati	AHL	18	4	8	12	37	...	...	...	—	—	—	—	—
—Anaheim	NHL	32	4	5	9	16	-1	0	0	—	—	—	—	—
98-99—Anaheim	NHL	80	5	4	9	34	-12	0	0	4	0	0	0	2
99-00—Anaheim	NHL	79	8	10	18	14	4	1	0	—	—	—	—	—
NHL Totals (4 years)		193	17	19	36	66	-10	1	0	4	0	0	0	2

NIEMI, ANTTI-JUSSI   D   MIGHTY DUCKS

PERSONAL: Born September 22, 1977, in Vantaa, Finland. ... 6-1/183. ... Shoots left.
TRANSACTIONS/CAREER NOTES: Selected by Ottawa Senators in fourth round (second Senators pick, 81st overall) of NHL entry draft (June 22, 1996). ... Traded by Senators with LW Ted Donato to Mighty Ducks of Anaheim for G Patrick Lalime (June 18, 1999).

			REGULAR SEASON							PLAYOFFS				
Season Team	League	Gms.	G	A	Pts.	PIM	+/-	PP	SH	Gms.	G	A	Pts.	PIM
93-94—Jokerit Helsinki	Finland Jr.	33	0	3	3	26	...	...	...	—	—	—	—	—
94-95—Jokerit Helsinki	Finland Jr.	24	4	8	12	74	...	...	...	—	—	—	—	—
95-96—Jokerit Helsinki	Finland Jr.	34	11	18	29	56	...	...	...	6	0	4	4	33
—Jokerit Helsinki	Finland	6	0	2	2	6	...	...	...	3	0	1	1	0
96-97—Jokerit Helsinki	Finland	44	2	9	11	38	...	...	...	9	0	2	2	2
97-98—Jokerit Helsinki	Finland	46	2	6	8	24	...	...	...	8	0	1	1	...
98-99—Jokerit Helsinki	Finland	53	3	7	10	107	...	...	...	3	0	0	0	2
99-00—Jokerit Helsinki	Finland	53	8	8	16	79	...	...	...	11	0	3	3	6

NIEMINEN, VILLE   LW   AVALANCHE

PERSONAL: Born April 6, 1977, in Tampere, Finland. ... 5-11/205. ... Shoots left.
TRANSACTIONS/CAREER NOTES: Selected by Colorado Avalanche in third round (fourth Avalanche pick, 78th overall) of NHL entry draft (June 21, 1997).

N

Season Team	League	REGULAR SEASON								PLAYOFFS				
		Gms.	G	A	Pts.	PIM	+/-	PP	SH	Gms.	G	A	Pts.	PIM
94-95—Tappara Tampere Jrs. .	Finland	16	11	21	32	47	...	...	...	—	—	—	—	—
—Tappara Tampere	Finland	16	0	0	0	0	...	...	...	—	—	—	—	—
95-96—Tappara Tampere Jrs. .	Finland	20	20	23	43	63	...	...	...	—	—	—	—	—
—Tappara Tampere	Finland	4	0	1	1	8	...	...	...	—	—	—	—	—
—KooVee Tampere	Finland	7	2	1	3	4	...	...	...	—	—	—	—	—
96-97—Tappara Tampere	Finland	49	10	13	23	120	...	...	...	3	1	0	1	8
97-98—Hershey	AHL	74	14	22	36	85	...	...	...	—	—	—	—	—
98-99—Hershey	AHL	67	24	19	43	127	...	...	...	3	0	1	1	0
99-00—Hershey	AHL	74	21	30	51	54	...	...	...	9	2	4	6	6
—Colorado	NHL	1	0	0	0	0	0	0	0	—	—	—	—	—
NHL Totals (1 year).............		1	0	0	0	0	0	0	0					

NIEUWENDYK, JOE — C — STARS

PERSONAL: Born September 10, 1966, in Oshawa, Ont. ... 6-1/205. ... Shoots left. ... Full Name: Joe T. Nieuwendyk. ... Nephew of Ed Kea, defenseman with Atlanta Flames (1973-74 through 1978-79) and St. Louis Blues (1979-80 through 1982-83); and cousin of Jeff Beukeboom, defenseman with Edmonton Oilers (1985-86 through 1991-92) and New York Rangers (1991-92 through 1998-99). ... Name pronounced NOO-ihn-dighk.

COLLEGE: Cornell.

TRANSACTIONS/CAREER NOTES: Selected by Calgary Flames in second round (second Flames pick, 27th overall) of NHL entry draft (June 15, 1985). ... Suffered concussion (November 1987). ... Bruised ribs (May 25, 1989). ... Tore left knee ligament (April 17, 1990). ... Underwent arthroscopic knee surgery (September 28, 1991); missed 12 games. ... Suffered from the flu (November 19, 1992); missed one game. ... Strained right knee (March 26, 1993); missed four games. ... Suffered charley horse (November 13, 1993); missed three games. ... Strained right knee ligaments (February 24, 1994); missed 17 games. ... Strained back (April 29, 1995); missed two games. ... Traded by Flames to Dallas Stars for C Corey Millen and rights to C/RW Jarome Iginla (December 19, 1995). ... Bruised chest (October 5, 1996); missed 12 games. ... Sprained knee (December 18, 1997); missed eight games. ... Reinjured knee (January 9, 1998); missed one game. ... Suffered inflammed knee (January 10, 1999); missed five games. ... Sprained ankle (February 23, 1999); missed one game. ... Suffered back spasms (March 16, 1999); missed one game. ... Injured knee (March 31, 1999); missed one game. ... Suffered back spasms (October 20, 1999); missed three games. ... Bruised chest (December 17, 1999); missed 10 games. ... Separated shoulder (January 19, 2000); missed 21 games.

HONORS: Won Ivy League Rookie of the Year Trophy (1984-85). ... Named to NCAA All-America (East) first team (1985-86 and 1986-87). ... Named to ECAC All-Star first team (1985-86 and 1986-87). ... Named ECAC Player of the Year (1986-87). ... Named NHL Rookie of the Year by The Sporting News (1987-88). ... Won Calder Memorial Trophy (1987-88). ... Won Dodge Ram Tough Award (1987-88). ... Named to NHL All-Rookie team (1987-88). ... Played in NHL All-Star Game (1988-1990 and 1994). ... Won King Clancy Trophy (1994-95). ... Won Conn Smythe Trophy (1998-99).

RECORDS: Shares NHL single-game record for most goals in one period—4 (January 11, 1989). ... Shares NHL single-season playoff record for most game-winning goals—6 (1999).

STATISTICAL PLATEAUS: Three-goal games: 1987-88 (2), 1988-89 (1), 1989-90 (1), 1992-93 (1), 1993-94 (1), 1994-95 (1), 1997-98 (1). Total: 8. ... Four-goal games: 1987-88 (2), 1997-98 (1). Total: 3. ... Five-goal games: 1988-89 (1). ... Total hat tricks: 12.

MISCELLANEOUS: Member of Stanley Cup championship team (1989 and 1999). ... Captain of Calgary Flames (1991-92 through 1994-95). ... Scored on a penalty shot (vs. Steve Weeks, December 16, 1988). ... Failed to score on a penalty shot (vs. Jeff Reese, December 12, 1988; vs. Ken Wregget, January 23, 1993).

STATISTICAL NOTES: Third player in NHL history to score 50 goals in each of his first two seasons. ... Led NHL with 11 game-winning goals (1988-89).

N

Season Team	League	REGULAR SEASON								PLAYOFFS				
		Gms.	G	A	Pts.	PIM	+/-	PP	SH	Gms.	G	A	Pts.	PIM
83-84—Pickering Jr. B	MTHL	38	30	28	58	35	...	...	...	—	—	—	—	—
84-85—Cornell University	ECAC	23	18	21	39	20	...	...	...	—	—	—	—	—
85-86—Cornell University	ECAC	21	21	21	42	45	...	...	...	—	—	—	—	—
86-87—Cornell University	ECAC	23	26	26	52	26	...	...	...	—	—	—	—	—
—Canadian nat'l team	Int'l	5	2	0	2	0	...	...	...	—	—	—	—	—
—Calgary	NHL	9	5	1	6	0	0	2	0	6	2	2	4	0
87-88—Calgary	NHL	75	51	41	92	23	20	*31	3	8	3	4	7	2
88-89—Calgary	NHL	77	51	31	82	40	26	19	3	22	10	4	14	10
89-90—Calgary	NHL	79	45	50	95	40	32	18	0	6	4	6	10	4
90-91—Calgary	NHL	79	45	40	85	36	19	22	4	7	4	1	5	10
91-92—Calgary	NHL	69	22	34	56	55	-1	7	0	—	—	—	—	—
92-93—Calgary	NHL	79	38	37	75	52	9	14	0	6	3	6	9	10
93-94—Calgary	NHL	64	36	39	75	51	19	14	1	6	2	2	4	0
94-95—Calgary	NHL	46	21	29	50	33	11	3	0	5	4	3	7	0
95-96—Dallas	NHL	52	14	18	32	41	-17	8	0	—	—	—	—	—
96-97—Dallas	NHL	66	30	21	51	32	-5	8	0	7	2	2	4	6
97-98—Dallas	NHL	73	39	30	69	30	16	14	0	1	1	0	1	0
—Can. Olympic team	Int'l	6	2	3	5	2	...	...	...	—	—	—	—	—
98-99—Dallas	NHL	67	28	27	55	34	11	8	0	23	*11	10	21	19
99-00—Dallas	NHL	48	15	19	34	26	-1	7	0	23	7	3	10	18
NHL Totals (14 years)..........		883	440	417	857	493	139	175	11	120	53	43	96	79

NIINIMAA, JANNE — D — OILERS

PERSONAL: Born May 22, 1975, in Raahe, Finland. ... 6-2/220. ... Shoots left. ... Name pronounced YAH-nee NEE-nuh-muh.

TRANSACTIONS/CAREER NOTES: Selected by Philadelphia Flyers in second round (first Flyers pick, 36th overall) of NHL entry draft (June 26, 1993). ... Traded by Flyers to Edmonton Oilers for D Dan McGillis and second-round pick (D Jason Beckett) in 1998 draft (March 24, 1998). ... Suffered back spasms (November 4, 1998); missed one game. ... Suffered back spasms (November 24, 1999); missed one game.

HONORS: Named to NHL All-Rookie team (1996-97).

MISCELLANEOUS: Member of bronze-medal-winning Finnish Olympic team (1998).

Season Team	League	Gms.	G	A	Pts.	PIM	+/-	PP	SH	Gms.	G	A	Pts.	PIM
			REGULAR SEASON								PLAYOFFS			
91-92—Karpat Oulu	Finland Div. 2	41	2	11	13	49	...	...	...	—	—	—	—	—
92-93—Karpat Oulu	Finland Div. 2	29	2	3	5	14	...	...	...	—	—	—	—	—
—Karpat Jr.	Finland	10	3	9	12	16	...	...	...	—	—	—	—	—
93-94—Jokerit Helsinki	Finland	45	3	8	11	24	...	...	...	12	1	1	2	4
94-95—Jokerit Helsinki	Finland	42	7	10	17	36	...	...	...	10	1	4	5	35
95-96—Jokerit Helsinki	Finland	49	5	15	20	79	...	...	...	11	0	2	2	12
96-97—Philadelphia	NHL	77	4	40	44	58	12	1	0	19	1	12	13	16
97-98—Philadelphia	NHL	66	3	31	34	56	6	2	0	—	—	—	—	—
—Fin. Olympic team	Int'l	6	0	3	3	8	...	...	...	—	—	—	—	—
—Edmonton	NHL	11	1	8	9	6	7	1	0	11	1	1	2	12
98-99—Edmonton	NHL	81	4	24	28	88	7	2	0	4	0	0	0	2
99-00—Edmonton	NHL	81	8	25	33	89	14	2	2	5	0	2	2	2
NHL Totals (4 years)		316	20	128	148	297	46	8	2	39	2	15	17	32

NIKOLISHIN, ANDREI — C — CAPITALS

PERSONAL: Born March 25, 1973, in Vorkuta, U.S.S.R. ... 6-0/214. ... Shoots left. ... Name pronounced nih-koh-LEE-shihn.
TRANSACTIONS/CAREER NOTES: Selected by Hartford Whalers in second round (second Whalers pick, 47th overall) of NHL entry draft (June 20, 1992). ... Played in Europe during 1994-95 NHL lockout. ... Sprained ankle (October 21, 1995); missed one game. ... Injured back (November 15, 1995); missed five games. ... Strained back (December 2, 1995); missed 15 games. ... Traded by Whalers to Washington Capitals for D Curtis Leschyshyn (November 9, 1996). ... Suffered bulging disc in back (February 2, 1997); missed eight games. ... Injured knee prior to 1997-98 season; missed first 42 games. ... Missed first nine games of 1998-99 season due to contract dispute; played in Russia. ... Strained abdominal muscle (March 28, 2000); missed four games.
HONORS: Named to CIS All-Star team (1993-94). ... Named CIS Player of the Year (1993-94).
MISCELLANEOUS: Member of gold-medal-winning Russian Olympic team (1994).

Season Team	League	Gms.	G	A	Pts.	PIM	+/-	PP	SH	Gms.	G	A	Pts.	PIM
			REGULAR SEASON								PLAYOFFS			
90-91—Dynamo Moscow	USSR	2	0	0	0	0	...	...	...	—	—	—	—	—
91-92—Dynamo Moscow	CIS	18	1	0	1	4	...	...	...	—	—	—	—	—
92-93—Dynamo Moscow	CIS	42	5	7	12	30	...	...	...	10	2	1	3	8
93-94—Dynamo Moscow	CIS	41	8	12	20	30	...	...	...	9	1	3	4	4
—Russian Oly. team	Int'l	8	2	5	7	6	...	...	...	—	—	—	—	—
94-95—Dynamo Moscow	CIS	12	7	2	9	6	...	...	...	—	—	—	—	—
—Hartford	NHL	39	8	10	18	10	7	1	1	—	—	—	—	—
95-96—Hartford	NHL	61	14	37	51	34	-2	4	1	—	—	—	—	—
96-97—Hartford	NHL	12	2	5	7	2	-2	0	0	—	—	—	—	—
—Washington	NHL	59	7	14	21	30	5	1	0	—	—	—	—	—
97-98—Portland	AHL	2	0	0	0	2	...	...	...	—	—	—	—	—
—Washington	NHL	38	6	10	16	14	1	1	0	21	1	13	14	12
98-99—Dynamo Moscow	Russian	4	0	0	0	0	...	...	...	—	—	—	—	—
—Washington	NHL	73	8	27	35	28	0	0	1	—	—	—	—	—
99-00—Washington	NHL	76	11	14	25	28	6	0	2	5	0	2	2	4
NHL Totals (6 years)		358	56	117	173	146	15	7	5	26	1	15	16	16

NILSON, MARCUS — C — PANTHERS

PERSONAL: Born March 1, 1978, in Balsta, Sweden. ... 6-2/193. ... Shoots right.
TRANSACTIONS/CAREER NOTES: Selected by Florida Panthers in first round (first Panthers pick, 20th overall) of NHL entry draft (June 22, 1996).

Season Team	League	Gms.	G	A	Pts.	PIM	+/-	PP	SH	Gms.	G	A	Pts.	PIM
			REGULAR SEASON								PLAYOFFS			
94-95—Djurgarden Jrs.	Sweden	24	7	8	15	22	...	...	...	—	—	—	—	—
95-96—Djurgarden Jrs.	Sweden	25	19	17	36	46	...	...	...	2	1	1	2	12
—Djurgarden Stockholm	Sweden	12	0	0	0	0	...	...	...	1	0	0	0	0
96-97—Djurgarden Stockholm	Sweden	37	0	3	3	33	...	...	...	4	0	0	0	0
97-98—Djurgarden Stockholm	Sweden	41	4	7	11	18	...	...	...	15	2	1	3	16
98-99—New Haven	AHL	69	8	25	33	10	...	...	...	—	—	—	—	—
—Florida	NHL	8	1	1	2	5	2	0	0	—	—	—	—	—
99-00—Louisville	AHL	64	9	23	32	52	...	...	...	4	0	0	0	2
—Florida	NHL	9	0	2	2	2	2	0	0	—	—	—	—	—
NHL Totals (2 years)		17	1	3	4	7	4	0	0					

N

NOLAN, OWEN — RW — SHARKS

PERSONAL: Born February 12, 1972, in Belfast, Northern Ireland. ... 6-1/210. ... Shoots right.
TRANSACTIONS/CAREER NOTES: Selected by Quebec Nordiques in first round (first Nordiques pick, first overall) of NHL entry draft (June 16, 1990). ... Suffered concussion, sore knee and sore back (October 1990). ... Suspended four off-days by NHL for cross-checking incident (December 7, 1992). ... Bruised hand (March 2, 1993); missed three games. ... Bruised shoulder (March 15, 1993); eight games. ... Injured right shoulder (October 19, 1993); missed 11 games. ... Dislocated left shoulder (November 12, 1993); missed remainder of season. ... Bruised shoulder (April 16, 1995); missed two games. ... Nordiques franchise moved to Colorado and renamed Avalanche for 1995-96 season (June 21, 1995). ... Traded by Avalanche to San Jose Sharks for D Sandis Ozolinsh (October 26, 1995). ... Suffered from the flu (March 5, 1996); missed two games. ... Suffered from an illness (November 27, 1996); missed one game. ... Bruised shoulder (January 9, 1997); missed two games. ... Suffered sore ankle (March 20, 1997); missed four games. ... Strained groin (April 7, 1997); missed three games. ... Strained shoulder (March 26, 1998); missed six games. ... Missed first two games of 1998-99 season due to contract dispute. ... Injured back (January 26, 1999); missed one game. ... Reinjured back (February 4, 1999); missed one game. ... Injured shoulder (March 29, 2000); missed four games.

HONORS: Won Emms Family Award (1988-89). ... Won Jim Mahon Memorial Trophy (1989-90). ... Named to OHL All-Star first team (1989-90). ... Played in NHL All-Star Game (1992, 1996, 1997 and 2000).
MISCELLANEOUS: Captain of San Jose Sharks (1998-99 and 1999-2000). ... Failed to score on a penalty shot (vs. Garth Snow, December 26, 1998). ... Shares San Jose Sharks all-time record for most goals (137).
STATISTICAL NOTES: Led NHL with eight game-winning goals (1994-95).
STATISTICAL PLATEAUS: Three-goal games: 1991-92 (2), 1992-93 (2), 1994-95 (3), 1996-97 (1), 1999-00 (1). Total: 9. ... Four-goal games: 1995-96 (1). ... Total hat tricks: 10.

			REGULAR SEASON								PLAYOFFS				
Season Team	League	Gms.	G	A	Pts.	PIM	+/-	PP	SH		Gms.	G	A	Pts.	PIM
88-89—Cornwall	OHL	62	34	25	59	213	...	...	...		18	5	11	16	41
89-90—Cornwall	OHL	58	51	59	110	240	...	...	...		6	7	5	12	26
90-91—Quebec	NHL	59	3	10	13	109	-19	0	0		—	—	—	—	—
—Halifax..................	AHL	6	4	4	8	11	...	...	...		—	—	—	—	—
91-92—Quebec	NHL	75	42	31	73	183	-9	17	0		—	—	—	—	—
92-93—Quebec	NHL	73	36	41	77	185	-1	15	0		5	1	0	1	2
93-94—Quebec	NHL	6	2	2	4	8	2	0	0		—	—	—	—	—
94-95—Quebec	NHL	46	30	19	49	46	21	13	2		6	2	3	5	6
95-96—Colorado	NHL	9	4	4	8	9	-3	4	0		—	—	—	—	—
—San Jose	NHL	72	29	32	61	137	-30	12	1		—	—	—	—	—
96-97—San Jose	NHL	72	31	32	63	155	-19	10	0		—	—	—	—	—
97-98—San Jose	NHL	75	14	27	41	144	-2	3	1		6	2	2	4	26
98-99—San Jose	NHL	78	19	26	45	129	16	6	2		6	1	1	2	6
99-00—San Jose	NHL	78	44	40	84	110	-1	*18	4		10	8	2	10	6
NHL Totals (10 years).........		643	254	264	518	1215	-45	98	10		33	14	8	22	46

NORONEN, MIKA   G   SABRES

PERSONAL: Born June 17, 1979, in Tampere, Finland. ... 6-1/191. ... Catches left.
TRANSACTIONS/CAREER NOTES: Selected by Buffalo Sabres in first round (first Sabres pick, 21st overall) of NHL entry draft (June 21, 1997).
HONORS: Won Dudley (Red) Garrett Memorial Trophy (1999-2000). ... Named to AHL All-Star second team (1999-2000).

			REGULAR SEASON								PLAYOFFS					
Season Team	League	Gms.	Min	W	L	T	GA	SO	Avg.		Gms.	Min.	W	L	GA	SO	Avg.
95-96—Tappara Tampere Jrs.....	Finland	16	962	...	...	...	37	2	2.31		—	—	—	—	—	—	—
96-97—Tappara Tampere..........	Finland	5	215	...	...	...	17	0	4.74		—	—	—	—	—	—	—
97-98—Tappara Tampere..........	Finland	47	1703	14	12	3	83	1	2.92		4	196	1	2	12	0	3.67
98-99—Tappara Tampere..........	Finland	43	2494	18	20	5	*135	2	3.25		—	—	—	—	—	—	—
99-00—Rochester..................	AHL	54	3089	*33	13	4	112	†6	*2.18		21	1235	13	*8	37	*6	*1.80

NORSTROM, MATTIAS   D   KINGS

PERSONAL: Born January 2, 1972, in Stockholm, Sweden. ... 6-2/201. ... Shoots left. ... Name pronounced muh-TEE-uhz NOHR-struhm.
TRANSACTIONS/CAREER NOTES: Selected by New York Rangers in second round (second Rangers pick, 48th overall) of NHL entry draft (June 20, 1992). ... Suffered from the flu (April 28, 1995); missed two games. ... Separated shoulder (December 30, 1995); missed six games. ... Traded by Rangers with C Ray Ferraro, C Ian Laperriere, C Nathan Lafayette and fourth-round pick (D Sean Blanchard) in 1997 draft to Los Angeles Kings for RW Shane Churla, LW Jari Kurri and D Marty McSorley (March 14, 1996). ... Bruised left wrist (November 7, 1996); missed one game. ... Suspended one game by NHL for illegal check (January 12, 1998). ... Bruised ribs (April 11, 1999); missed four games.
HONORS: Played in NHL All-Star Game (1999).

			REGULAR SEASON								PLAYOFFS				
Season Team	League	Gms.	G	A	Pts.	PIM	+/-	PP	SH		Gms.	G	A	Pts.	PIM
91-92—AIK Solna..................	Sweden	39	4	4	8	28	...	...	...		—	—	—	—	—
92-93—AIK Solna..................	Sweden	22	0	1	1	16	...	...	...		—	—	—	—	—
93-94—New York Rangers......	NHL	9	0	2	2	6	0	0	0		—	—	—	—	—
—Binghamton..................	AHL	55	1	9	10	70	...	...	...		—	—	—	—	—
94-95—Binghamton..................	AHL	63	9	10	19	91	...	...	...		—	—	—	—	—
—New York Rangers......	NHL	9	0	3	3	2	2	0	0		3	0	0	0	0
95-96—New York Rangers......	NHL	25	2	1	3	22	5	0	0		—	—	—	—	—
—Los Angeles..................	NHL	11	0	1	1	18	-8	0	0		—	—	—	—	—
96-97—Los Angeles..................	NHL	80	1	21	22	84	-4	0	0		—	—	—	—	—
97-98—Los Angeles..................	NHL	73	1	12	13	90	14	0	0		4	0	0	0	2
—Swedish Oly. team......	Int'l	4	0	1	1	2	...	...	...		—	—	—	—	—
98-99—Los Angeles..................	NHL	78	2	5	7	36	-10	0	1		—	—	—	—	—
99-00—Los Angeles..................	NHL	82	1	13	14	66	22	0	0		4	0	0	0	6
NHL Totals (7 years)...........		367	7	58	65	324	21	0	1		11	0	0	0	8

NORTON, BRAD   D   OILERS

PERSONAL: Born February 13, 1975, in Cambridge, Mass. ... 6-4/225. ... Shoots left. ... Full Name: Brad Joseph Norton. ... Brother of Jeff Norton, defenseman with six NHL teams (1987-88 through 1999-2000).
HIGH SCHOOL: Cushing Academy (Ashburnham, Mass.).
COLLEGE: Massachusetts.
TRANSACTIONS/CAREER NOTES: Selected by Edmonton Oilers in ninth round (ninth Oilers pick, 215th overall) of NHL entry draft (June 26, 1993).

Season Team	League	Gms.	G	A	Pts.	PIM	+/-	PP	SH	Gms.	G	A	Pts.	PIM
					REGULAR SEASON							PLAYOFFS		
92-93—Cushing Academy......	Mass. H.S.	31	10	26	36	36	...	...	...	—	—	—	—	—
93-94—Cushing Academy......	Mass. H.S.							Statistics unavailable.			—	—	—	—	—
94-95—Univ. of Mass.............	Hockey East	30	0	6	6	89	...	...	...	—	—	—	—	—
95-96—Univ. of Mass.............	Hockey East	34	4	12	16	99	...	...	...	—	—	—	—	—
96-97—Univ. of Mass.............	Hockey East	35	2	16	18	88	...	...	...	—	—	—	—	—
97-98—Univ. of Mass.............	Hockey East	20	2	13	15	28	...	...	...	—	—	—	—	—
—Detroit......................	IHL	33	1	4	5	56	...	...	...	22	0	2	2	87
98-99—Hamilton....................	AHL	58	1	8	9	134	...	...	...	11	0	1	1	6
99-00—Hamilton....................	AHL	40	5	12	17	104	...	...	...	10	1	4	5	26

NORTON, JEFF   D

PERSONAL: Born November 25, 1965, in Acton, Mass. ... 6-2/195. ... Shoots left. ... Full Name: Jeffrey Zaccari Norton. ... Brother of Brad Norton, defenseman, Edmonton Oilers.
HIGH SCHOOL: Cushing Academy (Ashburnham, Mass.).
COLLEGE: Michigan.
TRANSACTIONS/CAREER NOTES: Selected by New York Islanders in third round (third Islanders pick, 62nd overall) of NHL entry draft (June 9, 1984). ... Bruised ribs (November 16, 1988). ... Injured groin (February 1990). ... Strained groin and abdominal muscles (March 2, 1990); missed games. ... Suffered concussion (April 9, 1990). ... Suspended eight games by NHL for intentionally injuring another player in preseason game (September 30, 1990). ... Dislocated right shoulder (November 3, 1990); missed four games. ... Reinjured shoulder (December 27, 1990); missed five games. ... Reinjured shoulder and underwent surgery (February 23, 1991); missed remainder of season. ... Suffered concussion (October 26, 1991); missed one game. ... Tore ligaments in left wrist (January 3, 1992); missed remainder of season. ... Underwent surgery to left wrist (January 8, 1992). ... Suffered hip flexor (October 23, 1992); missed five games. ... Suffered sore shoulder (December 31, 1992); missed one game. ... Pulled groin (February 25, 1993); missed two games. ... Traded by Islanders to San Jose Sharks for third-round pick (D Jason Strudwick) in 1994 draft (June 20, 1993). ... Sprained ankle (December 11, 1993); missed nine games. ... Reinjured ankle (January 4, 1994); missed five games. ... Sprained ankle (February 19, 1994); missed five games. ... Suffered from the flu (January 28, 1995); missed one game. ... Traded by Sharks with third-round pick (traded to Colorado) in 1997 draft and future considerations to St. Louis Blues for C Craig Janney (March 6, 1995). ... Injured hand (March 7, 1995); missed one game. ... Traded by Blues with D Donald Dufresne to Edmonton Oilers for D Igor Kravchuck and D Ken Sutton (January 4, 1996). ... Fractured thumb (February 9, 1996); missed two games. ... Suffered back spasms (March 17, 1996); missed one game. ... Sprained left knee (March 24, 1996); missed nine games. ... Sprained ankle (October 15, 1996); missed six games. ... Injured right ankle (November 7, 1996); missed one game. ... Strained groin (January 7, 1997); missed one game. ... Traded by Oilers to Tampa Bay Lightning for D Drew Bannister and sixth-round pick (C Peter Sarno) in 1997 (March 18, 1997). ... Strained groin (October 5, 1997); missed three games. ... Traded by Lightning with RW Dino Ciccarelli to Florida Panthers for G Mark Fitzpatrick and RW Jody Hull (January 15, 1998). ... Suffered cracked sternum and bruised chest (March 21, 1998); missed remainder of season. ... Traded by Panthers to Sharks for LW Alex Hicks and fifth-round pick (traded to New York Islanders) in 1999 draft (November 11, 1998). ... Suffered back spasms (October 7, 1999); missed 10 games. ... Injured shoulder (January 11, 2000); missed two games. ... Suspended four games by NHL for stick-swinging incident (February 14, 2000).
HONORS: Named to CCHA All-Star second team (1986-87).

Season Team	League	Gms.	G	A	Pts.	PIM	+/-	PP	SH	Gms.	G	A	Pts.	PIM
					REGULAR SEASON							PLAYOFFS		
83-84—Cushing Academy......	Mass. H.S.	21	22	33	55	...	...	...	...	—	—	—	—	—
84-85—Univ. of Michigan........	CCHA	37	8	16	24	103	...	...	...	—	—	—	—	—
85-86—Univ. of Michigan........	CCHA	37	15	30	45	99	...	...	...	—	—	—	—	—
86-87—Univ. of Michigan........	CCHA	39	12	37	49	92	...	...	...	—	—	—	—	—
87-88—U.S. national team	Int'l	57	7	25	32	...	...	...	...	—	—	—	—	—
—U.S. Olympic team......	Int'l	6	0	4	4	4	...	...	...	—	—	—	—	—
—New York Islanders......	NHL	15	1	6	7	14	3	1	0	3	0	2	2	13
88-89—New York Islanders......	NHL	69	1	30	31	74	-24	1	0	—	—	—	—	—
89-90—New York Islanders......	NHL	60	4	49	53	65	-9	4	0	4	1	3	4	17
90-91—New York Islanders......	NHL	44	3	25	28	16	-13	2	1	—	—	—	—	—
91-92—New York Islanders......	NHL	28	1	18	19	18	2	0	1	—	—	—	—	—
92-93—New York Islanders......	NHL	66	12	38	50	45	-3	5	0	10	1	1	2	4
93-94—San Jose....................	NHL	64	7	33	40	36	16	1	0	14	1	5	6	20
94-95—San Jose....................	NHL	20	1	9	10	39	1	0	0	—	—	—	—	—
—St. Louis..................	NHL	28	2	18	20	33	21	0	0	7	1	1	2	11
95-96—St. Louis....................	NHL	36	4	7	11	26	4	0	0	—	—	—	—	—
—Edmonton..................	NHL	30	4	16	20	16	5	1	0	—	—	—	—	—
96-97—Edmonton..................	NHL	62	2	11	13	42	-7	0	0	—	—	—	—	—
—Tampa Bay...............	NHL	13	0	5	5	16	0	0	0	—	—	—	—	—
97-98—Tampa Bay...............	NHL	37	4	6	10	26	-25	4	0	—	—	—	—	—
—Florida......................	NHL	19	0	7	7	18	-7	0	0	—	—	—	—	—
98-99—Florida......................	NHL	3	0	0	0	2	0	0	0	—	—	—	—	—
—San Jose.................	NHL	69	4	18	22	42	2	2	0	6	0	7	7	10
99-00—San Jose....................	NHL	62	0	20	20	49	-2	0	0	12	0	1	1	7
NHL Totals (13 years).........		725	50	316	366	577	-36	21	2	56	4	20	24	82

NOVOSELTSEV, IVAN   C   PANTHERS

PERSONAL: Born January 23, 1979, in Golitsino, U.S.S.R. ... 6-1/183. ... Shoots left. ... Name pronounced noh-vuh-SEHLT-sehf.
TRANSACTIONS/CAREER NOTES: Selected by Florida Panthers in fourth round (fifth Panthers pick, 95th overall) of NHL entry draft (June 21, 1997).
HONORS: Named to OHL All-Star first team (1998-99).

Season Team	League	Gms.	G	A	Pts.	PIM	+/-	PP	SH	Gms.	G	A	Pts.	PIM
					REGULAR SEASON							PLAYOFFS		
95-96—Krylja Sov. Moscow.....	CIS	1	0	0	0	0	...	...	...	—	—	—	—	—
96-97—Kryla Sov. Moscow.....	Russian	30	0	3	3	18	...	...	...	2	0	0	0	4
—Kryla Sov. Moscow.....	Rus. Div. III	19	5	3	8	39	...	...	...	—	—	—	—	—
97-98—Sarnia	OHL	53	26	22	48	41	...	...	...	5	1	1	2	8
98-99—Sarnia	OHL	68	57	39	96	45	...	...	...	5	2	4	6	6
99-00—Louisville	AHL	47	14	21	35	22	...	...	...	4	1	0	1	6
—Florida......................	NHL	14	2	1	3	8	-3	2	0	—	—	—	—	—
NHL Totals (1 year)............		14	2	1	3	8	-3	2	0	—	—	—	—	—

N

PERSONAL: Born July 3, 1968, in Tampere, Finland. ... 6-2/199. ... Shoots right. ... Full Name: Teppo Kalevi Numminen. ... Name pronounced TEH-poh NOO-mih-nehn.

TRANSACTIONS/CAREER NOTES: Selected by Winnipeg Jets in second round (second Jets pick, 29th overall) of NHL entry draft (June 21, 1986). ... Separated shoulder (March 5, 1989). ... Fractured thumb (April 14, 1990). ... Fractured foot (January 28, 1993); missed 17 games. ... Dislocated thumb (February 9, 1994); missed remainder of season. ... Played in Europe during 1994-95 NHL lockout. ... Suffered from stomach flu (January 23, 1995); missed one game. ... Suffered stress fracture in right knee (February 22, 1995); missed five games. ... Separated shoulder (November 28, 1995); missed eight games. ... Jets franchise moved to Phoenix and renamed Coyotes for 1996-97 season; NHL approved move on January 18, 1996. ... Strained hip flexor (March 1, 2000); missed two games.

HONORS: Played in NHL All-Star Game (1999 and 2000).

MISCELLANEOUS: Member of silver-medal-winning Finnish Olympic team (1988). ... Member of bronze-medal-winning Finnish Olympic team (1998). ... Holds Phoenix Coyotes record for most games played (246).

					REGULAR SEASON							PLAYOFFS				
Season Team	League	Gms.	G	A	Pts.	PIM	+/-	PP	SH		Gms.	G	A	Pts.	PIM
84-85—Tappara	Finland	30	14	17	31	10	...	...	...		—	—	—	—	—
85-86—Tappara	Finland	39	2	4	6	6	...	...	...		8	0	0	0	0
86-87—Tappara	Finland	44	9	9	18	16	...	...	...		9	4	1	5	4
87-88—Tappara	Finland	44	10	10	20	29	...	...	...		10	6	6	12	6
—Fin. Olympic team	Int'l	6	1	4	5	0	...	...	...		—	—	—	—	—
88-89—Winnipeg	NHL	69	1	14	15	36	-11	0	1		—	—	—	—	—
89-90—Winnipeg	NHL	79	11	32	43	20	-4	1	0		7	1	2	3	10
90-91—Winnipeg	NHL	80	8	25	33	28	-15	3	0		—	—	—	—	—
91-92—Winnipeg	NHL	80	5	34	39	32	15	4	0		7	0	0	0	0
92-93—Winnipeg	NHL	66	7	30	37	33	4	3	1		6	1	1	2	2
93-94—Winnipeg	NHL	57	5	18	23	28	-23	4	0		—	—	—	—	—
94-95—TuTo Turku	Finland	12	3	8	11	4	...	...	...		—	—	—	—	—
—Winnipeg	NHL	42	5	16	21	16	12	2	0		—	—	—	—	—
95-96—Winnipeg	NHL	74	11	43	54	22	-4	6	0		6	0	0	0	2
96-97—Phoenix	NHL	82	2	25	27	28	-3	0	0		7	3	3	6	0
97-98—Phoenix	NHL	82	11	40	51	30	25	6	0		1	0	0	0	0
—Fin. Olympic team	Int'l	6	1	1	2	2	...	...	...		—	—	—	—	—
98-99—Phoenix	NHL	82	10	30	40	30	3	1	0		7	2	1	3	4
99-00—Phoenix	NHL	79	8	34	42	16	21	2	0		5	1	1	2	0
NHL Totals (12 years)		**872**	**84**	**341**	**425**	**319**	**20**	**32**	**2**		**46**	**8**	**8**	**16**	**18**

PERSONAL: Born March 29, 1969, in Turku, Finland. ... 6-1/198. ... Shoots left. ... Name pronounced KIGH NUHR-mih-nehn.

TRANSACTIONS/CAREER NOTES: Selected by Los Angeles Kings in eighth round (ninth Kings pick, 193rd overall) in NHL entry draft (June 22, 1996). ... Bruised thigh (January 15, 1997); missed two games. ... Bruised thigh (February 5, 1997); missed two games. ... Signed as free agent by Minnesota Wild (May 17, 2000).

					REGULAR SEASON							PLAYOFFS			
Season Team	League	Gms.	G	A	Pts.	PIM	+/-	PP	SH		Gms.	G	A	Pts.	PIM
89-90—TPS Turku Jr.	Finland	35	28	17	45	32	...	...	...		—	—	—	—	—
90-91—TuTo Turku	Finland	33	26	20	46	14	...	...	...		—	—	—	—	—
91-92—Kiekko-67	Finland Div. 2	44	44	19	63	34	...	...	...		—	—	—	—	—
92-93—Kiekko-67	Finland Div. 2	8	6	4	10	2	...	...	...		—	—	—	—	—
—TPS Turku	Finland	31	4	6	10	13	...	...	...		7	1	2	3	0
93-94—TPS Turku	Finland	45	23	12	35	20	...	...	...		11	0	3	3	4
94-95—HPK Hameenlinna	Finland	49	30	25	55	40	...	...	...		—	—	—	—	—
95-96—HV 71 Jonkoping	Sweden	40	31	24	55	32	...	...	...		4	3	1	4	8
96-97—Los Angeles	NHL	67	16	11	27	22	-3	4	0		—	—	—	—	—
97-98—Vastra Frolunda	Sweden	23	9	7	16	24	...	...	...		—	—	—	—	—
—Jokerit	Finland	20	7	9	16	30	...	...	...		—	—	—	—	—
98-99—Davos HC	Switzerland	42	26	14	40	26	...	...	...		—	—	—	—	—
99-00—TPS Turku	Finland	54	*41	37	*78	40	...	...	...		10	5	†9	*14	0
NHL Totals (1 year)		**67**	**16**	**11**	**27**	**22**	**-3**	**4**	**0**						

PERSONAL: Born October 3, 1972, in Stockholm, Sweden. ... 6-1/195. ... Shoots left. ... Full Name: Mikael Nylander. ... Name pronounced NEE-lan-duhr.

TRANSACTIONS/CAREER NOTES: Selected by Hartford Whalers in third round (fourth Whalers pick, 59th overall) of NHL entry draft (June 22, 1991). ... Fractured jaw (January 23, 1993); missed 15 games. ... Traded by Whalers with D Zarley Zalapski and D James Patrick to Calgary Flames for D Gary Suter, LW Paul Ranheim and C Ted Drury (March 10, 1994). ... Played in Europe during 1994-95 NHL lockout. ... Fractured left wrist and forearm (January 24, 1995); missed 42 games. ... Injured wrist (January 16, 1996); missed three games. ... Injured left knee (March 26, 1998); missed final 11 games of season and first 23 games of 1998-99 season. ... Traded by Flames to Tampa Bay Lightning for RW Andrei Nazarov (January 19, 1999). ... Suffered concussion (April 8, 1999); missed final five games of season. ... Traded by Lightning to Chicago Blackhawks for D Bryan Muir and LW Reid Simpson (November 12, 1999).

HONORS: Named Swedish League Rookie of the Year (1991-92).

STATISTICAL PLATEAUS: Three-goal games: 1992-93 (1). ... Four-goal games: 1999-00 (1). ... Total hat tricks: 2.

					REGULAR SEASON							PLAYOFFS			
Season Team	League	Gms.	G	A	Pts.	PIM	+/-	PP	SH		Gms.	G	A	Pts.	PIM
89-90—Huddinge	Sweden	31	7	15	22	4	...	...	...		—	—	—	—	—
90-91—Huddinge	Sweden	33	14	20	34	10	...	...	...		—	—	—	—	—
91-92—AIK Solna	Sweden	40	11	17	28	30	...	...	...		—	—	—	—	—
—Swedish Oly. team	Int'l	6	0	1	1	0	...	...	...		—	—	—	—	—

N

Season Team	League	REGULAR SEASON								PLAYOFFS				
		Gms.	G	A	Pts.	PIM	+/-	PP	SH	Gms.	G	A	Pts.	PIM
92-93—Hartford	NHL	59	11	22	33	36	-7	3	0	—	—	—	—	—
—Springfield	AHL	59	11	22	33	36	...	...	...	—	—	—	—	—
93-94—Hartford	NHL	58	11	33	44	24	-2	4	0	—	—	—	—	—
—Springfield	AHL	4	0	9	9	0	...	...	...	—	—	—	—	—
—Calgary	NHL	15	2	9	11	6	10	0	0	3	0	0	0	0
94-95—JyP HT	Finland	16	11	19	30	63	...	...	...	—	—	—	—	—
—Calgary	NHL	6	0	1	1	2	1	0	0	6	0	6	6	2
95-96—Calgary	NHL	73	17	38	55	20	0	4	0	4	0	0	0	0
96-97—Lugano	Switzerland	36	12	43	55	...	...	...	...	—	—	—	—	—
97-98—Calgary	NHL	65	13	23	36	24	10	0	0	—	—	—	—	—
—Swedish Oly. team	Int'l	4	0	0	0	6	...	...	...	—	—	—	—	—
98-99—Calgary	NHL	9	2	3	5	2	1	1	0	—	—	—	—	—
—Tampa Bay	NHL	24	2	7	9	6	-10	0	0	—	—	—	—	—
99-00—Tampa Bay	NHL	11	1	2	3	4	-3	1	0	—	—	—	—	—
—Chicago	NHL	66	23	28	51	26	9	4	0	—	—	—	—	—
NHL Totals (7 years)		386	82	166	248	150	9	17	0	13	0	6	6	2

OATES, ADAM — C — CAPITALS

PERSONAL: Born August 27, 1962, in Weston, Ont. ... 5-10/180. ... Shoots right. ... Full Name: Adam R. Oates. ... Name pronounced OHTS.
COLLEGE: Rensselaer Polytechnic Institute (N.Y.).
TRANSACTIONS/CAREER NOTES: Signed as non-drafted free agent by Detroit Red Wings (June 28, 1985). ... Pulled abdominal muscle (October 1987). ... Suffered from chicken pox (November 1988). ... Bruised thigh (December 1988). ... Traded by Red Wings with RW Paul MacLean to St. Louis Blues for LW Tony McKegney and C Bernie Federko (June 15, 1989). ... Tore rib and abdominal muscles (November 5, 1990); missed 18 games. ... Traded by Blues to Boston Bruins for C Craig Janney and D Stephane Quintal (February 7, 1992). ... Injured groin (January 6, 1994); missed seven games. ... Injured knee (October 28, 1995); missed 12 games. ... Traded by Bruins with RW Rick Tocchet and G Bill Ranford to Washington Capitals for G Jim Carey, C Jason Allison, C Anson Carter and third-round pick (RW Lee Goren) in 1997 draft (March 1, 1997). ... Injured back (April 10, 1997); missed two games. ... Strained groin (November 27, 1998); missed 23 games.
HONORS: Named to ECAC All-Star second team (1983-84). ... Named to NCAA All-America (East) first team (1984-85). ... Named to NCAA All-Tournament team (1984-85). ... Named to ECAC All-Star first team (1984-85). ... Named to THE SPORTING NEWS All-Star second team (1990-91). ... Named to NHL All-Star second team (1990-91). ... Played in NHL All-Star Game (1991-1994 and 1997).
RECORDS: Holds NHL All-Star Game record for most assists in one period—4 (first period, 1993).
STATISTICAL PLATEAUS: Three-goal games: 1992-93 (3), 1993-94 (2), 1997-98 (1). Total: 6. ... Four-goal games: 1995-96 (1). ... Total hat tricks: 7.
MISCELLANEOUS: Captain of Washington Capitals (1999-2000). ... Scored on a penalty shot (vs. Curtis Joseph, November 18, 1998).
STATISTICAL NOTES: Tied for NHL lead with 11 game-winning goals (1992-93).

Season Team	League	REGULAR SEASON								PLAYOFFS				
		Gms.	G	A	Pts.	PIM	+/-	PP	SH	Gms.	G	A	Pts.	PIM
82-83—R.P.I.	ECAC	22	9	33	42	8	...	...	...	—	—	—	—	—
83-84—R.P.I.	ECAC	38	26	57	83	15	...	...	...	—	—	—	—	—
84-85—R.P.I.	ECAC	38	31	60	91	29	...	...	...	—	—	—	—	—
85-86—Adirondack	AHL	34	18	28	46	4	...	...	...	17	7	14	21	4
—Detroit	NHL	38	9	11	20	10	1	0	-24	—	—	—	—	—
86-87—Detroit	NHL	76	15	32	47	21	0	4	0	16	4	7	11	6
87-88—Detroit	NHL	63	14	40	54	20	16	3	0	16	8	12	20	6
88-89—Detroit	NHL	69	16	62	78	14	-1	2	0	6	0	8	8	2
89-90—St. Louis	NHL	80	23	79	102	30	9	6	2	12	2	12	14	4
90-91—St. Louis	NHL	61	25	90	115	29	15	3	1	13	7	13	20	10
91-92—St. Louis	NHL	54	10	59	69	12	-4	3	0	—	—	—	—	—
—Boston	NHL	26	10	20	30	10	-5	3	0	15	5	14	19	4
92-93—Boston	NHL	84	45	*97	142	32	15	24	1	4	0	9	9	4
93-94—Boston	NHL	77	32	80	112	45	10	16	2	13	3	9	12	8
94-95—Boston	NHL	48	12	41	53	8	-11	4	1	5	1	0	1	2
95-96—Boston	NHL	70	25	67	92	18	16	7	1	5	2	5	7	2
96-97—Boston	NHL	63	18	52	70	10	-3	2	2	—	—	—	—	—
—Washington	NHL	17	4	8	12	4	-2	1	0	—	—	—	—	—
97-98—Washington	NHL	82	18	58	76	36	6	3	2	21	6	11	17	8
98-99—Washington	NHL	59	12	42	54	22	-1	3	0	—	—	—	—	—
99-00—Washington	NHL	82	15	56	71	14	13	5	0	5	0	3	3	4
NHL Totals (15 years)		1049	303	894	1197	335	74	89	-12	131	38	103	141	60

OBSUT, JAROSLAV — D — BLUES

PERSONAL: Born September 3, 1976, in Presov, Czechoslovakia. ... 6-1/185. ... Shoots left. ... Name pronounced ahb-SOOT.
TRANSACTIONS/CAREER NOTES: Selected by Winnipeg Jets in eighth round (ninth Jets pick, 188th overall) of NHL entry draft (July 8, 1995). ... Jets franchise moved to Phoenix and renamed Coyotes for 1996-97 season; NHL approved move on January 18, 1996. ... Signed as free agent by St. Louis Blues (May 25, 1999).

Season Team	League	REGULAR SEASON								PLAYOFFS				
		Gms.	G	A	Pts.	PIM	+/-	PP	SH	Gms.	G	A	Pts.	PIM
94-95—North Battleford	SJHL	55	21	30	51	126	...	...	...	—	—	—	—	—
95-96—Swift Current	WHL	72	10	11	21	57	...	...	...	6	0	0	0	2
96-97—Edmonton	WHL	13	2	9	11	4	...	...	...	—	—	—	—	—
—Medicine Hat	WHL	50	8	26	34	42	...	...	...	—	—	—	—	—
—Toledo	ECHL	3	1	0	1	0	...	...	...	5	0	1	1	6
97-98—Raleigh	ECHL	60	6	26	32	46	...	...	...	—	—	—	—	—
—Syracuse	AHL	4	0	1	1	4	...	...	...	—	—	—	—	—
98-99—Manitoba	IHL	2	0	0	0	0	...	...	...	—	—	—	—	—
—Augusta	ECHL	41	11	25	36	42	...	...	...	—	—	—	—	—
—Worcester	AHL	31	2	8	10	14	...	...	...	4	0	1	1	2
99-00—Worcester	AHL	7	0	2	2	4	...	...	...	—	—	—	—	—

PERSONAL: Born July 21, 1968, in Quill Lake, Sask. ... 6-0/210. ... Shoots right. ... Name pronounced OH-duh-lighn.
TRANSACTIONS/CAREER NOTES: Selected by Montreal Canadiens as underage junior in seventh round (eighth Canadiens pick, 141st overall) of NHL entry draft (June 21, 1986). ... Bruised right ankle (January 22, 1991); missed five games. ... Twisted right ankle (February 9, 1991). ... Suspended one game by NHL for game misconduct penalties (March 1, 1993). ... Bruised shoulder (January 24, 1994); missed three games. ... Suspended two games without pay and fined $1,000 by NHL for shooting puck into the opposing team's bench (April 3, 1996). ... Traded by Canadiens to New Jersey Devils for RW Stephane Richer (August 22, 1996). ... Bruised knee (January 21, 1997); missed three games. ... Bruised shoulder (November 12, 1997); missed one game. ... Suffered from the flu (January 11, 1999); missed two games. ... Bruised right knee (March 22, 1999); missed nine games. ... Injured back (November 5, 1999); missed three games. ... Suffered from the flu (January 14, 2000); missed three games. ... Traded by Devils to Phoenix Coyotes for D Deron Quint and conditional pick in 2001 draft (March 7, 2000). ... Selected by Columbus Blue Jackets in NHL expansion draft (June 23, 2000).
MISCELLANEOUS: Member of Stanley Cup championship team (1993).
STATISTICAL PLATEAUS: Three-goal games: 1993-94 (1).

				REGULAR SEASON							PLAYOFFS				
Season Team	League	Gms.	G	A	Pts.	PIM	+/-	PP	SH		Gms.	G	A	Pts.	PIM
85-86—Moose Jaw	WHL	67	9	37	46	117	...	...	...		13	1	6	7	34
86-87—Moose Jaw	WHL	59	9	50	59	70	...	...	...		9	2	5	7	26
87-88—Moose Jaw	WHL	63	15	43	58	166	...	...	...		—	—	—	—	—
88-89—Sherbrooke	AHL	33	3	4	7	120	...	...	...		3	0	2	2	5
—Peoria	IHL	36	2	8	10	116	...	...	...		—	—	—	—	—
89-90—Sherbrooke	AHL	68	7	24	31	265	...	...	...		12	6	5	11	79
—Montreal	NHL	8	0	2	2	33	...	0	0		—	—	—	—	—
90-91—Montreal	NHL	52	0	2	2	259	7	0	0		12	0	0	0	54
91-92—Montreal	NHL	71	1	7	8	212	15	0	0		7	0	0	0	11
92-93—Montreal	NHL	83	2	14	16	205	35	0	0		20	1	5	6	30
93-94—Montreal	NHL	79	11	29	40	276	8	6	0		7	0	0	0	17
94-95—Montreal	NHL	48	3	7	10	152	-13	0	0		—	—	—	—	—
95-96—Montreal	NHL	79	3	14	17	230	8	0	1		6	1	1	2	6
96-97—New Jersey	NHL	79	3	13	16	110	16	1	0		10	2	2	4	19
97-98—New Jersey	NHL	79	4	19	23	171	11	1	0		6	1	1	2	21
98-99—New Jersey	NHL	70	5	26	31	114	6	1	0		7	0	3	3	10
99-00—New Jersey	NHL	57	1	15	16	104	-10	0	0		—	—	—	—	—
—Phoenix	NHL	16	1	7	8	19	1	1	0		5	0	0	0	16
NHL Totals (11 years)		721	34	155	189	1885	...	10	1		80	5	12	17	184

PERSONAL: Born May 31, 1969, in Spy Hill, Sask. ... 6-0/200. ... Shoots right. ... Name pronounced AH-juhrs.
TRANSACTIONS/CAREER NOTES: Signed as non-drafted free agent by San Jose Sharks (September 3, 1991). ... Injured hand (December 21, 1991); missed four games. ... Fractured hand (November 5, 1992); missed 15 games. ... Suspended one game by NHL for accumulating three game-misconduct penalties (January 29, 1993). ... Suspended two games by NHL for accumulating four game-misconduct penalties (February 19, 1993). ... Traded by Sharks with fifth-round pick (D Elias Abrahamsson) in 1996 draft to Boston Bruins for D Al Iafrate (June 21, 1996). ... Injured neck (January 9, 1997); missed one game. ... Signed as free agent by Colorado Avalanche (October 24, 1997). ... Suffered from the flu (January 26, 1998); missed one game. ... Suffered from appendicitis (January 31, 1999); missed seven games. ... Selected by Minnesota Wild in NHL expansion draft (June 23, 2000).
MISCELLANEOUS: Captain of San Jose Sharks (1994-95 and 1995-96). ... Holds San Jose Sharks all-time record for most penalty minutes (1,001).

				REGULAR SEASON							PLAYOFFS				
Season Team	League	Gms.	G	A	Pts.	PIM	+/-	PP	SH		Gms.	G	A	Pts.	PIM
86-87—Brandon	WHL	70	7	14	21	150	...	...	...		—	—	—	—	—
87-88—Brandon	WHL	70	17	18	35	202	...	...	...		4	1	1	2	14
88-89—Brandon	WHL	71	31	29	60	277	...	...	...		—	—	—	—	—
89-90—Brandon	WHL	64	37	28	65	209	...	...	...		—	—	—	—	—
90-91—Kansas City	IHL	77	12	19	31	*318	...	...	...		—	—	—	—	—
91-92—Kansas City	IHL	12	2	2	4	56	...	...	...		9	3	0	3	13
—San Jose	NHL	61	7	4	11	217	-21	0	0		—	—	—	—	—
92-93—San Jose	NHL	66	12	15	27	253	-26	6	0		—	—	—	—	—
93-94—San Jose	NHL	81	13	8	21	222	-13	7	0		11	0	0	0	11
94-95—San Jose	NHL	48	4	3	7	117	-8	0	0		11	1	1	2	23
95-96—San Jose	NHL	78	12	4	16	192	-4	0	0		—	—	—	—	—
96-97—Boston	NHL	80	7	8	15	197	-15	1	0		—	—	—	—	—
97-98—Providence	AHL	4	0	0	0	31	...	...	...		—	—	—	—	—
—Colorado	NHL	68	5	8	13	213	5	0	0		6	0	0	0	25
98-99—Colorado	NHL	75	2	3	5	259	-3	1	0		15	1	0	1	14
99-00—Colorado	NHL	62	1	2	3	162	-7	0	0		4	0	0	0	0
NHL Totals (9 years)		619	63	55	118	1832	-92	15	0		47	2	1	3	73

PERSONAL: Born September 7, 1970, in Maniwaki, Que. ... 6-3/227. ... Shoots left. ... Name pronounced OH-jihk.
TRANSACTIONS/CAREER NOTES: Selected by Vancouver Canucks in fifth round (fifth Canucks pick, 86th overall) of NHL entry draft (June 16, 1990). ... Fractured cheekbone (February 27, 1991). ... Suspended six games by NHL for stick foul (November 26, 1991). ... Underwent knee surgery (February 11, 1993); missed five games. ... Suspended one game by NHL for accumulating three game misconduct penalties (January 27, 1993). ... Suspended one game by NHL for accumulating four game misconduct penalties (March 26, 1993). ... Suspended two games by NHL for stick incident (April 8, 1993). ... Separated shoulder (November 27, 1993); missed two games. ... Suspended by NHL for

O

10 games (September 1994); NHL reduced suspension to six games due to abbreviated 1994-95 season (January 19, 1995). ... Strained groin (March 10, 1995); missed six games. ... Strained abdomen (April 7, 1995); missed last 13 games of season. ... Injured knee (October 10, 1995); missed one game. ... Strained abdominal muscle (November 22, 1995); missed 24 games. ... Suspended four games and fined $1,000 by NHL for striking opposing player (November 29, 1995). ... Strained groin (January 20, 1997); missed five games. ... Fractured finger (April 4, 1997); missed remainder of season. ... Strained groin (November 8, 1997); missed nine games. ... Injured knee (January 24, 1998); missed seven games. ... Traded by Canucks to New York Islanders for D Jason Strudwick (March 23, 1998). ... Strained groin (October 24, 1998); missed two games. ... Strained abdominal muscle (December 2, 1998); missed three games. ... Reinjured abdominal muscle (December 12, 1998); missed remainder of season. ... Suspended nine games by NHL for striking opposing player (December 31, 1999). ... Traded by Islanders to Philadelphia Flyers for LW Mikael Andersson and fifth-round pick (F Kristofer Ottoson) in 2000 draft (February 15, 2000). ... Injured groin (February 19, 2000); missed five games.
MISCELLANEOUS: Scored on a penalty shot (vs. Mike Vernon, October 19, 1991). ... Holds Vancouver Canucks all-time record for most penalty minutes (2,127).

Season Team	League	REGULAR SEASON								PLAYOFFS				
		Gms.	G	A	Pts.	PIM	+/-	PP	SH	Gms.	G	A	Pts.	PIM
88-89—Laval	QMJHL	50	9	15	24	278	...	...	...	16	0	9	9	*129
89-90—Laval	QMJHL	51	12	26	38	280	...	...	...	13	6	5	11	*110
90-91—Milwaukee	IHL	17	7	3	10	102	...	...	...	—	—	—	—	—
—Vancouver	NHL	45	7	1	8	296	-6	0	0	6	0	0	0	18
91-92—Vancouver	NHL	65	4	6	10	348	-1	0	0	4	0	0	0	6
92-93—Vancouver	NHL	75	4	13	17	370	3	0	0	1	0	0	0	0
93-94—Vancouver	NHL	76	16	13	29	271	13	4	0	10	0	0	0	18
94-95—Vancouver	NHL	23	4	5	9	109	-3	0	0	5	0	0	0	47
95-96—Vancouver	NHL	55	3	4	7	181	-16	0	0	6	3	1	4	6
96-97—Vancouver	NHL	70	5	8	13	371	-5	1	0	—	—	—	—	—
97-98—Vancouver	NHL	35	3	2	5	181	-3	0	0	—	—	—	—	—
—New York Islanders	NHL	13	0	0	0	31	1	0	0	—	—	—	—	—
98-99—New York Islanders	NHL	23	4	3	7	133	-2	1	0	—	—	—	—	—
99-00—New York Islanders	NHL	46	5	10	15	90	-7	0	0	—	—	—	—	—
—Philadelphia	NHL	13	3	1	4	10	2	0	0	—	—	—	—	—
NHL Totals (10 years)		**539**	**58**	**66**	**124**	**2391**	**-24**	**6**	**0**	**32**	**3**	**1**	**4**	**95**

O'DONNELL, SEAN   D   WILD

PERSONAL: Born September 13, 1971, in Ottawa. ... 6-3/230. ... Shoots left.
TRANSACTIONS/CAREER NOTES: Selected by Buffalo Sabres in sixth round (sixth Sabres pick, 123rd overall) of NHL entry draft (June 22, 1991). ... Traded by Sabres to Los Angeles Kings for D Doug Houda (July 26, 1994). ... Bruised sternum (February 4, 1995); missed two games. ... Sprained left wrist (January 27, 1996); missed eight games. ... Sprained wrist (December 26, 1996); missed nine games. ... Suspended one game by NHL for an altercation while on the bench (January 30, 1997). ... Strained back (March 1, 1997); missed two games. ... Suspended two games by NHL for cross-checking and spearing incidents (April 14, 1999). ... Selected by Minnesota Wild in NHL expansion draft (June 23, 2000).

Season Team	League	REGULAR SEASON								PLAYOFFS				
		Gms.	G	A	Pts.	PIM	+/-	PP	SH	Gms.	G	A	Pts.	PIM
90-91—Sudbury	OHL	66	8	23	31	114	...	...	...	5	1	4	5	10
91-92—Rochester	AHL	73	4	9	13	193	...	...	...	16	1	2	3	21
92-93—Rochester	AHL	74	3	18	21	203	...	...	...	17	1	6	7	38
93-94—Rochester	AHL	64	2	10	12	242	...	...	...	4	0	1	1	21
94-95—Phoenix	IHL	61	2	18	20	132	...	...	...	9	0	1	1	21
—Los Angeles	NHL	15	0	2	2	49	-2	0	0	—	—	—	—	—
95-96—Los Angeles	NHL	71	2	5	7	127	3	0	0	—	—	—	—	—
96-97—Los Angeles	NHL	55	5	12	17	144	-13	2	0	—	—	—	—	—
97-98—Los Angeles	NHL	80	2	15	17	179	7	0	0	4	1	0	1	36
98-99—Los Angeles	NHL	80	1	13	14	186	1	0	0	—	—	—	—	—
99-00—Los Angeles	NHL	80	2	12	14	114	4	0	0	4	1	0	1	4
NHL Totals (6 years)		**381**	**12**	**59**	**71**	**799**	**0**	**2**	**0**	**8**	**2**	**0**	**2**	**40**

OHLUND, MATTIAS   D   CANUCKS

PERSONAL: Born September 9, 1976, in Pitea, Sweden. ... 6-3/210. ... Shoots left. ... Name pronounced muh-TEE-uhz OH-luhnd.
TRANSACTIONS/CAREER NOTES: Selected by Vancouver Canucks in first round (first Canucks pick, 13th overall) of NHL entry draft (June 28, 1994). ... Suffered concussion (March 26, 1998); missed four games. ... Sprained shoulder (February 23, 1999); missed three games. ... Suffered concussion (April 3, 1999); missed final five games of season. ... Injured eye (September 12, 1999); missed first 38 games of season. ... Injured groin (March 8, 2000); missed two games.
HONORS: Named to NHL All-Rookie team (1997-98). ... Played in NHL All-Star Game (1999).

O

Season Team	League	REGULAR SEASON								PLAYOFFS				
		Gms.	G	A	Pts.	PIM	+/-	PP	SH	Gms.	G	A	Pts.	PIM
92-93—Pitea	Sweden Dv. 2	22	0	6	6	16	...	...	...	—	—	—	—	—
93-94—Pitea	Sweden Dv. 2	28	7	10	17	62	...	...	...	—	—	—	—	—
94-95—Lulea	Sweden	34	6	10	16	34	...	...	...	9	4	0	4	16
95-96—Lulea	Sweden	38	4	10	14	26	...	...	...	13	0	1	1	47
96-97—Lulea	Sweden	47	7	9	16	38	...	...	...	10	1	2	3	8
97-98—Vancouver	NHL	77	7	23	30	76	3	1	0	—	—	—	—	—
—Swedish Oly. team	Int'l	4	0	1	1	4	...	...	...	—	—	—	—	—
98-99—Vancouver	NHL	74	9	26	35	83	-19	2	1	—	—	—	—	—
99-00—Vancouver	NHL	42	4	16	20	24	6	2	1	—	—	—	—	—
NHL Totals (3 years)		**193**	**20**	**65**	**85**	**183**	**-10**	**5**	**2**					

OLAUSSON, FREDRIK   D

PERSONAL: Born October 5, 1966, in Dadesjo, Sweden. ... 6-0/199. ... Shoots right. ... Name pronounced OHL-ih-suhn.
TRANSACTIONS/CAREER NOTES: Selected by Winnipeg Jets in fourth round (fourth Jets pick, 81st overall) of NHL entry draft (June 15, 1985). ... Dislocated shoulder (August 1987). ... Underwent shoulder surgery (November 1987). ... Signed five-year contract with Farjestad, Sweden (June 19, 1989); Farjestad agreed to allow Olausson to remain in Winnipeg. ... Sprained knee (January 22, 1993); missed 11 games. ... Lacerated ankle (November 8, 1993); missed two games. ... Suffered from the flu (January 18, 1993); missed one game. ... Sprained knee (January 23, 1993); missed 11 games. ... Suffered from the flu (March 4, 1993); missed one game. ... Traded by Jets with seventh-round pick (LW Curtis Sheptak) in 1994 draft to Edmonton Oilers for third-round pick (C Tavis Hansen) in 1994 draft (December 5, 1993). ... Strained knee (January 11, 1994). ... Played in Europe during 1994-95 NHL lockout. ... Suffered from the flu (February 17, 1995); missed one game. ... Suffered colitis (March 3, 1995); missed 10 games. ... Cracked ribs (November 4, 1995); missed 14 games. ... Suffered irregular heartbeat (December 6, 1995); missed five games. ... Claimed on waivers by Mighty Ducks of Anaheim (January 16, 1996). ... Traded by Mighty Ducks with C Alex Hicks to Pittsburgh Penguins for LW Shawn Antoski and D Dmitri Mironov (November 19, 1996). ... Fractured cheekbone (January 26, 1997); missed nine games. ... Strained groin (February 27, 1997); missed three games. ... Bruised foot (November 2, 1997); missed three games. ... Bruised wrist (December 9, 1997); missed two games. ... Signed as free agent by Mighty Ducks (August 29, 1998). ... Injured ribs (March 17, 1999); missed two games. ... Sprained ankle (October 15, 1999); missed two games. ... Suffered injury (November 13, 1999); missed one game. ... Suffered illness (December 15, 1999); missed two games. ... Suffered illness (April 3, 2000); missed one game. ... Announced retirement (April 10, 2000).
HONORS: Named to Swedish League All-Star team (1985-86).
MISCELLANEOUS: Scored on a penalty shot (vs. Martin Brodeur, November 24, 1999).

| | | | REGULAR SEASON | | | | | | | | PLAYOFFS | | | | |
Season Team	League	Gms.	G	A	Pts.	PIM	+/-	PP	SH	Gms.	G	A	Pts.	PIM
82-83—Nybro	Sweden	31	4	4	8	12	...	...	...	—	—	—	—	—
83-84—Nybro	Sweden	28	8	14	22	32	...	...	...	—	—	—	—	—
84-85—Farjestad Karlstad	Sweden	34	6	12	18	24	...	...	...	3	1	0	1	0
85-86—Farjestad Karlstad	Sweden	33	5	12	17	14	...	...	...	8	3	2	5	6
86-87—Winnipeg	NHL	72	7	29	36	24	-3	1	0	10	2	3	5	4
87-88—Winnipeg	NHL	38	5	10	15	18	3	2	0	5	1	1	2	0
88-89—Winnipeg	NHL	75	15	47	62	32	6	4	0	—	—	—	—	—
89-90—Winnipeg	NHL	77	9	46	55	32	-1	3	0	7	0	2	2	2
90-91—Winnipeg	NHL	71	12	29	41	24	-22	5	0	—	—	—	—	—
91-92—Winnipeg	NHL	77	20	42	62	34	-31	13	1	7	1	5	6	4
92-93—Winnipeg	NHL	68	16	41	57	22	-4	11	0	6	0	2	2	2
93-94—Winnipeg	NHL	18	2	5	7	10	-3	1	0	—	—	—	—	—
—Edmonton	NHL	55	9	19	28	20	-4	6	0	—	—	—	—	—
94-95—Ehrwald	Austria	10	4	3	7	8	...	...	...	—	—	—	—	—
—Edmonton	NHL	33	0	10	10	20	-4	0	0	—	—	—	—	—
95-96—Edmonton	NHL	20	0	6	6	14	-14	0	0	—	—	—	—	—
—Anaheim	NHL	36	2	16	18	24	7	1	0	—	—	—	—	—
96-97—Anaheim	NHL	20	2	9	11	8	-5	1	0	—	—	—	—	—
—Pittsburgh	NHL	51	7	20	27	24	21	2	0	4	0	1	1	0
97-98—Pittsburgh	NHL	76	6	27	33	42	13	2	0	6	0	3	3	2
98-99—Anaheim	NHL	74	16	40	56	30	17	10	0	4	0	2	2	4
99-00—Anaheim	NHL	70	15	19	34	28	-13	8	0	—	—	—	—	—
NHL Totals (14 years)		931	143	415	558	406	-37	70	1	49	4	19	23	18

OLCZYK, EDDIE   LW

PERSONAL: Born August 16, 1966, in Chicago. ... 6-1/205. ... Shoots left. ... Full Name: Ed Olczyk. ... Name pronounced OHL-chehk.
TRANSACTIONS/CAREER NOTES: Selected by Chicago Blackhawks in first round (first Blackhawks pick, third overall) of NHL entry draft (June 9, 1984). ... Hyperextended knee (September 3, 1984). ... Fractured bone in left foot (December 16, 1984). ... Traded by Blackhawks with LW Al Secord to Toronto Maple Leafs for RW Rick Vaive, LW Steve Thomas and D Bob McGill (September 1987). ... Pinched nerve in left knee (January 3, 1990). ... Traded by Maple Leafs with LW Mark Osborne to Winnipeg Jets for D Dave Ellett and LW Paul Fenton (November 10, 1990). ... Dislocated elbow and sprained ankle (January 8, 1992); missed 15 games. ... Sprained knee (November 24, 1992); missed nine games. ... Traded by Jets to New York Rangers for LW Kris King and RW Tie Domi (December 28, 1992). ... Fractured right thumb (January 31, 1994); missed 24 games. ... Suffered from kidney stones (January 24, 1995); missed six games. ... Suffered back spasms (March 3, 1995); missed three games. ... Traded by Rangers to Jets for fifth-round pick (D Alexei Vasiljev) in 1995 draft (April 7, 1995). ... Strained rib cage (October 28, 1995); missed four games. ... Strained back (January 3, 1996); missed four games. ... Sprained knee (March 7, 1996); missed 13 games. ... Signed as free agent by Los Angeles Kings (July 8, 1996). ... Suffered from the flu (December 12, 1996); missed two games. ... Traded by Kings to Pittsburgh Penguins for RW Glen Murray (March 18, 1997). ... Suffered concussion (October 4, 1997); missed five games. ... Suffered depressed fracture of zygomatic arch in neck (December 1, 1997); missed 18 games. ... Suffered back spasms (March 8, 1998); missed two games. ... Signed as free agent by Chicago Blackhawks (August 26, 1998). ... Suffered sore back prior to 1999-2000 season; missed first game of season. ... Suffered herniated disc in back (October 16, 1999) and underwent surgery; missed 25 games. ... Bruised ankle (January 15, 2000); missed three games. ... Strained groin (February 20, 2000); missed six games.
MISCELLANEOUS: Member of Stanley Cup championship team (1994).
STATISTICAL PLATEAUS: Three-goal games: 1988-89 (1), 1989-90 (1), 1992-93 (1), 1995-96 (1), 1996-97 (1). Total: 5.

| | | | REGULAR SEASON | | | | | | | | PLAYOFFS | | | | |
Season Team	League	Gms.	G	A	Pts.	PIM	+/-	PP	SH	Gms.	G	A	Pts.	PIM
83-84—U.S. national team	Int'l	56	19	40	59	36	...	...	...	—	—	—	—	—
—U.S. Olympic team	Int'l	6	2	6	8	0	...	...	...	—	—	—	—	—
84-85—Chicago	NHL	70	20	30	50	67	11	1	1	15	6	5	11	11
85-86—Chicago	NHL	79	29	50	79	47	2	8	1	3	0	0	0	0
86-87—Chicago	NHL	79	16	35	51	119	-4	2	1	4	1	1	2	4
87-88—Toronto	NHL	80	42	33	75	55	-22	14	4	6	5	4	9	2
88-89—Toronto	NHL	80	38	52	90	75	0	11	2	—	—	—	—	—
89-90—Toronto	NHL	79	32	56	88	78	0	6	0	5	1	2	3	14
90-91—Toronto	NHL	18	4	10	14	13	-7	0	0	—	—	—	—	—
—Winnipeg	NHL	61	26	31	57	69	-20	14	0	—	—	—	—	—
91-92—Winnipeg	NHL	64	32	33	65	67	11	12	0	6	2	1	3	4

Season Team	League	REGULAR SEASON								PLAYOFFS				
		Gms.	G	A	Pts.	PIM	+/-	PP	SH	Gms.	G	A	Pts.	PIM
92-93—Winnipeg	NHL	25	8	12	20	26	-11	2	0	—	—	—	—	—
—New York Rangers	NHL	46	13	16	29	26	9	0	0	—	—	—	—	—
93-94—New York Rangers	NHL	37	3	5	8	28	-1	0	0	1	0	0	0	0
94-95—New York Rangers	NHL	20	2	1	3	4	-2	1	0	—	—	—	—	—
—Winnipeg	NHL	13	2	8	10	8	1	1	0	—	—	—	—	—
95-96—Winnipeg	NHL	51	27	22	49	65	0	16	0	6	1	2	3	6
96-97—Los Angeles	NHL	67	21	23	44	45	-22	5	1	—	—	—	—	—
—Pittsburgh	NHL	12	4	7	11	6	8	0	0	5	1	0	1	12
97-98—Pittsburgh	NHL	56	11	11	22	35	-9	5	1	6	2	0	2	4
98-99—Chicago	NHL	61	10	15	25	29	-3	2	1	—	—	—	—	—
—Chicago	IHL	7	2	2	4	6	...	...	...	—	—	—	—	—
99-00—Chicago	NHL	33	2	2	4	12	-8	0	0	—	—	—	—	—
NHL Totals (16 years)		1031	342	452	794	874	-67	100	12	57	19	15	34	57

OLIVER, DAVID — RW

PERSONAL: Born April 17, 1971, in Sechelt, B.C. ... 5-11/190. ... Shoots right.
COLLEGE: Michigan.
TRANSACTIONS/CAREER NOTES: Selected by Edmonton Oilers in seventh round (seventh Oilers pick, 144th overall) of NHL entry draft (June 22, 1991). ... Suffered hip pointer (January 24, 1997); missed one game. ... Claimed on waivers by New York Rangers (February 22, 1997). ... Signed as free agent by Ottawa Senators (July 2, 1998). ... Signed as free agent by Phoenix Coyotes (July 16, 1999).
HONORS: Named to CCHA All-Star second team (1992-93). ... Named to NCAA All-America (West) first team (1993-94). ... Named CCHA Player of the Year (1993-94). ... Named to CCHA All-Star first team (1993-94).
STATISTICAL PLATEAUS: Three-goal games: 1994-95 (1).

Season Team	League	REGULAR SEASON								PLAYOFFS				
		Gms.	G	A	Pts.	PIM	+/-	PP	SH	Gms.	G	A	Pts.	PIM
90-91—Univ. of Michigan	CCHA	27	13	11	24	34	...	...	...	—	—	—	—	—
91-92—Univ. of Michigan	CCHA	44	31	27	58	32	...	...	...	—	—	—	—	—
92-93—Univ. of Michigan	CCHA	40	35	20	55	18	...	...	...	—	—	—	—	—
93-94—Univ. of Michigan	CCHA	41	28	40	68	16	...	...	...	—	—	—	—	—
94-95—Cape Breton	AHL	32	11	18	29	8	...	...	...	—	—	—	—	—
—Edmonton	NHL	44	16	14	30	20	-11	10	0	—	—	—	—	—
95-96—Edmonton	NHL	80	20	19	39	34	-22	14	0	—	—	—	—	—
96-97—Edmonton	NHL	17	1	2	3	4	-8	0	0	—	—	—	—	—
—New York Rangers	NHL	14	2	1	3	4	3	0	0	3	0	0	0	0
97-98—Houston	IHL	78	38	27	65	60	...	...	...	4	3	0	3	4
98-99—Ottawa	NHL	17	2	5	7	4	1	0	0	—	—	—	—	—
—Houston	IHL	37	18	17	35	30	...	...	...	19	10	6	16	22
99-00—Hartford	AHL	9	0	0	0	19	...	...	...	—	—	—	—	—
—Huntington	ECHL	26	6	9	15	151	...	...	...	5	0	1	1	17
—Phoenix	NHL	9	1	0	1	2	0	1	0	—	—	—	—	—
NHL Totals (5 years)		181	42	41	83	68	-37	25	0	3	0	0	0	0

OLIWA, KRZYSZTOF — RW — BLUE JACKETS

PERSONAL: Born April 12, 1973, in Tychy, Poland. ... 6-5/235. ... Shoots left. ... Name pronounced KRIH-stahf OH-lee-vuh.
TRANSACTIONS/CAREER NOTES: Selected by New Jersey Devils in third round (fourth Devils pick, 65th overall) of NHL entry draft (June 26, 1993). ... Injured foot (November 10, 1997); missed two games. ... Strained groin (November 28, 1998); missed one game. ... Sprained left knee (October 30, 1999); missed six games. ... Suffered from the flu (January 11, 2000); missed one game. ... Injured left knee (April 2, 2000); missed final three games of season. ... Traded by Devils to Columbus Blue Jackets for third-round pick in 2001 draft and future considerations (June 12, 2000); Devils acquired RW Turner Stevenson to complete deal (June 23, 2000).
MISCELLANEOUS: Member of Stanley Cup championship team (2000).

Season Team	League	REGULAR SEASON								PLAYOFFS				
		Gms.	G	A	Pts.	PIM	+/-	PP	SH	Gms.	G	A	Pts.	PIM
90-91—GKS Katowice	Poland Jrs.	5	4	4	8	10	...	...	...	—	—	—	—	—
91-92—GKS Tychy	Poland	10	3	7	10	6	...	...	...	—	—	—	—	—
92-93—Welland Jr. B	OHA	30	13	21	34	127	...	...	...	—	—	—	—	—
93-94—Albany	AHL	33	2	4	6	151	...	...	...	—	—	—	—	—
—Raleigh	ECHL	15	0	2	2	65	...	...	...	9	0	0	0	35
94-95—Albany	AHL	20	1	1	2	77	...	...	...	—	—	—	—	—
—Detroit	IHL	4	0	1	1	24	...	...	...	—	—	—	—	—
—Saint John	AHL	14	1	4	5	79	...	...	...	—	—	—	—	—
—Raleigh	ECHL	5	0	2	2	32	...	...	...	—	—	—	—	—
95-96—Albany	AHL	51	5	11	16	217	...	...	...	—	—	—	—	—
—Albany	ECHL	9	1	0	1	53	...	...	...	—	—	—	—	—
96-97—Albany	AHL	60	13	14	27	322	...	...	...	15	7	1	8	49
—New Jersey	NHL	1	0	0	0	5	-1	0	0	—	—	—	—	—
97-98—New Jersey	NHL	73	2	3	5	295	3	0	0	6	0	0	0	23
98-99—New Jersey	NHL	64	5	7	12	240	4	0	0	1	0	0	0	2
99-00—New Jersey	NHL	69	6	10	16	184	-2	1	0	—	—	—	—	—
NHL Totals (4 years)		207	13	20	33	724	4	1	0	7	0	0	0	25

O

O'NEILL, JEFF   C   HURRICANES

PERSONAL: Born February 23, 1976, in King City, Ont. ... 6-0/195. ... Shoots right.
HIGH SCHOOL: Bishop MacDonnell (Guelph, Ont.).
TRANSACTIONS/CAREER NOTES: Selected by Hartford Whalers in first round (first Whalers pick, fifth overall) of NHL entry draft (June 28, 1994). ... Bruised foot (December 30, 1995); missed four games. ... Reinjured foot (January 10, 1996); missed four games. ... Injured shoulder (February 17, 1996); missed four games. ... Injured groin (January 2, 1997); missed one game. ... Sprained wrist (April 2, 1997); missed four games. ... Whalers franchise moved to North Carolina and renamed Carolina Hurricanes for 1997-98 season; NHL approved move on June 25, 1997. ... Suffered concussion (December 20, 1997); missed one game. ... Fractured kneecap (April 13, 1998); missed three games. ... Strained neck (February 3, 1999); missed seven games. ... Suffered back spasms (November 24, 1999); missed two games.
HONORS: Won Emms Family Award (1992-93). ... Named to Can.HL All-Rookie team (1992-93). ... Named to OHL All-Rookie team (1992-93). ... Won Can.HL Top Draft Prospect Award (1993-94). ... Named to Can.HL All-Star second team (1994-95). ... Named to OHL All-Star first team (1994-95).
STATISTICAL PLATEAUS: Three-goal games: 1996-97 (1).

		REGULAR SEASON								PLAYOFFS				
Season Team	League	Gms.	G	A	Pts.	PIM	+/-	PP	SH	Gms.	G	A	Pts.	PIM
91-92—Thornhill	Tier II Jr. A	43	27	53	80	48	...	...	...	—	—	—	—	—
92-93—Guelph	OHL	65	32	47	79	88	...	...	...	5	2	2	4	6
93-94—Guelph	OHL	66	45	81	126	95	...	...	...	9	2	11	13	31
94-95—Guelph	OHL	57	43	81	124	56	...	...	...	14	8	18	26	34
95-96—Hartford	NHL	65	8	19	27	40	-3	1	0	—	—	—	—	—
96-97—Hartford	NHL	72	14	16	30	40	-24	2	1	—	—	—	—	—
—Springfield	AHL	1	0	0	0	0	...	...	...	—	—	—	—	—
97-98—Carolina	NHL	74	19	20	39	67	-8	7	1	—	—	—	—	—
98-99—Carolina	NHL	75	16	15	31	66	3	4	0	6	0	1	1	0
99-00—Carolina	NHL	80	25	38	63	72	-9	4	0	—	—	—	—	—
NHL Totals (5 years)		366	82	108	190	285	-41	18	2	6	0	1	1	0

ORSZAGH, VLADIMIR   RW   ISLANDERS

PERSONAL: Born May 24, 1977, in Banska Bystrica, Czechoslovakia. ... 5-11/173. ... Shoots left. ... Name pronounced OHR-sahg.
TRANSACTIONS/CAREER NOTES: Selected by New York Islanders in fifth round (fourth Islanders pick, 106th overall) of NHL entry draft (July 8, 1995). ... Suffered tendinitis (December 14, 1999); missed one game.

		REGULAR SEASON								PLAYOFFS				
Season Team	League	Gms.	G	A	Pts.	PIM	+/-	PP	SH	Gms.	G	A	Pts.	PIM
93-94—IS Banska Byst. Jrs.	Slovakia	...	38	27	65	...	...	...	...	—	—	—	—	—
94-95—Banska Bystrica	Slov. Div. II	38	18	12	30	...	...	...	...	—	—	—	—	—
—Martimex ZTS Martin..	Slovakia	1	0	0	0	0	...	...	...	—	—	—	—	—
95-96—Banska Bystrica	Slovakia	31	9	5	14	22	...	...	...	—	—	—	—	—
96-97—Utah	IHL	68	12	15	27	30	...	...	...	3	0	1	1	4
97-98—Utah	IHL	62	13	10	23	60	...	...	...	4	2	0	2	0
—New York Islanders	NHL	11	0	1	1	2	-3	0	0	—	—	—	—	—
98-99—Lowell	AHL	68	18	23	41	57	...	...	...	3	2	2	4	2
—New York Islanders	NHL	12	1	0	1	6	2	0	0	—	—	—	—	—
99-00—Lowell	AHL	55	8	12	20	22	...	...	...	7	3	3	6	2
—New York Islanders	NHL	11	2	1	3	4	1	0	0	—	—	—	—	—
NHL Totals (3 years)		34	3	2	5	12	0	0	0					

OSGOOD, CHRIS   G   RED WINGS

PERSONAL: Born November 26, 1972, in Peace River, Alta. ... 5-10/181. ... Catches left.
TRANSACTIONS/CAREER NOTES: Selected by Detroit Red Wings in third round (third Red Wings pick, 54th overall) of NHL entry draft (June 22, 1991). ... Strained hamstring (January 14, 1997); missed five games. ... Strained groin (March 14, 1998); missed four games. ... Strained hip flexor (November 19, 1998); missed six games. ... Injured right knee (April 27, 1999); missed four playoff games. ... Injured hand (November 24, 1999); missed 15 games.
HONORS: Named to WHL (East) All-Star second team (1990-91). ... Played in NHL All-Star Game (1996). ... Named to THE SPORTING NEWS All-Star first team (1995-96). ... Shared William M. Jennings Trophy with Mike Vernon (1995-96). ... Named to NHL All-Star second team (1995-96). ... Named to play in NHL All-Star Game (1997); replaced by G Guy Hebert due to injury.
RECORDS: Shares NHL single-season playoff record for most wins by goaltender—16 (1998).
MISCELLANEOUS: Member of Stanley Cup championship team (1997 and 1998). ... Holds Detroit Red Wings all-time record for goals-against average (2.35). ... Stopped a penalty shot attempt (vs. Peter Zezel, March 4, 1994; vs. Dave Gagner, April 1, 1995; vs. Mike Hudson, November 18, 1996). ... Allowed a penalty shot goal (vs. Alexander Mogilny, December 1, 1997; vs. Geoff Courtnall, October 29, 1998; vs. Pavel Bure, February 26, 1999).
STATISTICAL NOTES: Scored goal (March 6, 1996, vs. Hartford Whalers).

		REGULAR SEASON								PLAYOFFS					
Season Team	League	Gms.	Min.	W	L	T	GA	SO	Avg.	Gms.	Min.	W	L	GA	SO	Avg.
89-90—Medicine Hat	WHL	57	3094	24	28	2	228	0	4.42	3	173	3	4	17	0	5.90
90-91—Medicine Hat	WHL	46	2630	23	18	3	173	2	3.95	12	714	7	5	42	0	3.53
91-92—Medicine Hat	WHL	15	819	10	3	0	44	0	3.22	—						
—Brandon	WHL	16	890	3	10	1	60	1	4.04	—						
—Seattle	WHL	21	1217	12	7	1	65	1	3.20	15	904	9	6	51	0	3.38
92-93—Adirondack	AHL	45	2438	19	19	2	159	0	3.91	1	59	0	1	2	0	2.03
93-94—Adirondack	AHL	4	240	3	1	0	13	0	3.25	—						
—Detroit	NHL	41	2286	23	8	5	105	2	2.76	6	307	3	2	12	1	2.35
94-95—Adirondack	AHL	2	120	1	1	0	6	0	3.00	—						
—Detroit	NHL	19	1087	14	5	0	41	1	2.26	2	68	0	0	2	0	1.76
95-96—Detroit	NHL	50	2933	*39	6	5	106	5	2.17	15	936	8	7	33	2	2.12
96-97—Detroit	NHL	47	2769	23	13	9	106	6	2.30	2	47	0	0	2	0	2.55

O

Season Team	League	REGULAR SEASON								PLAYOFFS						
		Gms.	Min	W	L	T	GA	SO	Avg.	Gms.	Min.	W	L	GA	SO	Avg.
97-98—Detroit	NHL	64	3807	33	20	11	140	6	2.21	22	1361	16	6	48	2	2.12
98-99—Detroit	NHL	63	3691	34	25	4	149	3	2.42	6	358	4	2	14	1	2.35
99-00—Detroit	NHL	53	3148	30	14	8	126	6	2.40	9	547	5	4	18	2	1.97
NHL Totals (7 years)		337	19721	196	91	42	773	29	2.35	62	3624	36	21	129	8	2.14

O'SULLIVAN, CHRIS   D   MIGHTY DUCKS

PERSONAL: Born May 15, 1974, in Dorchester, Mass. ... 6-2/205. ... Shoots left.

HIGH SCHOOL: Catholic Memorial (Boston).

COLLEGE: Boston University.

TRANSACTIONS/CAREER NOTES: Selected by Calgary Flames in second round (second Flames pick, 30th overall) of NHL entry draft (June 20, 1992). ... Suffered concussion (December 20, 1997); missed three games. ... Traded by Flames to New York Rangers for D Lee Sorochan (March 23, 1999). ... Signed as free agent by Vancouver Canucks (August 11, 1999). ... Signed as free agent by Mighty Ducks of Anaheim (July 20, 2000).

HONORS: Named NCAA Tournament Most Valuable Player (1994-95). ... Named to NCAA All-Tournament team (1994-95). ... Named to NCAA All-America (East) second team (1994-95).

Season Team	League	REGULAR SEASON								PLAYOFFS				
		Gms.	G	A	Pts.	PIM	+/-	PP	SH	Gms.	G	A	Pts.	PIM
91-92—Catholic Memorial	Mass. H.S.	26	26	23	49	65	...	...	...	—	—	—	—	—
92-93—Boston University	Hockey East	5	0	2	2	4	...	...	...	—	—	—	—	—
93-94—Boston University	Hockey East	32	5	18	23	25	...	...	...	—	—	—	—	—
94-95—Boston University	Hockey East	40	23	33	56	48	...	...	...	—	—	—	—	—
95-96—Boston University	Hockey East	37	12	35	47	50	...	...	...	—	—	—	—	—
96-97—Calgary	NHL	27	2	8	10	2	0	1	0	—	—	—	—	—
—Saint John	AHL	29	3	8	11	17	...	...	...	5	0	4	4	0
97-98—Saint John	AHL	32	4	10	14	2	...	...	...	21	2	17	19	18
—Calgary	NHL	12	0	2	2	10	4	0	0	—	—	—	—	—
98-99—Saint John	AHL	41	7	29	36	24	...	...	...	—	—	—	—	—
—Calgary	NHL	10	0	1	1	2	-1	0	0	—	—	—	—	—
—Hartford	AHL	10	1	4	5	0	...	...	...	7	1	3	4	11
99-00—Syracuse	AHL	59	18	47	65	24	...	...	...	4	0	1	1	0
—Vancouver	NHL	11	0	5	5	2	2	0	0	—	—	—	—	—
NHL Totals (4 years)		60	2	16	18	16	5	1	0					

OUELLET, MAXIME   G   FLYERS

PERSONAL: Born June 17, 1981, in Beauport, Que. ... 6-0/180. ... Catches left.

TRANSACTIONS/CAREER NOTES: Selected by Philadelphia Flyers in first round (first Flyers pick, 22nd overall) of NHL entry draft (June 26, 1999).

HONORS: Named to QMJHL All-Star second team (1998-99 and 1999-2000). ... Won Mike Bossy Trophy (1998-99). ... Won Jacques Plante Trophy (1998-99).

Season Team	League	REGULAR SEASON								PLAYOFFS						
		Gms.	Min	W	L	T	GA	SO	Avg.	Gms.	Min.	W	L	GA	SO	Avg.
97-98—Quebec	QMJHL	24	1199	12	7	1	66	0	3.30	7	305	3	1	16	0	3.15
98-99—Quebec	QMJHL	*58	*3447	*40	12	*6	155	3	*2.70	13	803	6	7	41	†1	3.06
99-00—Quebec	QMJHL	53	2984	31	16	4	133	2	2.67	11	638	7	4	28	*2	*2.63

OZOLINSH, SANDIS   D   HURRICANES

PERSONAL: Born August 3, 1972, in Riga, U.S.S.R. ... 6-3/205. ... Shoots left. ... Name pronounced SAN-diz OH-zoh-lihnsh.

TRANSACTIONS/CAREER NOTES: Selected by San Jose Sharks in second round (third Sharks pick, 30th overall) of NHL entry draft (June 22, 1991). ... Strained back (November 7, 1992); missed one game. ... Tore anterior cruciate ligament in knee (December 30, 1992); missed remainder of season. ... Injured knee (December 11, 1993); missed one game. ... Traded by Sharks to Colorado Avalanche for RW Owen Nolan (October 26, 1995). ... Separated left shoulder (December 7, 1995); missed four games. ... Fractured finger (February 23, 1996); missed two games. ... Suffered back spasms (March 9, 1997); missed two games. ... Separated shoulder (October 7, 1997); missed two games. ... Injured knee (October 17, 1997) and underwent arthroscopic surgery; missed 13 games. ... Missed first 38 games of 1998-99 season due to contract dispute. ... Bruised sternum (February 9, 1999); missed two games. ... Traded by Avalanche with second-round pick (LW Tomas Kurka) in 2000 draft to Carolina Hurricanes for D Nolan Pratt, first-(C Vaclav Nedorost) and two second-round (C Jared Aulin and D Argis Saviels) picks in 2000 draft (June 24, 2000).

HONORS: Played in NHL All-Star Game (1994, 1997, 1998 and 2000). ... Named to NHL All-Star first team (1996-97).

MISCELLANEOUS: Member of Stanley Cup championship team (1996).

STATISTICAL PLATEAUS: Three-goal games: 1999-00 (1).

Season Team	League	REGULAR SEASON								PLAYOFFS				
		Gms.	G	A	Pts.	PIM	+/-	PP	SH	Gms.	G	A	Pts.	PIM
90-91—Dynamo Riga	USSR	44	0	3	3	49	...	...	...	—	—	—	—	—
91-92—HC Riga	CIS	30	5	0	5	42	...	...	...	—	—	—	—	—
—Kansas City	IHL	34	6	9	15	20	...	...	...	15	2	5	7	22
92-93—San Jose	NHL	37	7	16	23	40	-9	2	0	—	—	—	—	—
93-94—San Jose	NHL	81	26	38	64	24	16	4	0	14	0	10	10	8
94-95—San Jose	NHL	48	9	16	25	30	-6	3	1	11	3	2	5	6
95-96—San Francisco	IHL	2	1	0	1	0	...	...	...	—	—	—	—	—
—San Jose	NHL	7	1	3	4	4	2	1	0	—	—	—	—	—
—Colorado	NHL	66	13	37	50	50	0	7	1	22	5	14	19	16
96-97—Colorado	NHL	80	23	45	68	88	4	13	0	17	4	13	17	24
97-98—Colorado	NHL	66	13	38	51	65	-12	9	0	7	0	7	7	14
98-99—Colorado	NHL	39	7	25	32	22	10	4	0	19	4	8	12	22
99-00—Colorado	NHL	82	16	36	52	46	17	6	0	17	5	5	10	20
NHL Totals (8 years)		506	115	254	369	369	22	49	2	107	21	59	80	110

0

PAHLSSON, SAMUAL — C — BRUINS

PERSONAL: Born December 17, 1977, in Ornskoldsvik, Sweden. ... 5-11/190. ... Shoots left.
TRANSACTIONS/CAREER NOTES: Selected by Colorado Avalanche in seventh round (10th Avalanche pick, 176th overall) of NHL entry draft (June 22, 1996). ... Traded by Avalanche with LW Brian Rolston, D Martin Grenier and first-round pick (LW Martin Samuelsson) in 2000 draft to Boston Bruins for D Ray Bourque and LW Dave Andreychuk (March 6, 2000).

			REGULAR SEASON								PLAYOFFS				
Season Team	League	Gms.	G	A	Pts.	PIM	+/-	PP	SH		Gms.	G	A	Pts.	PIM
95-96—MoDo Ornskoldsvik	Sweden	36	1	3	4	8	...	...	...		—	—	—	—	—
96-97—MoDo Ornskoldsvik	Sweden	49	8	9	17	83	...	...	...		—	—	—	—	—
97-98—MoDo Ornskoldsvik	Sweden	23	6	11	17	24	...	...	...		9	3	0	3	6
98-99—MoDo Ornskoldsvik	Sweden	50	17	17	34	44	...	...	...		13	3	3	6	10
99-00—MoDo Ornskoldsvik	Sweden	47	16	11	27	67	...	...	...		13	3	3	6	8

PALFFY, ZIGMUND — RW — KINGS

PERSONAL: Born May 5, 1972, in Skalica, Czechoslovakia. ... 5-10/180. ... Shoots left. ... Name pronounced PAL-fee.
TRANSACTIONS/CAREER NOTES: Selected by New York Islanders in second round (second Islanders pick, 26th overall) of NHL entry draft (June 22, 1991). ... Suffered concussion (February 17, 1996); missed one game. ... Sprained shoulder (January 13, 1997); missed two games. ... Missed first 32 games of 1998-99 season due to contract dispute; played in Europe. ... Traded by Islanders with C Bryan Smolinski, G Marcel Cousineau and fourth-round pick (C Daniel Johansson) in 1999 draft to Los Angeles Kings for C Olli Jokinen, LW Josh Green, D Mathieu Biron and first-round pick (LW Taylor Pyatt) in 1999 draft (June 20, 1999). ... Suffered back spasms (December 4, 1999); missed four games. ... Suffered back spasms (January 4, 2000); missed one game. ... Strained right shoulder (March 15, 2000); missed final 12 games of regular season.
HONORS: Named Czechoslovakian League Rookie of the Year (1990-91). ... Named to Czechoslovakian League All-Star team (1991-92). ... Named to play in NHL All-Star Game (1997); replaced by D Scott Lachance due to injury. ... Played in NHL All-Star Game (1998).
STATISTICAL PLATEAUS: Three-goal games: 1995-96 (2), 1996-97 (1), 1997-98 (2), 1998-99 (1). Total: 6.

			REGULAR SEASON								PLAYOFFS				
Season Team	League	Gms.	G	A	Pts.	PIM	+/-	PP	SH		Gms.	G	A	Pts.	PIM
90-91—Nitra..........................	Czech.	50	34	16	50	18	...	...	...		—	—	—	—	—
91-92—Dukla Trencin..............	Czech.	32	23	25	*48	...	...	...	...		—	—	—	—	—
92-93—Dukla Trencin..............	Czech.	43	38	41	79	...	...	...	...		—	—	—	—	—
93-94—Salt Lake City..............	IHL	57	25	32	57	83	...	...	...		—	—	—	—	—
—Slovakian Oly. team	Int'l	8	3	7	10	8	...	...	...		—	—	—	—	—
—New York Islanders.....	NHL	5	0	0	0	0	-6	0	0		—	—	—	—	—
94-95—Denver........................	IHL	33	20	23	43	40	...	...	...		—	—	—	—	—
—New York Islanders.....	NHL	33	10	7	17	6	3	1	0		—	—	—	—	—
95-96—New York Islanders.....	NHL	81	43	44	87	56	-17	17	1		—	—	—	—	—
96-97—New York Islanders.....	NHL	80	48	42	90	43	21	6	4		—	—	—	—	—
97-98—New York Islanders.....	NHL	82	45	42	87	34	-2	*17	2		—	—	—	—	—
98-99—HK 36 Skalica	Slovakia	9	11	8	19	6	...	...	...		—	—	—	—	—
—New York Islanders.....	NHL	50	22	28	50	34	-6	5	2		—	—	—	—	—
99-00—Los Angeles................	NHL	64	27	39	66	32	18	4	0		4	2	0	2	0
NHL Totals (7 years)...........		395	195	202	397	205	11	50	9		4	2	0	2	0

PANDOLFO, JAY — LW — DEVILS

PERSONAL: Born December 27, 1974, in Winchester, Mass. ... 6-1/190. ... Shoots left.
HIGH SCHOOL: Burlington (Mass.).
COLLEGE: Boston University.
TRANSACTIONS/CAREER NOTES: Selected by New Jersey Devils in second round (second Devils pick, 32nd overall) of NHL entry draft (June 26, 1993). ... Suffered from the flu (January 14, 1999); missed two games. ... Bruised shoulder (March 17, 1999); missed 10 games. ... Suffered facial lacerations (January 29, 2000); missed three games.
HONORS: Named to NCAA All-America (East) first team (1995-96). ... Named Hockey East Player of the Year (1995-96). ... Named to Hockey East All-Star team (1995-96).
MISCELLANEOUS: Member of Stanley Cup championship team (2000). ... Failed to score on a penalty shot (vs. Rick Tabaracci, December 30, 1998).

			REGULAR SEASON								PLAYOFFS				
Season Team	League	Gms.	G	A	Pts.	PIM	+/-	PP	SH		Gms.	G	A	Pts.	PIM
90-91—Burlington H.S.	Mass. H.S.	20	19	27	46	10	...	...	...		—	—	—	—	—
91-92—Burlington H.S.	Mass. H.S.	20	35	34	69	14	...	...	...		—	—	—	—	—
92-93—Boston University	Hockey East	37	16	22	38	16	...	...	...		—	—	—	—	—
93-94—Boston University	Hockey East	37	17	25	42	27	...	...	...		—	—	—	—	—
94-95—Boston University	Hockey East	20	7	13	20	6	...	...	...		—	—	—	—	—
95-96—Boston University	Hockey East	39	38	29	67	6	...	...	...		—	—	—	—	—
—Albany.........................	AHL	5	3	1	4	0	...	...	...		3	0	0	0	0
96-97—Albany.........................	AHL	12	3	9	12	0	...	...	...		—	—	—	—	—
—New Jersey.................	NHL	46	6	8	14	6	-1	0	0		6	0	1	1	0
97-98—New Jersey.................	NHL	23	1	3	4	4	-4	0	0		3	0	2	2	0
—Albany.........................	AHL	51	18	19	37	24	...	...	...		—	—	—	—	—
98-99—New Jersey.................	NHL	70	14	13	27	10	3	1	1		7	1	0	1	0
99-00—New Jersey.................	NHL	71	7	8	15	4	0	0	0		23	0	5	5	0
NHL Totals (4 years)...........		210	28	32	60	24	-2	1	1		39	1	8	9	0

P

PAPINEAU, JUSTIN   C   BLUES

PERSONAL: Born January 15, 1980, in Ottawa. ... 5-10/160. ... Shoots left.
TRANSACTIONS/CAREER NOTES: Selected by Los Angeles Kings in second round (second Kings pick, 46th overall) of NHL entry draft (June 27, 1998). ... Returned to draft pool by Kings and selected by St. Louis Blues in third round (third Blues pick, 75th overall) of NHL entry draft (June 24, 2000).
HONORS: Named to OHL All-Rookie second team (1996-97).

		REGULAR SEASON								PLAYOFFS				
Season Team	League	Gms.	G	A	Pts.	PIM	+/-	PP	SH	Gms.	G	A	Pts.	PIM
95-96—Ottawa	OHA Jr. A	52	31	19	50	51	...	...	...	—	—	—	—	—
96-97—Belleville	OHL	40	10	32	42	32	...	...	...	—	—	—	—	—
97-98—Belleville	OHL	66	41	53	94	34	...	...	...	10	5	9	14	6
98-99—Belleville	OHL	68	52	47	99	28	...	...	...	21	*21	*30	*51	20
99-00—Belleville	OHL	60	40	36	76	52	...	...	...	16	4	12	16	16

PARENT, RICH   G   SENATORS

PERSONAL: Born January 12, 1973, in Montreal. ... 6-3/215. ... Catches left.
TRANSACTIONS/CAREER NOTES: Signed as non-drafted free agent by St. Louis Blues (July 17, 1997). ... Strained groin (October 1, 1997); missed three games. ... Suffered scrotal contusion and ruptured testicle (February 13, 1999); missed 11 games. ... Traded by Blues with D Chris McAlpine to Tampa Bay Lightning for RW Stephane Richer (January 13, 2000). ... Suffered from tendinitis (March 28, 2000); missed final seven games of season. ... Traded by Lightning to Ottawa Senators for seventh-round pick (traded to Buffalo) in 2000 draft (June 4, 2000).
HONORS: Won Norris Trophy (1996-97). ... Named Colonial Hockey League Goaltender of the year (1994-95 and 1995-96).

		REGULAR SEASON								PLAYOFFS						
Season Team	League	Gms.	Min	W	L	T	GA	SO	Avg.	Gms.	Min.	W	L	GA	SO	Avg.
94-95—Muskegon	Col.HL	35	1867	17	11	3	112	1	3.60	13	725	7	3	47	1	3.89
95-96—Muskegon	Col.HL	36	2086	23	7	4	85	2	2.44	—	—	—	—	—	—	—
—Detroit	IHL	19	1040	16	0	‡1	48	2	2.77	7	362	3	3	22	0	3.65
96-97—Detroit	IHL	53	2815	31	13	‡4	104	4	2.22	15	786	8	3	21	1	*1.60
97-98—Manitoba	IHL	26	1334	8	12	‡2	69	3	3.10	—	—	—	—	—	—	—
—St. Louis	NHL	1	12	0	0	0	0	0	...	—	—	—	—	—	—	—
—Detroit	IHL	7	418	4	0	‡3	15	0	2.15	5	157	1	0	6	0	2.29
98-99—Worcester	AHL	20	1100	8	8	2	56	1	3.05	—	—	—	—	—	—	—
—St. Louis	NHL	10	519	4	3	1	22	1	2.54	—	—	—	—	—	—	—
99-00—Utah	IHL	27	1571	21	7	‡3	58	1	2.22	—	—	—	—	—	—	—
—Tampa Bay	NHL	14	698	2	7	1	43	0	3.70	—	—	—	—	—	—	—
—Detroit	IHL	10	539	3	5	‡1	23	1	2.56	—	—	—	—	—	—	—
NHL Totals (3 years)		25	1229	6	10	2	65	1	3.17							

PARKER, SCOTT   RW   AVALANCHE

PERSONAL: Born January 29, 1978, in Hanford, Calif. ... 6-4/220. ... Shoots right.
TRANSACTIONS/CAREER NOTES: Selected by New Jersey Devils in third round (sixth Devils pick, 63rd overall) of NHL entry draft (June 22, 1996). ... Returned to draft pool by Devils and selected by Colorado Avalanche in first round (fourth Avalanche pick, 20th overall) of NHL entry draft (June 27, 1998). ... Suspended seven games by AHL for leaving the bench for an altercation (October 26, 1998). ... Suspended two games by AHL for receiving match penalty (April 6, 1999).

		REGULAR SEASON								PLAYOFFS				
Season Team	League	Gms.	G	A	Pts.	PIM	+/-	PP	SH	Gms.	G	A	Pts.	PIM
95-96—Kelowna	WHL	64	3	4	7	159	...	...	...	6	0	0	0	12
96-97—Kelowna	WHL	68	18	8	26	*330	...	...	...	6	0	2	2	4
97-98—Kelowna	WHL	71	30	22	52	243	...	...	...	7	6	0	6	23
98-99—Hershey	AHL	32	4	3	7	143	...	...	...	4	0	0	0	6
—Colorado	NHL	27	0	0	0	71	-3	0	0	—	—	—	—	—
99-00—Hershey	AHL	68	12	7	19	206	...	...	...	11	1	1	2	56
NHL Totals (1 year)		27	0	0	0	71	-3	0	0					

PARRISH, MARK   RW   ISLANDERS

PERSONAL: Born February 2, 1977, in Edina, Minn. ... 5-11/191. ... Shoots right.
HIGH SCHOOL: Thomas Jefferson Senior (Alexandria, Minn.).
COLLEGE: St. Cloud (Minn.) State.
TRANSACTIONS/CAREER NOTES: Selected by Colorado Avalanche in third round (third Avalanche pick, 79th overall) of NHL entry draft (June 22, 1996). ... Rights traded by Avalanche with third-round pick (D Lance Ward) in 1998 draft to Florida Panthers for RW/C Tom Fitzgerald (March 24, 1998). ... Strained back (February 14, 2000); missed one game. ... Traded by Panthers with LW Oleg Kvasha to New York Islanders for C Olli Jokinen and G Roberto Luongo (June 24, 2000).
HONORS: Named to NCAA All-America (West) second team (1996-97). ... Named to Can.HL All-Star second team (1997-98). ... Named to WHL (West) All-Star first team (1997-98).
STATISTICAL PLATEAUS: Four-goal games: 1998-99 (1).

		REGULAR SEASON								PLAYOFFS				
Season Team	League	Gms.	G	A	Pts.	PIM	+/-	PP	SH	Gms.	G	A	Pts.	PIM
94-95—Thomas Jefferson	Minn. H.S.	27	40	20	60	42	...	...	...	—	—	—	—	—
95-96—St. Cloud State	WCHA	38	15	14	29	28	...	...	...	—	—	—	—	—
96-97—St. Cloud State	WCHA	35	27	15	42	60	...	...	...	—	—	—	—	—
97-98—Seattle	WHL	54	54	38	92	29	...	...	...	5	2	3	5	2
—New Haven	AHL	1	1	0	1	2	...	...	...	—	—	—	—	—
98-99—Florida	NHL	73	24	13	37	25	-6	5	0	—	—	—	—	—
—New Haven	AHL	2	1	0	1	0	...	...	...	—	—	—	—	—
99-00—Florida	NHL	81	26	18	44	39	1	6	0	4	0	1	1	0
NHL Totals (2 years)		154	50	31	81	64	-5	11	0	4	0	1	1	0

P

PASSMORE, STEVE   G   KINGS

PERSONAL: Born January 29, 1973, in Thunder Bay, Ont. ... 5-9/165. ... Catches left.
TRANSACTIONS/CAREER NOTES: Selected by Quebec Nordiques in ninth round (10th Nordiques pick, 196th overall) of NHL entry draft (June 20, 1992). ... Traded by Nordiques to Edmonton Oilers for D Brad Werenka (March 21, 1994). ... Signed as free agent by Chicago Blackhawks (July 7, 1999). ... Traded by Blackhawks to Los Angeles Kings for fourth-round pick in 2000 or 2001 draft (May 1, 2000).
HONORS: Named to WHL (West) All-Star first team (1992-93 and 1993-94). ... Won Fred Hunt Memorial Award (1996-97). ... Named to AHL All-Star second team (1998-99).

Season Team	League	REGULAR SEASON								PLAYOFFS						
		Gms.	Min	W	L	T	GA	SO	Avg.	Gms.	Min.	W	L	GA	SO	Avg.
88-89—Tri-City	WHL	1	60	...	...	...	6	0	6.00	—	—	—	—	—	—	—
89-90—Tri-City	WHL	4	215	...	...	...	17	0	4.74	—	—	—	—	—	—	—
90-91—Victoria	WHL	35	1838	3	25	1	190	0	6.20	—	—	—	—	—	—	—
91-92—Victoria	WHL	*71	*4228	15	50	7	347	0	4.92	—	—	—	—	—	—	—
92-93—Victoria	WHL	43	2402	14	24	2	150	1	3.75	—	—	—	—	—	—	—
—Kamloops	WHL	25	1479	19	6	0	69	1	2.80	7	401	4	2	22	1	3.29
93-94—Kamloops	WHL	36	1927	22	9	2	88	1	*2.74	18	1099	†11	7	60	0	3.28
94-95—Cape Breton	AHL	25	1455	8	13	3	93	0	3.84	—	—	—	—	—	—	—
95-96—Cape Breton	AHL	2	90	1	0	0	2	0	1.33	—	—	—	—	—	—	—
96-97—Raleigh	ECHL	2	118	1	1	0	13	0	6.61	—	—	—	—	—	—	—
—Hamilton	AHL	27	1568	12	12	3	70	1	2.68	22	1325	12	*10	*61	†2	2.76
97-98—Hamilton	AHL	27	1656	11	10	6	87	2	3.15	3	133	0	2	14	0	6.32
—San Antonio	IHL	14	737	3	8	‡2	56	0	4.56	—	—	—	—	—	—	—
98-99—Hamilton	AHL	54	3148	24	21	†7	117	4	2.23	11	680	5	6	31	0	2.74
—Edmonton	NHL	6	362	1	4	1	17	0	2.82	—	—	—	—	—	—	—
99-00—Chicago	NHL	24	1388	7	12	3	63	1	2.72	—	—	—	—	—	—	—
—Cleveland	IHL	2	120	1	0	‡1	3	1	1.50	—	—	—	—	—	—	—
NHL Totals (2 years)		30	1750	8	16	4	80	1	2.74							

PATERA, PAVEL   C   WILD

PERSONAL: Born September 6, 1971, in Kladno, Czechoslovakia. ... 6-1/172. ... Shoots left.
TRANSACTIONS/CAREER NOTES: Selected by Dallas Stars in sixth round (fourth Stars pick, 153rd overall) of NHL entry draft (June 27, 1998). ... Traded by Stars with C Aaron Gavey, eighth-round pick (C Eric Johansson) in 2000 draft and fourth-round pick in 2002 draft to Minnesota Wild for D Brad Lukowich, third- and ninth-round picks in 2001 draft (June 25, 2000).

Season Team	League	REGULAR SEASON								PLAYOFFS				
		Gms.	G	A	Pts.	PIM	+/-	PP	SH	Gms.	G	A	Pts.	PIM
90-91—Poldi Kladno	Czech.	3	0	0	0	...	...	...	...	—	—	—	—	—
91-92—Poldi Kladno	Czech.	38	12	13	25	26	...	...	...	8	8	4	12	0
92-93—Poldi Kladno	Czech.	42	9	23	32	...	...	...	...	—	—	—	—	—
93-94—HC Kladno	Czech Rep.	43	21	39	60	...	...	...	...	11	5	10	15	...
94-95—HC Kladno	Czech Rep.	43	26	49	75	24	...	...	...	11	5	7	12	6
95-96—Poldi Kladno	Czech Rep.	40	24	31	55	38	...	...	...	8	3	1	4	34
96-97—AIK Solna	Sweden	50	19	24	43	44	...	...	...	7	2	3	5	6
97-98—AIK Solna	Sweden	46	8	17	25	50	...	...	...	—	—	—	—	—
98-99—Vsetin	Czech Rep.	52	16	37	53	58	...	...	...	12	5	*10	*15	...
99-00—Dallas	NHL	12	1	4	5	4	-1	0	0	—	—	—	—	—
—Vsetin	Czech Rep.	29	8	14	22	36	...	...	...	9	3	4	7	8
NHL Totals (1 year)		12	1	4	5	4	-1	0	0					

PATRICK, JAMES   D

PERSONAL: Born June 14, 1963, in Winnipeg. ... 6-2/200. ... Shoots right. ... Full Name: James A. Patrick. ... Brother of Steve Patrick, right winger with three NHL teams (1980-81 through 1985-86).
COLLEGE: North Dakota.
TRANSACTIONS/CAREER NOTES: Selected by New York Rangers as underage junior in first round (first Rangers pick, ninth overall) of NHL entry draft (June 10, 1981). ... Injured groin (October 1984). ... Pinched nerve (December 15, 1985). ... Strained left knee ligaments (March 1988). ... Bruised shoulder and chest (December 1988). ... Pulled groin (March 13, 1989). ... Sprained shoulder (November 4, 1992); missed three games. ... Bruised right shoulder (November 27, 1992); missed three games. ... Sprained left knee (January 27, 1993); missed four games. ... Suffered herniated disc (February 24, 1993); missed two games. ... Suffered herniated disc (March 28, 1993); missed remainder of season. ... Traded by Rangers with C Darren Turcotte to Hartford Whalers for RW Steve Larmer, LW Nick Kypreos and sixth-round pick (C Yuri Litvinov) in 1994 draft (November 2, 1993). ... Suffered herniated disc (December 7, 1993); missed five games. ... Traded by Whalers with C Michael Nylander and D Zarley Zalapski to Calgary Flames for D Gary Suter, LW Paul Ranheim and C Ted Drury (March 10, 1994). ... Strained left hip (March 10, 1995); missed five games. ... Suffered concussion (April 9, 1996); missed two games. ... Injured back (October 16, 1996); missed one game. ... Strained knee (October 24, 1996); missed five games. ... Suffered concussion (November 20, 1996); missed two games. ... Underwent knee surgery (December 12, 1996); missed remainder of season. ... Strained neck (October 22, 1997); missed six games. ... Reinjured neck (November 13, 1997); missed nine games. ... Suffered charley horse (January 5, 1998); missed one game. ... Signed as free agent by Buffalo Sabres (October 7, 1998). ... Suffered pinched nerve in neck (October 10, 1998); missed three games. ... Suffered concussion (February 24, 1999); missed one game. ... Suffered back spasms (February 17, 2000); missed two games.
HONORS: Named SJHL Player of the Year (1980-81). ... Named to SJHL All-Star first team (1980-81). ... Won WCHA Rookie of the Year Award (1981-82). ... Named to WCHA All-Star second team (1981-82). ... Named to NCAA All-Tournament team (1981-82). ... Named to NCAA All-America (West) team (1982-83). ... Named to WCHA All-Star first team (1982-83).

Season Team	League	REGULAR SEASON								PLAYOFFS				
		Gms.	G	A	Pts.	PIM	+/-	PP	SH	Gms.	G	A	Pts.	PIM
80-81—Prince Albert	SJHL	59	21	61	82	162	...	...	...	4	1	6	7	0
81-82—Univ. of North Dakota	WCHA	42	5	24	29	26	...	...	...	—	—	—	—	—
82-83—Univ. of North Dakota	WCHA	36	12	36	48	29	...	...	...	—	—	—	—	—
83-84—Can. Olympic team	Int'l	63	7	24	31	52	...	...	...	—	—	—	—	—
—New York Rangers	NHL	12	1	7	8	2	6	0	0	5	0	3	3	2

| Season Team | League | REGULAR SEASON | | | | | | | | PLAYOFFS | | | | |
		Gms.	G	A	Pts.	PIM	+/-	PP	SH	Gms.	G	A	Pts.	PIM
84-85—New York Rangers......	NHL	75	8	28	36	71	-17	4	1	3	0	0	0	4
85-86—New York Rangers......	NHL	75	14	29	43	88	14	2	1	16	1	5	6	34
86-87—New York Rangers......	NHL	78	10	45	55	62	13	5	0	6	1	2	3	2
87-88—New York Rangers......	NHL	70	17	45	62	52	16	9	0	—	—	—	—	—
88-89—New York Rangers......	NHL	68	11	36	47	41	3	6	0	4	0	1	1	2
89-90—New York Rangers......	NHL	73	14	43	57	50	4	9	0	10	3	8	11	0
90-91—New York Rangers......	NHL	74	10	49	59	58	-5	6	0	6	0	0	0	6
91-92—New York Rangers......	NHL	80	14	57	71	54	34	6	0	13	0	7	7	12
92-93—New York Rangers......	NHL	60	5	21	26	61	1	3	0	—	—	—	—	—
93-94—New York Rangers......	NHL	6	0	3	3	2	1	0	0	—	—	—	—	—
—Hartford	NHL	47	8	20	28	32	-12	4	1	—	—	—	—	—
—Calgary	NHL	15	2	2	4	6	6	1	0	7	0	1	1	6
94-95—Calgary	NHL	43	0	10	10	14	-3	0	0	5	0	1	1	0
95-96—Calgary	NHL	80	3	32	35	30	3	1	0	4	0	0	0	2
96-97—Calgary	NHL	19	3	1	4	6	2	1	0	—	—	—	—	—
97-98—Calgary	NHL	60	6	11	17	26	-2	1	0	—	—	—	—	—
98-99—Buffalo	NHL	45	1	7	8	16	12	0	0	20	0	1	1	12
99-00—Buffalo	NHL	66	5	8	13	22	8	0	0	5	0	1	1	2
NHL Totals (17 years)..........		1046	132	454	586	693	84	58	3	104	5	30	35	84

PEARSON, SCOTT   LW   ISLANDERS

PERSONAL: Born December 19, 1969, in Cornwall, Ont. ... 6-2/205. ... Shoots left.

TRANSACTIONS/CAREER NOTES: Selected by Toronto Maple Leafs in first round (first Maple Leafs pick, sixth overall) of NHL entry draft (June 11, 1988). ... Traded by Maple Leafs with second-round picks in 1991 draft (D Eric Lavigne) and 1992 draft (D Tuomas Gronman) to Quebec Nordiques for C/LW Aaron Broten, D Michel Petit and RW Lucien Deblois (November 17, 1990). ... Sprained left knee (September 27, 1992); missed first 22 games of season. ... Traded by Nordiques to Edmonton Oilers for LW Martin Gelinas and sixth-round pick (C Nicholas Checco) in 1993 draft (June 20, 1993). ... Sprained knee ligament (February 2, 1994); missed 11 games. ... Traded by Oilers to Buffalo Sabres for D Ken Sutton (April 7, 1995). ... Signed as free agent by Maple Leafs (July 8, 1996). ... Strained groin and abdominal muscle (October 19, 1996); missed 60 games. ... Signed as free agent by New York Islanders (July 30, 1999).

MISCELLANEOUS: Scored on a penalty shot (vs. Tom Barrasso, March 16, 1991). ... Failed to score on penalty shot (vs. Damian Rhodes, November 20, 1993).

| Season Team | League | REGULAR SEASON | | | | | | | | PLAYOFFS | | | | |
		Gms.	G	A	Pts.	PIM	+/-	PP	SH	Gms.	G	A	Pts.	PIM
85-86—Kingston	OHL	63	16	23	39	56	...	...	...	—	—	—	—	—
86-87—Kingston	OHL	62	30	24	54	101	...	...	...	9	3	3	6	42
87-88—Kingston	OHL	46	26	32	58	118	...	...	...	—	—	—	—	—
88-89—Kingston	OHL	13	9	8	17	34	...	...	...	—	—	—	—	—
—Niagara Falls	OHL	32	26	34	60	90	...	...	...	17	14	10	24	53
—Toronto	NHL	9	0	1	1	2	0	0	0	—	—	—	—	—
89-90—Newmarket	AHL	18	12	11	23	64	...	...	...	—	—	—	—	—
—Toronto	NHL	41	5	10	15	90	-7	0	0	2	2	0	2	10
90-91—Toronto	NHL	12	0	0	0	20	-5	0	0	—	—	—	—	—
—Quebec	NHL	35	11	4	15	86	-4	0	0	—	—	—	—	—
—Halifax	AHL	24	12	15	27	44	...	...	...	—	—	—	—	—
91-92—Quebec	NHL	10	1	2	3	14	-5	0	0	—	—	—	—	—
—Halifax	AHL	5	2	1	3	4	...	...	...	—	—	—	—	—
92-93—Halifax	AHL	5	3	1	4	25	...	...	...	—	—	—	—	—
—Quebec	NHL	41	13	1	14	95	3	0	0	3	0	0	0	0
93-94—Edmonton	NHL	72	19	18	37	165	4	3	0	—	—	—	—	—
94-95—Edmonton	NHL	28	1	4	5	54	-11	0	0	—	—	—	—	—
—Buffalo	NHL	14	2	1	3	20	-3	0	0	5	0	0	0	4
95-96—Rochester	AHL	26	8	8	16	113	...	...	...	—	—	—	—	—
—Buffalo	NHL	27	4	0	4	67	-4	0	0	—	—	—	—	—
96-97—Toronto	NHL	1	0	0	0	2	0	0	0	—	—	—	—	—
—St. John's....................	AHL	14	5	2	7	26	...	...	...	9	5	2	7	14
97-98—Chicago...................	IHL	78	34	17	51	225	...	...	...	22	12	6	18	50
98-99—Chicago...................	IHL	62	23	13	36	154	...	...	...	8	4	1	5	*50
99-00—Chicago...................	IHL	77	19	14	33	124	...	...	...	16	5	5	10	28
—New York Islanders	NHL	2	0	1	1	0	1	0	0	—	—	—	—	—
NHL Totals (10 years)..........		292	56	42	98	615	-39	3	0	10	2	0	2	14

PECA, MICHAEL   C   SABRES

PERSONAL: Born March 26, 1974, in Toronto. ... 5-11/181. ... Shoots right. ... Name pronounced PEH-kuh.

HIGH SCHOOL: LaSalle Secondary (Kinston, Ont.).

TRANSACTIONS/CAREER NOTES: Selected by Vancouver Canucks in second round (second Canucks pick, 40th overall) of NHL entry draft (June 20, 1992). ... Fractured cheek bone (February 9, 1995); missed 12 games. ... Injured wrist (April 26, 1995); missed one game. ... Traded by Canucks with D Mike Wilson and first-round pick (D Jay McKee) in 1995 draft to Buffalo Sabres for RW Alexander Mogilny and fifth-round pick (LW Todd Norman) in 1995 draft (July 8, 1995). ... Strained back (October 29, 1995); missed six games. ... Bruised sternum (December 2, 1995); missed one game. ... Sprained right knee (March 18, 1996); missed seven games. ... Injured shoulder (November 27, 1996); missed three games. ... Missed first 11 games of 1997-98 season due to contract dispute. ... Injured hip (November 6, 1997); missed three games. ... Suspended three games and fined $1,000 by NHL for elbowing incident (March 27, 1998). ... Reinjured hip (April 8, 1998); missed two games. ... Sprained knee (April 15, 1998); missed final two games of regular season and two playoff games. ... Dislocated shoulder (March 5, 2000); missed seven games. ... Suspended two games by NHL for elbowing incident (March 25, 2000).

HONORS: Won Frank J. Selke Trophy (1996-97).

MISCELLANEOUS: Captain of Buffalo Sabres (1997-98 through 1999-2000).

STATISTICAL PLATEAUS: Three-goal games: 1999-00 (1).

P

Season Team	League	REGULAR SEASON								PLAYOFFS				
		Gms.	G	A	Pts.	PIM	+/-	PP	SH	Gms.	G	A	Pts.	PIM
90-91—Sudbury	OHL	62	14	27	41	24	...	...	...	5	1	0	1	7
91-92—Sudbury	OHL	39	16	34	50	61	...	...	...	—	—	—	—	—
—Ottawa	OHL	27	8	17	25	32	...	...	...	11	6	10	16	6
92-93—Ottawa	OHL	55	38	64	102	80	...	...	...	—	—	—	—	—
—Hamilton	AHL	9	6	3	9	11	...	...	...	—	—	—	—	—
93-94—Ottawa	OHL	55	50	63	113	101	...	...	...	17	7	22	29	30
—Vancouver	NHL	4	0	0	0	2	-1	0	0	—	—	—	—	—
94-95—Syracuse	AHL	35	10	24	34	75	...	...	...	—	—	—	—	—
—Vancouver	NHL	33	6	6	12	30	-6	2	0	5	0	1	1	8
95-96—Buffalo	NHL	68	11	20	31	67	-1	4	3	—	—	—	—	—
96-97—Buffalo	NHL	79	20	29	49	80	26	5	*6	10	0	2	2	8
97-98—Buffalo	NHL	61	18	22	40	57	12	6	5	13	3	2	5	8
98-99—Buffalo	NHL	82	27	29	56	81	7	10	0	21	5	8	13	18
99-00—Buffalo	NHL	73	20	21	41	67	6	2	0	5	0	1	1	4
NHL Totals (7 years)		400	102	127	229	384	43	29	14	54	8	14	22	46

PEDERSON, DENIS   C   CANUCKS

PERSONAL: Born September 10, 1975, in Prince Albert, Sask. ... 6-2/205. ... Shoots right. ... Name pronounced PEE-duhr-suhn.

HIGH SCHOOL: Carlton Comprehensive (Prince Albert, Sask.).

TRANSACTIONS/CAREER NOTES: Selected by New Jersey Devils in first round (first Devils pick, 13th overall) of NHL entry draft (June 26, 1993). ... Bruised thigh (December 31, 1996); missed one game. ... Suffered head injury (February 19, 1997); missed one game. ... Suffered from the flu (March 11, 1997); missed one game. ... Injured back (January 21, 1999); missed one game. ... Reinjured back (March 28, 1999); missed three games. ... Reinjured back (April 10, 1999); missed two games. ... Injured groin (October 5, 1999); missed eight games. ... Reinjured groin (November 6, 1999); missed 14 games. ... Suffered illness (March 10, 2000); missed two games. ... Traded by Devils with C Brendan Morrison to Vancouver Canucks for RW Alexander Mogilny (March 14, 2000).

HONORS: Named to WHL All-Rookie team (1992-93). ... Named to WHL (East) All-Star second team (1993-94).

Season Team	League	REGULAR SEASON								PLAYOFFS				
		Gms.	G	A	Pts.	PIM	+/-	PP	SH	Gms.	G	A	Pts.	PIM
91-92—Prince Albert	WHL	10	0	0	0	6	...	...	...	7	0	1	1	13
92-93—Prince Albert	WHL	72	33	40	73	134	...	...	...	—	—	—	—	—
93-94—Prince Albert	WHL	71	53	45	98	157	...	...	...	—	—	—	—	—
94-95—Prince Albert	WHL	63	30	38	68	122	...	...	...	15	11	14	25	14
—Albany	AHL	—	—	—	—	—	...	...	...	3	0	0	0	2
95-96—Albany	AHL	68	28	43	71	104	...	...	...	4	1	2	3	0
—New Jersey	NHL	10	3	1	4	0	-1	1	0	—	—	—	—	—
96-97—Albany	AHL	3	1	3	4	7	...	...	...	—	—	—	—	—
—New Jersey	NHL	70	12	20	32	62	7	3	0	9	0	0	0	2
97-98—New Jersey	NHL	80	15	13	28	97	-6	7	0	6	1	1	2	2
98-99—New Jersey	NHL	76	11	12	23	66	-10	3	0	3	0	1	1	0
99-00—New Jersey	NHL	35	3	3	6	16	-7	0	0	—	—	—	—	—
—Vancouver	NHL	12	3	2	5	2	1	0	0	—	—	—	—	—
NHL Totals (5 years)		283	47	51	98	243	-16	14	0	18	1	2	3	4

PELLERIN, SCOTT   LW   WILD

PERSONAL: Born January 9, 1970, in Shediac, N.B. ... 5-11/190. ... Shoots left. ... Full Name: Jaque-Frederick Scott Pellerin. ... Name pronounced PEHL-ih-rihn.

HIGH SCHOOL: Athol Murray College of Notre Dame (Wilcox, Sask.).

COLLEGE: Maine.

TRANSACTIONS/CAREER NOTES: Selected by New Jersey Devils in third round (fourth Devils pick, 47th overall) of NHL entry draft (June 17, 1989). ... Signed as free agent by St. Louis Blues (July 3, 1996). ... Suffered sore ankle (March 9, 1998); missed one game. ... Suffered concussion (November 28, 1998); missed one game. ... Suffered from the flu (February 3, 2000); missed one game. ... Selected by Minnesota Wild in NHL expansion draft (June 23, 2000).

HONORS: Named Hockey East co-Rookie of the Year with Rob Gaudreau (1988-89). ... Named to Hockey East All-Rookie team (1988-89). ... Won Hobey Baker Memorial Award (1991-92). ... Named to NCAA All-America (East) first team (1991-92). ... Named Hockey East Player of the Year (1991-92). ... Named Hockey East Tournament Most Valuable Player (1991-92). ... Named to Hockey East All-Star first team (1991-92). ... Named to Hockey East All-Decade team (1994).

Season Team	League	REGULAR SEASON								PLAYOFFS				
		Gms.	G	A	Pts.	PIM	+/-	PP	SH	Gms.	G	A	Pts.	PIM
86-87—Notre Dame H.S.	SASK. H.S.	72	62	68	130	98	...	...	...	—	—	—	—	—
87-88—Notre Dame	SJHL	57	37	49	86	139	...	...	...	—	—	—	—	—
88-89—Univ. of Maine	Hockey East	45	29	33	62	92	...	...	...	—	—	—	—	—
89-90—Univ. of Maine	Hockey East	42	22	34	56	68	...	...	...	—	—	—	—	—
90-91—Univ. of Maine	Hockey East	43	23	25	48	60	...	...	...	—	—	—	—	—
91-92—Univ. of Maine	Hockey East	37	32	25	57	54	...	...	...	—	—	—	—	—
—Utica	AHL	—	—	—	—	—	...	...	...	3	1	0	1	0
92-93—Utica	AHL	27	15	18	33	33	...	...	...	2	0	1	1	0
—New Jersey	NHL	45	10	11	21	41	-1	1	2	—	—	—	—	—
93-94—Albany	IHL	73	28	46	74	84	...	...	...	5	2	1	3	11
—New Jersey	NHL	1	0	0	0	2	0	0	0	—	—	—	—	—
94-95—Albany	AHL	74	23	33	56	95	...	...	...	14	6	4	10	8
95-96—Albany	AHL	75	35	47	82	142	...	...	...	4	0	3	3	10
—New Jersey	NHL	6	2	1	3	0	1	0	0	—	—	—	—	—
96-97—Worcester	AHL	24	10	16	26	37	...	...	...	—	—	—	—	—
—St. Louis	NHL	54	8	10	18	35	12	0	2	6	0	0	0	6
97-98—St. Louis	NHL	80	8	21	29	62	14	1	1	10	0	2	2	10
98-99—St. Louis	NHL	80	20	21	41	42	1	0	†5	8	1	0	1	4
99-00—St. Louis	NHL	80	8	15	23	48	8	0	2	7	0	0	0	2
NHL Totals (7 years)		346	56	79	135	230	35	2	12	31	1	2	3	22

P

PELLETIER, JEAN-MARC   G   HURRICANES

PERSONAL: Born March 4, 1978, in Atlanta. ... 6-3/195. ... Catches left.
COLLEGE: Cornell.
TRANSACTIONS/CAREER NOTES: Selected by Philadelphia Flyers in second round (first Flyers pick, 30th overall) of NHL entry draft (June 21, 1997). ... Traded by Flyers with C Rod Brind'Amour and second-round pick (traded to Colorado) in 2000 draft to Carolina Hurricanes for rights to C Keith Primeau and fifth-round pick (traded to New York Islanders) in 2000 draft (January 23, 2000).
HONORS: Named to QMJHL All-Rookie Team (1997-98).

		REGULAR SEASON								PLAYOFFS					
Season Team	League	Gms.	Min	W	L	T	GA	SO	Avg.	Gms.	Min.	W	L	GA	SO	Avg.
95-96—Cornell University.........	ECAC	5	179	1	2	0	15	0	5.03	—	—	—	—	—	—	—
96-97—Cornell University.........	ECAC	11	678	5	2	3	28	1	2.48	—	—	—	—	—	—	—
97-98—Rimouski......................	QMJHL	34	1913	17	11	3	118	0	3.70	16	895	11	3	†51	1	3.42
98-99—Philadelphia	AHL	47	2636	25	16	4	122	2	2.78	1	27	0	0	0	0	...
—Philadelphia	NHL	1	60	0	1	0	5	0	5.00	—	—	—	—	—	—	—
99-00—Philadelphia	AHL	24	1405	14	10	0	58	3	2.48	—	—	—	—	—	—	—
—Cincinnati	IHL	22	1278	16	4	‡2	52	2	2.44	3	160	1	1	8	1	3.00
NHL Totals (1 year)..............		1	60	0	1	0	5	0	5.00							

PELTONEN, VILLE   LW   PREDATORS

PERSONAL: Born May 24, 1973, in Vantaa, Finland. ... 5-10/181. ... Shoots left. ... Name pronounced VIHL-lay PEHL-tuh-nehn.
TRANSACTIONS/CAREER NOTES: Selected by San Jose Sharks in third round (fourth Sharks pick, 58th overall) of NHL entry draft (June 26, 1993). ... Injured knee (October 15, 1996); missed 10 games. ... Signed as free agent by Nashville Predators (June 29, 1998). ... Separated shoulder (October 6, 1998); missed 10 games. ... Reinjured shoulder (December 5, 1998) and underwent surgery; missed remainder of season.
MISCELLANEOUS: Member of bronze-medal-winning Finnish Olympic team (1994 and 1998). ... Failed to score on a penalty shot (vs. Patrick Roy, March 5, 1996).

		REGULAR SEASON							PLAYOFFS				
Season Team	League	Gms.	G	A	Pts.	PIM	+/-	PP	SH	Gms.	G	A	Pts.	PIM
91-92—HIFK Helsinki	Finland	6	0	0	0	0	...	...	...	—	—	—	—	—
92-93—HIFK Helsinki	Finland	46	13	24	37	16	...	...	...	4	0	2	2	2
93-94—HIFK Helsinki	Finland	43	16	22	38	14	...	...	...	3	0	0	0	2
—Fin. Olympic team.......	Int'l	8	4	3	7	0	...	...	...	—	—	—	—	—
94-95—HIFK Helsinki	Finland	45	20	16	36	16	...	...	...	3	0	0	0	0
95-96—Kansas City	IHL	29	5	13	18	8	...	...	...	—	—	—	—	—
—San Jose....................	NHL	31	2	11	13	14	-7	0	0	—	—	—	—	—
96-97—San Jose....................	NHL	28	2	3	5	0	-8	1	0	—	—	—	—	—
—Kentucky....................	AHL	40	22	30	52	21	...	...	...	—	—	—	—	—
97-98—Vastra Frolunda	Sweden	44	22	29	*51	44	...	...	...	7	4	2	6	0
—Fin. Olympic team.......	Int'l	6	2	1	3	6	...	...	...	—	—	—	—	—
98-99—Nashville	NHL	14	5	5	10	2	1	1	0	—	—	—	—	—
99-00—Nashville	NHL	79	6	22	28	22	-1	2	0	—	—	—	—	—
NHL Totals (4 years)...........		152	15	41	56	38	-15	4	0					

PELUSO, MIKE   C   CAPITALS

PERSONAL: Born September 2, 1974, in Denver. ... 6-1/208. ... Shoots right. ... Full Name: Michael James Peluso. ... Cousin of Mike Peluso, left winger for six NHL teams (1989-90 through 1997-98).
HIGH SCHOOL: Bismarck (N.D.).
COLLEGE: Minnesota-Duluth.
TRANSACTIONS/CAREER NOTES: Selected by Calgary Flames in 10th round (11th Flames pick, 253rd overall) of NHL entry draft (June 29, 1994). ... Signed as free agent by Washington Capitals (February 10, 1999).
HONORS: Named to WCHA All-Rookie team (1994-95). ... Named to WCHA All-Star second team (1996-97).

		REGULAR SEASON							PLAYOFFS				
Season Team	League	Gms.	G	A	Pts.	PIM	+/-	PP	SH	Gms.	G	A	Pts.	PIM
91-92—Bismarck H.S.............	N.D. H.S.	23	50	49	99	...	...	...	...	—	—	—	—	—
92-93—Omaha	USHL				Statistics unavailable.									
93-94—Omaha	USHL	48	36	29	65	77	...	...	...	—	—	—	—	—
94-95—Minnesota-Duluth	WCHA	38	11	23	34	38	...	...	...	—	—	—	—	—
95-96—Minnesota-Duluth	WCHA	38	25	19	44	64	...	...	...	—	—	—	—	—
96-97—Minnesota-Duluth	WCHA	37	20	20	40	53	...	...	...	—	—	—	—	—
97-98—Minnesota-Duluth	WCHA	40	24	21	45	100	...	...	...	—	—	—	—	—
98-99—Portland	AHL	26	7	6	13	6	...	...	...	—	—	—	—	—
99-00—Portland	AHL	71	25	29	54	86	...	...	...	4	2	0	2	0

PERREAULT, YANIC   C   MAPLE LEAFS

PERSONAL: Born April 4, 1971, in Sherbrooke, Que. ... 5-10/185. ... Shoots left. ... Name pronounced YAH-nihk puh-ROH.
TRANSACTIONS/CAREER NOTES: Selected by Toronto Maple Leafs in third round (first Maple Leafs pick, 47th overall) of NHL entry draft (June 22, 1991). ... Signed as free agent by Los Angeles Kings (July 14, 1994). ... Strained abdominal muscle (December 13, 1996); missed 11 games. ... Underwent kidney surgery (February 3, 1997); missed remainder of season. ... Traded by Kings to Maple Leafs for C/RW Jason Podollan and third-round pick (G Cory Campbell) in 1999 draft (March 23, 1999). ... Fractured arm (December 4, 1999); missed 23 games.
HONORS: Won Can.HL Rookie of the Year Award (1988-89). ... Won Michel Bergeron Trophy (1988-89). ... Won Marcel Robert Trophy (1989-90). ... Won Michel Briere Trophy (1990-91). ... Won Jean Beliveau Trophy (1990-91). ... Won Frank J. Selke Trophy (1990-91). ... Won Shell Cup (1990-91). ... Named to QMJHL All-Star first team (1990-91).
STATISTICAL PLATEAUS: Three-goal games: 1997-98 (2). ... Four-goal games: 1998-99 (1). ... Total hat tricks: 3.

P

Season Team	League	REGULAR SEASON									PLAYOFFS				
		Gms.	G	A	Pts.	PIM	+/-	PP	SH		Gms.	G	A	Pts.	PIM
88-89—Trois-Rivieres	QMJHL	70	53	55	108	48	...	...	...		—	—	—	—	—
89-90—Trois-Rivieres	QMJHL	63	51	63	114	75	...	...	...		7	6	5	11	19
90-91—Trois-Rivieres	QMJHL	67	*87	98	*185	103	...	...	...		6	4	7	11	6
91-92—St. John's	AHL	62	38	38	76	19	...	...	...		16	7	8	15	4
92-93—St. John's	AHL	79	49	46	95	56	...	...	...		9	4	5	9	2
93-94—St. John's	AHL	62	45	60	105	38	...	...	...		11	*12	6	18	14
—Toronto	NHL	13	3	3	6	0	1	2	0		—	—	—	—	—
94-95—Phoenix	IHL	68	51	48	99	52	...	...	...		—	—	—	—	—
—Los Angeles	NHL	26	2	5	7	20	3	0	0		—	—	—	—	—
95-96—Los Angeles	NHL	78	25	24	49	16	-11	8	3		—	—	—	—	—
96-97—Los Angeles	NHL	41	11	14	25	20	0	1	1		—	—	—	—	—
97-98—Los Angeles	NHL	79	28	20	48	32	6	3	2		4	1	2	3	6
98-99—Los Angeles	NHL	64	10	17	27	30	-3	2	2		—	—	—	—	—
—Toronto	NHL	12	7	8	15	12	10	2	1		17	3	6	9	6
99-00—Toronto	NHL	58	18	27	45	22	3	5	0		1	0	1	1	0
NHL Totals (7 years)		371	104	118	222	152	9	23	9		22	4	9	13	12

PERSSON, RICARD — D — SENATORS

PERSONAL: Born August 24, 1969, in Ostersund, Sweden. ... 6-1/201. ... Shoots left. ... Full Name: Ricard Lars Persson. ... Name pronounced RIH-kahrd PEER-suhn.

TRANSACTIONS/CAREER NOTES: Selected by New Jersey Devils in second round (second Devils pick, 23rd overall) of NHL entry draft (June 13, 1987). ... Traded by Devils with LW Mike Peluso to St. Louis Blues for D Ken Sutton and second-round pick (LW Brett Clouthier) in 1999 draft (November 26, 1996). ... Sprained knee (October 9, 1999); missed 17 games. ... Injured shoulder (March 11, 2000); missed final 14 games of regular season. ... Signed as free agent by Ottawa Senators (July 12, 2000).

Season Team	League	REGULAR SEASON									PLAYOFFS				
		Gms.	G	A	Pts.	PIM	+/-	PP	SH		Gms.	G	A	Pts.	PIM
85-86—Ostersund	Sweden Dv. 2	24	2	2	4	16	...	...	...		—	—	—	—	—
86-87—Ostersund	Sweden Dv. 2	31	10	11	21	28	...	...	...		—	—	—	—	—
87-88—Leksand	Sweden	31	2	0	2	8	...	...	...		2	0	1	1	2
88-89—Leksand	Sweden	33	2	4	6	28	...	...	...		9	0	1	1	6
89-90—Leksand	Sweden	43	9	10	19	62	...	...	...		3	0	0	0	6
90-91—Leksand	Sweden	37	6	9	15	42	...	...	...		—	—	—	—	—
91-92—Leksand	Sweden	21	0	7	7	28	...	...	...		—	—	—	—	—
92-93—Leksand	Sweden	36	7	15	22	63	...	...	...		2	0	2	2	0
93-94—Malmo	Sweden	40	11	9	20	38	...	...	...		11	2	0	2	12
94-95—Malmo	Sweden	31	3	13	16	38	...	...	...		9	0	2	2	8
—Albany	AHL	—	—	—	—	—	...	...	...		9	3	5	8	7
95-96—New Jersey	NHL	12	2	1	3	8	5	1	0		—	—	—	—	—
—Albany	AHL	67	15	31	46	59	...	...	...		4	0	0	0	7
96-97—New Jersey	NHL	1	0	0	0	0	0	0	0		—	—	—	—	—
—Albany	AHL	13	1	4	5	8	...	...	...		—	—	—	—	—
—St. Louis	NHL	54	4	8	12	45	-2	1	0		6	0	0	0	27
97-98—Worcester	AHL	32	2	16	18	58	...	...	...		10	3	7	10	24
—St. Louis	NHL	1	0	0	0	0	0	0	0		—	—	—	—	—
98-99—Worcester	AHL	19	6	4	10	42	...	...	...		—	—	—	—	—
—St. Louis	NHL	54	1	12	13	94	4	0	0		13	0	3	3	17
99-00—St. Louis	NHL	41	0	8	8	38	-2	0	0		3	1	0	1	0
—Worcester	AHL	2	0	1	1	0	...	...	...		—	—	—	—	—
NHL Totals (5 years)		163	7	29	36	185	5	2	0		22	1	3	4	44

PETERS, ANDREW — LW — SABRES

PERSONAL: Born May 5, 1980, in St. Catharines, Ont. ... 6-4/195. ... Shoots left.

TRANSACTIONS/CAREER NOTES: Selected by Buffalo Sabres in second round (second Sabres pick, 34th overall) of NHL entry draft (June 27, 1998).

Season Team	League	REGULAR SEASON									PLAYOFFS				
		Gms.	G	A	Pts.	PIM	+/-	PP	SH		Gms.	G	A	Pts.	PIM
96-97—Georgetown	Tier II Jr. A	46	11	16	27	105	...	...	...		—	—	—	—	—
97-98—Oshawa	OHL	60	11	7	18	220	...	...	...		7	2	0	2	19
98-99—Oshawa	OHL	54	14	10	24	137	...	...	...		15	2	7	9	36
99-00—Kitchener	OHL	42	6	13	19	95	...	...	...		4	0	1	1	14

PETROV, OLEG — RW — CANADIENS

PERSONAL: Born April 18, 1971, in Moscow, U.S.S.R. ... 5-8/175. ... Shoots left. ... Name pronounced PAY-trahv.

TRANSACTIONS/CAREER NOTES: Selected by Montreal Canadiens in sixth round (ninth Canadiens pick, 127th overall) of NHL entry draft (June 22, 1991). ... Suffered injury (January 5, 1994); missed one game. ... Sprained ankle (April 6, 1994); missed three games. ... Torn medial collateral ligament in knee (December 11, 1999); missed 22 games.

HONORS: Named to NHL All-Rookie team (1993-94).

STATISTICAL PLATEAUS: Three-goal games: 1993-94 (1).

Season Team	League	Gms.	G	A	Pts.	PIM	+/-	PP	SH	Gms.	G	A	Pts.	PIM
					REGULAR SEASON							PLAYOFFS		
90-91—CSKA Moscow	USSR	43	7	4	11	8	...	...	...	—	—	—	—	—
91-92—CSKA Moscow	CIS	34	8	13	21	6	...	...	...	—	—	—	—	—
92-93—Montreal	NHL	9	2	1	3	10	2	0	0	1	0	0	0	0
—Fredericton	AHL	55	26	29	55	36	...	...	...	5	4	1	5	0
93-94—Fredericton	AHL	23	8	20	28	18	...	...	...	—	—	—	—	—
—Montreal	NHL	55	12	15	27	2	7	1	0	2	0	0	0	0
94-95—Montreal	NHL	12	2	3	5	4	-7	0	0	—	—	—	—	—
—Fredericton	AHL	17	7	11	18	12	...	...	...	17	5	6	11	10
95-96—Montreal	NHL	36	4	7	11	23	-9	0	0	5	0	1	1	0
—Fredericton	AHL	22	12	18	30	71	...	...	...	6	2	6	8	0
96-97—Ambri-Piotta	Switzerland	45	24	28	52	44	...	...	...	—	—	—	—	—
—HC Meran	Italy	12	5	12	17	4	...	...	...	—	—	—	—	—
97-98—Ambri-Piotta	Switzerland	40	30	*63	*93	60	...	...	...	14	11	11	22	40
98-99—Ambri Piotta	Switzerland	45	35	52	87	52	...	...	...	15	9	11	20	32
99-00—Quebec	AHL	16	7	7	14	4	...	...	...	—	—	—	—	—
—Montreal	NHL	44	2	24	26	8	10	1	0	—	—	—	—	—
NHL Totals (5 years)		156	22	50	72	47	3	2	0	8	0	1	1	0

PETROVICKY, ROBERT   C   ISLANDERS

PERSONAL: Born October 16, 1973, in Kosice, Czechoslovakia. ... 5-10/183. ... Shoots left. ... Name pronounced peht-roh-VIH-kee.
TRANSACTIONS/CAREER NOTES: Selected by Hartford Whalers in first round (first Whalers pick, ninth overall) of NHL entry draft (June 20, 1992). ... Sprained left ankle (February 28, 1993); missed five games. ... Loaned to Slovakian Olympic team (February 11, 1994). ... Returned to Whalers (February 28, 1994). ... Traded by Whalers to Dallas Stars for RW Dan Kesa (November 29, 1995). ... Signed as free agent by St. Louis Blues (September 6, 1996). ... Signed as free agent by Tampa Bay Lightning (February 14, 1999). ... Injured groin (October 28, 1999); missed two games. ... Strained neck (February 8, 2000); missed six games. ... Signed as free agent by New York Islanders (July 27, 2000).
HONORS: Named to Czechoslovakian League All-Star team (1991-92).

Season Team	League	Gms.	G	A	Pts.	PIM	+/-	PP	SH	Gms.	G	A	Pts.	PIM
					REGULAR SEASON							PLAYOFFS		
90-91—Dukla Trencin	Czech.	33	9	14	23	12	...	...	...	—	—	—	—	—
91-92—Dukla Trencin	Czech.	46	25	36	61	...	...	...	...	—	—	—	—	—
92-93—Hartford	NHL	42	3	6	9	45	-10	0	0	—	—	—	—	—
—Springfield	AHL	16	5	3	8	39	...	...	...	15	5	6	11	14
93-94—Hartford	NHL	33	6	5	11	39	-1	1	0	—	—	—	—	—
—Springfield	AHL	30	16	8	24	39	...	...	...	4	0	2	2	4
—Slovakian Oly. team	Int'l	8	1	6	7	18	...	...	...	—	—	—	—	—
94-95—Springfield	AHL	74	30	52	82	121	...	...	...	—	—	—	—	—
—Hartford	NHL	2	0	0	0	0	0	0	0	—	—	—	—	—
95-96—Springfield	AHL	9	4	8	12	18	...	...	...	—	—	—	—	—
—Detroit	IHL	12	5	3	8	16	...	...	...	—	—	—	—	—
—Michigan	IHL	50	23	23	46	63	...	...	...	7	3	1	4	16
—Dallas	NHL	5	1	1	2	0	1	1	0	—	—	—	—	—
96-97—Worcester	AHL	12	5	4	9	19	...	...	...	—	—	—	—	—
—St. Louis	NHL	44	7	12	19	10	2	0	0	2	0	0	0	0
97-98—Worcester	AHL	65	27	34	61	97	...	...	...	10	3	4	7	12
—Slovakian Oly. team	Int'l	4	2	1	3	0	...	...	...	—	—	—	—	—
98-99—Grand Rapids	IHL	49	26	32	58	87	...	...	...	—	—	—	—	—
—Tampa Bay	NHL	28	3	4	7	6	-8	0	0	—	—	—	—	—
99-00—Grand Rapids	IHL	7	5	3	8	4	...	...	...	—	—	—	—	—
—Tampa Bay	NHL	43	7	10	17	14	2	1	0	—	—	—	—	—
NHL Totals (7 years)		197	27	38	65	114	-14	3	0	2	0	0	0	0

PHILLIPS, CHRIS   D   SENATORS

PERSONAL: Born March 9, 1978, in Fort McMurray, Alta. ... 6-3/215. ... Shoots left. ... Nephew of Rod Phillips, Edmonton Oilers play-by-play announcer.
TRANSACTIONS/CAREER NOTES: Selected by Ottawa Senators in first round (first Senators pick, first overall) of NHL entry draft (June 22, 1996). ... Bruised knee (November 13, 1997); missed two games. ... Bruised eye (February 25, 1998); missed five games. ... Suffered back spasms (November 18, 1998); missed three games. ... Sprained right ankle (January 1, 1999); missed 21 games. ... Reinjured right ankle (February 20, 1999); missed 23 games. ... Injured right ankle (December 9, 1999) and underwent surgery; missed 17 games.
HONORS: Won Can.HL Top Draft Prospect Award (1995-96). ... Won Jim Piggott Memorial Trophy (1995-96). ... Named to Can.HL All-Rookie team (1995-96). ... Named to Memorial Cup All-Star Team (1996-97). ... Named to Can.HL All-Star first team (1996-97). ... Named to WHL (East) All-Star first team (1996-97). ... Won Bill Hunter Trophy (1996-97).

Season Team	League	Gms.	G	A	Pts.	PIM	+/-	PP	SH	Gms.	G	A	Pts.	PIM
					REGULAR SEASON							PLAYOFFS		
93-94—Fort McMurray	AJHL	56	6	16	22	72	...	...	...	—	—	—	—	—
94-95—Fort McMurray	AJHL	48	16	32	48	127	...	...	...	—	—	—	—	—
95-96—Prince Albert	WHL	61	10	30	40	97	...	...	...	18	2	12	14	30
96-97—Prince Albert	WHL	32	3	23	26	58	...	...	...	—	—	—	—	—
—Lethbridge	WHL	26	4	18	22	28	...	...	...	19	4	*21	25	20
97-98—Ottawa	NHL	72	5	11	16	38	2	2	0	11	0	2	2	2
98-99—Ottawa	NHL	34	3	3	6	32	-5	2	0	3	0	0	0	0
99-00—Ottawa	NHL	65	5	14	19	39	12	0	0	6	0	1	1	4
NHL Totals (3 years)		171	13	28	41	109	9	4	0	20	0	3	3	6

P

PHILLIPS, GREG — RW — KINGS

PERSONAL: Born March 27, 1978, in Winnipeg. ... 6-2/205. ... Shoots right.
TRANSACTIONS/CAREER NOTES: Selected by Los Angeles Kings in third round (third Kings pick, 57th overall) of NHL entry draft (June 22, 1996).

Season Team	League	REGULAR SEASON								PLAYOFFS				
		Gms.	G	A	Pts.	PIM	+/-	PP	SH	Gms.	G	A	Pts.	PIM
94-95—Saskatoon	WHL	64	3	5	8	94	...	...	...	10	0	0	0	4
95-96—Saskatoon	WHL	67	21	24	45	132	...	...	...	4	1	2	3	2
96-97—Saskatoon	WHL	34	17	19	36	64	...	...	...	—	—	—	—	—
97-98—Saskatoon	WHL	47	24	26	50	120	...	...	...	—	—	—	—	—
—Brandon	WHL	22	10	23	33	45	...	...	...	18	11	11	22	58
98-99—Springfield	AHL	63	16	13	29	74	...	...	...	3	0	0	0	4
99-00—Lowell	AHL	62	20	10	30	140	...	...	...	7	3	0	3	10

PICARD, MICHEL — LW

PERSONAL: Born November 7, 1969, in Beauport, Que. ... 5-11/202. ... Shoots left. ... Name pronounced pih-KAHRD.
TRANSACTIONS/CAREER NOTES: Selected by Hartford Whalers in ninth round (eighth Whalers pick, 178th overall) of NHL entry draft (June 17, 1989). ... Separated shoulder (November 14, 1991); missed seven games. ... Traded by Whalers to San Jose Sharks for future considerations (October 9, 1992); Whalers acquired LW Yvon Corriveau to complete deal (January 21, 1993). ... Signed as free agent by Ottawa Senators (June 23, 1994). ... Suspended two games and fined $1,000 by NHL for cross-checking (March 16, 1996). ... Traded by Senators to Washington Capitals for cash (May 21, 1996). ... Signed as free agent by St. Louis Blues (January 30, 1998). ... Signed as free agent by Edmonton Oilers (December 2, 1999).
HONORS: Named to QMJHL All-Star second team (1988-89). ... Named to AHL All-Star first team (1990-91 and 1994-95). ... Named to AHL All-Star second team (1993-94). ... Named to IHL All-Star first team (1996-97).

Season Team	League	REGULAR SEASON								PLAYOFFS				
		Gms.	G	A	Pts.	PIM	+/-	PP	SH	Gms.	G	A	Pts.	PIM
86-87—Trois-Rivieres	QMJHL	66	33	35	68	53	...	...	...	—	—	—	—	—
87-88—Trois-Rivieres	QMJHL	69	40	55	95	71	...	...	...	—	—	—	—	—
88-89—Trois-Rivieres	QMJHL	66	59	81	140	107	...	...	...	4	1	3	4	2
89-90—Binghamton	AHL	67	16	24	40	98	...	...	...	—	—	—	—	—
90-91—Hartford	NHL	5	1	0	1	2	-2	0	0	—	—	—	—	—
—Springfield	AHL	77	*56	40	96	61	...	...	...	18	8	13	21	18
91-92—Hartford	NHL	25	3	5	8	6	-2	1	0	—	—	—	—	—
—Springfield	AHL	40	21	17	38	44	...	...	...	11	2	0	2	34
92-93—Kansas City	IHL	33	7	10	17	51	...	...	...	12	3	2	5	20
—San Jose	NHL	25	4	0	4	24	-17	2	0	—	—	—	—	—
93-94—Portland	AHL	61	41	44	85	99	...	...	...	17	11	10	21	22
94-95—Prin. Edward Island	AHL	57	32	57	89	58	...	...	...	8	4	4	8	6
—Ottawa	NHL	24	5	8	13	14	-1	1	0	—	—	—	—	—
95-96—Prin. Edward Island	AHL	55	37	45	82	79	...	...	...	5	5	1	6	2
—Ottawa	NHL	17	2	6	8	10	-1	0	0	—	—	—	—	—
96-97—Grand Rapids	IHL	82	46	55	101	58	...	...	...	5	2	0	2	10
97-98—Grand Rapids	IHL	58	28	41	69	42	...	...	...	—	—	—	—	—
—St. Louis	NHL	16	1	8	9	29	3	0	0	—	—	—	—	—
98-99—St. Louis	NHL	45	11	11	22	16	5	0	0	5	0	0	0	2
—Grand Rapids	IHL	6	2	2	4	2	...	...	...	—	—	—	—	—
99-00—Edmonton	NHL	2	0	0	0	2	0	0	0	—	—	—	—	—
—Grand Rapids	IHL	65	33	35	68	50	...	...	...	17	8	10	†18	4
NHL Totals (8 years)		159	27	38	65	103	-15	4	0	5	0	0	0	2

PILON, RICH — D — RANGERS

PERSONAL: Born April 30, 1968, in Saskatoon, Sask. ... 6-2/220. ... Shoots left. ... Full Name: Richard Pilon. ... Name pronounced PEE-lahn.
TRANSACTIONS/CAREER NOTES: Selected by New York Islanders as underage junior in seventh round (ninth Islanders pick, 143rd overall) of NHL entry draft (June 21, 1986). ... Injured right leg (December 1988). ... Injured right eye (November 4, 1989); missed remainder of season. ... Injured left knee ligament (February 23, 1991). ... Suffered sore left shoulder (January 9, 1992); missed three games. ... Lacerated finger (January 30, 1992); missed four games. ... Bruised hand (October 31, 1992); missed two games. ... Bruised hand (November 22, 1992); missed four games. ... Sprained left knee (December 10, 1992); missed eight games. ... Injured lower back (January 10, 1993); missed 11 games. ... Injured left shoulder (November 13, 1993); missed seven games. ... Reinjured left shoulder (December 3, 1993); missed 32 games. ... Reinjured left shoulder (March 17, 1994); missed 14 games. ... Suffered sore groin (February 22, 1995); missed four games. ... Sprained ankle (March 5, 1995); missed 17 games. ... Fractured wrist (April 18, 1995); missed remainder of season. ... Injured wrist prior to 1995-96 season; missed first 26 games of season. ... Injured groin (December 12, 1995); missed four games. ... Injured wrist (January 9, 1996); missed one game. ... Strained hip flexor (February 4, 1996); missed four games. ... Strained hip flexor (March 3, 1996); missed last 18 games of regular season. ... Aggravated groin (October 9, 1996); missed 20 games. ... Suspended two games and fined $1,000 by NHL for slashing incident (January 11, 1997). ... Sprained knee ligament (February 11, 1997); missed three games. ... Injured foot (March 26, 1997); missed four games. ... Bruised knee (April 2, 1997); missed one game. ... Injured groin (October 19, 1997); missed one game. ... Injured foot (November 14, 1997); missed four games. ... Strained triceps (March 6, 1998); missed one game. ... Strained groin (October 10, 1998); missed two games. ... Reinjured groin (October 17, 1998); missed two games. ... Sprained wrist (December 2, 1998); missed two games. ... Sprained knee (January 5, 1999); missed seven games. ... Injured back (January 29, 1999); missed one game. ... Suffered sore back (March 6, 1999); missed one game. ... Suffered inflamed disk in back (March 14, 1999); missed final 14 games of season. ... Sprained medial collateral ligament in left knee (October 18, 1999); missed nine games. ... Sprained knee (November 23, 1999); missed two games. ... Claimed on waivers by New York Rangers (December 1, 1999). ... Strained left shoulder (February 9, 2000); missed two games. ... Reinjured left shoulder (February 15, 2000); missed six games. ... Reinjured left shoulder (March 1, 2000); missed five games. ... Reinjured left shoulder (April 3, 2000); missed one game.
HONORS: Named to WHL All-Star second team (1987-88).

P

Season Team	League	Gms.	G	A	Pts.	PIM	+/-	PP	SH	Gms.	G	A	Pts.	PIM
		REGULAR SEASON								PLAYOFFS				
85-86—Prince Albert	WHL	6	0	0	0	0	...	...	...	—	—	—	—	—
86-87—Prince Albert	WHL	68	4	21	25	192	...	...	...	7	1	6	7	17
87-88—Prince Albert	WHL	65	13	34	47	177	...	...	...	9	0	6	6	38
88-89—New York Islanders	NHL	62	0	14	14	242	-9	0	0	—	—	—	—	—
89-90—New York Islanders	NHL	14	0	2	2	31	2	0	0	—	—	—	—	—
90-91—New York Islanders	NHL	60	1	4	5	126	-12	0	0	—	—	—	—	—
91-92—New York Islanders	NHL	65	1	6	7	183	-1	0	0	—	—	—	—	—
92-93—New York Islanders	NHL	44	1	3	4	164	-4	0	0	15	0	0	0	50
—Capital District	AHL	6	0	1	1	8	...	...	...	—	—	—	—	—
93-94—New York Islanders	NHL	28	1	4	5	75	-4	0	0	—	—	—	—	—
—Salt Lake City	IHL	2	0	0	0	8	...	...	...	—	—	—	—	—
94-95—New York Islanders	NHL	20	1	1	2	40	-3	0	0	—	—	—	—	—
—Chicago	IHL	2	0	0	0	0	...	...	...	—	—	—	—	—
95-96—New York Islanders	NHL	27	0	3	3	72	-9	0	0	—	—	—	—	—
96-97—New York Islanders	NHL	52	1	4	5	179	4	0	0	—	—	—	—	—
97-98—New York Islanders	NHL	76	0	7	7	291	1	0	0	—	—	—	—	—
98-99—New York Islanders	NHL	52	0	4	4	88	-8	0	0	—	—	—	—	—
99-00—New York Islanders	NHL	9	0	2	2	34	-2	0	0	—	—	—	—	—
—New York Rangers	NHL	45	0	4	4	36	0	0	0	—	—	—	—	—
NHL Totals (12 years)		554	6	58	64	1561	-45	0	0	15	0	0	0	50

PITLICK, LANCE — D — PANTHERS

PERSONAL: Born November 5, 1967, in Fridley, Minn. ... 5-11/211. ... Shoots right.
HIGH SCHOOL: Cooper (New Hope, Minn.).
COLLEGE: Minnesota.
TRANSACTIONS/CAREER NOTES: Selected by Minnesota North Stars in ninth round (10th North Stars pick, 180th overall) of NHL entry draft (June 21, 1986). ... Severely pulled lower abdominal muscles (December 1, 1989). ... Underwent surgery to have tendons sewn onto his abdominal muscle for reinforcement (January 18, 1990). ... Signed as free agent by Philadelphia Flyers (September 5, 1990). ... Signed as free agent by Ottawa Senators (June 22, 1994). ... Bruised ribs (March 27, 1995); missed two games. ... Injured groin (January 5, 1996); missed one game. ... Injured groin during 1995-96 season; missed four games. ... Strained abdominal muscle (April 1, 1996); missed four games. ... Injured left knee (January 9, 1997); missed nine games. ... Strained groin (February 16, 1997); missed one game. ... Strained groin (December 2, 1997); missed one game. ... Bruised hip (December 12, 1998); missed 32 games. ... Signed as free agent by Florida Panthers (July 13, 1999). ... Fractured hand (October 24, 1999); missed five games. ... Fractured ankle (March 3, 2000); missed 14 games.

Season Team	League	Gms.	G	A	Pts.	PIM	+/-	PP	SH	Gms.	G	A	Pts.	PIM
		REGULAR SEASON								PLAYOFFS				
84-85—Cooper H.S.	Minn. H.S.	23	8	4	12		...	...	...	—	—	—	—	—
85-86—Cooper H.S.	Minn. H.S.	21	17	8	25		...	...	...	—	—	—	—	—
86-87—Univ. of Minnesota	WCHA	45	0	9	9	88	...	...	...	10	0	2	2	4
87-88—Univ. of Minnesota	WCHA	38	3	9	12	76	...	...	...	8	1	1	2	14
88-89—Univ. of Minnesota	WCHA	47	4	9	13	95	...	...	...	8	2	1	3	95
89-90—Univ. of Minnesota	WCHA	14	3	2	5	26	...	...	...	—	—	—	—	—
90-91—Hershey	AHL	64	6	15	21	75	...	...	...	3	0	0	0	9
91-92—U.S. national team	Int'l	19	0	1	1	38	...	...	...	—	—	—	—	—
—Hershey	AHL	4	0	0	0	6	...	...	...	3	0	0	0	4
92-93—Hershey	AHL	53	5	10	15	77	...	...	...	—	—	—	—	—
93-94—Hershey	AHL	58	4	13	17	93	...	...	...	11	1	0	1	11
94-95—Prin. Edward Island	AHL	61	8	19	27	55	...	...	...	11	1	4	5	10
—Ottawa	NHL	15	0	1	1	6	-5	0	0	—	—	—	—	—
95-96—Prin. Edward Island	AHL	29	4	10	14	39	...	...	...	5	0	0	0	0
—Ottawa	NHL	28	1	6	7	20	-8	0	0	—	—	—	—	—
96-97—Ottawa	NHL	66	5	5	10	91	2	0	0	7	0	0	0	4
97-98—Ottawa	NHL	69	2	7	9	50	8	0	0	11	0	1	1	17
98-99—Ottawa	NHL	50	3	6	9	33	7	0	0	2	0	0	0	0
99-00—Florida	NHL	62	3	5	8	44	7	0	0	4	0	1	1	0
NHL Totals (6 years)		290	14	30	44	244	11	0	0	24	0	2	2	21

PITTIS, DOMENIC — LW — OILERS

PERSONAL: Born October 1, 1974, in Calgary. ... 5-11/190. ... Shoots left. ... Name pronounced PIHT-ihz.
HIGH SCHOOL: Catholic Central (Lethbridge, Alta).
TRANSACTIONS/CAREER NOTES: Selected by Pittsburgh Penguins in second round (second Penguins pick, 52nd overall) of NHL entry draft (June 26, 1993). ... Signed as free agent by Buffalo Sabres (July 30, 1998). ... Suffered from the flu (October 27, 1999); missed one game. ... Injured ankle (November 9, 1999); missed three games. ... Signed as free agent by Edmonton Oilers (July 26, 2000).
HONORS: Named to WHL (East) All-Star second team (1993-94). ... Won John B. Sollenberger Trophy (1998-99).

Season Team	League	Gms.	G	A	Pts.	PIM	+/-	PP	SH	Gms.	G	A	Pts.	PIM
		REGULAR SEASON								PLAYOFFS				
91-92—Lethbridge	WHL	65	6	17	23	48	...	...	...	5	0	2	2	4
92-93—Lethbridge	WHL	66	46	73	119	69	...	...	...	4	3	3	6	8
93-94—Lethbridge	WHL	72	58	69	127	93	...	...	...	8	4	11	15	16
94-95—Cleveland	IHL	62	18	32	50	66	...	...	...	3	0	2	2	2
95-96—Cleveland	IHL	74	10	28	38	100	...	...	...	3	0	0	0	2
96-97—Pittsburgh	NHL	1	0	0	0	0	-1	0	0	—	—	—	—	—
—Long Beach	IHL	65	23	43	66	91	...	...	...	18	5	9	14	26
97-98—Syracuse	AHL	75	23	41	64	90	...	...	...	5	1	3	4	4
98-99—Rochester	AHL	76	38	66	*104	108	...	...	...	20	7	†14	*21	40
—Buffalo	NHL	3	0	0	0	2	0	0	0	—	—	—	—	—
99-00—Buffalo	NHL	7	1	0	1	6	1	0	0	—	—	—	—	—
—Rochester	AHL	53	17	48	65	85	...	...	...	21	4	*26	*30	28
NHL Totals (3 years)		11	1	0	1	8	0	0	0					

P

PLANTE, DEREK   C   FLYERS

PERSONAL: Born January 17, 1971, in Cloquet, Minn. ... 5-11/181. ... Shoots left. ... Full Name: Derek John Plante. ... Name pronounced PLANT.
HIGH SCHOOL: Cloquet (Minn.).
COLLEGE: Minnesota-Duluth.
TRANSACTIONS/CAREER NOTES: Selected by Buffalo Sabres in eighth round (seventh Sabres pick, 161st overall) of NHL entry draft (June 17, 1989). ... Bruised left shoulder (March 8, 1994); missed two games. ... Strained back (December 15, 1995); missed three games. ... Suffered back spasms (October 7, 1997); missed three games. ... Suffered back spasms (March 1, 1998); missed four games. ... Suffered back spasms and suffered from the flu (December 8, 1998); missed three games. ... Traded by Sabres to Dallas Stars for second-round pick (C Michael Zigomanis) in 1999 draft (March 23, 1999). ... Traded by Stars with D Kevin Dean and second-round pick in 2001 draft to Chicago Blackhawks for D Sylvain Cote and D Dave Manson (February 8, 2000). ... Signed as free agent by Philadelphia Flyers (July 26, 2000).
HONORS: Named to NCAA All-America (West) first team (1992-93). ... Named WCHA Player of the Year (1992-93). ... Named to WCHA All-Star first team (1992-93).
MISCELLANEOUS: Member of Stanley Cup championship team (1999).
STATISTICAL PLATEAUS: Three-goal games: 1993-94 (1).

		REGULAR SEASON								PLAYOFFS				
Season Team	League	Gms.	G	A	Pts.	PIM	+/-	PP	SH	Gms.	G	A	Pts.	PIM
87-88—Cloquet H.S.	Minn. H.S.	23	16	25	41	...	...	...	...	—	—	—	—	—
88-89—Cloquet H.S.	Minn. H.S.	24	30	33	63	...	...	...	...	—	—	—	—	—
89-90—Minnesota-Duluth	WCHA	28	10	11	21	12	...	...	...	—	—	—	—	—
90-91—Minnesota-Duluth	WCHA	36	23	20	43	6	...	...	...	—	—	—	—	—
91-92—Minnesota-Duluth	WCHA	37	27	36	63	28	...	...	...	—	—	—	—	—
92-93—Minnesota-Duluth	WCHA	37	*36	*56	*92	30	...	...	...	—	—	—	—	—
93-94—U.S. national team	Int'l	2	0	1	1	0	...	...	...	—	—	—	—	—
—Buffalo	NHL	77	21	35	56	24	4	8	1	7	1	0	1	0
94-95—Buffalo	NHL	47	3	19	22	12	-4	2	0	—	—	—	—	—
95-96—Buffalo	NHL	76	23	33	56	28	-4	4	0	—	—	—	—	—
96-97—Buffalo	NHL	82	27	26	53	24	14	5	0	12	4	6	10	4
97-98—Buffalo	NHL	72	13	21	34	26	8	5	0	11	0	3	3	10
98-99—Buffalo	NHL	41	4	11	15	12	3	0	0	6	1	0	1	4
—Dallas	NHL	10	2	3	5	4	1	1	0	6	1	0	1	4
99-00—Dallas	NHL	16	1	1	2	2	-4	1	0	—	—	—	—	—
—Michigan	IHL	13	0	4	4	2	...	...	...	—	—	—	—	—
—Chicago	IHL	4	2	1	3	2	...	...	...	8	3	1	4	6
—Chicago	NHL	17	1	1	2	2	-1	0	0	—	—	—	—	—
NHL Totals (7 years)		438	95	150	245	134	17	26	1	36	6	9	15	18

PODEIN, SHJON   LW   AVALANCHE

PERSONAL: Born March 5, 1968, in Eden Prairie, Minn. ... 6-2/200. ... Shoots left. ... Name pronounced SHAWN poh-DEEN.
COLLEGE: Minnesota-Duluth.
TRANSACTIONS/CAREER NOTES: Selected by Edmonton Oilers in eighth round (ninth Oilers pick, 166th overall) of NHL entry draft (June 11, 1988). ... Injured knee (March 9, 1994); missed five games. ... Signed as free agent by Philadelphia Flyers (July 27, 1994). ... Bruised right foot (February 22, 1996); missed three games. ... Traded by Flyers to Colorado Avalanche for RW Keith Jones (November 12, 1998). ... Fractured lower right leg (December 4, 1998); missed 25 games. ... Bruised foot (March 30, 1999); missed one game. ... Injured knee prior to start of 1999-2000 season; missed first five games of season. ... Fractured foot (January 7, 2000); missed two games.
STATISTICAL PLATEAUS: Three-goal games: 1999-00 (1).

		REGULAR SEASON								PLAYOFFS				
Season Team	League	Gms.	G	A	Pts.	PIM	+/-	PP	SH	Gms.	G	A	Pts.	PIM
87-88—Minnesota-Duluth	WCHA	30	4	4	8	48	...	...	...	—	—	—	—	—
88-89—Minnesota-Duluth	WCHA	36	7	5	12	46	...	...	...	—	—	—	—	—
89-90—Minnesota-Duluth	WCHA	35	21	18	39	36	...	...	...	—	—	—	—	—
90-91—Cape Breton	AHL	63	14	15	29	65	...	...	...	4	0	0	0	5
91-92—Cape Breton	AHL	80	30	24	54	46	...	...	...	5	3	1	4	2
92-93—Cape Breton	AHL	38	18	21	39	32	...	...	...	9	2	2	4	29
—Edmonton	NHL	40	13	6	19	25	-2	2	1	—	—	—	—	—
93-94—Edmonton	NHL	28	3	5	8	8	3	0	0	—	—	—	—	—
—Cape Breton	AHL	5	4	4	8	4	...	...	...	—	—	—	—	—
94-95—Philadelphia	NHL	44	3	7	10	33	-2	0	0	15	1	3	4	10
95-96—Philadelphia	NHL	79	15	10	25	89	25	0	4	12	1	2	3	50
96-97—Philadelphia	NHL	82	14	18	32	41	7	0	0	19	4	3	7	16
97-98—Philadelphia	NHL	82	11	13	24	53	8	1	1	5	0	0	0	10
98-99—Philadelphia	NHL	14	1	0	1	0	-2	0	0	—	—	—	—	—
—Colorado	NHL	41	2	6	8	24	-3	0	0	19	1	1	2	12
99-00—Colorado	NHL	75	11	8	19	29	12	0	1	17	5	0	5	8
NHL Totals (8 years)		485	73	73	146	302	46	3	7	87	12	9	21	106

PODKONICKY, ANDREI   C   BLUES

PERSONAL: Born May 9, 1978, in Zvolen, Czechoslovakia. ... 6-2/195. ... Shoots left. ... Name pronounced pahd-kah-NIH-kee.
TRANSACTIONS/CAREER NOTES: Selected by St. Louis Blues in eighth round (eighth Blues pick, 196th overall) of NHL entry draft (June 22, 1996).

		REGULAR SEASON								PLAYOFFS				
Season Team	League	Gms.	G	A	Pts.	PIM	+/-	PP	SH	Gms.	G	A	Pts.	PIM
94-95—Zvolen	Czech Rep.	17	0	4	4	6	...	...	...	—	—	—	—	—
95-96—ZTK Zvolen	Slov. Div. II	38	18	12	30	18	...	...	...	—	—	—	—	—
96-97—Portland	WHL	71	25	46	71	127	...	...	...	6	1	1	2	8
97-98—Portland	WHL	64	30	44	74	81	...	...	...	16	4	12	16	20
98-99—Worcester	AHL	61	19	24	43	52	...	...	...	4	0	0	0	4
99-00—Worcester	AHL	77	16	25	41	68	...	...	...	9	2	5	7	6

PODOLLAN, JASON   RW/C   KINGS

PERSONAL: Born February 18, 1976, in Vernon, B.C. ... 6-1/202. ... Shoots right. ... Name pronounced puh-DOH-lihn.
HIGH SCHOOL: University (Spokane, Wash.).
TRANSACTIONS/CAREER NOTES: Selected by Florida Panthers in second round (third Panthers pick, 31st overall) of NHL entry draft (June 28, 1994). ... Traded by Panthers to Toronto Maple Leafs for C Kirk Muller (March 18, 1997). ... Strained shoulder (March 19, 1997); missed two games. ... Traded by Maple Leafs with third-round pick (G Cory Campbell) in 1999 draft to Los Angeles Kings for C Yanic Perreault (March 23, 1999).
HONORS: Named to WHL (West) All-Star second team (1995-96).

Season Team	League	REGULAR SEASON								PLAYOFFS				
		Gms.	G	A	Pts.	PIM	+/-	PP	SH	Gms.	G	A	Pts.	PIM
91-92—Penticton	Jr. A	59	20	26	46	66	...	...	...	—	—	—	—	—
—Spokane	WHL	2	0	0	0	2	...	...	...	10	3	1	4	16
92-93—Spokane	WHL	72	36	33	69	108	...	...	...	10	4	4	8	14
93-94—Spokane	WHL	69	29	37	66	108	...	...	...	3	3	0	3	2
94-95—Spokane	WHL	72	43	41	84	102	...	...	...	11	5	7	12	18
—Cincinnati	IHL	—	—	—	—	—	...	...	...	3	0	0	0	2
95-96—Spokane	WHL	56	37	25	62	103	...	...	...	18	*21	12	33	28
96-97—Carolina	AHL	39	21	25	46	36	...	...	...	—	—	—	—	—
—Florida	NHL	19	1	1	2	4	-3	1	0	—	—	—	—	—
—St. John's	AHL	—	—	—	—	—	...	...	...	11	2	3	5	6
—Toronto	NHL	10	0	3	3	6	-2	0	0	—	—	—	—	—
97-98—St. John's	AHL	70	30	31	61	116	...	...	...	4	1	0	1	10
98-99—St. John's	AHL	68	42	26	68	65	...	...	...	—	—	—	—	—
—Toronto	NHL	4	0	0	0	0	0	0	0	—	—	—	—	—
—Long Beach	IHL	8	5	3	8	2	...	...	...	6	1	2	3	4
—Los Angeles	NHL	6	0	0	0	5	-3	0	0	—	—	—	—	—
99-00—Lowell	AHL	71	29	26	55	91	...	...	...	4	0	0	0	4
—Los Angeles	NHL	1	0	1	1	2	0	0	0	—	—	—	—	—
NHL Totals (3 years)		40	1	5	6	17	-8	1	0					

POESCHEK, RUDY   D

PERSONAL: Born September 29, 1966, in Kamloops, British Columbia ... 6-2/220. ... Shoots right. ... Full Name: Rudolph Leopold Poeschek. ... Name pronounced POH-shehk.
HIGH SCHOOL: North Kamloops (B.C.).
TRANSACTIONS/CAREER NOTES: Selected by New York Rangers as underage junior in 12th round (12th Rangers pick, 238th overall) of NHL entry draft (June 15, 1985). ... Injured shoulder (November 1986). ... Bruised right hand (February 1989). ... Suspended six games by AHL for pre-game fight (November 25, 1990). ... Traded by Rangers to Winnipeg Jets for C Guy Larose (January 22, 1991). ... Signed as free agent by Tampa Bay Lightning (August 13, 1993). ... Sprained ankle (February 7, 1995); missed two games. ... Reinjured ankle (February 14, 1995); missed nine games. ... Fractured thumb (April 16, 1995); missed final eight games of season. ... Injured knee (October 20, 1995); missed one game. ... Sprained left knee (October 22, 1996); missed 12 games. ... Signed as free agent by St. Louis Blues (July 7, 1997). ... Suffered back spasms (January 3, 1998); missed five games. ... Injured back (January 22, 1998); missed 27 games. ... Sprained ankle (January 28, 1999); missed 37 games.

Season Team	League	REGULAR SEASON								PLAYOFFS				
		Gms.	G	A	Pts.	PIM	+/-	PP	SH	Gms.	G	A	Pts.	PIM
83-84—Kamloops	WHL	47	3	9	12	93	...	...	...	8	0	2	2	7
84-85—Kamloops	WHL	34	6	7	13	100	...	...	...	15	0	3	3	56
85-86—Kamloops	WHL	32	3	13	16	92	...	...	...	16	3	7	10	40
86-87—Kamloops	WHL	54	13	18	31	153	...	...	...	15	2	4	6	37
87-88—New York Rangers	NHL	1	0	0	0	2	0	0	0	—	—	—	—	—
—Colorado	IHL	82	7	31	38	210	...	...	...	12	2	2	4	31
88-89—Denver	IHL	2	0	0	0	6	...	...	...	—	—	—	—	—
—New York Rangers	NHL	52	0	2	2	199	-8	0	0	—	—	—	—	—
89-90—Flint	IHL	38	8	13	21	109	...	...	...	4	0	0	0	16
—New York Rangers	NHL	15	0	0	0	55	-1	0	0	—	—	—	—	—
90-91—Binghamton	AHL	38	1	3	4	162	...	...	...	—	—	—	—	—
—Moncton	AHL	23	2	4	6	67	...	...	...	9	1	1	2	41
—Winnipeg	NHL	1	0	0	0	5	0	0	0	—	—	—	—	—
91-92—Moncton	AHL	63	4	18	22	170	...	...	...	11	0	2	2	46
—Winnipeg	NHL	4	0	0	0	17	-5	0	0	—	—	—	—	—
92-93—St. John's	AHL	78	7	24	31	189	...	...	...	9	0	4	4	13
93-94—Tampa Bay	NHL	71	3	6	9	118	3	0	0	—	—	—	—	—
94-95—Tampa Bay	NHL	25	1	1	2	92	0	0	0	—	—	—	—	—
95-96—Tampa Bay	NHL	57	1	3	4	88	-2	0	0	3	0	0	0	12
96-97—Tampa Bay	NHL	60	0	6	6	120	-3	0	0	—	—	—	—	—
97-98—St. Louis	NHL	50	1	7	8	64	-5	0	0	2	0	0	0	6
98-99—St. Louis	NHL	16	0	0	0	33	0	0	0	—	—	—	—	—
99-00—St. Louis	NHL	12	0	0	0	24	-3	0	0	—	—	—	—	—
—Worcester	AHL	5	0	0	0	4	...	...	...	—	—	—	—	—
—Houston	IHL	32	2	6	8	51	...	...	...	—	—	—	—	—
NHL Totals (12 years)		364	6	25	31	817	-24	0	0	5	0	0	0	18

POPOVIC, PETER   D   BRUINS

P

PERSONAL: Born February 10, 1968, in Koping, Sweden. ... 6-6/239. ... Shoots right. ... Name pronounced PAH-poh-vihk.
TRANSACTIONS/CAREER NOTES: Selected by Montreal Canadiens in fifth round (fifth Canadiens pick, 93rd overall) of NHL entry draft (June 11, 1988). ... Injured knee (November 20, 1993); missed six games. ... Bruised shoulder (December 22, 1993); missed seven games. ...

Played in Europe during 1994-95 NHL lockout. ... Suffered facial lacerations (March 11, 1995); missed six games. ... Fractured finger on right hand (December 23, 1995); missed six games. ... Bruised foot (February 17, 1997); missed one game. ... Injured rib (April 7, 1997); missed remainder of regular season and two playoff games. ... Suffered ankle infection (October 1, 1997); missed eight games. ... Traded by Canadiens to New York Rangers for LW Sylvain Blouin and sixth-round pick (traded to Phoenix) in 1999 draft (June 30, 1998). ... Bruised right eye (October 17, 1998); missed two games. ... Injured eye (February 14, 1999); missed 12 games. ... Traded by Rangers to Pittsburgh Penguins for D Kevin Hatcher (September 30, 1999). ... Injured groin (January 5, 2000); missed three games. ... Reinjured groin (January 23, 2000); missed four games. ... Fractured finger (February 1, 2000); missed 21 games. ... Signed as free agent by Boston Bruins (July 2, 2000).

			REGULAR SEASON								PLAYOFFS				
Season Team	League	Gms.	G	A	Pts.	PIM	+/-	PP	SH		Gms.	G	A	Pts.	PIM
86-87—Vasteras	Sweden	24	1	2	3	10	...	...	...		—	—	—	—	—
87-88—Vasteras	Sweden	28	3	17	20	16	...	...	...		—	—	—	—	—
88-89—Vasteras	Sweden	22	1	4	5	32	...	...	...		—	—	—	—	—
89-90—Vasteras	Sweden	30	2	10	12	24	...	...	...		2	0	1	1	2
90-91—Vasteras	Sweden	40	3	2	5	62	...	...	...		4	0	0	0	4
91-92—Vasteras	Sweden	34	7	10	17	30	...	...	...		—	—	—	—	—
92-93—Vasteras	Sweden	39	6	12	18	46	...	...	...		3	0	1	1	2
93-94—Montreal	NHL	47	2	12	14	26	10	1	0		6	0	1	1	0
94-95—Vasteras	Sweden	11	0	3	3	10	...	...	...		—	—	—	—	—
—Montreal	NHL	33	0	5	5	8	-10	0	0		—	—	—	—	—
95-96—Montreal	NHL	76	2	12	14	69	21	0	0		6	0	2	2	4
96-97—Montreal	NHL	78	1	13	14	32	9	0	0		3	0	0	0	2
97-98—Montreal	NHL	69	2	6	8	38	-6	0	0		10	1	1	2	2
98-99—New York Rangers	NHL	68	1	4	5	40	-12	0	0		—	—	—	—	—
99-00—Pittsburgh	NHL	54	1	5	6	30	-8	0	0		10	0	0	0	10
NHL Totals (7 years)		425	9	57	66	243	4	1	0		35	1	4	5	18

POSMYK, MAREK   D   LIGHTNING

PERSONAL: Born September 15, 1978, in Jihlava, Czechoslovakia. ... 6-5/209. ... Shoots right.
TRANSACTIONS/CAREER NOTES: Selected by Toronto Maple Leafs in second round (first Maple Leafs pick, 36th overall) of NHL entry draft (June 22, 1996). ... Traded by Maple Leafs with RW Mike Johnson and fifth-(RW Pavel Sedov) and sixth-round (D Aaron Gionet) picks in 2000 draft to Tampa Bay Lightning for C Darcy Tucker and fourth-round pick (RW Miguel Delisle) in 2000 draft (February 9, 2000). ... Strained medial collateral ligament in knee (March 19, 2000); missed three games. ... Injured neck (April 6, 2000); missed final two games of season.

			REGULAR SEASON								PLAYOFFS				
Season Team	League	Gms.	G	A	Pts.	PIM	+/-	PP	SH		Gms.	G	A	Pts.	PIM
94-95—Czech Rep.	Czech Rep.	16	1	3	4	...	...	...	...		—	—	—	—	—
95-96—Czech Rep.	Czech Rep.	16	6	5	11	...	...	...	...		—	—	—	—	—
—Dukla Jihlava	Czech Rep.	18	1	2	3	...	...	...	...		1	0	0	0	—
—Jihlava Jrs.	Czech Rep.	16	6	5	11	...	...	...	...		—	—	—	—	—
96-97—Dukla Jihlava	Czech Rep.	24	1	7	8	44	...	...	...		—	—	—	—	—
—St. John's	AHL	2	0	0	0	2	...	...	...		—	—	—	—	—
97-98—St. John's	AHL	3	0	0	0	4	...	...	...		—	—	—	—	—
—Sarnia	OHL	48	8	16	24	94	...	...	...		5	0	2	2	6
98-99—St. John's	AHL	41	1	0	1	36	...	...	...		—	—	—	—	—
99-00—St. John's	AHL	38	1	6	7	57	...	...	...		—	—	—	—	—
—Detroit	IHL	1	0	1	1	0	...	...	...		—	—	—	—	—
—Tampa Bay	NHL	18	1	2	3	20	1	0	0		—	—	—	—	—
NHL Totals (1 year)		18	1	2	3	20	1	0	0						

POTI, TOM   D   OILERS

PERSONAL: Born March 22, 1977, in Worcester, Mass. ... 6-3/215. ... Shoots left.
HIGH SCHOOL: Cushing Academy (Ashburnham, Mass.).
COLLEGE: Boston University.
TRANSACTIONS/CAREER NOTES: Selected by Edmonton Oilers in third round (fourth Oilers pick, 59th overall) of NHL entry draft (June 22, 1996). ... Bruised right knee (November 10, 1999); missed one game. ... Strained neck (December 4, 1999); missed two games. ... Bruised thumb (January 14, 2000); missed one game. ... Bruised ankle (February 13, 2000); missed one game. ... Reinjured ankle (February 29, 2000); missed one game.
HONORS: Named to NCAA All-Tournament team (1996-97). ... Named to Hockey East All-Rookie team (1996-97). ... Named to NCAA All-America (East) first team (1997-98). ... Named to Hockey East All-Star first team (1997-98). ... Named to NHL All-Rookie team (1998-99).

			REGULAR SEASON								PLAYOFFS				
Season Team	League	Gms.	G	A	Pts.	PIM	+/-	PP	SH		Gms.	G	A	Pts.	PIM
94-95—Cushing Academy	Mass. H.S.	36	16	47	63	35	...	...	...		—	—	—	—	—
95-96—Cushing Academy	Mass. H.S.	29	14	59	73	18	...	...	...		—	—	—	—	—
96-97—Boston University	Hockey East	38	4	17	21	54	...	...	...		—	—	—	—	—
97-98—Boston University	Hockey East	38	13	29	42	60	...	...	...		—	—	—	—	—
98-99—Edmonton	NHL	73	5	16	21	42	10	2	0		4	0	1	1	2
99-00—Edmonton	NHL	76	9	26	35	65	8	2	1		5	0	1	1	0
NHL Totals (2 years)		149	14	42	56	107	18	4	1		9	0	2	2	2

POTVIN, FELIX   G   CANUCKS

PERSONAL: Born June 23, 1971, in Anjou, Que. ... 6-1/190. ... Catches left. ... Name pronounced PAHT-vihn. ... Nickname: The Cat.
TRANSACTIONS/CAREER NOTES: Selected by Toronto Maple Leafs in second round (second Maple Leafs pick, 31st overall) of NHL entry draft (June 16, 1990). ... Traded by Maple Leafs with sixth-round pick (traded to Tampa Bay) in 1999 draft to New York Islanders for D Bryan Berard and sixth-round pick (RW Jan Sochor) in 1999 draft (January 9, 1999). ... Strained groin (February 13, 1999); missed 22 games. ... Traded by Islanders with second-(traded to Atlanta) and third-round (C Thatcher Bell) picks in 2000 draft to Vancouver Canucks for G Kevin Weekes,

P

C Dave Scatchard and RW Bill Muckalt (December 19, 1999). ... Injured knee (January 23, 2000); missed five games.

HONORS: Named to QMJHL All-Star second team (1989-90). ... Won Can.HL Goaltender of the Year Award (1990-91). ... Won Hap Emms Memorial Trophy (1990-91). ... Won Jacques Plante Trophy (1990-91). ... Won Shell Cup (1990-91). ... Won Guy Lafleur Trophy (1990-91). ... Named to Memorial Cup All-Star team (1990-91). ... Named to QMJHL All-Star first team (1990-91). ... Won Aldege (Baz) Bastien Trophy (1991-92). ... Won Dudley (Red) Garrett Memorial Trophy (1991-92). ... Named to AHL All-Star first team (1991-92). ... Named to NHL All-Rookie team (1992-93). ... Played in NHL All-Star Game (1994 and 1996).

MISCELLANEOUS: Stopped penalty shot attempt (vs. Brian Bradley, October 22, 1992; vs. Donald Audette, November 21, 1996).

			REGULAR SEASON								PLAYOFFS						
Season Team	League	Gms.	Min	W	L	T	GA	SO	Avg.	Gms.	Min.	W	L	GA	SO	Avg.
88-89—Chicoutimi	QMJHL	*65	*3489	25	31	1	*271	†2	4.66	—	—	—	—	—	—	—
89-90—Chicoutimi	QMJHL	*62	*3478	31	26	2	231	†2	3.99	—	—	—	—	—	—	—
90-91—Chicoutimi	QMJHL	54	3216	33	15	4	145	*6	†2.71	*16	*992	*11	5	46	0	*2.78
91-92—St. John's	AHL	35	2070	18	10	6	101	2	2.93	11	642	7	4	41	0	3.83
—Toronto	NHL	4	210	0	2	1	8	0	2.29	—	—	—	—	—	—	—
92-93—Toronto	NHL	48	2781	25	15	7	116	2	*2.50	21	1308	11	10	62	1	2.84
—St. John's	AHL	5	309	3	0	2	18	0	3.50	—	—	—	—	—	—	—
93-94—Toronto	NHL	66	3883	34	22	9	187	3	2.89	18	1124	9	†9	46	3	2.46
94-95—Toronto	NHL	36	2144	15	13	7	104	0	2.91	7	424	3	4	20	1	2.83
95-96—Toronto	NHL	69	4009	30	26	11	192	2	2.87	6	350	2	4	19	0	3.26
96-97—Toronto	NHL	*74	*4271	27	*36	7	*224	0	3.15	—	—	—	—	—	—	—
97-98—Toronto	NHL	67	3864	26	*33	7	176	5	2.73	—	—	—	—	—	—	—
98-99—Toronto	NHL	5	299	3	2	0	19	0	3.81	—	—	—	—	—	—	—
—New York Islanders	NHL	11	606	2	7	1	37	0	3.66	—	—	—	—	—	—	—
99-00—New York Islanders	NHL	22	1273	5	14	3	68	1	3.21	—	—	—	—	—	—	—
—Vancouver	NHL	34	1966	12	13	7	85	0	2.59	—	—	—	—	—	—	—
NHL Totals (9 years)		436	25306	179	183	60	1216	13	2.88	52	3206	25	27	147	5	2.75

POULIN, PATRICK　　　　C　　　　CANADIENS

PERSONAL: Born April 23, 1973, in Vanier, Que. ... 6-1/216. ... Shoots left. ... Name pronounced POO-lahn.

TRANSACTIONS/CAREER NOTES: Selected by Hartford Whalers in first round (first Whalers pick, ninth overall) of NHL entry draft (June 22, 1991). ... Traded by Whalers with D Eric Weinrich to Chicago Blackhawks for RW Steve Larmer and D Bryan Marchment (November 2, 1993). ... Sprained ankle (December 28, 1995); missed 19 games. ... Suffered back spasms (March 5, 1996); missed two games. ... Traded by Blackhawks with D Igor Ulanov and second-round pick (traded to New Jersey) to Tampa Bay Lightning for D Enrico Ciccone (March 20, 1996). ... Injured knee (January 13, 1997); missed one game. ... Injured knee (March 6, 1997); missed six games. ... Traded by Lightning with F Mick Vukota and D Igor Ulanov to Montreal Canadiens for F Stephane Richer, F Darcy Tucker and D David Wilkie (January 15, 1998). ... Sprained knee (November 19, 1998); missed one game.

HONORS: Won Jean Beliveau Trophy (1991-92). ... Named to Can.HL All-Star first team (1991-92). ... Named to QMJHL All-Star first team (1991-92).

			REGULAR SEASON							PLAYOFFS			
Season Team	League	Gms.	G	A	Pts.	PIM	+/-	PP	SH	Gms.	G	A	Pts.	PIM
89-90—St. Hyacinthe	QMJHL	60	25	26	51	55	...	...	...	12	1	9	10	5
90-91—St. Hyacinthe	QMJHL	56	32	38	70	82	...	...	...	4	0	2	2	23
91-92—St. Hyacinthe	QMJHL	56	52	86	*138	58	...	...	...	5	2	2	4	4
—Springfield	AHL	—	—	—	—	—	...	...	...	1	0	0	0	0
—Hartford	NHL	1	0	0	0	2	-1	0	0	7	2	1	3	0
92-93—Hartford	NHL	81	20	31	51	37	-19	4	0	—	—	—	—	—
93-94—Hartford	NHL	9	2	1	3	11	-8	1	0	—	—	—	—	—
—Chicago	NHL	58	12	13	25	40	0	1	0	4	0	0	0	0
94-95—Chicago	NHL	45	15	15	30	53	13	4	0	16	4	1	5	8
95-96—Chicago	NHL	38	7	8	15	16	7	1	0	—	—	—	—	—
—Indianapolis	IHL	1	0	1	1	0	...	...	...	—	—	—	—	—
—Tampa Bay	NHL	8	0	1	1	0	0	0	0	2	0	0	0	0
96-97—Tampa Bay	NHL	73	12	14	26	56	-16	2	3	—	—	—	—	—
97-98—Tampa Bay	NHL	44	2	7	9	19	-3	0	0	—	—	—	—	—
—Montreal	NHL	34	4	6	10	8	-1	0	1	3	0	0	0	0
98-99—Montreal	NHL	81	8	17	25	21	6	0	1	—	—	—	—	—
99-00—Montreal	NHL	82	10	5	15	17	-15	0	1	—	—	—	—	—
NHL Totals (9 years)		554	92	118	210	280	-37	13	6	32	6	2	8	8

PRATT, NOLAN　　　　D　　　　AVALANCHE

PERSONAL: Born August 14, 1975, in Fort McMurray, Alta. ... 6-2/208. ... Shoots left. ... Brother of Harlan Pratt, defenseman with Pittsburgh Penguins system (1997-98 and 1998-99).

HIGH SCHOOL: Sunset (Beaverton, Ore.).

TRANSACTIONS/CAREER NOTES: Selected by Hartford Whalers in fifth round (fourth Whalers pick, 115th overall) of NHL entry draft (June 26, 1993). ... Whalers franchise moved to North Carolina and renamed Carolina Hurricanes for 1997-98 season; NHL approved move on June 25, 1997. ... Suffered back spasms (December 21, 1998); missed eight games. ... Injured hip (December 20, 1999); missed two games. ... Injured hand (April 3, 2000); missed final two games of season. ... Traded by Hurricanes with first- (C Vaclav Nedorost) and two second-round (C Jared Aulin and D Argis Saviels) picks in 2000 draft to Colorado Avalanche for D Sandis Ozolinsh and second-round pick (LW Tomas Kurka) in 2000 draft (June 24, 2000).

			REGULAR SEASON							PLAYOFFS			
Season Team	League	Gms.	G	A	Pts.	PIM	+/-	PP	SH	Gms.	G	A	Pts.	PIM
91-92—Portland	WHL	22	2	9	11	13	...	...	...	6	1	3	4	12
92-93—Portland	WHL	70	4	19	23	97	...	...	...	16	2	7	9	31
93-94—Portland	WHL	72	4	32	36	105	...	...	...	10	1	2	3	14
94-95—Portland	WHL	72	6	37	43	196	...	...	...	9	1	6	7	10
95-96—Richmond	ECHL	4	1	0	1	2	...	...	...	—	—	—	—	—
—Springfield	AHL	62	2	6	8	72	...	...	...	2	0	0	0	0

P

Season Team	League	REGULAR SEASON								PLAYOFFS				
		Gms.	G	A	Pts.	PIM	+/-	PP	SH	Gms.	G	A	Pts.	PIM
96-97—Hartford	NHL	9	0	2	2	6	0	0	0	—	—	—	—	—
—Springfield	AHL	66	1	18	19	127	...	...	...	17	0	3	3	18
97-98—New Haven	AHL	54	3	15	18	135	...	...	...	—	—	—	—	—
—Carolina	NHL	23	0	2	2	44	-2	0	0	—	—	—	—	—
98-99—Carolina	NHL	61	1	14	15	95	15	0	0	3	0	0	0	2
99-00—Carolina	NHL	64	3	1	4	90	-22	0	0	—	—	—	—	—
NHL Totals (4 years)		157	4	19	23	235	-9	0	0	3	0	0	0	2

PRIMEAU, KEITH — C — FLYERS

PERSONAL: Born November 24, 1971, in Toronto. ... 6-5/220. ... Shoots left. ... Brother of Wayne Primeau, center, Tampa Bay Lightning. ... Name pronounced PREE-moh.

TRANSACTIONS/CAREER NOTES: Selected by Detroit Red Wings in first round (first Red Wings pick, third overall) of NHL entry draft (June 16, 1990). ... Suffered from the flu (January 13, 1993); missed two games. ... Sprained right shoulder (February 9, 1993); missed one game. ... Sprained right knee (March 2, 1993); missed two games. ... Sprained right knee (April 1, 1993); missed four games. ... Injured right thumb (February 10, 1995); missed one game. ... Suffered from the flu (February 25, 1995); missed one game. ... Reinjured thumb (March 2, 1995); missed one game. ... Injured ribs (November 1, 1995); missed eight games. ... Injured left knee (January 13, 1996); missed one game. ... Traded by Red Wings with D Paul Coffey and first-round pick (traded to San Jose) in 1997 draft to Hartford Whalers for LW Brendan Shanahan and D Brian Glynn (October 9, 1996). ... Suffered from the flu (December 3, 1996); missed one game. ... Suffered concussion (December 21, 1996); missed one game. ... Suspended two games by NHL for slashing incident (January 3, 1997). ... Suffered from asthma (February 12, 1997); missed one game. ... Whalers franchise moved to North Carolina and renamed Carolina Hurricanes for 1997-98 season; NHL approved move on June 25, 1997. ... Strained hip flexor (November 13, 1997); missed one game. ... Injured wrist (February 13, 1999); missed one game. ... Strained lower back (April 10, 1999); missed three games. ... Missed first 47 games of 1999-2000 season due to contract dispute. ... Rights traded by Hurricanes with fifth-round pick (traded to New York Islanders) in 2000 draft to Philadelphia Flyers for C Rod Brind'Amour, G Jean-Marc Pelletier and second-round pick (traded to Colorado) in 2000 draft (January 23, 2000). ... Fractured rib (February 12, 2000); missed nine games. ... Reinjured ribs (March 4, 2000); missed three games.

HONORS: Won Eddie Powers Memorial Trophy (1989-90). ... Named to OHL All-Star second team (1989-90). ... Played in NHL All-Star Game (1999).

MISCELLANEOUS: Captain of Carolina Hurricanes (1998-99). ... Holds Carolina Hurricanes franchise records for most goals (56) and points (125).

Season Team	League	REGULAR SEASON								PLAYOFFS				
		Gms.	G	A	Pts.	PIM	+/-	PP	SH	Gms.	G	A	Pts.	PIM
87-88—Hamilton	OHL	47	6	6	12	69	...	...	...	11	0	2	2	2
88-89—Niagara Falls	OHL	48	20	35	55	56	...	...	...	17	9	6	15	12
89-90—Niagara Falls	OHL	65	*57	70	*127	97	...	...	...	16	*16	17	*33	49
90-91—Detroit	NHL	58	3	12	15	106	-12	0	0	5	1	1	2	25
—Adirondack	AHL	6	3	5	8	8	...	...	...	—	—	—	—	—
91-92—Detroit	NHL	35	6	10	16	83	9	0	0	11	0	0	0	14
—Adirondack	AHL	42	21	24	45	89	...	...	...	9	1	7	8	27
92-93—Detroit	NHL	73	15	17	32	152	-6	4	1	7	0	2	2	26
93-94—Detroit	NHL	78	31	42	73	173	34	7	3	7	0	2	2	6
94-95—Detroit	NHL	45	15	27	42	99	17	1	0	17	4	5	9	45
95-96—Detroit	NHL	74	27	25	52	168	19	6	2	17	1	4	5	28
96-97—Hartford	NHL	75	26	25	51	161	-3	6	3	—	—	—	—	—
97-98—Carolina	NHL	81	26	37	63	110	19	7	3	—	—	—	—	—
—Can. Olympic team	Int'l	6	2	1	3	4	...	...	...	—	—	—	—	—
98-99—Carolina	NHL	78	30	32	62	75	8	9	1	6	0	3	3	6
99-00—Philadelphia	NHL	23	7	10	17	31	10	1	0	18	2	11	13	13
NHL Totals (10 years)		620	186	237	423	1158	95	41	13	88	8	28	36	163

PRIMEAU, WAYNE — C — LIGHTNING

PERSONAL: Born June 4, 1976, in Scarborough, Ont. ... 6-3/225. ... Shoots left. ... Brother of Keith Primeau, center, Philadelphia Flyers. ... Name pronounced PREE-moh.

HIGH SCHOOL: St. Mary's (Owen Sound, Ont.).

TRANSACTIONS/CAREER NOTES: Selected by Buffalo Sabres in first round (first Sabres pick, 17th overall) of NHL entry draft (June 28, 1994). ... Bruised shoulder (November 4, 1998); missed four games. ... Reinjured shoulder (December 5, 1998); missed four games. ... Reinjured shoulder (January 11, 1999); missed one game. ... Strained groin (March 7, 1999); missed one game. ... Injured hip (January 1, 2000); missed 20 games. ... Traded by Sabres with C/RW Brian Holzinger, D Cory Sarich and third-round pick (RW Alexandre Kharitonov) in 2000 draft to Tampa Bay Lightning for C Chris Gratton and second-round pick in 2001 draft (March 9, 2000).

Season Team	League	REGULAR SEASON								PLAYOFFS				
		Gms.	G	A	Pts.	PIM	+/-	PP	SH	Gms.	G	A	Pts.	PIM
92-93—Owen Sound	OHL	66	10	27	37	110	...	...	...	8	1	4	5	0
93-94—Owen Sound	OHL	65	25	50	75	75	...	...	...	9	1	6	7	8
94-95—Owen Sound	OHL	66	34	62	96	84	...	...	...	10	4	9	13	15
—Buffalo	NHL	1	1	0	1	0	-2	0	0	—	—	—	—	—
95-96—Buffalo	NHL	2	0	0	0	0	0	0	0	—	—	—	—	—
—Owen Sound	OHL	28	15	29	44	52	...	...	...	—	—	—	—	—
—Oshawa	OHL	24	12	13	25	33	...	...	...	3	2	3	5	2
—Rochester	AHL	8	2	3	5	6	...	...	...	17	3	1	4	11
96-97—Rochester	AHL	24	9	5	14	27	...	...	...	1	0	0	0	0
—Buffalo	NHL	45	2	4	6	64	-2	1	0	9	0	0	0	6
97-98—Buffalo	NHL	69	6	6	12	87	9	2	0	14	1	3	4	6
98-99—Buffalo	NHL	67	5	8	13	38	-6	0	0	19	3	4	7	6
99-00—Buffalo	NHL	41	5	7	12	38	-8	2	0	—	—	—	—	—
—Tampa Bay	NHL	17	2	3	5	25	-4	0	0	—	—	—	—	—
NHL Totals (6 years)		242	21	28	49	252	-13	5	0	42	4	7	11	18

P

PROBERT, BOB   LW   BLACKHAWKS

PERSONAL: Born June 5, 1965, in Windsor, Ont. ... 6-3/225. ... Shoots left. ... Full Name: Robert Probert. ... Name pronounced PROH-buhrt.
TRANSACTIONS/CAREER NOTES: Selected by Detroit Red Wings as underage junior in third round (third Red Wings pick, 46th overall) of NHL entry draft (June 8, 1983). ... Entered in-patient alcohol abuse treatment center (July 22, 1986). ... Suspended six games by NHL during the 1987-88 season for game misconduct penalties. ... Suspended without pay by Red Wings for skipping practice and missing team buses, flights and curfews (September 23, 1988). ... Reactivated by Red Wings (November 23, 1988). ... Suspended three games by NHL for hitting another player (December 10, 1988). ... Removed from team after showing up late for a game (January 26, 1989). ... Reactivated by Red Wings (February 15, 1989). ... Charged with smuggling cocaine into the United States (March 2, 1989). ... Expelled from the NHL (March 4, 1989). ... Reinstated by NHL (March 14, 1990). ... Unable to play any games in Canada while appealing deportation order by U.S. Immigration Department during 1990-91 and 1991-92 seasons. ... Fractured left wrist (December 1, 1990); missed 12 games. ... Suspended one game by NHL for game misconduct penalties (February 9, 1993). ... Bruised tailbone (November 20, 1993); missed eight games. ... Suspended four games by NHL for stick-swinging incident (October 16, 1993). ... Suspended two games and fined $500 by NHL for head-butting (April 7, 1994). ... Signed as free agent by Chicago Blackhawks (July 23, 1994). ... Placed on inactive status by NHL for violating substance abuse policies (September 2, 1994). ... Reinstated by NHL and declared eligible for 1995-96 season (April 28, 1995). ... Sprained knee (December 26, 1995); missed three games. ... Suspended one game by NHL for elbowing (February 10, 1996). ... Tore cartilage/sprained medial collateral ligament in right knee (October 9, 1997) and underwent surgery; missed 14 games. ... Tore rotator cuff (November 19, 1997); missed 54 games. ... Suspended four games by NHL for fighting incident (October 4, 1999). ... Strained elbow (November 27, 1999); missed one game. ... Suffered from the flu (February 23, 2000); missed one game.
HONORS: Played in NHL All-Star Game (1988).
MISCELLANEOUS: Holds Detroit Red Wings all-time record for most penalty minutes (2,090). ... Scored on a penalty shot (vs. Kari Takko, March 5, 1987).
STATISTICAL PLATEAUS: Three-goal games: 1987-88 (1).

		REGULAR SEASON								PLAYOFFS				
Season Team	League	Gms.	G	A	Pts.	PIM	+/-	PP	SH	Gms.	G	A	Pts.	PIM
82-83—Brantford	OHL	51	12	16	28	133	...	...	...	8	2	2	4	23
83-84—Brantford	OHL	65	35	38	73	189	...	...	...	6	0	3	3	16
84-85—Hamilton	OHL	4	0	1	1	21	...	...	...	—	—	—	—	—
—Sault Ste. Marie	OHL	44	20	52	72	172	...	...	...	15	6	11	17	*60
85-86—Adirondack	AHL	32	12	15	27	152	...	...	...	10	2	3	5	68
—Detroit	NHL	44	8	13	21	186	-14	3	0	—	—	—	—	—
86-87—Detroit	NHL	63	13	11	24	221	-6	2	0	16	3	4	7	63
—Adirondack	AHL	7	1	4	5	15	...	...	...	—	—	—	—	—
87-88—Detroit	NHL	74	29	33	62	*398	16	15	0	16	8	13	21	51
88-89—Detroit	NHL	25	4	2	6	106	-11	1	0	—	—	—	—	—
89-90—Detroit	NHL	4	3	0	3	21	0	0	0	—	—	—	—	—
90-91—Detroit	NHL	55	16	23	39	315	-3	4	0	6	1	2	3	50
91-92—Detroit	NHL	63	20	24	44	276	16	8	0	11	1	6	7	28
92-93—Detroit	NHL	80	14	29	43	292	-9	6	0	7	0	3	3	10
93-94—Detroit	NHL	66	7	10	17	275	-1	1	0	7	1	1	2	8
94-95—Chicago	NHL		Did not play.											
95-96—Chicago	NHL	78	19	21	40	237	15	1	0	10	0	2	2	23
96-97—Chicago	NHL	82	9	14	23	326	-3	1	0	6	2	1	3	41
97-98—Chicago	NHL	14	2	1	3	48	-7	2	0	—	—	—	—	—
98-99—Chicago	NHL	78	7	14	21	206	-11	0	0	—	—	—	—	—
99-00—Chicago	NHL	69	4	11	15	114	10	0	0	—	—	—	—	—
NHL Totals (15 years)		795	155	206	361	3021	-8	44	0	79	16	32	48	274

PROCHAZKA, MARTIN   LW   THRASHERS

PERSONAL: Born March 3, 1972, in Slany, Czechoslovakia. ... 5-11/180. ... Shoots left. ... Name pronounced pro-HAZ-kuh.
TRANSACTIONS/CAREER NOTES: Selected by Toronto Maple Leafs in seventh round (eighth Maple Leafs pick, 135th overall) of NHL entry draft (June 22, 1991). ... Traded by Maple Leafs to Atlanta Thrashers for sixth-round pick in 2001 draft (July 15, 1999).
MISCELLANEOUS: Member of gold-medal-winning Czech Republic Olympic team (1998).

		REGULAR SEASON								PLAYOFFS				
Season Team	League	Gms.	G	A	Pts.	PIM	+/-	PP	SH	Gms.	G	A	Pts.	PIM
89-90—Kladno	Czech.	49	18	12	30		...	...	...	—	—	—	—	—
90-91—Kladno	Czech.	50	19	10	29	21	...	...	...	—	—	—	—	—
91-92—Dukla Jihlava	Czech.	44	18	11	29	2	...	...	...	—	—	—	—	—
92-93—Kladno	Czech.	46	26	12	38	38	...	...	...	—	—	—	—	—
93-94—HC Kladno	Czech Rep.	43	24	16	40		...	...	...	2	2	0	2	...
94-95—HC Kladno	Czech Rep.	41	25	33	58		...	...	...	11	8	4	12	...
95-96—HC Kladno	Czech Rep.	37	15	27	42		...	...	...	8	2	4	6	...
96-97—AIK	Sweden	49	16	23	39	38	...	...	...	7	2	3	5	8
97-98—Toronto	NHL	29	2	4	6	8	-1	0	0	—	—	—	—	—
—Czech Rep. Oly. team..	Int'l	6	1	1	2	0	...	...	...	—	—	—	—	—
98-99—Vsetin	Czech Rep.	47	20	29	49	12	...	...	...	12	*10	9	19	...
99-00—Atlanta	NHL	3	0	1	1	0	-1	0	0	—	—	—	—	—
—Vsetin	Czech Rep.	31	10	10	20	16	...	...	...	9	2	0	2	0
NHL Totals (2 years)		32	2	5	7	8	-2	0	0					

PRONGER, CHRIS   D   BLUES

PERSONAL: Born October 10, 1974, in Dryden, Ont. ... 6-6/220. ... Shoots left. ... Full Name: Christopher Robert Pronger. ... Brother of Sean Pronger, center, Boston Bruins.
HIGH SCHOOL: Dryden (Ont.).
COLLEGE: Trent (Ont.).

P

TRANSACTIONS/CAREER NOTES: Selected by Hartford Whalers in first round (first Whalers pick, second overall) of NHL entry draft (June 26, 1993). ... Injured left wrist (March 29, 1994); missed three games. ... Injured left shoulder (January 21, 1995); missed five games. ... Traded by Whalers to St. Louis Blues for LW Brendan Shanahan (July 27, 1995). ... Suspended four games by NHL for slashing incident (November 1, 1995). ... Injured hand (February 15, 1997); missed one game. ... Suspended four games by NHL for slashing incident (December 19, 1998). ... Bruised ankle (February 11, 1999); missed 11 games. ... Suffered back spasms (March 12, 2000); missed one game.

HONORS: Named to Can.HL All-Rookie team (1991-92). ... Named to OHL Rookie All-Star team (1991-92). ... Won Can.HL Plus/Minus Award (1992-93). ... Won Can.HL Top Defenseman Award (1992-93). ... Won Max Kaminsky Award (1992-93). ... Named to Can.HL All-Star first team (1992-93). ... Named to OHL All-Star first team (1992-93). ... Named to NHL All-Rookie team (1993-94). ... Named to NHL All-Star second team (1997-98). ... Played in NHL All-Star Game (1999 and 2000). ... Named to THE SPORTING NEWS All-Star team (1999-2000). ... Named to NHL All-Star first team (1999-2000). ... Won Hart Memorial Trophy (1999-2000). ... Won James Norris Memorial Trophy (1999-2000).

MISCELLANEOUS: Captain of St. Louis Blues (1997-98 through 1999-2000).

			REGULAR SEASON								PLAYOFFS				
Season Team	League	Gms.	G	A	Pts.	PIM	+/-	PP	SH		Gms.	G	A	Pts.	PIM
90-91—Stratford	OPJHL	48	15	37	52	132	...	...	...		—	—	—	—	—
91-92—Peterborough	OHL	63	17	45	62	90	...	...	...		10	1	8	9	28
92-93—Peterborough	OHL	61	15	62	77	108	...	...	...		21	15	25	40	51
93-94—Hartford	NHL	81	5	25	30	113	-3	2	0		—	—	—	—	—
94-95—Hartford	NHL	43	5	9	14	54	-12	3	0		—	—	—	—	—
95-96—St. Louis	NHL	78	7	18	25	110	-18	3	1		13	1	5	6	16
96-97—St. Louis	NHL	79	11	24	35	143	15	4	0		6	1	1	2	22
97-98—St. Louis	NHL	81	9	27	36	180	*47	1	0		10	1	9	10	26
—Can. Olympic team	Int'l	6	0	0	0	4	...	...	...		—	—	—	—	—
98-99—St. Louis	NHL	67	13	33	46	113	3	8	0		13	1	4	5	28
99-00—St. Louis	NHL	79	14	48	62	92	*52	8	0		7	3	4	7	32
NHL Totals (7 years)		508	64	184	248	805	84	29	1		49	7	23	30	124

PRONGER, SEAN   C   BRUINS

PERSONAL: Born November 30, 1972, in Dryden, Ont. ... 6-3/210. ... Shoots left. ... Full Name: Sean James Pronger. ... Brother of Chris Pronger, defenseman, St. Louis Blues.

COLLEGE: Bowling Green State.

TRANSACTIONS/CAREER NOTES: Selected by Vancouver Canucks in third round (third Canucks pick, 51st overall) of NHL entry draft (June 22, 1991). ... Signed as free agent by Mighty Ducks of Anaheim (February 14, 1995). ... Strained abdominal muscle (February 17, 1997); missed two games. ... Traded by Mighty Ducks to Pittsburgh Penguins for rights to G Patrick Lalime (March 24, 1998). ... Fractured foot (April 4, 1998); missed seven games. ... Traded by Penguins with C Petr Nedved and D Chris Tamer to New York Rangers for LW Alexei Kovalev, C Harry York and future considerations (November 25, 1998). ... Traded by Rangers to Los Angeles Kings for LW Eric Lacroix (February 12, 1999). ... Tore medial collateral ligament in left knee (March 18, 1999); missed final 14 games of season. ... Signed as free agent by Boston Bruins (August 25, 1999).

			REGULAR SEASON								PLAYOFFS				
Season Team	League	Gms.	G	A	Pts.	PIM	+/-	PP	SH		Gms.	G	A	Pts.	PIM
89-90—Thunder Bay Flyers	USHL	48	18	34	52	61	...	...	...		—	—	—	—	—
90-91—Bowling Green	CCHA	40	3	7	10	30	...	...	...		—	—	—	—	—
91-92—Bowling Green	CCHA	34	9	7	16	28	...	...	...		—	—	—	—	—
92-93—Bowling Green	CCHA	39	23	23	46	35	...	...	...		—	—	—	—	—
93-94—Bowling Green	CCHA	38	17	17	34	38	...	...	...		—	—	—	—	—
94-95—Knoxville	ECHL	34	18	23	41	55	...	...	...		—	—	—	—	—
—Greensboro	ECHL	2	0	2	2	0	...	...	...		—	—	—	—	—
—San Diego	IHL	8	0	0	0	2	...	...	...		—	—	—	—	—
95-96—Baltimore	AHL	72	16	17	33	61	...	...	...		12	3	7	10	16
—Anaheim	NHL	7	0	1	1	6	0	0	0		—	—	—	—	—
96-97—Baltimore	AHL	41	26	17	43	17	...	...	...		—	—	—	—	—
—Anaheim	NHL	39	7	7	14	20	6	1	0		9	0	2	2	4
97-98—Anaheim	NHL	62	5	15	20	30	-9	1	0		—	—	—	—	—
—Pittsburgh	NHL	5	1	0	1	2	-1	0	0		5	0	0	0	4
98-99—Houston	IHL	16	11	7	18	32	...	...	...		—	—	—	—	—
—Pittsburgh	NHL	2	0	0	0	0	0	0	0		—	—	—	—	—
—New York Rangers	NHL	14	0	3	3	4	-3	0	0		—	—	—	—	—
—Los Angeles	NHL	13	0	1	1	4	2	0	0		—	—	—	—	—
99-00—Providence	AHL	51	11	18	29	26	...	...	...		—	—	—	—	—
—Boston	NHL	11	0	1	1	13	-4	0	0		—	—	—	—	—
—Manitoba	IHL	14	3	5	8	21	...	...	...		2	0	1	1	2
NHL Totals (5 years)		153	13	28	41	79	-9	2	0		14	0	2	2	8

PROSPAL, VACLAV   C   SENATORS

PERSONAL: Born February 17, 1975, in Ceske-Budejovice, Czechoslovakia. ... 6-2/195. ... Shoots left. ... Name pronounced VA-sla PRAHS-puhl.

TRANSACTIONS/CAREER NOTES: Selected by Philadelphia Flyers in third round (second Flyers pick, 71st overall) of NHL entry draft (June 26, 1993). ... Fractured left fibula (January 3, 1998); missed 18 games. ... Traded by Flyers with RW Pat Falloon and second round draft pick (LW Chris Bala) in 1998 draft to Ottawa Senators for RW Alexandre Daigle (January 17, 1998). ... Bruised thumb (April 2, 1998); missed two games. ... Bruised mouth (April 7, 1998); missed four games. ... Suffered from the flu (November 29, 1998); missed one game.

HONORS: Named to AHL All-Star first team (1996-97).

			REGULAR SEASON								PLAYOFFS				
Season Team	League	Gms.	G	A	Pts.	PIM	+/-	PP	SH		Gms.	G	A	Pts.	PIM
91-92—Motor-Ceske Bude.	Czech. Jrs.	36	16	16	32	12	...	...	...		—	—	—	—	—
92-93—Motor-Ceske Bude.	Czech. Jrs.	36	26	31	57	24	...	...	...		—	—	—	—	—
93-94—Hershey	AHL	55	14	21	35	38	...	...	...		2	0	0	0	2
94-95—Hershey	AHL	69	13	32	45	36	...	...	...		2	1	0	1	4
95-96—Hershey	AHL	68	15	36	51	59	...	...	...		5	2	4	6	2

P

Season Team	League	REGULAR SEASON								PLAYOFFS				
		Gms.	G	A	Pts.	PIM	+/-	PP	SH	Gms.	G	A	Pts.	PIM
96-97—Philadelphia	AHL	63	32	63	95	70	...	...	...	—	—	—	—	—
—Philadelphia	NHL	18	5	10	15	4	3	0	0	5	1	3	4	4
97-98—Philadelphia	NHL	41	5	13	18	17	-10	4	0	—	—	—	—	—
—Ottawa	NHL	15	1	6	7	4	-1	0	0	6	0	0	0	0
98-99—Ottawa	NHL	79	10	26	36	58	8	2	0	4	0	0	0	0
99-00—Ottawa	NHL	79	22	33	55	40	-2	5	0	6	0	4	4	4
NHL Totals (4 years)...........		232	43	88	131	123	-2	11	0	21	1	7	8	8

PROTSENKO, BORIS   RW   PENGUINS

PERSONAL: Born August 21, 1978, in Kiev, U.S.S.R. ... 5-11/192. ... Shoots right. ... Name pronounced praht-SEHN-koh.
TRANSACTIONS/CAREER NOTES: Selected by Pittsburgh Penguins in third round (fourth Penguins pick, 77th overall) of NHL entry draft (June 22, 1996).

Season Team	League	REGULAR SEASON								PLAYOFFS				
		Gms.	G	A	Pts.	PIM	+/-	PP	SH	Gms.	G	A	Pts.	PIM
94-95—Fernie........................	Tier II Jr. A	47	27	25	52	199	...	...	...	—	—	—	—	—
95-96—Calgary	WHL	71	46	29	75	68	...	...	...	—	—	—	—	—
96-97—Calgary	WHL	67	35	32	67	136	...	...	...	—	—	—	—	—
97-98—Calgary	WHL	70	40	47	87	124	...	...	...	18	6	8	14	30
98-99—Syracuse...................	AHL	65	24	24	48	84	...	...	...	—	—	—	—	—
99-00—Wilkes-Barre/Scranton	AHL	64	15	21	36	41	...	...	...	—	—	—	—	—

PRPIC, JOEL   C

PERSONAL: Born September 25, 1974, in Sudbury, Ont. ... 6-7/225. ... Shoots left. ... Full Name: Joel Melvin Prpic. ... Name pronounced PUHR-pihk.
COLLEGE: St. Lawrence (N.Y.).
TRANSACTIONS/CAREER NOTES: Selected by Boston Bruins in ninth round (ninth Bruins pick, 233rd overall) of NHL entry draft (June 26, 1993).

Season Team	League	REGULAR SEASON								PLAYOFFS				
		Gms.	G	A	Pts.	PIM	+/-	PP	SH	Gms.	G	A	Pts.	PIM
92-93—Waterloo Jr. B.............	OHA	45	17	43	60	160	...	...	...	—	—	—	—	—
93-94—St. Lawrence Univ.......	ECAC	31	2	4	6	90	...	...	...	—	—	—	—	—
94-95—St. Lawrence Univ.......	ECAC	32	7	10	17	62	...	...	...	—	—	—	—	—
95-96—St. Lawrence Univ.......	ECAC	32	3	10	13	77	...	...	...	—	—	—	—	—
96-97—St. Lawrence Univ.......	ECAC	34	10	8	18	57	...	...	...	—	—	—	—	—
97-98—Providence.................	AHL	73	17	18	35	53	...	...	...	—	—	—	—	—
—Boston	NHL	1	0	0	0	2	0	0	0	—	—	—	—	—
98-99—Providence.................	AHL	75	14	16	30	163	...	...	...	18	4	6	10	48
99-00—Providence.................	AHL	70	9	20	29	143	...	...	...	14	3	4	7	58
—Boston	NHL	14	0	3	3	0	-6	0	0	—	—	—	—	—
NHL Totals (2 years)...........		15	0	3	3	2	-6	0	0					

PUPPA, DAREN   G

PERSONAL: Born March 23, 1965, in Kirkland Lake, Ont. ... 6-4/205. ... Catches right. ... Full Name: Daren James Puppa. ... Name pronounced POO-puh.
COLLEGE: Rensselaer Polytechnic Institute (N.Y.).
TRANSACTIONS/CAREER NOTES: Selected by Buffalo Sabres in fourth round (sixth Sabres pick, 74th overall) of NHL entry draft (June 8, 1983). ... Injured knee (February 1986). ... Fractured left index finger (October 1987). ... Sprained right wrist (January 14, 1989). ... Fractured right arm (January 27, 1989). ... Injured back (November 20, 1990); missed nine games. ... Pulled groin and stomach muscles (February 19, 1991). ... Fractured arm (November 12, 1991); missed 16 games. ... Suffered sore knee (January 21, 1993); missed seven games. ... Traded by Sabres with LW Dave Andreychuk and first-round pick (D Kenny Jonsson) in 1993 draft to Toronto Maple Leafs for G Grant Fuhr and fifth-round pick (D Kevin Popp) in 1995 draft (February 2, 1993). ... Selected by Florida Panthers in NHL expansion draft (June 24, 1993). ... Selected by Tampa Bay Lightning in Phase II of NHL expansion draft (June 25, 1993). ... Suffered from tonsillitis (December 11, 1993); missed two games. ... Sprained lower back (February 5, 1994); missed two games. ... Injured hand (April 2, 1995); missed two games. ... Injured right forearm (November 5, 1995); missed one game. ... Injured right knee (November 29, 1995) and underwent surgery; missed 12 games. ... Strained groin (January 6, 1996); missed one game. ... Suffered back spasms (February 10, 1996); missed two games. ... Suffered back spasms (February 13, 1996); missed two games. ... Suffered back spasms (February 23, 1996); missed one game. ... Injured back (April 12, 1996); missed one game. ... Injured groin (October 5, 1996); missed nine games. ... Underwent back surgery (November 6, 1996); missed 41 games. ... Suffered sore back (April 5, 1997); missed one game. ... Suffered back spasms (December 27, 1997); missed remainder of season. ... Strained groin (November 21, 1998); missed remainder of season. ... Injured rib (November 2, 1999); missed final 71 games of season.
HONORS: Named to AHL All-Star first team (1986-87). ... Named to THE SPORTING NEWS All-Star second team (1989-90). ... Named to NHL All-Star second team (1989-90). ... Played in NHL All-Star Game (1990).
MISCELLANEOUS: Holds Tampa Bay Lightning all-time records for most games played by goaltender (206), wins (77), shutouts (12) and goals-against average (2.68). ... Stopped penalty shot attempt (vs. Ulf Dahlen, March 17, 1992; vs. Doug Weight, January 3, 1996; vs. Radek Bonk, January 13, 1996). ... Allowed penalty shot goal (vs. Steve Yzerman, January 29, 1992).

Season Team	League	REGULAR SEASON							PLAYOFFS					
		Gms.	Min.	W	L	T	GA	SO	Avg.	Gms.	Min.	W	L	GA	SO	Avg.
83-84—R.P.I.	ECAC	32	1816	24	6	0	89	...	2.94	—	—	—	—	—	—	—
84-85—R.P.I.	ECAC	32	1830	31	1	0	78	0	2.56	—	—	—	—	—	—	—
85-86—Buffalo	NHL	7	401	3	4	0	21	1	3.14	—	—	—	—	—	—	—
—Rochester..................	AHL	20	1092	8	11	0	79	0	4.34	—	—	—	—	—	—	—
86-87—Buffalo	NHL	3	185	0	2	1	13	0	4.22	—	—	—	—	—	—	—
—Rochester..................	AHL	57	3129	33	14	0	146	1	*2.80	*16	*944	10	6	*48	*1	3.05

P

Season Team	League	REGULAR SEASON								PLAYOFFS						
		Gms.	Min	W	L	T	GA	SO	Avg.	Gms.	Min.	W	L	GA	SO	Avg.
87-88—Rochester	AHL	26	1415	14	8	2	65	2	2.76	2	108	0	1	5	0	2.78
—Buffalo	NHL	17	874	8	6	1	61	0	4.19	3	142	1	1	11	0	4.65
88-89—Buffalo	NHL	37	1908	17	10	6	107	1	3.36	—						—
89-90—Buffalo	NHL	56	3241	31	16	6	156	1	2.89	6	370	2	4	15	0	2.43
90-91—Buffalo	NHL	38	2092	15	11	6	118	2	3.38	2	81	0	1	10	0	7.41
91-92—Buffalo	NHL	33	1757	11	14	4	114	0	3.89	—						—
—Rochester	AHL	2	119	0	2	0	9	0	4.54	—						—
92-93—Buffalo	NHL	24	1306	11	5	4	78	0	3.58	—						—
—Toronto	NHL	8	479	6	2	0	18	2	2.25	1	20	0	0	1	0	3.00
93-94—Tampa Bay	NHL	63	3653	22	33	6	165	4	2.71	—						—
94-95—Tampa Bay	NHL	36	2013	14	19	2	90	1	2.68	—						—
95-96—Tampa Bay	NHL	57	3189	29	16	9	131	5	2.46	4	173	1	3	14	0	4.86
96-97—Tampa Bay	NHL	6	325	1	1	2	14	0	2.58	—						—
—Adirondack	AHL	1	62	1	0	0	3	0	2.90	—						—
97-98—Tampa Bay	NHL	26	1456	5	14	6	66	0	2.72	—						—
98-99—Tampa Bay	NHL	13	691	5	6	1	33	2	2.87	—						—
99-00—Tampa Bay	NHL	5	249	1	2	0	19	0	4.58	—						—
NHL Totals (15 years)		429	23819	179	161	54	1204	19	3.03	16	786	4	9	51	0	3.89

PURINTON, DALE   D   RANGERS

PERSONAL: Born October 11, 1976, in Fort Wayne, Ind. ... 6-3/214. ... Shoots left.
TRANSACTIONS/CAREER NOTES: Selected by New York Rangers in fifth round (fourth Ranger pick, 117th overall) of NHL entry draft (July 8, 1995).

Season Team	League	REGULAR SEASON							PLAYOFFS				
		Gms.	G	A	Pts.	PIM	+/-	PP	SH	Gms.	G	A	Pts.	PIM
93-94—Vernon	Tier II Jr. A	42	1	6	7	194	...	...	...	—				—
94-95—Tacoma	WHL	65	0	8	8	291	...	...	...	3	0	0	0	13
95-96—Kelowna	WHL	22	1	4	5	88	...	...	...	—				—
—Lethbridge	WHL	37	3	6	9	144	...	...	...	4	1	1	2	25
96-97—Lethbridge	WHL	51	6	26	32	254	...	...	...	18	3	5	8	*88
97-98—Charlotte	ECHL	34	3	5	8	186	...	...	...	—				—
—Hartford	AHL	17	0	0	0	95	...	...	...	—				—
98-99—Hartford	AHL	45	1	3	4	306	...	...	...	7	0	2	2	24
99-00—Hartford	AHL	62	4	4	8	415	...	...	...	23	0	3	3	*87
—New York Rangers	NHL	1	0	0	0	7	-1	0	0	—				—
NHL Totals (1 year)		1	0	0	0	7	-1	0	0					

PUSHOR, JAMIE   D   BLUE JACKETS

PERSONAL: Born February 11, 1973, in Lethbridge, Alta. ... 6-3/220. ... Shoots right. ... Full Name: James Pushor. ... Name pronounced PUSH-uhr.
TRANSACTIONS/CAREER NOTES: Selected by Detroit Red Wings in second round (second Wings pick, 32nd overall) of NHL entry draft (June 22, 1991). ... Strained groin (November 21, 1997); missed three games. ... Traded by Red Wings with fourth-round pick (C Viktor Wallin) in 1998 draft to Mighty Ducks of Anaheim for D Dmitri Mironov (March 24, 1998). ... Fractured right finger (April 15, 1998); missed remainder of season. ... Suffered eye injury (January 6, 1999); missed two games. ... Bruised left shoulder and chest (February 14, 1999); missed four games. ... Selected by Atlanta Thrashers in NHL expansion draft (June 25, 1999). ... Traded by Thrashers to Dallas Stars for LW Jason Botterill (July 15, 1999). ... Selected by Columbus Blue Jackets in NHL expansion draft (June 23, 2000).
MISCELLANEOUS: Member of Stanley Cup championship team (1997).

Season Team	League	REGULAR SEASON							PLAYOFFS				
		Gms.	G	A	Pts.	PIM	+/-	PP	SH	Gms.	G	A	Pts.	PIM
89-90—Lethbridge	WHL	10	0	2	2	2	...	...	...	—				—
90-91—Lethbridge	WHL	71	1	13	14	193	...	...	...	—				—
91-92—Lethbridge	WHL	49	2	15	17	232	...	...	...	5	0	0	0	33
92-93—Lethbridge	WHL	72	6	22	28	200	...	...	...	4	0	1	1	9
93-94—Adirondack	AHL	73	1	17	18	124	...	...	...	12	0	0	0	22
94-95—Adirondack	AHL	58	2	11	13	129	...	...	...	4	0	1	1	0
95-96—Detroit	NHL	5	0	1	1	17	2	0	0	—				—
—Adirondack	AHL	65	2	16	18	126	...	...	...	3	0	0	0	5
96-97—Detroit	NHL	75	4	7	11	129	1	0	0	5	0	1	1	5
97-98—Detroit	NHL	54	2	5	7	71	2	0	0	—				—
—Anaheim	NHL	10	0	2	2	10	1	0	0	—				—
98-99—Anaheim	NHL	70	1	2	3	112	-20	0	0	4	0	0	0	6
99-00—Dallas	NHL	62	0	8	8	53	0	0	0	5	0	0	0	5
NHL Totals (5 years)		276	7	25	32	392	-14	0	0	14	0	1	1	16

PYATT, TAYLOR   LW   ISLANDERS

PERSONAL: Born August 19, 1981, in Thunder Bay, Ont. ... 6-4/220. ... Shoots left. ... Son of Nelson Pyatt, center/left winger with three NHL teams (1973-74 through 1979-80).
TRANSACTIONS/CAREER NOTES: Selected by New York Islanders in first round (second Islanders pick, eighth overall) of NHL entry draft (June 26, 1999).
HONORS: Named to OHL All-Rookie second team (1997-98). ... Named to OHL All-Star first team (1999-2000).

Season Team	League	REGULAR SEASON							PLAYOFFS				
		Gms.	G	A	Pts.	PIM	+/-	PP	SH	Gms.	G	A	Pts.	PIM
97-98—Sudbury	OHL	58	14	17	31	104	...	...	...	10	3	1	4	6
98-99—Sudbury	OHL	68	37	38	75	95	...	...	...	4	0	4	4	6
99-00—Sudbury	OHL	68	40	49	89	98	...	...	...	12	8	7	15	25

QUINT, DERON — D — BLUE JACKETS

PERSONAL: Born March 12, 1976, in Durham, N.H. ... 6-2/209. ... Shoots left.
HIGH SCHOOL: Meadowdale (Lynnwood, Wash.).
TRANSACTIONS/CAREER NOTES: Selected by Winnipeg Jets in second round (first Jets pick, 30th overall) of NHL entry draft (June 28, 1994). ... Suffered from the flu (January 29, 1996); missed two games. ... Jets franchise moved to Phoenix and renamed Coyotes for 1996-97 season; NHL approved move on January 18, 1996. ... Separated shoulder (November 27, 1997); missed six games. ... Suffered concussion (January 30, 1998); missed one game. ... Underwent hernia surgery (March 8, 1998); missed 11 games. ... Suffered concussion (October 6, 1998); missed first nine games of season. ... Separated shoulder (January 31, 1999); missed three games. ... Suffered concussion (March 30, 1999); missed final seven games of season. ... Traded by Coyotes with conditional pick in 2001 draft to New Jersey Devils for D Lyle Odelein (March 7, 2000). ... Traded by Devils to Columbus Blue Jackets for past considerations (June 25, 2000).
HONORS: Won WHL Top Draft Choice Award (1993-94). ... Named to Can.HL All-Rookie team (1993-94). ... Named to WHL (West) All-Star first team (1994-95).

		REGULAR SEASON								PLAYOFFS				
Season Team	League	Gms.	G	A	Pts.	PIM	+/-	PP	SH	Gms.	G	A	Pts.	PIM
90-91—Cardigan Prep School.	USHS (East)	31	67	54	121	...	...	...	...	—	—	—	—	—
91-92—Cardigan Prep School.	USHS (East)	32	111	68	179	...	...	...	...	—	—	—	—	—
92-93—Tabor Academy	Mass. H.S.	28	15	26	41	30	...	...	...	1	0	2	2	0
93-94—Seattle	WHL	63	15	29	44	47	...	...	...	9	4	12	16	8
94-95—Seattle	WHL	65	29	60	89	82	...	...	...	3	1	2	3	6
95-96—Winnipeg	NHL	51	5	13	18	22	-2	2	0	—	—	—	—	—
—Springfield	AHL	11	2	3	5	4	...	...	...	10	2	3	5	6
—Seattle	WHL	—	—	—	—	—	...	...	...	5	4	1	5	6
96-97—Springfield	AHL	43	6	18	24	20	...	...	...	12	2	7	9	4
—Phoenix	NHL	27	3	11	14	4	-4	1	0	7	0	2	2	0
97-98—Phoenix	NHL	32	4	7	11	16	-6	1	0	—	—	—	—	—
—Springfield	AHL	8	1	7	8	10	...	...	...	1	0	0	0	0
98-99—Phoenix	NHL	60	5	8	13	20	-10	2	0	—	—	—	—	—
99-00—Phoenix	NHL	50	3	7	10	22	0	0	0	—	—	—	—	—
—New Jersey	NHL	4	1	0	1	2	-2	0	0	—	—	—	—	—
NHL Totals (5 years)		224	21	46	67	86	-24	6	0	7	0	2	2	0

QUINTAL, STEPHANE — D — RANGERS

PERSONAL: Born October 22, 1968, in Boucherville, Que. ... 6-3/234. ... Shoots right. ... Name pronounced steh-FAN kahn-TAHL.
HIGH SCHOOL: Polyvalente de Mortagne (Boucherville, Que.).
TRANSACTIONS/CAREER NOTES: Fractured wrist (December 1985). ... Selected by Boston Bruins as underage junior in first round (second Bruins pick, 14th overall) of NHL entry draft (June 13, 1987). ... Fractured bone near eye (October 1988). ... Injured knee (January 1989). ... Sprained right knee (October 17, 1989); missed eight games. ... Fractured left ankle (April 9, 1991); missed remainder of playoffs. ... Traded by Bruins with C Craig Janney to St. Louis Blues for C Adam Oates (February 7, 1992). ... Traded by Blues with RW Nelson Emerson to Winnipeg Jets for D Phil Housley (September 24, 1993). ... Sprained wrist (January 16, 1994); missed two games. ... Sprained neck (April 6, 1994); missed one game. ... Sprained ankle (February 6, 1995); missed five games. ... Traded by Jets to Montreal Canadiens for second-round pick (D Jason Doig) in 1995 draft (July 8, 1995). ... Suffered concussion (November 11, 1995); missed one game. ... Sprained right knee (February 7, 1996); missed seven games. ... Underwent knee surgery (March 19, 1996); missed five games. ... Bruised foot (December 21, 1996); missed two games. ... Injured collarbone (January 1, 1997); missed two games. ... Sprained left knee (February 6, 1997); missed seven games. ... Suffered concussion (November 8, 1997); missed one game. ... Strained hip flexor (February 7, 1998); missed one game. ... Sprained ankle (April 1, 1998); missed nine games. ... Signed as free agent by New York Rangers (July 6, 1999). ... Suffered concussion (November 24, 1999); missed one game. ... Suffered neck spasms (January 4, 2000); missed one game.
HONORS: Named to QMJHL All-Star first team (1986-87).

		REGULAR SEASON								PLAYOFFS				
Season Team	League	Gms.	G	A	Pts.	PIM	+/-	PP	SH	Gms.	G	A	Pts.	PIM
85-86—Granby	QMJHL	67	2	17	19	144	...	...	...	—	—	—	—	—
86-87—Granby	QMJHL	67	13	41	54	178	...	...	...	8	0	9	9	10
87-88—Hull	QMJHL	38	13	23	36	138	...	...	...	19	7	12	19	30
88-89—Maine	AHL	16	4	10	14	28	...	...	...	—	—	—	—	—
—Boston	NHL	26	0	1	1	29	-5	0	0	—	—	—	—	—
89-90—Boston	NHL	38	2	2	4	22	-11	0	0	—	—	—	—	—
—Maine	AHL	37	4	16	20	27	...	...	...	—	—	—	—	—
90-91—Maine	AHL	23	1	5	6	30	...	...	...	—	—	—	—	—
—Boston	NHL	45	2	6	8	89	2	1	0	3	0	1	1	7
91-92—Boston	NHL	49	4	10	14	77	-8	0	0	—	—	—	—	—
—St. Louis	NHL	26	0	6	6	32	-3	0	0	4	1	2	3	6
92-93—St. Louis	NHL	75	1	10	11	100	-6	0	1	9	0	0	0	8
93-94—Winnipeg	NHL	81	8	18	26	119	-25	1	1	—	—	—	—	—
94-95—Winnipeg	NHL	43	6	17	23	78	0	3	0	—	—	—	—	—
95-96—Montreal	NHL	68	2	14	16	117	-4	0	1	6	0	1	1	6
96-97—Montreal	NHL	71	7	15	22	100	1	1	0	5	0	1	1	6
97-98—Montreal	NHL	71	6	10	16	97	13	0	0	9	0	2	2	4
98-99—Montreal	NHL	82	8	19	27	84	-23	1	1	—	—	—	—	—
99-00—New York Rangers	NHL	75	2	14	16	77	-10	0	0	—	—	—	—	—
NHL Totals (12 years)		750	48	142	190	1021	-79	7	4	36	1	7	8	37

RACHUNEK, KAREL — D — SENATORS

PERSONAL: Born August 27, 1979, in Gottwaldov, Czechoslovakia. ... 6-1/191. ... Shoots right.
TRANSACTIONS/CAREER NOTES: Selected by Ottawa Senators in ninth round (eighth Senators pick, 229th overall) of NHL entry draft (June 21, 1997). ... Suffered partially torn medial collateral ligament in right knee (November 17, 1999); missed 12 games.

Season Team	League	REGULAR SEASON Gms.	G	A	Pts.	PIM	+/-	PP	SH	PLAYOFFS Gms.	G	A	Pts.	PIM
95-96—ZPS Zlin Jrs.	Czech Rep.	38	8	11	19	...	...	...	...	—	—	—	—	—
96-97—ZPS Zlin Jrs.	Czech Rep.	27	2	11	13	...	...	...	...	—	—	—	—	—
97-98—ZPS Zlin	Czech Rep.	27	1	2	3	16	...	...	...	—	—	—	—	—
98-99—ZPS Zlin	Czech Rep.	39	3	9	12	88	...	...	...	6	0	0	0	...
99-00—Grand Rapids	IHL	62	6	20	26	64	...	...	...	9	0	5	5	6
—Ottawa	NHL	6	0	0	0	2	0	0	0	—	—	—	—	—
NHL Totals (1 year)		6	0	0	0	2	0	0	0					

RAFALSKI, BRIAN — D — DEVILS

PERSONAL: Born September 28, 1973, in Dearborn, Mich. ... 5-9/200. ... Shoots right.
COLLEGE: Wisconsin.
TRANSACTIONS/CAREER NOTES: Signed as non-drafted free agent by New Jersey Devils (June 18, 1999). ... Suffered illness (January 3, 2000); missed one game. ... Bruised ribs (March 17, 2000); missed five games.
HONORS: Named to NCAA All-America (West) first team (1994-95). ... Named to WCHA All-Star first team (1994-95). ... Named to NHL All-Rookie team (1999-2000).
MISCELLANEOUS: Member of Stanley Cup championship team (2000).

Season Team	League	REGULAR SEASON Gms.	G	A	Pts.	PIM	+/-	PP	SH	PLAYOFFS Gms.	G	A	Pts.	PIM
91-92—Univ. of Wisconsin	WCHA	34	3	14	17	34	...	...	...	—	—	—	—	—
92-93—Univ. of Wisconsin	WCHA	32	0	13	13	10	...	...	...	—	—	—	—	—
93-94—Univ. of Wisconsin	WCHA	37	6	17	23	26	...	...	...	—	—	—	—	—
94-95—Univ. of Wisconsin	WCHA	43	11	34	45	48	...	...	...	—	—	—	—	—
95-96—Brynas Gavle	Sweden Dv. 2	18	3	6	9	12	...	...	...	9	0	1	1	2
—Brynas Gavle	Sweden	22	1	8	9	14	...	...	...	—	—	—	—	—
96-97—HPK Hameenlinna	Finland	49	11	24	35	26	...	...	...	10	6	5	11	4
97-98—HIFK Helsinki	Finland	40	13	10	23	24	...	...	...	9	5	6	11	0
98-99—HIFK Helsinki	Finland	53	19	34	53	18	...	...	...	11	5	†9	14	4
99-00—New Jersey	NHL	75	5	27	32	28	21	1	0	23	2	6	8	8
NHL Totals (1 year)		75	5	27	32	28	21	1	0	23	2	6	8	8

RAGNARSSON, MARCUS — D — SHARKS

PERSONAL: Born August 13, 1971, in Ostervala, Sweden. ... 6-1/215. ... Shoots left. ... Name pronounced RAG-nuhr-suhn.
TRANSACTIONS/CAREER NOTES: Selected by San Jose Sharks in fifth round (fifth Sharks pick, 99th overall) of NHL entry draft (June 20, 1992). ... Injured foot (November 8, 1995); missed two games. ... Injured head (December 5, 1995); missed two games. ... Injured knee (January 10, 1996); missed one game. ... Suffered from the flu (January 16, 1996); missed one game. ... Injured hamstring (February 10, 1996); missed four games. ... Injured back (March 22, 1996); missed one game. ... Injured leg (November 1, 1996); missed two games. ... Fractured toe (December 9, 1996); missed two games. ... Suspended one game by NHL for high-sticking incident (November 3, 1997). ... Injured thumb (October 3, 1998); missed first eight games of season. ... Injured foot (October 19, 1999); missed 16 games. ... Suffered concussion (February 22, 2000); missed three games.

Season Team	League	REGULAR SEASON Gms.	G	A	Pts.	PIM	+/-	PP	SH	PLAYOFFS Gms.	G	A	Pts.	PIM
89-90—Djurgarden Stockholm	Sweden	13	0	2	2	0	...	...	...	1	0	0	0	0
90-91—Djurgarden Stockholm	Sweden	35	4	1	5	12	...	...	...	7	0	0	0	6
91-92—Djurgarden Stockholm	Sweden	40	8	5	13	14	...	...	...	—	—	—	—	—
92-93—Djurgarden Stockholm	Sweden	35	3	3	6	53	...	...	...	6	0	2	2	...
93-94—Djurgarden Stockholm	Sweden	19	0	4	4	24	...	...	...	—	—	—	—	—
94-95—Djurgarden Stockholm	Sweden	38	7	9	16	20	...	...	...	3	0	0	0	4
95-96—San Jose	NHL	71	8	31	39	42	-24	4	0	—	—	—	—	—
96-97—San Jose	NHL	69	3	14	17	63	-18	2	0	—	—	—	—	—
97-98—San Jose	NHL	79	5	20	25	65	-11	3	0	6	0	0	0	4
—Swedish Oly. team	Int'l	3	0	1	1	0	...	...	...	—	—	—	—	—
98-99—San Jose	NHL	74	0	13	13	66	7	0	0	6	0	1	1	6
99-00—San Jose	NHL	63	3	13	16	38	13	0	0	12	0	3	3	10
NHL Totals (5 years)		356	19	91	110	274	-33	9	0	24	0	4	4	20

RAJAMAKI, TOMMI — D — BLUE JACKETS

PERSONAL: Born February 29, 1976, in Pori, Finland. ... 6-2/180. ... Shoots left.
TRANSACTIONS/CAREER NOTES: Selected by Toronto Maple Leafs in seventh round (sixth Leafs pick, 178th overall) of NHL entry draft (June 29, 1994). ... Selected by Columbus Blue Jackets in NHL expansion draft (June 23, 2000).

Season Team	League	REGULAR SEASON Gms.	G	A	Pts.	PIM	+/-	PP	SH	PLAYOFFS Gms.	G	A	Pts.	PIM
93-94—Assat Pori	Finland				Statistics unavailable.									
94-95—Assat Jrs.	Finland	29	11	17	28	30	...	...	...	—	—	—	—	—
—Assat Pori	Finland	12	4	1	5	8	...	...	...	7	0	1	1	2
95-96—Assat Pori	Finland	45	5	2	7	26	...	...	...	3	0	0	0	6
96-97—Assat Pori	Finland	46	0	1	1	16	...	...	...	4	0	0	0	2
97-98—TPS Turku	Finland	46	1	1	2	24	...	...	...	4	0	0	0	0
98-99—TPS Turku	Finland	53	3	3	6	24	...	...	...	10	0	0	0	6
99-00—TPS Turku	Finland	53	2	6	8	48	...	...	...	11	0	1	1	2

RANFORD, BILL   G

PERSONAL: Born December 14, 1966, in Brandon, Man. ... 5-11/185. ... Catches left.
HIGH SCHOOL: New Westminster (B.C.).
TRANSACTIONS/CAREER NOTES: Selected by Boston Bruins as underage junior in third round (second Bruins pick, 52nd overall) of NHL entry draft (June 15, 1985). ... Traded by Bruins with LW Geoff Courtnall and second-round pick (C Petro Koivunen) in 1988 draft to Edmonton Oilers for G Andy Moog (March 1988). ... Sprained ankle (February 14, 1990); missed six games. ... Strained groin (January 4, 1992); missed two games. ... Strained hamstring (January 29, 1992); missed five games. ... Strained right quadriceps (November 12, 1992); missed two games. ... Strained left hamstring (April 7, 1993); missed two games. ... Bruised hand (March 23, 1993); missed one game. ... Strained hamstring (April 5, 1994); missed three games. ... Suffered back spasms (April 29, 1995); missed three games. ... Sprained ankle (January 3, 1996); missed two games. ... Traded by Oilers to Boston Bruins for D Sean Brown, RW Mariusz Czerkawski and first-round pick (D Matthieu Descoteaux) in 1996 draft (January 11, 1996). ... Suffered tendinitis in shoulder (December 29, 1996); missed 20 games. ... Traded by Bruins with C Adam Oates and RW Rick Tocchet to Washington Capitals for G Jim Carey, C Jason Allison, C Anson Carter and third-round pick (RW Lee Goren) in 1997 draft (March 1, 1997). ... Injured groin (October 1, 1997); missed three games. ... Injured back (October 9, 1997); missed six games. ... Strained hamstring (December 27, 1997); missed 10 games. ... Traded by Capitals to Tampa Bay Lightning for third-round pick (C Todd Hornung) in 1998 draft and second-round pick (C Michal Sivek) in 1999 draft (June 18, 1998). ... Strained groin (November 29, 1998); missed seven games. ... Injured shoulder (February 17, 1999); missed three games. ... Traded by Lightning with LW Wendal Clark and sixth-round pick (RW Kent McDonell) in 1999 draft to Detroit Red Wings for G Kevin Hodson and second-round pick (RW Sheldon Keefe) in 1999 draft (March 23, 1999). ... Signed as free agent by Oilers (August 4, 1999). ... Suffered inner ear infection (November 25, 1999); missed two games. ... Strained hamstring (April 3, 2000); missed three games. ... Announced retirement (April 24, 2000).
HONORS: Named to WHL All-Star second team (1985-86). ... Won Conn Smythe Trophy (1989-90). ... Played in NHL All-Star Game (1991).
RECORDS: Shares NHL single-season playoff record for most wins by a goaltender—16 (1990).
MISCELLANEOUS: Member of Stanley Cup championship teams (1988 and 1990). ... Holds Edmonton Oilers all-time record for most games played by a goaltender (449). ... Stopped penalty shot attempt (vs. Claude Loiselle, October 28, 1989; vs. Tom Kurvers, March 10, 1990; vs. Greg Adams, December 1, 1991; vs. Alexander Mogilny, January 10, 1992; vs. Mario Lemieux, March 17, 1992; vs. Dave Gagner, October 28, 1992; vs. C.J. Young, December 27, 1992; vs. Brett Hull, March 26, 1995; vs. Randy Burridge, February 3, 1996). ... Allowed penalty shot goal (vs. Robert Reichel, February 7, 1994; vs. John MacLean, January 10, 1999).
STATISTICAL NOTES: Tied for NHL lead with 30 regular-season losses (1995-96).

			REGULAR SEASON								PLAYOFFS					
Season Team	League	Gms.	Min	W	L	T	GA	SO	Avg.	Gms.	Min.	W	L	GA	SO	Avg.
83-84—New Westminster.........	WHL	27	1450	10	14	0	130	0	5.38	1	27	0	0	2	0	4.44
84-85—New Westminster.........	WHL	38	2034	19	17	0	142	0	4.19	7	309	2	3	26	0	5.05
85-86—New Westminster.........	WHL	53	2791	17	29	1	225	1	4.84	—	—	—	—	—	—	—
—Boston......................	NHL	4	240	3	1	0	10	0	2.50	2	120	0	2	7	0	3.50
86-87—Moncton...................	AHL	3	180	3	0	0	6	0	2.00	—	—	—	—	—	—	—
—Boston......................	NHL	41	2234	16	20	2	124	3	3.33	2	123	0	2	8	0	3.90
87-88—Maine.....................	AHL	51	2856	27	16	6	165	1	3.47	—	—	—	—	—	—	—
—Edmonton	NHL	6	325	3	0	2	16	0	2.95	—	—	—	—	—	—	—
88-89—Edmonton..................	NHL	29	1509	15	8	2	88	1	3.50	*22	*1401	*16	6	*59	1	2.53
89-90—Edmonton..................	NHL	56	3107	24	16	9	165	1	3.19	3	135	1	2	8	0	3.56
90-91—Edmonton..................	NHL	60	3415	27	27	3	182	0	3.20	16	909	8	*8	51	/d2	3.37
91-92—Edmonton..................	NHL	67	3822	27	26	10	228	1	3.58	—	—	—	—	—	—	—
92-93—Edmonton..................	NHL	67	3753	17	38	6	240	1	3.84	—	—	—	—	—	—	—
93-94—Edmonton..................	NHL	71	4070	22	34	11	236	1	3.48	—	—	—	—	—	—	—
94-95—Edmonton..................	NHL	40	2203	15	20	3	133	2	3.62	—	—	—	—	—	—	—
95-96—Edmonton..................	NHL	37	2015	13	†18	5	128	1	3.81	—	—	—	—	—	—	—
—Boston......................	NHL	40	2307	21	†12	4	109	1	2.83	4	239	1	3	16	0	4.02
96-97—Boston....................	NHL	37	2147	12	16	8	125	2	3.49	—	—	—	—	—	—	—
—Washington...............	NHL	18	1010	8	7	2	46	0	2.73	—	—	—	—	—	—	—
97-98—Washington...............	NHL	22	1183	7	12	2	55	0	2.79	—	—	—	—	—	—	—
98-99—Tampa Bay	NHL	32	1568	3	18	3	102	1	3.90	—	—	—	—	—	—	—
—Detroit....................	NHL	4	244	3	0	1	8	0	1.97	4	183	2	2	10	1	3.28
99-00—Edmonton..................	NHL	16	785	4	6	3	47	0	3.59	—	—	—	—	—	—	—
NHL Totals (15 years)...........		647	35937	240	279	76	2042	15	3.41	53	3110	28	25	159	4	3.07

RANHEIM, PAUL   LW   FLYERS

PERSONAL: Born January 25, 1966, in St. Louis. ... 6-1/210. ... Shoots right. ... Full Name: Paul Stephen Ranheim. ... Name pronounced RAN-highm.
HIGH SCHOOL: Edina (Minn.).
COLLEGE: Wisconsin.
TRANSACTIONS/CAREER NOTES: Selected by Calgary Flames in second round (third Flames pick, 38th overall) of NHL entry draft (June 8, 1983). ... Fractured right ankle (December 11, 1990); missed 41 games. ... Traded by Flames with D Gary Suter and C Ted Drury to Hartford Whalers for C Michael Nylander, D Zarley Zalapski and D James Patrick (March 10, 1994). ... Suffered finger infection on left hand (November 28, 1995); missed six games. ... Suffered abdominal strain (October 27, 1996); missed five games. ... Suffered sore groin (November 11, 1996); missed one game. ... Whalers franchise moved to North Carolina and renamed Carolina Hurricanes for 1997-98 season; NHL approved move on June 25, 1997. ... Injured back (March 22, 2000); missed two games. ... Traded by Hurricanes to Philadelphia Flyers for eigth-round pick in 2002 draft (May 31, 2000).
HONORS: Named to WCHA All-Star second team (1986-87). ... Named to NCAA All-America (West) first team (1987-88). ... Named to WCHA All-Star first team (1987-88). ... Won Garry F. Longman Memorial Trophy (1988-89). ... Won Ken McKenzie Trophy (1988-89). ... Named to IHL All-Star second team (1988-89).
MISCELLANEOUS: Scored on a penalty shot (vs. Bob Essensa, October 31, 1993).
STATISTICAL PLATEAUS: Three-goal games: 1991-92 (1).

			REGULAR SEASON							PLAYOFFS				
Season Team	League	Gms.	G	A	Pts.	PIM	+/-	PP	SH	Gms.	G	A	Pts.	PIM
82-83—Edina High School	Minn. H.S.	26	12	25	37	4	...	...	...	—	—	—	—	—
83-84—Edina High School	Minn. H.S.	26	16	24	40	6	...	...	...	—	—	—	—	—
84-85—Univ. of Wisconsin......	WCHA	42	11	11	22	40	...	...	...	—	—	—	—	—

Season Team	League	REGULAR SEASON								PLAYOFFS				
		Gms.	G	A	Pts.	PIM	+/-	PP	SH	Gms.	G	A	Pts.	PIM
85-86—Univ. of Wisconsin......	WCHA	33	17	17	34	34	...	...	...	—	—	—	—	—
86-87—Univ. of Wisconsin......	WCHA	42	24	35	59	54	...	...	...	—	—	—	—	—
87-88—Univ. of Wisconsin......	WCHA	44	36	26	62	63	...	...	...	—	—	—	—	—
88-89—Calgary	NHL	5	0	0	0	0	-3	0	0	—	—	—	—	—
—Salt Lake City..............	IHL	75	*68	29	97	16	...	...	...	14	5	5	10	8
89-90—Calgary	NHL	80	26	28	54	23	27	1	3	6	1	3	4	2
90-91—Calgary	NHL	39	14	16	30	4	20	2	0	7	2	2	4	0
91-92—Calgary	NHL	80	23	20	43	32	16	1	3	—	—	—	—	—
92-93—Calgary	NHL	83	21	22	43	26	-4	3	4	6	0	1	1	0
93-94—Calgary	NHL	67	10	14	24	20	-7	0	2	—	—	—	—	—
—Hartford	NHL	15	0	3	3	2	-11	0	0	—	—	—	—	—
94-95—Hartford	NHL	47	6	14	20	10	-3	0	0	—	—	—	—	—
95-96—Hartford	NHL	73	10	20	30	14	-2	0	1	—	—	—	—	—
96-97—Hartford	NHL	67	10	11	21	18	-13	0	3	—	—	—	—	—
97-98—Carolina	NHL	73	5	9	14	28	-11	0	1	—	—	—	—	—
98-99—Carolina	NHL	78	9	10	19	39	4	0	2	6	0	0	0	2
99-00—Carolina	NHL	79	9	13	22	6	-14	0	0	—	—	—	—	—
NHL Totals (12 years).........		786	143	180	323	222	-1	7	19	25	3	6	9	4

R

RASMUSSEN, ERIK — LW/C — SABRES

PERSONAL: Born March 28, 1977, in Minneapolis. ... 6-2/205. ... Shoots left. ... Name pronounced RAS-muh-suhn.
HIGH SCHOOL: Saint Louis Park (Minn.).
COLLEGE: Minnesota.
TRANSACTIONS/CAREER NOTES: Selected by Buffalo Sabres in first round (first Sabres pick, seventh overall) of NHL entry draft (June 22, 1996). ... Injured shoulder (October 26, 1997); missed one game. ... Injured foot (April 13, 1999); missed one game. ... Bruised hand (December 4, 1999); missed five games. ... Suffered back spasms (March 23, 2000); missed one game.
HONORS: Named to WCHA All-Rookie team (1995-96).

Season Team	League	REGULAR SEASON								PLAYOFFS				
		Gms.	G	A	Pts.	PIM	+/-	PP	SH	Gms.	G	A	Pts.	PIM
92-93—Saint Louis Park	Minn. H.S.	23	16	24	40	50	...	...	...	—	—	—	—	—
93-94—Saint Louis Park	Minn. H.S.	18	25	18	43	60	...	...	...	—	—	—	—	—
94-95—Saint Louis Park	Minn. H.S.	23	19	33	52	80	...	...	...	—	—	—	—	—
95-96—Univ. of Minnesota......	WCHA	40	16	32	48	55	...	...	...	—	—	—	—	—
96-97—Univ. of Minnesota......	WCHA	34	15	12	27	123	...	...	...	—	—	—	—	—
97-98—Buffalo	NHL	21	2	3	5	14	2	0	0	—	—	—	—	—
—Rochester	AHL	53	9	14	23	83	...	...	...	1	0	0	0	5
98-99—Rochester	AHL	37	12	14	26	47	...	...	...	—	—	—	—	—
—Buffalo	NHL	42	3	7	10	37	6	0	0	21	2	4	6	18
99-00—Buffalo	NHL	67	8	6	14	43	1	0	0	3	0	0	0	4
NHL Totals (3 years)...........		130	13	16	29	94	9	0	0	24	2	4	6	22

RATCHUK, PETER — D — PANTHERS

PERSONAL: Born September 10, 1977, in Buffalo. ... 6-1/185. ... Shoots left.
HIGH SCHOOL: Lawrence Academy (Groton, Mass.), then Shattuck-Saint Mary's School (Faribault, Minn.).
COLLEGE: Bowling Green State.
TRANSACTIONS/CAREER NOTES: Selected by Colorado Avalanche in first round (first Avalanche pick, 25th overall) of NHL entry draft (June 22, 1996). ... Signed as free agent by Florida Panthers (June 17, 1998).

Season Team	League	REGULAR SEASON								PLAYOFFS				
		Gms.	G	A	Pts.	PIM	+/-	PP	SH	Gms.	G	A	Pts.	PIM
94-95—Lawrence Academy.....	Mass. H.S.	31	8	15	23	18	...	...	...	—	—	—	—	—
95-96—Shattuck-Saint Mary's	Minn. H.S.	32	16	27	43	30	...	...	...	—	—	—	—	—
96-97—Bowling Green	CCHA	35	9	12	21	14	...	...	...	—	—	—	—	—
97-98—Hull....................	QMJHL	60	23	31	54	34	...	...	...	11	3	6	9	8
98-99—New Haven	AHL	53	7	20	27	44	...	...	...	—	—	—	—	—
—Florida.....................	NHL	24	1	1	2	10	-1	0	0	—	—	—	—	—
99-00—Louisville	AHL	76	9	17	26	64	...	...	...	4	1	2	3	0
NHL Totals (1 year)..............		24	1	1	2	10	-1	0	0					

RATHJE, MIKE — D — SHARKS

PERSONAL: Born May 11, 1974, in Mannville, Alta. ... 6-5/235. ... Shoots left. ... Full Name: Michael Rathje. ... Name pronounced RATH-jee.
HIGH SCHOOL: Medicine Hat (Alta.).
TRANSACTIONS/CAREER NOTES: Selected by San Jose Sharks in first round (first Sharks pick, third overall) of NHL entry draft (June 20, 1992). ... Strained abdominal muscle (February 19, 1994); missed three games. ... Sprained knee (February 26, 1994); missed four games. ... Sprained knee (February 2, 1995); missed three games. ... Injured foot (February 15, 1995); missed one game. ... Injured hip flexor (April 25, 1995); missed two games. ... Strained abdominal muscle (October 6, 1995); missed first two games of season. ... Injured shoulder (November 14, 1995); missed 12 games. ... Strained groin (November 8, 1996); missed 50 games. ... Injured groin (November 12, 1999); missed 16 games.
HONORS: Named to Can.HL All-Star second team (1992-93). ... Named to WHL (East) All-Star second team (1991-92 and 1992-93).

Season Team	League	REGULAR SEASON								PLAYOFFS				
		Gms.	G	A	Pts.	PIM	+/-	PP	SH	Gms.	G	A	Pts.	PIM
90-91—Medicine Hat	WHL	64	1	16	17	28	...	...	...	12	0	4	4	2
91-92—Medicine Hat	WHL	67	11	23	34	109	...	...	...	4	0	1	1	2
92-93—Medicine Hat	WHL	57	12	37	49	103	...	...	...	10	3	3	6	12
—Kansas City	IHL	—	—	—	—	—	...	...	...	5	0	0	0	12
93-94—San Jose	NHL	47	1	9	10	59	-9	1	0	1	0	0	0	0
—Kansas City	IHL	6	0	2	2	0	...	...	...	—	—	—	—	—
94-95—Kansas City	IHL	6	0	1	1	7	...	...	...	—	—	—	—	—
—San Jose	NHL	42	2	7	9	29	-1	0	0	11	5	2	7	4
95-96—Kansas City	IHL	36	6	11	17	34	...	...	...	—	—	—	—	—
—San Jose	NHL	27	0	7	7	14	-16	0	0	—	—	—	—	—
96-97—San Jose	NHL	31	0	8	8	21	-1	0	0	—	—	—	—	—
97-98—San Jose	NHL	81	3	12	15	59	-4	1	0	6	1	0	1	6
98-99—San Jose	NHL	82	5	9	14	36	15	2	0	6	0	0	0	4
99-00—San Jose	NHL	66	2	14	16	31	-2	0	0	12	1	3	4	8
NHL Totals (7 years)		376	13	66	79	249	-18	4	0	36	7	5	12	22

RAY, ROB — RW — SABRES

PERSONAL: Born June 8, 1968, in Stirling, Ont. ... 6-0/215. ... Shoots left.
TRANSACTIONS/CAREER NOTES: Selected by Buffalo Sabres in fifth round (fifth Sabres pick, 97th overall) of NHL entry draft (June 11, 1988). ... Tore right knee ligament (April 11, 1993); missed remainder of season. ... Suffered from the flu (March 11, 1995); missed one game. ... Fractured right cheekbone (November 27, 1995); missed eight games. ... Fractured thumb (November 22, 1997); missed 19 games. ... Suspended one playoff game by NHL for verbally abusing officials (April 26, 1998). ... Suspended four games by NHL for slew-footing incident (November 29, 1998). ... Bruised knee (February 6, 1999); missed one game.
HONORS: Won King Clancy Memorial Trophy (1998-99).
MISCELLANEOUS: Holds Buffalo Sabres all-time record for most penalty minutes (2,687).

Season Team	League	REGULAR SEASON								PLAYOFFS				
		Gms.	G	A	Pts.	PIM	+/-	PP	SH	Gms.	G	A	Pts.	PIM
84-85—Whitby Lawmen	OPJHL	35	5	10	15	318	...	...	...	—	—	—	—	—
85-86—Cornwall	OHL	53	6	13	19	253	...	...	...	6	0	0	0	26
86-87—Cornwall	OHL	46	17	20	37	158	...	...	...	5	1	1	2	16
87-88—Cornwall	OHL	61	11	41	52	179	...	...	...	11	2	3	5	33
88-89—Rochester	AHL	74	11	18	29	*446	...	...	...	—	—	—	—	—
89-90—Buffalo	NHL	27	2	1	3	99	-2	0	0	—	—	—	—	—
—Rochester	AHL	43	2	13	15	335	...	...	...	17	1	3	4	*115
90-91—Rochester	AHL	8	1	1	2	15	...	...	...	—	—	—	—	—
—Buffalo	NHL	66	8	8	16	*350	-11	0	0	6	1	1	2	56
91-92—Buffalo	NHL	63	5	3	8	354	-9	0	0	7	0	0	0	2
92-93—Buffalo	NHL	68	3	2	5	211	-3	1	0	—	—	—	—	—
93-94—Buffalo	NHL	82	3	4	7	274	2	0	0	7	1	0	1	43
94-95—Buffalo	NHL	47	0	3	3	173	-4	0	0	5	0	0	0	14
95-96—Buffalo	NHL	71	3	6	9	287	-8	0	0	—	—	—	—	—
96-97—Buffalo	NHL	82	7	3	10	286	3	0	0	12	0	1	1	28
97-98—Buffalo	NHL	63	2	4	6	234	2	1	0	10	0	0	0	24
98-99—Buffalo	NHL	76	0	4	4	*261	-2	0	0	5	1	0	1	0
99-00—Buffalo	NHL	69	1	3	4	158	0	0	0	—	—	—	—	—
NHL Totals (11 years)		714	34	41	75	2687	-32	2	0	52	3	2	5	167

RAYCROFT, ANDREW — G — BRUINS

PERSONAL: Born May 4, 1980, in Belleville, Ont. ... 6-0/150. ... Catches left.
TRANSACTIONS/CAREER NOTES: Selected by Boston Bruins in fifth round (fourth Bruins pick, 135th overall) of NHL entry draft (June 27, 1998).
HONORS: Named to OHL All-Star first team (1999-2000). ... Named to Can.HL All-Star first team (1999-2000). ... Won Can.HL Goaltender of the Year Award (1999-2000).

Season Team	League	REGULAR SEASON							PLAYOFFS					
		Gms.	Min	W	L	T	GA	SO	Avg.	Gms.	Min.	W	L	GA	SO	Avg.
96-97—Wellington	Tier II Jr. A	27	1402	...	...	...	92	0	3.94	—	—	—	—	—	—	—
97-98—Sudbury	OHL	33	1802	8	16	5	125	0	4.16	2	89	0	1	8	0	5.39
98-99—Sudbury	OHL	45	2528	17	22	†5	173	1	4.11	3	96	0	2	13	0	8.13
99-00—Kingston	OHL	*61	3340	33	20	5	191	0	3.43	5	300	1	4	21	0	4.20

REASONER, MARTY — C — BLUES

PERSONAL: Born February 26, 1977, in Rochester, N.Y. ... 6-0/203. ... Shoots left.
HIGH SCHOOL: Deerfield (Mass.) Academy.
COLLEGE: Boston College.
TRANSACTIONS/CAREER NOTES: Selected by St. Louis Blues in first round (first Blues pick, 14th overall) of NHL entry draft (June 22, 1996).
HONORS: Named to Hockey East All-Rookie team (1995-96). ... Named Hockey East Rookie of the Year (1995-96). ... Named to Hockey East All-Star team (1996-97). ... Named to NCAA All-America (East) first team (1997-98). ... Named to NCAA All-Tournament team (1997-98). ... Named Hockey East Tournament Most Valuable Player (1997-98). ... Named to Hockey East All-Star first team (1997-98).

Season Team	League	REGULAR SEASON								PLAYOFFS				
		Gms.	G	A	Pts.	PIM	+/-	PP	SH	Gms.	G	A	Pts.	PIM
93-94—Deerfield Academy	Mass. H.S.	22	27	24	51	...	...	...	...	—	—	—	—	—
94-95—Deerfield Academy	Mass. H.S.	26	25	32	57	14	...	...	...	—	—	—	—	—
95-96—Boston College	Hockey East	34	16	29	45	32	...	...	...	—	—	—	—	—

R

Season Team	League	REGULAR SEASON								PLAYOFFS				
		Gms.	G	A	Pts.	PIM	+/-	PP	SH	Gms.	G	A	Pts.	PIM
96-97—Boston College	Hockey East	35	20	24	44	31	...	...	...	—	—	—	—	—
97-98—Boston College	Hockey East	42	†33	40	*73	56	...	...	...	—	—	—	—	—
98-99—St. Louis	NHL	22	3	7	10	8	2	1	0	—	—	—	—	—
—Worcester	AHL	44	17	22	39	24	...	...	...	4	2	1	3	6
99-00—Worcester	AHL	44	23	28	51	39	...	...	...	—	—	—	—	—
—St. Louis	NHL	32	10	14	24	20	9	3	0	7	2	1	3	4
NHL Totals (2 years)		54	13	21	34	28	11	4	0	7	2	1	3	4

RECCHI, MARK   RW   FLYERS

PERSONAL: Born February 1, 1968, in Kamloops, B.C. ... 5-10/185. ... Shoots left. ... Name pronounced REH-kee.

TRANSACTIONS/CAREER NOTES: Selected by Pittsburgh Penguins in fourth round (fourth Penguins pick, 67th overall) of NHL entry draft (June 11, 1988). ... Injured left shoulder (December 23, 1990). ... Sprained right knee (March 30, 1991). ... Traded by Penguins with D Brian Benning and first-round pick (LW Jason Bowen) in 1992 draft to Philadelphia Flyers for RW Rick Tocchet, D Kjell Samuelsson, G Ken Wregget and third-round pick (C Dave Roche) in 1993 draft (February 19, 1992). ... Traded by Flyers with third-round pick (C Martin Hohenberger) in 1995 draft to Montreal Canadiens for D Eric Desjardins, LW Gilbert Dionne and LW John LeClair (February 9, 1995). ... Suffered from pneumonia (December 12, 1998); missed four games. ... Traded by Canadiens to Flyers for RW Dainius Zubrus and second-round pick (D Matt Carkner) in 1999 draft (March 10, 1999). ... Suffered concussion (March 22, 1999); missed three games. ... Suffered from headaches (April 1, 1999); missed two games. ... Suffered mild concussion (April 13, 1999); missed two games.

HONORS: Named to WHL (West) All-Star team (1987-88). ... Named to IHL All-Star second team (1988-89). ... Named to NHL All-Star second team (1991-92). ... Played in NHL All-Star Game (1991, 1993, 1994 and 1997-2000). ... Named All-Star Game Most Valuable Player (1997).

MISCELLANEOUS: Member of Stanley Cup championship team (1991). ... Failed to score on a penalty shot (vs. Don Beaupre, February 6, 1995; vs. Dominik Hasek, March 8, 1995).

STATISTICAL PLATEAUS: Three-goal games: 1991-92 (1), 1996-97 (1), 1997-98 (1). Total: 3.

Season Team	League	REGULAR SEASON								PLAYOFFS				
		Gms.	G	A	Pts.	PIM	+/-	PP	SH	Gms.	G	A	Pts.	PIM
84-85—Langley Eagles	BCJHL	51	26	39	65	39	...	...	...	—	—	—	—	—
85-86—New Westminster	WHL	72	21	40	61	55	...	...	...	—	—	—	—	—
86-87—Kamloops	WHL	40	26	50	76	63	...	...	...	13	3	16	19	17
87-88—Kamloops	WHL	62	61	*93	154	75	...	...	...	17	10	*21	†31	18
88-89—Pittsburgh	NHL	15	1	1	2	0	-2	0	0	—	—	—	—	—
—Muskegon	IHL	63	50	49	99	86	...	...	...	14	7	*14	†21	28
89-90—Muskegon	IHL	4	7	4	11	2	...	...	...	—	—	—	—	—
—Pittsburgh	NHL	74	30	37	67	44	6	6	2	—	—	—	—	—
90-91—Pittsburgh	NHL	78	40	73	113	48	0	12	0	24	10	24	34	33
91-92—Pittsburgh	NHL	58	33	37	70	78	-16	16	1	—	—	—	—	—
—Philadelphia	NHL	22	10	17	27	18	-5	4	0	—	—	—	—	—
92-93—Philadelphia	NHL	84	53	70	123	95	1	15	4	—	—	—	—	—
93-94—Philadelphia	NHL	84	40	67	107	46	-2	11	0	—	—	—	—	—
94-95—Philadelphia	NHL	10	2	3	5	12	-6	1	0	—	—	—	—	—
—Montreal	NHL	39	14	29	43	16	-3	8	0	—	—	—	—	—
95-96—Montreal	NHL	82	28	50	78	69	20	11	2	6	3	3	6	0
96-97—Montreal	NHL	82	34	46	80	58	-1	7	2	5	4	2	6	2
97-98—Montreal	NHL	82	32	42	74	51	11	9	1	10	4	8	12	6
—Can. Olympic team	Int'l	5	0	2	2	0	...	...	...	—	—	—	—	—
98-99—Montreal	NHL	61	12	35	47	28	-4	3	0	—	—	—	—	—
—Philadelphia	NHL	10	4	2	6	6	-3	0	0	6	0	1	1	2
99-00—Philadelphia	NHL	82	28	*63	91	50	20	7	1	18	6	12	18	6
NHL Totals (12 years)		863	361	572	933	619	16	110	13	69	27	50	77	49

REDDEN, WADE   D   SENATORS

PERSONAL: Born June 12, 1977, in Lloydminster, Sask. ... 6-2/205. ... Shoots left.

HIGH SCHOOL: Crocus Plaines (Brandon, Man.).

TRANSACTIONS/CAREER NOTES: Selected by New York Islanders in first round (first Islanders pick, second overall) of NHL entry draft (July 8, 1995). ... Traded by Islanders with G Damian Rhodes to Ottawa Senators for G Don Beaupre, D Bryan Berard and C Martin Straka (January 23, 1996). ... Bruised left foot (January 29, 1998); missed one game. ... Suffered back spasms (December 22, 1998); missed two games. ... Injured shoulder (March 4, 1999); missed eight games. ... Suffered illness (February 1, 2000); missed one game.

HONORS: Won Jim Piggott Memorial Trophy (1993-94). ... Won WHL Top Draft Prospect Award (1994-95). ... Named to Can.HL All-Star second team (1994-95 and 1995-96). ... Named to WHL (East) All-Star second team (1994-95). ... Named to WHL (Central/East) All-Star first team (1995-96). ... Named to Memorial Cup All-Star team (1995-96).

Season Team	League	REGULAR SEASON								PLAYOFFS				
		Gms.	G	A	Pts.	PIM	+/-	PP	SH	Gms.	G	A	Pts.	PIM
92-93—Lloydminster	SJHL	34	4	11	15	64	...	...	...	—	—	—	—	—
93-94—Brandon	WHL	64	4	35	39	98	...	...	...	14	2	4	6	10
94-95—Brandon	WHL	64	14	46	60	83	...	...	...	18	5	10	15	8
95-96—Brandon	WHL	51	9	45	54	55	...	...	...	19	5	10	15	19
96-97—Ottawa	NHL	82	6	24	30	41	1	2	0	7	1	3	4	2
97-98—Ottawa	NHL	80	8	14	22	27	17	3	0	9	0	2	2	2
98-99—Ottawa	NHL	72	8	21	29	54	7	3	0	4	1	2	3	2
99-00—Ottawa	NHL	81	10	26	36	49	-1	3	0	—	—	—	—	—
NHL Totals (4 years)		315	32	85	117	171	24	11	0	20	2	7	9	6

REEKIE, JOE   D   CAPITALS

PERSONAL: Born February 22, 1965, in Victoria, B.C. ... 6-3/225. ... Shoots left. ... Full Name: Joseph James Reekie.
TRANSACTIONS/CAREER NOTES: Selected by Hartford Whalers as underage junior in seventh round (eighth Whalers pick, 124th overall) of NHL entry draft (June 8, 1983). ... Returned to draft pool and selected by Buffalo Sabres in sixth round (sixth Sabres pick, 119th overall) of NHL entry draft (June 15, 1985). ... Injured ankle (March 14, 1987). ... Injured shoulder (October 1987). ... Fractured kneecap (November 15, 1987). ... Underwent surgery to left knee (September 1988). ... Traded by Sabres to New York Islanders for sixth-round pick (G Bill Pye) in 1989 draft (June 17, 1989). ... Sprained right knee (November 1989). ... Fractured two bones in left hand and suffered facial cuts in automobile accident and underwent surgery (December 7, 1989). ... Fractured left middle finger (March 21, 1990). ... Injured eye (January 12, 1991); missed six games. ... Fractured knuckle on left hand (January 3, 1992); missed 22 games. ... Selected by Tampa Bay Lightning in NHL expansion draft (June 18, 1992). ... Fractured left leg (January 16, 1993); missed remainder of season. ... Traded by Lightning to Washington Capitals for D Enrico Ciccone, third-round pick (RW Craig Reichert) in 1994 draft and conditional draft pick (March 21, 1994). ... Bruised foot (April 4, 1996); missed four games. ... Fractured heel (February 14, 1997); missed 17 games. ... Fractured foot (October 9, 1997); missed four games. ... Strained hip flexor (April 4, 1998); missed five games. ... Fractured foot (October 18, 1998); missed nine games. ... Lacerated finger (October 8, 1999); missed two games. ... Bruised foot (October 31, 1999); missed six games. ... Bruised foot (November 19, 1999); missed 10 games. ... Bruised foot (March 3, 2000); missed two games. ... Bruised foot (March 17, 2000); missed three games.

		REGULAR SEASON								PLAYOFFS				
Season Team	League	Gms.	G	A	Pts.	PIM	+/-	PP	SH	Gms.	G	A	Pts.	PIM
81-82—Nepean	COJHL	16	2	5	7	4	...	...	...	—	—	—	—	—
82-83—North Bay	OHL	59	2	9	11	49	...	...	...	8	0	1	1	11
83-84—North Bay	OHL	9	1	0	1	18	...	...	...	—	—	—	—	—
—Cornwall	OHL	53	6	27	33	166	...	...	...	3	0	0	0	4
84-85—Cornwall	OHL	65	19	63	82	134	...	...	...	9	4	13	17	18
85-86—Rochester	AHL	77	3	25	28	178	...	...	...	—	—	—	—	—
—Buffalo	NHL	3	0	0	0	14	-2	0	0	—	—	—	—	—
86-87—Buffalo	NHL	56	1	8	9	82	6	0	0	—	—	—	—	—
—Rochester	AHL	22	0	6	6	52	...	...	...	—	—	—	—	—
87-88—Buffalo	NHL	30	1	4	5	68	-3	0	0	2	0	0	0	4
88-89—Rochester	AHL	21	1	2	3	56	...	...	...	—	—	—	—	—
—Buffalo	NHL	15	1	3	4	26	6	1	0	—	—	—	—	—
89-90—New York Islanders	NHL	31	1	8	9	43	13	0	0	—	—	—	—	—
—Springfield	AHL	15	1	4	5	24	...	...	...	—	—	—	—	—
90-91—Capital District	AHL	2	1	0	1	0	...	...	...	—	—	—	—	—
—New York Islanders	NHL	66	3	16	19	96	17	0	0	—	—	—	—	—
91-92—New York Islanders	NHL	54	4	12	16	85	15	0	0	—	—	—	—	—
—Capital District	AHL	3	2	2	4	2	...	...	...	—	—	—	—	—
92-93—Tampa Bay	NHL	42	2	11	13	69	2	0	0	—	—	—	—	—
93-94—Tampa Bay	NHL	73	1	11	12	127	8	0	0	—	—	—	—	—
—Washington	NHL	12	0	5	5	29	7	0	0	11	2	1	3	29
94-95—Washington	NHL	48	1	6	7	97	10	0	0	7	0	0	0	2
95-96—Washington	NHL	78	3	7	10	149	7	0	0	—	—	—	—	—
96-97—Washington	NHL	65	1	8	9	107	8	0	0	—	—	—	—	—
97-98—Washington	NHL	68	2	8	10	70	15	0	0	21	1	2	3	20
98-99—Washington	NHL	73	0	10	10	68	11	0	0	—	—	—	—	—
99-00—Washington	NHL	59	0	7	7	50	21	0	0	5	0	1	1	2
NHL Totals (15 years)		773	21	124	145	1180	141	1	0	46	3	4	7	57

REGEHR, ROBYN   D   FLAMES

PERSONAL: Born April 19, 1980, in Recife, Brazil. ... 6-2/225. ... Shoots left. ... Name pronounced ruh-ZHEER.
TRANSACTIONS/CAREER NOTES: Selected by Colorado Avalanche in first round (third Avalanche pick, 19th overall) of NHL entry draft (June 27, 1998). ... Traded by Avalanche to Calgary Flames (March 27, 1999); completing deal in which Flames traded RW Theo Fleury and LW Chris Dingman to Avalanche for LW Rene Corbet, D Wade Belak and future considerations (February 28, 1999). ... Fractured legs prior to start of 1999-2000 season; missed first five games of season. ... Suffered concussion (January 11, 2000); missed 11 games.
HONORS: Named to WHL (West) All-Star first team (1998-99).

		REGULAR SEASON								PLAYOFFS				
Season Team	League	Gms.	G	A	Pts.	PIM	+/-	PP	SH	Gms.	G	A	Pts.	PIM
96-97—Kamloops	WHL	64	4	19	23	96	...	...	...	5	0	1	1	18
97-98—Kamloops	WHL	65	4	10	14	120	...	...	...	5	0	3	3	8
98-99—Kamloops	WHL	54	12	20	32	130	...	...	...	12	1	4	5	21
99-00—Saint John	AHL	5	0	0	0	0	...	...	...	—	—	—	—	—
—Calgary	NHL	57	5	7	12	46	-2	2	0	—	—	—	—	—
NHL Totals (1 year)		57	5	7	12	46	-2	2	0					

REICHEL, ROBERT   C   COYOTES

PERSONAL: Born June 25, 1971, in Litvinov, Czechoslovakia. ... 5-10/186. ... Shoots right. ... Brother of Martin Reichel, right winger, Edmonton Oilers system. ... Name pronounced RIGH-kuhl.
TRANSACTIONS/CAREER NOTES: Selected by Calgary Flames in fourth round (fifth Flames pick, 70th overall) of NHL entry draft (June 17, 1989). ... Strained right knee (March 16, 1993); missed three games. ... Played in Europe during 1994-95 NHL lockout. ... Traded by Flames to New York Islanders for LW Marty McInnis, G Tyrone Garner and sixth-round pick (D Ilja Demidov) in 1997 draft (March 18, 1997). ... Traded by Islanders with third- (C/LW Jason Jaspers) and fourth-round (C Preston Mizzi) picks in 1999 draft to Phoenix Coyotes for RW Brad Isbister and third-round pick (C Brian Collins) in 1999 draft (March 20, 1999). ... Missed entire 1999-2000 season due to contract dispute; played in Europe.
HONORS: Named to Czechoslovakian League All-Star team (1989-90).
MISCELLANEOUS: Member of gold-medal-winning Czech Republic Olympic team (1998). ... Scored on a penalty shot (vs. Bill Ranford, February 7, 1994; vs. Tom Barrasso, October 24, 1996; vs. Zac Bierk, January 14, 1998). ... Failed to score on a penalty shot (vs. Rick Tabaracci, March 25, 1999).
STATISTICAL NOTES: Led NHL with 83 games played (1998-99).
STATISTICAL PLATEAUS: Three-goal games: 1992-93 (2), 1993-94 (2), 1997-98 (1). Total: 5.

Season Team	League	REGULAR SEASON Gms.	G	A	Pts.	PIM	+/-	PP	SH	PLAYOFFS Gms.	G	A	Pts.	PIM
87-88—Litvinov	Czech.	36	17	10	27	8	...	...	...	—	—	—	—	—
88-89—Litvinov	Czech.	44	23	25	48	32	...	...	...	—	—	—	—	—
89-90—Litvinov	Czech.	52	49	34	83	...	...	...	...	—	—	—	—	—
90-91—Calgary	NHL	66	19	22	41	22	17	3	0	6	1	1	2	0
91-92—Calgary	NHL	77	20	34	54	32	1	8	0	—	—	—	—	—
92-93—Calgary	NHL	80	40	48	88	54	25	12	0	6	2	4	6	2
93-94—Calgary	NHL	84	40	53	93	58	20	14	0	7	0	5	5	0
94-95—Frankfurt	Germany	21	19	24	43	41	...	...	...	—	—	—	—	—
—Calgary	NHL	48	18	17	35	28	-2	5	0	7	2	4	6	4
95-96—Frankfurt	Germany	46	47	54	101	84	...	...	...	3	1	3	4	0
96-97—Calgary	NHL	70	16	27	43	22	-2	6	0	—	—	—	—	—
—New York Islanders....	NHL	12	5	14	19	4	7	0	1	—	—	—	—	—
97-98—New York Islanders....	NHL	82	25	40	65	32	-11	8	0	—	—	—	—	—
—Czech Rep. Oly. team..	Int'l	6	3	0	3	0	...	...	...	—	—	—	—	—
98-99—New York Islanders....	NHL	§70	19	37	56	50	-15	5	1	—	—	—	—	—
—Phoenix	NHL	§13	7	6	13	4	2	3	0	7	1	3	4	2
99-00—Litvinov	Czech Rep.	45	25	32	57	24	...	...	...	7	3	4	7	2
NHL Totals (8 years)		602	209	298	507	306	42	64	2	33	6	17	23	8

REID, DAVE LW AVALANCHE

PERSONAL: Born May 15, 1964, in Toronto. ... 6-1/217. ... Shoots left. ... Full Name: David Reid.

TRANSACTIONS/CAREER NOTES: Selected by Boston Bruins as underage junior in third round (fourth Bruins pick, 60th overall) of NHL entry draft (June 9, 1982). ... Underwent knee surgery (December 1986). ... Separated shoulder (November 1987); missed 10 games. ... Signed as free agent by Toronto Maple Leafs (August 1988). ... Suffered from pneumonia (March 1992); missed 10 games. ... Injured knee (March 25, 1993); missed remainder of season. ... Signed as free agent by Bruins (November 22, 1991). ... Injured hip (April 1995); missed two games. ... Fractured finger (February 1, 1996); missed 16 games. ... Signed as free agent by Dallas Stars (July 3, 1996). ... Strained lower back (January 29, 1998); missed three games. ... Strained lower back (February 7, 1998); missed 13 games. ... Suffered back spasms (February 21, 1999); missed one game. ... Strained lower back (March 25, 1999); missed three games. ... Signed as free agent by Colorado Avalanche (October 6, 1999). ... Bruised ankle (December 8, 1999); missed nine games. ... Injured knee (January 25, 2000); missed two games.

MISCELLANEOUS: Member of Stanley Cup championship team (1999).

STATISTICAL PLATEAUS: Three-goal games: 1995-96 (1), 1996-97 (1). Total: 2.

Season Team	League	REGULAR SEASON Gms.	G	A	Pts.	PIM	+/-	PP	SH	PLAYOFFS Gms.	G	A	Pts.	PIM
81-82—Peterborough	OHL	68	10	32	42	41	...	...	...	9	2	3	5	11
82-83—Peterborough	OHL	70	23	34	57	33	...	...	...	4	3	1	4	0
83-84—Peterborough	OHL	60	33	64	97	12	...	...	...	—	—	—	—	—
—Boston	NHL	8	1	0	1	2	1	0	0	—	—	—	—	—
84-85—Hershey	AHL	43	10	14	24	6	...	...	...	—	—	—	—	—
—Boston	NHL	35	14	13	27	27	-1	2	0	5	1	0	1	0
85-86—Moncton	AHL	26	14	18	32	4	...	...	...	—	—	—	—	—
—Boston	NHL	37	10	10	20	10	2	4	0	—	—	—	—	—
86-87—Boston	NHL	12	3	3	6	0	-1	0	0	2	0	0	0	0
—Moncton	AHL	40	12	22	34	23	...	...	...	5	0	1	1	0
87-88—Maine	AHL	63	21	37	58	40	...	...	...	10	6	7	13	0
—Boston	NHL	3	0	0	0	0	0	0	0	—	—	—	—	—
88-89—Toronto	NHL	77	9	21	30	22	12	1	1	—	—	—	—	—
89-90—Toronto	NHL	70	9	19	28	9	-8	0	4	3	0	0	0	0
90-91—Toronto	NHL	69	15	13	28	18	-10	1	*8	—	—	—	—	—
91-92—Maine	AHL	12	1	5	6	4	...	...	...	—	—	—	—	—
—Boston	NHL	43	7	7	14	27	5	2	1	15	2	5	7	4
92-93—Boston	NHL	65	20	16	36	10	12	1	5	—	—	—	—	—
93-94—Boston	NHL	83	6	17	23	25	10	0	2	13	2	1	3	2
94-95—Boston	NHL	38	5	5	10	10	8	0	0	5	0	0	0	0
—Providence	AHL	7	3	0	3	0	...	...	...	—	—	—	—	—
95-96—Boston	NHL	63	23	21	44	4	14	1	6	5	0	2	2	2
96-97—Dallas	NHL	82	19	20	39	10	12	1	1	7	1	0	1	4
97-98—Dallas	NHL	65	6	12	18	14	-15	3	0	5	0	3	3	2
98-99—Dallas	NHL	73	6	11	17	16	0	1	0	23	2	8	10	14
99-00—Colorado	NHL	65	11	7	18	28	12	0	0	17	1	3	4	0
NHL Totals (17 years)		888	164	195	359	232	53	17	28	100	9	22	31	28

REINPRECHT, STEVE KINGS

PERSONAL: Born May 7, 1976, in Edmonton. ... 6-1/195. ... Shoots left.

COLLEGE: Wisconsin.

TRANSACTIONS/CAREER NOTES: Signed as non-drafted free agent by Los Angeles Kings (March 31, 2000).

HONORS: Named to WCHA All-Star first team (1999-2000). ... Named to NCAA All-America (West) first team (1999-2000).

Season Team	League	REGULAR SEASON Gms.	G	A	Pts.	PIM	+/-	PP	SH	PLAYOFFS Gms.	G	A	Pts.	PIM
96-97—Wisconsin	WCHA	38	11	9	20	12	...	...	...	—	—	—	—	—
97-98—Wisconsin	WCHA	41	19	24	43	18	...	...	...	—	—	—	—	—
98-99—Wisconsin	WCHA	38	16	17	33	14	...	...	...	—	—	—	—	—
99-00—Univ. of Wisconsin	WCHA	37	26	40	*66	14	...	...	...	—	—	—	—	—
—Los Angeles	NHL	1	0	0	0	2	0	0	0	—	—	—	—	—
NHL Totals (1 year)		1	0	0	0	2	0	0	0					

PERSONAL: Born June 25, 1971, in Deerfield, Ill. ... 6-5/220. ... Shoots left.
COLLEGE: Bowling Green State.
TRANSACTIONS/CAREER NOTES: Selected by New Jersey Devils in 12th round (14th Devils pick, 242nd overall) of NHL entry draft (June 16, 1990). ... Signed as free agent by Edmonton Oilers (May 31, 1998). ... Claimed on waivers by St. Louis Blues (September 30, 1999). ... Strained shoulder (December 4, 1999); missed three games. ... Fractured foot (January 28, 2000); missed 18 games.

		REGULAR SEASON								PLAYOFFS				
Season Team	League	Gms.	G	A	Pts.	PIM	+/-	PP	SH	Gms.	G	A	Pts.	PIM
90-91—Bowling Green	CCHA	28	1	5	6	22	...	...	...	—	—	—	—	—
91-92—Bowling Green	CCHA	33	8	7	15	34	...	...	...	—	—	—	—	—
92-93—Bowling Green	CCHA	41	8	17	25	48	...	...	...	—	—	—	—	—
93-94—Bowling Green	CCHA	38	7	23	30	56	...	...	...	—	—	—	—	—
94-95—Albany	AHL	2	0	1	1	2	...	...	...	—	—	—	—	—
—Raleigh	ECHL	26	2	13	15	33	...	...	...	—	—	—	—	—
—Tallahassee	ECHL	43	5	25	30	61	...	...	...	13	2	5	7	10
95-96—Chicago	IHL	31	0	2	2	39	...	...	...	9	0	2	2	16
—Tallahassee	ECHL	7	1	3	4	10	...	...	...	—	—	—	—	—
—Jacksonville	ECHL	15	1	10	11	41	...	...	...	1	0	2	2	4
96-97—Chicago	IHL	57	3	10	13	108	...	...	...	—	—	—	—	—
—San Antonio	IHL	23	2	5	7	51	...	...	...	9	0	1	1	17
97-98—San Antonio	IHL	70	5	14	19	132	...	...	...	—	—	—	—	—
—Fort Wayne	IHL	11	2	2	4	16	...	...	...	4	0	2	2	4
98-99—Hamilton	AHL	58	9	25	34	84	...	...	...	11	0	5	5	6
—Edmonton	NHL	17	2	3	5	20	-1	0	0	—	—	—	—	—
99-00—St. Louis	NHL	56	4	21	25	32	18	0	0	4	0	1	1	0
NHL Totals (2 years)		73	6	24	30	52	17	0	0	4	0	1	1	0

PERSONAL: Born May 5, 1972, in Pitea, Sweden. ... 6-2/218. ... Shoots left.
TRANSACTIONS/CAREER NOTES: Selected by Philadelphia Flyers in second round (third Flyers pick, 40th overall) of NHL entry draft (June 16, 1990). ... Played in Europe during 1994-95 NHL lockout. ... Suffered sore shoulder (March 25, 1995); missed one game. ... Strained abdominal muscles (December 30, 1995); missed one game. ... Strained lower abdominal muscles (January 22, 1996); missed 17 games. ... Reinjured lower abdominal muscles (March 12, 1996); missed one game. ... Reinjured lower abdominal muscles (March 16, 1996); missed one game. ... Reinjured lower abdominal muscles (March 19, 1996); missed 11 games. ... Underwent abdominal surgery (May 1996). ... Strained groin (March 8, 1997); missed one game. ... Cut face (April 6, 1997); missed remainder of regular season. ... Traded by Flyers with D Karl Dykhuis to Tampa Bay Lightning for C Chris Gratton (August 20, 1997). ... Suffered from the flu (October 15, 1997); missed one game. ... Fractured wrist (December 13, 1997); missed 13 games. ... Fractured left thumb (November 10, 1998); missed seven games. ... Traded by Lightning with C Daymond Langkow to Flyers for C Chris Gratton and C/RW Mike Sillinger (December 12, 1998). ... Separated shoulder (December 23, 1998); missed nine games. ... Suffered from the flu (February 9, 2000); missed two games. ... Traded by Flyers to Phoenix Coyotes for RW Rick Tocchet (March 8, 2000). ... Strained hip flexor (March 15, 2000); missed six games. ... Suffered from the flu (February 9, 2000); missed two games. ... Signed by Lulea, Swedish Elite League (June 13, 2000).
HONORS: Named to NHL All-Rookie team (1993-94).
MISCELLANEOUS: Captain of Tampa Bay Lightning (1997-98).
STATISTICAL PLATEAUS: Three-goal games: 1993-94 (1), 1997-98 (1). Total: 2.

		REGULAR SEASON								PLAYOFFS				
Season Team	League	Gms.	G	A	Pts.	PIM	+/-	PP	SH	Gms.	G	A	Pts.	PIM
88-89—Pitea	Sweden	12	6	3	9	...	...	...	...	—	—	—	—	—
89-90—Pitea	Sweden	29	15	19	34	...	...	...	...	—	—	—	—	—
90-91—Lulea	Sweden	29	11	6	17	12	...	...	...	5	1	1	2	4
91-92—Lulea	Sweden	38	8	15	23	20	...	...	...	2	0	0	0	0
92-93—Lulea	Sweden	39	19	13	32	61	...	...	...	11	4	4	8	...
93-94—Philadelphia	NHL	83	38	44	82	36	8	9	0	—	—	—	—	—
94-95—Lulea	Sweden	10	9	4	13	16	...	...	...	—	—	—	—	—
—Philadelphia	NHL	47	26	31	57	20	20	8	0	15	6	7	13	6
95-96—Philadelphia	NHL	51	23	20	43	45	8	9	0	11	3	6	9	14
96-97—Philadelphia	NHL	77	22	37	59	65	36	1	0	18	5	6	11	4
97-98—Tampa Bay	NHL	68	16	22	38	34	-37	6	3	—	—	—	—	—
—Swedish Oly. team	Int'l	4	1	2	3	4	...	...	...	—	—	—	—	—
98-99—Tampa Bay	NHL	20	4	8	12	4	-2	2	0	—	—	—	—	—
—Philadelphia	NHL	46	11	15	26	14	7	4	0	6	0	1	1	0
99-00—Philadelphia	NHL	62	8	21	29	30	-1	3	0	—	—	—	—	—
—Phoenix	NHL	10	2	4	6	2	0	0	0	5	1	2	3	4
NHL Totals (7 years)		464	150	202	352	250	39	42	3	55	15	22	37	28

PERSONAL: Born June 21, 1973, in Quebec City. ... 6-1/209. ... Shoots left. ... Name pronounced ray-OHM. ... Nickname: Pass.
HIGH SCHOOL: Carpenter.
TRANSACTIONS/CAREER NOTES: Signed as non-drafted free agent by New Jersey Devils (October 1, 1992). ... Claimed by St. Louis Blues from Devils in NHL waiver draft (September 28, 1997). ... Suffered concussion (February 28, 1999); missed 10 games. ... Underwent shoulder surgery prior to 1999-2000 season; missed first 62 games of season.

Season Team	League	REGULAR SEASON									PLAYOFFS				
		Gms.	G	A	Pts.	PIM	+/-	PP	SH		Gms.	G	A	Pts.	PIM
91-92—Trois-Rivieres	QMJHL	65	17	20	37	84	...	...	...		14	5	4	9	23
92-93—Sherbrooke	QMJHL	65	28	34	62	88	...	...	...		14	6	5	11	31
93-94—Albany	AHL	55	17	18	35	43	...	...	...		5	0	1	1	0
94-95—Albany	AHL	78	19	25	44	46	...	...	...		14	3	6	9	19
95-96—Albany	AHL	68	26	42	68	50	...	...	...		4	1	2	3	2
96-97—Albany	AHL	51	22	23	45	40	...	...	...		16	2	8	10	16
—New Jersey	NHL	2	1	0	1	0	1	0	0		—	—	—	—	—
97-98—St. Louis	NHL	48	6	9	15	35	4	1	0		10	1	3	4	8
98-99—St. Louis	NHL	60	9	18	27	24	10	2	0		5	1	0	1	4
99-00—St. Louis	NHL	7	1	1	2	6	-2	0	0		—	—	—	—	—
—Worcester	AHL	7	1	1	2	4	...	...	...		—	—	—	—	—
NHL Totals (4 years)		117	17	28	45	65	13	3	0		15	2	3	5	12

RHODES, DAMIAN — G — THRASHERS

PERSONAL: Born May 28, 1969, in St. Paul, Minn. ... 6-0/180. ... Catches left. ... Full Name: Damian G. Rhodes.
HIGH SCHOOL: Richfield (Minn.).
COLLEGE: Michigan Tech.
TRANSACTIONS/CAREER NOTES: Selected by Toronto Maple Leafs in sixth round (sixth Maple Leafs pick, 112th overall) of NHL entry draft (June 13, 1987). ... Traded by Maple Leafs with LW Ken Belanger to New York Islanders for LW Kirk Muller (January 23, 1996). ... Traded by Islanders with D Wade Redden to Ottawa Senators for D Bryan Berard and C Martin Straka (January 23, 1996). ... Bruised calf (February 23, 1997); missed 10 games. ... Suffered from the flu (December 22, 1998); missed one game. ... Traded by Senators to Atlanta Thrashers for future considerations (June 18, 1999). ... Sprained ankle (November 17, 1999); missed 49 games.
MISCELLANEOUS: Holds Atlanta Thrashers all-time record for most wins (5). ... Shares Atlanta Thrashers all-time record for most shutouts (1). ... Holds Ottawa Senators all-time record for most games played by goaltender (181). ... Stopped a penalty shot attempt (vs. Scott Pearson, November 20, 1993; vs. Geoff Courtnall, March 21, 1995; vs. Martin Straka, April 3, 1996; vs. Todd Marchant, November 13, 1996; vs. Brad Isbister, March 16, 2000). ... Allowed a penalty shot goal (vs. Pavel Bure, February 28, 1998; vs. Dixon Ward, April 11, 1998; vs. Miroslav Satan, October 9, 1999; vs. Patrick Elias, March 10, 2000).

Season Team	League	REGULAR SEASON								PLAYOFFS						
		Gms.	Min	W	L	T	GA	SO	Avg.		Gms.	Min.	W	L	GA	SO	Avg.
85-86—Richfield H.S.	Minn. H.S.	16	720	...	...	...	56	0	4.67	—	—	—	—	—	—	—
86-87—Richfield H.S.	Minn. H.S.	19	673	...	...	...	51	1	4.55	—	—	—	—	—	—	—
87-88—Michigan Tech	WCHA	29	1623	16	10	1	114	0	4.21	—	—	—	—	—	—	—
88-89—Michigan Tech	WCHA	37	2216	15	22	0	163	0	4.41	—	—	—	—	—	—	—
89-90—Michigan Tech	WCHA	25	1358	6	17	0	119	0	5.26	—	—	—	—	—	—	—
90-91—Toronto	NHL	1	60	1	0	0	1	0	1.00	—	—	—	—	—	—	—
—Newmarket	AHL	38	2154	8	24	3	144	1	4.01	—	—	—	—	—	—	—
91-92—St. John's	AHL	43	2454	20	16	5	148	1	3.62	6	331	4	1	16	0	2.90
92-93—St. John's	AHL	52	*3074	27	16	8	184	1	3.59	9	538	4	5	37	0	4.13
93-94—Toronto	NHL	22	1213	9	7	3	53	0	2.62	1	0	0	0	0	0	...
94-95—Toronto	NHL	13	760	6	6	1	34	0	2.68	—	—	—	—	—	—	—
95-96—Toronto	NHL	11	624	4	5	1	29	0	2.79	—	—	—	—	—	—	—
—Ottawa	NHL	36	2123	10	22	4	98	2	2.77	—	—	—	—	—	—	—
96-97—Ottawa	NHL	50	2934	14	20	*14	133	1	2.72	—	—	—	—	—	—	—
97-98—Ottawa	NHL	50	2743	19	19	7	107	5	2.34	10	590	5	5	21	0	2.14
98-99—Ottawa	NHL	45	2480	22	13	7	101	3	2.44	2	150	0	2	6	0	2.40
99-00—Atlanta	NHL	28	1561	5	19	3	101	1	3.88	—	—	—	—	—	—	—
NHL Totals (8 years)		256	14498	90	111	40	657	12	2.72	13	740	5	7	27	0	2.19

RIBEIRO, MIKE — C — CANADIENS

PERSONAL: Born February 10, 1980, in Montreal. ... 5-11/150. ... Shoots left.
TRANSACTIONS/CAREER NOTES: Selected by Montreal Canadiens in second round (second Canadiens pick, 45th overall) of NHL entry draft (June 27, 1998).
HONORS: Won Michel Bergeron Trophy (1997-98). ... Named to QMJHL All-Star second team (1997-98). ... Named to QMJHL All-Rookie Team (1997-98). ... Named to QMJHL All-Star first team (1998-99). ... Won Jean Beliveau Trophy (1998-99). ... Named to Can.HL All-Star first team (1998-99).

Season Team	League	REGULAR SEASON									PLAYOFFS				
		Gms.	G	A	Pts.	PIM	+/-	PP	SH		Gms.	G	A	Pts.	PIM
97-98—Rouyn-Noranda	QMJHL	67	40	85	125	55	...	...	...		—	—	—	—	—
98-99—Rouyn-Noranda	QMJHL	69	67	*100	*167	137	...	...	...		11	5	11	16	12
—Fredericton	AHL	—	—	—	—	—	...	...	...		5	0	1	1	2
99-00—Montreal	NHL	19	1	1	2	2	-6	1	0		—	—	—	—	—
—Quebec	AHL	3	0	0	0	2	...	...	...		—	—	—	—	—
—Rouyn-Noranda	QMJHL	2	1	3	4	0	...	...	...		—	—	—	—	—
—Quebec	QMJHL	21	17	28	45	30	...	...	...		11	3	20	23	38
NHL Totals (1 year)		19	1	1	2	2	-6	1	0		—	—	—	—	—

RICCI, MIKE — C — SHARKS

PERSONAL: Born October 27, 1971, in Scarborough, Ont. ... 6-0/190. ... Shoots left. ... Name pronounced REE-chee.
TRANSACTIONS/CAREER NOTES: Selected by Philadelphia Flyers in first round (first Flyers pick, fourth overall) of NHL entry draft (June 16, 1990). ... Fractured right index finger and thumb (October 4, 1990); missed nine games. ... Traded by Flyers with G Ron Hextall, C Peter

Forsberg, D Steve Duchesne, D Kerry Huffman, first-round pick (G Jocelyn Thibault) in 1993 draft, cash and future considerations to Quebec Nordiques for C Eric Lindros (June 20, 1992); Nordiques acquired LW Chris Simon and first-round pick (traded to Toronto) in 1994 draft to complete deal (July 21, 1992). ... Sprained left wrist (November 3, 1992); missed four games. ... Suffered from the flu (January 5, 1993); missed two games. ... Nordiques franchise moved to Colorado and renamed Avalanche for 1995-96 season (July 21, 1995). ... Underwent sinus surgery (October 15, 1995); missed one game. ... Injured ankle (November 5, 1995); missed one game. ... Sprained left ankle (December 11, 1995); missed two games. ... Suffered back spasms (January 4, 1996); missed 16 games. ... Strained shoulder (October 30, 1996); missed 11 games. ... Fractured thumb (January 6, 1997); missed four games. ... Underwent shoulder surgery prior to 1997-98 season; missed first 16 games of season. ... Traded by Avalanche with second-round pick (RW Jonathan Cheechoo) in 1998 draft to San Jose Sharks for RW Shean Donovan and first-round pick (C Alex Tanguay) in 1998 draft (November 20, 1997).
HONORS: Named to OHL All-Star second team (1988-89). ... Won Can.HL Player of the Year Award (1989-90). ... Won Red Tilson Trophy (1989-90). ... Won William Hanley Trophy (1989-90). ... Named to OHL All-Star first team (1989-90).
MISCELLANEOUS: Member of Stanley Cup championship team (1996). ... Failed to score on a penalty shot (vs. Chris Terreri, November 17, 1990; vs. Stephane Fiset, October 24, 1999).
STATISTICAL PLATEAUS: Five-goal games: 1993-94 (1).

		REGULAR SEASON								PLAYOFFS				
Season Team	League	Gms.	G	A	Pts.	PIM	+/-	PP	SH	Gms.	G	A	Pts.	PIM
87-88—Peterborough	OHL	41	24	37	61	20	...	...	...	8	5	5	10	4
88-89—Peterborough	OHL	60	54	52	106	43	...	...	...	17	19	16	35	18
89-90—Peterborough	OHL	60	52	64	116	39	...	...	...	12	5	7	12	26
90-91—Philadelphia	NHL	68	21	20	41	64	-8	9	0	—	—	—	—	—
91-92—Philadelphia	NHL	78	20	36	56	93	-10	11	2	—	—	—	—	—
92-93—Quebec	NHL	77	27	51	78	123	8	12	1	6	0	6	6	8
93-94—Quebec	NHL	83	30	21	51	113	-9	13	3	—	—	—	—	—
94-95—Quebec	NHL	48	15	21	36	40	5	9	0	6	1	3	4	8
95-96—Colorado	NHL	62	6	21	27	52	1	3	0	22	6	11	17	18
96-97—Colorado	NHL	63	13	19	32	59	-3	5	0	17	2	4	6	17
97-98—Colorado	NHL	6	0	4	4	2	0	0	0	—	—	—	—	—
—San Jose	NHL	59	9	14	23	30	-4	5	0	6	1	3	4	6
98-99—San Jose	NHL	82	13	26	39	68	1	2	1	6	2	3	5	10
99-00—San Jose	NHL	82	20	24	44	60	14	10	0	12	5	1	6	2
NHL Totals (10 years)		708	174	257	431	704	-5	79	7	75	17	31	48	69

RICHARDS, BRAD   LW   LIGHTNING

PERSONAL: Born May 2, 1980, in Montague, P.E.I. ... 6-1/187. ... Shoots left.
TRANSACTIONS/CAREER NOTES: Selected by Tampa Bay Lightning in third round (second Lightning pick, 64th overall) of NHL entry draft (June 27, 1998).
HONORS: Named to QMJHL All-Rookie Team (1997-98). ... Named to QMJHL All-Star first team (1999-2000). ... Won Jean Beliveau Trophy (1999-2000). ... Won Michel Briere trophy (1999-2000). ... Won Guy Lafleur Trophy (1999-2000). ... Named to Can.HL All-Star first team (1999-2000). ... Won Can.HL Player of the Year Award (1999-2000). ... Won Can.HL Plus/Minus Award (1999-2000).

		REGULAR SEASON								PLAYOFFS				
Season Team	League	Gms.	G	A	Pts.	PIM	+/-	PP	SH	Gms.	G	A	Pts.	PIM
96-97—Notre Dame	SJHL	63	39	48	87	73	...	...	...	—	—	—	—	—
97-98—Rimouski	QMJHL	68	33	82	115	44	...	...	...	19	8	24	32	2
98-99—Rimouski	QMJHL	59	39	92	131	55	...	...	...	11	9	12	21	6
99-00—Rimouski	QMJHL	63	*71	*115	*186	69	...	...	...	12	13	*24	*37	16

RICHARDSON, LUKE   D   FLYERS

PERSONAL: Born March 26, 1969, in Kanata, Ont. ... 6-3/210. ... Shoots left. ... Full Name: Luke Glen Richardson.
TRANSACTIONS/CAREER NOTES: Selected by Toronto Maple Leafs as underage junior in first round (first Maple Leafs pick, seventh overall) of NHL entry draft (June 13, 1987). ... Traded by Maple Leafs with LW Vincent Damphousse, G Peter Ing, C Scott Thornton and future considerations to Edmonton Oilers for G Grant Fuhr, LW Glenn Anderson and LW Craig Berube (September 19, 1991). ... Strained clavicular joint (February 11, 1992); missed three games. ... Suffered from the flu (March 1993); missed one game. ... Fractured cheekbone (January 7, 1994); missed 15 games. ... Suffered from the flu (February 28, 1995); missed two games. ... Signed as free agent by Philadelphia Flyers (July 14, 1997). ... Suspended two games by NHL for fighting (January 30, 2000). ... Bruised shoulder (February 24, 2000); missed five games.

		REGULAR SEASON								PLAYOFFS				
Season Team	League	Gms.	G	A	Pts.	PIM	+/-	PP	SH	Gms.	G	A	Pts.	PIM
84-85—Ottawa Jr. B	ODHA	35	5	26	31	72	...	...	...	—	—	—	—	—
85-86—Peterborough	OHL	63	6	18	24	57	...	...	...	16	2	1	3	50
86-87—Peterborough	OHL	59	13	32	45	70	...	...	...	12	0	5	5	24
87-88—Toronto	NHL	78	4	6	10	90	-25	0	0	2	0	0	0	0
88-89—Toronto	NHL	55	2	7	9	106	-15	0	0	—	—	—	—	—
89-90—Toronto	NHL	67	4	14	18	122	-1	0	0	5	0	0	0	22
90-91—Toronto	NHL	78	1	9	10	238	-28	0	0	—	—	—	—	—
91-92—Edmonton	NHL	75	2	19	21	118	-9	0	0	16	0	5	5	45
92-93—Edmonton	NHL	82	3	10	13	142	-18	0	2	—	—	—	—	—
93-94—Edmonton	NHL	69	2	6	8	131	-13	0	0	—	—	—	—	—
94-95—Edmonton	NHL	46	3	10	13	40	-6	1	1	—	—	—	—	—
95-96—Edmonton	NHL	82	2	9	11	108	-27	0	0	—	—	—	—	—
96-97—Edmonton	NHL	82	1	11	12	91	9	0	0	12	0	2	2	14
97-98—Philadelphia	NHL	81	2	3	5	139	7	2	0	5	0	0	0	0
98-99—Philadelphia	NHL	78	0	6	6	106	-3	0	0	—	—	—	—	—
99-00—Philadelphia	NHL	74	2	5	7	140	14	0	0	18	0	1	1	41
NHL Totals (13 years)		947	28	115	143	1571	-115	3	3	58	0	8	8	122

RICHER, STEPHANE   RW

PERSONAL: Born June 7, 1966, in Buckingham, Que. ... 6-3/226. ... Shoots right. ... Full Name: Stephane Joseph Jean Richer. ... Name pronounced REE-shay.

TRANSACTIONS/CAREER NOTES: Selected by Montreal Canadiens as underage junior in second round (third Canadiens pick, 29th overall) of NHL entry draft (June 9, 1984). ... Sprained ankle (November 18, 1985); missed 13 games. ... Bruised right hand (March 12, 1988). ... Fractured right thumb (April 1988). ... Sprained right thumb (September 1988). ... Suspended 10 games by NHL for slashing (November 16, 1988). ... Suffered from the flu (March 15, 1989). ... Bruised right shoulder (September 1989). ... Bruised left foot (February 1990). ... Injured left ankle (April 21, 1990). ... Injured knee (December 12, 1990). ... Traded by Canadiens with RW Tom Chorske to New Jersey Devils for LW Kirk Muller and G Roland Melanson (September 20, 1991). ... Injured groin (October 22, 1991); missed two games. ... Injured left knee (March 24, 1992); missed three games. ... Injured back (December 6, 1992); missed two games. ... Pulled groin (March 14, 1995); missed two games. ... Reinjured groin (March 22, 1995); missed one game. ... Injured groin (October 17, 1995); missed one game. ... Bruised wrist (December 6, 1995); missed seven games. ... Suffered from the flu (February 11, 1996); missed one game. ... Traded by Devils to Canadiens for D Lyle Odelein (August 22, 1996). ... Suffered back spasms (November 25, 1996); missed six games. ... Bruised foot (January 20, 1997); missed five games. ... Suffered hairline fracture in foot (February 17, 1997); missed four games. ... Suffered back spasms (April 5, 1997); missed four games. ... Suffered lacerated calf (October 15, 1997); missed four games. ... Sprained ankle (November 8, 1997); missed one game. ... Sprained ankle (November 13, 1997); missed nine games. ... Sprained ankle (December 6, 1997); missed 17 games. ... Traded by Canadiens with C Darcy Tucker and D David Wilkie to Tampa Bay Lightning for C Patrick Poulin, RW Mick Vukota and D Igor Ulanov (January 15, 1998). ... Reinjured left ankle (April 2, 1998); missed final eight games of season. ... Injured ankle (October 16, 1998) and underwent surgery; missed 13 games. ... Sprained ankle (December 18, 1998); missed four games. ... Injured shoulder (February 20, 1999); missed one game. ... Strained muscle in rib cage (November 13, 1999); missed 15 games. ... Traded by Lightning to St. Louis Blues for D Chris McAlpine and G Rich Parent (January 13, 2000). ... Strained muscle in rib cage (February 11, 2000); missed two games.

HONORS: Won Michel Bergeron Trophy (1983-84). ... Named to QMJHL All-Star second team (1984-85). ... Played in NHL All-Star Game (1990).

MISCELLANEOUS: Member of Stanley Cup championship team (1986 and 1995).

STATISTICAL NOTES: Led NHL with 11 game-winning goals (1987-88).

STATISTICAL PLATEAUS: Three-goal games: 1987-88 (1), 1989-90 (2), 1990-91 (1), 1991-92 (1), 1992-93 (1), 1995-96 (1), 1999-00 (1). Total: 8. ... Four-goal games: 1985-86 (1), 1987-88 (1). Total: 2. ... Total hat tricks: 10.

Season Team	League	REGULAR SEASON								PLAYOFFS				
		Gms.	G	A	Pts.	PIM	+/-	PP	SH	Gms.	G	A	Pts.	PIM
83-84—Granby	QMJHL	67	39	37	76	58	...	...	...	3	1	1	2	4
84-85—Granby/Chicoutimi	QMJHL	57	61	59	120	71	...	...	...	12	13	13	26	25
—Montreal	NHL	1	0	0	0	0	0	0	0	—	—	—	—	—
—Sherbrooke	AHL	—	—	—	—	—	...	...	...	9	6	3	9	10
85-86—Montreal	NHL	65	21	16	37	50	1	5	0	16	4	1	5	23
86-87—Sherbrooke	AHL	12	10	4	14	11	...	...	...	—	—	—	—	—
—Montreal	NHL	57	20	19	39	80	11	4	0	5	3	2	5	0
87-88—Montreal	NHL	72	50	28	78	72	12	16	0	8	7	5	12	6
88-89—Montreal	NHL	68	25	35	60	61	4	11	0	21	6	5	11	14
89-90—Montreal	NHL	75	51	40	91	46	35	9	0	9	7	3	10	2
90-91—Montreal	NHL	75	31	30	61	53	0	9	0	13	9	5	14	6
91-92—New Jersey	NHL	74	29	35	64	25	-1	5	1	7	1	2	3	0
92-93—New Jersey	NHL	78	38	35	73	44	-1	7	1	5	2	2	4	2
93-94—New Jersey	NHL	80	36	36	72	16	31	7	3	20	7	5	12	6
94-95—New Jersey	NHL	45	23	16	39	10	8	1	2	19	6	15	21	2
95-96—New Jersey	NHL	73	20	12	32	30	-8	3	4	—	—	—	—	—
96-97—Montreal	NHL	63	22	24	46	32	0	2	0	5	0	0	0	0
97-98—Montreal	NHL	14	5	4	9	5	1	2	0	—	—	—	—	—
—Tampa Bay	NHL	26	9	11	20	36	-7	3	0	—	—	—	—	—
98-99—Tampa Bay	NHL	64	12	21	33	22	-10	3	2	—	—	—	—	—
99-00—Tampa Bay	NHL	20	7	5	12	4	2	1	0	—	—	—	—	—
—Detroit	IHL	2	0	0	0	0	...	...	...	—	—	—	—	—
—St. Louis	NHL	36	8	17	25	14	7	4	0	3	1	0	1	0
NHL Totals (16 years)		986	407	384	791	600	85	92	13	131	53	45	98	61

RICHTER, BARRY   D   CANADIENS

PERSONAL: Born September 11, 1970, in Madison, Wis. ... 6-2/200. ... Shoots left. ... Full Name: Barron Patrick Richter. ... Son of Pat Richter, tight end with Washington Redskins (1963-70). ... Name pronounced RIHK-tuhr.

HIGH SCHOOL: Culver (Ind.) Military Academy.

COLLEGE: Wisconsin.

TRANSACTIONS/CAREER NOTES: Selected by Hartford Whalers in second round (second Whalers pick, 32nd overall) of NHL entry draft (June 11, 1988). ... Traded by Whalers with RW Steve Larmer, LW Nick Kypreos and sixth-round pick (C Yuri Litvinov) in 1994 draft to New York Rangers for D James Patrick and C Darren Turcotte (November 2, 1993). ... Signed as free agent by Boston Bruins (July 17, 1996). ... Strained groin (November 4, 1996); missed four games. ... Signed as free agent by New York Islanders (August 19, 1998). ... Sprained shoulder (February 3, 1999); missed three games. ... Signed as free agent by Montreal Canadiens (August 6, 1999). ... Strained hip flexor (December 29, 1999); missed 19 games.

HONORS: Named to NCAA All-Tournament team (1991-92). ... Named to NCAA All-America (West) first team (1992-93). ... Named to WCHA All-Star first team (1992-93). ... Named to AHL All-Star first team (1995-96). ... Won Eddie Shore Plaque (1995-96).

Season Team	League	REGULAR SEASON								PLAYOFFS				
		Gms.	G	A	Pts.	PIM	+/-	PP	SH	Gms.	G	A	Pts.	PIM
86-87—Culver Military	Indiana H.S.	35	19	26	45	...	...	...	...	—	—	—	—	—
87-88—Culver Military	Indiana H.S.	35	24	29	53	18	...	...	...	—	—	—	—	—
88-89—Culver Military	Indiana H.S.	19	21	29	50	16	...	...	...	—	—	—	—	—
89-90—Univ. of Wisconsin	WCHA	42	13	23	36	26	...	...	...	—	—	—	—	—
90-91—Univ. of Wisconsin	WCHA	43	15	20	35	42	...	...	...	—	—	—	—	—
91-92—Univ. of Wisconsin	WCHA	39	10	25	35	62	...	...	...	—	—	—	—	—
92-93—Univ. of Wisconsin	WCHA	42	14	32	46	74	...	...	...	—	—	—	—	—

Season Team	League	REGULAR SEASON								PLAYOFFS				
		Gms.	G	A	Pts.	PIM	+/-	PP	SH	Gms.	G	A	Pts.	PIM
93-94—U.S. national team	Int'l	56	7	16	23	50	...	...	...	—	—	—	—	—
—U.S. Olympic team	Int'l	8	0	3	3	4	...	...	...	—	—	—	—	—
—Binghamton	AHL	21	0	9	9	12	...	...	...	—	—	—	—	—
94-95—Binghamton	AHL	73	15	41	56	54	...	...	...	11	4	5	9	12
95-96—Binghamton	AHL	69	20	61	81	64	...	...	...	3	0	3	3	0
—New York Rangers	NHL	4	0	1	1	0	2	0	0	—	—	—	—	—
96-97—Boston	NHL	50	5	13	18	32	-7	1	0	—	—	—	—	—
—Providence	AHL	19	2	6	8	4	...	...	...	10	4	4	8	4
97-98—Providence	AHL	75	16	29	45	47	...	...	...	—	—	—	—	—
98-99—New York Islanders	NHL	72	6	18	24	34	-4	0	0	—	—	—	—	—
99-00—Montreal	NHL	23	0	2	2	8	-5	0	0	—	—	—	—	—
—Quebec	AHL	2	0	0	0	0	...	...	...	—	—	—	—	—
—Manitoba	IHL	19	5	4	9	6	...	...	...	2	1	1	2	0
NHL Totals (4 years)		149	11	34	45	74	-14	1	0					

RICHTER, MIKE — G — RANGERS

PERSONAL: Born September 22, 1966, in Philadelphia. ... 5-11/185. ... Catches left. ... Full Name: Michael Thomas Richter. ... Name pronounced RIHK-tuhr.

HIGH SCHOOL: Northwood School (Lake Placid, N.Y.).

COLLEGE: Wisconsin.

TRANSACTIONS/CAREER NOTES: Selected by New York Rangers in second round (second Rangers pick, 28th overall) of NHL entry draft (June 15, 1985). ... Bruised thigh (January 30, 1992); missed 12 games. ... Injured groin (December 30, 1995); missed 15 games. ... Reinjured groin (February 18, 1996); missed eight games. ... Separated left shoulder (January 19, 1997); missed two games. ... Selected by Nashville Predators in NHL expansion draft (June 26, 1998). ... Signed as free agent by Rangers (July 14, 1998). ... Injured back (October 2, 1999); missed five games. ... Sprained left knee (February 5, 2000); missed two games. ... Reinjured left knee (February 18, 2000); missed two games. ... Reinjured left knee (March 13, 2000); missed one game ... Reinjured left knee (March 27, 2000); missed four games.

HONORS: Won WCHA Rookie of the Year Award (1985-86). ... Named to WCHA All-Star second team (1985-86 and 1986-87). ... Played in NHL All-Star Game (1992, 1994 and 2000). ... Named All-Star Game Most Valuable Player (1994).

RECORDS: Shares NHL single-season playoff record for most wins by goaltender—16 (1994). ... Shares NHL single-season playoff record for most shutouts—4 (1994).

MISCELLANEOUS: Member of Stanley Cup championship team (1994). ... Stopped a penalty shot attempt (vs. Kevin Dineen, October 19, 1989; vs. Pelle Eklund, January 14, 1990; vs. Troy Murray, November 27, 1991; vs. Steve Konowalchuk, March 5, 1995; vs. Ken Klee, March 12, 1997; vs. Marc Bureau, January 10, 1998; vs. Claude Lapointe, October 22, 1998; vs. Richard Zednik, November 11, 1999; vs. Randy Robitaille, January 31, 2000). ... Allowed a penalty shot goal (vs. Doug Weight, October 8, 1997).

Season Team	League	REGULAR SEASON								PLAYOFFS						
		Gms.	Min	W	L	T	GA	SO	Avg.	Gms.	Min.	W	L	GA	SO	Avg.
84-85—Northwood School	N.Y. H.S.	24	1374	...	...	...	52	2	2.27	—	—	—	—	—	—	—
85-86—Univ. of Wisconsin	WCHA	24	1394	14	9	0	92	1	3.96	—	—	—	—	—	—	—
86-87—Univ. of Wisconsin	WCHA	36	2136	19	16	1	126	0	3.54	—	—	—	—	—	—	—
87-88—U.S. national team	Int'l	29	1559	17	7	2	86	0	3.31	—	—	—	—	—	—	—
—U.S. Olympic team	Int'l	4	230	2	2	0	15	0	3.91	—	—	—	—	—	—	—
—Colorado	IHL	22	1298	16	5	0	68	1	3.14	10	536	5	3	35	0	3.92
88-89—Denver	IHL	*57	3031	23	26	0	*217	1	4.30	4	210	0	4	21	0	6.00
—New York Rangers	NHL	—	—	—	—	—	—	—	—	1	58	0	1	4	0	4.14
89-90—New York Rangers	NHL	23	1320	12	5	5	66	0	3.00	6	330	3	2	19	0	3.45
—Flint	IHL	13	782	7	4	‡2	49	0	3.76	—	—	—	—	—	—	—
90-91—New York Rangers	NHL	45	2596	21	13	7	135	0	3.12	6	313	2	4	14	†1	2.68
91-92—New York Rangers	NHL	41	2298	23	12	2	119	3	3.11	7	412	4	2	24	1	3.50
92-93—New York Rangers	NHL	38	2105	13	19	3	134	1	3.82	—	—	—	—	—	—	—
—Binghamton	AHL	5	305	*4	0	1	6	0	1.18	—	—	—	—	—	—	—
93-94—New York Rangers	NHL	68	3710	*42	12	6	159	5	2.57	23	1417	*16	7	49	†4	2.07
94-95—New York Rangers	NHL	35	1993	14	17	2	97	2	2.92	7	384	2	5	23	0	3.59
95-96—New York Rangers	NHL	41	2396	24	13	3	107	3	2.68	11	661	5	6	36	0	3.27
96-97—New York Rangers	NHL	61	3598	33	22	6	161	4	2.68	15	939	9	6	33	3	2.11
97-98—New York Rangers	NHL	72	4143	21	31	*15	†184	0	2.66	—	—	—	—	—	—	—
—U.S. Olympic team	Int'l	4	237	1	3	0	14	0	3.54	—	—	—	—	—	—	—
98-99—New York Rangers	NHL	68	3878	27	30	8	170	4	2.63	—	—	—	—	—	—	—
99-00—New York Rangers	NHL	61	3622	22	†31	8	173	0	2.87	—	—	—	—	—	—	—
NHL Totals (12 years)		553	31659	252	205	65	1505	22	2.85	76	4514	41	33	202	9	2.68

RIESEN, MICHEL — LW — OILERS

PERSONAL: Born April 11, 1979, in Oberbalm, Switzerland. ... 6-2/190. ... Shoots right. ... Name pronounced REE-sihn.

TRANSACTIONS/CAREER NOTES: Selected by Edmonton Oilers in first round (first Oilers pick, 14th overall) of NHL entry draft (June 21, 1997).

Season Team	League	REGULAR SEASON								PLAYOFFS				
		Gms.	G	A	Pts.	PIM	+/-	PP	SH	Gms.	G	A	Pts.	PIM
94-95—Biel-Bienne	Switzerland	12	0	2	2	0	...	...	...	6	2	0	2	0
95-96—Biel-Bienne	Switz. Div. 2	34	9	6	15	2	...	...	...	3	1	0	1	0
96-97—Biel-Bienne	Switz. Div. 2	38	16	16	32	49	...	...	...	—	—	—	—	—
97-98—Davos HC	Switzerland	32	16	9	25	8	...	...	...	18	5	5	10	4
98-99—Hamilton	AHL	60	6	17	23	6	...	...	...	3	0	0	0	0
99-00—Hamilton	AHL	73	29	31	60	20	...	...	...	10	3	5	8	4

RITA, JANI — LW/RW — OILERS

PERSONAL: Born July 25, 1981, in Helsinki, Finland. ... 6-1/206. ... Shoots right.
TRANSACTIONS/CAREER NOTES: Selected by Edmonton Oilers in first round (first Oilers pick, 13th overall) of NHL entry draft (June 26, 1999).

Season Team	League	Gms.	G	A	Pts.	PIM	+/-	PP	SH	Gms.	G	A	Pts.	PIM
		REGULAR SEASON								PLAYOFFS				
96-97—Jokerit Helsinki	Finland Jr.	3	0	0	0	0	...	...	...	—	—	—	—	—
97-98—Jokerit Helsinki	Finland Jr.	36	15	9	24	2	...	...	...	8	4	1	5	0
—Jokerit Helsinki	Finland	—								1	0	0	0	0
98-99—Jokerit Helsinki	Finland	41	3	2	5	39	...	...	...	—	—	—	—	—
—Jokerit Helsinki	Finland Jr.	20	9	13	22	8	...	...	...	—	—	—	—	—
99-00—Jokerit Helsinki	Finland	49	6	3	9	10	...	...	...	11	1	0	1	0

RITCHIE, BYRON — C — HURRICANES

PERSONAL: Born April 24, 1977, in Burnaby, B.C. ... 5-10/185. ... Shoots left.
TRANSACTIONS/CAREER NOTES: Selected by Hartford Whalers in seventh round (sixth Whalers pick, 165th overall) of NHL entry draft (July 8, 1995). ... Whalers franchise moved to North Carolina and renamed Carolina Hurricanes for 1997-98 season; NHL approved move on June 25, 1997.
HONORS: Named to WHL (East) All-Star second team (1995-96 and 1996-97). ... Named to Memorial Cup All-Star Team (1996-97).

Season Team	League	Gms.	G	A	Pts.	PIM	+/-	PP	SH	Gms.	G	A	Pts.	PIM
		REGULAR SEASON								PLAYOFFS				
93-94—Lethbridge	WHL	44	4	11	15	44	...	...	...	6	0	0	0	14
94-95—Lethbridge	WHL	58	22	28	50	132	...	...	...	—	—	—	—	—
95-96—Lethbridge	WHL	66	55	51	106	163	...	...	...	4	0	2	2	4
—Springfield	AHL	6	2	1	3	4	...	...	...	8	0	3	3	0
96-97—Lethbridge	WHL	63	50	76	126	115	...	...	...	18	16	12	*28	28
97-98—New Haven	AHL	65	13	18	31	97	...	...	...	—	—	—	—	—
98-99—New Haven	AHL	66	24	33	57	139	...	...	...	—	—	—	—	—
—Carolina	NHL	3	0	0	0	0	0	0	0	—	—	—	—	—
99-00—Carolina	NHL	26	0	2	2	17	-10	0	0	—	—	—	—	—
—Cincinnati	IHL	34	8	13	21	81	...	...	...	10	1	6	7	32
NHL Totals (2 years)		29	0	2	2	17	-10	0	0	—	—	—	—	—

RIVERS, JAMIE — D

PERSONAL: Born March 16, 1975, in Ottawa. ... 6-0/197. ... Shoots left. ... Brother of Shawn Rivers, defenseman with Tampa Bay Lightning (1992-93).
HIGH SCHOOL: Lasalle Secondary (Sudbury, Ont.).
TRANSACTIONS/CAREER NOTES: Selected by St. Louis Blues in third round (second Blues pick, 63rd overall) of NHL entry draft (June 26, 1993). ... Claimed by New York Islanders from Blues in NHL waiver draft (September 27, 1999). ... Bruised ankle (February 26, 2000); missed three games.
HONORS: Won Max Kaminsky Award (1993-94). ... Named to OHL All-Star first team (1993-94). ... Named to Can.HL All-Star second team (1993-94). ... Named to OHL All-Star second team (1994-95). ... Named to AHL All-Star second team (1996-97).

Season Team	League	Gms.	G	A	Pts.	PIM	+/-	PP	SH	Gms.	G	A	Pts.	PIM
		REGULAR SEASON								PLAYOFFS				
90-91—Ottawa	OHA Jr. A	55	4	30	34	74	...	...	...	—	—	—	—	—
91-92—Sudbury	OHL	55	3	13	16	20	...	...	...	8	0	0	0	0
92-93—Sudbury	OHL	62	12	43	55	20	...	...	...	14	7	19	26	4
93-94—Sudbury	OHL	65	32	*89	121	58	...	...	...	10	1	9	10	14
94-95—Sudbury	OHL	46	9	56	65	30	...	...	...	18	7	26	33	22
95-96—St. Louis	NHL	3	0	0	0	2	-1	0	0	—	—	—	—	—
—Worcester	AHL	75	7	45	52	130	...	...	...	4	0	1	1	4
96-97—Worcester	AHL	63	8	35	43	83	...	...	...	5	1	2	3	14
—St. Louis	NHL	15	2	5	7	6	-4	1	0	—	—	—	—	—
97-98—St. Louis	NHL	59	2	4	6	36	5	1	0	—	—	—	—	—
98-99—St. Louis	NHL	76	2	5	7	47	-3	1	0	9	1	1	2	2
99-00—New York Islanders	NHL	75	1	16	17	84	-4	1	0	—	—	—	—	—
NHL Totals (5 years)		228	7	30	37	175	-7	4	0	9	1	1	2	2

RIVET, CRAIG — D — CANADIENS

PERSONAL: Born September 13, 1974, in North Bay, Ont. ... 6-2/207. ... Shoots right. ... Name pronounced REE-vay.
TRANSACTIONS/CAREER NOTES: Selected by Montreal Canadiens in third round (fourth Canadiens pick, 68th overall) of NHL entry draft (June 20, 1992). ... Separated shoulder (January 20, 1997); missed six games. ... Bruised back (November 1, 1997); missed one game. ... Suffered concussion (December 19, 1997); missed seven games. ... Sprained shoulder (November 9, 1998); missed five games. ... Suffered back spasms and suffered from the flu (January 18, 1999); missed three games. ... Strained groin (March 13, 1999); missed three games. ... Reinjured groin (March 24, 1999); missed five games. ... Fractured cheekbone (October 8, 1999); missed nine games. ... Suffered illness (November 3, 1999); missed four games. ... Strained groin (January 4, 2000); missed eight games.

Season Team	League	Gms.	G	A	Pts.	PIM	+/-	PP	SH	Gms.	G	A	Pts.	PIM
		REGULAR SEASON								PLAYOFFS				
90-91—Barrie Jr. B	OHA	42	9	17	26	55	...	...	...	—	—	—	—	—
91-92—Kingston	OHL	66	5	21	26	97	...	...	...	—	—	—	—	—
92-93—Kingston	OHL	64	19	55	74	117	...	...	...	16	5	7	12	39
93-94—Fredericton	AHL	4	0	2	2	2	...	...	...	—	—	—	—	—
—Kingston	OHL	61	12	52	64	100	...	...	...	6	0	3	3	6

Season Team	League	REGULAR SEASON								PLAYOFFS				
		Gms.	G	A	Pts.	PIM	+/-	PP	SH	Gms.	G	A	Pts.	PIM
94-95—Fredericton	AHL	78	5	27	32	126	...	...	...	12	0	4	4	17
—Montreal	NHL	5	0	1	1	5	2	0	0	—	—	—	—	—
95-96—Fredericton	AHL	49	5	18	23	189	...	...	...	6	0	0	0	12
—Montreal	NHL	19	1	4	5	54	4	0	0	—	—	—	—	—
96-97—Montreal	NHL	35	0	4	4	54	7	0	0	5	0	1	1	14
—Fredericton	AHL	23	3	12	15	99	...	...	...	—	—	—	—	—
97-98—Montreal	NHL	61	0	2	2	93	-3	0	0	5	0	0	0	2
98-99—Montreal	NHL	66	2	8	10	66	-3	0	0	—	—	—	—	—
99-00—Montreal	NHL	61	3	14	17	76	11	0	0	—	—	—	—	—
NHL Totals (6 years)		247	6	33	39	348	18	0	0	10	0	1	1	16

ROBERTS, GARY   LW   MAPLE LEAFS

PERSONAL: Born May 23, 1966, in North York, Ont. ... 6-1/190. ... Shoots left.
TRANSACTIONS/CAREER NOTES: Selected by Calgary Flames as underage junior in first round (first Flames pick, 12th overall) of NHL entry draft (June 9, 1984). ... Injured back (January 1989). ... Suffered whiplash (November 9, 1991); missed one game. ... Suffered from the flu (January 19, 1993); missed one game. ... Suffered left quadricep hematoma (February 16, 1993); missed one game. ... Suspended one game by NHL for high-sticking (November 19, 1993). ... Suspended four games and fined $500 by NHL for two slashing incidents and fined $500 for high-sticking (January 7, 1994). ... Fractured thumb (March 20, 1994); missed one game. ... Fractured thumb (April 3, 1994); missed last five games of season. ... Suffered neck and spinal injury (February 4, 1995); underwent surgery and missed last 40 games of 1994-95 season and first 42 games of 1995-96 season. ... Injured neck (April 3, 1996); missed five games. ... Announced retirement (June 17, 1996); did not play during 1996-97 season. ... Traded by Flames with G Trevor Kidd to Carolina Hurricanes for G Jean-Sebastion Giguere and C Andrew Cassels (August 25, 1997). ... Strained abdominal muscle (November 12, 1997); missed six games. ... Strained rib muscle (January 11, 1998); missed 10 games. ... Suffered from the flu (March 31, 1998); missed one game. ... Injured groin (April 13, 1998); missed final three games of season. ... Sprained wrist (December 2, 1998); missed four games. ... Strained neck (April 14, 1999); missed one game. ... Strained shoulder (October 7, 1999); missed one game. ... Injured groin (October 23, 1999); missed four games. ... Suffered from the flu (January 18, 2000); missed one game. ... Injured groin (February 12, 2000); missed seven games. ... Signed as free agent by Toronto Maple Leafs (July 4, 2000).
HONORS: Named to OHL All-Star second team (1984-85 and 1985-86). ... Played in NHL All-Star Game (1992 and 1993). ... Won Bill Masterton Memorial Trophy (1995-96).
MISCELLANEOUS: Member of Stanley Cup championship team (1989). ... Holds Carolina Hurricanes record for most penalty minutes (281).
STATISTICAL PLATEAUS: Three-goal games: 1989-90 (1), 1991-92 (2), 1992-93 (2), 1993-94 (1), 1995-96 (3), 1997-98 (1). Total: 10. ... Four-goal games: 1993-94 (1). ... Total hat tricks: 11.

Season Team	League	REGULAR SEASON								PLAYOFFS				
		Gms.	G	A	Pts.	PIM	+/-	PP	SH	Gms.	G	A	Pts.	PIM
82-83—Ottawa	OHL	53	12	8	20	83	...	...	...	5	1	0	1	19
83-84—Ottawa	OHL	48	27	30	57	144	...	...	...	13	10	7	17	*62
84-85—Ottawa	OHL	59	44	62	106	186	...	...	...	5	2	8	10	10
—Moncton	AHL	7	4	2	6	7	...	...	...	—	—	—	—	—
85-86—Ottawa	OHL	24	26	25	51	83	...	...	...	—	—	—	—	—
—Guelph	OHL	23	18	15	33	65	...	...	...	20	18	13	31	43
86-87—Moncton	AHL	38	20	18	38	72	...	...	...	—	—	—	—	—
—Calgary	NHL	32	5	10	15	85	6	0	0	2	0	0	0	4
87-88—Calgary	NHL	74	13	15	28	282	24	0	0	9	2	3	5	29
88-89—Calgary	NHL	71	22	16	38	250	32	0	1	22	5	7	12	57
89-90—Calgary	NHL	78	39	33	72	222	31	5	0	6	2	5	7	41
90-91—Calgary	NHL	80	22	31	53	252	15	0	0	7	1	3	4	18
91-92—Calgary	NHL	76	53	37	90	207	32	15	0	—	—	—	—	—
92-93—Calgary	NHL	58	38	41	79	172	32	8	3	5	1	6	7	43
93-94—Calgary	NHL	73	41	43	84	145	37	12	3	7	2	6	8	24
94-95—Calgary	NHL	8	2	2	4	43	1	2	0	—	—	—	—	—
95-96—Calgary	NHL	35	22	20	42	78	15	9	0	—	—	—	—	—
96-97—							Did not play.							
97-98—Carolina	NHL	61	20	29	49	103	3	4	0	—	—	—	—	—
98-99—Carolina	NHL	77	14	28	42	178	2	1	1	6	1	1	2	8
99-00—Carolina	NHL	69	23	30	53	62	-10	12	0	—	—	—	—	—
NHL Totals (14 years)		792	314	335	649	2079	220	68	8	64	14	31	45	224

ROBERTSSON, BERT   D/LW   BLUE JACKETS

PERSONAL: Born June 30, 1974, in Sodertalje, Sweden. ... 6-3/210. ... Shoots left. ... Name pronounced ROH-behrt-suhn.
TRANSACTIONS/CAREER NOTES: Selected by Vancouver Canucks in 10th round (eighth Canucks pick, 254th overall) of NHL entry draft (June 29, 1993). ... Injured groin (April 1, 1999); missed four games. ... Signed as free agent by Edmonton Oilers (August 19, 1999). ... Selected by Columbus Blue Jackets in NHL expansion draft (June 23, 2000).

Season Team	League	REGULAR SEASON								PLAYOFFS				
		Gms.	G	A	Pts.	PIM	+/-	PP	SH	Gms.	G	A	Pts.	PIM
92-93—Sodertalje	Sweden Dv. 2	23	1	2	3	24	...	...	...	—	—	—	—	—
93-94—Sodertalje	Sweden Dv. 2	28	0	1	1	12	...	...	...	—	—	—	—	—
94-95—Sodertalje	Sweden Dv. 2	23	1	2	3	24	...	...	...	—	—	—	—	—
95-96—Syracuse	AHL	65	1	7	8	109	...	...	...	16	0	1	1	26
96-97—Syracuse	AHL	80	4	9	13	132	...	...	...	3	1	0	1	4
97-98—Syracuse	AHL	42	5	9	14	87	...	...	...	3	0	0	0	6
—Vancouver	NHL	30	2	4	6	24	2	0	0	—	—	—	—	—
98-99—Vancouver	NHL	39	2	2	4	13	-7	0	0	—	—	—	—	—
—Syracuse	AHL	8	1	0	1	21	...	...	...	—	—	—	—	—
99-00—Hamilton	AHL	6	0	3	3	12	...	...	...	—	—	—	—	—
—Edmonton	NHL	52	0	4	4	34	-3	0	0	5	0	0	0	0
NHL Totals (3 years)		121	4	10	14	71	-8	0	0	5	0	0	0	0

ROBIDAS, STEPHANE　　　　　D　　　　　CANADIENS

PERSONAL: Born March 3, 1973, in Sherbrooke, Que. ... 5-11/180. ... Shoots right.
TRANSACTIONS/CAREER NOTES: Selected by Montreal Canadiens in seventh round (seventh Canadiens pick, 164th overall) of NHL entry draft (June 26, 1995).
HONORS: Won Emile Bouchard Trophy (1996-97). ... Named to Can.HL All-Star second team (1996-97). ... Named to QMJHL All-Star first team (1996-97).

Season Team	League	REGULAR SEASON								PLAYOFFS				
		Gms.	G	A	Pts.	PIM	+/-	PP	SH	Gms.	G	A	Pts.	PIM
93-94—Shawinigan	QMJHL	67	3	18	21	33	...	...	...	1	0	0	0	0
94-95—Shawinigan	QMJHL	71	13	56	69	44	...	...	...	15	7	12	19	4
95-96—Shawinigan	QMJHL	67	23	56	79	53	...	...	...	6	1	5	6	10
96-97—Shawinigan	QMJHL	67	24	51	75	59	...	...	...	7	4	6	10	14
97-98—Fredericton	AHL	79	10	21	31	50	...	...	...	4	0	2	2	0
98-99—Fredericton	AHL	79	8	33	41	59	...	...	...	15	1	5	6	10
99-00—Quebec	AHL	76	14	31	45	36	...	...	...	3	0	1	1	0
—Montreal	NHL	1	0	0	0	0	0	0	0	—	—	—	—	—
NHL Totals (1 year)		1	0	0	0	0	0	0	0					

ROBITAILLE, LUC　　　　　LW　　　　　KINGS

PERSONAL: Born February 17, 1966, in Montreal. ... 6-1/205. ... Shoots left. ... Name pronounced ROH-bih-tigh.
TRANSACTIONS/CAREER NOTES: Selected by Los Angeles Kings as underage junior in ninth round (ninth Kings pick, 171st overall) of NHL entry draft (June 9, 1984). ... Suspended four games by NHL for crosschecking from behind (November 10, 1990). ... Underwent surgery to repair slight fracture of right ankle (June 15, 1994). ... Traded by Kings to Pittsburgh Penguins for RW Rick Tocchet and second-round pick (RW Pavel Rosa) in 1995 draft (July 29, 1994). ... Suspended by NHL for two games for high-sticking (February 7, 1995). ... Traded by Penguins with D Ulf Samuelsson to New York Rangers for D Sergei Zubov and C Petr Nedved (August 31, 1995). ... Suffered stress fracture in ankle (December 15, 1995); missed five games. ... Fractured foot (March 12, 1997); missed final 13 games of regular season. ... Traded by Rangers to Kings for LW Kevin Stevens (August 28, 1997). ... Injured right groin and abdomen (February 25, 1998) and underwent surgery; missed final 25 games of regular season. ... Fractured foot (November 3, 1999); missed 10 games.
HONORS: Named to QMJHL All-Star second team (1984-85). ... Won Can.HL Player of the Year Award (1985-86). ... Shared Guy Lafleur Trophy with Sylvain Cote (1985-86). ... Named to QMJHL All-Star first team (1985-86). ... Named to Memorial Cup All-Star team (1985-86). ... Won Calder Memorial Trophy (1986-87). ... Named to THE SPORTING NEWS All-Star second team (1986-87 and 1991-92). ... Named to NHL All-Star second team (1986-87 and 1991-92). ... Named to NHL All-Rookie team (1986-87). ... Named to THE SPORTING NEWS All-Star first team (1987-88 through 1990-91 and 1992-93). ... Played in NHL All-Star Game (1988-1993 and 1999). ... Named to NHL All-Star first team (1987-88 through 1990-91 and 1992-93).
RECORDS: Holds NHL single-season records for most points by a left-winger—125 (1992-93); and most goals by a left-winger—63 (1992-93).
STATISTICAL PLATEAUS: Three-goal games: 1986-87 (1), 1987-88 (3), 1988-89 (1), 1989-90 (2), 1992-93 (2), 1998-99 (1), 1999-00 (1). Total: 11. ... Four-goal games: 1991-92 (1), 1993-94 (1), 1994-95 (1). Total: 3. ... Total hat tricks: 14.
MISCELLANEOUS: Scored on a penalty shot (vs. Eldon Reddick, October 25, 1987; vs. Kay Whitmore, February 6, 1992). ... Failed to score on a penalty shot (vs. Sean Burke, February 2, 1989; vs. Jon Casey, April 3, 1993).

Season Team	League	REGULAR SEASON								PLAYOFFS				
		Gms.	G	A	Pts.	PIM	+/-	PP	SH	Gms.	G	A	Pts.	PIM
83-84—Hull	QMJHL	70	32	53	85	48	...	...	...	—	—	—	—	—
84-85—Hull	QMJHL	64	55	94	149	115	...	...	...	5	4	2	6	27
85-86—Hull	QMJHL	63	68	*123	†191	93	...	...	...	15	17	27	*44	28
86-87—Los Angeles	NHL	79	45	39	84	28	-18	18	0	5	1	4	5	2
87-88—Los Angeles	NHL	80	53	58	111	82	-9	17	0	5	2	5	7	18
88-89—Los Angeles	NHL	78	46	52	98	65	5	10	0	11	2	6	8	10
89-90—Los Angeles	NHL	80	52	49	101	38	8	20	0	10	5	5	10	10
90-91—Los Angeles	NHL	76	45	46	91	68	28	11	0	12	12	4	16	22
91-92—Los Angeles	NHL	80	44	63	107	95	-4	26	0	6	3	4	7	12
92-93—Los Angeles	NHL	84	63	62	125	100	18	24	2	24	9	13	22	28
93-94—Los Angeles	NHL	83	44	42	86	86	-20	24	0	—	—	—	—	—
94-95—Pittsburgh	NHL	46	23	19	42	37	10	5	0	12	7	4	11	26
95-96—New York Rangers	NHL	77	23	46	69	80	13	11	0	11	1	5	6	8
96-97—New York Rangers	NHL	69	24	24	48	48	16	5	0	15	4	7	11	4
97-98—Los Angeles	NHL	57	16	24	40	66	5	5	0	4	1	2	3	6
98-99—Los Angeles	NHL	82	39	35	74	54	-1	11	0	—	—	—	—	—
99-00—Los Angeles	NHL	71	36	38	74	68	11	13	0	4	2	2	4	6
NHL Totals (14 years)		1042	553	597	1150	915	62	200	2	119	49	61	110	152

ROBITAILLE, RANDY　　　　　C　　　　　PREDATORS

PERSONAL: Born October 12, 1975, in Ottawa. ... 5-11/198. ... Shoots left. ... Name pronounced ROH-bih-tigh.
COLLEGE: Miami of Ohio.
TRANSACTIONS/CAREER NOTES: Signed as free agent by Boston Bruins (March 27, 1997). ... Injured shoulder (March 27, 1997); missed remainder of season. ... Traded by Bruins to Atlanta Thrashers for RW Peter Ferraro (June 25, 1999). ... Traded by Thrashers to Nashville Predators for LW Denny Lambert (August 16, 1999).
HONORS: Named to CCHA All-Rookie team (1995-96). ... Named to CCHA All-Star first team (1996-97). ... Named to NCAA All-America (West) first team (1996-97). ... Named to AHL All-Star first team (1998-99). ... Won Les Cunningham Plaque (1998-99).
MISCELLANEOUS: Failed to score on a penalty shot (vs. Mike Richter, January 31, 2000).

Season Team	League	REGULAR SEASON								PLAYOFFS				
		Gms.	G	A	Pts.	PIM	+/-	PP	SH	Gms.	G	A	Pts.	PIM
94-95—Ottawa	CJHL	54	48	77	125	111	...	...	...	—	—	—	—	—
95-96—Miami of Ohio	CCHA	36	14	31	45	26	...	...	...	—	—	—	—	—
96-97—Miami of Ohio	CCHA	39	27	34	61	44	...	...	...	—	—	—	—	—
—Boston	NHL	1	0	0	0	0	0	0	0	—	—	—	—	—
97-98—Providence	AHL	48	15	29	44	16	...	...	...	—	—	—	—	—
—Boston	NHL	4	0	0	0	0	-2	0	0	—	—	—	—	—
98-99—Providence	AHL	74	28	*74	102	34	...	...	...	19	6	†14	20	20
—Boston	NHL	4	0	2	2	0	-1	0	0	1	0	0	0	0
99-00—Nashville	NHL	69	11	14	25	10	-13	2	0	—	—	—	—	—
NHL Totals (4 years)		78	11	16	27	10	-16	2	0	1	0	0	0	0

ROCHE, DAVE   LW   FLAMES   R

PERSONAL: Born June 13, 1975, in Lindsay, Ont. ... 6-4/230. ... Shoots left. ... Brother of Scott Roche, goaltender with St. Louis Blues system (1995-96 through 1998-99). ... Name pronounced ROHCH.

TRANSACTIONS/CAREER NOTES: Selected by Pittsburgh Penguins in third round (third Penguins pick, 62nd overall) of NHL entry draft (June 26, 1993). ... Sprained ankle (November 21, 1995); missed three games. ... Injured shoulder (April 10, 1996); missed eight games. ... Suspended one playoff game and fined $1,000 by NHL for butt-ending opponent (May 26, 1996). ... Traded by Penguins with G Ken Wregget to Calgary Flames for C German Titov and C Todd Hlushko (June 17, 1998). ... Injured knee (January 2, 1999); missed 18 games.

Season Team	League	REGULAR SEASON								PLAYOFFS				
		Gms.	G	A	Pts.	PIM	+/-	PP	SH	Gms.	G	A	Pts.	PIM
90-91—Peterborough Jr. B	OHA	40	22	17	39	85	...	...	...	—	—	—	—	—
91-92—Peterborough	OHL	62	10	17	27	105	...	...	...	10	0	0	0	34
92-93—Peterborough	OHL	56	40	60	100	105	...	...	...	21	14	15	29	42
93-94—Peterborough	OHL	34	15	22	37	127	...	...	...	—	—	—	—	—
—Windsor	OHL	29	14	20	34	73	...	...	...	4	1	1	2	15
94-95—Windsor	OHL	66	55	59	114	180	...	...	...	10	9	6	15	16
95-96—Pittsburgh	NHL	71	7	7	14	130	-5	0	0	16	2	7	9	26
96-97—Pittsburgh	NHL	61	5	5	10	155	-13	2	0	—	—	—	—	—
—Cleveland	IHL	18	5	5	10	25	...	...	...	13	6	3	9	*87
97-98—Syracuse	AHL	73	12	20	32	307	...	...	...	5	2	0	2	10
98-99—Calgary	NHL	36	3	3	6	44	-1	1	0	—	—	—	—	—
—Saint John	AHL	7	0	3	3	6	...	...	...	—	—	—	—	—
99-00—Saint John	AHL	67	22	21	43	130	...	...	...	3	0	1	1	8
—Calgary	NHL	2	0	0	0	5	-1	0	0	—	—	—	—	—
NHL Totals (4 years)		170	15	15	30	334	-20	3	0	16	2	7	9	26

RODGERS, MARC   RW   RED WINGS

PERSONAL: Born March 16, 1972, in Shawville, Que. ... 5-9/185. ... Shoots left.

TRANSACTIONS/CAREER NOTES: Signed as non-drafted free agent by Detroit Red Wings (August 3, 1998). ... Injured leg (December 11, 1999); missed 11 games.

Season Team	League	REGULAR SEASON								PLAYOFFS				
		Gms.	G	A	Pts.	PIM	+/-	PP	SH	Gms.	G	A	Pts.	PIM
89-90—Granby	QMJHL	61	24	31	55	155	...	...	...	—	—	—	—	—
90-91—Granby	QMJHL	64	28	49	77	41	...	...	...	—	—	—	—	—
91-92—Granby	QMJHL	36	30	57	87	49	...	...	...	—	—	—	—	—
—Verdun	QMJHL	29	14	19	33	0	...	...	...	18	3	13	16	26
92-93—Wheeling	ECHL	64	23	40	63	91	...	...	...	6	1	1	2	8
93-94—Las Vegas	IHL	40	7	7	14	110	...	...	...	4	0	2	2	17
94-95—Las Vegas	IHL	58	17	19	36	131	...	...	...	10	2	6	8	25
95-96—Las Vegas	IHL	51	13	16	29	65	...	...	...	21	4	4	8	16
—Utah	IHL	31	6	14	20	51	...	...	...	—	—	—	—	—
96-97—Utah	IHL	5	2	2	4	10	...	...	...	—	—	—	—	—
—Quebec	IHL	70	25	42	67	115	...	...	...	9	1	9	10	14
97-98—Quebec	IHL	61	20	22	42	61	...	...	...	—	—	—	—	—
—Chicago	IHL	11	5	5	10	22	...	...	...	22	9	9	18	10
98-99—Adirondack	AHL	80	19	38	57	66	...	...	...	3	0	0	0	10
99-00—Detroit	NHL	21	1	1	2	10	-3	0	0	—	—	—	—	—
—Manitoba	IHL	34	8	10	18	77	...	...	...	2	1	0	1	6
NHL Totals (1 year)		21	1	1	2	10	-3	0	0	—	—	—	—	—

ROENICK, JEREMY   C   COYOTES

PERSONAL: Born January 17, 1970, in Boston. ... 6-0/207. ... Shoots right. ... Brother of Trevor Roenick, center with Hartford Whalers/Carolina Hurricanes organization (1993-94 through 1996-97). ... Name pronounced ROH-nihk.

HIGH SCHOOL: Thayer Academy (Braintree, Mass.).

TRANSACTIONS/CAREER NOTES: Selected by Chicago Blackhawks in first round (first Blackhawks pick, eighth overall) of NHL entry draft (June 11, 1988). ... Sprained knee ligaments (January 9, 1989); missed one month. ... Played in Europe during 1994-95 NHL lockout. ... Sprained knee ligament (April 2, 1995); missed remainder of regular season and first eight games of playoffs. ... Pulled thigh muscle (March 4, 1996); missed three games. ... Sprained ankle (March 17, 1996); missed 12 games. ... Traded by Blackhawks to Phoenix Coyotes for C Alexei Zhamnov, RW Craig Mills and first-round pick (RW Ty Jones) in 1997 draft (August 16, 1996). ... Missed first four games of 1996-97 season due to contract dispute. ... Sprained knee (November 23, 1996); missed six games. ... Suffered mild concussion (December 5, 1997); missed one game. ... Suffered concussion (December 28, 1998); missed two games. ... Fractured jaw (April 14, 1999); missed final two games of regular season and six playoff games. ... Suspended five games by NHL for slashing incident (October 11, 1999). ... Suffered injury (March 3, 2000); missed one game.

HONORS: Named to QMJHL All-Star second team (1988-89). ... Named NHL Rookie of the Year by THE SPORTING NEWS (1989-90). ... Played in NHL All-Star Game (1991-1994, 1999 and 2000).

MISCELLANEOUS: Holds Phoenix Coyotes record for most assists (120). ... Scored on a penalty shot (vs. Dan Cloutier, December 2, 1999; vs. Tomas Vokoun, March 17, 2000). ... Failed to score on a penalty shot (vs. Andrei Trefilov, March 7, 1995).

STATISTICAL NOTES: Led NHL with 13 game-winning goals (1991-92).

STATISTICAL PLATEAUS: Three-goal games: 1989-90 (1), 1990-91 (2), 1992-93 (1), 1999-00 (2). Total: 6. ... Four-goal games: 1991-92 (1), 1993-94 (1). Total: 2. ... Total hat tricks: 8.

Season Team	League	REGULAR SEASON								PLAYOFFS				
		Gms.	G	A	Pts.	PIM	+/-	PP	SH	Gms.	G	A	Pts.	PIM
86-87—Thayer Academy	Mass. H.S.	24	31	34	65	...	...	...	...	—	—	—	—	—
87-88—Thayer Academy	Mass. H.S.	24	34	50	84	...	...	...	...	—	—	—	—	—
88-89—U.S. national team	Int'l	11	8	8	16	0	...	...	...	—	—	—	—	—
—Chicago	NHL	20	9	9	18	4	4	2	0	10	1	3	4	7
—Hull	QMJHL	28	34	36	70	14	...	...	...	—	—	—	—	—
89-90—Chicago	NHL	78	26	40	66	54	2	6	0	20	11	7	18	8
90-91—Chicago	NHL	79	41	53	94	80	38	15	4	6	3	5	8	4
91-92—Chicago	NHL	80	53	50	103	98	23	22	3	18	12	10	22	12
92-93—Chicago	NHL	84	50	57	107	86	15	22	3	4	1	2	3	2
93-94—Chicago	NHL	84	46	61	107	125	21	24	5	6	1	6	7	2
94-95—Koln	Germany	3	3	1	4	2	...	...	...	—	—	—	—	—
—Chicago	NHL	33	10	24	34	14	5	5	0	8	1	2	3	16
95-96—Chicago	NHL	66	32	35	67	109	9	12	4	10	5	7	12	2
96-97—Phoenix	NHL	72	29	40	69	115	-7	10	3	6	2	4	6	4
97-98—Phoenix	NHL	79	24	32	56	103	5	6	1	6	5	3	8	4
—U.S. Olympic team	Int'l	4	0	1	1	6	...	...	...	—	—	—	—	—
98-99—Phoenix	NHL	78	24	48	72	130	7	4	0	1	0	0	0	0
99-00—Phoenix	NHL	75	34	44	78	102	11	6	3	5	2	2	4	10
NHL Totals (12 years)		828	378	493	871	1020	133	134	26	100	44	51	95	71

ROEST, STACY   C   WILD

PERSONAL: Born March 15, 1974, in Lethbridge, Alta. ... 5-9/185. ... Shoots right.

TRANSACTIONS/CAREER NOTES: Signed as non-drafted free agent by Detroit Red Wings (June 9, 1997). ... Selected by Minnesota Wild in NHL expansion draft (June 23, 2000).

HONORS: Named to WHL All-Star (East) first team (1993-94). ... Named to WHL All-Star (East) second team (1994-95).

Season Team	League	REGULAR SEASON								PLAYOFFS				
		Gms.	G	A	Pts.	PIM	+/-	PP	SH	Gms.	G	A	Pts.	PIM
92-93—Medicine Hat	WHL	72	33	73	106	30	...	...	...	10	3	10	13	6
93-94—Medicine Hat	WHL	72	48	72	120	48	...	...	...	3	1	0	1	4
94-95—Medicine Hat	WHL	69	37	78	115	32	...	...	...	5	2	7	9	2
—Adirondack	AHL	3	0	0	0	0	...	...	...	—	—	—	—	—
95-96—Adirondack	AHL	76	16	39	55	40	...	...	...	3	0	0	0	0
96-97—Adirondack	AHL	78	25	41	66	30	...	...	...	4	1	1	2	0
97-98—Adirondack	AHL	80	34	58	92	30	...	...	...	3	2	1	3	6
98-99—Detroit	NHL	59	4	8	12	14	-7	0	0	—	—	—	—	—
—Adirondack	AHL	2	0	1	1	0	...	...	...	—	—	—	—	—
99-00—Detroit	NHL	49	7	9	16	12	-1	1	0	3	0	0	0	0
NHL Totals (2 years)		108	11	17	28	26	-8	1	0	3	0	0	0	0

ROLOSON, DWAYNE   G   BLUES

PERSONAL: Born October 12, 1969, in Simcoe, Ont. ... 6-1/190. ... Catches left. ... Name pronounced ROH-luh-suhn.

COLLEGE: Massachusetts-Lowell.

TRANSACTIONS/CAREER NOTES: Signed as non-drafted free agent by Calgary Flames (July 4, 1994). ... Signed as free agent by Buffalo Sabres (July 9, 1998). ... Selected by Columbus Blue Jackets in NHL expansion draft (June 23, 2000). ... Signed as free agent by St. Louis Blues (July 14, 2000).

HONORS: Named Hockey East Tournament Most Valuable Player (1993-94).

MISCELLANEOUS: Stopped a penalty shot attempt (vs. Rob Blake, April 13, 1998). ... Allowed a penalty shot goal (vs. Petr Sykora, January 6, 2000).

Season Team	League	REGULAR SEASON								PLAYOFFS						
		Gms.	Min.	W	L	T	GA	SO	Avg.	Gms.	Min.	W	L	GA	SO	Avg.
90-91—Mass.-Lowell	Hockey East	15	823	5	9	0	63	0	4.59	—	—	—	—	—	—	—
91-92—Mass.-Lowell	Hockey East	12	660	3	8	0	52	0	4.73	—	—	—	—	—	—	—
92-93—Mass.-Lowell	Hockey East	39	2342	20	17	2	150	0	3.84	—	—	—	—	—	—	—
93-94—Mass.-Lowell	Hockey East	40	2305	23	10	7	106	0	2.76	—	—	—	—	—	—	—
94-95—Saint John	AHL	46	2734	16	21	8	156	1	3.42	5	299	1	4	13	0	2.61
95-96—Saint John	AHL	67	4026	33	22	11	190	1	2.83	16	1027	10	6	49	1	2.86
96-97—Calgary	NHL	31	1618	9	14	3	78	1	2.89	—	—	—	—	—	—	—
—Saint John	AHL	8	481	6	2	0	22	1	2.74	—	—	—	—	—	—	—
97-98—Saint John	AHL	4	245	3	0	1	8	0	1.96	—	—	—	—	—	—	—
—Calgary	NHL	39	2205	11	16	8	110	0	2.99	—	—	—	—	—	—	—
98-99—Buffalo	NHL	18	911	6	8	2	42	1	2.77	4	139	1	1	10	0	4.32
—Rochester	AHL	2	120	2	0	0	4	0	2.00	—	—	—	—	—	—	—
99-00—Buffalo	NHL	14	677	1	7	3	32	0	2.84	—	—	—	—	—	—	—
NHL Totals (4 years)		102	5411	27	45	16	262	2	2.91	4	139	1	1	10	0	4.32

ROLSTON, BRIAN   C/LW   BRUINS

PERSONAL: Born February 21, 1973, in Flint, Mich. ... 6-2/205. ... Shoots left.
COLLEGE: Lake Superior State (Mich.).
TRANSACTIONS/CAREER NOTES: Selected by New Jersey Devils in first round (second Devils pick, 11th overall) of NHL entry draft (June 22, 1991). ... Loaned by Devils to U.S. Olympic Team (November 2, 1993). ... Fractured foot (October 17, 1995); missed 11 games. ... Injured hamstring (January 12, 1998); missed one game. ... Suffered from the flu (January 28, 1998); missed one game. ... Traded by Devils with a conditional third-round pick in the 2001 draft to Colorado Avalanche for RW Claude Lemieux, second-round pick (D Matt DeMarchi) in 2000 draft and swap of first-round picks in 2000 draft (November 3, 1999). ... Bruised ankle (January 27, 2000); missed three games. ... Traded by Avalanche with D Martin Grenier, C Samual Pahlsson and first-round pick (LW Martin Samuelsson) in 2000 draft to Boston Bruins for D Ray Bourque and LW Dave Andreychuk (March 6, 2000).
HONORS: Named to NCAA All-Tournament team (1991-92 and 1992-93). ... Named to NCAA All-America (West) second team (1992-93). ... Named to CCHA All-Star first team (1992-93).
MISCELLANEOUS: Member of Stanley Cup championship team (1995).
STATISTICAL PLATEAUS: Three-goal games: 1996-97 (1).

		REGULAR SEASON								PLAYOFFS				
Season Team	League	Gms.	G	A	Pts.	PIM	+/-	PP	SH	Gms.	G	A	Pts.	PIM
89-90—Detroit Compuware.....	NAJHL	40	36	37	73	57	...	...	...	—	—	—	—	—
90-91—Detroit Compuware.....	NAJHL	36	49	46	95	14	...	...	...	—	—	—	—	—
91-92—Lake Superior State ...	CCHA	41	18	28	46	16	...	...	...	—	—	—	—	—
92-93—Lake Superior State ...	CCHA	39	33	31	64	20	...	...	...	—	—	—	—	—
—U.S. Jr. national team .	Int'l	7	6	2	8	2	...	...	...	—	—	—	—	—
93-94—U.S. national team	Int'l	41	20	28	48	36	...	...	...	—	—	—	—	—
—U.S. Olympic team......	Int'l	8	7	0	7	8	...	...	...	—	—	—	—	—
—Albany......................	AHL	17	5	5	10	8	...	...	...	5	1	2	3	0
94-95—Albany......................	AHL	18	9	11	20	10	...	...	...	—	—	—	—	—
—New Jersey..............	NHL	40	7	11	18	17	5	2	0	6	2	1	3	4
95-96—New Jersey..............	NHL	58	13	11	24	8	9	3	1	—	—	—	—	—
96-97—New Jersey..............	NHL	81	18	27	45	20	6	2	2	10	4	1	5	6
97-98—New Jersey..............	NHL	76	16	14	30	16	7	0	2	6	1	0	1	2
98-99—New Jersey..............	NHL	82	24	33	57	14	11	5	†5	7	1	0	1	2
99-00—New Jersey..............	NHL	11	3	1	4	0	-2	1	0	—	—	—	—	—
—Colorado..................	NHL	50	8	10	18	12	-6	1	0	—	—	—	—	—
—Boston	NHL	16	5	4	9	6	-4	3	0	—	—	—	—	—
NHL Totals (6 years)...........		414	94	111	205	93	26	17	10	29	8	2	10	14

ROMINISKI, DALE   RW   LIGHTNING

PERSONAL: Born October 1, 1975, in Farmington Hills, Mich. ... 6-2/200. ... Shoots right.
HIGH SCHOOL: Brother Rice (Birmingham, Mich.).
COLLEGE: Michigan.
TRANSACTIONS/CAREER NOTES: Signed as non-drafted free agent by Tampa Bay Lightning (July 16, 1999).

		REGULAR SEASON								PLAYOFFS				
Season Team	League	Gms.	G	A	Pts.	PIM	+/-	PP	SH	Gms.	G	A	Pts.	PIM
94-95—Detroit Compuware.....	NAHL	40	21	21	42	30	...	...	...	—	—	—	—	—
95-96—Univ. of Michigan........	CCHA	42	8	8	16	39	...	...	...	—	—	—	—	—
96-97—Univ. of Michigan........	CCHA	44	7	9	16	62	...	...	...	—	—	—	—	—
97-98—Univ. of Michigan........	CCHA	54	10	17	27	106	...	...	...	—	—	—	—	—
98-99—Univ. of Michigan........	CCHA	47	18	8	26	86	...	...	...	—	—	—	—	—
99-00—Detroit......................	IHL	78	14	15	29	68	...	...	...	—	—	—	—	—
—Tampa Bay..................	NHL	3	0	1	1	2	1	0	0	—	—	—	—	—
NHL Totals (1 year).............		3	0	1	1	2	1	0	0	—	—	—	—	—

RONNING, CLIFF   C   PREDATORS

PERSONAL: Born October 1, 1965, in Vancouver. ... 5-8/165. ... Shoots left.
HIGH SCHOOL: Burnaby North (B.C.).
TRANSACTIONS/CAREER NOTES: Selected by St. Louis Blues as underage junior in seventh round (ninth Blues pick, 134th overall) of NHL entry draft (June 9, 1984). ... Injured groin (November 1988). ... Agreed to play in Italy for 1989-90 season (August 1989). ... Fractured right index finger (November 12, 1990); missed 12 games. ... Traded by Blues with LW Geoff Courtnall, D Robert Dirk, LW Sergio Momesso and fifth-round pick (RW Brian Loney) in 1992 draft to Vancouver Canucks for C Dan Quinn and D Garth Butcher (March 5, 1991). ... Sprained hand (January 4, 1993); missed five games. ... Separated shoulder (January 8, 1994); missed eight games. ... Strained groin (February 9, 1995); missed four games. ... Injured groin (October 8, 1995); missed two games. ... Signed as free agent by Phoenix Coyotes (July 2, 1996). ... Fractured hand (October 10, 1996); missed 12 games. ... Suffered from the flu (December 17, 1996); missed one game. ... Traded by Coyotes with D Richard Lintner to Nashville Predators for future considerations (October 31, 1998). ... Bruised knee (April 14, 1999); missed one game.
HONORS: Won Stewart (Butch) Paul Memorial Trophy (1983-84). ... Named to WHL All-Star second team (1983-84). ... Won WHL Most Valuable Player Trophy (1984-85). ... Won Bob Brownridge Memorial Trophy (1984-85). ... Won Frank Boucher Memorial Trophy (1984-85). ... Named to WHL (West) All-Star first team (1984-85).
MISCELLANEOUS: Holds Nashville Predators all-time records for most goals (44), assists (71) and most points (115).
STATISTICAL PLATEAUS: Three-goal games: 1986-87 (1), 1992-93 (1), 1995-96 (1). Total: 3.

		REGULAR SEASON								PLAYOFFS				
Season Team	League	Gms.	G	A	Pts.	PIM	+/-	PP	SH	Gms.	G	A	Pts.	PIM
82-83—New Westminster	BCJHL	52	82	68	150	42	...	...	...	—	—	—	—	—
83-84—New Westminster	WHL	71	69	67	136	10	...	...	...	9	8	13	21	10
84-85—New Westminster	WHL	70	*89	108	*197	20	...	...	...	11	10	14	24	4

R

Season Team	League	REGULAR SEASON								PLAYOFFS				
		Gms.	G	A	Pts.	PIM	+/-	PP	SH	Gms.	G	A	Pts.	PIM
85-86—Canadian nat'l team	Int'l	71	55	63	118	53	...	...	...	—	—	—	—	—
—St. Louis	NHL	—	—	—	—	—	—	—	—	5	1	1	2	2
86-87—Canadian nat'l team	Int'l	26	16	16	32	12	...	...	...	—	—	—	—	—
—St. Louis	NHL	42	11	14	25	6	-1	2	0	4	0	1	1	0
87-88—St. Louis	NHL	26	5	8	13	12	6	1	0	—	—	—	—	—
88-89—St. Louis	NHL	64	24	31	55	18	3	16	0	7	1	3	4	0
—Peoria	IHL	12	11	20	31	8	...	...	...	—	—	—	—	—
89-90—Asiago	Italy	42	76	60	136	30	...	...	...	6	7	12	19	4
90-91—St. Louis	NHL	48	14	18	32	10	2	5	0	—	—	—	—	—
—Vancouver	NHL	11	6	6	12	0	-2	2	0	6	6	3	9	12
91-92—Vancouver	NHL	80	24	47	71	42	18	6	0	13	8	5	13	6
92-93—Vancouver	NHL	79	29	56	85	30	19	10	0	12	2	9	11	6
93-94—Vancouver	NHL	76	25	43	68	42	7	10	0	24	5	10	15	16
94-95—Vancouver	NHL	41	6	19	25	27	-4	3	0	11	3	5	8	2
95-96—Vancouver	NHL	79	22	45	67	42	16	5	0	6	0	2	2	6
96-97—Phoenix	NHL	69	19	32	51	26	-9	8	0	7	0	7	7	12
97-98—Phoenix	NHL	80	11	44	55	36	5	3	0	6	1	3	4	4
98-99—Phoenix	NHL	7	2	5	7	2	3	2	0	—	—	—	—	—
—Nashville	NHL	72	18	35	53	40	-6	8	0	—	—	—	—	—
99-00—Nashville	NHL	82	26	36	62	34	-13	7	0	—	—	—	—	—
NHL Totals (14 years)		856	242	439	681	367	44	88	0	101	27	49	76	66

ROSA, PAVEL   RW/LW   KINGS

PERSONAL: Born June 7, 1977, in Most, Czechoslovakia. ... 5-11/188. ... Shoots right.
TRANSACTIONS/CAREER NOTES: Selected by Los Angeles Kings in second round (third Kings pick, 50th overall) of NHL entry draft (July 8, 1995).
HONORS: Won Michel Bergeron Trophy (1995-96). ... Named to QMJHL All-Rookie team (1995-96). ... Won Can.HL Top Scorer Award (1996-97). ... Won Jean Beliveau Trophy (1996-97). ... Named to Can.HL All-Star first team (1996-97). ... Named to QMJHL All-Star first team (1996-97).

Season Team	League	REGULAR SEASON								PLAYOFFS				
		Gms.	G	A	Pts.	PIM	+/-	PP	SH	Gms.	G	A	Pts.	PIM
94-95—Chem. Litvinov Jrs......	Czech Rep.	40	56	42	98	...	...	...	...	—	—	—	—	—
—Chem. Litvinov..........	Czech Rep.	—	—	—	—	—	...	...	...	1	0	0	0	0
95-96—Hull..................	QMJHL	61	46	70	116	39	...	...	...	18	14	22	36	25
96-97—Hull..................	QMJHL	68	*63	*89	*152	56	...	...	...	14	18	13	31	16
97-98—Fredericton	AHL	1	0	0	0	0	...	...	...	—	—	—	—	—
—Long Beach..............	IHL	2	0	1	1	0	...	...	...	1	1	1	2	0
98-99—Long Beach..........	IHL	31	17	13	30	28	...	...	...	6	1	2	3	0
—Los Angeles............	NHL	29	4	12	16	6	0	0	0	—	—	—	—	—
99-00—Long Beach..........	IHL	74	22	31	53	76	...	...	...	6	2	2	4	4
—Los Angeles............	NHL	3	0	0	0	0	-1	0	0	—	—	—	—	—
NHL Totals (2 years)..........		32	4	12	16	6	-1	0	0	—	—	—	—	—

ROUSE, BOB   D

PERSONAL: Born June 18, 1964, in Surrey, B.C. ... 6-2/225. ... Shoots right. ... Name pronounced ROWZ.
TRANSACTIONS/CAREER NOTES: Selected by Minnesota North Stars as underage junior in fourth round (third North Stars pick, 80th overall) of NHL entry draft (June 9, 1982). ... Bruised hip (January 1988). ... Traded by North Stars with RW Dino Ciccarelli to Washington Capitals for RW Mike Gartner and D Larry Murphy (March 7, 1989). ... Sprained right knee (December 12, 1989); missed eight games. ... Traded by Capitals with C Peter Zezel to Toronto Maple Leafs for D Al Iafrate (January 16, 1991). ... Fractured collarbone (February 16, 1991). ... Suspended four games by NHL for stick-swinging incident (October 14, 1993). ... Strained knee (December 29, 1993); missed three games. ... Tore knee cartilage (January 29, 1994); missed 14 games. ... Signed as free agent by Detroit Red Wings (August 5, 1994). ... Underwent hernia surgery (September 9, 1995); missed five games. ... Fractured orbital bone around eye (May 14, 1996); missed remainder of playoffs. ... Strained groin (December 27, 1996); missed four games. ... Suffered from the flu (March 26, 1997); missed two games. ... Signed as free agent by San Jose Sharks (July 13, 1998). ... Injured foot (March 28, 1999); missed five games. ... Released by Sharks (January 5, 2000).
HONORS: Won Top Defenseman Trophy (1983-84). ... Named to WHL (East) All-Star first team (1983-84).
MISCELLANEOUS: Member of Stanley Cup championship team (1997 and 1998). ... Captain of Minnesota North Stars (1988-89).

Season Team	League	REGULAR SEASON								PLAYOFFS				
		Gms.	G	A	Pts.	PIM	+/-	PP	SH	Gms.	G	A	Pts.	PIM
80-81—Billings..............	WHL	70	0	13	13	116	...	...	...	5	0	0	0	2
81-82—Billings..............	WHL	71	7	22	29	209	...	...	...	5	0	2	2	10
82-83—Nanaimo	WHL	29	7	20	27	86	...	...	...	—	—	—	—	—
—Lethbridge..............	WHL	42	8	30	38	82	...	...	...	20	2	13	15	55
83-84—Lethbridge..........	WHL	71	18	42	60	101	...	...	...	5	0	1	1	28
—Minnesota..............	NHL	1	0	0	0	0	0	0	0	—	—	—	—	—
84-85—Springfield..........	AHL	8	0	3	3	6	...	...	...	—	—	—	—	—
—Minnesota..............	NHL	63	2	9	11	113	-14	0	0	—	—	—	—	—
85-86—Minnesota..........	NHL	75	1	14	15	151	15	0	0	3	0	0	0	2
86-87—Minnesota..........	NHL	72	2	10	12	179	6	0	0	—	—	—	—	—
87-88—Minnesota..........	NHL	74	0	12	12	168	-30	0	0	—	—	—	—	—
88-89—Minnesota..........	NHL	66	4	13	17	124	-5	0	1	—	—	—	—	—
—Washington............	NHL	13	0	2	2	36	2	0	0	6	2	0	2	4
89-90—Washington........	NHL	70	4	16	20	123	-2	0	0	15	2	3	5	47
90-91—Washington........	NHL	47	5	15	20	65	-7	1	0	—	—	—	—	—
—Toronto................	NHL	13	2	4	6	10	-11	1	0	—	—	—	—	—
91-92—Toronto............	NHL	79	3	19	22	97	-20	1	0	—	—	—	—	—

Season Team	League	Gms.	G	A	Pts.	PIM	+/-	PP	SH	Gms.	G	A	Pts.	PIM
92-93—Toronto	NHL	82	3	11	14	130	7	0	1	21	3	8	11	29
93-94—Toronto	NHL	63	5	11	16	101	8	1	1	18	0	3	3	29
94-95—Detroit	NHL	48	1	7	8	36	14	0	0	18	0	3	3	8
95-96—Detroit	NHL	58	0	6	6	48	5	0	0	7	0	1	1	4
96-97—Detroit	NHL	70	4	9	13	58	8	0	2	20	0	0	0	55
97-98—Detroit	NHL	71	1	11	12	57	-9	0	0	22	0	3	3	16
98-99—San Jose	NHL	70	0	11	11	44	0	0	0	6	0	0	0	6
99-00—San Jose	NHL	26	0	1	1	19	-3	0	0	—	—	—	—	—
NHL Totals (17 years)		1061	37	181	218	1559	-36	4	5	136	7	21	28	200

ROUSSEL, DOMINIC — G — MIGHTY DUCKS

R

PERSONAL: Born February 22, 1970, in Hull, Que. ... 6-1/191. ... Catches left. ... Name pronounced roo-SEHL.

TRANSACTIONS/CAREER NOTES: Selected by Philadelphia Flyers as underage junior in third round (fourth Flyers pick, 63rd overall) of NHL entry draft (June 11, 1988). ... Pulled groin (November 29, 1992); missed three games. ... Reinjured groin (December 11, 1992); missed 11 games. ... Suffered from the flu (March 24, 1994); missed three games. ... Suffered inner ear infection (March 2, 1995); missed five games. ... Traded by Flyers to Winnipeg Jets for G Tim Cheveldae and third-round pick (RW Chester Gallant) in 1996 draft (February 27, 1996). ... Signed as free agent by Flyers (July 10, 1996). ... Traded by Flyers with D Jeff Staples to Nashville Predators for seventh-round pick (G Cam Ondrik) in 1998 draft (June 27, 1998). ... Traded by Predators to Mighty Ducks of Anaheim for G Chris Mason and D Marc Moro (October 5, 1998). ... Suffered back spasms (April 7, 1999); missed two games.

MISCELLANEOUS: Stopped a penalty shot attempt (vs. Stan Drulia, October 15, 1999).

Season Team	League	Gms.	Min	W	L	T	GA	SO	Avg.	Gms.	Min.	W	L	GA	SO	Avg.
87-88—Trois-Rivieres	QMJHL	51	2905	18	25	4	251	0	5.18	—	—	—	—	—	—	—
88-89—Shawinigan	QMJHL	46	2555	24	15	2	171	0	4.02	10	638	6	4	36	0	3.39
89-90—Shawinigan	QMJHL	37	1985	20	14	1	133	0	4.02	2	120	1	1	12	0	6.00
90-91—Hershey	AHL	45	2507	20	14	7	151	1	3.61	7	366	3	4	21	0	3.44
91-92—Hershey	AHL	35	2040	15	11	6	121	1	3.56	—	—	—	—	—	—	—
—Philadelphia	NHL	17	922	7	8	2	40	1	2.60	—	—	—	—	—	—	—
92-93—Philadelphia	NHL	34	1769	13	11	5	111	1	3.76	—	—	—	—	—	—	—
—Hershey	AHL	6	372	0	3	3	23	0	3.71	—	—	—	—	—	—	—
93-94—Philadelphia	NHL	60	3285	29	20	5	183	1	3.34	—	—	—	—	—	—	—
94-95—Philadelphia	NHL	19	1075	11	7	0	42	1	2.34	1	23	0	0	0	0	...
—Hershey	AHL	1	59	0	1	0	5	0	5.08	—	—	—	—	—	—	—
95-96—Philadelphia	NHL	9	456	2	3	2	22	1	2.89	—	—	—	—	—	—	—
—Hershey	AHL	12	689	4	4	3	32	0	2.79	—	—	—	—	—	—	—
—Winnipeg	NHL	7	285	2	2	0	16	0	3.37	—	—	—	—	—	—	—
96-97—Philadelphia	AHL	36	1852	18	9	3	82	2	2.66	1	26	0	0	3	0	6.92
97-98—Canadian nat'l team	Int'l	41	2307	25	12	1	86	5	2.24	—	—	—	—	—	—	—
98-99—Anaheim	NHL	18	884	4	5	4	37	1	2.51	—	—	—	—	—	—	—
99-00—Anaheim	NHL	20	988	6	5	3	52	1	3.16	—	—	—	—	—	—	—
NHL Totals (7 years)		184	9664	74	61	21	503	7	3.12	1	23	0	0	0	0	...

ROY, ANDRE — RW — SENATORS

PERSONAL: Born February 8, 1975, in Port Chester, N.Y. ... 6-4/213. ... Shoots left. ... Full Name: Andre Christopher Roy. ... Name pronounced WAH.

TRANSACTIONS/CAREER NOTES: Selected by Boston Bruins in sixth round (fifth Bruins pick, 151st overall) of NHL entry draft (June 29, 1994). ... Signed as free agent by Ottawa Senators (March 19, 1999). ... Injured right knee (November 18, 1999); missed one game.

Season Team	League	Gms.	G	A	Pts.	PIM	+/-	PP	SH	Gms.	G	A	Pts.	PIM
93-94—Beauport	QMJHL	33	6	7	13	125	...	...	...	—	—	—	—	—
—Chicoutimi	QMJHL	32	4	14	18	152	...	...	...	25	3	6	9	94
94-95—Chicoutimi	QMJHL	20	15	8	23	90	...	...	...	—	—	—	—	—
—Drummondville	QMJHL	34	18	13	31	233	...	...	...	4	2	0	2	34
95-96—Providence	AHL	58	7	8	15	167	...	...	...	1	0	0	0	10
—Boston	NHL	3	0	0	0	0	0	0	0	—	—	—	—	—
96-97—Providence	AHL	50	17	11	28	234	...	...	...	—	—	—	—	—
—Boston	NHL	10	0	2	2	12	-5	0	0	—	—	—	—	—
97-98—Providence	AHL	36	3	11	14	154	...	...	...	—	—	—	—	—
—Charlotte	ECHL	27	10	8	18	132	...	...	...	7	2	3	5	34
98-99—Fort Wayne	IHL	65	15	6	21	395	...	...	...	2	0	0	0	11
99-00—Ottawa	NHL	73	4	3	7	145	3	0	0	5	0	0	0	2
NHL Totals (3 years)		86	4	5	9	157	-2	0	0	5	0	0	0	2

ROY, PATRICK — G — AVALANCHE

PERSONAL: Born October 5, 1965, in Quebec City. ... 6-0/192. ... Catches left. ... Name pronounced WAH.

TRANSACTIONS/CAREER NOTES: Selected by Montreal Canadiens in third round (fourth Canadiens pick, 51st overall) of NHL entry draft (June 9, 1984). ... Suspended eight games by NHL for slashing (October 19, 1987). ... Sprained left knee ligaments (December 12, 1990); missed nine games. ... Tore left ankle ligaments (January 27, 1991); missed 14 games. ... Reinjured left ankle (March 16, 1991). ... Strained hip flexor (March 6, 1993); missed two games. ... Suffered stiff neck (December 11, 1993); missed two games. ... Strained neck (December 22, 1993); missed four games. ... Traded by Canadiens with RW Mike Keane to Colorado Avalanche for G Jocelyn Thibault, LW Martin Rucinsky and RW Andrei Kovalenko (December 6, 1995). ... Sprained thumb (January 23, 1997); missed two games. ... Injured shoulder (March 26, 1997); missed two games. ... Partially dislocated shoulder (November 17, 1997); missed two games. ... Injured left knee (December 26, 1998); missed four games. ... Suffered back spasms (January 4, 1999); missed four games. ... Injured groin (February 21, 1999); missed two games. ... Injured neck (February 15, 2000); missed one game. ... Injured groin (February 18, 2000); missed two games.

HONORS: Won Conn Smythe Trophy (1985-86 and 1992-93). ... Named to NHL All-Rookie team (1985-86). ... Shared William M. Jennings Trophy with Brian Hayward (1986-87 through 1988-89). ... Named to NHL All-Star second team (1987-88 and 1990-91). ... Named to THE SPORTING NEWS All-Star first team (1988-89, 1989-90 and 1991-92). ... Won Trico Goaltender Award (1988-89 and 1989-90). ... Named to NHL All-Star first team (1988-89, 1989-90 and 1991-92). ... Won Vezina Trophy (1988-89, 1989-90 and 1991-92). ... Played in NHL All-Star Game (1988, 1990-1994, 1997 and 1998). ... Named to THE SPORTING NEWS All-Star second team (1990-91). ... Won William M. Jennings Trophy (1991-92).

RECORDS: Holds NHL career record for most 30-or-more win seasons by goaltender—10. ... Holds NHL career playoff records for most games played by goaltender—196; most wins by goaltender—121; and most minutes played by goaltender —12,094. ... Shares NHL career playoff record for most shutouts—15. ... Shares NHL single-season playoff records for most wins by goaltender—16 (1993 and 1996); and most consecutive wins by goaltender—11 (1993).

MISCELLANEOUS: Member of Stanley Cup championship team (1986, 1993 and 1996). ... Holds Colorado Avalanche franchise all-time records for most games played in by a goalie (290), wins (155), shutouts (19) and goals-against average (2.37). ... Stopped a penalty shot attempt (vs. Dan Daoust, January 1, 1986; vs. Ville Peltonen, March 5, 1996; vs. Jamie Baker, March 28, 1996; vs. Andrew Cassels, November 30, 1999). ... Allowed a penalty shot goal (vs. Michel Goulet, January 10, 1987; vs. Jock Callender, March 18, 1989; vs. Pierre Turgeon, October 17, 1990; vs. Kevin Miller, October 10, 1991; vs. Theoren Fleury, October 22, 1996; vs. Tom Chorske, March 7, 1998).

STATISTICAL NOTES: Led NHL in save percentage with .900 in 1987-88, .908 in 1988-89, .912 in 1989-90 and .914 in 1991-92.

| | | | | REGULAR SEASON | | | | | | | | PLAYOFFS | | | | |
Season Team	League	Gms.	Min	W	L	T	GA	SO	Avg.	Gms.	Min.	W	L	GA	SO	Avg.
82-83—Granby	QMJHL	54	2808	13	35	1	293	0	6.26	—	—	—	—	—	—	—
83-84—Granby	QMJHL	61	3585	29	29	1	265	0	4.44	4	244	0	4	22	0	5.41
84-85—Granby	QMJHL	44	2463	16	25	1	228	0	5.55	—	—	—	—	—	—	—
—Montreal	NHL	1	20	1	0	0	0	0	...	—	—	—	—	—	—	—
—Sherbrooke	AHL	1	60	1	0	0	4	0	4.00	*13	*769	10	3	37	0	*2.89
85-86—Montreal	NHL	47	2651	23	18	3	148	1	3.35	20	1218	*15	5	39	†1	1.92
86-87—Montreal	NHL	46	2686	22	16	6	131	1	2.93	6	330	4	2	22	0	4.00
87-88—Montreal	NHL	45	2586	23	12	9	125	3	2.90	8	430	3	4	24	0	3.35
88-89—Montreal	NHL	48	2744	33	5	6	113	4	*2.47	19	1206	13	6	42	2	*2.09
89-90—Montreal	NHL	54	3173	31	16	5	134	3	2.53	11	641	5	6	26	1	2.43
90-91—Montreal	NHL	48	2835	25	15	6	128	1	2.71	13	785	7	5	40	0	3.06
91-92—Montreal	NHL	67	3935	36	22	8	155	†5	*2.36	11	686	4	7	30	1	2.62
92-93—Montreal	NHL	62	3595	31	25	5	192	2	3.20	20	1293	*16	4	46	0	*2.13
93-94—Montreal	NHL	68	3867	35	17	11	161	†7	2.50	6	375	3	3	16	0	2.56
94-95—Montreal	NHL	†43	2566	17	20	6	127	1	2.97	—	—	—	—	—	—	—
95-96—Montreal	NHL	22	1260	12	9	1	62	1	2.95	—	—	—	—	—	—	—
—Colorado	NHL	39	2305	22	15	1	103	1	2.68	22	*1454	*16	6	*51	*3	2.10
96-97—Colorado	NHL	62	3698	*38	15	7	143	7	2.32	17	1034	10	7	38	3	2.21
97-98—Colorado	NHL	65	3835	31	19	13	153	4	2.39	7	430	4	3	18	0	2.51
—Can. Olympic team	Int'l	6	369	4	2	0	9	1	1.46	—	—	—	—	—	—	—
98-99—Colorado	NHL	61	3648	32	19	8	139	5	2.29	19	1173	11	†8	*52	1	2.66
99-00—Colorado	NHL	63	3704	32	21	8	141	2	2.28	17	1039	11	6	31	3	1.79
NHL Totals (16 years)		841	49108	444	264	103	2155	48	2.63	196	12094	121	73	475	15	2.36

ROZSIVAL, MICHAL — D — PENGUINS

PERSONAL: Born September 3, 1978, in Vlasim, Czechoslovakia. ... 6-1/208. ... Shoots right. ... Name pronounced RAH-sih-vahl.

TRANSACTIONS/CAREER NOTES: Selected by Pittsburgh Penguins in fourth round (fifth Penguins pick, 105th overall) of NHL entry draft (June 22, 1996). ... Strained hip flexor (March 21, 2000); missed two games.

HONORS: Named to Can.HL All-Star second team (1997-98). ... Won Bill Hunter Trophy (1997-98). ... Named to WHL (East) All-Star first team (1997-98).

| | | | | REGULAR SEASON | | | | | | PLAYOFFS | | | | |
Season Team	League	Gms.	G	A	Pts.	PIM	+/-	PP	SH	Gms.	G	A	Pts.	PIM
94-95—Czech Rep.	Czech Rep.	31	8	13	21	...	...	...	...	—	—	—	—	—
95-96—Czech Rep.	Czech Rep.	36	3	4	7	...	...	...	...	—	—	—	—	—
96-97—Swift Current	WHL	63	8	31	39	80	...	...	...	10	0	6	6	15
97-98—Swift Current	WHL	71	14	55	69	122	...	...	...	12	0	5	5	33
98-99—Syracuse	AHL	49	3	22	25	72	...	...	...	—	—	—	—	—
99-00—Pittsburgh	NHL	75	4	17	21	48	11	1	0	2	0	0	0	4
NHL Totals (1 year)		75	4	17	21	48	11	1	0	2	0	0	0	4

RUCCHIN, STEVE — C — MIGHTY DUCKS

PERSONAL: Born July 4, 1971, in Thunder Bay, Ont. ... 6-2/212. ... Shoots left. ... Full Name: Steven Andrew Rucchin. ... Name pronounced ROO-chihn.

COLLEGE: Western Ontario.

TRANSACTIONS/CAREER NOTES: Selected by Mighty Ducks of Anaheim in first round (first Mighty Ducks pick, second overall) of NHL supplemental draft (June 28, 1994). ... Suffered from the flu (March 7, 1995); missed two games. ... Sprained left knee (November 27, 1995); missed 18 games. ... Strained groin (October 3, 1997); missed eight games. ... Strained left knee (April 9, 1998); missed two games. ... Injured groin (March 18, 1999); missed three games. ... Reinjured groin (March 31, 1999); missed seven games. ... Suffered infected left ankle (December 28, 1999); missed 11 games.

HONORS: Named OUAA Player of the Year (1993-94). ... Named to CIAU All-Star first team (1993-94).

| | | | | REGULAR SEASON | | | | | | PLAYOFFS | | | | |
Season Team	League	Gms.	G	A	Pts.	PIM	+/-	PP	SH	Gms.	G	A	Pts.	PIM
90-91—Univ. of W. Ontario	OUAA	34	13	16	29	14	...	...	...	—	—	—	—	—
91-92—Univ. of W. Ontario	OUAA	37	28	34	62	36	...	...	...	—	—	—	—	—
92-93—Univ. of W. Ontario	OUAA	34	22	26	48	16	...	...	...	—	—	—	—	—
93-94—Univ. of W. Ontario	OUAA	35	30	23	53	30	...	...	...	—	—	—	—	—
94-95—San Diego	IHL	41	11	15	26	14	...	...	...	—	—	—	—	—
—Anaheim	NHL	43	6	11	17	23	7	0	0	—	—	—	—	—

Season Team	League	REGULAR SEASON								PLAYOFFS				
		Gms.	G	A	Pts.	PIM	+/-	PP	SH	Gms.	G	A	Pts.	PIM
95-96—Anaheim	NHL	64	19	25	44	12	3	8	1	—	—	—	—	—
96-97—Anaheim	NHL	79	19	48	67	24	26	6	1	8	1	2	3	10
97-98—Anaheim	NHL	72	17	36	53	13	8	8	1	—	—	—	—	—
98-99—Anaheim	NHL	69	23	39	62	22	11	5	1	4	0	3	3	0
99-00—Anaheim	NHL	71	19	38	57	16	9	10	0	—	—	—	—	—
NHL Totals (6 years)		398	103	197	300	110	64	37	4	12	1	5	6	10

RUCINSKY, MARTIN — LW — CANADIENS

PERSONAL: Born March 11, 1971, in Most, Czechoslovakia. ... 6-1/205. ... Shoots left. ... Name pronounced roo-SHIHN-skee.

TRANSACTIONS/CAREER NOTES: Selected by Edmonton Oilers in first round (second Oilers pick, 20th overall) of NHL entry draft (June 22, 1991). ... Traded by Oilers to Quebec Nordiques for G Ron Tugnutt and LW Brad Zavisha (March 10, 1992). ... Suffered from the flu (February 28, 1993); missed one game. ... Bruised buttocks (December 3, 1994); missed one game. ... Sprained right wrist (January 11, 1994); missed one game. ... Fractured left cheekbone (January 30, 1994); missed four games. ... Suffered hairline fracture of right wrist (March 7, 1994); missed one game. ... Reinjured right wrist (March 21, 1994); missed six games. ... Reinjured right wrist (April 5, 1994); missed one game. ... Played in Europe during 1994-95 NHL lockout. ... Separated shoulder (February 25, 1995); missed 17 games. ... Reinjured shoulder (April 6, 1995); missed remainder of season. ... Nordiques franchise moved to Colorado and renamed Avalanche for 1995-96 season (June 21, 1995). ... Injured groin (November 28, 1995); missed one game. ... Traded by Avalanche with G Jocelyn Thibault and RW Andrei Kovalenko to Montreal Canadiens for G Patrick Roy and RW Mike Keane (December 6, 1995). ... Sprained right knee (April 6, 1996); missed two games. ... Injured hand (October 19, 1996); missed one game. ... Strained knee (November 25, 1996); missed one game. ... Separated shoulder (December 28, 1996); missed 10 games. ... Bruised foot (October 17, 1997); missed one game. ... Sprained ankle (April 4, 1998); missed three games. ... Injured shoulder (March 6, 1999); missed three games. ... Suffered concussion (November 16, 1999); missed one game. ... Suffered back spasms (March 25, 2000); missed one game.

HONORS: Played in NHL All-Star Game (2000).

MISCELLANEOUS: Mermber of gold-medal-winning Czech Republic Olympic team (1998). ... Failed to score on a penalty shot (vs. Corey Hirsch, January 2, 1999; vs. Jamie Storr, December 11, 1999).

STATISTICAL PLATEAUS: Three-goal games: 1995-96 (1), 1996-97 (1). Total: 2.

Season Team	League	REGULAR SEASON								PLAYOFFS				
		Gms.	G	A	Pts.	PIM	+/-	PP	SH	Gms.	G	A	Pts.	PIM
88-89—CHZ Litvinov	Czech.	3	1	0	1	2	...	...	...	—	—	—	—	—
89-90—CHZ Litvinov	Czech.	47	12	6	18	...	...	...	...	—	—	—	—	—
90-91—CHZ Litvinov	Czech.	49	23	18	41	79	...	...	...	—	—	—	—	—
—Czechoslovakia Jr.	Czech.	7	9	5	14	2	...	...	...	—	—	—	—	—
91-92—Cape Breton	AHL	35	11	12	23	34	...	...	...	—	—	—	—	—
—Edmonton	NHL	2	0	0	0	0	-3	0	0	—	—	—	—	—
—Halifax	AHL	7	1	1	2	6	...	...	...	—	—	—	—	—
—Quebec	NHL	4	1	1	2	2	1	0	0	—	—	—	—	—
92-93—Quebec	NHL	77	18	30	48	51	16	4	0	6	1	1	2	4
93-94—Quebec	NHL	60	9	23	32	58	4	4	0	—	—	—	—	—
94-95—Chem. Litvinov	Czech Rep.	13	12	10	22	34	...	...	...	—	—	—	—	—
—Quebec	NHL	20	3	6	9	14	5	0	0	—	—	—	—	—
95-96—Colorado	NHL	22	4	11	15	14	10	0	0	—	—	—	—	—
—Montreal	NHL	56	25	35	60	54	8	9	2	—	—	—	—	—
96-97—Montreal	NHL	70	28	27	55	62	1	6	3	5	0	0	0	4
97-98—Montreal	NHL	78	21	32	53	84	13	5	3	10	3	0	3	4
—Czech Rep. Oly. team	Int'l	6	3	1	4	4	...	...	...	—	—	—	—	—
98-99—Montreal	NHL	73	17	17	34	50	-25	5	0	—	—	—	—	—
99-00—Montreal	NHL	80	25	24	49	70	1	7	1	—	—	—	—	—
NHL Totals (9 years)		542	151	206	357	459	31	40	9	21	4	1	5	12

RUDKOWSKY, CODY — G — BLUES

PERSONAL: Born July 21, 1978, in Willingdon, Alta. ... 6-1/200. ... Catches left.

TRANSACTIONS/CAREER NOTES: Signed as non-drafted free agent by St. Louis Blues (March 25, 1999).

HONORS: Won Del Wilson Trophy (1998-99). ... Won Four Broncos Memorial Trophy (1998-99). ... Won Can.HL Goaltender of the Year Award (1998-99). ... Named to WHL (West) All-Star first team (1998-99). ... Named to Can.HL All-Star first team (1998-99).

Season Team	League	REGULAR SEASON							PLAYOFFS					
		Gms.	Min	W	L	T	GA	SO	Avg.	Gms.	Min.	W	L	GA	SO	Avg.
95-96—Seattle	WHL	2	21	0	0	0	3	0	8.57	—	—	—	—	—	—	—
96-97—Seattle	WHL	40	2162	19	16	1	124	0	3.44	1	30	1	0	0	0	...
97-98—Seattle	WHL	53	2805	20	22	3	175	1	3.74	5	278	1	4	18	0	3.88
98-99—Seattle	WHL	64	3665	34	17	*10	177	*7	2.90	11	637	5	*6	31	1	2.92
99-00—Worcester	AHL	28	1405	9	15	6	75	0	3.20	—	—	—	—	—	—	—
—Peoria	ECHL	11	599	7	4	0	32	0	3.21	2	119	1	1	6	0	3.03

RULLIER, JOE — D — KINGS

PERSONAL: Born January 28, 1980, in Montreal. ... 6-3/198. ... Shoots right.

TRANSACTIONS/CAREER NOTES: Selected by Los Angeles Kings in fifth round (fifth Kings pick, 133rd overall) of NHL entry draft (June 27, 1998).

Season Team	League	REGULAR SEASON								PLAYOFFS				
		Gms.	G	A	Pts.	PIM	+/-	PP	SH	Gms.	G	A	Pts.	PIM
96-97—Rimouski	QMJHL	23	0	3	3	77	...	...	...	4	0	0	0	11
97-98—Rimouski	QMJHL	55	1	10	11	176	...	...	...	16	1	4	5	34
98-99—Rimouski	QMJHL	54	7	32	39	202	...	...	...	11	2	3	5	26
99-00—Rimouski	QMJHL	49	3	32	35	161	...	...	...	14	1	8	9	34

R

RUPP, MICHAEL   LW   DEVILS

PERSONAL: Born January 13, 1980, in Cleveland. ... 6-5/218. ... Shoots left.
TRANSACTIONS/CAREER NOTES: Selected by New York Islanders in first round (first Islanders pick, ninth overall) of NHL entry draft (June 27, 1998). ... Returned to draft pool by Islanders and selected by New Jersey Devils in third round (seventh Devils pick, 76th overall) of NHL entry draft (June 24, 2000).

		REGULAR SEASON								PLAYOFFS				
Season Team	League	Gms.	G	A	Pts.	PIM	+/-	PP	SH	Gms.	G	A	Pts.	PIM
96-97—St. Edward's	USHS (East)	20	26	24	50	...				—	—	—	—	—
97-98—Windsor	OHL	38	9	8	17	60	...	...	...	—	—	—	—	—
—Erie	OHL	26	7	3	10	57	...	...	...	7	3	1	4	6
98-99—Erie	OHL	63	22	25	47	102	...	...	...	5	0	2	2	25
99-00—Erie	OHL	58	32	21	53	134	...	...	...	13	5	5	10	22

RUUTU, JARKKO   RW   CANUCKS

PERSONAL: Born August 23, 1975, in Vantaa, Finland. ... 6-2/194. ... Shoots left.
COLLEGE: Michigan Tech.
TRANSACTIONS/CAREER NOTES: Selected by Vancouver Canucks in third round (third Canucks pick, 68th overall) of NHL entry draft (June 27, 1998).

		REGULAR SEASON								PLAYOFFS				
Season Team	League	Gms.	G	A	Pts.	PIM	+/-	PP	SH	Gms.	G	A	Pts.	PIM
91-92—HIFK Helsinki	Finland Jr.	1	0	0	0	0	...	...	...	—	—	—	—	—
92-93—HIFK Helsinki	Finland Jr.	34	26	21	47	53	...	...	...	—	—	—	—	—
93-94—HIFK Helsinki	Finland Jr.	19	9	12	21	44	...	...	...	—	—	—	—	—
94-95—HIFK Helsinki	Finland Jr.	35	26	22	48	117	...	...	...	—	—	—	—	—
95-96—Michigan Tech	WCHA	39	12	10	22	96	...	...	...	—	—	—	—	—
96-97—HIFK Helsinki	Finland	48	11	10	21	155	...	...	...	—	—	—	—	—
97-98—HIFK Helsinki	Finland	37	10	10	20	87	...	...	...	8	7	4	11	10
98-99—HIFK Helsinki	Finland	25	10	4	14	136	...	...	...	9	0	2	2	43
99-00—Syracuse	AHL	65	26	32	58	164	...	...	...	4	3	1	4	8
—Vancouver	NHL	8	0	1	1	6	-1	0	0	—	—	—	—	—
NHL Totals (1 year)		8	0	1	1	6	-1	0	0					

RYAZANTSEV, ALEXANDER   D   AVALANCHE

PERSONAL: Born March 15, 1980, in Moscow, U.S.S.R. ... 5-11/200. ... Shoots right.
TRANSACTIONS/CAREER NOTES: Selected by Colorado Avalanche in sixth round (10th Avalanche pick, 167th overall) of NHL entry draft (June 27, 1998).

		REGULAR SEASON								PLAYOFFS				
Season Team	League	Gms.	G	A	Pts.	PIM	+/-	PP	SH	Gms.	G	A	Pts.	PIM
96-97—Spartak Moscow	Russian	20	1	2	3	4	...	...	...	—	—	—	—	—
—SAK Moscow	Rus. Div. III	18	0	0	0	8	...	...	...	—	—	—	—	—
97-98—Spartak-2 Moscow	Rus. Div. III	31	3	8	11	26	...	...	...	—	—	—	—	—
—Victoriaville	QMJHL	22	6	9	15	14	...	...	...	4	0	0	0	0
98-99—Victoriaville	QMJHL	64	17	40	57	57	...	...	...	6	0	3	3	10
—Hershey	AHL	2	0	0	0	0	...	...	...	—	—	—	—	—
99-00—Victoriaville	QMJHL	48	17	45	62	45	...	...	...	6	2	5	7	20
—Hershey	AHL	2	0	1	1	2	...	...	...	6	1	1	2	0

RYCROFT, MARK   RW   BLUES

PERSONAL: Born July 12, 1978, in Penticton, B.C. ... 6-0/197. ... Shoots right.
COLLEGE: University of Denver.
TRANSACTIONS/CAREER NOTES: Signed as non-drafted free agent by St. Louis Blues (May 15, 2000).

		REGULAR SEASON								PLAYOFFS				
Season Team	League	Gms.	G	A	Pts.	PIM	+/-	PP	SH	Gms.	G	A	Pts.	PIM
97-98—Univ. of Denver	WCHA	35	15	17	32	28	...	...	...	—	—	—	—	—
98-99—Univ. of Denver	WCHA	41	19	18	37	36	...	...	...	—	—	—	—	—
99-00—Univ. of Denver	WCHA	41	17	17	34		...	...	...	—	—	—	—	—

RYDER, MICHAEL   C   CANADIENS

PERSONAL: Born March 31, 1980, in St. John's, Nfld. ... 6-0/187. ... Shoots right.
TRANSACTIONS/CAREER NOTES: Selected by Montreal Canadiens in ninth round (ninth Canadiens pick, 216th overall) of NHL entry draft (June 27, 1998).
HONORS: Named to QMJHL All-Rookie Team (1997-98).

		REGULAR SEASON								PLAYOFFS				
Season Team	League	Gms.	G	A	Pts.	PIM	+/-	PP	SH	Gms.	G	A	Pts.	PIM
97-98—Hull	QMJHL	69	34	28	62	41	...	...	...	10	4	2	6	4
98-99—Hull	QMJHL	69	44	43	87	41	...	...	...	23	†20	16	36	39
99-00—Hull	QMJHL	63	50	58	108	50	...	...	...	15	11	17	28	28

PERSONAL: Born February 4, 1969, in Medford, Mass. ... 6-1/190. ... Shoots left. ... Full Name: Joseph William Sacco. ... Brother of David Sacco, left winger with Toronto Maple Leafs (1993-94) and Mighty Ducks of Anaheim (1994-95 and 1995-96). ... Name pronounced SA-koh.
HIGH SCHOOL: Medford (Mass.).
COLLEGE: Boston University.
TRANSACTIONS/CAREER NOTES: Selected by Toronto Maple Leafs in fourth round (fourth Maple Leafs pick, 71st overall) of NHL entry draft (June 13, 1987). ... Selected by Mighty Ducks of Anaheim in NHL expansion draft (June 24, 1993). ... Bruised left thumb (February 5, 1995); missed seven games. ... Strained chest muscle (January 22, 1997); missed five games. ... Traded by Mighty Ducks with D J.J. Daigneault and C Mark Janssens to New York Islanders for C Travis Green, D Doug Houda and RW Tony Tuzzolino (February 6, 1998). ... Strained hip flexor (March 14, 1998); missed one game. ... Injured wrist (November 12, 1998); missed four games. ... Injured shoulder (April 10, 1999) and underwent surgery; missed final three games of season. ... Signed as free agent by Washington Capitals (July 27, 1999). ... Bruised leg (November 26, 1999); missed two games. ... Suffered from the flu (February 3, 2000); missed one game.
MISCELLANEOUS: Holds Mighty Ducks of Anaheim all-time record for most games played (333). ... Scored on a penalty shot (vs. Jocelyn Thibault, November 12, 1997).

Season Team	League	REGULAR SEASON Gms.	G	A	Pts.	PIM	+/-	PP	SH	PLAYOFFS Gms.	G	A	Pts.	PIM
85-86—Medford H.S.	Mass. H.S.	20	30	30	60	...	...	...	...	—	—	—	—	—
86-87—Medford H.S.	Mass. H.S.	21	22	32	54	...	...	...	...	—	—	—	—	—
87-88—Boston University	Hockey East	34	14	22	36	38	...	...	...	—	—	—	—	—
88-89—Boston University	Hockey East	33	21	19	40	66	...	...	...	—	—	—	—	—
89-90—Boston University	Hockey East	44	28	24	52	70	...	...	...	—	—	—	—	—
90-91—Newmarket	AHL	49	18	17	35	24	...	...	...	—	—	—	—	—
—Toronto	NHL	20	0	5	5	2	-5	0	0	—	—	—	—	—
91-92—U.S. national team	Int'l	50	11	26	37	51	...	...	...	—	—	—	—	—
—U.S. Olympic team	Int'l	8	0	2	2	0	...	...	...	—	—	—	—	—
—Toronto	NHL	17	7	4	11	4	8	0	0	—	—	—	—	—
—St. John's	AHL	—	—	—	—	...	...	...	...	1	1	1	2	0
92-93—Toronto	NHL	23	4	4	8	8	-4	0	0	—	—	—	—	—
—St. John's	AHL	37	14	16	30	45	...	...	...	7	6	4	10	2
93-94—Anaheim	NHL	84	19	18	37	61	-11	3	1	—	—	—	—	—
94-95—Anaheim	NHL	41	10	8	18	23	-8	2	0	—	—	—	—	—
95-96—Anaheim	NHL	76	13	14	27	40	1	1	2	—	—	—	—	—
96-97—Anaheim	NHL	77	12	17	29	35	1	1	1	11	2	0	2	2
97-98—Anaheim	NHL	55	8	11	19	24	-1	0	2	—	—	—	—	—
—New York Islanders	NHL	25	3	3	6	10	1	0	0	—	—	—	—	—
98-99—New York Islanders	NHL	73	3	0	3	45	-24	0	1	—	—	—	—	—
99-00—Washington	NHL	79	7	16	23	50	7	0	0	5	0	0	0	4
NHL Totals (10 years)		570	86	100	186	302	-35	7	7	16	2	0	2	6

PERSONAL: Born February 26, 1981, in Leningrad, U.S.S.R. ... 6-2/196. ... Shoots left.
TRANSACTIONS/CAREER NOTES: Selected by Phoenix Coyotes in first round (second Coyotes pick, 19th overall) of NHL entry draft (June 26, 1999).
HONORS: Won Raymond Lagace Trophy (1999-2000).

Season Team	League	REGULAR SEASON Gms.	G	A	Pts.	PIM	+/-	PP	SH	PLAYOFFS Gms.	G	A	Pts.	PIM
96-97—SKA St. Petersburg	Russian	1	0	0	0	0	...	...	...	—	—	—	—	—
97-98—SKA St. Petersburg	Russian	9	0	1	1	4	...	...	...	—	—	—	—	—
—SKA-2 St. Petersburg	Rus. Div. III	34	4	3	7	36	...	...	...	—	—	—	—	—
98-99—SKA St. Petersburg	Russian	35	1	1	2	26	...	...	...	—	—	—	—	—
99-00—Quebec	QMJHL	55	11	32	43	95	...	...	...	11	2	4	6	14

PERSONAL: Born July 7, 1969, in Burnaby, B.C. ... 5-11/190. ... Shoots left. ... Full Name: Joseph Steve Sakic. ... Brother of Brian Sakic, left winger with Washington Capitals (1990-91 and 1991-92) and New York Rangers organizations (1992-93 through 1994-95). ... Name pronounced SAK-ihk.
TRANSACTIONS/CAREER NOTES: Selected by Quebec Nordiques as underage junior in first round (second Nordiques pick, 15th overall) of NHL entry draft (June 13, 1987). ... Sprained right ankle (November 28, 1988). ... Developed bursitis in left ankle (January 21, 1992); missed three games. ... Suffered recurrence of bursitis in left ankle (January 30, 1992); missed eight games. ... Injured eye (January 2, 1993); missed six games. ... Nordiques franchise moved to Colorado and renamed Avalanche for 1995-96 season (June 21, 1995). ... Lacerated calf (January 4, 1997); missed 17 games. ... Injured knee (February 18, 1998); missed 18 games. ... Suspended one game and fined $1,000 by NHL for kneeing incident (April 21, 1998). ... Sprained right shoulder (December 17, 1998); missed seven games. ... Injured rib cartilage (November 8, 1999); missed six games. ... Reinjured rib cartilage (November 26, 1999); missed 13 games. ... Suffered from the flu (January 18, 2000); missed one game. ... Injured groin (January 25, 2000); missed two games.
HONORS: Won WHL (East) Most Valuable Player Trophy (1986-87). ... Won WHL (East) Stewart (Butch) Paul Memorial Trophy (1986-87). ... Named to WHL All-Star second team (1986-87). ... Won Can.HL Player of the Year Award (1987-88). ... Won Four Broncos Memorial Trophy (1987-88). ... Shared Bob Clarke Trophy with Theoren Fleury (1987-88). ... Won WHL Player of the Year Award (1987-88). ... Named to WHL (East) All-Star first team (1987-88). ... Played in NHL All-Star Game (1990-1994, 1996, 1998 and 2000). ... Won Conn Smythe Trophy (1995-96). ... Named to play in NHL All-Star Game (1997); replaced by RW Teemu Selanne due to injury.
RECORDS: Shares NHL single-season playoff record for most game-winning goals—6 (1996).
STATISTICAL PLATEAUS: Three-goal games: 1988-89 (2), 1989-90 (1), 1990-91 (1), 1996-97 (1), 1998-99 (1), 1999-00 (2). Total: 8. ... Four-goal games: 1991-92 (1). ... Total hat tricks: 9.
MISCELLANEOUS: Member of Stanley Cup championship team (1996). ... Captain of Quebec Nordiques (1990-91 through 1994-95). ... Captain of Colorado Avalanche (1995-96 through 1999-2000). ... Holds Colorado Avalanche franchise all-time record for most points (1,060). ... Scored on a penalty shot (vs. Ken Wregget, December 9, 1989; vs. Trevor Kidd, January 14, 1996; vs. Tyler Moss, November 1, 1997).

Season Team	League	REGULAR SEASON								PLAYOFFS				
		Gms.	G	A	Pts.	PIM	+/-	PP	SH	Gms.	G	A	Pts.	PIM
86-87—Swift Current	WHL	72	60	73	133	31	...	...	...	4	0	1	1	0
87-88—Swift Current	WHL	64	†78	82	†160	64	...	...	...	10	11	13	24	12
88-89—Quebec	NHL	70	23	39	62	24	-36	10	0	—	—	—	—	—
89-90—Quebec	NHL	80	39	63	102	27	-40	8	1	—	—	—	—	—
90-91—Quebec	NHL	80	48	61	109	24	-26	12	3	—	—	—	—	—
91-92—Quebec	NHL	69	29	65	94	20	5	6	3	—	—	—	—	—
92-93—Quebec	NHL	78	48	57	105	40	-3	20	2	6	3	3	6	2
93-94—Quebec	NHL	84	28	64	92	18	-8	10	1	—	—	—	—	—
94-95—Quebec	NHL	47	19	43	62	30	7	3	2	6	4	1	5	0
95-96—Colorado	NHL	82	51	69	120	44	14	17	6	22	*18	16	*34	14
96-97—Colorado	NHL	65	22	52	74	34	-10	10	2	17	8	17	25	14
97-98—Colorado	NHL	64	27	36	63	50	0	12	1	6	2	3	5	6
—Can. Olympic team	Int'l	4	1	2	3	4	...	...	...	—	—	—	—	—
98-99—Colorado	NHL	73	41	55	96	29	23	12	†5	19	6	13	19	8
99-00—Colorado	NHL	60	28	53	81	28	30	5	1	17	2	7	9	8
NHL Totals (12 years)		852	403	657	1060	368	-44	125	27	93	43	60	103	52

SALEI, RUSLAN — D — MIGHTY DUCKS

PERSONAL: Born November 2, 1974, in Minsk, U.S.S.R. ... 6-1/206. ... Shoots left. ... Name pronounced ROO-slahn suh-LAY.

TRANSACTIONS/CAREER NOTES: Selected by Mighty Ducks of Anaheim in first round (first Mighty Ducks pick, ninth overall) of NHL entry draft (June 22, 1996). ... Suffered charley horse (November 22, 1997); missed one game. ... Fractured bone in left foot (December 10, 1997); missed one game. ... Suspended two games and fined $1,000 by NHL for head-butting incident (February 4, 1998). ... Suspended five games and fined $1,000 by NHL for illegal hit in preseason game (October 9, 1998). ... Injured shoulder (March 17, 1999); missed two games. ... Suspended 10 games by NHL for checking from behind incident (October 5, 1999).

Season Team	League	REGULAR SEASON								PLAYOFFS				
		Gms.	G	A	Pts.	PIM	+/-	PP	SH	Gms.	G	A	Pts.	PIM
92-93—Tivali Minsk	CIS	9	1	0	1	10	...	...	...	—	—	—	—	—
93-94—Tivali Minsk	CIS	39	2	3	5	50	...	...	...	—	—	—	—	—
94-95—Tivali Minsk	CIS	51	4	2	6	44	...	...	...	—	—	—	—	—
95-96—Las Vegas	IHL	76	7	23	30	123	...	...	...	15	3	7	10	18
96-97—Anaheim	NHL	30	0	1	1	37	-8	0	0	—	—	—	—	—
—Baltimore	AHL	12	1	4	5	12	...	...	...	—	—	—	—	—
—Las Vegas	IHL	8	0	2	2	24	...	...	...	3	2	1	3	6
97-98—Anaheim	NHL	66	5	10	15	70	7	1	0	—	—	—	—	—
—Cincinnati	AHL	6	3	6	9	14	...	...	...	—	—	—	—	—
—Belarus Oly. team	Int'l	7	1	0	1	4	...	...	...	—	—	—	—	—
98-99—Anaheim	NHL	74	2	14	16	65	1	1	0	3	0	0	0	4
99-00—Anaheim	NHL	71	5	5	10	94	3	1	0	—	—	—	—	—
NHL Totals (4 years)		241	12	30	42	266	3	3	0	3	0	0	0	4

SALO, SAMI — D — SENATORS

PERSONAL: Born September 2, 1974, in Turku, Finland. ... 6-3/192. ... Shoots right.

TRANSACTIONS/CAREER NOTES: Selected by Ottawa Senators in ninth round (seventh Senators pick, 239th overall) of NHL entry draft (June 22, 1996). ... Strained groin (October 17, 1998); missed five games. ... Strained groin (November 28, 1998); missed six games. ... Bruised thigh (February 18, 1999); missed one game. ... Strained shoulder (April 14, 1999); missed two games. ... Bruised chest (October 2, 1999); missed one game. ... Fractured left wrist (October 30, 1999); missed 23 games. ... Reinjured left wrist (December 29, 1999); missed 19 games. ... Sprained medial collateral ligament in right knee (February 29, 2000); missed one game.

HONORS: Named to NHL All-Rookie team (1998-99).

STATISTICAL PLATEAUS: Three-goal games: 1998-99 (1).

Season Team	League	REGULAR SEASON								PLAYOFFS				
		Gms.	G	A	Pts.	PIM	+/-	PP	SH	Gms.	G	A	Pts.	PIM
94-95—TPS Turku	Finland	7	1	2	3	6	...	...	...	—	—	—	—	—
—Kiekko-67	Finland Div. 2	19	4	2	6	4	...	...	...	—	—	—	—	—
95-96—TPS Turku	Finland	47	7	14	21	32	...	...	...	11	1	3	4	8
96-97—TPS Turku	Finland	48	9	6	15	10	...	...	...	10	2	3	5	4
97-98—Jokerit Helsinki	Finland	35	3	5	8	10	...	...	...	8	0	1	1	2
98-99—Ottawa	NHL	61	7	12	19	24	20	2	0	4	0	0	0	0
—Detroit	IHL	5	0	2	2	0	...	...	...	—	—	—	—	—
99-00—Ottawa	NHL	37	6	8	14	2	6	3	0	6	1	1	2	0
NHL Totals (2 years)		98	13	20	33	26	26	5	0	10	1	1	2	0

SALO, TOMMY — G — OILERS

PERSONAL: Born February 1, 1971, in Surahammar, Sweden. ... 5-11/173. ... Catches left. ... Name pronounced SAH-loh.

TRANSACTIONS/CAREER NOTES: Selected by New York Islanders in fifth round (fifth Islanders pick, 118th overall) of NHL entry draft (June 26, 1993). ... Suffered from tonsillitis (February 8, 1997); missed one game. ... Fractured finger (December 20, 1998); missed six games. ... Traded by Islanders to Edmonton Oilers for LW Mats Lindgren and eighth-round pick (F Radek Martinek) in 1999 draft (March 20, 1999).

HONORS: Won James Gatchene Memorial Trophy (1994-95). ... Won James Norris Memorial Trophy (1994-95). ... Won Garry F. Longman Memorial Trophy (1994-95). ... Named to IHL All-Star first team (1994-95). ... Won N.R. (Bud) Poile Trophy (1995-96). ... Played in NHL All-Star Game (2000).

MISCELLANEOUS: Member of gold-medal-winning Swedish Olympic team (1994). ... Stopped a penalty shot attempt (vs. Mike Sillinger, January 7, 2000). ... Allowed penalty shot goal (vs. Rob Zamuner, January 11, 1997). ... Holds Edmonton Oilers all-time record for goals-against average (2.33).

Season Team	League	REGULAR SEASON							PLAYOFFS					
		Gms.	Min	W	L	T	GA	SO	Avg.	Gms.	Min.	W	L	GA	SO	Avg.
90-91 —Vasteras	Sweden	2	100	...	...	...	11	0	6.60	—	—	—	—	—	—	—
91-92 —Vasteras	Sweden								Did not play.						
92-93 —Vasteras	Sweden	24	1431	...	...	...	59	2	2.47	—	—	—	—	—	—	—
93-94 —Vasteras	Sweden	32	1896	...	...	...	106	...	3.35	—	—	—	—	—	—	—
—Swedish Oly. team	Int'l	6	370	...	...	...	13	1	2.11	—	—	—	—	—	—	—
94-95 —Denver	IHL	65	*3810	*45	14	‡4	165	†3	*2.60	8	390	7	0	20	0	3.08
—New York Islanders	NHL	6	358	1	5	0	18	0	3.02	—	—	—	—	—	—	—
95-96 —New York Islanders	NHL	10	523	1	7	1	35	0	4.02	—	—	—	—	—	—	—
—Utah	IHL	45	2695	28	15	‡2	119	†4	2.65	22	1341	*15	7	51	*3	2.28
96-97 —New York Islanders	NHL	58	3208	20	27	8	151	5	2.82	—	—	—	—	—	—	—
97-98 —New York Islanders	NHL	62	3461	23	29	5	152	4	2.64	—	—	—	—	—	—	—
—Swedish Oly. team	Int'l	4	238	2	2	0	9	0	2.27	—	—	—	—	—	—	—
98-99 —New York Islanders	NHL	51	3018	17	26	7	132	5	2.62	—	—	—	—	—	—	—
—Edmonton	NHL	13	700	8	2	2	27	0	2.31	4	296	0	4	11	0	2.23
99-00 —Edmonton	NHL	70	4164	27	28	*13	162	2	2.33	5	297	1	4	14	0	2.83
NHL Totals (6 years)		270	15432	97	124	36	677	16	2.63	9	593	1	8	25	0	2.53

SALVADOR, BRYCE — D — BLUES

PERSONAL: Born February 11, 1976, in Brandon, Man. ... 6-1/194. ... Shoots left.
TRANSACTIONS/CAREER NOTES: Selected by Tampa Bay Lightning in sixth round (sixth Lightning pick, 138th overall) of NHL entry draft (June 29, 1994). ... Signed as free agent by St. Louis Blues (December 16, 1996).

Season Team	League	REGULAR SEASON								PLAYOFFS				
		Gms.	G	A	Pts.	PIM	+/-	PP	SH	Gms.	G	A	Pts.	PIM
92-93 —Lethbridge	WHL	64	1	4	5	29	...	...	...	4	0	0	0	0
93-94 —Lethbridge	WHL	61	4	14	18	36	...	...	...	9	0	1	1	2
94-95 —Lethbridge	WHL	67	1	9	10	88	...	...	...	—	—	—	—	—
95-96 —Lethbridge	WHL	56	4	12	16	75	...	...	...	3	0	1	1	2
96-97 —Lethbridge	WHL	63	8	32	40	81	...	...	...	19	0	7	7	14
97-98 —Worcester	AHL	46	2	8	10	74	...	...	...	11	0	1	1	45
98-99 —Worcester	AHL	69	5	13	18	129	...	...	...	4	0	1	1	2
99-00 —Worcester	AHL	55	0	13	13	53	...	...	...	9	0	1	1	2

SAMSONOV, SERGEI — LW — BRUINS

PERSONAL: Born October 27, 1978, in Moscow, U.S.S.R. ... 5-8/184. ... Shoots right. ... Name pronounced sam-SAH-nahf.
TRANSACTIONS/CAREER NOTES: Selected by Boston Bruins in first round (second Bruins pick, eighth overall) of NHL entry draft (June 21, 1997). ... Suffered from the flu (December 20, 1997); missed one game. ... Bruised thigh (February 12, 1998); missed one game. ... Suffered sinus infection (February 23, 1999); missed two games. ... Strained knee (January 4, 2000); missed five games.
HONORS: Won Garry F. Longman Memorial Trophy (1996-97). ... Named to IHL All-Rookie first team (1996-97). ... Named NHL Rookie of the Year by THE SPORTING NEWS (1997-98). ... Won Calder Memorial Trophy (1997-98). ... Named to NHL All-Rookie team (1997-98).
STATISTICAL PLATEAUS: Three-goal games: 1997-98 (1).

Season Team	League	REGULAR SEASON								PLAYOFFS				
		Gms.	G	A	Pts.	PIM	+/-	PP	SH	Gms.	G	A	Pts.	PIM
94-95 —CSKA Moscow	CIS	13	2	2	4	14	...	...	...	2	0	0	0	0
—CSKA Moscow Jrs.	CIS	50	110	72	182	...	...	...	...	—	—	—	—	—
95-96 —CSKA Moscow	CIS	51	21	17	38	12	...	...	...	3	1	1	2	4
96-97 —Detroit	IHL	73	29	35	64	18	...	...	...	19	8	4	12	12
97-98 —Boston	NHL	81	22	25	47	8	9	7	0	6	2	5	7	0
98-99 —Boston	NHL	79	25	26	51	18	-6	6	0	11	3	1	4	0
99-00 —Boston	NHL	77	19	26	45	4	-6	6	0	—	—	—	—	—
NHL Totals (3 years)		237	66	77	143	30	-3	19	0	17	5	6	11	0

SAMUELSSON, ULF — D — FLYERS

PERSONAL: Born March 26, 1964, in Fagersta, Sweden. ... 6-1/205. ... Shoots left. ... Name pronounced UHLF SAM-yuhl-suhn.
TRANSACTIONS/CAREER NOTES: Selected by Hartford Whalers in fourth round (fourth Whalers pick, 67th overall) of NHL entry draft (June 9, 1982). ... Suffered from the flu (December 1988); missed nine games. ... Tore ligaments in right knee and underwent surgery (August 1989); missed part of 1989-90 season. ... Traded by Whalers with C Ron Francis and D Grant Jennings to Pittsburgh Penguins for C John Cullen, D Zarley Zalapski and RW Jeff Parker (March 4, 1991). ... Injured hip flexor (October 29, 1991); missed six games. ... Underwent surgery to right elbow (December 1991); missed four games. ... Bruised left hand (February 8, 1992); missed one game. ... Suffered from the flu (February 1992); missed one game. ... Strained shoulder (November 10, 1992); missed two games. ... Fractured cheekbone (November 27, 1992); missed two games. ... Bruised knee (January 1993); missed one game. ... Suspended one game by NHL (February 1993). ... Suspended three off-days by NHL for stick-swinging incident (March 18, 1993). ... Suffered back spasms (April 4, 1993); missed one game. ... Injured knee (November 2, 1993); missed one game. ... Bruised foot (December 14, 1993); missed two games. ... Played in Europe during 1994-95 NHL lockout. ... Strained right elbow (March 21, 1995) and underwent elbow surgery; missed three games. ... Bruised knee (April 28, 1995); missed one game. ... Traded by Penguins with LW Luc Robitaille to New York Rangers for D Sergei Zubov and C Petr Nedved (August 31, 1995). ... Suffered mild concussion (October 14, 1995); missed two games. ... Separated shoulder (October 22, 1995); missed two games. ... Underwent elbow surgery (December 28, 1995); missed four games. ... Sprained knee (October 25, 1996); missed nine games. ... Suffered from the flu (October 3, 1997); missed one game. ... Strained rib muscle (November 28, 1997); missed one game. ... Sprained right knee (January 3, 1998); missed four games. ... Suffered laceration above left eye (March 28, 1998); missed two games. ... Suffered concussion (March 7, 1999); missed two games. ... Fractured foot (March 21, 1999); missed eight games. ... Traded by Rangers to Detroit Red Wings for second-round pick (C David Inman) in 1999 draft and third-round pick (C Dominic Moore) in 2000 draft (March 23, 1999). ... Traded by Red Wings to Atlanta Thrashers for future considerations (June 25, 1999). ... Signed as free agent by Philadelphia Flyers (October 18, 1999). ... Sprained left shoulder (December 5, 1999); missed four games. ... Suffered from the flu (February 12, 2000); missed one game. ... Injured shoulder (February 15, 2000); missed nine games. ... Sprained right knee (April 1, 2000); missed final six games of regular season.
MISCELLANEOUS: Member of Stanley Cup championship team (1991 and 1992).

Season Team	League	REGULAR SEASON Gms.	G	A	Pts.	PIM	+/-	PP	SH	PLAYOFFS Gms.	G	A	Pts.	PIM
81-82—Leksand	Sweden	31	3	1	4	40	...	...	...	—	—	—	—	—
82-83—Leksand	Sweden	33	9	6	15	72	...	...	...	—	—	—	—	—
83-84—Leksand	Sweden	36	5	10	15	53	...	...	...	—	—	—	—	—
84-85—Binghamton	AHL	36	5	11	16	92	...	...	...	—	—	—	—	—
—Hartford	NHL	41	2	6	8	83	-6	0	0	—	—	—	—	—
85-86—Hartford	NHL	80	5	19	24	174	8	0	1	10	1	2	3	38
86-87—Hartford	NHL	78	2	31	33	162	29	0	0	5	0	1	1	41
87-88—Hartford	NHL	76	8	33	41	159	-10	3	0	5	0	0	0	8
88-89—Hartford	NHL	71	9	26	35	181	23	3	0	4	0	2	2	4
89-90—Hartford	NHL	55	2	11	13	177	15	0	0	7	1	0	1	2
90-91—Hartford	NHL	62	3	18	21	174	13	0	0	—	—	—	—	—
—Pittsburgh	NHL	14	1	4	5	37	4	0	0	20	3	2	5	34
91-92—Pittsburgh	NHL	62	1	14	15	206	2	1	0	21	0	2	2	39
92-93—Pittsburgh	NHL	77	3	26	29	249	36	0	0	12	1	5	6	24
93-94—Pittsburgh	NHL	80	5	24	29	199	23	1	0	6	0	1	1	18
94-95—Leksand	Sweden	2	0	0	0	8	...	...	...	—	—	—	—	—
—Pittsburgh	NHL	44	1	15	16	113	11	0	0	7	0	2	2	8
95-96—New York Rangers	NHL	74	1	18	19	122	9	0	0	11	1	5	6	16
96-97—New York Rangers	NHL	73	6	11	17	138	3	1	0	15	0	2	2	30
97-98—New York Rangers	NHL	73	3	9	12	122	1	0	0	—	—	—	—	—
—Swedish Oly. team	Int'l	3	0	1	1	4	...	...	...	—	—	—	—	—
98-99—New York Rangers	NHL	67	4	8	12	93	6	0	0	—	—	—	—	—
—Detroit	NHL	4	0	0	0	6	-1	0	0	9	0	3	3	10
99-00—Philadelphia	NHL	49	1	2	3	58	8	0	0	—	—	—	—	—
NHL Totals (16 years)		1080	57	275	332	2453	174	9	1	132	7	27	34	272

S

SANDERSON, GEOFF   LW   BLUE JACKETS

PERSONAL: Born February 1, 1972, in Hay River, Northwest Territories. ... 6-0/190. ... Shoots left.

TRANSACTIONS/CAREER NOTES: Selected by Hartford Whalers in second round (second Whalers pick, 36th overall) of NHL entry draft (June 16, 1990). ... Bruised shoulder (October 14, 1991); missed one game. ... Injured groin (November 13, 1991); missed three games. ... Bruised knee (December 7, 1991); missed five games. ... Suffered from the flu (February 1, 1994). ... Played in Europe during 1994-95 NHL lockout. ... Whalers franchise moved to North Carolina and renamed Carolina Hurricanes for 1997-98 season; NHL approved move on June 25, 1997. ... Traded by Hurricanes to Vancouver Canucks with D Enrico Ciccone and G Sean Burke for LW Martin Gelinas and G Kirk McLean (January 3, 1998). ... Injured shoulder (January 21, 1998); missed eight games. ... Traded by Canucks to Buffalo Sabres for LW Brad May and third-round pick (traded to Tampa Bay) in 1999 draft (February 4, 1998). ... Bruised hip (April 13, 1998); missed one game. ... Injured back (January 18, 1999); missed one game. ... Injured hip (February 19, 1999); missed one game. ... Injured knee (March 1, 2000); missed five games. ... Selected by Columbus Blue Jackets in NHL expansion draft (June 23, 2000).

HONORS: Played in NHL All-Star Game (1994 and 1997).

STATISTICAL PLATEAUS: Three-goal games: 1992-93 (2), 1994-95 (1), 1995-96 (2), 1998-99 (1). Total: 6.

Season Team	League	REGULAR SEASON Gms.	G	A	Pts.	PIM	+/-	PP	SH	PLAYOFFS Gms.	G	A	Pts.	PIM
88-89—Swift Current	WHL	58	17	11	28	16	...	...	...	12	3	5	8	6
89-90—Swift Current	WHL	70	32	62	94	56	...	...	...	4	1	4	5	8
90-91—Swift Current	WHL	70	62	50	112	57	...	...	...	3	1	2	3	4
—Hartford	NHL	2	1	0	1	0	-2	0	0	3	0	0	0	0
—Springfield	AHL	—	—	—	—	—	...	...	...	1	0	0	0	2
91-92—Hartford	NHL	64	13	18	31	18	5	2	0	7	1	0	1	2
92-93—Hartford	NHL	82	46	43	89	28	-21	21	2	—	—	—	—	—
93-94—Hartford	NHL	82	41	26	67	42	-13	15	1	—	—	—	—	—
94-95—HPK Hameenlinna	Finland	12	6	4	10	24	...	...	...	—	—	—	—	—
—Hartford	NHL	46	18	14	32	24	-10	4	0	—	—	—	—	—
95-96—Hartford	NHL	81	34	31	65	40	0	6	0	—	—	—	—	—
96-97—Hartford	NHL	82	36	31	67	29	-9	12	1	—	—	—	—	—
97-98—Carolina	NHL	40	7	10	17	14	-4	2	0	—	—	—	—	—
—Vancouver	NHL	9	0	3	3	4	-1	0	0	—	—	—	—	—
—Buffalo	NHL	26	4	5	9	20	6	0	0	14	3	1	4	4
98-99—Buffalo	NHL	75	12	18	30	22	8	1	0	19	4	6	10	14
99-00—Buffalo	NHL	67	13	13	26	22	4	4	0	5	0	2	2	8
NHL Totals (10 years)		656	225	212	437	263	-37	67	4	48	8	9	17	28

SAPRYKIN, OLEG   C/LW   FLAMES

PERSONAL: Born February 12, 1981, in Moscow, U.S.S.R. ... 6-0/187. ... Shoots left.

TRANSACTIONS/CAREER NOTES: Selected by Calgary Flames in first round (first Flames pick, 11th overall) of NHL entry draft (June 26, 1999).

HONORS: Named to WHL (West) All-Star second team (1998-99 and 1999-2000).

Season Team	League	REGULAR SEASON Gms.	G	A	Pts.	PIM	+/-	PP	SH	PLAYOFFS Gms.	G	A	Pts.	PIM
97-98—HC CSKA	Rus. Div. II	15	0	3	3	6	...	...	...	—	—	—	—	—
98-99—Seattle	WHL	66	47	46	93	107	...	...	...	11	5	11	16	36
99-00—Calgary	NHL	4	0	1	1	2	-4	0	0	—	—	—	—	—
—Seattle	WHL	48	30	36	66	89	...	...	...	6	3	3	6	37
NHL Totals (1 year)		4	0	1	1	2	-4	0	0	—	—	—	—	—

SARAULT, YVES   LW   THRASHERS

PERSONAL: Born December 23, 1972, in Valleyfield, Que. ... 6-1/183. ... Shoots left. ... Name pronounced EEV suh-ROH.
TRANSACTIONS/CAREER NOTES: Selected by Montreal Canadiens in third round (third Canadiens pick, 61st overall) of NHL entry draft (June 22, 1991). ... Traded by Canadiens with RW Craig Ferguson to Calgary Flames for eighth-round pick (D Petr Kubos) in 1997 draft (November 25, 1995). ... Signed as free agent by Colorado Avalanche (September 7, 1996). ... Signed as free agent by Ottawa Senators (July 28, 1998). ... Sprained wrist (October 29, 1998); missed 29 games. ... Suffered back spasms (February 26, 2000); missed two games. ... Signed as free agent by Atlanta Thrashers (July 20, 2000).
HONORS: Named to QMJHL All-Star second team (1991-92).

		REGULAR SEASON								PLAYOFFS				
Season Team	League	Gms.	G	A	Pts.	PIM	+/-	PP	SH	Gms.	G	A	Pts.	PIM
89-90—Victoriaville	QMJHL	70	12	28	40	140	...	...	...	16	0	3	3	26
90-91—St. Jean	QMJHL	56	22	24	46	113	...	...	...	—	—	—	—	—
91-92—St. Jean	QMJHL	50	28	38	66	96	...	...	...	—	—	—	—	—
—Trois-Rivieres	QMJHL	18	16	14	30	10	...	...	...	15	10	10	20	18
92-93—Fredericton	AHL	59	14	17	31	41	...	...	...	3	0	1	1	2
—Wheeling	ECHL	2	1	3	4	0	...	...	...	—	—	—	—	—
93-94—Fredericton	AHL	60	13	14	27	72	...	...	...	—	—	—	—	—
94-95—Fredericton	AHL	69	24	21	45	96	...	...	...	13	2	1	3	33
—Montreal	NHL	8	0	1	1	0	-1	0	0	—	—	—	—	—
95-96—Montreal	NHL	14	0	0	0	4	-7	0	0	—	—	—	—	—
—Calgary	NHL	11	2	1	3	4	-2	0	0	—	—	—	—	—
—Saint John	AHL	26	10	12	22	34	...	...	...	16	6	2	8	33
96-97—Colorado	NHL	28	2	1	3	6	0	0	0	5	0	0	0	2
—Hershey	AHL	6	2	3	5	8	...	...	...	—	—	—	—	—
97-98—Hershey	AHL	63	23	36	59	43	...	...	...	7	1	2	3	14
—Colorado	NHL	2	1	0	1	0	1	0	0	—	—	—	—	—
98-99—Detroit	IHL	36	11	12	23	52	...	...	...	11	7	2	9	40
—Ottawa	NHL	11	0	1	1	4	1	0	0	—	—	—	—	—
99-00—Grand Rapids	IHL	62	17	26	43	77	...	...	...	17	7	4	11	32
—Ottawa	NHL	11	0	2	2	7	-3	0	0	—	—	—	—	—
NHL Totals (6 years)		85	5	6	11	25	-11	0	0	5	0	0	0	2

SARICH, CORY   D   LIGHTNING

PERSONAL: Born August 16, 1978, in Saskatoon, Sask. ... 6-3/193. ... Shoots right. ... Name pronounced SAIRCH.
TRANSACTIONS/CAREER NOTES: Selected by Buffalo Sabres in second round (second Sabres pick, 27th overall) of NHL entry draft (June 22, 1996). ... Traded by Sabres with C Wayne Primeau, C/RW Brian Holzinger and third-round pick (RW Alexandre Kharitonov) in 2000 draft to Tampa Bay Lightning for C Chris Gratton and second-round pick in 2001 draft (March 9, 2000).
HONORS: Named to WHL (West) All-Star second team (1997-98).

		REGULAR SEASON								PLAYOFFS				
Season Team	League	Gms.	G	A	Pts.	PIM	+/-	PP	SH	Gms.	G	A	Pts.	PIM
94-95—Saskatoon	WHL	6	0	0	0	4	...	...	...	3	0	1	1	0
95-96—Saskatoon	WHL	59	5	18	23	54	...	...	...	3	0	0	0	4
96-97—Saskatoon	WHL	58	6	27	33	158	...	...	...	—	—	—	—	—
97-98—Seattle	WHL	46	8	40	48	137	...	...	...	—	—	—	—	—
98-99—Rochester	AHL	77	3	26	29	82	...	...	...	20	2	4	6	14
—Buffalo	NHL	4	0	0	0	0	3	0	0	—	—	—	—	—
99-00—Buffalo	NHL	42	0	4	4	35	2	0	0	—	—	—	—	—
—Rochester	AHL	15	0	6	6	44	...	...	...	—	—	—	—	—
—Tampa Bay	NHL	17	0	2	2	42	-8	0	0	—	—	—	—	—
NHL Totals (2 years)		63	0	6	6	77	-3	0	0					

SATAN, MIROSLAV   RW   SABRES

PERSONAL: Born October 22, 1974, in Topolcany, Czechoslovakia. ... 6-1/195. ... Shoots left. ... Name pronounced shuh-TAN.
TRANSACTIONS/CAREER NOTES: Selected by Edmonton Oilers in fifth round (sixth Oilers pick, 111th overall) of NHL entry draft (June 26, 1993). ... Suffered collapsed lung (October 1, 1995); missed two games. ... Separated right shoulder (January 13, 1996); missed four games. ... Suffered from the flu (March 9, 1997); missed one game. ... Traded by Oilers to Buffalo Sabres for D Craig Millar and LW Barrie Moore (March 18, 1997). ... Fined $1,000 by NHL for high-sticking incident (May 28, 1998). ... Suffered from the flu (November 28, 1998); missed one game. ... Injured foot (April 25, 1999); missed nine playoff games.
HONORS: Played in NHL All-Star Game (2000).
MISCELLANEOUS: Scored on a penalty shot (vs. Damian Rhodes, October 9, 1999). ... Failed to score on a penalty shot (vs. Ken Wregget, December 28, 1999; vs. Kevin Weekes, March 4, 2000).
STATISTICAL NOTES: Led NHL with 21.0 shooting percentage (1996-97).
STATISTICAL PLATEAUS: Three-goal games: 1996-97 (1), 1997-98 (1), 1999-00 (1). Total: 3.

		REGULAR SEASON								PLAYOFFS				
Season Team	League	Gms.	G	A	Pts.	PIM	+/-	PP	SH	Gms.	G	A	Pts.	PIM
91-92—VTJ Topolcany	Czech Dv.II	9	2	1	3	6	...	...	...	—	—	—	—	—
—VTJ Topolcany Jrs	Czech. Jrs.	31	30	22	52		...	...	...	—	—	—	—	—
92-93—Dukla Trencin	Czech.	38	11	6	17		...	...	...	—	—	—	—	—
93-94—Dukla Trencin	Slovakia	30	32	16	48	16	...	...	...	—	—	—	—	—
—Slovakian Oly. team	Int'l	8	9	0	9	0	...	...	...	—	—	—	—	—
94-95—Detroit	IHL	8	1	3	4	4	...	...	...	—	—	—	—	—
—San Diego	IHL	6	0	2	2	6	...	...	...	—	—	—	—	—
—Cape Breton	AHL	25	24	16	40	15	...	...	...	—	—	—	—	—
95-96—Edmonton	NHL	62	18	17	35	22	0	6	0	—	—	—	—	—
96-97—Edmonton	NHL	64	17	11	28	22	-4	5	0	—	—	—	—	—
—Buffalo	NHL	12	8	2	10	4	1	2	0	7	0	0	0	0
97-98—Buffalo	NHL	79	22	24	46	34	2	9	0	14	5	4	9	4
98-99—Buffalo	NHL	81	40	26	66	44	24	13	3	12	3	5	8	2
99-00—Dukla Trencin	Slovakia	3	2	8	10	2	...	...	...	—	—	—	—	—
—Buffalo	NHL	81	33	34	67	32	16	5	3	5	3	2	5	0
NHL Totals (5 years)		379	138	114	252	158	39	40	6	38	11	11	22	6

S

SAUVE, PHILIPPE   G   AVALANCHE

PERSONAL: Born February 27, 1980, in Buffalo. ... 6-0/175. ... Catches left.
TRANSACTIONS/CAREER NOTES: Selected by Colorado Avalanche in second round (sixth Avalanche pick, 38th overall) of NHL entry draft (June 27, 1998).
HONORS: Won Can.HL Humanitarian Award (1998-99).

Season Team	League	REGULAR SEASON								PLAYOFFS						
		Gms.	Min	W	L	T	GA	SO	Avg.	Gms.	Min.	W	L	GA	SO	Avg.
96-97 —Rimouski	QMJHL	26	1332	11	9	2	84	0	3.78	1	14	0		3	0	12.86
97-98 —Rimouski	QMJHL	40	2326	23	16	0	131	1	3.38	7	262	0	5	33	0	7.56
98-99 —Rimouski	QMJHL	44	2401	16	19	4	155	0	3.87	11	595	6	4	30	†1	3.03
99-00 —Drummondville	QMJHL	28	1526	12	12	2	106	0	4.17	—	—	—	—	—	—	—
—Hull	QMJHL	17	992	9	7	1	57	0	3.45	12	735	6	6	47	0	3.84

SAVAGE, ANDRE   C   BRUINS

PERSONAL: Born May 27, 1975, in Ottawa. ... 6-0/195. ... Shoots right. ... Full Name: Andre Ronald Savage. ... Name pronounced suh-VAHJ.
COLLEGE: Michigan Tech.
TRANSACTIONS/CAREER NOTES: Signed as non-drafted free agent by Boston Bruins (June 12, 1998). ... Bruised sternum (March 8, 2000); missed two games. ... Strained trapezius muscle (April 1, 2000); missed final four games of season.
HONORS: Named to WCHA All-Star first team (1997-98).

Season Team	League	REGULAR SEASON								PLAYOFFS				
		Gms.	G	A	Pts.	PIM	+/-	PP	SH	Gms.	G	A	Pts.	PIM
94-95 —Michigan Tech	WCHA	39	7	17	24	56	...	...	...	—	—	—	—	—
95-96 —Michigan Tech	WCHA	40	13	27	40	42	...	...	...	—	—	—	—	—
96-97 —Michigan Tech	WCHA	37	18	20	38	34	...	...	...	—	—	—	—	—
97-98 —Michigan Tech	WCHA	33	14	27	41	34	...	...	...	—	—	—	—	—
98-99 —Providence	AHL	63	27	42	69	54	...	...	...	5	0	1	1	0
—Boston	NHL	6	1	0	1	0	2	0	0	—	—	—	—	—
99-00 —Providence	AHL	30	15	17	32	22	...	...	...	14	6	7	13	22
—Boston	NHL	43	7	13	20	10	-8	2	0	—	—	—	—	—
NHL Totals (2 years)		49	8	13	21	10	-6	2	0					

SAVAGE, BRIAN   RW   CANADIENS

PERSONAL: Born February 24, 1971, in Sudbury, Ont. ... 6-2/192. ... Shoots left.
HIGH SCHOOL: Lo-Ellen Park Secondary (Sudbury, Ont.).
COLLEGE: Miami of Ohio.
TRANSACTIONS/CAREER NOTES: Selected by Montreal Canadiens in eighth round (11th Canadiens pick, 171st overall) of NHL entry draft (June 22, 1991). ... Bruised knee (February 4, 1995); missed 10 games. ... Bruised knee (April 5, 1995); missed one game. ... Suffered hip pointer (February 17, 1996); missed six games. ... Suffered from the flu (April 1, 1996); missed one game. ... Injured groin (October 26, 1996); missed one game. ... Fractured hand (October 1, 1997); missed seven games. ... Bruised thigh (November 26, 1997); missed one game. ... Fractured thumb (March 21, 1998); missed 10 games. ... Strained groin (November 4, 1998); missed one game. ... Reinjured groin (December 9, 1998); missed 11 games. ... Tore muscle in rib cage (January 21, 1999); missed 11 games. ... Fractured vertebrae in neck (November 20, 1999); missed 44 games.
HONORS: Named to NCAA All-America (West) second team (1992-93). ... Named CCHA Player of the Year (1992-93). ... Named to CCHA All-Star first team (1992-93).
MISCELLANEOUS: Member of silver-medal-winning Canadian Olympic team (1994).
STATISTICAL PLATEAUS: Three-goal games: 1995-96 (1), 1996-97 (1), 1999-00 (2). Total: 4. ... Four-goal games: 1997-98 (1). ... Total hat tricks: 5.

Season Team	League	REGULAR SEASON								PLAYOFFS				
		Gms.	G	A	Pts.	PIM	+/-	PP	SH	Gms.	G	A	Pts.	PIM
90-91 —Miami of Ohio	CCHA	28	5	6	11	26	...	...	...	—	—	—	—	—
91-92 —Miami of Ohio	CCHA	40	24	16	40	43	...	...	...	—	—	—	—	—
92-93 —Miami of Ohio	CCHA	38	37	21	58	44	...	...	...	—	—	—	—	—
—Canadian nat'l team	Int'l	9	3	0	3	12	...	...	...	—	—	—	—	—
93-94 —Canadian nat'l team	Int'l	51	20	26	46	38	...	...	...	—	—	—	—	—
—Can. Olympic team	Int'l	8	2	2	4	6	...	...	...	—	—	—	—	—
—Fredericton	AHL	17	12	15	27	4	...	...	...	—	—	—	—	—
—Montreal	NHL	3	1	0	1	0	0	0	0	3	0	2	2	0
94-95 —Montreal	NHL	37	12	7	19	27	5	0	0	—	—	—	—	—
95-96 —Montreal	NHL	75	25	8	33	28	-8	4	0	6	0	2	2	2
96-97 —Montreal	NHL	81	23	37	60	39	-14	5	0	5	1	1	2	0
97-98 —Montreal	NHL	64	26	17	43	36	11	8	0	9	0	2	2	6
98-99 —Montreal	NHL	54	16	10	26	20	-14	5	0	—	—	—	—	—
99-00 —Montreal	NHL	38	17	12	29	19	-4	6	1	—	—	—	—	—
NHL Totals (7 years)		352	120	91	211	169	-24	28	1	23	1	7	8	8

SAVAGE, REGGIE   RW   BLUE JACKETS

PERSONAL: Born May 1, 1970, in Montreal. ... 5-10/197. ... Shoots left. ... Full Name: Reginald David Savage.
TRANSACTIONS/CAREER NOTES: Selected by Washington Capitals in first round (first Capitals pick, 15th overall) of NHL entry draft (June 11, 1988). ... Traded by Capitals with RW Paul MacDermid to Quebec Nordiques for LW Mike Hough (June 20, 1993). ... Suffered charley horse (October 20, 1993); missed one game. ... Fractured left wrist (February 14, 1994); missed remainder of season. ... Signed as free agent by Phoenix Coyotes (August 28, 1996). ... Signed as free agent by Columbus Blue Jackets (June 1, 2000).
MISCELLANEOUS: Scored on a penalty shot (vs. Jon Casey, November 18, 1992).

Season Team	League	Gms.	G	A	Pts.	PIM	+/-	PP	SH	Gms.	G	A	Pts.	PIM
87-88—Victoriaville	QMJHL	68	68	54	122	77	...	...	...	5	2	3	5	8
88-89—Victoriaville	QMJHL	54	58	55	113	178	...	...	...	16	15	13	28	52
89-90—Victoriaville	QMJHL	63	51	43	94	79	...	...	...	16	13	10	23	40
90-91—Baltimore	AHL	62	32	29	61	10	...	...	...	6	1	1	2	6
—Washington	NHL	1	0	0	0	0	...	...	...	—	—	—	—	—
91-92—Baltimore	AHL	77	42	28	70	51	...	...	...	—	—	—	—	—
92-93—Baltimore	AHL	40	37	18	55	28	...	...	...	—	—	—	—	—
—Washington	NHL	16	2	3	5	12	-4	2	0	—	—	—	—	—
93-94—Quebec	NHL	17	3	4	7	16	3	1	0	—	—	—	—	—
—Cornwall	AHL	33	21	13	34	56	...	...	...	—	—	—	—	—
94-95—Cornwall	AHL	34	13	7	20	56	...	...	...	14	5	6	11	40
95-96—Syracuse	AHL	10	9	5	14	28	...	...	...	16	9	6	15	54
—Atlanta	IHL	66	22	14	36	118	...	...	...	—	—	—	—	—
96-97—Springfield	AHL	68	32	25	57	103	...	...	...	17	6	7	13	24
97-98—Kansas City	IHL	51	6	10	16	60	...	...	...	—	—	—	—	—
—San Antonio	IHL	22	6	12	18	24	...	...	...	—	—	—	—	—
—Orlando	IHL	10	5	5	10	18	...	...	...	17	2	9	11	60
98-99—Asiago	Italy	44	44	47	91	80	...	...	...	—	—	—	—	—
99-00—Syracuse	AHL	78	36	34	70	135	...	...	...	4	0	0	0	8
NHL Totals (3 years)		34	5	7	12	28	-1	3	0					

SAVARD, MARC   C   FLAMES

PERSONAL: Born July 17, 1977, in Ottawa. ... 5-10/184. ... Shoots left. ... Name pronounced suh-VAHRD.
HIGH SCHOOL: Henry Street (Whitby, Ont.).
TRANSACTIONS/CAREER NOTES: Selected by New York Rangers in fourth round (third Rangers pick, 91st overall) of NHL entry draft (July 8, 1995). ... Traded by Rangers with first-round pick (C/LW Oleg Saprykin) in 1999 draft to Calgary Flames for rights to LW Jan Hlavac and first- (C Jamie Lundmark) and third-round (D Pat Aufiero) picks in 1999 draft (June 26, 1999). ... Suffered concussion (January 8, 2000); missed two games.
HONORS: Won Can.HL Top Scorer Award (1994-95). ... Won Eddie Powers Memorial Trophy (1994-95). ... Named to OHL All-Star second team (1994-95).
STATISTICAL PLATEAUS: Four-goal games: 1999-00 (1).

Season Team	League	Gms.	G	A	Pts.	PIM	+/-	PP	SH	Gms.	G	A	Pts.	PIM
92-93—Metcalfe	Jr. B	31	46	53	99	26	...	...	...	—	—	—	—	—
93-94—Oshawa	OHL	61	18	39	57	24	...	...	...	5	4	3	7	8
94-95—Oshawa	OHL	66	43	96	*139	78	...	...	...	7	5	6	11	8
95-96—Oshawa	OHL	48	28	59	87	77	...	...	...	5	4	5	9	6
96-97—Oshawa	OHL	64	43	*87	*130	94	...	...	...	18	13	†24	*37	20
97-98—New York Rangers	NHL	28	1	5	6	4	-4	0	0	—	—	—	—	—
—Hartford	AHL	58	21	53	74	66	...	...	...	15	8	19	27	24
98-99—Hartford	AHL	9	3	10	13	16	...	...	...	7	1	12	13	16
—New York Rangers	NHL	70	9	36	45	38	-7	4	0	—	—	—	—	—
99-00—Calgary	NHL	78	22	31	53	56	-2	4	0	—	—	—	—	—
NHL Totals (3 years)		176	32	72	104	98	-13	8	0					

SAWYER, KEVIN   LW   MIGHTY DUCKS

PERSONAL: Born February 18, 1974, in Christina Lake, B.C. ... 6-2/205. ... Shoots left.
TRANSACTIONS/CAREER NOTES: Signed as non-drafted free agent by St. Louis Blues (February 16, 1995). ... Traded by Blues with D Steve Staios to Boston Bruins for RW Steve Leach (March 8, 1996). ... Signed as free agent by Dallas Stars (July 25, 1997). ... Signed as free agent by St. Louis Blues (September 4, 1998). ... Signed as free agent by Phoenix Coyotes (August 15, 1999). ... Signed as free agent by Mighty Ducks of Anaheim (July 13, 2000).

Season Team	League	Gms.	G	A	Pts.	PIM	+/-	PP	SH	Gms.	G	A	Pts.	PIM
92-93—Spokane	WHL	62	4	3	7	274	...	...	...	—	—	—	—	—
93-94—Spokane	WHL	60	10	15	25	350	...	...	...	3	0	1	1	6
94-95—Spokane	WHL	54	7	9	16	365	...	...	...	11	2	0	2	58
—Peoria	IHL	—	—	—	—	—	...	...	...	2	0	0	0	12
95-96—Worcester	AHL	41	3	4	7	268	...	...	...	—	—	—	—	—
—St. Louis	NHL	6	0	0	0	23	-2	0	0	—	—	—	—	—
—Providence	AHL	4	0	0	0	29	...	...	...	4	0	1	1	9
—Boston	NHL	2	0	0	0	5	1	0	0	—	—	—	—	—
96-97—Providence	AHL	60	8	9	17	367	...	...	...	6	0	0	0	32
—Boston	NHL	2	0	0	0	0	0	0	0	—	—	—	—	—
97-98—Michigan	IHL	60	2	5	7	*398	...	...	...	3	0	0	0	23
98-99—Worcester	AHL	70	8	14	22	299	...	...	...	4	0	1	1	4
99-00—Phoenix	NHL	3	0	0	0	12	1	0	0	—	—	—	—	—
—Springfield	AHL	56	4	8	12	321	...	...	...	4	0	0	0	6
NHL Totals (3 years)		13	0	0	0	40	0	0	0					

SCATCHARD, DAVE   C   ISLANDERS

PERSONAL: Born February 20, 1976, in Hinton, Alta. ... 6-2/220. ... Shoots right. ... Name pronounced SKATCH-uhrd.
TRANSACTIONS/CAREER NOTES: Selected by Vancouver Canucks in second round (third Canucks pick, 42nd overall) of NHL entry draft (June 28, 1994). ... Suffered hip pointer (December 15, 1997); missed two games. ... Bruised ankle (October 13, 1999); missed five games. ... Traded by Canucks with G Kevin Weekes and RW Bill Muckalt to New York Islanders for G Felix Potvin, second- (traded to Atlanta) and third-round (C Thatcher Bell) picks in 2000 draft (December 19, 1999). ... Suffered concussion (March 22, 2000); missed final eight games of season.

Season Team	League	REGULAR SEASON								PLAYOFFS				
		Gms.	G	A	Pts.	PIM	+/-	PP	SH	Gms.	G	A	Pts.	PIM
92-93—Kimberley	RMJHL	51	20	23	43	61	...	...	...	—	—	—	—	—
93-94—Portland	WHL	47	9	11	20	46	...	...	...	10	2	1	3	4
94-95—Portland	WHL	71	20	30	50	148	...	...	...	8	0	3	3	21
95-96—Portland	WHL	59	19	28	47	146	...	...	...	7	1	8	9	14
—Syracuse	AHL	1	0	0	0	0	...	...	...	15	2	5	7	29
96-97—Syracuse	AHL	26	8	7	15	65	...	...	...	—	—	—	—	—
97-98—Vancouver	NHL	76	13	11	24	165	-4	0	0	—	—	—	—	—
98-99—Vancouver	NHL	82	13	13	26	140	-12	0	2	—	—	—	—	—
99-00—Vancouver	NHL	21	0	4	4	24	-3	0	0	—	—	—	—	—
—New York Islanders	NHL	44	12	14	26	93	0	0	1	—	—	—	—	—
NHL Totals (3 years)		223	38	42	80	422	-19	0	3					

SCHAEFER, PETER — LW — CANUCKS

PERSONAL: Born July 12, 1977, in Yellow Grass, Sask. ... 5-11/195. ... Shoots left.
HIGH SCHOOL: Crocus Plains (Brandon, Man.).
TRANSACTIONS/CAREER NOTES: Selected by Vancouver Canucks in third round (third Canucks pick, 66th overall) of NHL entry draft (July 8, 1995). ... Sprained shoulder (April 2, 1999); missed final six games of season. ... Suffered illness (November 20, 1999); missed one game. ... Injured knee (February 14, 2000); missed three games. ... Reinjured knee (February 23, 2000); missed four games. ... Suffered from the flu (April 2, 2000); missed one game.
HONORS: Named to WHL (East) All-Star first team (1995-96 and 1996-97). ... Won Four Broncos Memorial Trophy (1996-97). ... Named to Can.HL All-Star first team (1996-97).

Season Team	League	REGULAR SEASON								PLAYOFFS				
		Gms.	G	A	Pts.	PIM	+/-	PP	SH	Gms.	G	A	Pts.	PIM
93-94—Brandon	WHL	2	1	0	1	0	...	...	...	—	—	—	—	—
94-95—Brandon	WHL	68	27	32	59	34	...	...	...	18	5	3	8	18
95-96—Brandon	WHL	69	47	61	108	53	...	...	...	19	10	13	23	5
96-97—Brandon	WHL	61	49	74	123	85	...	...	...	6	1	4	5	4
—Syracuse	AHL	5	0	3	3	0	...	...	...	3	1	3	4	14
97-98—Syracuse	AHL	73	19	44	63	41	...	...	...	5	2	1	3	2
98-99—Syracuse	AHL	41	10	19	29	66	...	...	...	—	—	—	—	—
—Vancouver	NHL	25	4	4	8	8	-1	1	0	—	—	—	—	—
99-00—Vancouver	NHL	71	16	15	31	20	0	2	2	—	—	—	—	—
—Syracuse	AHL	2	0	0	0	2	...	...	...	—	—	—	—	—
NHL Totals (2 years)		96	20	19	39	28	-1	3	2					

SCHASTLIVY, PETR — LW — SENATORS

PERSONAL: Born April 18, 1979, in Angarsk, U.S.S.R. ... 6-1/204. ... Shoots left.
TRANSACTIONS/CAREER NOTES: Selected by Ottawa Senators in fourth round (fifth Senators pick, 101st overall) of NHL entry draft (June 27, 1998).

Season Team	League	REGULAR SEASON								PLAYOFFS				
		Gms.	G	A	Pts.	PIM	+/-	PP	SH	Gms.	G	A	Pts.	PIM
96-97—Yermak Angarsk	Rus. Div. III					Statistics unavailable.								
97-98—Torpedo-2 Yaroslavl	Rus. Div. II	47	15	9	24	34	...	...	...	—	—	—	—	—
—Torpedo Yaroslavl	Russian	4	0	0	0	0	...	...	...	—	—	—	—	—
98-99—Torpedo Yaroslavl	Russian	40	6	1	7	28	...	...	...	6	0	0	0	2
99-00—Grand Rapids	IHL	46	16	12	28	10	...	...	...	17	8	7	15	6
—Ottawa	NHL	13	2	5	7	2	4	1	0	1	0	0	0	0
NHL Totals (1 year)		13	2	5	7	2	4	1	0	1	0	0	0	0

SCHILL, JONATHAN — LW — BLUE JACKETS

PERSONAL: Born June 28, 1979, in Kitchener, Ont. ... 6-1/201. ... Shoots left.
TRANSACTIONS/CAREER NOTES: Signed as non-drafted free agent by Columbus Blue Jackets (May 8, 2000).

Season Team	League	REGULAR SEASON								PLAYOFFS				
		Gms.	G	A	Pts.	PIM	+/-	PP	SH	Gms.	G	A	Pts.	PIM
96-97—Kingston	OHL	52	3	7	10	16	...	...	...	4	0	0	0	0
97-98—Kingston	OHL	67	14	17	31	34	...	...	...	12	1	1	2	4
98-99—Kingston	OHL	68	32	27	59	93	...	...	...	5	2	1	3	6
99-00—Kingston	OHL	65	39	48	87	79	...	...	...	3	1	1	2	6

SCHNEIDER, MATHIEU — D

PERSONAL: Born June 12, 1969, in New York. ... 5-10/192. ... Shoots left.
HIGH SCHOOL: Mount St. Charles Academy (Woonsocket, R.I.).
TRANSACTIONS/CAREER NOTES: Selected by Montreal Canadiens in third round (fourth Canadiens pick, 44th overall) of NHL entry draft (June 13, 1987). ... Bruised left shoulder (February 1990). ... Sprained left ankle (January 26, 1991); missed nine games. ... Sprained ankle (January 27, 1993); missed 24 games. ... Separated shoulder (April 18, 1993); missed seven playoff games. ... Injured ankle (December 6, 1993); missed two games. ... Underwent elbow surgery (March 29, 1994); missed five games. ... Suffered illness (February 27, 1995); missed one game. ... Traded by Canadiens with LW Kirk Muller and C Craig Darby to New York Islanders for D Vladimir Malakhov and C Pierre Turgeon (April 5, 1995). ... Bruised ribs (October 28, 1995); missed one game. ... Traded by Islanders with LW Wendel Clark and D D.J. Smith to Toronto Maple Leafs for LW Sean Haggerty, C Darby Hendrickson, D Kenny Jonsson and first-round pick (G Roberto Luongo) in 1997 draft

S

(March 13, 1996). ... Suspended three games by NHL for elbowing incident (November 14, 1996). ... Strained groin (December 12, 1996); missed 27 games. ... Reinjured groin (February 12, 1997) and underwent surgery; and missed final 26 games of season. ... Suffered concussion and facial lacerations (December 2, 1997); missed two games. ... Bruised shoulder (January 6, 1998); missed two games. ... Strained upper abdominal muscle (February 2, 1998); missed one game. ... Strained groin (April 6, 1998); missed one game. ... Traded by Maple Leafs to New York Rangers for D Alexander Karpovtsev and fourth-round pick (LW Mirko Murovic) in 1999 draft (October 14, 1998). ... Suffered from the flu (January 27, 2000); missed one game. ... Suffered from the flu (March 26, 2000); missed one game. ... Selected by Columbus Blue Jackets in NHL expansion draft (June 23, 2000).

HONORS: Named to OHL All-Star first team (1987-88 and 1988-89). ... Played in NHL All-Star Game (1996).

MISCELLANEOUS: Member of Stanley Cup championship team (1993). ... Captain of New York Islanders (1995-March 13, 1996).

		REGULAR SEASON								PLAYOFFS				
Season Team	League	Gms.	G	A	Pts.	PIM	+/-	PP	SH	Gms.	G	A	Pts.	PIM
85-86—Mt. St. Charles H.S.	R.I.H.S.	19	3	27	30	...	...	...	...	—	—	—	—	—
86-87—Cornwall	OHL	63	7	29	36	75	...	...	...	5	0	0	0	22
87-88—Montreal	NHL	4	0	0	0	2	-2	0	0	—	—	—	—	—
—Cornwall	OHL	48	21	40	61	85	...	...	...	11	2	6	8	14
—Sherbrooke	AHL	—	—	—	—	—	...	...	...	3	0	3	3	12
88-89—Cornwall	OHL	59	16	57	73	96	...	...	...	18	7	20	27	30
89-90—Sherbrooke	AHL	28	6	13	19	20	...	...	...	—	—	—	—	—
—Montreal	NHL	44	7	14	21	25	2	5	0	9	1	3	4	31
90-91—Montreal	NHL	69	10	20	30	63	7	5	0	13	2	7	9	18
91-92—Montreal	NHL	78	8	24	32	72	10	2	0	10	1	4	5	6
92-93—Montreal	NHL	60	13	31	44	91	8	3	0	11	1	2	3	16
93-94—Montreal	NHL	75	20	32	52	62	15	11	0	1	0	0	0	0
94-95—Montreal	NHL	30	5	15	20	49	-3	2	0	—	—	—	—	—
—New York Islanders	NHL	13	3	6	9	30	-5	1	0	—	—	—	—	—
95-96—New York Islanders	NHL	65	11	36	47	93	-18	7	0	—	—	—	—	—
—Toronto	NHL	13	2	5	7	10	-2	0	0	6	0	4	4	8
96-97—Toronto	NHL	26	5	7	12	20	3	1	0	—	—	—	—	—
97-98—Toronto	NHL	76	11	26	37	44	-12	4	1	—	—	—	—	—
—U.S. Olympic team	Int'l	4	0	0	0	6	...	...	...	—	—	—	—	—
98-99—New York Rangers	NHL	75	10	24	34	71	-19	5	0	—	—	—	—	—
99-00—New York Rangers	NHL	80	10	20	30	78	-6	3	0	—	—	—	—	—
NHL Totals (12 years)		708	115	260	375	710	-22	49	1	50	5	20	25	79

SCHULTZ, RAY — D — ISLANDERS

PERSONAL: Born November 14, 1976, in Red Deer, Alta. ... 6-2/200. ... Shoots left. ... Cousin of Rene Chapdelaine, defenseman with Los Angeles Kings (1990-91 through 1992-93).

TRANSACTIONS/CAREER NOTES: Selected by Ottawa Senators in eighth round (eighth Senators pick, 184th overall) of NHL entry draft (July 8, 1995). ... Signed as free agent by New York Islanders (June 17, 1997). ... Suspended two games by AHL for being assessed a match penalty in a game (February 19, 1999).

		REGULAR SEASON								PLAYOFFS				
Season Team	League	Gms.	G	A	Pts.	PIM	+/-	PP	SH	Gms.	G	A	Pts.	PIM
93-94—Tri-City	WHL	3	0	0	0	11	...	...	...	—	—	—	—	—
94-95—Tri-City	WHL	63	1	8	9	209	...	...	...	11	0	0	0	16
95-96—Calgary	WHL	66	3	17	20	282	...	...	...	—	—	—	—	—
96-97—Calgary	WHL	32	3	17	20	141	...	...	...	—	—	—	—	—
—Kelowna	WHL	23	3	11	14	63	...	...	...	6	0	2	2	12
97-98—Kentucky	AHL	51	2	4	6	179	...	...	...	1	0	0	0	25
—New York Islanders	NHL	13	0	1	1	45	3	0	0	—	—	—	—	—
98-99—Lowell	AHL	54	0	3	3	184	...	...	...	1	0	0	0	4
—New York Islanders	NHL	4	0	0	0	7	-2	0	0	—	—	—	—	—
99-00—Kansas City	IHL	65	5	5	10	208	...	...	...	—	—	—	—	—
—New York Islanders	NHL	9	0	1	1	30	1	0	0	—	—	—	—	—
NHL Totals (3 years)		26	0	2	2	82	2	0	0					

SCHWAB, COREY — G — CANUCKS

PERSONAL: Born November 4, 1970, in North Battleford, Sask. ... 6-0/180. ... Catches left. ... Name pronounced SHWAHB.

TRANSACTIONS/CAREER NOTES: Selected by New Jersey Devils in 10th round (12th Devils pick, 200th overall) of NHL entry draft (June 16, 1990). ... Injured groin (October 12, 1995); missed six games. ... Traded by Devils to Tampa Bay Lightning for G Jeff Reese and second-(LW Pierre Dagenais) and eighth-(RW Jason Bertsch) round picks in 1996 draft (June 22, 1996). ... Injured groin (January 9, 1997); missed one game. ... Injured groin (December 23, 1997); missed one game. ... Injured ankle (December 31, 1997); missed remainder of season. ... Selected by Atlanta Thrashers in NHL expansion draft (June 25, 1999). ... Traded by Thrashers to Vancouver Canucks for conditional pick in 2000 draft (October 29, 1999).

HONORS: Shared Harry (Hap) Holmes Memorial Trophy with Mike Dunham (1994-95). ... Shared Jack Butterfield Trophy with Mike Dunham (1994-95). ... Named to AHL All-Star second team (1994-95).

MISCELLANEOUS: Stopped a penalty shot attempt (vs. Steve Heinze, December 17, 1997).

		REGULAR SEASON							PLAYOFFS					
Season Team	League	Gms.	Min	W	L	T	GA	SO	Avg.	Gms.	Min.	W	L	GA	SO	Avg.
88-89—Seattle	WHL	10	386	2	2	0	31	0	4.82	—	—	—	—	—	—	—
89-90—Seattle	WHL	27	1150	15	2	1	69	0	3.60	3	49	0	0	2	0	2.45
90-91—Seattle	WHL	58	3289	32	18	3	224	0	4.09	6	382	1	5	25	0	3.93
91-92—Utica	AHL	24	1322	9	12	1	95	1	4.31	—	—	—	—	—	—	—
—Cincinnati	AHL	8	450	6	0	1	31	0	4.13	9	540	6	3	29	0	3.22
92-93—Cincinnati	IHL	3	185	1	2	0	17	0	5.51	—	—	—	—	—	—	—
—Utica	AHL	40	2387	18	16	5	169	2	4.25	1	59	0	1	6	0	6.10
93-94—Albany	AHL	51	3059	27	21	3	184	0	3.61	5	298	1	4	20	0	4.03

Season Team	League	REGULAR SEASON								PLAYOFFS						
		Gms.	Min	W	L	T	GA	SO	Avg.	Gms.	Min.	W	L	GA	SO	Avg.
94-95—Albany	AHL	45	2711	25	10	9	117	3	*2.59	7	425	6	1	19	0	2.68
95-96—Albany	AHL	5	298	3	2	0	13	0	2.62	—	—	—	—	—	—	—
—New Jersey	NHL	10	331	0	3	0	12	0	2.18	—	—	—	—	—	—	—
96-97—Tampa Bay	NHL	31	1462	11	12	1	74	2	3.04	—	—	—	—	—	—	—
97-98—Tampa Bay	NHL	16	821	2	9	1	40	1	2.92	—	—	—	—	—	—	—
98-99—Cleveland	IHL	8	477	1	6	‡1	31	0	3.90	—	—	—	—	—	—	—
—Tampa Bay	NHL	40	2146	8	25	3	126	0	3.52	—	—	—	—	—	—	—
99-00—Orlando	IHL	16	868	13	4	‡2	31	1	2.14	—	—	—	—	—	—	—
—Vancouver	NHL	6	269	2	1	1	16	0	3.57	—	—	—	—	—	—	—
—Syracuse	AHL	12	720	7	5	0	42	0	3.50	4	246	1	3	11	1	2.68
NHL Totals (5 years)		103	5029	23	50	6	268	3	3.20							

SCOVILLE, DARRYL — D — FLAMES

PERSONAL: Born October 13, 1975, in Regina, Sask. ... 6-3/215. ... Shoots left.
COLLEGE: Merrimack College (Mass.).
TRANSACTIONS/CAREER NOTES: Signed as non-drafted free agent by Calgary Flames (June 12, 1998).

Season Team	League	REGULAR SEASON							PLAYOFFS				
		Gms.	G	A	Pts.	PIM	+/-	PP	SH	Gms.	G	A	Pts.	PIM
95-96—Merrimack College	Hockey East	34	6	20	26	54	...	...	...	—	—	—	—	—
96-97—Merrimack College	Hockey East	35	7	16	23	71	...	...	...	—	—	—	—	—
97-98—Merrimack College	Hockey East	38	4	26	30	84	...	...	...	—	—	—	—	—
98-99—Saint John	AHL	61	1	7	8	66	...	...	...	7	1	2	3	13
99-00—Saint John	AHL	64	11	25	36	99	...	...	...	3	1	2	3	0
—Calgary	NHL	6	0	0	0	2	1	0	0	—	—	—	—	—
NHL Totals (1 year)		6	0	0	0	2	1	0	0					

SEDIN, DANIEL — LW — CANUCKS

PERSONAL: Born September 26, 1980, in Ornskoldsvik, Sweden. ... 6-1/194. ... Shoots left. ... Twin brother of Henrik Sedin, center, Vancouver Canucks.
TRANSACTIONS/CAREER NOTES: Selected by Vancouver Canucks in first round (first Canucks pick, second overall) of NHL entry draft (June 26, 1999).

Season Team	League	REGULAR SEASON							PLAYOFFS				
		Gms.	G	A	Pts.	PIM	+/-	PP	SH	Gms.	G	A	Pts.	PIM
96-97—MoDo Ornsk. Jrs.	Sweden Jr.	26	26	14	40	...	...	...	...	—	—	—	—	—
97-98—MoDo Ornskoldsvik	Sweden	45	4	8	12	26	...	...	...	9	0	0	0	2
—MoDo Ornsk. Jrs.	Sweden Jr.	4	3	3	6	4	...	...	...	—	—	—	—	—
98-99—MoDo Ornskoldsvik	Sweden	50	21	21	42	20	...	...	...	13	4	8	12	14
99-00—MoDo Ornskoldsvik	Sweden	50	19	26	45	28	...	...	...	13	†8	6	14	18

SEDIN, HENRIK — C — CANUCKS

PERSONAL: Born September 26, 1980, in Ornskoldsvik, Sweden. ... 6-2/196. ... Shoots left. ... Twin brother of Daniel Sedin, left winger, Vancouver Canucks.
TRANSACTIONS/CAREER NOTES: Selected by Vancouver Canucks in first round (second Canucks pick, third overall) of NHL entry draft (June 26, 1999).

Season Team	League	REGULAR SEASON							PLAYOFFS				
		Gms.	G	A	Pts.	PIM	+/-	PP	SH	Gms.	G	A	Pts.	PIM
96-97—MoDo Ornsk. Jrs.	Sweden Jr.	26	14	22	36	...	...	...	...	—	—	—	—	—
97-98—MoDo Ornskoldsvik	Sweden	39	1	4	5	8	...	...	...	7	0	0	0	0
—MoDo Ornsk. Jrs.	Sweden Jr.	8	4	7	11	8	...	...	...	—	—	—	—	—
98-99—MoDo Ornskoldsvik	Sweden	49	12	22	34	32	...	...	...	13	2	8	10	6
99-00—MoDo Ornskoldsvik	Sweden	50	9	38	47	22	...	...	...	13	5	9	14	2

SEELEY, RICHARD — D — KINGS

PERSONAL: Born April 30, 1979, in Powell River, B.C. ... 6-2/199. ... Shoots left.
TRANSACTIONS/CAREER NOTES: Selected by Los Angeles Kings in sixth round (sixth Kings pick, 137th overall) of NHL entry draft (June 21, 1997).

Season Team	League	REGULAR SEASON							PLAYOFFS				
		Gms.	G	A	Pts.	PIM	+/-	PP	SH	Gms.	G	A	Pts.	PIM
95-96—Powell River	BCJHL	44	1	8	9	42	...	...	...	—	—	—	—	—
96-97—Lethbridge	WHL	3	0	0	0	11	...	...	...	—	—	—	—	—
—Prince Albert	WHL	18	0	1	1	9	...	...	...	4	0	0	0	2
97-98—Prince Albert	WHL	65	8	21	29	114	...	...	...	—	—	—	—	—
98-99—Prince Albert	WHL	61	10	48	58	110	...	...	...	14	1	11	12	14
99-00—Lowell	AHL	36	5	1	6	37	...	...	...	—	—	—	—	—

SELANNE, TEEMU — RW — MIGHTY DUCKS

PERSONAL: Born July 3, 1970, in Helsinki, Finland. ... 6-0/200. ... Shoots right. ... Name pronounced TAY-moo suh-LAH-nay. ... Nickname: The Finnish Flash.
TRANSACTIONS/CAREER NOTES: Selected by Winnipeg Jets in first round (first Jets pick, 10th overall) of NHL entry draft (June 11, 1988). ... Fractured left leg (October 19, 1989). ... Severed Achilles' tendon (January 26, 1994); missed 33 games. ... Played in Europe during 1994-95 NHL lockout. ... Suffered from patella tendonitis (February 28, 1995); missed one game. ... Suspended two games and fined $500 by NHL (March 28, 1995). ... Traded by Jets with C Marc Chouinard and fourth-round pick (traded to Toronto) in 1996 draft to Mighty Ducks of

Anaheim for C Chad Kilger, D Oleg Tverdovsky and third-round pick (D Per-Anton Lundstrom) in 1996 draft (Febraury 7, 1996). ... Strained abdominal muscle (March 23, 1997); missed four games. ... Strained abdominal muscle (February 7, 1998); missed five games. ... Strained groin (April 9, 1998); missed final four games of season. ... Strained thigh muscle (November 11,1998); missed six games. ... Reinjured thigh muscle (December 3, 1998); missed one game. ... Strained groin (November 14, 1999); missed three games.

HONORS: Named to Finnish League All-Star team (1990-91 and 1991-92). ... Named NHL Rookie of the Year by THE SPORTING NEWS (1992-93). ... Won Calder Memorial Trophy (1992-93). ... Named to THE SPORTING NEWS All-Star first team (1992-93). ... Named to NHL All-Star first team (1992-93 and 1996-97). ... Named to NHL All-Rookie team (1992-93). ... Played in NHL All-Star Game (1993, 1994 and 1996-2000). ... Named to THE SPORTING NEWS All-Star team (1996-97 and 1997-98). ... Named All-Star Game Most Valuable Player (1998). ... Named to NHL All-Star second team (1997-98 and 1998-99). ... Won Maurice "Rocket" Richard Trophy (1998-99).

RECORDS: Holds NHL rookie-season records for most points—132; and goals—76 (1993).

STATISTICAL PLATEAUS: Three-goal games: 1992-93 (4), 1993-94 (2), 1995-96 (2), 1996-97 (1), 1997-98 (3), 1998-99 (1), 1999-00 (1). Total: 14. ... Four-goal games: 1992-93 (1), 1995-96 (1). Total: 2. ... Total hat tricks: 16.

MISCELLANEOUS: Member of bronze-medal-winning Finnish Olympic team (1998). ... Captain of Mighty Ducks of Anaheim (October 1-December 10, 1997 and February 4, 1998 through remainder of season). ... Scored on a penalty shot (vs. Wendell Young, March 9, 1993). ... Failed to score on a penalty shot (vs. Trevor Kidd, February 6, 1995; vs. Jean-Sebastien Aubin, October 27, 1999).

STATISTICAL NOTES: Tied for NHL lead with three game-tying goals (1997-98).

		REGULAR SEASON							PLAYOFFS				
Season Team	League	Gms.	G	A	Pts.	PIM	+/-	PP	SH	Gms.	G	A	Pts.	PIM
87-88—Jokerit Helsinki	Finland Jr.	33	43	23	66	18	...	...	...	5	4	3	7	2
—Jokerit Helsinki	Finland	5	1	1	2	0	...	...	...	—	—	—	—	—
88-89—Jokerit Helsinki	Finland	34	35	33	68	12	...	...	...	5	7	3	10	4
89-90—Jokerit Helsinki	Finland	11	4	8	12	0	...	...	...	—	—	—	—	—
90-91—Jokerit Helsinki	Finland	42	*33	25	58	12	...	...	...	—	—	—	—	—
91-92—Fin. Olympic team	Int'l	8	7	4	11	...	...	...	...	—	—	—	—	—
—Jokerit Helsinki	Finland	44	39	23	62	20	...	...	...	—	—	—	—	—
92-93—Winnipeg	NHL	84	†76	56	132	45	8	24	0	6	4	2	6	2
93-94—Winnipeg	NHL	51	25	29	54	22	-23	11	0	—	—	—	—	—
94-95—Jokerit Helsinki	Finland	20	7	12	19	6	...	...	...	—	—	—	—	—
—Winnipeg	NHL	45	22	26	48	2	1	8	2	—	—	—	—	—
95-96—Winnipeg	NHL	51	24	48	72	18	3	6	1	—	—	—	—	—
—Anaheim	NHL	28	16	20	36	4	2	3	0	—	—	—	—	—
96-97—Anaheim	NHL	78	51	58	109	34	28	11	1	11	7	3	10	4
97-98—Anaheim	NHL	73	†52	34	86	30	12	10	1	—	—	—	—	—
—Fin. Olympic team	Int'l	5	4	6	10	8	...	...	...	—	—	—	—	—
98-99—Anaheim	NHL	75	*47	60	107	30	18	*25	0	4	2	2	4	2
99-00—Anaheim	NHL	79	33	52	85	12	6	8	0	—	—	—	—	—
NHL Totals (8 years)		564	346	383	729	197	55	106	5	21	13	7	20	8

SELIVANOV, ALEX RW

PERSONAL: Born March 23, 1971, in Moscow, U.S.S.R. ... 6-0/206. ... Shoots left. ... Full Name: Alexander Selivanov. ... Name pronounced sehl-ih-VAH-nahf.

TRANSACTIONS/CAREER NOTES: Selected by Philadelphia Flyers in sixth round (sixth Flyers pick, 140th overall) of NHL entry draft (June 29, 1994). ... Rights traded by Flyers to Tampa Bay Lightning for fourth-round pick (LW Radovan Somik) in 1995 draft (September 6, 1994). ... Sprained ankle (February 10, 1996); missed two games. ... Injured back (November 25, 1996); missed one game. ... Injured wrist (December 14, 1996); missed one game. ... Sprained knee (February 4, 1997); missed one game. ... Underwent knee surgery (February 25, 1997); missed eight games. ... Suffered a partial facial fracture (April 2, 1998); missed final eight games of season. ... Injured wrist (January 26, 1999); missed one game. ... Traded by Lightning to Edmonton Oilers for C/RW Alexandre Daigle (January 29, 1999).

STATISTICAL PLATEAUS: Three-goal games: 1998-99 (1), 1999-00 (1). Total: 2. ... Four-goal games: 1999-00 (1). ... Total hat tricks: 3.

		REGULAR SEASON							PLAYOFFS				
Season Team	League	Gms.	G	A	Pts.	PIM	+/-	PP	SH	Gms.	G	A	Pts.	PIM
88-89—Spartak Moscow	USSR	1	0	0	0	0	...	...	...	—	—	—	—	—
89-90—Spartak Moscow	USSR	4	0	0	0	0	...	...	...	—	—	—	—	—
90-91—Spartak Moscow	USSR	21	3	1	4	6	...	...	...	—	—	—	—	—
91-92—Spartak Moscow	CIS	31	6	7	13	16	...	...	...	—	—	—	—	—
92-93—Spartak Moscow	CIS	42	12	19	31	16	...	...	...	3	2	0	2	2
93-94—Spartak Moscow	CIS	45	30	11	41	50	...	...	...	6	5	1	6	2
94-95—Atlanta	IHL	4	0	3	3	2	...	...	...	—	—	—	—	—
—Chicago	IHL	14	4	1	5	8	...	...	...	—	—	—	—	—
—Tampa Bay	NHL	43	10	6	16	14	-2	4	0	—	—	—	—	—
95-96—Tampa Bay	NHL	79	31	21	52	93	3	13	0	6	2	2	4	6
96-97—Tampa Bay	NHL	69	15	18	33	61	-3	3	0	—	—	—	—	—
97-98—Tampa Bay	NHL	70	16	19	35	85	-38	4	0	—	—	—	—	—
98-99—Cleveland	IHL	2	0	1	1	4	...	...	...	—	—	—	—	—
—Tampa Bay	NHL	43	6	13	19	18	-8	1	0	—	—	—	—	—
—Edmonton	NHL	29	8	6	14	24	0	1	0	2	0	1	1	2
99-00—Edmonton	NHL	67	27	20	47	46	2	10	0	5	0	0	0	8
NHL Totals (6 years)		400	113	103	216	341	-46	36	0	13	2	3	5	16

SEMENOV, ALEXEI D OILERS

PERSONAL: Born April 10, 1981, in Murmansk, U.S.S.R. ... 6-6/210. ... Shoots left.

TRANSACTIONS/CAREER NOTES: Selected by Edmonton Oilers in second round (second Oilers pick, 36th overall) of NHL entry draft (June 26, 1999).

		REGULAR SEASON							PLAYOFFS				
Season Team	League	Gms.	G	A	Pts.	PIM	+/-	PP	SH	Gms.	G	A	Pts.	PIM
97-98—Krylja Sovetov-2 Mos.	Rus. Div. III	52	1	2	3	48	...	...	...	—	—	—	—	—
98-99—Sudbury	OHL	28	0	3	3	28	...	...	...	2	0	0	0	4
99-00—Sudbury	OHL	65	9	35	44	135	...	...	...	12	1	3	4	23
—Hamilton	AHL	—	—	—	—	—	...	...	...	3	0	0	0	0

SHANAHAN, BRENDAN   LW   RED WINGS

PERSONAL: Born January 23, 1969, in Mimico, Ont. ... 6-3/215. ... Shoots right. ... Full Name: Brendan Frederick Shanahan.
HIGH SCHOOL: Michael Power/St. Joseph's (Islington, Ont.).
TRANSACTIONS/CAREER NOTES: Bruised tendons in shoulder (January 1987). ... Selected by New Jersey Devils as underage junior in first round (first Devils pick, second overall) of NHL entry draft (June 13, 1987). ... Fractured nose (December 1987). ... Suffered back spasms (March 1989). ... Suspended five games by NHL for stick-fighting (January 13, 1990). ... Suffered lower abdominal strain (February 1990). ... Suffered lacerations to lower right side of face and underwent surgery (January 8, 1991); missed five games. ... Signed as free agent by St. Louis Blues (July 25, 1991); D Scott Stevens awarded to Devils as compensation (September 3, 1991). ... Pulled groin (October 24, 1992); missed 12 games. ... Suspended six off-days and fined $500 by NHL for hitting another player in face with his stick (January 7, 1993). ... Suspended one game by NHL for high-sticking incident (February 23, 1993). ... Suffered viral infection (November 18, 1993); missed one game. ... Injured hamstring (March 22, 1994); missed two games. ... Played in Europe during 1994-95 NHL lockout. ... Suffered viral infection (January 20, 1995); missed three games. ... Fractured ankle (May 15, 1995); missed last two games of playoffs. ... Traded by Blues to Hartford Whalers for D Chris Pronger (July 27, 1995). ... Sprained wrist (November 11, 1995); missed eight games. ... Traded by Whalers with D Brian Glynn to Detroit Red Wings for C Keith Primeau, D Paul Coffey and first-round pick (traded to San Jose) in 1997 draft (October 9, 1996). ... Suspended one game and fined $1,000 by NHL for cross-checking incident (October 11, 1996). ... Strained groin (October 30, 1996); missed one game. ... Suffered stiff neck (October 12, 1997); missed four games. ... Suffered back spasms (April 15, 1998); missed final game of regular season and two playoff games. ... Suspended two games by NHL for stick-swinging incident (November 9, 1999).
HONORS: Played in NHL All-Star Game (1994 and 1996-2000). ... Named to NHL All-Star first team (1993-94 and 1999-2000).
MISCELLANEOUS: Member of Stanley Cup championship team (1997 and 1998). ... Captain of Hartford Whalers (1995-96). ... Failed to score on a penalty shot (vs. Grant Fuhr, December 27, 1992; vs. Trevor Kidd, November 5, 1997).
STATISTICAL PLATEAUS: Three-goal games: 1992-93 (1), 1993-94 (4), 1995-96 (1), 1996-97 (3), 1998-99 (2). Total: 11.

		REGULAR SEASON								PLAYOFFS				
Season Team	League	Gms.	G	A	Pts.	PIM	+/-	PP	SH	Gms.	G	A	Pts.	PIM
84-85—Mississauga	MTHL	36	20	21	41	26	...	...	...	—	—	—	—	—
85-86—London	OHL	59	28	34	62	70	...	...	...	5	5	5	10	5
86-87—London	OHL	56	39	53	92	128	...	...	...	—	—	—	—	—
87-88—New Jersey	NHL	65	7	19	26	131	-20	2	0	12	2	1	3	44
88-89—New Jersey	NHL	68	22	28	50	115	2	9	0	—	—	—	—	—
89-90—New Jersey	NHL	73	30	42	72	137	15	8	0	6	3	3	6	20
90-91—New Jersey	NHL	75	29	37	66	141	4	7	0	7	3	5	8	12
91-92—St. Louis	NHL	80	33	36	69	171	-3	13	0	6	2	3	5	14
92-93—St. Louis	NHL	71	51	43	94	174	10	18	0	11	4	3	7	18
93-94—St. Louis	NHL	81	52	50	102	211	-9	15	*7	4	2	5	7	4
94-95—Dusseldorf	Germany	3	5	3	8	4	...	...	...	—	—	—	—	—
—St. Louis	NHL	45	20	21	41	136	7	6	2	5	4	5	9	14
95-96—Hartford	NHL	74	44	34	78	125	2	17	2	—	—	—	—	—
96-97—Hartford	NHL	2	1	0	1	0	1	0	1	—	—	—	—	—
—Detroit	NHL	79	46	41	87	131	31	†20	2	20	9	8	17	43
97-98—Detroit	NHL	75	28	29	57	154	6	15	1	20	5	4	9	22
—Can. Olympic team	Int'l	6	2	0	2	0	...	...	...	—	—	—	—	—
98-99—Detroit	NHL	81	31	27	58	123	2	5	0	10	3	7	10	6
99-00—Detroit	NHL	78	41	37	78	105	24	13	1	9	3	2	5	10
NHL Totals (13 years)		947	435	444	879	1854	72	148	16	110	40	46	86	207

SHANNON, DARRYL   D

PERSONAL: Born June 21, 1968, in Barrie, Ont. ... 6-2/208. ... Shoots left. ... Brother of Darrin Shannon, left winger with three NHL teams (1988-89 through 1997-98).
TRANSACTIONS/CAREER NOTES: Selected by Toronto Maple Leafs in second round (second Maple Leafs pick, 36th overall) of NHL entry draft (June 21, 1986). ... Fractured right leg and right thumb, bruised chest and suffered slipped disk in automobile accident (June 20, 1990). ... Signed as free agent with Winnipeg Jets (July 8, 1993). ... Traded by Jets with LW Michael Grosek to Buffalo Sabres for D Craig Muni (February 15, 1996). ... Injured right knee (April 10, 1996); missed one game. ... Bruised knee (December 29, 1997); missed four games. ... Selected by Atlanta Thrashers in NHL expansion draft (June 25, 1999). ... Traded by Thrashers with LW Jason Botterill to Calgary Flames for C Hnat Domenichelli and LW Dmitri Vlasenkov (February 11, 2000).
HONORS: Named to OHL All-Star second team (1986-87). ... Won Max Kaminsky Trophy (1987-88). ... Named to OHL All-Star first team (1987-88). ... Named to Memorial Cup All-Star team (1987-88).

		REGULAR SEASON								PLAYOFFS				
Season Team	League	Gms.	G	A	Pts.	PIM	+/-	PP	SH	Gms.	G	A	Pts.	PIM
84-85—Barrie Jr. B	OHA	39	5	23	28	50	...	...	...	—	—	—	—	—
85-86—Windsor	OHL	57	6	21	27	52	...	...	...	16	5	6	11	22
86-87—Windsor	OHL	64	23	27	50	83	...	...	...	14	4	8	12	18
87-88—Windsor	OHL	60	16	70	86	116	...	...	...	12	3	8	11	17
88-89—Toronto	NHL	14	1	3	4	6	5	0	0	—	—	—	—	—
—Newmarket	AHL	61	5	24	29	37	...	...	...	5	0	3	3	10
89-90—Newmarket	AHL	47	4	15	19	58	...	...	...	—	—	—	—	—
—Toronto	NHL	10	0	1	1	12	-10	0	0	—	—	—	—	—
90-91—Toronto	NHL	10	0	1	1	0	1	0	0	—	—	—	—	—
—Newmarket	AHL	47	2	14	16	51	...	...	...	—	—	—	—	—
91-92—Toronto	NHL	48	2	8	10	23	-17	1	0	—	—	—	—	—
92-93—Toronto	NHL	16	0	0	0	11	-5	0	0	—	—	—	—	—
—St. John's	AHL	7	1	1	2	4	...	...	...	—	—	—	—	—
93-94—Moncton	AHL	37	1	10	11	62	...	...	...	20	1	7	8	32
—Winnipeg	NHL	20	0	4	4	18	-6	0	0	—	—	—	—	—
94-95—Winnipeg	NHL	40	5	9	14	48	1	0	1	—	—	—	—	—
95-96—Winnipeg	NHL	48	2	7	9	72	5	0	0	—	—	—	—	—
—Buffalo	NHL	26	2	6	8	20	10	0	0	—	—	—	—	—
96-97—Buffalo	NHL	82	4	19	23	112	23	1	0	12	2	3	5	8
97-98—Buffalo	NHL	76	3	19	22	56	26	1	0	15	2	4	6	8
98-99—Buffalo	NHL	71	3	12	15	52	28	1	0	2	0	0	0	0
99-00—Atlanta	NHL	49	5	13	18	65	-14	1	0	—	—	—	—	—
—Calgary	NHL	27	1	8	9	22	-13	0	0	—	—	—	—	—
NHL Totals (12 years)		537	28	110	138	517	34	5	1	29	4	7	11	16

SHANTZ, JEFF — C — FLAMES

PERSONAL: Born October 10, 1973, in Edmonton. ... 6-0/195. ... Shoots right.
HIGH SCHOOL: Robert Usher (Regina, Sask.).
TRANSACTIONS/CAREER NOTES: Selected by Chicago Blackhawks in second round (second Blackhawks pick, 36th overall) of NHL entry draft (June 20, 1992). ... Bruised right shoulder (1993-94 season); missed six games. ... Suffered swollen eye (November 30, 1996); missed one game. ... Sprained knee (February 25, 1997); missed 10 games. ... Separated shoulder (January 4, 1998); missed six games. ... Tore anterior cruciate ligament in left knee (March 19, 1998); missed final 14 games of season. ... Traded by Blackhawks with C/LW Steve Dubinsky to Calgary Flames for D Jamie Allison, C/LW Marty McInnis and RW Erik Andersson (October 27, 1998). ... Suffered concussion (November 14, 1998); missed two games. ... Injured shoulder (March 25, 1999); missed four games. ... Bruised ribs (December 6, 1999); missed eight games.
HONORS: Named to WHL (East) All-Star first team (1992-93).

		REGULAR SEASON								PLAYOFFS				
Season Team	League	Gms.	G	A	Pts.	PIM	+/-	PP	SH	Gms.	G	A	Pts.	PIM
89-90—Regina	WHL	1	0	0	0	0	...	...	...	—	—	—	—	—
—Medicine Hat	AMHL	36	18	31	49	30	...	...	...	—	—	—	—	—
90-91—Regina	WHL	69	16	21	37	22	...	...	...	8	2	2	4	2
91-92—Regina	WHL	72	39	50	89	75	...	...	...	—	—	—	—	—
92-93—Regina	WHL	64	29	54	83	75	...	...	...	13	2	12	14	14
93-94—Chicago	NHL	52	3	13	16	30	-14	0	0	6	0	0	0	6
—Indianapolis	IHL	19	5	9	14	20	...	...	...	—	—	—	—	—
94-95—Indianapolis	IHL	32	9	15	24	20	...	...	...	—	—	—	—	—
—Chicago	NHL	45	6	12	18	33	11	0	2	16	3	1	4	2
95-96—Chicago	NHL	78	6	14	20	24	12	1	2	10	2	3	5	6
96-97—Chicago	NHL	69	9	21	30	28	11	0	1	6	0	4	4	6
97-98—Chicago	NHL	61	11	20	31	36	0	1	2	—	—	—	—	—
98-99—Chicago	NHL	7	1	0	1	4	-1	0	0	—	—	—	—	—
—Calgary	NHL	69	12	17	29	40	15	1	1	—	—	—	—	—
99-00—Calgary	NHL	74	13	18	31	30	-13	6	0	—	—	—	—	—
NHL Totals (7 years)		455	61	115	176	225	21	9	8	38	5	8	13	20

SHARIFIJANOV, VADIM — RW — CANUCKS

PERSONAL: Born December 23, 1975, in Ufa, U.S.S.R. ... 6-0/205. ... Shoots left. ... Name pronounced vah-DEEM shuh-RIH-fee-AH-nahf.
TRANSACTIONS/CAREER NOTES: Selected by New Jersey Devils in first round (first Devils pick, 25th overall) of NHL entry draft (June 28, 1994). ... Strained groin (October 10, 1998); missed one game. ... Suffered from the flu (January 18, 1999); missed one game. ... Traded by Devils with third-round pick (D Tim Branham) in 2000 draft to Vancouver Canucks for third-round pick (LW Max Birbraer) in 2000 draft and third round pick in 2001 draft (January 14, 2000). ... Injured hip (February 17, 2000); missed seven games.

		REGULAR SEASON								PLAYOFFS				
Season Team	League	Gms.	G	A	Pts.	PIM	+/-	PP	SH	Gms.	G	A	Pts.	PIM
92-93—Salavat Yulayev Ufa	CIS	37	6	4	10	16	...	...	...	2	1	0	1	0
93-94—Salavat Yulayev Ufa	CIS	46	10	6	16	36	...	...	...	5	3	0	3	4
94-95—CSKA Moscow	CIS	34	7	3	10	26	...	...	...	2	0	0	0	0
—Albany	AHL	1	1	1	2	0	...	...	...	9	3	3	6	10
95-96—Albany	AHL	69	14	28	42	28	...	...	...	—	—	—	—	—
96-97—Albany	AHL	70	14	27	41	89	...	...	...	10	3	3	6	6
—New Jersey	NHL	2	0	0	0	0	0	0	0	—	—	—	—	—
97-98—Albany	AHL	72	23	27	50	69	...	...	...	12	4	9	13	6
98-99—New Jersey	NHL	53	11	16	27	28	11	1	0	4	0	0	0	0
—Albany	AHL	2	1	1	2	0	...	...	...	—	—	—	—	—
99-00—New Jersey	NHL	20	3	4	7	8	-6	0	0	—	—	—	—	—
—Vancouver	NHL	17	2	1	3	14	-7	1	0	—	—	—	—	—
NHL Totals (3 years)		92	16	21	37	50	-2	2	0	4	0	0	0	0

SHEFER, ANDREI — LW — KINGS

PERSONAL: Born July 26, 1981, in Sverdlovsk, U.S.S.R. ... 6-1/180. ... Shoots left.
TRANSACTIONS/CAREER NOTES: Selected by Los Angeles Kings in second round (first Kings pick, 43rd overall) of NHL entry draft (June 26, 1999).

		REGULAR SEASON								PLAYOFFS				
Season Team	League	Gms.	G	A	Pts.	PIM	+/-	PP	SH	Gms.	G	A	Pts.	PIM
97-98—Dyn.-Energiya-2 Yek.	Rus. Div. III	16	3	3	6	18	...	...	...	—	—	—	—	—
98-99—Severstal Cherepovets	Russian	8	1	0	1	4	...	...	...	—	—	—	—	—
99-00—Halifax	QMJHL	72	34	42	76	30	...	...	...	10	0	5	5	4

SHEPPARD, RAY — RW

PERSONAL: Born May 27, 1966, in Pembroke, Ont. ... 6-1/195. ... Shoots right.
TRANSACTIONS/CAREER NOTES: Selected by Buffalo Sabres as underage junior in third round (third Sabres pick, 60th overall) of NHL entry draft (June 9, 1984). ... Injured left knee (September 1986); missed Sabres training camp. ... Bruised back during training camp (September 1988). ... Suffered facial lacerations (November 25, 1988). ... Suffered facial lacerations (November 27, 1988). ... Suffered from the flu (December 1988). ... Sprained ankle (January 30, 1989). ... Injured left knee (March 16, 1990). ... Traded by Sabres to New York Rangers for future considerations and cash (July 10, 1990). ... Sprained medial collateral ligaments in right knee (February 18, 1991); missed 13 games. ... Dislocated left shoulder (March 24, 1991). ... Signed as free agent by Detroit Red Wings (August 5, 1991). ... Strained lower abdominal muscle (March 20, 1992); missed five games. ... Injured knee (October 8, 1992); missed five games. ... Reinjured knee (October 28, 1992); missed two games. ... Suffered back spasms (February 13, 1993); missed three games. ... Strained back (March 2, 1993); missed two games. ... Injured left knee (October 6, 1995); missed two games. ... Injured back (February 22, 1995); missed two games. ... Traded by Red Wings to San Jose Sharks for C Igor Larionov and second-round pick (traded to St. Louis) in 1998 draft (October 25, 1995). ... Injured groin

S

(November 2, 1995); missed one game. ... Injured knee (December 16, 1995); missed two games. ... Injured shoulder (February 5, 1996); missed nine games. ... Traded by Sharks with fourth-round pick (D Joey Tetarenko) in 1996 draft to Florida Panthers for second-(traded to Chicago) and fourth-round (RW Matt Bradley) picks in 1996 draft (March 16, 1996). ... Sprained right shoulder (September 27, 1996); missed two games. ... Sprained knee ligament (February 1, 1997); missed 11 games. ... Sprained knee (January 7, 1998); missed one game. ... Traded by Panthers to Carolina Hurricanes for G Kirk McLean (March 24, 1998). ... Pulled groin (April 13, 1998); missed final three games of season. ... Suffered back spasms (December 21, 1998); missed one game. ... Pulled groin (January 4, 1999); missed two games. ... Bruised foot (February 26, 1999); missed three games. ... Signed as free agent by Panthers (November 16, 1999). ... Suffered from the flu and inner ear infection (January 12, 2000); missed four games. ... Strained groin (March 21, 2000); missed three games.

HONORS: Won Red Tilson Trophy (1985-86). ... Won Eddie Powers Memorial Trophy (1985-86). ... Won Jim Mahon Memorial Trophy (1985-86). ... Named to OHL All-Star first team (1985-86). ... Named to NHL All-Rookie team (1987-88).
STATISTICAL PLATEAUS: Three-goal games: 1987-88 (2), 1991-92 (1), 1993-94 (2), 1994-95 (1), 1995-96 (1), 1995-96 (1), 1996-97 (3), 1997-98 (1). Total: 12.

Season Team	League	REGULAR SEASON									PLAYOFFS				
		Gms.	G	A	Pts.	PIM	+/-	PP	SH		Gms.	G	A	Pts.	PIM
82-83—Brockville	COJHL	48	27	36	63	81	...	...	...		—	—	—	—	—
83-84—Cornwall	OHL	68	44	36	80	69	...	...	...		—	—	—	—	—
84-85—Cornwall	OHL	49	25	33	58	51	...	...	...		9	2	12	14	4
85-86—Cornwall	OHL	63	*81	61	*142	25	...	...	...		6	7	4	11	0
86-87—Rochester	AHL	55	18	13	31	11	...	...	...		15	12	3	15	2
87-88—Buffalo	NHL	74	38	27	65	14	-6	15	0		6	1	1	2	2
88-89—Buffalo	NHL	67	22	21	43	15	-7	7	0		1	0	1	1	0
89-90—Buffalo	NHL	18	4	2	6	0	3	1	0		—	—	—	—	—
—Rochester	AHL	5	3	5	8	2	...	...	...		17	8	7	15	9
90-91—New York Rangers	NHL	59	24	23	47	21	8	7	0		—	—	—	—	—
91-92—Detroit	NHL	74	36	26	62	27	7	11	1		11	6	2	8	4
92-93—Detroit	NHL	70	32	34	66	29	7	10	0		7	2	3	5	0
93-94—Detroit	NHL	82	52	41	93	26	13	19	0		7	2	1	3	4
94-95—Detroit	NHL	43	30	10	40	17	11	11	0		17	4	3	7	5
95-96—Detroit	NHL	5	2	2	4	2	0	0	0		—	—	—	—	—
—San Jose	NHL	51	27	19	46	10	-19	12	0		—	—	—	—	—
—Florida	NHL	14	8	2	10	4	0	2	0		21	8	8	16	0
96-97—Florida	NHL	68	29	31	60	4	4	13	0		5	2	0	2	0
97-98—Florida	NHL	61	14	17	31	21	-13	5	0		—	—	—	—	—
—Carolina	NHL	10	4	2	6	2	2	2	0		—	—	—	—	—
98-99—Carolina	NHL	74	25	33	58	16	4	5	0		6	5	1	6	2
99-00—Florida	NHL	47	10	10	20	4	-4	5	0		—	—	—	—	—
NHL Totals (13 years)		817	357	300	657	212	10	125	1		81	30	20	50	17

SHEVALIER, JEFF — LW/C

PERSONAL: Born March 14, 1974, in Mississauga, Ont. ... 6-0/185. ... Shoots left. ... Name pronounced shuh-VAHL-yay.
HIGH SCHOOL: Chippewa Secondary (North Bay, Ont.).
TRANSACTIONS/CAREER NOTES: Selected by Los Angeles Kings in fifth round (fourth Kings pick, 111th overall) of NHL entry draft (June 20, 1992). ... Suffered concussion (March 24, 1997); missed one game. ... Strained groin (April 7, 1997); missed three games. ... Signed as free agent by Tampa Bay Lightning (July 12, 1999). ... Traded by Lightning to Ottawa Senators for future considerations (March 8, 2000).
HONORS: Named to OHL All-Star first team (1993-94).

Season Team	League	REGULAR SEASON									PLAYOFFS				
		Gms.	G	A	Pts.	PIM	+/-	PP	SH		Gms.	G	A	Pts.	PIM
90-91—Oakville Jr.B	OHA	5	1	4	5	0	...	...	...		—	—	—	—	—
—Georgetown Jr. B	OHA	12	11	11	22	8	...	...	...		—	—	—	—	—
—Acton Jr. C	OHA	28	29	31	60	62	...	...	...		—	—	—	—	—
91-92—North Bay	OHL	64	28	29	57	26	...	...	...		21	5	11	16	25
92-93—North Bay	OHL	62	59	54	113	46	...	...	...		2	1	2	3	4
93-94—North Bay	OHL	64	52	49	101	52	...	...	...		17	8	14	22	18
94-95—Phoenix	IHL	68	31	39	70	44	...	...	...		9	5	4	9	0
—Los Angeles	NHL	1	1	0	1	0	1	0	0		—	—	—	—	—
95-96—Phoenix	IHL	79	29	38	67	72	...	...	...		4	2	2	4	2
96-97—Phoenix	IHL	46	16	21	37	26	...	...	...		—	—	—	—	—
—Los Angeles	NHL	26	4	9	13	6	-6	1	0		—	—	—	—	—
97-98—Springfield	AHL	66	23	30	53	38	...	...	...		4	1	1	2	0
98-99—Cincinnati	IHL	76	29	34	63	57	...	...	...		3	1	1	2	0
99-00—Detroit	IHL	46	11	25	36	42	...	...	...		—	—	—	—	—
—Tampa Bay	NHL	5	0	0	0	2	-1	0	0		—	—	—	—	—
—Grand Rapids	IHL	2	0	0	0	0	...	...	...		—	—	—	—	—
—Quebec	AHL	5	0	2	2	2	...	...	...		—	—	—	—	—
NHL Totals (3 years)		32	5	9	14	8	-6	1	0						

SHIELDS, STEVE — G — SHARKS

PERSONAL: Born July 19, 1972, in Toronto. ... 6-3/215. ... Catches left.
COLLEGE: Michigan.
TRANSACTIONS/CAREER NOTES: Selected by Buffalo Sabres in fifth round (fifth Sabres pick, 101st overall) of NHL entry draft (June 22, 1991). ... Traded by Sabres with fourth-round pick (RW Miroslav Zalesak) in 1998 draft to San Jose Sharks for G Kay Whitmore, second-round pick (RW Jaroslav Kristek) in 1998 draft and fifth-round pick (traded to Columbus) in 2000 draft (June 18, 1998).
HONORS: Named to NCCA All-America (West) second team (1992-93 and 1993-94). ... Named to CCHA All-Star first team (1992-93 and 1993-94).
MISCELLANEOUS: Stopped a penalty shot attempt (vs. Terry Yake, January 26, 1999; vs. Pierre Turgeon, December 30, 1999). ... Allowed penalty shot goal (vs. Eric Lindros, May 11, 1997 (playoffs)).

Season Team	League	Gms.	Min	W	L	T	GA	SO	Avg.	Gms.	Min.	W	L	GA	SO	Avg.
90-91—Univ. of Michigan	CCHA	37	1963	26	6	3	106	0	3.24	—	—	—	—	—	—	—
91-92—Univ. of Michigan	CCHA	37	2091	27	7	2	98	1	2.81	—	—	—	—	—	—	—
92-93—Univ. of Michigan	CCHA	39	2027	30	6	2	75	...	2.22	—	—	—	—	—	—	—
93-94—Univ. of Michigan	CCHA	36	1961	28	6	1	87	2	2.66	—	—	—	—	—	—	—
94-95—South Carolina	ECHL	21	1158	11	5	‡2	52	2	2.69	3	144	0	2	11	0	4.58
—Rochester	AHL	13	673	3	8	0	53	0	4.73	1	20	0	0	3	0	9.00
95-96—Rochester	AHL	43	2356	20	17	2	140	1	3.57	*19	*1126	*15	3	47	1	2.50
—Buffalo	NHL	2	75	1	0	0	4	0	3.20	—	—	—	—	—	—	—
96-97—Rochester	AHL	23	1331	14	6	2	60	1	2.70	—	—	—	—	—	—	—
—Buffalo	NHL	13	789	3	8	2	39	0	2.97	10	570	4	6	26	1	2.74
97-98—Buffalo	NHL	16	785	3	6	4	37	0	2.83	—	—	—	—	—	—	—
—Rochester	AHL	1	59	0	1	0	3	0	3.05	—	—	—	—	—	—	—
98-99—San Jose	NHL	37	2162	15	11	8	80	4	2.22	1	60	0	1	6	0	6.00
99-00—San Jose	NHL	67	3797	27	30	8	162	4	2.56	12	696	5	7	36	0	3.10
NHL Totals (5 years)		135	7608	49	55	22	322	8	2.54	23	1326	9	14	68	1	3.08

SHTALENKOV, MIKHAIL   G

PERSONAL: Born October 20, 1965, in Moscow, U.S.S.R. ... 6-1/184. ... Catches left. ... Name pronounced mih-KIGHL shtuh-LEHN-kahf.
TRANSACTIONS/CAREER NOTES: Selected by Mighty Ducks of Anaheim in fifth round (fifth Mighty Ducks pick, 108th overall) of NHL entry draft (June 26, 1993). ... Selected by Nashville Predators in NHL expansion draft (June 26, 1998). ... Traded by Predators with F Jim Dowd to Edmonton Oilers for G Eric Fichaud, D Drake Berehowsky and D Greg de Vries (October 1, 1998). ... Traded by Oilers to Phoenix Coyotes for fifth-round pick (traded to Nashville) in 2000 draft (March 11, 1999). ... Traded by Coyotes with fourth-round pick (D Chris Eade) in 2000 draft to Florida Panthers for G Sean Burke and fifth-round pick (D Nate Kiser) in 2000 draft (November 19, 1999).
HONORS: Named Soviet League Rookie of the Year (1986-87). ... Won Garry F. Longman Memorial Trophy (1992-93).
MISCELLANEOUS: Member of silver-medal-winning Russian Olympic team (1998). ... Stopped penalty shot attempt (vs. Peter Bondra, December 13, 1996). ... Allowed penalty shot goal (vs. Dan Quinn, March 21, 1995).

Season Team	League	Gms.	Min	W	L	T	GA	SO	Avg.	Gms.	Min.	W	L	GA	SO	Avg.
86-87—Dynamo Moscow	USSR	17	893	...	...	...	36	1	2.42	—	—	—	—	—	—	—
87-88—Dynamo Moscow	USSR	25	1302	...	...	...	72	1	3.32	—	—	—	—	—	—	—
88-89—Dynamo Moscow	USSR	4	80	...	...	...	3	0	2.25	—	—	—	—	—	—	—
89-90—Dynamo Moscow	USSR	6	20	...	...	...	1	0	3.00	—	—	—	—	—	—	—
90-91—Dynamo Moscow	USSR	31	1568	...	...	...	56	2	2.14	—	—	—	—	—	—	—
91-92—Dynamo Moscow	CIS	27	1268	...	...	...	45	1	2.13	—	—	—	—	—	—	—
—Unif. Olympic team	Int'l	8	440	...	...	...	12	3	1.64	—	—	—	—	—	—	—
92-93—Milwaukee	IHL	47	2669	26	14	‡5	135	2	3.03	3	209	1	1	11	0	3.16
93-94—San Diego	IHL	28	1616	15	11	‡2	93	0	3.45	—	—	—	—	—	—	—
—Anaheim	NHL	10	543	3	4	1	24	0	2.65	—	—	—	—	—	—	—
94-95—Anaheim	NHL	18	810	4	7	1	49	0	3.63	—	—	—	—	—	—	—
95-96—Anaheim	NHL	30	1637	7	16	3	85	0	3.12	—	—	—	—	—	—	—
96-97—Anaheim	NHL	24	1079	7	8	1	52	2	2.89	4	211	0	3	10	0	2.84
97-98—Anaheim	NHL	40	2049	13	18	5	110	1	3.22	—	—	—	—	—	—	—
—Russian Oly. team	Int'l	5	290	4	1	0	8	0	1.66	—	—	—	—	—	—	—
98-99—Edmonton	NHL	34	1819	12	17	3	81	3	2.67	—	—	—	—	—	—	—
—Phoenix	NHL	4	243	1	2	1	9	0	2.22	—	—	—	—	—	—	—
99-00—Phoenix	NHL	15	904	7	6	2	36	2	2.39	—	—	—	—	—	—	—
—Florida	NHL	15	882	8	4	2	34	0	2.31	—	—	—	—	—	—	—
NHL Totals (7 years)		190	9966	62	82	19	480	8	2.89	4	211	0	3	10	0	2.84

SHULMISTRA, RICH   G   PANTHERS

PERSONAL: Born April 1, 1971, in Sudbury, Ont. ... 6-2/185. ... Catches right. ... Full Name: Richard Shulmistra. ... Name pronounced SHOOL-mih-struh.
HIGH SCHOOL: LaSalle Secondary (Kingston, Ont.).
COLLEGE: Miami of Ohio.
TRANSACTIONS/CAREER NOTES: Selected by Quebec Nordiques in NHL supplemental draft (June 19, 1992). ... Nordiques franchise moved to Colorado and renamed Avalanche for 1995-96 season (June 21, 1995). ... Signed as free agent by New Jersey Devils (December 31, 1997). ... Signed as free agent by Florida Panthers (July 21, 1999).
HONORS: Named to CCHA All-Star second team (1992-93). ... Named to AHL All-Star second team (1997-98).

Season Team	League	Gms.	Min	W	L	T	GA	SO	Avg.	Gms.	Min.	W	L	GA	SO	Avg.
90-91—Miami of Ohio	CCHA	20	920	2	12	2	80	0	5.22	—	—	—	—	—	—	—
91-92—Miami of Ohio	CCHA	19	850	3	5	2	67	0	4.73	—	—	—	—	—	—	—
92-93—Miami of Ohio	CCHA	33	1949	22	6	4	88	...	2.71	—	—	—	—	—	—	—
93-94—Miami of Ohio	CCHA	27	1521	13	12	1	74	0	2.92	—	—	—	—	—	—	—
94-95—Cornwall	AHL	20	937	4	9	2	58	0	3.71	8	447	4	3	22	0	2.95
95-96—Cornwall	AHL	36	1844	9	18	2	100	0	3.25	1	8	0	0	1	0	7.50
96-97—Albany	AHL	23	1063	5	9	2	43	2	2.43	2	77	1	0	2	0	1.56
97-98—Fort Wayne	IHL	11	657	3	8	0	34	1	3.11	—	—	—	—	—	—	—
—Albany	AHL	35	2022	20	8	4	78	2	*2.31	13	696	8	3	32	1	2.76
—New Jersey	NHL	1	62	0	1	0	2	0	1.94	—	—	—	—	—	—	—
98-99—Albany	AHL	12	596	6	4	0	34	0	3.42	2	64	0	2	3	0	2.81
—Manitoba	IHL	44	2469	25	11	‡7	117	2	2.84	—	—	—	—	—	—	—
99-00—Louisville	AHL	27	1447	12	11	2	80	2	3.32	—	—	—	—	—	—	—
—Florida	NHL	1	60	1	0	0	1	0	1.00	—	—	—	—	—	—	—
—Orlando	IHL	9	520	6	1	‡3	16	1	1.85	1	30	0	1	3	0	6.00
NHL Totals (2 years)		2	122	1	1	0	3	0	1.48							

SHVIDKI, DENIS   RW   PANTHERS

PERSONAL: Born November 21, 1980, in Kharkov, U.S.S.R. ... 6-0/205. ... Shoots left.
TRANSACTIONS/CAREER NOTES: Selected by Florida Panthers in first round (first Panthers pick, 12th overall) of NHL entry draft (June 26, 1999).
HONORS: Named to OHL All-Star second team (1998-99).

Season Team	League	REGULAR SEASON Gms.	G	A	Pts.	PIM	+/-	PP	SH	PLAYOFFS Gms.	G	A	Pts.	PIM
96-97—Torpedo-Yaroslavl	Russian	17	3	2	5	6	...	...	...	—	—	—	—	—
97-98—Torpedo-Yaroslavl	Russian	15	1	1	2	2	...	...	...	—	—	—	—	—
—Torpedo-2 Yaroslavl	Rus. Div. II	32	20	13	33	20	...	...	...	—	—	—	—	—
98-99—Barrie	OHL	61	35	59	94	8	...	...	...	12	7	9	16	2
99-00—Barrie	OHL	61	41	65	106	55	...	...	...	9	3	1	4	2

SILLINGER, MIKE   C   PANTHERS

PERSONAL: Born June 29, 1971, in Regina, Sask. ... 5-11/191. ... Shoots right. ... Name pronounced SIHL-in-juhr.
TRANSACTIONS/CAREER NOTES: Selected by Detroit Red Wings in first round (first Red Wings pick, 11th overall) of NHL entry draft (June 17, 1989). ... Fractured rib in training camp (September 1990). ... Suffered from the flu (March 5, 1993); missed three games. ... Strained rotator cuff (October 9, 1993); missed four games. ... Played in Europe during 1994-95 NHL lockout. ... Injured eye (January 17, 1995); missed four games. ... Traded by Red Wings with D Jason York to Mighty Ducks of Anaheim for LW Stu Grimson, D Mark Ferner and sixth-round pick (LW Magnus Nilsson) in 1996 draft (April 4, 1995). ... Traded by Mighty Ducks to Vancouver Canucks for RW Roman Oksuita (March 15, 1996). ... Suffered concussion (March 26, 1997); missed two games. ... Traded by Canucks to Flyers for sixth-round pick (traded back to Philadelphia) in 1998 draft (February 5, 1998). ... Sprained left knee (October 22, 1998); missed one game. ... Traded by Flyers with C Chris Gratton to Tampa Bay Lightning for RW Mikael Renberg and C Daymond Langkow (December 12, 1998). ... Traded by Lightning to Florida Panthers for C Ryan Johnson and LW Dwayne Hay (March 14, 2000).
HONORS: Named to WHL All-Star second team (1989-90). ... Named to WHL (East) All-Star first team (1990-91).
MISCELLANEOUS: Scored on a penalty shot (vs. Mark Fitzpatrick, January 14, 1997). ... Failed to score on a penalty shot (vs. Tommy Salo, January 7, 2000).
STATISTICAL NOTES: Led NHL with 21.9 shooting percentage (1997-98).

Season Team	League	REGULAR SEASON Gms.	G	A	Pts.	PIM	+/-	PP	SH	PLAYOFFS Gms.	G	A	Pts.	PIM
87-88—Regina	WHL	67	18	25	43	17	...	...	...	4	2	2	4	0
88-89—Regina	WHL	72	53	78	131	52	...	...	...	—	—	—	—	—
89-90—Regina	WHL	70	57	72	129	41	...	...	...	11	12	10	22	2
—Adirondack	AHL	—	—	—	—	—	...	...	...	1	0	0	0	0
90-91—Regina	WHL	57	50	66	116	42	...	...	...	8	6	9	15	4
—Detroit	NHL	3	0	1	1	0	-2	0	0	3	0	1	1	0
91-92—Adirondack	AHL	64	25	41	66	26	...	...	...	15	9	*19	*28	12
—Detroit	NHL	—	—	—	—	—	...	...	...	8	2	2	4	2
92-93—Detroit	NHL	51	4	17	21	16	0	0	0	—	—	—	—	—
—Adirondack	AHL	15	10	20	30	31	...	...	...	11	5	13	18	10
93-94—Detroit	NHL	62	8	21	29	10	2	0	1	—	—	—	—	—
94-95—Wien	Austria	13	13	14	27	10	...	...	...	—	—	—	—	—
—Detroit	NHL	13	2	6	8	2	3	0	0	—	—	—	—	—
—Anaheim	NHL	15	2	5	7	6	1	2	0	—	—	—	—	—
95-96—Anaheim	NHL	62	13	21	34	32	-20	7	0	—	—	—	—	—
—Vancouver	NHL	12	1	3	4	6	2	0	1	6	0	0	0	2
96-97—Vancouver	NHL	78	17	20	37	25	-3	3	3	—	—	—	—	—
97-98—Vancouver	NHL	48	10	9	19	34	-14	1	2	—	—	—	—	—
—Philadelphia	NHL	27	11	11	22	16	3	1	2	3	1	0	1	0
98-99—Philadelphia	NHL	25	0	3	3	8	-9	0	0	—	—	—	—	—
—Tampa Bay	NHL	54	8	2	10	28	-20	0	2	—	—	—	—	—
99-00—Tampa Bay	NHL	67	19	25	44	86	-29	6	3	—	—	—	—	—
—Florida	NHL	13	4	4	8	16	-1	2	0	4	2	1	3	2
NHL Totals (10 years)		530	99	148	247	285	-87	22	14	24	5	4	9	6

SIM, JON   LW   STARS

PERSONAL: Born September 29, 1977, in New Glasgow, Nova Scotia. ... 5-10/184. ... Shoots left. ... Full Name: Jonathan Sim.
TRANSACTIONS/CAREER NOTES: Selected by Dallas Stars in third round (second Stars pick, 70th overall) of NHL entry draft (June 22, 1996).
HONORS: Named to OHL All-Star second team (1997-98).
MISCELLANEOUS: Member of Stanley Cup championship team (1999).

Season Team	League	REGULAR SEASON Gms.	G	A	Pts.	PIM	+/-	PP	SH	PLAYOFFS Gms.	G	A	Pts.	PIM
94-95—Sarnia	OHL	25	9	12	21	19	...	...	...	4	3	2	5	2
95-96—Sarnia	OHL	63	56	46	102	130	...	...	...	10	8	7	15	26
96-97—Sarnia	OHL	64	†56	39	95	109	...	...	...	12	9	5	14	32
97-98—Sarnia	OHL	59	44	50	94	95	...	...	...	5	1	4	5	14
98-99—Michigan	IHL	68	24	27	51	91	...	...	...	5	3	1	4	18
—Dallas	NHL	7	1	0	1	12	1	0	0	4	0	0	0	0
99-00—Michigan	IHL	35	14	16	30	65	...	...	...	—	—	—	—	—
—Dallas	NHL	25	5	3	8	10	4	2	0	7	1	0	1	6
NHL Totals (2 years)		32	6	3	9	22	5	2	0	11	1	0	1	6

SIMON, CHRIS   LW   CAPITALS

PERSONAL: Born January 30, 1972, in Wawa, Ont. ... 6-4/231. ... Shoots left. ... Name pronounced SIGH-muhn.

TRANSACTIONS/CAREER NOTES: Selected by Philadelphia Flyers in second round (second Flyers pick, 25th overall) of NHL entry draft (June 16, 1990). ... Underwent surgery to repair left rotator cuff and torn muscle (September 1990). ... Traded by Flyers with first-round pick (traded to Toronto) in 1994 draft to Quebec Nordiques (July 21, 1992) to complete deal in which Flyers sent G Ron Hextall, C Mike Ricci, C Peter Forsberg, D Steve Duchesne, first-round pick (G Jocelyn Thibault) in 1993 draft and cash to Nordiques for C Eric Lindros (June 20, 1992). ... Suffered from the flu (March 13, 1993); missed one game. ... Injured back (December 1, 1993); missed 31 games. ... Injured back (February 16, 1994); missed one game. ... Injured back (March 6, 1994); missed one game. ... Injured back (March 18, 1994); missed remainder of season. ... Injured back (January 31, 1995); missed six games. ... Injured shoulder (March 22, 1995); missed 13 games. ... Nordiques franchise moved to Colorado and renamed Avalanche for 1995-96 season (June 21, 1995). ... Suffered back spasms (January 6, 1996); missed two games. ... Injured shoulder (February 5, 1996); missed four games. ... Traded by Avalanche with D Curtis Leschyshyn to Washington Capitals for RW Keith Jones and first- (D Scott Parker) and fourth-round (traded back to Washington) picks in 1998 draft (November 2, 1996). ... Injured arm (December 20, 1996); missed two games. ... Suffered back spasms (January 24, 1997); missed 17 games. ... Suffered back spasms (March 22, 1997); missed one game. ... Strained shoulder (March 29, 1997); missed six games. ... Suspended three games by NHL for alleged racial remarks (November 9, 1997). ... Bruised shoulder (October 25, 1997); missed five games. ... Reinjured shoulder (December 20, 1997) and underwent shoulder surgery; missed remainder of regular season. ... Strained shoulder (December 5, 1998) and underwent shoulder surgery; missed remainder of season. ... Strained neck (November 27, 1999); missed six games. ... Reinjured neck (December 21, 1999); missed one game. ... Suspended one playoff game by NHL for cross-checking incident (April 14, 2000).

MISCELLANEOUS: Member of Stanley Cup championship team (1996).

		REGULAR SEASON								PLAYOFFS				
Season Team	League	Gms.	G	A	Pts.	PIM	+/-	PP	SH	Gms.	G	A	Pts.	PIM
87-88—Sault Ste. Marie	OHA	55	42	36	78	172	...	...	...	—	—	—	—	—
88-89—Ottawa	OHL	36	4	2	6	31	...	...	...	—	—	—	—	—
89-90—Ottawa	OHL	57	36	38	74	146	...	...	...	3	2	1	3	4
90-91—Ottawa	OHL	20	16	6	22	69	...	...	...	17	5	9	14	59
91-92—Ottawa	OHL	2	1	1	2	24	...	...	...	—	—	—	—	—
—Sault Ste. Marie	OHL	31	19	25	44	143	...	...	...	11	5	8	13	49
92-93—Halifax	AHL	36	12	6	18	131	...	...	...	—	—	—	—	—
—Quebec	NHL	16	1	1	2	67	-2	0	0	5	0	0	0	26
93-94—Quebec	NHL	37	4	4	8	132	-2	0	0	—	—	—	—	—
94-95—Quebec	NHL	29	3	9	12	106	14	0	0	6	1	1	2	19
95-96—Colorado	NHL	64	16	18	34	250	10	4	0	12	1	2	3	11
96-97—Washington	NHL	42	9	13	22	165	-1	3	0	—	—	—	—	—
97-98—Washington	NHL	28	7	10	17	38	-1	4	0	18	1	0	1	26
98-99—Washington	NHL	23	3	7	10	48	-4	0	0	—	—	—	—	—
99-00—Washington	NHL	75	29	20	49	146	11	7	0	4	2	0	2	24
NHL Totals (8 years)		314	72	82	154	952	25	18	0	45	5	3	8	106

SIMPSON, REID   LW

PERSONAL: Born May 21, 1969, in Flin Flon, Man. ... 6-2/220. ... Shoots left.

TRANSACTIONS/CAREER NOTES: Selected by Philadelphia Flyers in fourth round (third Flyers pick, 72nd overall) of NHL entry draft (June 17, 1989). ... Signed as free agent by Minnesota North Stars (December 13, 1992). ... North Stars franchise moved from Minnesota to Dallas and renamed Stars for 1993-94 season. ... Traded by Stars with D Roy Mitchell to New Jersey Devils for future considerations (March 21, 1994). ... Bruised right shoulder (November 27, 1995); missed six games. ... Strained groin (September 9, 1996); missed first two games of season. ... Reinjured groin (October 16, 1996); underwent groin surgery (November 22, 1996) and missed 38 games. ... Injured hamstring (November 8, 1997); missed 13 games. ... Traded by Devils to Chicago Blackhawks for fourth-round pick (D Mikko Jokela) in 1998 draft and future considerations (January 8, 1998). ... Strained hip flexor (March 12, 1998); missed two games. ... Fractured hand (September 20, 1998); missed first eight games of season. ... Suspended two games and fined $1,000 by NHL for actions toward a spectator (November 14, 1998). ... Traded by Blackhawks with D Bryan Muir to Tampa Bay Lightning for C Michael Nylander (November 12, 1999). ... Fractured jaw (January 13, 2000); missed final 40 games of regular season.

		REGULAR SEASON								PLAYOFFS				
Season Team	League	Gms.	G	A	Pts.	PIM	+/-	PP	SH	Gms.	G	A	Pts.	PIM
85-86—Flin Flon	MJHL	40	20	21	41	200	...	...	...	—	—	—	—	—
—New Westminster	WHL	2	0	0	0	0	...	...	...	—	—	—	—	—
86-87—Prince Albert	WHL	47	3	8	11	105	...	...	...	—	—	—	—	—
87-88—Prince Albert	WHL	72	13	14	27	164	...	...	...	10	1	0	1	43
88-89—Prince Albert	WHL	59	26	29	55	264	...	...	...	4	2	1	3	30
89-90—Prince Albert	WHL	29	15	17	32	121	...	...	...	14	4	7	11	34
—Hershey	AHL	28	2	2	4	175	...	...	...	—	—	—	—	—
90-91—Hershey	AHL	54	9	15	24	183	...	...	...	1	0	0	0	0
91-92—Hershey	AHL	60	11	7	18	145	...	...	...	—	—	—	—	—
—Philadelphia	NHL	1	0	0	0	0	0	0	0	—	—	—	—	—
92-93—Kalamazoo	IHL	45	5	5	10	193	...	...	...	—	—	—	—	—
—Minnesota	NHL	1	0	0	0	5	0	0	0	—	—	—	—	—
93-94—Kalamazoo	IHL	5	0	0	0	16	...	...	...	—	—	—	—	—
—Albany	AHL	37	9	5	14	135	...	...	...	5	1	1	2	18
94-95—Albany	AHL	70	18	25	43	268	...	...	...	14	1	8	9	13
—New Jersey	NHL	9	0	0	0	27	-1	0	0	—	—	—	—	—
95-96—New Jersey	NHL	23	1	5	6	79	2	0	0	—	—	—	—	—
—Albany	AHL	6	1	3	4	17	...	...	...	—	—	—	—	—
96-97—Albany	AHL	3	0	0	0	10	...	...	...	—	—	—	—	—
—New Jersey	NHL	27	0	4	4	60	0	0	0	5	0	0	0	29
97-98—New Jersey	NHL	6	0	0	0	16	-2	0	0	—	—	—	—	—
—Chicago	NHL	38	3	2	5	102	-1	1	0	—	—	—	—	—
98-99—Chicago	NHL	53	5	4	9	145	2	1	0	—	—	—	—	—
99-00—Cleveland	IHL	12	2	2	4	56	...	...	...	—	—	—	—	—
—Tampa Bay	NHL	26	1	0	1	103	-3	0	0	—	—	—	—	—
NHL Totals (8 years)		184	10	15	25	537	-3	2	0	5	0	0	0	29

SIMPSON, TODD   D   PANTHERS

PERSONAL: Born May 28, 1973, in Edmonton. ... 6-3/215. ... Shoots left.
COLLEGE: Brown.
TRANSACTIONS/CAREER NOTES: Signed as non-drafted free agent by Calgary Flames (July 6, 1994). ... Injured knee (October 1, 1997) and underwent surgery; missed 10 games. ... Injured shoulder (November 15, 1997); missed four games. ... Suffered concussion (March 19, 1998); missed final 15 games of season. ... Suffered facial injury (March 13, 1999); missed nine games. ... Traded by Flames to Florida Panthers for LW Bill Lindsay (September 30, 1999).
MISCELLANEOUS: Captain of Calgary Flames (1997-98 and 1998-99).

		REGULAR SEASON								PLAYOFFS				
Season Team	League	Gms.	G	A	Pts.	PIM	+/-	PP	SH	Gms.	G	A	Pts.	PIM
91-92—Brown University	ECAC	14	1	3	4	18	...	...	...	—	—	—	—	—
92-93—Tri-City	WHL	69	5	18	23	196	...	...	...	4	0	0	0	13
93-94—Tri-City	WHL	12	2	3	5	32	...	...	...	—	—	—	—	—
—Saskatoon	WHL	51	7	19	26	175	...	...	...	16	1	5	6	42
94-95—Saint John	AHL	80	3	10	13	321	...	...	...	5	0	0	0	4
95-96—Calgary	NHL	6	0	0	0	32	0	0	0	—	—	—	—	—
—Saint John	AHL	66	4	13	17	277	...	...	...	16	2	3	5	32
96-97—Calgary	NHL	82	1	13	14	208	-14	0	0	—	—	—	—	—
97-98—Calgary	NHL	53	1	5	6	109	-10	0	0	—	—	—	—	—
98-99—Calgary	NHL	73	2	8	10	151	18	0	0	—	—	—	—	—
99-00—Florida	NHL	82	1	6	7	202	5	0	0	4	0	0	0	4
NHL Totals (5 years)		296	5	32	37	702	-1	0	0	4	0	0	0	4

SIVEK, MICHAL   C   CAPITALS

PERSONAL: Born January 21, 1981, in Nachod, Czechoslovakia. ... 6-3/209. ... Shoots left.
TRANSACTIONS/CAREER NOTES: Selected by Washington Capitals in second round (second Capitals pick, 29th overall) of NHL entry draft (June 26, 1999).

		REGULAR SEASON								PLAYOFFS				
Season Team	League	Gms.	G	A	Pts.	PIM	+/-	PP	SH	Gms.	G	A	Pts.	PIM
96-97—Sparta Praha Jrs.	Czech Rep.	38	18	11	29	...	...	...	...	—	—	—	—	—
97-98—Sparta Praha	Czech Rep.	25	1	1	2	10	...	...	...	5	1	0	1	0
—Sparta Praha Jrs.	Czech Rep.	31	13	8	21	...	...	...	...	—	—	—	—	—
98-99—Sparta Praha	Czech Rep.	1	1	0	1	2	...	...	...	—	—	—	—	—
—Velvana Kladno	Czech Rep.	34	3	8	11	24	...	...	...	—	—	—	—	—
99-00—Prince Albert	WHL	53	23	37	60	65	...	...	...	6	1	4	5	10

SKOPINTSEV, ANDREI   D

PERSONAL: Born September 28, 1971, in Moscow, U.S.S.R. ... 6-0/185. ... Shoots right.
TRANSACTIONS/CAREER NOTES: Selected by Tampa Bay Lightning in sixth round (seventh Lightning pick, 153rd overall) of NHL entry draft (June 21, 1997). ... Strained abdominal muscle (November 29, 1998); missed 19 games. ... Injured shoulder (March 6, 1999); missed four games.

		REGULAR SEASON								PLAYOFFS				
Season Team	League	Gms.	G	A	Pts.	PIM	+/-	PP	SH	Gms.	G	A	Pts.	PIM
89-90—Krylja Sov. Moscow	USSR	20	0	0	0	10	...	...	...	—	—	—	—	—
90-91—Krylja Sov. Moscow	USSR	16	0	1	1	2	...	...	...	—	—	—	—	—
91-92—Krylja Sov. Moscow	CIS	36	1	1	2	14	...	...	...	—	—	—	—	—
92-93—Krylja Sov. Moscow	CIS	12	1	0	1	4	...	...	...	7	1	0	1	2
93-94—Krylja Sov. Moscow	CIS	43	4	8	12	14	...	...	...	3	1	0	1	0
94-95—Krylja Sov. Moscow	CIS	52	8	12	20	55	...	...	...	4	1	1	2	0
95-96—Augsburg	Germany	46	10	20	30	32	...	...	...	7	3	2	5	22
96-97—TPS Turku	Finland	46	3	6	9	80	...	...	...	10	1	1	2	4
97-98—TPS Turku	Finland	48	2	9	11	8	...	...	...	4	0	1	1	4
98-99—Cleveland	IHL	19	3	2	5	8	...	...	...	—	—	—	—	—
—Tampa Bay	NHL	19	1	1	2	10	1	0	0	—	—	—	—	—
99-00—Detroit	IHL	51	4	15	19	44	...	...	...	—	—	—	—	—
—Tampa Bay	NHL	4	0	0	0	6	-4	0	0	—	—	—	—	—
NHL Totals (2 years)		23	1	1	2	16	-3	0	0					

SKOULA, MARTIN   D   AVALANCHE

PERSONAL: Born October 28, 1979, in Litvinov, Czechoslovakia. ... 6-3/218. ... Shoots left.
TRANSACTIONS/CAREER NOTES: Selected by Colorado Avalanche in first round (second Avalanche pick, 17th overall) of NHL entry draft (June 27, 1998). ... Injured shoulder (January 5, 2000); missed two games.
HONORS: Named to OHL All-Star second team (1998-99).

		REGULAR SEASON								PLAYOFFS				
Season Team	League	Gms.	G	A	Pts.	PIM	+/-	PP	SH	Gms.	G	A	Pts.	PIM
95-96—Litvinov Jrs.	Czech Rep.	38	0	4	4	...	...	...	...	—	—	—	—	—
—Litvinov	Czech Rep.	—	—	—	—	...	...	...	...	1	0	0	0	0
96-97—Litvinov Jrs.	Czech Rep.	38	2	9	11	...	...	...	...	—	—	—	—	—
—Litvinov	Czech Rep.	1	0	0	0	0	...	...	...	—	—	—	—	—
97-98—Barrie	COJHL	66	8	36	44	36	...	...	...	6	1	3	4	4
98-99—Barrie	OHL	67	13	46	59	46	...	...	...	12	3	10	13	13
—Hershey	AHL	—	—	—	—	...	...	...	...	1	0	0	0	0
99-00—Colorado	NHL	80	3	13	16	20	5	2	0	17	0	2	2	4
NHL Totals (1 year)		80	3	13	16	20	5	2	0	17	0	2	2	4

SKRASTINS, KARLIS — D — PREDATORS

PERSONAL: Born July 9, 1974, in Riga, U.S.S.R. ... 6-1/205. ... Shoots left.
TRANSACTIONS/CAREER NOTES: Selected by Nashville Predators in ninth round (eighth Predators pick, 230th overall) of 1998 NHL entry draft (June 27, 1998).

		REGULAR SEASON								PLAYOFFS				
Season Team	League	Gms.	G	A	Pts.	PIM	+/-	PP	SH	Gms.	G	A	Pts.	PIM
96-97—TPS Turku	Finland	50	2	8	10	20	...	...	...	—	—	—	—	—
97-98—TPS Turku	Finland	48	4	15	19	67	...	...	...	—	—	—	—	—
98-99—Milwaukee	IHL	75	8	36	44	47	...	...	...	2	0	1	1	2
—Nashville	NHL	2	0	1	1	0	0	0	0	—	—	—	—	—
99-00—Milwaukee	IHL	19	3	8	11	10	...	...	...	—	—	—	—	—
—Nashville	NHL	59	5	6	11	20	-7	1	0	—	—	—	—	—
NHL Totals (2 years)		61	5	7	12	20	-7	1	0					

SKRBEK, PAVEL — D — PREDATORS

PERSONAL: Born August 9, 1978, in Kladno, Czechoslovakia. ... 6-3/213. ... Shoots left.
TRANSACTIONS/CAREER NOTES: Selected by Pittsburgh Penguins in second round (second Penguins pick, 28th overall) of NHL entry draft (June 22, 1996). ... Traded by Penguins to Nashville Predators for D Bob Boughner (March 13, 2000).

		REGULAR SEASON								PLAYOFFS				
Season Team	League	Gms.	G	A	Pts.	PIM	+/-	PP	SH	Gms.	G	A	Pts.	PIM
94-95—Poldi Kladno	Czech Rep.	29	7	6	13	...	...	...	...	—	—	—	—	—
95-96—HC Kladno Jrs.	Czech Rep.	29	10	12	22	...	...	...	...	—	—	—	—	—
—HC Kladno	Czech Rep.	13	0	1	1	...	...	...	...	5	0	0	0	...
96-97—Poldi Kladno	Czech Rep.	35	1	5	6	26	...	...	...	3	0	0	0	4
97-98—Poldi Kladno	Czech Rep.	47	4	10	14	126	...	...	...	—	—	—	—	—
98-99—Syracuse	AHL	64	6	16	22	38	...	...	...	—	—	—	—	—
—Pittsburgh	NHL	4	0	0	0	2	2	0	0	—	—	—	—	—
99-00—Wilkes-Barre/Scranton	AHL	51	7	16	23	50	...	...	...	—	—	—	—	—
—Milwaukee	IHL	6	0	0	0	0	...	...	...	—	—	—	—	—
NHL Totals (1 year)		4	0	0	0	2	2	0	0					

SKRUDLAND, BRIAN — C

PERSONAL: Born July 31, 1963, in Peace River, Alta. ... 6-0/200. ... Shoots left. ... Cousin of Barry Pederson, center with four NHL teams (1980-81 through 1991-92). ... Name pronounced SKROOD-luhnd.
TRANSACTIONS/CAREER NOTES: Signed as non-drafted free agent by Montreal Canadiens (September 13, 1983). ... Injured groin (February 1988). ... Strained left knee ligaments (December 27, 1988). ... Bruised right foot (January 1989). ... Sprained right ankle (October 7, 1989); missed 21 games. ... Pulled hip muscle (November 4, 1990); missed six games. ... Fractured foot (January 17, 1991); missed 14 games including All-Star Game. ... Fractured left thumb (October 5, 1991); missed five games. ... Sprained knee (October 26, 1991); missed 25 games. ... Fractured nose (January 25, 1992); missed eight games. ... Tore right knee ligaments (October 6, 1992); missed 27 games. ... Injured shoulder (January 14, 1993); missed one game. ... Traded by Canadiens to Calgary Flames for RW Gary Leeman (January 28, 1993). ... Sprained ankle (February 16, 1993); missed four games. ... Fractured thumb (March 2, 1993); missed 12 games. ... Lacerated right ear (April 11, 1993); missed one game. ... Selected by Florida Panthers in NHL expansion draft (June 24, 1993). ... Sprained right ankle (April 4, 1994); missed five games. ... Injured left hip flexor (March 22, 1995); missed one game. ... Suspended one game for high-sticking (February 13, 1996). ... Injured left hip flexor (April 12, 1996); missed one game. ... Fractured rib (October 30, 1996); missed three games. ... Suffered from the flu (December 10, 1996); missed one game. ... Bruised right shoulder (January 23, 1997); missed five games. ... Fractured ribs (February 7, 1997); missed six games. ... Sprained knee ligament (March 7, 1997); missed remainder of season. ... Signed as free agent by New York Rangers (July 7, 1997). ... Traded by Rangers with RW Mike Keane and sixth-round pick (RW Pavel Patera) in 1998 draft to Dallas Stars for LW Bob Errey, RW Todd Harvey and fourth-round pick (LW Boyd Kane) in 1998 draft (March 24, 1998). ... Injured kneecap (October 5, 1998); missed first five games of season. ... Strained back (December 23, 1998); missed two games. ... Fractured finger (January 1, 1999); missed two games. ... Tore cartilage in ribcage and bruised chest (February 7, 1999); missed 30 games. ... Bruised chest (October 8, 1999); missed 17 games. ... Reinjured chest (January 3, 2000); missed remainder of season.
HONORS: Won Jack Butterfield Trophy (1984-85).
MISCELLANEOUS: Member of Stanley Cup championship team (1986 and 1999). ... Captain of Florida Panthers (1994-95 through 1996-97).

		REGULAR SEASON								PLAYOFFS				
Season Team	League	Gms.	G	A	Pts.	PIM	+/-	PP	SH	Gms.	G	A	Pts.	PIM
80-81—Saskatoon	WHL	66	15	27	42	97	...	...	...	—	—	—	—	—
81-82—Saskatoon	WHL	71	27	29	56	135	...	...	...	5	0	1	1	2
82-83—Saskatoon	WHL	71	35	59	94	42	...	...	...	6	1	3	4	19
83-84—Nova Scotia	AHL	56	13	12	25	55	...	...	...	12	2	8	10	14
84-85—Sherbrooke	AHL	70	22	28	50	109	...	...	...	17	9	8	17	23
85-86—Montreal	NHL	65	9	13	22	57	3	2	0	20	2	4	6	76
86-87—Montreal	NHL	79	11	17	28	107	18	0	1	14	1	5	6	29
87-88—Montreal	NHL	79	12	24	36	112	44	0	1	11	1	5	6	24
88-89—Montreal	NHL	71	12	29	41	84	22	1	1	21	3	7	10	40
89-90—Montreal	NHL	59	11	31	42	56	21	4	0	11	3	5	8	30
90-91—Montreal	NHL	57	15	19	34	85	12	1	1	13	3	10	13	42
91-92—Montreal	NHL	42	3	3	6	36	-4	0	0	11	1	1	2	20
92-93—Montreal	NHL	23	5	3	8	55	1	0	2	—	—	—	—	—
—Calgary	NHL	16	2	4	6	10	3	0	0	6	0	3	3	12
93-94—Florida	NHL	79	15	25	40	136	13	0	2	—	—	—	—	—
94-95—Florida	NHL	47	5	9	14	88	0	1	0	—	—	—	—	—
95-96—Florida	NHL	79	7	20	27	129	6	0	1	21	1	3	4	18
96-97—Florida	NHL	51	5	13	18	48	4	0	0	—	—	—	—	—
97-98—New York Rangers	NHL	59	5	6	11	39	-4	0	0	—	—	—	—	—
—Dallas	NHL	13	2	0	2	10	-2	0	0	17	0	1	1	16
98-99—Dallas	NHL	40	4	1	5	33	2	0	0	19	0	2	2	16
99-00—Dallas	NHL	22	1	2	3	22	0	0	0	—	—	—	—	—
NHL Totals (15 years)		881	124	219	343	1107	139	9	9	164	15	46	61	323

S

SKUDRA, PETER   G

PERSONAL: Born April 24, 1973, in Riga, U.S.S.R. ... 6-1/189. ... Catches left. ... Name pronounced SKOO-druh.
TRANSACTIONS/CAREER NOTES: Signed as non-drafted free agent by Pittsburgh Penguins (September 25, 1997). ... Separated shoulder (September 8, 1998); missed first two games of season. ... Bruised lower left leg (November 3, 1998); missed 14 games. ... Injured ankle (November 6, 1999); missed three games. ... Suffered concussion (December 26, 1999); missed two games. ... Suffered from the flu (February 11, 2000); missed two games.
MISCELLANEOUS: Stopped a penalty shot attempt (vs. Doug Gilmour, October 16, 1999).

Season Team	League	REGULAR SEASON								PLAYOFFS						
		Gms.	Min.	W	L	T	GA	SO	Avg.	Gms.	Min.	W	L	GA	SO	Avg.
92-93—Pardaugava Riga	CIS	27	1498	...	...	...	74	...	2.96	1	60	...	...	5	0	5.00
93-94—Pardaugava Riga	CIS	14	783	...	...	...	42	...	3.22	1	55	...	...	4	0	4.36
94-95—Greensboro	ECHL	33	1612	13	9	‡5	113	0	4.21	6	341	2	2	28	0	4.93
95-96—Erie	ECHL	12	681	3	8	‡1	47	0	4.14	—	—	—	—	—	—	—
—Johnstown	ECHL	30	1657	12	11	‡4	98	0	3.55	—	—	—	—	—	—	—
96-97—Johnstown	ECHL	4	200	2	1	‡1	11	0	3.30	—	—	—	—	—	—	—
—Hamilton	AHL	32	1615	8	16	2	101	0	3.75	—	—	—	—	—	—	—
97-98—Houston	IHL	9	499	5	3	‡1	23	0	2.77	—	—	—	—	—	—	—
—Pittsburgh	NHL	17	851	6	4	3	26	0	1.83	—	—	—	—	—	—	—
—Kansas City	IHL	13	776	10	3	0	37	0	2.86	8	513	4	4	20	1	*2.34
98-99—Pittsburgh	NHL	37	1914	15	11	5	89	3	2.79	—	—	—	—	—	—	—
99-00—Pittsburgh	NHL	20	922	5	7	3	48	1	3.12	1	20	0	0	1	0	3.00
NHL Totals (3 years)		74	3687	26	22	11	163	4	2.65	1	20	0	0	1	0	3.00

SLANEY, JOHN   D   PENGUINS

PERSONAL: Born February 7, 1972, in St. John's, Nfld. ... 6-0/185. ... Shoots left. ... Full Name: John G. Slaney.
TRANSACTIONS/CAREER NOTES: Selected by Washington Capitals in first round (first Capitals pick, ninth overall) of NHL entry draft (June 16, 1990). ... Sprained right ankle (March 9, 1994); missed six games. ... Traded by Capitals to Colorado Avalanche for third-round pick (C Shawn McNeil) in 1996 draft (July 12, 1995). ... Traded by Avalanche to Los Angeles Kings for sixth-round pick (RW Brian Willsie) in 1996 draft (December 28, 1995). ... Fractured right hand (March 6, 1996); missed 12 games. ... Suffered concussion (November 17, 1996); missed one game. ... Signed as free agent by Phoenix Coyotes (August 18, 1997). ... Bruised thigh (October 30, 1997); missed one game. ... Suffered from the flu (December 10, 1997); missed one game. ... Fractured thumb (January 24, 1998); missed seven games. ... Injured hamstring (April 18, 1998); missed one game. ... Selected by Nashville Predators in NHL expansion draft (June 26, 1998). ... Bruised thumb (January 28, 1999); missed two games. ... Sprained wrist (February 5, 1999); missed three games. ... Injured rib (March 28, 1999); missed final nine games of season. ... Signed as free agent by Pittsburgh Penguins (September 30, 1999).
HONORS: Won Max Kaminsky Trophy (1989-90). ... Named to OHL All-Star first team (1989-90). ... Named to OHL All-Star second team (1990-91).

Season Team	League	REGULAR SEASON								PLAYOFFS				
		Gms.	G	A	Pts.	PIM	+/-	PP	SH	Gms.	G	A	Pts.	PIM
88-89—Cornwall	OHL	66	16	43	59	23	...	...	...	18	8	16	24	10
89-90—Cornwall	OHL	64	38	59	97	60	...	...	...	6	0	8	8	11
90-91—Cornwall	OHL	34	21	25	46	28	...	...	...	—	—	—	—	—
91-92—Cornwall	OHL	34	19	41	60	43	...	...	...	6	3	8	11	0
—Baltimore	AHL	6	2	4	6	0	...	...	...	—	—	—	—	—
92-93—Baltimore	AHL	79	20	46	66	60	...	...	...	7	0	7	7	8
93-94—Portland	AHL	29	14	13	27	17	...	...	...	—	—	—	—	—
—Washington	NHL	47	7	9	16	27	3	3	0	11	1	1	2	2
94-95—Washington	NHL	16	0	3	3	6	-3	0	0	—	—	—	—	—
—Portland	AHL	8	3	10	13	4	...	...	...	7	1	3	4	4
95-96—Colorado	NHL	7	0	3	3	4	2	0	0	—	—	—	—	—
—Cornwall	AHL	5	0	4	4	2	...	...	...	—	—	—	—	—
—Los Angeles	NHL	31	6	11	17	10	5	3	1	—	—	—	—	—
96-97—Los Angeles	NHL	32	3	11	14	4	-10	1	0	—	—	—	—	—
—Phoenix	IHL	35	9	25	34	8	...	...	...	—	—	—	—	—
97-98—Las Vegas	IHL	5	2	2	4	10	...	...	...	—	—	—	—	—
—Phoenix	NHL	55	3	14	17	24	-3	1	0	—	—	—	—	—
98-99—Nashville	NHL	46	2	12	14	14	-12	0	0	—	—	—	—	—
—Milwaukee	IHL	7	0	1	1	0	...	...	...	—	—	—	—	—
99-00—Pittsburgh	NHL	29	1	4	5	10	-10	1	0	2	1	0	1	2
—Wilkes-Barre/Scranton	AHL	49	30	30	60	25	...	...	...	—	—	—	—	—
NHL Totals (7 years)		263	22	67	89	99	-28	9	1	13	2	1	3	4

SLEGR, JIRI   D   PENGUINS

PERSONAL: Born May 30, 1971, in Jihlava, Czechoslovakia. ... 6-0/206. ... Shoots left. ... Son of Jiri Bubla, defenseman with Vancouver Canucks (1981-82 through 1985-86). ... Name pronounced YIH-ree SLAY-guhr.
TRANSACTIONS/CAREER NOTES: Selected by Vancouver Canucks in second round (third Canucks pick, 23rd overall) of NHL entry draft (June 16, 1990). ... Played in Europe during 1994-95 NHL lockout. ... Traded by Canucks to Edmonton Oilers for RW Roman Oksiuta (April 7, 1995). ... Sprained ligaments in left knee (December 27, 1995); missed 19 games. ... Traded by Oilers to Pittsburgh Penguins for third-round pick (traded to New Jersey) in 1998 draft (August 12, 1997). ... Suffered hip pointer (November 14, 1997); missed four games. ... Suffered from the flu (December 16, 1997); missed one game. ... Injured shoulder (March 2, 1998); missed one game. ... Fractured hand (November 5, 1998); missed 13 games. ... Bruised knee (April 1, 1999); missed one game. ... Sprained ankle (October 8, 1999); missed five games. ... Suffered from the flu (November 20, 1999); missed one game. ... Sprained knee (November 26, 1999); missed two games.
HONORS: Named to Czechoslovakian League All-Star team (1990-91).
MISCELLANEOUS: Member of gold-medal-winning Czech Republic Olympic team (1998).

Season Team	League	REGULAR SEASON								PLAYOFFS				
		Gms.	G	A	Pts.	PIM	+/-	PP	SH	Gms.	G	A	Pts.	PIM
87-88—Litvinov	Czech Rep.	4	1	1	2	0	...	...	...	—	—	—	—	—
88-89—Litvinov	Czech.	8	0	0	0	0	...	...	...	—	—	—	—	—
89-90—Litvinov	Czech.	51	4	15	19	...	...	...	...	—	—	—	—	—
90-91—Litvinov	Czech.	39	10	33	43	26	...	...	...	—	—	—	—	—
91-92—Litvinov	Czech.	38	7	22	29	30	...	...	...	—	—	—	—	—
—Czech. Olympic Team	Int'l	8	1	1	2	...	...	...	...	—	—	—	—	—
92-93—Vancouver	NHL	41	4	22	26	109	16	2	0	5	0	3	3	4
—Hamilton	AHL	21	4	14	18	42	...	...	...	—	—	—	—	—
93-94—Vancouver	NHL	78	5	33	38	86	0	1	0	—	—	—	—	—
94-95—Chem. Litvinov	Czech Rep.	11	3	10	13	43	...	...	...	—	—	—	—	—
—Vancouver	NHL	19	1	5	6	32	0	0	0	—	—	—	—	—
—Edmonton	NHL	12	1	5	6	14	-5	1	0	—	—	—	—	—
95-96—Edmonton	NHL	57	4	13	17	74	-1	0	1	—	—	—	—	—
—Cape Breton	AHL	4	1	2	3	4	...	...	...	—	—	—	—	—
96-97—Chem. Litvinov	Czech Rep.	1	0	0	0	0	...	...	...	—	—	—	—	—
—Sodertalje SK	Sweden	30	4	14	18	62	...	...	...	—	—	—	—	—
97-98—Pittsburgh	NHL	73	5	12	17	109	10	1	1	6	0	4	4	2
—Czech Rep. Oly. team	Int'l	6	1	0	1	8	...	...	...	—	—	—	—	—
98-99—Pittsburgh	NHL	63	3	20	23	86	13	1	0	13	1	3	4	12
99-00—Pittsburgh	NHL	74	11	20	31	82	20	0	0	10	2	3	5	19
NHL Totals (7 years)		417	34	130	164	592	53	6	2	34	3	13	16	37

S

SLOAN, BLAKE   RW   STARS

PERSONAL: Born July 27, 1975, in Park Ridge, Ill. ... 5-10/196. ... Shoots right.
COLLEGE: Michigan.
TRANSACTIONS/CAREER NOTES: Signed as non-drafted free agent by Dallas Stars (March 10, 1999). ... Sprained ankle (February 21, 2000); missed 15 games.
MISCELLANEOUS: Member of Stanley Cup championship team (1999). ... Played defense (1993-94 through 1998-99).

Season Team	League	REGULAR SEASON								PLAYOFFS				
		Gms.	G	A	Pts.	PIM	+/-	PP	SH	Gms.	G	A	Pts.	PIM
93-94—Univ. of Michigan	CCHA	38	2	4	6	48	...	...	...	—	—	—	—	—
94-95—Univ. of Michigan	CCHA	39	2	15	17	60	...	...	...	—	—	—	—	—
95-96—Univ. of Michigan	CCHA	41	6	24	30	57	...	...	...	—	—	—	—	—
96-97—Univ. of Michigan	CCHA	41	2	15	17	52	...	...	...	—	—	—	—	—
97-98—Houston	IHL	70	2	13	15	86	...	...	...	2	0	0	0	0
98-99—Houston	IHL	62	8	10	18	76	...	...	...	19	0	2	2	8
—Dallas	NHL	14	0	0	0	10	-1	0	0	16	0	0	0	12
99-00—Dallas	NHL	67	4	13	17	50	11	0	0	35	0	2	2	20
NHL Totals (2 years)		81	4	13	17	60	10	0	0	35	0	2	2	20

SMEHLIK, RICHARD   D   SABRES

PERSONAL: Born January 23, 1970, in Ostrava, Czechoslovakia. ... 6-3/222. ... Shoots left. ... Name pronounced SHMEHL-ihk.
TRANSACTIONS/CAREER NOTES: Selected by Buffalo Sabres in fifth round (third Sabres pick, 97th overall) of NHL entry draft (June 16, 1990). ... Injured hip (October 30, 1992); missed two games. ... Played in Europe during 1994-95 NHL lockout. ... Bruised shoulder (January 27, 1995); missed six games. ... Tore knee ligaments (August 10, 1995); missed entire 1995-96 season. ... Suffered tendonitis in knee (January 12, 1996); missed five games. ... Suffered sore knee (November 19, 1996); missed six games. ... Suffered sore knee (February 23, 1997); missed one game. ... Strained groin (March 30, 1997); missed three games. ... Injured wrist (February 4, 1998); missed two games. ... Bruised eye (February 25, 1998); missed seven games. ... Suspended one game and fined $1,000 by NHL for high-sticking incident (October 15, 1998). ... Bruised quadricep muscle (November 21, 1998); missed seven games. ... Injured rib (December 17, 1999); missed nine games. ... Suffered back spasms (February 17, 2000); missed three games.
MISCELLANEOUS: Member of gold-medal-winning Czech Republic Olympic team (1998).

Season Team	League	REGULAR SEASON								PLAYOFFS				
		Gms.	G	A	Pts.	PIM	+/-	PP	SH	Gms.	G	A	Pts.	PIM
88-89—Vitkovice	Czech.	38	2	5	7	12	...	...	...	—	—	—	—	—
89-90—Vitkovice	Czech.	43	4	3	7	...	...	...	...	—	—	—	—	—
90-91—Dukla Jihlava	Czech.	51	4	2	6	22	...	...	...	—	—	—	—	—
91-92—Vitkovice	Czech.	47	9	10	19	...	...	...	...	—	—	—	—	—
—Czech. Olympic Team	Int'l	8	0	1	1	2	...	...	...	—	—	—	—	—
92-93—Buffalo	NHL	80	4	27	31	59	9	0	0	8	0	4	4	2
93-94—Buffalo	NHL	84	14	27	41	69	22	3	3	7	0	2	2	10
94-95—HC Vitkovice	Czech Rep.	13	5	2	7	12	...	...	...	—	—	—	—	—
—Buffalo	NHL	39	4	7	11	46	5	0	1	5	0	0	0	2
95-96—Buffalo	NHL							Did not play.						
96-97—Buffalo	NHL	62	11	19	30	43	19	2	0	12	0	2	2	4
97-98—Buffalo	NHL	72	3	17	20	62	11	0	1	15	0	2	2	6
—Czech Rep. Oly. team	Int'l	6	0	1	1	4	...	...	...	—	—	—	—	—
98-99—Buffalo	NHL	72	3	11	14	44	-9	0	0	21	0	3	3	10
99-00—Buffalo	NHL	64	2	9	11	50	13	0	0	5	1	0	1	0
NHL Totals (8 years)		473	41	117	158	373	70	5	5	73	1	13	14	34

SMITH, BRANDON — D — BRUINS

PERSONAL: Born February 25, 1973, in Hazelton, B.C. ... 6-1/196. ... Shoots left. ... Full Name: Brandon Stuart Smith.
TRANSACTIONS/CAREER NOTES: Signed as non-drafted free agent by Detroit Red Wings (July 28, 1997). ... Signed as free agent by Boston Bruins (July 22, 1998).
HONORS: Named to AHL All-Star first team (1998-99).

Season Team	League	REGULAR SEASON								PLAYOFFS				
		Gms.	G	A	Pts.	PIM	+/-	PP	SH	Gms.	G	A	Pts.	PIM
89-90—Portland	WHL	59	2	17	19	16	...	...	...	—	—	—	—	—
90-91—Portland	WHL	17	8	5	13	8	...	...	...	—	—	—	—	—
91-92—Portland	WHL	70	12	32	44	63	...	...	...	—	—	—	—	—
92-93—Portland	WHL	72	20	54	74	38	...	...	...	16	4	9	13	6
93-94—Portland	WHL	72	19	63	82	47	...	...	...	10	2	10	12	8
94-95—Dayton	ECHL	60	16	49	65	57	...	...	...	4	2	3	5	0
—Adirondack	AHL	14	1	2	3	7	...	...	...	3	0	0	0	2
95-96—Adirondack	AHL	48	4	13	17	22	...	...	...	3	0	1	1	2
96-97—Adirondack	AHL	80	8	26	34	30	...	...	...	4	0	0	0	0
97-98—Adirondack	AHL	64	9	27	36	26	...	...	...	1	0	1	1	0
98-99—Providence	AHL	72	16	46	62	32	...	...	...	19	1	9	10	12
—Boston	NHL	5	0	0	0	0	2	0	0	—	—	—	—	—
99-00—Providence	AHL	55	8	30	38	20	...	...	...	14	1	11	12	2
—Boston	NHL	22	2	4	6	10	-4	0	0	—	—	—	—	—
NHL Totals (2 years)		27	2	4	6	10	-2	0	0					

SMITH, D.J. — D — MAPLE LEAFS

PERSONAL: Born May 13, 1977, in Windsor, Ont. ... 6-2/205. ... Shoots right. ... Full Name: Denis Smith.
HIGH SCHOOL: Holy Names (Windsor, Ont.).
TRANSACTIONS/CAREER NOTES: Selected by New York Islanders in second round (third Islanders pick, 41st overall) of NHL entry draft (July 8, 1995). ... Rights traded by Islanders with LW Wendel Clark and D Mathieu Schneider to Toronto Maple Leafs for LW Sean Haggerty, C Darby Hendrickson, D Kenny Jonsson and first-round pick (G Roberto Luongo) in 1997 draft (March 13, 1996).
HONORS: Named to OHL All-Star second team (1996-97).

Season Team	League	REGULAR SEASON								PLAYOFFS				
		Gms.	G	A	Pts.	PIM	+/-	PP	SH	Gms.	G	A	Pts.	PIM
92-93—Belle River	Jr. C	50	11	29	40	101	...	...	...	—	—	—	—	—
93-94—Windsor	Jr. B	51	8	34	42	267	...	...	...	—	—	—	—	—
94-95—Windsor	OHL	61	4	13	17	201	...	...	...	10	1	3	4	41
95-96—Windsor	OHL	64	14	45	59	260	...	...	...	7	1	7	8	23
96-97—Windsor	OHL	63	15	52	67	190	...	...	...	5	1	7	8	11
—Toronto	NHL	8	0	1	1	7	-5	0	0	—	—	—	—	—
—St. John's	AHL	—	—	—	—	—	...	...	...	1	0	0	0	0
97-98—St. John's	AHL	65	4	11	15	237	...	...	...	4	0	0	0	4
98-99—St. John's	AHL	79	7	28	35	216	...	...	...	5	0	1	1	0
99-00—St. John's	AHL	74	6	22	28	197	...	...	...	—	—	—	—	—
—Toronto	NHL	3	0	0	0	5	-1	0	0	—	—	—	—	—
NHL Totals (2 years)		11	0	1	1	12	-6	0	0					

SMITH, DAN — D — AVALANCHE

PERSONAL: Born October 19, 1976, in Fernie, B.C. ... 6-2/195. ... Shoots left.
COLLEGE: British Columbia.
TRANSACTIONS/CAREER NOTES: Selected by Colorado Avalanche in seventh round (seventh Avalanche pick, 181st overall) of NHL entry draft (July 8, 1995).

Season Team	League	REGULAR SEASON								PLAYOFFS				
		Gms.	G	A	Pts.	PIM	+/-	PP	SH	Gms.	G	A	Pts.	PIM
94-95—British Columbia	CWUAA	28	1	2	3	26	...	...	...	—	—	—	—	—
95-96—Tri-City	WHL	58	1	21	22	70	...	...	...	11	1	3	4	14
96-97—Tri-City	WHL	72	5	19	24	174	...	...	...	—	—	—	—	—
97-98—Hershey	AHL	50	1	2	3	71	...	...	...	6	0	0	0	4
98-99—Hershey	AHL	54	5	7	12	72	...	...	...	5	0	1	1	0
—Colorado	NHL	12	0	0	0	9	5	0	0	—	—	—	—	—
99-00—Hershey	AHL	49	7	15	22	56	...	...	...	—	—	—	—	—
—Colorado	NHL	3	0	0	0	0	2	0	0	—	—	—	—	—
NHL Totals (2 years)		15	0	0	0	9	7	0	0					

SMITH, JASON — D — OILERS

PERSONAL: Born November 2, 1973, in Calgary. ... 6-3/208. ... Shoots right.
TRANSACTIONS/CAREER NOTES: Selected by New Jersey Devils in first round (first Devils pick, 18th overall) of NHL entry draft (June 20, 1992). ... Injured right knee (November 5, 1994); missed 37 games. ... Bruised hand (November 5, 1995); missed 15 games. ... Traded by Devils with C Steve Sullivan and C Alyn McCauley to Toronto Maple Leafs for C Doug Gilmour, D Dave Ellett and third-round pick (D Andre Lakos) in 1999 draft (February 25, 1997). ... Fractured toe (March 30, 1998); missed one game. ... Traded by Maple Leafs to Edmonton Oilers for fourth-round pick (D Jonathan Zion) in 1999 draft and second-round pick (C Kris Vernarsky) in 2000 (March 23, 1999). ... Bruised shoulder (February 23, 2000); missed one game.
HONORS: Named to Can.HL All-Rookie team (1991-92). ... Won Bill Hunter Trophy (1992-93). ... Named to Can.HL All-Star first team (1992-93). ... Named to WHL (East) All-Star first team (1992-93).

Season Team	League	REGULAR SEASON								PLAYOFFS				
		Gms.	G	A	Pts.	PIM	+/-	PP	SH	Gms.	G	A	Pts.	PIM
90-91—Calgary Canucks	AJHL	45	3	15	18	69	...	...	...	—	—	—	—	—
—Regina	WHL	2	0	0	0	7	...	...	...	—	—	—	—	—
91-92—Regina	WHL	62	9	29	38	168	...	...	...	1	0	0	0	2
92-93—Utica	AHL	—	—	—	—	...	...	...	...	—	—	—	—	—
—Regina	WHL	64	14	52	66	175	...	...	...	13	4	8	12	39
93-94—New Jersey	NHL	41	0	5	5	43	7	0	0	6	0	0	0	7
—Albany	AHL	20	6	3	9	31	...	...	...	—	—	—	—	—
94-95—Albany	AHL	7	0	2	2	15	...	...	...	11	2	2	4	19
—New Jersey	NHL	2	0	0	0	0	-3	0	0	—	—	—	—	—
95-96—New Jersey	NHL	64	2	1	3	86	5	0	0	—	—	—	—	—
96-97—New Jersey	NHL	57	1	2	3	38	-8	0	0	—	—	—	—	—
—Toronto	NHL	21	0	5	5	16	-4	0	0	—	—	—	—	—
97-98—Toronto	NHL	81	3	13	16	100	-5	0	0	—	—	—	—	—
98-99—Toronto	NHL	60	2	11	13	40	-9	0	0	—	—	—	—	—
—Edmonton	NHL	12	1	1	2	11	0	0	0	4	0	1	1	4
99-00—Edmonton	NHL	80	3	11	14	60	16	0	0	5	0	1	1	4
NHL Totals (7 years)		418	12	49	61	394	-1	0	0	15	0	2	2	15

SMITH, MARK — C — SHARKS

PERSONAL: Born October 24, 1977, in Eyebrow, Sask. ... 5-10/200. ... Shoots left.
TRANSACTIONS/CAREER NOTES: Selected by San Jose Sharks in ninth round (seventh Sharks pick, 219th overall) in NHL entry draft (June 21, 1997).
HONORS: Named to WHL (East) All-Star second team (1997-98).

Season Team	League	REGULAR SEASON								PLAYOFFS				
		Gms.	G	A	Pts.	PIM	+/-	PP	SH	Gms.	G	A	Pts.	PIM
94-95—Lethbridge	WHL	49	3	4	7	25	...	...	...	—	—	—	—	—
95-96—Lethbridge	WHL	71	11	24	35	59	...	...	...	19	7	13	20	51
96-97—Lethbridge	WHL	62	19	38	57	125	...	...	...	19	7	13	20	51
97-98—Lethbridge	WHL	70	42	67	109	206	...	...	...	3	0	2	2	18
98-99—Kentucky	AHL	78	18	21	39	101	...	...	...	12	2	7	9	16
99-00—Kentucky	AHL	79	21	45	66	153	...	...	...	9	0	5	5	22

SMITH, STEVE — D — FLAMES

PERSONAL: Born April 30, 1963, in Glasgow, Scotland. ... 6-4/215. ... Shoots left. ... Full Name: James Stephen Smith.
TRANSACTIONS/CAREER NOTES: Selected by Edmonton Oilers as underage junior in sixth round (fifth Oilers pick, 111th overall) of NHL entry draft (June 10, 1981). ... Strained right shoulder (November 1, 1985). ... Pulled stomach muscle (February 1986). ... Separated left shoulder (September 20, 1988). ... Aggravated shoulder injury (October 1988). ... Dislocated left shoulder and tore cartilage (January 2, 1989). ... Underwent surgery to left shoulder (January 23, 1989); missed 45 games. ... Traded by Oilers to Chicago Blackhawks for D Dave Manson and third-round pick in either 1992 or 1993 draft; Oilers used third-round pick in 1992 draft to select RW Kirk Maltby (September 26, 1991). ... Pulled rib-cage muscle (December 31, 1991); missed three games. ... Strained back muscle (December 27, 1992); missed four games. ... Suspended four games and fined $500 by NHL for slashing (November 22, 1993). ... Fractured left leg (February 24, 1994); missed remainder of season. ... Suffered back spasms (October 5, 1995); missed 14 games. ... Suffered sore back (November 22, 1995); missed 11 games. ... Suffered sore back (January 2, 1996); missed 11 games. ... Suffered sore back (January 28, 1996); missed six games. ... Fractured left fibula (April 7, 1996); missed seven games. ... Injured nerve in leg (October 5, 1996); missed 10 games. ... Suffered sore back (November 17, 1996); missed three games. ... Suffered sore back (November 27, 1996); missed 13 games. ... Suffered sore back (December 31, 1996); missed 28 games. ... Announced retirement (August 14, 1997). ... Activated from retirement and signed by Calgary Flames (August 17, 1998). ... Injured ankle (March 13, 1999); missed seven games. ... Suffered laceration on neck (April 3, 1999); missed final six games of season. ... Suffered dislocated elbow (November 6, 1999); missed 22 games. ... Bruised spinal cord (January 8, 2000); missed final 40 games of season.
HONORS: Played in NHL All-Star Game (1991).
MISCELLANEOUS: Member of Stanley Cup championship team (1987, 1988 and 1990). ... Captain of Calgary Flames (1999-2000).

Season Team	League	REGULAR SEASON								PLAYOFFS				
		Gms.	G	A	Pts.	PIM	+/-	PP	SH	Gms.	G	A	Pts.	PIM
80-81—London	OMJHL	62	4	12	16	141	...	...	...	4	1	2	3	13
81-82—London	OHL	58	10	36	46	207	...	...	...	3	1	0	1	10
82-83—London	OHL	50	6	35	41	133	...	...	...	—	—	—	—	—
—Moncton	AHL	2	0	0	0	0	...	...	...	—	—	—	—	—
83-84—Moncton	AHL	64	1	8	9	176	...	...	...	—	—	—	—	—
84-85—Nova Scotia	AHL	68	2	28	30	161	...	...	...	5	0	3	3	40
—Edmonton	NHL	2	0	0	0	2	-2	0	0	—	—	—	—	—
85-86—Nova Scotia	AHL	4	0	2	2	11	...	...	...	—	—	—	—	—
—Edmonton	NHL	55	4	20	24	166	30	1	0	6	0	1	1	14
86-87—Edmonton	NHL	62	7	15	22	165	11	2	0	15	1	3	4	45
87-88—Edmonton	NHL	79	12	43	55	286	40	5	0	19	1	11	12	55
88-89—Edmonton	NHL	35	3	19	22	97	5	0	0	7	2	2	4	20
89-90—Edmonton	NHL	75	7	34	41	171	6	3	0	22	5	10	15	37
90-91—Edmonton	NHL	77	13	41	54	193	14	4	0	18	1	2	3	45
91-92—Chicago	NHL	76	9	21	30	304	23	3	0	18	1	11	12	16
92-93—Chicago	NHL	78	10	47	57	214	12	7	1	4	0	0	0	10
93-94—Chicago	NHL	57	5	22	27	174	-5	1	0	—	—	—	—	—
94-95—Chicago	NHL	48	1	12	13	128	6	0	0	16	0	1	1	26
95-96—Chicago	NHL	37	0	9	9	71	12	0	0	6	0	0	0	16
96-97—Chicago	NHL	21	0	0	0	29	4	0	0	3	0	0	0	4
97-98—		Did not play.												
98-99—Calgary	NHL	69	1	14	15	80	3	0	0	—	—	—	—	—
99-00—Calgary	NHL	20	0	4	4	42	-13	0	0	—	—	—	—	—
NHL Totals (16 years)		791	72	301	373	2122	146	26	1	134	11	41	52	288

S

SMITH, WYATT   C

PERSONAL: Born February 13, 1977, in Thief River Falls, Minn. ... 5-11/200. ... Shoots left.
COLLEGE: Minnesota.
TRANSACTIONS: Selected by Phoenix Coyotes in ninth round (sixth Coyotes pick, 233rd overall) of NHL entry draft (June 21, 1997).

			REGULAR SEASON								PLAYOFFS				
Season Team	League	Gms.	G	A	Pts.	PIM	+/-	PP	SH		Gms.	G	A	Pts.	PIM
95-96—Univ. of Minnesota......	WCHA	32	4	5	9	32	...	...	...		—	—	—	—	—
96-97—Univ. of Minnesota......	WCHA	39	24	23	47	62	...	...	...		—	—	—	—	—
97-98—Univ. of Minnesota......	WCHA	39	24	23	47	62	...	...	...		—	—	—	—	—
98-99—Univ. of Minnesota......	WCHA	43	23	20	43	37	...	...	...		—	—	—	—	—
99-00—Springfield	AHL	60	14	26	40	26	...	...	...		5	2	3	5	13
—Phoenix.....................	NHL	2	0	0	0	0	-2	0	0		—	—	—	—	—
NHL Totals (1 year)..............		2	0	0	0	0	-2	0	0						

SMOLINSKI, BRYAN   C   KINGS

PERSONAL: Born December 27, 1971, in Toledo, Ohio. ... 6-1/208. ... Shoots right. ... Full Name: Bryan Anthony Smolinski.
COLLEGE: Michigan State.
TRANSACTIONS/CAREER NOTES: Selected by Boston Bruins in first round (first Bruins pick, 21st overall) of NHL entry draft (June 16, 1990). ... Injured knee (April 14, 1994); missed one game. ... Suffered charley horse (April 1995); missed four games. ... Traded by Bruins with RW Glen Murray to Pittsburgh Penguins for LW Kevin Stevens and C Shawn McEachern (August 2, 1995). ... Bruised knee (January 16, 1996); missed one game. ... Traded by Penguins to New York Islanders for D Darius Kasparaitis and C Andreas Johansson (November 17, 1996). ... Traded by Islanders with RW Zigmund Palffy, G Marcel Cousineau and fourth-round pick (C Daniel Johansson) in 1999 draft to Los Angeles Kings for C Olli Jokinen, LW Josh Green, D Mathieu Biron and first-round pick (LW Taylor Pyatt) in 1999 draft (June 20, 1999). ... Sprained knee (April 3, 1999); missed final three games of season.
HONORS: Named to CCHA All-Rookie team (1989-90). ... Named to NCAA All-America (West) first team (1992-93). ... Named to CCHA All-Star first team (1992-93).
STATISTICAL PLATEAUS: Three-goal games: 1994-95 (1).

			REGULAR SEASON								PLAYOFFS				
Season Team	League	Gms.	G	A	Pts.	PIM	+/-	PP	SH		Gms.	G	A	Pts.	PIM
87-88—Detroit Little Caesars ..	MNHL	80	43	77	120	...	...	...	...		—	—	—	—	—
88-89—Stratford Jr. B	OHA	46	32	62	94	132	...	...	...		—	—	—	—	—
89-90—Michigan State............	CCHA	39	10	17	27	45	...	...	...		—	—	—	—	—
90-91—Michigan State............	CCHA	35	9	12	21	24	...	...	...		—	—	—	—	—
91-92—Michigan State............	CCHA	44	30	35	65	59	...	...	...		—	—	—	—	—
92-93—Michigan State............	CCHA	40	31	37	68	93	...	...	...		—	—	—	—	—
—Boston	NHL	9	1	3	4	0	3	0	0		4	1	0	1	2
93-94—Boston	NHL	83	31	20	51	82	4	4	3		13	5	4	9	4
94-95—Boston	NHL	44	18	13	31	31	-3	6	0		5	0	1	1	4
95-96—Pittsburgh	NHL	81	24	40	64	69	6	8	2		18	5	4	9	10
96-97—Detroit......................	IHL	6	5	7	12	10	...	...	...		—	—	—	—	—
—New York Islanders.....	NHL	64	28	28	56	25	9	9	0		—	—	—	—	—
97-98—New York Islanders.....	NHL	81	13	30	43	34	-16	3	0		—	—	—	—	—
98-99—New York Islanders.....	NHL	82	16	24	40	49	-7	7	0		—	—	—	—	—
99-00—Los Angeles...............	NHL	79	20	36	56	48	2	2	0		4	0	0	0	2
NHL Totals (8 years)...........		523	151	194	345	338	-2	39	5		44	11	9	20	22

SMREK, PETER   D   BLUES

PERSONAL: Born February 16, 1979, in Martin, Czechoslovakia. ... 6-1/194. ... Shoots left.
TRANSACTIONS/CAREER NOTES: Selected by St. Louis Blues in third round (second Blues pick, 85th overall) of NHL entry draft (June 26, 1999).

			REGULAR SEASON								PLAYOFFS				
Season Team	League	Gms.	G	A	Pts.	PIM	+/-	PP	SH		Gms.	G	A	Pts.	PIM
97-98—Martimex Martin Jrs. ..	Slov. Jr.	23	0	5	5	24	...	...	...		—	—	—	—	—
98-99—Des Moines.................	USHL	52	6	26	32	59	...	...	...		—	—	—	—	—
99-00—Worcester	AHL	64	5	19	24	26	...	...	...		2	0	0	0	4
—Peoria	ECHL	4	1	1	2	2	...	...	...		—	—	—	—	—

SMYTH, RYAN   LW   OILERS

PERSONAL: Born February 21, 1976, in Banff, Alta. ... 6-1/195. ... Shoots left. ... Brother of Kevin Smyth, left winger with Hartford Whalers (1993-94 through 1995-96). ... Name pronounced SMIHTH.
HIGH SCHOOL: Vanier Comm. Catholic (Edson, Alta.).
TRANSACTIONS/CAREER NOTES: Selected by Edmonton Oilers in first round (second Oilers pick, sixth overall) of NHL entry draft (June 28, 1994). ... Tore medial collateral ligament in knee (January 20, 1998); missed 15 games. ... Bruised thigh (December 27, 1998); missed one game. ... Fractured jaw (March 10, 1999); missed seven games.
HONORS: Named to Can.HL All-Star first team (1994-95). ... Named to WHL (East) All-Star second team (1994-95).
STATISTICAL PLATEAUS: Three-goal games: 1996-97 (1), 1999-00 (1). Total: 2.

			REGULAR SEASON								PLAYOFFS				
Season Team	League	Gms.	G	A	Pts.	PIM	+/-	PP	SH		Gms.	G	A	Pts.	PIM
91-92—Moose Jaw	WHL	2	0	0	0	0	...	...	...		—	—	—	—	—
92-93—Moose Jaw	WHL	64	19	14	33	59	...	...	...		—	—	—	—	—
93-94—Moose Jaw	WHL	72	50	55	105	88	...	...	...		—	—	—	—	—
94-95—Moose Jaw	WHL	50	41	45	86	66	...	...	...		10	6	9	15	22
—Edmonton	NHL	3	0	0	0	0	-1	0	0		—	—	—	—	—
95-96—Edmonton	NHL	48	2	9	11	28	-10	1	0		—	—	—	—	—
—Cape Breton...............	AHL	9	6	5	11	4	...	...	...		—	—	—	—	—

S

Season Team	League	REGULAR SEASON								PLAYOFFS				
		Gms.	G	A	Pts.	PIM	+/-	PP	SH	Gms.	G	A	Pts.	PIM
96-97—Edmonton	NHL	82	39	22	61	76	-7	†20	0	12	5	5	10	12
97-98—Edmonton	NHL	65	20	13	33	44	-24	10	0	12	1	3	4	16
98-99—Edmonton	NHL	71	13	18	31	62	0	6	0	3	3	0	3	0
99-00—Edmonton	NHL	82	28	26	54	58	-2	11	0	5	1	0	1	6
NHL Totals (6 years)		351	102	88	190	268	-44	48	0	32	10	8	18	34

SNOW, GARTH — G

PERSONAL: Born July 28, 1969, in Wrentham, Mass. ... 6-3/210. ... Catches left.
HIGH SCHOOL: Mount St. Charles Academy (Woonsocket, R.I.).
COLLEGE: Maine.
TRANSACTIONS/CAREER NOTES: Selected by Quebec Nordiques in sixth round (sixth Nordiques pick, 114th overall) of NHL entry draft (June 13, 1987). ... Nordiques franchise moved to Colorado and renamed Avalanche for 1995-96 season (June 21, 1995). ... Rights traded by Avalanche to Philadelphia Flyers for third-(traded to Washington) and sixth-(G Kai Fischer) round picks in 1996 draft (July 12, 1995). ... Pulled groin (March 27, 1997); missed three games. ... Traded by Flyers to Vancouver Canucks for G Sean Burke (March 4, 1998). ... Strained hip flexor (March 18, 1998); missed three games. ... Strained hip flexor (October 31, 1998); missed two games. ... Injured finger (September 21, 1999); missed two games. ... Fractured finger (October 13, 1999); missed 15 games.
HONORS: Named to NCAA All-Tournament team (1992-93). ... Named to Hockey East All-Star second team (1992-93).
MISCELLANEOUS: Holds Vancouver Canucks all-time record for goals-against average (2.87). ... Stopped a penalty shot attempt (vs. Owen Nolan, December 26, 1998).

Season Team	League	REGULAR SEASON							PLAYOFFS					
		Gms.	Min	W	L	T	GA	SO	Avg.	Gms.	Min.	W	L	GA	SO	Avg.
88-89—Univ. of Maine	Hockey East	5	241	2	2	0	14	1	3.49	—	—	—	—	—	—	—
89-90—Univ. of Maine	Hockey East						Did not play.									
90-91—Univ. of Maine	Hockey East	25	1290	18	4	0	64	0	2.98	—	—	—	—	—	—	—
91-92—Univ. of Maine	Hockey East	31	1792	25	4	2	73	2	2.44	—	—	—	—	—	—	—
92-93—Univ. of Maine	Hockey East	23	1210	21	0	1	42	1	2.08	—	—	—	—	—	—	—
93-94—U.S. national team	Int'l	23	1324	13	5	3	71	1	3.22	—	—	—	—	—	—	—
—Quebec	NHL	5	279	3	2	0	16	0	3.44	—	—	—	—	—	—	—
—U.S. Olympic team	Int'l	5	299	1	2	2	17	0	3.41	—	—	—	—	—	—	—
—Cornwall	AHL	16	927	6	5	3	51	0	3.30	13	790	8	5	42	0	3.19
94-95—Cornwall	AHL	62	3558	*32	20	7	162	3	2.73	8	402	4	3	14	†2	*2.09
—Quebec	NHL	2	119	1	1	0	11	0	5.55	1	9	0	0	1	0	6.67
95-96—Philadelphia	NHL	26	1437	12	8	4	69	0	2.88	1	1	0	0	0	0	...
96-97—Philadelphia	NHL	35	1884	14	8	8	79	2	2.52	12	699	8	4	33	0	2.83
97-98—Philadelphia	NHL	29	1651	14	9	4	67	1	2.43	—	—	—	—	—	—	—
—Vancouver	NHL	12	504	3	6	0	26	0	3.10	—	—	—	—	—	—	—
98-99—Vancouver	NHL	65	3501	20	†31	8	†171	6	2.93	—	—	—	—	—	—	—
99-00—Vancouver	NHL	32	1712	10	15	3	76	0	2.66	—	—	—	—	—	—	—
NHL Totals (7 years)		206	11087	77	80	27	515	9	2.79	14	709	8	4	34	0	2.88

SONNENBERG, MARTIN — LW — PENGUINS

PERSONAL: Born January 23, 1978, in Wetaskiwin, Alta. ... 6-0/184. ... Shoots left.
TRANSACTIONS/CAREER NOTES: Signed as non-drafted free agent by Pittsburgh Penguins (October 9, 1998).

Season Team	League	REGULAR SEASON								PLAYOFFS				
		Gms.	G	A	Pts.	PIM	+/-	PP	SH	Gms.	G	A	Pts.	PIM
95-96—Saskatoon	WHL	58	8	7	15	24	...	...	...	3	0	0	0	2
96-97—Saskatoon	WHL	72	38	26	64	79	...	...	...	—	—	—	—	—
97-98—Saskatoon	WHL	72	40	52	92	87	...	...	...	6	1	3	4	9
98-99—Syracuse	AHL	37	16	9	25	31	...	...	...	—	—	—	—	—
—Pittsburgh	NHL	44	1	1	2	19	-2	0	0	7	0	0	0	0
99-00—Pittsburgh	NHL	14	1	2	3	0	0	1	0	—	—	—	—	—
—Wilkes-Barre/Scranton	AHL	62	20	33	53	109	...	...	...	—	—	—	—	—
NHL Totals (2 years)		58	2	3	5	19	-2	1	0	7	0	0	0	0

SOPEL, BRENT — D — CANUCKS

PERSONAL: Born January 7, 1977, in Saskatoon, Sask. ... 6-1/205. ... Shoots right. ... Name pronounced SOH-puhl.
TRANSACTIONS/CAREER NOTES: Selected by Vancouver Canucks in sixth round (sixth Canucks pick, 144th overall) of NHL entry draft (July 8, 1995).

Season Team	League	REGULAR SEASON								PLAYOFFS				
		Gms.	G	A	Pts.	PIM	+/-	PP	SH	Gms.	G	A	Pts.	PIM
93-94—Saskatoon	WHL	11	2	2	4	2	...	...	...	—	—	—	—	—
94-95—Saskatoon	WHL	22	1	10	11	31	...	...	...	—	—	—	—	—
—Swift Current	WHL	41	4	19	23	50	...	...	...	3	0	3	3	0
95-96—Swift Current	WHL	71	13	48	61	87	...	...	...	6	1	2	3	4
—Syracuse	AHL	1	0	0	0	0	...	...	...	—	—	—	—	—
96-97—Swift Current	WHL	62	15	41	56	109	...	...	...	10	5	11	16	32
—Syracuse	AHL	2	0	0	0	0	...	...	...	3	0	0	0	0
97-98—Syracuse	AHL	76	10	33	43	70	...	...	...	5	0	7	7	12
98-99—Syracuse	AHL	53	10	21	31	59	...	...	...	—	—	—	—	—
—Vancouver	NHL	5	1	0	1	4	-1	1	0	—	—	—	—	—
99-00—Syracuse	AHL	50	6	25	31	67	...	...	...	4	0	2	2	8
—Vancouver	NHL	18	2	4	6	12	9	0	0	—	—	—	—	—
NHL Totals (2 years)		23	3	4	7	16	8	1	0					

SOROCHAN, LEE — D

PERSONAL: Born September 9, 1975, in Edmonton. ... 5-11/210. ... Shoots left. ... Name pronounced SAWR-ih-kihn.
HIGH SCHOOL: Gibbons (Alta.).
TRANSACTIONS/CAREER NOTES: Selected by New York Rangers in second round (second Rangers pick, 34th overall) of NHL entry draft (June 26, 1993). ... Traded by Rangers to Calgary Flames for D Chris O'Sullivan (March 23, 1999).

Season Team	League	REGULAR SEASON								PLAYOFFS				
		Gms.	G	A	Pts.	PIM	+/-	PP	SH	Gms.	G	A	Pts.	PIM
91-92—Lethbridge	WHL	67	2	9	11	105	...	...	...	5	0	2	2	6
92-93—Lethbridge	WHL	69	8	32	40	208	...	...	...	4	0	1	1	12
93-94—Lethbridge	WHL	46	5	27	32	123	...	...	...	9	4	3	7	16
94-95—Lethbridge	WHL	29	4	15	19	93	...	...	...	—	—	—	—	—
—Saskatoon	WHL	24	5	13	18	63	...	...	...	10	3	6	9	34
—Binghamton	AHL	—	—	—	—	—	...	...	...	8	0	0	0	11
95-96—Binghamton	AHL	45	2	8	10	26	...	...	...	1	0	0	0	0
96-97—Binghamton	AHL	77	4	27	31	160	...	...	...	4	0	2	2	18
97-98—Hartford	AHL	73	7	11	18	197	...	...	...	13	0	2	2	51
98-99—Fort Wayne	IHL	45	0	10	10	204	...	...	...	—	—	—	—	—
—Hartford	AHL	16	0	2	2	33	...	...	...	—	—	—	—	—
—Calgary	NHL	2	0	0	0	0	-3	0	0	—	—	—	—	—
—Saint John	AHL	3	1	3	4	4	...	...	...	7	3	3	6	29
99-00—Saint John	AHL	60	4	37	41	124	...	...	...	3	2	1	3	12
—Calgary	NHL	1	0	0	0	0	0	0	0	—	—	—	—	—
NHL Totals (2 years)		3	0	0	0	0	-3	0	0					

SOURAY, SHELDON — D — CANADIENS

PERSONAL: Born July 13, 1976, in Elk Point, Alta. ... 6-4/230. ... Shoots left. ... Name pronounced SOOR-ay.
TRANSACTIONS/CAREER NOTES: Selected by New Jersey Devils in third round (third Devils pick, 71st overall) of NHL entry draft (June 29, 1994). ... Suffered head injury (September 27, 1997); missed five games. ... Bruised right wrist (October 17, 1997); missed four games. ... Suffered from the flu (December 18, 1997); missed one game. ... Suffered from the flu (January 30, 1998); missed one game. ... Traded by Devils with D Josh DeWolf and second-round pick in 2001 draft to Montreal Canadiens for D Vladimir Malakhov (March 1, 2000).
HONORS: Named to WHL (West) All-Star second team (1995-96).

Season Team	League	REGULAR SEASON								PLAYOFFS				
		Gms.	G	A	Pts.	PIM	+/-	PP	SH	Gms.	G	A	Pts.	PIM
92-93—Fort Saskatchewan	AJHL	35	0	12	12	125	...	...	...	—	—	—	—	—
—Tri-City	WHL	2	0	0	0	0	...	...	...	—	—	—	—	—
93-94—Tri-City	WHL	42	3	6	9	122	...	...	...	—	—	—	—	—
94-95—Tri-City	WHL	40	2	24	26	140	...	...	...	—	—	—	—	—
—Prince George	WHL	11	2	3	5	23	...	...	...	—	—	—	—	—
—Albany	AHL	7	0	2	2	8	...	...	...	—	—	—	—	—
95-96—Prince George	WHL	32	9	18	27	91	...	...	...	—	—	—	—	—
—Kelowna	WHL	27	7	20	27	94	...	...	...	6	0	5	5	2
—Albany	AHL	6	0	2	2	12	...	...	...	4	0	1	1	4
96-97—Albany	AHL	70	2	11	13	160	...	...	...	16	2	3	5	47
97-98—New Jersey	NHL	60	3	7	10	85	18	0	0	3	0	1	1	2
—Albany	AHL	6	0	0	0	8	...	...	...	—	—	—	—	—
98-99—New Jersey	NHL	70	1	7	8	110	5	0	0	2	0	1	1	0
99-00—New Jersey	NHL	52	0	8	8	70	-6	0	0	—	—	—	—	—
—Montreal	NHL	19	3	0	3	44	7	0	0	—	—	—	—	—
NHL Totals (3 years)		201	7	22	29	309	24	0	0	5	0	2	2	2

SPACEK, JAROSLAV — D — PANTHERS

PERSONAL: Born February 11, 1974, in Rokycany, Czechoslovakia. ... 5-11/198. ... Shoots left.
TRANSACTIONS/CAREER NOTES: Selected by Florida Panthers in fifth round (fifth Panthers pick, 117th overall) of NHL entry draft (June 27, 1998). ... Suffered from the flu (April 7, 1999); missed three games.

Season Team	League	REGULAR SEASON								PLAYOFFS				
		Gms.	G	A	Pts.	PIM	+/-	PP	SH	Gms.	G	A	Pts.	PIM
92-93—Skoda Plzen	Czech.	16	1	3	4		...	...	...	—	—	—	—	—
93-94—Skoda Plzen	Czech Rep.	34	2	10	12		...	...	...	—	—	—	—	—
94-95—Interconex Plzen	Czech Rep.	38	4	8	12	14	...	...	...	3	1	0	1	2
95-96—ZKZ Plzen	Czech Rep.	40	3	10	13	42	...	...	...	3	0	1	1	4
96-97—ZKZ Plzen	Czech Rep.	52	9	29	38	44	...	...	...	—	—	—	—	—
97-98—Farjestad Karlstad	Sweden	45	10	16	26	63	...	...	...	12	2	5	7	14
98-99—Florida	NHL	63	3	12	15	28	15	2	1	—	—	—	—	—
—New Haven	AHL	14	4	8	12	15	...	...	...	—	—	—	—	—
99-00—Florida	NHL	82	10	26	36	53	7	4	0	4	0	0	0	0
NHL Totals (2 years)		145	13	38	51	81	22	6	1	4	0	0	0	0

SPANHEL, MARTIN — LW — BLUE JACKETS

PERSONAL: Born July 1, 1977, in Gottwaldov, Czechoslovakia. ... 6-2/202. ... Shoots left. ... Name pronounced spah-NEHL.
TRANSACTIONS/CAREER NOTES: Selected by Philadelphia Flyers in sixth round (fifth Flyers pick, 152nd overall) of NHL entry draft (July 8, 1995). ... Traded by Flyers with first (traded to Winnipeg)- and fourth-round (traded to Buffalo) picks in 1996 draft to San Jose Sharks for RW Pat Falloon (November 16, 1995). ... Signed as free agent by Columbus Blue Jackets (June 7, 2000).

Season Team	League	Gms.	G	A	Pts.	PIM	+/-	PP	SH	Gms.	G	A	Pts.	PIM
94-95—ZPS Zlin Jrs.	Czech. Jrs.	33	25	16	41	...	...	...	...	—	—	—	—	—
—ZPS Zlin Jrs.	Czech. Jrs.	33	25	16	41	...	...	...	...	—	—	—	—	—
—ZPS Zlin	Czech Rep.	1	0	0	0	...				—	—	—	—	—
95-96—Moose Jaw	WHL	61	4	12	16	33	...			—	—	—	—	—
—Lethbridge	WHL	6	1	0	1	0	...			—	—	—	—	—
96-97—ZPS Zlin	Czech Rep.	22	3	6	9	20	...			—	—	—	—	—
—ZPS Zlin Jrs.	Czech. Jrs.	6	6	3	9	2	...			—	—	—	—	—
—Karlovy Vary	Czech. D-II	7	4	3	7	...				—	—	—	—	—
97-98—ZPS Zlin	Czech Rep.	40	7	9	16	70	...			—	—	—	—	—
98-99—HC Keramika Plzen	Czech Rep.	49	13	13	26	60	...			5	2	1	3	...
99-00—HC Keramika Plzen	Czech Rep.	52	21	27	48	86	...			7	1	4	5	12

ST. LOUIS, MARTIN　　　　RW　　　　LIGHTNING

PERSONAL: Born September 8, 1971, in Laval, Que. ... 5-9/185. ... Shoots left.
COLLEGE: Vermont.
TRANSACTIONS/CAREER NOTES: Signed as non-drafted free agent by Calgary Flames (February 18, 1998). ... Suffered concussion (March 15, 2000); missed two games. ... Signed as free agent by Tampa Bay Lightning (July 31, 2000).
HONORS: Named to NCAA All-America (East) first team (1994-95 through 1996-97). ... Named to ECAC All-Star first team (1994-95 through 1996-97).

		REGULAR SEASON								PLAYOFFS				
Season Team	League	Gms.	G	A	Pts.	PIM	+/-	PP	SH	Gms.	G	A	Pts.	PIM
93-94—Vermont	ECAC	33	15	36	51	24	...	...	...	—	—	—	—	—
94-95—Vermont	ECAC	35	23	48	71	36	...	...	...	—	—	—	—	—
95-96—Vermont	ECAC	35	29	56	85	36	...	...	...	—	—	—	—	—
96-97—Vermont	ECAC	35	24	26	50	65	...	...	...	—	—	—	—	—
97-98—Cleveland	IHL	56	16	34	50	24	...	...	...	—	—	—	—	—
—Saint John	AHL	25	15	11	26	20	...	...	...	20	5	15	20	16
98-99—Calgary	NHL	13	1	1	2	10	-2	0	0	—	—	—	—	—
—Saint John	AHL	53	28	34	62	30	...	...	...	7	4	4	8	2
99-00—Saint John	AHL	17	15	11	26	14	...	...	...	—	—	—	—	—
—Calgary	NHL	56	3	15	18	22	-5	0	0	—	—	—	—	—
NHL Totals (2 years)		69	4	16	20	32	-7	0	0	—	—	—	—	—

STAIOS, STEVE　　　　RW/D　　　　THRASHERS

PERSONAL: Born July 28, 1973, in Hamilton, Ont. ... 6-1/200. ... Shoots right. ... Name pronounced STAY-ohz.
TRANSACTIONS/CAREER NOTES: Selected by St. Louis Blues in second round (first Blues pick, 27th overall) of NHL entry draft (June 22, 1991). ... Traded by Blues with LW Kevin Sawyer to Boston Bruins for RW Steve Leach (March 8, 1996). ... Strained groin (November 6, 1996); missed 13 games. ... Claimed on waivers by Vancouver Canucks (March 18, 1997). ... Injured knee (February 24, 1999); missed 16 games. ... Selected by Atlanta Thrashers in NHL expansion draft (June 25, 1999). ... Sprained medial collateral ligament in right knee (November 20, 1999); missed four games. ... Injured groin (December 30, 1999); missed 16 games. ... Reinjured groin (February 15, 2000); missed final 27 games of season. ... Traded by Thrashers to New Jersey Devils for ninth-round pick (C Simon Gamache) in 2000 draft (June 12, 2000). ... Traded by Devils to Thrashers for future considerations (July 10, 2000).

		REGULAR SEASON								PLAYOFFS				
Season Team	League	Gms.	G	A	Pts.	PIM	+/-	PP	SH	Gms.	G	A	Pts.	PIM
89-90—Hamilton Jr. B	OHA	40	9	27	36	66	...	...	...	—	—	—	—	—
90-91—Niagara Falls	OHL	66	17	29	46	115	...	...	...	12	2	3	5	10
91-92—Niagara Falls	OHL	65	11	42	53	122	...	...	...	17	7	8	15	27
92-93—Niagara Falls	OHL	12	4	14	18	30	...	...	...	—	—	—	—	—
—Sudbury	OHL	53	13	44	57	67	...	...	...	11	5	6	11	22
93-94—Peoria	IHL	38	3	9	12	42	...	...	...	—	—	—	—	—
94-95—Peoria	IHL	60	3	13	16	64	...	...	...	6	0	0	0	10
95-96—Peoria	IHL	6	0	1	1	14	...	...	...	—	—	—	—	—
—Worcester	AHL	57	1	11	12	114	...	...	...	—	—	—	—	—
—Providence	AHL	7	1	4	5	8	...	...	...	—	—	—	—	—
—Boston	NHL	12	0	0	0	4	-5	0	0	3	0	0	0	0
96-97—Boston	NHL	54	3	8	11	71	-26	0	0	—	—	—	—	—
—Vancouver	NHL	9	0	6	6	20	2	0	0	—	—	—	—	—
97-98—Vancouver	NHL	77	3	4	7	134	-3	0	0	—	—	—	—	—
98-99—Vancouver	NHL	57	0	2	2	54	-12	0	0	—	—	—	—	—
99-00—Atlanta	NHL	27	2	3	5	66	-5	0	0	—	—	—	—	—
NHL Totals (5 years)		236	8	23	31	349	-49	0	0	3	0	0	0	0

STAPLETON, MIKE　　　　C　　　　ISLANDERS

PERSONAL: Born May 5, 1966, in Sarnia, Ont. ... 5-10/185. ... Shoots right. ... Son of Pat Stapleton, defenseman with Boston Bruins (1961-62 and 1962-63), Chicago Blackhawks (1965-66 through 1972-73) and three WHA teams (1973-74 through 1977-78).
TRANSACTIONS/CAREER NOTES: Selected by Chicago Blackhawks in seventh round (seventh Blackhawks pick, 132nd overall) of NHL entry draft (June 9, 1984). ... Signed as free agent by Pittsburgh Penguins (September 4, 1992). ... Claimed on waivers by Edmonton Oilers (February 19, 1994). ... Signed as free agent by Winnipeg Jets (August 9, 1995). ... Suffered charley horse (October 12, 1995); missed one game. ... Fractured jaw (November 1, 1995); missed 16 games. ... Strained groin (March 27, 1996); missed five games. ... Jets franchise moved to Phoenix and renamed Coyotes for 1996-97 season; NHL approved move on January 18, 1996. ... Suffered eye abrasion (January 30, 1998); missed four games. ... Fractured foot (March 28, 1998); missed five games. ... Suffered from the flu (November 1, 1998); missed one game. ... Suffered charley horse (January 17, 1999); missed one game. ... Suffered facial lacerations (February 14, 1999); missed four games. ... Selected by Atlanta Thrashers in NHL expansion draft (June 25, 1999). ... Injured ribs (January 12, 2000); missed 13 games. ... Signed as free agent by New York Islanders (July 3, 2000).

Season Team	League	REGULAR SEASON								PLAYOFFS				
		Gms.	G	A	Pts.	PIM	+/-	PP	SH	Gms.	G	A	Pts.	PIM
82-83—Strathroy Jr. B	OHA	40	39	38	77	99	...	...	...	—	—	—	—	—
83-84—Cornwall	OHL	70	24	45	69	94	...	...	...	3	1	2	3	4
84-85—Cornwall	OHL	56	41	44	85	68	...	...	...	9	2	4	6	23
85-86—Cornwall	OHL	56	39	65	104	74	...	...	...	6	2	3	5	2
86-87—Canadian nat'l team	Int'l	21	2	4	6	4	...			—	—	—	—	—
—Chicago	NHL	39	3	6	9	6	-9	0	0	4	0	0	0	2
87-88—Saginaw	IHL	31	11	19	30	52	...			10	5	6	11	10
—Chicago	NHL	53	2	9	11	59	-10	0	0	—	—	—	—	—
88-89—Chicago	NHL	7	0	1	1	7	-1	0	0	—	—	—	—	—
—Saginaw	IHL	69	21	47	68	162	...			6	1	3	4	4
89-90—Arvika	Sweden	30	15	18	33	...				—	—	—	—	—
—Indianapolis	IHL	16	5	10	15	6	...			13	9	10	19	38
90-91—Chicago	NHL	7	0	1	1	2	0	0	0	—	—	—	—	—
—Indianapolis	IHL	75	29	52	81	76	...			7	1	4	5	0
91-92—Indianapolis	IHL	59	18	40	58	65	...			—	—	—	—	—
—Chicago	NHL	19	4	4	8	8	0	1	0	—	—	—	—	—
92-93—Pittsburgh	NHL	78	4	9	13	10	-8	0	1	4	0	0	0	0
93-94—Pittsburgh	NHL	58	7	4	11	18	-4	3	0	—	—	—	—	—
—Edmonton	NHL	23	5	9	14	28	-1	1	0	—	—	—	—	—
94-95—Edmonton	NHL	46	6	11	17	21	-12	3	0	—	—	—	—	—
95-96—Winnipeg	NHL	58	10	14	24	37	-4	3	1	6	0	0	0	21
96-97—Phoenix	NHL	55	4	11	15	36	-4	2	0	7	0	0	0	14
97-98—Phoenix	NHL	64	5	5	10	36	-4	1	1	6	0	0	0	2
98-99—Phoenix	NHL	76	9	9	18	34	-6	0	2	7	1	0	1	0
99-00—Atlanta	NHL	62	10	12	22	30	-29	4	0	—	—	—	—	—
NHL Totals (13 years)		645	69	105	174	332	-92	18	5	34	1	0	1	39

STEFAN, PATRIK · C · THRASHERS

PERSONAL: Born September 16, 1980, in Pribram, Czechoslovakia. ... 6-3/200. ... Shoots left.
TRANSACTIONS/CAREER NOTES: Selected by Atlanta Thrashers in first round (first Thrashers pick, first overall) of NHL entry draft (June 26, 1999). ... Suffered concussion (November 19, 1999); missed two games. ... Suffered back spasms (February 29, 2000); missed three games. ... Suffered from the flu (March 22, 2000); missed two games.

Season Team	League	REGULAR SEASON								PLAYOFFS				
		Gms.	G	A	Pts.	PIM	+/-	PP	SH	Gms.	G	A	Pts.	PIM
96-97—Sparta Praha	Czech Rep.	5	0	1	1	2	...	...	...	7	1	0	1	0
97-98—Sparta Praha	Czech Rep.	27	2	6	8	16	...			—	—	—	—	—
—Long Beach	IHL	25	5	15	20	10	...			10	1	1	2	2
98-99—Long Beach	IHL	33	11	24	35	26	...			—	—	—	—	—
99-00—Atlanta	NHL	72	5	20	25	30	-20	1	0	—	—	—	—	—
NHL Totals (1 year)		72	5	20	25	30	-20	1	0					

STEPHENS, CHARLIE · C/RW · CAPITALS

PERSONAL: Born April 5, 1981, in Nilestown, Ont. ... 6-4/225. ... Shoots right.
TRANSACTIONS/CAREER NOTES: Selected by Washington Capitals in second round (third Capitals pick, 31st overall) of NHL entry draft (June 26, 1999).

Season Team	League	REGULAR SEASON								PLAYOFFS				
		Gms.	G	A	Pts.	PIM	+/-	PP	SH	Gms.	G	A	Pts.	PIM
97-98—Toronto St. Michael's	OHL	58	9	21	30	38	...	...	...	—	—	—	—	—
98-99—Toronto St. Michael's	OHL	7	2	4	6	8	...	...	...	—	—	—	—	—
—Guelph	OHL	61	24	28	52	72	...	...	...	11	3	5	8	19
99-00—Guelph	OHL	56	16	34	50	87	...	...	...	6	1	3	4	15

STERN, RONNIE · RW · SHARKS

PERSONAL: Born January 11, 1967, in Ste. Agatha Des Mont, Que. ... 6-0/205. ... Shoots right. ... Full Name: Ronald Stern.
TRANSACTIONS/CAREER NOTES: Selected by Vancouver Canucks as underage junior in fourth round (third Canucks pick, 70th overall) of NHL entry draft (June 21, 1986). ... Bruised shoulder (April 1989). ... Suffered laceration near eye and dislocated shoulder (March 19, 1990). ... Fractured wrist (October 30, 1990); missed 10 weeks. ... Traded by Canucks with D Kevan Guy and option to switch fourth-round picks in 1992 draft to Calgary Flames for D Dana Murzyn; Flames did not exercise option (March 5, 1991). ... Suffered back spasms (October 15, 1992); missed 11 games. ... Fractured bone in right foot (October 11, 1993); missed three games. ... Bruised shoulder (December 7, 1993); missed one game. ... Bruised shoulder (December 28, 1993); missed six games. ... Sprained left ankle (February 6, 1995); missed four games. ... Strained thigh (April 25, 1995); missed three games. ... Suspended two games by NHL for accumulating four game misconduct penalties (March 22, 1995). ... Suspended four games and fined $1,000 by NHL for slashing (December 19, 1995). ... Suffered back spasms (December 27, 1995); missed five games. ... Injured neck and shoulder (January 14, 1996); missed 21 games. ... Injured lower back (October 19, 1996); missed three games. ... Injured knee (September 14, 1997) and underwent surgery (October 7, 1997); missed entire season. ... Signed as free agent by San Jose Sharks (August 25, 1998). ... Injured back (November 16, 1999); missed five games.
STATISTICAL PLATEAUS: Three-goal games: 1991-92 (1), 1992-93 (1), 1994-95 (1). Total: 3.

Season Team	League	REGULAR SEASON								PLAYOFFS				
		Gms.	G	A	Pts.	PIM	+/-	PP	SH	Gms.	G	A	Pts.	PIM
84-85—Longueuil	QMJHL	67	6	14	20	176	...	...	...	—	—	—	—	—
85-86—Longueuil	QMJHL	70	39	33	72	317	...	...	...	—	—	—	—	—
86-87—Longueuil	QMJHL	56	32	39	71	266	...	...	...	19	11	9	20	55

		REGULAR SEASON								PLAYOFFS				
Season Team	League	Gms.	G	A	Pts.	PIM	+/-	PP	SH	Gms.	G	A	Pts.	PIM
87-88—Fredericton	AHL	2	1	0	1	4	...	...	...	—	—	—	—	—
—Flint	IHL	55	14	19	33	294	...	...	...	16	8	8	16	94
—Vancouver	NHL	15	0	0	0	52	-7	0	0	—	—	—	—	—
88-89—Milwaukee	IHL	45	19	23	42	280	...	...	...	5	1	0	1	11
—Vancouver	NHL	17	1	0	1	49	-6	0	0	3	0	1	1	17
89-90—Milwaukee	IHL	26	8	9	17	165	...	...	...	—	—	—	—	—
—Vancouver	NHL	34	2	3	5	208	-17	0	0	—	—	—	—	—
90-91—Milwaukee	IHL	7	2	2	4	81	...	...	...	—	—	—	—	—
—Vancouver	NHL	31	2	3	5	171	-14	0	0	—	—	—	—	—
—Calgary	NHL	13	1	3	4	69	0	0	0	7	1	3	4	14
91-92—Calgary	NHL	72	13	9	22	338	0	0	1	—	—	—	—	—
92-93—Calgary	NHL	70	10	15	25	207	4	0	0	6	0	0	0	43
93-94—Calgary	NHL	71	9	20	29	243	6	0	1	7	2	0	2	12
94-95—Calgary	NHL	39	9	4	13	163	4	1	0	7	3	1	4	8
95-96—Calgary	NHL	52	10	5	15	111	2	0	0	4	0	2	2	8
96-97—Calgary	NHL	79	7	10	17	157	-4	0	1	—	—	—	—	—
97-98—Calgary	NHL						Did not play.							
98-99—San Jose	NHL	78	7	9	16	158	-3	1	0	6	0	0	0	6
99-00—San Jose	NHL	67	4	5	9	151	-9	0	0	3	1	0	1	11
NHL Totals (13 years).........		638	75	86	161	2077	-44	2	3	43	7	7	14	119

STEVENS, KEVIN — LW — FLYERS

S

PERSONAL: Born April 15, 1965, in Brockton, Mass. ... 6-3/230. ... Shoots left. ... Full Name: Kevin Michael Stevens.

HIGH SCHOOL: Silver Lake (Mass.).

COLLEGE: Boston College.

TRANSACTIONS/CAREER NOTES: Selected by Los Angeles Kings in sixth round (sixth Kings pick, 108th overall) of NHL entry draft (June 8, 1983). ... Traded by Kings to Pittsburgh Penguins for LW Anders Hakansson (September 9, 1983). ... Injured left knee (November 5, 1992) and underwent surgery; missed nine games. ... Suspended one game by NHL (March 1993). ... Suffered from bronchitis (April 3, 1993); missed two games. ... Fractured left ankle (February 4, 1995); missed 21 games. ... Traded by Penguins with C Shawn McEachern to Boston Bruins for C Bryan Smolinski and RW Glen Murray (August 2, 1995). ... Traded by Bruins to Los Angeles Kings for RW Rick Tocchet (January 25, 1996). ... Fractured left fibula (February 29, 1996); missed 10 games. ... Suffered concussion (October 15, 1996); missed one game. ... Suffered back spasms (November 27, 1996); missed one game. ... Bruised ankle (February 20, 1997); missed seven games. ... Injured knee (April 9, 1997); missed two games. ... Traded by Kings to New York Rangers for LW Luc Robitaille (August 28, 1997). ... Strained groin (October 8, 1997); missed one game. ... Suffered from the flu (March 21, 1998); missed one game. ... Suffered from the flu (November 6, 1999); missed two games. ... Signed as free agent by Philadelphia Flyers (July 7, 2000).

HONORS: Named to NCAA All-America (East) second team (1986-87). ... Named to Hockey East All-Star first team (1986-87). ... Named to The Sporting News All-Star second team (1990-91 and 1992-93). ... Named to NHL All-Star second team (1990-91 and 1992-93). ... Named to The Sporting News All-Star first team (1991-92). ... Named to NHL All-Star first team (1991-92). ... Played in NHL All-Star Game (1991-1993).

MISCELLANEOUS: Member of Stanley Cup championship team (1991 and 1992). ... Failed to score on a penalty shot (vs. Nikolai Khabibulin, February 26, 1996; vs. Sean Burke, March 22, 1998).

STATISTICAL PLATEAUS: Three-goal games: 1989-90 (1), 1990-91 (1), 1991-92 (3), 1992-93 (2), 1993-94 (1), 1998-99 (1). Total: 9. ... Four-goal games: 1991-92 (1), 1992-93 (1). Total: 2. ... Total hat tricks: 11.

		REGULAR SEASON								PLAYOFFS				
Season Team	League	Gms.	G	A	Pts.	PIM	+/-	PP	SH	Gms.	G	A	Pts.	PIM
82-83—Silver Lake H.S.	Minn. H.S.	18	24	27	51	...	...	...	...	—	—	—	—	—
83-84—Boston College	ECAC	37	6	14	20	36	...	...	...	—	—	—	—	—
84-85—Boston College	Hockey East	40	13	23	36	36	...	...	...	—	—	—	—	—
85-86—Boston College	Hockey East	42	17	27	44	56	...	...	...	—	—	—	—	—
86-87—Boston College	Hockey East	39	*35	35	70	54	...	...	...	—	—	—	—	—
87-88—U.S. national team	Int'l	44	22	23	45	52	...	...	...	—	—	—	—	—
—U.S. Olympic team......	Int'l	5	1	3	4	2	...	...	...	—	—	—	—	—
—Pittsburgh..................	NHL	16	5	2	7	8	-6	2	0	—	—	—	—	—
88-89—Pittsburgh..................	NHL	24	12	3	15	19	-8	4	0	11	3	7	10	16
—Muskegon..................	IHL	45	24	41	65	113	...	...	...	—	—	—	—	—
89-90—Pittsburgh..................	NHL	76	29	41	70	171	-13	12	0	—	—	—	—	—
90-91—Pittsburgh..................	NHL	80	40	46	86	133	-1	18	0	24	*17	16	33	53
91-92—Pittsburgh..................	NHL	80	54	69	123	254	8	19	0	21	13	15	28	28
92-93—Pittsburgh..................	NHL	72	55	56	111	177	17	26	0	12	5	11	16	22
93-94—Pittsburgh..................	NHL	83	41	47	88	155	-24	21	0	6	1	1	2	10
94-95—Pittsburgh..................	NHL	27	15	12	27	51	0	6	0	12	4	7	11	21
95-96—Boston..................	NHL	41	10	13	23	49	1	3	0	—	—	—	—	—
—Los Angeles..................	NHL	20	3	10	13	22	-11	3	0	—	—	—	—	—
96-97—Los Angeles..................	NHL	69	14	20	34	96	-27	4	0	—	—	—	—	—
97-98—New York Rangers	NHL	80	14	27	41	130	-7	5	0	—	—	—	—	—
98-99—New York Rangers	NHL	81	23	20	43	64	-10	8	0	—	—	—	—	—
99-00—New York Rangers	NHL	38	3	5	8	43	-7	1	0	—	—	—	—	—
NHL Totals (13 years).........		787	318	371	689	1372	-88	132	0	86	43	57	100	150

STEVENS, SCOTT — D — DEVILS

PERSONAL: Born April 1, 1964, in Kitchener, Ont. ... 6-1/215. ... Shoots left. ... Brother of Mike Stevens, center/left winger with four NHL teams (1984-85 and 1987-88 through 1989-90).

TRANSACTIONS/CAREER NOTES: Selected by Washington Capitals as underage junior in first round (first Capitals pick, fifth overall) of NHL entry draft (June 9, 1982). ... Bruised right knee (November 6, 1985); missed seven games. ... Fractured right index finger (December 14, 1986). ... Bruised shoulder (April 1988). ... Suffered from poison oak (November 1988). ... Fractured left foot (December 29, 1989); missed 17 games. ... Suspended three games by NHL for scratching (February 27, 1990). ... Bruised left shoulder (March 27, 1990). ... Dislocated left shoulder (May 3, 1990). ... Signed as free agent by St. Louis Blues (July 9, 1990); Blues owed Capitals two first-round draft picks among the top seven over next two years and $100,000 cash; upon failing to get a pick in the top seven in 1991, Blues forfeited their first-round pick in 1991 (LW Trevor Halverson), 1992 (D Sergei Gonchar), 1993 (D Brendan Witt) (traded to Toronto Maple Leafs) and 1995 (LW Miikka Elomo) drafts to Capitals (July 9, 1990). ... Awarded to New Jersey Devils as compensation for Blues signing free agent RW/LW Brendan Shanahan (September 3, 1991). ... Strained right knee (February 20, 1992); missed 12 games. ... Suffered concussion (December 27, 1992); missed three games. ... Strained knee (November 19, 1993); missed one game. ... Suspended one game by NHL for highsticking incident (October 7, 1996). ... Suffered from the flu (December 23, 1996); missed one game. ... Suffered hip pointer (February 28, 1998); missed one game. ... Suffered from the flu (December 8, 1998); missed one game. ... Suffered back spasms (December 19, 1998); missed one game. ... Strained groin (March 15, 1999); missed five games. ... Suffered from the flu (January 8, 2000); missed two games. ... Suffered from the flu (March 24, 2000); missed one game.

HONORS: Named to NHL All-Rookie team (1982-83). ... Named to THE SPORTING NEWS All-Star second team (1987-88). ... Named to NHL All-Star first team (1987-88 and 1993-94). ... Named to NHL All-Star second team (1991-92 and 1996-97). ... Played in NHL All-Star Game (1985, 1989, 1991-1994 and 1996-2000). ... Named to THE SPORTING NEWS All-Star first team (1993-94).

MISCELLANEOUS: Member of Stanley Cup championship team (1995 and 2000). ... Captain of St. Louis Blues (1990-91). ... Captain of New Jersey Devils (1992-93 and 1995-96 through 1999-2000).

		REGULAR SEASON								PLAYOFFS				
Season Team	League	Gms.	G	A	Pts.	PIM	+/-	PP	SH	Gms.	G	A	Pts.	PIM
80-81—Kitchener Jr. B	OHA	39	7	33	40	82	...	...	...	—	—	—	—	—
—Kitchener	OHL	1	0	0	0	0	...	...	...	—	—	—	—	—
81-82—Kitchener	OHL	68	6	36	42	158	...	...	...	15	1	10	11	71
82-83—Washington	NHL	77	9	16	25	195	15	0	0	4	1	0	1	26
83-84—Washington	NHL	78	13	32	45	201	26	7	0	8	1	8	9	21
84-85—Washington	NHL	80	21	44	65	221	19	16	0	5	0	1	1	20
85-86—Washington	NHL	73	15	38	53	165	0	3	0	9	3	8	11	12
86-87—Washington	NHL	77	10	51	61	283	13	2	0	7	0	5	5	19
87-88—Washington	NHL	80	12	60	72	184	14	5	1	13	1	11	12	46
88-89—Washington	NHL	80	7	61	68	225	1	6	0	6	1	4	5	11
89-90—Washington	NHL	56	11	29	40	154	1	7	0	15	2	7	9	25
90-91—St. Louis	NHL	78	5	44	49	150	23	1	0	13	0	3	3	36
91-92—New Jersey	NHL	68	17	42	59	124	24	7	1	7	2	1	3	29
92-93—New Jersey	NHL	81	12	45	57	120	14	8	0	5	2	2	4	10
93-94—New Jersey	NHL	83	18	60	78	112	*53	5	1	20	2	9	11	42
94-95—New Jersey	NHL	48	2	20	22	56	4	1	0	20	1	7	8	24
95-96—New Jersey	NHL	82	5	23	28	100	7	2	1	—	—	—	—	—
96-97—New Jersey	NHL	79	5	19	24	70	26	0	0	10	0	4	4	2
97-98—New Jersey	NHL	80	4	22	26	80	19	1	0	6	1	0	1	8
—Can. Olympic team	Int'l	6	0	0	0	2	...	...	...	—	—	—	—	—
98-99—New Jersey	NHL	75	5	22	27	64	29	0	0	7	2	1	3	10
99-00—New Jersey	NHL	78	8	21	29	103	30	0	1	23	3	8	11	6
NHL Totals (18 years)		1353	179	649	828	2607	318	71	5	178	22	79	101	347

STEVENSON, JEREMY — LW

PERSONAL: Born July 28, 1974, in San Bernardino, Calif. ... 6-2/217. ... Shoots left. ... Full Name: Jeremy Joseph Stevenson.
HIGH SCHOOL: St. Lawrence (Cornwall, Ont.).
TRANSACTIONS/CAREER NOTES: Selected by Winnipeg Jets in third round (third Jets pick, 60th overall) of NHL entry draft (June 20, 1992). ... Returned to draft pool by Jets and selected by Mighty Ducks of Anaheim in 11th round (10th Mighty Ducks pick, 262nd overall) of NHL entry draft (June 28, 1994). ... Fractured ankle (October 24, 1996); missed 33 games. ... Suffered concussion prior to 1997-98 season; missed first four games of season. ... Suspended one game by AHL for receiving match penalty (April 6, 1999).

		REGULAR SEASON								PLAYOFFS				
Season Team	League	Gms.	G	A	Pts.	PIM	+/-	PP	SH	Gms.	G	A	Pts.	PIM
90-91—Cornwall	OHL	58	13	20	33	124	...	...	...	—	—	—	—	—
91-92—Cornwall	OHL	63	15	23	38	176	...	...	...	6	3	1	4	4
92-93—Newmarket	OHL	54	28	28	56	144	...	...	...	5	5	1	6	28
93-94—Newmarket	OHL	9	2	4	6	27	...	...	...	—	—	—	—	—
—Sault Ste. Marie	OHL	48	18	19	37	183	...	...	...	14	1	1	2	23
94-95—Greensboro	ECHL	43	14	13	27	231	...	...	...	17	6	11	17	64
95-96—Baltimore	AHL	60	11	10	21	295	...	...	...	12	4	2	6	23
—Anaheim	NHL	3	0	1	1	12	1	0	0	—	—	—	—	—
96-97—Baltimore	AHL	25	8	8	16	125	...	...	...	3	0	0	0	8
—Anaheim	NHL	5	0	0	0	14	-1	0	0	—	—	—	—	—
97-98—Anaheim	NHL	45	3	5	8	101	-4	0	0	—	—	—	—	—
—Cincinnati	AHL	10	5	0	5	34	...	...	...	—	—	—	—	—
98-99—Cincinnati	AHL	22	4	4	8	83	...	...	...	3	1	0	1	2
99-00—Cincinnati	AHL	41	11	14	25	100	...	...	...	—	—	—	—	—
—Anaheim	NHL	3	0	0	0	7	-1	0	0	—	—	—	—	—
NHL Totals (4 years)		56	3	6	9	134	-5	0	0					

STEVENSON, TURNER — RW — DEVILS

PERSONAL: Born May 18, 1972, in Port Alberni, B.C. ... 6-3/226. ... Shoots right.
TRANSACTIONS/CAREER NOTES: Selected by Montreal Canadiens in first round (first Canadiens pick, 12th overall) of NHL entry draft (June 16, 1990). ... Suffered from the flu (October 21, 1995); missed two games. ... Sprained knee (October 7, 1996); missed five games. ... Sprained knee (October 26, 1996); missed four games. ... Sprained knee (November 11, 1996); missed seven games. ... Sprained left shoulder (November 12, 1997); missed eight games. ... Tore cartilage in ribs (December 19, 1997); missed five games. ... Strained hamstring (April 15, 1998); missed three games. ... Suspended two games and fined $1,000 by NHL for elbowing incident (October 19, 1998). ... Suffered back spasms (December 29, 1998); missed one game. ... Sprained ankle (December 31, 1998); missed 10 games. ... Suffered back spasms (October 9, 1999); missed two games. ... Strained back (November 16, 1999); missed 13 games. ... Suffered from the flu (January 11, 2000); missed three games. ... Selected by Columbus Blue Jackets in NHL expansion draft (June 23, 2000). ... Traded by Blue Jackets to New Jersey Devils (June 23, 2000), completing deal in which Devils traded RW Krzysztof Oliwa to Blue Jackets for third-round pick in 2001 draft and future considerations (June 12, 2000).

Season Team	League	REGULAR SEASON								PLAYOFFS				
		Gms.	G	A	Pts.	PIM	+/-	PP	SH	Gms.	G	A	Pts.	PIM
88-89—Seattle	WHL	69	15	12	27	84	...	...	...	—	—	—	—	—
89-90—Seattle	WHL	62	29	32	61	276	...	...	...	13	3	2	5	35
90-91—Seattle	WHL	57	36	27	63	222	...	...	...	6	1	5	6	15
—Fredericton	AHL	—	—	—	—	—	...	...	...	4	0	0	0	5
91-92—Seattle	WHL	58	20	32	52	264	...	...	...	15	9	3	12	55
92-93—Fredericton	AHL	79	25	34	59	102	...	...	...	5	2	3	5	11
—Montreal	NHL	1	0	0	0	0	-1	0	0	—	—	—	—	—
93-94—Fredericton	AHL	66	19	28	47	155	...	...	...	—	—	—	—	—
—Montreal	NHL	2	0	0	0	2	-2	0	0	3	0	2	2	0
94-95—Fredericton	AHL	37	12	12	24	109	...	...	...	—	—	—	—	—
—Montreal	NHL	41	6	1	7	86	0	0	0	—	—	—	—	—
95-96—Montreal	NHL	80	9	16	25	167	-2	0	0	6	0	1	1	2
96-97—Montreal	NHL	65	8	13	21	97	-14	1	0	5	1	1	2	2
97-98—Montreal	NHL	63	4	6	10	110	-8	1	0	10	3	4	7	12
98-99—Montreal	NHL	69	10	17	27	88	6	0	0	—	—	—	—	—
99-00—Montreal	NHL	64	8	13	21	61	-1	0	0	—	—	—	—	—
NHL Totals (8 years)		385	45	66	111	611	-22	2	0	24	4	8	12	16

STEWART, CAM — LW — WILD

S

PERSONAL: Born September 18, 1971, in Kitchener, Ont. ... 5-11/196. ... Shoots left. ... Full Name: Cameron G. Stewart.
COLLEGE: Michigan.
TRANSACTIONS/CAREER NOTES: Selected by Boston Bruins in third round (second Bruins pick, 63rd overall) of NHL entry draft (June 16, 1990). ... Fractured finger (November 13, 1993); missed seven games. ... Injured neck (January 11, 1997); missed two games. ... Suffered back spasms (January 20, 1997); missed six games. ... Signed as free agent by Florida Panthers (July 19, 1999). ... Suffered concussion (October 30, 1999); missed nine games. ... Bruised thigh (November 27, 1999); missed one game. ... Strained hip flexor (April 1, 2000); missed three games. ... Selected by Minnesota Wild in NHL expansion draft (June 23, 2000).

Season Team	League	REGULAR SEASON								PLAYOFFS				
		Gms.	G	A	Pts.	PIM	+/-	PP	SH	Gms.	G	A	Pts.	PIM
88-89—Elmira Jr. B	OHA	43	38	50	88	138	...	...	...	—	—	—	—	—
89-90—Elmira Jr. B	OHA	46	44	95	139	172	...	...	...	—	—	—	—	—
90-91—Univ. of Michigan	CCHA	44	8	24	32	122	...	...	...	—	—	—	—	—
91-92—Univ. of Michigan	CCHA	44	13	15	28	106	...	...	...	—	—	—	—	—
92-93—Univ. of Michigan	CCHA	39	20	39	59	69	...	...	...	—	—	—	—	—
93-94—Boston	NHL	57	3	6	9	66	-6	0	0	8	0	3	3	7
—Providence	AHL	14	3	2	5	5	...	...	...	—	—	—	—	—
94-95—Boston	NHL	5	0	0	0	2	0	0	0	—	—	—	—	—
—Providence	AHL	31	13	11	24	38	...	...	...	9	2	5	7	0
95-96—Providence	AHL	54	17	25	42	39	...	...	...	—	—	—	—	—
—Boston	NHL	6	0	0	0	0	-2	0	0	5	1	0	1	2
96-97—Boston	NHL	15	0	1	1	4	-2	0	0	—	—	—	—	—
—Providence	AHL	18	4	3	7	37	...	...	...	—	—	—	—	—
—Cincinnati	IHL	7	3	2	5	8	...	...	...	1	0	0	0	0
97-98—Houston	IHL	63	18	27	45	51	...	...	...	4	0	1	1	18
98-99—Houston	IHL	61	36	26	62	75	...	...	...	19	10	5	15	26
99-00—Florida	NHL	65	9	7	16	30	-2	0	0	—	—	—	—	—
NHL Totals (5 years)		148	12	14	26	102	-12	0	0	13	1	3	4	9

STILLMAN, CORY — LW — FLAMES

PERSONAL: Born December 20, 1973, in Peterborough, Ont. ... 6-0/194. ... Shoots left.
HIGH SCHOOL: Herman E. Fawcett (Brantford, Ont.).
TRANSACTIONS/CAREER NOTES: Selected by Calgary Flames in first round (first Flames pick, sixth overall) of NHL entry draft (June 20, 1992). ... Suspended four games by AHL for incident involving on-ice official (March 29, 1995). ... Suffered from the flu (October 8, 1995); missed one game. ... Bruised knee (January 14, 1996); missed two games. ... Injured shoulder (December 16, 1996); missed five games. ... Bruised ribs (October 11, 1997); missed six games. ... Strained knee (December 27, 1998); missed five games. ... Injured shoulder (December 27, 1999); missed final 45 games of season.
HONORS: Won Emms Family Award (1990-91).
STATISTICAL PLATEAUS: Three-goal games: 1997-98 (1).

Season Team	League	REGULAR SEASON								PLAYOFFS				
		Gms.	G	A	Pts.	PIM	+/-	PP	SH	Gms.	G	A	Pts.	PIM
89-90—Peterborough Jr. B	OHA	41	30	54	84	76	...	...	...	—	—	—	—	—
90-91—Windsor	OHL	64	31	70	101	31	...	...	...	11	3	6	9	8
91-92—Windsor	OHL	53	29	61	90	59	...	...	...	7	2	4	6	8
92-93—Peterborough	OHL	61	25	55	80	55	...	...	...	18	3	8	11	18
—Canadian nat'l team	Int'l	1	0	0	0	0	...	...	...	—	—	—	—	—
93-94—Saint John	AHL	79	35	48	83	52	...	...	...	7	2	4	6	16
94-95—Saint John	AHL	63	28	53	81	70	...	...	...	5	0	2	2	2
—Calgary	NHL	10	0	2	2	2	1	0	0	—	—	—	—	—
95-96—Calgary	NHL	74	16	19	35	41	-5	4	1	2	1	1	2	0
96-97—Calgary	NHL	58	6	20	26	14	-6	2	0	—	—	—	—	—
97-98—Calgary	NHL	72	27	22	49	40	-9	9	4	—	—	—	—	—
98-99—Calgary	NHL	76	27	30	57	38	7	9	3	—	—	—	—	—
99-00—Calgary	NHL	37	12	9	21	12	-9	6	0	—	—	—	—	—
NHL Totals (6 years)		327	88	102	190	147	-21	30	8	2	1	1	2	0

STOCK, P.J.　　　　　　　　　C　　　　　　　　CANADIENS

PERSONAL: Born May 26, 1975, in Victoriaville, Que. ... 5-10/190. ... Shoots left.
TRANSACTIONS/CAREER NOTES: Signed as non-drafted free agent by New York Rangers (September 2, 1997). ... Suspended three games by AHL for leaving bench and starting altercation (December 31, 1998). ... Signed as free agent by Montreal Canadiens (July 7, 2000).

		REGULAR SEASON								PLAYOFFS				
Season Team	League	Gms.	G	A	Pts.	PIM	+/-	PP	SH	Gms.	G	A	Pts.	PIM
94-95—Victoriaville	QMJHL	70	9	46	55	386	...	...	...	4	0	0	0	60
95-96—Victoriaville	QMJHL	67	19	43	62	432	...	...	...	12	5	4	9	79
96-97—St. Francis Xavier	CIAU	27	11	20	31	110	...	...	...	3	0	4	4	14
97-98—Hartford	AHL	41	8	8	16	202	...	...	...	11	1	3	4	79
—New York Rangers	NHL	38	2	3	5	114	4	0	0	—	—	—	—	—
98-99—New York Rangers	NHL	5	0	0	0	6	-1	0	0	—	—	—	—	—
—Hartford	AHL	55	4	14	18	250	...	...	...	6	0	1	1	35
99-00—Hartford	AHL	64	13	23	36	290	...	...	...	23	1	11	12	69
—New York Rangers	NHL	11	0	1	1	11	1	0	0	—	—	—	—	—
NHL Totals (3 years)		54	2	4	6	131	4	0	0					

STORR, JAMIE　　　　　　　　　G　　　　　　　　KINGS

PERSONAL: Born December 28, 1975, in Brampton, Ont. ... 6-2/198. ... Catches left. ... Name pronounced STOHR.
HIGH SCHOOL: West Hill (Owen Sound, Ont.).
TRANSACTIONS/CAREER NOTES: Selected by Los Angeles Kings in first round (first Kings pick, seventh overall) of NHL entry draft (June 28, 1994). ... Strained right groin (October 1, 1997); missed 12 games. ... Strained left groin (October 18, 1998); missed 16 games. ... Sprained ankle (April 2, 1999); missed final eight games of season. ... Strained right groin (November 23, 1999); missed one game. ... Suffered concussion (December 16, 1999); missed 10 games.
HONORS: Named to OHL All-Star first team (1993-94). ... Named to NHL All-Rookie team (1997-98).
MISCELLANEOUS: Holds Los Angeles Kings record for goals-against average (2.51). ... Stopped a penalty shot attempt (vs. Todd White, February 26, 1999; vs. Martin Rucinsky, December 11, 1999).

		REGULAR SEASON								PLAYOFFS						
Season Team	League	Gms.	Min	W	L	T	GA	SO	Avg.	Gms.	Min.	W	L	GA	SO	Avg.
90-91—Brampton	Jr. B	24	1145	...	...	...	91	0	4.77	—						
91-92—Owen Sound	OHL	34	1733	11	16	1	128	0	4.43	5	299	1	4	28	0	5.62
92-93—Owen Sound	OHL	41	2362	20	17	3	180	0	4.57	8	454	4	4	35	0	4.63
93-94—Owen Sound	OHL	35	2004	21	11	1	120	1	3.59	9	547	4	5	44	0	4.83
94-95—Owen Sound	OHL	17	977	5	9	2	64	0	3.93	—						
—Los Angeles	NHL	5	263	1	3	1	17	0	3.88	—						
—Windsor	OHL	4	241	3	1	0	8	1	1.99	10	520	6	3	34	1	3.92
95-96—Los Angeles	NHL	5	262	3	1	0	12	0	2.75	—						
—Phoenix	IHL	48	2711	22	20	‡4	139	2	3.08	2	118	1	1	4	1	2.03
96-97—Phoenix	IHL	44	2441	16	22	‡4	147	0	3.61	—						
—Los Angeles	NHL	5	265	2	1	1	11	0	2.49	—						
97-98—Los Angeles	NHL	17	920	9	5	1	34	2	2.22	3	145	0	2	9	0	3.72
—Long Beach	IHL	11	629	7	2	‡1	31	0	2.96	—						
98-99—Los Angeles	NHL	28	1525	12	12	2	61	4	2.40	—						
99-00—Los Angeles	NHL	42	2206	18	15	5	93	1	2.53	1	36	0	1	2	0	3.33
NHL Totals (6 years)		102	5441	45	37	10	228	7	2.51	4	181	0	3	11	0	3.65

STRAKA, MARTIN　　　　　　　　　C　　　　　　　　PENGUINS

PERSONAL: Born September 3, 1972, in Plzen, Czechoslovakia. ... 5-9/176. ... Shoots left. ... Name pronounced STRAH-kuh.
TRANSACTIONS/CAREER NOTES: Selected by Pittsburgh Penguins in first round (first Penguins pick, 19th overall) of NHL entry draft (June 20, 1992). ... Played in Europe during 1994-95 NHL lockout. ... Suffered from the flu (February 14, 1995); missed four games. ... Traded by Penguins to Ottawa Senators for D Norm Maciver and C Troy Murray (April 7, 1995). ... Strained knee (April 19, 1995); missed remainder of season. ... Injured hamstring (November 11, 1995); missed one game. ... Traded by Senators with D Bryan Berard to New York Islanders for D Wade Redden and G Damian Rhodes (January 23, 1996). ... Claimed on waivers by Florida Panthers (March 15, 1996). ... Bruised buttocks (April 10, 1996); missed final two games of season. ... Strained groin (January 1, 1997); missed one game. ... Strained groin (January 8, 1997); missed two games. ... Strained groin (January 22, 1997); missed four games. ... Strained groin (March 5, 1997); missed nine games. ... Signed as free agent by Penguins (August 7, 1997). ... Fractured foot (December 29, 1997); missed seven games. ... Bruised shoulder (March 3, 1999); missed one game. ... Bruised shoulder (April 8, 1999); missed one game. ... Bruised knee (October 16, 1999); missed one games. ... Reinjured knee (October 27, 1999); missed two games. ... Bruised ribs (December 15, 1999); missed seven games. ... Bruised shin (April 5, 2000); missed one game.
HONORS: Named to Czechoslovakian League All-Star team (1991-92). ... Played in NHL All-Star Game (1999).
MISCELLANEOUS: Member of gold-medal-winning Czech Republic Olympic team (1998). ... Scored on a penalty shot (vs. Roman Turek, January 19, 2000). ... Failed to score on a penalty shot (vs. Jocelyn Thibault, March 16, 1995; vs. Damian Rhodes, April 3, 1996).
STATISTICAL PLATEAUS: Three-goal games: 1993-94 (1), 1997-98 (1), 1998-99 (1). Total: 3.

		REGULAR SEASON								PLAYOFFS				
Season Team	League	Gms.	G	A	Pts.	PIM	+/-	PP	SH	Gms.	G	A	Pts.	PIM
89-90—Skoda Plzen	Czech.	1	0	3	3	...	...	...	...	—	—	—	—	—
90-91—Skoda Plzen	Czech.	47	7	24	31	6	...	...	...	—	—	—	—	—
91-92—Skoda Plzen	Czech.	50	27	28	55	20	...	...	...	—	—	—	—	—
92-93—Pittsburgh	NHL	42	3	13	16	29	2	0	0	11	2	1	3	2
—Cleveland	IHL	4	4	3	7	0	...	...	...	—	—	—	—	—
93-94—Pittsburgh	NHL	84	30	34	64	24	24	2	0	6	1	0	1	2
94-95—Interconex Plzen	Czech Rep.	19	10	11	21	18	...	...	...	—	—	—	—	—
—Pittsburgh	NHL	31	4	12	16	16	0	0	0	—	—	—	—	—
—Ottawa	NHL	6	1	1	2	0	-1	0	0	—	—	—	—	—
95-96—Ottawa	NHL	43	9	16	25	29	-14	5	0	—	—	—	—	—
—New York Islanders	NHL	22	2	10	12	6	-6	0	0	—	—	—	—	—
—Florida	NHL	12	2	4	6	6	1	1	0	13	2	2	4	2

Season Team	League	REGULAR SEASON								PLAYOFFS				
		Gms.	G	A	Pts.	PIM	+/-	PP	SH	Gms.	G	A	Pts.	PIM
96-97—Florida........................	NHL	55	7	22	29	12	9	2	0	4	0	0	0	0
97-98—Pittsburgh..................	NHL	75	19	23	42	28	-1	4	3	6	2	0	2	2
—Czech Rep. Oly. team..	Int'l	6	1	2	3	0	...	...	...	—	—	—	—	—
98-99—Pittsburgh..................	NHL	80	35	48	83	26	12	5	4	13	6	9	15	6
99-00—Pittsburgh..................	NHL	71	20	39	59	26	24	3	1	11	3	9	12	10
NHL Totals (8 years)...........		521	132	222	354	202	50	22	8	64	16	21	37	24

STRUDWICK, JASON   D   CANUCKS

PERSONAL: Born July 17, 1975, in Edmonton. ... 6-3/220. ... Shoots left. ... Name pronounced STRUHD-wihk.
COLLEGE: Cariboo University-College (Kamloops, B.C.).
TRANSACTIONS/CAREER NOTES: Selected by New York Islanders in third round (third Islanders pick, 63rd overall) of NHL entry draft (June 29, 1994). ... Traded by Islanders to Vancouver Canucks for LW Gino Odjick (March 23, 1998). ... Injured back (November 17, 1999); missed 10 games.

Season Team	League	REGULAR SEASON								PLAYOFFS				
		Gms.	G	A	Pts.	PIM	+/-	PP	SH	Gms.	G	A	Pts.	PIM
93-94—Kamloops	WHL	61	6	8	14	118	...	...	...	19	0	4	4	24
94-95—Kamloops	WHL	72	3	11	14	183	...	...	...	21	1	1	2	39
95-96—Worcester	AHL	60	2	7	9	119	...	...	...	4	0	1	1	0
—New York Islanders.....	NHL	1	0	0	0	7	0	0	0	—	—	—	—	—
96-97—Kentucky...................	AHL	80	1	9	10	198	...	...	...	4	0	0	0	0
97-98—Kentucky...................	AHL	39	3	1	4	87	...	...	...	—	—	—	—	—
—New York Islanders.....	NHL	17	0	1	1	36	1	0	0	—	—	—	—	—
—Vancouver..................	NHL	11	0	1	1	29	-3	0	0	—	—	—	—	—
—Syracuse....................	AHL	—				...	...	...	...	3	0	0	0	6
98-99—Vancouver	NHL	65	0	3	3	114	-19	0	0	—	—	—	—	—
99-00—Vancouver	NHL	63	1	3	4	64	-13	0	0	—	—	—	—	—
NHL Totals (4 years)...........		157	1	8	9	250	-34	0	0					

S

STUART, BRAD   D   SHARKS

PERSONAL: Born November 6, 1979, in Rocky Mountain House, Alta. ... 6-2/210. ... Shoots left.
TRANSACTIONS/CAREER NOTES: Selected by San Jose Sharks in first round (first Sharks pick, third overall) of NHL entry draft (June 27, 1998).
HONORS: Named to WHL (East) All-Star second team (1997-98). ... Won Bill Hunter Trophy (1998-99). ... Won Can.HL Defenseman of the Year Award (1998-99). ... Named to WHL (East) All-Star first team (1998-99). ... Named to Can.HL All-Star first team (1998-99). ... Named to NHL All-Rookie team (1999-2000).

Season Team	League	REGULAR SEASON								PLAYOFFS				
		Gms.	G	A	Pts.	PIM	+/-	PP	SH	Gms.	G	A	Pts.	PIM
96-97—Regina	WHL	57	7	36	43	58	...	...	...	5	0	4	4	14
97-98—Regina	WHL	72	20	45	65	82	...	...	...	9	3	4	7	10
98-99—Regina	WHL	29	10	19	29	43	...	...	...	—	—	—	—	—
—Calgary	WHL	30	11	22	33	26	...	...	...	21	8	15	23	59
99-00—San Jose...................	NHL	82	10	26	36	32	3	5	1	12	1	0	1	6
NHL Totals (1 year)............		82	10	26	36	32	3	5	1	12	1	0	1	6

STUMPEL, JOZEF   C   KINGS

PERSONAL: Born July 20, 1972, in Nitra, Czechoslovakia. ... 6-3/216. ... Shoots right. ... Name pronounced JOH-sehf STUHM-puhl.
TRANSACTIONS/CAREER NOTES: Selected by Boston Bruins in second round (second Bruins pick, 40th overall) of NHL entry draft (June 22, 1991). ... Injured shoulder (December 1992); missed nine games. ... Injured knee (March 17, 1994); missed nine games. ... Played in Europe during 1994-95 NHL lockout. ... Injured knee (April 1995). ... Fractured cheek bone (February 27, 1996); missed three games. ... Suffered back spasms (January 4, 1997); missed one game. ... Suffered back spasms (February 1, 1997); missed three games. ... Traded by Bruins with RW Sandy Moger and fourth-round pick (traded to New Jersey) in 1998 draft to Los Angeles Kings for LW Dimitri Khristich and G Byron Dafoe (August 29, 1997). ... Suffered from the flu (February 7, 1998); missed one game. ... Bruised kidney (March 5, 1998); missed four games. ... Strained hip flexor and strained abdominal muscle (October 18, 1998); missed 10 games. ... Sprained right ankle (November 16, 1998); missed three games. ... Sprained right knee (April 8, 1999); missed final five games of season. ... Suffered hernia (November 3, 1999); missed 18 games. ... Bruised left knee (January 3, 2000); missed seven games.
STATISTICAL PLATEAUS: Three-goal games: 1995-96 (1), 1997-98 (1). Total: 2.

Season Team	League	REGULAR SEASON								PLAYOFFS				
		Gms.	G	A	Pts.	PIM	+/-	PP	SH	Gms.	G	A	Pts.	PIM
89-90—Nitra.........................	Czech.	38	12	11	23	0	...	...	...	—	—	—	—	—
90-91—Nitra.........................	Czech.	49	23	22	45	14	...	...	...	—	—	—	—	—
91-92—Boston	NHL	4	1	0	1	0	1	0	0	—	—	—	—	—
—Koln	Germany	33	19	18	37	35	...	...	...	—	—	—	—	—
92-93—Providence................	AHL	56	31	61	92	26	...	...	...	6	4	4	8	0
—Boston	NHL	13	1	3	4	4	-3	0	0	—	—	—	—	—
93-94—Boston	NHL	59	8	15	23	14	4	0	0	13	1	7	8	4
—Providence................	AHL	17	5	12	17	4	...	...	...	—	—	—	—	—
94-95—Koln	Germany	25	16	23	39	18	...	...	...	—	—	—	—	—
—Boston	NHL	44	5	13	18	8	4	1	0	5	0	0	0	0
95-96—Boston	NHL	76	18	36	54	14	-8	5	0	5	1	2	3	0
96-97—Boston	NHL	78	21	55	76	14	-22	6	0	—	—	—	—	—
97-98—Los Angeles	NHL	77	21	58	79	53	17	4	0	4	1	2	3	2
98-99—Los Angeles	NHL	64	13	21	34	10	-18	1	0	—	—	—	—	—
99-00—Los Angeles	NHL	57	17	41	58	10	23	3	0	4	0	4	4	8
NHL Totals (9 years)...........		472	105	242	347	127	-2	20	0	31	3	15	18	14

STURM, MARCO   LW   SHARKS

PERSONAL: Born September 8, 1978, in Dingolfing, West Germany. ... 6-0/195. ... Shoots left.
TRANSACTIONS/CAREER NOTES: Selected by San Jose Sharks in first round (second Sharks pick, 21st overall) of NHL entry draft (June 22, 1996). ... Sprained wrist (April 1, 1998); missed six games. ... Injured foot (March 3, 1999); missed two games. ... Suffered concussion (December 2, 1999); missed four games.
HONORS: Played in NHL All-Star Game (1999).
STATISTICAL PLATEAUS: Three-goal games: 1998-99 (1).

			REGULAR SEASON								PLAYOFFS			
Season Team	League	Gms.	G	A	Pts.	PIM	+/-	PP	SH	Gms.	G	A	Pts.	PIM
95-96—Landshut	Germany	47	12	20	32	50	...	...	...	—	—	—	—	—
96-97—Landshut	Germany	46	16	27	43	40	...	...	...	7	1	4	5	6
97-98—San Jose	NHL	74	10	20	30	40	-2	2	0	2	0	0	0	0
—German Oly. team	Int'l	2	0	0	0	0	...	...	...	—	—	—	—	—
98-99—San Jose	NHL	78	16	22	38	52	7	3	2	6	2	2	4	4
99-00—San Jose	NHL	74	12	15	27	22	4	2	4	12	1	3	4	6
NHL Totals (3 years)		226	38	57	95	114	9	7	6	20	3	5	8	10

SUCHY, RADOSLAV   D   COYOTES

PERSONAL: Born April 7, 1976, in Poprad, Czechoslovakia. ... 6-1/191. ... Shoots left.
TRANSACTIONS/CAREER NOTES: Signed as non-drafted free agent by Phoenix Coyotes (September 25, 1997).
HONORS: Won George Parsons Trophy (1996-97). ... Named to QMJHL All-Star second team (1996-97).

			REGULAR SEASON								PLAYOFFS			
Season Team	League	Gms.	G	A	Pts.	PIM	+/-	PP	SH	Gms.	G	A	Pts.	PIM
93-94—Poprad	Slovakia						Statistics unavailable.							
94-95—Sherbrooke	QMJHL	69	12	32	44	30	...	...	...	7	0	3	3	2
95-96—Sherbrooke	QMJHL	68	15	53	68	68	...	...	...	7	0	3	3	2
96-97—Sherbrooke	QMJHL	32	6	34	40	14	...	...	...	—	—	—	—	—
—Chicoutimi	QMJHL	28	5	24	29	24	...	...	...	19	6	15	21	12
97-98—Las Vegas	IHL	26	1	4	5	10	...	...	...	—	—	—	—	—
—Springfield	AHL	41	6	15	21	16	...	...	...	4	0	1	1	2
98-99—Springfield	AHL	69	4	32	36	10	...	...	...	3	0	1	1	0
99-00—Springfield	AHL	2	0	1	1	0	...	...	...	—	—	—	—	—
—Phoenix	NHL	60	0	6	6	16	2	0	0	5	0	1	1	0
NHL Totals (1 year)		60	0	6	6	16	2	0	0	5	0	1	1	0

SULLIVAN, MIKE   C   COYOTES

PERSONAL: Born February 28, 1968, in Marshfield, Mass. ... 6-2/201. ... Shoots left. ... Full Name: Michael Barry Sullivan.
HIGH SCHOOL: Boston College High.
COLLEGE: Boston University.
TRANSACTIONS/CAREER NOTES: Selected by New York Rangers in fourth round (fourth Rangers pick, 69th overall) of NHL entry draft (June 13, 1987). ... Traded by Rangers with D Mark Tinordi, D Paul Jerrard, RW Brett Barnett and third-round pick (C Murray Garbutt) in 1989 draft to Minnesota North Stars for LW Igor Liba, C Brian Lawton and rights to LW Eric Bennett (October 11, 1988). ... Signed as free agent by San Jose Sharks (August 9, 1991). ... Sprained left knee (April 6, 1993); missed remainder of season. ... Claimed on waivers by Calgary Flames (January 6, 1994). ... Pulled groin (January 29, 1994); missed 13 games. ... Bruised knee (April 6, 1994); missed one game. ... Bruised left foot (March 17, 1995); missed two games. ... Sprained right ankle (April 13, 1995); missed final eight games of season. ... Suffered concussion (February 15, 1997); missed two games. ... Suffered back spasms (March 16, 1997); missed two games. ... Traded by Flames to Boston Bruins for seventh-round pick (RW Radek Duda) in 1998 draft (June 21, 1997). ... Injured wrist (February 4, 1998); missed two games. ... Selected by Nashville Predators in NHL expansion draft (June 26, 1998). ... Traded by Predators to Phoenix Coyotes for seventh-round pick (G Kyle Kettles) in 1999 draft (June 30, 1998). ... Fractured toe (December 17, 1998); missed three games. ... Fractured rib (January 11, 1999); missed 12 games. ... Separated shoulder (February 26, 1999); missed four games. ... Bruised ankle (January 12, 2000); missed three games.

			REGULAR SEASON								PLAYOFFS			
Season Team	League	Gms.	G	A	Pts.	PIM	+/-	PP	SH	Gms.	G	A	Pts.	PIM
85-86—Boston College H.S.	Mass. H.S.	22	26	33	59	...				—	—	—	—	—
86-87—Boston University	Hockey East	37	13	18	31	18	...			—	—	—	—	—
87-88—Boston University	Hockey East	30	18	22	40	30	...			—	—	—	—	—
88-89—Boston University	Hockey East	36	19	17	36	30	...			—	—	—	—	—
—Virginia	ECHL	2	0	0	0	0	...			—	—	—	—	—
89-90—Boston University	Hockey East	38	11	20	31	26	...			—	—	—	—	—
90-91—San Diego	IHL	74	12	23	35	27	...			—	—	—	—	—
91-92—Kansas City	IHL	10	2	8	10	8	...			—	—	—	—	—
—San Jose	NHL	64	8	11	19	15	-18	1	0	—	—	—	—	—
92-93—San Jose	NHL	81	6	8	14	30	-42	0	2	—	—	—	—	—
93-94—San Jose	NHL	26	2	2	4	4	-3	0	2	—	—	—	—	—
—Kansas City	IHL	6	3	3	6	0	...			—	—	—	—	—
—Saint John	AHL	5	2	0	2	4	...			—	—	—	—	—
—Calgary	NHL	19	2	3	5	6	2	0	0	7	1	1	2	8
94-95—Calgary	NHL	38	4	7	11	14	-2	0	0	7	3	5	8	2
95-96—Calgary	NHL	81	9	12	21	24	-6	0	1	4	0	0	0	0
96-97—Calgary	NHL	67	5	6	11	10	-11	0	3	—	—	—	—	—
—Adirondack	AHL	17	1	3	4	2	...			—	—	—	—	—
97-98—Boston	NHL	77	5	13	18	34	-1	0	0	6	0	1	1	2
98-99—Phoenix	NHL	63	2	4	6	24	-11	0	1	5	0	0	0	2
99-00—Phoenix	NHL	79	5	10	15	10	-4	0	2	5	0	1	1	0
NHL Totals (9 years)		595	48	76	124	171	-96	1	11	34	4	8	12	14

SULLIVAN, STEVE   RW   BLACKHAWKS

PERSONAL: Born July 6, 1974, in Timmins, Ont. ... 5-9/160. ... Shoots right.
TRANSACTIONS/CAREER NOTES: Selected by New Jersey Devils in ninth round (10th Devils pick, 233rd overall) of NHL entry draft (June 29, 1994). ... Traded by Devils with D Jason Smith and C Alyn McCauley to Toronto Maple Leafs for C Doug Gilmour, D Dave Ellett and third-round pick (D Andre Lakos) in 1999 draft (February 25, 1997). ... Suffered from the flu (March 7, 1998); missed three games. ... Back spasms (May 11, 1999); missed one playoff game. ... Claimed on waivers by Chicago Blackhawks (October 23, 1999). ... Suffered from the flu (February 18, 2000); missed one game.
HONORS: Named to AHL All-Star first team (1995-96).
MISCELLANEOUS: Failed to score on a penalty shot (vs. Ron Tugnutt, March 6, 1999).
STATISTICAL PLATEAUS: Four-goal games: 1998-99 (1).

		REGULAR SEASON							PLAYOFFS				
Season Team	League	Gms.	G	A	Pts.	PIM	+/-	PP	SH	Gms.	G	A	Pts.	PIM
92-93—Sault Ste. Marie	OHL	62	36	27	63	44	...	...	...	16	3	8	11	18
93-94—Sault Ste. Marie	OHL	63	51	62	113	82	...	...	...	14	9	16	25	22
94-95—Albany	AHL	75	31	50	81	124	...	...	...	14	4	7	11	10
95-96—Albany	AHL	53	33	42	75	127	...	...	...	4	3	0	3	6
—New Jersey	NHL	16	5	4	9	8	3	2	0	—	—	—	—	—
96-97—Albany	AHL	15	8	7	15	16	...	...	...	—	—	—	—	—
—New Jersey	NHL	33	8	14	22	14	9	2	0	—	—	—	—	—
—Toronto	NHL	21	5	11	16	23	5	1	0	—	—	—	—	—
97-98—Toronto	NHL	63	10	18	28	40	-8	1	0	—	—	—	—	—
98-99—Toronto	NHL	63	20	20	40	28	12	4	0	13	3	3	6	14
99-00—Toronto	NHL	7	0	1	1	4	-1	0	0	—	—	—	—	—
—Chicago	NHL	73	22	42	64	52	20	2	1	—	—	—	—	—
NHL Totals (5 years)		276	70	110	180	169	40	12	1	13	3	3	6	14

SUNDIN, MATS   C   MAPLE LEAFS

PERSONAL: Born February 13, 1971, in Bromma, Sweden. ... 6-5/220. ... Shoots right. ... Full Name: Mats Johan Sundin. ... Name pronounced suhn-DEEN.
TRANSACTIONS/CAREER NOTES: Selected by Quebec Nordiques in first round (first Nordiques pick, first overall) of NHL entry draft (June 17, 1989). ... Separated right shoulder (January 2, 1993); missed three games. ... Suspended one game by NHL for second stick-related infraction (March 2, 1993). ... Traded by Nordiques with D Garth Butcher, LW Todd Warriner and first-round pick (traded to Washington Capitals) in 1994 draft to Toronto Maple Leafs for LW Wendel Clark, D Sylvain Lefebvre, RW Landon Wilson and first-round pick (D Jeffrey Kealty) in 1994 draft (June 28, 1994). ... Played in Europe during 1994-95 NHL lockout. ... Sprained shoulder (March 25, 1995); missed one game. ... Suffered slight tear of knee cartilage (October 24, 1995); missed four games. ... Fractured ankle (October 9, 1999); missed nine games.
HONORS: Named to Swedish League All-Star team (1990-91 and 1991-92). ... Played in NHL All-Star Game (1996-2000).
MISCELLANEOUS: Captain of Toronto Maple Leafs (1997-98 through 1999-2000). ... Scored on a penalty shot (vs. Tom Draper, March 3, 1992; vs. Arturs Irbe, March 15, 1995; vs. Dominik Hasek, May 29, 1999 (playoffs)). ... Failed to score on a penalty shot (vs. Kelly Hrudey, February 2, 1993; vs. Andrei Trefilov, January 10, 1998; vs. John Vanbiesbrouck, April 22, 1999 (playoffs)).
STATISTICAL PLATEAUS: Three-goal games: 1990-91 (2), 1992-93 (1), 1996-97 (1), 1998-99 (1). Total: 5. ... Five-goal games: 1991-92 (1). ... Total hat tricks: 6.

		REGULAR SEASON							PLAYOFFS				
Season Team	League	Gms.	G	A	Pts.	PIM	+/-	PP	SH	Gms.	G	A	Pts.	PIM
88-89—Nacka	Sweden	25	10	8	18	18	...	...	...	—	—	—	—	—
89-90—Djurgarden Stockholm	Sweden	34	10	8	18	16	...	...	...	8	7	0	7	4
90-91—Quebec	NHL	80	23	36	59	58	-24	4	0	—	—	—	—	—
91-92—Quebec	NHL	80	33	43	76	103	-19	8	2	—	—	—	—	—
92-93—Quebec	NHL	80	47	67	114	96	21	13	4	6	3	1	4	6
93-94—Quebec	NHL	84	32	53	85	60	1	6	2	—	—	—	—	—
94-95—Djurgarden Stockholm	Sweden	12	7	2	9	14	...	...	...	—	—	—	—	—
—Toronto	NHL	47	23	24	47	14	-5	9	0	7	5	4	9	4
95-96—Toronto	NHL	76	33	50	83	46	8	7	6	6	3	1	4	4
96-97—Toronto	NHL	82	41	53	94	59	6	7	4	—	—	—	—	—
97-98—Toronto	NHL	82	33	41	74	49	-3	9	1	—	—	—	—	—
—Swedish Oly. team	Int'l	4	3	0	3	4	...	...	...	—	—	—	—	—
98-99—Toronto	NHL	82	31	52	83	58	22	4	0	17	8	8	16	16
99-00—Toronto	NHL	73	32	41	73	46	16	10	2	12	3	5	8	10
NHL Totals (10 years)		766	328	460	788	589	23	77	21	48	22	19	41	40

SUNDSTROM, NIKLAS   LW   SHARKS

PERSONAL: Born January 6, 1975, in Ornskoldsvik, Sweden. ... 6-0/195. ... Shoots left.
TRANSACTIONS/CAREER NOTES: Selected by New York Rangers in first round (first Rangers pick, eighth overall) of NHL entry draft (June 26, 1993). ... Fractured finger and sprained knee (December 5, 1997); missed 10 games. ... Traded by Rangers with G Dan Cloutier and first- (RW Nikita Alexeev) and third-round (traded to San Jose) picks in 2000 draft to Tampa Bay Lightning for first-round pick (RW Pavel Brendl) in 1999 draft (June 26, 1999). ... Traded by Lightning with third-round pick (traded to Chicago) in 2000 draft to San Jose Sharks for D Andrei Zyuzin, D Bill Houlder, LW Shawn Burr and C Steve Guolla (August 4, 1999).
STATISTICAL NOTES: Tied for NHL lead with three game-tying goals (1999-2000).

		REGULAR SEASON							PLAYOFFS				
Season Team	League	Gms.	G	A	Pts.	PIM	+/-	PP	SH	Gms.	G	A	Pts.	PIM
91-92—MoDo Ornskoldsvik	Sweden	9	1	3	4	0	...	...	...	—	—	—	—	—
92-93—MoDo Ornskoldsvik	Sweden	40	7	11	18	18	...	...	...	—	—	—	—	—
93-94—MoDo Ornskoldsvik	Sweden	37	7	12	19	28	...	...	...	11	4	3	7	2
94-95—MoDo Ornskoldsvik	Sweden	33	8	13	21	30	...	...	...	—	—	—	—	—
95-96—New York Rangers	NHL	82	9	12	21	14	2	1	1	11	4	3	7	4
96-97—New York Rangers	NHL	82	24	28	52	20	23	5	1	9	0	5	5	2

			REGULAR SEASON								PLAYOFFS				
Season Team	League	Gms.	G	A	Pts.	PIM	+/-	PP	SH		Gms.	G	A	Pts.	PIM
97-98—New York Rangers......	NHL	70	19	28	47	24	0	4	0		—	—	—	—	—
—Swedish Oly. team......	Int'l	4	1	1	2	2	...	...	...		—	—	—	—	—
98-99—New York Rangers......	NHL	81	13	30	43	20	-2	1	2		—	—	—	—	—
99-00—San Jose....................	NHL	79	12	25	37	22	9	2	1		12	0	2	2	2
NHL Totals (5 years)............		394	77	123	200	100	32	13	5		32	4	10	14	8

SUTER, GARY   D   SHARKS

PERSONAL: Born June 24, 1964, in Madison, Wis. ... 6-0/215. ... Shoots left. ... Full Name: Gary Lee Suter. ... Name pronounced SOO-tuhr.
COLLEGE: Wisconsin.
TRANSACTIONS/CAREER NOTES: Selected by Calgary Flames in ninth round (ninth Flames pick, 180th overall) of NHL entry draft (June 9, 1984). ... Stretched knee ligament (December 1986). ... Suspended first four games of regular season and next six international games in which NHL participates for high-sticking during Canada Cup (September 4, 1987). ... Injured left knee (February 1988). ... Pulled hamstring (February 1989). ... Ruptured appendix (February 22, 1989); missed 16 games. ... Fractured jaw (April 11, 1989). ... Bruised knee (December 12, 1991); missed 10 games. ... Injured ribs (March 16, 1993); missed one game. ... Suffered from the flu (March 30, 1993); missed one game. ... Tore left knee ligaments (November 4, 1993); missed 33 games. ... Strained left leg muscle (January 24, 1994); missed 10 games. ... Traded by Flames with LW Paul Ranheim and C Ted Drury to Hartford Whalers for C Michael Nylander, D Zarley Zalapski and D James Patrick (March 10, 1994). ... Traded by Hartford with LW Randy Cunneyworth and third-round pick (traded to Vancouver) in 1995 draft to Chicago Blackhawks for D Frantisek Kucera and LW Jocelyn Lemieux (March 11, 1994). ... Fractured bone in hand (May 25, 1995); missed four playoff games. ... Strained groin (December 14, 1997); missed five games. ... Suspended four games and fined $1,000 by NHL for cross-checking incident (February 3, 1998). ... Signed as free agent by San Jose Sharks (July 1, 1998). ... Injured elbow during offseason; missed first five games of season. ... Reinjured elbow (October 24, 1998); missed remainder of season. ... Injured knee (February 23, 2000); missed six games.
HONORS: Named USHL Top Defenseman (1982-83). ... Named to USHL All-Star first team (1982-83). ... Won Calder Memorial Trophy (1985-86). ... Named to NHL All-Rookie team (1985-86). ... Played in NHL All-Star Game (1986, 1988, 1989 and 1991). ... Named to THE SPORTING NEWS All-Star first team (1987-88). ... Named to NHL All-Star second team (1987-88). ... Named to THE SPORTING NEWS All-Star second team (1988-89). ... Named to play in NHL All-Star Game (1996); replaced by D Larry Murphy due to injury.
RECORDS: Shares NHL single-game record for most assists by a defenseman—6 (April 4, 1986).
MISCELLANEOUS: Member of Stanley Cup championship team (1989).

			REGULAR SEASON								PLAYOFFS				
Season Team	League	Gms.	G	A	Pts.	PIM	+/-	PP	SH		Gms.	G	A	Pts.	PIM
81-82—Duquque....................	USHL	18	3	4	7	32	...	...	...		—	—	—	—	—
82-83—Dubuque....................	USHL	41	9	10	19	112	...	...	...		—	—	—	—	—
83-84—Univ. of Wisconsin......	WCHA	35	4	18	22	68	...	...	...		—	—	—	—	—
84-85—Univ. of Wisconsin......	WCHA	39	12	39	51	110	...	...	...		—	—	—	—	—
85-86—Calgary....................	NHL	80	18	50	68	141	11	9	0		10	2	8	10	8
86-87—Calgary....................	NHL	68	9	40	49	70	-10	4	0		6	0	3	3	10
87-88—Calgary....................	NHL	75	21	70	91	124	39	6	1		9	1	9	10	6
88-89—Calgary....................	NHL	63	13	49	62	78	26	8	0		5	0	3	3	10
89-90—Calgary....................	NHL	76	16	60	76	97	4	5	0		6	0	1	1	14
90-91—Calgary....................	NHL	79	12	58	70	102	26	6	0		7	1	6	7	12
91-92—Calgary....................	NHL	70	12	43	55	128	1	4	0		—	—	—	—	—
92-93—Calgary....................	NHL	81	23	58	81	112	-1	10	1		6	2	3	5	8
93-94—Calgary....................	NHL	25	4	9	13	20	-3	2	1		—	—	—	—	—
—Chicago......................	NHL	16	2	3	5	18	-9	2	0		6	3	2	5	6
94-95—Chicago....................	NHL	48	10	27	37	42	14	5	0		12	2	5	7	10
95-96—Chicago....................	NHL	82	20	47	67	80	3	12	2		10	3	3	6	8
96-97—Chicago....................	NHL	82	7	21	28	70	-4	3	0		6	1	4	5	8
97-98—Chicago....................	NHL	73	14	28	42	74	1	5	2		—	—	—	—	—
—U.S. Olympic team......	Int'l	4	0	0	0	2	...	...	...		—	—	—	—	—
98-99—San Jose....................	NHL	1	0	0	0	0	0	0	0		—	—	—	—	—
99-00—San Jose....................	NHL	76	6	28	34	52	7	2	1		12	2	5	7	12
NHL Totals (15 years).........		995	187	591	778	1208	105	83	8		95	17	52	69	112

SUTTER, RON   C

PERSONAL: Born December 2, 1963, in Viking, Alta. ... 6-0/185. ... Shoots right. ... Full Name: Ronald Sutter. ... Brother of Brian Sutter, left winger with St. Louis Blues (1976-77 through 1987-88) and head coach with Blues (1988-89 through 1991-92), Boston Bruins (1992-93 through 1994-95), and Calgary Flames (1997-98 through 1999-2000); brother of Brent Sutter, center with New York Islanders (1980-81 through 1991-92) Chicago Blackhawks (1991-92 through 1997-98); brother of Darryl Sutter, head coach, San Jose Sharks and left winger with Blackhawks (1979-80 through 1986-87); brother of Duane Sutter, right winger with Islanders (1979-80 through 1986-87) and Blackhawks (1987-88 through 1989-90); and twin brother of Rich Sutter, right winger with seven NHL teams (1982-83 through 1994-95). ... Name pronounced SUH-tuhr.
HIGH SCHOOL: Winston Churchill (Lethbridge, Ont.).
TRANSACTIONS/CAREER NOTES: Selected by Philadelphia Flyers as underage junior in first round (first Flyers pick, fourth overall) of NHL entry draft (June 9, 1982). ... Fractured ankle (November 27, 1981). ... Bruised ribs (March 1985). ... Suffered stress fracture in lower back (January 1987). ... Tore rib cartilage (March 1988). ... Fractured jaw (October 29, 1988). ... Pulled groin (March 1989). ... Traded by Flyers with D Murray Baron to St. Louis Blues for C Rod Brind'Amour and C Dan Quinn (September 22, 1991). ... Strained ligament in right knee (February 1, 1992); missed 10 games. ... Suffered abdominal pain (September 1992); missed first 18 games of season. ... Separated shoulder (March 30, 1993); missed remainder of season. ... Underwent abdominal surgery during off-season; missed nine games. ... Traded by Blues with C Bob Bassen and D Garth Butcher to Quebec Nordiques for D Steve Duchesne and RW Denis Chasse (January 23, 1994). ... Suffered sore neck (November 16, 1993); missed two games. ... Traded by Nordiques with first-round pick (RW Brett Lindros) in 1994 draft to New York Islanders for D Uwe Krupp and first-round pick (D Wade Belak) in 1994 draft (June 28, 1994). ... Sprained right ankle (February 7, 1995); missed 18 games. ... Signed as free agent by Boston Bruins (March 8, 1996). ... Signed as free agent by San Jose Sharks (October 12, 1996). ... Strained groin (November 10, 1997); missed eight games. ... Injured groin (December 2, 1997); missed eight games. ... Injured back (November 7, 1998); missed 12 games. ... Injured eye (February 15, 1999); missed four games. ... Suffered from the flu (November 27, 1999); missed two games.
MISCELLANEOUS: Captain of Philadelphia Flyers (1989-90 and 1990-91). ... Failed to score on a penalty shot (vs. Kelly Hrudey, November 18, 1984; vs. Grant Fuhr, May 28, 1985 (playoffs)).

Season Team	League	REGULAR SEASON								PLAYOFFS				
		Gms.	G	A	Pts.	PIM	+/-	PP	SH	Gms.	G	A	Pts.	PIM
79-80—Red Deer	AJHL	60	12	33	45	44	...	...	...	—	—	—	—	—
80-81—Lethbridge	WHL	72	13	32	45	152	...	...	...	9	2	5	7	29
81-82—Lethbridge	WHL	59	38	54	92	207	...	...	...	12	6	5	11	28
82-83—Lethbridge	WHL	58	35	48	83	98	...	...	...	20	*22	†19	*41	45
—Philadelphia	NHL	10	1	1	2	9	0	0	0	—	—	—	—	—
83-84—Philadelphia	NHL	79	19	32	51	101	4	5	3	3	0	0	0	22
84-85—Philadelphia	NHL	73	16	29	45	94	13	2	0	19	4	8	12	28
85-86—Philadelphia	NHL	75	18	42	60	159	26	0	0	5	0	2	2	10
86-87—Philadelphia	NHL	39	10	17	27	69	10	0	0	16	1	7	8	12
87-88—Philadelphia	NHL	69	8	25	33	146	-9	1	0	7	0	1	1	26
88-89—Philadelphia	NHL	55	26	22	48	80	25	4	1	19	1	9	10	51
89-90—Philadelphia	NHL	75	22	26	48	104	2	0	2	—	—	—	—	—
90-91—Philadelphia	NHL	80	17	28	45	92	2	2	0	—	—	—	—	—
91-92—St. Louis	NHL	68	19	27	46	91	9	5	4	6	1	3	4	8
92-93—St. Louis	NHL	59	12	15	27	99	-11	4	0	—	—	—	—	—
93-94—St. Louis	NHL	36	6	12	18	46	-1	1	0	—	—	—	—	—
—Quebec	NHL	37	9	13	22	44	3	4	0	—	—	—	—	—
94-95—New York Islanders	NHL	27	1	4	5	21	-8	0	0	—	—	—	—	—
95-96—Phoenix	IHL	25	6	13	19	28	...	...	...	—	—	—	—	—
—Boston	NHL	18	5	7	12	24	10	0	1	5	0	0	0	8
96-97—San Jose	NHL	78	5	7	12	65	-8	1	2	—	—	—	—	—
97-98—San Jose	NHL	57	2	7	9	22	-2	0	0	6	1	0	1	14
98-99—San Jose	NHL	59	3	6	9	40	-8	0	0	6	0	0	0	4
99-00—San Jose	NHL	78	5	6	11	34	-3	0	1	12	0	2	2	10
NHL Totals (18 years)		1072	204	326	530	1340	54	29	14	104	8	32	40	193

SUTTER, SHAUN   C   FLAMES

PERSONAL: Born June 2, 1980, in Red Deer, Alta. ... 5-11/160. ... Shoots right. ... Son of Brian Sutter, head coach with Calgary Flames (1997-98 through 1999-2000) and left winger with St. Louis Blues (1976-77 through 1987-88); Nephew of Darryl Sutter, head coach, San Jose Sharks and left winger with Chicago Blackhawks (1979-80 through 1986-87); nephew of Brent Sutter, center with New York Islanders (1980-81 through 1991-92) and Blackhawks (1991-92 through 1997-98); nephew of Ron Sutter, center, San Jose Sharks; nephew of Rich Sutter, right winger with seven teams (1982-83 through 1994-95); and nephew of Duane right winger with Islanders (1979-80 through 1986-87) and Blackhawks (1987-88 through 1989-90).

TRANSACTIONS/CAREER NOTES: Selected by Calgary Flames in fourth round (fourth Flames pick, 102nd overall) of NHL entry draft (June 27, 1998).

Season Team	League	REGULAR SEASON								PLAYOFFS				
		Gms.	G	A	Pts.	PIM	+/-	PP	SH	Gms.	G	A	Pts.	PIM
96-97—Red Deer	AMHL	33	15	24	39	143	...	...	...	—	—	—	—	—
97-98—Lethbridge	WHL	69	11	9	20	146	...	...	...	4	0	0	0	4
98-99—Lethbridge	WHL	35	8	4	12	43	...	...	...	—	—	—	—	—
—Medicine Hat	WHL	23	9	5	14	38	...	...	...	—	—	—	—	—
99-00—Medicine Hat	WHL	29	1	7	8	43	...	...	...	—	—	—	—	—
—Calgary	WHL	6	0	1	1	8	...	...	...	—	—	—	—	—

SUTTON, ANDY   D   WILD

PERSONAL: Born March 10, 1975, in Kingston, Ont. ... 6-6/245. ... Full Name: Andy Cameron Sutton.
HIGH SCHOOL: St. Michael's (Toronto).
COLLEGE: Michigan Tech.
TRANSACTIONS/CAREER NOTES: Signed as non-drafted free agent by San Jose Sharks (March 20, 1998). ... Injured wrist (November 27, 1999); missed three games. ... Reinjured wrist (December 8, 1999); missed three games. ... Reinjured wrist (December 20, 1999); missed seven games. ... Reinjured wrist (January 12, 2000); missed 10 games. ... Traded by Sharks with seventh-round pick (RW/LW Peter Bartos) in 2000 draft and third round pick in 2001 draft to Minnesota Wild for eighth-round pick in 2001 draft and future considerations (June 12, 2000).
HONORS: Named to WCHA All-Star second team (1997-98).

Season Team	League	REGULAR SEASON								PLAYOFFS				
		Gms.	G	A	Pts.	PIM	+/-	PP	SH	Gms.	G	A	Pts.	PIM
94-95—Michigan Tech	WCHA	19	2	1	3	42	...	...	...	—	—	—	—	—
95-96—Michigan Tech	WCHA	32	2	2	4	38	...	...	...	—	—	—	—	—
96-97—Michigan Tech	WCHA	32	2	7	9	73	...	...	...	—	—	—	—	—
97-98—Michigan Tech	WCHA	38	16	24	40	97	...	...	...	—	—	—	—	—
—Kentucky	AHL	7	0	0	0	33	...	...	...	—	—	—	—	—
98-99—San Jose	NHL	31	0	3	3	65	-4	0	0	—	—	—	—	—
—Kentucky	AHL	21	5	10	15	53	...	...	...	5	0	0	0	23
99-00—San Jose	NHL	40	1	1	2	80	-5	0	0	—	—	—	—	—
—Kentucky	AHL	3	0	1	1	0	...	...	...	—	—	—	—	—
NHL Totals (2 years)		71	1	4	5	145	-9	0	0					

SUTTON, KEN   D   DEVILS

PERSONAL: Born November 5, 1969, in Edmonton. ... 6-1/205. ... Shoots left. ... Full Name: Kenneth Sutton.
TRANSACTIONS/CAREER NOTES: Selected by Buffalo Sabres in fifth round (fourth Sabres pick, 98th overall) of NHL entry draft (June 17, 1989). ... Separated shoulder (March 3, 1992); missed six games. ... Fractured ankle (September 15, 1992); missed first 19 games of season. ... Fractured finger (February 15, 1995); missed 10 games. ... Traded by Sabres to Edmonton Oilers for LW Scott Pearson (April 7, 1995). ... Traded by Oilers with D Igor Kravchuk to St. Louis Blues for D Donald Dufresne and D Jeff Norton (January 4, 1996). ... Traded by Blues with second-round pick (LW Brett Clouthier) in 1999 draft to New Jersey Devils for LW Mike Peluso and D Ricard Persson (November 26, 1996). ... Traded by Devils with RW John MacLean to San Jose Sharks for D Doug Bodger and LW Dody Wood (December 7, 1997). ... Traded by

S

Sharks to Devils for fifth-round pick (RW Nicholas Dimitrakos) in 1999 draft (August 26, 1998). ... Claimed by Washington Capitals from Devils in NHL waiver draft (September 27, 1999). ... Traded by Capitals to Devils for future considerations (October 5, 1999).
HONORS: Named to Memorial Cup All-Star team (1988-89). ... Named to AHL All-Star first team (1998-99). ... Won Eddie Shore Award (1998-99).
MISCELLANEOUS: Member of Stanley Cup championship team (2000).

		REGULAR SEASON								PLAYOFFS				
Season Team	League	Gms.	G	A	Pts.	PIM	+/-	PP	SH	Gms.	G	A	Pts.	PIM
87-88—Calgary Canucks.........	AJHL	53	13	43	56	228	...	...	...	—	—	—	—	—
88-89—Saskatoon..................	WHL	71	22	31	53	104	...	...	...	8	2	5	7	12
89-90—Rochester	AHL	57	5	14	19	83	...	...	...	11	1	6	7	15
90-91—Buffalo	NHL	15	3	6	9	13	2	2	0	6	0	1	1	2
—Rochester	AHL	62	7	24	31	65	...	...	...	3	1	1	2	14
91-92—Buffalo	NHL	64	2	18	20	71	5	0	0	7	0	2	2	4
92-93—Buffalo	NHL	63	8	14	22	30	-3	1	0	8	3	1	4	8
93-94—Buffalo	NHL	78	4	20	24	71	-6	1	0	4	0	0	0	2
94-95—Buffalo	NHL	12	1	2	3	30	-2	0	0	—	—	—	—	—
—Edmonton	NHL	12	3	1	4	12	-1	0	0	—	—	—	—	—
95-96—Edmonton	NHL	32	0	8	8	39	-12	0	0	—	—	—	—	—
—St. Louis	NHL	6	0	0	0	4	-1	0	0	1	0	0	0	0
—Worcester	AHL	32	4	16	20	60	...	...	...	4	0	2	2	21
96-97—Manitoba..................	IHL	20	3	10	13	48	...	...	...	—	—	—	—	—
—Albany	AHL	61	6	13	19	79	...	...	...	16	4	8	12	55
97-98—Albany	AHL	10	0	7	7	15	...	...	...	—	—	—	—	—
—New Jersey	NHL	13	0	0	0	6	1	0	0	—	—	—	—	—
—San Jose	NHL	8	0	0	0	15	-4	0	0	—	—	—	—	—
98-99—Albany	AHL	75	13	42	55	118	...	...	...	5	0	2	2	12
—New Jersey	NHL	5	1	0	1	0	1	0	0	—	—	—	—	—
99-00—New Jersey	NHL	6	0	2	2	2	2	0	0	—	—	—	—	—
—Albany	AHL	57	5	16	21	129	...	...	...	—	—	—	—	—
NHL Totals (9 years)..........		314	22	71	93	293	-18	4	0	26	3	4	7	16

SVARTVADET, PER — LW — THRASHERS

PERSONAL: Born May 17, 1975, in Solleftea, Sweden. ... 6-1/190. ... Shoots left. ... Name pronounced PAIR SVAHRT-vuh-deht.
TRANSACTIONS/CAREER NOTES: Selected by Dallas Stars in sixth round (fifth Stars pick, 139th overall) of NHL entry draft (June 26, 1993). ... Traded by Stars to Atlanta Thrashers for sixth-round pick (RW Justin Cox) in 1999 draft (June 26, 1999). ... Fractured finger (October 16, 1999); missed one game.

		REGULAR SEASON								PLAYOFFS				
Season Team	League	Gms.	G	A	Pts.	PIM	+/-	PP	SH	Gms.	G	A	Pts.	PIM
91-92—MoDo Hockey Jrs......	Sweden Jr.	30	17	19	36	36	...	...	...	—	—	—	—	—
92-93—MoDo Ornskoldsvik	Sweden	2	0	0	0	0	...	...	...	—	—	—	—	—
—MoDo Hockey Jrs......	Sweden Jr.	22	19	27	46	38	...	...	...	—	—	—	—	—
93-94—MoDo Ornskoldsvik	Sweden	36	2	1	3	4	...	...	...	11	0	0	0	6
94-95—MoDo Ornskoldsvik	Sweden	40	6	9	15	31	...	...	...	—	—	—	—	—
95-96—MoDo Ornskoldsvik	Sweden	40	9	14	23	26	...	...	...	8	2	3	5	0
96-97—MoDo Ornskoldsvik	Sweden	50	7	18	25	38	...	...	...	—	—	—	—	—
97-98—MoDo Ornskoldsvik	Sweden	46	6	12	18	28	...	...	...	7	3	2	5	2
98-99—MoDo Ornskoldsvik	Sweden	50	9	23	32	30	...	...	...	13	3	6	9	6
99-00—Atlanta	NHL	38	3	4	7	6	-8	0	0	—	—	—	—	—
—Orlando	IHL	27	4	6	10	10	...	...	...	5	0	1	1	0
NHL Totals (1 year)..............		38	3	4	7	6	-8	0	0					

SVEHLA, ROBERT — D — PANTHERS

PERSONAL: Born January 2, 1969, in Martin, Czechoslovakia. ... 6-1/210. ... Shoots right. ... Name pronounced SVAY-luh.
TRANSACTIONS/CAREER NOTES: Selected by Calgary Flames in fourth round (fourth Flames pick, 78th overall) of NHL entry draft (June 20, 1992). ... Traded by Flames with D Magnus Svensson to Florida Panthers for third-round pick (LW Dmitri Vlasenkov) in 1996 draft and fourth-round pick (LW Ryan Ready) in 1997 draft (September 29, 1994). ... Sprained left rotator cuff (April 22, 1995); missed two games. ... Reinjured left rotator cuff (April 28, 1995); missed one game. ... Suffered back spasms (March 4, 1998); missed three games.
HONORS: Named Czechoslovakian League Player of the Year (1991-92). ... Named to Czechoslovakian League All-Star team (1991-92). ... Played in NHL All-Star Game (1997).
MISCELLANEOUS: Member of bronze-medal-winning Czechoslovakian Olympic team (1992).

		REGULAR SEASON								PLAYOFFS				
Season Team	League	Gms.	G	A	Pts.	PIM	+/-	PP	SH	Gms.	G	A	Pts.	PIM
89-90—Dukla Trencin..............	Czech.	29	4	3	7	...	...	...	...	—	—	—	—	—
90-91—Dukla Trencin..............	Czech.	58	16	9	25	...	...	...	...	—	—	—	—	—
91-92—Dukla Trencin..............	Czech.	51	23	28	51	0	...	...	...	—	—	—	—	—
—Czech. Olympic Team .	Int'l	8	2	1	3	...	...	...	...	—	—	—	—	—
92-93—Malmo	Sweden	40	19	10	29	86	...	...	...	6	0	1	1	14
93-94—Malmo	Sweden	37	14	25	39	*127	...	...	...	10	5	1	6	23
—Slovakian Oly. team	Int'l	8	2	4	6	26	...	...	...	—	—	—	—	—
94-95—Malmo	Sweden	32	11	13	24	83	...	...	...	9	2	3	5	6
—Florida......................	NHL	5	1	1	2	0	3	1	0	—	—	—	—	—
95-96—Florida......................	NHL	81	8	49	57	94	-3	7	0	22	0	6	6	32
96-97—Florida......................	NHL	82	13	32	45	86	2	5	0	5	1	4	5	4
97-98—Florida......................	NHL	79	9	34	43	113	-3	3	0	—	—	—	—	—
—Slovakian Oly. team	Int'l	2	0	1	1	0	...	...	...	—	—	—	—	—
98-99—Florida......................	NHL	80	8	29	37	83	-13	4	0	—	—	—	—	—
99-00—Florida......................	NHL	82	9	40	49	64	23	3	0	4	0	1	1	4
NHL Totals (6 years)..........		409	48	185	233	440	9	23	0	31	1	11	12	40

S

SVEJKOVSKY, JAROSLAV   RW   LIGHTNING

PERSONAL: Born October 1, 1976, in Plzen, Czechoslovakia. ... 6-1/193. ... Shoots right. ... Name pronounced svay-KAHF-skee.
TRANSACTIONS/CAREER NOTES: Selected by Washington Capitals in first round (second Capitals pick, 17th overall) of NHL entry draft (June 22, 1996). ... Sprained ankle (October 23, 1997); missed 14 games. ... Reinjured ankle (November 26, 1997); missed 29 games. ... Sprained ankle (October 24, 1998); missed 37 games. ... Suffered concussion (March 15, 1999); missed final 15 games of season. ... Strained groin (October 12, 1999); missed one game. ... Bruised shoulder (October 26, 1999); missed seven games. ... Traded by Capitals to Tampa Bay Lightning for seventh-round pick (traded to Los Angeles) in 2000 draft and third-round pick in 2001 draft (January 17, 2000). ... Bruised right knee (February 8, 2000); missed nine games.
HONORS: Named to WHL (West) All-Star second team (1995-96). ... Won Dudley (Red) Garrett Memorial Trophy (1996-97). ... Named to AHL All-Rookie team (1996-97).
STATISTICAL PLATEAUS: Four-goal games: 1996-97 (1).

		REGULAR SEASON								PLAYOFFS				
Season Team	League	Gms.	G	A	Pts.	PIM	+/-	PP	SH	Gms.	G	A	Pts.	PIM
93-94—Plzen Jrs.	Czech Rep.	8	0	0	0	8	...	...	...	—	—	—	—	—
94-95—Plzen Jrs.	Czech Rep.	25	18	19	37	30	...	...	...	—	—	—	—	—
—Ta'Bor	Czech Rep.	11	6	7	13		...	...	...	—	—	—	—	—
95-96—Tri-City	WHL	70	58	43	101	118	...	...	...	11	10	9	19	8
96-97—Portland	AHL	54	38	28	66	56	...	...	...	5	2	0	2	6
—Washington	NHL	19	7	3	10	4	-1	2	0	—	—	—	—	—
97-98—Washington	NHL	17	4	1	5	10	-5	2	0	1	0	0	0	4
—Portland	AHL	16	12	7	19	16	...	...	...	7	1	2	3	2
98-99—Washington	NHL	25	6	8	14	12	-2	4	0	—	—	—	—	—
99-00—Washington	NHL	23	1	2	3	2	-7	1	0	—	—	—	—	—
—Tampa Bay	NHL	29	5	5	10	28	-7	0	0	—	—	—	—	—
NHL Totals (4 years)		113	23	19	42	56	-22	9	0	1	0	0	0	4

SVOBODA, PETR   D   LIGHTNING

PERSONAL: Born February 14, 1966, in Most, Czechoslovakia. ... 6-2/198. ... Shoots left. ... Name pronounced svuh-BOH-duh.
TRANSACTIONS/CAREER NOTES: Selected by Montreal Canadiens in first round (first Canadiens pick, fifth overall) of NHL entry draft (June 9, 1984). ... Suffered back spasms (January 1988). ... Suffered hip pointer (March 1988). ... Sprained right wrist (November 21, 1988); missed five games. ... Injured back (March 1989). ... Separated shoulder (November 1989). ... Pulled groin (November 22, 1989). ... Reinjured groin (December 11, 1989); missed 15 games. ... Bruised left foot (March 11, 1990). ... Suffered stomach disorder (November 28, 1990); missed five games. ... Fractured left foot (January 15, 1991); missed 15 games. ... Injured mouth (December 14, 1991). ... Sprained ankle (February 17, 1992); missed seven games. ... Traded by Canadiens to Buffalo Sabres for D Kevin Haller (March 10, 1992). ... Bruised knee (October 28, 1992); missed four games. ... Tore ligament in right knee (January 17, 1993); missed remainder of season. ... Injured knee (October 12, 1993); missed three games. ... Suffered knee inflammation (October 16, 1993); missed seven games. ... Sprained left knee (March 17, 1994); missed 12 games. ... Played in Europe during 1994-95 NHL lockout. ... Separated shoulder (March 2, 1995); missed two games. ... Fractured jaw (March 16, 1995); missed one game. ... Traded by Sabres to Philadelphia Flyers for D Garry Galley (April 7, 1995). ... Strained neck (April 26, 1995); missed one game. ... Injured groin (October 31, 1995); missed one game. ... Suffered pinched nerve in neck (November 16, 1995); missed three games. ... Pulled hamstring (January 11, 1996); missed two games. ... Suffered concussion (February 2, 1996); missed one game. ... Strained shoulder (April 4, 1996); missed one game. ... Separated left shoulder (October 15, 1996); missed six games. ... Strained groin (December 31, 1996); missed four games. ... Suffered pinched nerve in neck (January 28, 1997); missed three games. ... Strained groin (March 13, 1997); missed two games. ... Fractured finger (October 1, 1997); missed 11 games. ... Strained neck (January 3, 1998); missed four games. ... Strained right elbow (March 5, 1998); missed four games. ... Bruised left thumb (March 24, 1998); missed seven games. ... Suffered hip flexor (October 31, 1998); missed three games. ... Sprained left knee (December 10, 1998); missed two games. ... Suffered from the flu (December 23, 1998); missed two games. ... Traded by Flyers to Tampa Bay Lightning for D Karl Dykhuis (December 28, 1998). ... Strained groin (January 29, 1999); missed five games. ... Reinjured groin (February 13, 1999); missed two games. ... Injured knee (March 24, 1999); missed two games. ... Injured shoulder (April 16, 1999); missed final game of season. ... Injured shoulder (January 5, 2000); missed one game. ... Injured shoulder (January 17, 2000); missed two games. ... Injured thumb (February 17, 2000); missed one game. ... Sprained thumb (March 1, 2000); missed two games. ... Strained muscle in abdomen (March 30, 2000); missed final five games of season.
HONORS: Played in NHL All-Star Game (2000).
MISCELLANEOUS: Member of Stanley Cup championship team (1986). ... Member of gold-medal-winning Czech Republic Olympic team (1998).

		REGULAR SEASON								PLAYOFFS				
Season Team	League	Gms.	G	A	Pts.	PIM	+/-	PP	SH	Gms.	G	A	Pts.	PIM
83-84—Czechoslovakia Jr.	Czech.	40	15	21	36	14	...	...	...	—	—	—	—	—
84-85—Montreal	NHL	73	4	27	31	65	16	0	0	7	1	1	2	12
85-86—Montreal	NHL	73	1	18	19	93	24	0	0	8	0	0	0	21
86-87—Montreal	NHL	70	5	17	22	63	14	1	0	14	0	5	5	10
87-88—Montreal	NHL	69	7	22	29	149	46	2	0	10	0	5	5	12
88-89—Montreal	NHL	71	8	37	45	147	28	4	0	21	1	11	12	16
89-90—Montreal	NHL	60	5	31	36	98	20	2	0	10	0	5	5	2
90-91—Montreal	NHL	60	4	22	26	52	5	3	0	2	0	1	1	2
91-92—Montreal	NHL	58	5	16	21	94	9	1	0	—	—	—	—	—
—Buffalo	NHL	13	1	6	7	52	-8	0	0	7	1	4	5	6
92-93—Buffalo	NHL	40	2	24	26	59	3	1	0	—	—	—	—	—
93-94—Buffalo	NHL	60	2	14	16	89	11	1	0	3	0	0	0	4
94-95—Chem. Litvinov	Czech Rep.	8	2	0	2	40	...	...	...	—	—	—	—	—
—Buffalo	NHL	26	0	5	5	60	-5	0	0	—	—	—	—	—
—Philadelphia	NHL	11	0	3	3	10	0	0	0	14	0	4	4	8
95-96—Philadelphia	NHL	73	1	28	29	105	28	0	0	12	0	6	6	22
96-97—Philadelphia	NHL	67	2	12	14	94	10	1	0	16	1	2	3	16
97-98—Philadelphia	NHL	56	3	15	18	83	19	2	0	3	0	1	1	4
—Czech Rep. Oly. team	Int'l	6	1	1	2	39	...	...	...	—	—	—	—	—
98-99—Philadelphia	NHL	25	4	2	6	28	5	1	1	—	—	—	—	—
—Tampa Bay	NHL	34	1	16	17	53	-4	0	0	—	—	—	—	—
99-00—Tampa Bay	NHL	70	2	23	25	170	-11	2	0	—	—	—	—	—
NHL Totals (16 years)		1009	57	338	395	1564	210	21	1	127	4	45	49	135

S

SWANSON, BRIAN — C — OILERS

PERSONAL: Born March 24, 1976, in Eagle River, Alaska. ... 5-10/185. ... Shoots left.
COLLEGE: Colorado College.
TRANSACTIONS/CAREER NOTES: Selected by San Jose Sharks in fifth round (fifth Sharks pick, 115th overall) of NHL entry draft (June 29, 1994). ... Traded by Sharks with D Jayson More and fourth-round pick (D Tomi Kallarsson) in 1997 draft to New York Rangers for D Marty McSorley (August 20, 1996). ... Signed as free agent by Edmonton Oilers (August 20, 1999).
HONORS: Named to WCHA All-Star second team (1995-96). ... Named WCHA Rookie of the Year (1995-96). ... Named to WCHA All-Rookie team (1995-96). ... Named to WCHA All-Star first team (1996-97 through 1998-99). ... Named to NCAA All-America (West) second team (1997-98). ... Named to NCAA All-America (West) first team (1998-99).

				REGULAR SEASON							PLAYOFFS				
Season Team	League	Gms.	G	A	Pts.	PIM	+/-	PP	SH		Gms.	G	A	Pts.	PIM
93-94—Omaha	USHL	47	38	42	80	40	...	...	...		—	—	—	—	—
94-95—Portland	WHL	65	3	18	21	91	...	...	...		9	2	1	3	18
95-96—Colorado College	WCHA	40	26	33	59	24	...	...	...		—	—	—	—	—
96-97—Colorado College	WCHA	43	19	32	51	47	...	...	...		—	—	—	—	—
97-98—Colorado College	WCHA	42	18	*38	*56	26	...	...	...		—	—	—	—	—
98-99—Colorado College	WCHA	42	25	†41	66	28	...	...	...		—	—	—	—	—
—Hartford	AHL	4	0	0	0	4	...	...	...		—	—	—	—	—
99-00—Hamilton	AHL	69	19	40	59	18	...	...	...		10	2	5	7	6

SWEENEY, DON — D — BRUINS

S

PERSONAL: Born August 17, 1966, in St. Stephen, N.B. ... 5-10/184. ... Shoots left. ... Full Name: Donald Clark Sweeney.
HIGH SCHOOL: St. Paul (N.B.).
COLLEGE: Harvard.
TRANSACTIONS/CAREER NOTES: Selected by Boston Bruins in eighth round (eighth Bruins pick, 166th overall) of NHL entry draft (June 9, 1984). ... Injured knee (October 12, 1991); missed four games. ... Sprained knee (October 5, 1993); missed six games. ... Injured ribs (December 15, 1993); missed three games. ... Injured shoulder (October 17, 1995); missed three games. ... Injured shoulder (October 31, 1995); missed two games. ... Fractured shoulder (March 1, 1998); missed remainder of season. ... Suffered from the flu (January 13, 2000); missed one game.
HONORS: Named to NCAA All-America (East) second team (1987-88). ... Named to ECAC All-Star first team (1987-88).

				REGULAR SEASON							PLAYOFFS				
Season Team	League	Gms.	G	A	Pts.	PIM	+/-	PP	SH		Gms.	G	A	Pts.	PIM
83-84—St. Paul N.B. H.S.	N.B. H.S.	22	33	26	59	...	...	...	...		—	—	—	—	—
84-85—Harvard University	ECAC	29	3	7	10	30	...	...	...		—	—	—	—	—
85-86—Harvard University	ECAC	31	4	5	9	29	...	...	...		—	—	—	—	—
86-87—Harvard University	ECAC	34	7	14	21	22	...	...	...		—	—	—	—	—
87-88—Harvard University	ECAC	30	6	23	29	37	...	...	...		—	—	—	—	—
—Maine	AHL	—	—	—	—	...	...	...	...		6	1	3	4	0
88-89—Maine	AHL	42	8	17	25	24	...	...	...		—	—	—	—	—
—Boston	NHL	36	3	5	8	20	-6	0	0		—	—	—	—	—
89-90—Boston	NHL	58	3	5	8	58	11	0	0		21	1	5	6	18
—Maine	AHL	11	0	8	8	8	...	...	...		—	—	—	—	—
90-91—Boston	NHL	77	8	13	21	67	2	0	1		19	3	0	3	25
91-92—Boston	NHL	75	3	11	14	74	-9	0	0		15	0	0	0	10
92-93—Boston	NHL	84	7	27	34	68	34	0	1		4	0	0	0	4
93-94—Boston	NHL	75	6	15	21	50	29	1	2		12	2	1	3	4
94-95—Boston	NHL	47	3	19	22	24	6	1	0		5	0	0	0	4
95-96—Boston	NHL	77	4	24	28	42	-4	2	0		5	0	2	2	6
96-97—Boston	NHL	82	3	23	26	39	-5	0	0		—	—	—	—	—
97-98—Boston	NHL	59	1	15	16	24	12	0	0		—	—	—	—	—
98-99—Boston	NHL	81	2	10	12	64	14	0	0		11	3	0	3	6
99-00—Boston	NHL	81	1	13	14	48	-14	0	0		—	—	—	—	—
NHL Totals (12 years)		832	44	180	224	578	70	4	4		92	9	8	17	77

SYDOR, DARRYL — D — STARS

PERSONAL: Born May 13, 1972, in Edmonton. ... 6-1/205. ... Shoots left. ... Full Name: Darryl Marion Sydor. ... Name pronounced sih-DOHR.
TRANSACTIONS/CAREER NOTES: Selected by Los Angeles Kings in first round (first Kings pick, seventh overall) of NHL entry draft (June 16, 1990). ... Bruised hip (November 27, 1992); missed two games. ... Sprained right shoulder (March 15, 1993); missed two games. ... Traded by Kings with seventh-round pick (G Eoin McInerney) in 1996 draft to Dallas Stars for RW Shane Churla and D Doug Zmolek (February 17, 1996). ... Sprained knee (February 21, 1999); missed three games. ... Reinjured knee (March 7, 1999); missed five games. ... Fractured eye socket (October 2, 1999); missed three games. ... Injured groin (October 20, 2000); missed three games. ... Injured neck (March 26, 2000); missed two games.
HONORS: Named to WHL (West) All-Star first team (1989-90 through 1991-92). ... Won Bill Hunter Trophy (1990-91). ... Named to Can.HL All-Star second team (1991-92) ... Played in NHL All-Star Game (1998 and 1999).
MISCELLANEOUS: Member of Stanley Cup championship team (1999).
STATISTICAL PLATEAUS: Three-goal games: 1997-98 (1).

				REGULAR SEASON							PLAYOFFS				
Season Team	League	Gms.	G	A	Pts.	PIM	+/-	PP	SH		Gms.	G	A	Pts.	PIM
88-89—Kamloops	WHL	65	12	14	26	86	...	...	...		15	1	4	5	19
89-90—Kamloops	WHL	67	29	66	95	129	...	...	...		17	2	9	11	28
90-91—Kamloops	WHL	66	27	78	105	88	...	...	...		12	3	*22	25	10
91-92—Kamloops	WHL	29	9	39	48	43	...	...	...		17	3	15	18	18
—Los Angeles	NHL	18	1	5	6	22	-3	0	0		—	—	—	—	—
92-93—Los Angeles	NHL	80	6	23	29	63	-2	0	0		24	3	8	11	16

Season Team	League	REGULAR SEASON								PLAYOFFS				
		Gms.	G	A	Pts.	PIM	+/-	PP	SH	Gms.	G	A	Pts.	PIM
93-94—Los Angeles	NHL	84	8	27	35	94	-9	1	0	—	—	—	—	—
94-95—Los Angeles	NHL	48	4	19	23	36	-2	3	0	—	—	—	—	—
95-96—Los Angeles	NHL	58	1	11	12	34	-11	1	0	—	—	—	—	—
—Dallas	NHL	26	2	6	8	41	-1	1	0	—	—	—	—	—
96-97—Dallas	NHL	82	8	40	48	51	37	2	0	7	0	2	2	0
97-98—Dallas	NHL	79	11	35	46	51	17	4	1	17	0	5	5	14
98-99—Dallas	NHL	74	14	34	48	50	-1	9	0	23	3	9	12	16
99-00—Dallas	NHL	74	8	26	34	32	6	5	0	23	1	6	7	6
NHL Totals (9 years)		623	63	226	289	474	31	26	1	94	7	30	37	52

SYKORA, PETR   RW   DEVILS

PERSONAL: Born November 19, 1976, in Plzen, Czechoslovakia. ... 6-0/190. ... Shoots left. ... Name pronounced sih-KOHR-uh.
TRANSACTIONS/CAREER NOTES: Selected by New Jersey Devils in first round (first Devils pick, 18th overall) of NHL entry draft (July 8, 1995). ... Injured back (February 21, 1996); missed two games. ... Injured groin (October 5, 1996); missed two games. ... Reinjured groin (November 9, 1996); missed four games. ... Reinjured groin (November 30, 1996); missed three games. ... Bruised shoulder (November 5, 1997); missed two games. ... Sprained left ankle (November 29, 1997); missed 20 games. ... Suffered from food poisoning (January 2, 1999); missed two games ... Suffered from the flu (March 2, 2000); missed three games.
HONORS: Named to NHL All-Rookie team (1995-96).
MISCELLANEOUS: Member of Stanley Cup championship team (2000). ... Scored on a penalty shot (vs. Dwayne Roloson, January 6, 2000).

Season Team	League	REGULAR SEASON								PLAYOFFS				
		Gms.	G	A	Pts.	PIM	+/-	PP	SH	Gms.	G	A	Pts.	PIM
91-92—Skoda Plzen	Czech.	30	50	50	100	...	...	...	...	—	—	—	—	—
92-93—Skoda Plzen	Czech.	19	12	5	17	...	...	...	...	—	—	—	—	—
93-94—Skoda Plzen	Czech Rep.	37	10	16	26	...	...	...	...	4	0	1	1	...
—Cleveland	IHL	13	4	5	9	8	...	...	...	—	—	—	—	—
94-95—Detroit	IHL	29	12	17	29	16	...	...	...	—	—	—	—	—
95-96—Albany	AHL	5	4	1	5	0	...	...	...	—	—	—	—	—
—New Jersey	NHL	63	18	24	42	32	7	8	0	—	—	—	—	—
96-97—New Jersey	NHL	19	1	2	3	4	-8	0	0	2	0	0	0	2
—Albany	AHL	43	20	25	45	48	...	...	...	4	1	4	5	2
97-98—New Jersey	NHL	58	16	20	36	22	0	3	1	2	0	0	0	0
—Albany	AHL	2	4	1	5	0	...	...	...	—	—	—	—	—
98-99—New Jersey	NHL	80	29	43	72	22	16	15	0	7	3	3	6	4
99-00—New Jersey	NHL	79	25	43	68	26	24	5	1	23	9	8	17	10
NHL Totals (5 years)		299	89	132	221	106	39	31	2	34	12	11	23	16

SYLVESTER, DEAN   RW   THRASHERS

PERSONAL: Born December 30, 1972, in Hanson, Mass. ... 6-2/210. ... Shoots right.
HIGH SCHOOL: Boston College High.
COLLEGE: Kent.
TRANSACTIONS/CAREER NOTES: Selected by San Jose Sharks in NHL supplemental draft (June 25, 1993). ... Signed as free agent by Buffalo Sabres (September 10, 1998). ... Traded by Sabres to Atlanta Thrashers for future considerations (June 25, 1999). ... Suffered back spasms (February 14, 2000); missed three games. ... Suffered back spasms (February 23, 2000); missed six games.
STATISTICAL PLATEAUS: Three-goal games: 1999-00 (1).

Season Team	League	REGULAR SEASON								PLAYOFFS				
		Gms.	G	A	Pts.	PIM	+/-	PP	SH	Gms.	G	A	Pts.	PIM
90-91—Boston College H.S.	Mass. H.S.	18	19	13	32	...	...	...	...	—	—	—	—	—
91-92—Kent	Indep.	31	7	21	28	10	...	...	...	—	—	—	—	—
92-93—Kent	CCHA	38	33	20	53	28	...	...	...	—	—	—	—	—
93-94—Kent	CCHA	39	22	24	46	28	...	...	...	—	—	—	—	—
94-95—Michigan State	CCHA	40	15	15	30	38	...	...	...	—	—	—	—	—
95-96—Mobile	ECHL	44	24	27	51	35	...	...	...	—	—	—	—	—
—Kansas City	IHL	36	11	10	21	15	...	...	...	4	0	0	0	2
96-97—Kansas City	IHL	77	23	22	45	47	...	...	...	3	1	1	2	0
97-98—Kansas City	IHL	77	33	20	53	63	...	...	...	11	5	2	7	4
98-99—Rochester	AHL	76	35	30	65	46	...	...	...	18	†12	5	17	8
—Buffalo	NHL	1	0	0	0	0	-1	0	0	4	0	0	0	2
99-00—Orlando	IHL	16	4	3	7	43	...	...	...	—	—	—	—	—
—Atlanta	NHL	52	16	10	26	24	-14	1	0	—	—	—	—	—
NHL Totals (2 years)		53	16	10	26	24	-15	1	0	4	0	0	0	2

TABARACCI, RICK   G   STARS

PERSONAL: Born January 2, 1969, in Toronto. ... 5-11/181. ... Catches left. ... Full Name: Richard Stephen Tabaracci. ... Name pronounced TA-buh-RA-chee.
TRANSACTIONS/CAREER NOTES: Selected by Pittsburgh Penguins as underage junior in second round (second Penguins pick, 26th overall) of NHL entry draft (June 13, 1987). ... Traded by Penguins with C/LW Randy Cunneyworth and RW Dave McLlwain to Winnipeg Jets for RW Andrew McBain, D Jim Kyte and LW Randy Gilhen (June 17, 1989). ... Pulled right hamstring (December 11, 1990); missed seven games. ... Strained (October 10, 1992); missed one game. ... Suffered back spasms (December 1, 1992); missed one game. ... Suffered back spasms (January 19, 1993); missed seven games. ... Traded by Jets to Washington Capitals for G Jim Hrivnak and second-round pick (C Alexei Budayev) in 1993 draft (March 22, 1993). ... Tore knee ligaments (September 16, 1993); missed seven games. ... Sprained knee (February 20, 1994); missed 21 games. ... Strained hamstring (February 13, 1995). ... Traded by Capitals to Calgary Flames for fifth-round pick (D Joel Cort) in 1995 draft (April 7, 1995). ... Traded by Flames to Tampa Bay Lightning for C Aaron Gavey (November 19, 1996). ... Bruised sternum

S
T

(January 8, 1997); missed one game. ... Traded by Lightning to Flames for fourth-round pick (LW Eric Beaudoin) in 1998 draft (June 21, 1997). ... Separated shoulder (January 9, 1998); missed six games. ... Injured knee (January 31, 1998); missed three games. ... Pulled groin (April 9, 1998); missed final five games of season. ... Traded by Flames to Washington Capitals for conditional draft pick and future considerations (August 7, 1998). ... Strained groin (October 30, 1998); missed four games. ... Signed as free agent by Atlanta Thrashers (November 3, 1999). ... Traded by Thrashers to Colorado Avalanche for RW Shean Donovan (December 8, 1999). ... Selected by Columbus Blue Jackets in NHL expansion draft (June 23, 2000). ... Signed as free agent by Dallas Stars (July 12, 2000).

HONORS: Named to OHL All-Star first team (1987-88). ... Named to OHL All-Star second team (1988-89).

MISCELLANEOUS: Stopped a penalty shot attempt (vs. Jeff Beukeboom, October 6, 1990; vs. Darren Turcotte, March 22, 1998; vs. Mariusz Czerkawski, December 4, 1998; vs. Jay Pandolfo, December 30, 1998; vs. Robert Reichel, March 25, 1999). ... Allowed a penalty shot goal (vs. Pavel Bure, February 28, 1992).

						REGULAR SEASON								PLAYOFFS				
Season Team	League	Gms.	Min	W	L	T	GA	SO	Avg.	Gms.	Min.	W	L	GA	SO	Avg.
85-86—Markham Jr. B	OHA	40	2176	...	...	...	188	1	5.18	—	—	—	—	—	—	—
86-87—Cornwall	OHL	*59	*3347	23	32	3	*290	1	5.20	5	303	1	4	26	0	5.15
87-88—Cornwall	OHL	58	3448	33	18	6	200	†3	3.48	11	642	5	6	37	0	3.46
—Muskegon	IHL	—	—	—	—	—	—	—	—	1	13	0	0	1	0	4.62
88-89—Cornwall	OHL	50	2974	24	20	5	*210	1	4.24	18	1080	10	8	65	†1	3.61
—Pittsburgh	NHL	1	33	0	0	0	4	0	7.27	—	—	—	—	—	—	—
89-90—Moncton	AHL	27	1580	10	15	2	107	2	4.06	—	—	—	—	—	—	—
—Fort Wayne	IHL	22	1064	8	9	‡1	73	0	4.12	3	159	1	2	19	0	7.17
90-91—Moncton	AHL	11	645	4	5	2	41	0	3.81	—	—	—	—	—	—	—
—Winnipeg	NHL	24	1093	4	9	4	71	1	3.90	—	—	—	—	—	—	—
91-92—Moncton	AHL	23	1313	10	11	1	80	0	3.66	—	—	—	—	—	—	—
—Winnipeg	NHL	18	966	6	7	3	52	0	3.23	7	387	3	4	26	0	4.03
92-93—Winnipeg	NHL	19	959	5	10	0	70	0	4.38	—	—	—	—	—	—	—
—Moncton	AHL	5	290	2	1	2	18	0	3.72	—	—	—	—	—	—	—
—Washington	NHL	6	343	3	2	0	10	2	1.75	4	304	1	3	14	0	2.76
93-94—Washington	NHL	32	1770	13	14	2	91	2	3.08	2	111	0	2	6	0	3.24
—Portland	AHL	3	177	3	0	0	8	0	2.71	—	—	—	—	—	—	—
94-95—Washington	NHL	8	394	1	3	2	16	0	2.44	—	—	—	—	—	—	—
—Chicago	IHL	2	120	1	1	0	9	0	4.50	—	—	—	—	—	—	—
—Calgary	NHL	5	202	2	0	1	5	0	1.49	1	19	0	0	0	0	...
95-96—Calgary	NHL	43	2391	19	16	3	117	3	2.94	3	204	0	3	7	0	2.06
96-97—Calgary	NHL	7	361	2	4	0	14	1	2.33	—	—	—	—	—	—	—
—Tampa Bay	NHL	55	3012	20	25	6	138	4	2.75	—	—	—	—	—	—	—
97-98—Calgary	NHL	42	2419	13	22	6	116	0	2.88	—	—	—	—	—	—	—
98-99—Washington	NHL	23	1193	4	12	3	50	2	2.51	—	—	—	—	—	—	—
99-00—Atlanta	NHL	1	59	0	1	0	4	0	4.07	—	—	—	—	—	—	—
—Orlando	IHL	21	1231	15	6	‡4	53	1	2.58	—	—	—	—	—	—	—
—Colorado	NHL	2	60	1	0	0	2	0	2.00	—	—	—	—	—	—	—
—Cleveland	IHL	10	568	7	5	0	28	0	2.96	—	—	—	—	—	—	—
—Utah	IHL	11	626	4	4	‡3	24	1	2.30	3	179	1	2	7	0	2.35
NHL Totals (11 years)		286	15255	93	130	30	760	15	2.99	17	1025	4	12	53	0	3.10

TALLAS, ROB — G — BLACKHAWKS

PERSONAL: Born March 20, 1973, in Edmonton. ... 6-0/163. ... Catches left. ... Name pronounced TAL-ihz.

TRANSACTIONS/CAREER NOTES: Signed as non-drafted free agent by Boston Bruins (September 13, 1995). ... Injured ankle (March 24, 1997); missed eight games. ... Strained hamstring (January 24, 1998); missed eight games. ... Lacerated finger (November 24, 1999); missed two games. ... Signed as free agent by Chicago Blackhawks (July 31, 2000).

MISCELLANEOUS: Stopped a penalty shot attempt (vs. Daymond Langkow, November 24, 1998).

						REGULAR SEASON								PLAYOFFS				
Season Team	League	Gms.	Min	W	L	T	GA	SO	Avg.	Gms.	Min.	W	L	GA	SO	Avg.
91-92—Seattle	WHL	14	708	4	7	0	52	0	4.41	—	—	—	—	—	—	—
92-93—Seattle	WHL	52	3151	24	23	3	194	2	3.69	5	333	1	4	18	0	3.24
93-94—Seattle	WHL	51	2849	23	21	3	188	0	3.96	9	567	5	4	40	0	4.23
94-95—Charlotte	ECHL	36	2011	21	9	‡3	114	0	3.40	—	—	—	—	—	—	—
—Providence	AHL	2	82	1	0	0	4	1	2.93	—	—	—	—	—	—	—
95-96—Boston	NHL	1	60	1	0	0	3	0	3.00	—	—	—	—	—	—	—
—Providence	AHL	37	2136	12	16	7	117	1	3.29	2	135	0	2	9	0	4.00
96-97—Providence	AHL	24	1423	9	14	1	83	0	3.50	—	—	—	—	—	—	—
—Boston	NHL	28	1244	8	12	1	69	1	3.33	—	—	—	—	—	—	—
97-98—Providence	AHL	10	575	1	8	1	39	0	4.07	—	—	—	—	—	—	—
—Boston	NHL	14	788	6	3	3	24	1	1.83	—	—	—	—	—	—	—
98-99—Boston	NHL	17	987	7	7	2	43	1	2.61	—	—	—	—	—	—	—
99-00—Boston	NHL	27	1363	4	13	4	72	0	3.17	—	—	—	—	—	—	—
NHL Totals (5 years)		87	4442	26	35	10	211	3	2.85							

TALLINDER, HENRIK — D — SABRES

PERSONAL: Born January 10, 1979, in Stockholm, Sweden. ... 6-3/194. ... Shoots left.

TRANSACTIONS/CAREER NOTES: Selected by Buffalo Sabres in second round (second Sabres pick, 48th overall) of NHL entry draft (June 21, 1997).

					REGULAR SEASON					PLAYOFFS			
Season Team	League	Gms.	G	A	Pts.	PIM	+/-	PP	SH	Gms.	G	A	Pts.	PIM
95-96—AIK Solna Jrs.	Sweden	40	4	13	17	55	...	...	...	—	—	—	—	—
96-97—AIK Solna Jrs.	Sweden						Statistics unavailable.							
—AIK Solna	Sweden	1	0	0	0	0	...	...	...	—	—	—	—	—
97-98—AIK Solna	Sweden	34	0	0	0	26	...	...	...	—	—	—	—	—
98-99—AIK Solna	Sweden	36	0	0	0	30	...	...	...	—	—	—	—	—
99-00—AIK Solna	Sweden	50	0	2	2	59	...	...	...	—	—	—	—	—

TAMER, CHRIS   D   THRASHERS

PERSONAL: Born November 17, 1970, in Dearborn, Mich. ... 6-2/208. ... Shoots left. ... Full Name: Chris Thomas Tamer. ... Name pronounced TAY-muhr.
COLLEGE: Michigan.
TRANSACTIONS/CAREER NOTES: Selected by Pittsburgh Penguins in fourth round (third Penguins pick, 68th overall) of NHL entry draft (June 16, 1990). ... Injured shoulder (March 27, 1994); missed four games. ... Fractured ankle (May 6, 1995); missed eight playoff games. ... Pulled abdominal muscle (December 17, 1995); missed five games. ... Sprained wrist (December 30, 1995); missed five games. ... Fractured jaw (January 17, 1996); missed two games. ... Pulled abdominal muscle (November 22, 1996); missed 20 games. ... Strained hip flexor (January 4, 1997); missed 13 games. ... Strained hip flexor (March 4, 1997); missed four games. ... Traded by Penguins with C Petr Nedved and C Sean Pronger to New York Rangers for RW Alexei Kovalev, C Harry York and future considerations (November 25, 1998). ... Selected by Atlanta Thrashers in NHL expansion draft (June 25, 1999). ... Sprained medial collateral ligament in knee (February 29, 2000); missed six games.

		REGULAR SEASON								PLAYOFFS				
Season Team	League	Gms.	G	A	Pts.	PIM	+/-	PP	SH	Gms.	G	A	Pts.	PIM
87-88—Redford	NAJHL	40	10	20	30	217	...	...	...	—	—	—	—	—
88-89—Redford	NAJHL	31	6	13	19	79	...	...	...	—	—	—	—	—
89-90—Univ. of Michigan	CCHA	42	2	7	9	147	...	...	...	—	—	—	—	—
90-91—Univ. of Michigan	CCHA	45	8	19	27	130	...	...	...	—	—	—	—	—
91-92—Univ. of Michigan	CCHA	43	4	15	19	125	...	...	...	—	—	—	—	—
92-93—Univ. of Michigan	CCHA	39	5	18	23	113	...	...	...	—	—	—	—	—
93-94—Cleveland	IHL	53	1	2	3	160	...	...	...	—	—	—	—	—
—Pittsburgh	NHL	12	0	0	0	9	3	0	0	5	0	0	0	2
94-95—Cleveland	IHL	48	4	10	14	204	...	...	...	—	—	—	—	—
—Pittsburgh	NHL	36	2	0	2	82	0	0	0	4	0	0	0	18
95-96—Pittsburgh	NHL	70	4	10	14	153	20	0	0	18	0	7	7	24
96-97—Pittsburgh	NHL	45	2	4	6	131	-25	0	1	4	0	0	0	4
97-98—Pittsburgh	NHL	79	0	7	7	181	4	0	0	6	0	1	1	4
98-99—Pittsburgh	NHL	11	0	0	0	32	-2	0	0	—	—	—	—	—
—New York Rangers	NHL	52	1	5	6	92	-12	0	0	—	—	—	—	—
99-00—Atlanta	NHL	69	2	8	10	91	-32	0	0	—	—	—	—	—
NHL Totals (7 years)		374	11	34	45	771	-44	0	1	37	0	8	8	52

TANABE, DAVID   D   HURRICANES

PERSONAL: Born July 19, 1980, in Minneapolis. ... 6-1/195. ... Shoots right. ... Full Name: David Michael Tanabe. ... Name pronounced tuh-nah-BEE.
COLLEGE: Wisconsin.
TRANSACTIONS/CAREER NOTES: Selected by Carolina Hurricanes in first round (first Hurricanes pick, 16th overall) of NHL entry draft (June 26, 1999).

		REGULAR SEASON								PLAYOFFS				
Season Team	League	Gms.	G	A	Pts.	PIM	+/-	PP	SH	Gms.	G	A	Pts.	PIM
97-98—U.S. National	NAHL	73	8	21	29	96	...	...	...	—	—	—	—	—
98-99—Univ. of Wisconsin	WCHA	35	10	12	22	44	...	...	...	—	—	—	—	—
99-00—Carolina	NHL	31	4	0	4	14	-4	3	0	—	—	—	—	—
—Cincinnati	IHL	32	0	13	13	14	...	...	...	11	1	4	5	6
NHL Totals (1 year)		31	4	0	4	14	-4	3	0					

TANGUAY, ALEX   LW   AVALANCHE

PERSONAL: Born November 21, 1979, in Ste.-Justine, Que. ... 6-0/190. ... Shoots left. ... Name pronounced tan-GAY.
TRANSACTIONS/CAREER NOTES: Selected by Colorado Avalanche in first round (first Avalanche pick, 12th overall) of NHL entry draft (June 27, 1998). ... Strained neck (March 14, 2000); missed six games.
HONORS: Named to Can.HL All-Rookie team (1996-97). ... Named to QMJHL All-Rookie team (1996-97).

		REGULAR SEASON								PLAYOFFS				
Season Team	League	Gms.	G	A	Pts.	PIM	+/-	PP	SH	Gms.	G	A	Pts.	PIM
96-97—Halifax	QMJHL	70	27	41	68	50	...	...	...	12	4	8	12	8
97-98—Halifax	QMJHL	51	47	38	85	32	...	...	...	5	7	6	13	4
98-99—Halifax	QMJHL	31	27	34	61	30	...	...	...	5	1	2	3	2
—Hershey	AHL	5	1	2	3	2	...	...	...	5	0	2	2	0
99-00—Colorado	NHL	76	17	34	51	22	6	5	0	17	2	1	3	2
NHL Totals (1 year)		76	17	34	51	22	6	5	0	17	2	1	3	2

TAYLOR, CHRIS   C   SABRES

PERSONAL: Born March 6, 1972, in Stratford, Ont. ... 6-0/189. ... Shoots left. ... Brother of Tim Taylor, center, New York Rangers.
TRANSACTIONS/CAREER NOTES: Selected by New York Islanders in second round (second Islanders pick, 27th overall) of NHL entry draft (June 16, 1990). ... Signed as free agent by Los Angeles Kings (August 1, 1997). ... Signed as free agent by Boston Bruins (July 22, 1998). ... Signed as free agent by Buffalo Sabres (August 13, 1999).

		REGULAR SEASON								PLAYOFFS				
Season Team	League	Gms.	G	A	Pts.	PIM	+/-	PP	SH	Gms.	G	A	Pts.	PIM
88-89—London	OHL	62	7	16	23	52	...	...	...	15	0	2	2	15
89-90—London	OHL	66	45	60	105	60	...	...	...	6	3	2	5	6
90-91—London	OHL	65	50	78	128	50	...	...	...	7	4	8	12	6
91-92—London	OHL	66	48	74	122	57	...	...	...	10	8	16	24	9
92-93—Roanoke	ECHL	5	2	1	3	0	...	...	...	—	—	—	—	—
—Capital District	AHL	77	19	43	62	32	...	...	...	4	0	1	1	2

Season Team	League	Gms.	G	A	Pts.	PIM	+/-	PP	SH	Gms.	G	A	Pts.	PIM
93-94—Raleigh	ECHL	2	0	0	0	0	...	...	...	—	—	—	—	—
—Salt Lake City	IHL	79	21	20	41	38	...	...	...	—	—	—	—	—
94-95—Denver	IHL	78	38	48	86	47	...	...	...	14	7	6	13	10
—Roanoke	ECHL	1	0	0	0	2	...	...	...	—	—	—	—	—
—New York Islanders	NHL	10	0	3	3	2	1	0	0	—	—	—	—	—
95-96—Utah	IHL	50	18	23	41	60	...	...	...	22	5	11	16	26
—New York Islanders	NHL	11	0	1	1	2	1	0	0	—	—	—	—	—
96-97—Utah	IHL	71	27	40	67	24	...	...	...	7	1	2	3	0
—New York Islanders	NHL	1	0	0	0	0	0	0	0	—	—	—	—	—
97-98—Utah	IHL	79	28	56	84	66	...	...	...	4	0	2	2	6
98-99—Boston	NHL	37	3	5	8	12	-3	0	1	—	—	—	—	—
—Providence	AHL	21	6	11	17	6	...	...	...	—	—	—	—	—
—Las Vegas	IHL	14	3	12	15	2	...	...	...	—	—	—	—	—
99-00—Rochester	AHL	49	21	28	49	21	...	...	...	—	—	—	—	—
—Buffalo	NHL	11	1	1	2	2	-2	0	0	2	0	0	0	2
NHL Totals (5 years)		70	4	10	14	18	-3	0	1	2	0	0	0	2

TAYLOR, TIM   C   RANGERS

PERSONAL: Born February 6, 1969, in Stratford, Ont. ... 6-1/188. ... Shoots left. ... Full Name: Tim Robertson Taylor. ... Brother of Chris Taylor, center, Buffalo Sabres.

TRANSACTIONS/CAREER NOTES: Selected by Washington Capitals in second round (second Capitals pick, 36th overall) of NHL entry draft (June 11, 1988). ... Traded by Capitals to Vancouver Canucks for C Eric Murano (January 29, 1993). ... Signed as free agent by Detroit Red Wings (July 28, 1993). ... Injured right shoulder (April 5, 1996); missed three games. ... Sprained shoulder (October 15, 1996); missed 16 games. ... Suffered from an illness (April 9, 1997); missed two games. ... Selected by Boston Bruins from Red Wings in NHL waiver draft (September 28, 1997). ... Injured ribs (March 21, 1998); missed one game. ... Injured hip (March 22, 1998); missed two games. ... Sprained ankle (October 14, 1998); missed two games. ... Reinjured ankle (November 13, 1998); missed six games. ... Reinjured ankle (December 10, 1998); missed 14 games. ... Strained groin (April 17, 1999); missed final game of season. ... Signed as free agent by New York Rangers (July 15, 1999). ... Suffered concussion (October 2, 1999); missed two games. ... Injured hand (October 20, 1999); missed one game. ... Injured rib (November 24, 1999); missed one game. ... Suffered from the flu (February 13, 2000); missed two games.

HONORS: Won John B. Sollenberger Trophy (1993-94). ... Named to AHL All-Star first team (1993-94).

MISCELLANEOUS: Member of Stanley Cup championship team (1997). ... Scored on a penalty shot (vs. Jocelyn Thibault, April 15, 1998).

Season Team	League	Gms.	G	A	Pts.	PIM	+/-	PP	SH	Gms.	G	A	Pts.	PIM
86-87—London	OHL	34	7	9	16	11	...	...	...	—	—	—	—	—
87-88—London	OHL	64	46	50	96	66	...	...	...	12	9	9	18	26
88-89—London	OHL	61	34	80	114	93	...	...	...	21	*21	25	*46	58
89-90—Baltimore	AHL	74	22	21	43	63	...	...	...	9	2	2	4	13
90-91—Baltimore	AHL	79	25	42	67	75	...	...	...	5	0	1	1	4
91-92—Baltimore	AHL	65	9	18	27	131	...	...	...	—	—	—	—	—
92-93—Baltimore	AHL	41	15	16	31	49	...	...	...	—	—	—	—	—
—Hamilton	AHL	36	15	22	37	37	...	...	...	—	—	—	—	—
93-94—Adirondack	AHL	79	36	*81	117	86	...	...	...	12	2	10	12	12
—Detroit	NHL	1	1	0	1	0	-1	0	0	—	—	—	—	—
94-95—Detroit	NHL	22	0	4	4	16	3	0	0	6	0	1	1	12
95-96—Detroit	NHL	72	11	14	25	39	11	1	1	18	0	4	4	4
96-97—Detroit	NHL	44	3	4	7	52	-6	0	1	2	0	0	0	0
97-98—Boston	NHL	79	20	11	31	57	-16	1	3	6	0	0	0	10
98-99—Boston	NHL	49	4	7	11	55	-10	0	0	12	0	3	3	8
99-00—New York Rangers	NHL	76	9	11	20	72	-4	0	0	—	—	—	—	—
NHL Totals (7 years)		343	48	51	99	291	-23	2	5	44	0	8	8	34

TENKRAT, PETR   RW   MIGHTY DUCKS

PERSONAL: Born May 31, 1977, in Kladno, Czechoslovakia. ... 6-1/185. ... Shoots right.

TRANSACTIONS/CAREER NOTES: Selected by Mighty Ducks of Anaheim in eighth round (sixth Mighty Ducks pick, 230th overall) of NHL entry draft (June 26, 1999).

Season Team	League	Gms.	G	A	Pts.	PIM	+/-	PP	SH	Gms.	G	A	Pts.	PIM
94-95—Poldi Kladno	Czech Rep.	—	—	—	—	—	...	...	...	1	0	0	0	...
95-96—Poldi Kladno	Czech Rep.	18	0	3	3	...	...	...	...	3	0	0	0	...
96-97—Poldi Kladno	Czech Rep.	43	5	9	14	6	...	...	...	3	0	1	1	0
97-98—Poldi Kladno	Czech Rep.	52	9	10	19	24	...	...	...	—	—	—	—	—
98-99—Velvana Kladno	Czech Rep.	50	21	14	35	32	...	...	...	—	—	—	—	—
99-00—Ilves Tampere	Finland	53	35	14	49	75	...	...	...	3	1	1	2	14

TERRERI, CHRIS   G   DEVILS

PERSONAL: Born November 15, 1964, in Providence, R.I. ... 5-9/170. ... Catches left. ... Full Name: Christopher Arnold Terreri. ... Name pronounced tuh-RAIR-ee.

COLLEGE: Providence.

TRANSACTIONS/CAREER NOTES: Selected by New Jersey Devils in fifth round (third Devils pick, 87th overall) of NHL entry draft (June 8, 1983). ... Strained knee (October 1986). ... Strained lower back (March 21, 1992); missed five games. ... Traded by Devils to San Jose Sharks for second-round pick (traded to Pittsburgh) in 1996 draft (November 14, 1995). ... Injured elbow (March 15, 1996); missed 12 games. ...

Injured wrist (October 20, 1996); missed 12 games. ... Traded by Sharks with D Michal Sykora and RW Ulf Dahlen to Chicago Blackhawks for G Ed Belfour (January 25, 1997). ... Fractured finger (November 11, 1997); missed 20 games. ... Strained groin (January 1, 1998); missed 23 games. ... Traded by Blackhawks to Devils for second-round pick (D Stepan Mokhov) in 1999 draft (August 25, 1998). ... Suffered from the flu (January 14, 1999); missed two games. ... Selected by Minnesota Wild in NHL expansion draft (June 23, 2000). ... Traded by Wild to Devils with ninth-round pick in 2001 draft for D Brad Bombardir (June 23, 2000).

HONORS: Named NCAA Tournament Most Valuable Player (1984-85). ... Named Hockey East Player of the Year (1984-85). ... Named Hockey East Tournament Most Valuable Player (1984-85). ... Named to NCAA All-Tournament team (1984-85). ... Named to NCAA All-America (East) first team (1984-85). ... Named to Hockey East All-Star first team (1984-85). ... Named to NCAA All-America (East) second team (1985-86). ... Named to Hockey East All-Decade team (1994).

MISCELLANEOUS: Member of Stanley Cup championship team (1995 and 2000). ... Stopped a penalty shot attempt (vs. Mike Ricci, November 17, 1990; vs. Murray Craven, October 13, 1991; vs. Rob Zamuner, October 9, 1997). ... Allowed a penalty shot goal (vs. Mario Lemieux, December 31, 1988; vs. Bob Errey, January 5, 1991; vs. Ray Bourque, March 19, 1994).

		REGULAR SEASON								PLAYOFFS						
Season Team	League	Gms.	Min	W	L	T	GA	SO	Avg.	Gms.	Min.	W	L	GA	SO	Avg.
82-83 —Providence College	ECAC	11	529	7	1	0	17	2	1.93	—	—	—	—	—	—	—
83-84 —Providence College	ECAC	10	391	4	2	0	20	0	3.07	—	—	—	—	—	—	—
84-85 —Providence College	Hockey East	41	2515	15	13	5	131	1	3.13	—	—	—	—	—	—	—
85-86 —Providence College	Hockey East	27	1540	6	16	0	96	0	3.74	—	—	—	—	—	—	—
86-87 —Maine	AHL	14	765	4	9	1	57	0	4.47	—	—	—	—	—	—	—
—New Jersey	NHL	7	286	0	3	1	21	0	4.41	—	—	—	—	—	—	—
87-88 —U.S. national team	Int'l	26	1430	17	7	2	81	0	3.40	—	—	—	—	—	—	—
—U.S. Olympic team	Int'l	3	128	1	1	0	14	0	6.56	—	—	—	—	—	—	—
—Utica...........................	AHL	7	399	5	1	0	18	0	2.71	—	—	—	—	—	—	—
88-89 —New Jersey	NHL	8	402	0	4	2	18	0	2.69	—	—	—	—	—	—	—
—Utica...........................	AHL	39	2314	20	15	3	132	0	3.42	2	80	0	1	6	0	4.50
89-90 —New Jersey	NHL	35	1931	15	12	3	110	0	3.42	4	238	2	2	13	0	3.28
90-91 —New Jersey	NHL	53	2970	24	21	7	144	1	2.91	7	428	3	4	21	0	2.94
91-92 —New Jersey	NHL	54	3186	22	22	10	169	1	3.18	7	386	3	3	23	0	3.58
92-93 —New Jersey	NHL	48	2672	19	21	3	151	2	3.39	4	219	1	3	17	0	4.66
93-94 —New Jersey	NHL	44	2340	20	11	4	106	2	2.72	4	200	3	0	9	0	2.70
94-95 —New Jersey	NHL	15	734	3	7	2	31	0	2.53	1	8	0	0	0	0	—
95-96 —New Jersey	NHL	4	210	3	0	0	9	0	2.57	—	—	—	—	—	—	—
—San Jose	NHL	46	2516	13	29	1	155	0	3.70	—	—	—	—	—	—	—
96-97 —San Jose	NHL	22	1200	6	10	3	55	0	2.75	—	—	—	—	—	—	—
—Chicago........................	NHL	7	429	4	1	2	19	0	2.66	2	44	0	0	3	0	4.09
97-98 —Chicago........................	NHL	21	1222	8	10	2	49	2	2.41	—	—	—	—	—	—	—
—Indianapolis	IHL	3	180	2	0	1	3	1	1.00	—	—	—	—	—	—	—
98-99 —New Jersey	NHL	12	726	8	3	1	30	1	2.48	—	—	—	—	—	—	—
99-00 —New Jersey	NHL	12	649	2	9	0	37	0	3.42	—	—	—	—	—	—	—
NHL Totals (13 years)...........		388	21473	147	163	41	1104	9	3.08	29	1523	12	12	86	0	3.39

TEZIKOV, ALEXEI — D — CAPITALS

PERSONAL: Born June 22, 1978, in Togliatti, U.S.S.R. ... 6-1/198. ... Shoots left. ... Name pronounced TEHS-ih-kahf.
TRANSACTIONS/CAREER NOTES: Selected by Buffalo Sabres in fifth round (seventh Sabres pick, 115th overall) of NHL entry draft (June 22, 1996). ... Traded by Sabres with future considerations to Washington Capitals for C Joe Juneau and third-round pick (LW Tim Preston) in 1999 draft (March 23, 1999). ... Suffered back spasms (November 11, 1999); missed three games. ... Suffered from the flu (March 9, 2000); missed two games.
HONORS: Named to QMJHL All-Star second team (1997-98). ... Named to QMJHL All-Rookie Team (1997-98). ... Won Raymond Lagace Trophy (1997-98).

		REGULAR SEASON								PLAYOFFS				
Season Team	League	Gms.	G	A	Pts.	PIM	+/-	PP	SH	Gms.	G	A	Pts.	PIM
95-96 —Lada Togliatti	CIS	14	0	0	0	8	...	...	...	—	—	—	—	—
96-97 —Lada Togliatti	Russian	7	0	0	0	4	...	...	...	—	—	—	—	—
—Tor. Nichny Nov.	Russian	5	0	2	2	2	...	...	...	—	—	—	—	—
97-98 —Moncton	QMJHL	60	15	33	48	144	...	...	...	10	3	8	11	20
98-99 —Moncton	QMJHL	25	9	21	30	52	...	...	...	—	—	—	—	—
—Rochester	AHL	31	3	7	10	41	...	...	...	—	—	—	—	—
—Cincinnati	IHL	5	0	0	0	2	...	...	...	3	0	0	0	10
—Washington	NHL	5	0	0	0	0	-1	0	0	—	—	—	—	—
99-00 —Portland	AHL	53	6	9	15	70	...	...	...	—	—	—	—	—
—Washington	NHL	23	1	1	2	2	-2	1	0	—	—	—	—	—
NHL Totals (2 years)...........		28	1	1	2	2	-3	1	0					

THEODORE, JOSE — G — CANADIENS

PERSONAL: Born September 13, 1976, in Laval, Que. ... 5-11/185. ... Catches right. ... Name pronounced JO-zhay TAY-uh-dohr.
TRANSACTIONS/CAREER NOTES: Selected by Montreal Canadiens in second round (second Canadiens pick, 44th overall) of NHL entry draft (June 28, 1994). ... Strained groin (March 29, 2000); missed three games.
HONORS: Named to QMJHL All-Star second team (1994-95 and 1995-96).
MISCELLANEOUS: Allowed a penalty shot goal (vs. Scott Niedermayer, November 11, 1998).
STATISTICAL NOTES: Tied for NHL lead with .919 save percentage (1999-2000).

		REGULAR SEASON								PLAYOFFS						
Season Team	League	Gms.	Min	W	L	T	GA	SO	Avg.	Gms.	Min.	W	L	GA	SO	Avg.
92-93 —St. Jean......................	QMJHL	34	1776	12	16	2	112	0	3.78	3	175	0	2	11	0	3.77
93-94 —St. Jean......................	QMJHL	57	3225	20	29	6	194	0	3.61	5	296	1	4	18	1	3.65
94-95 —Hull	QMJHL	58	3348	32	22	2	193	5	3.46	21	1263	15	6	59	1	2.80
—Fredericton..................	AHL	—	—	—	—	—	—	—	—	1	60	0	1	3	0	3.00

Season Team	League	REGULAR SEASON								PLAYOFFS						
		Gms.	Min	W	L	T	GA	SO	Avg.	Gms.	Min.	W	L	GA	SO	Avg.
95-96—Hull	QMJHL	48	2803	33	11	2	158	0	3.38	5	300	2	3	20	0	4.00
—Montreal	NHL	1	9	0	0	0	1	0	6.67	—	—	—	—	—	—	—
96-97—Fredericton	AHL	26	1469	12	12	0	87	0	3.55	—	—	—	—	—	—	—
—Montreal	NHL	16	821	5	6	2	53	0	3.87	2	168	1	1	7	0	2.50
97-98—Fredericton	AHL	53	3053	20	23	8	145	2	2.85	4	237	1	3	13	0	3.29
—Montreal	NHL	—	—	—	—	—	—	—	—	3	120	0	1	1	0	.50
98-99—Montreal	NHL	18	913	4	12	0	50	1	3.29	—	—	—	—	—	—	—
—Fredericton	AHL	27	1609	12	13	2	77	2	2.87	13	694	8	5	35	†1	3.03
99-00—Montreal	NHL	30	1655	12	13	2	58	5	2.10	—	—	—	—	—	—	—
NHL Totals (5 years)		65	3398	21	31	4	162	6	2.86	5	288	1	2	8	0	1.67

THERIEN, CHRIS   D   FLYERS

PERSONAL: Born December 14, 1971, in Ottawa. ... 6-4/230. ... Shoots left. ... Name pronounced TAIR-ee-uhn.

HIGH SCHOOL: Northwood School (Lake Placid, N.Y.).

COLLEGE: Providence.

TRANSACTIONS/CAREER NOTES: Selected by Philadelphia Flyers in third round (seventh Flyers pick, 47th overall) of NHL entry draft (June 16, 1990). ... Suffered from the flu (November 3, 1997); missed one game. ... Sprained left knee (April 8, 1998); missed three games. ... Strained shoulder (October 9, 1998); missed first three games of season. ... Bruised left thigh (December 13, 1998); missed three games.

HONORS: Named to Hockey East All-Rookie Team (1990-91). ... Named to Hockey East All-Star second team (1992-93). ... Named to NHL All-Rookie team (1994-95).

Season Team	League	REGULAR SEASON								PLAYOFFS				
		Gms.	G	A	Pts.	PIM	+/-	PP	SH	Gms.	G	A	Pts.	PIM
89-90—Northwood School	N.Y. H.S.	31	35	37	72	54	...	...	...	—	—	—	—	—
90-91—Providence College	Hockey East	36	4	18	22	36	...	...	...	—	—	—	—	—
91-92—Providence College	Hockey East	36	16	25	41	38	...	...	...	—	—	—	—	—
92-93—Providence College	Hockey East	33	8	11	19	52	...	...	...	—	—	—	—	—
—Canadian nat'l team	Int'l	8	1	4	5	8	...	...	...	—	—	—	—	—
93-94—Canadian nat'l team	Int'l	59	7	15	22	46	...	...	...	—	—	—	—	—
—Can. Olympic team	Int'l	4	0	0	0	4	...	...	...	—	—	—	—	—
—Hershey	AHL	6	0	0	0	2	...	...	...	—	—	—	—	—
94-95—Hershey	AHL	34	3	13	16	27	...	...	...	—	—	—	—	—
—Philadelphia	NHL	48	3	10	13	38	8	1	0	15	0	0	0	10
95-96—Philadelphia	NHL	82	6	17	23	89	16	3	0	12	0	0	0	18
96-97—Philadelphia	NHL	71	2	22	24	64	27	0	0	19	1	6	7	6
97-98—Philadelphia	NHL	78	3	16	19	80	5	1	0	5	0	1	1	4
98-99—Philadelphia	NHL	74	3	15	18	48	16	1	0	6	0	0	0	6
99-00—Philadelphia	NHL	80	4	9	13	66	11	1	0	18	0	1	1	12
NHL Totals (6 years)		433	21	89	110	385	83	7	0	75	1	8	9	56

THIBAULT, JOCELYN   G   BLACKHAWKS

PERSONAL: Born January 12, 1975, in Montreal. ... 5-11/170. ... Catches left. ... Name pronounced TEE-boh.

TRANSACTIONS/CAREER NOTES: Selected by Quebec Nordiques in first round (first Nordiques pick, 10th overall) of NHL entry draft (June 26, 1993). ... Sprained shoulder (March 28, 1995); missed 10 games. ... Nordiques franchise moved to Colorado and renamed Avalanche for 1995-96 season (June 21, 1995). ... Traded by Avalanche with LW Martin Rucinsky and RW Andrei Kovalenko to Montreal Canadiens for G Patrick Roy and RW Mike Keane (December 6, 1995). ... Bruised right hand (February 21, 1996); missed two games. ... Fractured finger (October 24, 1996); missed nine games. ... Suffered from the flu (February 3, 1997); missed two games. ... Bruised collarbone (January 8, 1998); missed one game. ... Traded by Canadiens with D Dave Manson and D Brad Brown to Chicago Blackhawks for G Jeff Hackett, D Eric Weinrich, D Alain Nasreddine and fourth-round pick (D Chris Dyment) in 1999 draft (November 16, 1998). ... Fractured finger (November 27, 1999); missed six games.

HONORS: Named to QMJHL All-Rookie team (1991-92). ... Won Can.HL Goaltender-of-the-Year Award (1992-93). ... Won Jacques Plante Trophy (1992-93). ... Won Michel Briere Trophy (1992-93). ... Won Marcel Robert Trophy (1992-93). ... Named to Can.HL All-Star first team (1992-93). ... Named to QMJHL All-Star first team (1992-93).

MISCELLANEOUS: Stopped a penalty shot attempt (vs. Tony Granato, November 25, 1993; vs. Martin Straka, March 16, 1995). ... Allowed a penalty shot goal (vs. Joe Sacco, November 12, 1997; vs. Tim Taylor, April 15, 1998).

Season Team	League	REGULAR SEASON								PLAYOFFS						
		Gms.	Min	W	L	T	GA	SO	Avg.	Gms.	Min.	W	L	GA	SO	Avg.
91-92—Trois-Rivieres	QMJHL	30	1497	14	7	1	77	0	3.09	3	110	1	1	4	0	2.19
92-93—Sherbrooke	QMJHL	56	3190	34	14	5	159	*3	*2.99	15	883	9	6	57	0	3.87
93-94—Quebec	NHL	29	1504	8	13	3	83	0	3.31	—	—	—	—	—	—	—
—Cornwall	AHL	4	240	4	0	0	9	1	2.25	—	—	—	—	—	—	—
94-95—Sherbrooke	QMJHL	13	776	6	6	1	38	1	2.94	—	—	—	—	—	—	—
—Quebec	NHL	18	898	12	2	2	35	1	2.34	3	148	1	2	8	0	3.24
95-96—Colorado	NHL	10	558	3	4	2	28	0	3.01	—	—	—	—	—	—	—
—Montreal	NHL	40	2334	23	13	3	110	3	2.83	6	311	2	4	18	0	3.47
96-97—Montreal	NHL	61	3397	22	24	11	164	1	2.90	3	179	0	3	13	0	4.36
97-98—Montreal	NHL	47	2652	19	15	8	109	2	2.47	2	43	0	0	4	0	5.58
98-99—Montreal	NHL	10	529	3	4	2	23	1	2.61	—	—	—	—	—	—	—
—Chicago	NHL	52	3014	21	26	5	136	4	2.71	—	—	—	—	—	—	—
99-00—Chicago	NHL	60	3438	25	26	7	158	3	2.76	—	—	—	—	—	—	—
NHL Totals (7 years)		327	18324	136	127	43	846	15	2.77	14	681	3	9	43	0	3.79

THINEL, MARC-ANDRE — RW — CANADIENS

PERSONAL: Born March 24, 1981, in St. Jerome, Que. ... 5-11/158. ... Shoots left.

TRANSACTIONS/CAREER NOTES: Selected by Montreal Canadiens in fifth round (sixth Canadiens pick, 145th overall) of NHL entry draft (June 26, 1999).

HONORS: Named to QMJHL All-Star first team (1999-2000).

		REGULAR SEASON								PLAYOFFS				
Season Team	League	Gms.	G	A	Pts.	PIM	+/-	PP	SH	Gms.	G	A	Pts.	PIM
97-98—Victoriaville	QMJHL	58	7	10	17	20	...	...	...	6	0	3	3	4
98-99—Victoriaville	QMJHL	66	45	58	103	16	...	...	...	6	5	3	8	4
99-00—Victoriaville	QMJHL	71	59	73	132	55	...	...	...	6	5	6	11	18

THOMAS, STEVE — RW — MAPLE LEAFS

PERSONAL: Born July 15, 1963, in Stockport, England. ... 5-10/185. ... Shoots left.

TRANSACTIONS/CAREER NOTES: Signed as non-drafted free agent by Toronto Maple Leafs (May 12, 1984). ... Fractured wrist during training camp (September 1984). ... Traded by Maple Leafs with RW Rick Vaive and D Bob McGill to Chicago Blackhawks for LW Al Secord and RW Ed Olczyk (September 3, 1987). ... Pulled stomach muscle (October 1987). ... Separated left shoulder (February 20, 1988) and underwent surgery. ... Pulled back muscle (October 18, 1988). ... Separated right shoulder (December 21, 1988). ... Underwent surgery to repair chronic shoulder separation problem (January 25, 1989). ... Strained right shoulder (September 1990); missed first 11 games of season. ... Traded by Blackhawks with C Adam Creighton to New York Islanders for C Brent Sutter and RW Brad Lauer (October 25, 1991). ... Bruised ribs (March 10, 1992); missed one game. ... Bruised ribs (November 21, 1992); missed three games. ... Suffered neck muscle spasms (January 4, 1994); missed five games. ... Injured back and thumb (January 24, 1995); missed one game. ... Traded by Islanders to New Jersey Devils for RW Claude Lemieux (October 3, 1995). ... Injured head (February 1, 1996); missed one game. ... Suffered from the flu (October 24, 1996); missed two games. ... Strained ankle (November 30, 1996); missed 10 games. ... Strained knee (December 31, 1996); missed 12 games. ... Strained groin (October 23, 1997); missed 20 games. ... Bruised ribs (January 5, 1998); missed four games. ... Suffered back spasms (April 5, 1998); missed three games. ... Signed as free agent by Toronto Maple Leafs (July 12, 1998). ... Suffered back spasms (March 1, 1999); missed one game. ... Fractured toe (March 9, 1999); missed three games. ... Suffered injury (February 29, 2000); missed one game.

HONORS: Won Dudley (Red) Garrett Memorial Trophy (1984-85). ... Named to AHL All-Star first team (1984-85).

RECORDS: Holds NHL career record for most overtime goals—11.

		REGULAR SEASON								PLAYOFFS				
Season Team	League	Gms.	G	A	Pts.	PIM	+/-	PP	SH	Gms.	G	A	Pts.	PIM
81-82—Markham Tier II Jr. A..	OHA	48	68	57	125	113	...	...	...	—	—	—	—	—
82-83—Toronto	OHL	61	18	20	38	42	...	...	...	—	—	—	—	—
83-84—Toronto	OHL	70	51	54	105	77	...	...	...	—	—	—	—	—
84-85—Toronto	NHL	18	1	1	2	2	-13	0	0	—	—	—	—	—
—St. Catharines	AHL	64	42	48	90	56	...	...	...	—	—	—	—	—
85-86—St. Catharines	AHL	19	18	14	32	35	...	...	...	—	—	—	—	—
—Toronto	NHL	65	20	37	57	36	-15	5	0	10	6	8	14	9
86-87—Toronto	NHL	78	35	27	62	114	-3	3	0	13	2	3	5	13
87-88—Chicago	NHL	30	13	13	26	40	1	5	0	3	1	2	3	6
88-89—Chicago	NHL	45	21	19	40	69	-2	8	0	12	3	5	8	10
89-90—Chicago	NHL	76	40	30	70	91	-3	13	0	20	7	6	13	33
90-91—Chicago	NHL	69	19	35	54	129	8	2	0	6	1	2	3	15
91-92—Chicago	NHL	11	2	6	8	26	-3	0	0	—	—	—	—	—
—New York Islanders....	NHL	71	28	42	70	71	11	3	0	—	—	—	—	—
92-93—New York Islanders....	NHL	79	37	50	87	111	3	12	0	18	9	8	17	37
93-94—New York Islanders....	NHL	78	42	33	75	139	-9	17	0	4	1	0	1	8
94-95—New York Islanders....	NHL	47	11	15	26	60	-14	3	0	—	—	—	—	—
95-96—New Jersey	NHL	81	26	35	61	98	-2	6	0	—	—	—	—	—
96-97—New Jersey	NHL	57	15	19	34	46	9	1	0	10	1	1	2	18
97-98—New Jersey	NHL	55	14	10	24	32	4	3	0	6	0	3	3	2
98-99—Toronto	NHL	78	28	45	73	33	26	11	0	17	6	3	9	12
99-00—Toronto	NHL	81	26	37	63	68	1	9	0	12	6	3	9	10
NHL Totals (16 years)		1019	378	454	832	1165	-1	101	0	131	43	44	87	173

THORNTON, JOE — C — BRUINS

PERSONAL: Born July 2, 1979, in London, Ont. ... 6-4/225. ... Shoots left. ... Cousin of Scott Thornton, left winger, San Jose Sharks.

TRANSACTIONS/CAREER NOTES: Selected by Boston Bruins in first round (first Bruins pick, first overall) of NHL entry draft (June 21, 1997). ... Suffered broken forearm prior to 1997-98 season; missed first three games. ... Injured ankle (December 13, 1997); missed 10 games. ... Suffered from viral infection (March 28, 1998); missed six games. ... Suffered chest injury (April 17, 1999); missed final game of regular season and one playoff game. ... Bruised knee (November 20, 1999); missed one game.

HONORS: Won Can.HL Rookie of the Year Award (1995-96). ... Won Emms Family Trophy (1995-96). ... Won Can.HL Top Prospect Award (1996-97). ... Named to Can.HL All-Star second team (1996-97). ... Named to OHL All-Star second team (1996-97).

		REGULAR SEASON								PLAYOFFS				
Season Team	League	Gms.	G	A	Pts.	PIM	+/-	PP	SH	Gms.	G	A	Pts.	PIM
94-95—St. Thomas	Jr. B	50	40	64	104	53	...	...	...	—	—	—	—	—
95-96—Sault Ste. Marie	OHL	66	30	46	76	51	...	...	...	4	1	1	2	11
96-97—Sault Ste. Marie	OHL	59	41	81	122	123	...	...	...	11	11	8	19	24
97-98—Boston	NHL	55	3	4	7	19	-6	0	0	6	0	0	0	9
98-99—Boston	NHL	81	16	25	41	69	3	7	0	11	3	6	9	4
99-00—Boston	NHL	81	23	37	60	82	-5	5	0	—	—	—	—	—
NHL Totals (3 years)		217	42	66	108	170	-8	12	0	17	3	6	9	13

THORNTON, SCOTT   LW   SHARKS

PERSONAL: Born January 9, 1971, in London, Ont. ... 6-3/216. ... Shoots left. ... Full Name: Scott C. Thornton. ... Cousin of Joe Thornton, center, Boston Bruins.

TRANSACTIONS/CAREER NOTES: Selected by Toronto Maple Leafs in first round (first Maple Leafs pick, third overall) of NHL entry draft (June 17, 1989). ... Separated shoulder (January 24, 1991); missed eight games. ... Traded by Maple Leafs with LW Vincent Damphousse, D Luke Richardson, G Peter Ing and future considerations to Edmonton Oilers for G Grant Fuhr, RW/LW Glenn Anderson and LW Craig Berube (September 19, 1991). ... Suffered concussion (November 23, 1991); missed one game. ... Sprained ankle (October 6, 1993); missed 13 games. ... Suffered back spasms (November 21, 1993); missed one game. ... Suffered wrist contusion (April 14, 1994); missed one game. ... Suffered from Cytomegalo virus (January 9, 1996); missed three games. ... Traded by Oilers to Montreal Canadiens for RW Andrei Kovalenko (September 6, 1996). ... Bruised hand (December 28, 1996); missed three games. ... Suffered from the flu (February 10, 1997); missed one game. ... Underwent arthroscopic knee surgery (March 6, 1997); missed five games. ... Separated shoulder (January 3, 1998); missed two games. ... Injured neck (February 7, 1998); missed one game. ... Fractured rib (March 18, 1998); missed eight games. ... Injured shoulder (April 15, 1998); missed three games. ... Strained abdominal muscle (November 3, 1998) and underwent surgery; missed 31 games. ... Suffered from migraines (February 2, 1999); missed three games. ... Suffered back spasms (April 13, 1999); missed one game. ... Injured tricep (September 20, 1999); missed first two games of 1999-2000 season. ... Reinjured tricep (October 8, 1999); missed three games. ... Strained groin (December 12, 1999); missed one game. ... Traded by Canadiens to Dallas Stars for LW Juha Lind (January 22, 2000). ... Suffered from the flu (March 8, 2000); missed one game. ... Suspended for three games for by NHL for high-sticking incident (March 22, 2000). ... Signed as free agent by San Jose Sharks (July 1, 2000).

			REGULAR SEASON								PLAYOFFS				
Season Team	League	Gms.	G	A	Pts.	PIM	+/-	PP	SH		Gms.	G	A	Pts.	PIM
86-87—London Diamonds	OPJHL	31	10	7	17	10	...	...	...		—	—	—	—	—
87-88—Belleville	OHL	62	11	19	30	54	...	...	...		6	0	1	1	2
88-89—Belleville	OHL	59	28	34	62	103	...	...	...		5	1	1	2	6
89-90—Belleville	OHL	47	21	28	49	91	...	...	...		11	2	10	12	15
90-91—Belleville	OHL	3	2	1	3	2	...	...	...		6	0	7	7	14
—Newmarket	AHL	5	1	0	1	4	...	...	...		—	—	—	—	—
—Toronto	NHL	33	1	3	4	30	-15	0	0		—	—	—	—	—
91-92—Edmonton	NHL	15	0	1	1	43	-6	0	0		1	0	0	0	0
—Cape Breton	AHL	49	9	14	23	40	...	...	...		5	1	0	1	8
92-93—Cape Breton	AHL	58	23	27	50	102	...	...	...		16	1	2	3	35
—Edmonton	NHL	9	0	1	1	0	-4	0	0		—	—	—	—	—
93-94—Edmonton	NHL	61	4	7	11	104	-15	0	0		—	—	—	—	—
—Cape Breton	AHL	2	1	1	2	31	...	...	...		—	—	—	—	—
94-95—Edmonton	NHL	47	10	12	22	89	-4	0	1		—	—	—	—	—
95-96—Edmonton	NHL	77	9	9	18	149	-25	0	2		—	—	—	—	—
96-97—Montreal	NHL	73	10	10	20	128	-19	1	1		5	1	0	1	2
97-98—Montreal	NHL	67	6	9	15	158	0	1	0		9	0	2	2	10
98-99—Montreal	NHL	47	7	4	11	87	-2	1	0		—	—	—	—	—
99-00—Montreal	NHL	35	2	3	5	70	-7	0	0		—	—	—	—	—
—Dallas	NHL	30	6	3	9	38	-5	1	0		†23	2	7	9	28
NHL Totals (10 years)		**494**	**55**	**62**	**117**	**896**	**-102**	**4**	**4**		**38**	**3**	**9**	**12**	**40**

TIMANDER, MATTIAS   D   BLUE JACKETS

PERSONAL: Born April 16, 1974, in Solleftea, Sweden. ... 6-3/215. ... Shoots left. ... Name pronounced tih-MAN-duhr.

TRANSACTIONS/CAREER NOTES: Selected by Boston Bruins in seventh round (seventh Bruins pick, 208th overall) of NHL entry draft (June 21, 1992). ... Injured shoulder (November 26, 1996); missed four games. ... Injured finger (November 17, 1997); missed two games. ... Injured shoulder (March 2, 1999); missed two games. ... Reinjured shoulder (March 13, 1999); missed one game. ... Injured shoulder (November 22, 1999); missed 11 games. ... Selected by Columbus Blue Jackets in NHL expansion draft (June 23, 2000).

			REGULAR SEASON								PLAYOFFS				
Season Team	League	Gms.	G	A	Pts.	PIM	+/-	PP	SH		Gms.	G	A	Pts.	PIM
92-93—MoDo Ornskoldsvik	Sweden	1	0	0	0	0	...	...	...		—	—	—	—	—
93-94—MoDo Ornskoldsvik	Sweden	23	2	2	4	6	...	...	...		11	2	0	2	10
94-95—MoDo Ornskoldsvik	Sweden	39	8	9	17	24	...	...	...		—	—	—	—	—
95-96—MoDo Ornskoldsvik	Sweden	37	4	10	14	34	...	...	...		7	1	1	2	8
96-97—Boston	NHL	41	1	8	9	14	-9	0	0		—	—	—	—	—
—Providence	AHL	32	3	11	14	20	...	...	...		10	1	1	2	12
97-98—Boston	NHL	23	1	1	2	6	-9	0	0		—	—	—	—	—
—Providence	AHL	31	3	7	10	25	...	...	...		—	—	—	—	—
98-99—Providence	AHL	43	2	22	24	24	...	...	...		—	—	—	—	—
—Boston	NHL	22	0	6	6	10	4	0	0		4	1	1	2	2
99-00—Boston	NHL	60	0	8	8	22	-11	0	0		—	—	—	—	—
—Hershey	AHL	1	0	0	0	2	...	...	...		—	—	—	—	—
NHL Totals (4 years)		**146**	**2**	**23**	**25**	**52**	**-25**	**0**	**0**		**4**	**1**	**1**	**2**	**2**

TIMONEN, KIMMO   D   PREDATORS

PERSONAL: Born March 18, 1975, in Kuopio, Finland. ... 5-10/196. ... Shoots left. ... Name pronounced KEE-moh TEE-muh-nehn.

TRANSACTIONS/CAREER NOTES: Selected by Los Angeles Kings in 10th round (11th Kings pick, 250th overall) of NHL entry draft (June 26, 1993). ... Rights traded by Kings with D Jan Vopat to Nashville Predators for future considerations (June 26, 1998). ... Lacerated lip (January 26, 1999); missed one game. ... Strained abdominal muscle (December 18, 1999); missed four games. ... Fractured wrist (January 11, 2000); missed 15 games. ... Fractured ankle (March 14, 2000); missed final 12 games of season.

HONORS: Named to play in NHL All-Star Game (2000).

MISCELLANEOUS: Scored on a penalty shot (vs. Jeff Hackett, November 18, 1999).

Season Team	League	REGULAR SEASON								PLAYOFFS				
		Gms.	G	A	Pts.	PIM	+/-	PP	SH	Gms.	G	A	Pts.	PIM
91-92—KalPa Kuopio	Finland	5	0	0	0	0	...	...	...	—	—	—	—	—
92-93—KalPa Kuopio	Finland	33	0	2	2	4	...	...	...	—	—	—	—	—
93-94—KalPa Kuopio	Finland	46	6	7	13	55	...	...	...	—	—	—	—	—
94-95—TPS Turku	Finland	45	3	4	7	10	...	...	...	13	0	1	1	6
95-96—TPS Turku	Finland	48	3	21	24	22	...	...	...	9	1	2	3	12
96-97—TPS Turku	Finland	50	10	14	24	18	...	...	...	12	2	7	9	8
97-98—HIFK Helsinki	Finland	45	10	15	25	59	...	...	...	9	3	4	7	8
—Fin. Olympic team	Int'l	6	0	1	1	2	...	...	...	—	—	—	—	—
98-99—Milwaukee	IHL	29	2	13	15	22	...	...	...	—	—	—	—	—
—Nashville	NHL	50	4	8	12	30	-4	1	0	—	—	—	—	—
99-00—Nashville	NHL	51	8	25	33	26	-5	2	1	—	—	—	—	—
NHL Totals (2 years)		101	12	33	45	56	-9	3	1					

TITOV, GERMAN — C — MIGHTY DUCKS

PERSONAL: Born October 15, 1965, in Moscow, U.S.S.R. ... 6-1/201. ... Shoots left. ... Name pronounced GAIR-muhn TEE-tahf.

TRANSACTIONS/CAREER NOTES: Selected by Calgary Flames in 10th round (10th Flames pick, 252nd overall) of NHL entry draft (June 26, 1993). ... Fractured nose (December 31, 1993); missed four games. ... Bruised hand (February 18, 1994); missed two games. ... Bruised hand (April 2, 1994); missed one game. ... Played in Europe during 1994-95 NHL lockout. ... Pulled groin (March 28, 1995); missed eight games. ... Sore lower back (October 13, 1996); missed one game. ... Injured ankle (January 22, 1997); missed one game. ... Reinjured ankle (March 7, 1997); missed one game. ... Bruised hand (March 11, 1998); missed two games. ... Injured knee (April 7, 1998); missed final six games of season. ... Traded by Flames with C Todd Hlushko to Pittsburgh Penguins for G Ken Wregget and LW Dave Roche (June 17, 1998). ... Injured finger (November 19, 1998); missed one game. ... Bruised knee (November 25, 1998); missed two games. ... Strained hamstring (March 25, 1999); missed three games. ... Reinjured hamstring (April 5, 1999); missed three games. ... Strained groin and suffered from the flu (January 31, 2000); missed six games. ... Traded by Penguins to Edmonton Oilers for C Josef Beranek (March 14, 2000). ... Strained shoulder (March 25, 2000); missed five games. ... Signed as free agent by Mighty Ducks of Anaheim (July 1, 2000).

MISCELLANEOUS: Member of silver-medal-winning Russian Olympic team (1998).

STATISTICAL PLATEAUS: Three-goal games: 1994-95 (1), 1996-97 (1). Total: 2.

Season Team	League	REGULAR SEASON								PLAYOFFS				
		Gms.	G	A	Pts.	PIM	+/-	PP	SH	Gms.	G	A	Pts.	PIM
82-83—Khimik	USSR	16	0	2	2	4	...			—	—	—	—	—
83-84—Khimik	USSR							Did not play.						
84-85—Khimik	USSR							Did not play.						
85-86—Khimik	USSR							Did not play.						
86-87—Khimik	USSR	23	1	0	1	10	...	...	...	—	—	—	—	—
87-88—Khimik	USSR	39	6	5	11	10	...	...	...	—	—	—	—	—
88-89—Khimik	USSR	44	10	3	13	24	...	...	...	—	—	—	—	—
89-90—Khimik	USSR	44	6	14	20	19	...	...	...	—	—	—	—	—
90-91—Khimik	USSR	45	13	11	24	28	...	...	...	—	—	—	—	—
91-92—Khimik	CIS	42	18	13	31	35	...	...	...	—	—	—	—	—
92-93—TPS Turku	Finland	47	25	19	44	49	...	...	...	7	2	1	3	4
93-94—Calgary	NHL	76	27	18	45	28	20	8	3	7	2	1	3	4
94-95—TPS Turku	Finland	14	6	6	12	20	...	...	...	—	—	—	—	—
—Calgary	NHL	40	12	12	24	16	6	3	2	7	5	3	8	10
95-96—Calgary	NHL	82	28	39	67	24	9	13	2	4	0	2	2	0
96-97—Calgary	NHL	79	22	30	52	36	-12	12	0	—	—	—	—	—
97-98—Calgary	NHL	68	18	22	40	38	-1	6	1	—	—	—	—	—
—Russian Oly. team	Int'l	6	1	0	1	6	...	...	...	—	—	—	—	—
98-99—Pittsburgh	NHL	72	11	45	56	34	18	3	1	11	3	5	8	4
99-00—Pittsburgh	NHL	63	17	25	42	34	-3	4	2	—	—	—	—	—
—Edmonton	NHL	7	0	4	4	4	2	0	0	5	1	1	2	0
NHL Totals (7 years)		487	135	195	330	214	39	49	11	34	11	12	23	18

TKACHUK, KEITH — LW — COYOTES

PERSONAL: Born March 28, 1972, in Melrose, Mass. ... 6-2/225. ... Shoots left. ... Full Name: Keith Matthew Tkachuk. ... Name pronounced kuh-CHUHK.

HIGH SCHOOL: Malden (Mass.) Catholic.

COLLEGE: Boston University.

TRANSACTIONS/CAREER NOTES: Selected by Winnipeg Jets in first round (first Jets pick, 19th overall) of NHL entry draft (June 16, 1990). ... Lacerated forearm (November 12, 1993); missed one game. ... Strained groin (October 9, 1995); missed three games. ... Suffered concussion (November 26, 1995); missed one game. ... Suspended two games and fined $1,000 by NHL for stick-swinging incident (March 16, 1996). ... Jets franchise moved to Phoenix and renamed Coyotes for 1996-97 season; NHL approved move on January 18, 1996. ... Suffered from the flu (March 5, 1997); missed one game. ... Injured groin (March 2, 1998); missed two games. ... Suffered hairline fracture of rib (March 12, 1998); missed seven games. ... Injured groin (December 14, 1998); missed two games. ... Fractured ribs (December 20, 1998); missed eight games. ... Strained lower back (February 2, 1999); missed two games. ... Injured neck (December 4, 1999); missed three games. ... Suffered back spasms (December 26, 1999); missed four games. ... Sprained ankle (January 31, 2000); missed one game. ... Sprained ankle (February 12, 2000); missed 16 games. ... Suspended two games by NHL for high-sticking incident (March 24, 2000). ... Sprained ankle (March 29, 2000); missed final six games of regular season.

HONORS: Named to Hockey East All-Rookie team (1990-91). ... Named to NHL All-Star second team (1994-95 and 1997-98). ... Named to THE SPORTING NEWS All-Star first team (1995-96). ... Played in NHL All-Star Game (1997-1999).

MISCELLANEOUS: Captain of Winnipeg Jets (1993-94 and 1994-95). ... Captain of Phoenix Coyotes (1996-97 through 1999-2000). ... Holds Phoenix Coyotes franchise all-time record for penalty minutes (1,400). ... Scored on a penalty shot (vs. Jean-Sebastien Aubin, January 12, 2000). ... Failed to score on a penalty shot (vs. Bob Essensa, January 24, 1998).

STATISTICAL PLATEAUS: Three-goal games: 1993-94 (1), 1996-97 (1), 1997-98 (3), 1998-99 (1). Total: 6. ... Four-goal games: 1995-96 (1), 1996-97 (1). Total: 2. ... Total hat tricks: 8.

T

Season Team	League	REGULAR SEASON								PLAYOFFS				
		Gms.	G	A	Pts.	PIM	+/-	PP	SH	Gms.	G	A	Pts.	PIM
88-89—Malden Catholic H.S. ...	Mass. H.S.	21	30	16	46	...		...		—	—	—	—	—
89-90—Malden Catholic H.S. ...	Mass. H.S.	6	12	14	26	...		...		—	—	—	—	—
90-91—Boston University	Hockey East	36	17	23	40	70		...		—	—	—	—	—
91-92—U.S. national team	Int'l	45	10	10	20	141		...		—	—	—	—	—
—U.S. Olympic team	Int'l	8	1	1	2	12		...		—	—	—	—	—
—Winnipeg	NHL	17	3	5	8	28	0	2	0	7	3	0	3	30
92-93—Winnipeg	NHL	83	28	23	51	201	-13	12	0	6	4	0	4	14
93-94—Winnipeg	NHL	84	41	40	81	255	-12	22	3	—	—	—	—	—
94-95—Winnipeg	NHL	48	22	29	51	152	-4	7	2	—	—	—	—	—
95-96—Winnipeg	NHL	76	50	48	98	156	11	20	2	6	1	2	3	22
96-97—Phoenix..................	NHL	81	*52	34	86	228	-1	9	2	7	6	0	6	7
97-98—Phoenix..................	NHL	69	40	26	66	147	9	11	0	6	3	3	6	10
—U.S. Olympic team	Int'l	4	0	2	2	6		...		—	—	—	—	—
98-99—Phoenix..................	NHL	68	36	32	68	151	22	11	2	7	1	3	4	13
99-00—Phoenix..................	NHL	50	22	21	43	82	7	5	1	5	1	1	2	4
NHL Totals (9 years)..........		576	294	258	552	1400	19	99	12	44	19	9	28	100

TKACZUK, DANIEL   C   FLAMES

PERSONAL: Born June 10, 1979, in Toronto. ... 6-1/197. ... Shoots left. ... Name pronounced kuh-CHOOK.

TRANSACTIONS/CAREER NOTES: Selected by Calgary Flames in first round (first Flames pick, sixth overall) of NHL entry draft (June 21, 1997).

HONORS: Named to OHL All-Star first team (1998-99). ... Named to Can.HL All-Star second team (1998-99).

Season Team	League	REGULAR SEASON								PLAYOFFS				
		Gms.	G	A	Pts.	PIM	+/-	PP	SH	Gms.	G	A	Pts.	PIM
95-96—Barrie........................	OHL	61	22	39	61	38		...		7	1	2	3	8
96-97—Barrie........................	OHL	62	45	48	93	49		...		9	7	2	9	2
97-98—Barrie........................	OHL	57	35	40	75	38		...		6	2	3	5	8
98-99—Barrie........................	OHL	58	43	62	105	58		...		12	7	8	15	10
99-00—Saint John	AHL	80	25	41	66	56		...		3	0	0	0	0

TOCCHET, RICK   RW   FLYERS

PERSONAL: Born April 9, 1964, in Scarborough, Ont. ... 6-0/210. ... Shoots right. ... Name pronounced TAH-kiht.

TRANSACTIONS/CAREER NOTES: Selected by Philadelphia Flyers as underage junior in sixth round (fifth Flyers pick, 121st overall) of NHL entry draft (June 8, 1983). ... Bruised right knee (November 23, 1985); missed seven games. ... Separated left shoulder (February 1988). ... Suspended 10 games by NHL for injuring an opposing player during a fight (October 27, 1988). ... Hyperextended right knee (April 21, 1989). ... Suffered viral infection (November 1989). ... Tore tendon in left groin (January 26, 1991); missed five games. ... Reinjured groin (March 1991); missed five games. ... Sprained knee (November 29, 1991); missed five games. ... Bruised heel (January 18, 1991); missed 10 games. ... Traded by Flyers with G Ken Wregget, D Kjell Samuelsson and third-round pick (C Dave Roche) in 1993 draft to Pittsburgh Penguins for RW Mark Recchi, D Brian Benning and first-round pick (LW Jason Bowen) in 1992 draft (February 19, 1992). ... Fractured jaw (March 15, 1992); missed three games. ... Bruised left foot (October 10, 1992); missed two games. ... Bruised foot (February 8, 1993); missed two games. ... Bruised ribs (November 13, 1993); missed two games. ... Suffered back spasms (December 2, 1993); missed two games. ... Suffered back spasms (December 31, 1993); missed 12 games. ... Injured back (February 21, 1994); missed one game. ... Injured back (February 28, 1994); missed 10 games. ... Traded by Penguins with second-round pick (RW Pavel Rosa) in 1995 draft to Los Angeles Kings for LW Luc Robitaille (July 29, 1994). ... Strained lower back (April 1, 1995); missed five games. ... Suffered back spasms (April 17, 1995); missed six games. ... Suffered back spasms (May 3, 1995); missed one game. ... Traded by Kings to Boston Bruins for LW Kevin Stevens (January 25, 1996). ... Bruised shoulder (November 7, 1996); missed two games. ... Injured knee (November 29, 1996); missed 17 games. ... Traded by Bruins with C Adam Oates and G Bill Ranford to Washington Capitals for G Jim Carey, C Jason Allison, C Anson Carter and third-round pick (RW Lee Goren) in 1997 draft (March 1, 1997). ... Bruised foot (March 1, 1997); missed three games. ... Strained back (April 6, 1997); missed four games. ... Signed as free agent by Phoenix Coyotes (July 8, 1997). ... Injured thumb (October 13, 1997); missed four games. ... Suspended two games and fined $1,000 by NHL for injuring another player (January 23, 1998). ... Suspended five games by NHL for illegal check (January 30, 1998). ... Suspended two games and fined $1,000 by NHL for high-sticking incident (April 14, 1998). ... Traded by Coyotes to Flyers for RW Mikael Renberg (March 8, 2000).

HONORS: Played in NHL All-Star Game (1989-1991 and 1993).

RECORDS: Shares NHL All-Star Game record for fastest goal from start of period—19 seconds (1993, second period).

STATISTICAL PLATEAUS: Three-goal games: 1987-88 (2), 1988-89 (2), 1989-90 (1), 1990-91 (1), 1991-92 (1), 1992-93 (2), 1994-95 (1), 1995-96 (2). Total: 12. ... Four-goal games: 1987-88 (1), 1989-90 (1). Total: 2. ... Total hat tricks: 14.

MISCELLANEOUS: Member of Stanley Cup championship team (1992). ... Captain of Philadelphia Flyers (1991-92). ... Holds Philadelphia Flyers all-time record for most penalty minutes (1,683). ... Failed to score on a penalty shot (vs. Craig Billington, January 6, 1987; vs. Geoff Sarjeant, March 18, 1996).

Season Team	League	REGULAR SEASON								PLAYOFFS				
		Gms.	G	A	Pts.	PIM	+/-	PP	SH	Gms.	G	A	Pts.	PIM
81-82—Sault Ste. Marie	OHL	59	7	15	22	184		...		11	1	1	2	28
82-83—Sault Ste. Marie	OHL	66	32	34	66	146		...		16	4	13	17	*67
83-84—Sault Ste. Marie	OHL	64	44	64	108	209		...		16	*22	14	†36	41
84-85—Philadelphia	NHL	75	14	25	39	181	6	0	0	19	3	4	7	72
85-86—Philadelphia	NHL	69	14	21	35	284	12	3	0	5	1	2	3	26
86-87—Philadelphia	NHL	69	21	26	47	288	16	1	1	26	11	10	21	72
87-88—Philadelphia	NHL	65	31	33	64	301	3	10	2	5	1	4	5	55
88-89—Philadelphia	NHL	66	45	36	81	183	-1	16	1	16	6	6	12	69
89-90—Philadelphia	NHL	75	37	59	96	196	4	15	1	—	—	—	—	—
90-91—Philadelphia	NHL	70	40	31	71	150	2	8	0	—	—	—	—	—
91-92—Philadelphia	NHL	42	13	16	29	102	3	4	0	—	—	—	—	—
—Pittsburgh	NHL	19	14	16	30	49	12	4	1	14	6	13	19	24
92-93—Pittsburgh	NHL	80	48	61	109	252	28	20	4	12	7	6	13	24
93-94—Pittsburgh	NHL	51	14	26	40	134	-15	5	1	6	2	3	5	20

Season Team	League	REGULAR SEASON								PLAYOFFS				
		Gms.	G	A	Pts.	PIM	+/-	PP	SH	Gms.	G	A	Pts.	PIM
94-95—Los Angeles	NHL	36	18	17	35	70	-8	7	1	—	—	—	—	—
95-96—Los Angeles	NHL	44	13	23	36	117	3	4	0	—	—	—	—	—
—Boston	NHL	27	16	8	24	64	7	6	0	5	4	0	4	21
96-97—Boston	NHL	40	16	14	30	67	-3	3	0	—	—	—	—	—
—Washington	NHL	13	5	5	10	31	0	1	0	—	—	—	—	—
97-98—Phoenix	NHL	68	26	19	45	157	1	8	0	6	6	2	8	25
98-99—Phoenix	NHL	81	26	30	56	147	5	6	1	7	0	3	3	8
99-00—Phoenix	NHL	64	12	17	29	67	-5	2	0	—	—	—	—	—
—Philadelphia	NHL	16	3	3	6	23	4	2	0	18	5	6	11	*49
NHL Totals (16 years)		1070	426	486	912	2863	74	125	13	139	52	59	111	465

TOMS, JEFF — LW — ISLANDERS

PERSONAL: Born June 4, 1974, in Swift Current, Sask. ... 6-5/213. ... Shoots left.
TRANSACTIONS/CAREER NOTES: Selected by New Jersey Devils in ninth round (10th Devils pick, 210th overall) of NHL entry draft (June 26, 1993). ... Traded by Devils to Tampa Bay Lightning for fourth-round pick (traded to Calgary) in 1994 draft (May 31, 1994). ... Claimed on waivers by Washington Capitals (November 19, 1997). ... Sprained knee (December 12, 1997); missed 11 games. ... Strained abdominal muscle (January 7, 1999); missed 30 games. ... Signed as free agent by New York Islanders (July 27, 2000).

Season Team	League	REGULAR SEASON								PLAYOFFS				
		Gms.	G	A	Pts.	PIM	+/-	PP	SH	Gms.	G	A	Pts.	PIM
91-92—Sault Ste. Marie	OHL	36	9	5	14	0	...	...	...	16	0	1	1	2
92-93—Sault Ste. Marie	OHL	59	16	23	39	20	...	...	...	16	4	4	8	7
93-94—Sault Ste. Marie	OHL	64	52	45	97	19	...	...	...	14	11	4	15	2
94-95—Atlanta	IHL	40	7	8	15	10	...	...	...	4	0	0	0	4
95-96—Atlanta	IHL	68	16	18	34	18	...	...	...	1	0	0	0	0
—Tampa Bay	NHL	1	0	0	0	0	0	0	0	—	—	—	—	—
96-97—Adirondack	AHL	37	11	16	27	8	...	...	...	4	1	2	3	0
—Tampa Bay	NHL	34	2	8	10	10	2	0	0	—	—	—	—	—
97-98—Tampa Bay	NHL	13	1	2	3	7	-6	0	0	—	—	—	—	—
—Washington	NHL	33	3	4	7	8	-11	0	0	1	0	0	0	0
98-99—Portland	AHL	20	3	7	10	8	...	...	...	—	—	—	—	—
—Washington	NHL	21	1	5	6	2	0	0	0	—	—	—	—	—
99-00—Washington	NHL	20	1	2	3	4	-1	0	0	—	—	—	—	—
—Portland	AHL	33	16	21	37	16	...	...	...	4	1	1	2	2
NHL Totals (5 years)		122	8	21	29	31	-16	0	0	1	0	0	0	0

TORGAJEV, PAVEL — LW

PERSONAL: Born January 25, 1966, in Gorky, U.S.S.R. ... 6-0/207. ... Shoots left. ... Name pronounced PA-vuhl tohr-GAY-ehv.
TRANSACTIONS/CAREER NOTES: Selected by Calgary Flames in 11th round (12th Flames pick, 279th overall) of NHL entry draft (June 29, 1994). ... Bruised hip (November 24, 1995). missed three games. ... Released by Flames (September 30, 1999). ... Resigned by Flames (October 17, 1999). ... Claimed on waivers by Tampa Bay Lightning (November 26, 1999).

Season Team	League	REGULAR SEASON								PLAYOFFS				
		Gms.	G	A	Pts.	PIM	+/-	PP	SH	Gms.	G	A	Pts.	PIM
93-94—TPS Turku	Finland	47	19	11	30	60	...	...	...	—	—	—	—	—
94-95—JyP HT	Finland	50	13	18	31	44	...	...	...	—	—	—	—	—
95-96—Saint John	AHL	16	11	6	17	18	...	...	...	—	—	—	—	—
—Calgary	NHL	41	6	10	16	14	2	0	0	1	0	0	0	0
96-97—Saint John	AHL	5	1	2	3	4	...	...	...	—	—	—	—	—
—Lugan	Switzerland	34	18	21	39	87	...	...	...	—	—	—	—	—
97-98—HC Davos	Switzerland	38	20	27	47	85	...	...	...	17	6	9	15	14
98-99—Fribourg-Gotteron	Switzerland	26	15	11	26	36	...	...	...	—	—	—	—	—
99-00—Calgary	NHL	9	0	2	2	4	0	0	0	—	—	—	—	—
—Tampa Bay	NHL	5	0	2	2	2	1	0	0	—	—	—	—	—
—Long Beach	IHL	36	8	9	17	47	...	...	...	—	—	—	—	—
NHL Totals (2 years)		55	6	14	20	20	3	0	0	1	0	0	0	0

TORY, JEFF — D — STARS

PERSONAL: Born May 9, 1973, in Burnaby, B.C. ... 5-11/190. ... Shoots right.
COLLEGE: Maine.
TRANSACTIONS/CAREER NOTES: Signed as non-drafted free agent by Philadelphia Flyers (July 13, 1999). ... Signed as free agent by Dallas Stars (July 26, 2000).
HONORS: Named to Hockey East All-Star second team (1994-95). ... Named to NCAA All-America (East) second team (1994-95). ... Named to Hockey East All-Star team (1995-96). ... Named to NCAA All-America (East) first team (1995-96). ... Signed as free agent by Philadelphia Flyers (July 26, 2000).

Season Team	League	REGULAR SEASON								PLAYOFFS				
		Gms.	G	A	Pts.	PIM	+/-	PP	SH	Gms.	G	A	Pts.	PIM
94-95—Univ. of Maine	Hockey East	40	13	42	55	22	...	...	...	—	—	—	—	—
95-96—Univ. of Maine	Hockey East	38	4	37	41	36	...	...	...	—	—	—	—	—
96-97—Canadian nat'l team	Int'l	54	8	37	45	30	...	...	...	—	—	—	—	—
—Kentucky	AHL	3	0	2	2	0	...	...	...	—	—	—	—	—
97-98—Houston	IHL	74	11	27	38	35	...	...	...	4	0	1	1	2
98-99—Houston	IHL	79	19	36	55	46	...	...	...	18	2	6	8	8
99-00—Philadelphia	AHL	76	17	41	58	44	...	...	...	5	1	3	4	4

TRAVERSE, PATRICK — D — MIGHTY DUCKS

PERSONAL: Born March 14, 1974, in Montreal. ... 6-4/200. ... Shoots left.
TRANSACTIONS/CAREER NOTES: Selected by Ottawa Senators in third round (third Senators pick, 50th overall) of NHL entry draft (June 20, 1992). ... Suffered concussion (January 30, 1999); missed three games. ... Sprained shoulder (February 20, 1999); missed 13 games. ... Bruised right shoulder (February 17, 2000); missed seven games. ... Traded by Senators to Mighty Ducks of Anaheim for D Joel Kwiatkowski (June 12, 2000).

		REGULAR SEASON								PLAYOFFS				
Season Team	League	Gms.	G	A	Pts.	PIM	+/-	PP	SH	Gms.	G	A	Pts.	PIM
91-92—Shawinigan	QMJHL	59	3	11	14	12	...	...	...	10	0	0	0	4
92-93—Shawinigan	QMJHL	53	5	24	29	24	...	...	...	—	—	—	—	—
—New Haven	AHL	2	0	0	0	2	...	...	...	—	—	—	—	—
—St. Jean	QMJHL	15	1	6	7	0	...	...	...	4	0	1	1	2
93-94—Prin. Edward Island	AHL	3	0	1	1	2	...	...	...	—	—	—	—	—
—St. Jean	QMJHL	66	15	37	52	30	...	...	...	5	0	4	4	4
94-95—Prin. Edward Island	AHL	70	5	13	18	19	...	...	...	7	0	2	2	0
95-96—Prin. Edward Island	AHL	55	4	21	25	32	...	...	...	5	1	2	3	2
—Ottawa	NHL	5	0	0	0	2	-1	0	0	—	—	—	—	—
96-97—Worcester	AHL	24	0	4	4	23	...	...	...	—	—	—	—	—
—Grand Rapids	IHL	10	2	1	3	10	...	...	...	2	0	1	1	2
97-98—Hershey	AHL	71	14	15	29	67	...	...	...	7	1	3	4	4
98-99—Ottawa	NHL	46	1	9	10	22	12	0	0	—	—	—	—	—
99-00—Ottawa	NHL	66	6	17	23	21	17	1	0	6	0	0	0	2
NHL Totals (3 years)		117	7	26	33	45	28	1	0	6	0	0	0	2

TREBIL, DAN — D — ISLANDERS

PERSONAL: Born April 10, 1974, in Bloomington, Minn. ... 6-4/212. ... Shoots right. ... Full Name: Daniel Trebil. ... Name pronounced TREH-buhl.
HIGH SCHOOL: Thomas Jefferson (Bloomington, Minn.).
COLLEGE: Minnesota.
TRANSACTIONS/CAREER NOTES: Selected by New Jersey Devils in sixth round (seventh Devils pick, 138th overall) of NHL entry draft (June 20, 1992). ... Signed as free agent by Mighty Ducks of Anaheim (May 30, 1996). ... Fractured right thumb (December 10, 1997); missed 16 games. ... Traded by Mighty Ducks to Pittsburgh Penguins for fifth-round pick (D Bill Cass) in 2000 draft (March 14, 2000). ... Signed as free agent by New York Islanders (July 28, 2000).
HONORS: Named to NCAA All-America (West) second team (1995-96). ... Named to WCHA All-Star second team (1995-96).

		REGULAR SEASON								PLAYOFFS				
Season Team	League	Gms.	G	A	Pts.	PIM	+/-	PP	SH	Gms.	G	A	Pts.	PIM
89-90—Thomas Jefferson	Minn. H.S.	22	3	6	9	10	...	...	...	—	—	—	—	—
90-91—Thomas Jefferson	Minn. H.S.	23	4	12	16	8	...	...	...	—	—	—	—	—
91-92—Thomas Jefferson	Minn. H.S.	28	7	26	33	6	...	...	...	—	—	—	—	—
92-93—Univ. of Minnesota	WCHA	36	2	11	13	16	...	...	...	—	—	—	—	—
93-94—Univ. of Minnesota	WCHA	42	1	21	22	24	...	...	...	—	—	—	—	—
94-95—Univ. of Minnesota	WCHA	44	10	33	43	10	...	...	...	—	—	—	—	—
95-96—Univ. of Minnesota	WCHA	42	11	35	46	36	...	...	...	—	—	—	—	—
96-97—Baltimore	AHL	49	4	20	24	38	...	...	...	—	—	—	—	—
—Anaheim	NHL	29	3	3	6	23	5	0	0	9	0	1	1	6
97-98—Anaheim	NHL	21	0	1	1	2	-8	0	0	—	—	—	—	—
—Cincinnati	AHL	32	5	15	20	21	...	...	...	—	—	—	—	—
98-99—Cincinnati	AHL	52	6	15	21	31	...	...	...	—	—	—	—	—
—Anaheim	NHL	6	0	0	0	0	-2	0	0	1	0	0	0	2
99-00—Cincinnati	AHL	52	7	21	28	48	...	...	...	—	—	—	—	—
—Pittsburgh	NHL	3	1	0	1	0	2	0	0	—	—	—	—	—
NHL Totals (4 years)		59	4	4	8	25	-3	0	0	10	0	1	1	8

TREMBLAY, YANNICK — D — THRASHERS

PERSONAL: Born November 15, 1975, in Pointe-aux-Trembles, Que. ... 6-2/200. ... Shoots right.
COLLEGE: St. Thomas (N.B.).
TRANSACTIONS/CAREER NOTES: Selected by Toronto Maple Leafs in sixth round (fourth Maple Leafs pick, 145th overall) of NHL entry draft (July 8, 1995). ... Selected by Atlanta Thrashers in NHL expansion draft (June 25, 1999). ... Strained groin (October 23, 1999); missed one game. ... Injured hip (December 8, 1999); missed one game. ... Strained hip flexor (February 7, 2000); missed one game. ... Suffered from the flu (April 8, 2000); missed two games.

		REGULAR SEASON								PLAYOFFS				
Season Team	League	Gms.	G	A	Pts.	PIM	+/-	PP	SH	Gms.	G	A	Pts.	PIM
93-94—St. Thomas Univ.	AUAA	25	2	3	5	10	...	...	...	—	—	—	—	—
94-95—Beauport	QMJHL	70	10	32	42	22	...	...	...	17	6	8	14	6
95-96—Beauport	QMJHL	61	12	33	45	42	...	...	...	20	3	16	19	18
—St. John's	AHL	3	0	1	1	0	...	...	...	—	—	—	—	—
96-97—Sherbrooke	QMJHL	42	21	25	46	212	...	...	...	—	—	—	—	—
—St. John's	AHL	67	7	25	32	34	...	...	...	11	2	9	11	0
—Toronto	NHL	5	0	0	0	0	-4	0	0	—	—	—	—	—
97-98—St. John's	AHL	17	3	6	9	4	...	...	...	4	0	1	1	5
—Toronto	NHL	38	2	4	6	6	-6	1	0	—	—	—	—	—
98-99—Toronto	NHL	35	2	7	9	16	0	0	0	—	—	—	—	—
99-00—Atlanta	NHL	75	10	21	31	22	-42	4	1	—	—	—	—	—
NHL Totals (4 years)		153	14	32	46	44	-52	5	1					

TREPANIER, PASCAL　　　　　　　D/RW　　　　　　　MIGHTY DUCKS

PERSONAL: Born April 9, 1973, in Gaspe, Que. ... 6-0/210. ... Shoots right. ... Name pronounced TREH-puhn-yeh.
TRANSACTIONS/CAREER NOTES: Signed as free agent by Colorado Avalanche (August 30, 1996). ... Selected by Mighty Ducks of Anaheim from Avalanche in NHL waiver draft (October 5, 1998). ... Bruised left leg (March 3, 1999); missed one game. ... Injured anterior cruciate ligament and meniscus in right knee (April 6, 1999) and underwent knee surgery; missed remainder of season. ... Suspended five games by NHL for elbowing incident (October 5, 1999). ... Suffered head injury (December 17, 1999); missed six games. ... Bruised left ankle (March 3, 2000); missed nine games.
HONORS: Named to AHL All-Star second team (1996-97).

		REGULAR SEASON								PLAYOFFS				
Season Team	League	Gms.	G	A	Pts.	PIM	+/-	PP	SH	Gms.	G	A	Pts.	PIM
90-91—Hull	QMJHL	46	3	3	6	56	...	...	...	4	0	2	2	7
91-92—Trois-Rivieres	QMJHL	53	4	18	22	125	...	...	...	15	3	5	8	21
92-93—Sherbrooke	QMJHL	59	15	33	48	130	...	...	...	15	5	7	12	36
93-94—Sherbrooke	QMJHL	48	16	41	57	67	...	...	...	12	1	8	9	14
94-95—Cornwall	AHL	4	0	0	0	9	...	...	...	—	—	—	—	—
—Dayton	ECHL	36	16	28	44	113	...	...	...	—	—	—	—	—
—Kalamazoo	IHL	14	1	2	3	47	...	...	...	—	—	—	—	—
95-96—Cornwall	AHL	70	13	20	33	142	...	...	...	8	1	2	3	24
96-97—Hershey	AHL	73	14	39	53	151	...	...	...	23	6	13	19	59
97-98—Colorado	NHL	15	0	1	1	18	-2	0	0	—	—	—	—	—
—Hershey	AHL	43	13	18	31	105	...	...	...	7	4	2	6	8
98-99—Anaheim	NHL	45	2	4	6	48	0	0	0	—	—	—	—	—
99-00—Anaheim	NHL	37	0	4	4	54	2	0	0	—	—	—	—	—
NHL Totals (3 years)		97	2	9	11	120	0	0	0					

TRNKA, PAVEL　　　　　　　　　D　　　　　　　　　MIGHTY DUCKS

PERSONAL: Born July 27, 1976, in Plzen, Czechoslovakia. ... 6-3/200. ... Shoots left. ... Name pronounced TRIHN-kuh.
TRANSACTIONS/CAREER NOTES: Selected by Mighty Ducks of Anaheim in fifth round (fifth Mighty Ducks pick, 106th overall) of NHL entry draft (June 29, 1994). ... Suffered concussion (January 12, 1998); missed one game. ... Strained groin (December 8, 1999); missed five games. ... Sprained ankle (March 17, 2000); missed final nine games of season.

		REGULAR SEASON								PLAYOFFS				
Season Team	League	Gms.	G	A	Pts.	PIM	+/-	PP	SH	Gms.	G	A	Pts.	PIM
92-93—Skoda Plzen Jrs.	Czech.						Statistics unavailable.							
93-94—Skoda Plzen	Czech Rep.	12	0	1	1	...	...	...	...	—	—	—	—	—
94-95—HC Kladno	Czech Rep.	28	0	5	5	...	...	...	...	—	—	—	—	—
—Interconex Plzen	Czech Rep.	6	0	0	0	...	...	...	...	—	—	—	—	—
95-96—Baltimore	AHL	69	2	6	8	44	...	...	...	6	0	0	0	2
96-97—Baltimore	AHL	69	6	14	20	86	...	...	...	3	0	0	0	2
97-98—Cincinnati	AHL	23	3	5	8	28	...	...	...	—	—	—	—	—
—Anaheim	NHL	48	3	4	7	40	-4	1	0	—	—	—	—	—
98-99—Anaheim	NHL	63	0	4	4	60	-6	0	0	4	0	1	1	2
99-00—Anaheim	NHL	57	2	15	17	34	12	0	0	—	—	—	—	—
NHL Totals (3 years)		168	5	23	28	134	2	1	0	4	0	1	1	2

TROSCHINSKY, ANDREI　　　　　C　　　　　　　　　　　BLUES

PERSONAL: Born February 14, 1978, in Ust-Kamenogorsk, U.S.S.R. ... 6-5/187. ... Shoots left.
TRANSACTIONS/CAREER NOTES: Selected by St. Louis Blues in sixth round (fifth Blues pick, 170th overall) of NHL entry draft (June 27, 1998).

		REGULAR SEASON								PLAYOFFS				
Season Team	League	Gms.	G	A	Pts.	PIM	+/-	PP	SH	Gms.	G	A	Pts.	PIM
95-96—Dynamo-2 Moscow	CIS Div. III						Statistics unavailable.							
96-97—Torpedo Ust-Kam.	Rus. Div. II	9	1	1	2	8	...	...	...	—	—	—	—	—
97-98—Torpedo Ust-Kam.	Rus. Div. II	47	10	16	26	34	...	...	...	—	—	—	—	—
98-99—							Statistics unavailable.							
98-99—Ust-Kamengoresk	Rus. Div. II	16	0	3	3	20	...	...	...	—	—	—	—	—

TRUDEL, JEAN-GUY　　　　　　　　　　　　　　　COYOTES

PERSONAL: Born October 18, 1975, in Cadillac, Que. ... 6-0/190. ... Shoots right.
TRANSACTIONS/CAREER NOTES: Signed as non-drafted free agent by Phoenix Coyotes (July 16, 1999).
HONORS: Named to ECHL All-Star first team (1997-98). ... Named to AHL All-Star second team (1999-2000).

		REGULAR SEASON								PLAYOFFS				
Season Team	League	Gms.	G	A	Pts.	PIM	+/-	PP	SH	Gms.	G	A	Pts.	PIM
95-96—Hull	QMJHL	70	50	71	121	96	...	...	...	17	11	18	29	8
96-97—Peoria	ECHL	37	25	29	54	47	...	...	...	9	9	10	19	22
—San Antonio	IHL	12	1	5	6	4	...	...	...	—	—	—	—	—
—Chicago	IHL	6	1	2	3	2	...	...	...	—	—	—	—	—
97-98—Peoria	ECHL	62	39	74	113	147	...	...	...	3	0	0	0	2
98-99—Kansas City	IHL	76	24	25	49	66	...	...	...	3	1	0	1	0
99-00—Springfield	AHL	72	34	39	73	80	...	...	...	3	0	1	1	4
—Phoenix	NHL	1	0	0	0	0	-1	0	0	—	—	—	—	—
NHL Totals (1 year)		1	0	0	0	0	-1	0	0					

TSELIOS, NIKOS — D — HURRICANES

PERSONAL: Born January 20, 1979, in Oak Park, Ill. ... 6-4/187. ... Shoots left. ... Cousin of Chris Chelios, defenseman, Detroit Red Wings. ... Name pronounced NEE-kohz CHEL-yoz.
TRANSACTIONS/CAREER NOTES: Selected by Carolina Hurricanes in first round (first Hurricanes pick, 22nd overall) of NHL entry draft (June 21, 1997).
HONORS: Named to Can.HL All-Rookie team (1996-97). ... Named to OHL All-Rookie first team (1996-97).

		REGULAR SEASON								PLAYOFFS				
Season Team	League	Gms.	G	A	Pts.	PIM	+/-	PP	SH	Gms.	G	A	Pts.	PIM
95-96—Chicago	MNHL	27	5	8	13	40	...	...	...	—	—	—	—	—
96-97—Belleville	OHL	64	9	37	46	61	...	...	...	—	—	—	—	—
97-98—Belleville	OHL	20	2	10	12	16	...	...	...	—	—	—	—	—
—Plymouth	OHL	41	8	20	28	27	...	...	...	15	1	8	9	27
98-99—Plymouth	OHL	60	21	39	60	60	...	...	...	11	4	10	14	8
99-00—Cincinnati	IHL	80	3	19	22	75	...	...	...	10	0	2	2	4

TSYPLAKOV, VLADIMIR — LW

PERSONAL: Born April 18, 1969, in Moscow, U.S.S.R. ... 6-1/210. ... Shoots left. ... Name pronounced SIHP-luh-kahf.
TRANSACTIONS/CAREER NOTES: Selected by Los Angeles Kings in third round (fourth Kings pick, 59th overall) of NHL entry draft (July 8, 1995). ... Underwent reconstructive surgery on right shoulder (December 14, 1995); missed 45 games. ... Strained abdominal muscle prior to 1995-96 season; missed first nine games of season. ... Strained groin (February 13, 1997); missed three games. ... Fractured right hand (November 11, 1997); missed two games. ... Sprained left knee (February 19, 1999); missed 12 games. ... Traded by Kings to Buffalo Sabres for eighth-round pick (RW Dan Welch) in 2000 draft (January 24, 2000).

		REGULAR SEASON								PLAYOFFS				
Season Team	League	Gms.	G	A	Pts.	PIM	+/-	PP	SH	Gms.	G	A	Pts.	PIM
88-89—Dynamo Minsk	USSR	19	6	1	7	4	...	...	...	—	—	—	—	—
89-90—Dynamo Minsk	USSR	47	11	6	17	20	...	...	...	—	—	—	—	—
90-91—Dynamo Minsk	USSR	28	6	5	11	14	...	...	...	—	—	—	—	—
91-92—Dynamo Minsk	CIS	29	10	9	19	16	...	...	...	—	—	—	—	—
92-93—Detroit	Col.HL	44	33	43	76	20	...	...	...	6	5	4	9	6
—Indianapolis	IHL	11	6	7	13	4	...	...	...	5	1	1	2	2
93-94—Fort Wayne	IHL	63	31	32	63	51	...	...	...	14	6	8	14	16
94-95—Fort Wayne	IHL	79	38	40	78	39	...	...	...	4	2	4	6	2
95-96—Las Vegas	IHL	9	5	6	11	4	...	...	...	—	—	—	—	—
—Los Angeles	NHL	23	5	5	10	4	1	0	0	—	—	—	—	—
96-97—Los Angeles	NHL	67	16	23	39	12	8	1	0	—	—	—	—	—
97-98—Los Angeles	NHL	73	18	34	52	18	15	2	0	4	0	1	1	8
—Belarus Oly. team	Int'l	5	1	1	2	2	...	...	...	—	—	—	—	—
98-99—Los Angeles	NHL	69	11	12	23	32	-7	0	2	—	—	—	—	—
99-00—Los Angeles	NHL	29	6	7	13	4	6	1	0	—	—	—	—	—
—Buffalo	NHL	34	6	13	19	10	17	0	0	5	0	1	1	4
NHL Totals (5 years)		295	62	94	156	80	40	4	2	9	0	2	2	12

TUCKER, DARCY — C — MAPLE LEAFS

PERSONAL: Born March 15, 1975, in Castor, Alta. ... 5-11/185. ... Shoots left.
TRANSACTIONS/CAREER NOTES: Selected by Montreal Canadiens in sixth round (eighth Canadiens pick, 151st overall) of NHL entry draft (June 26, 1993). ... Bruised knee (December 16, 1996); missed one game. ... Traded by Canadiens with RW Stephane Richer and D David Wilkie to Tampa Bay Lightning for C Patrick Poulin, RW Mick Vukota and D Igor Ulanov (January 15, 1998). ... Suspended two games by NHL for spearing incident (December 28, 1999). ... Traded by Lightning with fourth-round pick (RW Miguel Delisle) in 2000 draft to Toronto Maple Leafs for RW Mike Johnson, D Marek Posmyk and fifth- (RW Pavel Sedov) and sixth-round (D Aaron Gionet) picks in 2000 draft (February 9, 2000).
HONORS: Won Stafford Smythe Memorial Trophy (1993-94). ... Named to Can.HL All-Star first team (1993-94). ... Named to WHL (West) All-Star first team (1993-94 and 1994-95). ... Named to Memorial Cup All-Star team (1993-94 and 1994-95). ... Won Dudley (Red) Garrett Memorial Trophy (1995-96).

		REGULAR SEASON								PLAYOFFS				
Season Team	League	Gms.	G	A	Pts.	PIM	+/-	PP	SH	Gms.	G	A	Pts.	PIM
91-92—Kamloops	WHL	26	3	10	13	42	...	...	...	9	0	1	1	16
92-93—Kamloops	WHL	67	31	58	89	155	...	...	...	13	7	6	13	34
93-94—Kamloops	WHL	66	52	88	140	143	...	...	...	19	9	*18	*27	43
94-95—Kamloops	WHL	64	64	73	137	94	...	...	...	21	16	15	31	19
95-96—Fredericton	AHL	74	29	64	93	174	...	...	...	7	7	3	10	14
—Montreal	NHL	3	0	0	0	0	-1	0	0	—	—	—	—	—
96-97—Montreal	NHL	73	7	13	20	110	-5	1	0	4	0	0	0	0
97-98—Montreal	NHL	39	1	5	6	57	-6	0	0	—	—	—	—	—
—Tampa Bay	NHL	35	6	8	14	89	-8	1	1	—	—	—	—	—
98-99—Tampa Bay	NHL	82	21	22	43	176	-34	8	2	—	—	—	—	—
99-00—Tampa Bay	NHL	50	14	20	34	108	-15	1	0	—	—	—	—	—
—Toronto	NHL	27	7	10	17	55	3	0	2	12	4	2	6	15
NHL Totals (5 years)		309	56	78	134	595	-66	11	5	16	4	2	6	15

TUGNUTT, RON — G — BLUE JACKETS

PERSONAL: Born October 22, 1967, in Scarborough, Ont. ... 5-11/160. ... Catches left. ... Full Name: Ronald Frederick Bradley Tugnutt.
TRANSACTIONS/CAREER NOTES: Selected by Quebec Nordiques as underage junior in fourth round (fourth Nordiques pick, 81st overall) of NHL entry draft (June 21, 1986). ... Sprained ankle (March 1989). ... Sprained knee (January 13, 1990). ... Injured hamstring (January 29, 1991); missed 11 games. ... Traded by Nordiques with LW Brad Zavisha to Edmonton Oilers for LW Martin Rucinsky (March 10, 1992). ... Selected by Mighty Ducks of Anaheim in NHL expansion draft (June 24, 1993). ... Traded by Mighty Ducks to Montreal Canadiens for C

Stephan Lebeau (February 20, 1994). ... Strained knee (January 28, 1995); missed five games. ... Signed as free agent by Washington Capitals (September 20, 1995). ... Signed as free agent by Ottawa Senators (July 17, 1996). ... Strained hip flexor (January 31, 1998); missed two games. ... Injured right knee (March 6, 1999); missed two games. ... Strained left knee prior to 1999-2000 season; missed two games. ... Reinjured left knee (November 28, 1999); missed three games. ... Suffered illness (January 28, 2000); missed three games. ... Traded by Senators with D Janne Laukkanen to Pittsburgh Penguins for G Tom Barrasso (March 14, 2000). ... Signed as free agent by Columbus Blue Jackets (July 4, 2000).

HONORS: Won F.W. (Dinty) Moore Trophy (1984-85). ... Shared Dave Pinkney Trophy with Kay Whitmore (1985-86). ... Named to OHL All-Star first team (1986-87). ... Played in NHL All-Star Game (1999).

MISCELLANEOUS: Holds Ottawa Senators all-time records for wins (72), goals-against average (2.32) and shutouts (13). ... Stopped penalty shot attempt (vs. Dave McLlwain, October 12, 1991; vs. Cam Neely, October 15, 1993; vs. Brett Harkins, March 22, 1997; vs. Steve Sullivan, March 6, 1999). ... Allowed penalty shot goal (vs. Benoit Hogue, February 16, 1993; vs. Jason Allison, March 24, 1999).

			REGULAR SEASON							PLAYOFFS					
Season Team	League	Gms.	Min	W	L	T	GA	SO	Avg.	Gms.	Min.	W	L	GA	SO	Avg.
84-85—Peterborough	OHL	18	938	7	4	2	59	0	3.77	—	—	—	—	—	—	—
85-86—Peterborough	OHL	26	1543	18	7	0	74	1	2.88	3	133	2	0	6	0	2.71
86-87—Peterborough	OHL	31	1891	21	7	2	88	2	*2.79	6	374	3	3	21	1	3.37
87-88—Quebec	NHL	6	284	2	3	0	16	0	3.38	—	—	—	—	—	—	—
—Fredericton	AHL	34	1962	20	9	4	118	1	3.61	4	204	1	2	11	0	3.24
88-89—Quebec	NHL	26	1367	10	10	3	82	0	3.60	—	—	—	—	—	—	—
—Halifax	AHL	24	1368	14	7	2	79	1	3.46	—	—	—	—	—	—	—
89-90—Quebec	NHL	35	1978	5	24	3	152	0	4.61	—	—	—	—	—	—	—
—Halifax	AHL	6	366	1	5	0	23	0	3.77	—	—	—	—	—	—	—
90-91—Halifax	AHL	2	100	0	1	0	8	0	4.80	—	—	—	—	—	—	—
—Quebec	NHL	56	3144	12	†29	10	212	1	4.05	—	—	—	—	—	—	—
91-92—Quebec	NHL	30	1583	6	17	3	106	1	4.02	—	—	—	—	—	—	—
—Halifax	AHL	8	447	3	3	1	30	0	4.03	—	—	—	—	—	—	—
—Edmonton	NHL	3	124	1	1	0	10	0	4.84	2	60	0	0	3	0	3.00
92-93—Edmonton	NHL	26	1338	9	12	2	93	0	4.17	—	—	—	—	—	—	—
93-94—Anaheim	NHL	28	1520	10	15	1	76	1	3.00	—	—	—	—	—	—	—
—Montreal	NHL	8	378	2	3	1	24	0	3.81	1	59	0	1	5	0	5.08
94-95—Montreal	NHL	7	346	1	3	1	18	0	3.12	—	—	—	—	—	—	—
95-96—Portland	AHL	58	3067	21	23	6	171	2	3.35	13	781	7	6	36	1	2.77
96-97—Ottawa	NHL	37	1991	17	15	1	93	3	2.80	7	425	3	4	14	1	1.98
97-98—Ottawa	NHL	42	2236	15	14	8	84	3	2.25	2	74	0	1	6	0	4.86
98-99—Ottawa	NHL	43	2508	22	10	8	75	3	*1.79	2	118	0	2	6	0	3.05
99-00—Ottawa	NHL	44	2435	18	12	8	103	4	2.54	—	—	—	—	—	—	—
—Pittsburgh	NHL	7	374	4	2	0	15	0	2.41	11	746	6	5	22	2	1.77
NHL Totals (12 years)		398	21606	134	170	49	1159	15	3.22	25	1482	9	13	56	3	2.27

TUOMAINEN, MARKO   RW

PERSONAL: Born April 25, 1972, in Kuopio, Finland. ... 6-3/218. ... Shoots right. ... Name pronounced too-oh-MIGH-nehn.
COLLEGE: Clarkson (N.Y.).
TRANSACTIONS/CAREER NOTES: Selected by Edmonton Oilers in ninth round (10th Oilers pick, 205th overall) of NHL entry draft (June 20, 1992). ... Signed as free agent by Los Angeles Kings (June 1, 1999). ... Suffered eye injury (October 20, 1999); missed seven games.
HONORS: Named to ECAC All-Star first team (1992-93 and 1994-95). ... Named to NCAA All-America (East) second team (1994-95).

			REGULAR SEASON							PLAYOFFS				
Season Team	League	Gms.	G	A	Pts.	PIM	+/-	PP	SH	Gms.	G	A	Pts.	PIM
89-90—KalPa Kuopio	Finland	5	0	0	0	0	...	...	...	—	—	—	—	—
90-91—KalPa Kuopio	Finland	30	2	1	3	2	...	...	...	8	0	0	0	6
91-92—Clarkson	ECAC	29	11	13	24	34	...	...	...	—	—	—	—	—
92-93—Clarkson	ECAC	35	25	30	55	26	...	...	...	—	—	—	—	—
93-94—Clarkson	ECAC	34	23	29	52	60	...	...	...	—	—	—	—	—
94-95—Clarkson	ECAC	37	23	37	60	34	...	...	...	—	—	—	—	—
—Edmonton	NHL	4	0	0	0	0	0	0	0	—	—	—	—	—
95-96—Cape Breton	AHL	58	25	35	60	71	...	...	...	—	—	—	—	—
96-97—Hamilton	AHL	79	31	21	52	130	...	...	...	22	7	5	12	4
97-98—HIFK Helsinki	Finland	46	13	9	22	20	...	...	...	9	0	3	3	0
98-99—HIFK Helsinki	Finland	48	11	17	28	*173	...	...	...	11	1	3	4	*46
99-00—Los Angeles	NHL	63	9	8	17	80	-12	2	1	1	0	0	0	0
NHL Totals (2 years)		67	9	8	17	80	-12	2	1	1	0	0	0	0

TURCO, MARTY   G   STARS

PERSONAL: Born August 13, 1975, in Sault Ste. Marie, Ont. ... 5-11/183. ... Catches left.
HIGH SCHOOL: St. Mary's College (Sault Ste. Marie, Ont.).
COLLEGE: Michigan.
TRANSACTIONS/CAREER NOTES: Selected by Dallas Stars in fifth round (fourth Stars pick, 124th overall) of NHL entry draft (June 29, 1994).
HONORS: Named CCHA Rookie of the Year (1994-95). ... Named to NCAA All-Tournament team (1995-96 and 1997-98). ... Named to CCHA All-Star first team (1996-1997). ... Named to NCAA All-America (West) first team (1996-97). ... Named NCAA Tournament Most Valuable Player (1997-98). ... Named to CCHA All-Star second team (1997-98). ... Won Garry F. Longman Memorial Trophy (1998-99).

			REGULAR SEASON							PLAYOFFS					
Season Team	League	Gms.	Min	W	L	T	GA	SO	Avg.	Gms.	Min.	W	L	GA	SO	Avg.
93-94—Cambridge Jr. B	OHA	34	1937	...	...	...	114	0	3.53	—	—	—	—	—	—	—
94-95—Univ. of Michigan	CCHA	37	2064	27	7	1	95	1	2.76	—	—	—	—	—	—	—
95-96—Univ. of Michigan	CCHA	42	2334	34	7	1	84	5	2.16	—	—	—	—	—	—	—
96-97—Univ. of Michigan	CCHA	41	2296	33	4	4	87	4	2.27	—	—	—	—	—	—	—
97-98—Univ. of Michigan	CCHA	*45	*2640	*33	10	1	95	3	2.16	—	—	—	—	—	—	—
98-99—Michigan	IHL	54	3127	24	17	‡10	136	1	2.61	5	300	2	3	14	0	2.80
99-00—Michigan	IHL	60	3399	28	*27	‡7	*139	*7	2.45	—	—	—	—	—	—	—

TURCOTTE, DARREN　　　　C

PERSONAL: Born March 2, 1968, in Boston. ... 6-0/183. ... Shoots left. ... Name pronounced TUHR-kaht.

TRANSACTIONS/CAREER NOTES: Selected by New York Rangers as underage junior in sixth round (sixth Rangers pick, 114th overall) of NHL entry draft (June 21, 1986). ... Separated shoulder (October 1987); missed 34 games. ... Suffered concussion (March 1989). ... Sprained left ankle (October 1989). ... Injured knee (April 11, 1990). ... Broke left foot (April 27, 1990). ... Suffered contusion above left ankle (November 13, 1991); missed two games. ... Bruised right foot (March 4, 1992); missed one game. ... Reinjured right foot (March 9, 1992); missed two games. ... Sprained ankle (January 2, 1993); missed one game. ... Suffered hairline fracture in foot (February 10, 1993); missed 11 games. ... Traded by Rangers with D James Patrick to Hartford Whalers for RW Steve Larmer, LW Nick Kypreos and sixth-round pick (C Yuri Litvinov) in 1994 draft (November 2, 1993). ... Underwent medial collateral ligament surgery (December 9, 1993); missed 50 games. ... Traded by Whalers to Winnipeg Jets for RW Nelson Emerson (October 6, 1995). ... Injured hand (December 19, 1995); missed one game. ... Strained right thumb (February 13, 1996); missed six games. ... Traded by Jets with second-round pick (traded to Chicago) in 1996 draft to San Jose Sharks for C Craig Janney (March 18, 1996). ... Injured back (April 6, 1996); missed one game. ... Strained knee (October 5, 1996); missed three games. ... Injured ear (January 24, 1997); missed 13 games. ... Suffered from an illness (March 11, 1997); missed one game. ... Traded by Sharks to St. Louis Blues for LW Stephane Matteau (July 25, 1997). ... Bruised shoulder (October 11, 1997); missed 11 games. ... Suffered from the flu (December 18, 1997); missed one game. ... Suffered from the flu (January 10, 1998); missed one game. ... Bruised hand (March 1, 1998); missed two games. ... Traded by Blues to Nashville Predators for second-round pick (traded to Florida) in 1999 draft (June 27, 1998). ... Suffered back spasms (October 17, 1998); missed two games. ... Suffered back spasms (December 19, 1998); missed one game. ... Tore medial collateral ligament in knee (January 14, 1999); missed 24 games. ... Tore anterior cruciate ligament in knee (March 14, 1999); missed final 15 games of season. ... Injured knee (November 30, 1999); missed 51 games. ... Announced retirement (March 27, 2000).

HONORS: Played in NHL All-Star Game (1991).

MISCELLANEOUS: Failed to score on a penalty shot (vs. Wendell Young, December 29, 1991; vs. Rick Tabaracci, March 22, 1998).

STATISTICAL PLATEAUS: Three-goal games: 1988-89 (1), 1989-90 (1), 1990-91 (1), 1991-92 (1). Total: 4.

Season Team	League		REGULAR SEASON									PLAYOFFS			
		Gms.	G	A	Pts.	PIM	+/-	PP	SH		Gms.	G	A	Pts.	PIM
84-85—North Bay	OHL	62	33	32	65	28	...	...	...		8	0	2	2	0
85-86—North Bay	OHL	62	35	37	72	35	...	...	...		10	3	4	7	8
86-87—North Bay	OHL	55	30	48	78	20	...	...	...		18	12	8	20	6
87-88—Colorado	IHL	8	4	3	7	9	...	...	...		6	2	6	8	8
—North Bay	OHL	32	30	33	63	16	...	...	...		4	3	0	3	4
88-89—Denver	IHL	40	21	28	49	32	...	...	...		—	—	—	—	—
—New York Rangers	NHL	20	7	3	10	4	0	2	0		1	0	0	0	0
89-90—New York Rangers	NHL	76	32	34	66	32	3	10	1		10	1	6	7	4
90-91—New York Rangers	NHL	74	26	41	67	37	-5	15	2		6	1	2	3	0
91-92—New York Rangers	NHL	71	30	23	53	57	11	13	1		8	4	0	4	6
92-93—New York Rangers	NHL	71	25	28	53	40	-3	7	3		—	—	—	—	—
93-94—New York Rangers	NHL	13	2	4	6	13	-2	0	0		—	—	—	—	—
—Hartford	NHL	19	2	11	13	4	-11	0	0		—	—	—	—	—
94-95—Hartford	NHL	47	17	18	35	22	1	3	1		—	—	—	—	—
95-96—Winnipeg	NHL	59	16	16	32	26	-3	2	0		—	—	—	—	—
—San Jose	NHL	9	6	5	11	4	8	0	1		—	—	—	—	—
96-97—San Jose	NHL	65	16	21	37	16	-8	3	1		—	—	—	—	—
97-98—St. Louis	NHL	62	12	6	18	26	6	3	0		10	0	0	0	2
98-99—Nashville	NHL	40	4	5	9	16	-11	0	0		—	—	—	—	—
99-00—Nashville	NHL	9	0	1	1	4	0	0	0		—	—	—	—	—
NHL Totals (12 years)		635	195	216	411	301	-14	58	10		35	6	8	14	12

TUREK, ROMAN　　　　G　　　　BLUES

PERSONAL: Born May 21, 1970, in Pisek, Czechoslovakia. ... 6-3/200. ... Catches right. ... Name pronounced ROH-mahn TOOR-ihk.

TRANSACTIONS/CAREER NOTES: Selected by Minnesota North Stars in sixth round (sixth North Stars pick, 113th overall) of NHL entry draft (June 16, 1990). ... North Stars franchise moved from Minnesota to Dallas and renamed Stars for 1993-94 season. ... Strained groin (January 8, 1997); missed three games. ... Injured knee (March 31, 1997); missed seven games. ... Strained groin (November 15, 1997); missed 12 games. ... Strained groin (December 10, 1998); missed three games. ... Sprained knee (April 14, 1999); missed final three games of season. ... Traded by Stars to St. Louis Blues for second-round pick (D Dan Jancevski) in 1999 draft (June 20, 1999).

HONORS: Shared William M. Jennings Trophy with Ed Belfour (1998-99). ... Played in NHL All-Star Game (2000). ... Named to THE SPORTING NEWS All-Star Team (1999-2000). ... Named to NHL All-Star second team (1999-2000). ... Won William M. Jennings Trophy (1999-2000).

MISCELLANEOUS: Member of Stanley Cup championship team (1999). ... Stopped a penalty shot attempt (vs. Jeff Friesen, December 30, 1999). ... Allowed a penalty shot goal (vs. Alexander Korolyuk, January 11, 2000; vs. Martin Straka, January 19, 2000). ... Holds St. Louis Blues all-time record for goals-against average (1.95).

STATISTICAL NOTES: Led NHL in winning percentage with .627 (1999-2000).

Season Team	League		REGULAR SEASON								PLAYOFFS					
		Gms.	Min	W	L	T	GA	SO	Avg.		Gms.	Min.	W	L	GA	SO	Avg.
90-91—Budejovice	Czech.	26	1244	...	...	...	98	0	4.73		—	—	—	—	—	—	—
91-92—Budejovice	Czech Dv.II						Did not play.									
92-93—Budejovice	Czech.	43	2555	...	...	...	121	...	2.84		—	—	—	—	—	—	—
93-94—Budejovice	Czech Rep.	44	2584	...	...	...	111	...	2.58		3	180	...	...	12	...	4.00
—Czech Rep. Oly. team	Int'l	2	120	2	0	0	4	2	2.00		—	—	—	—	—	—	—
94-95—Budejovice	Czech Rep.	44	2587	...	...	...	119	...	2.76		9	498	...	...	25	...	3.01
95-96—Nurnberg	Germany	48	2787	...	...	...	154	...	3.32		5	338	...	...	14	...	2.49
96-97—Michigan	IHL	29	1555	8	13	‡4	77	0	2.97		—	—	—	—	—	—	—
—Dallas	NHL	6	263	3	1	0	9	0	2.05		—	—	—	—	—	—	—
97-98—Dallas	NHL	23	1324	11	10	1	49	1	2.22		—	—	—	—	—	—	—
—Michigan	IHL	2	119	1	1	0	5	0	2.52		—	—	—	—	—	—	—
98-99—Dallas	NHL	26	1382	16	3	3	48	1	2.08		—	—	—	—	—	—	—
99-00—St. Louis	NHL	67	3960	42	15	9	129	*7	1.95		7	415	3	4	19	0	2.75
NHL Totals (4 years)		122	6929	72	29	13	235	9	2.03		7	415	3	4	19	0	2.75

TURGEON, PIERRE — C — BLUES

PERSONAL: Born August 28, 1969, in Rouyn, Que. ... 6-1/199. ... Shoots left. ... Brother of Sylvain Turgeon, left winger with four NHL teams (1983-84 through 1994-95). ... Name pronounced TUHR-zhaw.

TRANSACTIONS/CAREER NOTES: Selected by Buffalo Sabres as underage junior in first round (first Sabres pick, first overall) of NHL entry draft (June 13, 1987). ... Traded by Sabres with RW Benoit Hogue, D Uwe Krupp and C Dave McLlwain to New York Islanders for C Pat LaFontaine, LW Randy Wood, D Randy Hillier and future considerations; Sabres later received fourth-round pick (D Dean Melanson) in 1992 draft to complete deal (October 25, 1991). ... Injured right knee (January 3, 1992); missed three games. ... Separated shoulder (April 28, 1993); missed six playoff games. ... Suffered from tendinitis in right wrist (October 5, 1993); missed one game. ... Suffered from the flu (December 29, 1993); missed one game. ... Fractured cheekbone (January 26, 1994); missed 12 games. ... Traded by Islanders with D Vladimir Malakhov to Montreal Canadiens for LW Kirk Muller, D Mathieu Schneider and C Craig Darby (April 5, 1995). ... Strained shoulder (November 8, 1995); missed thigh (October 24, 1996); missed one game. ... Traded by Canadiens with C Craig Conroy and D Rory Fitzpatrick to St. Louis Blues for LW Shayne Corson, D Murray Baron and fifth-round pick (D Gennady Razin) in 1997 draft (October 29, 1996). ... Fractured right forearm (October 4, 1997); missed 22 games. ... Fractured hand (December 14, 1998); missed 14 games. ... Suffered back spasms (November 20, 1999); missed four games. ... Suffered from the flu (January 11, 2000); missed one game. ... Injured thumb (January 29, 2000); missed 24 games.

HONORS: Won Michel Bergeron Trophy (1985-86). ... Won Michael Bossy Trophy (1986-87). ... Played in NHL All-Star Game (1990, 1993, 1994 and 1996). ... Won Lady Byng Memorial Trophy (1992-93). ... Named to play in NHL All-Star Game (2000); replaced by LW Ray Whitney due to injury.

MISCELLANEOUS: Captain of Montreal Canadiens (1995-96 through October 29, 1996). ... Scored on a penalty shot (vs. Patrick Roy, October 17, 1990; vs. Pat Jablonski, November 7, 1992). ... Failed to score on a penalty shot (vs. Steve Shields, December 30, 1999).

STATISTICAL PLATEAUS: Three-goal games: 1989-90 (1), 1990-91 (1), 1991-92 (2), 1992-93 (4), 1993-94 (2), 1994-95 (1), 1995-96 (1), 1998-99 (1), 1999-00 (1). Total: 14.

Season Team	League	REGULAR SEASON								PLAYOFFS				
		Gms.	G	A	Pts.	PIM	+/-	PP	SH	Gms.	G	A	Pts.	PIM
85-86—Granby	QMJHL	69	47	67	114	31	...	...	...	—	—	—	—	—
86-87—Granby	QMJHL	58	69	85	154	8	...	...	...	7	9	6	15	15
87-88—Buffalo	NHL	76	14	28	42	34	-8	8	0	6	4	3	7	4
88-89—Buffalo	NHL	80	34	54	88	26	-2	19	0	5	3	5	8	2
89-90—Buffalo	NHL	80	40	66	106	29	10	17	1	6	2	4	6	2
90-91—Buffalo	NHL	78	32	47	79	26	14	13	2	6	3	1	4	6
91-92—Buffalo	NHL	8	2	6	8	4	-1	0	0	—	—	—	—	—
—New York Islanders	NHL	69	38	49	87	16	8	13	0	—	—	—	—	—
92-93—New York Islanders	NHL	83	58	74	132	26	-1	24	0	11	6	7	13	0
93-94—New York Islanders	NHL	69	38	56	94	18	14	10	4	4	0	1	1	0
94-95—New York Islanders	NHL	34	13	14	27	10	-12	3	2	—	—	—	—	—
—Montreal	NHL	15	11	9	20	4	12	2	0	—	—	—	—	—
95-96—Montreal	NHL	80	38	58	96	44	19	17	1	6	2	4	6	2
96-97—Montreal	NHL	9	1	10	11	2	4	0	0	—	—	—	—	—
—St. Louis	NHL	69	25	49	74	12	4	5	0	5	1	1	2	2
97-98—St. Louis	NHL	60	22	46	68	24	13	6	0	10	4	4	8	2
98-99—St. Louis	NHL	67	31	34	65	36	4	10	0	13	4	9	13	6
99-00—St. Louis	NHL	52	26	40	66	8	30	8	0	7	0	7	7	0
NHL Totals (13 years)		929	423	640	1063	319	108	155	10	79	29	46	75	26

TVERDOVSKY, OLEG — D — MIGHTY DUCKS

PERSONAL: Born May 18, 1976, in Donetsk, U.S.S.R. ... 6-0/200. ... Shoots left. ... Name pronounced OH-lehg teh-vuhr-DAHV-skee.

TRANSACTIONS/CAREER NOTES: Selected by Mighty Ducks of Anaheim in first round (first Mighty Ducks pick, second overall) of NHL entry draft (June 28, 1994). ... Suffered from pink eye (March 15, 1995); missed two games. ... Traded by Mighty Ducks with C Chad Kilger and third-round pick (D Per-Anton Lundstrom) in 1996 draft to Winnipeg Jets for C Marc Chouinard, RW Teemu Selanne and fourth-round pick (traded to Toronto) in 1996 draft (February 7, 1996). ... Jets franchise moved to Phoenix and renamed Coyotes for 1996-97 season; NHL approved move on January 18, 1996. ... Pulled rib muscle (December 23, 1997); missed one game. ... Traded by Coyotes to Mighty Ducks for C Travis Green and first-round pick (C Scott Kelman) in 1999 draft (June 26, 1999).

HONORS: Played in NHL All-Star Game (1997).

Season Team	League	REGULAR SEASON								PLAYOFFS				
		Gms.	G	A	Pts.	PIM	+/-	PP	SH	Gms.	G	A	Pts.	PIM
92-93—Soviet Wings	CIS	21	0	1	1	6	...	...	...	6	0	0	0	...
93-94—Soviet Wings	CIS	46	4	10	14	22	...	...	...	3	1	0	1	2
94-95—Brandon	WHL	7	1	4	5	4	...	...	...	—	—	—	—	—
—Anaheim	NHL	36	3	9	12	14	-6	1	1	—	—	—	—	—
95-96—Anaheim	NHL	51	7	15	22	35	0	2	0	—	—	—	—	—
—Winnipeg	NHL	31	0	8	8	6	-7	0	0	6	0	1	1	0
96-97—Phoenix	NHL	82	10	45	55	30	-5	3	1	7	0	1	1	0
97-98—Hamilton	AHL	9	8	6	14	2	...	...	...	—	—	—	—	—
—Phoenix	NHL	46	7	12	19	12	1	4	0	6	0	7	7	0
98-99—Phoenix	NHL	82	7	18	25	32	11	2	0	6	0	2	2	6
99-00—Anaheim	NHL	82	15	36	51	30	5	5	0	—	—	—	—	—
NHL Totals (6 years)		410	49	143	192	159	-1	17	2	25	0	11	11	6

ULANOV, IGOR — D — OILERS

PERSONAL: Born October 1, 1969, in Kraskokamsk, U.S.S.R. ... 6-3/211. ... Shoots right. ... Name pronounced EE-gohr yoo-LAH-nahf.

TRANSACTIONS/CAREER NOTES: Selected by Winnipeg Jets in 10th round (eighth Jets pick, 203rd overall) of NHL entry draft (June 22, 1991). ... Suffered back spasms (March 7, 1992); missed five games. ... Fractured foot (March 16, 1995); missed 19 games. ... Traded by Jets with C Mike Eagles to Washington Capitals for third-round (traded to Dallas Stars) and fifth-round (G Brian Elder) picks in 1995 draft (April 7, 1995). ... Traded by Capitals to Chicago Blackhawks for third-round pick (G Dave Weninger) in 1996 draft (October 17, 1995). ... Traded by Blackhawks with LW Patrick Poulin and second-round pick (D Jeff Paul) in 1996 draft to Tampa Bay Lightning for D Enrico Ciccone (March

T

U

20, 1996). ... Injured ribs (October 5, 1996); missed three games. ... Strained groin (February 14, 1997); missed six games. ... Traded by Lightning with C Patrick Poulin and RW Mick Vukota to Montreal Canadiens for RW Stephane Richer, C Darcy Tucker and D David Wilkie (January 15, 1998). ... Tore ligaments in left knee (January 21, 1998); missed remainder of season. ... Fractured left foot (November 3, 1999); missed 13 games. ... Traded by Canadiens with D Alain Nasreddine to Edmonton Oilers for D Christian LaFlamme and D Mathieu Descoteaux (March 9, 2000).

Season Team	League	REGULAR SEASON								PLAYOFFS				
		Gms.	G	A	Pts.	PIM	+/-	PP	SH	Gms.	G	A	Pts.	PIM
90-91 —Khimik	USSR	41	2	2	4	52	...	...	...	—	—	—	—	—
91-92 —Khimik	CIS	27	1	4	5	24	...	...	...	—	—	—	—	—
—Winnipeg	NHL	27	2	9	11	67	5	0	0	7	0	0	0	39
—Moncton	AHL	3	0	1	1	16	...	...	...	—	—	—	—	—
92-93 —Moncton	AHL	9	1	3	4	26	...	...	...	—	—	—	—	—
—Fort Wayne	IHL	3	0	1	1	29	...	...	...	—	—	—	—	—
—Winnipeg	NHL	56	2	14	16	124	6	0	0	4	0	0	0	4
93-94 —Winnipeg	NHL	74	0	17	17	165	-11	0	0	—	—	—	—	—
94-95 —Winnipeg	NHL	19	1	3	4	27	-2	0	0	—	—	—	—	—
—Washington	NHL	3	0	1	1	2	3	0	0	2	0	0	0	4
95-96 —Indianapolis	IHL	1	0	0	0	0	...	...	...	—	—	—	—	—
—Chicago	NHL	53	1	8	9	92	12	0	0	—	—	—	—	—
—Tampa Bay	NHL	11	2	1	3	24	-1	0	0	5	0	0	0	15
96-97 —Tampa Bay	NHL	59	1	7	8	108	2	0	0	—	—	—	—	—
97-98 —Tampa Bay	NHL	45	2	7	9	85	-5	1	0	—	—	—	—	—
—Montreal	NHL	4	0	1	1	12	-2	0	0	10	1	4	5	12
98-99 —Montreal	NHL	76	3	9	12	109	-3	0	0	—	—	—	—	—
99-00 —Montreal	NHL	43	1	5	6	76	-11	0	0	—	—	—	—	—
—Edmonton	NHL	14	0	3	3	10	-3	0	0	5	0	0	0	6
NHL Totals (9 years)		484	15	85	100	901	-10	1	0	33	1	4	5	80

VAIC, LUBOMIR   C   CANUCKS

PERSONAL: Born March 6, 1977, in Spisska Nova Ves, Czechoslovakia. ... 5-9/165. ... Shoots left. ... Name pronounced VAZ.
TRANSACTIONS/CAREER NOTES: Selected by Vancouver Canucks in ninth round (eighth Canucks pick, 227th overall) of the NHL entry draft (June 22, 1996). ... Injured shoulder (January 15, 2000); missed nine games.

Season Team	League	REGULAR SEASON								PLAYOFFS				
		Gms.	G	A	Pts.	PIM	+/-	PP	SH	Gms.	G	A	Pts.	PIM
93-94 —Poprad	Slovakia	28	10	6	16	10	...	...	...	—	—	—	—	—
94-95 —Spisska Nova Ves	Slovakia	19	5	4	9	2	...	...	...	—	—	—	—	—
95-96 —HC Kosice	Slovakia	36	7	19	26	10	...	...	...	—	—	—	—	—
96-97 —HC Kosice	Slovakia	36	13	12	25	...	...	...	...	7	2	0	2	...
97-98 —Syracuse	AHL	50	12	15	27	22	...	...	...	3	0	0	0	4
—Vancouver	NHL	5	1	1	2	2	-2	0	0	—	—	—	—	—
98-99 —Spisska Nova Ves	Slovakia	35	20	22	42	42	...	...	...	—	—	—	—	—
—HC Kosice	Slovakia	—	—	—	—	—	...	...	...	11	2	3	5	8
99-00 —Syracuse	AHL	63	13	29	42	42	...	...	...	4	0	3	3	8
—Vancouver	NHL	4	0	0	0	0	0	0	0	—	—	—	—	—
NHL Totals (2 years)		9	1	1	2	2	-2	0	0					

VALICEVIC, ROB   C   PREDATORS

PERSONAL: Born January 6, 1971, in Detroit. ... 6-2/192. ... Shoots right. ... Full Name: Robert Valicevic.
COLLEGE: Lake Superior State (Mich.).
TRANSACTIONS/CAREER NOTES: Selected by New York Islanders in sixth round (sixth Islanders pick, 114th overall) of NHL entry draft (June 22, 1991). ... Signed as free agent by Nashville Predators (June 8, 1998). ... Suffered concussion (January 31, 2000); missed two games.
STATISTICAL PLATEAUS: Three-goal games: 1999-00 (1).

Season Team	League	REGULAR SEASON								PLAYOFFS				
		Gms.	G	A	Pts.	PIM	+/-	PP	SH	Gms.	G	A	Pts.	PIM
91-92 —Lake Superior State	CCHA	32	8	4	12	12	...	...	...	—	—	—	—	—
92-93 —Lake Superior State	CCHA	43	21	20	41	28	...	...	...	—	—	—	—	—
93-94 —Lake Superior State	CCHA	45	18	20	38	46	...	...	...	—	—	—	—	—
94-95 —Lake Superior State	CCHA	37	10	22	32	40	...	...	...	—	—	—	—	—
95-96 —Louisiana	ECHL	60	42	20	62	85	...	...	...	5	2	3	5	8
—Springfield	AHL	2	0	0	0	2	...	...	...	—	—	—	—	—
96-97 —Houston	IHL	58	11	12	23	42	...	...	...	12	1	3	4	11
—Louisiana	ECHL	8	7	2	9	21	...	...	...	—	—	—	—	—
97-98 —Houston	IHL	72	29	28	57	47	...	...	...	4	2	0	2	2
98-99 —Houston	IHL	57	16	33	49	62	...	...	...	19	7	10	17	8
—Nashville	NHL	19	4	2	6	2	4	0	0	—	—	—	—	—
99-00 —Nashville	NHL	80	14	11	25	21	-11	2	1	—	—	—	—	—
NHL Totals (2 years)		99	18	13	31	23	-7	2	1					

VALIQUETTE, STEPHEN   G   ISLANDERS

PERSONAL: Born August 20, 1977, in Etobicoke, Ont. ... 6-5/205. ... Catches left.
TRANSACTIONS/CAREER NOTES: Selected by Los Angeles Kings in eighth round (14th Kings pick, 190th overall) of NHL entry draft (June 22, 1996). ... Signed as free agent by New York Islanders (September 9, 1998).

Season Team	League	Gms.	Min	W	L	T	GA	SO	Avg.	Gms.	Min.	W	L	GA	SO	Avg.
94-95—Sudbury	OHL	4	138	2	0	0	6	0	2.61	—	—	—	—	—	—	—
95-96—Sudbury	OHL	39	1887	13	16	2	123	0	3.91	—	—	—	—	—	—	—
96-97—Sudbury	OHL	61	3311	21	29	7	*232	1	4.20	—	—	—	—	—	—	—
97-98—Sudbury	OHL	14	807	5	7	1	50	0	3.72	—	—	—	—	—	—	—
—Erie	OHL	28	1525	16	7	3	65	3	2.56	7	467	3	4	15	1	1.93
98-99—Hampton Roads	ECHL	31	1713	18	7	‡3	84	1	2.94	2	60	0	1	7	0	7.00
—Lowell	AHL	1	59	0	1	0	3	0	3.05	—	—	—	—	—	—	—
99-00—Providence	AHL	1	60	1	0	0	3	0	3.00	—	—	—	—	—	—	—
—Trenton	ECHL	12	692	5	6	‡1	36	1	3.12	—	—	—	—	—	—	—
—Lowell	AHL	14	727	8	5	0	36	0	2.97	—	—	—	—	—	—	—
—New York Islanders	NHL	6	193	2	0	0	6	0	1.87	—	—	—	—	—	—	—
NHL Totals (1 year)		6	193	2	0	0	6	0	1.87							

VALK, GARRY   LW   MAPLE LEAFS

PERSONAL: Born November 27, 1967, in Edmonton. ... 6-1/200. ... Shoots left. ... Full Name: Garry P. Valk. ... Name pronounced VAHLK.
COLLEGE: North Dakota.
TRANSACTIONS/CAREER NOTES: Selected by Vancouver Canucks in sixth round (fifth Canucks pick, 108th overall) of NHL entry draft (June 13, 1987). ... Sprained thumb (November 24, 1991); missed one game. ... Sprained shoulder (January 21, 1992); missed eight games. ... Sprained knee (February 26, 1993); missed 12 games. ... Selected by Mighty Ducks of Anaheim in NHL waiver draft (October 3, 1993). ... Suffered concussion (December 5, 1993); missed one game. ... Suffered post-concussion syndrome (December 5, 1993); missed four games. ... Sprained left knee (January 16, 1995); missed 10 games. ... Injured right eye (December 7, 1995); missed one game. ... Injured ear (December 22, 1995); missed one game. ... Traded by Mighty Ducks to Pittsburgh Penguins for D J.J. Daigneault (February 21, 1997). ... Bruised ribs (March 16, 1997); missed five games. ... Injured knee (April 11, 1997); missed one game. ... Suffered charley horse (October 1, 1997); missed two games. ... Injured groin (October 24, 1997); missed three games. ... Strained muscle in abdomen (March 5, 1998); missed 13 games. ... Signed as free agent by Toronto Maple Leafs (October 6, 1998). ... Strained neck (November 25, 1998); missed two games. ... Strained abdominal muscle (January 20, 1999); missed two games. ... Strained back (February 6, 1999); missed one game. ... Suffered injury (November 9, 1999); missed two games. ... Suffered injury (March 18, 2000); missed one game. ... Suffered injury (March 25, 2000); missed five games.
STATISTICAL PLATEAUS: Three-goal games: 1995-96 (1).

Season Team	League	Gms.	G	A	Pts.	PIM	+/-	PP	SH	Gms.	G	A	Pts.	PIM
85-86—Sherwood Park	AJHL	40	20	26	46	116	...	...	...	—	—	—	—	—
86-87—Sherwood Park	AJHL	59	42	44	86	204	...	...	...	—	—	—	—	—
87-88—Univ. of North Dakota	WCHA	38	23	12	35	64	...	...	...	—	—	—	—	—
88-89—Univ. of North Dakota	WCHA	40	14	17	31	71	...	...	...	—	—	—	—	—
89-90—Univ. of North Dakota	WCHA	43	22	17	39	92	...	...	...	—	—	—	—	—
90-91—Vancouver	NHL	59	10	11	21	67	-23	1	0	5	0	0	0	20
—Milwaukee	IHL	10	12	4	16	13	...	...	...	3	0	0	0	2
91-92—Vancouver	NHL	65	8	17	25	56	3	2	1	4	0	0	0	5
92-93—Vancouver	NHL	48	6	7	13	77	6	0	0	7	0	1	1	12
—Hamilton	AHL	7	3	6	9	6	...	...	...	—	—	—	—	—
93-94—Anaheim	NHL	78	18	27	45	100	8	4	1	—	—	—	—	—
94-95—Anaheim	NHL	36	3	6	9	34	-4	0	0	—	—	—	—	—
95-96—Anaheim	NHL	79	12	12	24	125	8	1	1	—	—	—	—	—
96-97—Anaheim	NHL	53	7	7	14	53	-2	0	0	—	—	—	—	—
—Pittsburgh	NHL	17	3	4	7	25	-6	0	0	—	—	—	—	—
97-98—Pittsburgh	NHL	39	2	1	3	33	-3	0	0	—	—	—	—	—
98-99—Toronto	NHL	77	8	21	29	53	8	1	0	17	3	4	7	22
99-00—Toronto	NHL	73	10	14	24	44	-2	0	1	12	1	2	3	14
NHL Totals (10 years)		624	87	127	214	667	-7	9	4	45	4	7	11	73

VALTONEN, TOMEK   LW   RED WINGS

PERSONAL: Born January 8, 1980, in Piotrkow Trybunalski, Poland. ... 6-1/198. ... Shoots left.
TRANSACTIONS/CAREER NOTES: Selected by Detroit Red Wings in second round (third Red Wings pick, 56th overall) of NHL entry draft (June 27, 1998).

Season Team	League	Gms.	G	A	Pts.	PIM	+/-	PP	SH	Gms.	G	A	Pts.	PIM
95-96—Ilves Tampere	Finland Jr.	12	7	7	14	28	...	...	...	—	—	—	—	—
96-97—Ilves Tampere	Finland Jr.	27	10	9	19	82	...	...	...	3	0	1	1	6
97-98—Ilves Tampere	Finland	19	1	0	1	14	...	...	...	3	0	0	0	0
—Kiek.-Karhut Joensuu	Finland Div. 2	6	1	2	3	39	...	...	...	—	—	—	—	—
—Ilves Tampere	Finland Jr.	13	3	2	5	36	...	...	...	—	—	—	—	—
98-99—Plymouth	OHL	43	8	16	24	53	...	...	...	7	1	0	1	0
99-00—Jokerit	Finland	41	0	3	3	63	...	...	...	9	1	0	1	8

VAN ACKER, ERIC   D   BRUINS

PERSONAL: Born March 1, 1979, in St. Jean, Que. ... 6-5/220. ... Shoots left.
TRANSACTIONS/CAREER NOTES: Selected by Boston Bruins in ninth round (11th Bruins pick, 218th overall) in NHL entry draft (June 21, 1997).

Season Team	League	Gms.	G	A	Pts.	PIM	+/-	PP	SH	Gms.	G	A	Pts.	PIM
96-97—Chicoutimi	QMJHL	69	1	5	6	141	...	...	...	16	0	0	0	4
97-98—Chicoutimi	QMJHL	49	1	5	6	136	...	...	...	6	0	0	0	14
98-99—Baie-Comeau	QMJHL	65	1	6	7	192	...	...	...	—	—	—	—	—
99-00—Providence	AHL	4	0	0	0	2	...	...	...	—	—	—	—	—
—Greenville	ECHL	46	0	8	8	112	...	...	...	13	1	0	1	37

VAN ALLEN, SHAUN — C — STARS

PERSONAL: Born August 29, 1967, in Calgary. ... 6-1/204. ... Shoots left. ... Full Name: Shaun Kelly Van Allen.
HIGH SCHOOL: Walter Murray (Saskatoon, Sask.).
TRANSACTIONS/CAREER NOTES: Selected by Edmonton Oilers in fifth round (fifth Oilers pick, 105th overall) of NHL entry draft (June 13, 1987). ... Suffered concussion (January 9, 1993); missed 11 games. ... Signed as free agent by Mighty Ducks of Anaheim (July 22, 1993). ... Suffered back spasms (February 7, 1995); missed two games. ... Suffered from the flu (May 1, 1995); missed one game. ... Dislocated right thumb (November 15, 1995); missed 21 games. ... Suffered back spasms (February 7, 1996); missed four games. ... Traded by Mighty Ducks with D Jason York to Ottawa Senators for C Ted Drury and rights to D Marc Moro (October 1, 1996). ... Suffered back spasms (February 2, 1998); missed one game. ... Strained left knee (December 30, 1999); missed one game. ... Strained muscle in abdomen (January 12, 2000); missed five games. ... Signed as free agent by Dallas Stars (July 12, 2000).
HONORS: Named to AHL All-Star second team (1990-91). ... Won John B. Sollenberger Trophy (1991-92). ... Named to AHL All-Star first team (1991-92).
MISCELLANEOUS: Failed to score on a penalty shot (vs. Eric Fichaud, December 1, 1998).

Season Team	League		REGULAR SEASON								PLAYOFFS			
		Gms.	G	A	Pts.	PIM	+/-	PP	SH		Gms.	G	A	Pts.	PIM
84-85—Swift Current	SAJHL	61	12	20	32	136	...	...	...		—	—	—	—	—
85-86—Saskatoon	WHL	55	12	11	23	43	...	...	...		13	4	8	12	28
86-87—Saskatoon	WHL	72	38	59	97	116	...	...	...		11	4	6	10	24
87-88—Nova Scotia	AHL	19	4	10	14	17	...	...	...		4	1	1	2	4
—Milwaukee	IHL	40	14	28	42	34	...	...	...		—	—	—	—	—
88-89—Cape Breton	AHL	76	32	42	74	81	...	...	...		—	—	—	—	—
89-90—Cape Breton	AHL	61	25	44	69	83	...	...	...		4	0	2	2	8
90-91—Edmonton	NHL	2	0	0	0	0	0	0	0		—	—	—	—	—
—Cape Breton	AHL	76	25	75	100	182	...	...	...		4	0	1	1	8
91-92—Cape Breton	AHL	77	29	*84	*113	80	...	...	...		5	3	7	10	14
92-93—Cape Breton	AHL	43	14	62	76	68	...	...	...		15	8	9	17	18
—Edmonton	NHL	21	1	4	5	6	-2	0	0		—	—	—	—	—
93-94—Anaheim	NHL	80	8	25	33	64	0	2	2		—	—	—	—	—
94-95—Anaheim	NHL	45	8	21	29	32	-4	1	1		—	—	—	—	—
95-96—Anaheim	NHL	49	8	17	25	41	13	0	0		—	—	—	—	—
96-97—Ottawa	NHL	80	11	14	25	35	-8	1	1		7	0	1	1	4
97-98—Ottawa	NHL	80	4	15	19	48	4	0	0		11	0	1	1	10
98-99—Ottawa	NHL	79	6	11	17	30	3	0	1		4	0	0	0	0
99-00—Ottawa	NHL	75	9	19	28	37	20	0	2		6	0	1	1	9
NHL Totals (9 years)		**511**	**55**	**126**	**181**	**293**	**26**	**4**	**7**		**28**	**0**	**3**	**3**	**23**

VAN DRUNEN, DAVID — D

PERSONAL: Born January 31, 1976, in Sherwood Park, Alta. ... 5-11/206. ... Shoots right. ... Name pronounced van DROO-nehn.
TRANSACTIONS/CAREER NOTES: Signed as non-drafted free agent by Ottawa Senators (May 2, 1997).
HONORS: Named to WHL (East) All-Star second team (1996-97).

Season Team	League		REGULAR SEASON								PLAYOFFS			
		Gms.	G	A	Pts.	PIM	+/-	PP	SH		Gms.	G	A	Pts.	PIM
92-93—Sherwood Park	AJHL	32	3	16	19	114	...	...	...		—	—	—	—	—
93-94—Prince Albert	WHL	63	3	10	13	95	...	...	...		—	—	—	—	—
94-95—Prince Albert	WHL	71	2	14	16	132	...	...	...		15	3	4	7	36
95-96—Prince Albert	WHL	70	10	23	33	172	...	...	...		18	1	5	6	37
96-97—Prince Albert	WHL	72	18	47	65	216	...	...	...		0	0	4	4	24
97-98—Baton Rouge	ECHL	59	8	22	30	107	...	...	...		—	—	—	—	—
—Detroit	IHL	1	0	0	0	2	...	...	...		—	—	—	—	—
—Hershey	AHL	5	0	0	0	2	...	...	...		—	—	—	—	—
—Portland	AHL	4	0	0	0	2	...	...	...		—	—	—	—	—
98-99—Saginaw	UHL	63	5	17	22	126	...	...	...		—	—	—	—	—
—Cincinnati	IHL	1	0	0	0	0	...	...	...		—	—	—	—	—
—Dayton	ECHL	9	2	4	6	12	...	...	...		4	0	0	0	12
99-00—Mobile	ECHL	29	1	9	10	78	...	...	...		5	1	1	2	14
—Grand Rapids	IHL	36	0	6	6	76	...	...	...		1	0	0	0	2
—Ottawa	NHL	1	0	0	0	0	0	0	0		—	—	—	—	—
NHL Totals (1 year)		**1**	**0**	**0**	**0**	**0**	**0**	**0**	**0**		—	—	—	—	—

VAN IMPE, DARREN — D — BRUINS

PERSONAL: Born May 18, 1973, in Saskatoon, Sask. ... 6-1/205. ... Shoots left. ... Name pronounced VAN-IHMP.
TRANSACTIONS/CAREER NOTES: Selected by New York Islanders in seventh round (seventh Islanders pick, 170th overall) of NHL entry draft (June 26, 1993). ... Traded by Islanders to Mighty Ducks of Anaheim for ninth-round pick (LW Mike Broda) in 1995 draft (September 2, 1994). ... Claimed on waivers by Boston Bruins (November 26, 1997). ... Strained shoulder (January 7, 1998); missed one game. ... Hyperextended elbow (November 29, 1998); missed two games. ... Separated shoulder (February 9, 1999); missed 12 games. ... Sprained ankle (March 25, 1999); missed four games. ... Suffered concussion (April 4, 2000); missed final three games of season.
HONORS: Named to WHL (East) All-Star first team (1992-93 and 1993-94).

Season Team	League		REGULAR SEASON								PLAYOFFS			
		Gms.	G	A	Pts.	PIM	+/-	PP	SH		Gms.	G	A	Pts.	PIM
90-91—Prince Albert	WHL	70	15	45	60	57	...	...	...		3	1	1	2	2
91-92—Prince Albert	WHL	69	9	37	46	129	...	...	...		8	1	5	6	10
92-93—Red Deer	WHL	54	23	47	70	118	...	...	...		4	2	5	7	16
93-94—Red Deer	WHL	58	20	64	84	125	...	...	...		4	2	4	6	6
94-95—San Diego	IHL	76	6	17	23	74	...	...	...		5	0	0	0	0
—Anaheim	NHL	1	0	1	1	4	0	0	0		—	—	—	—	—

Season Team	League	REGULAR SEASON								PLAYOFFS				
		Gms.	G	A	Pts.	PIM	+/-	PP	SH	Gms.	G	A	Pts.	PIM
95-96—Baltimore	AHL	63	11	47	58	79	...	...	...	—	—	—	—	—
—Anaheim	NHL	16	1	2	3	14	8	0	0	—	—	—	—	—
96-97—Anaheim	NHL	74	4	19	23	90	3	2	0	9	0	2	2	16
97-98—Anaheim	NHL	19	1	3	4	4	-10	0	0	—	—	—	—	—
—Boston	NHL	50	2	8	10	36	4	2	0	6	2	1	3	0
98-99—Boston	NHL	60	5	15	20	66	-5	4	0	11	1	2	3	4
99-00—Boston	NHL	79	5	23	28	73	-19	4	0	—	—	—	—	—
NHL Totals (6 years)		299	18	71	89	287	-19	12	0	26	3	5	8	20

VAN OENE, DARREN   LW   SABRES

PERSONAL: Born January 18, 1978, in Edmonton. ... 6-3/207. ... Shoots left. ... Name pronounced van OH-ihn.
TRANSACTIONS/CAREER NOTES: Selected by Buffalo Sabres in second round (third Sabres pick, 33rd overall) of NHL entry draft (June 22, 1996).

Season Team	League	REGULAR SEASON								PLAYOFFS				
		Gms.	G	A	Pts.	PIM	+/-	PP	SH	Gms.	G	A	Pts.	PIM
94-95—Brandon	WHL	59	5	13	18	108	...	...	...	18	1	1	2	34
95-96—Brandon	WHL	47	10	18	28	126	...	...	...	18	1	6	7	*78
96-97—Brandon	WHL	56	21	27	48	139	...	...	...	6	2	3	5	19
97-98—Brandon	WHL	51	23	24	47	161	...	...	...	17	6	7	13	51
98-99—Rochester	AHL	73	11	20	31	143	...	...	...	12	2	4	6	8
99-00—Rochester	AHL	80	20	18	38	153	...	...	...	21	1	3	4	24

VANBIESBROUCK, JOHN   G   ISLANDERS

PERSONAL: Born September 4, 1963, in Detroit. ... 5-8/176. ... Catches left. ... Name pronounced van-BEES-bruk.
TRANSACTIONS/CAREER NOTES: Selected by New York Rangers in fourth round (fifth Rangers pick, 72nd overall) of NHL entry draft (June 10, 1981). ... Fractured jaw (October 1987). ... Severely lacerated wrist (June 1988). ... Underwent knee surgery (May 11, 1990). ... Suffered lower back spasms (February 25, 1992); missed 11 games. ... Pulled groin (November 2, 1992); missed four games. ... Traded by Rangers to Vancouver Canucks for future considerations (June 20, 1993); Rangers acquired D Doug Lidster to complete deal (June 25, 1993). ... Selected by Florida Panthers in NHL expansion draft (June 24, 1993). ... Lacerated hand (February 1, 1994); missed seven games. ... Signed as free agent by Philadelphia Flyers (July 7, 1998). ... Traded by Flyers to New York Islanders for fourth-round pick in 2001 draft (June 25, 2000).
HONORS: Won F.W. (Dinty) Moore Trophy (1980-81). ... Shared Dave Pinkney Trophy with Marc D'Amour (1981-82). ... Named to OHL All-Star second team (1982-83). ... Shared Tommy Ivan Trophy with D Bruce Affleck (1983-84). ... Shared Terry Sawchuk Trophy with Ron Scott (1983-84). ... Named to CHL All-Star first team (1983-84). ... Won Vezina Trophy (1985-86). ... Named to THE SPORTING NEWS All-Star first team (1985-86 and 1993-94). ... Named to NHL All-Star first team (1985-86). ... Played in NHL All-Star Game (1994, 1996 and 1997). ... Named to NHL All-Star second team (1993-94).
MISCELLANEOUS: Holds Florida Panthers all-time records for most games played by goalie (268), most wins (106), most shutouts (13) and goals-against average (2.58). ... Holds Philadelphia Flyers all-time record for goals-against average (2.18). ... Stopped a penalty shot attempt (vs. Petr Klima, February 17, 1987; vs. Ray Bourque, November 11, 1988; vs. Pavel Bure, February 17, 1992; vs. Trent Klatt, October 1, 1997; vs. Mats Sundin, April 22, 1999 (playoffs)). ... Allowed a penalty shot goal (vs. Pat Verbeek, March 27, 1988; vs. Keith Acton, March 25, 1990; vs. Mario Lemieux, April 11, 1997; vs. Derek King, February 7, 1998).

Season Team	League	REGULAR SEASON								PLAYOFFS						
		Gms.	Min.	W	L	T	GA	SO	Avg.	Gms.	Min.	W	L	GA	SO	Avg.
80-81—Sault Ste. Marie	OMJHL	56	2941	31	16	1	203	0	4.14	11	457	3	3	24	1	3.15
81-82—Sault Ste. Marie	OHL	31	1686	12	12	2	102	0	3.63	7	276	1	4	20	0	4.35
—New York Rangers	NHL	1	60	1	0	0	1	0	1.00	—	—	—	—	—	—	—
82-83—Sault Ste. Marie	OHL	*62	3471	39	21	1	209	0	3.61	16	944	7	6	56	*1	3.56
83-84—New York Rangers	NHL	3	180	2	1	0	10	0	3.33	1	1	0	0	0	0	...
—Tulsa	CHL	37	2153	20	13	2	124	*3	3.46	4	240	4	0	10	0	*2.50
84-85—New York Rangers	NHL	42	2358	12	24	3	166	1	4.22	1	20	0	0	0	0	...
85-86—New York Rangers	NHL	61	3326	31	21	5	184	3	3.32	16	899	8	8	49	*1	3.27
86-87—New York Rangers	NHL	50	2656	18	20	5	161	0	3.64	4	195	1	3	11	1	3.38
87-88—New York Rangers	NHL	56	3319	27	22	7	187	0	3.38	—	—	—	—	—	—	—
88-89—New York Rangers	NHL	56	3207	28	21	4	197	0	3.69	2	107	0	1	6	0	3.36
89-90—New York Rangers	NHL	47	2734	19	19	7	154	1	3.38	6	298	2	3	15	0	3.02
90-91—New York Rangers	NHL	40	2257	15	18	6	126	3	3.35	1	52	0	0	1	0	1.15
91-92—New York Rangers	NHL	45	2526	27	13	3	120	2	2.85	7	368	2	5	23	0	3.75
92-93—New York Rangers	NHL	48	2757	20	18	7	152	4	3.31	—	—	—	—	—	—	—
93-94—Florida	NHL	57	3440	21	25	11	145	1	2.53	—	—	—	—	—	—	—
94-95—Florida	NHL	37	2087	14	15	4	86	4	2.47	—	—	—	—	—	—	—
95-96—Florida	NHL	57	3178	26	20	7	142	2	2.68	22	1332	12	*10	50	1	2.25
96-97—Florida	NHL	57	3347	27	19	10	128	2	2.29	5	328	1	4	13	1	2.38
97-98—Florida	NHL	60	3451	18	29	11	165	4	2.87	—	—	—	—	—	—	—
—U.S. Olympic team	Int'l	1	1	0	0	0	0	0	0	—	—	—	—	—	—	—
98-99—Philadelphia	NHL	62	3712	27	18	*15	135	6	2.18	6	369	2	4	9	1	1.46
99-00—Philadelphia	NHL	50	2950	25	15	9	108	3	2.20	—	—	—	—	—	—	—
NHL Totals (18 years)		829	47545	358	318	114	2367	38	2.99	71	3969	28	38	177	5	2.68

V

VANDENBUSSCHE, RYAN   RW   BLACKHAWKS

PERSONAL: Born February 28, 1973, in Simcoe, Ontario. ... 6-0/200. ... Shoots right. ... Name pronounced VAN-dihn-bush.
TRANSACTIONS/CAREER NOTES: Selected by Toronto Maple Leafs in eighth round (173rd overall) of NHL entry draft (June 20, 1992). ... Signed as free agent by New York Rangers (August 22, 1995). ... Traded by Rangers to Chicago Blackhawks for D Ryan Risidore (March 24, 1998). ... Suspended one game by NHL for head-butting incident (March 28, 1999). ... Underwent elbow surgery prior to 1999-2000 season; missed first six games of season. ... Suffered sore back (December 3, 1999); missed five games. ... Lacerated left hand (March 3, 2000); missed 10 games.

Season Team	League	REGULAR SEASON								PLAYOFFS				
		Gms.	G	A	Pts.	PIM	+/-	PP	SH	Gms.	G	A	Pts.	PIM
90-91—Cornwall	OHL	49	3	8	11	139	...	...	...	—	—	—	—	—
91-92—Cornwall	OHL	61	13	15	28	232	...	...	...	6	0	2	2	9
92-93—Newmarket	OHL	30	15	12	27	161	...	...	...	—	—	—	—	—
—Guelph	OHL	29	3	14	17	99	...	...	...	5	1	3	4	13
—St. John's	AHL	1	0	0	0	0	...	...	...	—	—	—	—	—
93-94—St. John's	AHL	44	4	10	14	124	...	...	...	—	—	—	—	—
—Springfield	AHL	9	1	2	3	29	...	...	...	5	0	0	0	16
94-95—St. John's	AHL	53	2	13	15	239	...	...	...	—	—	—	—	—
95-96—Binghamton	AHL	68	3	17	20	240	...	...	...	4	0	0	0	9
96-97—Binghamton	AHL	38	8	11	19	133	...	...	...	—	—	—	—	—
—New York Rangers	NHL	11	1	0	1	30	-2	0	0	—	—	—	—	—
97-98—New York Rangers	NHL	16	1	0	1	38	-2	0	0	—	—	—	—	—
—Hartford	AHL	15	2	0	2	45	...	...	...	—	—	—	—	—
—Chicago	NHL	4	0	1	1	5	0	0	0	—	—	—	—	—
—Indianapolis	IHL	3	1	1	2	4	...	...	...	—	—	—	—	—
98-99—Indianapolis	IHL	34	3	10	13	130	...	...	...	—	—	—	—	—
—Portland	AHL	37	4	1	5	119	...	...	...	—	—	—	—	—
—Chicago	NHL	6	0	0	0	17	0	0	0	—	—	—	—	—
99-00—Chicago	NHL	52	0	1	1	143	-3	0	0	—	—	—	—	—
NHL Totals (4 years)		89	2	2	4	233	-7	0	0					

VARADA, VACLAV   RW   SABRES

PERSONAL: Born April 26, 1976, in Vsetin, Czechoslovakia. ... 6-0/200. ... Shoots left. ... Name pronounced vuh-RAH-duh.
TRANSACTIONS/CAREER NOTES: Selected by San Jose Sharks in fourth round (fourth Sharks pick, 89th overall) of NHL entry draft (June 29, 1994). ... Traded by Sharks with LW Martin Spahnel and fourth-round pick (D Mike Martone) in 1996 draft to Buffalo Sabres for D Doug Bodger (November 16, 1995). ... Fractured left hand (February 2, 1997); missed 15 games. ... Sprained ankle (February 9, 1999); missed 10 games. ... Suffered ear injury (January 18, 2000); missed three games.

Season Team	League	REGULAR SEASON								PLAYOFFS				
		Gms.	G	A	Pts.	PIM	+/-	PP	SH	Gms.	G	A	Pts.	PIM
92-93—TJ Vitkovice	Czech.	1	0	0	0		...	...	...	—	—	—	—	—
93-94—HC Vitkovice	Czech Rep.	24	6	7	13		...	...	...	5	1	1	2	...
94-95—Tacoma	WHL	68	50	38	88	108	...	...	...	4	4	3	7	11
—Czech. Jr. nat'l team	Int'l	7	6	4	10	25	...	...	...	—	—	—	—	—
95-96—Kelowna	WHL	59	39	46	85	100	...	...	...	6	3	3	6	16
—Rochester	AHL	5	3	0	3	4	...	...	...	—	—	—	—	—
—Buffalo	NHL	1	0	0	0	0	0	0	0	—	—	—	—	—
—Czech. Jr. nat'l team	Int'l	6	5	1	6	8	...	...	...	—	—	—	—	—
96-97—Rochester	AHL	53	23	25	48	81	...	...	...	10	1	6	7	27
—Buffalo	NHL	5	0	0	0	2	0	0	0	—	—	—	—	—
97-98—Rochester	AHL	45	30	26	56	74	...	...	...	—	—	—	—	—
—Buffalo	NHL	27	5	6	11	15	0	0	0	15	3	4	7	18
98-99—Buffalo	NHL	72	7	24	31	61	11	1	0	21	5	4	9	14
99-00—HC Vitkovice	Czech Rep.	5	2	3	5	12	...	...	...	—	—	—	—	—
—Buffalo	NHL	76	10	27	37	62	12	0	0	5	0	0	0	8
NHL Totals (5 years)		181	22	57	79	140	23	1	0	41	8	8	16	40

VARLAMOV, SERGEI   RW   FLAMES

PERSONAL: Born July 21, 1978, in Kiev, U.S.S.R. ... 5-11/195. ... Shoots left. ... Name pronounced VAHR-luh-mahf.
TRANSACTIONS/CAREER NOTES: Signed as non-drafted free agent by Calgary Flames (September 18, 1996).
HONORS: Won Can.HL Player of the Year Award (1997-98). ... Named to Can.HL All-Star first team (1997-98). ... Won Bob Clarke Trophy (1997-98). ... Won Four Broncos Memorial Trophy (1997-98). ... Named to WHL (East) All-Star first team (1997-98).

Season Team	League	REGULAR SEASON								PLAYOFFS				
		Gms.	G	A	Pts.	PIM	+/-	PP	SH	Gms.	G	A	Pts.	PIM
95-96—Swift Current	WHL	55	23	21	44	65	...	...	...	—	—	—	—	—
96-97—Swift Current	WHL	72	46	39	85	94	...	...	...	—	—	—	—	—
—Saint John	AHL	1	0	0	0	2	...	...	...	—	—	—	—	—
97-98—Swift Current	WHL	72	*66	53	*119	132	...	...	...	12	10	5	15	28
—Calgary	NHL	1	0	0	0	0	0	0	0	—	—	—	—	—
—Saint John	AHL	—	—	—	—	—	...	...	...	3	0	0	0	0
98-99—Saint John	AHL	76	24	33	57	66	...	...	...	7	0	4	4	8
99-00—Saint John	AHL	68	20	21	41	88	...	...	...	3	0	0	0	24
—Calgary	NHL	7	3	0	3	0	0	0	0	—	—	—	—	—
NHL Totals (2 years)		8	3	0	3	0	0	0	0					

VASILIEV, ALEXEI   D   RANGERS

PERSONAL: Born September 1, 1977, in Yaroslavl, U.S.S.R. ... 6-1/192. ... Shoots left. ... Name pronounced vuh-SIHL-yehf.
TRANSACTIONS/CAREER NOTES: Selected by New York Rangers in fifth round (fourth Rangers pick, 110th overall) of NHL entry draft (July 8, 1995).

V

Season Team	League	REGULAR SEASON								PLAYOFFS				
		Gms.	G	A	Pts.	PIM	+/-	PP	SH	Gms.	G	A	Pts.	PIM
93-94—Yaroslavl	CIS	2	0	1	1	4	...	...	...	—	—	—	—	—
94-95—Yaroslavl 2	CIS.2					Statistics unavailable.								
95-96—Yaroslavl	CIS	40	4	7	11	4	...	...	...	—	—	—	—	—
96-97—Torpedo-Yaroslavl	Russian	44	2	8	10	10	...	...	...	9	1	1	2	8
97-98—Hartford	AHL					Did not play.								
98-99—Hartford	AHL	75	8	19	27	24	...	...	...	6	0	1	1	2
99-00—Hartford	AHL	75	10	28	38	20	...	...	...	15	3	1	4	2
—New York Rangers	NHL	1	0	0	0	2	-1	0	0	—	—	—	—	—
NHL Totals (1 year)		1	0	0	0	2	-1	0	0					

VASILJEVS, HERBERT   C   THRASHERS

PERSONAL: Born May 27, 1976, in Rigo, U.S.S.R. ... 5-11/180. ... Shoots right.
TRANSACTIONS/CAREER NOTES: Signed as free agent by Florida Panthers (October 3, 1997). ... Traded by Panthers with D Gord Murphy, D Daniel Tjarnqvist and sixth-round pick (traded to Dallas) in 1999 draft to Atlanta Thrashers for G Trevor Kidd (June 25, 1999).

Season Team	League	REGULAR SEASON								PLAYOFFS				
		Gms.	G	A	Pts.	PIM	+/-	PP	SH	Gms.	G	A	Pts.	PIM
95-96—Guelph	OHL	65	34	33	67	63	...	...	...	16	6	13	19	6
96-97—Carolina	AHL	54	13	18	31	30	...	...	...	—	—	—	—	—
—Port Huron	Col.HL	3	3	2	5	4	...	...	...	—	—	—	—	—
97-98—New Haven	AHL	76	36	30	66	60	...	...	...	3	1	0	1	2
98-99—Kentucky	AHL	76	28	48	76	66	...	...	...	12	2	1	3	4
—Florida	NHL	5	0	0	0	2	-1	0	0	—	—	—	—	—
99-00—Orlando	IHL	73	25	35	60	60	...	...	...	6	2	2	4	6
—Atlanta	NHL	7	1	0	1	4	-3	0	0	—	—	—	—	—
NHL Totals (2 years)		12	1	0	1	6	-4	0	0					

VERBEEK, PAT   RW   RED WINGS

PERSONAL: Born May 24, 1964, in Sarnia, Ont. ... 5-9/192. ... Shoots right.
TRANSACTIONS/CAREER NOTES: Selected by New Jersey Devils as underage junior in third round (third Devils pick, 43rd overall) of NHL entry draft (June 9, 1982). ... Suffered severed left thumb between knuckles in a corn-planting machine on his farm and underwent surgery to have thumb reconnected (May 15, 1985). ... Pulled side muscle (March 1987). ... Bruised chest (October 28, 1988). ... Traded by Devils to Hartford Whalers for LW Sylvain Turgeon (June 17, 1989). ... Missed first three games of 1991-92 season due to contract dispute. ... Traded by Whalers to New York Rangers for D Glen Featherstone, D Michael Stewart, first-round pick (G Jean-Sebastien Giguere) in 1995 draft and fourth-round pick (C Steve Wasylko) in 1996 draft (March 23, 1995). ... Injured knee (February 17, 1996); missed two games. ... Separated shoulder (March 1, 1996); missed nine games. ... Suffered back spasms (April 7, 1996); missed two games. ... Signed as free agent by Dallas Stars (July 3, 1996). ... Sprained knee (January 4, 1997); missed one game. ... Sprained knee (April 14, 1999); missed final three games of regular season and four playoff games. ... Suspended one playoff game by NHL for slashing incident (May 7, 1999). ... Signed as free agent by Detroit Red Wings (November 10, 1999).
HONORS: Won Emms Family Award (1981-82). ... Played in NHL All-Star Game (1991 and 1996).
MISCELLANEOUS: Member of Stanley Cup championship team (1999). ... Scored on a penalty shot (vs. John Vanbiesbrouck, March 27, 1988).
STATISTICAL NOTES: Only player in NHL history to lead team in goals scored and penalty minutes (1989-90 and 1990-91). ... Captain of Hartford Whalers (1992-93 through 1993-94).
STATISTICAL PLATEAUS: Three-goal games: 1985-86 (1), 1986-87 (1), 1987-88 (1), 1988-89 (1), 1992-93 (2), 1993-94 (2), 1995-96 (2), 1997-98 (1). Total: 11. ... Four-goal games: 1987-88 (1). ... Total hat tricks: 12.

Season Team	League	REGULAR SEASON								PLAYOFFS				
		Gms.	G	A	Pts.	PIM	+/-	PP	SH	Gms.	G	A	Pts.	PIM
80-81—Petrolia Jr. B	OPJHL	42	44	44	88	155	...	...	...	—	—	—	—	—
81-82—Sudbury	OHL	66	37	51	88	180	...	...	...	—	—	—	—	—
82-83—Sudbury	OHL	61	40	67	107	184	...	...	...	—	—	—	—	—
—New Jersey	NHL	6	3	2	5	8	-2	0	0	—	—	—	—	—
83-84—New Jersey	NHL	79	20	27	47	158	-19	5	1	—	—	—	—	—
84-85—New Jersey	NHL	78	15	18	33	162	-24	5	1	—	—	—	—	—
85-86—New Jersey	NHL	76	25	28	53	79	-25	4	1	—	—	—	—	—
86-87—New Jersey	NHL	74	35	24	59	120	-23	17	0	—	—	—	—	—
87-88—New Jersey	NHL	73	46	31	77	227	29	13	0	20	4	8	12	51
88-89—New Jersey	NHL	77	26	21	47	189	-18	9	0	—	—	—	—	—
89-90—Hartford	NHL	80	44	45	89	228	1	14	0	7	2	2	4	26
90-91—Hartford	NHL	80	43	39	82	246	0	15	0	6	3	2	5	40
91-92—Hartford	NHL	76	22	35	57	243	-16	10	0	7	0	2	2	12
92-93—Hartford	NHL	84	39	43	82	197	-7	16	0	—	—	—	—	—
93-94—Hartford	NHL	84	37	38	75	177	-15	15	1	—	—	—	—	—
94-95—Hartford	NHL	29	7	11	18	53	0	3	0	—	—	—	—	—
—New York Rangers	NHL	19	10	5	15	18	-2	4	0	10	4	6	10	20
95-96—New York Rangers	NHL	69	41	41	82	129	29	17	0	11	3	6	9	12
96-97—Dallas	NHL	81	17	36	53	128	3	5	0	7	1	3	4	16
97-98—Dallas	NHL	82	31	26	57	170	15	9	0	17	3	2	5	26
98-99—Dallas	NHL	78	17	17	34	133	11	8	0	18	3	4	7	14
99-00—Detroit	NHL	68	22	26	48	95	22	7	0	9	1	1	2	2
NHL Totals (18 years)		1293	500	513	1013	2760	-41	176	4	112	24	36	60	219

V

VERNON, MIKE   G   FLAMES

PERSONAL: Born February 24, 1963, in Calgary. ... 5-9/180. ... Catches left.

TRANSACTIONS/CAREER NOTES: Selected by Calgary Flames in third round (second Flames pick, 56th overall) of NHL entry draft (June 10, 1981). ... Injured hip (March 2, 1988). ... Suffered back spasms (February 1989). ... Suffered back spasms (March 1990); missed 10 games. ... Suffered lacerated forehead (October 25, 1992); missed five games. ... Suffered from the flu (November 15, 1993); missed two games. ... Twisted knee (December 30, 1993); missed 14 games. ... Traded by Flames to Detroit Red Wings for D Steve Chiasson (June 29, 1994). ... Pulled groin (December 29, 1995); missed 12 games. ... Suffered from the flu (October 23, 1996); missed three games. ... Injured knee (March 12, 1997); missed three games. ... Traded by Red Wings to San Jose Sharks for second-round pick in 1998 draft and second-round pick (traded to Tampa Bay) in 1999 draft (August 18, 1997). ... Injured groin (March 1, 1999); missed six games. ... Suffered from the flu (December 19, 1999); missed two games. ... Traded by Sharks with third-round pick (RW Sean O'Connor) in 2000 draft to Florida Panthers for RW Radek Dvorak (December 30, 1999). ... Selected by Minnesota Wild in NHL expansion draft (June 23, 2000). ... Traded by Wild to Flames for rights to C Dan Cavanaugh and eighth-round pick in 2001 draft (June 23, 2000).

HONORS: Won WHL Most Valuable Player Trophy (1981-82 and 1982-83). ... Won WHL Top Goaltender Trophy (1981-82 and 1982-83). ... Won WHL Player of the Year Award (1981-82). ... Named to WHL All-Star first team (1981-82 and 1982-83). ... Named to CHL All-Star second team (1983-84). ... Named to THE SPORTING NEWS All-Star second team (1988-89). ... Named to NHL All-Star second team (1988-89). ... Played in NHL All-Star Game (1988-1991 and 1993). ... Shared William M. Jennings Trophy with Chris Osgood (1995-96). ... Won Conn Smythe Trophy (1996-97).

RECORDS: Shares NHL single-season playoff record for most wins by a goaltender—16 (1989 and 1997).

MISCELLANEOUS: Member of Stanley Cup championship team (1989 and 1997). ... Holds Calgary Flames all-time records for games played by a goaltender (467) and wins (248). ... Holds San Jose Sharks all-time records for most shutouts (9) and lowest goals-against average (2.39). ... Stopped a penalty shot attempt (vs. Kirk Muller, March 14, 1989; vs. Jim Cummins, April 7, 1996; vs. Claude Lapointe, January 12, 2000). ... Allowed a penalty shot goal (vs. Stan Smyl, January 16, 1987; vs. Craig MacTavish, December 23, 1988; vs. Gino Odjick, October 19, 1991; vs. Paul Broten, January 16, 1992; vs. Pavel Bure, November 12, 1997).

Season Team	League	Gms.	Min	W	L	T	GA	SO	Avg.	Gms.	Min.	W	L	GA	SO	Avg.
80-81—Calgary	WHL	59	3154	33	17	1	198	1	3.77	22	1271	...	...	82	1	3.87
81-82—Calgary	WHL	42	2329	22	14	2	143	*3	*3.68	9	527	...	...	30	0	*3.42
—Oklahoma City	CHL	—								1	70	0	1	4	0	3.43
82-83—Calgary	WHL	50	2856	19	18	2	155	*3	*3.26	16	925	9	7	60	0	3.89
—Calgary	NHL	2	100	0	2	0	11	0	6.60	—						
83-84—Calgary	NHL	1	11	0	1	0	4	0	21.82	—						
—Colorado	CHL	*46	*2648	30	13	2	148	1	*3.35	6	347	2	4	21	0	3.63
84-85—Moncton	AHL	41	2050	10	20	4	134	0	3.92	—						
85-86—Salt Lake City	IHL	10	601	6	4	0	34	1	3.39	—						
—Moncton	AHL	6	374	3	1	2	21	0	3.37	—						
—Calgary	NHL	18	921	9	3	3	52	1	3.39	*21	*1229	12	*9	*60	0	2.93
86-87—Calgary	NHL	54	2957	30	21	1	178	1	3.61	5	263	2	3	16	0	3.65
87-88—Calgary	NHL	64	3565	39	16	7	210	1	3.53	9	515	4	4	34	0	3.96
88-89—Calgary	NHL	52	2938	*37	6	5	130	0	2.65	*22	*1381	*16	5	*52	*3	2.26
89-90—Calgary	NHL	47	2795	23	14	9	146	0	3.13	6	342	2	3	19	0	3.33
90-91—Calgary	NHL	54	3121	31	19	3	172	1	3.31	7	427	3	4	21	0	2.95
91-92—Calgary	NHL	63	3640	24	30	9	217	0	3.58	—						
92-93—Calgary	NHL	64	3732	29	26	9	203	2	3.26	4	150	1	1	15	0	6.00
93-94—Calgary	NHL	48	2798	26	17	5	131	3	2.81	7	466	3	4	23	0	2.96
94-95—Detroit	NHL	30	1807	19	6	4	76	1	2.52	18	1063	12	6	41	1	2.31
95-96—Detroit	NHL	32	1855	21	7	2	70	3	2.26	4	243	2	2	11	0	2.72
96-97—Detroit	NHL	33	1952	13	11	8	79	0	2.43	20	1229	16	4	36	1	1.76
97-98—San Jose	NHL	62	3564	30	22	8	146	5	2.46	6	348	2	4	14	1	2.41
98-99—San Jose	NHL	49	2831	16	22	10	107	4	2.27	5	321	2	3	13	0	2.43
99-00—San Jose	NHL	15	772	6	5	1	32	0	2.49	—						
—Florida	NHL	34	2019	18	13	2	83	1	2.47	4	237	0	4	12	0	3.04
NHL Totals (17 years)		722	41378	371	241	86	2047	23	2.97	138	8214	77	56	367	6	2.68

VIRTUE, TERRY   D   RANGERS

PERSONAL: Born August 8, 1970, in Scarborough, Ont. ... 6-0/197. ... Shoots right.

TRANSACTIONS/CAREER NOTES: Signed as non-drafted free agent by St. Louis Blues (January 29, 1996). ... Signed as free agent by Boston Bruins (August 28, 1998). ... Signed as free agent by New York Rangers (July 29, 1999).

HONORS: Named to AHL All-Star second team (1998-99).

Season Team	League	Gms.	G	A	Pts.	PIM	+/-	PP	SH	Gms.	G	A	Pts.	PIM
88-89—Victoria	WHL	8	1	1	2	13	...	...	...	—				
89-90—Tri-City	WHL	58	2	19	21	167	...	...	...	—				
90-91—Tri-City	WHL	11	1	8	9	24	...	...	...	—				
—Portland	WHL	59	9	44	53	127	...	...	...	—				
91-92—Roanoke	ECHL	38	4	22	26	165	...	...	...	—				
—Louisville	ECHL	23	1	15	16	58	...	...	...	13	0	8	8	49
92-93—Louisville	ECHL	28	0	17	17	84	...	...	...	—				
—Wheeling	ECHL	31	3	15	18	86	...	...	...	16	3	5	8	18
93-94—Wheeling	ECHL	34	5	28	33	61	...	...	...	6	2	2	4	4
—Cape Breton	AHL	26	4	6	10	10	...	...	...	5	0	0	0	17
94-95—Worcester	AHL	73	14	25	39	183	...	...	...	—				
95-96—Worcester	AHL	76	7	31	38	234	...	...	...	4	0	0	0	4
96-97—Worcester	AHL	80	16	26	42	220	...	...	...	5	0	4	4	8
97-98—Worcester	AHL	74	8	26	34	233	...	...	...	11	1	4	5	41
98-99—Providence	AHL	76	8	48	56	117	...	...	...	17	2	12	14	29
—Boston	NHL	4	0	0	0	0	2	0	0	—				
99-00—Hartford	AHL	67	5	22	27	166	...	...	...	23	3	7	10	51
—New York Rangers	NHL	1	0	0	0	0	-2	0	0	—				
NHL Totals (2 years)		5	0	0	0	0	0	0	0	—				

VISHNEVSKI, VITALI — D — MIGHTY DUCKS

PERSONAL: Born March 18, 1980, in Kharkov, U.S.S.R. ... 6-2/190. ... Shoots left.
TRANSACTIONS/CAREER NOTES: Selected by Mighty Ducks of Anaheim in first round (first Mighty Ducks pick, fifth overall) of NHL entry draft (June 27, 1998). ... Suffered injury (April 5, 2000); missed final two games of season.

Season Team	League	REGULAR SEASON								PLAYOFFS				
		Gms.	G	A	Pts.	PIM	+/-	PP	SH	Gms.	G	A	Pts.	PIM
95-96—Torpedo-2 Yaroslavl....	CIS Div. II	40	4	4	8	20	...	...	...	—	—	—	—	—
96-97—Torpedo-2 Yaroslavl....	Rus. Div. III	45	0	2	2	30	...	...	...	—	—	—	—	—
97-98—Torpedo-2 Yaroslavl....	Rus. Div. II	47	8	9	17	164	...	...	...	—	—	—	—	—
98-99—Torpedo Yaroslavl.......	Russian	34	3	4	7	38	...	...	...	10	0	0	0	4
99-00—Cincinnati..................	AHL	35	1	3	4	45	...	...	...	—	—	—	—	—
—Anaheim..................	NHL	31	1	1	2	26	0	1	0	—	—	—	—	—
NHL Totals (1 year).............		31	1	1	2	26	0	1	0					

VLASAK, TOMAS — C — KINGS

PERSONAL: Born February 1, 1975, in Prague, Czechoslovakia. ... 5-10/161. ... Shoots right. ... Name pronounced VLA-sihk.
TRANSACTIONS/CAREER NOTES: Selected by Los Angeles Kings in fifth round (sixth Kings pick, 120th overall) of NHL entry draft (June 26, 1993).

Season Team	League	REGULAR SEASON								PLAYOFFS				
		Gms.	G	A	Pts.	PIM	+/-	PP	SH	Gms.	G	A	Pts.	PIM
91-92—Slavia Praha Jrs.........	Czech.	69	49	43	92	24	...	...	...	—	—	—	—	—
92-93—Slavia Praha...............	Czech Dv.II	31	17	6	23	6	...	...	...	—	—	—	—	—
93-94—Litvinov.....................	Czech Rep.	41	16	11	27	0	...	...	...	4	0	1	1	...
94-95—Litvinov.....................	Czech Rep.	35	6	14	20	4	...	...	...	4	0	0	0	4
95-96—Litvinov.....................	Czech Rep.	35	10	22	32	...	...	...	...	15	5	5	10	6
96-97—Litvinov.....................	Czech Rep.	52	26	34	60	16	...	...	...	—	—	—	—	—
97-98—Chem. Litvinov..........	Czech Rep.	51	22	44	66	40	...	...	...	4	1	2	3	2
98-99—HPK Hameenlinna.......	Finland	54	28	29	57	36	...	...	...	8	2	*9	11	0
99-00—HPK Hameenlinna.......	Finland	48	24	39	63	63	...	...	...	8	3	4	7	6

VOKOUN, TOMAS — G — PREDATORS

PERSONAL: Born July 2, 1976, in Karlovy Vary, Czechoslovakia. ... 6-3/183. ... Catches right. ... Name pronounced TOH-mahz voh-KOON.
TRANSACTIONS/CAREER NOTES: Selected by Montreal Canadiens in ninth round (11th Canadiens pick, 226th overall) of NHL entry draft (June 29, 1994). ... Selected by Nashville Predators in NHL expansion draft (June 26, 1998). ... Strained neck (January 19, 1999); missed one game. ... Suffered injury (March 31, 2000); missed final four games of season.
MISCELLANEOUS: Holds Nashville Predators all-time records for most shutouts (2) and goals-against average (2.86). ... Allowed a penalty shot goal (vs. Jeremy Roenick, March 17, 2000).

Season Team	League	REGULAR SEASON								PLAYOFFS						
		Gms.	Min	W	L	T	GA	SO	Avg.	Gms.	Min.	W	L	GA	SO	Avg.
93-94—Poldi Kladno.................	Czech Rep.	1	20	...	...	...	2	0	6.00	—	—	—	—	—	—	—
94-95—Poldi Kladno.................	Czech Rep.	26	1368	...	...	...	70	...	3.07	5	240	...	...	19	...	4.75
95-96—Wheeling...................	ECHL	35	1911	20	10	‡2	117	0	3.67	7	436	4	3	19	0	2.61
—Fredericton...............	AHL	—	—	—	—	—	—	—	—	1	59	0	1	4	0	4.07
96-97—Fredericton...............	AHL	47	2645	12	26	7	154	2	3.49	—	—	—	—	—	—	—
—Montreal..................	NHL	1	20	0	0	0	4	0	12.00	—	—	—	—	—	—	—
97-98—Fredericton...............	AHL	31	1735	13	13	2	90	0	3.11	—	—	—	—	—	—	—
98-99—Milwaukee	IHL	9	539	3	2	‡4	22	1	2.45	2	149	0	2	8	0	3.22
—Nashville	NHL	37	1954	12	18	4	96	1	2.95	—	—	—	—	—	—	—
99-00—Nashville	NHL	33	1879	9	20	1	87	1	2.78	—	—	—	—	—	—	—
—Milwaukee	IHL	7	364	6	2	0	17	0	2.80	—	—	—	—	—	—	—
NHL Totals (3 years).............		71	3853	21	38	5	187	2	2.91							

VOLCHKOV, ALEXANDRE — LW — OILERS

PERSONAL: Born September 15, 1977, in Moscow, U.S.S.R. ... 6-2/205. ... Shoots left. ... Name pronounced VOHLCH-kahv.
TRANSACTIONS/CAREER NOTES: Selected by Washington Capitals in first round (first Capitals pick, fourth overall) of NHL entry draft (June 22, 1996). ... Traded by Capitals to Edmonton Oilers for future considerations (February 4, 2000).
HONORS: Named to Can.HL All-Rookie team (1995-96). ... Named to OHL All-Rookie first team (1995-96). ... Named to OHL All-Star second team (1996-97).

Season Team	League	REGULAR SEASON								PLAYOFFS				
		Gms.	G	A	Pts.	PIM	+/-	PP	SH	Gms.	G	A	Pts.	PIM
94-95—CSKA Moscow Jrs......	CIS	50	20	30	50	20	...	...	...	—	—	—	—	—
95-96—Barrie........................	OHL	47	37	27	64	36	...	...	...	7	2	3	5	12
96-97—Barrie........................	OHL	56	29	53	82	76	...	...	...	9	6	9	15	12
—Portland..................	AHL	—	—	—	—	—	...	...	...	4	0	0	0	0
97-98—Portland..................	AHL	34	2	5	7	20	...	...	...	1	0	0	0	0
98-99—Portland..................	AHL	27	3	8	11	24	...	...	...	—	—	—	—	—
—Cincinnati...............	IHL	25	1	3	4	8	...	...	...	—	—	—	—	—
99-00—Portland..................	AHL	35	11	15	26	47	...	...	...	—	—	—	—	—
—Washington	NHL	3	0	0	0	0	-2	0	0	—	—	—	—	—
—Hamilton	AHL	25	2	6	8	11	...	...	...	—	—	—	—	—
NHL Totals (1 year).............		3	0	0	0	0	-2	0	0					

VOPAT, JAN   D   PREDATORS

PERSONAL: Born March 22, 1973, in Most, Czechoslovakia. ... 6-0/210. ... Shoots left. ... Brother of Roman Vopat, center with four NHL teams (1995-96 through 1998-99). ... Name pronounced YAHN VOH-paht.

TRANSACTIONS/CAREER NOTES: Selected by Hartford Whalers in third round (third Whalers pick, 57th overall) of NHL entry draft (June 20, 1992). ... Traded by Whalers to Los Angeles Kings for fourth-round pick (C Ian MacNeil) in 1995 draft (May 31, 1995). ... Underwent back surgery (October 22, 1996); missed 30 games. ... Sprained ankle (January 24, 1997); missed six games. ... Sprained ankle (Febraury 15, 1997); missed one game. ... Bruised thigh (April 7, 1997); missed one game. ... Traded by Kings with rights to D Kimmo Timonen to Nashville Predators for future considerations (June 26, 1998). ... Bruised thumb (October 2, 1998); missed first five games of season. ... Suffered from the flu (January 21, 1999); missed one game. ... Suffered concussion (February 5, 1999); missed four games. ... Suffered concussion (February 19, 1999); missed five games. ... Suffered illness (March 12, 1999); missed five games. ... Suffered illness (October 2, 1999); missed first two games of season. ... Suffered illness (November 11, 1999); missed final 68 games of season.

Season Team	League	REGULAR SEASON								PLAYOFFS				
		Gms.	G	A	Pts.	PIM	+/-	PP	SH	Gms.	G	A	Pts.	PIM
90-91—CHZ Litvinov	Czech.	25	1	4	5	4	...	...	...	—	—	—	—	—
91-92—Chemopetrol Litvinov .	Czech.	46	4	2	6	6	...	...	...	—	—	—	—	—
92-93—Chemopetrol Litvinov .	Czech.	45	12	10	22		...	...	...	—	—	—	—	—
93-94—Chem. Litvinov	Czech Rep.	41	9	19	28		...	...	...	4	1	1	2	—
—Czech Rep. Oly. team	Int'l	8	0	1	1	8				—	—	—	—	—
94-95—Chem. Litvinov	Czech Rep.	42	7	18	25		...	...	...	4	0	2	2	—
95-96—Phoenix	IHL	47	0	9	9	34	...	...	...	4	0	2	2	4
—Los Angeles	NHL	11	1	4	5	4	3	0	0	—	—	—	—	—
96-97—Los Angeles	NHL	33	4	5	9	22	3	0	0	—	—	—	—	—
—Phoenix	IHL	4	0	6	6	6	...	...	...	—	—	—	—	—
97-98—Los Angeles	NHL	21	1	5	6	10	8	0	0	2	0	1	1	2
—Utah	IHL	38	8	13	21	24	...	...	...	—	—	—	—	—
98-99—Nashville	NHL	55	5	6	11	28	0	0	0	—	—	—	—	—
99-00—Nashville	NHL	6	0	0	0	6	1	0	0	—	—	—	—	—
—Milwaukee	IHL	2	1	0	1	2	...	...	...	—	—	—	—	—
NHL Totals (5 years)		126	11	20	31	70	15	0	0	2	0	1	1	2

VUJTEK, VLADIMIR   LW   THRASHERS

PERSONAL: Born February 17, 1972, in Ostrava, Czechoslovakia. ... 6-1/190. ... Shoots left. ... Name pronounced VWEE-tehk.

TRANSACTIONS/CAREER NOTES: Selected by Montreal Canadiens in fourth round (fifth Canadiens pick, 73rd overall) of NHL entry draft (June 22, 1991). ... Traded by Canadiens with LW Shayne Corson and C Brent Gilchrist to Edmonton Oilers for LW Vincent Damphousse and fourth-round pick (D Adam Wiesel) in 1993 draft (August 27, 1992). ... Suffered charley horse (October 6, 1992); missed eight games. ... Suspended by Oilers after failing to report to assigned team (January 4, 1993). ... Strained lower back (March 17, 1993); missed five games. ... Injured shoulder (January 11, 1994); missed seven games. ... Injured shoulder and underwent surgery (February 14, 1994); missed remainder of season. ... Played in Europe during 1994-95 NHL lockout. ... Traded by Oilers to Tampa Bay Lightning for RW Brantt Myhres and conditional draft pick (July 16, 1997). ... Suffered from the flu (October 3, 1997); missed one game. ... Suffered from chest virus (November 8, 1997); missed 42 games. ... Signed as free agent by Atlanta Thrashers (July 19, 1999). ... Lacerated face (September 18, 1999); missed first six games of 1999-2000 season.

HONORS: Named to WHL (West) All-Star first team (1991-92).

Season Team	League	REGULAR SEASON								PLAYOFFS				
		Gms.	G	A	Pts.	PIM	+/-	PP	SH	Gms.	G	A	Pts.	PIM
89-90—Vitkovice	Czech.	29	3	4	7		...	...	...	—	—	—	—	—
90-91—Tri-City	WHL	37	26	18	44	25	...	...	...	—	—	—	—	—
—Vitkovice	Czech.	26	7	4	11		...	...	...	—	—	—	—	—
91-92—Tri-City	WHL	53	41	61	102	114	...	...	...	—	—	—	—	—
—Montreal	NHL	2	0	0	0	0	...	...	...	—	—	—	—	—
92-93—Edmonton	NHL	30	1	10	11	8	-1	0	0	—	—	—	—	—
—Cape Breton	AHL	20	10	9	19	14	...	...	...	1	0	0	0	0
93-94—Edmonton	NHL	40	4	15	19	14	-7	1	0	—	—	—	—	—
—Cape Breton	AHL	30	10	11	21	30	...	...	...	—	—	—	—	—
—Las Vegas	IHL	1	0	0	0	0	...	...	...	—	—	—	—	—
94-95—HC Vitkovice	Czech Rep.	18	5	7	12	51	...	...	...	—	—	—	—	—
95-96—TJ Vitkovice	Czech Rep.	26	6	7	13	0	...	...	...	4	1	1	2	0
96-97—Assat Pori	Finland	50	27	31	58	48	...	...	...	4	1	2	3	2
97-98—Tampa Bay	NHL	30	2	4	6	16	-2	0	0	—	—	—	—	—
—Adirondack	AHL	2	1	2	3	0	...	...	...	—	—	—	—	—
98-99—HC Vitkovice	Czech Rep.	47	20	35	55	75	...	...	...	—	—	—	—	—
99-00—Atlanta	NHL	3	0	0	0	0	0	0	0	—	—	—	—	—
—Sparta Praha	Czech Rep.	21	12	19	31	10	...	...	...	8	2	3	5	10
NHL Totals (5 years)		105	7	29	36	38	-10	1	0	—	—	—	—	—

VYBORNY, DAVID   C   BLUE JACKETS

PERSONAL: Born January 22, 1975, in Jihlava, Czechoslovakia. ... 5-10/183. ... Shoots left. ... Name pronounced vigh-BOHR-nee.

TRANSACTIONS/CAREER NOTES: Selected by Edmonton Oilers in second round (third Oilers pick, 33rd overall) of NHL entry draft (June 26, 1993). ... Signed as free agent by Columbus Blue Jackets (June 7, 2000).

HONORS: Named Czechoslovakian League Rookie of the Year (1991-92).

Season Team	League	REGULAR SEASON								PLAYOFFS				
		Gms.	G	A	Pts.	PIM	+/-	PP	SH	Gms.	G	A	Pts.	PIM
90-91—Sparta Prague	Czech.	3	0	0	0	0	...	...	...	—	—	—	—	—
91-92—Sparta Prague	Czech.	32	6	9	15	2	...	...	...	—	—	—	—	—
92-93—Sparta Prague	Czech.	52	20	24	44		...	...	...	—	—	—	—	—

Season Team	League	REGULAR SEASON								PLAYOFFS				
		Gms.	G	A	Pts.	PIM	+/-	PP	SH	Gms.	G	A	Pts.	PIM
93-94—Sparta Prague.............	Czech Rep.	44	15	20	35	...	...	...	...	6	4	7	11	...
94-95—Cape Breton.............	AHL	76	23	38	61	30	...	...	...	—	—	—	—	—
95-96—Sparta Praha.............	Czech Rep.	52	19	36	55	42	...	...	...	—	—	—	—	—
96-97—Sparta Praha.............	Czech Rep.	47	20	29	49	14	...	...	...	—	—	—	—	—
97-98—MoDo Ornskoldsvik	Sweden	45	16	21	37	34	...	...	...	—	—	—	—	—
98-99—Sparta Praha.............	Czech Rep.	52	24	†46	*70	22	...	...	...	8	1	3	4	...
99-00—Sparta Praha.............	Czech Rep.	50	25	38	63	30	...	...	...	9	3	8	*11	4

VYSHEDKEVICH, SERGEI   D   THRASHERS

PERSONAL: Born January 3, 1975, in Moscow, U.S.S.R. ... 6-0/195. ... Shoots left. ... Name pronounced vih-shuh-KEH-vihch.

TRANSACTIONS/CAREER NOTES: Selected by New Jersey Devils in third round (third Devils pick, 70th overall) of NHL entry draft (July 8, 1995). ... Traded by Devils to Atlanta Thrashers for future considerations (June 25, 1999).

Season Team	League	REGULAR SEASON								PLAYOFFS				
		Gms.	G	A	Pts.	PIM	+/-	PP	SH	Gms.	G	A	Pts.	PIM
93-94—Dynamo Moscow........	CIS	—								4	0	2	2	2
94-95—Dynamo Moscow........	CIS	49	6	7	13	67	...	...	...	14	2	0	2	12
95-96—Dynamo Moscow........	CIS	49	5	4	9	12	...	...	...	13	1	1	2	6
96-97—Albany......................	AHL	65	8	27	35	16	...	...	...	12	0	6	6	0
97-98—Albany......................	AHL	54	12	16	28	12	...	...	...	13	0	10	10	4
98-99—Albany......................	AHL	79	11	38	49	28	...	...	...	5	0	3	3	0
99-00—Orlando....................	IHL	69	11	24	35	32	...	...	...	6	3	3	6	8
—Atlanta	NHL	7	1	3	4	2	-3	1	0	—	—	—	—	—
NHL Totals (1 year).............		7	1	3	4	2	-3	1	0					

WAITE, JIMMY   G   MAPLE LEAFS

PERSONAL: Born April 15, 1969, in Sherbrooke, Que. ... 6-1/190. ... Catches left. ... Full Name: Jim Waite. ... Name pronounced WAYT.

TRANSACTIONS/CAREER NOTES: Selected by Chicago Blackhawks as underage junior in first round (first Blackhawks pick, eighth overall) of NHL entry draft (June 13, 1987). ... Fractured collarbone (December 6, 1988). ... Sprained ankle (October 12, 1991); missed one game. ... Traded by Blackhawks to San Jose Sharks for future considerations (June 18, 1993); Blackhawks aquired D Neil Wilkinson to complete deal (July 9, 1993). ... Sprained knee (January 11, 1994); missed two games. ... Underwent arthroscopic knee surgery (March 7, 1994); missed eight games. ... Traded by Sharks to Blackhawks for fourth-round pick (traded to New York Rangers) in 1997 draft (February 6, 1995). ... Selected by Phoenix Coyotes from Blackhawks in NHL waiver draft (September 28, 1997). ... Sprained thumb (January 9, 1998); missed 18 games. ... Bruised hand (February 6, 1999); missed two games. ... Signed as free agent by Toronto Maple Leafs (August 19, 1999).

HONORS: Won Raymond Lagace Trophy (1986-87). ... Named to QMJHL All-Star second team (1986-87). ... Won James Norris Memorial Trophy (1989-90). ... Named to IHL All-Star first team (1989-90).

Season Team	League	REGULAR SEASON							PLAYOFFS					
		Gms.	Min.	W	L	T	GA	SO	Avg.	Gms.	Min.	W	L	GA	SO	Avg.
86-87—Chicoutimi..................	QMJHL	50	2569	23	17	3	209	†2	4.88	11	576	4	6	54	*1	5.63
87-88—Chicoutimi..................	QMJHL	36	2000	17	16	1	150	0	4.50	4	222	1	2	17	0	4.59
88-89—Chicago......................	NHL	11	494	0	7	1	43	0	5.22	—	—	—	—	—	—	—
—Saginaw........................	IHL	5	304	3	1	0	10	0	1.97	—	—	—	—	—	—	—
89-90—Indianapolis................	IHL	54	*3207	34	14	‡5	135	*5	*2.53	†10	*602	9	1	19	†1	*1.89
—Chicago........................	NHL	4	183	2	0	0	14	0	4.59	—	—	—	—	—	—	—
90-91—Indianapolis................	IHL	49	2888	26	18	‡4	167	3	3.47	6	369	2	4	20	0	3.25
—Chicago........................	NHL	1	60	1	0	0	2	0	2.00	—	—	—	—	—	—	—
91-92—Chicago......................	NHL	17	877	4	7	4	54	0	3.69	—	—	—	—	—	—	—
—Indianapolis..................	IHL	13	702	4	7	‡1	53	0	4.53	—	—	—	—	—	—	—
—Hershey........................	AHL	11	631	6	4	1	44	0	4.18	6	360	2	4	19	0	3.17
92-93—Chicago......................	NHL	20	996	6	7	1	49	2	2.95	—	—	—	—	—	—	—
93-94—San Jose....................	NHL	15	697	3	7	0	50	0	4.30	2	40	0	0	3	0	4.50
94-95—Chicago......................	NHL	2	119	1	1	0	5	0	2.52	—	—	—	—	—	—	—
—Indianapolis..................	IHL	4	239	2	1	‡1	13	0	3.26	—	—	—	—	—	—	—
95-96—Indianapolis................	IHL	56	3157	28	18	‡6	179	0	3.40	5	297	2	3	15	1	3.03
—Chicago........................	NHL	1	31	0	0	0	0	0	0	—	—	—	—	—	—	—
96-97—Chicago......................	NHL	2	105	0	1	1	7	0	4.00	—	—	—	—	—	—	—
—Indianapolis..................	IHL	41	2450	22	15	‡4	112	2	2.74	4	222	1	3	13	0	3.51
97-98—Phoenix.....................	NHL	17	793	5	6	1	28	1	2.12	4	171	0	3	11	0	3.86
98-99—Phoenix.....................	NHL	16	898	6	5	4	41	1	2.74	—	—	—	—	—	—	—
—Utah............................	IHL	11	622	6	3	‡2	30	0	2.89	—	—	—	—	—	—	—
—Springfield....................	AHL	8	483	3	4	1	19	0	2.36	2	118	0	2	6	0	3.05
99-00—St. John's..................	AHL	*62	*3461	20	*37	4	176	0	3.05	—	—	—	—	—	—	—
NHL Totals (11 years)...........		106	5253	28	41	12	293	4	3.35	6	211	0	3	14	0	3.98

WALKER, SCOTT   RW   PREDATORS

PERSONAL: Born July 19, 1973, in Cambridge, Ont. ... 5-10/190. ... Shoots right.

TRANSACTIONS/CAREER NOTES: Selected by Vancouver Canucks in fifth round (fourth Canucks pick, 124th overall) of NHL entry draft (June 26, 1993). ... Strained abdominal muscle (October 12, 1996); missed eight games. ... Strained groin (December 13, 1996); missed six games. ... Fractured nasal bone (November 16, 1997); missed four games. ... Selected by Nashville Predators in NHL expansion draft (June 26, 1998). ... Separated shoulder (November 19, 1998); missed nine games. ... Suffered ear infection (January 26, 1999); missed two games. ... Suffered concussion (December 6, 1999); missed 10 games. ... Bruised foot (January 21, 2000); missed three games.

HONORS: Named to OHL All-Star second team (1992-93).

V
W

Season Team	League	REGULAR SEASON								PLAYOFFS				
		Gms.	G	A	Pts.	PIM	+/-	PP	SH	Gms.	G	A	Pts.	PIM
89-90—Kitch.-Cambridge Jr.	OHA	33	7	27	34	91	...	...	...	—	—	—	—	—
90-91—Cambridge Jr. B	OHA	45	10	27	37	241	...	...	...	—	—	—	—	—
91-92—Owen Sound	OHL	53	7	31	38	128	...	...	...	5	0	7	7	8
92-93—Owen Sound	OHL	57	23	68	91	110	...	...	...	8	1	5	6	16
—Canadian nat'l team	Int'l	2	3	0	3	0	...	...	...	—	—	—	—	—
93-94—Hamilton	AHL	77	10	29	39	272	...	...	...	4	0	1	1	25
94-95—Syracuse	AHL	74	14	38	52	334	...	...	...	—	—	—	—	—
—Vancouver	NHL	11	0	1	1	33	0	0	0	—	—	—	—	—
95-96—Vancouver	NHL	63	4	8	12	137	-7	0	1	—	—	—	—	—
—Syracuse	AHL	15	3	12	15	52	...	...	...	16	9	8	17	39
96-97—Vancouver	NHL	64	3	15	18	132	2	0	0	—	—	—	—	—
97-98—Vancouver	NHL	59	3	10	13	164	-8	0	1	—	—	—	—	—
98-99—Nashville	NHL	71	15	25	40	103	0	0	1	—	—	—	—	—
99-00—Nashville	NHL	69	7	21	28	90	-16	0	1	—	—	—	—	—
NHL Totals (6 years)		337	32	80	112	659	-29	0	4					

WALLIN, JESSE — D — RED WINGS

PERSONAL: Born March 10, 1978, in Saskatoon, Sask. ... 6-2/190. ... Shoots left. ... Name pronounced WAH-lihn.

TRANSACTIONS/CAREER NOTES: Selected by Detroit Red Wings in first round (first Red Wings pick, 26th overall) of NHL entry draft (June 22, 1996).

HONORS: Won Can.HL Humanitarian of the Year Award (1996-97). ... Won WHL Humanitarian Award (1996-97).

Season Team	League	REGULAR SEASON								PLAYOFFS				
		Gms.	G	A	Pts.	PIM	+/-	PP	SH	Gms.	G	A	Pts.	PIM
94-95—Prince Albert	WHL	72	4	20	24	72	...	...	...	—	—	—	—	—
95-96—Red Deer	WHL	70	5	19	24	61	...	...	...	9	0	3	3	4
96-97—Red Deer	WHL	59	6	33	39	70	...	...	...	16	1	4	5	10
97-98—Red Deer	WHL	14	1	6	7	17	...	...	...	5	0	1	1	2
98-99—Adirondack	AHL	76	4	12	16	34	...	...	...	3	0	2	2	2
99-00—Cincinnati	AHL	75	3	14	17	61	...	...	...	—	—	—	—	—
—Detroit	NHL	1	0	0	0	0	-2	0	0	—	—	—	—	—
NHL Totals (1 year)		1	0	0	0	0	-2	0	0					

WALLIN, RICKARD — C — WILD

PERSONAL: Born April 9, 1980, in Stockholm, Sweden. ... 6-2/183. ... Shoots left.

TRANSACTIONS/CAREER NOTES: Selected by Phoenix Coyotes in sixth round (eighth Coyotes pick, 160th overall) of NHL entry draft (June 27, 1998). ... Traded by Coyotes to Minnesota Wild for C Joe Juneau (June 23, 2000).

Season Team	League	REGULAR SEASON								PLAYOFFS				
		Gms.	G	A	Pts.	PIM	+/-	PP	SH	Gms.	G	A	Pts.	PIM
96-97—Vasteras	Sweden Jr.	26	3	3	6		...	...	...	—	—	—	—	—
97-98—Farjestad Karlstad	Sweden Jr.	29	20	20	40	32	...	...	...	2	1	1	2	2
98-99—Farjestad Karlstad	Sweden Jr.	5	0	0	0	0	...	...	...	—	—	—	—	—
99-00—Troja-Ljungby	Sweden	46	15	22	37	54	...	...	...	—	—	—	—	—

WALZ, WES — C — WILD

W

PERSONAL: Born May 15, 1970, in Calgary. ... 5-10/185. ... Shoots right.

TRANSACTIONS/CAREER NOTES: Selected by Boston Bruins in third round (third Bruins pick, 57th overall) of NHL entry draft (June 17, 1989). ... Traded by Bruins with D Garry Galley and future considerations to Philadelphia Flyers for D Gord Murphy, RW Brian Dobbin and third-round pick (LW Sergei Zholtok) in 1992 draft (January 2, 1992). ... Signed as free agent by Calgary Flames (August 31, 1993). ... Strained hip (February 26, 1995); missed one game. ... Signed as free agent by Detroit Red Wings (August 11, 1995). ... Signed as free agent by Minnesota Wild (June 28, 2000).

HONORS: Won Jim Piggott Memorial Trophy (1988-89). ... Won WHL Player of the Year Award (1989-90). ... Named to WHL (East) All-Star first team (1989-90).

MISCELLANEOUS: Failed to score on a penalty shot (vs. Tim Cheveldae, November 2, 1991).

Season Team	League	REGULAR SEASON								PLAYOFFS				
		Gms.	G	A	Pts.	PIM	+/-	PP	SH	Gms.	G	A	Pts.	PIM
87-88—Prince Albert	WHL	1	1	1	2	0		...	...	—	—	—	—	—
88-89—Lethbridge	WHL	63	29	75	104	32	...	...	...	8	1	5	6	6
89-90—Boston	NHL	2	1	1	2	0	-1	1	0	—	—	—	—	—
—Lethbridge	WHL	56	54	86	140	69	...	...	...	19	13	*24	†37	33
90-91—Maine	AHL	20	8	12	20	19	...	...	...	2	0	0	0	21
—Boston	NHL	56	8	8	16	32	-14	1	0	2	0	0	0	0
91-92—Boston	NHL	15	0	3	3	12	-3	0	0	—	—	—	—	—
—Maine	AHL	21	13	11	24	38	...	...	...	—	—	—	—	—
—Hershey	AHL	41	13	28	41	37	...	...	...	6	1	2	3	0
—Philadelphia	NHL	2	1	0	1	0	1	0	0	—	—	—	—	—
92-93—Hershey	AHL	78	35	45	80	106	...	...	...	—	—	—	—	—
93-94—Calgary	NHL	53	11	27	38	16	20	1	0	6	3	0	3	2
—Saint John	AHL	15	6	6	12	14	...	...	...	—	—	—	—	—
94-95—Calgary	NHL	39	6	12	18	11	7	4	0	1	0	0	0	0
95-96—Adirondack	AHL	38	20	35	55	58	...	...	...	—	—	—	—	—
—Detroit	NHL	2	0	0	0	0	0	0	0	—	—	—	—	—
96-97—Zug	Switzerland	41	24	22	46	67	...	...	...					

Season Team	League	REGULAR SEASON								PLAYOFFS				
		Gms.	G	A	Pts.	PIM	+/-	PP	SH	Gms.	G	A	Pts.	PIM
97-98—							Did not play.							
98-99—Zug	Switzerland	42	22	27	49	75	...	...	...	10	3	9	12	2
99-00—Long Beach	IHL	6	4	3	7	8	...	...	...	—	—	—	—	—
—Lugano	Switzerland	13	7	11	18	14	...	...	...	5	3	4	7	4
NHL Totals (6 years)		169	27	51	78	71	10	7	0	9	3	0	3	2

WANVIG, KYLE — RW — BRUINS

PERSONAL: Born January 29, 1981, in Calgary. ... 6-2/197. ... Shoots right.
TRANSACTIONS/CAREER NOTES: Selected by Boston Bruins in third round (third Bruins pick, 89th overall) of NHL entry draft (June 26, 1999).

Season Team	League	REGULAR SEASON								PLAYOFFS				
		Gms.	G	A	Pts.	PIM	+/-	PP	SH	Gms.	G	A	Pts.	PIM
97-98—Edmonton	WHL	62	17	12	29	69	...	...	...	—	—	—	—	—
98-99—Kootenay	WHL	71	12	20	32	119	...	...	...	7	1	3	4	18
99-00—Kootenay	WHL	6	2	2	4	12	...	...	...	—	—	—	—	—
—Red Deer	WHL	58	21	18	39	123	...	...	...	4	1	0	1	4

WARD, AARON — D — RED WINGS

PERSONAL: Born January 17, 1973, in Windsor, Ont. ... 6-2/225. ... Shoots right. ... Full Name: Aaron Christian Ward.
COLLEGE: Michigan.
TRANSACTIONS/CAREER NOTES: Selected by Winnipeg Jets in first round (first Jets pick, fifth overall) of NHL entry draft (June 22, 1991). ... Traded by Jets with fourth-round pick (D John Jakopin) in 1993 draft and future considerations to Detroit Red Wings for RW Paul Ysebaert (June 11, 1993); Red Wings acquired RW Alan Kerr to complete deal (June 18, 1993). ... Suffered bronchitis (December 22, 1996); missed three games. ... Suffered from the flu (October 26, 1997); missed two games. ... Bruised knee (November 26, 1997); missed one game. ... Fractured right foot (December 3, 1997); missed 19 games. ... Sprained shoulder (February 7, 1998); missed two games. ... Strained rotator cuff (November 21, 1998); missed two games. ... Injured ribs (October 22, 1999); missed one game. ... Suffered injury (December 4, 1999); missed four games. ... Injured shoulder (January 22, 2000); missed final 35 games of regular season.
HONORS: Named to CCHA All-Rookie Team (1990-91).
MISCELLANEOUS: Member of Stanley Cup championship team (1997 and 1998).

Season Team	League	REGULAR SEASON								PLAYOFFS				
		Gms.	G	A	Pts.	PIM	+/-	PP	SH	Gms.	G	A	Pts.	PIM
88-89—Nepean	COJHL	56	2	17	19	44	...	...	...	—	—	—	—	—
89-90—Nepean	COJHL	52	6	33	39	85	...	...	...	—	—	—	—	—
90-91—Univ. of Michigan	CCHA	46	8	11	19	126	...	...	...	—	—	—	—	—
91-92—Univ. of Michigan	CCHA	42	7	12	19	64	...	...	...	—	—	—	—	—
92-93—Univ. of Michigan	CCHA	30	5	8	13	73	...	...	...	—	—	—	—	—
—Canadian nat'l team	Int'l	4	0	0	0	8	...	...	...	—	—	—	—	—
93-94—Detroit	NHL	5	1	0	1	4	2	0	0	—	—	—	—	—
—Adirondack	AHL	58	4	12	16	87	...	...	...	9	2	6	8	6
94-95—Adirondack	AHL	76	11	24	35	87	...	...	...	4	0	1	1	0
—Detroit	NHL	1	0	1	1	2	1	0	0	—	—	—	—	—
95-96—Adirondack	AHL	74	5	10	15	133	...	...	...	3	0	0	0	6
96-97—Detroit	NHL	49	2	5	7	52	-9	0	0	19	0	0	0	17
97-98—Detroit	NHL	52	5	5	10	47	-1	0	0	8	0	1	1	8
98-99—Detroit	NHL	60	3	8	11	52	-5	0	0	3	0	0	0	0
99-00—Detroit	NHL	36	1	3	4	24	-4	0	0	3	0	0	0	0
NHL Totals (6 years)		203	12	22	34	181	-16	0	0	30	0	1	1	25

WARD, DIXON — RW/LW

PERSONAL: Born September 23, 1968, in Leduc, Alta. ... 6-0/200. ... Shoots right. ... Full Name: Dixon M. Ward Jr.
COLLEGE: North Dakota.
TRANSACTIONS/CAREER NOTES: Selected by Vancouver Canucks in seventh round (sixth Canucks pick, 128th overall) of NHL entry draft (June 11, 1988). ... Separated left shoulder (December 1990). ... Sprained ankle (March 14, 1993); missed four games. ... Suspended three games and fined $500 by NHL for checking from behind (October 15, 1993). ... Traded by Canucks to Los Angeles Kings for C Jimmy Carson (January 8, 1994). ... Traded by Kings with C Guy Leveque, RW Shayne Toporowski and C Kelly Fairchild to Toronto Maple Leafs for LW Eric Lacroix, D Chris Snell and fourth-round pick (C Eric Belanger) in 1996 draft (October 3, 1994). ... Signed as free agent by Buffalo Sabres (August 24, 1995). ... Bruised sternum (April 10, 1999); missed two games. ... Injured neck (November 4, 1999); missed three games.
HONORS: Named to WCHA All-Star second team (1990-91 and 1991-92). ... Won Jack Butterfield Trophy (1995-96).
MISCELLANEOUS: Scored on a penalty shot (vs. Damian Rhodes, April 11, 1998).
STATISTICAL PLATEAUS: Three-goal games: 1998-99 (1).

Season Team	League	REGULAR SEASON								PLAYOFFS				
		Gms.	G	A	Pts.	PIM	+/-	PP	SH	Gms.	G	A	Pts.	PIM
86-87—Red Deer	AJHL	59	46	40	86	153	...	...	...	—	—	—	—	—
87-88—Red Deer	AJHL	51	60	71	131	167	...	...	...	—	—	—	—	—
88-89—Univ. of North Dakota	WCHA	37	8	9	17	26	...	...	...	—	—	—	—	—
89-90—Univ. of North Dakota	WCHA	45	35	34	69	44	...	...	...	—	—	—	—	—
90-91—Univ. of North Dakota	WCHA	43	34	35	69	84	...	...	...	—	—	—	—	—
91-92—Univ. of North Dakota	WCHA	38	33	31	64	90	...	...	...	—	—	—	—	—
92-93—Vancouver	NHL	70	22	30	52	82	34	4	1	9	2	3	5	0
93-94—Vancouver	NHL	33	6	1	7	37	-14	2	0	—	—	—	—	—
—Los Angeles	NHL	34	6	2	8	45	-8	2	0	—	—	—	—	—

W

Season Team	League	REGULAR SEASON								PLAYOFFS				
		Gms.	G	A	Pts.	PIM	+/-	PP	SH	Gms.	G	A	Pts.	PIM
94-95—Toronto	NHL	22	0	3	3	31	-4	0	0	—				
—St. John's	AHL	6	3	3	6	19	...	...	...	—				
—Detroit	IHL	7	3	6	9	7				5	3	0	3	7
95-96—Rochester	AHL	71	38	56	94	74	...	...	...	19	11	*24	*35	8
—Buffalo	NHL	8	2	2	4	6	1	0	0	—				
96-97—Buffalo	NHL	79	13	32	45	36	17	1	2	12	2	3	5	6
97-98—Buffalo	NHL	71	10	13	23	42	9	0	2	15	3	8	11	6
98-99—Buffalo	NHL	78	20	24	44	44	10	2	1	21	7	5	12	32
99-00—Buffalo	NHL	71	11	9	20	41	1	1	2	5	0	1	1	2
NHL Totals (8 years)		466	90	116	206	364	46	12	8	62	14	20	34	46

WARD, ED   RW   DEVILS

PERSONAL: Born November 10, 1969, in Edmonton. ... 6-3/220. ... Shoots right. ... Full Name: Edward John Ward.
COLLEGE: Northern Michigan.
TRANSACTIONS/CAREER NOTES: Selected by Quebec Nordiques in sixth round (seventh Nordiques pick, 108th overall) of NHL entry draft (June 11, 1988). ... Traded by Nordiques to Calgary Flames for D Francois Groleau (March 24, 1995). ... Bruised ribs (December 3, 1995); missed one game. ... Lacerated elbow (December 13, 1995); missed one game. ... Selected by Atlanta Thrashers in NHL expansion draft (June 25, 1999). ... Sprained ankle (February 15, 2000); missed nine games. ... Traded by Thrashers to Mighty Ducks of Anaheim for future considerations (March 14, 2000). ... Traded by Mighty Ducks to New Jersey Devils for seventh-round pick in 2001 draft (June 12, 2000).

Season Team	League	REGULAR SEASON								PLAYOFFS				
		Gms.	G	A	Pts.	PIM	+/-	PP	SH	Gms.	G	A	Pts.	PIM
86-87—Sherwood Park	AJHL	60	18	28	46	272	...	...	...	—				
87-88—N. Michigan Univ.	WCHA	25	0	2	2	40	...	...	...	—				
88-89—N. Michigan Univ.	WCHA	42	5	15	20	36	...	...	...	—				
89-90—N. Michigan Univ.	WCHA	39	5	11	16	77	...	...	...	—				
90-91—N. Michigan Univ.	WCHA	46	13	18	31	109	...	...	...	—				
91-92—Halifax	AHL	51	7	11	18	65	...	...	...	—				
—Greensboro	ECHL	12	4	8	12	21	...	...	...	—				
92-93—Halifax	AHL	70	13	19	32	56	...	...	...	—				
93-94—Cornwall	AHL	60	12	30	42	65	...	...	...	12	1	3	4	14
—Quebec	NHL	7	1	0	1	5	0	0	0	—				
94-95—Cornwall	AHL	56	10	14	24	118	...	...	...	—				
—Saint John	AHL	11	4	5	9	20	...	...	...	5	1	0	1	10
—Calgary	NHL	2	1	1	2	2	-2	0	0	—				
95-96—Saint John	AHL	12	1	2	3	45	...	...	...	16	4	4	8	27
—Calgary	NHL	41	3	5	8	44	-2	0	0	—				
96-97—Saint John	AHL	1	0	0	0	0	...	...	...	—				
—Detroit	IHL	31	7	6	13	45	...	...	...	—				
—Calgary	NHL	40	5	8	13	49	-3	0	0	—				
97-98—Calgary	NHL	64	4	5	9	122	-1	0	0	—				
98-99—Calgary	NHL	68	3	5	8	67	-4	0	0	—				
99-00—Atlanta	NHL	44	5	1	6	44	-5	0	2	—				
—Anaheim	NHL	8	1	0	1	15	-2	0	0	—				
NHL Totals (7 years)		274	23	25	48	348	-19	0	2					

WARD, JASON   RW/C   CANADIENS

PERSONAL: Born January 16, 1979, in Chapleau, Ont. ... 6-2/193. ... Shoots right.
TRANSACTIONS/CAREER NOTES: Selected by Montreal Canadiens in first round (first Canadiens pick, 11th overall) of NHL entry draft (June 21, 1997). ... Fractured cheekbone (February 10, 2000); missed seven games.

Season Team	League	REGULAR SEASON								PLAYOFFS				
		Gms.	G	A	Pts.	PIM	+/-	PP	SH	Gms.	G	A	Pts.	PIM
94-95—Oshawa	Tier II Jr. A	47	30	31	61	75	...	...	...	—				
95-96—Niagara Falls	OHL	64	15	35	50	139	...	...	...	10	6	4	10	23
96-97—Erie	OHL	58	25	39	64	137	...	...	...	5	1	2	3	2
97-98—Erie	OHL	21	7	9	16	42	...	...	...	—				
—Windsor	OHL	26	19	27	46	34	...	...	...	—				
—Fredericton	AHL	7	1	0	1	2	...	...	...	1	0	0	0	2
98-99—Windsor	OHL	12	8	11	19	25	...	...	...	—				
—Plymouth	OHL	23	14	13	27	28	...	...	...	11	6	8	14	12
—Fredericton	AHL	—					...	...	...	10	4	2	6	22
99-00—Quebec	AHL	40	14	12	26	30	...	...	...	3	2	1	3	4
—Montreal	NHL	32	2	1	3	10	-1	1	0	—				
NHL Totals (1 year)		32	2	1	3	10	-1	1	0					

WARRENER, RHETT   D   SABRES

PERSONAL: Born January 27, 1976, in Shaunavon, Sask. ... 6-1/210. ... Shoots right. ... Name pronounced REHT WAHR-uh-nuhr.
TRANSACTIONS/CAREER NOTES: Selected by Florida Panthers in second round (second Panthers pick, 27th overall) of NHL entry draft (June 28, 1994). ... Strained groin (October 20, 1996); missed four games. ... Reinjured groin (November 11, 1996); missed two games. ... Reinjured groin (December 22, 1996); missed 10 games. ... Strained groin (November 2, 1998); missed 12 games. ... Traded by Panthers with fifth-round pick (G Ryan Miller) in 1999 draft to Buffalo Sabres for D Mike Wilson (March 23, 1999). ... Injured shoulder (October 30, 1999); missed two games. ... Strained hip muscle (January 1, 2000); missed four games. ... Injured groin (February 21, 2000); missed eight games.

Season Team	League	Gms.	G	A	Pts.	PIM	+/-	PP	SH	Gms.	G	A	Pts.	PIM
		REGULAR SEASON								**PLAYOFFS**				
91-92—Saskatoon	WHL	2	0	0	0	0	...	...	...	—	—	—	—	—
92-93—Saskatoon	WHL	68	2	17	19	100	...	...	...	9	0	0	0	14
93-94—Saskatoon	WHL	61	7	19	26	131	...	...	...	16	0	5	5	33
94-95—Saskatoon	WHL	66	13	26	39	137	...	...	...	10	0	3	3	6
95-96—Carolina	AHL	9	0	0	0	4	...	...	...	—	—	—	—	—
—Florida	NHL	28	0	3	3	46	4	0	0	21	0	3	3	10
96-97—Florida	NHL	62	4	9	13	88	20	1	0	5	0	0	0	0
97-98—Florida	NHL	79	0	4	4	99	-16	0	0	—	—	—	—	—
98-99—Florida	NHL	48	0	7	7	64	-1	0	0	—	—	—	—	—
—Buffalo	NHL	13	1	0	1	20	3	0	0	20	1	3	4	32
99-00—Buffalo	NHL	61	0	3	3	89	18	0	0	5	0	0	0	2
NHL Totals (5 years)		291	5	26	31	406	28	1	0	51	1	6	7	44

WARRINER, TODD   LW   LIGHTNING

PERSONAL: Born January 3, 1974, in Blenheim, Ont. ... 6-1/200. ... Shoots left. ... Name pronounced WAHR-ih-nuhr.

HIGH SCHOOL: Herman E. Fawcett (Brantford, Ont.).

TRANSACTIONS/CAREER NOTES: Selected by Quebec Nordiques in first round (first Nordiques pick, fourth overall) of NHL entry draft (June 20, 1992). ... Traded by Nordiques with C Mats Sundin, D Garth Butcher and first-round pick (traded to Washington Capitals) in 1994 draft to Toronto Maple Leafs for LW Wendel Clark, D Sylvain Lefebvre, RW Landon Wilson and first-round pick (D Jeffrey Kealty) in 1994 draft (June 28, 1994). ... Suffered hip pointer (December 7, 1995); missed eight games. ... Injured hip flexor (October 3, 1996); missed one game. ... Injured hip flexor (November 19, 1996); missed four games. ... Suffered from the flu (April 2, 1997); missed one game. ... Sprained shoulder (October 15, 1997); missed three games. ... Bruised thigh (November 17, 1997); missed 27 games. ... Sprained knee (March 4, 1999); missed four games. ... Traded by Maple Leafs to Tampa Bay Lightning for third-round pick (G Mikael Tellqvist) in 2000 draft (November 29, 1999). ... Injured hip (January 15, 2000); missed two games. ... Strained groin (March 8, 2000); missed one game.

HONORS: Won Can.HL Top Draft Prospect Award (1991-92). ... Won OHL Top Draft Prospect Award (1991-92). ... Named to Can.HL All-Star second team (1991-92). ... Named to OHL All-Star first team (1991-92).

MISCELLANEOUS: Member of silver-medal-winning Canadian Olympic team (1994).

Season Team	League	Gms.	G	A	Pts.	PIM	+/-	PP	SH	Gms.	G	A	Pts.	PIM
		REGULAR SEASON								**PLAYOFFS**				
88-89—Blenheim Jr. C	OHA	10	1	4	5	0	...			—	—	—	—	—
89-90—Chatham Jr. B	OHA	40	24	21	45	12	...			—	—	—	—	—
90-91—Windsor	OHL	57	36	28	64	26	...			11	5	6	11	12
91-92—Windsor	OHL	50	41	42	83	66	...			7	5	4	9	6
92-93—Windsor	OHL	23	13	21	34	29	...			—	—	—	—	—
—Kitchener	OHL	32	19	24	43	35	...			7	5	14	19	14
93-94—Canadian nat'l team	Int'l	50	11	20	31	33	...			—	—	—	—	—
—Can. Olympic team	Int'l	4	1	1	2	0	...			—	—	—	—	—
—Kitchener	OHL	—	—	—	—	—	...			1	0	1	1	0
—Cornwall	AHL	—	—	—	—	—	...			10	1	4	5	4
94-95—St. John's	AHL	46	8	10	18	22	...			4	1	0	1	2
—Toronto	NHL	5	0	0	0	0	-3	0	0	—	—	—	—	—
95-96—St. John's	AHL	11	5	6	11	16	...			—	—	—	—	—
—Toronto	NHL	57	7	8	15	26	-11	1	0	6	1	1	2	2
96-97—Toronto	NHL	75	12	21	33	41	-3	2	2	—	—	—	—	—
97-98—Toronto	NHL	45	5	8	13	20	5	0	0	—	—	—	—	—
98-99—Toronto	NHL	53	9	10	19	28	-6	1	0	9	0	0	0	2
99-00—Toronto	NHL	18	3	1	4	2	6	0	0	—	—	—	—	—
—Tampa Bay	NHL	55	11	13	24	34	-14	3	1	—	—	—	—	—
NHL Totals (6 years)		308	47	61	108	151	-26	7	3	15	1	1	2	4

WASHBURN, STEVE   C   FLYERS

W

PERSONAL: Born April 10, 1975, in Ottawa. ... 6-2/198. ... Shoots left.

TRANSACTIONS/CAREER NOTES: Selected by Florida Panthers in third round (fifth Panthers pick, 78th overall) of NHL entry draft (June 26, 1993). ... Sprained knee (April 11, 1997); missed remainder of season. ... Separated right shoulder (October 28, 1997); missed nine games. ... Fractured finger (October 3, 1998); missed first five games of season. ... Tore right groin (November 7, 1998); missed 12 games. ... Strained groin (December 27, 1998); missed eight games. ... Claimed on waivers by Vancouver Canucks (February 18, 1999). ... Signed as free agent by Nashville Predators (August 10, 1999). ... Traded by Predators to Philadelphia Flyers for conditional pick in 2001 draft (November 16, 1999).

Season Team	League	Gms.	G	A	Pts.	PIM	+/-	PP	SH	Gms.	G	A	Pts.	PIM
		REGULAR SEASON								**PLAYOFFS**				
90-91—Gloucester	OPJHL	56	21	30	51	47	...			—	—	—	—	—
91-92—Ottawa	OHL	59	5	17	22	10	...			11	2	3	5	4
92-93—Ottawa	OHL	66	20	38	58	54	...			—	—	—	—	—
93-94—Ottawa	OHL	65	30	50	80	88	...			17	7	16	23	10
94-95—Ottawa	OHL	63	43	63	106	72	...			9	1	3	4	4
—Cincinnati	IHL	6	3	1	4	0	...			—	—	—	—	—
95-96—Carolina	AHL	78	29	54	83	45	...			—	—	—	—	—
—Florida	NHL	1	0	1	1	0	1	0	0	1	0	1	1	0
96-97—Carolina	AHL	60	23	40	63	66	...			—	—	—	—	—
—Florida	NHL	18	3	6	9	4	2	1	0	—	—	—	—	—
97-98—Florida	NHL	58	11	8	19	32	-6	4	0	—	—	—	—	—
—New Haven	AHL	6	3	5	8	4	...			3	2	0	2	15
98-99—Florida	NHL	4	0	0	0	0	-1	0	0	—	—	—	—	—
—New Haven	AHL	10	4	3	7	6	...			—	—	—	—	—
—Vancouver	NHL	8	0	0	0	2	0	0	0	—	—	—	—	—
—Syracuse	AHL	13	1	6	7	6	...			—	—	—	—	—
99-00—Milwaukee	IHL	12	0	4	4	16	...			—	—	—	—	—
—Philadelphia	AHL	61	19	52	71	93	...			5	0	2	2	8
—Philadelphia	NHL	1	0	0	0	0	0	0	0	—	—	—	—	—
NHL Totals (5 years)		90	14	15	29	42	-4	5	0	1	0	1	1	0

WATSON, DAN D BLUE JACKETS

PERSONAL: Born October 5, 1979, in Glencoe, Ont. ... 6-2/221. ... Shoots left.
TRANSACTIONS/CAREER NOTES: Signed as non-drafted free agent by Columbus Blue Jackets (May 16, 2000).

Season Team	League	REGULAR SEASON Gms.	G	A	Pts.	PIM	+/-	PP	SH	PLAYOFFS Gms.	G	A	Pts.	PIM
96-97—Sarnia	OHL	10	0	2	2	7	...	...	...	—	—	—	—	—
97-98—Sarnia	OHL	66	6	15	21	19	...	...	...	5	0	1	1	4
98-99—Sarnia	OHL	68	2	18	20	27	...	...	...	6	0	0	0	4
99-00—Sarnia	OHL	68	1	15	16	40	...	...	...	7	0	0	0	4

WATT, MIKE LW/C PREDATORS

PERSONAL: Born March 31, 1976, in Seaforth, Ont. ... 6-2/208. ... Shoots left.
COLLEGE: Michigan State.
TRANSACTIONS/CAREER NOTES: Selected by Edmonton Oilers in second round (third Oilers pick, 32nd overall) of NHL entry draft (June 28, 1994). ... Traded by Oilers to New York Islanders for G Eric Fichaud (June 18, 1998). ... Suffered charley horse (October 24, 1998); missed one game. ... Strained hand (November 6, 1999); missed three games. ... Claimed on waivers by Nashville Predators (May 23, 2000).

Season Team	League	REGULAR SEASON Gms.	G	A	Pts.	PIM	+/-	PP	SH	PLAYOFFS Gms.	G	A	Pts.	PIM
91-92—Stratford Jr. B	OHA	46	5	26	31	...	...	...	...	—	—	—	—	—
92-93—Stratford Jr. B	OHA	45	20	35	55	100	...	...	...	—	—	—	—	—
93-94—Stratford Jr. B	OHA	48	34	34	68	165	...	...	...	—	—	—	—	—
94-95—Michigan State	CCHA	39	12	6	18	64	...	...	...	—	—	—	—	—
95-96—Michigan State	CCHA	37	17	22	39	60	...	...	...	—	—	—	—	—
96-97—Michigan State	CCHA	39	24	17	41	109	...	...	...	—	—	—	—	—
97-98—Hamilton	AHL	63	24	25	49	65	...	...	...	9	2	2	4	8
—Edmonton	NHL	14	1	2	3	4	-4	0	0	—	—	—	—	—
98-99—New York Islanders	NHL	75	8	17	25	12	-2	0	0	—	—	—	—	—
99-00—New York Islanders	NHL	45	5	6	11	17	-8	0	1	—	—	—	—	—
—Lowell	AHL	16	6	11	17	6	...	...	...	7	1	1	2	4
NHL Totals (3 years)		134	14	25	39	33	-14	0	1					

WEBB, STEVE RW ISLANDERS

PERSONAL: Born April 30, 1975, in Peterborough, Ont. ... 6-0/208. ... Shoots right.
TRANSACTIONS/CAREER NOTES: Selected by Buffalo Sabres in seventh round (eighth Sabres pick, 176th overall) of NHL entry draft (June 29, 1994). ... Signed as free agent by New York Islanders (October 14, 1996). ... Injured lower back (October 27, 1999); missed one game. ... Injured back (November 4, 1999); missed four games. ... Suffered from the flu (April 9, 2000); missed final game of season.

Season Team	League	REGULAR SEASON Gms.	G	A	Pts.	PIM	+/-	PP	SH	PLAYOFFS Gms.	G	A	Pts.	PIM
91-92—Peterborough	Jr. B	37	9	9	18	195	...	...	...	—	—	—	—	—
92-93—Windsor	OHL	63	14	25	39	181	...	...	...	—	—	—	—	—
93-94—Windsor	OHL	33	6	15	21	117	...	...	...	—	—	—	—	—
—Peterborough	OHL	2	0	1	1	9	...	...	...	—	—	—	—	—
94-95—Peterborough	OHL	42	8	16	24	109	...	...	...	11	3	3	6	22
95-96—Muskegon	Col.HL	58	18	24	42	263	...	...	...	5	1	2	3	22
—Detroit	IHL	4	0	0	0	24	...	...	...	—	—	—	—	—
96-97—Kentucky	AHL	25	6	6	12	103	...	...	...	2	0	0	0	19
—New York Islanders	NHL	41	1	4	5	144	-10	1	0	—	—	—	—	—
97-98—Kentucky	AHL	37	5	13	18	139	...	...	...	3	0	1	1	10
—New York Islanders	NHL	20	0	0	0	35	-2	0	0	—	—	—	—	—
98-99—Lowell	AHL	23	2	4	6	80	...	...	...	—	—	—	—	—
—New York Islanders	NHL	45	0	0	0	32	-10	0	0	—	—	—	—	—
99-00—New York Islanders	NHL	65	1	3	4	103	-4	0	0	—	—	—	—	—
NHL Totals (4 years)		171	2	7	9	314	-26	1	0					

WEEKES, KEVIN G LIGHTNING

PERSONAL: Born April 4, 1975, in Toronto. ... 6-0/195. ... Catches left. ... Name pronounced WEEKS.
HIGH SCHOOL: West Hill (Ont.) Secondary.
TRANSACTIONS/CAREER NOTES: Selected by Florida Panthers in second round (second Panthers pick, 41st overall) of NHL entry draft (June 26, 1993). ... Sprained right knee (March 19, 1998); missed remainder of season. ... Traded by Panthers with D Ed Jovanovski, C Dave Gagner, C Mike Brown and first-round pick (C Nathan Smith) in 2000 draft to Vancouver Canucks for RW Pavel Bure, D Bret Hedican, D Brad Ference and third-round pick (RW Robert Fried) in 2000 draft (January 17, 1999). ... Injured knee (October 28, 1999); missed three games. ... Traded by Canucks with C Dave Scatchard and RW Bill Muckalt to New York Islanders for G Felix Potvin, second-(traded to Atlanta) and third-round (C Thatcher Bell) picks in 2000 draft (December 19, 1999). ... Sore neck (April 9, 2000); missed final game of season. ... Traded by Islanders with rights to D Kristian Kudroc and second-round pick in 2001 draft to Tampa Bay Lightning for first-(LW Raffi Torres), fourth-(RW/LW Vladimir Gorbunov) and seventh-round (D Ryan Caldwell) picks in 2000 draft (June 24, 2000).
MISCELLANEOUS: Stopped a penalty shot attempt (vs. Miroslav Satan, March 4, 2000). ... Allowed a penalty shot goal (vs. Paul Kariya, January 21, 1998).

W

Season Team	League	Gms.	Min	W	L	T	GA	SO	Avg.	Gms.	Min.	W	L	GA	SO	Avg.
91-92—St. Michael's	Tier II Jr. A	2	127	...	...	...	11	0	5.20	—	—	—	—	—	—	—
92-93—Owen Sound	OHL	29	1645	9	12	5	143	0	5.22	1	26	0	0	5	0	11.54
93-94—Owen Sound	OHL	34	1974	13	19	1	158	0	4.80	—	—	—	—	—	—	—
94-95—Ottawa	OHL	41	2266	13	23	4	154	1	4.08	—	—	—	—	—	—	—
95-96—Carolina	AHL	60	3403	24	25	8	229	2	4.04	—	—	—	—	—	—	—
96-97—Carolina	AHL	51	2899	17	†28	4	172	1	3.56	—	—	—	—	—	—	—
97-98—Fort Wayne	IHL	12	719	9	2	‡1	34	1	2.84	—	—	—	—	—	—	—
—Florida	NHL	11	485	0	5	1	32	0	3.96	—	—	—	—	—	—	—
98-99—Detroit	IHL	33	1857	19	5	‡7	64	*4	*2.07	—	—	—	—	—	—	—
—Vancouver	NHL	11	532	0	8	1	34	0	3.83	—	—	—	—	—	—	—
99-00—Vancouver	NHL	20	987	6	7	4	47	1	2.86	—	—	—	—	—	—	—
—New York Islanders	NHL	36	2026	10	20	4	115	1	3.41	—	—	—	—	—	—	—
NHL Totals (3 years)		78	4030	16	40	10	228	2	3.39							

WEIGHT, DOUG — C — OILERS

PERSONAL: Born January 21, 1971, in Warren, Mich. ... 5-11/200. ... Shoots left. ... Full Name: Douglas D. Weight. ... Name pronounced WAYT.

COLLEGE: Lake Superior State (Mich.).

TRANSACTIONS/CAREER NOTES: Selected by New York Rangers in second round (second Rangers pick, 34th overall) of NHL entry draft (June 16, 1990). ... Sprained elbow (October 14, 1991); missed three games. ... Damaged ligaments (January 11, 1991). ... Suspended four off-days and fined $500 by NHL for cross-checking (November 5, 1992). ... Traded by Rangers to Edmonton Oilers for LW Esa Tikkanen (March 17, 1993). ... Played in Europe during 1994-95 NHL lockout. ... Sprained ankle (February 15, 1997); missed one game. ... Injured ankle (February 21, 1997); missed one game. ... Sprained left shoulder (March 15, 1998); missed two games. ... Tore medial collateral ligament in right knee (October 28, 1998); missed 34 games. ... Fractured ribs (December 14, 1999); missed five games.

HONORS: Named to CCHA All-Rookie team (1989-90). ... Named to NCAA All-America (West) second team (1990-91). ... Named to CCHA All-Star first team (1990-91). ... Played in NHL All-Star Game (1996 and 1998).

MISCELLANEOUS: Captain of Edmonton Oilers (1999-2000). ... Scored on a penalty shot (vs. Mike Richter, October 8, 1997).

STATISTICAL PLATEAUS: Three-goal games: 1995-96 (1).

Season Team	League	Gms.	G	A	Pts.	PIM	+/-	PP	SH	Gms.	G	A	Pts.	PIM
88-89—Bloomfield	NAJHL	34	26	53	79	105	...	...	...	—	—	—	—	—
89-90—Lake Superior State	CCHA	46	21	48	69	44	...	...	...	—	—	—	—	—
90-91—Lake Superior State	CCHA	42	29	46	75	86	...	...	...	1	0	0	0	0
—New York Rangers	NHL	—	—	—	—	—	—	—	—	7	2	2	4	0
91-92—New York Rangers	NHL	53	8	22	30	23	-3	0	0	4	1	4	5	6
—Binghamton	AHL	9	3	14	17	2	...	...	...	—	—	—	—	—
92-93—New York Rangers	NHL	65	15	25	40	55	4	3	0	—	—	—	—	—
—Edmonton	NHL	13	2	6	8	10	-2	0	0	—	—	—	—	—
93-94—Edmonton	NHL	84	24	50	74	47	-22	4	1	—	—	—	—	—
94-95—Rosenheim	Germany	8	2	3	5	18	...	...	...	—	—	—	—	—
—Edmonton	NHL	48	7	33	40	69	-17	1	0	—	—	—	—	—
95-96—Edmonton	NHL	82	25	79	104	95	-19	9	0	—	—	—	—	—
96-97—Edmonton	NHL	80	21	61	82	80	1	4	0	12	3	8	11	8
97-98—Edmonton	NHL	79	26	44	70	69	1	9	0	12	2	7	9	14
—U.S. Olympic team	Int'l	4	0	2	2	2	...	...	...	—	—	—	—	—
98-99—Edmonton	NHL	43	6	31	37	12	-8	1	0	4	1	1	2	15
99-00—Edmonton	NHL	77	21	51	72	54	6	3	1	5	3	2	5	4
NHL Totals (10 years)		624	155	402	557	514	-59	34	2	41	11	20	31	41

WEINRICH, ERIC — D — CANADIENS

W

PERSONAL: Born December 19, 1966, in Roanoke, Va. ... 6-1/213. ... Shoots left. ... Full Name: Eric John Weinrich. ... Name pronounced WIGHN-rihch.

HIGH SCHOOL: North Yarmouth (Maine) Academy.

COLLEGE: Maine.

TRANSACTIONS/CAREER NOTES: Selected by New Jersey Devils in second round (third Devils pick, 32nd overall) of NHL entry draft (June 15, 1985). ... Traded by Devils with G Sean Burke to Hartford Whalers for RW Bobby Holik, second-round pick (LW Jay Pandolfo) in 1993 draft and future considerations (August 28, 1992). ... Suffered concussion (November 25, 1992); missed two games. ... Sprained knee (September 22, 1993); missed five games. ... Signed as free agent by Hartford Whalers (September 25, 1993). ... Injured right knee (October 5, 1993); missed five games. ... Traded with LW Patrick Poulin by Whalers to the Chicago Blackhawks for RW Steve Larmer and D Bryan Marchment (November 2, 1993). ... Fractured jaw (February 24, 1994); missed 17 games. ... Cut eye (November 1, 1995); missed three games. ... Cut thigh (December 31, 1996); missed one game. ... Traded by Blackhawks with G Jeff Hackett, D Alain Nasreddine and fourth-round pick (D Chris Dyment) in 1999 draft to Montreal Canadiens for G Jocelyn Thibault, D Dave Manson and D Brad Brown (November 16, 1998). ... Fractured foot (March 22, 2000); missed five games.

HONORS: Named to NCAA All-America (East) second team (1986-87). ... Named to Hockey East All-Star first team (1986-87). ... Won Eddie Shore Plaque (1989-90). ... Named to AHL All-Star first team (1989-90). ... Named to NHL All-Rookie team (1990-91).

Season Team	League	Gms.	G	A	Pts.	PIM	+/-	PP	SH	Gms.	G	A	Pts.	PIM
83-84—North Yarmouth Acad.	Maine H.S.	17	23	33	56	...	...	...	...	—	—	—	—	—
84-85—North Yarmouth Acad.	Maine H.S.	20	6	21	27	...	...	...	...	—	—	—	—	—
85-86—Univ. of Maine	Hockey East	34	0	15	15	26	...	...	...	—	—	—	—	—
86-87—Univ. of Maine	Hockey East	41	12	32	44	59	...	...	...	—	—	—	—	—
87-88—Univ. of Maine	Hockey East	8	4	7	11	22	...	...	...	—	—	—	—	—
—U.S. national team	Int'l	39	3	9	12	24	...	...	...	—	—	—	—	—
—U.S. Olympic team	Int'l	3	0	0	0	24	...	...	...	—	—	—	—	—

Season Team	League	REGULAR SEASON								PLAYOFFS				
		Gms.	G	A	Pts.	PIM	+/-	PP	SH	Gms.	G	A	Pts.	PIM
88-89—Utica	AHL	80	17	27	44	70	...	...	...	5	0	1	1	8
—New Jersey	NHL	2	0	0	0	0	-1	0	0	—	—	—	—	—
89-90—Utica	AHL	57	12	48	60	38	...	...	...	—	—	—	—	—
—New Jersey	NHL	19	2	7	9	11	1	1	0	6	1	3	4	17
90-91—New Jersey	NHL	76	4	34	38	48	10	1	0	7	1	2	3	6
91-92—New Jersey	NHL	76	7	25	32	55	10	5	0	7	0	2	2	4
92-93—Hartford	NHL	79	7	29	36	76	-11	1	2	—	—	—	—	—
93-94—Hartford	NHL	8	1	1	2	2	-5	1	0	—	—	—	—	—
—Chicago	NHL	54	3	23	26	31	6	1	0	6	0	2	2	6
94-95—Chicago	NHL	48	3	10	13	33	1	1	0	16	1	5	6	4
95-96—Chicago	NHL	77	5	10	15	65	14	0	0	10	1	4	5	10
96-97—Chicago	NHL	81	7	25	32	62	19	1	0	6	0	1	1	4
97-98—Chicago	NHL	82	2	21	23	106	10	0	0	—	—	—	—	—
98-99—Chicago	NHL	14	1	3	4	12	-13	0	0	—	—	—	—	—
—Montreal	NHL	66	6	12	18	77	-12	4	0	—	—	—	—	—
99-00—Montreal	NHL	77	4	25	29	39	4	2	0	—	—	—	—	—
NHL Totals (12 years)		759	52	225	277	617	33	17	2	58	4	19	23	51

WELLS, CHRIS — C/LW — STARS

PERSONAL: Born November 12, 1975, in Calgary. ... 6-6/223. ... Shoots left.
HIGH SCHOOL: Meadowdale (Lynnwood, Wash.).
TRANSACTIONS/CAREER NOTES: Selected by Pittsburgh Penguins in first round (first Penguins pick, 24th overall) of NHL entry draft (June 28, 1994). ... Suffered tendinitis in knee (October 9, 1995); missed two games. ... Traded by Penguins to Florida Panthers for C Stu Barnes and D Jason Woolley (November 19, 1996). ... Strained groin (March 15, 1998); missed one game. ... Reinjured groin (March 26, 1998); missed final 12 games of season. ... Suffered hernia (September 12, 1998); missed first 32 games of season. ... Suspended four games by NHL for cross-checking incident (November 3, 1999). ... Traded by Panthers to New York Rangers for future considerations (March 13, 2000). ... Signed as free agent by Dallas Stars (July 28, 2000).
HONORS: Named to WHL (West) All-Star first team (1994-95).

Season Team	League	REGULAR SEASON								PLAYOFFS				
		Gms.	G	A	Pts.	PIM	+/-	PP	SH	Gms.	G	A	Pts.	PIM
90-91—Calgary Royals	AJHL	35	13	14	27	33	...	...	...	—	—	—	—	—
91-92—Seattle	WHL	64	13	8	21	70	...	...	...	11	0	0	0	15
92-93—Seattle	WHL	63	18	37	55	111	...	...	...	5	2	3	5	4
93-94—Seattle	WHL	69	30	44	74	150	...	...	...	9	6	5	11	23
94-95—Seattle	WHL	69	45	63	108	148	...	...	...	3	0	1	1	4
—Cleveland	IHL	3	0	1	1	2	...	...	...	—	—	—	—	—
95-96—Pittsburgh	NHL	54	2	2	4	59	-6	0	1	—	—	—	—	—
96-97—Cleveland	IHL	15	4	6	10	9	...	...	...	—	—	—	—	—
—Florida	NHL	47	2	6	8	42	5	0	0	3	0	0	0	0
97-98—Florida	NHL	61	5	10	15	47	4	0	1	—	—	—	—	—
98-99—Florida	NHL	20	0	2	2	31	-4	0	0	—	—	—	—	—
—New Haven	AHL	9	3	1	4	28	...	...	...	—	—	—	—	—
99-00—Florida	NHL	13	0	0	0	14	-5	0	0	—	—	—	—	—
—Louisville	AHL	31	8	10	18	20	...	...	...	—	—	—	—	—
—Hartford	AHL	14	2	2	4	6	...	...	...	20	3	4	7	38
NHL Totals (5 years)		195	9	20	29	193	-6	0	2	3	0	0	0	0

WERENKA, BRAD — D — FLAMES

W

PERSONAL: Born February 12, 1969, in Two Hills, Alta. ... 6-1/218. ... Shoots left. ... Full Name: John Bradley Werenka. ... Name pronounced wuh-REHN-kuh.
HIGH SCHOOL: Fort Saskatchewan (Alta.).
COLLEGE: Northern Michigan.
TRANSACTIONS/CAREER NOTES: Selected by Edmonton Oilers as underage junior in second round (second Oilers pick, 42nd overall) of NHL entry draft (June 13, 1987). ... Traded by Oilers to Quebec Nordiques for G Steve Passmore (March 21, 1994). ... Signed as free agent by Chicago Blackhawks (August 10, 1995). ... Signed as free agent by Pittsburgh Penguins (July 31, 1997). ... Sprained ankle (October 17, 1997); missed 10 games. ... Bruised shoulder (November 22, 1997); missed one game. ... Suspended one game by NHL for high-sticking incident (March 28, 1999). ... Fractured orbital bone (December 26, 1999); missed two games. ... Traded by Penguins to Calgary Flames for LW Rene Corbet and G Tyler Moss (March 14, 2000).
HONORS: Named to NCAA All-America (West) first team (1990-91). ... Named to NCAA All-Tournament team (1990-91). ... Named to WCHA All-Star first team (1990-91). ... Won Governors Trophy (1996-97). ... Named to IHL All-Star first team (1996-97).
MISCELLANEOUS: Member of silver-medal-winning Canadian Olympic team (1994).

Season Team	League	REGULAR SEASON								PLAYOFFS				
		Gms.	G	A	Pts.	PIM	+/-	PP	SH	Gms.	G	A	Pts.	PIM
85-86—Fort Saskatchewan	AJHL	29	12	23	35	24	...	...	...	—	—	—	—	—
86-87—N. Michigan Univ.	WCHA	30	4	4	8	35	...	...	...	—	—	—	—	—
87-88—N. Michigan Univ.	WCHA	34	7	23	30	26	...	...	...	—	—	—	—	—
88-89—N. Michigan Univ.	WCHA	28	7	13	20	16	...	...	...	—	—	—	—	—
89-90—N. Michigan Univ.	WCHA	8	2	5	7	8	...	...	...	—	—	—	—	—
90-91—N. Michigan Univ.	WCHA	47	20	43	63	36	...	...	...	—	—	—	—	—
91-92—Cape Breton	AHL	66	6	21	27	95	...	...	...	5	0	3	3	6
92-93—Canadian nat'l team	Int'l	18	3	7	10	10	...	...	...	—	—	—	—	—
—Edmonton	NHL	27	5	3	8	24	1	0	1	—	—	—	—	—
—Cape Breton	AHL	4	1	1	2	4	...	...	...	16	4	17	21	12

Season Team	League	REGULAR SEASON								PLAYOFFS				
		Gms.	G	A	Pts.	PIM	+/-	PP	SH	Gms.	G	A	Pts.	PIM
93-94—Cape Breton	AHL	25	6	17	23	19	...	...	...	—	—	—	—	—
—Edmonton	NHL	15	0	4	4	14	-1	0	0	—	—	—	—	—
—Can. Olympic team	Int'l	8	2	2	4	8	...	...	...	—	—	—	—	—
—Quebec	NHL	11	0	7	7	8	4	0	0	—	—	—	—	—
—Cornwall	AHL	—	—	—	—	—	...	...	...	12	2	10	12	36
94-95—Milwaukee	IHL	80	8	45	53	161	...	...	...	15	3	10	13	36
95-96—Indianapolis	IHL	73	15	42	57	85	...	...	...	5	1	3	4	8
—Chicago	NHL	9	0	0	0	8	-2	0	0	—	—	—	—	—
96-97—Indianapolis	IHL	82	20	56	76	83	...	...	...	4	1	4	5	6
97-98—Pittsburgh	NHL	71	3	15	18	46	15	2	0	6	1	0	1	8
98-99—Pittsburgh	NHL	81	6	18	24	93	17	1	0	13	1	1	2	6
99-00—Pittsburgh	NHL	61	3	8	11	69	15	0	0	—	—	—	—	—
—Calgary	NHL	12	1	1	2	21	-2	0	0	—	—	—	—	—
NHL Totals (6 years)		287	18	56	74	283	47	3	1	19	2	1	3	14

WESENBERG, BRIAN   RW   THRASHERS

PERSONAL: Born May 9, 1977, in Peterborough, Ont. ... 6-3/173. ... Shoots right.
HIGH SCHOOL: Bishop MacDonnell (Guelph, Ont.).
TRANSACTIONS/CAREER NOTES: Selected by Mighty Ducks of Anaheim in second round (second Mighty Ducks pick, 29th overall) of NHL entry draft (July 8, 1995). ... Traded by Mighty Ducks to Philadelphia Flyers for C Anatoli Semenov and D Mike Crowley (March 19, 1996). ... Suffered concussion (April 10, 1999); missed final three games of season. ... Traded by Flyers to Atlanta Thrashers for LW Eric Bertrand (December 9, 1999).

Season Team	League	REGULAR SEASON								PLAYOFFS				
		Gms.	G	A	Pts.	PIM	+/-	PP	SH	Gms.	G	A	Pts.	PIM
93-94—Cobourg	Tier II Jr. A	40	14	18	32	81	...	...	...	—	—	—	—	—
94-95—Guelph	OHL	66	17	27	44	81	...	...	...	14	2	3	5	18
95-96—Guelph	OHL	66	25	33	58	161	...	...	...	16	4	11	15	34
96-97—Guelph	OHL	64	37	43	80	186	...	...	...	18	4	9	13	59
—Philadelphia	AHL	—	—	—	—	—	...	...	...	3	0	0	0	7
97-98—Philadelphia	AHL	74	17	22	39	93	...	...	...	19	1	4	5	34
98-99—Philadelphia	AHL	71	23	20	43	169	...	...	...	16	5	3	8	28
—Philadelphia	NHL	1	0	0	0	5	1	0	0	—	—	—	—	—
99-00—Philadelphia	AHL	22	3	5	8	44	...	...	...	—	—	—	—	—
—Orlando	IHL	31	9	3	12	50	...	...	...	4	0	0	0	9
NHL Totals (1 year)		1	0	0	0	5	1	0	0					

WESLEY, GLEN   D   HURRICANES

PERSONAL: Born October 2, 1968, in Red Deer, Alta. ... 6-1/201. ... Shoots left.
TRANSACTIONS/CAREER NOTES: Selected by Boston Bruins as underage junior in first round (first Bruins pick, third overall) of NHL entry draft (June 13, 1987). ... Sprained left knee (October 1988). ... Fractured foot (November 24, 1992); missed 14 games. ... Injured groin (February 1993); missed one game. ... Injured groin (March 1993); missed three games. ... Injured groin (April 1993); missed two games. ... Injured kidney (March 3, 1994); missed three games. ... Traded by Bruins to Hartford Whalers for first-round picks in 1995 (D Kyle McLaren), 1996 (D Johnathan Aitken) and 1997 (C Sergei Samsonov) drafts (August 26, 1994). ... Bruised shin (November 4, 1995); missed two games. ... Injured groin (December 28, 1995); missed three games. ... Sprained knee (January 6, 1996); missed three games. ... Injured groin (January 17, 1996); missed four games. ... Injured groin (January 25, 1996); missed three games. ... Strained hip flexor (November 4, 1996); missed one game. ... Fractured foot (November 16, 1996); missed 10 games. ... Suffered from the flu (February 5, 1997); missed one game. ... Whalers franchise moved to North Carolina and renamed Carolina Hurricanes for 1997-98 season; NHL approved move on June 25, 1997. ... Sprained ankle (March 24, 1999); missed eight games. ... Strained groin (November 22, 1999); missed two games. ... Suffered eye injury (February 17, 2000); missed two games.
HONORS: Won WHL (West) Top Defenseman Trophy (1985-86 and 1986-87). ... Named to WHL (West) All-Star first team (1985-86 and 1986-87). ... Named to NHL All-Rookie team (1987-88). ... Played in NHL All-Star Game (1989).
MISCELLANEOUS: Captain of Hartford Whalers (1994-95).
STATISTICAL PLATEAUS: Three-goal games: 1993-94 (1).

Season Team	League	REGULAR SEASON								PLAYOFFS				
		Gms.	G	A	Pts.	PIM	+/-	PP	SH	Gms.	G	A	Pts.	PIM
83-84—Red Deer	AJHL	57	9	20	29	40	...	...	...	—	—	—	—	—
—Portland	WHL	3	1	2	3	0	...	...	...	—	—	—	—	—
84-85—Portland	WHL	67	16	52	68	76	...	...	...	6	1	6	7	8
85-86—Portland	WHL	69	16	75	91	96	...	...	...	15	3	11	14	29
86-87—Portland	WHL	63	16	46	62	72	...	...	...	20	8	18	26	27
87-88—Boston	NHL	79	7	30	37	69	21	1	2	23	6	8	14	22
88-89—Boston	NHL	77	19	35	54	61	23	8	1	10	0	2	2	4
89-90—Boston	NHL	78	9	27	36	48	6	5	0	21	2	6	8	36
90-91—Boston	NHL	80	11	32	43	78	0	5	1	19	2	9	11	19
91-92—Boston	NHL	78	9	37	46	54	-9	4	0	15	2	4	6	16
92-93—Boston	NHL	64	8	25	33	47	-2	4	1	4	0	0	0	0
93-94—Boston	NHL	81	14	44	58	64	1	6	1	13	3	3	6	12
94-95—Hartford	NHL	48	2	14	16	50	-6	1	0	—	—	—	—	—
95-96—Hartford	NHL	68	8	16	24	88	-9	6	0	—	—	—	—	—
96-97—Hartford	NHL	68	6	26	32	40	0	3	1	—	—	—	—	—
97-98—Carolina	NHL	82	6	19	25	36	7	1	0	—	—	—	—	—
98-99—Carolina	NHL	74	7	17	24	44	14	0	0	6	0	0	0	2
99-00—Carolina	NHL	78	7	15	22	38	-4	1	0	—	—	—	—	—
NHL Totals (13 years)		955	113	337	450	717	42	45	7	111	15	32	47	111

W

WESTLUND, TOMMY — RW — HURRICANES

PERSONAL: Born December 29, 1974, in Fors, Sweden. ... 6-0/202. ... Shoots right.
TRANSACTIONS/CAREER NOTES: Selected by Carolina Hurricanes in fourth round (fifth Hurricanes pick, 93rd overall) of NHL entry draft (June 27, 1998).

Season Team	League	Gms.	G	A	Pts.	PIM	+/-	PP	SH	Gms.	G	A	Pts.	PIM
91-92—Avesta	Sweden Dv. 3	27	11	9	20	8	...			—	—	—	—	—
92-93—Avesta	Sweden Dv. 2	32	9	5	14	32	...			—	—	—	—	—
93-94—Avesta	Sweden Dv. 2	31	20	11	31	34	...			—	—	—	—	—
94-95—Avesta	Sweden Dv. 2	32	17	13	30	22	...			—	—	—	—	—
95-96—Brynas Gavle	Sweden	18	2	1	3	2	...			—	—	—	—	—
—Brynas Gavle	Sweden Dv. 2	18	10	10	20	4	...			8	1	0	1	4
96-97—Brynas Gavle	Sweden	50	21	13	34	16	...			—	—	—	—	—
97-98—Brynas Gavle	Sweden	46	29	9	38	45	...			3	0	1	1	0
98-99—New Haven	AHL	50	8	18	26	31	...			—	—	—	—	—
99-00—Carolina	NHL	81	4	8	12	19	-10	0	1	—	—	—	—	—
NHL Totals (1 year)		81	4	8	12	19	-10	0	1	—	—	—	—	—

WHITE, BRIAN — D — AVALANCHE

PERSONAL: Born February 7, 1976, in Winchester, Mass. ... 6-1/180. ... Shoots right.
HIGH SCHOOL: Arlington (Mass.) Catholic.
COLLEGE: Maine.
TRANSACTIONS/CAREER NOTES: Selected by Tampa Bay Lightning in 11th round (11th Lightning pick, 268th overall) of NHL entry draft (June 29, 1994). ... Signed as free agent by Colorado Avalanche (July 1, 1998).

Season Team	League	Gms.	G	A	Pts.	PIM	+/-	PP	SH	Gms.	G	A	Pts.	PIM
92-93—Arlington Catholic	Mass. H.S.	...	7	25	32	...	...	...	...	—	—	—	—	—
93-94—Arlington Catholic	Mass. H.S.	26	10	29	39	...	...	...	...	—	—	—	—	—
94-95—Univ. of Maine	Hockey East	28	1	1	2	16	...	...	...	—	—	—	—	—
95-96—Univ. of Maine	Hockey East	39	0	4	4	18	...	...	...	—	—	—	—	—
96-97—Univ. of Maine	Hockey East	35	4	12	16	36	...	...	...	—	—	—	—	—
97-98—Univ. of Maine	Hockey East	33	0	12	12	45	...	...	...	—	—	—	—	—
—Long Beach	IHL	1	0	0	0	0	...	...	...	—	—	—	—	—
98-99—Hershey	AHL	71	4	8	12	41	...	...	...	4	0	1	1	2
—Colorado	NHL	2	0	0	0	0	0	0	0	—	—	—	—	—
99-00—Hershey	AHL	79	3	19	22	78	...	...	...	14	0	3	3	21
NHL Totals (1 year)		2	0	0	0	0	0	0	0					

WHITE, COLIN — D — DEVILS

PERSONAL: Born December 12, 1977, in New Glasgow, Nova Scotia. ... 6-4/210. ... Shoots left. ... Full Name: John Colin White.
TRANSACTIONS/CAREER NOTES: Selected by New Jersey Devils in second round (fifth Devils pick, 49th overall) of NHL entry draft (June 22, 1996). ... Suffered injury (January 28. 2000); missed two games. ... Suffered stiff neck (March 10, 2000); missed three games.
HONORS: Named to QMJHL All-Rookie team (1995-96).
MISCELLANEOUS: Member of Stanley Cup championship team (2000).

Season Team	League	Gms.	G	A	Pts.	PIM	+/-	PP	SH	Gms.	G	A	Pts.	PIM
94-95—Laval	QMJHL	7	0	1	1	32	...	...	...	—	—	—	—	—
—Hull	QMJHL	5	0	1	1	4	...	...	...	12	0	0	0	23
95-96—Hull	QMJHL	62	2	8	10	303	...	...	...	18	0	4	4	42
96-97—Hull	QMJHL	63	3	12	15	297	...	...	...	14	3	12	15	65
97-98—Albany	AHL	76	3	13	16	235	...	...	...	13	0	0	0	55
98-99—Albany	AHL	77	2	12	14	265	...	...	...	5	0	1	1	8
99-00—Albany	AHL	52	5	21	26	176	...	...	...	—	—	—	—	—
—New Jersey	NHL	21	2	1	3	40	3	0	0	23	1	5	6	18
NHL Totals (1 year)		21	2	1	3	40	3	0	0	23	1	5	6	18

WHITE, PETER — C — FLYERS

PERSONAL: Born March 15, 1969, in Montreal. ... 5-11/200. ... Shoots left. ... Full Name: Peter Toby White.
COLLEGE: Michigan State.
TRANSACTIONS/CAREER NOTES: Selected by Edmonton Oilers in fifth round (fourth Oilers pick, 92nd overall) of NHL entry draft (June 17, 1989). ... Traded by Oilers with fourth-round pick (RW Jason Sessa) in 1996 draft to Toronto Maple Leafs for LW Kent Manderville (December 4, 1995). ... Signed as free agent by Philadelphia Flyers (July 17, 1996).
HONORS: Named to CCHA All-Rookie team (1988-89). ... Named CCHA Playoff Most Valuable Player (1989-90). ... Won John B. Sellenberger Trophy (1994-95 and 1996-97). ... Named to AHL All-Star second team (1994-95, 1996-97 and 1997-98).

Season Team	League	Gms.	G	A	Pts.	PIM	+/-	PP	SH	Gms.	G	A	Pts.	PIM
87-88—Pembroke	COJHL	56	90	136	226	32	...	...	...	—	—	—	—	—
88-89—Michigan State	CCHA	46	20	33	53	17	...	...	...	—	—	—	—	—
89-90—Michigan State	CCHA	45	22	40	62	6	...	...	...	—	—	—	—	—
90-91—Michigan State	CCHA	37	7	31	38	28	...	...	...	—	—	—	—	—
91-92—Michigan State	CCHA	44	26	51	77	32	...	...	...	—	—	—	—	—
92-93—Cape Breton	AHL	64	12	28	40	10	...	...	...	16	3	3	6	12

Season Team	League	REGULAR SEASON								PLAYOFFS				
		Gms.	G	A	Pts.	PIM	+/-	PP	SH	Gms.	G	A	Pts.	PIM
93-94—Cape Breton	AHL	45	21	49	70	12	...	...	...	5	2	3	5	2
—Edmonton	NHL	26	3	5	8	2	1	0	0	—	—	—	—	—
94-95—Cape Breton	AHL	65	36	†69	*105	30	...	...	...	—	—	—	—	—
—Edmonton	NHL	9	2	4	6	0	1	2	0	—	—	—	—	—
95-96—Edmonton	NHL	26	5	3	8	0	-14	1	0	—	—	—	—	—
—Toronto	NHL	1	0	0	0	0	0	0	0	—	—	—	—	—
—St. John's	AHL	17	6	7	13	6	...			—	—	—	—	—
—Atlanta	IHL	36	21	20	41	4	...	...	...	3	0	3	3	2
96-97—Philadelphia	AHL	80	*44	61	*105	28	...	...	...	10	6	8	14	6
97-98—Philadelphia	AHL	80	27	*78	*105	28	...	...	...	20	9	9	18	6
98-99—Philadelphia	AHL	77	31	59	90	20	...	...	...	16	4	13	17	12
—Philadelphia	NHL	3	0	0	0	0	0	0	0	—	—	—	—	—
99-00—Philadelphia	AHL	62	20	41	61	38	...	...	...	—	—	—	—	—
—Philadelphia	NHL	21	1	5	6	6	1	0	0	16	0	2	2	0
NHL Totals (5 years)		86	11	17	28	8	-11	3	0	16	0	2	2	0

WHITE, TODD   C   SENATORS

PERSONAL: Born May 21, 1975, in Kanata, Ont. ... 5-10/180. ... Shoots left.
COLLEGE: Clarkson (N.Y.).
TRANSACTIONS/CAREER NOTES: Signed as free agent by Chicago Blackhawks (August 6, 1997). ... Suffered charley horse (October 4, 1997); missed one game. ... Bruised ribs prior to 1998-99 season; missed first six games of season. ... Traded by Blackhawks to Philadelphia Flyers for conditional pick in 2001 draft (January 26, 2000). ... Signed as free agent by Ottawa Senators (July 12, 2000).
HONORS: Named to ECAC All-Star second team (1995-96). ... Named to NCAA All-America (East) first team (1996-97). ... Named to ECAC All-Star first team (1996-97). ... Won Garry F. Longman Trophy (1997-98).
MISCELLANEOUS: Failed to score on a penalty shot (vs. Jamie Storr, Februaury 26, 1999).

Season Team	League	REGULAR SEASON								PLAYOFFS				
		Gms.	G	A	Pts.	PIM	+/-	PP	SH	Gms.	G	A	Pts.	PIM
93-94—Clarkson	ECAC	33	10	12	22	28	...	...	...	—	—	—	—	—
94-95—Clarkson	ECAC	34	13	16	29	44	...	...	...	—	—	—	—	—
95-96—Clarkson	ECAC	38	29	43	72	36	...	...	...	—	—	—	—	—
96-97—Clarkson	ECAC	37	38	36	74	22	...	...	...	—	—	—	—	—
97-98—Chicago	NHL	7	1	0	1	2	0	0	0	—	—	—	—	—
—Indianapolis	IHL	65	†46	36	82	28	...	...	...	5	2	3	5	4
98-99—Chicago	IHL	25	11	13	24	8	...	...	...	10	1	4	5	8
—Chicago	NHL	35	5	8	13	20	-1	2	0	—	—	—	—	—
99-00—Cleveland	IHL	42	21	30	51	32	...	...	...	—	—	—	—	—
—Chicago	NHL	1	0	0	0	0	0	0	0	—	—	—	—	—
—Philadelphia	AHL	32	19	24	43	12	...	...	...	5	2	1	3	8
—Philadelphia	NHL	3	1	0	1	0	-1	0	0	—	—	—	—	—
NHL Totals (3 years)		46	7	8	15	22	-2	2	0	—	—	—	—	—

WHITFIELD, TRENT   C   CAPITALS

PERSONAL: Born June 17, 1977, in Estevan, Sask. ... 5-11/199. ... Shoots left.
TRANSACTIONS/CAREER NOTES: Selected by Boston Bruins in fourth round (fifth Bruins pick, 100th overall) of NHL entry draft (June 22, 1996). ... Signed as free agent by Washington Capitals (September 1, 1998).
HONORS: Named to WHL (West) All-Star first team (1996-97). ... Named to WHL (West) All-Star second team (1997-98).

Season Team	League	REGULAR SEASON								PLAYOFFS				
		Gms.	G	A	Pts.	PIM	+/-	PP	SH	Gms.	G	A	Pts.	PIM
93-94—Spokane	WHL	5	1	1	2	0	...	...	...	11	7	6	13	5
94-95—Spokane	WHL	48	8	17	25	26	...	...	...	18	8	10	18	10
95-96—Spokane	WHL	72	33	51	84	75	...	...	...	9	5	7	12	10
96-97—Spokane	WHL	58	34	42	76	74	...	...	...	18	9	10	19	15
97-98—Spokane	WHL	65	38	44	82	97	...	...	...					
98-99—Portland	AHL	50	10	8	18	20	...	...	...					
—Hampton Roads	ECHL	19	13	12	25	12	...	...	...	4	2	0	2	14
99-00—Portland	AHL	79	18	35	53	52	...	...	...	3	1	1	2	2
—Washington	NHL	—	—	—	—	—	—	—	—	3	0	0	0	0
NHL Totals (1 year)		0	0	0	0	0	0	0	0	3	0	0	0	0

WHITNEY, RAY   LW   PANTHERS

PERSONAL: Born May 8, 1972, in Fort Saskatchewan, Alta. ... 5-10/175. ... Shoots right.
TRANSACTIONS/CAREER NOTES: Selected by San Jose Sharks in second round (second Sharks pick, 23rd overall) of NHL entry draft (June 22, 1991). ... Sprained knee (October 30, 1993); missed 18 games. ... Suffered from the flu (December 15, 1993); missed one game. ... Injured ankle (February 20, 1995) and suffered eye infection (February 28, 1995); missed seven games. ... Suffered eye infection (March 21, 1995); missed one game. ... Suffered from the flu (April 9, 1995); missed one game. ... Injured groin (December 15, 1995); missed three games. ... Injured wrist (February 18, 1996); missed 17 games. ... Signed as free agent by Edmonton Oilers (October 1, 1997). ... Claimed on waivers by Florida Panthers (November 6, 1997). ... Strained groin (October 22, 1999); missed one game.
HONORS: Won Four Broncos Memorial Trophy (1990-91). ... Won Bob Clarke Trophy (1990-91). ... Won WHL (West) Player of the Year Award (1990-91). ... Won George Parsons Trophy (1990-91). ... Named to Memorial Cup All-Star team (1990-91). ... Named to WHL (West) All-Star first team (1990-91). ... Played in NHL All-Star Game (2000).
MISCELLANEOUS: Scored on a penalty shot (vs. Guy Hebert, March 21, 1999).

W

Season Team	League	REGULAR SEASON								PLAYOFFS				
		Gms.	G	A	Pts.	PIM	+/-	PP	SH	Gms.	G	A	Pts.	PIM
88-89—Spokane	WHL	71	17	33	50	16	...	...	...	—	—	—	—	—
89-90—Spokane	WHL	71	57	56	113	50	...	...	...	6	3	4	7	6
90-91—Spokane	WHL	72	67	118	*185	36	...	...	...	15	13	18	*31	12
91-92—San Diego	IHL	63	36	54	90	12	...	...	...	4	0	0	0	0
—San Jose	NHL	2	0	3	3	0	-1	0	0	—	—	—	—	—
—Koln	Germany	10	3	6	9	4	...	...	...	—	—	—	—	—
92-93—Kansas City	IHL	46	20	33	53	14	...	...	...	12	5	7	12	2
—San Jose	NHL	26	4	6	10	4	-14	1	0	—	—	—	—	—
93-94—San Jose	NHL	61	14	26	40	14	2	1	0	14	0	4	4	8
94-95—San Jose	NHL	39	13	12	25	14	-7	4	0	11	4	4	8	2
95-96—San Jose	NHL	60	17	24	41	16	-23	4	2	—	—	—	—	—
96-97—Kentucky	AHL	9	1	7	8	2	...	...	...	—	—	—	—	—
—Utah	IHL	43	13	35	48	34	...	...	...	7	3	1	4	6
—San Jose	NHL	12	0	2	2	4	-6	0	0	—	—	—	—	—
97-98—Edmonton	NHL	9	1	3	4	0	-1	0	0	—	—	—	—	—
—Florida	NHL	68	32	29	61	28	10	12	0	—	—	—	—	—
98-99—Florida	NHL	81	26	38	64	18	-3	7	0	—	—	—	—	—
99-00—Florida	NHL	81	29	42	71	35	16	5	0	4	1	0	1	4
NHL Totals (9 years)		439	136	185	321	133	-27	34	2	29	5	8	13	14

WIEMER, JASON   C   FLAMES

PERSONAL: Born April 14, 1976, in Kimberley, B.C. ... 6-1/220. ... Shoots left. ... Name pronounced WEE-muhr.
TRANSACTIONS/CAREER NOTES: Selected by Tampa Bay Lightning in first round (first Lightning pick, eighth overall) of NHL entry draft (June 28, 1994). ... Suffered from the flu (March 2, 1995); missed one game. ... Injured jaw (November 3, 1995); missed one game. ... Injured back (April 12, 1996); missed one game. ... Broke bursa sac in elbow (November 30, 1996); missed 14 games. ... Traded by Lightning to Calgary Flames for RW Sandy McCarthy and third- (LW Brad Richards) and fifth-round (D Curtis Rich) picks in 1998 draft (March 24, 1998). ... Injured hand (March 30, 1999); missed three games. ... Injured knee prior to start of 1999-2000 season; missed first 10 games of season. ... Reinjured knee (October 28, 1999); missed three games. ... Suffered injury (March 31, 2000); missed final five games of season.
STATISTICAL PLATEAUS: Three-goal games: 1995-96 (1).

Season Team	League	REGULAR SEASON								PLAYOFFS				
		Gms.	G	A	Pts.	PIM	+/-	PP	SH	Gms.	G	A	Pts.	PIM
91-92—Kimberley	RMJHL	45	34	33	67	211	...	...	...	—	—	—	—	—
—Portland	WHL	2	0	1	1	0	...	...	...	—	—	—	—	—
92-93—Portland	WHL	68	18	34	52	159	...	...	...	16	7	3	10	27
93-94—Portland	WHL	72	45	51	96	236	...	...	...	10	4	4	8	32
94-95—Portland	WHL	16	10	14	24	63	...	...	...	—	—	—	—	—
—Tampa Bay	NHL	36	1	4	5	44	-2	0	0	—	—	—	—	—
95-96—Tampa Bay	NHL	66	9	9	18	81	-9	4	0	6	1	0	1	28
96-97—Tampa Bay	NHL	63	9	5	14	134	-13	2	0	—	—	—	—	—
—Adirondack	AHL	4	1	0	1	7	...	...	...	—	—	—	—	—
97-98—Tampa Bay	NHL	67	8	9	17	132	-9	2	0	—	—	—	—	—
—Calgary	NHL	12	4	1	5	29	-1	0	0	—	—	—	—	—
98-99—Calgary	NHL	78	8	13	21	177	-12	1	0	—	—	—	—	—
99-00—Calgary	NHL	64	11	11	22	120	-10	2	0	—	—	—	—	—
NHL Totals (6 years)		386	50	52	102	716	-56	12	0	6	1	0	1	28

WILLIAMS, JEFF   LW   BLUE JACKETS

W

PERSONAL: Born February 11, 1976, in Pointe-Claire, Que. ... 6-1/200. ... Shoots left.
HIGH SCHOOL: Bishop MacDonnell (Guelph, Ont.).
TRANSACTIONS/CAREER NOTES: Selected by New Jersey Devils in seventh round (eighth Devils pick, 181st overall) of NHL entry draft (June 29, 1994). ... Claimed by Atlanta Thrashers from Devils in NHL waiver draft (September 27, 1999). ... Traded by Thrashers with C Sylvain Cloutier to Devils for LW Eric Bertrand, LW Wes Mason and seventh-round pick (LW Ken Magowan) in 2000 draft (November 1, 1999). ... Selected by Columbus Blue Jackets in NHL expansion draft (June 23, 2000).
HONORS: Won William Hanley Trophy (1995-96). ... Named to AHL All-Star second team (1998-99).

Season Team	League	REGULAR SEASON								PLAYOFFS				
		Gms.	G	A	Pts.	PIM	+/-	PP	SH	Gms.	G	A	Pts.	PIM
91-92—Newmarket	Jr. B	4	1	1	2	4	...	...	...	—	—	—	—	—
92-93—Newmarket	Jr. B	45	28	35	63	18	...	...	...	—	—	—	—	—
93-94—Guelph	OHL	62	14	12	26	19	...	...	...	9	2	1	3	4
94-95—Guelph	OHL	52	15	32	47	21	...	...	...	14	5	5	10	0
95-96—Guelph	OHL	63	15	49	64	42	...	...	...	16	13	15	28	10
96-97—Albany	AHL	46	13	20	33	12	...	...	...	15	1	2	3	15
—Raleigh	ECHL	20	4	8	12	8	...	...	...	—	—	—	—	—
97-98—Albany	AHL	58	13	12	25	20	...	...	...	12	5	6	11	2
98-99—Albany	AHL	74	*46	27	73	39	...	...	...	5	1	2	3	0
99-00—Orlando	IHL	6	2	4	6	0	...	...	...	—	—	—	—	—
—Albany	AHL	71	29	20	49	24	...	...	...	5	0	0	0	2

WILLIS, SHANE   RW   HURRICANES

PERSONAL: Born June 13, 1977, in Edmonton. ... 6-0/176. ... Shoots right.
TRANSACTIONS/CAREER NOTES: Selected by Tampa Bay Lightning in third round (third Lightning pick, 56th overall) of NHL entry draft (July 8, 1995). ... Returned to draft pool by Lightning and selected by Carolina Hurricanes in fourth round (fourth Hurricanes pick, 88th overall) of NHL entry draft (June 21, 1997).
HONORS: Named to Can.HL All-Rookie team (1994-95). ... Named to WHL (East) All-Star first team (1996-97 and 1997-98). ... Named to AHL All-Star first team (1998-99). ... Won Dudley (Red) Garrett Memorial Trophy (1998-99).

Season Team	League	REGULAR SEASON								PLAYOFFS				
		Gms.	G	A	Pts.	PIM	+/-	PP	SH	Gms.	G	A	Pts.	PIM
94-95—Prince Albert	WHL	65	24	19	43	38	...	...	...	13	3	4	7	6
95-96—Prince Albert	WHL	69	41	40	81	47	...	...	...	18	11	10	21	18
96-97—Prince Albert	WHL	41	34	22	56	63	...	...	...	—	—	—	—	—
—Lethbridge	WHL	26	22	17	39	24	...	...	...	19	13	11	24	20
97-98—New Haven	AHL	1	0	1	1	2	...	...	...	—	—	—	—	—
—Lethbridge	WHL	64	58	54	112	73	...	...	...	4	2	3	5	6
98-99—New Haven	AHL	73	31	50	81	49	...	...	...	—	—	—	—	—
—Carolina	NHL	7	0	0	0	0	-2	0	0	—	—	—	—	—
99-00—Cincinnati	IHL	80	35	25	60	64	...	...	...	11	5	3	8	8
—Carolina	NHL	2	0	0	0	0	-1	0	0	—	—	—	—	—
NHL Totals (2 years)		9	0	0	0	0	-3	0	0					

WILLSIE, BRIAN — RW — AVALANCHE

PERSONAL: Born March 16, 1978, in London, Ont. ... 6-0/190. ... Shoots right.
TRANSACTIONS/CAREER NOTES: Selected by Colorado Avalanche in sixth round (seventh Avalanche pick, 146th overall) of NHL entry draft (June 22, 1996).
HONORS: Named to OHL All-Star first team (1997-98).

Season Team	League	REGULAR SEASON								PLAYOFFS				
		Gms.	G	A	Pts.	PIM	+/-	PP	SH	Gms.	G	A	Pts.	PIM
95-96—Guelph	OHL	65	13	21	34	18	...	...	...	16	4	2	6	6
96-97—Guelph	OHL	64	37	31	68	37	...	...	...	18	15	4	19	10
97-98—Guelph	OHL	57	45	31	76	41	...	...	...	12	9	5	14	18
98-99—Hershey	AHL	72	19	10	29	28	...	...	...	3	1	0	1	0
99-00—Hershey	AHL	78	20	39	59	44	...	...	...	12	2	6	8	8
—Colorado	NHL	1	0	0	0	0	0	0	0	—	—	—	—	—
NHL Totals (1 year)		1	0	0	0	0	0	0	0					

WILM, CLARKE — C — FLAMES

PERSONAL: Born October 24, 1976, in Central Butte, Sask. ... 6-0/202. ... Shoots left. ... Name pronounced WIHLM.
TRANSACTIONS/CAREER NOTES: Selected by Calgary Flames in sixth round (fifth Flames pick, 150th overall) of NHL entry draft (July 8, 1995). ... Suffered concussion (November 27, 1998); missed two games.

Season Team	League	REGULAR SEASON								PLAYOFFS				
		Gms.	G	A	Pts.	PIM	+/-	PP	SH	Gms.	G	A	Pts.	PIM
91-92—Saskatoon	WHL	—	—	—	—	—	...	...	...	1	0	0	0	0
92-93—Saskatoon	WHL	69	14	19	33	71	...	...	...	9	4	2	6	13
93-94—Saskatoon	WHL	70	18	32	50	181	...	...	...	16	0	9	9	19
94-95—Saskatoon	WHL	71	20	39	59	179	...	...	...	10	6	1	7	21
95-96—Saskatoon	WHL	72	49	61	110	83	...	...	...	4	1	1	2	4
96-97—Saint John	AHL	62	9	19	28	107	...	...	...	5	2	0	2	15
97-98—Saint John	AHL	68	13	26	39	112	...	...	...	21	5	9	14	8
98-99—Calgary	NHL	78	10	8	18	53	11	2	2	—	—	—	—	—
99-00—Calgary	NHL	78	10	12	22	67	-6	1	3	—	—	—	—	—
NHL Totals (2 years)		156	20	20	40	120	5	3	5					

WILSON, LANDON — RW — COYOTES

W

PERSONAL: Born March 15, 1975, in St. Louis. ... 6-2/216. ... Shoots right. ... Son of Rick Wilson, defenseman with three NHL teams (1973-74 through 1976-77).
COLLEGE: North Dakota.
TRANSACTIONS/CAREER NOTES: Selected by Toronto Maple Leafs in first round (second Maple Leafs pick, 19th overall) of NHL entry draft (June 26, 1993). ... Traded by Maple Leafs with LW Wendel Clark, D Sylvain Lefebvre and first-round pick (D Jeffrey Kealty) in 1994 draft to Quebec Nordiques for C Mats Sundin, D Garth Butcher, LW Todd Warriner and first-round pick (traded to Washington Capitals) in 1994 draft (June 28, 1994). ... Nordiques franchise moved to Colorado and renamed Avalanche for 1995-96 season (June 21, 1995). ... Traded by Avalanche with D Anders Myrvold to Boston Bruins for first-round pick (D Robyn Regehr) in 1998 draft (November 22, 1996). ... Sprained shoulder (December 12, 1996); missed 10 games. ... Suffered charley horse (January 7, 1997); missed 12 games. ... Suffered concussion (March 9, 1999); missed two games. ... Strained abdominal muscle (April 15, 1999); missed one game. ... Strained shoulder (April 28, 1999); missed remainder of playoffs. ... Injured shoulder (November 4, 1999); missed seven games. ... Signed as free agent by Phoenix Coyotes (July 7, 2000).
HONORS: Named WCHA Rookie of the Year (1993-94). ... Named to WCHA All-Rookie team (1993-94). ... Named to AHL All-Star first team (1998-99).
MISCELLANEOUS: Failed to score on a penalty shot (vs. Curtis Joseph, March 17, 1999).

Season Team	League	REGULAR SEASON								PLAYOFFS				
		Gms.	G	A	Pts.	PIM	+/-	PP	SH	Gms.	G	A	Pts.	PIM
92-93—Dubuque	USHL	43	29	36	65	284	...	...	...	—	—	—	—	—
93-94—Univ. of North Dakota	WCHA	35	18	15	33	147	...	...	...	—	—	—	—	—
94-95—Univ. of North Dakota	WCHA	31	7	16	23	141	...	...	...	—	—	—	—	—
—Cornwall	AHL	8	4	4	8	25	...	...	...	13	3	4	7	68
95-96—Cornwall	AHL	53	21	13	34	154	...	...	...	8	1	3	4	22
—Colorado	NHL	7	1	0	1	6	3	0	0	—	—	—	—	—
96-97—Colorado	NHL	9	1	2	3	23	1	0	0	—	—	—	—	—
—Boston	NHL	40	7	10	17	49	-6	0	0	—	—	—	—	—
—Providence	AHL	2	2	1	3	2	...	...	...	10	3	4	7	16

Season Team	League	REGULAR SEASON								PLAYOFFS				
		Gms.	G	A	Pts.	PIM	+/-	PP	SH	Gms.	G	A	Pts.	PIM
97-98—Boston	NHL	28	1	5	6	7	3	0	0	1	0	0	0	0
—Providence	AHL	42	18	10	28	146	...	...	...					
98-99—Providence	AHL	48	31	22	53	89	...	...	...	11	7	1	8	19
—Boston	NHL	22	3	3	6	17	0	0	0	8	1	1	2	8
99-00—Boston	NHL	40	1	3	4	18	-6	0	0					
—Providence	AHL	17	5	5	10	45	...	...	...	9	2	3	5	38
NHL Totals (5 years)		146	14	23	37	120	-5	0	0	9	1	1	2	8

WILSON, MIKE D PANTHERS

PERSONAL: Born February 26, 1975, in Brampton, Ont. ... 6-6/212. ... Shoots left.

TRANSACTIONS/CAREER NOTES: Selected by Vancouver Canucks in first round (first Canucks pick, 20th overall) of NHL entry draft (June 26, 1993). ... Traded by Canucks with RW Michael Peca and first-round pick (D Jay McKee) in 1995 draft to Buffalo Sabres for RW Alexander Mogilny and fifth-round pick (LW Todd Norman) in 1995 draft (July 8, 1995). ... Suffered concussion (January 26, 1996); missed two games. ... Bruised chest (November 13, 1997); missed one game. ... Suffered mild concussion (January 8, 1998); missed two games. ... Missed first 19 games of 1998-99 season due to contract dispute; played with Las Vegas of IHL. ... Traded by Sabres to Florida Panthers for D Rhett Warrener and fifth-round pick (G Ryan Miller) in 1999 draft (March 23, 1999). ... Suffered concussion (March 31, 1999); missed final nine games of season.

HONORS: Named to Can.HL All-Rookie team (1992-93). ... Named to OHL All-Rookie team (1992-93).

Season Team	League	REGULAR SEASON								PLAYOFFS				
		Gms.	G	A	Pts.	PIM	+/-	PP	SH	Gms.	G	A	Pts.	PIM
91-92—Georgetown Jr. B	OHA	41	9	13	22	65	...	...	...					
92-93—Sudbury	OHL	53	6	7	13	58	...	...	...	14	1	1	2	21
93-94—Sudbury	OHL	60	4	22	26	62	...	...	...	9	1	3	4	8
94-95—Sudbury	OHL	64	13	34	47	46	...	...	...	18	1	8	9	10
95-96—Rochester	AHL	15	0	5	5	38	...	...	...	—	—	—	—	—
—Buffalo	NHL	58	4	8	12	41	13	1	0	—	—	—	—	—
96-97—Buffalo	NHL	77	2	9	11	51	13	0	0	10	0	1	1	2
97-98—Buffalo	NHL	66	4	4	8	48	13	0	0	15	0	1	1	13
98-99—Las Vegas	IHL	6	3	1	4	6	...	...	...	—	—	—	—	—
—Buffalo	NHL	30	1	2	3	47	10	0	0	—	—	—	—	—
—Florida	NHL	4	0	0	0	0	2	0	0	—	—	—	—	—
99-00—Florida	NHL	60	4	16	20	35	10	0	0	4	0	0	0	0
NHL Totals (5 years)		295	15	39	54	222	61	1	0	29	0	2	2	15

WITEHALL, JOHAN RW RANGERS

PERSONAL: Born January 7, 1972, in Goteborg, Sweden. ... 6-1/198. ... Shoots left.

TRANSACTIONS/CAREER NOTES: Selected by New York Rangers in eighth round (eighth Rangers pick, 207th overall) of NHL entry draft (June 27, 1998).

Season Team	League	REGULAR SEASON								PLAYOFFS				
		Gms.	G	A	Pts.	PIM	+/-	PP	SH	Gms.	G	A	Pts.	PIM
97-98—Leksand	Sweden	42	12	4	16	34	...	...	...	2	0	0	0	2
98-99—Hartford	AHL	62	14	15	29	56	...	...	...	7	1	2	3	6
—New York Rangers	NHL	4	0	0	0	0	0	0	0	—	—	—	—	—
99-00—Hartford	AHL	73	17	24	41	65	...	...	...	17	6	7	13	10
—New York Rangers	NHL	9	1	1	2	2	0	0	0	—	—	—	—	—
NHL Totals (2 years)		13	1	1	2	2	0	0	0					

W

WITT, BRENDAN D CAPITALS

PERSONAL: Born February 20, 1975, in Humboldt, Sask. ... 6-2/224. ... Shoots left.

HIGH SCHOOL: Meadowdale (Lynnwood, Wash.).

TRANSACTIONS/CAREER NOTES: Selected by Washington Capitals in first round (first Capitals pick, 11th overall) of NHL entry draft (June 26, 1993). ... Missed entire 1994-95 season due to contract dispute. ... Fractured wrist (January 28, 1996); missed 34 games. ... Suffered from the flu (November 15, 1996); missed five games. ... Bruised shoulder (November 27, 1997); missed seven games. ... Suffered illness (January 6, 1998); missed three games. ... Injured wrist (April 6, 1998); missed final six games of regular season and five playoff games. ... Sprained knee (October 18, 1998); missed one game. ... Strained hip flexor (October 28, 1998); missed five games. ... Missed game for personal reasons (January 26, 1999). ... Sprained wrist (February 3, 1999); missed 15 games. ... Sprained knee (October 16, 1999); missed two games. ... Strained back (November 26, 1999); missed one game. ... Strained groin (March 11, 2000); missed one game. ... Injured thigh (March 25, 2000); missed one game.

HONORS: Named to WHL (West) All-Star first team (1992-93 and 1993-94). ... Won Bill Hunter Trophy (1993-94). ... Named to Can.HL All-Star first team (1993-94).

Season Team	League	REGULAR SEASON								PLAYOFFS				
		Gms.	G	A	Pts.	PIM	+/-	PP	SH	Gms.	G	A	Pts.	PIM
90-91—Seattle	WHL	—					...	...	...	1	0	0	0	...
91-92—Seattle	WHL	67	3	9	12	212	...	...	...	15	1	1	2	84
92-93—Seattle	WHL	70	2	26	28	239	...	...	...	5	1	2	3	30
93-94—Seattle	WHL	56	8	31	39	235	...	...	...	9	3	8	11	23
94-95—								Did not play.						
95-96—Washington	NHL	48	2	3	5	85	-4	0	0	—	—	—	—	—
96-97—Washington	NHL	44	3	2	5	88	-20	0	0	—	—	—	—	—
—Portland	AHL	30	2	4	6	56	...	...	...	5	1	0	1	30
97-98—Washington	NHL	64	1	7	8	112	-11	0	0	16	1	0	1	14
98-99—Washington	NHL	54	2	5	7	87	-6	0	0	—	—	—	—	—
99-00—Washington	NHL	77	1	7	8	114	5	0	0	3	0	0	0	0
NHL Totals (6 years)		287	9	24	33	486	-36	0	0	19	1	0	1	14

WOOLLEY, JASON   D   SABRES

PERSONAL: Born July 27, 1969, in Toronto. ... 6-1/207. ... Shoots left. ... Full Name: Jason Douglas Woolley.
COLLEGE: Michigan State.
TRANSACTIONS/CAREER NOTES: Selected by Washington Capitals in third round (fourth Capitals pick, 61st overall) of NHL entry draft (June 17, 1989). ... Fractured wrist (October 12, 1992); missed 24 games. ... Tore abdominal muscle (January 2, 1994). ... Signed as free agent by Detroit Vipers (October 7, 1994). ... Contract sold by Vipers to Florida Panthers (February 14, 1995). ... Separated left shoulder (October 15, 1995); missed two games. ... Fractured left thumb (November 18, 1995); missed 13 games. ... Traded by Panthers with C Stu Barnes to Pittsburgh Penguins for C Chris Wells (November 19, 1996). ... Injured groin (November 22, 1996); missed one game. ... Strained groin (February 27, 1997); missed one game. ... Strained groin (March 4, 1997); missed two games. ... Bruised wrist (March 18, 1997); missed two games. ... Traded by Penguins to Buffalo Sabres for fifth-round pick (D Robert Scuderi) in 1998 draft (September 24, 1997). ... Fractured thumb (October 1, 1997); missed nine games. ... Suffered from the flu (February 15, 1999); missed one game. ... Strained groin (April 14, 1999); missed one game. ... Injured rib (November 12, 1999); missed four games. ... Suffered from the flu (March 4, 2000); missed two games.
HONORS: Named to CCHA All-Rookie team (1988-89). ... Named to NCAA All-America (West) first team (1990-91). ... Named to CCHA All-Star first team (1990-91).
MISCELLANEOUS: Member of silver-medal-winning Canadian Olympic team (1992).

| | | REGULAR SEASON | | | | | | | | | PLAYOFFS | | | | |
Season Team	League	Gms.	G	A	Pts.	PIM	+/-	PP	SH		Gms.	G	A	Pts.	PIM
87-88—St. Michael's Jr. B	ODHA	31	19	37	56	22	...	...	...		—	—	—	—	—
88-89—Michigan State	CCHA	47	12	25	37	26	...	...	...		—	—	—	—	—
89-90—Michigan State	CCHA	45	10	38	48	26	...	...	...		—	—	—	—	—
90-91—Michigan State	CCHA	40	15	44	59	24	...	...	...		—	—	—	—	—
91-92—Canadian nat'l team	Int'l	60	14	30	44	36	...	...	...		—	—	—	—	—
—Can. Olympic team	Int'l	8	0	5	5	4	...	...	...		—	—	—	—	—
—Baltimore	AHL	15	1	10	11	6	...	...	...		—	—	—	—	—
—Washington	NHL	1	0	0	0	0	1	0	0		—	—	—	—	—
92-93—Baltimore	AHL	29	14	27	41	22	...	...	...		1	0	2	2	0
—Washington	NHL	26	0	2	2	10	3	0	0		—	—	—	—	—
93-94—Portland	AHL	41	12	29	41	14	...	...	...		9	2	2	4	4
—Washington	NHL	10	1	2	3	4	2	0	0		4	1	0	1	4
94-95—Detroit	IHL	48	8	28	36	38	...	...	...		—	—	—	—	—
—Florida	NHL	34	4	9	13	18	-1	1	0		—	—	—	—	—
95-96—Florida	NHL	52	6	28	34	32	-9	3	0		13	2	6	8	14
96-97—Florida	NHL	3	0	0	0	2	1	0	0		—	—	—	—	—
—Pittsburgh	NHL	57	6	30	36	28	3	2	0		5	0	3	3	0
97-98—Buffalo	NHL	71	9	26	35	35	8	3	0		15	2	9	11	12
98-99—Buffalo	NHL	80	10	33	43	62	16	4	0		21	4	11	15	10
99-00—Buffalo	NHL	74	8	25	33	52	14	2	0		5	0	2	2	2
NHL Totals (9 years)		408	44	155	199	243	38	15	0		63	9	31	40	42

WORRELL, PETER   LW   PANTHERS

PERSONAL: Born August 18, 1977, in Pierrefonds, Que. ... 6-6/235. ... Shoots left. ... Name pronounced wuh-REHL.
TRANSACTIONS/CAREER NOTES: Selected by Florida Panthers in seventh round (seventh Panthers pick, 166th overall) of NHL entry draft (July 8, 1995). ... Suspended three games and fined $1,000 by NHL for elbowing incident (November 18, 1998). ... Sprained knee (September 21, 1999); missed nine games. ... Partially tore anterior collateral ligament in right knee (October 29, 1999); missed 12 games. ... Sprained knee (January 14, 2000); missed six games. ... Suffered head injury (March 19, 2000); missed six games.

| | | REGULAR SEASON | | | | | | | | | PLAYOFFS | | | | |
Season Team	League	Gms.	G	A	Pts.	PIM	+/-	PP	SH		Gms.	G	A	Pts.	PIM
94-95—Hull	QMJHL	56	1	8	9	243	...	...	...		21	0	1	1	91
95-96—Hull	QMJHL	63	23	36	59	464	...	...	...		18	11	8	19	81
96-97—Hull	QMJHL	62	18	45	63	*495	...	...	...		14	3	13	16	83
97-98—New Haven	AHL	50	15	12	27	309	...	...	...		1	0	1	1	6
—Florida	NHL	19	0	0	0	153	-4	0	0		—	—	—	—	—
98-99—Florida	NHL	62	4	5	9	258	0	0	0		—	—	—	—	—
—New Haven	AHL	10	3	1	4	65	...	...	...		—	—	—	—	—
99-00—Florida	NHL	48	3	6	9	169	-7	2	0		4	1	0	1	8
NHL Totals (3 years)		129	7	11	18	580	-11	2	0		4	1	0	1	8

WREGGET, KEN   G   RED WINGS

PERSONAL: Born March 25, 1964, in Brandon, Man. ... 6-1/210. ... Catches left.
TRANSACTIONS/CAREER NOTES: Selected by Toronto Maple Leafs as underage junior in third round (fourth Maple Leafs pick, 45th overall) of NHL entry draft (June 9, 1982). ... Injured knee (December 26, 1985). ... Traded by Maple Leafs to Philadelphia Flyers for two first-round picks (RW Rob Pearson and D Steve Bancroft) in 1989 draft (March 6, 1989). ... Tore hamstring (November 1, 1989); missed seven games. ... Pulled hamstring (March 24, 1990). ... Strained right hip flexor (November 4, 1990); missed 15 games. ... Traded by Flyers with RW Rick Tocchet, D Kjell Samuelsson and third-round pick (C Dave Roche) in 1993 draft to Pittsburgh Penguins for RW Mark Recchi, D Brian Benning and first-round pick (LW Jason Bowen) in 1992 draft (February 19, 1992). ... Bruised right knee (February 27, 1993); missed one game. ... Injured foot (April 4, 1994); missed five games. ... Strained ankle (March 24, 1995); missed two games. ... Reinjured ankle (April 5, 1995); missed four games. ... Pulled hamstring (December 26, 1996); missed 19 games. ... Reinjured hamstring (March 18, 1997); missed four games. ... Reinjured hamstring (April 5, 1997); missed three games. ... Bruised knee (October 25, 1997); missed one game. ... Herniated disk in back (November 5, 1997); missed 23 games. ... Bruised knee and back (March 14, 1998); missed five games. ... Traded by Penguins with C Dave Roche to Calgary Flames for C German Titov and LW/C Todd Hlushko (June 17, 1998). ... Suffered back spasms (November 3, 1998); missed 41 games. ... Signed as free agent by Detroit Red Wings (July 9, 1999).
HONORS: Won WHL Top Goaltender Trophy (1983-84). ... Named to WHL (East) All-Star first team (1983-84).
MISCELLANEOUS: Member of Stanley Cup championship team (1992). ... Stopped a penalty shot attempt (vs. Christian Ruuttu, November 15, 1987; vs. Lane Lambert, March 15, 1988; vs. Joe Nieuwendyk, January 23, 1993; vs. Scott Niedermayer, February 7, 1996; vs. Miroslav Satan, December 28, 1999). ... Allowed a penalty shot goal (vs. Rick Meagher, December 7, 1986; vs. Joe Sakic, December 9, 1989; vs. Doug Brown, November 23, 1991; vs. Chris Drury, March 18, 2000).

Season Team	League	REGULAR SEASON								PLAYOFFS						
		Gms.	Min	W	L	T	GA	SO	Avg.	Gms.	Min.	W	L	GA	SO	Avg.
81-82 —Lethbridge...................	WHL	36	1713	19	12	0	118	1	4.13	3	84	...	...	3	0	2.14
82-83 —Lethbridge...................	WHL	48	2696	26	17	1	157	1	3.49	*20	*1154	14	5	58	*1	*3.02
83-84 —Lethbridge...................	WHL	53	*3053	32	20	0	161	0	*3.16	4	210	1	3	18	0	5.14
—Toronto	NHL	3	165	1	1	1	14	0	5.09	—	—	—	—	—	—	—
84-85 —Toronto	NHL	23	1278	2	15	3	103	0	4.84	—	—	—	—	—	—	—
—St. Catharines	AHL	12	688	2	8	1	48	0	4.19	—	—	—	—	—	—	—
85-86 —St. Catharines	AHL	18	1058	8	9	0	78	1	4.42	—	—	—	—	—	—	—
—Toronto	NHL	30	1566	9	13	4	113	0	4.33	10	607	6	4	32	†1	3.16
86-87 —Toronto	NHL	56	3026	22	28	3	200	0	3.97	13	761	7	6	29	1	*2.29
87-88 —Toronto	NHL	56	3000	12	35	4	222	0	4.44	2	108	0	1	11	0	6.11
88-89 —Toronto	NHL	32	1888	9	20	2	139	0	4.42	—	—	—	—	—	—	—
—Philadelphia	NHL	3	130	1	1	0	13	0	6.00	5	268	2	2	10	0	2.24
89-90 —Philadelphia	NHL	51	2961	22	24	3	169	0	3.42	—	—	—	—	—	—	—
90-91 —Philadelphia	NHL	30	1484	10	14	3	88	0	3.56	—	—	—	—	—	—	—
91-92 —Philadelphia	NHL	23	1259	9	8	3	75	0	3.57	—	—	—	—	—	—	—
—Pittsburgh..............	NHL	9	448	5	3	0	31	0	4.15	1	40	0	0	4	0	6.00
92-93 —Pittsburgh..............	NHL	25	1368	13	7	2	78	0	3.42	—	—	—	—	—	—	—
93-94 —Pittsburgh..............	NHL	42	2456	21	12	7	138	1	3.37	—	—	—	—	—	—	—
94-95 —Pittsburgh..............	NHL	38	2208	*25	9	2	118	0	3.21	11	661	5	6	33	1	3.00
95-96 —Pittsburgh..............	NHL	37	2132	20	13	2	115	3	3.24	9	599	7	2	23	0	2.30
96-97 —Pittsburgh..............	NHL	46	2514	17	17	6	136	2	3.25	5	297	1	4	18	0	3.64
97-98 —Pittsburgh..............	NHL	15	611	3	6	2	28	0	2.75	—	—	—	—	—	—	—
98-99 —Calgary..............	NHL	27	1590	10	12	4	67	1	2.53	—	—	—	—	—	—	—
99-00 —Detroit..............	NHL	29	1579	14	10	2	70	0	2.66	—	—	—	—	—	—	—
NHL Totals (17 years)...........		575	31663	225	248	53	1917	9	3.63	56	3341	28	25	160	3	2.87

WRIGHT, JAMIE   LW   STARS

PERSONAL: Born May 13, 1976, in Kitchener, Ont. ... 6-0/195. ... Shoots right.
HIGH SCHOOL: Bishop MacDonnell (Guelph, Ont.).
TRANSACTIONS/CAREER NOTES: Selected by Dallas Stars in fourth round (third Stars pick, 98th overall) of NHL entry draft (June 29, 1994).
HONORS: Won Bobby Smith Trophy (1994-95).

Season Team	League	REGULAR SEASON							PLAYOFFS				
		Gms.	G	A	Pts.	PIM	+/-	PP	SH	Gms.	G	A	Pts.	PIM
91-92 —Elmira Jr. B.................	OHA	44	17	11	28	46	...	...	...	—	—	—	—	—
92-93 —Elmira Jr. B.................	OHA	47	22	32	54	52	...	...	...	—	—	—	—	—
93-94 —Guelph	OHL	65	17	15	32	34	...	...	...	8	2	1	3	10
94-95 —Guelph	OHL	65	43	39	82	34	...	...	...	14	6	8	14	6
95-96 —Guelph	OHL	55	30	36	66	45	...	...	...	16	10	12	22	35
96-97 —Michigan....................	IHL	60	6	8	14	34	...	...	...	1	0	0	0	0
97-98 —Michigan....................	IHL	53	15	11	26	31	...	...	...	—	—	—	—	—
—Dallas....................	NHL	21	4	2	6	2	8	0	0	5	0	0	0	0
98-99 —Dallas....................	NHL	11	0	0	0	0	-3	0	0	—	—	—	—	—
—Michigan....................	IHL	64	16	15	31	92	...	...	...	2	0	0	0	2
99-00 —Michigan....................	IHL	49	12	4	16	64	...	...	...	—	—	—	—	—
—Dallas....................	NHL	23	1	4	5	16	4	0	0	—	—	—	—	—
NHL Totals (3 years)...........		55	5	6	11	18	9	0	0	5	0	0	0	0

WRIGHT, TYLER   C   BLUE JACKETS

PERSONAL: Born April 6, 1973, in Canora, Sask. ... 5-11/187. ... Shoots right.
TRANSACTIONS/CAREER NOTES: Selected by Edmonton Oilers in first round (first Oilers pick, 12th overall) of NHL entry draft (June 22, 1991). ... Traded by Oilers to Pittsburgh Penguins for seventh-round pick (RW Brandon LaFrance) in 1996 draft (June 22, 1996). ... Bruised ribs (December 13, 1996); missed one game. ... Suffered back spasms (January 18, 2000); missed two games. ... Strained knee (April 3, 2000); missed two games. ... Selected by Columbus Blue Jackets in NHL expansion draft (June 23, 2000).

Season Team	League	REGULAR SEASON							PLAYOFFS				
		Gms.	G	A	Pts.	PIM	+/-	PP	SH	Gms.	G	A	Pts.	PIM
89-90 —Swift Current	WHL	67	14	18	32	119	...	...	...	4	0	0	0	12
90-91 —Swift Current	WHL	66	41	51	92	157	...	...	...	3	0	0	0	6
91-92 —Swift Current	WHL	63	36	46	82	295	...	...	...	8	2	5	7	16
92-93 —Swift Current	WHL	37	24	41	65	76	...	...	...	17	9	17	26	49
—Edmonton..................	NHL	7	1	1	2	19	-4	0	0	—	—	—	—	—
93-94 —Cape Breton..............	AHL	65	14	27	41	160	...	...	...	5	2	0	2	11
—Edmonton	NHL	5	0	0	0	4	-3	0	0	—	—	—	—	—
94-95 —Cape Breton..............	AHL	70	16	15	31	184	...	...	...	—	—	—	—	—
—Edmonton	NHL	6	1	0	1	14	1	0	0	—	—	—	—	—
95-96 —Edmonton	NHL	23	1	0	1	33	-7	0	0	—	—	—	—	—
—Cape Breton..............	AHL	31	6	12	18	158	...	...	...	—	—	—	—	—
96-97 —Pittsburgh..............	NHL	45	2	2	4	70	-7	0	0	—	—	—	—	—
—Cleveland..................	IHL	10	4	3	7	34	...	...	...	14	4	2	6	44
97-98 —Pittsburgh..............	NHL	82	3	4	7	112	-3	1	0	6	0	1	1	4
98-99 —Pittsburgh..............	NHL	61	0	0	0	90	-2	0	0	13	0	0	0	19
99-00 —Wilkes-Barre/Scranton	AHL	25	5	15	20	86	...	...	...	—	—	—	—	—
—Pittsburgh..............	NHL	50	12	10	22	45	4	0	0	11	3	1	4	17
NHL Totals (8 years)...........		279	20	17	37	387	-21	1	0	30	3	2	5	40

W

YACHMENEV, VITALI   RW   PREDATORS

PERSONAL: Born January 8, 1975, in Chelyabinsk, U.S.S.R. ... 5-9/190. ... Shoots left. ... Name pronounced vee-TAL-ee YAHCH-mih-nehf.
TRANSACTIONS/CAREER NOTES: Selected by Los Angeles Kings in third round (third Kings pick, 59th overall) of NHL entry draft (June 29, 1994). ... Sprained left shoulder (October 4, 1996); missed eight games. ... Sprained ankle (December 27, 1996); missed seven games. ... Suffered from the flu (February 11, 1997); missed one game. ... Traded by Kings to Nashville Predators for future considerations (July 7, 1998). ... Partially dislocated shoulder (February 4, 1999); missed 10 games. ... Sprained wrist (November 3, 1999); missed three games. ... Reinjured wrist (November 13, 2000); missed four games.
HONORS: Named Can.HL Rookie of the Year (1993-94). ... Won Emms Family Award (1993-94). ... Named to Can.HL All-Rookie team (1993-94). ... Named to OHL All-Rookie team (1993-94). ... Won William Hanley Trophy (1994-95).
STATISTICAL PLATEAUS: Three-goal games: 1995-96 (1).

		REGULAR SEASON								PLAYOFFS				
Season Team	League	Gms.	G	A	Pts.	PIM	+/-	PP	SH	Gms.	G	A	Pts.	PIM
90-91—Traktor Chelyabinsk	USSR	80	88	60	148	72	...	...	...	—	—	—	—	—
91-92—Traktor Chelyabinsk....	CIS	80	82	70	152	20	...	...	...	—	—	—	—	—
92-93—Mechel Chelyabinsk....	CIS Div. II	51	23	20	43	12	...	...	...	—	—	—	—	—
93-94—North Bay	OHL	66	*61	52	113	18	...	...	...	18	13	19	32	12
94-95—North Bay	OHL	59	53	52	105	8	...	...	...	6	1	8	9	2
—Phoenix	IHL	—	—	—	—	—	...	...	...	4	1	0	1	0
95-96—Los Angeles	NHL	80	19	34	53	16	-3	6	1	—	—	—	—	—
96-97—Los Angeles	NHL	65	10	22	32	10	-9	2	0	—	—	—	—	—
97-98—Los Angeles	NHL	4	0	1	1	4	1	0	0	—	—	—	—	—
—Long Beach................	IHL	59	23	28	51	14	...	...	...	17	8	9	17	4
98-99—Milwaukee................	IHL	16	7	6	13	0	...	...	...	—	—	—	—	—
—Nashville	NHL	55	7	10	17	10	-10	0	1	—	—	—	—	—
99-00—Nashville	NHL	68	16	16	32	12	5	1	1	—	—	—	—	—
NHL Totals (5 years)...........		272	52	83	135	52	-16	9	3					

YAKE, TERRY   C   CAPITALS

PERSONAL: Born October 22, 1968, in New Westminster, B.C. ... 5-11/190. ... Shoots right.
TRANSACTIONS/CAREER NOTES: Selected by Hartford Whalers in fourth round (third Whalers pick, 81st overall) of NHL entry draft (June 13, 1987). ... Selected by Mighty Ducks of Anaheim in NHL expansion draft (June 24, 1993). ... Traded by Mighty Ducks to Toronto Maple Leafs for RW David Sacco (September 28, 1994). ... Signed as free agent by Buffalo Sabres (August 5, 1996). ... Signed as free agent by St. Louis Blues (August 12, 1997). ... Selected by Atlanta Thrashers in NHL expansion draft (June 25, 1999). ... Claimed by Blues from Thrashers in NHL waiver draft (September 27, 1999). ... Strained groin (November 17, 1999); missed nine games. ... Claimed on waivers by Washington Capitals (January 18, 2000).
MISCELLANEOUS: Failed to score on a penalty shot (vs. Steve Shields, January 26, 1999; vs. Sean Burke, November 18, 1999).
STATISTICAL PLATEAUS: Three-goal games: 1993-94 (1).

		REGULAR SEASON								PLAYOFFS				
Season Team	League	Gms.	G	A	Pts.	PIM	+/-	PP	SH	Gms.	G	A	Pts.	PIM
84-85—Brandon	WHL	11	1	1	2	0	...	...	...	—	—	—	—	—
85-86—Brandon	WHL	72	26	26	52	49	...	...	...	—	—	—	—	—
86-87—Brandon	WHL	71	44	58	102	64	...	...	...	—	—	—	—	—
87-88—Brandon	WHL	72	55	85	140	59	...	...	...	3	4	2	6	7
88-89—Hartford	NHL	2	0	0	0	0	1	0	0	—	—	—	—	—
—Binghamton	AHL	75	39	56	95	57	...	...	...	—	—	—	—	—
89-90—Hartford	NHL	2	0	1	1	0	-1	0	0	—	—	—	—	—
—Binghamton	AHL	77	13	42	55	37	...	...	...	—	—	—	—	—
90-91—Hartford	NHL	19	1	4	5	10	-3	0	0	6	1	1	2	16
—Springfield	AHL	60	35	42	77	56	...	...	...	15	9	9	18	10
91-92—Hartford	NHL	15	1	1	2	4	-2	0	0	—	—	—	—	—
—Springfield	AHL	53	21	34	55	63	...	...	...	8	3	4	7	2
92-93—Springfield	AHL	16	8	14	22	27	...	...	...	—	—	—	—	—
—Hartford	NHL	66	22	31	53	46	3	4	1	—	—	—	—	—
93-94—Anaheim	NHL	82	21	31	52	44	2	5	0	—	—	—	—	—
94-95—Toronto	NHL	19	3	2	5	2	1	1	0	—	—	—	—	—
—Denver	IHL	2	0	3	3	2	...	...	...	17	4	11	15	16
95-96—Milwaukee................	IHL	70	32	56	88	70	...	...	...	5	3	6	9	4
96-97—Rochester	AHL	78	34	*67	101	77	...	...	...	10	8	8	16	2
97-98—St. Louis	NHL	65	10	15	25	38	1	3	1	10	2	1	3	6
98-99—Worcester	AHL	24	8	11	19	26	...	...	...	—	—	—	—	—
—St. Louis	NHL	60	9	18	27	34	-9	3	0	13	1	2	3	14
99-00—St. Louis	NHL	26	4	9	13	22	2	2	0	—	—	—	—	—
—Washington	NHL	35	6	5	11	12	2	1	0	3	0	0	0	0
NHL Totals (10 years).........		391	77	117	194	212	-3	19	2	32	4	4	8	36

YAKUSHIN, DMITRI   D   MAPLE LEAFS

PERSONAL: Born January 21, 1978, in Kharkov, Ukraine. ... 6-0/200. ... Shoots left.
TRANSACTIONS/CAREER NOTES: Selected by Toronto Maple Leafs in sixth round (ninth Maple Leafs pick, 140th overall) of NHL entry draft (June 22, 1996).

		REGULAR SEASON								PLAYOFFS				
Season Team	League	Gms.	G	A	Pts.	PIM	+/-	PP	SH	Gms.	G	A	Pts.	PIM
95-96—Pembroke	CJHL	31	8	5	13	62	...	...	...	—	—	—	—	—
96-97—Edmonton	WHL	63	3	14	17	103	...	...	...	—	—	—	—	—
97-98—Edmonton	WHL	29	1	10	11	41	...	...	...	—	—	—	—	—
—Regina	WHL	42	1	24	25	57	...	...	...	9	2	8	10	12
98-99—St. John's	AHL	71	2	6	8	65	...	...	...	4	0	0	0	0
99-00—St. John's	AHL	64	1	13	14	106	...	...	...	—	—	—	—	—
—Toronto	NHL	2	0	0	0	2	0	0	0	—	—	—	—	—
NHL Totals (1 year).............		2	0	0	0	2	0	0	0					

Y

YASHIN, ALEXEI   C   SENATORS

PERSONAL: Born November 5, 1973, in Sverdlovsk, U.S.S.R. ... 6-3/225. ... Shoots right. ... Name pronounced uh-LEK-see YA-shin.
TRANSACTIONS/CAREER NOTES: Selected by Ottawa Senators in first round (first Senators pick, second overall) of NHL entry draft (June 20, 1992). ... Suffered strep throat (December 4, 1993); missed one game. ... Missed entire 1999-2000 season due to contract dispute.
HONORS: Named to CIS All-Star team (1992-93). ... Played in NHL All-Star Game (1994 and 1999). ... Named to THE SPORTING NEWS All-Star team (1998-99). ... Named to NHL All-Star second team (1998-99).
MISCELLANEOUS: Member of silver-medal-winning Russian Olympic team (1998). ... Captain of Ottawa Senators (1998-99). ... Holds Ottawa Senators all-time records for most games played (422), goals (178), assists (225) and points (403).
STATISTICAL PLATEAUS: Three-goal games: 1993-94 (1), 1994-95 (1), 1995-96 (1), 1997-98 (1), 1998-99 (1). Total: 5.

Season Team	League	REGULAR SEASON								PLAYOFFS				
		Gms.	G	A	Pts.	PIM	+/-	PP	SH	Gms.	G	A	Pts.	PIM
90-91—Avtomo. Sverdlovsk....	USSR	26	2	1	3	10	...	...	...	—	—	—	—	—
91-92—Dynamo Moscow........	CIS	35	7	5	12	19	...	...	...	—	—	—	—	—
92-93—Dynamo Moscow........	CIS	27	10	12	22	18	...	...	...	10	7	3	10	18
93-94—Ottawa	NHL	83	30	49	79	22	-49	11	2	—	—	—	—	—
94-95—Las Vegas	IHL	24	15	20	35	32	...	...	...	—	—	—	—	—
—Ottawa	NHL	47	21	23	44	20	-20	11	0	—	—	—	—	—
95-96—Ottawa	NHL	46	15	24	39	28	-15	8	0	—	—	—	—	—
96-97—Ottawa	NHL	82	35	40	75	44	-7	10	0	7	1	5	6	2
97-98—Ottawa	NHL	82	33	39	72	24	6	5	0	11	5	3	8	8
—Russian Oly. team.......	Int'l	6	3	3	6	0	...	...	...	—	—	—	—	—
98-99—Ottawa	NHL	82	44	50	94	54	16	19	0	4	0	0	0	10
99-00—Ottawa	NHL					Did not play.								
NHL Totals (6 years)...........		422	178	225	403	192	-69	64	2	22	6	8	14	20

YELLE, STEPHANE   C   AVALANCHE

PERSONAL: Born May 9, 1974, in Ottawa. ... 6-1/190. ... Shoots left. ... Name pronounced YEHL.
TRANSACTIONS/CAREER NOTES: Selected by New Jersey Devils in eighth round (ninth Devils pick, 186th overall) of NHL entry draft (June 20, 1992). ... Traded by Devils with 11th-round pick (D Stephen Low) in 1994 draft to Quebec Nordiques for 11th-round pick (C Mike Hansen) in 1994 draft (June 1, 1994). ... Nordiques franchise moved to Colorado and renamed Avalanche for 1995-96 season (June 21, 1995). ... Pulled groin (February 15, 1996); missed nine games. ... Strained hip flexor (December 14, 1996); missed three games. ... Sprained right wrist (November 28, 1998); missed nine games. ... Sprained knee (May 3, 1999); missed nine playoff games. ... Injured sternum (January 25, 2000); missed two games. ... Strained hip flexor (March 7, 2000); missed one game.
MISCELLANEOUS: Member of Stanley Cup championship team (1996). ... Shares Colorado Avalanche record for most games played (303) with Sylvain Lefebvre.

Season Team	League	REGULAR SEASON								PLAYOFFS				
		Gms.	G	A	Pts.	PIM	+/-	PP	SH	Gms.	G	A	Pts.	PIM
91-92—Oshawa......................	OHL	55	12	14	26	20	...	...	...	7	2	0	2	1
92-93—Oshawa......................	OHL	66	24	50	74	20	...	...	...	10	2	4	6	4
93-94—Oshawa......................	OHL	66	35	69	104	22	...	...	...	5	1	7	8	2
94-95—Cornwall	AHL	40	18	15	33	22	...	...	...	13	7	7	14	8
95-96—Colorado	NHL	71	13	14	27	30	15	0	2	22	1	4	5	8
96-97—Colorado	NHL	79	9	17	26	38	1	0	1	12	1	6	7	2
97-98—Colorado	NHL	81	7	15	22	48	-10	0	1	7	1	0	1	12
98-99—Colorado	NHL	72	8	7	15	40	-8	1	0	10	0	1	1	6
99-00—Colorado	NHL	79	8	14	22	28	9	0	1	17	1	2	3	4
NHL Totals (5 years)...........		382	45	67	112	184	7	1	5	68	4	13	17	32

YLONEN, JUHA   C   COYOTES

PERSONAL: Born February 13, 1972, in Helsinki, Finland. ... 6-1/189. ... Shoots left. ... Name pronounced YOO-hah yee-LOH-nehn.
TRANSACTIONS/CAREER NOTES: Selected by Winnipeg Jets in fifth round (fifth Jets pick, 91st overall) of NHL entry draft (June 22, 1991). ... Jets franchise moved to Phoenix and renamed Coyotes for 1996-97 season; NHL approved move on January 18, 1996. ... Bruised foot (March 10, 1998); missed two games. ... Fractured leg (March 19, 1998); missed 14 games. ... Sprained knee (February 19, 1999); missed 14 games. ... Sprained knee (March 23, 1999); missed nine games. ... Suffered hip flexor (April 1, 2000); missed final four games of regular season.
MISCELLANEOUS: Member of bronze-medal-winning Finnish Olympic team (1998).

Season Team	League	REGULAR SEASON								PLAYOFFS				
		Gms.	G	A	Pts.	PIM	+/-	PP	SH	Gms.	G	A	Pts.	PIM
90-91—Kiekko-Espoo.............	Finland Div. 2	40	12	21	33	4	...	...	...	—	—	—	—	—
91-92—HPK Hameenlinna.......	Finland	43	7	11	18	8	...	...	...	—	—	—	—	—
92-93—HPK Hameenlinna.......	Finland	48	8	18	26	22	...	...	...	12	3	5	8	2
93-94—Jokerit Helsinki	Finland	37	5	11	16	2	...	...	...	12	1	3	4	8
94-95—Jokerit Helsinki	Finland	50	13	15	28	10	...	...	...	11	3	2	5	0
95-96—Jokerit Helsinki	Finland	24	3	13	16	20	...	...	...	11	4	5	9	4
96-97—Springfield	AHL	70	20	41	61	6	...	...	...	17	5	†16	21	4
—Phoenix......................	NHL	2	0	0	0	0	0	0	0	—	—	—	—	—
97-98—Phoenix......................	NHL	55	1	11	12	10	-3	0	1	—	—	—	—	—
—Fin. Olympic team.......	Int'l	6	0	0	0	8	...	...	...	—	—	—	—	—
98-99—Phoenix......................	NHL	59	6	17	23	20	18	2	0	2	0	2	2	2
99-00—Phoenix......................	NHL	76	6	23	29	12	-6	0	1	1	0	0	0	0
NHL Totals (4 years)...........		192	13	51	64	42	9	2	2	3	0	2	2	2

YORK, HARRY — C

PERSONAL: Born April 16, 1974, in Ponoka, Alta. ... 6-2/220. ... Shoots left.
TRANSACTIONS/CAREER NOTES: Signed as non-drafted free agent by St. Louis Blues (May 1, 1996). ... Traded by Blues to New York Rangers for C Mike Eastwood (March 24, 1998). ... Partially dislocated right shoulder (March 26, 1998); missed 10 games. ... Traded by Rangers with RW Alexei Kovalev and future considerations to Pittsburgh Penguins for C Petr Nedved, C Sean Pronger and D Chris Tamer (November 25, 1998). ... Claimed on waivers by Vancouver Canucks (December 8, 1998). ... Sprained shoulder (March 11, 1999); missed six games. ... Injured hip (December 6, 1999); missed four games.

		REGULAR SEASON								PLAYOFFS				
Season Team	League	Gms.	G	A	Pts.	PIM	+/-	PP	SH	Gms.	G	A	Pts.	PIM
94-95 —Fort McMurray	AJHL	54	35	73	108	...	...	...	...	—	—	—	—	—
95-96 —Nashville	ECHL	64	33	50	83	122	...	...	...	—	—	—	—	—
—Atlanta	IHL	2	0	0	0	15	...	...	...	—	—	—	—	—
—Worcester	AHL	13	8	5	13	2	...	...	...	4	0	4	4	4
96-97 —St. Louis	NHL	74	14	18	32	24	1	3	1	5	0	0	0	2
97-98 —St. Louis	NHL	58	4	6	10	31	0	0	0	—	—	—	—	—
—New York Rangers	NHL	2	0	0	0	0	-1	0	0	—	—	—	—	—
98-99 —New York Rangers	NHL	5	0	0	0	4	-1	0	0	—	—	—	—	—
—Pittsburgh	NHL	2	0	0	0	0	0	0	0	—	—	—	—	—
—Vancouver	NHL	49	7	9	16	20	-2	1	0	—	—	—	—	—
99-00 —Vancouver	NHL	54	4	13	17	20	-4	1	1	—	—	—	—	—
—Syracuse	AHL	1	0	0	0	15	...	...	...	—	—	—	—	—
NHL Totals (4 years)		244	29	46	75	99	-7	5	2	5	0	0	0	2

YORK, JASON — D — SENATORS

PERSONAL: Born May 20, 1970, in Nepean, Ont. ... 6-1/200. ... Shoots right.
TRANSACTIONS/CAREER NOTES: Selected by Detroit Red Wings in seventh round (sixth Red Wings pick, 129th overall) of NHL entry draft (June 16, 1990). ... Traded by Red Wings with C/RW Mike Sillinger to Mighty Ducks of Anaheim for LW Stu Grimson, D Mark Ferner and sixth-round pick (LW Magnus Nilsson) in 1996 draft (April 4, 1995). ... Sprained right ankle (December 1, 1995); missed two games. ... Traded by Mighty Ducks with C Shaun Van Allen to Ottawa Senators for C Ted Drury and rights to D Marc Moro (October 1, 1996). ... Strained groin (December 4, 1996); missed six games. ... Suffered concussion (January 3, 1998); missed four games. ... Injured right eye (April 13, 1998); missed three games. ... Strained shoulder (October 1, 1998); missed first two games of season. ... Strained groin (December 8, 1999); missed three games.
HONORS: Named to AHL All-Star first team (1993-94).

		REGULAR SEASON								PLAYOFFS				
Season Team	League	Gms.	G	A	Pts.	PIM	+/-	PP	SH	Gms.	G	A	Pts.	PIM
89-90 —Windsor	OHL	39	9	30	39	38	...	...	...	—	—	—	—	—
—Kitchener	OHL	25	11	25	36	17	...	...	...	17	3	19	22	10
90-91 —Windsor	OHL	66	13	80	93	40	...	...	...	11	3	10	13	12
91-92 —Adirondack	AHL	49	4	20	24	32	...	...	...	5	0	1	1	0
92-93 —Adirondack	AHL	77	15	40	55	86	...	...	...	11	0	3	3	18
—Detroit	NHL	2	0	0	0	0	0	0	0	—	—	—	—	—
93-94 —Adirondack	AHL	74	10	56	66	98	...	...	...	12	3	11	14	22
—Detroit	NHL	7	1	2	3	2	0	0	0	—	—	—	—	—
94-95 —Adirondack	AHL	5	1	3	4	4	...	...	...	—	—	—	—	—
—Detroit	NHL	10	1	2	3	2	0	0	0	—	—	—	—	—
—Anaheim	NHL	15	0	8	8	12	4	0	0	—	—	—	—	—
95-96 —Anaheim	NHL	79	3	21	24	88	-7	0	0	—	—	—	—	—
96-97 —Ottawa	NHL	75	4	17	21	67	-8	1	0	7	0	0	0	4
97-98 —Ottawa	NHL	73	3	13	16	62	8	0	0	7	1	1	2	7
98-99 —Ottawa	NHL	79	4	31	35	48	17	2	0	4	1	1	2	4
99-00 —Ottawa	NHL	79	8	22	30	60	-3	1	0	6	0	2	2	2
NHL Totals (8 years)		419	24	116	140	341	11	4	0	24	2	4	6	17

YORK, MIKE — C — RANGERS

PERSONAL: Born January 3, 1978, in Pontiac, Mich. ... 5-10/185. ... Shoots right. ... Full Name: Michael York.
COLLEGE: Michigan State.
TRANSACTIONS/CAREER NOTES: Selected by New York Rangers in sixth round (seventh Rangers pick, 136th overall) of NHL entry draft (June 21, 1997).
HONORS: Named to CCHA All-Rookie team (1995-96). ... Named to NCAA All-America (West) first team (1997-98 and 1998-99). ... Named CCHA Tournament Most Valuable Player (1997-98). ... Named to CCHA All-Star second team (1997-98). ... Named to CCHA All-Star first team (1998-99). ... Named to NHL All-Rookie team (1999-2000).

		REGULAR SEASON								PLAYOFFS				
Season Team	League	Gms.	G	A	Pts.	PIM	+/-	PP	SH	Gms.	G	A	Pts.	PIM
95-96 —Michigan State	CCHA	39	12	27	39	20	...	...	...	—	—	—	—	—
96-97 —Michigan State	CCHA	37	18	29	47	42	...	...	...	—	—	—	—	—
97-98 —Michigan State	CCHA	40	27	34	61	38	...	...	...	—	—	—	—	—
98-99 —Michigan State	CCHA	42	22	32	*54	41	...	...	...	—	—	—	—	—
—Hartford	AHL	3	2	2	4	0	...	...	...	6	3	1	4	0
99-00 —New York Rangers	NHL	82	26	24	50	18	-17	8	0	—	—	—	—	—
NHL Totals (1 year)		82	26	24	50	18	-17	8	0					

Y

YOUNG, B.J.   RW   RED WINGS

PERSONAL: Born July 23, 1977, in Anchorage, Alaska. ... 5-10/178. ... Shoots right.
TRANSACTIONS/CAREER NOTES: Selected by Detroit Red Wings in sixth round (fifth Red Wings pick, 157th overall) of NHL entry draft (June 21, 1997).
HONORS: Named to WHL (East) All-Star first team (1996-97).

Season Team	League	REGULAR SEASON								PLAYOFFS				
		Gms.	G	A	Pts.	PIM	+/-	PP	SH	Gms.	G	A	Pts.	PIM
93-94—Tri-City	WHL	54	19	24	43	66	...	...	...	2	1	1	2	2
94-95—Tri-City	WHL	30	6	3	9	39	...	...	...	—	—	—	—	—
—Red Deer	WHL	21	5	9	14	33	...	...	...	—	—	—	—	—
95-96—Red Deer	WHL	67	49	45	94	144	...	...	...	8	4	9	13	12
96-97—Red Deer	WHL	63	58	56	114	97	...	...	...	16	8	14	22	26
97-98—Adirondack	AHL	65	15	22	37	191	...	...	...	3	0	2	2	6
98-99—Adirondack	AHL	58	13	17	30	150	...	...	...	3	1	0	1	6
99-00—Cincinnati	AHL	71	25	26	51	147	...	...	...	—	—	—	—	—
—Detroit	NHL	1	0	0	0	0	0	0	0	—	—	—	—	—
NHL Totals (1 year)		1	0	0	0	0	0	0	0					

YOUNG, SCOTT   RW   BLUES

PERSONAL: Born October 1, 1967, in Clinton, Mass. ... 6-1/200. ... Shoots right. ... Full Name: Scott Allen Young.
HIGH SCHOOL: St. Mark's (Southborough, Mass.).
COLLEGE: Boston University.
TRANSACTIONS/CAREER NOTES: Selected by Hartford Whalers in first round (first Whalers pick, 11th overall) of NHL entry draft (June 21, 1986). ... Suffered lacerations above right eye (October 8, 1988). ... Lacerated face (February 18, 1990). ... Traded by Whalers to Pittsburgh Penguins for RW Rob Brown (December 21, 1990). ... Traded by Penguins to Quebec Nordiques for D Bryan Fogarty (March 10, 1992). ... Injured rib (February 14, 1993); missed one game. ... Bruised ribs (February 23, 1993); missed one game. ... Sprained right ankle (October 5, 1993); missed eight games. ... Played in Europe during 1994-95 NHL lockout. ... Nordiques franchise moved to Colorado and renamed Avalanche for 1995-96 season (June 21, 1995). ... Bruised right shoulder (December 23, 1996); missed five games. ... Traded by Avalanche to Mighty Ducks of Anaheim for third-round pick (traded to Florida) in 1998 draft (September 17, 1997). ... Bruised right foot (November 22, 1997); missed two games. ... Bruised right foot (November 29, 1997); missed five games. ... Suffered eye abrasion (March 9, 1998); missed two games. ... Signed as free agent by St. Louis Blues (July 16, 1998). ... Suffered sore back (February 8, 1999); missed one game. ... Injured back (January 28, 2000); missed three games. ... Separated shoulder (April 5, 2000); missed final two games of regular season.
HONORS: Named Hockey East Rookie of the Year (1985-86).
MISCELLANEOUS: Member of Stanley Cup championship team (1991 and 1996).
STATISTICAL PLATEAUS: Three-goal games: 1992-93 (1), 1993-94 (1), 1994-95 (1), 1996-97 (1). Total: 4.

Season Team	League	REGULAR SEASON								PLAYOFFS				
		Gms.	G	A	Pts.	PIM	+/-	PP	SH	Gms.	G	A	Pts.	PIM
84-85—St. Marks H.S.	Mass. H.S.	23	28	41	69	...	...	...	...	—	—	—	—	—
85-86—Boston University	Hockey East	38	16	13	29	31	...	...	...	—	—	—	—	—
86-87—Boston University	Hockey East	33	15	21	36	24	...	...	...	—	—	—	—	—
87-88—U.S. Olympic team	Int'l	59	13	53	66	...	...	...	...	—	—	—	—	—
—Hartford	NHL	7	0	0	0	2	-6	0	0	4	1	0	1	0
88-89—Hartford	NHL	76	19	40	59	27	-21	6	0	4	2	0	2	4
89-90—Hartford	NHL	80	24	40	64	47	-24	10	2	7	2	0	2	2
90-91—Hartford	NHL	34	6	9	15	8	-9	3	1	—	—	—	—	—
—Pittsburgh	NHL	43	11	16	27	33	3	3	1	17	1	6	7	2
91-92—U.S. national team	Int'l	10	2	4	6	21	...	...	...	—	—	—	—	—
—U.S. Olympic team	Int'l	8	2	1	3	2	...	...	...	—	—	—	—	—
—Bolzano	Italy	18	22	17	39	6	...	...	...	—	—	—	—	—
92-93—Quebec	NHL	82	30	30	60	20	5	9	6	6	4	1	5	0
93-94—Quebec	NHL	76	26	25	51	14	-4	6	1	—	—	—	—	—
94-95—Frankfurt	Germany	1	1	0	1	0	...	...	...	—	—	—	—	—
—Landshut	Germany	4	6	1	7	6	...	...	...	—	—	—	—	—
—Quebec	NHL	48	18	21	39	14	9	3	3	6	3	3	6	2
95-96—Colorado	NHL	81	21	39	60	50	2	7	0	22	3	12	15	10
96-97—Colorado	NHL	72	18	19	37	14	-5	7	0	17	4	2	6	14
97-98—Anaheim	NHL	73	13	20	33	22	-13	4	2	—	—	—	—	—
98-99—St. Louis	NHL	75	24	28	52	27	8	8	0	13	4	7	11	10
99-00—St. Louis	NHL	75	24	15	39	18	12	6	1	6	6	2	8	8
NHL Totals (12 years)		822	234	302	536	296	-43	72	17	102	30	33	63	52

YUSHKEVICH, DMITRY   D   MAPLE LEAFS

PERSONAL: Born November 19, 1971, in Yaroslavl, U.S.S.R. ... 5-11/208. ... Shoots right. ... Name pronounced yoosh-KAY-vihch.
TRANSACTIONS/CAREER NOTES: Selected by Philadelphia Flyers in sixth round (sixth Flyers pick, 122nd overall) of NHL entry draft (June 22, 1991). ... Sprained wrist (January 28, 1993); missed two games. ... Strained groin (February 18, 1994); missed four games. ... Played in Europe during 1994-95 NHL lockout. ... Suffered from sore back (February 23, 1995); missed three games. ... Sprained left knee (April 16, 1995); missed five games. ... Traded by Flyers with second-round pick (G Francis Larivee) in 1996 draft to Toronto Maple Leafs for first-(RW Dainius Zubrus) and fourth-round (traded to Los Angeles) picks in 1996 draft and second-round pick (G Jean-Marc Pelletier) in 1997 draft (August 30, 1995). ... Sprained knee (October 26, 1995); missed eight games. ... Bruised knee (December 30, 1995); missed two games. ... Pulled hamstring (December 14, 1996); missed four games. ... Injured knee (March 22, 1997); missed two games. ... Fractured toe (October 15, 1997); missed six games. ... Sprained knee (December 31, 1997); missed two games. ... Strained groin (December 12, 1998); missed three games.
HONORS: Played in NHL All-Star Game (2000).
MISCELLANEOUS: Member of silver-medal-winning Russian Olympic team (1998).

Season Team	League	REGULAR SEASON Gms.	G	A	Pts.	PIM	+/-	PP	SH	PLAYOFFS Gms.	G	A	Pts.	PIM
88-89—Torpedo Yaroslavl	USSR	23	2	1	3	8	...	...	...	—	—	—	—	—
89-90—Torpedo Yaroslavl	USSR	41	2	3	5	39	...	...	...	—	—	—	—	—
90-91—Torpedo Yaroslavl	USSR	43	10	4	14	22	...	...	...	—	—	—	—	—
91-92—Dynamo Moscow	CIS	41	6	7	13	14	...	...	...	—	—	—	—	—
—Unif. Olympic team	Int'l	8	1	2	3	4	...	...	...	—	—	—	—	—
92-93—Philadelphia	NHL	82	5	27	32	71	12	1	0	—	—	—	—	—
93-94—Philadelphia	NHL	75	5	25	30	86	-8	1	0	—	—	—	—	—
94-95—Torpedo Yaroslavl	CIS	10	3	4	7	8	...	...	...	—	—	—	—	—
—Philadelphia	NHL	40	5	9	14	47	-4	3	1	15	1	5	6	12
95-96—Toronto	NHL	69	1	10	11	54	-14	1	0	4	0	0	0	0
96-97—Toronto	NHL	74	4	10	14	56	-24	1	1	—	—	—	—	—
97-98—Toronto	NHL	72	0	12	12	78	-13	0	0	—	—	—	—	—
—Russian Oly. team	Int'l	6	0	0	0	2	...	...	...	—	—	—	—	—
98-99—Toronto	NHL	78	6	22	28	88	25	2	1	17	1	5	6	22
99-00—Toronto	NHL	77	3	24	27	55	2	2	1	12	1	1	2	4
NHL Totals (8 years)		567	29	139	168	535	-24	11	4	48	3	11	14	38

YZERMAN, STEVE   C   RED WINGS

PERSONAL: Born May 9, 1965, in Cranbrook, B.C. ... 5-10/185. ... Shoots right. ... Name pronounced IGH-zuhr-muhn.

TRANSACTIONS/CAREER NOTES: Selected by Detroit Red Wings as underage junior in first round (first Red Wings pick, fourth overall) of NHL entry draft (June 8, 1983). ... Fractured collarbone (January 31, 1986). ... Injured ligaments of right knee (March 1, 1988) and underwent surgery. ... Injured right knee in playoff game (April 8, 1991). ... Suffered herniated disc (October 21, 1993); missed 26 games. ... Sprained knee (May 27, 1995); missed three playoff games. ... Suffered from the flu (March 17, 1996); missed one game. ... Bruised ankle (April 9, 1997); missed one game. ... Sprained medial collateral ligament in knee (January 28, 1998); missed three games. ... Strained groin (April 11, 1998); missed three games. ... Suffered lacerations to forehead and nose and fractured nose (January 21, 1999); missed one game. ... Sprained knee (March 29, 2000); missed final four games of regular season.

HONORS: Named NHL Rookie of the Year by THE SPORTING NEWS (1983-84). ... Named to NHL All-Rookie team (1983-84). ... Played in NHL All-Star Game (1984, 1988-1993, 1997 and 2000). ... Won Lester B. Pearson Award (1988-89). ... Won Conn Smythe Trophy (1997-98). ... Named to play in NHL All-Star Game (1999); replaced by LW Luc Robitaille due to injury. ... Named to THE SPORTING NEWS All-Star team (1999-2000). ... Named to NHL All-Star first team (1999-2000). ... Won Frank J. Selke Trophy (1999-2000).

MISCELLANEOUS: Member of Stanley Cup championship team (1997 and 1998). ... Captain of Detroit Red Wings (1986-87 through 1999-2000). ... Scored on a penalty shot (vs. Bob Essensa, February 13, 1989; vs. Grant Fuhr, January 3, 1992; vs. Daren Puppa, January 29, 1992). ... Failed to score on a penalty shot (vs. Doug Keans, November 22, 1987; vs. Darcy Wakaluk, March 19, 1993; vs. Blaine Lacher, November 2, 1995). ... Became youngest player (18 years old) to play in NHL All-Star Game (January 31, 1984).

STATISTICAL PLATEAUS: Three-goal games: 1983-84 (1), 1984-85 (1), 1987-88 (2), 1988-89 (2), 1989-90 (2), 1990-91 (3), 1991-92 (3), 1992-93 (3). Total: 17. ... Four-goal games: 1989-90 (1). ... Total hat tricks: 18.

Season Team	League	REGULAR SEASON Gms.	G	A	Pts.	PIM	+/-	PP	SH	PLAYOFFS Gms.	G	A	Pts.	PIM
81-82—Peterborough	OHL	58	21	43	64	65	...	...	...	6	0	1	1	16
82-83—Peterborough	OHL	56	42	49	91	33	...	...	...	4	1	4	5	0
83-84—Detroit	NHL	80	39	48	87	33	-17	13	0	4	3	3	6	0
84-85—Detroit	NHL	80	30	59	89	58	-17	9	0	3	2	1	3	2
85-86—Detroit	NHL	51	14	28	42	16	-24	3	0	—	—	—	—	—
86-87—Detroit	NHL	80	31	59	90	43	-1	9	1	16	5	13	18	8
87-88—Detroit	NHL	64	50	52	102	44	30	10	6	3	1	3	4	6
88-89—Detroit	NHL	80	65	90	155	61	17	17	3	6	5	5	10	2
89-90—Detroit	NHL	79	62	65	127	79	-6	16	†7	—	—	—	—	—
90-91—Detroit	NHL	80	51	57	108	34	-2	12	6	7	3	3	6	4
91-92—Detroit	NHL	79	45	58	103	64	26	9	*8	11	3	5	8	12
92-93—Detroit	NHL	84	58	79	137	44	33	13	†7	7	4	3	7	4
93-94—Detroit	NHL	58	24	58	82	36	11	7	3	3	1	3	4	0
94-95—Detroit	NHL	47	12	26	38	40	6	4	0	15	4	8	12	0
95-96—Detroit	NHL	80	36	59	95	64	29	16	2	18	8	12	20	4
96-97—Detroit	NHL	81	22	63	85	78	22	8	0	20	7	6	13	4
97-98—Detroit	NHL	75	24	45	69	46	3	6	2	22	6	18	24	22
—Can. Olympic team	Int'l	6	1	1	2	10	...	...	...	—	—	—	—	—
98-99—Detroit	NHL	80	29	45	74	42	8	13	2	10	9	4	13	0
99-00—Detroit	NHL	78	35	44	79	34	28	15	2	8	0	4	4	0
NHL Totals (17 years)		1256	627	935	1562	816	146	180	49	153	61	91	152	68

ZALAPSKI, ZARLEY   D   FLYERS

PERSONAL: Born April 22, 1968, in Edmonton. ... 6-1/215. ... Shoots left. ... Name pronounced zuh-LAP-skee.

TRANSACTIONS/CAREER NOTES: Selected by Pittsburgh Penguins in first round (first Penguins pick, fourth overall) of NHL entry draft (June 21, 1986). ... Suffered from Spondylosis, deterioration of the structure of the spine (October 1987). ... Tore ligaments in right knee (December 29, 1988). ... Broke right collarbone (October 25, 1989). ... Sprained right knee (February 24, 1990); missed 13 games. ... Traded by Penguins with C John Cullen and RW Jeff Parker to Hartford Whalers for C Ron Francis, D Ulf Samuelsson and D Grant Jennings (March 4, 1991). ... Suffered from the flu (March 3, 1993); missed one game. ... Sprained knee (October 14, 1993); missed 10 games. ... Traded by Hartford Whalers with C Michael Nylander and D James Patrick to Calgary Flames for D Gary Suter, LW Paul Ranheim and C Ted Drury (March 10, 1994). ... Bruised thigh (February 16, 1994); missed one game. ... Suffered from the flu (November 8, 1995); missed two games. ... Tore knee ligament (October 6, 1996); underwent surgery (December 10, 1996); missed remainder of season. ... Injured knee (November 22, 1997); missed one game. ... Traded by Flames to Canadiens with RW Jonas Hoglund for RW Valeri Bure and fourth-round draft pick (C Shaun Sutter) in 1998 draft (February 1, 1998). ... Signed as free agent by New York Rangers (August 31, 1998). ... Signed as free agent by Philadelphia Flyers (February 13, 2000).

HONORS: Named to NHL All-Rookie team (1988-89). ... Played in NHL All-Star Game (1993).

Season Team	League	REGULAR SEASON								PLAYOFFS				
		Gms.	G	A	Pts.	PIM	+/-	PP	SH	Gms.	G	A	Pts.	PIM
84-85—Fort Saskatchewan	AJHL	23	17	30	47	14	...	...	...	—	—	—	—	—
85-86—Fort Saskatchewan	AJHL	27	20	33	53	46	...	...	...	—	—	—	—	—
—Canadian nat'l team	Int'l	32	2	4	6	10	...	...	...	—	—	—	—	—
86-87—Canadian nat'l team	Int'l	74	11	29	40	28	...	...	...	—	—	—	—	—
87-88—Canadian nat'l team	Int'l	47	3	13	16	32	...	...	...	—	—	—	—	—
—Can. Olympic team	Int'l	8	1	3	4	2	...	...	...	—	—	—	—	—
—Pittsburgh	NHL	15	3	8	11	7	10	0	0	—	—	—	—	—
88-89—Pittsburgh	NHL	58	12	33	45	57	9	5	1	11	1	8	9	13
89-90—Pittsburgh	NHL	51	6	25	31	37	-14	5	0	—	—	—	—	—
90-91—Pittsburgh	NHL	66	12	36	48	59	15	5	1	—	—	—	—	—
—Hartford	NHL	11	3	3	6	6	-7	3	0	6	1	3	4	8
91-92—Hartford	NHL	79	20	37	57	120	-7	4	0	7	2	3	5	6
92-93—Hartford	NHL	83	14	51	65	94	-34	8	1	—	—	—	—	—
93-94—Hartford	NHL	56	7	30	37	56	-6	0	0	—	—	—	—	—
—Calgary	NHL	13	3	7	10	18	0	1	0	7	0	3	3	2
94-95—Calgary	NHL	48	4	24	28	46	9	1	0	7	0	4	4	4
95-96—Calgary	NHL	80	12	17	29	115	11	5	0	4	0	1	1	10
96-97—Calgary	NHL	2	0	0	0	0	-1	0	0	—	—	—	—	—
97-98—Calgary	NHL	35	2	7	9	41	-12	2	0	—	—	—	—	—
—Montreal	NHL	28	1	5	6	22	-1	0	1	6	0	1	1	4
98-99—ZSC Lions Zurich	Switzerland	11	1	5	6	37	...	...	...	3	1	0	1	4
99-00—Long Beach	IHL	7	0	5	5	6	...	...	...	—	—	—	—	—
—Utah	IHL	56	4	24	28	69	...	...	...	5	1	1	2	4
—Philadelphia	NHL	12	0	2	2	6	0	0	0	—	—	—	—	—
NHL Totals (12 years)		637	99	285	384	684	-28	39	4	48	4	23	27	47

ZALESAK, MIROSLAV   RW   SHARKS

PERSONAL: Born January 2, 1980, in Skalica, Czechoslovakia. ... 6-0/185. ... Shoots left.
TRANSACTIONS/CAREER NOTES: Selected by San Jose Sharks in fourth round (fifth Sharks pick, 104th overall) of NHL entry draft (June 27, 1998).

Season Team	League	REGULAR SEASON								PLAYOFFS				
		Gms.	G	A	Pts.	PIM	+/-	PP	SH	Gms.	G	A	Pts.	PIM
95-96—HC Nitra	Slovakia Jrs.	49	53	29	82		...	...	...	—	—	—	—	—
96-97—HC Nitra	Slovakia Jrs.	58	51	31	82		...	...	...	—	—	—	—	—
97-98—HC Nitra	Slovakia Jrs.	23	33	23	56	16	...	...	...	—	—	—	—	—
—Plastika Nitra	Slovakia	30	8	6	14	0	...	...	...	—	—	—	—	—
98-99—Plastika Nitra	Slovakia	15	4	3	7	10	...	...	...	—	—	—	—	—
—Drummondville	QMJHL	45	24	27	51	18	...	...	...	—	—	—	—	—
99-00—Drummondville	QMJHL	60	50	61	111	40	...	...	...	16	7	11	18	4

ZAMUNER, ROB   LW   SENATORS

PERSONAL: Born September 17, 1969, in Oakville, Ont. ... 6-3/203. ... Shoots left. ... Name pronounced ZAM-uh-nuhr.
TRANSACTIONS/CAREER NOTES: Selected by New York Rangers in third round (third Rangers pick, 45th overall) of NHL entry draft (June 17, 1989). ... Signed as free agent by Tampa Bay Lightning (July 14, 1992); Rangers awarded third-round pick in 1993 draft as compensation (July 23, 1992). ... Hyperextended elbow (March 19, 1995); missed five games. ... Sprained knee (October 4, 1995); missed 10 games. ... Suffered sore back (April 1, 1998); missed five games. ... Strained groin (October 30, 1998); missed three games. ... Strained groin (November 8, 1998); missed 18 games. ... Strained groin (February 26, 1999); missed three games. ... Traded by Lightning with second-round pick in 2000, 2001 or 2002 draft to Ottawa Senators for C/LW Andreas Johansson to complete deal that allowed Tampa Bay to sign general manager Rick Dudley (June 30, 1999). ... Strained groin (October 28, 1999); missed five games. ... Sprained medial collateral ligament in left knee (December 23, 1999); missed 19 games.
MISCELLANEOUS: Captain of Tampa Bay Lightning (1998-99). ... Holds Tampa Bay Lightning all-time record for most games played (475). ... Scored on a penalty shot (vs. Tommy Salo, January 11, 1997). ... Failed to score on a penalty shot (vs. Chris Terreri, October 9, 1997).
STATISTICAL PLATEAUS: Three-goal games: 1997-98 (1).

Season Team	League	REGULAR SEASON								PLAYOFFS				
		Gms.	G	A	Pts.	PIM	+/-	PP	SH	Gms.	G	A	Pts.	PIM
86-87—Guelph	OHL	62	6	15	21	8	...	...	...	—	—	—	—	—
87-88—Guelph	OHL	58	20	41	61	18	...	...	...	—	—	—	—	—
88-89—Guelph	OHL	66	46	65	111	38	...	...	...	7	5	5	10	9
89-90—Flint	IHL	77	44	35	79	32	...	...	...	4	1	0	1	6
90-91—Binghamton	AHL	80	25	58	83	50	...	...	...	9	7	6	13	35
91-92—Binghamton	AHL	61	19	53	72	42	...	...	...	11	8	9	17	8
—New York Rangers	NHL	9	1	2	3	2	0	0	0	—	—	—	—	—
92-93—Tampa Bay	NHL	84	15	28	43	74	-25	1	0	—	—	—	—	—
93-94—Tampa Bay	NHL	59	6	6	12	42	-9	0	0	—	—	—	—	—
94-95—Tampa Bay	NHL	43	9	6	15	24	-3	0	3	—	—	—	—	—
95-96—Tampa Bay	NHL	72	15	20	35	62	11	0	3	6	2	3	5	10
96-97—Tampa Bay	NHL	82	17	33	50	56	3	0	4	—	—	—	—	—
97-98—Tampa Bay	NHL	77	14	12	26	41	-31	0	3	—	—	—	—	—
—Can. Olympic team	Int'l	6	1	0	1	8	...	...	...	—	—	—	—	—
98-99—Tampa Bay	NHL	58	8	11	19	24	-15	1	1	—	—	—	—	—
99-00—Ottawa	NHL	57	9	12	21	32	-6	0	1	6	2	0	2	2
NHL Totals (9 years)		541	94	130	224	357	-75	2	15	12	4	3	7	12

ZEDNIK, RICHARD   RW   CAPITALS

PERSONAL: Born January 6, 1976, in Bystrica, Czechoslovakia. ... 6-0/199. ... Shoots left. ... Name pronounced ZEHD-nihk.
TRANSACTIONS/CAREER NOTES: Selected by Washington Capitals in 10th round (10th Capitals pick, 249th overall) of NHL entry draft (June 29, 1994). ... Suffered from the flu (November 6, 1996); missed two games. ... Suffered from the flu (December 12, 1997); missed one game. ... Suffered concussion (March 18, 1998); missed six games. ... Strained abdominal muscle (April 2, 1998); missed final eight games of regular season and four playoff games. ... Bruised shoulder (October 21, 1998); missed 10 games. ... Suspended four games and fined $1,000 by NHL for high-sticking incident (November 20, 1998). ... Strained groin (December 19, 1998); missed 19 games. ... Suffered concussion (February 23, 2000); missed 13 games.
HONORS: Named to WHL (West) All-Star second team (1995-96).
MISCELLANEOUS: Failed to score on a penalty shot (vs. Mike Richter, November 11, 1999).
STATISTICAL NOTES: Tied for NHL lead with three game-tying goals (1999-2000).

		REGULAR SEASON								PLAYOFFS				
Season Team	League	Gms.	G	A	Pts.	PIM	+/-	PP	SH	Gms.	G	A	Pts.	PIM
93-94—Banska Bystrica	Slovakia	25	3	6	9	...	...	...	...	—	—	—	—	—
94-95—Portland	WHL	65	35	51	86	89	...	...	...	9	5	5	10	20
95-96—Portland	WHL	61	44	37	81	154	...	...	...	7	8	4	12	23
—Portland	AHL	1	1	1	2	0	...	...	...	21	4	5	9	26
—Washington	NHL	1	0	0	0	0	0	0	0	—	—	—	—	—
96-97—Washington	NHL	11	2	1	3	4	-5	1	0	—	—	—	—	—
—Portland	AHL	56	15	20	35	70	...	...	...	5	1	0	1	6
97-98—Washington	NHL	65	17	9	26	28	-2	2	0	17	7	3	10	16
98-99—Washington	NHL	49	9	8	17	50	-6	1	0	—	—	—	—	—
99-00—Washington	NHL	69	19	16	35	54	6	1	0	5	0	0	0	5
NHL Totals (5 years)		195	47	34	81	136	-7	5	0	22	7	3	10	21

ZEHR, JEFF   LW   BRUINS

PERSONAL: Born December 10, 1978, in Woodstock, Ont. ... 6-3/195. ... Shoots left. ... Name pronounced ZAIR.
TRANSACTIONS/CAREER NOTES: Selected by New York Islanders in second round (third Islanders pick, 31st overall) of NHL entry draft (June 21, 1997). ... Signed as free agent by Boston Bruins (June 21, 1999).

		REGULAR SEASON								PLAYOFFS				
Season Team	League	Gms.	G	A	Pts.	PIM	+/-	PP	SH	Gms.	G	A	Pts.	PIM
94-95—Stratford	OPJHL	44	26	32	58	143	...	...	...	—	—	—	—	—
95-96—Windsor	OHL	56	4	21	25	103	...	...	...	7	0	1	1	2
96-97—Windsor	OHL	57	27	32	59	196	...	...	...	5	2	1	3	4
97-98—Windsor	OHL	20	12	18	30	67	...	...	...	—	—	—	—	—
—Erie	OHL	32	15	24	39	91	...	...	...	5	0	3	3	24
98-99—Erie	OHL	28	20	23	43	78	...	...	...	—	—	—	—	—
—Sarnia	OHL	14	4	10	14	43	...	...	...	6	3	4	7	27
99-00—Providence	AHL	12	3	3	6	37	...	...	...	—	—	—	—	—
—Boston	NHL	4	0	0	0	2	-1	0	0	—	—	—	—	—
NHL Totals (1 year)		4	0	0	0	2	-1	0	0					

ZELEPUKIN, VALERI   LW   BLACKHAWKS

PERSONAL: Born September 17, 1968, in Voskresensk, U.S.S.R. ... 6-1/200. ... Shoots left. ... Name pronounced vuh-LAIR-ee zehl-ih-POO-kihn.
TRANSACTIONS/CAREER NOTES: Selected by New Jersey Devils in 11th round (13th Devils pick, 221st overall) of NHL entry draft (June 22, 1990). ... Bruised shoulder (January 22, 1993); missed five games. ... Bruised left shoulder (December 22, 1993); missed one game. ... Injured chest (April 14, 1994); missed one game. ... Injured eye (January 24, 1995); missed first 42 games of season. ... Bruised finger (April 26, 1995); missed one game. ... Injured eye (October 7, 1995); missed first two games of season. ... Injured calf (November 27, 1995); missed two games. ... Injured foot (February 18, 1996); missed one game. ... Bruised right knee (March 23, 1996); missed six games. ... Suffered from the flu (November 14, 1996); missed three games. ... Suffered infected elbow (January 2, 1997); missed four games. ... Traded by Devils with RW Bill Guerin to Edmonton Oilers for C Jason Arnott and D Bryan Muir (January 4, 1998). ... Traded by Oilers to Philadelphia Flyers for C Dan Lacroix (October 5, 1998). ... Strained right shoulder (November 1, 1998); missed one game. ... Reinjured right shoulder (November 7, 1998); missed three games. ... Reinjured right shoulder (November 17, 1998); missed one game. ... Strained lower back (November 18, 1999); missed one game. ... Bruised right ankle (March 18, 2000); missed four games. ... Signed as free agent by Chicago Blackhawks (July 18, 2000).
MISCELLANEOUS: Member of Stanley Cup championship team (1995). ... Member of silver-medal-winning Russian Olympic team (1998). ... Failed to score on a penalty shot (vs. Martin Brodeur, October 30, 1999).

		REGULAR SEASON								PLAYOFFS				
Season Team	League	Gms.	G	A	Pts.	PIM	+/-	PP	SH	Gms.	G	A	Pts.	PIM
84-85—Khimik	USSR	5	0	0	0	2	...	...	...	—	—	—	—	—
85-86—Khimik	USSR	33	2	2	4	10	...	...	...	—	—	—	—	—
86-87—Khimik	USSR	19	1	0	1	4	...	...	...	—	—	—	—	—
87-88—SKA Leningrad	USSR	18	18	6	24	...	...	...	...	—	—	—	—	—
—CSKA Moscow	USSR	19	3	1	4	8	...	...	...	—	—	—	—	—
88-89—CSKA Moscow	USSR	17	2	3	5	2	...	...	...	—	—	—	—	—
89-90—Khimik	USSR	46	17	14	31	26	...	...	...	—	—	—	—	—
90-91—Khimik	USSR	46	12	19	31	22	...	...	...	—	—	—	—	—
91-92—Utica	AHL	22	20	9	29	8	...	...	...	—	—	—	—	—
—New Jersey	NHL	44	13	18	31	28	11	3	0	4	1	1	2	—
92-93—New Jersey	NHL	78	23	41	64	70	19	5	1	5	0	2	2	0
93-94—New Jersey	NHL	82	26	31	57	70	36	8	0	20	5	2	7	14
94-95—New Jersey	NHL	4	1	2	3	6	3	0	0	18	1	2	3	12
95-96—New Jersey	NHL	61	6	9	15	107	-10	3	0	—	—	—	—	—
96-97—New Jersey	NHL	71	14	24	38	36	-10	3	0	8	3	2	5	2
97-98—New Jersey	NHL	35	2	8	10	32	0	0	0	—	—	—	—	—
—Edmonton	NHL	33	2	10	12	57	-2	0	0	8	1	2	3	2
—Russian Oly. team	Int'l	6	1	2	3	0	...	...	...	—	—	—	—	—
98-99—Philadelphia	NHL	74	16	9	25	48	0	0	0	4	1	0	1	4
99-00—Philadelphia	NHL	77	11	21	32	55	-3	2	0	18	1	2	3	12
NHL Totals (9 years)		559	114	173	287	509	44	24	1	85	13	13	26	48

Z

ZETTLER, ROB   D

PERSONAL: Born March 8, 1968, in Sept-Iles, Que. ... 6-3/197. ... Shoots left.

TRANSACTIONS/CAREER NOTES: Selected by Minnesota North Stars as underage junior in fifth round (fifth North Stars pick, 55th overall) of NHL entry draft (June 21, 1986). ... Tore hip flexor (January 21, 1991); missed 11 games. ... Selected by San Jose Sharks in NHL dispersal draft (May 30, 1991). ... Strained back (October 20, 1992); missed three games. ... Injured groin (April 8, 1993); missed one game. ... Traded by Sharks to Philadelphia Flyers for C Viacheslav Butsayev (February 1, 1994). ... Traded by Flyers to Toronto Maple Leafs for fifth-round pick (G Per-Ragna Bergqvist) in 1996 draft (July 8, 1995). ... Suspended two games by NHL for checking from behind (January 4, 1996). ... Strained groin (April 3, 1997); missed three games. ... Dislocated thumb (November 11, 1997); missed three games. ... Selected by Nashville Predators in NHL expansion draft (June 26, 1998). ... Signed as free agent by Washington Capitals (September 7, 1999).

Season Team	League	REGULAR SEASON								PLAYOFFS				
		Gms.	G	A	Pts.	PIM	+/-	PP	SH	Gms.	G	A	Pts.	PIM
84-85—Sault Ste. Marie	OHL	60	2	14	16	37	...	...	...	—	—	—	—	—
85-86—Sault Ste. Marie	OHL	57	5	23	28	92	...	...	...	—	—	—	—	—
86-87—Sault Ste. Marie	OHL	64	13	22	35	89	...	...	...	4	0	0	0	0
87-88—Sault Ste. Marie	OHL	64	7	41	48	77	...	...	...	6	2	2	4	9
—Kalamazoo	IHL	2	0	1	1	0	...	...	...	7	0	2	2	2
88-89—Minnesota	NHL	2	0	0	0	0	1	0	0	—	—	—	—	—
—Kalamazoo	IHL	80	5	21	26	79	...	...	...	6	0	1	1	26
89-90—Minnesota	NHL	31	0	8	8	45	-7	0	0	—	—	—	—	—
—Kalamazoo	IHL	41	6	10	16	64	...	...	...	7	0	0	0	6
90-91—Kalamazoo	IHL	1	0	0	0	2	...	...	...	—	—	—	—	—
—Minnesota	NHL	47	1	4	5	119	-10	0	0	—	—	—	—	—
91-92—San Jose	NHL	74	1	8	9	99	-23	0	0	—	—	—	—	—
92-93—San Jose	NHL	80	0	7	7	150	-50	0	0	—	—	—	—	—
93-94—San Jose	NHL	42	0	3	3	65	-7	0	0	—	—	—	—	—
—Philadelphia	NHL	33	0	4	4	69	-19	0	0	—	—	—	—	—
94-95—Philadelphia	NHL	32	0	1	1	34	-3	0	0	1	0	0	0	2
95-96—Toronto	NHL	29	0	1	1	48	-1	0	0	2	0	0	0	0
96-97—Utah	IHL	30	0	10	10	60	...	...	...	—	—	—	—	—
—Toronto	NHL	48	2	12	14	51	8	0	0	—	—	—	—	—
97-98—Toronto	NHL	59	0	7	7	108	-8	0	0	—	—	—	—	—
98-99—Utah	IHL	77	2	16	18	136	...	...	...	—	—	—	—	—
—Nashville	NHL	2	0	0	0	2	-2	0	0	—	—	—	—	—
99-00—Portland	AHL	23	2	2	4	27	...	...	...	—	—	—	—	—
—Washington	NHL	12	0	2	2	19	-1	0	0	5	0	0	0	2
NHL Totals (12 years)		491	4	57	61	809	-122	0	0	8	0	0	0	4

ZEVAKHIN, ALEXANDER   C   PENGUINS

PERSONAL: Born June 4, 1980, in Perm, U.S.S.R. ... 6-0/187. ... Shoots left.

TRANSACTIONS/CAREER NOTES: Selected by Pittsburgh Penguins in second round (second Penguins pick, 54th overall) of NHL entry draft (June 27, 1998).

Season Team	League	REGULAR SEASON								PLAYOFFS				
		Gms.	G	A	Pts.	PIM	+/-	PP	SH	Gms.	G	A	Pts.	PIM
95-96—CSKA	CIS Jr.	65	52	30	82	30	...	...	...	—	—	—	—	—
96-97—CSKA Moscow	Rus. Div. II	29	7	3	10	10	...	...	...	—	—	—	—	—
—CSKA-2 Moscow	Rus. Div. III	30	15	18	33	10	...	...	...	—	—	—	—	—
97-98—CSKA-2 Moscow	Rus. Div. III	32	13	14	27	20	...	...	...	—	—	—	—	—
—CSKA Moscow	Russian	10	1	0	1	0	...	...	...	—	—	—	—	—
98-99—CSKA Moscow	Russian	42	7	4	11	16	...	...	...	3	0	0	0	0
99-00—CSKA Moscow	Russian	15	1	0	1	6	...	...	...	—	—	—	—	—

ZHAMNOV, ALEXEI   C   BLACKHAWKS

PERSONAL: Born October 1, 1970, in Moscow, U.S.S.R. ... 6-1/200. ... Shoots left. ... Name pronounced ZHAM-nahf.

TRANSACTIONS/CAREER NOTES: Selected by Winnipeg Jets in fourth round (fifth Jets pick, 77th overall) of NHL entry draft (June 16, 1990). ... Suffered hip flexor (November 2, 1992); missed two games. ... Suffered back spasms (January 27, 1993); missed one game. ... Suffered back spasms (February 3, 1993); missed one game. ... Suffered back spasms (February 12, 1993); missed 12 games. ... Suffered left quad contusion (October 26, 1993); missed three games. ... Sprained back (December 27, 1993); missed eight games. ... Suffered back spasms (March 19, 1994); missed remainder of season. ... Suffered stress fracture in leg (October 12, 1995); missed eight games. ... Suffered from the flu (January 5, 1996); missed one game. ... Bruised back (March 7, 1996); missed four games. ... Injured back (March 16, 1996); missed remainder of regular season. ... Jets franchise moved to Phoenix and renamed Coyotes for 1996-97 season; NHL approved move on January 18, 1996. ... Traded by Coyotes with RW Craig Mills and first-round pick (RW Ty Jones) in 1997 draft to Chicago Blackhawks for C Jeremy Roenick (August 16, 1996). ... Fractured toe (November 2, 1997); missed four games. ... Suffered concussion (November 29, 1997); missed one game. ... Suffered concussion (March 3, 1998); missed four games. ... Bruised back (April 4, 1998); missed one game. ... Fractured finger (April 15, 1998); missed two games. ... Bruised ankle (November 10, 1998); missed one game. ... Suffered from the flu (December 26, 1998); missed one game. ... Injured back (February 6, 1999); missed four games. ... Strained groin (November 7, 1999); missed three games. ... Strained hamstring (January 15, 2000); missed eight games.

HONORS: Named to NHL All-Star second team (1994-95).

MISCELLANEOUS: Member of gold-medal-winning Unified Olympic team (1992). ... Member of silver-medal-winning Russian Olympic team (1998).

STATISTICAL PLATEAUS: Three-goal games: 1993-94 (2), 1994-95 (1), 1995-96 (1), 1996-97 (1). Total: 5. ... Five-goal games: 1994-95 (1). ... Total hat tricks: 6.

Z

Season Team	League	REGULAR SEASON								PLAYOFFS				
		Gms.	G	A	Pts.	PIM	+/-	PP	SH	Gms.	G	A	Pts.	PIM
88-89—Dynamo Moscow	USSR	4	0	0	0	0	...	...	...	—	—	—	—	—
89-90—Dynamo Moscow	USSR	43	11	6	17	23	...	...	...	—	—	—	—	—
90-91—Dynamo Moscow	USSR	46	16	12	28	24	...	...	...	—	—	—	—	—
91-92—Dynamo Moscow	CIS	39	15	21	36	28	...	...	...	—	—	—	—	—
—Unif. Olympic team	Int'l	8	0	3	3	8	...	...	...	—	—	—	—	—
92-93—Winnipeg	NHL	68	25	47	72	58	7	6	1	6	0	2	2	2
93-94—Winnipeg	NHL	61	26	45	71	62	-20	7	0	—	—	—	—	—
94-95—Winnipeg	NHL	48	30	35	65	20	5	9	0	—	—	—	—	—
95-96—Winnipeg	NHL	58	22	37	59	65	-4	5	0	6	2	1	3	8
96-97—Chicago	NHL	74	20	42	62	56	18	6	1	—	—	—	—	—
97-98—Chicago	NHL	70	21	28	49	61	16	6	2	—	—	—	—	—
—Russian Oly. team	Int'l	6	2	1	3	2	...	...	...	—	—	—	—	—
98-99—Chicago	NHL	76	20	41	61	50	-10	8	1	—	—	—	—	—
99-00—Chicago	NHL	71	23	37	60	61	7	5	0	—	—	—	—	—
NHL Totals (8 years)		526	187	312	499	433	19	52	5	12	2	3	5	10

ZHITNIK, ALEXEI — D — SABRES

PERSONAL: Born October 10, 1972, in Kiev, U.S.S.R. ... 5-11/215. ... Shoots left. ... Name pronounced ZHIHT-nihk.

TRANSACTIONS/CAREER NOTES: Selected by Los Angeles Kings in fourth round (third Kings pick, 81st overall) of NHL entry draft (June 22, 1991). ... Suffered from the flu (January 12, 1993); missed five games. ... Suspended one game by NHL for cross-checking (November 30, 1993). ... Traded by Kings with D Charlie Huddy, G Robb Stauber and fifth-round pick (D Marian Menhart) in 1995 draft to Buffalo Sabres for G Grant Fuhr, D Philippe Boucher and D Denis Tsygurov (February 14, 1995). ... Fractured thumb (February 19, 1995); missed three games. ... Reinjured thumb (March 8, 1995); missed one game. ... Ruptured calf muscle (March 19, 1995); missed 11 games. ... Suspended two games and fined $1,000 by NHL for high-sticking incident (November 1, 1996). ... Missed first four games of 1997-98 season due to contract dispute. ... Bruised chest (November 29, 1998); missed one game. ... Suffered eye injury (October 17, 1999); missed one game. ... Fractured finger (March 8, 2000); missed six games. ... Suspended one playoff game by NHL for high-sticking incident (April 19, 2000).

HONORS: Played in NHL All-Star Game (1999).

MISCELLANEOUS: Member of gold-medal-winning Unified Olympic team (1992). ... Member of silver-medal-winning Russian Olympic team (1998).

Season Team	League	REGULAR SEASON								PLAYOFFS				
		Gms.	G	A	Pts.	PIM	+/-	PP	SH	Gms.	G	A	Pts.	PIM
89-90—Sokol Kiev	USSR	31	3	4	7	16	...	...	...	—	—	—	—	—
90-91—Sokol Kiev	USSR	40	1	4	5	46	...	...	...	—	—	—	—	—
91-92—CSKA Moscow	CIS	36	2	7	9	48	...	...	...	—	—	—	—	—
—Unif. Olympic team	Int'l	8	1	0	1	0	...	...	...	—	—	—	—	—
92-93—Los Angeles	NHL	78	12	36	48	80	-3	5	0	24	3	9	12	26
93-94—Los Angeles	NHL	81	12	40	52	101	-11	11	0	—	—	—	—	—
94-95—Los Angeles	NHL	11	2	5	7	27	-3	2	0	—	—	—	—	—
—Buffalo	NHL	21	2	5	7	34	-3	1	0	5	0	1	1	14
95-96—Buffalo	NHL	80	6	30	36	58	-25	5	0	—	—	—	—	—
96-97—Buffalo	NHL	80	7	28	35	95	10	3	1	12	1	0	1	16
97-98—Buffalo	NHL	78	15	30	45	102	19	2	3	15	0	3	3	36
—Russian Oly. team	Int'l	6	0	2	2	2	...	...	...	—	—	—	—	—
98-99—Buffalo	NHL	81	7	26	33	96	-6	3	1	21	4	11	15	*52
99-00—Buffalo	NHL	74	2	11	13	95	-6	1	0	4	0	0	0	8
NHL Totals (8 years)		584	65	211	276	688	-28	33	5	81	8	24	32	152

ZHOLTOK, SERGEI — C — CANADIENS

PERSONAL: Born December 2, 1972, in Riga, U.S.S.R. ... 6-1/191. ... Shoots right. ... Name pronounced SAIR-gay ZOHL-tahk.

TRANSACTIONS/CAREER NOTES: Selected by Boston Bruins in third round (second Bruins pick, 56th overall) of NHL entry draft (June 20, 1992). ... Signed as free agent by Ottawa Senators (June 25, 1996). ... Signed as free agent by Montreal Canadiens (September 9, 1998). ... Sprained knee (November 30, 1998); missed one game. ... Bruised hip (April 6, 1999); missed three games. ... Injured shoulder prior to start of 1999-2000 season; missed first 11 games of season. ... Suffered injury (December 3, 1999); missed one game.

Season Team	League	REGULAR SEASON								PLAYOFFS				
		Gms.	G	A	Pts.	PIM	+/-	PP	SH	Gms.	G	A	Pts.	PIM
90-91—Dynamo Riga	USSR	39	4	0	4	16	...	...	...	—	—	—	—	—
91-92—HC Riga	CIS	27	6	3	9	6	...	...	...	—	—	—	—	—
92-93—Providence	AHL	64	31	35	66	57	...	...	...	6	3	5	8	4
—Boston	NHL	1	0	1	1	0	1	0	0	—	—	—	—	—
93-94—Providence	AHL	54	29	33	62	16	...	...	...	—	—	—	—	—
—Boston	NHL	24	2	1	3	2	-7	1	0	—	—	—	—	—
94-95—Providence	AHL	78	23	35	58	42	...	...	...	13	8	5	13	6
95-96—Las Vegas	IHL	82	51	50	101	30	...	...	...	15	7	13	20	6
96-97—Las Vegas	IHL	19	13	14	27	20	...	...	...	—	—	—	—	—
—Ottawa	NHL	57	12	16	28	19	2	5	0	7	1	1	2	0
97-98—Ottawa	NHL	78	10	13	23	16	-7	7	0	11	0	2	2	0
98-99—Montreal	NHL	70	7	15	22	6	-12	2	0	—	—	—	—	—
—Fredericton	AHL	7	3	4	7	0	...	...	...	—	—	—	—	—
99-00—Quebec	AHL	1	0	1	1	2	...	...	...	—	—	—	—	—
—Montreal	NHL	68	26	12	38	28	2	9	0	—	—	—	—	—
NHL Totals (6 years)		298	57	58	115	71	-21	24	0	18	1	3	4	0

Z

ZMOLEK, DOUG — D — BLACKHAWKS

PERSONAL: Born November 3, 1970, in Rochester, Minn. ... 6-2/220. ... Shoots left. ... Full Name: Doug Allan Zmolek. ... Name pronounced ZMOH-lehk.
HIGH SCHOOL: John Marshall (Rochester, Minn.).
COLLEGE: Minnesota.
TRANSACTIONS/CAREER NOTES: Selected by Minnesota North Stars in first round (first North Stars pick, seventh overall) of NHL entry draft (June 17, 1989). ... Selected by San Jose Sharks in NHL dispersal draft (May 30, 1991). ... Traded by Sharks with D Mike Lalor and cash to Dallas Stars for RW Ulf Dahlen and seventh-round pick (RW Brad Mehalko) in 1995 draft (March 19, 1994). ... Sprained thumb (March 12, 1994); missed one game. ... Separated shoulder (March 31, 1994); missed five games. ... Bruised kneecap (April 7, 1995); missed six games. ... Injured shoulder (November 9, 1995); missed five games. ... Traded by Stars with RW Shane Churla to Los Angeles Kings for Darryl Sydor and seventh-round pick (G Eoin McInerney) in 1996 draft (February 17, 1996). ... Sprained left knee (March 23, 1996); missed last eight games of season. ... Bruised thigh (October 26, 1996); missed one game. ... Strained right shoulder (November 7, 1996); missed one game. ... Sprained right shoulder (December 9, 1996); missed six games. ... Bruised hand (January 14, 1997); missed one game. ... Suffered irregular heartbeat (February 17, 1997); missed five games. ... Bruised left foot (November 11, 1997); missed one game. ... Suffered concussion (January 5, 1998); missed two games. ... Sprained right shoulder (March 7, 1998); missed eight games. ... Traded by Kings to Chicago Blackhawks for third-round pick (D Frantisek Kaberle) in 1999 draft (September 3, 1998). ... Strained groin (January 2, 1999); missed six games. ... Suffered concussion (February 15, 1999); missed one game. ... Bruised chest (March 10, 1999); missed three games. ... Strained groin (October 21, 1999); missed three games. ... Strained groin (January 16, 2000); missed two games. ... Injured hamstring (February 22, 2000); missed 12 games.
HONORS: Named to NCAA All-America (West) second team (1991-92). ... Named to WCHA All-Star second team (1991-92).

		REGULAR SEASON								PLAYOFFS				
Season Team	League	Gms.	G	A	Pts.	PIM	+/-	PP	SH	Gms.	G	A	Pts.	PIM
87-88—John Marshall............	Minn. H.S.	27	4	32	36	...	...	...	...	—	—	—	—	—
88-89—John Marshall............	Minn. H.S.	29	17	41	58	...	...	...	...	—	—	—	—	—
89-90—Univ. of Minnesota......	WCHA	40	1	10	11	52	...	...	...	—	—	—	—	—
90-91—Univ. of Minnesota......	WCHA	42	3	15	18	94	...	...	...	—	—	—	—	—
91-92—Univ. of Minnesota......	WCHA	44	6	21	27	88	...	...	...	—	—	—	—	—
92-93—San Jose....................	NHL	84	5	10	15	229	-50	2	0	—	—	—	—	—
93-94—San Jose....................	NHL	68	0	4	4	122	-9	0	0	—	—	—	—	—
—Dallas.......................	NHL	7	1	0	1	11	1	0	0	7	0	1	1	4
94-95—Dallas.......................	NHL	42	0	5	5	67	-6	0	0	5	0	0	0	10
95-96—Dallas.......................	NHL	42	1	5	6	65	1	0	0	—	—	—	—	—
—Los Angeles................	NHL	16	1	0	1	22	-6	0	0	—	—	—	—	—
96-97—Los Angeles..............	NHL	57	1	0	1	116	-22	0	0	—	—	—	—	—
97-98—Los Angeles..............	NHL	46	0	8	8	111	0	0	0	2	0	0	0	2
98-99—Chicago.....................	NHL	62	0	14	14	102	1	0	0	—	—	—	—	—
99-00—Chicago.....................	NHL	43	2	7	9	60	6	0	0	—	—	—	—	—
NHL Totals (8 years)...........		**467**	**11**	**53**	**64**	**905**	**-84**	**2**	**0**	**14**	**0**	**1**	**1**	**16**

ZUBOV, SERGEI — D — STARS

PERSONAL: Born July 22, 1970, in Moscow, U.S.S.R. ... 6-1/200. ... Shoots right. ... Name pronounced SAIR-gay ZOO-bahf.
TRANSACTIONS/CAREER NOTES: Selected by New York Rangers in fifth round (sixth Rangers pick, 85th overall) of NHL entry draft (June 16, 1990). ... Suffered concussion (February 26, 1993); missed one game. ... Suffered from the flu (February 4, 1995); missed one game. ... Underwent wrist surgery (February 27, 1995); missed nine games. ... Traded by Rangers with C Petr Nedved to Pittsburgh Penguins for LW Luc Robitaille and D Ulf Samuelsson (August 31, 1995). ... Fractured finger (October 9, 1995); missed nine games. ... Reinjured finger (November 11, 1995); missed seven games. ... Bruised shoulder (March 31, 1996); missed one game. ... Traded by Penguins to Dallas Stars for D Kevin Hatcher (June 22, 1996). ... Suffered from the flu (November 20, 1996); missed one game. ... Suffered back spasms (January 24, 1997); missed two games. ... Sprained neck (March 4, 1998); missed nine games. ... Bruised wrist (April 14, 1999); missed one game. ... Sprained medial collateral ligament in knee (March 29, 2000); missed final five games of season.
HONORS: Played in NHL All-Star Game (1998-2000).
MISCELLANEOUS: Member of Stanley Cup championship team (1994 and 1999). ... Member of gold-medal-winning Unified Olympic team (1992).

		REGULAR SEASON								PLAYOFFS				
Season Team	League	Gms.	G	A	Pts.	PIM	+/-	PP	SH	Gms.	G	A	Pts.	PIM
88-89—CSKA Moscow............	USSR	29	1	4	5	10	...	...	...	—	—	—	—	—
89-90—CSKA Moscow............	USSR	48	6	2	8	16	...	...	...	—	—	—	—	—
90-91—CSKA Moscow............	USSR	41	6	5	11	12	...	...	...	—	—	—	—	—
91-92—CSKA Moscow............	CIS	36	4	7	11	6	...	...	...	—	—	—	—	—
—Unif. Olympic team.....	Int'l	8	0	1	1	0	...	...	...	—	—	—	—	—
92-93—CSKA Moscow............	CIS	1	0	1	1	0	...	...	...	—	—	—	—	—
—Binghamton................	AHL	30	7	29	36	14	...	...	...	11	5	5	10	2
—New York Rangers......	NHL	49	8	23	31	4	-1	3	0	—	—	—	—	—
93-94—New York Rangers......	NHL	78	12	77	89	39	20	9	0	22	5	14	19	0
—Binghamton................	AHL	2	1	2	3	0	...	...	...	—	—	—	—	—
94-95—New York Rangers......	NHL	38	10	26	36	18	-2	6	0	10	3	8	11	2
95-96—Pittsburgh..................	NHL	64	11	55	66	22	28	3	2	18	1	14	15	26
96-97—Dallas.......................	NHL	78	13	30	43	24	19	1	0	7	0	3	3	2
97-98—Dallas.......................	NHL	73	10	47	57	16	16	5	1	17	4	5	9	2
98-99—Dallas.......................	NHL	81	10	41	51	20	9	5	0	23	1	12	13	4
99-00—Dallas.......................	NHL	77	9	33	42	18	-2	3	1	18	2	7	9	6
NHL Totals (8 years)...........		**538**	**83**	**332**	**415**	**161**	**87**	**35**	**4**	**115**	**16**	**63**	**79**	**42**

Z

ZUBRUS, DAINIUS　　　　　RW　　　　　CANADIENS

PERSONAL: Born June 16, 1978, in Elektrenai, U.S.S.R. ... 6-4/224. ... Shoots left. ... Name pronounced DIGH-nuhz ZOO-bruhz.
TRANSACTIONS/CAREER NOTES: Selected by Philadelphia Flyers in first round (first Flyers pick, 15th overall) of NHL entry draft (June 22, 1996). ... Bruised right hand (October 8, 1997); missed two games. ... Reinjured right hand (October 15, 1997); missed five games. ... Suspended two games and fined $1,000 by NHL for slashing incident (April 2, 1998). ... Strained left hamstring (December 15, 1997); missed one game. ... Traded by Flyers with second-round pick (D Matt Carkner) in 1999 draft to Montreal Canadiens for RW Mark Recchi (March 10, 1999). ... Strained hip flexor (October 20, 1999); missed one game. ... Injured back (October 27, 1999); missed one game. ... Suffered back spasms (January 4, 2000); missed one game. ... Suffered concussion (February 27, 2000); missed six games.

Season Team	League	Gms.	G	A	Pts.	PIM	+/-	PP	SH	Gms.	G	A	Pts.	PIM
					REGULAR SEASON						PLAYOFFS			
95-96—Pembroke	CJHL	28	19	13	32	73	...	...	...	—	—	—	—	—
—Caledon	Jr. A	7	3	7	10	2	...	...	...	17	11	12	23	4
96-97—Philadelphia	NHL	68	8	13	21	22	3	1	0	19	5	4	9	12
97-98—Philadelphia	NHL	69	8	25	33	42	29	1	0	5	0	1	1	2
98-99—Philadelphia	NHL	63	3	5	8	25	-5	0	1	—	—	—	—	—
—Montreal	NHL	17	3	5	8	4	-3	0	0	—	—	—	—	—
99-00—Montreal	NHL	73	14	28	42	54	-1	3	0	—	—	—	—	—
NHL Totals (4 years)		290	36	76	112	147	23	5	1	24	5	5	10	14

ZYUZIN, ANDREI　　　　　D　　　　　LIGHTNING

PERSONAL: Born January 21, 1978, in Ufa, U.S.S.R. ... 6-1/210. ... Shoots left. ... Name pronounced ZYOO-zihn.
TRANSACTIONS/CAREER NOTES: Selected by San Jose Sharks in first round (first Sharks pick, second overall) of NHL entry draft (June 22, 1996). ... Suspended two playoff games by NHL for slashing incident (April 19, 1999). ... Traded by Sharks with D Bill Houlder, LW Shawn Burr and C Steve Guolla to Tampa Bay Lightning for LW Niklas Sundstrom and third-round pick (traded to Chicago) in 2000 draft (August 4, 1999). ... Injured shoulder (October 28, 1999); missed five games. ... Injured shoulder (January 11, 2000); missed remainder of season.

Season Team	League	Gms.	G	A	Pts.	PIM	+/-	PP	SH	Gms.	G	A	Pts.	PIM
					REGULAR SEASON						PLAYOFFS			
94-95—Salavat Yulayev Ufa	CIS	30	3	0	3	16	...	...	...	—	—	—	—	—
95-96—Salavat Yulayev Ufa	CIS	41	6	3	9	24	...	...	...	2	0	0	0	4
96-97—Salavet Yulayev Ufa	USSR	32	7	10	17	28	...	...	...	7	1	1	2	4
97-98—San Jose	NHL	56	6	7	13	66	8	2	0	6	1	0	1	14
—Kentucky	AHL	17	4	5	9	28	...	...	...	—	—	—	—	—
98-99—San Jose	NHL	25	3	1	4	38	5	2	0	—	—	—	—	—
—Kentucky	AHL	23	2	12	14	42	...	...	...	—	—	—	—	—
99-00—Tampa Bay	NHL	34	2	9	11	33	-11	0	0	—	—	—	—	—
NHL Totals (3 years)		115	11	17	28	137	2	4	0	6	1	0	1	14

Z

2000 TOP DRAFT PICKS

ALEXEEV, NIKITA   RW   LIGHTNING

PERSONAL: Born December 27, 1981, in Murmansk, U.S.S.R. ... 6-5/215. ... Shoots left.
TRANSACTIONS/CAREER NOTES: Selected by Tampa Bay Lightning in first round (first Lightning pick, eighth overall) of NHL entry draft (June 24, 2000).

		REGULAR SEASON					PLAYOFFS				
Season Team	League	Gms.	G	A	Pts.	PIM	Gms.	G	A	Pts.	PIM
97-98—Soviet Wings	Russian Jr.	...	15	10	25	8	—	—	—	—	—
98-99—Erie	OHL	61	17	18	35	15	5	1	1	2	4
99-00—Erie	OHL	64	24	29	53	42	13	4	3	7	6

AULIN, JARED   C   AVALANCHE

PERSONAL: Born March 15, 1982, in Calgary. ... 5-11/175. ... Shoots right.
TRANSACTIONS/CAREER NOTES: Selected by Colorado Avalanche in second round (second Avalanche pick, 47th overall) of NHL entry draft (June 24, 2000).

		REGULAR SEASON					PLAYOFFS				
Season Team	League	Gms.	G	A	Pts.	PIM	Gms.	G	A	Pts.	PIM
98-99—Kamloops	WHL	55	7	19	26	23	13	1	3	4	2
99-00—Kamloops	WHL	57	17	38	55	70	4	0	1	1	6

BOYES, BRAD   C   MAPLE LEAFS

PERSONAL: Born April 17, 1982, in Mississauga, Ont. ... 6-0/181. ... Shoots right.
TRANSACTIONS/CAREER NOTES: Selected by Toronto Maple Leafs in first round (first Maple Leafs pick, 24th overall) of NHL entry draft (June 24, 2000).
HONORS: Won Can.HL Scholastic Player of the Year Award (1999-2000).

		REGULAR SEASON					PLAYOFFS				
Season Team	League	Gms.	G	A	Pts.	PIM	Gms.	G	A	Pts.	PIM
98-99—Erie	OHL	59	24	36	60	30	5	1	2	3	10
99-00—Erie	OHL	68	36	46	82	38	13	6	8	14	10

BRYZGALOV, ILJA   G   MIGHTY DUCKS

PERSONAL: Born June 22, 1980, in Togliatti, U.S.S.R. ... 6-3/196. ... Catches left.

		REGULAR SEASON							PLAYOFFS						
Season Team	League	Gms.	Min	W	L	T	GA	SO	Avg.	Gms.	Min.	W	L	GA	SO	Avg.
99-00—Lada Togliatti	Russian	14	796	...	...	...	18	3	1.36	7	407	...	...	10	1	1.47

CUTTA, JAKUB   D   CAPITALS

PERSONAL: Born December 29, 1981, in Yablonec, Czechoslovakia. ... 6-3/195. ... Shoots left.
TRANSACTIONS/CAREER NOTES: Selected by Washington Capitals in second round (third Capitals pick, 61st overall) of NHL entry draft (June 24, 2000).

		REGULAR SEASON					PLAYOFFS				
Season Team	League	Gms.	G	A	Pts.	PIM	Gms.	G	A	Pts.	PIM
98-99—Swift Current	WHL	59	3	3	6	63	—	—	—	—	—
99-00—Swift Current	WHL	71	2	12	14	114	12	0	2	2	24

DEMARCHI, MATT   D   DEVILS

PERSONAL: Born May 4, 1981, in Bemidji, Minn. ... 6-3/180.
COLLEGE: Minnesota.
TRANSACTIONS/CAREER NOTES: Selected by New Jersey Devils in second round (fourth Devils pick, 57th overall) of NHL entry draft (June 24, 2000).

		REGULAR SEASON					PLAYOFFS				
Season Team	League	Gms.	G	A	Pts.	PIM	Gms.	G	A	Pts.	PIM
98-99—North Iowa	USHL	53	4	14	18	131	—	—	—	—	—
99-00—Univ. of Minnesota	WCHA	34	0	4	4	72	—	—	—	—	—

DICAIRE, GERARD   D   SABRES

PERSONAL: Born September 14, 1982, in Faro, Yukon. ... 6-2/190. ... Shoots left.
TRANSACTIONS/CAREER NOTES: Selected by Buffalo Sabres in second round (second Sabres pick, 48th pick overall) of NHL entry draft (June 24, 2000).

		REGULAR SEASON					PLAYOFFS				
Season Team	League	Gms.	G	A	Pts.	PIM	Gms.	G	A	Pts.	PIM
99-00—Seattle	WHL	68	11	25	36	38	7	0	1	1	6

DiPIETRO, RICK   G   ISLANDERS

PERSONAL: Born September 19, 1981, in Lewiston, Maine. ... 6-0/185. ... Catches right.
COLLEGE: Boston University.
TRANSACTIONS/CAREER NOTES: Selected by New York Islanders in first round (first Islanders pick, first overall) of NHL entry draft (June 24, 2000).
HONORS: Named to Hockey East All-Star second team (1999-2000).

		REGULAR SEASON								PLAYOFFS					
Season Team	League	Gms.	Min	W	L	T	GA	SO	Avg.	Gms.	Min.	W	L	GA	SO	Avg.
97-98—U.S. Jr. national team....	Int'l	46	2526	21	19	0	131	2	3.11	—	—	—	—	—	—	—
98-99—U.S. Jr. national team....	Int'l	30	1733	22	6	2	67	3	2.32	—	—	—	—	—	—	—
99-00—Boston University.........	Hockey East	30	1791	18	5	5	73	2	2.45	—	—	—	—	—	—	—

ELLIS, DAN   G   STARS

PERSONAL: Born June 19, 1980, in Saskatoon, Sask. ... 6-0/180. ... Catches left.
TRANSACTIONS/CAREER NOTES: Selected by Dallas Stars in second round (second Stars pick, 60th overall) of NHL entry draft (June 24, 2000).

		REGULAR SEASON								PLAYOFFS					
Season Team	League	Gms.	Min	W	L	T	GA	SO	Avg.	Gms.	Min.	W	L	GA	SO	Avg.
98-99—Newmarket..................	OPJHL	30	...	...	...	...	...	3	...	—	—	—	—	—	—	—
99-00—Omaha	USHL	55	...	34	16	4	...	11	...	—	—	—	—	—	—	—

ENDICOTT, SHANE   C   PENGUINS

PERSONAL: Born December 21, 1981, in Saskatoon, Sask. ... 6-4/200. ... Shoots left.
TRANSACTIONS/CAREER NOTES: Selected by Pittsburgh Penguins in second round (second Penguins pick, 52nd overall) of NHL entry draft (June 24, 2000).

		REGULAR SEASON					PLAYOFFS				
Season Team	League	Gms.	G	A	Pts.	PIM	Gms.	G	A	Pts.	PIM
97-98—Seattle	WHL	5	0	0	0	0	5	0	0	0	0
98-99—Seattle	WHL	72	13	26	39	27	11	0	1	1	0
99-00—Seattle	WHL	70	23	32	55	62	7	1	6	7	6

FOSTER, KURTIS   D   FLAMES

PERSONAL: Born November 24, 1981, in Carp, Ont. ... 6-5/205. ... Shoots right.
TRANSACTIONS/CAREER NOTES: Selected by Calgary Flames in second round (second Flames pick, 40th overall) of NHL entry draft (June 24, 2000).

		REGULAR SEASON					PLAYOFFS				
Season Team	League	Gms.	G	A	Pts.	PIM	Gms.	G	A	Pts.	PIM
97-98—Peterborough..........................	OHL	39	1	1	2	45	4	0	0	0	2
98-99—Peterborough..........................	OHL	54	2	13	15	59	5	0	0	0	6
99-00—Peterborough..........................	OHL	68	6	18	24	116	5	1	2	3	4

FROLOV, ALEXANDER   LW   KINGS

PERSONAL: Born June 19, 1982, in Moscow, U.S.S.R. ... 6-3/191. ... Shoots right.
TRANSACTIONS/CAREER NOTES: Selected by Los Angeles Kings in first round (first Kings pick, 20th overall) of NHL entry draft (June 24, 2000).

		REGULAR SEASON					PLAYOFFS				
Season Team	League	Gms.	G	A	Pts.	PIM	Gms.	G	A	Pts.	PIM
98-99—Torpedo-2 Yaroslavl...............	Rus. Div. II				Statistics unavailable.						
99-00—Torpedo-2 Yaroslavl...............	Rus. Div. II				Statistics unavailable.						

GABORIK, MARIAN   LW   WILD

PERSONAL: Born February 14, 1982, in Trencin, Czechoslovakia. ... 6-1/183. ... Shoots left.
TRANSACTIONS/CAREER NOTES: Selected by Minnesota Wild in first round (first Wild pick, third overall) of NHL entry draft (June 24, 2000).

		REGULAR SEASON					PLAYOFFS				
Season Team	League	Gms.	G	A	Pts.	PIM	Gms.	G	A	Pts.	PIM
98-99—Dukla Trencin........................	Slovakia	33	11	9	20	6	3	1	0	1	2
99-00—Dukla Trencin........................	Slovakia	50	25	21	46	34	5	1	2	3	2

HAINSEY, RON   D   CANADIENS

PERSONAL: Born March 24, 1981, in Bolton, Conn. ... 6-2/187. ... Shoots left.
COLLEGE: Massachusetts-Lowell.
TRANSACTIONS/CAREER NOTES: Selected by Montreal Canadiens in first round (first Canadiens pick, 13th overall) of NHL entry draft (June 24, 2000).

2000 TOP DRAFT PICKS

Season Team	League	REGULAR SEASON					PLAYOFFS				
		Gms.	G	A	Pts.	PIM	Gms.	G	A	Pts.	PIM
98-99—U.S. National	USHL	48	5	12	17	45	—	—	—	—	—
99-00—Mass.-Lowell	Hockey East	30	3	8	11	20	—	—	—	—	—

HALE, DAVID   D   DEVILS

PERSONAL: Born June 18, 1981, in Colorado Springs, Colo. ... 6-2/204. ... Shoots left.
COLLEGE: North Dakota.
TRANSACTIONS/CAREER NOTES: Selected by New Jersey Devils in first round (first Devils pick, 22nd overall) of NHL entry draft (June 24, 2000).

Season Team	League	REGULAR SEASON					PLAYOFFS				
		Gms.	G	A	Pts.	PIM	Gms.	G	A	Pts.	PIM
98-99—Sioux City	USHL	56	3	15	18	127	—	—	—	—	—
99-00—Sioux City	USHL	54	6	18	24	187	—	—	—	—	—

HARTNELL, SCOTT   RW   PREDATORS

PERSONAL: Born April 18, 1982, in Regina, Sask. ... 6-2/192. ... Shoots left. ... Cousin of Mark Deyell, center, Toronto Maple Leafs system.
TRANSACTIONS/CAREER NOTES: Selected by Nashville Predators in first round (first Predators pick, sixth overall) of NHL entry draft (June 24, 2000).

Season Team	League	REGULAR SEASON					PLAYOFFS				
		Gms.	G	A	Pts.	PIM	Gms.	G	A	Pts.	PIM
97-98—Lloydminster	Jr. A	...	9	16	25	82	—	—	—	—	—
—Prince Albert	WHL	1	0	1	1	2	—	—	—	—	—
98-99—Prince Albert	WHL	65	10	34	44	104	14	0	5	5	22
99-00—Prince Albert	WHL	62	27	55	82	124	6	3	2	5	6

HEATLEY, DANY   LW   THRASHERS

PERSONAL: Born January 21, 1981, in Freiburg, Germany. ... 6-1/200. ... Shoots left.
COLLEGE: Wisconsin.
TRANSACTIONS/CAREER NOTES: Selected by Atlanta Thrashers in first round (first Thrashers pick, second overall) of NHL entry draft (June 24, 2000).
HONORS: Named to WCHA All-Star first team (1999-2000). ... Named to NCAA All-America (West) second team (1999-2000).

Season Team	League	REGULAR SEASON					PLAYOFFS				
		Gms.	G	A	Pts.	PIM	Gms.	G	A	Pts.	PIM
98-99—Calgary Royals	AJHL	60	70	57	127	91	—	—	—	—	—
99-00—Univ. of Wisconsin	WCHA	38	28	28	56	32	—	—	—	—	—

HILBERT, ANDY   C   BRUINS

PERSONAL: Born February 6, 1981, in Howell, Mich. ... 5-11/190. ... Shoots left.
COLLEGE: Michigan.
TRANSACTIONS/CAREER NOTES: Selected by Boston Bruins in second round (third Bruins pick, 37th overall) of NHL entry draft (June 24, 2000).

Season Team	League	REGULAR SEASON					PLAYOFFS				
		Gms.	G	A	Pts.	PIM	Gms.	G	A	Pts.	PIM
98-99—U.S. National	USHL	46	23	35	58	140	—	—	—	—	—
99-00—Univ. of Michigan	CCHA	35	17	15	32	39	—	—	—	—	—

HOSSA, MARCEL   C   CANADIENS

PERSONAL: Born October 12, 1981, in Ilava, Czechoslovakia. ... 6-1/200. ... Shoots left. ... Brother of Marian Hossa, left winger, Ottawa Senators.
TRANSACTIONS/CAREER NOTES: Selected by Montreal Canadiens in first round (second Canadiens pick, 16th overall) of NHL entry draft (June 24, 2000).

Season Team	League	REGULAR SEASON					PLAYOFFS				
		Gms.	G	A	Pts.	PIM	Gms.	G	A	Pts.	PIM
97-98—Dukla Trencin Jrs.	Slovakia Jrs.				Statistics unavailable.						
98-99—Portland	WHL	70	7	14	21	66	2	0	0	0	0
99-00—Portland	WHL	60	24	29	53	58	—	—	—	—	—

HUML, IVAN   LW   BRUINS

PERSONAL: Born September 6, 1981, in Kladno, Czechoslovakia. ... 6-2/183. ... Shoots left.
TRANSACTIONS/CAREER NOTES: Selected by Boston Bruins in second round (fourth Bruins pick, 59th overall) of NHL entry draft (June 24, 2000).

Season Team	League	REGULAR SEASON					PLAYOFFS				
		Gms.	G	A	Pts.	PIM	Gms.	G	A	Pts.	PIM
98-99—Langley	BCHL	33	23	17	40	41	—	—	—	—	—
99-00—Langley	BCHL	49	53	51	104	72	—	—	—	—	—

JONSSON, LARS — D — BRUINS

PERSONAL: Born January 2, 1982, in Borlange, Sweden. ... 6-1/198. ... Shoots left.
TRANSACTIONS/CAREER NOTES: Selected by Boston Bruins in first round (first Bruins pick, seventh overall) of NHL entry draft (June 24, 2000).

		REGULAR SEASON					PLAYOFFS				
Season Team	League	Gms.	G	A	Pts.	PIM	Gms.	G	A	Pts.	PIM
98-99—Leksand	Sweden Jr.	40	4	8	12	42	—	—	—	—	—
99-00—Leksand	Sweden Jr.	34	16	22	38	50	—	—	—	—	—
—Leksand	Sweden	5	0	0	0	4	—	—	—	—	—

KLESLA, ROSTISLAV — D — BLUE JACKETS

PERSONAL: Born March 21, 1982, in Novy Jicin, Czechoslovakia. ... 6-2/198. ... Shoots left.
TRANSACTIONS/CAREER NOTES: Selected by Columbus Blue Jackets in first round (first Blue Jackets pick, fourth overall) of NHL entry draft (June 24, 2000).
HONORS: Won Can.HL Top Draft Prospect Award (1999-2000).

		REGULAR SEASON					PLAYOFFS				
Season Team	League	Gms.	G	A	Pts.	PIM	Gms.	G	A	Pts.	PIM
97-98—Opava	Czech. Jrs.	40	11	16	27	...	—	—	—	—	—
98-99—Sioux City	USHL	54	4	12	16	100	—	—	—	—	—
99-00—Brampton	OHL	67	16	29	45	174	6	1	1	2	21

KOLANOS, KRYS — C — COYOTES

PERSONAL: Born July 27, 1981, in Calgary. ... 6-2/196. ... Shoots right.
TRANSACTIONS/CAREER NOTES: Selected by Phoenix Coyotes in first round (first Coyotes pick, 19th overall) of NHL entry draft (June 24, 2000).

		REGULAR SEASON					PLAYOFFS				
Season Team	League	Gms.	G	A	Pts.	PIM	Gms.	G	A	Pts.	PIM
98-99—Calgary Royals	AJHL	58	43	67	110	98	—	—	—	—	—
99-00—Boston College	Hockey East	34	14	13	27	44	—	—	—	—	—

KOPECKY, TOMAS — C/LW — RED WINGS

PERSONAL: Born February 2, 1982, in Ilava, Czechoslovakia. ... 6-3/187. ... Shoots left.
TRANSACTIONS/CAREER NOTES: Selected by Detroit Red Wings in second round (second Red Wings pick, 38th overall) of NHL entry draft (June 24, 2000).

		REGULAR SEASON					PLAYOFFS				
Season Team	League	Gms.	G	A	Pts.	PIM	Gms.	G	A	Pts.	PIM
98-99—Dukla Trencin Jrs.	Slovakia Jrs.	44	13	16	29	...	—	—	—	—	—
99-00—Dukla Trencin	Slovakia	52	3	4	7	24	5	0	0	0	0
—Dukla Trencin Jrs.	Slovakia Jrs.	12	11	13	24	10	—	—	—	—	—

KRAHN, BRENT — G — FLAMES

PERSONAL: Born April 2, 1982, in Winnipeg. ... 6-4/200. ... Catches left.
TRANSACTIONS/CAREER NOTES: Selected by Calgary Flames in first round (first Flames pick, ninth overall) of NHL entry draft (June 24, 2000).

		REGULAR SEASON								PLAYOFFS						
Season Team	League	Gms.	Min	W	L	T	GA	SO	Avg.	Gms.	Min.	W	L	GA	SO	Avg.
99-00—Calgary	WHL	39	2315	33	6	0	92	4	2.38	5	266	2	2	13	0	2.93

KRIUKOV, ARTEM — C — SABRES

PERSONAL: Born March 5, 1982, in U.S.S.R. ... 6-3/180. ... Shoots left.
TRANSACTIONS/CAREER NOTES: Selected by Buffalo Sabres in first round (first Sabres pick, 15th overall) of NHL entry draft (June 24, 2000).

		REGULAR SEASON					PLAYOFFS				
Season Team	League	Gms.	G	A	Pts.	PIM	Gms.	G	A	Pts.	PIM
98-99—Torpedo-2 Yaroslavl	Rus. Div. II	20	2	2	4	6	—	—	—	—	—
99-00—Torpedo Yaroslavl	Russian	3	0	0	0	4	—	—	—	—	—

KRONVALL, NIKLAS — D — RED WINGS

PERSONAL: Born January 12, 1981, in Stockholm, Sweden. ... 5-11/165. ... Shoots left.
TRANSACTIONS/CAREER NOTES: Selected by Detroit Red Wings in first round (first Red Wings pick, 29th overall) of NHL entry draft (June 24, 2000).

		REGULAR SEASON					PLAYOFFS				
Season Team	League	Gms.	G	A	Pts.	PIM	Gms.	G	A	Pts.	PIM
98-99—Huddinge	Sweden	14	0	1	1	10	—	—	—	—	—
99-00—Djurgarden Stockholm	Sweden	37	1	4	5	16	8	0	0	0	8

KURKA, TOMAS — LW — HURRICANES

PERSONAL: Born December 14, 1981, in Litvinov, Czechoslovakia. ... 5-11/190. ... Shoots left.
TRANSACTIONS/CAREER NOTES: Selected by Carolina Hurricanes in second round (first Hurricanes pick, 32nd overall) of NHL entry draft (June 24, 2000).

		REGULAR SEASON					PLAYOFFS				
Season Team	League	Gms.	G	A	Pts.	PIM	Gms.	G	A	Pts.	PIM
97-98—Litvinov	Czech. Jrs.	44	38	23	61	...	—	—	—	—	—
98-99—Litvinov	Czech. Jrs.	48	60	42	102	38	—	—	—	—	—
—Litvinov	Czech.	6	0	0	0	0	—	—	—	—	—
99-00—Plymouth	OHL	64	36	28	64	37	17	7	6	13	6

LAINE, TEEMU — RW — DEVILS

PERSONAL: Born August 9, 1982, in Helsinki, Finland. ... 6-0/194. ... Shoots left.
TRANSACTIONS/CAREER NOTES: Selected by New Jersey Devils in second round (second Devils pick, 39th overall) of NHL entry draft (June 24, 2000).

		REGULAR SEASON					PLAYOFFS				
Season Team	League	Gms.	G	A	Pts.	PIM	Gms.	G	A	Pts.	PIM
98-99—Jokerit Helsinki	Finland Jr. B	34	20	19	39	87	—	—	—	—	—
99-00—Jokerit Helsinki	Finland	14	1	1	2	8	—	—	—	—	—
—Jokerit Helsinki	Finland Jr.	23	5	9	14	14	—	—	—	—	—

LILJA, ANDREAS — D — KINGS

PERSONAL: Born July 13, 1975, in Sweden. ... 6-3/220. ... Shoots left.
TRANSACTIONS/CAREER NOTES: Selected by Los Angeles Kings in second round (second Kings pick, 54th overall) of NHL entry draft (June 24, 2000).

		REGULAR SEASON					PLAYOFFS				
Season Team	League	Gms.	G	A	Pts.	PIM	Gms.	G	A	Pts.	PIM
99-00—Malmo	Sweden	49	8	11	19	88	6	0	0	0	8

MAATTA, TERO — D — SHARKS

PERSONAL: Born January 2, 1982, in Vantaa, Finland. ... 6-1/205. ... Shoots left.
TRANSACTIONS/CAREER NOTES: Selected by San Jose Sharks in second round (first Sharks pick, 41st overall) of NHL entry draft (June 24, 2000).

		REGULAR SEASON					PLAYOFFS				
Season Team	League	Gms.	G	A	Pts.	PIM	Gms.	G	A	Pts.	PIM
98-99—Jokerit Helsinki	Finland Jr.	20	0	0	0	30	—	—	—	—	—
—Jokerit Helsinki	Finland Jr. B	33	5	11	16	53	—	—	—	—	—
99-00—Jokerit Helsinki	Finland Jr.	31	4	4	8	53	—	—	—	—	—

MARTIN, PAUL — D — DEVILS

PERSONAL: Born March 5, 1981, in Minneapolis, Minn. ... 6-1/170. ... Shoots left.
HIGH SCHOOL: Elk River (Minn.).
TRANSACTIONS/CAREER NOTES: Selected by New Jersey Devils in second round (fifth Devils pick, 62nd overall) of NHL entry draft (June 24, 2000).

		REGULAR SEASON					PLAYOFFS				
Season Team	League	Gms.	G	A	Pts.	PIM	Gms.	G	A	Pts.	PIM
98-99—Elk River	USHS (West)	25	9	21	30	28	—	—	—	—	—
99-00—Elk River	USHS (West)	24	15	35	50	26	—	—	—	—	—

MIKHNOV, ALEXEI — LW/RW — OILERS

PERSONAL: Born August 31, 1982, in U.S.S.R. ... 6-5/194. ... Shoots left.
TRANSACTIONS/CAREER NOTES: Selected by Edmonton Oilers in first round (first Oilers pick, 17th overall) of NHL entry draft (June 24, 2000).

		REGULAR SEASON					PLAYOFFS				
Season Team	League	Gms.	G	A	Pts.	PIM	Gms.	G	A	Pts.	PIM
98-99—Torpedo-2 Yaroslavl	Rus. Div. II	14	2	2	4	4	—	—	—	—	—
99-00—Torpedo-2 Yaroslavl	Rus. Div. II				Statistics unavailable.						

MORISSET, DAVID — RW — BLUES

PERSONAL: Born April 6, 1981, in Langley, B.C. ... 6-2/195. ... Shoots right.
TRANSACTIONS/CAREER NOTES: Selected by St. Louis Blues in second round (second Blues pick, 65th overall) of NHL entry draft (June 24, 2000).

Season Team	League	REGULAR SEASON					PLAYOFFS				
		Gms.	G	A	Pts.	PIM	Gms.	G	A	Pts.	PIM
97-98—Seattle	WHL	58	6	2	8	104	5	1	0	1	6
98-99—Seattle	WHL	17	4	0	4	31	11	1	1	2	22
99-00—Seattle	WHL	60	23	34	57	71	7	3	4	7	12

NEDOROST, VACLAV — C — AVALANCHE

PERSONAL: Born March 16, 1982, in Budejovice, Czechoslovakia. ... 6-1/187. ... Shoots left.
TRANSACTIONS/CAREER NOTES: Selected by Colorado Avalanche in first round (first Avalanche pick, 14th overall) of NHL entry draft (June 24, 2000).

Season Team	League	REGULAR SEASON					PLAYOFFS				
		Gms.	G	A	Pts.	PIM	Gms.	G	A	Pts.	PIM
98-99—Budejovice	Czech. Jrs.	35	5	13	18	10	—	—	—	—	—
99-00—Budejovice	Czech Rep.	38	8	6	14	6	3	0	0	0	0
—Budejovice	Czech. Jrs.	7	2	5	7	6	—	—	—	—	—

NIKULIN, ILYA — D — THRASHERS

PERSONAL: Born March 12, 1982, in Moscow, U.S.S.R. ... 6-3/211. ... Shoots left.
TRANSACTIONS/CAREER NOTES: Selected by Atlanta Thrashers in second round (second Thrashers pick, 31st overall) of NHL entry draft (June 24, 2000).

Season Team	League	REGULAR SEASON					PLAYOFFS				
		Gms.	G	A	Pts.	PIM	Gms.	G	A	Pts.	PIM
98-99—Dynamo-2 Moscow	Rus. Div. II	23	0	2	2	18	—	—	—	—	—
99-00—Tver	Russian			Statistics unavailable.			—	—	—	—	—

NORDQVIST, JONAS — C — BLACKHAWKS

PERSONAL: Born April 26, 1982, in Leksand, Sweden. ... 6-2/191. ... Shoots left.
TRANSACTIONS/CAREER NOTES: Selected by Chicago Blackhawks in second round (third Blackhawks pick, 49th overall) of NHL entry draft (June 24, 2000).

Season Team	League	REGULAR SEASON					PLAYOFFS				
		Gms.	G	A	Pts.	PIM	Gms.	G	A	Pts.	PIM
98-99—Leksand	Sweden Jr.	32	14	25	39	...	—	—	—	—	—
99-00—Leksand	Sweden Jr.	34	15	24	39	32	—	—	—	—	—
—Leksand	Sweden	3	0	0	0	0	—	—	—	—	—

NOVAK, FILIP — D — RANGERS

PERSONAL: Born May 7, 1982, in Ceske Budejovice, Czechoslovakia. ... 6-0/174. ... Shoots left.
TRANSACTIONS/CAREER NOTES: Selected by New York Rangers in second round (first Rangers pick, 64th overall) of NHL entry draft (June 24, 2000).

Season Team	League	REGULAR SEASON					PLAYOFFS				
		Gms.	G	A	Pts.	PIM	Gms.	G	A	Pts.	PIM
98-99—Budejovice	Czech. Jrs.	68	8	10	18	34	—	—	—	—	—
99-00—Regina	WHL	47	7	32	39	70	7	1	4	5	5

ORPIK, BROOKS — D — PENGUINS

PERSONAL: Born September 26, 1980, in Amherst, N.Y. ... 6-3/217. ... Shoots left.
HIGH SCHOOL: Thayer Academy (Braintree, Mass.).
COLLEGE: Boston College.
TRANSACTIONS/CAREER NOTES: Selected by Pittsburgh Penguins in first round (first Penguins pick, 18th overall) of NHL entry draft (June 24, 2000).

Season Team	League	REGULAR SEASON					PLAYOFFS				
		Gms.	G	A	Pts.	PIM	Gms.	G	A	Pts.	PIM
97-98—Thayer Academy	Mass. H.S.	22	0	7	7	...	—	—	—	—	—
98-99—Boston College	Hockey East	41	1	10	11	96	—	—	—	—	—
99-00—Boston College	Hockey East	38	1	9	10	100	—	—	—	—	—

OTT, STEVE — C/LW — STARS

PERSONAL: Born August 19, 1982, in Stoney Point, Ont. ... 5-11/160. ... Shoots left.
TRANSACTIONS/CAREER NOTES: Selected by Dallas Stars in first round (first Stars pick, 25th overall) of NHL entry draft (June 24, 2000).

Season Team	League	REGULAR SEASON					PLAYOFFS				
		Gms.	G	A	Pts.	PIM	Gms.	G	A	Pts.	PIM
98-99—Leamington	Jr. B	48	14	30	44	110	—	—	—	—	—
99-00—Windsor	OHL	66	23	39	62	131	12	3	5	8	21

PETTINGER, MATT — LW — CAPITALS

PERSONAL: Born October 22, 1980, in Victoria, B.C. ... 6-0/205. ... Shoots left. ... Nephew of Gord Pettinger, center with three NHL teams (1932-33 through 1939-40).
COLLEGE: University of Denver.
TRANSACTIONS/CAREER NOTES: Selected by Washington Capitals in second round (second Capitals pick, 43rd overall) of NHL entry draft (June 24, 2000).

Season Team	League	REGULAR SEASON					PLAYOFFS				
		Gms.	G	A	Pts.	PIM	Gms.	G	A	Pts.	PIM
98-99—Univ. of Denver	WCHA	38	14	6	20	52	—	—	—	—	—
99-00—Univ. of Denver	WCHA	19	2	6	8	...	—	—	—	—	—
—Calgary	WHL	27	14	6	20	41	11	2	6	8	30

RONNQVIST, JONAS — LW/RW — MIGHTY DUCKS

PERSONAL: Born August 22, 1973, in Sweden. ... 6-1/200. ... Shoots left.
TRANSACTIONS/CAREER NOTES: Selected by Mighty Ducks of Anaheim in fourth round (third Mighty Ducks pick, 98th overall) of NHL entry draft (June 24, 2000).

Season Team	League	REGULAR SEASON					PLAYOFFS				
		Gms.	G	A	Pts.	PIM	Gms.	G	A	Pts.	PIM
99-00—Lulea	Sweden	49	15	24	39	42	—	—	—	—	—

SAMUELSSON, MARTIN — RW/LW — BRUINS

PERSONAL: Born January 25, 1982, in Upperlands Vasby, Sweden. ... 6-2/189. ... Shoots left.
TRANSACTIONS/CAREER NOTES: Selected by Boston Bruins in first round (second Bruins pick, 27th overall) of NHL entry draft (June 24, 2000).

Season Team	League	REGULAR SEASON					PLAYOFFS				
		Gms.	G	A	Pts.	PIM	Gms.	G	A	Pts.	PIM
98-99—MoDo Ornskoldsvik Jrs.	Sweden Jr.				Statistics unavailable.						
99-00—MoDo Ornskoldsvik Jrs.	Sweden Jr.	19	9	8	17	18	—	—	—	—	—

SAPOZHNIKOV, VLADIMIR — D — PANTHERS

PERSONAL: Born August 2, 1982, in Seversk, U.S.S.R. ... 6-3/205. ... Shoots left.
TRANSACTIONS/CAREER NOTES: Selected by Florida Panthers in second round (second Panthers pick, 58th overall) of NHL entry draft (June 24, 2000).

Season Team	League	REGULAR SEASON					PLAYOFFS				
		Gms.	G	A	Pts.	PIM	Gms.	G	A	Pts.	PIM
98-99—Novokuznetsk	Rus. Div. II				Statistics unavailable.						
99-00—Novokuznetsk	Rus. Div. II				Statistics unavailable.						

SAVIELS, ARGIS — D — AVALANCHE

PERSONAL: Born January 15, 1982, in Riga, U.S.S.R. ... 6-1/192. ... Shoots left.
TRANSACTIONS/CAREER NOTES: Selected by Colorado Avalanche in second round (fourth Avalanche pick, 63rd pick overall) of NHL entry draft (June 24, 2000).

Season Team	League	REGULAR SEASON					PLAYOFFS				
		Gms.	G	A	Pts.	PIM	Gms.	G	A	Pts.	PIM
99-00—Owen Sound	OHL	65	7	25	32	56	—	—	—	—	—

SCHULTZ, NICK — D — WILD

PERSONAL: Born August 25, 1982, in Strasbourg, Sask. ... 6-0/187. ... Shoots left.
TRANSACTIONS/CAREER NOTES: Selected by Minnesota Wild in second round (second Wild pick, 33rd overall) of NHL entry draft (June 24, 2000).

Season Team	League	REGULAR SEASON					PLAYOFFS				
		Gms.	G	A	Pts.	PIM	Gms.	G	A	Pts.	PIM
99-00—Prince Albert	WHL	72	11	33	44	38	6	0	3	3	2

SMIRNOV, ALEXEI — LW — MIGHTY DUCKS

PERSONAL: Born January 28, 1982, in Tver, U.S.S.R. ... 6-3/211. ... Shoots left.
TRANSACTIONS/CAREER NOTES: Selected by Might Ducks of Anaheim in first round (first Mighty Ducks pick, 12th overall) of NHL entry draft (June 24, 2000).

Season Team	League	REGULAR SEASON					PLAYOFFS				
		Gms.	G	A	Pts.	PIM	Gms.	G	A	Pts.	PIM
98-99—Dynamo Moscow	Russian	1	0	0	0	0	—	—	—	—	—
—Dynamo-2 Moscow	Rus. Div. II	27	9	3	12	24	—	—	—	—	—
99-00—Dynamo Moscow	Russian	1	0	0	0	0	—	—	—	—	—
—Tver	Russian				Statistics unavailable.						

SMITH, NATHAN — C — CANUCKS

PERSONAL: Born February 9, 1982, in Strathcona, Alta. ... 6-1/192. ... Shoots left. ... Brother of Jarrett Smith, center, Mighty Ducks of Anaheim system.
TRANSACTIONS/CAREER NOTES: Selected by Vancouver Canucks in first round (first Canucks pick, 23rd overall) of NHL entry draft (June 24, 2000).

		REGULAR SEASON					PLAYOFFS				
Season Team	League	Gms.	G	A	Pts.	PIM	Gms.	G	A	Pts.	PIM
98-99—Swift Current	WHL	47	5	8	13	26	—	—	—	—	—
99-00—Swift Current	WHL	70	21	28	49	72	12	1	6	7	4

SOIN, SERGEI — C/LW — AVALANCHE

PERSONAL: Born March 31, 1982, in Moscow, U.S.S.R. ... 6-0/176. ... Shoots left.
TRANSACTIONS/CAREER NOTES: Selected by Colorado Avalanche in second round (third Avalanche pick, 50th overall) of NHL entry draft (June 24, 2000).

		REGULAR SEASON					PLAYOFFS				
Season Team	League	Gms.	G	A	Pts.	PIM	Gms.	G	A	Pts.	PIM
98-99—Kryla Sov. Moscow	Russian	20	1	2	3	4					
99-00—Kryla Sov. Moscow	Russian				Statistics unavailable.						

STOLL, JARRETT — C — FLAMES

PERSONAL: Born June 24, 1982, in Melville, Sask. ... 6-1/199. ... Shoots right.
TRANSACTIONS/CAREER NOTES: Selected by Calgary Flames in second round (third Flames pick, 46th overall) of NHL entry draft (June 24, 2000).

		REGULAR SEASON					PLAYOFFS				
Season Team	League	Gms.	G	A	Pts.	PIM	Gms.	G	A	Pts.	PIM
98-99—Kootenay	WHL	57	13	21	34	40	4	0	0	0	2
99-00—Kootenay	WHL	71	37	38	75	64	20	7	9	16	24

SUGLOBOV, ALEKSANDER — RW/LW — DEVILS

PERSONAL: Born January 15, 1982, in U.S.S.R. ... 6-0/176. ... Shoots left.
TRANSACTIONS/CAREER NOTES: Selected by New Jersey Devils in second round (third Devils pick, 56th overall) of NHL entry draft (June 24, 2000).

		REGULAR SEASON					PLAYOFFS				
Season Team	League	Gms.	G	A	Pts.	PIM	Gms.	G	A	Pts.	PIM
99-00—Torpedo-2 Yaroslavl	Rus. Div. II				Statistics unavailable.						

SUTHERBY, BRIAN — C — CAPITALS

PERSONAL: Born March 1, 1982, in Edmonton. ... 6-2/180. ... Shoots left.
TRANSACTIONS/CAREER NOTES: Selected by Washington Capitals in first round (first Capitals pick, 26th overall) of NHL entry draft (June 24, 2000).

		REGULAR SEASON					PLAYOFFS				
Season Team	League	Gms.	G	A	Pts.	PIM	Gms.	G	A	Pts.	PIM
98-99—Moose Jaw	WHL	66	9	12	21	47	11	0	1	1	0
99-00—Moose Jaw	WHL	47	18	17	35	102	4	1	1	2	12

TAFFE, JEFF — C — BLUES

PERSONAL: Born February 19, 1981, in Hastings, Minn. ... 6-1/180. ... Shoots left. ... Name pronounced TAYFE.
HIGH SCHOOL: Hastings (Minn.).
COLLEGE: Minnesota.
TRANSACTIONS/CAREER NOTES: Selected by St. Louis Blues in first round (first Blues pick, 30th overall) of NHL entry draft (June 24, 2000).

		REGULAR SEASON					PLAYOFFS				
Season Team	League	Gms.	G	A	Pts.	PIM	Gms.	G	A	Pts.	PIM
98-99—Hastings H.S.	USHS (West)	25	38	48	86	26	—	—	—	—	—
99-00—Univ. of Minnesota	WCHA	34	9	10	19	16	—	—	—	—	—

TATARINOV, ALEXANDER — RW — COYOTES

PERSONAL: Born April 14, 1982, in Yekaterinburg, U.S.S.R. ... 5-11/176. ... Shoots left.
TRANSACTIONS/CAREER NOTES: Selected by Phoenix Coyotes in second round (second Coyotes pick, 53rd overall) of NHL entry draft (June 24, 2000).

		REGULAR SEASON					PLAYOFFS				
Season Team	League	Gms.	G	A	Pts.	PIM	Gms.	G	A	Pts.	PIM
97-98—Ottawa	OHL	53	4	19	23	20	—	—	—	—	—
98-99—					Did not play.						
99-00—Torpedo-2 Yaroslavl	Rus. Div. II				Statistics unavailable.						

2000 TOP DRAFT PICKS

TORRES, RAFFI — LW — ISLANDERS

PERSONAL: Born October 8, 1981, in Toronto. ... 6-0/207. ... Shoots left.
TRANSACTIONS/CAREER NOTES: Selected by New York Islanders in first round (second Islanders pick, fifth overall) of NHL entry draft (June 24, 2000).
HONORS: Named to OHL All-Star second team (1999-2000).

Season Team	League	REGULAR SEASON					PLAYOFFS				
		Gms.	G	A	Pts.	PIM	Gms.	G	A	Pts.	PIM
97-98—Thornhill	Jr. A	46	17	16	33	90	—	—	—	—	—
98-99—Brampton	OHL	62	35	27	62	32	—	—	—	—	—
99-00—Brampton	OHL	68	43	48	91	40	6	5	2	7	23

USTRNUL, LIBOR — D — THRASHERS

PERSONAL: Born February 20, 1982, in Olomouc, Czechoslovakia. ... 6-5/228. ... Shoots left.
TRANSACTIONS/CAREER NOTES: Selected by Atlanta Thrashers in second round (third Thrashers pick, 42nd overall) of NHL entry draft (June 24, 2000).

Season Team	League	REGULAR SEASON					PLAYOFFS				
		Gms.	G	A	Pts.	PIM	Gms.	G	A	Pts.	PIM
98-99—Thunder Bay Flyers	USHL	52	2	5	7	65	—	—	—	—	—
99-00—Plymouth	OHL	68	0	15	15	208	23	0	3	3	29

VERMETTE, ANTOINE — C — SENATORS

PERSONAL: Born July 20, 1982, in St-Agapit, Que. ... 6-0/184. ... Shoots left.
TRANSACTIONS/CAREER NOTES: Selected by Ottawa Senators in second round (third Senators pick, 55th overall) of NHL entry draft (June 24, 2000).
HONORS: Won Mike Bossy Trophy (1999-2000).

Season Team	League	REGULAR SEASON					PLAYOFFS				
		Gms.	G	A	Pts.	PIM	Gms.	G	A	Pts.	PIM
98-99—Quebec	QMJHL	57	9	17	26	32	13	0	0	0	2
99-00—Victoriaville	QMJHL	71	30	41	71	87	6	0	1	1	6

VERNARSKY, KRIS — C — MAPLE LEAFS

PERSONAL: Born April 5, 1982, in Warren, Mich. ... 6-2/201. ... Shoots left.
TRANSACTIONS/CAREER NOTES: Selected by Toronto Maple Leafs in second round (second Maple Leafs pick, 51st overall) of NHL entry draft (June 24, 2000).

Season Team	League	REGULAR SEASON					PLAYOFFS				
		Gms.	G	A	Pts.	PIM	Gms.	G	A	Pts.	PIM
98-99—Plymouth	OHL	45	3	14	17	30	11	0	0	0	2
99-00—Plymouth	OHL	64	16	22	38	63	19	3	6	9	24

VOLCHENKOV, ANTON — D — SENATORS

PERSONAL: Born February 25, 1982, in Moscow, U.S.S.R. ... 6-0/209. ... Shoots left.
TRANSACTIONS/CAREER NOTES: Selected by Ottawa Senators in first round (first Senators pick, 21st overall) of NHL entry draft (June 24, 2000).

Season Team	League	REGULAR SEASON					PLAYOFFS				
		Gms.	G	A	Pts.	PIM	Gms.	G	A	Pts.	PIM
99-00—CSKA	Rus. Div. II					Statistics unavailable.					

VOROBIEV, PAVEL — RW — BLACKHAWKS

PERSONAL: Born May 5, 1982, in Karaganda, U.S.S.R. ... 6-0/183. ... Shoots left.
TRANSACTIONS/CAREER NOTES: Selected by Chicago Blackhawks in first round (second Blackhawks pick, 11th overall) of NHL entry draft (June 24, 2000).

Season Team	League	REGULAR SEASON					PLAYOFFS				
		Gms.	G	A	Pts.	PIM	Gms.	G	A	Pts.	PIM
98-99—Torpedo-2 Yaroslavl	Rus. Div. II	17	0	1	1	0	—	—	—	—	—
99-00—Torpedo Yaroslavl	Russian	8	2	0	2	4	—	—	—	—	—

WIDING, DANIEL — RW — PREDATORS

PERSONAL: Born April 13, 1982, in Gavle, Sweden. ... 6-0/185. ... Shoots right.
TRANSACTIONS/CAREER NOTES: Selected by Nashville Predators in second round (second Predators pick, 36th overall) of NHL entry draft (June 24, 2000).

Season Team	League	REGULAR SEASON					PLAYOFFS				
		Gms.	G	A	Pts.	PIM	Gms.	G	A	Pts.	PIM
99-00—Leksand	Sweden Jr.	34	15	12	27	65	—	—	—	—	—
—Leksand	Sweden	3	0	0	0	2	—	—	—	—	—

WILLIAMS, JUSTIN   RW   FLYERS

PERSONAL: Born October 4, 1981, in Cobourg, Ont. ... 6-1/176. ... Shoots right.
TRANSACTIONS/CAREER NOTES: Selected by Philadelphia Flyers in first round (first Flyers pick, 28th overall) of NHL entry draft (June 24, 2000).

		REGULAR SEASON					PLAYOFFS				
Season Team	League	Gms.	G	A	Pts.	PIM	Gms.	G	A	Pts.	PIM
97-98—Colborne	Jr. C	36	32	35	67	26	—	—	—	—	—
—Cobourg	Tier II Jr. A	17	0	3	3	5	—	—	—	—	—
98-99—Plymouth	OHL	47	4	8	12	28	7	1	2	3	0
99-00—Plymouth	OHL	68	37	46	83	46	23	*14	16	*30	10

WINCHESTER, BRAD   LW   OILERS

PERSONAL: Born March 1, 1981, in Madison, Wis. ... 6-5/208. ... Shoots left.
COLLEGE: Wisconsin.
TRANSACTIONS/CAREER NOTES: Selected by Edmonton Oilers in second round (second Oilers pick, 35th overall) of NHL entry draft (June 24, 2000).

		REGULAR SEASON					PLAYOFFS				
Season Team	League	Gms.	G	A	Pts.	PIM	Gms.	G	A	Pts.	PIM
98-99—U.S. National	USHL	48	14	23	37	103	—	—	—	—	—
99-00—Univ. of Wisconsin	WCHA	29	8	8	16	48	—	—	—	—	—

YAKUBOV, MIKHAIL   C   BLACKHAWKS

PERSONAL: Born February 16, 1982, in Bamaul, U.S.S.R. ... 6-3/185. ... Shoots left.
TRANSACTIONS/CAREER NOTES: Selected by Chicago Blackhawks in first round (first Blackhawks pick, 10th overall) of NHL entry draft (June 24, 2000).

		REGULAR SEASON					PLAYOFFS				
Season Team	League	Gms.	G	A	Pts.	PIM	Gms.	G	A	Pts.	PIM
99-00—Togliatti	Rus .Div. II				Statistics unavailable.						

ZAINULLIN, RUSLAN   RW   LIGHTNING

PERSONAL: Born February 14, 1982, in Kazan, U.S.S.R. ... 6-2/202. ... Shoots left.
TRANSACTIONS/CAREER NOTES: Selected by Tampa Bay Lightning in second round (second Lightning pick, 34th pick overall) of NHL entry draft (June 24, 2000).

		REGULAR SEASON					PLAYOFFS				
Season Team	League	Gms.	G	A	Pts.	PIM	Gms.	G	A	Pts.	PIM
97-98—Ak Bars-2 Kazan	Rus. Div. II	36	13	8	21	22	—	—	—	—	—
99-00—Ak Bars Kazan	Russian	14	1	1	2	4	—	—	—	—	—

2000 TOP DRAFT PICKS

BOWMAN, SCOTTY

RED WINGS

PERSONAL: Born September 18, 1933, in Montreal. ... Full Name: William Scott Bowman.
HONORS: Inducted into Hall of Fame (1991).

HEAD COACHING RECORD

BACKGROUND: Minor league hockey supervisor, Montreal Canadiens organization (1954-55 through 1956-57). ... Coach, Team Canada (1976 and 1981). ... Director of hockey operations/general manager, Buffalo Sabres (1979-80 through 1986-87). ... Director of player development, Pittsburgh Penguins (1990-91). ... Director of player personnel, Detroit Red Wings (1994-95 through 1996-97).
HONORS: Won Jack Adams Award (1976-77 and 1995-96). ... Named NHL Executive of the Year by THE SPORTING NEWS (1979-80). ... Named NHL Coach of the Year by THE SPORTING NEWS (1995-96).
RECORDS: Holds NHL career regular-season records for wins—1,144; and winning percentage—.653. ... Holds NHL career playoff records for wins—205; and games—324.

Season Team	League	W	L	T	RT	Pct.	Finish	W	L	Pct.
67-68—St. Louis	NHL	23	21	14	—	.517	3rd/Western Division	8	10	.444
68-69—St. Louis	NHL	37	25	14	—	.579	1st/Western Division	8	4	.667
69-70—St. Louis	NHL	37	27	12	—	.566	1st/Western Division	8	8	.500
70-71—St. Louis	NHL	13	10	5	—	.554	2nd/West Division	2	4	.333
71-72—Montreal	NHL	46	16	16	—	.692	3rd/Eastern Division	2	4	.333
72-73—Montreal	NHL	52	10	16	—	.769	1st/East Division	12	5	.706
73-74—Montreal	NHL	45	24	9	—	.635	2nd/East Division	2	4	.333
74-75—Montreal	NHL	47	14	19	—	.706	1st/Adams Division	6	5	.545
75-76—Montreal	NHL	58	11	11	—	.794	1st/Adams Division	12	1	.923
76-77—Montreal	NHL	60	8	12	—	.825	1st/Adams Division	12	2	.857
77-78—Montreal	NHL	59	10	11	—	.806	1st/Adams Division	12	3	.800
78-79—Montreal	NHL	52	17	11	—	.719	1st/Adams Division	12	4	.750
79-80—Buffalo	NHL	47	17	16	—	.688	1st/Adams Division	9	5	.643
81-82—Buffalo	NHL	18	10	7	—	.614	3rd/Adams Division	1	3	.250
82-83—Buffalo	NHL	38	29	13	—	.556	3rd/Adams Division	6	4	.600
83-84—Buffalo	NHL	48	25	7	—	.644	2nd/Adams Division	0	3	.000
84-85—Buffalo	NHL	38	28	14	—	.563	3rd/Adams Division	2	3	.400
85-86—Buffalo	NHL	18	18	1	—	.500	5th/Adams Division	—	—	—
86-87—Buffalo	NHL	3	7	2	—	.333	5th/Adams Division	—	—	—
91-92—Pittsburgh	NHL	39	32	9	—	.544	3rd/Patrick Division	16	5	.762
92-93—Pittsburgh	NHL	56	21	7	—	.708	1st/Patrick Division	7	5	.583
93-94—Detroit	NHL	46	30	8	—	.595	1st/Central Division	3	4	.429
94-95—Detroit	NHL	33	11	4	—	.729	1st/Central Division	12	6	.667
95-96—Detroit	NHL	62	13	7	—	.799	1st/Central Division	10	9	.526
96-97—Detroit	NHL	38	26	18	—	.573	2nd/Central Division	16	4	.800
97-98—Detroit	NHL	44	23	15	—	.628	2nd/Central Division	16	6	.727
98-99—Detroit	NHL	39	31	7	—	.552	1st/Central Division	6	4	.600
99-00—Detroit	NHL	48	24	10	2	.646	2nd/Central Division	5	4	.556
NHL Totals (28 years)		1144	538	295	2	.653	**NHL Totals (26 years)**	205	119	.633

NOTES:

67-68—Defeated Philadelphia in Western Division finals; defeated Minnesota in Stanley Cup semifinals; lost to Montreal in Stanley Cup finals.
68-69—Defeated Philadelphia in Stanley Cup quarterfinals; defeated Los Angeles in Stanley Cup semifinals; lost to Montreal in Stanley Cup finals.
69-70—Defeated Minnesota in Stanley Cup quarterfinals; defeated Pittsburgh in Stanley Cup semifinals; lost to Montreal in Stanley Cup finals.
70-71—Lost to Minnesota in Stanley Cup quarterfinals.
71-72—Lost to New York Rangers in Stanley Cup quarterfinals.
72-73—Defeated Buffalo in Stanley Cup quarterfinals; defeated Philadelphia in Stanley Cup semifinals; defeated Chicago in Stanley Cup finals.
73-74—Lost to New York Rangers in Stanley Cup quarterfinals.
74-75—Defeated Vancouver in Stanley Cup quarterfinals; lost to Buffalo in Stanley Cup semifinals.
75-76—Defeated Chicago in Stanley Cup quarterfinals; defeated New York Islanders in Stanley Cup semifinals; defeated Philadelphia in Stanley Cup finals.
76-77—Defeated St. Louis in Stanley Cup quarterfinals; defeated New York Islanders in Stanley Cup semifinals; defeated Boston in Stanley Cup finals.
77-78—Defeated Detroit in Stanley Cup quarterfinals; defeated Toronto in Stanley Cup semifinals; defeated Boston in Stanley Cup finals.
78-79—Defeated Toronto in Stanley Cup quarterfinals; defeated Boston in Stanley Cup semifinals; defeated New York Rangers in Stanley Cup finals.
79-80—Defeated Vancouver in Stanley Cup preliminary round; defeated Chicago in Stanley Cup quarterfinals; lost to New York Islanders in Stanley Cup semifinals.
81-82—Lost to Boston in Stanley Cup preliminary round.
82-83—Defeated Montreal in Adams Division semifinals; lost to Boston in Adams Division finals.
83-84—Lost to Quebec in Adams Division semifinals.
84-85—Lost to Quebec in Adams Division semifinals.
86-87—Replaced on interim basis by Craig Ramsay (November 1986).
91-92—Defeated Washington in Patrick Division semifinals; defeated New York Rangers in Patrick Division finals; defeated Boston in Wales Conference finals; defeated Chicago in Stanley Cup finals.
92-93—Defeated New Jersey in Patrick Division semifinals; lost to New York Islanders in Patrick Division finals.
93-94—Lost to San Jose in Western Conference quarterfinals.
94-95—Defeated Dallas in Western Conference quarterfinals; defeated San Jose in Western Conference semifinals; defeated Chicago in Western Conference finals; lost to New Jersey in Stanley Cup finals.
95-96—Defeated Winnipeg in Western Conference quarterfinals; defeated St. Louis in Western Conference semifinals; lost to Colorado in Western Conference finals.
96-97—Defeated St. Louis in Western Conference quarterfinals; defeated Anaheim in Western Conference semifinals; defeated Colorado in Western Conference finals; defeated Philadelphia in Stanley Cup finals.
97-98—Defeated Phoenix in Western Conference quarterfinals; defeated St. Louis in Western Conference semifinals; defeated Dallas in Western Conference finals; defeated Washington in Stanley Cup finals.
98-99—Missed first five games of season due to illness; defeated Anaheim in Western Conference quarterfinals; lost to Colorado in Western Conference semifinals.
99-00—Defeated Los Angeles in Western Conference quarterfinals; lost to Colorado in Western Conference semifinals.

BURNS, PAT — BRUINS

PERSONAL: Born April 4, 1952, in St.-Henri, Que.
MISCELLANEOUS: Served 17 years with the Gatineau (Quebec) and Ottawa Police Departments before assuming a professional hockey coaching career.

HEAD COACHING RECORD

BACKGROUND: Assistant coach, Canadian National team (1986). ... Assistant coach, Canadian Junior National team (1987).
HONORS: Named NHL Coach of the Year by THE SPORTING NEWS (1988-89, 1992-93 and 1997-98). ... Won Jack Adams Award (1988-89, 1992-93 and 1997-98). ... Only coach in NHL history to win Coach of the Year award for three different NHL teams.

Season Team	League	W	L	T	RT	Pct.	Finish	W	L	Pct.
83-84—Hull	QMJHL	25	45	0	—	.357	6th/LeBel Division			
84-85—Hull	QMJHL	33	34	1	—	.493	2nd/LeBel Division	1	4	.200
85-86—Hull	QMJHL	54	18	0	—	.750	1st/LeBel Division	15	0	1.000
86-87—Hull	QMJHL	26	39	5	—	.407	4th/LeBel Division	4	4	.500
87-88—Sherbrooke	AHL	42	34	4	—	.550	3rd/North Division	2	4	.333
88-89—Montreal	NHL	53	18	9	—	.719	1st/Adams Division	14	7	.667
89-90—Montreal	NHL	41	28	11	—	.581	3rd/Adams Division	5	6	.455
90-91—Montreal	NHL	39	30	11	—	.556	2nd/Adams Division	7	6	.538
91-92—Montreal	NHL	41	28	11	—	.581	1st/Adams Division	4	7	.364
92-93—Toronto	NHL	44	29	11	—	.589	3rd/Norris Division	11	10	.524
93-94—Toronto	NHL	43	29	12	—	.583	2nd/Central Division	9	9	.500
94-95—Toronto	NHL	21	19	8	—	.521	4th/Central Division	3	4	.429
95-96—Toronto	NHL	25	30	10	—	.462	—	—	—	—
97-98—Boston	NHL	39	30	13	—	.555	2nd/Northeast Division	2	4	.333
98-99—Boston	NHL	39	30	13	—	.555	3rd/Northeast Division	6	6	.500
99-00—Boston	NHL	24	39	19	6	.409	5th/Northeast Division	—	—	—
NHL Totals (11 years)		**409**	**310**	**128**	**6**	**.558**	**NHL Totals (9 years)**	**61**	**59**	**.508**

NOTES:
84-85—Lost to Verdun in quarterfinals of President Cup playoffs.
85-86—Defeated Shawinigan in quarterfinals of President Cup playoffs; defeated St. Jean in semifinals of President Cup playoffs; defeated Drummondville in President Cup finals.
86-87—Eliminated in President Cup quarterfinal round-robin series.
87-88—Lost to Fredericton in quarterfinals of Calder Cup playoffs.
88-89—Defeated Hartford in Adams Division semifinals; defeated Boston in Adams Division finals; defeated Philadelphia in Wales Conference finals; lost to Calgary in Stanley Cup finals.
89-90—Defeated Buffalo in Adams Division semifinals; lost to Boston in Adams Division finals.
90-91—Defeated Buffalo in Adams Division semifinals; lost to Boston in Adams Division finals.
91-92—Defeated Hartford in Adams Division semifinals; lost to Boston in Adams Division finals.
92-93—Defeated Detroit in Norris Division semifinals; defeated St. Louis in Norris Division finals; lost to Los Angeles in Campbell Conference finals.
93-94—Defeated Chicago in Western Conference quarterfinals; defeated San Jose in Western Conference semifinals; lost to Vancouver in Western Conference finals.
94-95—Lost to Chicago in Western Conference quarterfinals.
95-96—Replaced as head coach by Nick Beverley (March 4) with club in fifth place.
97-98—Lost to Washington in Eastern Conference quarterfinals.
98-99—Defeated Carolina in Eastern Conference quarterfinals; lost to Buffalo in Eastern Conference semifinals.

CRAWFORD, MARC — CANUCKS

PERSONAL: Born February 13, 1961, in Belleville, Ont. ... Shot left. ... Full Name: Marc Joseph John Crawford. ... Brother of Bob Crawford, right winger with four NHL teams (1979-80 and 1981-82 through 1986-87).
TRANSACTIONS/CAREER NOTES: Selected by Vancouver Canucks in fourth round (third Canucks pick, 70th overall) of NHL entry draft (June 11, 1980). ... Suspended three games by NHL for leaving bench to fight (February 3, 1987).
MISCELLANEOUS: Played left wing.

Season Team	League	Gms.	G	A	Pts.	PIM	+/-	PP	SH	Gms.	G	A	Pts.	PIM
79-80—Cornwall	OHL	54	27	36	63	127	...	...	...	18	8	20	28	48
80-81—Cornwall	OHL	63	42	57	99	242	...	...	...	19	20	15	35	27
81-82—Dallas	CHL	34	13	21	34	71	...	...	...	—	—	—	—	—
—Vancouver	NHL	40	4	8	12	29	0	0	0	14	1	0	1	11
82-83—Vancouver	NHL	41	4	5	9	28	-3	0	0	3	0	1	1	25
—Fredericton	AHL	30	15	9	24	59	...	...	...	9	1	3	4	10
83-84—Vancouver	NHL	19	0	1	1	9	0	0	0	—	—	—	—	—
—Fredericton	AHL	56	9	22	31	96	...	...	...	7	4	2	6	23
84-85—Vancouver	NHL	1	0	0	0	4	-4	0	0	—	—	—	—	—
85-86—Vancouver	NHL	54	11	14	25	92	-7	0	0	3	0	1	1	8
—Fredericton	AHL	26	10	14	24	55	...	...	...	—	—	—	—	—
86-87—Vancouver	NHL	21	0	3	3	67	-8	0	0	—	—	—	—	—
—Fredericton	AHL	25	8	11	19	21	...	...	...	—	—	—	—	—
87-88—Fredericton	AHL	43	5	13	18	90	...	...	...	2	0	0	0	14
88-89—Milwaukee	IHL	53	23	30	53	166	...	...	...	11	2	5	7	26
NHL Totals (6 years)		**176**	**19**	**31**	**50**	**229**	**-22**	**0**	**0**	**20**	**1**	**2**	**3**	**44**

HEAD COACHING RECORD

BACKGROUND: Player/assistant coach, Fredericton Express of AHL (1987-88). ... Nordiques franchise moved to Denver for 1995-96 season and renamed Colorado Avalanche. ... Hockey analyst, CBC television (1998-January 24, 1999).
HONORS: Won Louis A.R. Pieri Memorial Award (1992-93). ... Named NHL Coach of the Year by THE SPORTING NEWS (1994-95). ... Won Jack Adams Award (1994-95).

Season Team	League	W	L	T	RT	Pct.	Finish	W	L	Pct.
						REGULAR SEASON			**PLAYOFFS**	
89-90—Cornwall	OHL	24	38	4	—	.394	6th/Leyden Division	2	4	.333
90-91—Cornwall	OHL	23	42	1	—	.356	7th/Leyden Division	—	—	—
91-92—St. John's	AHL	39	29	12	—	.563	2nd/Atlantic Division	11	5	.688
92-93—St. John's	AHL	41	26	13	—	.594	1st/Atlantic Division	4	5	.444
93-94—St. John's	AHL	45	23	12	—	.638	1st/Atlantic Division	6	5	.545
94-95—Quebec	NHL	30	13	5	—	.677	1st/Northeast Division	2	4	.333
95-96—Colorado	NHL	47	25	10	—	.634	1st/Pacific Division	16	6	.727
96-97—Colorado	NHL	49	24	9	—	.652	1st/Pacific Division	10	7	.588
97-98—Colorado	NHL	39	26	17	—	.579	1st/Pacific Division	3	4	.429
98-99—Vancouver	NHL	8	23	6	—	.297	4th/Northwest Division	—	—	—
99-00—Vancouver	NHL	30	37	15	8	.457	3rd/Northwest Division	—	—	—
NHL Totals (6 years)		203	148	62	8	.567	**NHL Totals (4 years)**	31	21	.596

NOTES:

89-90—Lost to Oshawa in Leyden Division quarterfinals.

91-92—Defeated Cape Breton in first round of Calder Cup playoffs; defeated Moncton in second round of Calder Cup playoffs; lost to Adirondack in Calder Cup finals.

92-93—Defeated Moncton in first round of Calder Cup playoffs; lost to Cape Breton in second round of Calder Cup playoffs.

93-94—Defeated Cape Breton in first round of Calder Cup playoffs; lost to Moncton in second round of Calder Cup playoffs.

94-95—Lost to New York Rangers in Eastern Conference quarterfinals.

95-96—Defeated Vancouver in Western Conference quarterfinals; defeated Chicago in Western Conference semifinals; defeated Detroit in Western Conference finals; defeated Florida in Stanley Cup finals.

96-97—Defeated Chicago in Western Conference quarterfinals; defeated Edmonton in Western Conference semifinals; lost to Detroit in Western Conference finals.

97-98—Lost to Edmonton in Western Conference quarterfinals.

98-99—Replaced Mike Keenan as head coach (January 24) with club in third place.

FRANCIS, BOBBY   COYOTES

PERSONAL: Born December 5, 1958, in North Battleford, Sask. ... Son of Emile Francis, goaltender with Chicago Blackhawks (1946-47 and 1947-48) and New York Rangers (1948-49 through 1951-52); and head coach with New York Rangers (1965-66 through 1974-75) and St. Louis Blues (1976-77, 1981-82 and 1982-83).

COLLEGE: New Hampshire.

TRANSACTIONS/CAREER NOTES: Signed as non-drafted free agent by Calgary Flames (October 27, 1980). ... Traded by Flames to Detroit Red Wings for the rights to RW Yves Courteau (December 2, 1982).

HONORS: Named to CHL All-Star first team (1981-82). ... Won Ken McKenzie Trophy (1981-82). ... Won Tommy Ivan Trophy (1981-82).

MISCELLANEOUS: Played center.

Season Team	League	Gms.	G	A	Pts.	PIM	+/-	PP	SH	Gms.	G	A	Pts.	PIM
				REGULAR SEASON								**PLAYOFFS**		
72-73—Brooklyn	NYJHL	38	36	34	70	44	...	...	...	—	—	—	—	—
73-74—Brooklyn	NYJHL	41	41	53	94	63	...	...	...	12	17	11	28	24
74-75—Bronx	NYJHL	40	53	59	112	71	...	...	...	—	—	—	—	—
75-76—Beawick	NEJHL	40	62	74	136	61	...	...	...	—	—	—	—	—
76-77—Univ. of New Hamp.	Hockey East						Did not play.							
77-78—Univ. of New Hamp.	Hockey East	40	9	44	53	...				—	—	—	—	—
78-79—Univ. of New Hamp.	Hockey East	35	20	46	66	44	...			—	—	—	—	—
79-80—Univ. of New Hamp.	Hockey East	28	19	23	42	30	...			—	—	—	—	—
80-81—Birmingham	CHL	18	6	21	27	20	...			—	—	—	—	—
—Muskegon	IHL	27	16	17	33	33	...			—	—	—	—	—
81-82—Oklahoma City	CHL	80	48	66	114	76	...	...	...	4	1	2	3	11
82-83—Colorado	CHL	26	20	16	36	24	...	...	...	—	—	—	—	—
—Detroit	NHL	14	2	0	2	0	-1	0	0	—	—	—	—	—
—Adirondack	AHL	17	3	8	11	0	...			—	—	—	—	—
83-84—Colorado	CHL	68	32	50	82	53	...	...	...	1	0	1	1	0
84-85—Salt Lake City	IHL	53	24	16	40	36	...	...	...	6	1	1	2	0
85-86—Salt Lake City	IHL	82	32	44	76	163	...	...	...	5	0	4	4	10
86-87—Salt Lake City	IHL	82	29	69	98	86	...	...	...	17	9	8	17	13
NHL Totals (1 year)		14	2	0	2	0	-1	0	0					

HEAD COACHING RECORD

BACKGROUND: Assistant coach, Salt Lake City Golden Eagles of IHL (1986-87 through 1988-89). ... Assistant coach, Boston Bruins (1997-98 and 1998-99).

Season Team	League	W	L	T	RT	Pct.	Finish	W	L	Pct.
						REGULAR SEASON			**PLAYOFFS**	
89-90—Salt Lake City	IHL	37	36	9	—	.506	2nd/West Division	5	6	.455
90-91—Salt Lake City	IHL	50	28	5	—	.633	2nd/West Division	0	4	.000
91-92—Salt Lake City	IHL	33	40	9	—	.457	4th/West Division	1	4	.200
92-93—Salt Lake City	IHL	38	39	5	—	.494	2nd/Pacific Division	—	—	—
93-94—Saint John	AHL	37	33	10	—	.525	2nd/Atlantic Division	3	4	.429
94-95—Saint John	AHL	27	40	13	—	.419	4th/Atlantic Division	1	4	.200
95-96—Providence	AHL	30	40	10	—	.438	4th/Northern Division	1	3	.250
96-97—Providence	AHL	35	40	5	—	.469	4th/New England Division	4	6	.400
99-00—Phoenix	NHL	39	35	8	4	.524	3rd/Pacific Division	1	4	.200
NHL Totals (1 year)		39	35	8	4	.524	**NHL Totals (1 year)**	1	4	.200

NOTES:

89-90—Defeated Milwaukee in quarterfinals of Turner Cup playoffs; lost to Indianapolis in semifinals of Turner Cup playoffs.

90-91—Lost to Phoenix in Turner Cup quarterfinals.

91-92—Lost to Kansas City in West Division quarterfinals.
93-94—Lost to Moncton in Atlantic Division semifinals.
94-95—Lost to Prince Edward Island in Atlantic Division semifinals.
95-96—Lost to Springfield in Eastern Conference quarterfinals.
96-97—Defeated Worcester in Southern Conference quarterfinals; lost to Springfield in Southern Conference semifinals.
99-00—Lost to Colorado in Western Conference quarterfinals.

FRASER, CURT — THRASHERS

PERSONAL: Born January 12, 1958, in Cincinnati. ... Shot left.
TRANSACTIONS/CAREER NOTES: Selected by Vancouver Canucks in second round of 1978 amateur draft. ... Traded by Canucks to Chicago Blackhawks for RW Tony Tanti (January 3, 1983). ... Tore knee ligaments (November 1983). ... Fractured bone in face (January 13, 1985). ... Sprained shoulder (December 14, 1985); missed 19 games. ... Bruised ribs (October 1987). ... Suffered from virus (November 1987). ... Traded by Blackhawks to Minnesota North Stars for LW Dirk Graham (January 4, 1988). ... Injured ribs (October 1988). ... Injured wrist (January 1989). ... Injured shoulder and underwent surgery (January 15, 1989). ... Missed most of 1989-90 season due to shoulder rehabilitation.
MISCELLANEOUS: Played left wing.

		REGULAR SEASON								PLAYOFFS				
Season Team	League	Gms.	G	A	Pts.	PIM	+/-	PP	SH	Gms.	G	A	Pts.	PIM
73-74—Kelowna	JR.ABCHL	52	32	32	64	85	...	...	...	—	—	—	—	—
74-75—Victoria	WCHL	68	17	32	49	105	...	...	...	—	—	—	—	—
75-76—Victoria	WCHL	71	43	64	107	167	...	...	...	—	—	—	—	—
76-77—Victoria	WCHL	60	34	41	75	82	...	...	...	4	4	2	6	4
77-78—Victoria	WCHL	66	48	44	92	256	...	...	...	13	10	7	17	28
78-79—Vancouver	NHL	78	16	19	35	116	-7	2	0	3	0	2	2	6
79-80—Vancouver	NHL	78	17	25	42	143	7	0	0	4	0	0	0	2
80-81—Vancouver	NHL	77	25	24	49	118	-19	7	0	3	1	0	1	2
81-82—Vancouver	NHL	79	28	39	67	175	2	11	0	17	3	7	10	98
82-83—Vancouver	NHL	36	6	7	13	99	-7	2	0	—	—	—	—	—
—Chicago	NHL	38	6	13	19	77	2	0	0	13	4	4	8	18
83-84—Chicago	NHL	29	5	12	17	26	9	1	0	5	0	0	0	14
84-85—Chicago	NHL	73	25	25	50	109	3	4	0	15	6	3	9	36
85-86—Chicago	NHL	61	29	39	68	84	11	7	0	3	0	1	1	12
86-87—Chicago	NHL	75	25	25	50	182	5	3	0	2	1	1	2	10
87-88—Chicago	NHL	27	4	6	10	57	-13	1	0	—	—	—	—	—
—Minnesota	NHL	10	1	1	2	20	-7	0	0	—	—	—	—	—
88-89—Minnesota	NHL	35	5	5	10	76	-15	1	0	—	—	—	—	—
89-90—Minnesota	NHL	8	1	0	1	22	-5	0	0	—	—	—	—	—
NHL Totals (12 years)		704	193	240	433	1304	-34	39	0	65	15	18	33	198

HEAD COACHING RECORD
BACKGROUND: Assistant coach, Milwaukee Admirals of IHL (1990-91 and 1991-92). ... Associate coach, Syracuse Crunch of AHL (1994-95).

		REGULAR SEASON						PLAYOFFS		
Season Team	League	W	L	T	RT	Pct.	Finish	W	L	Pct.
92-93—Milwaukee	IHL	49	23	10	—	.659	1st/Midwest Division	2	4	.333
93-94—Milwaukee	IHL	40	24	17	—	.599	2nd/Midwest Division	0	4	.000
95-96—Orlando	IHL	52	24	6	—	.671	1st/Central Division	11	12	.478
96-97—Orlando	IHL	53	24	5	—	.677	2nd/Northeast Division	4	6	.400
97-98—Orlando	IHL	42	30	10	—	.573	2nd/Northeast Division	9	8	.529
98-99—Orlando	IHL	45	33	4	—	.573	2nd/Northeast Division	10	7	.588
99-00—Atlanta	NHL	14	61	7	4	.213	5th/Southeast Division	—	—	—
NHL Totals (1 year)		14	61	7	4	.213				

NOTES:
92-93—Lost to Kansas City in Western Conference quarterfinals.
93-94—Lost to Atlanta in Western Conference quarterfinals.
95-96—Defeated Fort Wayne in Eastern Conference quarterfinals; defeated Detroit in Eastern Conference semifinals; defeated Cincinnati in Eastern Conference finals; lost to Utah in Turner Cup Finals.
96-97—Defeated Grand Rapids in Eastern Conference quarterfinals; lost to Cleveland in Eastern Conference semifinals.
97-98—Defeated Indianapolis in Eastern Conference quarterfinals; defeated Cleveland in Eastern Conference semifinals; lost to Detroit in Eastern Conference finals.
98-99—Defeated Michigan in Eastern Conference semifinals; defeated Detroit in Eastern Conference finals; lost to Houston in Turner Cup finals.

GORING, BUTCH — ISLANDERS

PERSONAL: Born October 22, 1949, in St. Boniface, Man. ... Full Name: Robert Thomas Goring.
TRANSACTIONS/CAREER NOTES: Selected by Los Angeles Kings in fifth round of 1969 NHL amateur draft. ... Missed part of 1970-71 season with mononucleosis. ... Missed part of 1972-73 season with severe laceration on right leg. ... Missed part of 1973-74 season with shoulder separation. ... Missed part of 1974-75 season with eye injury. ... Traded by Kings to New York Islanders for RW Billy Harris and D Dave Lewis (March 10, 1980). ... Claimed on waivers by Boston Bruins (January 8, 1985). ... Announced retirement (May 1985).
HONORS: Won Bill Masterson Trophy (1977-78). ... Won Lady Byng Memorial Trophy (1977-78). ... Played in NHL All-Star Game (1980). ... Won Conn Smythe Trophy (1980-81).
MISCELLANEOUS: Member of Stanley Cup championship team (1980, 1981, 1982 and 1983). ... Played center.

		REGULAR SEASON								PLAYOFFS				
Season Team	League	Gms.	G	A	Pts.	PIM	+/-	PP	SH	Gms.	G	A	Pts.	PIM
65-66—Winnipeg Rangers	MJHL	3	0	0	0	0	...	...	...	3	0	1	1	0
66-67—Winnipeg Rangers	MJHL	51	35	31	66	2	...	...	...	8	2	6	8	0
67-68—Hull	QSHL	39	16	41	57	4	...	...	...					

Season Team	League	Gms.	G	A	Pts.	PIM	+/-	PP	SH	Gms.	G	A	Pts.	PIM
		REGULAR SEASON								**PLAYOFFS**				
68-69—Winnipeg	WCJHL	39	42	33	75	0	...	...	...	—	—	—	—	—
—Dauphin	MJHL	—	—	—	—	—	...	...	...	12	8	8	16	5
—Regina	SJHL	—	—	—	—	—	...	...	...	4	3	1	4	0
69-70—Springfield	AHL	19	13	7	20	0	...	...	...	—	—	—	—	—
—Los Angeles	NHL	59	13	23	36	8	-15	2	0	—	—	—	—	—
70-71—Springfield	AHL	40	23	32	55	4	...	...	...	12	11	14	25	0
—Los Angeles	NHL	19	2	5	7	2	4	0	0	—	—	—	—	—
71-72—Los Angeles	NHL	74	21	29	50	2	-10	3	0	—	—	—	—	—
72-73—Los Angeles	NHL	67	28	31	59	2	0	4	1	—	—	—	—	—
73-74—Los Angeles	NHL	70	28	33	61	2	2	5	3	5	0	1	1	0
74-75—Los Angeles	NHL	60	27	33	60	6	26	6	3	3	0	0	0	0
75-76—Los Angeles	NHL	80	33	40	73	8	0	5	5	9	2	3	5	4
76-77—Los Angeles	NHL	78	30	55	85	6	10	13	0	9	7	5	12	0
77-78—Los Angeles	NHL	80	37	36	73	2	-4	9	3	2	0	0	0	2
78-79—Los Angeles	NHL	80	36	51	87	16	-20	13	4	2	0	0	0	0
79-80—Los Angeles	NHL	69	20	48	68	12	-21	2	1	—	—	—	—	—
—New York Islanders	NHL	12	6	5	11	2	7	0	1	21	7	12	19	2
80-81—New York Islanders	NHL	78	23	37	60	0	4	4	1	18	10	10	20	6
81-82—New York Islanders	NHL	67	15	17	32	10	-3	1	5	19	6	5	11	12
82-83—New York Islanders	NHL	75	19	20	39	8	10	2	5	20	4	8	12	4
83-84—New York Islanders	NHL	71	22	24	46	8	9	0	5	21	1	5	6	2
84-85—New York Islanders	NHL	29	2	5	7	2	-11	0	1	—	—	—	—	—
—Boston	NHL	39	13	21	34	6	-8	2	2	5	1	1	2	0
86-87—Nova Scotia	AHL	10	3	5	8	2	...	...	...	—	—	—	—	—
NHL Totals (16 years)		1107	375	513	888	102	-20	71	40	134	38	50	88	32

HEAD COACHING RECORD

BACKGROUND: General Manager, Utah Grizzlies of IHL (1995-96 through 1998-99).

HONORS: Won Commissioner's Trophy (1994-95 and 1995-96).

Season Team	League	W	L	T	RT	Pct.	Finish	W	L	Pct.
		REGULAR SEASON						**PLAYOFFS**		
85-86—Boston	NHL	37	31	12	—	.538	3rd/Adams Division	0	3	.000
86-87—Boston	NHL	5	7	1	—	.423	—	—	—	—
87-88—Spokane	WHL	37	32	3	—	.535	2nd/West Division	7	8	.467
88-89—Spokane	WHL	2	9	0	—	.182	—	—	—	—
90-91—Capital District	AHL	28	43	9	—	.406	7th/South Division	—	—	—
91-92—Capital District	AHL	32	37	11	—	.469	4th/Northern Division	3	4	.429
92-93—Capital District	AHL	34	34	12	—	.500	3rd/Northern Division	0	4	.000
93-94—Las Vegas	IHL	52	18	11	—	.710	1st/Pacific Division	1	4	.200
94-95—Denver	IHL	57	18	6	—	.741	1st/Southwest Division	15	2	.882
95-96—Utah	IHL	49	29	4	—	.622	2nd/Southwest Division	15	7	.682
96-97—Utah	IHL	43	33	6	—	.561	3rd/Southwest Division	3	4	.429
97-98—Utah	IHL	47	27	8	—	.622	3rd/Southwest Division	1	3	.250
98-99—Utah	IHL	39	34	9	—	.530	3rd/Southwest Division	—	—	—
99-00—New York Islanders	NHL	24	49	9	1	.348	5th/Atlantic Division	—	—	—
NHL Totals (3 years)		66	87	22	1	.440	**NHL Totals (1 year)**	0	3	.000

NOTES:

85-86—Lost to Montreal in Adams Division semifinals.
86-87—Replaced by Terry O'Reilly as head coach (November 5).
87-88—Defeated Victoria in West Division semifinals; lost to Kamloops in West Division finals.
91-92—Lost to Springfield in first round of Calder Cup playoffs.
92-93—Lost to Adirondack in first round of Calder Cup playoffs.
93-94—Lost to San Diego in Western Conference quarterfinals.
94-95—Defeated Minnesota in Western Conference quarterfinals; defeated Phoenix in Western Conference semifinals; defeated Milwaukee in Western Conference finals; defeated Kansas City in Turner Cup finals.
95-96—Defeated Kansas City in Western Conference quarterfinals; defeated Peoria in Western Conference semifinals; defeated Las Vegas in Western Conference finals; defeated Orlando in Turner Cup finals.
96-97—Defeated Kansas City in Western Conference quarterfinals; lost to Long Beach in Western Conference semifinals.
97-98—Lost to Kansas City in Western Conference quarterfinals.

HARTLEY, BOB — AVALANCHE

PERSONAL: Born September 7, 1960, in Hawksbury, Ont. ... Full Name: Robert Hartley.

HEAD COACHING RECORD

Season Team	League	W	L	T	RT	Pct.	Finish	W	L	Pct.
		REGULAR SEASON						**PLAYOFFS**		
92-93—Laval	QMJHL	43	25	2	—	.629	1st/Robert Le Bel Division	12	1	.923
94-95—Cornwall	AHL	38	33	9	—	.531	2nd/Southern Division	8	6	.571
95-96—Cornwall	AHL	34	39	7	—	.469	4th/Central Division	3	5	.375
96-97—Hershey	AHL	43	22	10	—	.640	2nd/Mid-Atlantic Division	15	8	.652
97-98—Hershey	AHL	36	31	7	—	.534	2nd/Mid-Atlantic Division	3	4	.429
98-99—Colorado	NHL	44	28	10	—	.598	1st/ Northwest Division	11	8	.579
99-00—Colorado	NHL	42	29	11	1	.579	1st/Northwest Division	11	6	.647
NHL Totals (2 years)		86	57	21	1	.588	**NHL Totals (2 years)**	22	14	.611

NOTES:

92-93—Defeated Verdun in quarterfinals of President Cup playoffs; defeated Drummondville in semifinals of President Cup playoffs; defeated Sherbrooke in finals of President Cup playoffs.

94-95—Defeated Hershey in division semifinals in Calder Cup playoffs; defeated Binghamton in division finals in Calder Cup playoffs; lost to Fredericton in league semifinals in Calder Cup playoffs.

95-96—Defeated Albany in conference quarterfinals in Calder Cup playoffs; lost to Rochester in conference finals in Calder Cup playoffs.

96-97—Defeated Kentucky in conference quarterfinals in Calder Cup playoffs; defeated Phliadelphia in conference semifinals in Calder Cup playoffs; defeated Springfield in conference finals in Calder Cup playoffs; defeated Hamilton in Calder Cup finals.

97-98—Defeated Kentucky in conference quarterfinals in Calder Cup playoffs; lost to Philadelphia in conference semifinals in Calder Cup playoffs.

98-99—Defeated San Jose in Western Conference quarterfinals; defeated Detroit in Western Conference semifinals; lost to Dallas in Western Conference finals.

99-00—Defeated Phoenix in Western Conference quarterfinals; defeated Detroit in Western Conference semifinals; lost to Dallas in Western Conference finals.

HARTSBURG, CRAIG — MIGHTY DUCKS

PERSONAL: Born June 29, 1959, in Stratford, Ont. ... Shot left.

TRANSACTIONS/CAREER NOTES: Selected by Minnesota North Stars in first round (first North Stars pick, sixth overall) of NHL entry draft (August 9, 1979). ... Tore ligaments in left knee (September 1977). ... Separated shoulder (September 1980). ... Underwent surgery to remove bone spur on knee (October 10, 1983). ... Injured ligaments in left knee (January 10, 1984). ... Suffered hip pointer (October 1984). ... Fractured femur (December 1984). ... Injured groin (January 16, 1986); missed four games. ... Suffered herniated disc (February 1987). ... Strained knee ligaments (March 1987). ... Suffered concussion (November 7, 1987). ... Injured left hip and separated shoulder (March 1988). ... Underwent shoulder surgery (March 1988). ... Suffered staph infection on right ankle and required hospitalization (October 11, 1988). ... Reinjured right ankle (January 2, 1989).

HONORS: Won Max Kaminsky Memorial Trophy (1976-77). ... Named to OHA All-Star second team (1976-77). ... Played in NHL All-Star game (1980, 1982 and 1983).

MISCELLANEOUS: Captain of Minnesota North Stars (1982-83 through 1987-88). ... Played defense.

STATISTICAL PLATEAUS: Three-goal games: 1986-87 (1).

		REGULAR SEASON								PLAYOFFS				
Season Team	League	Gms.	G	A	Pts.	PIM	+/-	PP	SH	Gms.	G	A	Pts.	PIM
75-76—Sault Ste. Marie	OHA	64	9	19	28	65	...	...	...	—	—	—	—	—
76-77—Sault Ste. Marie	OHA	61	29	64	93	142	...	...	...	9	0	11	11	27
77-78—Sault Ste. Marie	OHA	36	15	42	57	101	...	...	...	13	4	8	12	24
78-79—Birmingham	WHA	77	9	40	49	73	...	...	...	—	—	—	—	—
79-80—Minnesota	NHL	79	14	30	44	81	-2	7	0	15	3	1	4	17
80-81—Minnesota	NHL	74	13	30	43	124	-9	8	0	19	3	12	15	16
81-82—Minnesota	NHL	76	17	60	77	117	11	5	0	4	1	2	3	14
82-83—Minnesota	NHL	78	12	50	62	109	7	3	1	9	3	8	11	7
83-84—Minnesota	NHL	26	7	7	14	37	-2	5	0	—	—	—	—	—
84-85—Minnesota	NHL	32	7	11	18	54	-5	1	1	9	5	3	8	14
85-86—Minnesota	NHL	75	10	47	57	127	7	4	0	5	0	1	1	2
86-87—Minnesota	NHL	73	11	50	61	93	-2	4	0	—	—	—	—	—
87-88—Minnesota	NHL	27	3	16	19	29	-2	2	0	—	—	—	—	—
88-89—Minnesota	NHL	30	4	14	18	47	-8	1	0	—	—	—	—	—
WHA Totals (1 year)		77	9	40	49	73	...	...	...					
NHL Totals (10 years)		570	98	315	413	818	-5	40	2	61	15	27	42	70

HEAD COACHING RECORD

BACKGROUND: Assistant coach, Minnesota North Stars (1989-90). ... Assistant coach, Philadelphia Flyers (1990-91 through 1993-94).

		REGULAR SEASON						PLAYOFFS		
Season Team	League	W	L	T	RT	Pct.	Finish	W	L	Pct.
94-95—Guelph	OHL	47	14	5	—	.750	1st/Central Division	10	4	.714
95-96—Chicago	NHL	40	28	14	—	.573	2nd/Central Division	6	4	.600
96-97—Chicago	NHL	34	35	13	—	.494	5th/Central Division	2	4	.333
97-98—Chicago	NHL	30	39	13	—	.445	5th/Central Division	—	—	—
98-99—Anaheim	NHL	35	34	13	—	.506	3rd/Pacific Division	0	4	.000
99-00—Anaheim	NHL	34	36	12	3	.488	5th/Pacific Division	—	—	—
NHL Totals (5 years)		173	172	65	3	.501	NHL Totals (3 years)	8	12	.400

NOTES:

94-95—Defeated Owen Sound in second round of OHL playoffs; defeated Belleville in third round of OHL playoffs; lost to Detroit in J. Ross Robertson Cup finals.

95-96—Defeated Calgary in Western Conference quarterfinals; lost to Colorado in Western Conference semifinals.

96-97—Lost to Colorado in Western Conference quarterfinals.

98-99—Lost to Detroit in Western Conference quarterfinals.

HAY, DON — FLAMES

PERSONAL: Born March 13, 1954, in Kamloops, B.C.

HEAD COACHING RECORD

BACKGROUND: Assistant coach, Kamloops Blazers of WHL (1985-86 through 1991-92). ... Assistant coach, Calgary Flames (1995-96). ... Assistant coach, Mighty Ducks of Anaheim (1997-98). ... General Manager, Tri-City Americans of WHL (1998-99 and 1999-2000).

HONORS: Won Dunc McCallum Memorial Trophy (1998-99).

Season Team	League	W	L	T	RT	Pct.	Finish	W	L	Pct.
92-93—Kamloops	WHL	42	28	2	—	.597	3rd/West Division	8	5	.615
93-94—Kamloops	WHL	50	16	6	—	.736	1st/West Division	12	7	.632
94-95—Kamloops	WHL	52	14	6	—	.764	1st/West Division	12	5	.706
96-97—Phoenix	NHL	38	37	7	—	.506	3rd/Central Division	3	4	.429
98-99—Tri-City	WHL	43	23	6	—	.639	2nd/West Division	7	5	.583
99-00—Tri-City	WHL	24	41	7	2	.382	6th/West Division	0	4	.000

NOTES:
92-93—Defeated Seattle in West Division preliminary round; defeated Spokane in West Division semifinals; lost to Portland in West Division finals.
93-94—Defeated Seattle in West Division semifinals; defeated Portland in West Division finals; defeated Saskatoon in WHL finals.
94-95—Defeated Portland in West Division semifinals; defeated Tri-City in West Division finals; defeated Brandon in WHL finals.
96-97—Lost to Anaheim in Western Conference quarterfinals.
98-99—Defeated Portland in first round of President Cup playoffs; defeated Seattle in second round of President Cup playoffs; lost to Kamloops in third round of President Cup playoffs.
99-00—Lost to Spokane in first round of President Cup playoffs.

HITCHCOCK, KEN — STARS

PERSONAL: Born December 17, 1951, in Edmonton.
COLLEGE: University of Alberta.

HEAD COACHING RECORD
BACKGROUND: Assistant coach, Philadelphia Flyers (1990-91 through 1992-93).
HONORS: Named NHL Coach of the Year by THE SPORTING NEWS (1996-97).

		REGULAR SEASON						PLAYOFFS		
Season Team	League	W	L	T	RT	Pct.	Finish	W	L	Pct.
84-85—Kamloops	WHL	52	17	2	—	.746	1st/West Division	10	5	.667
85-86—Kamloops	WHL	49	19	4	—	.708	1st/West Division	14	2	.875
86-87—Kamloops	WHL	55	14	3	—	.785	1st/West Division	8	5	.615
87-88—Kamloops	WHL	45	26	1	—	.632	1st/West Division	12	6	.667
88-89—Kamloops	WHL	34	33	5	—	.507	3rd/West Division	8	8	.500
89-90—Kamloops	WHL	56	16	0	—	.778	1st/West Division	14	3	.824
93-94—Kalamazoo	IHL	48	26	7	—	.636	1st/Atlantic Division	1	4	.200
94-95—Kalamazoo	IHL	43	24	14	—	.617	2nd/Northern Division	10	6	.625
95-96—Michigan	IHL	19	10	11	—	.613	—	—	—	—
—Dallas	NHL	15	23	5	—	.407	6th/Central Division	—	—	—
96-97—Dallas	NHL	48	26	8	—	.634	1st/Central Division	2	4	.333
97-98—Dallas	NHL	49	22	11	—	.665	1st/Central Division	10	7	.588
98-99—Dallas	NHL	51	19	12	—	.695	1st/Pacific Division	16	7	.696
99-00—Dallas	NHL	43	29	10	6	.585	1st/Pacific Division	14	9	.609
NHL Totals (5 years)		206	119	46	6	.617	**NHL Totals (4 years)**	42	27	.609

NOTES:
84-85—Defeated Portland in West Division semifinals; defeated New Westminster in West Division finals; lost to Prince Albert in WHL finals.
85-86—Defeated Seattle in West Division semifinals; defeated Portland in West Division finals; defeated Medicine Hat in WHL finals.
86-87—Defeated Victoria in West Division semifinals; lost to Portland in West Division finals.
87-88—Defeated New Westminster in West Division semifinals; defeated Spokane in West Division finals; lost to Medicine Hat in WHL finals.
88-89—Defeated Victoria in West Division semifinals; lost to Portland in West Division finals.
89-90—Defeated Spokane in West Division semifinals; defeated Seattle in West Division finals; defeated Lethbridge in WHL finals.
93-94—Lost to Cincinnati in Eastern Conference quarterfinals.
94-95—Defeated Chicago in Eastern Conference quarterfinals; defeated Cincinnati in Eastern Conference semifinals; lost to Kansas City in Eastern Conference finals.
95-96—Replaced Bob Gainey as head coach (January 8) with club in sixth place.
96-97—Lost to Edmonton in Western Conference quarterfinals.
97-98—Defeated San Jose in Western Conference quarterfinals; defeated Edmonton in Western Conference semifinals; lost to Detroit in Western Conference finals.
98-99—Defeated Edmonton in Western Conference quarterfinals; defeated St. Louis in Western Conference semifinals; defeated Colorado in Western Conference finals; defeated Buffalo in Stanley Cup finals.
99-00—Defeated Edmonton in Western Conference quarterfinals; defeated San Jose in Western Conference semifinals; defeated Colorado in Western Conference finals; lost to New Jersey in Stanley Cup finals.

HLINKA, IVAN — PENGUINS

PERSONAL: Born January 26, 1950, in Most, Czechoslovakia. ... Played center. ... Shot left.
TRANSACTIONS/CAREER NOTES: Rights traded by Winnipeg Jets to Vancouver Canucks for LW Brent Ashton and fourth-round pick (LW Tom Martin) in 1982 draft (July 15, 1981).

		REGULAR SEASON								PLAYOFFS				
Season Team	League	Gms.	G	A	Pts.	PIM	+/-	PP	SH	Gms.	G	A	Pts.	PIM
74-75—CHZ Litvinov	Czech.	...	36	42	78	...	...	...	...	—	—	—	—	—
75-76—CHZ Litvinov	Czech.						Statistics unavailable.							
76-77—CHZ Litvinov	Czech.						Statistics unavailable.							
77-78—CHZ Litvinov	Czech.						Statistics unavailable.							
78-79—Trencin-Litinov	Czech	...	17	20	37	...	...	...	...	13	4	8	12	...
79-80—CHZ Litvinov	Czech.						Statistics unavailable.							
80-81—CHZ Litvinov	Czech.	41	25	35	60	...	...	...	...	28	5	15	20	...
81-82—Vancouver	NHL	72	23	37	60	16	21	7	0	12	2	6	8	4
82-83—Vancouver	NHL	65	19	44	63	12	-3	8	0	4	1	4	5	4
NHL Totals (2 years)		137	42	81	123	28	18	15	0	16	3	10	13	8

HEAD COACHING RECORD
BSCKGROUND: Head coach, Czechoslovakian National Team. ... Head coach, Litvinov of Czechoslovakian League. ... Associate head coach, Pittsburgh Penguins (February 20, 2000-remainder of season).

PERSONAL: Born December 22, 1947, in North Battleford, Sask. ... Full Name: W. David King.
COLLEGE: University of Sasketchewan (degree in education, 1971).

HEAD COACHING RECORD

BACKGROUND: Head coach, University of Sasketchewan (1972-73 and 1978-79 through 1982-83). ... Head coach, Saskatoon Junior B Quakers (1973-74 through 1975-76). ... Vice-President/General Manager and head coach, Canadian National Teams (1983-84 through 1991-92). ... Consultant to Japanese Ice Hockey Federation and Nagano Olympic Games (1995-96 and 1996-97). ... Assistant coach, Montreal Canadiens (1997-98 and 1998-99). ... Director of European Scouting, Canadiens (1999-2000).
HONORS: Named CIAU Coach of the Year (1979-80).

		REGULAR SEASON						PLAYOFFS		
Season Team	League	W	L	T	RT	Pct.	Finish	W	L	Pct.
76-77—Saskatoon	WCHL	30	30	12	—	.500	2nd/Eastern Division	2	4	.333
77-78—Billings	WHL	32	31	9	—	.507	2nd/Central Division	7	5	.583
92-93—Calgary	NHL	43	30	11	—	.577	2nd/Smythe Division	2	4	.333
93-94—Calgary	NHL	42	29	13	—	.577	1st/Pacific Division	3	4	.429
94-95—Calgary	NHL	24	17	7	—	.573	1st/Pacific Division	3	4	.429
NHL Totals (3 years)		109	76	31	0	.576	**NHL Totals (3 years)**	8	12	.400

NOTES:
76-77—Lost to Lethbridge in first round of WCHL playoffs.
77-78—Defeated Medicine Hat in Central Division Final; eliminated Flin Flon in Round Robin League Semifinals; lost to New Westminster in League Finals.
92-93—Lost to Los Angeles in Smythe Division semifinals.
93-94—Lost to Vancouver in Western Conference quarterfinals.
94-95—Lost to San Jose in Western Conference quarterfinals.

PERSONAL: Born September 7, 1945, in Ville LaSalle, Que. ... Full Name: Jacques Gerard Lemaire. ... Uncle of Manny Fernandez, goaltender, Minnesota Wild. ... Name pronounced luh-MAIR.
HONORS: Inducted into Hall of Fame (1984).
MISCELLANEOUS: Played center and left wing. ... Member of Stanley Cup championship teams (1968, 1969, 1971, 1973 and 1976-1979). Total: 3.
STATISTICAL PLATEAUS: Three-goal games: 1977-78 (1), 1978-79 (2). Total: 3.

		REGULAR SEASON							PLAYOFFS				
Season Team	League	Gms.	G	A	Pts.	PIM	+/-	PP	SH	Gms.	G	A	Pts.	PIM
62-63—Lachine	QJHL	42	41	63	104	...	...	...	...	—	—	—	—	—
63-64—Montreal Jr. Canadiens	OHA Jr. A	42	25	30	55	...	...	...	...	—	—	—	—	—
64-65—Montreal Jr. Canadiens	OHA Jr. A	56	25	47	72	...	...	...	...	—	—	—	—	—
—Quebec	AHL	1	0	0	0	0	...	...	...	—	—	—	—	—
65-66—Montreal Jr. Canadiens	OHA Jr. A	48	41	52	93	69	...	...	...	—	—	—	—	—
66-67—Houston	CPHL	69	19	30	49	19	...	...	...	6	0	1	1	0
67-68—Montreal	NHL	69	22	20	42	16	...	...	...	13	7	6	13	6
68-69—Montreal	NHL	75	29	34	63	29	...	...	...	14	4	2	6	6
69-70—Montreal	NHL	69	32	28	60	16	...	...	...	—	—	—	—	—
70-71—Montreal	NHL	78	28	28	56	18	...	...	...	20	9	10	19	17
71-72—Montreal	NHL	77	32	49	81	26	...	...	...	6	2	1	3	2
72-73—Montreal	NHL	77	44	51	95	16	...	...	...	17	7	13	20	2
73-74—Montreal	NHL	66	29	38	67	10	...	...	...	6	0	4	4	2
74-75—Montreal	NHL	80	36	56	92	20	...	...	...	11	5	7	12	4
75-76—Montreal	NHL	61	20	32	52	20	...	...	...	13	3	3	6	2
76-77—Montreal	NHL	75	34	41	75	22	...	...	...	14	7	12	19	6
77-78—Montreal	NHL	75	36	61	97	14	...	...	...	15	6	8	14	10
78-79—Montreal	NHL	50	24	31	55	10	...	...	...	16	11	12	23	6
NHL Totals (12 years)		852	366	469	835	217	...	...	...	145	61	78	139	63

HEAD COACHING RECORD

BACKGROUND: Assistant coach, University of Plattsburgh (1981-82). ... Assistant coach, Montreal Canadiens (October 1982-February 1983). ... Assistant to managing director/director of player personnel, Canadiens (1985-86 through 1987-88). ... Assistant to managing director of Verdun, Canadiens organization (1988-89). ... Assistant to managing director, Canadiens (1989-90 and 1990-91). ... Assistant to managing director of Fredericton, Canadiens organization (1991-92 and 1992-93). ... Served as interim coach of Montreal Canadiens while Jacques Demers was hospitalized with chest pains (March 10 and 11, 1993; team was 1-1 during that time). ... Consultant to General Manager, Canadiens (1998-99 and 1999-2000).
HONORS: Named NHL Coach of the Year by The Sporting News (1993-94). ... Won Jack Adams Award (1993-94).

		REGULAR SEASON						PLAYOFFS		
Season Team	League	W	L	T	RT	Pct.	Finish	W	L	Pct.
79-80—Sierre	Swiss						Record unavailable.			
80-81—Sierre	Swiss						Record unavailable.			
82-83—Longueuil	QMJHL	37	29	4	—	.557	3rd/LeBel Division	8	7	.533
83-84—Montreal	NHL	7	10	0	—	.412	4th/Adams Division	9	6	.600
84-85—Montreal	NHL	41	27	12	—	.588	1st/Adams Division	6	6	.500
93-94—New Jersey	NHL	47	25	12	—	.631	2nd/Atlantic Division	11	9	.550
94-95—New Jersey	NHL	22	18	8	—	.542	2nd/Atlantic Division	16	4	.800
95-96—New Jersey	NHL	37	33	12	—	.524	5th/Atlantic Division	—	—	
96-97—New Jersey	NHL	45	23	14	—	.634	1st/Atlantic Division	5	5	.500
97-98—New Jersey	NHL	48	23	11	—	.652	1st/Atlantic Division	2	4	.333
NHL Totals (7 years)		247	159	69		.593	**NHL Totals (6 years)**	49	34	.590

NOTES:

82-83—Defeated Chicoutimi in President Cup quarterfinals; defeated Laval in President Cup semifinals; lost to Verdun in President Cup finals.
83-84—Defeated Boston in Adams Division semifinals; defeated Quebec in Adams Division finals; lost to New York Islanders in Wales Conference finals.
84-85—Defeated Boston in Adams Division semifinals; lost to Quebec in Adams Division finals.
93-94—Defeated Buffalo in Eastern Conference quarterfinals; defeated Boston in Eastern Conference semifinals; lost to New York Rangers in Eastern Conference finals.
94-95—Defeated Boston in Eastern Conference quarterfinals; defeated Pittsburgh in Eastern Conference semifinals; defeated Philadelphia in Eastern Conference finals; defeated Detroit in Stanley Cup finals.
96-97—Defeated Montreal in Eastern Conference quarterfinals; lost to New York Rangers in Eastern Conference semifinals.
97-98—Lost to Ottawa in Eastern Conference quarterfinals.

LOW, RON — RANGERS

PERSONAL: Born June 21, 1950, in Birtle, Man. ... Caught right. ... Full Name: Ron Albert Low. ... Name pronounced LOH.
TRANSACTIONS/CAREER NOTES: Selected by Toronto Maple Leafs in eighth round (eighth Maple Leafs pick, 103rd overall) of NHL amateur draft (June 11, 1970). ... Claimed by Washington Capitals from Maple Leafs in expansion draft (June 12, 1974). ... Signed as free agent by Detroit Red Wings (August 17, 1977). ... Claimed by Quebec Nordiques from Red Wings in expansion draft (June 13, 1979). ... Traded by Nordiques to Edmonton Oilers for C Ron Chipperfield (March 11, 1980). ... Traded by Oilers to New Jersey Devils with D Jim McTaggart for G Lindsay Middlebrook and C Paul Miller (February 19, 1983).
HONORS: Named to CHL All-Star second team (1973-74). ... Won Tommy Ivan Trophy (1978-79). ... Named to CHL All-Star first team (1978-79).
MISCELLANEOUS: Played goaltender.

Season Team	League	REGULAR SEASON								PLAYOFFS						
		Gms.	Min	W	L	T	GA	SO	Avg.	Gms.	Min.	W	L	GA	SO	Avg.
70-71—Jacksonville	EHL	49	2940	...	...	...	293	1	5.98	—	—	—	—	—	—	—
—Tulsa	CHL	4	192	...	...	...	11	0	3.44	—	—	—	—	—	—	—
71-72—Richmond	AHL	1	60	...	...	...	2	0	2.00	—	—	—	—	—	—	—
—Tulsa	CHL	43	2428	...	...	...	135	1	3.34	8	474	...	...	15	1	1.90
72-73—Toronto	NHL	42	2343	12	24	4	152	1	3.89	—	—	—	—	—	—	—
73-74—Tulsa	CHL	56	3213	...	...	...	169	1	3.16	—	—	—	—	—	—	—
74-75—Washington	NHL	48	2588	8	36	2	235	1	5.45	—	—	—	—	—	—	—
75-76—Washington	NHL	43	2289	6	31	2	208	0	5.45	—	—	—	—	—	—	—
76-77—Washington	NHL	54	2918	16	27	5	188	0	3.87	—	—	—	—	—	—	—
77-78—Detroit	NHL	32	1816	9	12	9	102	1	3.37	4	240	1	3	17	0	4.25
78-79—Kansas City	CHL	63	3795	...	...	...	244	0	3.86	4	237	...	...	15	0	3.80
79-80—Syracuse	AHL	15	905	5	9	1	70	0	4.64	—	—	—	—	—	—	—
—Quebec	NHL	15	828	5	7	2	51	0	3.70	—	—	—	—	—	—	—
—Edmonton	NHL	11	650	8	2	1	37	0	3.42	3	212	0	3	12	...	3.40
80-81—Edmonton	NHL	24	1260	5	13	3	93	0	4.43	—	—	—	—	—	—	—
—Wichita	CHL	2	120	0	2	0	10	0	5.00	—	—	—	—	—	—	—
81-82—Edmonton	NHL	29	1554	17	7	1	100	0	3.86	—	—	—	—	—	—	—
82-83—Edmonton	NHL	3	104	0	1	0	10	0	5.77	—	—	—	—	—	—	—
—New Jersey	NHL	11	608	2	7	1	41	0	4.05	—	—	—	—	—	—	—
83-84—New Jersey	NHL	44	2218	8	25	4	161	0	4.36	—	—	—	—	—	—	—
84-85—New Jersey	NHL	26	1326	6	11	4	85	1	3.85	—	—	—	—	—	—	—
NHL Totals (11 years)		382	20502	102	203	38	1463	4	4.28	7	452	1	6	29	0	3.85

HEAD COACHING RECORD

BACKGROUND: Player/assistant coach, Nova Scotia Oilers (1985-86). ... Assistant coach, Nova Scotia Oilers (1986-87). ... Assistant coach, Edmonton Oilers (August 3, 1989 through 1994-95).

Season Team	League	REGULAR SEASON						PLAYOFFS		
		W	L	T	RT	Pct.	Finish	W	L	Pct.
87-88—Nova Scotia	AHL	35	36	9	—	.494	4th/Northern Division	—	—	—
88-89—Cape Breton	AHL	27	47	6	—	.375	7th/Northern Division	—	—	—
94-95—Edmonton	NHL	5	7	1	—	.423	5th/Pacific Division	—	—	—
95-96—Edmonton	NHL	30	44	8	—	.415	5th/Pacific Division	—	—	—
96-97—Edmonton	NHL	36	37	9	—	.494	3rd/Pacific Division	5	6	.455
97-98—Edmonton	NHL	35	37	10	—	.488	3rd/Pacific Division	5	7	.417
98-99—Edmonton	NHL	33	37	12	—	.476	2nd/Northwest Division	0	4	.000
99-00—Houston	IHL	44	29	9	—	.591	3rd/West Division	6	5	.545
NHL Totals (5 years)		139	162	40		.466	**NHL Totals (3 years)**	10	17	.370

NOTES:

96-97—Defeated Dallas in Western Conference quarterfinals; lost to Colorado in Western Conferenece semifinals.
97-98—Defeated Colorado in Western Conference quarterfinals; lost to Dallas in Western Conference semifinals.
98-99—Lost to Dallas in Western Conference quarterfinals.
99-00—Defeated Utah in conference semifinals; lost to Chicago in conference finals.

LUDZIK, STEVE — LIGHTNING

PERSONAL: Born April 3, 1962, in Toronto. ... Shot left. ... Full Name: Steven Ludzik.
TRANSACTIONS/CAREER NOTES: Selected by Chicago Blackhawks as underage junior in second round (third Blackhawks pick, 28th overall) of NHL entry draft (June 11, 1980). ... Fractured left foot (October 19, 1985). ... Fractured collarbone (January 26, 1987). ... Traded by Blackhawks with sixth-round pick (C Derek Edgerly) in 1990 draft to Buffalo Sabres to complete earlier deal involving G Jacques Cloutier (September 28, 1989). ... Injured eye (November 12, 1989); missed 10 games. ... Suspended six games by AHL for a pre-game fight (November 25, 1990).
MISCELLANEOUS: Played center.

Season Team	League	REGULAR SEASON								PLAYOFFS				
		Gms.	G	A	Pts.	PIM	+/-	PP	SH	Gms.	G	A	Pts.	PIM
77-78—Markham Waxers	OPJHL	34	15	24	39	20	...	...	...	—	—	—	—	—
78-79—Niagara Falls	OMJHL	68	32	65	97	138	...	...	...	—	—	—	—	—
79-80—Niagara Falls	OMJHL	67	43	76	119	102	...	...	...	10	6	6	12	16
80-81—Niagara Falls	OMJHL	58	50	92	142	108	...	...	...	12	5	9	14	40
81-82—Chicago	NHL	8	2	1	3	2	1	0	0	—	—	—	—	—
—New Brunswick	AHL	75	21	41	62	142	...	...	...	15	3	7	10	6
82-83—Chicago	NHL	66	6	19	25	63	7	0	0	13	3	5	8	20
83-84—Chicago	NHL	80	9	20	29	73	-5	0	0	4	0	1	1	9
84-85—Chicago	NHL	79	11	20	31	86	5	0	1	15	1	1	2	16
85-86—Chicago	NHL	49	6	5	11	21	-2	0	1	3	0	0	0	12
86-87—Chicago	NHL	52	5	12	17	34	-3	0	0	4	0	0	0	0
87-88—Chicago	NHL	73	6	15	21	40	-14	1	0	5	0	1	1	13
88-89—Chicago	NHL	6	1	0	1	8	0	0	0	—	—	—	—	—
—Saginaw	IHL	65	21	57	78	129	...	...	...	6	0	1	1	17
89-90—Rochester	AHL	54	25	29	54	71	...	...	...	16	5	6	11	57
—Buffalo	NHL	11	0	1	1	6	-2	0	0	—	—	—	—	—
90-91—Rochester	AHL	65	22	29	51	137	...	...	...	8	3	5	8	6
91-92—Rochester	AHL	45	6	22	28	88	...	...	...	14	2	1	3	8
NHL Totals (9 years)		424	46	93	139	333	-13	1	2	44	4	8	12	70

HEAD COACHING RECORD

BACKGROUND: Associate coach, Detroit Vipers of IHL (1995-96).

Season Team	League	REGULAR SEASON						PLAYOFFS		
		W	L	T	RT	Pct.	Finish	W	L	Pct.
94-95—Muskegon	Col.HL	42	27	5	—	.601	2nd/West Division	10	7	.588
96-97—Detroit	IHL	57	17	8	—	.744	1st/Northeast Division	18	6	.750
97-98—Detroit	IHL	47	20	15	—	.665	1st/Northeast Division	14	9	.609
98-99—Detroit	IHL	50	21	11	—	.677	1st/Northeast Division	6	5	.545
99-00—Tampa Bay	NHL	19	54	9	7	.287	4th/Southeast Division	—	—	—
NHL Totals (1 year)		19	54	9	7	.287				

NOTES:

94-95—Defeated London in Preliminary Round of Colonial Cup playoffs; defeated Detroit in semifinals of Colonial Cup playoffs; lost to Thunder Bay in Colonial Cup finals.

96-97—Defeated Michigan in Eastern Conference quarterfinals; defeated Quebec in Eastern Conference semifinals; defeated Cleveland in Eastern Conference Finals; defeated Long Beach in Turner Cup finals.

97-98—Defeated Michigan in Eastern Conference quarterfinals; defeated Cincinnati in Eastern Conference semifinals; defeated Orlando in Eastern Conference finals; lost to Chicago in Turner Cup finals.

98-99—Defeated Indianapolis in Eastern Conference semifinals; lost to Orlando in Eastern Conference finals.

MacTAVISH, CRAIG   OILERS

PERSONAL: Born August 15, 1958, in London, Ont. ... Shot left.

HIGH SCHOOL: Westminster (London, Ont.).

COLLEGE: Lowell (Mass.).

TRANSACTIONS/CAREER NOTES: Selected by Boston Bruins in ninth round (ninth Bruins pick, 153rd overall) of NHL amateur draft (June 15, 1978). ... Involved in automobile accident in which another driver was killed (January 25, 1984); pleaded guilty to vehicular homicide, driving while under the influence of alcohol and reckless driving and sentenced to a year in prison (May 1984); missed 1984-85 season. ... Signed as free agent by Edmonton Oilers (February 1, 1985). ... Strained lower back (January 1993); missed one game. ... Suffered concussion (March 10, 1993); missed one game. ... Strained wrist (October 18, 1993); missed one game. ... Reinjured wrist (December 7, 1993); missed one game. ... Suffered whiplash (December 15, 1993); missed four games. ... Bruised foot (December 30, 1993); missed one game. ... Traded by Oilers to New York Rangers for C Todd Marchant (March 21, 1994). ... Signed as free agent by Philadelphia Flyers (July 6, 1994). ... Injured foot (January 24, 1995); missed one game. ... Bruised foot (April 14, 1995); missed two games. ... Underwent knee surgery (September 25, 1995); missed first eight games of season. ... Traded by Flyers to St. Louis Blues for C Dale Hawerchuk (March 15, 1996). ... Announced retirement (April 29, 1997).

HONORS: Named ECAC Division II Rookie of the Year (1977-78). ... Named to ECAC Division II All-Star second team (1977-78). ... Named to NCAA All-America East (College Division) first team (1978-79). ... Named ECAC Division II Player of the Year (1978-79). ... Named to ECAC Division II All-Star first team (1978-79). ... Played in NHL All-Star Game (1996).

MISCELLANEOUS: Member of Stanley Cup championship teams (1987, 1988, 1990 and 1994). ... Captain of Edmonton Oilers (1992-93 and 1993-94). ... Scored on a penalty shot (vs. Mike Vernon, December 23, 1988). ... Played center.

STATISTICAL PLATEAUS: Three-goal games: 1985-86 (1), 1990-91 (1). Total: 2.

Season Team	League	REGULAR SEASON								PLAYOFFS				
		Gms.	G	A	Pts.	PIM	+/-	PP	SH	Gms.	G	A	Pts.	PIM
77-78—University of Lowell	ECAC-II	24	26	19	45	...	...	...	...	—	—	—	—	—
78-79—University of Lowell	ECAC-II	31	36	52	88	...	...	...	...	—	—	—	—	—
79-80—Binghamton	AHL	34	17	15	32	20	...	...	...	—	—	—	—	—
—Boston	NHL	46	11	17	28	8	...	0	0	10	2	3	5	7
80-81—Boston	NHL	24	3	5	8	13	-1	0	0	—	—	—	—	—
—Springfield	AHL	53	19	24	43	89	...	...	...	7	5	4	9	8
81-82—Erie	AHL	72	23	32	55	37	...	...	...	—	—	—	—	—
—Boston	NHL	2	0	1	1	0	...	...	...	—	—	—	—	—
82-83—Boston	NHL	75	10	20	30	18	15	0	0	17	3	1	4	18
83-84—Boston	NHL	70	20	23	43	35	9	7	0	1	0	0	0	0
84-85—Boston	NHL	Did not play.												
85-86—Edmonton	NHL	74	23	24	47	70	17	4	1	10	4	4	8	11
86-87—Edmonton	NHL	79	20	19	39	55	9	1	4	21	1	9	10	16
87-88—Edmonton	NHL	80	15	17	32	47	-3	0	3	19	0	1	1	31
88-89—Edmonton	NHL	80	21	31	52	55	10	2	4	7	0	1	1	8

Season Team	League	REGULAR SEASON								PLAYOFFS				
		Gms.	G	A	Pts.	PIM	+/-	PP	SH	Gms.	G	A	Pts.	PIM
89-90 —Edmonton	NHL	80	21	22	43	89	13	1	6	22	2	6	8	29
90-91 —Edmonton	NHL	80	17	15	32	76	-1	2	6	18	3	3	6	20
91-92 —Edmonton	NHL	80	12	18	30	98	-1	0	2	16	3	0	3	28
92-93 —Edmonton	NHL	82	10	20	30	110	-16	0	3	—	—	—	—	—
93-94 —Edmonton	NHL	66	16	10	26	80	-20	0	0	—	—	—	—	—
—New York Rangers	NHL	12	4	2	6	11	6	1	0	23	1	4	5	22
94-95 —Philadelphia	NHL	45	3	9	12	23	2	0	0	15	1	4	5	20
95-96 —Philadelphia	NHL	55	5	8	13	62	-3	0	0	—	—	—	—	—
—St. Louis	NHL	13	0	1	1	8	-6	0	0	13	0	2	2	6
96-97 —St. Louis	NHL	50	2	5	7	33	-12	0	0	1	0	0	0	2
NHL Totals (18 years)		1093	213	267	480	891	...	...	...	193	20	38	58	218

HEAD COACHING RECORD
BACKGROUND: Assistant coach, New York Rangers (1997-98 and 1998-99). ... Assistant coach, Edmonton Oilers (1999-2000).

MARTIN, JACQUES   SENATORS

PERSONAL: Born October 1, 1952, in Rockland, Ont.

HEAD COACHING RECORD
BACKGROUND: Assistant coach, Chicago Blackhawks (1988-89 through 1989-90). ... Assistant coach, Quebec Nordiques (1990-91 through 1992-93 and 1994-95). ... Assistant coach, Colorado Avalanche (1995 through January 24, 1996).
HONORS: Named NHL Coach of the Year by THE SPORTING NEWS (1998-99). ... Won Jack Adams Award (1998-99).

Season Team	League	REGULAR SEASON						PLAYOFFS		
		W	L	T	RT	Pct.	Finish	W	L	Pct.
85-86 —Guelph	OHL	41	23	2	—	.636	2nd/Emms Division	15	3	.833
86-87 —St. Louis	NHL	32	33	15	—	.494	1st/Norris Division	2	4	.333
87-88 —St. Louis	NHL	34	38	8	—	.475	2nd/Norris Division	5	5	.500
93-94 —Cornwall	AHL	33	36	11	—	.481	T3rd/Southern Division	4	2	.667
95-96 —Ottawa	NHL	10	24	4	—	.316	6th/Northeast Division	—	—	—
96-97 —Ottawa	NHL	31	36	15	—	.470	T3rd/Northeast Division	3	4	.429
97-98 —Ottawa	NHL	34	33	15	—	.506	5th/Northeast Division	5	6	.455
98-99 —Ottawa	NHL	44	23	15	—	.628	1st/Northeast Division	0	4	.000
99-00 —Ottawa	NHL	41	30	11	2	.567	2nd/Northeast Division	2	4	.333
NHL Totals (7 years)		226	217	83	2	.509	**NHL Totals (6 years)**	17	27	.386

NOTES:
85-86—Defeated Sudbury in OHL quarterfinals; defeated Windsor in OHL semifinals; defeated Belleville in J. Ross Robertson Cup finals.
86-87—Lost to Toronto in Norris Division semifinals.
87-88—Defeated Chicago in Norris Division semifinals; lost to Detroit in Norris Division finals.
93-94—Defeated Hamilton in quarterfinals of Calder Cup playoffs; defeated Hershey in division finals of Calder Cup playoffs; lost to Moncton in semifinals of Calder Cup playoffs.
95-96—Replaced Rick Bowness as head coach (January 24) with club in sixth place.
96-97—Lost to Buffalo in Eastern Conference quarterfinals.
97-98—Defeated New Jersey in Eastern Conference quarterfinals; lost to Washington in Eastern Conference semifinals.
98-99—Lost to Buffalo in Eastern Conference quarterfinals.
99-00—Lost to Toronto in Eastern Conference quarterfinals.

MAURICE, PAUL   HURRICANES

PERSONAL: Born January 30, 1967, in Sault Ste. Marie, Ont.

HEAD COACHING RECORD
BACKGROUND: Assistant coach, Hartford Whalers (June 9-November 6, 1995). ... Whalers franchise moved to North Carolina and renamed Carolina Hurricanes for 1997-98 season; NHL approved move on June 25, 1997.

Season Team	League	REGULAR SEASON						PLAYOFFS		
		W	L	T	RT	Pct.	Finish	W	L	Pct.
93-94 —Detroit	OHL	42	20	4	—	.667	1st/West Division	11	6	.647
94-95 —Detroit	OHL	44	18	4	—	.697	1st/West Division	16	5	.762
95-96 —Hartford	NHL	29	33	8	—	.471	4th/Northeast Division	—	—	—
96-97 —Hartford	NHL	32	39	11	—	.457	5th/Northeast Division	—	—	—
97-98 —Carolina	NHL	33	41	8	—	.451	6th/Northeast Division	—	—	—
98-99 —Carolina	NHL	34	30	18	—	.524	1st/Southeast Division	2	4	.333
99-00 —Carolina	NHL	37	35	10	0	.512	3rd/Southeast Division	—	—	—
NHL Totals (5 years)		165	178	55	0	.484	**NHL Totals (1 year)**	2	4	.333

NOTES:
93-94—Defeated Owen Sound in quarterfinals of OHL playoffs; defeated Sault Ste. Marie in semifinals of OHL playoffs; lost to North Bay in OHL finals.
94-95—Defeated London in first round of OHL playoffs; defeated Peterborough in second round of OHL playoffs; defeated Sudbury in third round of OHL playoffs; defeated Guelph in J. Ross Robertson Cup finals.
95-96—Replaced Paul Homgren as head coach (November 6) with club in third place.
98-99—Lost to Boston in Eastern Conference quarterfinals.

MURRAY, ANDY   KINGS

PERSONAL: Born March 3, 1951, in Gladstone, Man.
COLLEGE: Brandon (Man.) University (degree in political science/sociology, 1972); then University of Manitoba; then Simon Fraser University (B.C.); then University of North Dakota; then St. Thomas University, Miami (master's degree in sports management, 1986).

HEAD COACHING RECORD
BACKGROUND: Assistant coach, Brandon University (1973-74). ... Head coach, Brandon Travelers of Manitoba Junior A Hockey League (1974-75 through 1977-78). ... Head coach, Brandon University (1978-79 through 1980-81). ... Served as head coach for several of Switzerland Division-A teams (1981-82 through 1987-88). ... Assistant coach, Hershey Bears of AHL (1986-87 and 1987-88). ... Assistant coach, Philadelphia Flyers (1988-89 and 1989-90). ... Assistant coach, Minnesota North Stars (1990-91 and 1991-92). ... Head coach, Lugano of Swiss League (1991-92). ... Head coach, Eisbaren Berlin of German League (1992-93). ... Assistant coach, Winnipeg Jets (1993-94 and 1994-95). ... Head coach, Canadian national team (1996-97 and 1997-98). ... Head coach, Shattuck-St. Mary's (Fairbault, Minn.) HS (1998-99).

Season Team	League	W	L	T	RT	Pct.	Finish	W	L	Pct.
				REGULAR SEASON					**PLAYOFFS**	
99-00—Los Angeles	NHL	39	31	12	4	.549	2nd/Pacific Division	0	4	.000

NOTES:
99-00—Lost to Detroit in Western Conference quarterfinals.

MURRAY, TERRY   PANTHERS

PERSONAL: Born July 20, 1950, in Shawville, Que. ... Shot right. ... Full Name: Terry Rodney Murray. ... Brother of Bryan Murray, general manager, Florida Panthers.
HIGH SCHOOL: Shawville (Que.).
TRANSACTIONS/CAREER NOTES: Selected by Oakland Seals from in seventh round (seventh Seals pick, 88th overall) of NHL amateur draft (June 11, 1970). ... Fractured leg (1973-74). ... Signed as free agent by Philadelphia Flyers (September 23, 1975). ... Traded by Philadelphia Flyers with RW Dave Kelly, RW Steve Coates and LW Bob Ritchie to Detroit Red Wings for D Mike Korney and D Rick LaPointe (February 1977). ... Contract sold by Red Wings to Flyers (November 1977). ... Selected by Washington Capitals in NHL waiver draft (October 1981).
HONORS: Won Eddie Shore Plaque (1977-78 and 1978-79). ... Named to AHL All-Star first team (1975-76, 1977-78 and 1978-79).
MISCELLANEOUS: Played defense.

		REGULAR SEASON								PLAYOFFS				
Season Team	League	Gms.	G	A	Pts.	PIM	+/-	PP	SH	Gms.	G	A	Pts.	PIM
67-68—Ottawa	OHA Jr. A	52	0	4	4	59	...	...	...	—	—	—	—	—
68-69—Ottawa	OHA Jr. A	50	1	16	17	39	...	...	...	—	—	—	—	—
69-70—Ottawa	OHA Jr. A	50	4	24	28	43	...	...	...	—	—	—	—	—
70-71—Providence	AHL	57	1	22	23	47	...	...	...	10	0	1	1	5
71-72—Baltimore	AHL	30	0	5	5	13	...	...	...	—	—	—	—	—
—Boston	AHL	9	0	0	0	0	...	...	...	—	—	—	—	—
—Oklahoma City	CPHL	17	1	1	2	19	...	...	...	6	0	0	0	2
72-73—Salt Lake City	WHL	39	3	8	11	30	...	...	...	9	0	6	6	14
—California	NHL	23	0	3	3	4	-14	0	0	—	—	—	—	—
73-74—California	NHL	58	0	12	12	48	-43	0	0	—	—	—	—	—
74-75—Salt Lake City	CHL	62	5	30	35	122	...	...	...	11	2	2	4	30
—California	NHL	9	0	2	2	8	2	0	0	—	—	—	—	—
75-76—Richmond	AHL	67	8	48	56	95	...	...	...	6	1	4	5	2
—Philadelphia	NHL	3	0	0	0	2	0	0	0	6	0	1	1	0
76-77—Philadelphia	NHL	36	0	13	13	14	21	0	0	—	—	—	—	—
—Detroit	NHL	23	0	7	7	10	-18	0	0	—	—	—	—	—
77-78—Philadelphia	AHL	7	2	1	3	13	...	...	...	—	—	—	—	—
—Maine	AHL	68	9	40	49	53	...	...	...	12	1	7	8	28
78-79—Philadelphia	NHL	5	0	0	0	0	0	0	0	—	—	—	—	—
—Maine	AHL	55	14	23	37	14	...	...	...	10	1	5	6	6
79-80—Maine	AHL	68	3	19	22	26	...	...	...	12	2	2	4	10
80-81—Maine	AHL	2	0	1	1	0	...	...	...	—	—	—	—	—
—Philadelphia	NHL	71	1	17	18	53	46	0	0	12	2	1	3	10
81-82—Washington	NHL	74	3	22	25	60	-14	0	0	—	—	—	—	—
NHL Totals (8 years)		302	4	76	80	199	-20	0	0	18	2	2	4	10

HEAD COACHING RECORD
BACKGROUND: Assistant coach, Washington Capitals (1982-83 through 1987-88). ... Scout, Philadelphia Flyers (1997-98).

		REGULAR SEASON						PLAYOFFS		
Season Team	League	W	L	T	RT	Pct.	Finish	W	L	Pct.
88-89—Baltimore	AHL	30	46	4	—	.400	6th/South Division	—	—	—
89-90—Baltimore	AHL	26	17	1	—	.602	—	—	—	—
—Washington	NHL	18	14	2	—	.559	3rd/Patrick Division	8	7	.533
90-91—Washington	NHL	37	36	7	—	.506	3rd/Patrick Division	5	6	.455
91-92—Washington	NHL	45	27	8	—	.613	2nd/Patrick Division	3	4	.429
92-93—Washington	NHL	43	34	7	—	.554	2nd/Patrick Division	2	4	.333
93-94—Washington	NHL	20	23	4	—	.468	—	—	—	—
—Cincinnati	ECHL	17	7	4	—	.679	2nd/Central Division	6	5	.545
94-95—Philadelphia	NHL	28	16	4	—	.625	1st/Atlantic Division	10	5	.667
95-96—Philadelphia	NHL	45	24	13	—	.628	1st/Atlantic Division	6	6	.500
96-97—Philadelphia	NHL	45	24	13	—	.628	2nd/Atlantic Division	12	7	.632
98-99—Florida	NHL	30	34	18	—	.476	2nd/Southeast Division	—	—	—
99-00—Florida	NHL	43	33	6	6	.561	2nd/Southeast Division	0	4	.000
NHL Totals (10 years)		354	265	82	6	.563	**NHL Totals (8 years)**	46	43	.517

NOTES:

89-90—Replaced Bryan Murray as head coach (January 15) with club in fourth place; defeated New Jersey in Patrick Division semifinals; defeated New York Rangers in Patrick Division finals; lost to Boston in Wales Conference finals.

90-91—Defeated New York Rangers in Patrick Division semifinals; lost to Pittsburgh in Patrick Division finals.

91-92—Lost to Pittsburgh in Patrick Division semifinals.

92-93—Lost to New York Islanders in Patrick Division semifinals.

93-94—Replaced as head coach by Jim Schoenfeld (January 27) with club in fifth place. Loaned to Florida Panthers (February 18) to coach Cincinnati Cyclones of IHL.

94-95—Defeated Buffalo in Atlantic Division quarterfinals; defeated New York Rangers in Atlantic Division semifinals; lost to New Jersey in Atlantic Division finals.

95-96—Defeated Tampa Bay in Eastern Conference quarterfinals; lost to Florida in Eastern Conference semifinals.

96-97—Defeated Pittsburgh in Eastern Conference quarterfinals; defeated Sabres in Eastern Conference semifinals; defeated New York Rangers in Eastern Conference finals; lost to Detroit in Stanley Cup finals.

99-00—Lost to New Jersey in Eastern Conference quarterfinals.

QUENNEVILLE, JOEL   BLUES

PERSONAL: Born September 15, 1958, in Windsor, Ont. ... Shot left. ... Full Name: Joel Norman Quenneville.

TRANSACTIONS/CAREER NOTES: Selected by Toronto Maple Leafs in second round (first Maple Leafs pick, 21st overall) of NHL amateur draft (June 15, 1978). ... Traded by Maple Leafs with RW Lanny McDonald to Colorado Rockies for RW Wilf Paiement and LW Pat Hickey (December 1979). ... Injured ribcage (March 1980). ... Underwent surgery to repair torn ligaments in ring finger of left hand (March 1980). ... Sprained ankle, twisted knee and suffered facial lacerations (January 4, 1982). ... Rockies franchise moved to New Jersey and became the Devils (June 30, 1982). ... Traded by Devils with C Steve Tambellini to Calgary Flames for C Mel Bridgman and D Phil Russell (July 1983). ... Traded by Flames with D Richie Dunn to Hartford Whalers for D Mickey Volcan and third-round pick in 1984 draft (August 1983). ... Fractured right shoulder (December 18, 1986); missed 42 games. ... Separated left shoulder (January 19, 1989); missed nine games. ... Traded by Whalers to Washington Capitals for cash (October 3, 1990). ... Signed as free agent by Maple Leafs (July 30, 1991).

HONORS: Named to OMJHL All-Star second team (1977-78). ... Named to AHL All-Star second team (1991-92).

MISCELLANEOUS: Played defense.

			REGULAR SEASON								PLAYOFFS				
Season Team	League	Gms.	G	A	Pts.	PIM	+/-	PP	SH		Gms.	G	A	Pts.	PIM
75-76—Windsor	OHA Mj. Jr.	66	15	33	48	61	...	...	...		—	—	—	—	—
76-77—Windsor	OMJHL	65	19	59	78	169	...	...	...		9	6	5	11	112
77-78—Windsor	OMJHL	66	27	76	103	114	...	...	...		6	2	3	5	17
78-79—Toronto	NHL	61	2	9	11	60	7	0	0		6	0	1	1	4
—New Brunswick	AHL	16	1	10	11	10	...	...	...		—	—	—	—	—
79-80—Toronto	NHL	32	1	4	5	24	-2	1	0		—	—	—	—	—
—Colorado Rockies	NHL	35	5	7	12	26	-21	1	0		—	—	—	—	—
80-81—Colorado Rockies	NHL	71	10	24	34	86	-24	3	0		—	—	—	—	—
81-82—Colorado Rockies	NHL	64	5	10	15	55	-29	0	0		—	—	—	—	—
82-83—New Jersey	NHL	74	5	12	17	46	-13	0	1		—	—	—	—	—
83-84—Hartford	NHL	80	5	8	13	95	-11	0	2		—	—	—	—	—
84-85—Hartford	NHL	79	6	16	22	96	-15	0	0		—	—	—	—	—
85-86—Hartford	NHL	71	5	20	25	83	20	1	0		10	0	2	2	12
86-87—Hartford	NHL	37	3	7	10	24	8	0	1		6	0	0	0	0
87-88—Hartford	NHL	77	1	8	9	44	-13	0	0		6	0	2	2	2
88-89—Hartford	NHL	69	4	7	11	32	3	0	0		4	0	3	3	4
89-90—Hartford	NHL	44	1	4	5	34	9	0	0		—	—	—	—	—
90-91—Washington	NHL	9	1	0	1	0	-8	0	0		—	—	—	—	—
—Baltimore	AHL	59	6	13	19	58	...	...	...		6	1	1	2	6
91-92—St. John's	AHL	73	7	23	30	58	...	...	...		16	0	1	1	10
NHL Totals (13 years)		**803**	**54**	**136**	**190**	**705**	**-89**	**6**	**4**		**32**	**0**	**8**	**8**	**22**

HEAD COACHING RECORD

BACKGROUND: Player/coach, St. John's of the AHL (1991-92). ... Assistant coach, St. John's (1992-93). ... Assistant coach, Quebec Nordiques (1994-95). ... Quebec franchise moved to Denver and renamed Colorado Avalanche for 1995-96 season. ... Assistant coach, Colorado Avalanche (1995-96 through January 5, 1997).

HONORS: Named NHL Coach of the Year by THE SPORTING NEWS (1999-2000). ... Won Jack Adams Award (1999-2000).

		REGULAR SEASON						PLAYOFFS		
Season Team	League	W	L	T	RT	Pct.	Finish	W	L	Pct.
93-94—Springfield	AHL	29	38	13	—	.444	4th/Northern Division	2	4	.333
96-97—St. Louis	NHL	18	15	7	—	.538	4th/Central Division	2	4	.333
97-98—St. Louis	NHL	45	29	8	—	.598	3rd/Central Division	6	4	.600
98-99—St. Louis	NHL	37	32	13	—	.530	2nd/Central Division	6	7	.462
99-00—St. Louis	NHL	51	20	11	1	.689	1st/Central Division	3	4	.429
NHL Totals (4 years)		**151**	**96**	**39**	**1**	**.596**	**NHL Totals (4 years)**	**17**	**19**	**.472**

NOTES:

93-94—Lost to Adirondack in division semifinals of Calder Cup playoffs.

96-97—Replaced Mike Keenan as coach (January 6); lost to Detroit in Western Conference quarterfinals.

97-98—Defeated Los Angeles in Western Conference quarterfinals; lost to Detroit in Western Conference semifinals.

98-99—Defeated Phoenix in Western Conference quarterfinals; lost to Dallas in Western Conference semifinals.

99-00—Lost to San Jose in Western Conference quarterfinals.

QUINN, PAT   MAPLE LEAFS

PERSONAL: Born January 29, 1943, in Hamilton, Ont. ... Shot left. ... Full Name: John Brian Patrick Quinn.

HIGH SCHOOL: Central (Hamilton, Ont.).

COLLEGE: UC San Diego, then Widener University (degree in law).

TRANSACTIONS/CAREER NOTES: Loaned by Detroit Red Wings to Tulsa Oilers for 1964-65 season. ... Fractured ankle (1965). ... Selected by Montreal Canadiens from Red Wings in intraleague draft (June 1966). ... Sold by Canadiens to St. Louis Blues (June 1967). ... Traded by Blues to Toronto Maple Leafs for rights to LW Dickie Moore (March 1968). ... Selected by Vancouver Canucks in NHL expansion draft (June 1970). ... Selected by Atlanta Flames in NHL expansion draft (June 1972). ... Fractured leg (1976). ... Played defense.
MISCELLANEOUS: Captain of Atlanta Flames (1975-76 through 1976-77). ... Played defense.

		REGULAR SEASON								PLAYOFFS				
Season Team	League	Gms.	G	A	Pts.	PIM	+/-	PP	SH	Gms.	G	A	Pts.	PIM
58-59—Hamilton Jr. A............	OHA	20	0	1	1	...	...	...	...	—	—	—	—	—
59-60—Hamilton Jr. A............	OHA	27	0	1	1	...	...	...	...	—	—	—	—	—
60-61—Hamilton Jr. B............	OHA					Statistics unavailable.				—	—	—	—	—
61-62—						Did not play.								
62-63—Edmonton..................	CAHL					Statistics unavailable.								
63-64—Knoxville....................	EHL	72	6	31	37	217	...	...	...	3	0	0	0	9
64-65—Tulsa........................	CPHL	70	3	32	35	202	...	...	...	—	—	—	—	—
65-66—Memphis....................	CPHL	67	2	16	18	135	...	...	...	—	—	—	—	—
66-67—Houston.....................	CPHL	15	0	3	3	66	...	...	...	—	—	—	—	—
—Seattle......................	WHL	35	1	3	4	49	...	...	...	5	0	0	0	2
67-68—Tulsa........................	CPHL	51	3	15	18	178	...	...	...	11	1	4	5	19
68-69—Tulsa........................	CHL	17	0	6	6	25	...	...	...	—	—	—	—	—
—Toronto....................	NHL	40	2	7	9	95	10	0	0	4	0	0	0	13
69-70—Tulsa........................	CHL	2	0	1	1	6	...	...	...	—	—	—	—	—
—Toronto....................	NHL	59	0	5	5	88	-14	0	0	—	—	—	—	—
70-71—Vancouver.................	NHL	76	2	11	13	149	2	0	0	—	—	—	—	—
71-72—Vancouver.................	NHL	57	2	3	5	63	-28	0	0	—	—	—	—	—
72-73—Atlanta......................	NHL	78	2	18	20	113	2	0	1	—	—	—	—	—
73-74—Atlanta......................	NHL	77	5	27	32	94	15	0	0	4	0	0	0	6
74-75—Atlanta......................	NHL	80	2	19	21	156	12	0	0	—	—	—	—	—
75-76—Atlanta......................	NHL	80	2	11	13	134	5	0	1	2	0	1	1	2
76-77—Atlanta......................	NHL	59	1	12	13	58	-7	0	0	1	0	0	0	0
NHL Totals (10 years).........		606	18	113	131	950	-3	0	2	11	0	1	1	21

HEAD COACHING RECORD

BACKGROUND: Assistant coach, Philadelphia Flyers (1977-78). ... Coach, Team Canada (1986). ... President/general manager, Vancouver Canucks (1987-88 through November 4, 1997). ... Assistant general manager, Team Canada (1996 and 1997).
HONORS: Named NHL Coach of the Year by The Sporting News (1979-80 and 1991-92). ... Won Jack Adams Award (1979-80 and 1991-92).

		REGULAR SEASON						PLAYOFFS		
Season Team	League	W	L	T	RT	Pct.	Finish	W	L	Pct.
78-79—Philadelphia	NHL	18	8	4	—	.667	2nd/Patrick Division	3	5	.375
79-80—Philadelphia	NHL	48	12	20	—	.725	1st/Patrick Division	13	6	.684
80-81—Philadelphia	NHL	41	24	15	—	.606	2nd/Patrick Division	6	6	.500
81-82—Philadelphia	NHL	34	29	9	—	.535	3rd/Patrick Division	—	—	—
84-85—Los Angeles	NHL	34	32	14	—	.513	4th/Smythe Division	0	3	.000
85-86—Los Angeles	NHL	23	49	8	—	.338	5th/Smythe Division	—	—	—
86-87—Los Angeles	NHL	18	20	4	—	.476	4th/Smythe Division	—	—	—
90-91—Vancouver	NHL	9	13	4	—	.423	4th/Smythe Division	2	4	.333
91-92—Vancouver	NHL	42	26	12	—	.600	1st/Smythe Division	6	7	.462
92-93—Vancouver	NHL	46	29	9	—	.601	1st/Smythe Division	6	6	.500
93-94—Vancouver	NHL	41	40	3	—	.506	2nd/Pacific Division	15	9	.625
95-96—Vancouver	NHL	3	3	0	—	.500	3rd/Pacific Division	2	4	.333
98-99—Toronto	NHL	45	30	7	—	.591	2nd/Northeast Division	9	8	.529
99-00—Toronto	NHL	45	30	7	3	.591	1st/Northeast Division	6	6	.500
NHL Totals (14 years)		447	345	116	3	.556	**NHL Totals (11 years)**	68	64	.515

NOTES:
78-79—Defeated Vancouver in Stanley Cup preliminary round; lost to New York Rangers in Stanley Cup quarterfinals.
79-80—Defeated Edmonton in Stanley Cup preliminary round; defeated New York Rangers in Stanley Cup quarterfinals; defeated Minnesota in Stanley Cup semifinals; lost to New York Islanders in Stanley Cup finals.
80-81—Defeated Quebec in Stanley Cup preliminary round; lost to Calgary in Stanley Cup quarterfinals.
84-85—Lost to Edmonton in Smythe Division semifinals.
90-91—Replaced Bob McCammon as head coach (January) with club in fifth place; lost to Los Angeles in Smythe Division semifinals.
91-92—Defeated Winnipeg in Smythe Division semifinals; lost to Edmonton in Smythe Division finals.
92-93—Defeated Winnipeg in Smythe Division semifinals; lost to Los Angeles in Smythe Division finals.
93-94—Defeated Calgary in Western Conference quarterfinals; defeated Dallas in Western Conference semifinals; defeated Toronto in Western Conference finals; lost to New York Rangers in Stanley Cup finals.
95-96—Replaced Rick Ley as head coach (March 28) with club in third place; lost to Colorado in Western Conference quarterfinals.
98-99—Defeated Philadelphia in Eastern Conference quarterfinals; defeated Pittsburgh in Eastern Conference semifinals; lost to Buffalo in Eastern Conference finals.
99-00—Defeated Ottawa in Eastern Conference quarterfinals; lost to New Jersey in Eastern Conference semifinals.

RAMSAY, CRAIG   FLYERS

PERSONAL: Born March 17, 1951, in Weston, Ont. ... Full Name: Craig Edward Ramsay.
TRANSACTIONS/CAREER NOTES: Selected by Buffalo Sabres in second round (19th pick overall) of 1971 amateur draft.
HONORS: Played in NHL All-Star Game (1976). ... Won Frank J. Selke Trophy (1984-85).
MISCELLANEOUS: Played left wing.

		REGULAR SEASON								PLAYOFFS				
Season Team	League	Gms.	G	A	Pts.	PIM	+/-	PP	SH	Gms.	G	A	Pts.	PIM
67-68—Peterborough..............	OHA	40	6	13	19	21	...	...	...	5	0	0	0	4
68-69—Peterborough..............	OHA	54	11	28	39	20	...	...	...	10	1	2	3	9
69-70—Peterborough..............	OHA	54	27	41	68	18	...	...	...	—	—	—	—	—
70-71—Peterborough..............	OHA	58	30	76	106	25	...	...	...	—	—	—	—	—

Season Team	League	REGULAR SEASON								PLAYOFFS				
		Gms.	G	A	Pts.	PIM	+/-	PP	SH	Gms.	G	A	Pts.	PIM
71-72—Cincinnati	AHL	19	5	7	12	4	...	...	...	—	—	—	—	—
—Buffalo	NHL	57	6	10	16	0	5	0	0	—	—	—	—	—
72-73—Buffalo	NHL	76	11	17	28	15	13	0	1	6	1	1	2	0
73-74—Buffalo	NHL	78	20	26	46	0	17	1	2	—	—	—	—	—
74-75—Buffalo	NHL	80	26	38	64	26	51	1	7	17	5	7	12	2
75-76—Buffalo	NHL	80	22	49	71	34	44	1	1	9	1	2	3	2
76-77—Buffalo	NHL	80	41	20	61	37	2	3	2	6	0	4	4	0
77-78—Buffalo	NHL	80	28	43	71	18	38	2	5	8	3	1	4	9
78-79—Buffalo	NHL	80	26	31	57	10	21	4	3	3	1	0	1	2
79-80—Buffalo	NHL	80	21	39	60	18	15	5	0	10	0	6	6	2
80-81—Buffalo	NHL	80	24	35	59	12	39	12	1	8	2	4	6	4
81-82—Buffalo	NHL	80	16	35	51	8	14	0	1	4	1	1	2	0
82-83—Buffalo	NHL	64	11	18	29	7	14	0	3	10	2	3	5	4
83-84—Buffalo	NHL	76	9	17	26	17	3	0	0	3	0	1	1	0
84-85—Buffalo	NHL	79	12	21	33	16	17	0	0	5	1	1	2	0
NHL Totals (14 years)		1070	273	399	672	218	293	29	26	89	17	31	48	27

HEAD COACHING RECORD

BACKGROUND: Player/assistant coach, Buffalo Sabres (1984-85). ... Assistant coach, Sabres (1984-85 through November 1986). ... Assistant to General Manager, Sabres (December 1986 through 1991-92). ... Associate coach, Florida Panthers (1993-94 and 1994-95). ... Scout, Dallas Stars (1995-96). ... Assistant coach, Ottawa Senators (1996-97 and 1997-98). ... Assistant coach, Philadelphia Flyers (1998-99).

Season Team	League	REGULAR SEASON						PLAYOFFS		
		W	L	T	RT	Pct.	Finish	W	L	Pct.
86-87—Buffalo	NHL	4	15	2	—	.238	—	—	—	—
99-00—Philadelphia	NHL	16	8	1	0	.660	1st/Atlantic Division	11	7	.611
NHL Totals (2 years)		20	23	3	0	.467	**NHL Totals (1 year)**	11	7	.611

NOTES:
86-87—Replaced Scotty Bowman as head coach on interim basis (November 1986).
99-00—Replaced Roger Nielson as head coach due to illness (February 20); defeated Buffalo in Eastern Conference quarterfinals; defeated Pittsburgh in Eastern Conference semifinals; lost to New Jersey in Eastern Conference finals.

ROBINSON, LARRY — DEVILS

PERSONAL: Born June 2, 1951, in Winchester, Ont. ... Full Name: Larry Clark Robinson. ... Brother of Moe Robinson, defenseman with Montreal Canadiens (1979-80).

TRANSACTIONS/CAREER NOTES: Selected by Montreal Canadiens from Kitchener Rangers in second round (fourth Canadiens pick, 20th overall) of NHL amateur draft (June 10, 1971). ... Injured knee; missed part of 1978-79 season. ... Separated right shoulder (March 6, 1980). ... Injured groin (October 1980). ... Separated left shoulder (November 14, 1980). ... Fractured nose (January 8, 1981). ... Injured left shoulder (October 1982). ... Suffered skin infection behind right knee (October 1983). ... Hyperextended left elbow (March 1985). ... Strained ligaments in right ankle (March 9, 1987). ... Fractured right leg (August 1987). ... Sprained right wrist (December 1987). ... Hyperextended knee (May 23, 1989). ... Signed as free agent by Los Angeles Kings (July 26, 1989). ... Suffered food poisoning (March 1990). ... Injured eye (November 26, 1991); missed two games.

HONORS: Named to COJHL All-Star first team (1969-70). ... Played in NHL All-Star Game (1974, 1976-1978, 1980, 1982, 1986, 1988, 1989 and 1992). ... Won James Norris Memorial Trophy (1976-77 and 1979-80). ... Named to THE SPORTING NEWS All-Star first team (1976-77 through 1979-80). ... Named to NHL All-Star first team (1976-77, 1978-79 and 1979-80). ... Won Conn Smythe Trophy (1977-78). ... Named to NHL All-Star second team (1977-78, 1980-81 and 1985-86). ... Named to THE SPORTING NEWS All-Star second team (1980-81, 1981-82 and 1985-86).

RECORDS: Holds NHL career playoff record for most consecutive years in playoffs—20 (1972-73 through 1991-92). ... Shares NHL career playoff record for most years in playoffs—20 (1972-73 through 1991-92).

STATISTICAL PLATEAUS: Three-goal games: 1985-86 (1).

MISCELLANEOUS: Member of Stanley Cup championship team (1973, 1976-1979 and 1986). ... Played defense.

Season Team	League	REGULAR SEASON								PLAYOFFS				
		Gms.	G	A	Pts.	PIM	+/-	PP	SH	Gms.	G	A	Pts.	PIM
68-69—Brockville	COJHL						Statistics unavailable.							
69-70—Brockville	COJHL	40	22	29	51	74	...	...	...	—	—	—	—	—
70-71—Kitchener	OHA Jr. A	61	12	39	51	65	...	...	...	—	—	—	—	—
71-72—Nova Scotia	AHL	74	10	14	24	54	...	...	...	15	2	10	12	31
72-73—Nova Scotia	AHL	38	6	33	39	33	...	...	...	—	—	—	—	—
—Montreal	NHL	36	2	4	6	20	3	0	0	11	1	4	5	9
73-74—Montreal	NHL	78	6	20	26	66	32	0	0	6	0	1	1	26
74-75—Montreal	NHL	80	14	47	61	76	61	1	0	11	0	4	4	27
75-76—Montreal	NHL	80	10	30	40	59	50	2	0	13	3	3	6	10
76-77—Montreal	NHL	77	19	66	85	45	*120	3	0	14	2	10	12	12
77-78—Montreal	NHL	80	13	52	65	39	71	3	2	15	4	17	21	6
78-79—Montreal	NHL	67	16	45	61	33	50	4	0	16	6	9	15	8
79-80—Montreal	NHL	72	14	61	75	39	38	6	0	10	0	4	4	2
80-81—Montreal	NHL	65	12	38	50	37	46	7	0	3	0	1	1	2
81-82—Montreal	NHL	71	12	47	59	41	57	5	1	5	0	1	1	8
82-83—Montreal	NHL	71	14	49	63	33	33	6	0	3	0	0	0	2
83-84—Montreal	NHL	74	9	34	43	39	4	4	0	15	0	5	5	22
84-85—Montreal	NHL	76	14	33	47	44	32	6	0	12	3	8	11	8
85-86—Montreal	NHL	78	19	63	82	39	29	10	0	20	0	13	13	22
86-87—Montreal	NHL	70	13	37	50	44	24	6	0	17	3	17	20	6
87-88—Montreal	NHL	53	6	34	40	30	26	2	0	11	1	4	5	4
88-89—Montreal	NHL	74	4	26	30	22	23	0	0	21	2	8	10	12
89-90—Los Angeles	NHL	64	7	32	39	34	7	1	0	10	2	3	5	10
90-91—Los Angeles	NHL	62	1	22	23	16	22	0	0	12	1	4	5	15
91-92—Los Angeles	NHL	56	3	10	13	37	1	0	0	2	0	0	0	0
NHL Totals (20 years)		1384	208	750	958	793	730	66	3	227	28	116	144	211

HEAD COACHING RECORD

BACKGROUND: Assistant coach, New Jersey Devils (1993-94, 1994-95 and 1999-March 23, 2000).

		REGULAR SEASON						PLAYOFFS		
Season Team	League	W	L	T	RT	Pct.	Finish	W	L	Pct.
95-96—Los Angeles	NHL	24	40	18	—	.402	6th/Pacific Division	—	—	—
96-97—Los Angeles	NHL	28	43	11	—	.409	6th/Pacific Division	—	—	—
97-98—Los Angeles	NHL	38	33	11	—	.530	2nd/Pacific Division	0	4	.000
98-99—Los Angeles	NHL	32	45	5	—	.421	5th/Pacific Division	—	—	—
99-00—New Jersey	NHL	4	4	0	0	.500	2nd/Atlantic Division	16	7	.696
NHL Totals (5 years)		126	165	45	0	.442	**NHL Totals (2 years)**	16	11	.593

NOTES:

97-98—Lost to St. Louis in Western Conference quarterfinals.

99-00—Replaced Robbie Ftorek as head coach (March 23) with team in first place; defeated Florida in Eastern Conference quarterfinals; defeated Toronto in Eastern Conference semifinals; defeated Philadelphia in Eastern Conference finals; defeated Dallas in Stanley Cup finals.

RUFF, LINDY   SABRES

PERSONAL: Born February 17, 1960, in Warburg, Alta. ... Shot left. ... Full Name: Lindy Cameron Ruff.

TRANSACTIONS/CAREER NOTES: Selected by Buffalo Sabres as underage junior in second round (second Sabres pick, 32nd overall) of NHL entry draft (August 9, 1979). ... Fractured ankle (December 1980). ... Fractured hand (March 1983). ... Injured shoulder (January 14, 1984). ... Separated shoulder (October 26, 1984). ... Fractured left clavicle (March 5, 1986). ... Sprained shoulder (November 1988). ... Traded by Sabres to New York Rangers for fifth-round pick (D Richard Smehlik) in 1990 draft (March 7, 1989). ... Fractured rib (January 23, 1990); missed seven games. ... Fractured nose (March 21, 1990). ... Bruised left thigh (April 1990). ... Signed as free agent by Sabres (September 1991).

HONORS: Named to IHL All-Star team (1992-93).

MISCELLANEOUS: Captain of Buffalo Sabres (1986-87 through 1988-89). ... Scored on a penalty shot (vs. Mario Brunetta, November 26, 1989). ... Played defense.

		REGULAR SEASON							PLAYOFFS				
Season Team	League	Gms.	G	A	Pts.	PIM	+/-	PP	SH	Gms.	G	A	Pts.	PIM
76-77—Taber	AJHL	60	13	33	46	112	...	...	...	—	—	—	—	—
—Lethbridge	WCHL	2	0	2	2	0	...	...	...	—	—	—	—	—
77-78—Lethbridge	WCHL	66	9	24	33	219	...	...	...	8	2	8	10	4
78-79—Lethbridge	WHL	24	9	18	27	108	...	...	...	6	0	1	1	0
79-80—Buffalo	NHL	63	5	14	19	38	-2	1	0	8	1	1	2	19
80-81—Buffalo	NHL	65	8	18	26	121	3	1	0	6	3	1	4	23
81-82—Buffalo	NHL	79	16	32	48	194	1	3	0	4	0	0	0	28
82-83—Buffalo	NHL	60	12	17	29	130	14	2	0	10	4	2	6	47
83-84—Buffalo	NHL	58	14	31	45	101	15	3	0	3	1	0	1	9
84-85—Buffalo	NHL	39	13	11	24	45	-1	2	0	5	2	4	6	15
85-86—Buffalo	NHL	54	20	12	32	158	8	5	1	—	—	—	—	—
86-87—Buffalo	NHL	50	6	14	20	74	-12	0	0	—	—	—	—	—
87-88—Buffalo	NHL	77	2	23	25	179	-9	0	0	6	0	2	2	23
88-89—Buffalo	NHL	63	6	11	17	86	-17	0	0	—	—	—	—	—
—New York Rangers	NHL	13	0	5	5	31	-6	0	0	2	0	0	0	17
89-90—New York Rangers	NHL	56	3	6	9	80	-10	0	0	8	0	3	3	12
90-91—New York Rangers	NHL	14	0	1	1	27	-2	0	0	—	—	—	—	—
91-92—Rochester	AHL	62	10	24	34	110	...	...	...	13	0	4	4	16
92-93—San Diego	IHL	81	10	32	42	100	...	...	...	14	1	6	7	26
NHL Totals (12 years)		691	105	195	300	1264	-18	17	1	52	11	13	24	193

HEAD COACHING RECORD

BACKGROUND: Assistant coach, Florida Panthers (1993-94 through 1996-97).

		REGULAR SEASON						PLAYOFFS		
Season Team	League	W	L	T	RT	Pct.	Finish	W	L	Pct.
97-98—Buffalo	NHL	36	29	17	—	.543	3rd/Northeast Division	10	5	.667
98-99—Buffalo	NHL	37	28	17	—	.555	3rd/Northeast Division	14	7	.667
99-00—Buffalo	NHL	35	36	11	4	.494	3rd/Northeast Division	1	4	.200
NHL Totals (3 years)		108	93	45	4	.530	**NHL Totals (3 years)**	25	16	.610

NOTES:

97-98—Defeated Philadelphia in Eastern Conference quarterfinals; defeated Montreal in Eastern Conference semifinals; lost to Washington in Eastern Conference finals.

98-99—Defeated Ottawa in Eastern Conference quarterfinals; defeated Boston in Eastern Conference semifinals; defeated Toronto in Eastern Conference finals; lost to Dallas in Stanley Cup finals.

99-00—Lost to Philadelphia in Eastern Conference quarterfinals.

SUHONEN, ALPO   BLACKHAWKS

PERSONAL: Born in Valkeakoski, Finland.

TRANSACTIONS/CAREER NOTES: Played with Jokerit and Pori of Finnish Elite League (1965-66 through 1970-71). ... Player/assistant coach Forssa of Finnish Elite League (1971-72 and 1972-73).

HEAD COACHING RECORD

BACKGROUND: Coach, Forssa of Finnish Elite League (1973-74 through 1976-77). ... Director of Finland National Under-18 and Under-20 teams (1977-78 through 1985-86). ... Head coach, Swiss Elite League (1978-79, 1986-87 and 1987-88). ... Guest coach, Hartford Whalers (need years). ... Head coach, Finnish National Team (1982-83 through 1985-86). ... Assistant coach, Winnipeg Jets (1989-90 and 1992-93).

... Out of professional hockey (1989-90 through 1991-92, 1993-94 and 1994-95). ... Head coach, Kloten of Swiss Elite League (1995-96 and 1996-97). ... Broadcaster, European Hockey League (1997-98). ... Head coach, HPK Hameelinna of Finnish Elite League (1998). ... Assistant coach, Toronto Maple Leafs (1998-99).

Season Team	League	REGULAR SEASON						PLAYOFFS		
		W	L	T	RT	Pct.	Finish	W	L	Pct.
88-89—Moncton	AHL						Record unavailable.			
96-97—Chicago	IHL	9	5	1	—	.633	3rd/Midwest Division	1	3	.250

NOTES:
88-89—Named head coach in February.
96-97—Lost to San Antonio, 3-1, in conference quarterfinals.

SUTTER, DARRYL — SHARKS

PERSONAL: Born August 19, 1958, in Viking, Alta. ... Shot left. ... Brother of Brian Sutter, left winger with St. Louis Blues (1976-77 through 1987-88) and head coach with Blues (1988-89 through 1991-92), Boston Bruins (1992-93 through 1994-95) and Calgary Flames (1997-98 through 1999-2000); brother of Duane Sutter, right winger with New York Islanders (1979-80 through 1986-87) and Chicago Blackhawks (1987-88 through 1989-90); brother of Rich Sutter, right winger, with seven NHL teams (1982-83 through 1994-95); brother of Ron Sutter, center, San Jose Sharks; and brother of Brent Sutter, center with Islanders (1980-81 through 1991-92) and Blackhawks (1991-92 through 1997-98). ... Name pronounced SUH-tuhr.

TRANSACTIONS/CAREER NOTES: Selected by Chicago Blackhawks in 11th round (11th Blackhawks pick, 179th overall) of NHL amateur draft (June 1978). ... Lacerated left elbow, developed infection and underwent surgery (November 27, 1981). ... Fractured nose (November 7, 1982). ... Fractured ribs (November 1983). ... Fracture left cheekbone and injured left eye (January 2, 1984). ... Underwent arthroscopic surgery to right knee (September 1984). ... Bruised ribs (October 1984). ... Fractured left ankle (December 26, 1984). ... Separated right shoulder and underwent surgery (November 13, 1985); missed 30 games. ... Injured knee (February 1987). ... Retired as player to become assistant coach of Blackhawks (June 1987).

HONORS: Named top rookie of Japan National League (1978-79). ... Won Dudley (Red) Garrett Memorial Trophy (1979-80). ... Named to AHL All-Star second team (1979-80).

MISCELLANEOUS: Captain of Chicago Blackhawks (1982-83 through 1986-87). ... Played left wing.

Season Team	League	REGULAR SEASON								PLAYOFFS				
		Gms.	G	A	Pts.	PIM	+/-	PP	SH	Gms.	G	A	Pts.	PIM
74-75—Red Deer	AJHL	60	16	20	36	43	...	...	...	—	—	—	—	—
75-76—Red Deer	AJHL	60	43	93	136	82	...	...	...	—	—	—	—	—
76-77—Red Deer	AJHL	56	55	78	133	131	...	...	...	—	—	—	—	—
—Lethbridge	WCHL	1	1	0	1	0	...	...	...	15	3	7	10	13
77-78—Lethbridge	WCHL	68	33	48	81	119	...	...	...	8	4	9	13	2
78-79—New Brunswick	AHL	19	7	6	13	6	...	...	...	5	1	2	3	0
—Iwakura	Japan	20	28	13	41	0	...	...	...	—	—	—	—	—
79-80—New Brunswick	AHL	69	35	31	66	69	...	...	...	12	6	6	12	8
—Chicago	NHL	8	2	0	2	2	1	0	0	7	3	1	4	2
80-81—Chicago	NHL	76	40	22	62	86	-1	14	0	3	3	1	4	2
81-82—Chicago	NHL	40	23	12	35	31	0	4	3	3	0	1	1	2
82-83—Chicago	NHL	80	31	30	61	53	18	10	0	13	4	6	10	8
83-84—Chicago	NHL	59	20	20	40	44	-18	8	0	5	1	1	2	0
84-85—Chicago	NHL	49	20	18	38	12	8	2	0	15	12	7	19	12
85-86—Chicago	NHL	50	17	10	27	44	-15	3	0	3	1	2	3	0
86-87—Chicago	NHL	44	8	6	14	16	-3	1	0	2	0	0	0	0
NHL Totals (8 years)		**406**	**161**	**118**	**279**	**288**	**-10**	**42**	**3**	**51**	**24**	**19**	**43**	**26**

HEAD COACHING RECORD

BACKGROUND: Assistant coach, Chicago Blackhawks (1987-88). ... Associate coach, Blackhwaks (1991-92). ... Special assistant to general manager, Blackhawks (1995-96 and 1996-97).

Season Team	League	REGULAR SEASON						PLAYOFFS		
		W	L	T	RT	Pct.	Finish	W	L	Pct.
88-89—Saginaw	IHL	46	26	10	—	.622	2nd/East Division	2	4	.333
89-90—Indianapolis	IHL	53	21	8	—	.695	1st/West Division	12	2	.857
90-91—Indianapolis	IHL	48	29	5	—	.616	2nd/East Division	3	4	.429
92-93—Chicago	NHL	47	25	12	—	.631	1st/Norris Division	0	4	.000
93-94—Chicago	NHL	39	36	9	—	.518	5th/Central Division	2	4	.333
94-95—Chicago	NHL	24	19	5	—	.552	3rd/Central Division	9	7	.563
97-98—San Jose	NHL	34	38	10	—	.476	4th/Pacific Division	2	4	.333
98-99—San Jose	NHL	31	33	18	—	.488	3rd/Pacific Division	2	4	.333
99-00—San Jose	NHL	35	37	10	7	.488	4th/Pacific Division	5	7	.417
NHL Totals (6 years)		**210**	**188**	**64**	**7**	**.524**	**NHL Totals (6 years)**	**20**	**30**	**.400**

NOTES:
88-89—Lost to Fort Wayne in quarterfinals of Turner Cup playoffs.
89-90—Defeated Peoria in quarterfinals of Turner Cup playoffs; defeated Salt Lake City in semifinals of Turner Cup playoffs; defeated Muskegon in Turner Cup finals.
90-91—Lost to Fort Wayne in quarterfinals of Turner Cup playoffs.
92-93—Lost to St. Louis in Norris Division semifinals.
93-94—Lost to Toronto in Western Conference quarterfinals.
94-95—Defeated Toronto in Western Conference quarterfinals; defeated Vancouver in Western Conference semifinals; lost to Detroit in Western Conference finals.
97-98—Lost to Dallas in Western Conference quarterfinals.
98-99—Lost to Colorado in Western Conference quarterfinals.
99-00—Defeated St. Louis in Western Conference quarterfinals; lost to Dallas in Western Conference semifinals.

NHL HEAD COACHES

PERSONAL: Born July 15, 1962, in Winnipeg.

Season Team	League	Gms.	G	A	Pts.	PIM	+/-	PP	SH	Gms.	G	A	Pts.	PIM
				REGULAR SEASON								PLAYOFFS		
79-80—Regina	WHL	41	4	8	12	42	...	...	...	—	—	—	—	—
80-81—Regina	WHL	62	4	13	17	115	...	...	...	—	—	—	—	—
81-82—Regina	WHL	50	6	28	34	155	...	...	...	20	1	7	8	79

HEAD COACHING RECORD

BACKGROUND: Player/assistant coach, University of Manitoba (1983-84). ... Head coach/general manager, Dauphin Kings junior team (1984-85 through 1986-87). ... Assistant coach, University of Manitoba (1987-88). ... Scout, Washington Capitals (1988-89 through 1990-91). ... Assistant coach, Baltimore Skipjacks of the AHL (1991-92). ... Scout, Nashville Predators (1997-98).
HONORS: Named AHL Coach of the Year (1993-94).

Season Team	League	W	L	T	RT	Pct.	Finish	W	L	Pct.
				REGULAR SEASON					PLAYOFFS	
92-93—Baltimore	AHL	28	40	12	—	.425	4th/Southern Division	3	4	.429
93-94—Portland	AHL	43	27	10	—	.600	2nd/Northern Division	12	5	.706
94-95—Portland	AHL	46	22	12	—	.650	2nd/Northern Division	3	4	.429
95-96—Portland	AHL	32	38	10	—	.463	3rd/Northern Division	14	10	.583
96-97—Portland	AHL	37	26	10	—	.575	3rd/New England Division	2	3	.400
98-99—Nashville	NHL	28	47	7	—	.384	4th/Central Division	—	—	—
99-00—Nashville	NHL	28	47	7	7	.384	4th/Central Division	—	—	—
NHL Totals (2 years)		56	94	14	7	.384				

NOTES:
92-93—Lost to Binghamton in the first round of Calder Cup playoffs.
93-94—Defeated Albany in Northern Division semifinals; defeated Adirondack in Northern Division finals; defeated Moncton in Calder Cup finals.
94-95—Lost to Providence in Northern Division semifinals.
95-96—Defeated Worcester in Eastern Conference quarterfinals; defeated Springfield in Eastern Conference semifinals; defeated Saint John in Eastern Conference finals; lost to Rochester in Calder Cup finals.
96-97—Lost to Springfield in Southern Conference quarterfinals.

PERSONAL: Born May 14, 1961, in Quebec City. ... Shot right.
TRANSACTIONS/CAREER NOTES: Selected by St. Louis Blues in eighth round (seventh Blues pick, 167th overall) of NHL entry draft (June 1981).
MISCELLANEOUS: Played defense.

Season Team	League	Gms.	G	A	Pts.	PIM	+/-	PP	SH	Gms.	G	A	Pts.	PIM
				REGULAR SEASON								PLAYOFFS		
79-80—Hull	QJHL	35	5	34	39	82	...	...	...	—	—	—	—	—
—Trois Riv. Flambeaux	QJHL	28	6	19	25	93	...	...	...	—	—	—	—	—
80-81—Trois Riv. Flambeaux	QJHL	67	7	55	62	181	...	...	...	—	—	—	—	—
81-82—Salt Lake City	CHL	64	2	10	12	266	...	...	...	—	—	—	—	—
—St. Louis	NHL	14	1	2	3	43	-1	0	0	—	—	—	—	—
82-83—Salt Lake City	CHL	33	1	4	5	189	...	...	...	—	—	—	—	—
—St. Louis	NHL	28	1	3	4	39	-4	0	0	—	—	—	—	—
83-84—Montana	CHL	47	2	14	16	139	...	...	...	—	—	—	—	—
—Maine	AHL	11	0	1	1	46	...	...	...	—	—	—	—	—
NHL Totals (2 years)		42	2	5	7	82	-5	0	0					

HEAD COACHING RECORD

BACKGROUND: Assistant coach, Canadian junior national team (1989 and 1991). ... Assistant coach, Ottawa Senators (1992-93 through November 20, 1995).
HONORS: Canadian Coach of the Year (1987-88).

Season Team	League	W	L	T	RT	Pct.	Finish	W	L	Pct.
				REGULAR SEASON					PLAYOFFS	
86-87—Trois-Rivieres	QMJHL	26	37	2	—	.415	5th/Frank Dilio Division	—	—	—
87-88—Hull	QMJHL	43	23	4	—	.643	1st Robert Le Bel Division	12	7	.632
88-89—Hull	QMJHL	40	25	5	—	.607	3rd/Robert Le Bel Division	5	4	.556
89-90—Hull	QMJHL	36	29	5	—	.550	T5th/Robert Le Bel Division	4	7	.364
90-91—Hull	QMJHL	33	25	7	—	.562	2nd/Robert Le Bel Division	2	4	.333
91-92—Hull	QMJHL	40	23	5	—	.625	2nd/Robert Le Bel Division	2	4	.333
95-96—Beauport	QMJHL	19	7	5	—	.694	1st/Frank Dilio Division	13	7	.650
96-97—Beauport	QMJHL	24	44	2	—	.357	6th/Frank Dilio Division	1	3	.250
97-98—Montreal	NHL	37	32	13	—	.530	4th/Northeast Division	4	6	.400
98-99—Montreal	NHL	32	39	11	—	.457	5th/Northeast Division	—	—	—
99-00—Montreal	NHL	35	38	9	4	.482	4th/Northeast Division	—	—	—
NHL Totals (3 years)		104	109	33	4	.490	**NHL Totals (1 year)**	4	6	.400

NOTES:
87-88—Defeated Granby in quarterfinals of President Cup playoffs; defeated Laval in semifinals of President Cup playoffs; defeated Drummondville in President Cup finals.
88-89—Defeated St. Jean in quarterfinals of President Cup playoffs; lost to Victoriaville in semifinals of President Cup playoffs.
89-90—Defeated Longueuil in quarterfinals of President Cup playoffs; lost to Laval in semifinals of President Cup playoffs.
90-91—Lost to Laval in quarterfinals of President Cup playoffs.
91-92—Lost to Laval in quarterfinals of President Cup playoffs.
95-96—Defeated Rimouski in quarterfinals of President Cup playoffs; defeated Hull in semifinals of President Cup playoffs; lost to Granby in President Cup finals.
96-97—Lost to Halifax in quarterfinals of President Cup playoffs.
97-98—Defeated Pittsburgh in Eastern Conference quarterfinals; lost to Buffalo in Eastern Conference semifinals.

NHL HEAD COACHES

PERSONAL: Born May 28, 1955, in Windsor, Ont. ... Shot right. ... Full Name: Ronald Lawrence Wilson. ... Son of Larry Wilson, center with Detroit Red Wings (1949-50, 1951-52 and 1952-53) and Chicago Blackhawks (1953-54 through 1955-56) and coach with Red Wings (1976-77); and nephew of Johnny Wilson, left winger with four NHL teams (1949-50 through 1961-62) and coach with four NHL teams and two WHA teams (1969-70 through 1979-80).

COLLEGE: Providence (degree in economics).

TRANSACTIONS/CAREER NOTES: Selected by Toronto Maple Leafs in seventh round (seventh Maple Leafs pick, 132nd overall) in NHL entry draft (June 3, 1975). ... Loaned by Davos HC to Minnesota North Stars for remainder of NHL season and playoffs (March 1985). ... Loaned by Davos HC to Minnesota North Stars for remainder of NHL season and playoffs (March 1986). ... Traded by Davos HC to Minnesota North Stars for D Craig Levie (May 1986). ... Separated shoulder (March 9, 1987).

HONORS: Named to NCAA All-America (East) first team (1974-75 and 1975-76). ... Named to ECAC All-Star team (1973-74 through 1976-77). ... Named ECAC Player of the Year (1974-75).

MISCELLANEOUS: Played defense.

		REGULAR SEASON								PLAYOFFS				
Season Team	League	Gms.	G	A	Pts.	PIM	+/-	PP	SH	Gms.	G	A	Pts.	PIM
73-74—Providence College.....	ECAC	26	16	22	38	...	...	...	...	—	—	—	—	—
74-75—Providence College.....	ECAC	27	26	61	87	12	...	...	...	—	—	—	—	—
—U.S. national team	Int'l	27	5	32	37	42	...	...	...	—	—	—	—	—
75-76—Providence College.....	ECAC	28	19	47	66	44	...	...	...	—	—	—	—	—
76-77—Providence College.....	ECAC	30	17	42	59	62	...	...	...	—	—	—	—	—
—Dallas........................	CHL	4	1	0	1	2	...	...	...	—	—	—	—	—
77-78—Dallas....................	CHL	67	31	38	69	18	...	...	...	—	—	—	—	—
—Toronto	NHL	13	2	1	3	0	-5	1	0	—	—	—	—	—
78-79—New Brunswick..........	AHL	31	11	20	31	13	...	...	...	—	—	—	—	—
—Toronto	NHL	46	5	12	17	4	-10	4	0	3	0	1	1	0
79-80—New Brunswick..........	AHL	43	20	43	63	10	...	...	...	—	—	—	—	—
—Toronto	NHL	5	0	2	2	0	-2	0	0	3	1	2	3	2
80-81—EHC Kloten	Switzerland	38	22	23	45	...	...	...	...	—	—	—	—	—
81-82—Davos HC..................	Switzerland	38	24	23	47	...	...	...	...	—	—	—	—	—
82-83—Davos HC..................	Switzerland	36	32	32	64	...	...	...	...	—	—	—	—	—
83-84—Davos HC..................	Switzerland	36	33	39	72	...	...	...	...	—	—	—	—	—
84-85—Davos HC..................	Switzerland	38	39	62	101	...	...	...	...	—	—	—	—	—
—Minnesota..................	NHL	13	4	8	12	2	-1	0	0	9	1	6	7	2
85-86—Davos HC..................	Switzerland	27	28	41	69	...	...	...	...	—	—	—	—	—
—Minnesota..................	NHL	11	1	3	4	8	-2	1	0	5	2	4	6	4
86-87—Minnesota.................	NHL	65	12	29	41	36	-9	6	0	—	—	—	—	—
87-88—Minnesota.................	NHL	24	2	12	14	16	-4	1	0	—	—	—	—	—
NHL Totals (7 years)...........		**177**	**26**	**67**	**93**	**66**	**-33**	**13**	**0**	**20**	**4**	**13**	**17**	**8**

HEAD COACHING RECORD

BACKGROUND: Assistant coach, Milwaukee Admirals of IHL (1989-90). ... Served as interim coach of Milwaukee while Ron Lapointe was hospitalized for cancer treatments (February and March 1990; team went 9-10). ... Assistant coach, Vancouver Canucks (1990-91 through 1992-93).

		REGULAR SEASON						PLAYOFFS		
Season Team	League	W	L	T	RT	Pct.	Finish	W	L	Pct.
93-94—Anaheim............................	NHL	33	46	5	—	.423	4th/Pacific Division	—	—	—
94-95—Anaheim............................	NHL	16	27	5	—	.385	6th/Pacific Division	—	—	—
95-96—Anaheim............................	NHL	35	39	8	—	.476	4th/Pacific Division	—	—	—
96-97—Anaheim............................	NHL	36	33	13	—	.518	2nd/Pacific Division	4	7	.364
97-98—Washington.........................	NHL	40	30	12	—	.561	3rd/Atlantic Division	12	9	.571
98-99—Washington.........................	NHL	31	45	6	—	.415	3rd/Southeast Division	—	—	—
99-00—Washington.........................	NHL	44	26	12	2	.610	1st/Southeast Division	1	4	.200
NHL Totals (7 years)		**235**	**246**	**61**	**2**	**.490**	**NHL Totals (3 years)**......................	**17**	**20**	**.459**

NOTES:

96-97—Defeated Phoenix in Western Conference quarterfinals; lost to Detroit in Western Conference semifinals.

97-98—Defeated Boston in Eastern Conference quarterfinals; defeated Ottawa in Eastern Conference semifinals; defeated Buffalo in Eastern Conference finals; lost to Detroit in Stanley Cup finals.

99-00—Lost to Pittsburgh in Eastern Conference quarterfinals.

BIG SAVINGS

From
The Sporting News

Because you are a reader of *The Sporting News* books
we are pleased to offer you the opportunity to purchase any of the books
in our ultimate sports library at substantial savings off the retail prices...

Item	Title	Retail Price	Your Price
#608	TSN Selects Baseball's 100 Greatest Players	$29.95	$19.95
#609	Sports Crosswords & Games	$ 9.95	$ 7.95
#621	Celebrating 70: Mark McGwire's Historic Season	$29.95	$19.95
#624	TSN Selects Football's 100 Greatest Players	$29.95	$19.95
#625	Cleveland Browns: The Illustrated History	$29.95	$19.95
#626	TSN Selects Baseball's 25 Greatest Moments	$29.95	$19.95
#627	2000 Baseball Record Book	$15.95	$12.95
#628	2000 Baseball Guide	$15.95	$12.95

Turn page for more selections and ordering information...

#629	2000 Baseball Register	$15.95	$12.95
#630	2000 Official Major League Baseball Fact Book	$15.95	$12.95
#631	2000 Official Baseball Rules	$ 6.95	$ 5.95
#632	TSN Selects 50 Greatest Sluggers (NEW)	$29.95	$19.95
#633	The Ballpark Book (NEW)	$39.95	$24.95
#634	2000 Official WNBA Guide and Register (NEW)	$15.95	$12.95
#635	2000 Pro Football Guide	$15.95	$12.95
#636	2000 Pro Football Register	$15.95	$12.95
#637	2000-01 Hockey Guide	$15.95	$12.95
#638	2000-01 Hockey Register	$15.95	$12.95
#639	2000-01 NBA Guide (Available September)	$15.95	$12.95
#640	2000-01 NBA Register (Available September)	$15.95	$12.95
#641	2000-01 NBA Rules (Available September)	$ 6.95	$ 5.95

To Order Call Toll-Free

1-800-825-8508 Dept. HR00

Or fax your order to 515-699-3738 Dept. HR00

Credit card only for phone or fax orders.

Or send check or money order to The Sporting News,
Attn: Book Dept., P.O. Box 11229, Des Moines, IA 50340.

Postage & Handling: Please include $3.75 for the first books and $1.50 for each additional
book. For Canadian orders, $6.76 for the first books and $1.50 for each additional book.

Book Publishing Group